BORDER AND TERRITORIAL
DISPUTES OF THE WORLD

Other current affairs reference titles from John Harper Publishing include:

Revolutionary and Dissident Movements of the World
The Council of the European Union
Directory of European Union Political Parties
The European Commission
The European Courts
The European Parliament
Political Parties of the World
Trade Unions of the World
Treaties and Alliances of the World

BORDER AND TERRITORIAL DISPUTES OF THE WORLD

4th edition

Edited by Peter Calvert

with contributions by: Antony Alcock, Peter Beck, Alan Collins, Stephen Day, Mohammed Faal, Jane Freedman, John Glenn, Olexander Hryb, Lawrence Joffe, Kimmo Katajala, Jez Littlewood, Robert Lowe, Simon Massey, David Scott Mathieson, R J May, Alexandra McLeod, Nadia Milanova, Paul Nugent, Robert G Patman, Charlie Pericleous, Lloyd Pettiford, Steven Ratuva, Christopher Saunders, Mark Smith, Roger Southall and Nebojsa Vladisavljevic

JOHN HARPER PUBLISHING

Border and Territorial Disputes of the World, 4th edition

Published by John Harper Publishing, 27 Palace Gates Road, London N22 7BW, United Kingdom

Distributed outside North America by Extenza-Turpin, Stratton Business Park, Pegasus Drive, Biggleswade, SG18 8QB, UK
Distributed exclusively in the United States and Canada, and non-exclusively outside North America, by Gale Group Inc., 27500 Drake Rd., Farmington Hills, Michigan 48331, USA

1st edition (1982)
2nd edition (1987)
3rd edition (1992)

This edition first published 2004
© John Harper Publishing 2004
ISBN 0-9543811-3-0

Printed in Great Britain by the Cromwell Press

Table of Contents

MAPS

Introduction

At the time of publication of the third edition of this work (1992)—in the immediate aftermath of the collapse of communism in Europe and the dissolution of the Soviet Union in 1991—there was understandable concern that Europe might once more become a focus of conflict and tension.

And so, to some degree, it did: for much of the 1990s conflict between the various territories of the former Yugoslavia proved a major concern for the international community. These conflicts cost thousands of lives and reached such an intensity that they led for the first time to the active deployment of forces by NATO, something which had been avoided throughout the Cold War itself. A series of wars also broke out in the former Soviet republics in the Caucasus, conflicts which today remain suspended rather than settled.

Yet tensions between the territories of the former Soviet Union, the collapse of which had led both to the revival of boundary disputes long believed to be extinct and to the emergence of new ones, have not in general had the serious consequences that were feared a decade ago. A helpful factor in Eastern Europe has been the eastward expansion of the European Union, with applicant states proving willing to put territorial grievances to one side for the sake of achieving acceptance into the broader European community. This was not inevitable, as other examples show. In April 2004, for instance, at the last moment, the Greek Cypriot community rejected by referendum the settlement that had been so painstakingly worked out in recent months, and so only part of Cyprus has entered the Union.

In the Middle East, for different reasons, the future of the Occupied Territories remains in doubt but the capacity of the issue to arouse anger on all sides is greater than ever. Iraq's territorial ambitions led to war with Iran in the 1980s and its invasion of Kuwait in 1990 and the subsequent Gulf War; the issue of Iraq's borders has effectively been suppressed for the time being as a consequence of the US-led invasion of 2003, but its borders remain problematic and the border with Turkey has achieved new sensitivity with the creation of a semi-autonomous Kurdish entity within northern Iraq. In the Arabian peninsula, in contrast, a number of disputes have been settled in the last few years, though this at the same time as the regimes of the region have come under increasing internal pressure.

The level of international interest and engagement with the disputes described in this volume tends to depend very much on the strategic importance of the disputed territory. In Africa the Western Sahara question remains open, but is no longer seen as likely to lead to violence, and conflicts elsewhere in that continent often evoke only a muted international response. In Latin America, Peru and Ecuador have reached agreement and the El Salvador-Honduras dispute has been settled, though most disputes remain unresolved, if not actively prosecuted.

In Asia, the major disputes documented in the last edition have remained unsettled and in some cases have loomed even larger. In the case of Kashmir, the issue achieved renewed salience from the late 1990s with both India and Pakistan becoming declared nuclear powers, and the underlying dispute between the states has been exacerbated by intensified conflict within Kashmir itself. Following the attack on the Indian parliament in December 2001, which India blamed on groups sponsored by Pakistan, both countries deployed vast forces along the Line of Control in Kashmir, and while ritualistic sabre-rattling was evident from both parties, the dangers of the situation provoked frantic international diplomacy over a period of several months. The nuclear dimension has also emerged since the 1990s in the Korean conflict, with the USA seeking to prevent North Korea's threatened development of nuclear weapons by a mix of threats and rewards. And, while China has sought to persuade Taiwan that it could enjoy the status of Hong Kong if it accepted Beijing's sovereignty, and economic relations between the two countries have flourished, political relations have been complicated and at times soured by the the decline of the old Kuomintang ruling party in Taiwan and the rise of advocates of a "two-China" solution—anathema to Beijing. The possibility of serious conflict is being skirted around rather than receding into the distance.

Sadly, so few of the disputes that existed in 1992 have reached resolution that the present volume is again substantially larger than its predecessor, in the hope that when the next "unexpected" conflict arises, the necessary background information will be easily available. As the record of major wars in the twentieth century linked directly to border and territorial disputes shows, while such disputes are perhaps fewer than conflicts arising from domestic insurgencies, their potential for large-scale violence, engaging rival states and their allies, can be vastly greater.

The same general principles for inclusion of disputes have been applied as in previous editions. Boundary demarcation problems are only included where they involve contentious territorial claims by one state against another. Maritime boundary disputes are not covered except where they arise from or are relevant to landward claims. Where a dispute appears to have been settled since the last edition appeared a full account has been included; it is hoped, for the last time. The principle adopted in previous editions of including certain historically significant disputes which now appear settled or dormant has, however, again been followed as experience has shown that they may be unexpectedly revived, as in the case of the recent confrontation between Morocco and Spain. Readers seeking further information on situations where inter-governmental disputes as such are not involved, but rebel movements or other dissidents include territorial adjustments among their demands, should consult the publishers' *Revolutionary and Dissident Movements of the World* (ed. Bogdan Szajkowski, 4th edn., 2004).

The editor wishes to express his warmest thanks to all the contributors who responded to his appeal for help with this project, sometimes at very short notice. Their names are listed on the title page, and further details given in the Notes about the Contributors, and the credit for the book's merits belongs to them.

Peter Calvert

THE CONTRIBUTORS

The following have originated or updated entries for the present edition, as indicated at the end of each entry.

Antony Alcock is Emeritus Professor of European Studies at the University of Ulster, and has been researching and writing about the South Tyrol since the mid-1960s.

Peter Beck is Professor of International History at Kingston University. He is the author of *Antarctica in International Politics*; *The Falkland Islands as an International Problem*; and numerous articles in *Polar Record*.

Peter Calvert is Emeritus Professor of Comparative and International Politics, University of Southampton. His most recent publications include (with Susan Calvert) *Politics and Society in the Third World* (2nd edn, 2001); *Comparative Politics: an Introduction* (2002); and (co-edited with Peter Burnell) *Civil Society in Democratization* (2004).

Alan Collins is a Lecturer in the Department of Politics and International Relations at the University of Wales, Swansea. His area of research is security in Southeast Asia and his publications include *Security & Southeast Asia: Domestic, Regional and Global Issues* (Lynne Rienner).

Stephen Day is a Lecturer in European Politics at the University of Newcastle. His research and teaching interests centre around comparative politics and include European and Japanese politics, communist and social democratic parties, citizenship and suffrage rights.

Mohammed Faal is a Lecturer in Peace Studies in the Department of Peace Studies, University of Bradford, with a specialist interest in African security studies, and holds a PhD from the University of Southampton.

Jane Freedman is a Lecturer in Politics at the University of Southampton. She has published books and articles on French politics and on gender and politics.

John Glenn is a Lecturer in International Relations at the University of Southampton. He has published on several aspects of Central Asia, including the new security challenges confronting these states since the dissolution of the Soviet Union and the difficulties they have experienced in the transition to a market economy.

Olexander Hryb is a BBC World Service radio producer. Born in Lviv (Ukraine), he completed his doctoral studies at the Graduate School for Social Research (Polish Academy of Science) and the University of Sussex. He has published on Eastern European nationalism, Cossack revival, and media in Ukraine.

Lawrence Joffe is a writer on Middle Eastern affairs, contributing to a range of newspapers and magazines. His publications include *Keesing's Guide to the Middle East Peace Process* (1996).

Kimmo Katajala is Academy Research Fellow at the Karelian Institute, Department of Human Sciences, University of Joensuu, Finland, and has a specialist interest in Russian-Finnish border issues from the medieval to the modern period.

Jez Littlewood is a Research Fellow at the Mountbatten Centre for International Studies, University of Southampton. He specializes in issues related to international security, particularly weapons of mass destruction and terrorism.

Robert Lowe is the Manager of the Middle East Programme at the Royal Institute of International Affairs in London. He previously worked for the British Council and *The Times of Central Asia* and gained an MA in Asian History from the School of Oriental and African Studies, University of London, and an MA in Scottish History from Edinburgh University.

Simon Massey is a Senior Research Fellow at the African Studies Centre at Coventry University. His main research area is international security, in particular the political and ethical bases for peacekeeping intervention. Other research interests include francophone and lusophone Africa and the democratization process in Africa.

David Scott Mathieson is a doctoral student at the Australian National University. He has written on Burmese political economy and the civil war and his current research is on the economics of conflict in modern Burma.

Ronald J May is a Senior Fellow, Research School of Pacific and Asian Studies, and convenor of the Centre for Conflict and Post-Conflict Studies, Asia Pacific, at the Australian National University. He has written extensively on topics including the Philippines, Papua New Guinea, and ethnicity.

Alexandra McLeod is currently a doctoral candidate at the University of Southampton, researching and analyzing the politics of human rights and democracy promotion. She has conducted research for a number of projects in the field of global security and defence.

Nadia Milanova is Programme Director for the non-governmental organization Human Rights Without Frontiers International and a former head of the Prague office of the OSCE Secretariat. She holds a PhD from the University of Exeter for a thesis on the conflict over Nagorno Karabakh and the conflict resolution activities of the OSCE.

Paul Nugent is Reader in African History and member of the Centre of African Studies, University of Edinburgh. His publications include (edited with A. I. Asiwaju) *African Boundaries: Barriers, Conduits and Opportunities* (Pinter, 1996) and *Smugglers, Secessionists and Loyal Citizens on the Ghana-Togo Frontier: The Lie of the Land Since 1914* (James Currey, 2002).

Robert G Patman is an Associate Professor in the Department of Political Studies at the University of Otago, New Zealand. His research interests centre on international relations, the Horn of Africa, the ending of the Cold War and the relationship between order and justice in a globalizing world. His publications include *The Soviet Union in the Horn of Africa: the Diplomacy of Intervention and Disengagement* (Cambridge University Press, 1990) *Security in a Post-Cold War World* (Macmillan and St Martin's Press, 1999) and *Universal Human Rights?* (Macmillan and St Martin's Press, 2000).

Charlie Pericleous is a doctoral candidate in International Relations at the University of Southampton, with a special interest in territorial disputes and counter-terrorist policies in the European Union.

Lloyd Pettiford is currently Acting Head of Department for International Studies at Nottingham Trent University, having gained a PhD from the

University of Southampton in 1994 for a thesis entitled *Changing Conceptions of Security in Central America*. He has since published widely on topics including the politics and security challenges of Central America.

Steven Ratuva is a visiting fellow at the Australian National University and also a fellow at the Pacific Institute of Advanced Studies for Governance and Development at the University of the South Pacific in Fiji. His areas of research and publications are state-civil relations, ethnic politics, security, conflict resolution, post-colonial development and affirmative action.

Christopher Saunders lectures in the Department of Historical Studies at the University of Cape Town, South Africa. He has published widely on aspects of the recent history of South Africa and Namibia.

Mark Smith is a Research Fellow at the Mountbatten centre for International Studies, University of Southampton, and has a PhD from the University of Wales, Aberystwyth. He has written on issues including arms control, non-proliferation, and NATO.

Roger Southall is Distinguished Research Fellow, Democracy and Governance, Human Sciences Research Council, Pretoria, South Africa. He was formerly Professor of Political Studies at Rhodes University, having previously taught in universities in Lesotho, Canada and the UK. He has published widely on African, particularly southern African, topics.

Nebojsa Vladisavljevic teaches comparative politics in the Department of Government, London School of Economics and Political Science (LSE). He has published in the field of nationalist mobilization and regime change, especially on the former Yugoslavia.

AFRICA

1.1 Burkina Faso - Mali

An area extending along the border between the West African Republics of Burkina Faso (known as Upper Volta until August 1984) and Mali for about 90 miles (145 km) and of a width of between nine and 12 miles came into dispute between the two states after their achievement of independence in April and July 1960 respectively. At the end of 1985 the two sides fought a brief war over the disputed territory, but subsequently accepted a demarcation judgment of the International Court of Justice which came into effect at the end of 1987. (Map 1 on p.493 illustrates this dispute.)

Geographical and Historical Background of the Dispute

The area disputed between Burkina Faso and Mali contains a chain of pools in the Dori district (*cercle*), through which flows the Béli river, the only source of fresh water in the region. It includes pasture and agricultural land and has therefore attracted settlers as well as nomads who have seasonally migrated to the area with their livestock.

The colony of Upper Volta was first created by France under a decree of March 1, 1919, which laid down that seven districts (including that of Dori) which had until then been part of Upper Senegal-Niger (renamed the French Sudan on Dec. 4, 1920) would constitute the new colony. Its creation was officially motivated by the "particularly homogeneous ethnic and linguistic character of the region", which was said to be inhabited by "Mossis, Bobos and other related ethnic groups". However, under a further French decree of Sept. 5, 1932, the Governor-General of French West Africa dissolved the colony of Upper Volta and distributed its territory among the French colonies of Niger, the French Sudan and Côte d'Ivoire, with the Dori district being allocated to Niger (except for one canton which went to the French Sudan).

This 1932 decree was in turn revoked under a French law of Sept. 4, 1947, which restored Upper Volta, laying down that its frontiers should be those which had existed on Sept. 5, 1932, but that adjustments to these frontiers could be made later by consultation among the local assemblies concerned. The frontiers created by France were in principle accepted by both Mali (the former French Sudan) and Upper Volta in their 1960 declarations of independence.

Inconclusive Discussions about the Border Problem, 1961-74

The border problem was first discussed at a bilateral meeting at San (Mali) on Nov. 18-19, 1961, when it was agreed to have the frontier demarcated by a mixed commission of heads of border districts of the two states. This mixed commission agreed on Dec. 7, 1961, at Ansongo (Mali) that the frontier was as shown on a 1925 colonial map (of a 1:500,000 scale), and the Ansongo commander accepted that on all maps the Béli region was shown as being in Upper Volta. The San decision was, however, superseded by the creation of a new bipartisan commission set up in Bamako (the capital of Mali) on Feb. 24, 1964, and charged with proposing the demarcation of the frontier on the basis of the work done by the district heads.

The problem was again discussed at a meeting at Bobo-Diolassou (Upper Volta) in 1966 and at a meeting of the two heads of state at Orodara (Upper Volta) in May 1968, when two bodies were created—a permanent bipartisan commission to study the problems of co-operation between the two states and a mixed technical commission to explore the frontier on the basis of pre-independence documents held by the two states. On Sept. 29-30, 1968, it was agreed in Bamako that, if no texts could be found to support the frontier demarcation, then reference should be made to maps to solve the problem. The mixed technical commission was later instructed to explore the situation on the ground in certain areas, but in 1974 Mali declared that the commission had failed to carry out all its instructions fully, and it also rejected a 1926 atlas submitted by Upper Volta as a means of settling the question. All discussion was thereupon broken off.

Claims made by both Governments

As set out in a memorandum of Dec. 11, 1972, the thesis of the Malian government has been that the Béli region had geographically and historically always been part of the French Sudan and hence of Mali, in particular as part of the subdivision of Ansongo. In particular, Mali asserted in its memorandum that the delineation of a frontier on a map must be based on legal documents; that the maps available are often in conflict with existing legal documents and with each other; and that the people who inhabited the disputed area were of Malian origin and had contributed significantly to the development of the area during the colonial era.

The Mali government newspaper *L'Essor* declared at that time that, as the area was inhabited by Malians, the desire to keep the Béli region was "not a territorial claim" but was "simply an historically and geographically incontrovertible fact" and that "the claims of a state can be founded only on those of its population [who] have possessed and inhabited the zone". Radio Mali reiterated the claim to the region of Béli as Malian territory on Dec. 20, 1974, when it declared that Malian people had been settled there for centuries, had been born and had grown up there and had "possessed and inhabited the zone". It also stated that an additional strip extending for 140 kilometres between Coro and Bouanza was similarly in dispute.

Burkina Faso (Upper Volta) based its claim on the following principal considerations: (i) the provisions of the French law of Sept. 5, 1947, restoring Upper Volta with its frontiers as at Sept. 5, 1932; (ii) the prin-

3

ciples of the Charter of the Organization of African Unity (OAU), which include "respect for the sovereignty and territorial integrity of each member state and for its inalienable right to independent existence" (Article III, Para. 3 of the Charter) and "unreserved condemnation…of subversive activities on the part of neighbouring states" (Article II, Para. 5); and (iii) Resolution AGH/RES.16 (1) on intangibility of frontiers adopted by the OAU Assembly of Heads of State and Government in July 1964. According to this Resolution, member states undertook to respect the frontiers existing at the moment of their achievement of independence. In this context, Upper Volta quoted a speech made at the inaugural OAU Assembly in 1963 by the then President of Mali, endorsing the maintenance of existing frontiers and calling for a multilateral non-aggression pact guaranteed by all states represented at the Assembly.

The Upper Volta point of view was set out in detail in a 58-page memorandum submitted to an OAU mediation commission appointed in December 1974. In this memorandum Upper Volta adduced historical, geographical and demographic arguments in support of its thesis that the disputed area had never been part of Mali (or of the earlier French Sudan).

With regard to earlier frontiers, Upper Volta, while not excluding legal texts, considered maps to be the only objective documents because they were drawn on the basis of legal texts and by an official organ (the cartographic service of French West Africa). At the same time, Upper Volta rejected a 1925 map showing part of the Béli pools to be in the French Sudan, on the ground that this map was only provisional and was replaced by later maps showing all Béli pools to be inside Upper Volta.

On the issue of migration, Upper Volta pointed out that, according to official documents, migrants had moved mainly from the north to the south, the majority of these migrants being Tuaregs and Bellahs (population groups also represented in Algeria, Mauritania and Niger); that under conventions concluded between the French Sudan (or Mali) and Upper Volta also after their achievement of independence, to facilitate migration into the Béli region, the latter was recognized as part of Upper Volta and as not having always been inhabited by Malians; and that Mali had no right to use the presence of people of Malian origin as a basis for territorial claims as "to change the frontiers so as to embrace homogeneous groups would inevitably upset the present configuration of all African states". Upper Volta therefore considered the Malian thesis to be indefensible in law, even if it was conceivable on the strictly human level, and also to be dangerous because other states might claim sovereignty over Malian villages inhabited by Tuaregs. It also rejected Mali's claim based on the achievements of Malians in the region, pointing out that Upper Volta was not making any claims in respect of regions in neighbouring countries where people from Upper Volta had worked.

Border Incidents and Mediation Efforts, 1974-76

Armed clashes broke out on Nov. 25, 1974, and continued into December of that year. The continued hostilities were the subject of talks held at the frontier village of Aramana on Dec. 4 by Presidents Moussa Traore of Mali and Lamizana of Upper Volta. These talks did not lead to peace, however, and on Dec. 17, 1974, it was claimed in Bamako that Upper Volta had launched a general offensive against Mali, whereas it was announced in Ouagadougou (the capital of Burkina Faso/Upper Volta) on Dec. 18 that Malian forces had taken up positions in Upper Volta territory along the whole length of the disputed frontier. Mali claimed at the same time that it was merely taking possession of territory which was legally its own.

Following mediation efforts by Presidents Senghor of Senegal and Eyadema of Togo, a meeting was held on Dec. 26, 1974, in Lomé, Togo, at which a joint communiqué (issued on the following day) was signed by the Presidents of Mali, Niger, Togo and Upper Volta. In this communiqué it was agreed that a mediation commission was to be set up, with Guinea, Niger, Senegal and Togo as members, to guarantee the safety of the two countries' nationals on each other's territories, as well as their property; to supervise the effective withdrawal of troops from the border zone; and to seek a solution to the dispute.

The mediation commission subsequently carried out this work, under the auspices of the OAU, in two sub-committees—a juridical one examining the arguments on the two sides and a military one which visited the disputed area but was not admitted to Mali. The commission eventually recommended the independent demarcation of the border by a neutral technical commission which would determine sovereignty over certain villages in the disputed area, but as a result of Mali's refusal to admit the OAU's military committee such a commission was never set up.

Fresh border incidents were reported early in June 1975, when Mali alleged that Upper Volta forces had raided two villages and killed two people on June 3. The government of Guinea appealed to both sides on June 5 to halt hostilities and to evacuate their troops from the contested zone pending a settlement agreement. At a further meeting held in Lomé on June 18 and attended also by the Presidents of Guinea, Niger, Senegal and Togo, the Presidents of Mali and of Upper Volta undertook to "end their dispute on the basis of recommendations of the mediation commission", which was to appoint a neutral committee (including a cartographer and an ethnologist) to determine the position of several villages, while the government of Mali agreed to "restore to Upper Volta the equipment belonging to it and seized during the events of December 1974" and also to release two Upper Volta prisoners held in Mali. This undertaking was honoured on June 24, and on July 5 President Lamizana of Upper Volta announced that he had set free three detained Malians.

On July 11, 1975, the two Presidents signed, jointly with President Sekou Touré of Guinea, an agreement in which they undertook "to renounce the use of force" in any dispute between them. The following year, at a meeting of ministers from the two countries held in Upper Volta on March 9, it was agreed that the two Presidents should instruct the joint commission to resume its work with the aim of achieving a final settlement of the problem of the border area between specified villages, and that the administrative officers in the border districts should meet frequently to educate the population.

Agreed Recommendations of 1979

At a meeting between the Upper Volta and Malian Interior Ministers held in Ségou (Mali) on Nov. 21-22, 1979, the two sides agreed on recommendations for continued meetings of the administrative and local authorities in order to settle any border incidents; on empowering a technical joint commission to set up a programme of action and to define its working procedures; and on the adoption of a policy of consultation to find adequate solutions to the problem. The Malian minister was quoted as saying that there was "no point of divergence between Upper Volta and Mali" and that "we could and must settle our problems without any foreign intervention".

Agreement to Submit Dispute to International Court of Justice—Renewed Fighting in December 1985

In a joint communiqué issued on Sept. 16, 1983, the two countries' heads of state agreed to submit the border dispute to the International Court of Justice (ICJ) "while continuing the bilateral dialogue within the existing ad hoc structures". An ICJ chamber to hear the case was formed on April 3, 1985, and by September 1985 the two countries' border commissions had reached agreement on the demarcation of some 1,000 kilometres of the common border. (Meanwhile, on Aug. 4, 1984, Upper Volta had been renamed Burkina Faso, meaning "a country of people with integrity".)

However, fighting broke out in the border area on Dec. 25, 1985, apparently as the result of an attempt by Burkina Faso to carry out (between Dec. 10 and 20, 1985) a census operation in four villages in the disputed border region. According to Malian reports, villagers who refused to submit to the census had been mistreated, but the Burkinabé authorities claimed that the census operations in the villages (three of which were, according to maps in current usage, in Burkina territory) had been obstructed by Malian troops.

Malian airborne attacks were carried out on Dec. 25, 1985, on various towns far south of the border, and on Dec. 26 Burkina Faso launched an air attack on Sikasso, a Malian town some 700 kilometres southwest of the area of conflict, whereupon Mali retaliated by attacking Koloko in Burkina Faso. The fighting was ended by a truce negotiated by the member governments of the Non-Aggression and Defence Aid Agreement (ANAD, embracing Burkina Faso, Côte d'Ivoire, Mali, Mauritania, Niger, Senegal and Togo). After being formally endorsed by the two heads of state, the truce came into force on Dec. 31, 1985. In Burkina Faso it was announced in mid-January 1986 that 41 of its nationals had been killed in the fighting, among them 21 civilians. No official casualty figures were given by Mali.

The ICJ chamber dealing with the border dispute held an emergency meeting on Jan. 9, 1986, and called on both parties to observe the truce, to take no action which might aggravate the situation and to effect, within 20 days, a troop withdrawal behind lines to be agreed by both governments. Such an agreement was concluded at an ANAD meeting held in Côte d'Ivoire on Jan. 17-18, 1986, when the heads of state of Burkina Faso and Mali effected a public reconciliation. Exchanges of prisoners took place between the two sides between Jan. 9 and Feb. 27, 1986.

Diplomatic relations between the two countries were resumed in June 1986. On Aug. 9 of that year Captain Thomas Sankara, Chairman of the National Recovery Council of Burkina Faso, said his country had not gained by the war which he described as "something very dangerous and even fatal". In November 1986 a Malian defence delegation, led by the Malian Minister of National Defence, General Sekou Ly, visited Burkina Faso.

Decision of the International Court of Justice

On Dec. 22, 1986, the ICJ chamber (consisting of Judge Mohammed Bedjaoui as president and Judges Manfred Lachs and José Maria Ruda, as well as Judges ad hoc François Luchaire and Georges Abi-Saab) unanimously agreed on the frontier line between the two states (although the two ad hoc judges dissociated themselves from some of the reasons and conclusions). The judgment had the effect of that of the full Court and was accepted as binding and to be effected within a year by the two parties. The Court was asked to nominate three experts to assist in the demarcation of the border.

In the judgment the disputed area of some 1,200 square miles was divided into roughly equal parts on both sides of a 124½-mile border line, with Mali obtaining a bigger part of the disputed territory's western zone and Burkina Faso a lesser portion in the eastern zone. In its judgment the ICJ chamber came to the following conclusions:

Historical background. Both states derived their existence from the process of decolonization which had been unfolding in Africa during the past 30 years. Their territories and that of Niger were formerly part of French West Africa. Burkina Faso corresponded to the colony of Upper Volta and Mali to Sudan (formerly French Sudan). Both parties stated that the settlement should be based on respect for the principle of the intangibility of frontiers inherited from colonization.

The principle. In those circumstances, the Court could not disregard the principle of *uti possidetis juris* (i.e. the presumption that post-colonial states possessed sovereignty within antecedent colonial boundaries). It emphasized the general scope of the principle in matters of decolonization and its exceptional importance for the African continent. Although invoked for the first time in Spanish America, the principle was not a rule pertaining solely to one specific system of international law. It was a general principle logically connected with the phenomenon of the obtaining of independence and its obvious purpose was to prevent the independence and stability of new states being endangered by fratricidal struggles provoked by the challenging of frontiers following the withdrawal of the administering power. The principle accorded pre-eminence to legal title over effective possession as a basis of sovereignty. Its primary aim was to secure respect for the territorial boundaries which existed when independence was achieved. When those boundaries were delimitations between different administrative divisions or colonies subject to the same sovereign, the application of the principle resulted in their being transformed into international boundaries, as in the instant case. The principle appeared in conflict with the right of peoples to self-determination; however, the maintenance of territorial status quo in Africa was often seen as the wisest course. The essential requirement of stability in order to survive and develop had induced African states to consent to the maintenance of colonial frontiers.

French colonial law. The parties agreed that the delimitation of the frontier had to be appraised in the light of the French colonial law. The line to be determined as that which existed in 1959-60 was originally no more than an administrative boundary dividing two former French overseas territories and as such was defined at that time not according to international law but according to the relevant French legislation. International law, and therefore the principle of *uti possidetis*, applied as from the accession of independence but had no retroactive effect. The principle froze the territorial title; it stopped the clock but it did not put back the hands. International law did not effect any return to the law of the colonizing state, which was but one factual element among others, evidence indicative of the colonial heritage at the critical date.

Administrative heritage. French West Africa was headed by a governor-general and divided into colonies, headed by a lieutenant-governor. Colonies were subdivided into *cercles* headed by a commandant. Mali gained its independence in 1960, succeeding the Sudanese Republic which had emerged from the French Sudan. Upper Volta came into being in 1919, was abolished in 1932 and reconstituted in 1947, with the 1932 boundaries, and gained independence in 1960. The problem for the Court was to ascertain what in the disputed area was the frontier that existed in 1959-60 between Sudan and Upper Volta. Both parties agreed that when they became independent there was a definite frontier and both accepted that no modifica-

tion had taken place since.

Tripoint problem. The easternmost point of the disputed frontier, the tripoint Niger-Mali-Burkina Faso, gave rise to conflict between the parties. Mali claimed that it could not be determined without Niger's agreement, and Burkina Faso considered that the Court had to reach a decision. The Court held that its jurisdiction was not restricted merely because the end-point of the disputed frontier lay on the frontier of a third state not a party to the proceedings. The rights of Niger were in any event safeguarded by Article 59 of the Statute of the Court which provided that the decision of the Court had no binding force except between the parties and in respect of that particular case. In any event, the Court was not required to fix a tripoint, which would require the consent of all three states, but to ascertain in the light of the evidence which the parties had made available how far the frontier they had inherited from the colonial power extended. Such a finding implied that the territory of a third state lay beyond the end-point and that the parties had exclusive sovereign rights up to that point. However, since the parties had contended that they possessed a common frontier with the other as far as a specific point, neither could change its position to rely on sovereignty of a third state. The Court would merely define the end-point where the frontier ceased to divide the territories of Burkina Faso and Mali but that would not amount to a decision that that was a tripoint which affected Niger.

Evidence. The parties relied on different types of evidence. (1) They referred to legislative and regulative texts or administrative documents. However, as those contained no complete description of the disputed area they were limited in scope and the correct interpretation of them was a matter of dispute between the parties. (2) Both produced an abundant collection of cartographic materials (maps). But the Court noted that in frontier delimitations maps merely constituted information and never constituted territorial titles in themselves. They were merely extrinsic evidence which might be used along with other evidence to establish the real facts. Their value depended on their technical reliability and their neutrality to the parties in the dispute. None of the maps available could provide an official illustration of any of the texts produced although it was clear from their wording that two of the texts were intended to be accompanied by maps. Further, no indisputable boundary line could be discerned from the documents. One map, issued between 1958 and 1960 by the French Institut Géographique National (IGN), was drawn up by a body neutral towards the parties. Although it did not possess the status of a legal title, it was a visual portrayal both of the available texts and of information available on the ground. Where other evidence was lacking or not sufficient to show an exact line, the probative force of the IGN map had to be viewed as compelling. (3) The parties also invoked the conduct of the administrative authorities as proof of the effective exercise of territorial jurisdiction in the region during the colonial period. The role played by such conduct was complex and the Court had to make a careful evaluation of their legal force in each particular instance.

The Court emphasized that the present case was decidedly unusual as concerned the facts to be proved or the evidence to be produced. Although the parties had produced as complete a case file as possible, the Court could not be certain of deciding the case on a basis of full knowledge of facts. The case file showed inconsistencies and shortcomings. The Court considered what relationship could be established among the pieces of information provided by the various texts of which it had to make use and reached a number of conclusions. In certain points the sources agreed and bore one another out, but in some respects, in view of the shortcomings of some of the older maps, they tended to conflict. The western end-point was already agreed between the parties and the Court drew in a series of straight lines between co-ordinates the boundary from there to the frontier of Niger. At one place, the pool of In Abao, the co-ordinates were not specified but it was left to the three experts who were to be appointed to define them. The Court considered it inappropriate to appoint those experts in the judgment, but said they would be appointed later by an order of the Court.

The Court noted with satisfaction the agreement in January 1986 of the heads of state of Burkina Faso and Mali to withdraw all their armed forces from either side of the disputed area and to effect their return to their respective territories. The Court finally noted that the parties had declared that they would accept the judgment as binding upon them and was happy to record the attachment of both parties to the international judicial process and to the peaceful settlement of disputes.

The dispute has been regarded as settled since the ICJ judgement.

Mohammed Faal

1.2 Cameroon - Nigeria

The question of sovereignty over the Bakassi Peninsula, an area of 665 sq km lying between the adjoining coastal regions of Cameroon and Nigeria, became a matter of contention between the two states, resulting in sporadic skirmishes in the 1980s and 1990s and being the subject of an International Court of Justice ruling in 2002. (The region is shown on Map 1, p. 493.)

Background to the Dispute

Cameroon was a German colony until the end of World War I when the eastern part was put under French administration and the western part under British administration. After World War II, a United Nations trusteeship plan continued the division. On Jan. 1, 1960, the French section of the trusteeship achieved independence, becoming the Republic of Cameroon. On Feb. 11, 1961, the UN organized a plebiscite whereby North British Cameroon voted for incorporation into Nigeria (which had attained its independence from Britain the previous year) while West Cameroon to the south, by a majority of 233,571 to 97,741, opted for merger with the Republic of Cameroon. West Cameroon consequently united with the rest of Cameroon to form the Federal Republic of Cameroon. A section of the population of West Cameroon, however, remained opposed to the incorporation of their area in Cameroon. In particular, the Bakassi peninsula, situated on the Cameroon side of the border and to the west of the Rio del Rey river, was largely inhabited by Nigerians who had settled there prior to 1961. Many of these Nigerians were fishermen and some were engaged in smuggling, and they tended to seek protection from the authorities of the Nigerian Cross River State.

A maritime border agreement signed at the northern Cameroon town of Maroua on June 1, 1975, by Gen. Yakubu Gowon (then Nigeria's head of state) and President Ahmadou Ahidjo of Cameroon, left the access channel to the port of Calabar in Nigerian territorial waters and also provided that the lawful activities of Nigerian fishermen in a two-kilometre-wide strip should not affect the territorial waters issue. However, Gen. Gowon was deposed in July 1975 and the agreement was never ratified by Nigeria on the grounds that it was "defective in parts".

On the question of the two countries' common border, President Ahidjo stated in July 1976 that although Cameroon had strongly challenged the correctness of the 1961 plebiscite resulting in the transfer of Northern Cameroon to Nigeria, and had unsuccessfully tried to appeal to the United Nations and the International Court of Justice, his government had bowed to the facts and preferred to refrain from making any territorial claims. He added that where Cameroon's boundaries with any of its six neighbours (Nigeria and Chad to the north, the Central African Republic to the east and Congo, Gabon and Equatorial Guinea in the south) were imprecisely delimited the problem would be solved amicably.

Escalation of Tension in 1981

On May 18, 1981, Prof. Ishaya Audu, the Nigerian Minister of External Affairs, announced that, although the Nigerian President had recently visited Cameroon as "part of the exercise of defusing the tension along this border and generally trying to settle issues by peaceful means", the situation had taken "a different turn". He maintained that at a Nigerian village in Cross River State, well within Nigerian territory and separated from the Cameroon border by the Akpa Yafi river (also referred to as the Ate Akate or Agpa Yafe river) on May 15, 1981, "a platoon of Nigerian soldiers and five support boats were fired upon by a Cameroonian support boat" and five Nigerian soldiers had been killed and three others seriously wounded, whereupon the Cameroonians had fled. The minister added that his government had sent the Cameroonian government "a very stern note of protest"; that it reserved the right to take any appropriate action to protect the lives and property of Nigerians; and that it would report the matter to the Organization of African Unity (OAU).

Prof. Audu later contended that there had been "regular harassment" of Nigerians living in the border area and also incursions by Cameroonians into Nigerian villages. The Cameroonians, on the other hand, alleged that the incident of May 15 had taken place on the Rio del Rey river, i.e. in Cameroonian territorial waters 20 miles to the east of the boundary, while on May 22 President Ahidjo was reported to have ordered an inquiry into an earlier exchange of artillery fire on the Rio del Rey river. In a message delivered in Lagos on May 24 by a delegation led by Paul Dontsop (Cameroon's Foreign Minister), President Ahidjo expressed his regrets at the incident of May 15 and made proposals for working out a peaceful solution to the border problem, but the National Security Council of Nigeria found that these proposals did not cover all the issues referred to in Nigeria's protest note.

There followed strong expressions of hostility to Cameroon in the Nigerian press, where it was claimed that Cameroon was massing forces for a military confrontation and was prospecting for oil in Nigerian waters. Alhaji Akanbi Oniyangi (the Minister of Defence) refused to rule out the possibility of war, and demonstrating university students called for war and caused damage to Cameroon's embassy in Lagos.

Ayissi Mvodo, Cameroonian Minister of State for Territorial Administration, said in an interview published on June 3 that many other incidents had occurred in the past and had been settled peacefully by the authorities of both countries, and that the position of the Cameroonian government was always to seek such a settlement without recourse to force, in particular because the two "brotherly and neighbouring countries" harboured "huge numbers of each other's citizens".

With regard to Nigeria's appeal to the OAU, the Secretariat of the OAU declined to place the matter on the agenda of the OAU Assembly of Heads of State and Government held in Nairobi on June 24-28, 1981, and President Shehu Shagari thereupon refused to attend the session. Following mediation efforts by various African leaders, it was reported on July 15, 1981, that an OAU ministerial committee would be set up to look into the situation. President Ahidjo had earlier (on July 7) been reported to have emphasized that calm had been restored to the area; that Cameroon would not be the origin of any eventual conflict with its neighbours; and that it was ready to take part in any mediation efforts.

In Lagos it was announced on July 20, 1981, that President Ahidjo had promised that his country would pay compensation to the families of the five Nigerian soldiers killed on May 15, and that he had tendered an unreserved apology. President Shagari, in accepting this offer (as reported on July 24), suggested the establishment of "an arbitration tribunal comprising countries acceptable to both nations to look into the entire boundary question with a view to forestalling further unrest".

In a joint communiqué issued on Jan. 13, 1982, at the end of a visit by President Ahidjo to Lagos, it was stated inter alia that the two countries' Presidents had expressed their regret at the border clash of May 1981, had resolved not to allow the incident to affect co-operation between them, and had decided to reactivate a Nigeria-Cameroon joint commission to strengthen co-operation in all fields.

Although Nigeria had early in 1983 expelled an estimated 120,000 Cameroonians as "illegal aliens", the two countries' Presidents agreed on April 21, 1983, to establish a new Nigeria-Cameroon joint commission and to "pursue, intensify and consolidate" the co-operation between their countries.

On May 2, 1987, there was an incursion into Borno State (Nigeria) by a number of Cameroonian gendarmes; the incursion was described as a "minor incident" by Nigeria's President Babangida although subsequently, when Nigeria opened 100 new border posts, the governors of border states were ordered to take reprisals against any belligerent neighbouring country. During Sept. 20-25, 1987, there was an official visit to Cameroon by the Nigerian Chief of Army Staff Maj.-Gen. Abacha which led to the announcement (Sept. 26) of the formation of a joint military border patrol to check border incursions.

In June 1991 a number of Cameroonian incursions occurred in isolated areas of eastern Nigeria and included the occupation of nine small fishing settlements on offshore islands. However, on July 17, 1991, Nigeria's Vice-President, Augustus Aikhomu, ruled out the possibility of war with Cameroon over the border dispute and it was agreed that representatives of the two countries should meet to discuss the question. In 1992 the government of Nigeria published an official map locating Bakassi in Nigerian territory. The presence of Nigerian troops in several localities of the Peninsula led to protests by the Republic of Cameroon and from the end of 1993, several incidents were reported between the armed forces of the two countries when Nigerian troops invaded the Cameroonian localities of Jabane and Diamond Island in the Bakassi Peninsula.

On March 29, 1994, the Cameroon government filed an application to the International Court of Justice (ICJ) instituting proceedings against Nigeria regarding sovereignty over the Bakassi Peninsula and part of Cameroonian territory in the area of Lake Chad. In September 2002 the Presidents of Cameroon and Nigeria agreed at UN-brokered talks, following a re-escalation of tension in the prelude to the announcement of the ICJ decision, that they would abide by the Court's ruling and refrain from inflammatory statements, and they also agreed on the need for eventual demilitarization of the Peninsula.

The following month, the Court ruled in favour of Cameroon in respect of its sovereignty over the Bakassi Peninsula and areas around Lake Chad, while awarding some other territories near the land border to Nigeria. However, the judgement also found in favour of Nigeria's call for the retention of existing maritime boundaries between it and Cameroon (and also Equatorial Guinea), ensuring Nigeria's continued access to large offshore oil reserves in the Gulf of Guinea and the continuation of offshore oilfield division agreements previously reached with Equatorial Guinea and São Tomé and Príncipe. The latter result was seen as likely to prove more significant to Nigeria than the confirmation of Cameroonian sovereignty over Bakassi. By 2002, the USA imported close to 15 per cent of its crude oil from the Gulf of Guinea region.

Mohammed Faal

1.3 Chad - Libya

In 1973 the Libyan government of Col. Moamer al Kadhafi annexed an area south of the existing border between Libya and Chad known as the Aozou strip (see Map 2, p. 493). Whereas the Libyan action met with no opposition from the then government of Chad led by President Ngarta (François) Tombalbaye nor from other states in the area, objections to the annexation were first raised by Gen. Félix Malloum, who had become President of Chad after the overthrow of President Tombalbaye in April 1975. In 1980, by which time Chad had been devastated by civil war, Libyan forces, invited into the country by a provisional "government of national unity" formed in November 1979 under the presidency of Goukouni Oueddei, temporarily occupied the greater part of Chad. President Goukouni Oueddei accepted the Libyan annexation of the Aozou strip as "an accomplished fact", whereas rebel groups, especially that led by Hissène Habré, continued to dispute Libya's right to the strip. Thus Hissène Habré's eventual military victory and assumption of power in Chad in June 1982 reopened the dispute over the Aozou strip, which advancing Chadian government forces succeeded in penetrating in early August 1987, when the town of Aozou was captured from the Libyans.

History of Chad's Northern Boundary

The boundary between Libya and Chad was first laid down under a convention signed in Paris by France and the United Kingdom on June 14, 1898 (with ratifications being exchanged in Paris on June 13, 1899), with the object of delimiting the spheres of influence of France and the United Kingdom east of the Niger river. Under an Anglo-French declaration of March 21, 1899, the French zone was delimited to the north-east and east by a line starting "from the point of intersection of the Tropic of Cancer with the 16th degree of longitude east of Greenwich" and running "thence to the north until it meets the 24th degree of longitude east of Greenwich". Italy concurred with the above line in an exchange of notes with France on Nov. 1, 1902. Under a convention of Sept. 8, 1919, France and the United Kingdom determined the line's point of intersection with the 24th meridian (which had not been specified in the 1899 declaration) at 19°30′N.

Whereas the territory to the north of this line had been under Turkish suzerainty as part of the Ottoman empire, Italy occupied the region of Tripoli in September 1911, and in the Treaty of Ouchy of Oct. 18, 1912, the Ottoman empire recognized Italian sovereignty over the territory which became officially known as Libya after 1934. Following Libya's declaration of independence on Dec. 24, 1951, the boundary between Libya and French Equatorial Africa was recognized in a Franco-Libyan treaty of Aug. 10, 1955, as fixed under the above-mentioned agreements. Chad, which had been part of French Equatorial Africa, became independent on Aug. 11, 1960.

Libya's Annexation of the Aozou Strip

In June 1973 the Libyan government of Col. Kadhafi annexed the Aozou strip, basing its action on the provisions of a Franco-Italian protocol signed in Rome on Jan. 7, 1935. This protocol, dealing with the delimitation of "the frontier between Libya and the French colonies" (and also "between Eritrea and the French coast of Somaliland", i.e. Djibouti), defined the proposed southern frontier of Libya (as described in an official communiqué of Jan. 8, 1935) as follows: "The frontier separating Libya from French West Africa and French Equatorial Africa is determined by the line which runs from Tummo, the terminating point of the line traced in the Italo-French agreement of Sept. 12, 1919, meeting the western frontier of the Anglo-Egyptian Sudan at 24°E, 18°45′N. This line leaves (in Italian territory) Aozou and Guezendi, and in French territory Bardai and Tecro. The size of the territories thus recognized as belonging to Italian Libya is approximately 114,000 square kilometres (43,000 square miles)".

This protocol was agreed to "in application of Article 13 of the Treaty of London", which had been concluded by France, Italy, Russia and the United Kingdom in 1915 with the object of inducing Italy to join the Allies in World War I. The article in question read as follows: "In the event of France and Great Britain increasing their colonial territories in Africa at the expense of Germany, those two powers agree in principle that Italy may claim some equitable compensation, particularly as regards the settlement in her favour of the questions relative to the frontiers of the Italian colonies of Eritrea, Somaliland and Libya and the neighbouring colonies belonging to France and Great Britain". However, France never ratified the protocol (which was said to have been interpreted by Mussolini as giving him, as far as France was concerned, a free hand in his invasion of Abyssinia in October 1935).

The timing of Libya's annexation of the Aozou strip was widely regarded as being connected with the existence of uranium deposits in the strip (in the same geological formation which included uranium deposits in Gabon). Although consisting (according to the European Nuclear Energy Agency) of low-grade, high-cost ores, the deposits were considered adequate to complete the required basis for the nuclear independence of Libya, which had concluded an agreement with the Soviet Union for the supply of a 10-megawatt nuclear reactor and associated technology to Libya.

The annexation of the Aozou strip was not officially announced in Libya until early September 1975 (in the Tripoli newspaper *Al Fateh*).

Reactions in Chad to the Annexation

At the time of the annexation of the Aozou strip Chad had close relations with Libya. Following a visit to Tripoli by President Tombalbaye, the Libyan government had, on Dec. 23, 1972, undertaken to "contribute to the strengthening of unity" in Chad, to grant Chad development credits and (reportedly) also to hand over to the government of Chad any members of the rebel *Front de libération nationale* (Frolinat) who might be in Libya. During a visit to Chad by Col. Kadhafi on March 5-6, 1974, the Aozou strip was not officially referred to. However, on April 26, 1976, President Malloum, who accused both Libya and Algeria of supporting the Frolinat rebels, denounced Libya for having illegally occupied the Aozou strip. On Oct. 16 of that year Chad closed its border with Libya, and a few days later President Malloum notified Col. Kadhafi that there could be no talk of co-operation between the two countries until Libya had withdrawn from the Aozou strip.

At a meeting of the Council of Ministers of the Organization of African Unity (OAU) in Libreville (Gabon) in June 1977, the Foreign Minister of Chad accused Libya of arming and aiding rebels in northern Chad, and he asked the OAU to use all its authority "to restore Chad's rights in the Aozou strip". The Libyan representative at the meeting asserted in turn that the strip was in fact "not northern Chad" but "southern Libya". The OAU Assembly of Heads of State and Government, meeting also in Libreville early in July 1977, thereupon set up a commission to deal with the dispute. On Feb. 6, 1978, the government of President Malloum suspended its diplomatic relations with Libya.

At an OAU Assembly of Heads of State and Government, meeting in Khartoum, President Malloum on July 20, 1978, denounced Libya's "expansionist desires" and called on the OAU to demand

Libya's withdrawal from Chad and to set up a mission to be sent to northern Chad to ascertain that it had been invaded by Libyan forces. The OAU subsequently established a committee of five African Presidents to investigate Chad's allegations and also Libyan accusations to the effect that Chad had been relying on French "colonial forces" to suppress a popular uprising in Chad by "genocidal methods". Subsequent OAU efforts were directed mainly at the prevention of further escalation of the civil war in Chad and had no bearing on the status of the Aozou strip, which remained firmly under Libyan control.

President Malloum resigned on March 23, 1979, and after lengthy negotiations a provisional "government of national unity" was established under the presidency of Goukouni Oueddei on Nov. 10, 1979. On June 15, 1980, this government signed a treaty of friendship with Libya, under which both sides undertook "mutually to defend each other in the event of one of the two parties being threatened by direct or indirect aggression". On Jan. 6, 1981, the two governments announced, at the end of a visit to Tripoli by President Goukouni Oueddei, their intention to work towards "full unity" between the two countries, with Libya sending military personnel to Chad to help preserve security and maintain peace. After it had become apparent that there was widespread opposition to any eventual merger between Libya and Chad (not only outside but also inside Chad), it was stated in Libya and in Chad that no such merger was intended.

The Vice-President of Chad, in particular, said in a broadcast on Jan. 11, 1981, that the Tripoli announcement did not represent a treaty with Libya but concerned only "complete unity of the two peoples in historical, ethnical and ideological terms" and not a merger of the two countries. President Goukouni Oueddei had stated on Dec. 26, 1980, that the Libyan occupation of the Aozou strip had placed him before an "accomplished fact" inherited from the Tombalbaye regime, and he added: "Nobody will be able to intervene to disunite Chad and Libya".

Civil War and Libyan Intervention in Chad

In November 1981 the Libyan troops which had entered Chad at the invitation of President Goukouni Oueddei were withdrawn from the country at his request. This withdrawal was followed by the advance of the *Forces armées du nord* (FAN) led by Hissène Habré, which gradually occupied all major towns in Chad and finally overthrew the Goukouni Oueddei government in June 1982. While the ex-President attempted to regroup his forces in northern Chad, where Libya continued to maintain a military presence, the Foreign Minister in Hissène Habré's government declared on Sept. 13, 1982, that Chad would seek to expel the Libyans from the Aozou strip by resorting to the United Nations, the Organization of African Unity and, if necessary, the International Court of Justice. The Libyan government, however, denied on Sept. 20 that the Aozou strip was Chadian territory.

Early in October 1982 it was announced in Libya that eight different factions had formed a 15-member "national peace government" under the leadership of Goukouni Oueddei and based in Bardai (northern Chad). There ensued heavy fighting between the two sides' forces. At the request of President Habré, French troops entered Chad and launched, on Aug. 13, 1983, an operation designed to form a defensive line at the southern limit of the range of Libyan aircraft operating from bases in southern Libya and northern Chad, and with French fighter aircraft standing by at a base in the Central African Republic.

In January 1984 the French declared the area of Chad south of the 16th parallel to be an exclusive zone in which no Libyan-backed forces would be tolerated. In April of that year France and Libya began to discuss a mutual withdrawal of forces from Chad. In this context the French Defence Minister (Charles Hernu) issued a warning that France would "not leave Chad as long as there was one Libyan soldier remaining south of the Aozou strip", which President Habré still regarded as part of Chad.

The mutual troop withdrawal was finally agreed on Sept. 17, 1984 (although Hernu stated that the Aozou strip was not included in the withdrawal and that its future sovereignty was a matter for the United Nations). On Nov. 10, 1984, both France and Libya stated that withdrawal had been completed by both sides; however, by Nov. 16, 1984, it became clear that there still remained strong Libyan forces inside Chad. Subsequent efforts by the opposing Chadian sides to reach an agreement remained fruitless.

After renewed fighting had broken out in northern Chad in February 1986, French fighter bombers from the Central African Republic bombed a northern air-base on Feb. 16 and, in response to a Libyan air attack on the airport of N'Djaména (the Chadian capital), the French government announced that it would send "a deterrent force" to Chad. In October 1986, however, Goukouni Oueddei was ousted as leader of the Libyan-backed government and thereupon directed his forces, estimated at 3,000 men, to form an alliance with the government of President Habré. (Goukouni Oueddei himself was later reported to have been placed under house arrest in Tripoli for having advocated a peaceful settlement of the conflict in Chad.) In December 1986 the United States approved an extra US$15 million in military aid to the Habré government, in addition to US$5 million for 1987.

By January 1987 some 1,400 French troops were said to be deployed in Chad south of the 16th parallel. Following a Libyan air raid on government positions south of the line on Jan. 4, 1987, the forces of the Habré government, with French logistical support, launched a major offensive against Libyan positions south of the Aozou strip. Peace talks between Chad and Libya were initiated in Khartoum (Sudan) in early March but failed to make any progress. Later that month Chadian government forces achieved major military successes by recapturing Ouadi-Doum (on March 22) and Faya Largeau (March 27) from the

Libyans, taking many prisoners and capturing large quantities of armaments. In consequence of this defeat, Libya became virtually restricted to the Aozou strip.

During a visit to France (July 12-15, 1987) President Habré stated his determination "to liberate the Aozou strip by one means or another". On Aug. 8, 1987, Chad forces captured the town of Aozou, inflicting heavy casualties on the Libyans. President François Mitterrand of France subsequently advised Habré not to proceed with the attack and other African leaders called for a peaceful solution. On Aug. 28 Libyan forces recaptured the town of Aozou although a week later (Sept. 5-6) Chad forces carried out unprecedented raids into southern Libya and attacked the Maatar as Sarra air base 100 kilometres north of the border, killing an estimated 1,700 Libyans and destroying 20 Libyan aircraft on the ground. This attack was widely criticized by neutral African countries and France and it was suggested that the USA had encouraged it.

On Sept. 17, 1987, Col. Kadhafi said he was prepared to regard the war as over if Chad ceded the Aozou strip to Libya after which, he said, Libya would never again interfere in Chad. The offer was rejected by President Habré. In September 1988 Libya conceded that the conflict had been a mistake and on Oct. 3 Chad and Libya formally ended their war and agreed to work towards a peaceful settlement of the Aozou conflict and establish diplomatic relations at once.

On July 20, 1989, Kadhafi and Habré met for the first time in Bamako (Mali) at a mini-summit under the chairmanship of President Moussa Traore; also present were Presidents Omar Bongo (Gabon), Ibrahim Babangida (Nigeria) and Chadli Bendjedid (Algeria). The meeting broke down after a day over the question of repatriating Libyan prisoners of war and because of reports that Libya was arming anti-Habré dissidents in the Darfur province of Sudan.

However, on Aug. 31, 1989, an agreement between Chad and Libya to resolve the Aozou strip dispute was signed by the Chad and Libyan Foreign Ministers, Acheikh bin Oumar and Jadallah Azouz al Talhi, assisted by Algerian mediation. The status of the strip was to be resolved in a year but if no firm decision could be reached it would then go to the International Court of Justice (ICJ) for binding arbitration. Meanwhile, both countries agreed to end hostile media campaigns and sign a treaty of friendship and co-operation. Further talks were held in Tripoli (Dec. 18-21, 1989), at which Libya insisted upon the return of prisoners: it accused Chad of training some 2,000 prisoners of war in a camp near N'Djaména (with US help) as part of a rebel National Front for the Liberation of Libya.

In 1990 (Aug. 22-23) Kadhafi and Habré met in Rabat (Morocco) for further talks hosted by King Hassan where they agreed to submit the Aozou dispute to arbitration by the ICJ at The Hague. They also agreed to hold further talks to resolve outstanding differences.

On Feb. 3, 1994, the ICJ delivered its judgement on the Aozou strip dispute. It found that the boundary between Chad and Libya was defined by the Treaty of Friendship and Good-Neighbourliness concluded on Aug. 10, 1955, between the French Republic and the United Kingdom of Libya. On April 4, 1994, representatives of Chad and Libya signed an agreement at Surt (Libya) concerning the implementation of the ICJ judgement. The agreement also called for the withdrawal of the Libyan administration and forces from the Aozou strip.

The United Nations Security Council adopted Resolution 915 (1994) welcoming the signing of the Surt agreement, noting that the agreement provided that UN observers should be present during all the Libyan withdrawal operations and should establish that the withdrawal was actually effected. Furthermore, Resolution 915 provided for the creation of the United Nations Aozou Strip Observer Group (UNASOG) and authorized the deployment for a single period of up to forty days, of nine UN Observers and six support staff to observe the implementation of the Surt agreement. The work carried out by UNASOG went according to plan with both parties' full co-operation. After receiving the Secretary-General's report of June 6, 1994, and satisfied that UNASOG had accomplished its mission, the Security Council adopted Resolution 926 (1994) terminating the mandate of UNASOG with immediate effect.

Mohammed Faal

1.4 Chad - Nigeria

A dispute concerning sovereignty over a number of islands in Lake Chad led to a series of clashes between Chadian and Nigerian troops in April–May 1983.

In addition to Chad to the east and Nigeria to the west, both Cameroon to the south and Niger to the north extend to the shores of Lake Chad, sovereignty over which is thus divided between the four countries.

As a result of the 1983 clashes, the border between Chad and Nigeria was closed for several months. Although an agreement to end the fighting was signed on May 7, clashes continued. In Nigeria it was claimed on May 16 that over 300 Chadian soldiers had been killed in a Nigerian counter-attack. On July 11, 1983, the two countries' Presidents agreed to end the fighting and to reopen the border. The border was nevertheless closed again temporarily until the heads of state of the two countries agreed on May 15, 1984, to reopen it.

After there were further cross border clashes between Nigerian and Chadian forces in the Lake Chad region in September 1998, Chad, Niger and Nigeria agreed on joint border patrols.

Regional governments have co-operated in the work of managing the water and other resources and environ-ment of Lake Chad, and to resolve disputes concerning the Lake, in the Lake Chad Basin Commission, established in 1964 by Cameroon, Chad, Niger and Nigeria (the Central African Republic and Sudan also now being members). A border demarcation exercise was carried out under Commission auspices from 1988-92, but the member states have thus far failed to ratify the delimitation treaty over the Lake region.

Mohammed Faal

1.5 Comoros - France (Mayotte)

A dispute between Comoros and France over the island of Mayotte in the Indian Ocean arose when the people of Mayotte opted by a large majority in favour of remaining a French dependency rather than joining the other Comoro islands on their assumption of independence in 1975. Since Mayotte had previously been part of the French overseas territory of the Comoro Islands, the Comoro government has consistently asserted that the island is part of its national territory, whereas the French government has upheld the right of its people to determine their own future status.

The Comoro Islands, situated in the Indian Ocean some 300-500 kilometres (200-320 miles) north-west of Madagascar, consist of four main islands—Grande Comore (also known as Njazidja or Grand Comoro), Anjouan (Nzwani), Mohéli (Mwali) and Mayotte (or Mahoré)—as well as numerous smaller islands, covering 2,236 square kilometres (or 833 square miles). (See Map 3, p. 494.)

The islands were an Arab sultanate until the 1840s, when they became a French protectorate, with Mayotte being declared a French colony in 1843, and the three other islands on July 21, 1912. Between 1914 and 1946 the Comoros were attached to the French government-general of Madagascar but on May 9, 1946, they were granted administrative autonomy. Under a French *loi-cadre* of June 26, 1956, the Comoros were given the status of a French overseas territory with their own Council of Government and with wider powers for their Territorial Assembly. Under a French law promulgated on Dec. 29, 1961, the Comoros were granted full internal autonomy, with the existing Territorial Assembly becoming a Chamber of Deputies, which elected the President of the territorial Council of Government, and with France retaining responsibility for foreign affairs, defence, currency and external economic relations—these arrangements coming into effect in April 1962. In January 1968 the islands were given a new statute, extending the powers of the Chamber of Deputies vis-à-vis the government and the local councils, and also in regard to courts administering both Islamic and territorial law, and giving the Prime Minister sole responsibility for internal security.

The Character of Mayotte

The population of Mayotte (which covers about 375 square kilometres or 145 square miles) has a tradition of independence from the other islands of the archipelago. In 1590 the people of Mayotte refused to recognize the authority of the successor of Sultan Mohamed ben Haissa of Anjouan, who had died, and there followed a four-year war between the two islands. In modern times, their differences with the other islanders have been exacerbated by the fact that they are mainly Christians, whereas Islam predominates elsewhere in the archipelago. At the time of Comoran independence, the island's total population numbered about 40,000 (compared with 430,000 for the Comoros islands as a whole) of whom only 10 per cent spoke French, the main language being Swahili.

Politically the people of Mayotte, in their majority, have followed Mahoré People's Movement (*Mouvement populaire mahorais*, MPM), which was founded in 1958 and which has normally been linked with the centrist current in French metropolitan politics. The Party for the Mahoran Democratic Rally (*Parti pour le rassemblement démocratique des Mahorais*, PRDM), was founded in 1978 to support the return of Mayotte to the Comoros, but has found little support.

In 1961 the MPM strongly criticized the Comoro government for moving the islands' capital from Dzaoudzi (Mayotte) to Moroni (Grande Comore), and from then onwards the movement campaigned for complete integration with France. It held four of 31 seats in the Comoros Chamber of Deputies until 1972, and five seats in the 39-member Chamber elected thereafter. The conflict between the government of the Comoros and the majority of the inhabitants of Mayotte came into the open in 1972, when the majority parties in the Chamber of Deputies joined forces, on Sept. 10, 1972, in order to promote independence for the islands "in friendship and co-operation with France", against the votes of the five members from Mayotte. In consequence, the French government soon found itself in the position of a third party to the conflict.

Unilateral Declaration of Independence by Comoro Government

Following negotiations between the Comoro and French governments, a joint declaration was signed in Paris on June 15, 1973, by Ahmed Abdallah, then Prime Minister of the Comoros, and the French Minister of Overseas Departments and Territories, providing for independence for the Comoro Islands within five years, provided approval of independence was obtained "in consultation with the populations of the archipelago".

The MPM, however, strongly condemned any moves towards a negotiated independence which did not provide for a referendum on an island-by-island basis. Ahmed Abdallah had stated on June 7, 1973, that in the independence referendum the four islands would be consulted collectively, since according to the terms of the law they constituted a single territorial entity. The referendum itself was held on Dec. 22, 1974, when a total of 154,184 votes (or 95.96 per cent of the valid votes) was cast in favour of independence, compared with only 8,854 votes against it. On Mayotte, however, 63 per cent of those who went to the polls were understood to have come out against and about 25 per cent of the 16,000 registered electors did not vote.

After a visit to the Comoros by a French parliamentary mission in March 1975 and the submission of its report, the French National Assembly adopted, on June 26, 1975 (by 291 votes to 184, the latter including the Socialists and Communists), a Comoro Islands Independence Bill. This bill provided for independence for the islands and for the creation, within six months from the promulgation of the act, of a constitutional committee (consisting of representatives of all political groups which had been allowed to take part in the December 1974 referendum campaign, the territory's representatives in the French National Assembly and Senate and the members of the Comoro Chamber of Deputies) to draw up a constitution guaranteeing the democratic freedom of citizens and the political and administrative individuality of the islands comprising the future state. This draft constitution was to be approved "island by island" by a majority of votes cast in a referendum; if one or several of the islands rejected the draft, the committee would have to submit a new text within three months, and if the new draft was not approved by all the islands it would apply only to those islands which had adopted it.

The bill was, on June 27, 1975, rejected as "unacceptable and inapplicable" by Ahmed Abdallah, then President of the Comoro Council of Government, and subsequently also by ministers of his government and by his *Oudzima* (Unity) party, but it was nevertheless approved by the French Senate and enacted on June 30, 1975. A week later the Comoro Chamber of Deputies (on July 6) voted by 33 votes to none (with one member being absent and the five MPM members taking no part in the vote) in favour of immediate independence. The President of the Chamber thereupon announced the islands' independence on the same day, while Ahmed Abdallah subsequently declared "the independence of the Comoros within their colonial borders". On July 7 the Chamber elected Ahmed Abdallah as head of state by 32 votes to one (with the MPM members again taking no part in the vote) and it also constituted itself as the new state's National Assembly and decided to set up a constitutional committee composed of representatives of all parties and charged with drafting a new constitution, which would have to be approved by the electorate as a whole and not "island by island".

Meanwhile, the five MPM deputies telegraphed the French President, placing their island "under the protection of the French Republic" and declaring that the population of Mayotte would refuse to recognize Ahmed Abdallah's government. In a statement issued on July 9, the French government took note of the declaration of independence of deputies from Grande Comore, Anjouan and Mohéli, expressed readiness to engage in talks on the transfer of power, but added that the French government would have to take account of the desire of Mayotte to follow the procedure approved by the French National Assembly involving approval of the accession to independence "island by island".

President Abdallah declared on the same day that France had "shattered the unity" of the new state and that he would call on the International Court of Justice to arbitrate; he also claimed that France wished to retain control of Mayotte in order to establish a military base on it, and he called for the earliest possible withdrawal of French armed forces from the Comoro Islands. In response, the French Secretary of State for Overseas Departments and Territories (Olivier Stirn) stated on July 10 that it was the unilateral declaration of independence by the other three islands which had created the "secession" of Mayotte; that France could grant independence but not unity; and that French law continued to apply on Mayotte.

On July 22, 1975, the French government announced that it had decided to withdraw from Grande Comore the last remaining military detachment of 26 men. However, some 200 soldiers of the French Foreign Legion remained stationed on Mayotte, to which the French government had appointed a representative on July 14. On Aug. 1 pro-French demonstrators entered the French administration offices on Mayotte, asked officials of the newly-established independence government to leave, and installed members of the local council in these offices and also appointed Younoussa Bamana (one of the MPM leaders) as prefect.

Developments following Deposition of President Abdallah

On Aug. 3, 1975, the government of President Abdallah was overthrown by armed supporters of the *Front uni national*, which combined four (pro-independence) opposition parties under the leadership of Ali Soilih. The latter declared on Aug. 3 that he wished to preserve the territorial integrity of the archipelago and to "maintain the ties of friendship and co-operation with France which have been broken by President Abdallah", whom he also accused of having "provoked" the break-up of the Comoros. On Aug. 10 the Revolutionary Council formed by Ali Soilih handed over its powers to a 12-member National Executive Council which included two members from Mayotte, one being a member of the MPM.

On Oct. 27, 1975, the National Executive Council claimed that 2,000 people, who had many years earlier moved from Anjouan to Mayotte, had been expelled

from the latter island by the MPM. According to reports from Mayotte itself, at least 200 people had been forcibly expelled by the MPM, which had threatened to use the French troops stationed on the island against them. The French authorities declared on Oct. 28 that no ships leaving Mayotte would be allowed to carry passengers and that earlier deportations would be the subject of an inquiry.

The following month, on Nov. 21, 1975, a total of 160 men led by Ali Soilih flew from Grande Comore to Mayotte in an attempt to persuade the inhabitants of Mayotte to end their "secession", but they were met by a hostile crowd and withdrew from Mayotte after a few hours. At the same time, the National Executive Council decided to launch a "general mobilization for the cause of national liberation", and on Nov. 26 the Council declared that all property of the French administration on the Comoro Islands was the property of the new state. Two days later, the Comoro authorities announced that all French nationals would be repatriated; the last of some 400 French nationals to leave was the French delegate-general (Henri Beaux) on Dec. 14.

A bill approved by the French government on Oct. 29, 1975, recognized the independence of Grande Comore, Anjouan and Mohéli and provided for a referendum to be held on Mayotte within two months from the promulgation of the act in order to determine that island's future. If the referendum proved in favour of Mayotte's remaining part of the French Republic, a second referendum was to be held within another two months to decide whether Mayotte was to be a French overseas department or an overseas territory. The bill was approved by the National Assembly (in amended form) on Dec. 10, 1975, by 300 votes to 179, and by the Senate on Dec. 31 by 198 votes to 78, and it was enacted on Dec. 31, 1975, when the three islands ceased to be part of the French Republic. During the proceedings, the then left-wing opposition claimed that the bill did not conform to the French constitution and violated the UN Charter, and pointed out that the new state "of four islands" had been admitted to the United Nations (see below).

Comoro-French Relations following Ahmed Abdallah's Return to Power

On the three islands of the independent Comoro state, the Ali Soilih regime attempted to introduce a radical socialist system on the Chinese model, involving the suppression of traditional Islamic practices. However, the regime was overthrown on May 12-13, 1978, in a coup organized with the help of Col. Robert (Bob) Denard, a French mercenary. A new government of the state, henceforth to be known as the Federal and Islamic Republic of the Comoros, was set up by May 24 with the participation of ex-President Ahmed Abdallah as one of two co-presidents of a Political-Military Directory. Later that year, on Oct. 22, Ahmed Abdallah was, as the sole candidate, elected head of state with 99.95 per cent of the votes cast.

In a referendum held on the three islands on Oct. 1, 1978, a new constitution was approved by 99.31 per cent of the 187,124 voters. With regard to the situation of Mayotte, the constitution stated (in Article 44) that "where the regular functioning of the constitutional institutions is interrupted by force the present constitution's provisions relating to these institutions are suspended and the island [concerned] will provisionally exercise on its territory all powers previously held by the Federal Republic". In an order of Sept. 16 it had been stated that the constitution, when approved in the referendum, would be applied to Mayotte ''as soon as the administration of Mayotte returns to the Comoro community".

Between the new government and France a treaty of friendship and co-operation and four co-operation agreements, including a military one, were signed on Nov. 10, 1978. Under the military agreement France was to supply aid in the event of external aggression against the Federal and Islamic Republic of the Comoros and to provide technical assistance in the training of the Comoro Army.

French Government's Position in the Dispute

The French government's attitude to the MPM's demand for continued close links between Mayotte and France was, generally speaking, that France was not opposed to such links but did not consider the granting of the status of a French department to Mayotte as appropriate. Pierre Messmer, then French Minister of State for Overseas Departments and Territories, declared during a visit to Mayotte in January 1972: "Mayotte, which has been French for 130 years, can remain French for as many years as it wishes. The population will be consulted to this end, and on that occasion a referendum will be held island by island".

In the event, however, the proposals approved by the government on Oct. 2, 1974, were for a global referendum on all four islands as one entity, although the government accepted amendments to its proposals, moved in the National Assembly and the Senate in November 1974, to the effect, inter alia, that parliamentary ratification of independence should not be sought until Mayotte had received a measure of regional autonomy as proposed by the Comoro Chamber of Deputies in January 1974.

President Giscard d'Estaing made a strong case for the unity of the Comoros at a press conference on Oct. 24, 1974, as follows: "The population of the Comoros is homogeneous, with a virtually non-existent or very limited element of French descent.

Was it reasonable, confronted with the request for independence presented by the government of the islands, to imagine part of the archipelago becoming independent and one island, however much one may sympathize with its inhabitants, retaining a different status? I think we have to accept contemporary realities. The Comoros are and always have been an entity, and it is natural for them to share a common destiny, even though some of them might have wanted a differ-

ent solution, a fact that naturally touches us although we were not to act in consequence. It is not for us, on the occasion of a territory's independence, to propose to break up the unity of what has always been one Comoro archipelago".

During a visit to all four islands of the Comoros on Feb. 24-26, 1975, Olivier Stirn, then French Secretary of State for Overseas Departments and Territories, described the question of Mayotte as "an internal problem of the Comoros" which could be "settled within the framework of an agreement between the different parties on a draft constitution" which would embody "the maximum respect for a very broad autonomy of the islands". Subsequently, during the debate on the 1975 bill, Olivier Stirn denied that there was any link between the government's position and the maintenance of a naval base on Mayotte (the island's large lagoon offering exceptionally good shelter to ships and serving as a staging post for French naval units in the Indian Ocean.)

The French government's objectives in Mayotte were redefined during a visit to the island on Sept. 10-11, 1980, by Paul Dijoud, Secretary of State for Overseas Departments and Territories since April 1978. He stated that the "irreversible" status of a department was not suitable for the conditions of the island; and that it ought to improve its relations with the rest of the archipelago.

French Legislation and Administrative Measures concerning Mayotte

On Mayotte the first referendum provided for under the French act of Dec. 31, 1975, was held on Feb. 8, 1976, and (according to official results published on March 13) 18,061 voters, or 83.3 per cent of the registered electorate of 21,671, took part in it; there were 17,949 valid votes, of which 17,845 (or 99.4 per cent of the votes cast) were for remaining with France and only 104 for union with the other Comoro islands.

In a second referendum held on April 11, 1976, Mayotte's voters were asked whether they wished the island "to retain its status as an overseas territory" or to abandon that status. As the voters were not expressly asked whether they favoured the status of an overseas department for Mayotte, the MPM had a third ballot paper printed (in addition to the two official ones, one for each alternative) containing the demand for overseas departmental status. The MPM realized that these additional ballot papers would be declared invalid, and it therefore instructed voters in certain areas to use the official ballot paper rejecting territorial status (to ensure the defeat of those who favoured maintenance of the existing territorial status), while massive casting of the unofficial ballot paper would make it clear that there was a majority in favour of departmental status.

In the event, the official result (announced on April 2) showed that of 21,659 registered voters, 17,384 had taken part in the poll; 13,837 papers (or 79.59 per cent) had been blank or invalid; 3,547 (or 20.4 per cent) had been valid; and of those 3,457 (or 97.46 per cent of the valid votes) had been in favour of abandoning the overseas territory status and only 90 (or 2.53 per cent) in favour of maintaining it. Olivier Stirn commented afterwards that the result had shown that Mayotte wished to be given departmental status "now".

Following the introduction of the French franc as legal tender in Mayotte in February 1976, under a bill approved by the French government on Dec. 1, 1976, and passed, with amendments, by the National Assembly on Dec. 14 and by the Senate on Dec. 18, Mayotte was given a special status as a collectivité territoriale. According to this new status Mayotte was administered by a 17-member conseil-général elected by direct universal suffrage; a representative of the French government with the rank of prefect was in charge of national interests (including defence), administrative control and respect for the law; and laws which had applied in the Comoros before their independence remained valid on Mayotte. After at least three years from the date of the bill's promulgation the people of Mayotte would, if the conseil-général demanded it by a two-thirds majority, be consulted on the statute which they wished to adopt. Under another bill passed at the same time a senator from Mayotte was to be elected to the French Senate in 1977.

Hostile Attitude of UN and OAU to French status of Mayotte

The continued adherence of Mayotte to the French Republic was strongly opposed by a majority of the member states of the United Nations and by the Organization of African Unity (OAU). Thus the UN General Assembly unanimously decided on Nov. 12, 1974, with France not taking part in the vote, to approve a recommendation by the UN Security Council to accept the Comoros as a whole as a member of the United Nations. The French permanent representative at the United Nations explained that France did not wish to oppose the Comoros' admission but had to reconcile the need to facilitate the creation of the new state with the procedure required by the French constitution.

Upon an urgent call by Ali Soilih (then head of state of the Comoros) the UN Security Council met on Feb. 4-6, 1976, and eventually formulated a draft resolution declaring the proposed referendum on Mayotte to constitute interference in the Comoros' internal affairs, and calling on France to abandon the referendum and to hold immediate talks with the Comoro government on safeguarding that country's unity and territorial integrity. However, the draft resolution was vetoed by France, which had argued that the principle of self-determination would override that of territorial integrity, while Italy, the United Kingdom and the United States abstained from voting on the resolution.

A commission of inquiry sent to the Comoros in June 1976 by the UN General Assembly reported that the "French occupation" of Mayotte involved "atrocities", including the enforced marriage of women to French soldiers ("to make the island white") and the expulsion of Comoro citizens opposed to Mayotte's "illegal occupation", and that there existed a French military base on the island. The French Ministry of Defence stated, however, that it had no intention of establishing such a base on Mayotte.

On Oct. 21, 1976, the UN General Assembly called, by 102 votes to one (France) with 28 abstentions, on France to withdraw from Mayotte. The resolution condemned the Mayotte referenda as "null and void" and asked France to negotiate with the Comoro government on the integration of Mayotte in the independent Republic of the Comoros. The French permanent representative at the United Nations, however, declared that Mayotte was an integral part of France, that its inhabitants had freely chosen to remain so, and that France had no strategic ambitions in Mayotte, did not wish to recolonize it and would give it an "evolutionary" status.

On Dec. 6, 1979, the UN General Assembly adopted, by 112 votes to one (France) with 23 abstentions, a further resolution reaffirming the sovereignty of the Comoro Islands over Mayotte and calling on the French government to enter into early negotiations with the Comoro government in order to comply with UN resolutions in this matter. However, the French permanent representative rejected the resolution as "impermissible interference in the internal affairs" of his country. On Nov. 28, 1980, the UN General Assembly reaffirmed "the sovereignty of the Islamic Federal Republic of the Comoros over the island of Mayotte" in a resolution adopted by 100 votes to one (France) with 26 abstentions. Virtually identical resolutions were adopted at subsequent Assembly sessions.

After the Comoros had, early in July 1975, been admitted as a member of the OAU, the latter also repeatedly condemned France for its continued "occupation" of Mayotte. On Dec. 15, 1976, the OAU rejected the bill passed by the French National Assembly on Dec. 14 granting Mayotte a special status within the French Republic. On July 8, 1978, however, the OAU Council of Ministers excluded the new Comoro government from current OAU sessions on the grounds that it had been installed with the help of a white mercenary. Nevertheless, the subsequent Assembly of Heads of State and Government of the OAU, held on July 18-22, 1978, again condemned the continuing presence of France on Mayotte.

At its session held in Freetown (Sierra Leone) on July 1-4, 1980, the OAU Assembly of Heads of State and Government decided to send to Moroni a committee of seven members to discuss with the Comorian government "appropriate means likely to speed up the settlement of the question". At its Assembly of Heads of State and Government held on July 28-30, 1986, the OAU again called for Mayotte's return to the Comoros.

December 1979 French Law on Status of Mayotte

In a further law, approved by the French Senate and the National Assembly and promulgated on Dec. 22, 1979, it was laid down that the island of Mayotte was "part of the French Republic and cannot cease to belong to it without the consent of its population"; and that within five years the people of Mayotte would be consulted, following the opinion of their conseil-général, as to whether the statute defined in the law of Dec. 26, 1976, should be maintained, or Mayotte should be made a department, or possibly a different status should be adopted. Meanwhile, the government was authorized to extend by order, before Sept. 30, 1982, existing laws on internal affairs with amendments as deemed necessary. While the then left-wing opposition in the National Assembly abstained from voting on the legislation, the then deputy for Mayotte (Younoussa Bamana) voted against it and again called for departmental status for Mayotte.

Before the Assembly's law commission Paul Dijoud, Secretary of State for Overseas Departments and Territories, had earlier stated that the obstacles to giving departmental status to an island of whose population only 10 per cent spoke French, were the lack of sanitary, social, economic and cultural structures, illiteracy, the specific character of its Muslim culture and customs, and underdevelopment.

French Reaffirmations of Status of Mayotte

On the relations between France and Mayotte the French Minister for External Relations stated in the French National Assembly on April 4, 1983, that the French government's objectives were to promote balanced and harmonious economic development in the Comoro archipelago while taking account of the specific needs of each island, and envisaged the implementation of co-operation projects corresponding to the aspirations of the whole population of the Comoros.

The French Prime Minister, Jacques Chirac, visited Mayotte on Oct. 1, 1986, when he reaffirmed his government's decision to maintain Mayotte's status as a French territory as long as the island's population wished it; he added that he would make this clear to the President of the Comoros in talks with him the same day. Chirac also undertook to carry out in Mayotte a five-year programme to bring the island to the level of development necessary for the status of an overseas department.

Following the assassination of President Abdallah in November 1989, the Comoros Islands were ruled briefly by the French mercenary Bob Denard with members of the former Presidential Guard. However, he was deported, on Dec. 15, under joint French and South African pressure. The Presidential Guard was then replaced by 50 French paratroopers at the request of the Comoros authorities.

Expansion of the Dispute to Anjouan and Mohéli

Relations between France and the Comoros have been further complicated by the growth of separatist movements in the other islands of Anjouan and Mohéli. These separatist movements have demanded independence from rule from Moroni and either return to French rule, or the status of micro-states in association with France. The underlying causes of these secessionist movements have been, firstly, the economic stagnation of the islands compared with the relative economic success of French controlled Mayotte; and secondly, political attempts by the government in Moroni to centralize the administration of the Comoros, which has been seen by some as a bid for political and administrative supremacy by Grande Comore.

In 1997 a secessionist rebellion took place in Anjouan, and in September of that year, when troops were sent from Grande Comore to try and regain control of the island, they were beaten off and a separatist government was set up, led by Abdallah Ibrahim. A locally organized referendum in Anjouan on a separatist constitution, held in October 1997, was reportedly carried by 99.5 per cent of the votes. However, in 1998 splits emerged within the Anjouan political leadership, which led to violent clashes between those favouring union with France and those supporting independence. In June 1999, Abderermane Said Abeid formed a government of national unity on the island.

France has repeatedly stated that it rejects all demands for re-incorporation of the islands of Anjouan and Mohéli under French administration. However, the government in Moroni views France as attempting to undermine Comoros national unity.

The Antananarivo and Fomboni Agreements

In April 1999 the OAU sponsored an inter-island conference in Antananarivo, Madagascar. An agreement was reached to re-unite the islands of the Comoros Republic within one year as the Union of the Comoros Islands, with the presidency to rotate amongst the islands. However, the Anjouan representative refused to sign the agreement. This led to renewed violence, with the Anjouanese community in Moroni being targeted. In response to this chaos Colonel Assoumani Azzali seized power in Moroni in a bloodless coup on April 30, 1999.

The OAU threatened sanctions if Anjouan did not sign the Antananarivo accord by Feb. 1, 2000. The Anjouan leadership responded to this by holding a referendum in January 2000, in which it claimed 94.7 per cent voted for full independence for the island. The OAU refused to accept the result of this referendum, claiming it had been brought about by intimidation, and backed the imposition of sanctions on Anjouan by the Moroni government. The OAU summit in 2000 recommended military action to end Anjouan's secession, and in August 2000 plans were prepared for a naval blockade led by South Africa.

A new round of negotiations was opened following these threats, and a deal was brokered by the OAU and the organisation of the Francophonie (French speaking countries). These negotiations, held in Fomboni, the main town of Mohéli, built on the Antananarivo framework. The Fomboni agreement was finally signed in

February 2001 by the political leaders of Grande Comore, Anjouan and Mohéli. It stipulates the adoption of a new constitution clarifying the relationship between the governments of each island and the central government. The accord offers wide autonomy for each island in return for national unity.

The secessionist movements in Anjouan and Mohéli complicated French relationships with the Comoros as it was believed by many in Moroni that France was somehow implicated in demands for re-integration of these islands into France. In the midst of these difficulties in the Comoros, France passed laws to confirm the status of Mayotte as part of the French Republic.

On Jan 27, 2000, an agreement was signed between the French government and the principal political parties on Mayotte. This agreement fixed common objectives relating to the relationship between the French state and Mayotte. A referendum was held on July 2, 2000, in which the population of Mayotte had an opportunity to vote on this agreement. It was accepted by 72.94 per cent of voters.

In July 2001 a law was passed by the French National Assembly which gave Mayotte the status of a "Departmental Collectivity". This law reaffirmed that Mayotte was a part of the French Republic and could not cease to be so without the consent of its population. The law also contained provisions relating to the economic and social development of the island.

Jane Freedman

1.6 Ethiopia - Eritrea

Ethiopia and Eritrea, two of the ten poorest countries in the world, waged a two-year border war between 1998 and 2000. The conflict erupted on May 6, 1998, when Eritrean troops occupied a town called Badme, which is located in a 400-sq km triangle of rocky scrubland claimed by both countries (see map 4, p. 494).

The outbreak of the border war seemed generally unexpected, including by the Ethiopian Prime Minister, Meles Zenawi. It ended what many outsiders considered to be model relations between the two countries. Previously, the Eritrean People's Liberation Front (EPLF), led by Eritrean President Isaya Afewerki, had stood shoulder to shoulder with Meles Zenawi's Ethiopian People's Revolutionary Democratic Front (EPRDF) party to overthrow the 14-year military dictatorship in Ethiopia of Mengistu Haile Mariam in May 1991. The two sides then reached agreement on Eritrea's independence from Ethiopia, a decision that was overwhelmingly endorsed in a UN-supervised referendum in Eritrea in 1993.

Yet on closer examination, this dispute was not so surprising, nor was it only about a border. The historical and political context of this widely deplored family quarrel between two closely linked regimes in Ethiopia and Eritrea makes this clear.

The Evolution of a Troubled Relationship

Historically, the division between Ethiopia and Eritrea can be traced to the Italian penetration of the Horn of Africa during the latter part of the nineteenth century. In 1889, differences developed between Ethiopia and Italy over the Treaty of Ucciali. Italy interpreted the treaty as providing legal grounds for declaring a protectorate over Ethiopia. But while Emperor Menelik forced Italy to recognize Ethiopian independence after achieving a comprehensive military victory at Adowa in 1896, he did not regain control of Eritrea from Italy.

Eritrea remained an Italian colony until 1941 when British and Commonwealth troops, assisted by Ethiopian resistance, reversed Italy's 1935 conquest of Ethiopia and restored Emperor Haile Selassie to the throne. However, the British retained temporary responsibility for the administration of Eritrea. Because the British permitted a measure of freedom of speech and association previously denied, Eritrea experienced a considerable upsurge of political activity during this period. By 1945, several political parties had emerged in the territory, with a sharp division between those that favoured union with Ethiopia, in the Unionist Party, and those favouring independence, in the Islamic League.

Viewed from Addis Ababa, the stirring of national political activity in Eritrea was a most unwelcome development. For Emperor Haile Selassie, the absence of a direct say in the future of the former Italian colony, and the need to dislodge the British from territory, emphasized the importance of US diplomatic support in the region. To the USA, Ethiopia appeared to be an important bulwark in Africa against the apparent global threat of Soviet communism.

The Cold War Context

The convergence of Ethiopian and US interests had a significant impact on the post-World War II settlement of Eritrea. After the Four Powers had failed to reach any agreement on Eritrea's future, the issue was placed in the hands of the UN General Assembly. Eventually, and after some lobbying by Washington, UN Resolution 390 A (V) stipulated that Eritrea was to be an autonomous unit federated with Ethiopia under the sovereignty of the Ethiopian Crown.

In 1952, the implementation of the UN resolution on Eritrea paved the way for a strategic alliance between Ethiopia and the USA. An agreement signed in May 1953 gave Washington a 25-year lease on a communications station near Asmara, Eritrea. This station, known as Kagnew, became the "linchpin" in the Ethiopian-American relationship. John Foster Dulles, then US Secretary of State, made clear that such strategic considerations took precedence over local rights:

"From the point of view of justice, the opinion of the Eritrean people must receive consideration. Nevertheless, the strategic interests of the United States in the Red Sea basin and considerations of security and world peace make it necessary that the country has to be linked with our ally, Ethiopia".

Over the next two decades, Addis Ababa received 20 per cent of all US economic aid ($350 million) and 50 per cent of all US military aid to black Africa ($278.6 million). Certainly, Emperor Haile Selassie never made any secret of his contempt for the UN-sponsored federation arrangement. His representative in Eritrea, Andargachew Mesai, declared on March 22, 1955, that "there are no internal or external affairs, as far as the Office of His Imperial Majesty's Representative is concerned, and there will be none in the future". In 1952, the Emperor suspended the Eritrean constitution and acquired the power to veto the decision of the Eritrean Assembly. In 1956, the Eritrean National Assembly was suspended. A year later, the locally spoken languages of Tigrinya and Arabic were replaced by Amharic as the official language. In 1959, the Eritrean flag was finally removed. Finally, in 1962, Addis Ababa terminated the federal arrangement and annexed Eritrea. The fact that Ethiopia's action violated the provision specifying that only the UN General Assembly had the power to change the status of the Federal Act, was apparently not deemed sufficient reason for objection by either the USA or the Soviet Union.

The Eritrean Rebellion

In 1959, an underground organization, the Eritrean Liberation Movement (ELM), was formed to resist absorption by Addis Ababa. By 1961, a new organization, the Eritrean Liberation Front (ELF), began military operations against Ethiopian forces in the territory. Thanks to Syrian and indirect Soviet support, the ELF forces between 1964 and 1967 grew from a few hundred with antiquated weapons to about 2,000 with relatively modern weapons.

While the Eritrean rebellion was hampered by the political impact of the Six Day War in 1967 and internal divisions in the early 1970s, it continued to widen in the last years of Emperor Haile Selassie's rule. Rather than engage in conventional military operations which they could not win, the ELF resorted to hit and run tactics. In August 1969, in two separate ambushes, the ELF killed 113 soldiers in the Massawa area. Then, on Nov. 21, 1970, the commander of the Ethiopian Second Division, General Teshome Erghetu, was assassinated during an inspection visit to the province. A State of Emergency was declared on Dec. 17, 1970, thus placing much of Eritrea under martial law.

Outside Ethiopia, the ELF initiated a series of bombings and hijackings aimed at Ethiopian Airlines (EAL). On March 11, 1969, the ELF bombed and badly damaged an EAL jet at Frankfurt airport, West Germany. On June 18, 1969, the ELF struck again at Karachi airport, badly damaging a second jet.

Similarly, on Sept. 13, 1969, three ELF members hijacked an EAL jet to Aden, interrupting an Addis Ababa-Djibouti flight. Angered by the publicity generated through these incidents, the Ethiopian government blamed the "Syrian Liberation Front of Eritrea" for the terrorist acts.

Despite such bellicose rhetoric, the worsening security situation in Eritrea spurred Emperor Haile Selassie into efforts to contain rising external support for the rebels. In October 1973, Addis Ababa attempted to make a virtue out of necessity by announcing the phasing out of the US communications station at Kagnew. A combination of rapid advances in satellite communications technology and the availability of an alternative facility at Diego Garcia in the Indian Ocean effectively ended America's need for Kagnew. At the same time, the Emperor severed diplomatic relations with Israel following the Yom Kippur war. That move officially ended what had been an extremely close relationship. It was, amongst other things, a desperate attempt to improve relations with those Arab states sympathetic to Eritrean nationalism.

The Ethiopian revolution of 1974, in which Haile Selassie was overthrown, brought a brief lull in hostilities in Eritrea. But once it became clear that the new revolutionary government in Addis Ababa was as determined as the former regime to hang on to this territory, the Eritrean conflict escalated. In November 1974, the Dergue (the Amharic term for the Co-ordinating Committee of the Armed Forces) dispatched an extra 5,000 troops to the province in a renewed attempt to enforce a military solution. The two main Eritrean movements, the ELF, and its offshoot, the Eritrean People's Liberation Front (EPLF), boosted by a new influx of arms from states like Saudi Arabia, Egypt, Sudan and Kuwait, responded in kind and launched a joint offensive on Asmara, the provincial capital of Eritrea.

By the spring of 1976, the Dergue adopted a "carrot and stick" approach towards the Eritrean insurrection. The "carrot" was a nine-point peace plan, announced on May 16, 1976. The plan offered, amongst other things, "immediate autonomy" to Eritrea and the lifting of the state of emergency that was in force. The "stick" was the mobilization of a poorly trained and ill-equipped 40,000 Ethiopian peasant militia to enforce the new plan. But, in what was a major disaster for Addis Ababa's peace initiative, this rag-tag militia was decimated before it even entered Eritrea. The rebels made it clear they would accept nothing short of self-determination for the province.

From mid-1976, practically all of the Ethiopian garrisons in Eritrea found themselves under active siege. On Jan. 5, 1977, Karora became the first Eritrean town to be captured by the EPLF. About a month later, Um Hager fell to the ELF. Then, on March 23, 1977, the EPLF, for the first time, extended nationalist control over a district capital, Nacfa, in the Sahel province.

Meanwhile, the Soviet Union distanced itself from "separatist cliques" in Eritrea. Conscious of a new opportunity to replace the United States as Ethiopia's main external ally, Moscow sought to advance in March 1977 a Marxist-Leninist confederation consisting of Ethiopia, Somalia, South Yemen and Djibouti. Under this plan, Eritrea (and the Ogaden, for which see Section 1.7) would be granted the status of autonomous regions within the existing border arrangements of Ethiopia. But this diplomatic initiative failed. President Siad of Somalia argued that a federation was fruitless unless all peoples within it had been granted the right to national self-determination, including the Eritreans. The Soviets disagreed. On May 5, 1977, Moscow completed its displacement of the USA in Ethiopia by signing a declaration of friendship and cooperation with Addis Ababa.

Soviet support for Ethiopia's territorial integrity placed it in direct opposition to its old allies in Somalia and in the Eritrean liberation movements. In November 1977, the USSR launched a massive military intervention to thwart a Somali attempt to "liberate" the Ogaden. Then, following the Somali defeat in March 1978, the USSR turned its attention to backing Mengistu's renewed effort to destroy the Eritrean rebels. Between 1978 and 1987, the Soviets supplied Addis Ababa with more than $7 billion in military aid and transformed the Ethiopian military into the largest and best equipped in sub-Saharan Africa. But despite periodic "final" offensives, Mengistu's army failed to quell the EPLF guerrilla threat outside the major urban centres in Eritrea.

The End of the Cold War—Eritrean Independence

Shortly after becoming Soviet leader in March 1985, Mikhail Gorbachev urged Mengistu to embrace "new political thinking" in his policy toward Eritrea. He also made it clear that Moscow was not prepared to underwrite Mengistu's burgeoning military requirements indefinitely. In 1988, amid signs of growing Soviet disquiet, Mengistu's army suffered reverses on the battlefield that effectively marked the beginning of the end for Ethiopian control of Eritrea. From March 17-19, 1988, the EPLF routed the Ethiopians at Afabet, the main garrison for the country's crack troops. Altogether, the EPLF put out of action three Ethiopian divisions (18,000 troops) and captured an enormous quantity of Soviet arms. Moreover, for the first time since the start of Soviet involvement, the EPLF captured three Soviet officers.

From a Soviet standpoint, the need for a negotiated settlement to the Ethiopian–Eritrean conflict had become urgent. New military cooperation between the Ethiopian People's Revolutionary Democratic Front (EPRDF), a broad coalition of resistance groups formed in May 1988, and the EPLF strengthened the rebel challenge. At the same time, an abortive coup attempt in May 1989 robbed Mengistu of his entire military high command, most of whom were summarily executed for their part in the plot. Nevertheless, Mengistu ruled out the possibility of discussing Eritrean independence with rebel groups.

Meanwhile, the EPRDF and EPLF made spectacular gains as the demoralized Ethiopian army fell apart. In February 1990, Mengistu's regime lost control of the key Red Sea port of Massawa to the EPLF and then suffered a succession of defeats by the EPRDF in early 1991 in provinces like Gojjam, Gondar and Wollo. In May 1991, barely six months after Gorbachev had cut off all military aid to Ethiopia, the Mengistu regime collapsed.

Following Mengistu's downfall, it was left to the USA to play a crucial role in facilitating the transition arrangements in Ethiopia and Eritrea. At US-brokered peace talks in London, Herman Cohen, the US Assistant Secretary of State for African affairs, endorsed the EPRDF takeover of central government in Addis Ababa and also, in a sudden departure from previous US policy, announced Washington's support for an EPLF proposal concerning a UN-supervised referendum to decide the issue of Eritrean independence. The referendum, which took place between April 23-25, 1993, saw an overwhelming endorsement for Eritrean independence, confirmed in May with the country's entry into the UN.

From Friendship to War

The relationship between the two countries remained a cordial one for five years. Both regimes had emerged from armed insurgent movements, the EPRDF and EPLF, which for many years were comrades in arms against the Mengistu regime. They shared a similar mix of ethno-regionalist–nationalist ideology and both their political elites hailed from the same ethno-linguistic group, the Tigrinya-speakers of northern Ethiopia and southern Eritrea. Indeed, the leaders of the two states, Meles Zenawi and Isaya Afewerki, were actually linked by distant family ties.

In Ethiopia, President Meles and members of his transitional government pledged to oversee the formation of a multi-party democracy. The election for a 547-member constituent assembly was held in June 1994, and this assembly adopted the constitution of the Federal Democratic Republic of Ethiopia in December. The elections for Ethiopia's first popularly elected national parliament and regional legislatures were held in May and June 1995. Most opposition parties chose to boycott these elections. As a consequence, the EPRDF won a landslide victory and an EPRDF-led government under Prime Minister Meles Zenawi took office in August 1995.

Meanwhile, the EPLF converted itself from a national liberation movement into a political party, taking the designation the People's Front for Democracy and Justice (PFDJ) in February 1994. Plans were also made for an eventual multi-party system and general elections. In the interim, the transitional National Assembly, dominated by the Central Committee of the PFDJ, elected Isaya Afewerki as President of Eritrea.

Economically, Ethiopia and Eritrea adopted broadly complementary approaches to national development. These were oriented towards liberal market-economy reforms and closer integration with the international community, especially the West. The Addis Ababa government opened itself up to international loans while continuing to rely on the Eritrean ports of Assab and Massawa for its foreign trade. For its part, Eritrea concentrated on export-led growth and Ethiopia loomed large in this strategy. In 1996, for example, 65% of Eritrean exports were destined for Ethiopia.

With regard to international relations, both countries maintained close links with the USA and received substantial aid from Washington and the Western donor community generally. Meles Zenawi and Isaya Afewerki were hailed as pragmatic "new-style" African leaders who had a crucial role to play in maintaining stability in the otherwise volatile Horn of Africa region. However, the new boundary between Ethiopia and Eritrea was left vague after 1991. The old Italian colonial border of Eritrea, established in 1890, was taken as a point of departure, with the proviso that a final agreement would have to be achieved through further bilateral discussions. To this end, an Ethiopian-Eritrean border commission continued to work on this issue right up to the sudden outbreak of hostilities.

On May 6, 1998, Eritrean troops took over the remote town of Badme, situated southwest of Asmara. Ethiopia demanded an immediate withdrawal, but the Eritrean government claimed it was simply occupying its sovereign territory. Each side accused the other of invasion. Fighting quickly spread from Badme to fronts along the common border at Zalambessa and Burie, and developed into a full-scale war.

"Bewildering", "absurd" and "bizarre" were among the descriptions used by diplomats to characterize the conflict. In any event, the international community struggled to advance a peace process. Despite almost immediate appeals from the Organization of African Unity (OAU) and the UN Security Council, as well as a joint US-Rwandan peace plan, this brutal border war lasted for two years. It resulted in the deaths of more than 70,000 people and hundreds of thousands of citizens on both sides were either displaced or forced to flee across the borders.

Peace Agreement

In June 2000, Ethiopia and Eritrea signed a cessation of hostilities agreement brokered by Algeria, the OAU and the USA. Six months later, the two sides signed a comprehensive peace agreement in Algiers which provided, inter alia, for a permanent end to hostilities and the establishment of an independent commission to decide the border question. The June accord paved the way, in September 2000, for establishing a UN peacekeeping force, the UN Mission in Ethiopia and Eritrea (UNMEE) to monitor the ceasefire and assist in ensuring observance of security commitments. UNMEE has consisted of some 4,200 military personnel from 40 countries. Since the deployment of UNMEE, the armed forces of Ethiopia and Eritrea have been separated by a 25-kilometre wide Temporary Security Zone

(TSZ) along the disputed border. That arrangement remains in place at the time of writing because of the periodic renewal of UNMEE's mandate by the UN. It should be added that the December 2000 ceasefire has held, and there has been a return of substantial numbers of people displaced by the border conflict.

While both Ethiopia and Eritrea insist they will not instigate a resumption of fighting, there is little evidence to suggest that the underlying grievances are close to being resolved. Under the terms of the Algiers accord, a five-member Independent Boundary Commission issued a "final and binding" decision on April 13, 2002, stating where the border would fall. Both sides gained and lost territory, but the wrangling has centred on the Commission's ruling that the symbolic town of Badme lies in Eritrea. The Commission's ruling was reaffirmed in March 2003. In late May 2003, Ethiopian Prime Minister Meles Zenawi said the border ruling on Badme was "wrong and unjust", and called for changes to the decision. But the Eritrean government dismissed any notion of dialogue on the border ruling as "unthinkable". It also warned of "consequences" if Ethiopia did not abide by the Badme ruling. Since Badme was the starting point of the two-year war between the two countries, the perception seems to be that whichever country is awarded Badme will be seen as having "won" the war. To date, the two sides have not agreed to a final demarcation of the border.

It must be emphasized that the border conflict has been symptomatic of much deeper sources of tension in the Ethiopian-Eritrean relationship. First, apart from periods of Italian and British administration, Ethiopia and Eritrea had little tradition of being separate entities before 1991. Ethnically, culturally, and historically much of what is now known as Eritrea was administered from Ethiopia. There was, therefore, considerable irritation in Addis Ababa when Eritrea in November 1997 introduced its own currency, the nafka, to replace the birr, which it had shared with Ethiopia until that time. That decision, according to the Eritrean government, was made in the interests of the national economy. But in practice it severely complicated cross-border trade arrangements and prompted Addis Ababa not only to insist that all bilateral trade with Eritrea should be conducted in hard currency, but also to divert much of its trade to the port of Djibouti. These developments were mutually damaging, in economic terms, and increased unemployment in both countries.

Second, geopolitical rivalry in the Horn of Africa has played a part in fuelling tension. As the largest state in the region, Ethiopia is conscious that it is now landlocked and cut off from the Red Sea by tiny Eritrea. On the other hand, Isaya's government, caught up in several other territorial conflicts with its neighbours, including Djibouti and the Sudan, has been determined that this fledgling state will not be reduced to satellite status by its much larger neighbour. At the same time, both countries, though extremely poor, have spent heavily on defence, supplementing the arms acquired from Mengistu's well-stocked armouries, to support these national aspirations.

Third, domestic politics have contributed to the Ethiopian-Eritrean stand-off. Quasi-democratization in both countries created environments in which political elites were able to bolster their popular legitimacy by utilizing nationalist and aggressive foreign policy rhetoric. The leadership of Isaya Afewerki in Eritrea evidently believed that a rapid escalation of the border clash to full-scale war would undermine domestic popular support and topple the EPRDF regime. But war escalation had precisely the opposite effect. It provided an ideal opportunity for Meles Zenawi, a northerner from Tigre, to counter criticisms from some members of the Amhara community that his government had not been robust enough in defending the national interest. By launching massive Ethiopian retaliation to the Eritrean military move in Badme, Meles was able to parade his nationalist credentials and strengthen the EPRDF's position domestically. The border war thus served nation- and state-building goals in both countries.

Relations between Ethiopia and Eritrea have been practically non-existent since they signed the December 2000 peace deal officially ending their two-year border conflict. While a return to large-scale war between the two countries is unlikely, ongoing tensions and unresolved underlying issues are likely to require the continued presence of UN peacekeepers for, at least, the immediate future. In July 2003, Addis Ababa launched a strategy of "peaceful containment" of Eritrea while Asmara retorted that this new policy was "tantamount to declaring aggression".

Nevertheless, the new US-led global war against terrorism may yet increase the pressures for a thaw in Ethiopian-Eritrean relations. Given their location in the Horn of Africa, both Ethiopia and Eritrea play a strategic role in US thinking. US Defence Secretary, Donald Rumsfeld, visited Ethiopia and Eritrea in December 2002, and US military officials have made a number of visits for talks with Prime Minister Meles Zenawi and President Isayas Aferwerki. The desire to secure US bases (and the perceived economic and political benefits that flow from such facilities) might be a powerful incentive for Ethiopia and Eritrea to improve their troubled relationship.

Robert Patman

1.7 Ethiopia - Somalia

The status of the Ogaden region, encompassing Ethiopia's eastern provinces of Hararghe, Bale and Sidamo, has been the subject of a long-standing dispute between Ethiopia and neighbouring Somalia. This border dispute pre-dates Somalia's independence in 1960. The Somalis generally refer to the area as Western Somalia, and regard it as a Somali-inhabited region under foreign (Ethiopian) domination where the principle of self-determination has yet to be applied.

The Ogaden is a geographical metaphor rather than a clearly demarcated political entity (see Map 5, p. 495). It has no precise boundaries but is often thought to comprise the Ogaden desert and a sub-area known as the Haud or Reserve region, located on the southern side of the border of former British Somaliland. Inasmuch as the disputed area can be defined, it is an area inhabited by nomadic pastoral peoples that are predominately ethnic Somalis. Their population has been variously estimated at between one and three million.

Historically, Somali irredentist claims are grounded in the idea that the Somali tribes of the Horn of Africa constituted one political system before the colonial division of that territory in the late 19th century. Prior to 1886, according to the Somali view, effective Ethiopian sovereignty extended no further eastward than the line of the Awash river. That is to say, Ethiopian sovereignty fell short of the towns of Diredawa, Harar and Jijiga and the whole of the now-disputed area. It was only in the last part of the 19th century, as the European powers established their authority over what became British and Italian Somaliland, that the Ethiopian empire extended its control eastwards, to the limits codified in subsequent agreements with the British and Italians (see below).

Origins of the Ogaden Dispute

The emergence of the Ogaden dispute was broadly linked to the expansion of European influence in the Horn of Africa in the second half of the 19th century. In particular, the arrival of the British served to re-define the geopolitics of the region. In 1868 a British expeditionary force defeated Ethiopia in the Battle of Magdala. At the same time, the British exerted control over Egypt, a long-standing player in the Horn. In 1875, London purchased a controlling share in the Suez Canal Company and within seven years consolidated its dominance of Egypt though a military occupation of that country. Then, in a series of treaties concluded with local Somali tribes in 1884-86, the British established a protectorate on the northern Somali coast.

Meanwhile, Tsarist Russia, concerned by the European penetration of the area, supported Ethiopian nationalism as a way of undermining rival powers in the Horn. Indeed, Russian military aid not only helped Ethiopia to resist foreign encroachment—in 1896, Emperor Menelik's army achieved an historic victory over the Italians at Adowa—but also facilitated a significant expansion of the Ethiopian empire. In 1887 Ethiopia annexed Harar, following the Egyptian withdrawal, and then absorbed the Somali-populated lands of the Haud and the Ogaden, both of which were officially under British protection. By 1897, Ethiopia's new frontiers were codified, at least theoretically, through treaties with Britain and Italy. These treaties, however, were signed without the consent of the Somali clansman (who had earlier placed themselves under British protection) and left a legacy of confusion for future Ethiopian-Somali relations.

The treaty concluded between Britain and Ethiopia on May 14, 1897, established the southern boundary of British Somaliland. This was subsequently demarcated by an Anglo-Ethiopian boundary commission between 1932 and 1935. The treaty stipulated that certain Somali tribespeople would come under Ethiopian jurisdiction. In Annex I of the 1897 treaty, the British envoy required and obtained from the Ethiopian Emperor a recognition that "in the event of a possible occupation by Ethiopia of territories inhabited by tribes who have formerly accepted and enjoyed British protection in the districts excluded from the British protectorate…it will be your special care that these tribes receive equitable treatment and are thus no losers by this transfer of suzerainty". In Annex III, both sides agreed that "the tribes occupying either side of the line shall have the right to use the grazing grounds on the other side, but during their migrations it is understood that they shall be subject to the jurisdiction of the territorial authority". These treaty-based grazing rights were in existence until Somalia's independence in 1960.

As for the border between Ethiopia and Italian Somaliland, neither the Ethiopian Treaty of 1897 or the Ethiopian-Italian Convention of 1908 succeeded in defining its exact location. Essentially, the Ethiopians maintained that a frontier line agreed in negotiations in 1897 between Emperor Menelek and the Italian representative, Maj. Nerazzini, ran more or less parallel with the coast and 140 miles (225 kilometres) from it, to a tripoint with British Somaliland. The Ethiopian contention was that the southern part of this frontier (from Dolo to the Uebi Scebeli river) was then pushed northward in favour of Italy in return for the payment of 3,000,000 lire, as stipulated in an Additional Act to the 1908 treaty. The Italian interpretation was that the Menelek-Nerazzini agreement in 1897 (to which the 1908 treaty refers only as "the line accepted by the Italian government in 1897") covered only the frontier north of the Uebi Scebeli river and that this frontier ran at a distance of some 180 miles (290 kilometres) from the coast.

This indeterminacy, temporarily superseded by the Italian conquest of Ethiopia in 1935, introduced serious strains into the British-Ethiopian relationship after the British defeated the Italians in 1941 and took control of the Horn of Africa. The British restored Emperor Haile Selassie to his throne in Ethiopia, but retained temporary responsibility for the administration of the Reserved Area and the Ogaden, under the terms of an Anglo-Ethiopian treaty concluded in December 1944. However, this was not an ideal arrangement as far as Addis Ababa was concerned.

Many of the territories under British military administration, the Haud, the Ogaden and the former Italian colonies, Italian Somaliland and Eritrea, experienced a dramatic upswing in political activity during the war years. This was possible because the British permitted a measure of freedom of speech and association, previously denied. Moreover, in the Somali territories, the British administration took an explicit pro-Somali stand. The then British Foreign Secretary, Ernest Bevin, suggested in 1948 the creation in these territories of a unified Somali nation as a United Nations trust territory under British administration. However, the idea failed to win international support and was strongly opposed by Ethiopia. Suspicious of British intentions in the region, Emperor Haile Selassie sought new allies.

In 1944, the United States and Ethiopia established full diplomatic relations. Within months, an American citizen, John Spencer, was appointed as Emperor Haile Selassie's foreign policy adviser. And despite the British presence in the Ogaden, the first concession for oil exploration there was granted to a US company, Sinclair. The Ethiopian-American connection grew out of mutual need. For the Emperor, the absence of a direct say in the settlement of the old Italian colonies, and the need to dislodge the British from the Ogaden and the Haud, made Washington the most likely guardian of its local interests. To the United States, Ethiopia appeared to be an important buffer in Africa against the perceived global threat of Soviet communism.

The convergence of Ethiopian and US interests had a profound effect on the post-war situation in the Horn of Africa. In September 1948, Britain bowed to joint Ethiopian-US pressure and withdrew from the Ogaden. Amongst other things, Emperor Haile Selassie skilfully exploited Washington's economic interest in the area to pressurize Britain. Without the support of its closest ally, and lacking the financial wherewithal to continue the military occupation, Britain decided to leave despite the known strength of Somali feeling on the matter. The president of the Somali Youth League, formed in 1947, had already formulated a programme of Somali reunification that was to include the Ogaden. When the British decision to "return" the territory was announced, a riot ensued in which 25 Somalis lost their lives. The eventual transfer of the territory was eased through a British disbursement of £91,000 amongst the Ogaden clansmen.

British military administration over the former Italian Somaliland was ended in 1950 when Italy took over the administration of what had become the UN Trust Territory of Somaliland. Four years later, Britain decided to end its administration in the Haud and Reserve Areas, and return these vital grazing lands to Ethiopian control. However, when the Anglo-Ethiopian agreement of Nov. 29, 1954, became public knowledge, there was an immediate and widespread Somali outcry. A belated British attempt to redress the situation by buying back the disputed territory failed. Thereafter Somali unrest in the Ogaden intensified. Ethiopian tax-collecting forays were often resisted, sometimes forcibly, and subsequent Ethiopian attempts to make Somali nomads accept Ethiopian citizenship only heightened anti-Ethiopian feeling.

The situation was not helped by the failure of Ethiopia and the former Italian Somaliland to reach agreement on their mutual frontier which, in practice, remained the provisional administration line left by the British in that territory in 1950. After the failure of direct negotiations, the UN General Assembly recommended arbitration in 1957. However, neither Ethiopia nor Italy, representing the former Italian Somaliland territory, could agree on an "independent" person to draw up the tribunal's terms of reference. Eventually, on the initiative of the UN, Trygve Lie was appointed. He failed, though, to secure any agreement, and no resolution was passed on the eastern frontier before Somalia's independence.

The Parameters of the Ethiopian-Somali Dispute

1960 was an important year for the Ogaden dispute. It marked the end of a period of relative tranquillity and the beginning of a phase dominated by strife and tension. The catalyst in this transformation was the birth of an independent Somalia. The country was formed on July 1, 1960, through the unification of the former British Somaliland Protectorate and the former Italian Trust Territory. Yet such independence did not fully correspond to the aspirations of Somali nationalism. Over one million Somalis, sharing a common language, a common religion, a common culture and a common understanding of themselves as a political community, were left outside the borders of the new state. These Somalis lived in three contiguous regions: French Somaliland (later to become Djibouti), the Northern Frontier District of Kenya and the Ogaden region of Ethiopia. (See also Section 1.11 on the related dispute between Kenya and Somalia.)

From the very beginning of its existence, Somalia refused to accept the existing borders as valid. These were seen as artificial and arbitrary, and simply a legacy of the colonial era. The task thus confronting the new Republic in 1960 was to expand the boundaries of the state so that they coincided with those of the "nation". This fundamental goal was enshrined both in the new state's constitution (which declared that: "The Somali Republic shall promote, by legal and peaceful means, the union of Somali territories") and a five-pointed star flag, with each point representing one of the segments into which the colonial powers had divided Somalia.

According to the Somali perspective, the Ogaden area or "Western Somalia" (like French Somaliland and the Northern Frontier District of Kenya) still had not been decolonized. The fact that the colonial conquest was not by a European power but by an African one, Ethiopia, made, in the Somali view, no difference. The first government of Somalia, therefore, saw itself as a champion of the right of self-determination for the people of the Ogaden.

However, if the realization of the Somali nation-state depended on a revision of existing frontiers, it was equally true that the survival of the Ethiopian state was seen to depend on their preservation. Ethiopia believed that the Ogaden area was an integral part of its territory and saw the Somali stance as an unwarranted interference in its internal affairs. The Ethiopians insisted that Somalia must accept the territorial boundaries that existed at the time of its independence in 1960. They considered that the northern sector of the boundary was clearly delineated by the Anglo-Ethiopian treaty of 1897. (However, the Ethiopian government took the position in 1960 that trans-border grazing rights provided by the 1897 treaty no longer applied after Somalia became independent.) With regard to the southern sector of the boundary, the Ethiopians argued that this had been largely defined by the 1908 treaty between Ethiopia and Italy.

More generally, as a multi-ethnic state, Ethiopia feared that if the right to secede were granted in the Ogaden, such a grant would stimulate secessionist demands from other groups and thus culminate in the disintegration of the state itself. In other words, Ethiopian and Somali approaches to the border question were irreconcilable. There was little or no room for compromise. Somali self-determination could only be exercised at the expense of Ethiopian territorial integrity and vice versa.

The Cold War and the Escalation of the Ogaden Dispute

Fighting in the border region erupted almost immediately after Somali independence. On Jan. 1, 1961, in the confused aftermath of an abortive coup in Ethiopia, there was a brutal clash between armed Somali tribesmen and Ethiopian soldiers in Damot. In what was a portent for future clashes, the US-equipped and US-trained Ethiopian forces emerged triumphant. This, however, did not stop the Somali President, Aden Abdullah Osman, from threatening war if Ethiopian mistreatment of indigenous Somalis did not cease. For its part, Ethiopia demanded an end to armed Somali infiltration into the Ogaden.

In November 1963, Somalia refused a tripartite offer of Western military assistance, valued at US$10 million and, instead, accepted Soviet military aid, said to be worth US$35 million. While this military aid package was a modest deal by Soviet standards, it was a substantial one in local terms: it provided for the expansion of the Somali army from 2,000 to 10,000 and included an assortment of MiG-15 aircraft and T-34 tanks.

The Soviet-Somali arms deal increased tensions in Ethiopian-Somali relations. In February 1964, full-scale fighting broke out between Ethiopia and Somalia in the Ogaden border area. The border war continued until March 30, 1964, when both Ethiopia and Somalia agreed to respect a cease-fire resolution adopted by the Organization of African Unity (OAU). After seeing its army virtually routed by the larger Ethiopian forces, Somalia experienced a major diplomatic reverse. In July 1964, a Tanzanian resolution at the OAU Summit in Cairo, to reaffirm the principle concerning the preservation of the existing territorial frontiers at independence, was passed by the overwhelming majority of the Heads of State present.

While Somalia declared it did not feel bound by the resolution, it was undoubtedly a set-back for any hopes of pressing Somali territorial claims through peaceful means. In March 1965, for instance, a Somali request for the dispatch of an OAU "fact-finding commission" to examine the causes of the unrest in the Ogaden was ignored after Ethiopia objected. Between 1964 and 1966, a number of armed skirmishes involving Ethiopian forces and Ogaden nomads were reported.

Faced with the fact that a policy of confrontation had done little to realize the pan-Somali goal, the new Somali government of President Abdirashid Ali Shermarke and Prime Minister Mohammed Ibrahim Egal, formed in July 1967, decided to pursue a policy of dialogue with Ethiopia. According to a communiqué published simultaneously in Addis Ababa and Mogadishu on Sept. 22, 1967, both countries agreed to the normalization of diplomatic relations; the establishment of an Ethiopian-Somali joint military commission to examine complaints by either side; and to seek to remove the "conditions which affect adversely relations between the two countries".

Détente was achieved, however, without any progress on the major issues originally causing the border dispute. Ethiopia interpreted the new agreements as fully consistent with the preservation of its territorial integrity. Somalia, on the other hand, rationalized the détente strategy in terms of economic expediency and vigorously denied there had been any compromise on the principle of Somali unification. Moreover, political changes in Somalia and Ethiopia soon exposed the limitations of the détente strategy. A military coup on Oct. 21, 1969, brought Major-General Siad Barre to power and within a year Somalia renamed itself the Somali Democratic Republic, and pledged its allegiance to "scientific socialism". Relations between Mogadishu and the USSR expanded rapidly. On July 11, 1974, the two countries signed a twenty-year Treaty of Friendship and Co-operation. Between 1974 and 1976, Soviet largesse transformed little Somalia into the fourth most heavily armed state in black Africa after Nigeria, Zaire and Ethiopia. In addition, Somalia joined the Arab League in 1974 and also built good relations with Communist China during this period.

While the new military regime in Somalia pledged to continue the policy of détente with Ethiopia, it also declared that it regarded "the Somali people's right to self-determination as a sacred right". Border tensions increased with the announcement in December 1972 that a US oil company, Tenneco, had discovered substantial quantities of natural gas in the Bale region of the Ogaden. In May 1973, the Ethiopian Foreign Minister vigorously rejected a Somali call at the OAU Council of Ministers Summit for a solution of the "territorial dispute" on the grounds that no such dispute existed. An OAU "good offices" committee set up in 1973 failed to reconcile Ethiopia and Somalia.

Developments in Somalia, especially the massive Soviet-backed military build up, were a source of deep concern in Addis Ababa. That concern did not diminish with the military overthrow of Emperor Haile Selassie's regime in 1974. The new military regime in Addis Ababa, known as the Dergue, showed itself no less intent than had its imperial predecessor on retaining possession of the Ogaden, especially when it found itself courted by the Soviet Union.

Anxious to replace the USA as Ethiopia's main external ally, the Kremlin advanced a proposal in March 1977 to establish a Marxist-Leninist confederation of Ethiopia, Somalia, Djibouti and South Yemen. It also promised to underwrite the scheme economically and militarily. Under this plan, the Ogaden, after minor frontier rectifications in the Hararghe province, would be granted the status of autonomous region with the existing border arrangements. While the new Ethiopian leader, Colonel Mengistu Haile Mariam, welcomed what was essentially a status quo solution, President Siad angrily rebuffed the Soviet initiative. He argued that an ideological federation was fruitless unless all peoples within it had been granted the right to national self-determination. According to Siad, the Ogaden or "Western Somalia" was entitled to the option of joining as an independent unit or as part of Somalia.

Meanwhile, the USSR completed its displacement of the USA in Ethiopia. In April 1977, the Dergue announced the closure of the Kagnew Communications Station in Asmara and other US facilities. On May 5, 1977, Mengistu signed a declaration in Moscow on friendship and cooperation, and signed a major arms deal worth US$400 million. The arms agreement represented a turning point in Soviet-Somali relations. Siad described the delivery of Soviet arms to Addis Ababa as a "danger" and openly questioned Soviet advice to be patient on the "lost lands".

On July 23, 1977, the Somali army launched a general offensive in the Ogaden in support of Western Somali Liberation Front (WSLF) insurgents. Between July and September 1977, the Somali campaign in the Ogaden was extremely successful. By mid-September 1977, the Somali side had gained control, even by Addis Ababa's own admission, of 90 per cent of the disputed area. The most telling blow came on Sept. 13 when the Somalis overran Jijiga, Ethiopia's main tank and radar base and gateway to Dire Dawa and Harar, two strategic towns in the Hararghe region.

However, if Somalia was initially successful on the battlefield, the opposite was true on the diplomatic front. In August 1977, the eight-nation OAU mediation committee passed a resolution reaffirming the inviolability of African frontiers and, in effect, upholding the Ethiopian position. At the same time, the United States, "shocked" by the scale of the Ogaden fighting and conscious that two of its key allies, Israel and Kenya, were supporting Ethiopia, promptly rescinded an offer to supply Somalia with arms. In view of the participation of Somali regular forces in the conflict, the USA argued it could not make arms available to

Mogadishu until the territorial integrity of Ethiopia was restored. Furthermore, the Soviet Union, after some hesitation, publicly condemned Somalia's "armed intervention" and said that even "the noble pretext of exercising the principle of self-determination" did not justify such an act. On Oct. 20, 1977, Moscow publicly announced the cessation of all arms deliveries to Somalia.

In a desperate effort to obtain Western arms, President Siad on Nov. 13, 1977, abrogated the 1974 Soviet-Somali Treaty of Friendship and Co-operation, expelled Soviet advisers and severed relations with Cuba. But Siad's action failed to move the West and on Nov. 26, 1977, the USSR launched a massive air and sea-lift of military equipment and personnel to Ethiopia. Overall, the Soviet Union ferried in over US$1 billion-worth of armaments, 12,000 Cuban combat troops and 750 soldiers from South Yemen, as well as General Vasily Petrov, Deputy Commander-in-Chief of Soviet Ground Forces, to direct the war against the Somalis.

From the moment that the Soviet-backed Ethiopian-Cuban counter-offensive was launched in January 1978, the Ogaden conflict became a predictable endgame. The assault took place on four fronts between Dire Dawa and Harar, and the Somalis were rapidly driven back towards the key town of Jijiga. The final blow was delivered in early March 1978 when Ethiopia regained control of Jijiga. On March 9, Siad announced the withdrawal of all regular Somali forces from the Ogaden. Two weeks later, Addis Ababa officially confirmed it had regained control of the disputed province.

The Aftermath of the 1977-78 Ogaden War

The Soviet-Cuban intervention did not end the Ogaden dispute, but it dealt a devastating blow to the Somali cause. Fighting broke out again in the Ogaden just nine months after the announcement of the Somali withdrawal. By May 1980, the conflict had significantly escalated. For the first time since the 1977-78 war, Somali regular soldiers entered the fray alongside the WSLF guerrillas. The response of Mengistu's regime was both immediate and overwhelming. It launched a series of air-strikes on northern Somali border towns suspected of being stop-off points for Somali infiltrators and deployed newly imported Hind Mi24 helicopter gunships from the USSR against rebel-held positions. The result was that, by August 1980, the second foray of Somali troops, perhaps 14,000-strong, collapsed. To make matters worse, the OAU 18th Assembly of Heads of State and Government, held in Nairobi on June 24-28, 1981, adopted a resolution reaffirming that the Ogaden was "an integral part of Ethiopia", and condemning all subversion and use of force against Ethiopia.

Ironically, these set-backs qualified Somalia for defensive military aid from the United States. On Aug. 22, 1980, the USA and Somalia finally signed an agreement for the use of military facilities at the port of Berbera by the new US Rapid Deployment Force

(RDF). In return, Somalia was to receive $20 million in military credits, $5 million in budgetary support and a further $20 million in general credits.

The conflict entered a new stage in July 1982. In an attempt to end the almost constant Somali threat to the Ogaden, Ethiopia launched a limited offensive in central Somalia. The operation involved about 7,000 Ethiopian troops and a dissident Somali group, the Somali Democratic Salvation Front (SDSF). There was probably some Soviet involvement, too. But, contrary to Ethiopian and Soviet hopes, Siad's government survived the crisis. An airlift of US military equipment helped, as did widespread Somali antipathy towards Ethiopia.

After the flare-up in the summer of 1982, sporadic clashes in the Ethiopian-Somali border area continued. On each occasion, however, Ethiopia largely dominated the exchanges. Having captured two Somali border towns, Balamballe and Galdogob, in 1982 Ethiopia ensured most of the action took place on Somali soil. In July 1983 and again in January 1985, Mogadishu announced that it had repulsed attacks from Ethiopian "invaders". Then on Feb. 12, 1987, a more serious incident occurred. An Ethiopian brigade and some guerrillas from the Somali National Movement (SNM) launched a joint offensive on six towns in the Togdheer region in north-west Somalia. The attack was supported by twenty-two T-55 tanks and a squadron of MiG-23 fighter-bombers. Around 300 Ethiopian soldiers were killed and vast quantities of Soviet-supplied military equipment, including eleven T-55 tanks, were lost in what was a firm rebuff. Meanwhile, the Ogaden province itself remained comparatively quiet. The well-equipped Ethiopian army had squeezed the WSLF to little more than a nuisance value.

Nevertheless, there were new pressures on Ethiopia to reach an accommodation with Somalia. First, Mikhail Gorbachev, who succeeded Konstantin Chernenko in March 1985 as Soviet leader, made it clear to Mengistu that there were limits to Soviet military aid. Between 1978 and 1987, Moscow gave more than $7 billion in arms to Ethiopia and it signed a new $2 billion arms agreement in November 1987. However, the Gorbachev government told Mengistu that he could not expect similar arms deals after 1991, and publicly urged "the speediest establishment of a stable peace and good-neighbourly relations between Ethiopia and Somalia".

It was against this background that Mengistu and Siad held their first face-to-face talks for nearly a decade in Djibouti in mid-January 1986. At the meeting, the sides agreed to set up a joint ministerial committee to improve bilateral relations. Between January 1986 and April 1987, the newly formed Ethiopian–Somali joint ministerial committee met three times. The main sticking point seemed to be procedural. Ethiopia insisted that Somalia recognize the existing international border before discussing other issues such as the re-establishment of diplomatic relations. The atmosphere was further strained by the aforementioned bloody Ethiopian-Somali border clash on Feb. 12. As an upshot, the third round of peace talks in April 1987 was suspended.

Second, the position of the Ethiopian army in Eritrea sharply deteriorated in the late 1980s. In fact, from March 17-19, 1988, the rebel Eritrean People's Liberation Front (EPLF) scored its single biggest military victory ever by routing the Ethiopians at Afabet. This town was the Ethiopian regional headquarters in Eritrea, and the main garrison for the country's crack troops. Altogether, the EPLF put out of action three Ethiopian divisions (about 18,000 troops), captured an enormous quantity of Soviet arms and, for the first time, captured two Soviet officers.

After the Afabet debacle, Mengistu had little choice but to improve relations with Somalia. Only in that event could he re-deploy in Eritrea a major part of the 60,000 troops based in the Ogaden. On April 4, 1988, following a face-to-face meeting between the leaders of Ethiopia and Somalia, a new ten point bilateral agreement was announced. Under this plan, the two sides resolved to restore diplomatic relations after a break of eleven years; "prevent all acts of destabilization and subversive activities against each other"; implement a phased withdrawal of their troops from the existing border; and "refrain from using or threatening force against the territorial integrity and political independence of the other".

The Ethiopian-Somali peace accord confirmed that Mengistu had retreated on the basic issue dividing the two countries. Somalia was not required to abandon its territorial claim to the Ogaden. According to the agreement, the two sides merely agreed to discuss the boundary issue at some future unspecified date. The paramount concern for the Mengistu government was to obtain an assurance of security on Ethiopia's eastern borders. Indeed, the ink on the agreement was barely dry before Ethiopia stared airlifting troops from the Somali border to the battle zones in the north in preparation for a counter-offensive there. For the Siad regime, too, the peace agreement was something of an exercise in political expediency. The withdrawal of Ethiopian troops from the border zone meant that the embattled Somali government automatically regained control of the towns of Galdogob and Balamballe for the first time since 1982. Additionally, the peace pact terminated all Ethiopian financial and logistical support for Somali rebel groups such as the SNM. This agreement, however, had an unexpected sting. It seemed to prompt an SNM invasion of the northern region of Somalia in May 1988 from bases previously used in Ethiopia. Fierce fighting, centred on the provincial capital of Hargeisa, ensued. It marked the beginnings of a civil war that would eventually topple the Siad dictatorship in January 1991 and leave the country without a recognized central government.

The New Global Context

The end of the Cold War in the late 1980s played a significant part in reducing the prominence of the Ethiopian-Somali border dispute. While the Cold War did not cause the Ogaden conflict, both parties to the dispute exploited superpower rivalry to advance their interests. However, with the removal of this structural condition, the repressive regimes in Ethiopia and Somalia lost their superpower life-support systems and collapsed.

In Ethiopia, barely six months after Gorbachev cut off military aid, spectacular military gains by the Eritrean People's Liberation Front (EPLF) and the Ethiopian People's Revolutionary Democratic Front (EPRDF), a broad coalition of resistance groups, forced Mengistu to flee Addis Ababa. With US support, the EPRDF took power in Addis Ababa in May 1991 and accepted an EPLF proposal for a UN-supervised referendum to decide the issue of Eritrean independence. As a consequence, Eritrea became an independent country in 1993.

Meanwhile, the US Congress, citing human rights violations by Siad's regime against rebels in northern Somalia, forced the Bush administration to suspend its military and economic aid programme to Somalia in 1989. In January 1991, Siad was ousted from power by the United Somali Congress (USC). But instead of heralding stability, the overthrow of Siad accelerated the disintegration of the Somali state. The leaders of the USC became absorbed in a bloody power struggle that spread chaos and starvation throughout southern Somalia.

In 1992, constant civil war and drought combined to produce a catastrophic famine resulting in the deaths of an estimated 300,000 Somalis. The international response included the establishment of a US-led UN military presence in an effort to restore stability and ensure the distribution of humanitarian supplies. However, instead of presiding over the political reconstruction of Somalia, the US-UN force became embroiled in hostilities with the most formidable of the Somali warlords, General Mohamed Farah Aideed. The confrontation effectively ended the operation and led to the humiliating withdrawal of US-UN troops in March 1995.

The conditions that led to the UN-US intervention in Somalia—civil war in a failed state—still endure in 2003. Somalia has been without an internationally recognized or effective government for more than 12 years. But this state of affairs has re-defined, rather than eliminated, border tensions between Ethiopia and its neighbour. Attempts to establish a new authority, based in Mogadishu, have increased Ethiopian-Somali tensions. The Transitional National Government (TNG), established following the Arta peace conference in Djibouti in August 2000, failed to extend its rule beyond a portion of Mogadishu, despite recognition by the United Nations.

Ethiopia has opposed the TNG and accused it of having links with armed "terrorist" movements such as the Ogaden National Liberation Front (ONLF), a separatist organization that grew out of the WSLF in the early 1990s, and a militant Islamist group, *Al-Ittihaad*. According to Meles Zenawi, the Ethiopian Prime Minister, *Al-Ittihaad* has links to Osama bin Laden's *Al-Qaeda* terrorist organization. Furthermore, Ethiopia has backed the Somali Reconstruction and Restoration Council (SRRC), a loose coalition of warlords from southern Somalia, which opposes the TNG. The TNG leadership has for its part consistently denied any links with Islamic extremist groups, and recently alleged Ethiopia was trying to prevent the emergence of a strong united Somalia. Speaking at the Africa Union summit in Maputo in July 2003, TNG President Abdulkassim Salat Hassan said his government in Mogadishu "could have done far more in the three years of its existence had it not been for the daily interference of Ethiopia in Somalia's internal affairs".

Assessing the accuracy of these allegations traded between the two countries is not easy. But several things are fairly clear. First, there was a significant increase in ONLF activity in the late 1990s and the beginning of the 21st century. A number of foreign aid workers were reportedly kidnapped by the ONLF in the Ogaden region and there were also reports of small-scale clashes with Ethiopian troops in the area. The increase in ONLF activity was almost certainly linked to Eritrean efforts to deflect Addis Ababa's attention from its border war with Asmara.

Second, Ethiopia has made a number of cross-border incursions into Somalia. In February 2003, the Ethiopian Prime Minister, Meles Zenawi, admitted in a BBC interview that he occasionally sent troops into Somalia to attack members of *Al-Ittihaad*. Since 1996, Ethiopian troops have made a number of incursions, occupying Dolo and Luq in Somalia's Gedo region for most of 1997. Most of these operations seemed to be aimed at *Al-Ittihaad* but sometimes included support for Somali groups like the Rahanwein Resistance Army (RRA) deemed to be supportive of Ethiopian interests in that country.

Third, following the Sept. 11, 2001, attacks on the United States, Washington turned its attention to possible links between *Al-Qaeda* and Somalia. The US administration placed *Al-Ittihaad* on its list of terrorist organizations and in November 2001 closed the Somali bank and remittance firm Al-Barakaat and seized its assets. The actions reflected growing US concern that Somalia might provide a refuge for Bin Laden and other *Al-Qaeda* members fleeing Afghanistan. Although by January 2002, it appeared that Washington had concluded that the *Al-Qaeda* presence in Somalia was negligible, Ethiopia has emerged as a key partner for the USA in the war against terrorism in the Horn of Africa. In July 2003, the US counter-terrorism force in the Horn began a three-month training exercise with the Ethiopian defence force. The USA has also acknowledged that some of its military intelligence comes from Ethiopia. Heightened post-Sept. 11 concerns in Washington about Somalia's potential for significant terrorist activity is likely to produce more sustained US engagement in the Horn of Africa. The USA is unlikely to wish to allow Somalia to continue indefinitely as a failed state, and any serious attempt to re-establish stability and central control in that country will involve, at some stage, tackling the Ogaden issue.

Robert Patman

1.8 France-Madagascar

A dispute between the governments of France and Madagascar concerns sovereignty over a number of small islands, originally uninhabited, off the coast of Madagascar, and having a total area of 28 square kilometres (about 11 square miles). These islands are the Glorioso Islands (Iles Glorieuses) to the north of Madagascar, as well as the three islets of Juan de Nova, Bassas da India and Europa, situated in the Mozambique Channel. (Map 3, p. 494 illustrates this dispute.)

The islands in question have been under French sovereignty since 1896 and are administered by the prefect of the French overseas department of Réunion (east of Madagascar and southwest of Mauritius) through the intermediary of Réunion's Director of Meteorological Services, who has stationed personnel on them for weather observation (except on Bassas da India, which is almost totally submerged at high tide). From December 1973 the French government maintained small "symbolic" contingents drawn from a parachute regiment (itself stationed on Réunion) on each of these islands (again except Bassas da India), and an airstrip on Juan de Nova has been enlarged so as to enable transport aircraft to use it. The government of Madagascar, however, has forbidden such aircraft to overfly Malagasy territory.

The government of Madagascar has persisted in claiming sovereignty over the islands. In September 1973 Madagascar announced that it had extended its territorial waters limit to 90 kilometres (56 miles) and that of its continental shelf to 180 kilometres (112 miles) from its coasts so as to include the above-mentioned islands, and it accordingly informed the United Nations in 1976. In an interview given in June 1976 President Didier Ratsiraka of Madagascar said: "We are not giving up hope that one day these islands will revert to us. I do not see why France should not surrender them seeing that it has granted independence to all its former colonies in Asia and Africa". The French government, on the other hand, under a decree of Feb. 3, 1978, declared exclusive 200-mile (320-km) economic zones around its dependencies in the Indian Ocean, expressly including the contested islands.

On March 21 of that year the government of Madagascar officially protested against the French decision to include the islands in France's exclusive economic zone and affirmed that the Iles Glorieuses, Juan de Nova, Bassas da India and Europa were "an integral part of Madagascar's territory". In this protest no mention was made of the island of Tromelin, about 560 kilometres, or 360 miles, north of Réunion, also included in the French government decree of

Feb. 3, 1978; the government of Madagascar had in fact ceded its claim for this island to Mauritius, which had claimed it for itself (see Section 1.9).

Endorsement of Madagascar's Claim by the UN General Assembly

At the request of Madagascar the United Nations General Assembly took up the question of the sovereignty over these islands in 1979 and 1980. The UN General Assembly, in a resolution (34/91) adopted on Dec. 12, 1979, noted Madagascar's claim for the "reintegration" in its territory of the Iles Glorieuses, Juan de Nova, Bassas da India and Europa; requested the government of France to repeal measures which "infringe the sovereignty and territorial integrity of Madagascar"; and called on the French government to initiate negotiations with Madagascar on the reintegration of these islands in Madagascar. The resolution was approved by 93 votes to seven (Belgium, France, Italy, Luxembourg, Senegal, the United Kingdom and the United States) with 36 abstentions (including other Western countries).

The Special Political Committee of the UN General Assembly (having the same composition as the Assembly) adopted on Nov. 25, 1980, a resolution demanding that the islands, which, the committee claimed, had been "arbitrarily separated" from Madagascar, should be returned to that country. The resolution was passed by 83 votes to 13 (Belgium, France, the Federal Republic of Germany, Greece, Guatemala, Honduras, Italy, Luxembourg, Morocco, the Netherlands, Senegal, the United Kingdom and the United States) with 32 abstentions.

In a further resolution (35/123), adopted on Dec. 11, 1980, by 81 votes to 13 with 37 abstentions, the UN General Assembly expressed regret that the negotiations envisaged in its previous resolution had not been initiated; took note of a report of the UN Secretary-General on the subject; and again invited France urgently to initiate negotiations with Madagascar in order to settle the question "in accordance with the purposes and principles of the United Nations". Those voting against this resolution included all the then member states of the European Community except Denmark and Ireland (which both abstained) and also the United States. Thereafter the question of the disputed islands remained on the Assembly's agenda, although after 1981 active consideration of the issue was repeatedly deferred with the consent of Madagascar.

Madagascar's Appeals to the OAU and theNon-Aligned Movement

In an explanatory statement deposited with the Organization of African Unity (OAU) the government of the Democratic Republic of Madagascar declared inter alia that on April 1, 1960 (on the eve of Madagascar's achievement of independence), France had presented Madagascar with a *fait accompli* by arbitrarily detaching the islands from Madagascar and transferring them to the direct control of the French Ministry of Overseas Departments and Territories; that under a decree of Sept. 19, 1960 (confirmed on March 11, 1972, and April 17, 1973), the French government had entrusted the administration of the islands to the prefect of Réunion; but that until 1960 France had consistently confirmed the "organic unity" of Madagascar and the islands; that under international law a state had "a natural right of sovereignty" over nearby small islands; that the government of Madagascar therefore intended to denounce all measures taken by France in relation to the disputed islands, to ask for the opening of significant negotiations on the subject, and to inform regional and national organizations accordingly.

The government of Madagascar also stated that it had denounced the progressive militarization of the islands and their inclusion in a strategy which was incompatible with the demands of national and regional security and with the creation of a zone of peace in the Indian Ocean; had protested against the French declaration of 200-mile economic zones round the islands; had taken part in the work of a joint Franco-Malagasy commission from March to June 1979, without result; had placed the question before the OAU in July 1979 and before the Non-Aligned Movement in September 1979, with the result that (i) the 16th OAU Assembly of Heads of State and Government (in Monrovia on July 12-17, 1979) had approved a resolution stating that the islands were an integral part of the territory of the Democratic Republic of Madagascar and inviting the French government to restore them to Madagascar, and (ii) the sixth conference of heads of state and government of Non-Aligned countries (in Havana on Sept. 3-9, 1979) had similarly demanded the restoration of the islands to Madagascar.

French Rejection of UN Resolutions

In a statement made in reply to claims made by the permanent representative of Madagascar at the UN General Assembly, Jacques Leprette, the French permanent representative at the United Nations, said before the vote of Dec. 11, 1980, inter alia: "The territories concerned have been part of the French Republic since the last century. These small islands, with a total area of about 11 square miles, were 'vacant lands without owner' and without any population. They were taken possession of under international law within the legal forms required and without any protest from the international community. These territories were [on April 1, 1960] placed under the authority of the [French] Minister of Overseas Departments and Territories. The government of Madagascar took note of this situation on April 2, 1960, when the first series of co-operation agreements with France was concluded. On the legal level, French sovereignty, which had been uncontested until recent years, has never been interrupted since its inception. It has been expressed by the effective and continued exercise of state functions".

Stating that Madagascar's claim to the islands was

in conflict with Article 2, Paragraph 7, of the UN Charter (laying down that "nothing in the Charter shall authorize the United Nations to intervene in matters which are essentially within the domestic jurisdiction of any state"), the French representative also rejected the argument of "contiguity" (advanced by the representative of Madagascar) as not being recognized in international law and as inapplicable to territories at a distance of 150 to 380 kilometres (about 90 to 240 miles). The delimitation of such territories, he said, must be effected in agreement between neighbouring states, and he continued: "If any coastal state were able to claim all the islands situated at less than 200 miles off its coasts the world's political map would be overturned and world peace would be threatened".

The French representative also rejected the Malagasy argument that the islands were part of the continental shelf of Madagascar, stating that in fact they were separated from Madagascar by ocean depths of more than 3,000 metres. In this context he referred to a decision by the International Court of Justice laying down that parts of the continental shelf situated at about 100 miles (160 kilometres) from a coast, or separated from these coasts by a trench, could not be regarded as lying adjacent to the coast.

On the constitutional aspect he said that the decision of Oct. 15, 1958 (when Madagascar became an autonomous republic within the French Community), which rendered void the law on the annexation of Madagascar, contained no mention of the islands in question; that they had not been annexed at the same time as Madagascar but had been the object of a direct occupation; and that they could therefore not be regarded as dependencies of Madagascar. He also emphasized that the question was not one of decolonization, as these islands lacked all resources, even drinking water, and had never been able to sustain any living soul.

Following Madagascar's achievement of full independence on June 26, 1960, the property records of the Iles Glorieuses and of Juan de Nova (there being none for Bassas da India, Europa or Tromelin), which had been held by the French authorities in Madagascar, were transferred to the French ambassador to Madagascar; the French government regarded this fact as implying recognition of French sovereignty over the islands by Madagascar.

French Statements of Intent, 1981 and 1984

On Oct. 1, 1981, it was reported that President Ratsiraka had stated that France was ready to negotiate on the question of the disputed islands in the Indian Ocean and that his government was "satisfied with this promise". The French Minister for External Relations thereupon declared in the French Senate on Nov. 4, 1981, that the Malagasy position on the islands was "essentially based on an argument not recognized in international law", i.e. that of proximity; that the French government "must look after France's interests in that region of the world and the development of her

relations of co-operation and friendship both with Madagascar and with the region's other states"; and that France would "be committed only by her own official statements on this subject".

On June 11, 1984, the minister declared in the French National Assembly: "The government is intent on conducting in the Indian Ocean an active policy both as regards development aid and increasing France's influence in the cultural and other fields in that region, particularly as a result of the spread of francophony. To this end, it is according priority to giving greater substance to its relations with the various partners in the area, which are currently developing in a climate of restored trust. It is in that spirit that it is looking at the question of the scattered islands and it does not intend refusing a dialogue, once our partners have expressed a desire to start discussions on that issue. The fact that, since 1981, the Malagasy authorities have agreed to postpone the debate on that question at every session of the United Nations General Assembly, bears witness to the spirit in which they now intend to see that aspect of our friendly relations evolve. The government considers that the conditions appear right for finding a solution to the question of the scattered islands that can take into account all the legitimate interests of the partners involved, particularly those which France regards as fundamental".

In January 1986, the government of Madagascar decreed the extension of its exclusive economic zone to 200 nautical miles from the shore and a reduction in its territorial waters limit from 56 to 12 miles "in accordance with the new International Law of the Sea". The decree was intended in part to reassert Madagascar's claim to the disputed islands.

Jane Freedman

1.9 France - Mauritius (Tromelin Island)

The government of Mauritius formally claimed sovereignty, with retroactive effect from 1814, over the island of Tromelin in a document presented to the French ambassador to Mauritius by the latter's Prime Minister on April 2, 1976, and the French government officially rejected this claim on Dec. 17, 1976. (Map 3, p. 494, illustrates this dispute.)

History of the Dispute

The island of Tromelin, situated about 450 kilometres (280 miles) east of Madagascar and 550 kilometres (340 miles) north of Mauritius and the island of Réunion (a French overseas department), consists of a volcano which is crowned by a coral plateau and the ocean floor around which is about 4,000 metres deep.

Its total area is only about one square kilometre, and its highest point rises to only seven metres above sea-level. The island has had no economic importance (except for the export of turtles), there is no fresh water and no agriculture is possible. It is difficult of access by sea but has a landing strip suitable for light aircraft only.

Tromelin was discovered by French seafarers in 1722 and was named after a Frenchman who landed there in 1776. There is no evidence that the French government ever announced its occupation or notified foreign powers of such occupation but the island's status was not disputed. At the first session of the regional association of the World Meteorological Organization (WMO), held in Antananarivo (Madagascar) in January 1953, France was asked to examine the possibility of setting up a weather observation station on Tromelin. A permanent observation station was eventually set up on the island by France on May 7, 1954, which thus constituted a date of effective French occupation of Tromelin.

Until 1960 Tromelin was administered from Madagascar, which after its achievement of independence from France that year laid claim to the island. After 1976, however, this claim was waived in favour of Mauritius (which achieved independence from Britain in 1968), as confirmed by President Didier Ratsiraka during a visit to Madagascar by Paul Berenger, a leader of the left-wing Mauritian Militant Movement, which had emerged as the strongest political party in general elections held in Mauritius in 1976.

The government of Mauritius based its claim to Tromelin on its own interpretation of the first Treaty of Paris of May 30, 1814, under which Britain restored to France certain Indian Ocean islands which it had taken in 1810, "except the Isle of France [i.e. Mauritius] and its dependencies, especially Rodrigues and the Seychelles" (over which France ceded sovereignty to Britain). In its claim of April 2, 1976, the Mauritian government interpreted the word "especially" as meaning "in particular, among others or notably" and asserted that in addition to Rodrigues and the Seychelles the exception included also "minor dependencies" (among them Tromelin) such as the Chagos Archipelago, Agalega and the Cargados-Carajos (St Brandon) islands, which had in fact, with French acquiescence, remained under British sovereignty. The Mauritian government also referred to certain administrative acts carried out by the Port Louis authorities after 1814—in particular to leases issued between 1901 and 1956 to Mauritian nationals for the exploitation of guano. According to French sources, however, there was no guano on Tromelin and the leases had never been taken up.

The government of Mauritius reiterated its claim during an international conference on radio diffusion by satellite in Geneva in February 1977, when it called for individual receiving installations to be erected on Tromelin. The French delegation at the conference insisted on the inclusion in the final protocol of the conference of an express restatement of the French position in regard to continued sovereignty over the island. The Mauritian government's claim was also reaffirmed on June 20, 1980, when it was announced that the constitution of Mauritius would be amended so as to include Tromelin in a list of dependencies.

The French Minister for External Relations stated in the French National Assembly on April 4, 1983, that the question of French sovereignty over Tromelin was to be reviewed in the context of France's global policy in the region of the south-western Indian Ocean; that "an important financial effort" begun in 1983 would be continued in favour of Mauritius; and that a constructive dialogue had begun "on the different aspects of our presence in the region".

The minister also said that the government's plans implied an active policy of aid for the economic development of the countries concerned, and that a climate of dialogue and co-operation between France and the states in the south-western region of the Indian Ocean was essential for the success of the policy, which would contribute to the perpetuity of the French presence in the region.

More recently France has expressed the view that there is potential for settlement of the dispute through an agreement on co-management of the islands.

Jane Freedman

1.10 Ghana - Togo

Relations between the neighbouring West African Republics of Ghana and Togo have been impaired, especially between 1957 and 1962 and again between 1972 and 1977, by a dispute which has its origins in the colonial era. The dispute has centred on (i) the division of the former German colony of Togoland under a 1920 League of Nations mandate into French-administered and British-administered territories, the former eventually becoming present-day Togo and the latter being now part of Ghana, and (ii) the separation of the Ewe between the two countries, with the majority residing in Togo and the remainder in Ghana—although not all in the area which was once part of German Togoland. However, the view that the Ewe always constituted a single "tribe" is historically problematic and has indeed been contested by elements within the Ewe group itself. A sense of "Ewe-ness" did not exist prior to the drawing of the border lines; on the contrary, it arose out of the act of colonial partition. Even then, there was a lack of consensus, in both halves of partitioned Togoland, as to where the boundaries of the Ewe area really ran, which in large part explains the limitations of the unification movement.

In the mid-1970s, it seemed that Ghana and

Togo, both of which were then ruled by military regimes, might come to blows over the issue. But since 1978 the dispute has receded. Relations between the governments have often been fraught since that time, but the Togolese authorities have effectively ceased to advance the case for the reintegration of former British Togoland and/or the Ewe. Although it is conceivable that the dispute could be reactivated in the future, the fact that the Togolese have come to accept a fait accompli makes this rather unlikely. (Map 1, p. 493 illustrates this dispute.)

Origins of the Dispute

At the beginning of World War I Togoland, which had been a German colony effectively since 1884 (formally from Dec. 24, 1885), was occupied by both British and French forces. They made a temporary division of the territory which was very much to the advantage of the former. However, on July 10, 1919, Britain and France agreed to re-partition the territory between them, with France now obtaining two-thirds, including the entire coastline, the capital and the railways, and Britain obtaining the remainder which was contiguous with the (British) Gold Coast Colony. This division was confirmed in 1920, when the League of Nations granted Britain and France mandates for the administration of their respective parts of Togoland. The division affected principally the Ewe, who had first been divided between British and German colonial territories and would have been placed under one flag if the wartime dispensation had survived. On the other hand, the Dagomba in the north were now reunified.

It is estimated that, before European intervention, the Ewe had been divided politically into about 120 sub-groups, located in the pre-colonial borderlands between the centralized kingdoms of Dahomey and Ashanti. During periods of warfare, the Ewe groups had formed temporary alliances (most notably against the Ashanti) but these had been dissolved in times of peace. Significantly, no complaints had been recorded from the various Ewe groups when they were first divided in 1884, as they did not see themselves as an ethnic group at this time. Opposition to partition after World War I among some Ewe in the Lomé area was unsuccessful. The Ewe in French Togoland were encouraged to embrace French culture, were conscripted (for local defence) and were ruled by a centralized government, albeit one which consulted local opinion far more systematically than in the colonies proper. In British Togoland, the Ewe were taught in their own language, were encouraged to maintain their traditions, were not conscripted and were administered through recognized Native Authorities.

At the end of World War II the two Togolands were converted into UN trust territories and remained under French and British administration, with unchanged boundaries. At this stage, an All-Ewe Conference made explicit demands for Ewe reunification and momentarily won international approval. However, its standing was rapidly undercut by a rival Togoland Union, led by British Togoland Ewe, who demanded Togoland unification and the exclusion of Gold Coast Ewe from any new dispensation. This stance reflected enmities carried down from the nineteenth century, which were reinforced by the uneven spread of mission education to the advantage of the coastal zone. A UN commission stated in 1950 inter alia: "the problem has attained the force and dimensions of a nationalistic movement and a solution should be sought with urgency in the interests of peace and stability in that part of the world". In 1952 the Ewe areas in British Togoland and the Gold Coast were finally constituted into a single Trans-Volta Togoland region.

The British government announced in 1955 that British Togoland would cease to be a UN trust territory when the Gold Coast attained its independence, for which preparations were then being made. Upon a recommendation by a United Nations mission which had visited the Togolands, a plebiscite was held in British Togoland on May 9, 1956. The question was whether the territory should be integrated with the Gold Coast on the latter's achievement of independence or whether it should remain a UN trust territory pending the ultimate determination of its future. The plebiscite resulted in 93,095 votes being cast for integration with the Gold Coast and 67,492 for separation. Of the territory's six districts four showed majorities for integration, whereas in the other two districts—Ho and Kpandu (inhabited by Ewes of whom many wished for eventual unification of their territory with the French-administered Togoland)—there was a majority of 36,010 votes in favour of continued trusteeship as against only 15,798 votes for integration with the Gold Coast. Crucially for the subsequent development of the dispute, the majority of voters in Southern British Togoland had cast their votes in favour of separation from the Gold Coast.

The United Nations General Assembly, in a resolution of Dec. 13, 1956, noted the result of the plebiscite and the proposed granting of independence to Ghana (the Gold Coast) by Britain with effect from March 6, 1957. It declared that as from that date the UN trusteeship over British Togoland would cease and the territory would be united with an independent Ghana. The UN declined to consider the votes of Northern and Southern British Togoland separately, which might otherwise have permitted the latter to re-unite with French Togoland. By contrast, when the Cameroons plebiscite results were interpreted a few years later, the northern and southern sectors were permitted to go their separate ways. This presented the Togolese (French Togolanders) with what they regarded as a legitimate grievance.

In French Togoland, a new statute published by the French government early in August 1956 conferred self-government on the territory within the French Union. This new statute was approved in a referendum held on Oct. 28, 1956, by a total of 313,458 of the territory's 438,175 registered voters (this majority varying from about 62 per cent in the south to 80 per cent in the north). The principal opposition to the new statute came from those Ewes who recognized that the French were angling for termination of UN trusteeship, which would make a future union of all the Ewe people or the two Togolands very difficult. The UN General Assembly, however, declined to comply with a French request for the ending of the trusteeship and instead appointed a commission to examine the situation on Dec. 13, 1956. As a result of this commission's report the Assembly decided in December 1957 that elections should be held in French Togoland in 1958 to enable its inhabitants to decide on their future. These elections were held under UN supervision in April 1958, which presented a genuinely level playing field for the first time (the French had previously hobbled the opposition). They resulted in a majority vote for the termination of UN trusteeship and for the full independence of the territory. The General Assembly agreed to its independence on Nov. 14, 1958, and the Republic of Togo became fully independent, outside the French Community, on April 27, 1960.

Irredentist and Secessionist Rumblings, 1957-63

Within Ghana the integration of former British Togoland continued to be opposed by the Togoland Congress (formerly the Togoland Union), although many Ewe had come to accept the virtues of being part of the newly independent state. Riots with fatal results occurred in the Ho and Kpandu districts in March 1957, and two military training camps with ammunition and explosives were said to have been discovered by the police. Four leaders of the (by then defunct) Togoland Congress were sentenced to six years' hard labour for conspiring to show that the integration of British Togoland with Ghana had been a failure and to persuade the United Nations to intervene; three other defendants were given three-year prison sentences at the same time.

Dr Kwame Nkrumah, then Prime Minister of Ghana, said at Ho on Oct. 28, 1959, that, speaking "for our kinsmen on the other side of the border" he would enter into discussions with Togolese leaders on the integration of the two countries after the achievement of independence by Togo. Given that Nkrumah had covertly assisted the electoral victory of Sylvanus Olympio (the Togolese Prime Minister) in 1958, and that the latter was the most articulate spokesman for Ewe unification, the chances for a deal should have been good. However, Olympio increasingly took the view that Togo should not surrender its hard-won independence by merging its sovereignty with Ghana. Nkrumah's efforts to force his hand only made him more intractable. At the end of January 1960, Nkrumah said that integration should be achieved by peaceful means, based on the wishes of the people involved. The suggestion was, however, rejected as "an insult" by Olympio, who said on Feb. 4 that his government would never accept a unitary state with Ghana, and that he himself had always opposed the union of British Togoland with Ghana and had sought the formation of a reunified Togolese state. His attitude was supported by Nicolas Grunitzky, the former Prime Minister and then leader of the principal opposition party.

On March 15, 1960, the Ghanaian Foreign Ministry published the text of a note sent to the French government alleging that "a draft constitution" circulated in French Togoland defined a considerable area of Ghana as part of Togo, and that "certain steps" were being taken in Togoland "with a view to creating disturbances in Ghana". In the note the Ghanaian government requested France to take steps to prevent the territory from being used as "a base for an armed attack on Ghana". These allegations were wholly rejected by the Togoland government on March 16, while the French government categorically denied that there existed any Togolese "draft constitution". By 1961 several thousand refugees were said to have fled from Ghana to Togo for fear of being detained under the Preventive Detention Act because of their membership of the (opposition) United Party or because of being opposed to the incorporation of the former British Togoland within Ghana.

The attitude of the government of Ghana towards the Republic of Togo was set out in a White Paper published on Dec. 11, 1961. Here it was stated that the partition of German Togoland after World War I had produced "a continuing source of trouble". It alleged that a current plot consisted in part of "an attempt to repeat what was unsuccessfully tried in 1957, this time with the support of the Republic of Togo", which was described as "one of the countries on the African continent where neocolonialism has its strongest hold". The White Paper implicitly reiterated Ghanaian territorial claims to the Republic of Togo and stated that a plebiscite on the issue of union with Ghana was desirable in Togo. The White Paper also accused Dr Kofi A. Busia, the leader of Ghana's opposition United Party, of planning to set up a government-in-exile in Lomé.

During 1962 the Ghanaian government made further accusations against Togo, alleging in particular that it had given asylum to persons responsible for attempts to assassinate President Nkrumah, and that it tolerated the existence of a "subversive organization" among Ghanaian refugees in Togo. The Togolese government, however, stated on Dec. 19, 1962, that Ghanaian exiles were allowed to remain in Togo only on condition of taking no part in political activities. On Jan. 6, 1963, the government of Ghana demanded the extradition of Busia and other Ghanaian exiles. On Jan. 13, however, Olympio was suddenly killed in Africa's first successful military coup. Upon a request by the newly-appointed President Grunitzky, the Ghanaian government recognized the new regime on Jan. 21 and reopened the border between the two countries which had been virtually closed to road traffic for about a year. However, relations subsequently deteriorated and the border was closed again by Togo, and was not officially reopened until April 23, 1966—that is, after the overthrow of Nkrumah himself on Feb. 24 of that year.

The Last Reprise, 1972-78

Since the fall of Nkrumah, no Ghanaian government has repeated the demands for the incorporation of Togo into Ghana. But in 1972 a movement calling itself the National Liberation Movement for Western Togoland (TOLIMO) despatched a secessionist petition to the Organization of African Unity. By this point, Ghana was under a military regime, led by Colonel Ignatius Kutu Acheampong. In July 1973, the government of Ghana disclosed that a number of Ewe chiefs had been temporarily arrested for their implication in a secessionist conspiracy. It appears that the chiefs had begun attending meetings of a cultural nature, celebrating the supposed migration of all the Ewes from the town of Notsie (in Togo), but that these had subsequently assumed a political hue.

In February 1974, TOLIMO caused considerable embarrassment to the Ghanaian government when its members greeted the UN Secretary-General, Kurt Waldheim, with placards and bearing a petition demanding a revisitation of the 1956 plebiscite as he passed through Lomé. On Feb. 21, 1975, a delegation of chiefs and others from the Volta Region of Ghana reported to Acheampong that a resolution had been adopted by some chiefs on Dec. 28, 1974, calling for negotiations between the government of Ghana and TOLIMO. Early in 1975 the government offered an amnesty to all TOLIMO members who ended their secessionist activities by Dec. 1, 1975. It stated that they would not be punished and that those in voluntary exile could return to Ghana and live there as law-abiding citizens. The regime made a particular effort to win support from the chiefs, who were offered various favours in return for expressions of loyalty. On Dec. 23, Acheampong declared before a delegation of chiefs from the Region that the deadline of the amnesty had been extended to the end of January 1976. He also stated that the authorities had recently uncovered a plot to overthrow the government and that the persons involved, whom he described as "a small group of political agitators in the Volta Region" who wished part of that region to be joined to the neighbouring Togo, would be prosecuted.

While many TOLIMO members were reported to have taken advantage of the amnesty, some 22 leading members of the movement (some of them employees of the Togolese government) remained in Togo. TOLIMO had responded to the amnesty offer in an open letter to Acheampong, asking for negotiations "directly or through the Organization of African Unity in order that permanent peace should exist in the territory, if necessary by handing over this problem, which cannot be done away with by the mere granting of an amnesty, to an arbitration which shall find a means by which it can be solved permanently".

On Jan. 13, 1976, the government of Togo revealed where the real impetus for this campaign was emanating from. An advertisement in *The Times* (of London) called upon Acheampong to "show his statesmanship and restore Togo as she was before the Europeans got

to work" and asserted that "no one could call the 'plebiscite' of 1956 fair or a thoughtful reflection of the aspirations of the local inhabitants". The Ghanaian authorities stiffened their own position accordingly. They officially terminated the amnesty on March 3, 1976, under a decree (amended on March 18) which banned "any organization whose objects include advocating and promoting the secession from Ghana of the former British-mandated territory of Togoland or any part of it, or the integration of this territory with any foreign territory", and specifically TOLIMO, under pain of a fine up to 5,000 cedis (£2,000) or imprisonment for up to five years, or both, for any activities carried out on behalf of the movement.

During a treason trial held in Accra between May 19 and July 28, 1976, the chief accused, Capt. (retd.) Kojo Tsikata, was reported to have said that the Acheampong government had "a psychosis of an Ewe plot against it" which, he claimed, was being played out at this trial. The eight defendants in the trial, all Ewes, pleaded not guilty, but seven of them were sentenced (five to death and two to 20 and 15 years' imprisonment respectively). There was, however, no plausible link with the secessionist agenda of TOLIMO. Tsikata and his colleagues were southern Ewes (from the former Gold Coast) who regarded themselves as good Ghanaians. Their problem was with the composition of the regime in Accra.

On Jan. 28, 1977, the government of Togo took up the border issue once again by issuing a statement, published as an advertisement in *The Times*, in which it claimed that the plebiscite of "May 9, 1957" (which in fact took place a year earlier), had "not completely resolved" the problem and that "the question of reunification" had "never ceased to affect relations between Ghana and independent Togo". The statement continued: "Border problems are common in Africa, of course. Throughout the world, except in a few privileged nations, there are no natural frontiers to separate nations, large or small. Borders have always been created by men. It is hardly surprising, but in Togo men have flouted principles which have been defended at such high cost elsewhere...Many arguments are advanced in favour of maintaining the status quo, both in the Organization of African Unity and at the international level. The principle that the frontiers inherited from colonialism are sacrosanct undoubtedly prevents Africa from tearing itself apart, but general principles have never ruled out consideration of individual cases. Togo existed as an entity before and during colonization. In view of the reunification of British and French Cameroons, the Togolese wonder why there should be one law for one nation and another for the other". The statement alleged unfair British pressure to influence the 1956 plebiscite result (for which there is actually some evidence).

The Togolese statement elicited a bellicose response from the Ghanaian side. In November 1977, Acheampong warned that his country was "prepared to shed blood to the last drop to defend the territorial integrity of the nation". Moreover, the Ghanaians accused their Togolese counterparts of encouraging smuggling in order to bleed the country dry and so to hasten the date when former British Togoland could be reclaimed. The tone of Ghanaian rhetoric seems to have induced the government of President Gnassingbe Eyadema to back off from pushing its claims as forcefully as before. In addition, as Eyadema headed a northern-centered regime which encountered the most stubborn opposition from the Ewe south, the incorporation of former British Togoland would have swung the demographic balance to the disadvantage of the regime. Whatever the reasons, the Togolese government turned off the funding for TOLIMO and moderated its official position over the course of 1977. From 1978 onwards, the Ewe/Togoland dispute receded into the background, having failed to excite any real sympathy from amongst the peoples of the Volta region of Ghana. TOLIMO was in many respects a Togolese government creation that had outlived its usefulness. After 1978, it was allowed to wither on the vine.

Border Developments Since 1978

During the 1980s and 1990s, the borders were repeatedly closed as inter-governmental relations remained poor. However, the periodic disputes had only a limited connection to issues concerning the border as such. The Ghanaians complained about Togolese encroachment on their land in the Nkwanta area, and they continued to prioritize the war against the smuggling of cocoa and other commodities by vigorous policing of the border. However, most of the tension lay in mutual accusations of bad neighbourliness.

A military coup brought Flt.-Lt. Jerry Rawlings to power in Ghana on Dec. 31, 1981. In June 1983, the Rawlings regime was almost overthrown by rebels who infiltrated Accra, having crossed through the Togo border. On the other side, an attempted coup against Eyadema in September 1986 led to strained relations with Ghana, which was accused (with Burkina Faso) of having been actively complicit in the plot. The border was consequently closed in October 1986. Although Togo reopened its border in February 1987, Ghana kept its side closed, probably because it assisted in the reduction of smuggling activity. On March 18, the Ghanaian Ministry of Foreign Affairs made strong representations to the Togolese government over (i) alleged border incidents during the previous six months; (ii) reports of Togo's intention to build a concrete wall along parts of the border and to erect a barbed wire fence along another parts; and (iii) arrests of Ghanaians in border villages by Togolese soldiers and officials crossing into Ghana. These allegations were categorically denied by the Togolese Foreign Ministry which stated that Togo had merely taken measures to ensure its security and had no intention of building a wall along part of the border. The spokesman also said that Togo would be quite happy to discuss the border issue peacefully within the framework of the two countries' existing joint commission. The following day, however, the Togolese Ministry of

Foreign Affairs confirmed that a barbed wire fence had been erected along a section of the border and added that the Ghanaian authorities had been informed of this beforehand. On May 22, Ghana reopened the border posts that had been closed since October 1986.

In January 1989 relations between the two countries were again put under strain when Togo arrested and repatriated 124 Ghanaians living in Togo (a further 10 were arrested and deported later that month) without explanation. But on Oct. 4, 1991, Ghana and Togo signed a communiqué under which they jointly agreed "to promote close and mutually beneficial co-operation" and the following day land, sea and air borders were opened for the free movement of goods and personnel.

The impact of the wave of democratization which swept across Africa after 1989 tended to further complicate relations between the Eyadema and Rawlings regimes. The most significant challenger to Eyadema was Gilchrist Olympio (the son of the murdered first President) to whom Rawlings offered a safe haven in Ghana. Given that Rawlings' mother was Ewe, this was widely interpreted as a manifestation of ethnic solidarity.

The determination of the Eyadema dictatorship to face down the southern opposition by any means, foul or fair, led to bouts of violence in Togo that had repercussions across the border. In January 1993, Eyadema unleashed the army on protesters in Lomé, leading to many deaths and the flight of some 100,000 refugees into Ghana. In January 1994, the Togolese accused the Ghanaians of direct complicity in an attempt to overthrow the government. During the fierce fighting which took place in Lomé, the Ghanaian border town of Aflao was fired upon and a number of people were killed. Thereafter, repeating a familiar cycle, the two governments sough to de-escalate the crisis. It was agreed to reactivate a Joint Commission for Co-operation and the Ghanaians re-appointed an ambassador to Lomé. However, the unwillingness of the Ghanaians to abandon Olympio's cause set limits on the rapprochement. Moreover, some 5,000 Togolese refugees still remained in Ghana, most of whom were located at Klikor, in close proximity to the border.

Given the lack of any genuine rapport between Rawlings and Eyadema, an element of suspicion was bound to remain for as long as they remained their countries' leaders. However, in 2000 Rawlings served out his final term of office as elected President. In the elections which ensued in December, Eyadema is alleged to have given active support to J.A. Kufuor of the opposition New Patriotic Party (NPP) which enabled him to defeat Rawlings' chosen successor. Kufuor repaid the favour by immediately paying an official visit to Lomé. The Eyadema-Kufuor pact subsequently blossomed, to the dismay of many Ghanaian democrats, and culminated in further efforts to harmonize relations between the two countries.

In May 2002, the two governments agreed in principle to open the border on a 24-hour basis and to convene the Joint Commission as quickly as possible. The fact that both countries are signatories to Economic Community of West African States (ECOWAS) protocols covering the freedom of movement of citizens and the liberalization of trade, provides a regional framework for closer co-operation. In January 2003, Ghana and Togo were amongst the signatories to the West African Gas Pipeline Project, which will pump natural gas from Nigeria through Togo to Ghana. This is a sign of the willingness to think regionally and to place old disputes on one side. By then it was a long time since the issue of Ewe/Togoland unification had been raised and it currently enjoyed almost no support in either country.

Divided border communities, such as that of Agotime, are taking advantage of the unprecedented harmony in inter-state relations to promote their own forms of cross-border co-operation. Local festivals which would have been inconceivable at the start of the 1990s, such was the paranoia of the two sets of authorities, have become a popular feature of the local calendar. The organizers do not imagine that the border will ever be erased, except possibly in the context of West African integration, and they do think of themselves as Ghanaian and Togolese respectively. However, they also see these festivals as a chance to foster their own sense of being Agotime as well. As governments realize that these events do not need to threaten state sovereignty, they are making a modest contribution to turning the border into a bridge rather than a barrier.

Paul Nugent

1.11 Kenya - Somalia

The boundaries of the former British colony of Kenya at independence on Dec. 12, 1963, encompassed an area of approximately 50,000 square miles or 130,000 square kilometres (defined as the country's North-Eastern province) whose population was predominantly Somali-speaking (the number of ethnic Somalis being estimated at approximately 200,000).

Somalis have regarded this population as one of the five elements of the historic Somali nation. From 1960, when the Republic of Somalia became independent, its successive governments espoused the goal of unification of the Somali nation, of which the Republic comprises only two of the five elements, namely the former British Somaliland Protectorate and Italian-administered Somalia (which had latterly been a United Nations trust territory). Somali irredentism was expressed as a demand for the right of self-determination for the three categories of Somali-speaking peoples under foreign administration. These were, firstly, those in Kenya, the subject of this section; and secondly those in Ethiopia, for

which see Section 1.7. (Map 5 on p. 495 illustrates the region.)

The third dispute related to the fifth element of the "historic Somali people", the Issa, who form the largest population group in Djibouti. Djibouti was known for most of the colonial period as French Somaliland, before being renamed in 1967 as the French Territory of the Afars and Issas. Somali demands for its self-determination were effectively ended after Djibouti gained independence from France on June 26, 1977, with a governing coalition in which the Issas were in a majority. Somalia recognized and established diplomatic relations with the new Republic of Djibouti. The Ethiopian and Kenyan governments, in calling for the explicit renunciation by Somalia of all territorial claims against its neighbours, continued to refer to the existence of a Somali territorial claim on Djibouti, although Somalia has not actually done anything to pursue such a claim.

The demand for self-determination for Somalis within Kenya, as expressed by leaders of the local population and supported by the government of Somalia, was addressed in the first instance to Britain as the colonial authority prior to Kenyan independence, and was subsequently pursued in the form of a dispute between Somalia and Kenya. The position adopted by the government of Somalia has been that this does not constitute a territorial dispute as such since Somalia did not desire to annex the territory in question, although if the population should desire union with Somalia, having once achieved self-determination, such a union would be encouraged by Somalia.

Historical background

The situation in Kenya prior to independence was that ethnic Somalis formed approximately half the population of the Northern Frontier District (NFD), an area of 150,000 square miles (388,000 square kilometres) which in fact comprised six administrative districts, the eastern three of which (Garissa, Wajir and Mandera) were inhabited almost entirely by Somali-speaking people. The border demarcation between Kenya (specifically the NFD) and Somalia was not recognized by the latter, its alignment having been determined by a commission in 1930 on the basis of a treaty of July 15, 1924, between Britain and Italy whereby the territory known as Jubaland was detached from the British Kenya Colony and incorporated within Italian Somaliland. The NFD was administered by the British as a "closed district", entry from and exit to the rest of Kenya being subject to permit, and Somali nationalist aspirations as expressed notably by the Somali Youth League (SYL, formed in 1943) were affected by a ban on all political activity in the NFD from 1948 to 1960.

Harold Macmillan, the British Prime Minister, said

in the House of Commons on April 11, 1960, that "Her Majesty's government does not and will not encourage or support any claim affecting the territorial integrity of French Somaliland, Kenya or Ethiopia; this is a matter which could only be considered if that were the wishes of the governments and peoples concerned". This was apparently interpreted by Somali leaders to mean that a claim for self-determination for the NFD would indeed be considered if that were the wish of the British government (then responsible for governing Kenya) and the Somali people.

Local Somali chiefs made clear their demand for secession from Kenya at a meeting in November 1961 with Reginald Maudling, the then British Colonial Secretary, and further representations to the same effect were made by an NFD delegation to the Kenya Constitutional Conference held in London in February-April 1962. This delegation met with a special representative group of the conference, its direct participation having been strongly opposed by Kenyan nationalist leaders.

Without acceding to Somali demands for a referendum on the NFD, the British government proposed instead the establishment of an independent fact-finding commission, which was subsequently set up with the brief that it should ascertain and report on public opinion in the NFD "regarding arrangements to be made for the future of the area". The commission visited the NFD in October-November 1962 and reported in December that the population was divided but vigorous and determined in its opinions, with the largest areas (in both population and size) seeking secession when Kenya became independent, and ultimate union with the Republic of Somalia.

Duncan Sandys, Reginald Maudling's successor as the British Colonial Secretary, issued a statement on March 8, 1963, at a session of the Kenyan Council of Ministers in Nairobi, containing the British government's decision on the NFD. While the Somali-populated areas would not be allowed to secede, he said, they were to be formed into a separate, seventh (North-Eastern) province of Kenya; this decision was incorporated into the Kenyan constitution, which was laid before Parliament in London in the form of an Order in Council on April 18, 1963. Although the decision was represented by the British government as an interim rather than a final one, there seemed little prospect in the foreseeable future of a Kenyan government allowing the Somali-speaking area to secede. Kenyan leaders had already made clear their opposition to any such secession, during visits which they made to Somalia in the latter part of 1962, and Jomo Kenyatta (subsequently the first Prime Minister and later President of Kenya) reiterated on March 14, 1963, that Kenya would not entertain "any secession or handing over of one inch of our territory" to Somalia or to any other country. Talks between Kenyan and Somali government representatives, held in Rome on Aug. 25-28, 1963, did nothing to alter this position. Britain made it known during this meeting that it would not take responsibility for a final deci-

sion, although legally Britain remained the responsible authority until Kenyan independence.

Meanwhile the Republic of Somalia had on March 12, 1963, broken off diplomatic relations with Britain in view of what it described as the British failure "to recognize the wishes expressed by the overwhelming majority of the peoples inhabiting the NFD of Kenya". This marked the end of Somali attempts to obtain from Britain the satisfaction of their demands for the self-determination of the NFD. The issue thereafter became one between Somalia and Kenya, in the context of relations between independent African states in the post-colonial period.

The definition of the precise area in dispute was complicated by the Kenyan regional administrative reorganization implemented during the transition to independence. The NFD, to which Somalia continued to refer, officially ceased to exist, being subdivided in such a way that ethnic Somali peoples within Kenya were for the most part incorporated within the new North-Eastern province.

In the period immediately following the independence of Kenya, the Kenyan government held the Somali government responsible for rebel activity in the North-Eastern province, as a consequence of which activity a state of emergency was declared in the region on Dec. 25, 1963. In the same month a defence pact was ratified between Kenya and Ethiopia, the pact having been concluded in July 1963 with a view to safeguarding the integrity of the existing borders between the two countries and Somalia. Kenyan-Somali border hostilities continued sporadically until 1967, when (in September of that year) a degree of reconciliation was achieved following prolonged attempts at mediation by other African states.

The Kenya-Somali Dispute and the OAU

From its foundation in 1963, and indeed from its antecedents in the pan-African movement, the Organization of African Unity (OAU) has generally been associated with the doctrine that independent African states should adhere to the boundaries existing at the time of their independence. The principle of mutual respect for the territorial integrity of African states was expressly reaffirmed by a resolution adopted in Cairo on July 21, 1964, at the first ordinary session of the OAU Assembly of Heads of State or Government. The resolution included a solemn declaration that all member states pledged themselves "to respect the borders existing on their achievement of national independence". The representative of Somalia had been absent for the vote on this resolution, however, and he made it clear in a statement on July 23 that his government did not consider itself bound by its terms. Moreover, he said, Somalia opposed the perpetuation in independent Africa of what he described as "the uncorrected mistakes which still existed" with regard to state borders inherited from the colonial era.

The substantive issue of border hostilities between Kenya and Somalia was removed from the agenda of the OAU's 1964 Cairo summit meeting and referred to bilateral talks. Such attempts as were made at mediation (notably talks arranged in Tanzania in December 1965) failed to resolve the matter, and violent border incidents continued, accompanied by a further deterioration in relations between the two countries and the imposition of restrictions on trade between them in July 1966. Kenyan government sources in late 1966 estimated that 1,650 Somali "shifta" (bandits) had been killed in the border area in clashes over a three-year period, during which time it was said that 69 Kenyan forces personnel, police and administrators had also died along with over 500 Kenyan civilians.

A list of "prerequisites for normalizing relations", which the Kenyans put forward in December 1965 and subsequently reiterated, stipulated in particular that Somalia should recognize the former NFD area as an integral part of Kenya and cease all material and propaganda support for ethnic Somali shifta insurgents in the area. Rather to the contrary, however, a new Somali government established in July 1967 issued an explicit statement of its position in the form of a speech by Mohammed Ibrahim Egal, the new Prime Minister and Minister of Foreign Affairs. While stating that "we in the Somali Republic make no claims on the territory of any of our neighbours", the new Prime Minister went on to say that "what we are after is simply independence through the proper process of self-determination for our brothers" and that "we do intend to champion the cause of Somali territories under foreign domination, in order that they may attain sovereign independent status through the process of self-determination". After such independence it was envisaged that unions would be arranged "out of discussion and mutual agreement between independent Somali states".

Notwithstanding these divergent positions, however, on Sept. 13, 1967 (i.e. only two months after the change of government in Somalia), the Kenyan and Somali governments issued a joint declaration at the OAU Assembly in Kinshasa, undertaking to end the violent clashes and expressing the desire to respect each other's sovereignty and territorial integrity and to resolve their outstanding differences.

The following month a further Memorandum of Agreement was signed by President Kenyatta of Kenya and Prime Minister Egal of Somalia. Known as the Arusha Agreement, this was concluded at a meeting held in Arusha (Tanzania) on Oct. 8, 1967, under OAU auspices with the mediation of President Kaunda of Zambia. It called for the ending of clashes, the resumption of normal relations, the gradual suspension of emergency measures on both sides, the ending of hostile propaganda, and the formation of a joint committee (with Zambian mediation) to supervise the implementation of these processes and to seek solutions to outstanding differences. The agreement formed the basis for the establishment of diplomatic relations between Somalia and Kenya in January 1968, when trade restrictions were also lifted. In the same month Somalia re-established diplomatic relations with Britain, broken off over the NFD issue at the time

of Kenyan independence. Continuing bilateral contacts between Kenya and Somalia led to the lifting by Kenya on March 15, 1969, of the state of emergency in the North-Eastern province, and it was also agreed that restrictions on the movement of livestock across the border (i.e. by nomadic herdsmen) would be relaxed.

The essence of the Kenyan-Somali accommodation was not that their disagreement had moved towards being resolved, but rather that it had been allowed to become dormant under the mutually convenient ambiguity of the Arusha formula. The Somalis could interpret the call for a working committee "to examine ways and means of bringing about a satisfactory solution to major and minor differences between Kenya and Somalia" as an acceptance that what they continued to call "the NFD question" remained on the agenda to be settled in future negotiations. The Kenyans, meanwhile, interpreted the commitment at Arusha to respect each other's territorial integrity "in the spirit of paragraph 3 of Article III of the OAU Charter" to mean that Kenya's borders at independence, encompassing the North-Eastern province with its majority ethnic Somali population, would no longer be called into question. There was thus no further need, according to this interpretation, for Kenya to insist as a precondition for any negotiation that Somalia explicitly declare its recognition of the North-Eastern province as an integral and de jure part of the Kenya Republic.

Course of Kenyan-Somali Relations, 1967-79

The Somali government's acceptance of the Arusha formula did not pass entirely without domestic criticism; indeed, hostile demonstrations met Prime Minister Egal on his return to Mogadishu, and former Prime Minister Abdirizak Hadji Hussein denounced the agreements. The government responded by closing down the Mogadishu branch of the Somali Youth League, of which Abdirizak Hussein was the secretary-general, and Egal (although the SYL central committee voted to expel him from the party) won the support of Parliament in a vote on Nov. 23, 1967, endorsing his efforts to settle outstanding differences between Somalia and her neighbours.

This policy approach continued essentially unchanged under the military government of Gen. Siad Barre, installed after a coup in Somalia in October 1969. Although a Revolutionary Charter, promulgated following the suspension of the 1960 constitution, reaffirmed a commitment to "the fight for the unity of the Somali nation", assurances were given to Kenya that the new regime would continue its predecessor's policy of seeking co-operation to solve outstanding differences.

Reports of incidents in the area in 1977 and early 1978 were accompanied by renewed Kenyan pressure for the Somali government to make a formal renunciation of any territorial claims against its neighbours. The first of the new series of incidents occurred on June 27, 1977, when (according to the Kenyan government announcement) Somali troops believed to be passing through on their way into Ethiopia were involved in clashes at the Ramu border post in northern Kenya in which six Kenyan police and seven Somalis were killed. Kenyan complaints over this incident at the OAU ministerial meeting in Gabon on June 30 were met by Somali denials; the Somalis insisted that Somalia had no intention of attacking Kenya and that there had been no clashes in the area since the 1967 agreement. A Somali assertion that the attack had in fact come from Ethiopia, was in turn denied by the Ethiopians.

A meeting was held on July 19, 1977, between Daniel arap Moi, then Kenyan Vice-President, and his Somali counterpart, Hussein Kulmia Afrah, following which a joint communiqué was issued stating that both sides had pledged to maintain the peace and to set up a border commission to "normalize and restore tranquillity" in the region. However, according to President Kenyatta of Kenya in a speech in Nairobi on Oct. 20, 1977, official Somali maps "still lay false claim on Kenyan territory", and it was reported at this time that the Kenyan government had conveyed to the Somalis by way of the Egyptian government as intermediary a renewed demand for the public renunciation of any Somali territorial claims against Kenya. It was further reported that the governments of the United Kingdom and the United States were unwilling to provide military assistance sought by Somalia, unless and until Somalia formally declared that it had no territorial claims against Ethiopia, Kenya and Djibouti.

Meanwhile, Vice-President Moi of Kenya had announced on Oct. 15, 1977, his government's intention of carrying out a census to establish the number of Kenyans of Somali origin, any of whom regarded as "favourable to Somalia" would be expelled from Kenyan territory. On the same day the Somali ambassador to Kenya replied to allegations that Somali travel documents had been furnished to Kenyans of Somali origin, and that the recipients of such documents had then gone abroad for military training. The issue of travel documents, he said, had occurred only for humanitarian reasons when individuals without Kenyan papers had wanted to travel abroad, and he stated that this would not happen again. In an announcement on Dec. 12, 1978, on the occasion of the release of 26 political detainees by the new Kenyan government (now under President Moi following President Kenyatta's death), it was stated that the majority of those released were ethnic Somalis arrested in the border area for alleged subversive activities.

On Sept. 10, 1979, the first ever meeting between a Kenyan and a Somali head of state (Presidents Moi and Siad Barre) was arranged in the Saudi Arabian city of Taif. At this meeting the Kenyans reportedly unsuccessfully pressed their demand for a public Somali renunciation of support for the self-determination of ethnic Somalis in Kenya. Shortly after returning from this meeting, President Siad Barre gave on Sept. 23 his assent to the new Somali constitution, as drawn up by the ruling Somali Revolutionary Socialist Party in January 1979, and approved in a national referendum on Aug. 25. Article 15 stated that "the Somali Democratic Republic shall firmly uphold the principle of self-determination of peoples and fully support the national liberation movements and all peoples fighting for their freedom and independence", while Article 16 stipulated that the Republic "adopting peaceful and legal means shall support the liberation of Somali territories under colonial occupation and shall encourage the unity of the Somali people through their own free will".

Further Incidents in 1980—Somali Denial of Territorial Aspirations

In November 1980 further violent incidents were reported near the Kenyan-Somali border, and the provincial commissioner of the North-Eastern province of Kenya announced on Nov. 10 that a curfew would be imposed throughout the province and all Kenyan citizens of Somali origin would be confined in security villages. The following day the Somali government denied any involvement in the disturbances (in which six Kenyan officials were reportedly killed). On Nov. 13, according to Kenyan radio, President Moi sent a message to President Siad Barre welcoming "assurances given yesterday by the Somali ambassador to Kenya that Somalia had no territorial claim in Kenya whatever", and President Siad said on Nov. 30 in a speech in Mogadishu (as reported on Somali radio) that Somalia was not seeking any Kenyan territory and that it would be to the mutual benefit of both countries if Kenya understood Somalia's desire for a peaceful relationship. He stated that Kenya was responsible for the future and the rights of the people of Kenya's North-Eastern province, but that Somalia in turn "would not tolerate the killing and the denial to these people of their rights". He repeated also the Somali claim that it was the Ethiopians who were responsible for creating disturbances in the area, with the intention of marring relations between Kenya and Somalia.

December 1980 Ethiopian-Kenyan Joint Communiqué

The Kenyan-Somali dispute, being one facet of the wider issue of Somali nationalist aspirations, was intimately connected with the most salient issue for irredentist Somali policy, namely the territorial dispute with Ethiopia over the Ogaden region (see Section 1.7). Since January 1979 Ethiopia and Kenya had had a 10-year treaty of friendship and co-operation (concluded on Jan. 31 during an official visit to Addis Ababa by President Moi) which included a pledge to maintain the inviolability of their frontiers and of mutual defence to resist "the expansionist policies of any country or group of countries".

Lt.-Col. Mengistu Haile Mariam, the Ethiopian head of state, made an official visit to Nairobi in December 1980, during which (on Dec. 1) he described Somalia's policies as "a thorn in the flesh of both Ethiopia and Kenya". An Ethiopian-Kenyan joint communiqué issued on Dec. 4 called on Somalia "to renounce publicly and unconditionally all claim to the territories of Ethiopia, Kenya and Djibouti". According to Addis Ababa radio the communiqué set out a series of conditions which Somalia must fulfil, including (besides the payment of reparations for war damages to Ethiopia) the renunciation of territorial claims, the acceptance of the inviolability of existing state frontiers and the withdrawal of Somalia's reservation entered when this principle had been reiterated at the OAU in 1964. The two leaders reportedly agreed that "non-acceptance of these conditions by Somalia would mean the perpetuation of the existing tension and insecurity in the area" and that active Kenyan-Ethiopian collaboration should be intensified, and they called for an end to all international military aid to Somalia.

The Somali government responded vehemently to this communiqué, calling an emergency joint meeting on Dec. 7 of the Supreme Revolutionary Council, the SRSP central committee, the People's Assembly and the Council of Ministers. This meeting condemned the communiqué as provocative and threatening and tantamount to a declaration of war, and urged "the Somali people wherever they are to be ready to defend their motherland and national sovereignty". The President's Office issued a statement on Dec. 8 (which was substantially reiterated in a speech by President Siad Barre the next day) warning that the Abyssinians (i.e. Ethiopians) planned a systematic liquidation of Somalis under their rule. With Kenyan collaboration, it was alleged, Ethiopia intended to declare war on Somalia. The statement distinguished between "Abyssinian colonialism" and the Somali-Kenya issue, which it described as "a colonial legacy needing a just and responsible solution, in accordance with the OAU Charter". With regard to former colonial boundaries, Somalia "continued to uphold its 1964 principle" and to oppose "the uncorrected mistakes which still existed".

Improvement in Relations—1984 Border Security Agreement

Bilateral talks on June 29, 1981, between Presidents Moi and Siad Barre led to an improvement in Kenyan-Somali relations; a joint communiqué referred to a "commitment to promote better understanding and collaboration in the interest and welfare of the two nations". Subsequent meetings included discussions in August 1981 of a Somali offer to assist Kenya in controlling border violence. The Nairobi *Standard* newspaper on Sept. 8, 1981, quoted President Siad Barre as stating: "We in Somalia have no claim whatsoever on any part of Kenya's territory…It is of course a historical fact that there are people of Somali origin in Kenya. But we regard them as Kenyans".

The continuing problem of violent incidents involving ethnic Somalis in northern Kenya nevertheless remained a potential source of friction. In the Wajir area in early 1984, many members of the Somali-speaking Degodia tribe were killed as Kenyan forces

moved in to disarm them after they had been involved in clashes with another local Somali-speaking group. However, the absence of Somali government support for local irredentism was illustrated in mid-September 1984 by the announcement of the closure of the headquarters in Somalia of the Northern Frontier District Liberation Front (NFDLF, a group whose existence had first been reported in April 1981) and the return to Kenya of 331 NFDLF members under the terms of an amnesty announced by the Kenyan authorities in December 1983.

Meanwhile, President Moi had visited Somalia in July 1984 (appealing on July 24 for peace between Somalia and Ethiopia), and later that year a Somali delegation visited Nairobi, where on Dec. 2 it was announced that a border security agreement had been signed. Under this agreement, both countries would grant entry visas to the nationals of the other, thereby facilitating the free movement of peoples across their common border.

The Kenyan government, particularly in the context of meetings with Ethiopian delegations, continued to make reference on occasion to the importance of all African states accepting formally their boundaries as at independence. Thus for example on March 5, 1987, a joint communiqué issued after an Ethiopian-Kenyan ministerial committee meeting (and coinciding with heightened Ethiopian-Somali tensions) praised the Ethiopian-Somali dialogue of the past year but said that the acceptance of boundaries established at independence was "a fundamental principle for the promotion of mutual trust and co-operation" and "the foundation of lasting peace among states".

On Nov. 18, 1987, a Kenya government delegation led by Justus Ole Tipis, Minister of State in the President's Office, visited Mogadishu where it held four days of meetings at ministerial level. Justus Ole Tipis then announced that the two governments would co-operate to combat poaching and to encourage cross-border movement. He stressed his awareness that Somalia harboured no territorial claims to northern Kenya. In May 1988 General Cheruiyat, head of Kenya's military academy, visited installations in Hargeisa and Berbera.

On Sept. 20, 1989, four Kenyan policemen were killed in a clash on the Kenya-Somali border at the Hare Hare settlement and four others injured. Somalia claimed that its forces had been in pursuit of anti-government rebels. However, following a visit by the Somali Defence Minister, Hussein Abdurahman Malu, to Nairobi on Sept. 29, the two countries agreed to take action against poachers and "bandits" in the border region.

Somali Civil War—Border Tensions

The Siad Barre regime fell in January 1991. A decade of civil conflict ensued during which Somalia was left without effective government. Tension along the border remained high during this period of inter-clan civil war with regular violent incidents. In September 1991 the Somali Democratic Movement (SDM), representing the interests of the Darood and Hariwe clans, complained that the Kenyan army continued to support forces still loyal to Siad Barre. The following month saw Kenya reinforce the border following cattle raids that left four Kenyans dead.

Border tension increased markedly in April 1992. Following a failed advance on Mogadishu by Siad Barre loyalists, the former President fled to Kenya. Fighters loyal to Mohammed Farah Aideed's United Somali Congress (USC) crossed the border in "hot pursuit" of Siad Barre's forces. The Kenyan government warned the USC that any further incursions would be "decisively dealt with". The warning was largely ignored and fighting spilled over the border. USC fighters entered several Kenyan border towns. The inhabitants of Kiunga in Lamu district were forced to flee their homes for several days, while Kenyan security forces engaged USC forces at El Wak, 80 km south of Mandera.

The upsurge in fighting led to increased refugee flows and lawlessness in towns on the Kenyan side of the border. By the end of 1992 Kenya hosted approximately 420,000 refugees, the majority of whom came from Somalia. The problem of refugees and internally displaced persons was dealt with differently by the government in Kenya and the United Nations High Commission for Refugees (UNHCR) in Somalia. In late 1992, President Moi announced that Kenya intended to repatriate all Somali refugees. However, as a short-term measure the Kenyan government allowed the UNHCR and non-governmental organizations to construct refugee camps in North-Eastern province and on the coast near Mombassa. Somali refugees were restricted to these camps and were not allowed to travel to, or seek work in, cities or towns. Even so, the refugees faced hostility from the local nomadic population. The camps were located in arid areas with no real potential for agricultural development. As such the refugees, unable to work or grow their own food, became wholly dependent on international aid for their survival.

With continued insecurity in Somalia precluding large-scale repatriation, the camps, in particular Dadaab in Garissa district, have assumed a state of semi-permanence. As of December 2002, 130,000 Somali refugees remained in the country. In Somalia, the UNHCR established the Cross-Border Operation intended to protect internally displaced persons, to stem the flow of refugees into Kenya and tempt those who had already crossed the border to return home. Outposts were created about 100 miles from the Kenya-Somalia border along the Juba river. This strip of land was designated a "preventive zone". In December 1992 the UN Security Council mandated a US-led peacekeeping intervention to ensure the safe delivery of humanitarian aid throughout Somalia. The conduct of the mission, however, was misjudged, leading to UN and US disillusionment with the intractability of the Somali conflict and the premature withdrawal of the peacekeepers by early 1995.

Insecurity in Somalia ensured continued tension along the border leading to the Kenyan government sporadically closing border points. On June 29, 1999, a serious incursion by militiamen loyal to Hassan Aideed's Somali National Alliance (SNA) resulted in a robust response by the Kenyan armed forces. Around 400 SNA fighters took control of a Kenyan army and police post at Amuma and seized rifles, ammunition and communications equipment. The government responded by closing the border to all Somalis, including refugees, and by sending tanks and other military equipment to the border. Five Kenyan navy vessels were also deployed to patrol the maritime border. As a result of this show of strength the SNA commander made an apology and returned the commandeered materiel.

Despite the establishment in October 2000 of a Transitional National Government (TNG) in Somalia under Abdulkasim Hassan, insecurity along the border persisted. In March 2001 17,000 refugees fled across the border. Despite 10,000 people being spontaneously repatriated and the UNHCR negotiating further repatriation there remained a residual population of 5,000 Somalis from this influx. In May 2001, in response to continued border insecurity, President Moi closed the border and called on Hassan and the TNG "to act like a national government" and to take measures against illegal activities, notably arms trafficking, along the border. The border was reopened in July 2001.

Tension between the two states increased following a terrorist attack in Mombassa widely believed to have been carried out by *Al-Ittihaad al-Islamiya*, a group operating out of Somalia. In October 2002 Kenya hosted talks aimed at ending the inter-clan violence in Somalia. In July 2003 the new Kenyan government of Mwai Kibaki appointed Mohammed Affey, an ethnic Somali, as the first ambassador to Somalia for thirteen years.

Simon Massey

1.12 Lesotho - South Africa

The Kingdom of Lesotho, an enclave of territory completely surrounded by the territory of the Republic of South Africa (the length of the border being in all some 565 miles or 900 km), attained independence from the United Kingdom on Oct. 4, 1966. The validity of the country's borders, as inherited from the colonial era, has been called into question by the country's politicians on the grounds that these borders perpetuate an unjust arrangement imposed on the Basotho (Basuto) or South Sotho people in the 19th century. This section gives an account of the historical background to Lesotho's territorial claims, which relate to substantial if imprecisely defined areas generally described as "the conquered territories", as well as of cross-border relations between Lesotho and South Africa in more recent times. (Map 6 on p. 495 illustrates this dispute.)

Lesotho's Existing Boundaries

Lesotho's boundaries today are essentially as defined in the Second Convention of Aliwal North, which was concluded on Feb. 12, 1869, and which brought to an end a series of wars between the Basotho and neighbouring Boer settlers. This treaty, although it was signed by the Basotho ruler King Moshoeshoe, had actually been negotiated between the British governor of the Cape of Good Hope (to whom Moshoeshoe had successfully appealed for protection) and the (Boer) authorities of the Orange Free State. The new boundary was adjusted the following year to include in Basutoland a parcel of territory (Chief Molapo's territory) in the north-west around Butha Buthe. The revised border ran from the confluence of the Caledon and Putisani (or Phuthiatsana) rivers eastwards to the Drakensberg following the centre of the Caledon river rather than the centre of the more southerly Putisani.

The British high commissioner's Notice of May 13, 1870, as amended by Government Notice No.74 of Nov. 6, 1871, defines the borders of Basutoland (now Lesotho) as follows: "From the junction of the Cornetspruit [Makhaleng] with the Orange river, along the centre of the former to the point nearest to Olifantsbeen; from that point, by Olifantsbeen, to the southern point of Langeberg to its north-western extremity; from thence to the eastern point of Jammerberg; along the top of Jammerberg to its north-western extremity; from thence by a prolongation of the same, to the Caledon river; along the centre of the Caledon river to the heads of the Orange river at the Mount aux Sources; thence westward [in fact first south-eastward and then south-westward] along the Drakensberg, between the watersheds of the Orange river and the St John's river [Umzimvubu] to the source of the Tees [Telle]; down the centre of the river to its junction with the Orange river, and down the centre of the latter river to its junction with the Cornetspruit".

Extent of Earlier Basotho Settlement and Authority

Moshoeshoe I had succeeded, in the period to 1835, in establishing his authority as king over the Basotho people, whose area of settlement extended into areas to the north and west of the Caledon river as well as to the south-west of Lesotho's modern boundaries. Other tribes migrating into the northern part of the Basotho-dominated area were brought into a vassal relationship as tributaries of King Moshoeshoe. (See below, however, for dispute over the status of the Barolong tribe in the Thaba Nchu area.)

From the late 1830s the position of the Basotho was affected by the migration into this area of Afrikaner, or Boer, farmers from the south, notably in the Boer treks which began on a large scale in 1836. By these treks the Boers aimed to remove themselves from British colonial rule (the colony of the Cape of Good Hope having been ceded by the Netherlands to Britain in 1814) and to establish themselves anew in what later became the South African territories of the Orange Free State, Transvaal and parts of Natal.

King Moshoeshoe signed a treaty with the British governor of Cape Colony on Oct. 5, 1843, in which the extent of Moshoeshoe's territory was described in Article III. According to this description (known as the Napier line) the territory extended westward to the junction of the Caledon and Orange rivers, south to the Orange river, east to the Drakensberg and north to "a line extending from about 25 to 30 miles north of the Caledon river, excepting near its source and at its junction with the Gariep [Orange]". However, neither this description, nor a series of disputed attempts to give greater precision to the boundary definition (including the so-called Maitland, Southey and Warden lines), prevented continual cross-border conflict, cattle raiding and similar disturbances between Basotho and Boers.

First, Second and Third Basotho Wars with Orange Free State

Soon after the formal establishment of the independent Boer republic of the Orange Free State (the British having proclaimed their sovereignty over the new Boer settlements in 1848 but having established a separate administration for the Orange River Territory in 1851 and allowed independence on Feb. 23, 1854), a conflict known as the First Basotho (Basuto) War or Senekal's War began in 1856 between Basutoland and the Orange Free State. This war was officially concluded by the First Treaty (or Convention) of Aliwal North on Sept. 29, 1858.

As shown on Map 6, the territorial limits of Basutoland as defined in this treaty were based on the Warden line proposals of 1849. Although the territory thus defined does not include the full extent of all areas of Basotho settlement (and notably omits an area in the south-west which had been described as part of King Moshoeshoe's territory in his 1843 treaty with the Cape Colony—see above), it is to this territory, substantially larger than modern Lesotho, that the claims expressed by Lesotho's leaders generally relate.

A subsequent Second Basotho War (Sequiti War) from 1865 to 1866 ended with the Basotho becoming subject to the Orange Free State as well as ceding part of their territory. The terms of the peace were accepted by Moshoeshoe's son Molapo in the Imperani Treaty, which was confirmed a month later by the Treaty of Thaba Bosiu, concluded between King Moshoeshoe and the Orange Free State authorities on April 3, 1866.

The Basotho, who had already sought British protection against the Boers in 1861 but without success, renewed their appeal after the outbreak of the Third

Basotho War in 1867. As a result of a petition from King Moshoeshoe in January 1868, the British governor of the Cape on March 12, 1868, proclaimed the Basotho to be British subjects and their land to be British territory. The governor subsequently concluded a treaty with the Orange Free State (the Second Treaty or Convention of Aliwal North of Feb. 12, 1869) by which a new boundary was delimited (the agreement also being accepted by King Moshoeshoe on behalf of his people—see above).

Complexities affecting Lesotho's Territorial Claims

Although, as already indicated, the principal basis for Lesotho's territorial claims is that the Basotho lands were unjustly taken from them by force, a more general claim to lands south and east of the Drakensberg has also been expressed. The areas in question, in particular the districts of North and South Maluti, later lying within Griqualand East and the former "African homeland" of Transkei (incorporated since 1994 into the Eastern Cape Province of South Africa), were settled by 19th-century Basotho migrants, with the support of the British authorities in the 1880s.

A different complication affects the Thaba Nchu area in the north-west, where an enclave within the Orange Free State was apportioned by South Africa as part of the so-called Bophuthatswana African homeland (before it was incorporated into the province of the Free State in 1994). The area was inhabited by the Barolong tribe migrating southward in 1833, and it has been disputed whether the tribal chief did or did not become a vassal of King Moshoeshoe at this time, as did other tribal chiefs. The claim that he did not do so would affect Lesotho's historical claim to that particular enclave, which falls geographically within the area regarded by Lesotho as "the conquered territories".

Lesotho's Claims following Independence

Basutoland, transferred to be part of the Cape Colony from 1871 to 1884 and thereafter administered as a British High Commission Territory, attained independence as Lesotho on Oct. 4, 1966, as already noted above. Prior to independence, certain members of the Legislative Assembly had demanded (on Nov. 2, 1965) that the British should secure the return to Basutoland of areas of South Africa in Orange Free State, Natal and eastern Cape Province, this demand reportedly being generally supported by all political parties in the country.

Although reference to seeking the return of the "conquered territories" was included in the programme of the Basotho National Party (BNP)—which ruled the country from independence until it was ousted by a military coup in January 1986—as well as that of the opposition Basotho Congress Party (BCP), the government adopted an attitude of restraint on the issue, at least until 1973. In June of that year, the Lesotho government requested legal advice from the United Nations to pre-pare for negotiations which it was seeking with South Africa, and in January 1975 Chief Leabua Jonathan, the Prime Minister, declared that he would press his country's claims at the UN and, if necessary, at the International Court of Justice. The then Foreign Minister, Joseph Kotsokoane, said at the UN in November 1975 that there could soon be a confrontation with South Africa over the border issue, and his successor, Charles Molapo, told the UN General Assembly in October 1976 that the South African government should open talks on the return of land which he said had been "illegally ceded" during the colonial era.

From late 1976 the position was complicated by a dispute which arose from the Lesotho government's refusal to recognize the sovereignty of the African homeland of the Transkei, bordering on southern Lesotho and including areas claimed by Lesotho. In a move which received no international recognition, South Africa on Oct. 26, 1976, granted "political independence" to the Transkei, which consisted of territory formerly administered as a homeland within South Africa. Transkei authorities thereupon assumed jurisdiction over the territory's borders and border crossing points, which included three crossing points into Lesotho.

The Lesotho government refused to comply with Transkeian border formalities, on the ground that this might imply recognition of Transkeian sovereignty (Lesotho allegedly being the target of South African pressure to this end). Lesotho successfully appealed at the United Nations for international assistance to compensate for what was described as the effective closure of the border crossings in question (even though international journalists reported that the dispute had not in practice affected free movement of people across the border). The real objection of the Lesotho government was to Transkei's insistence that Lesotho citizens should have Transkei visas rather than those of South Africa, as formerly. In consequence, the 33 other border crossings between Lesotho and South Africa, lying along the remaining sections of the border between the two countries, were not affected directly. The three affected crossing points were quietly officially reopened in 1980.

In the wake of the dispute over the Transkei issue and its border implications for Lesotho, Chief Jonathan in February 1977 asserted his country's territorial claims in very broad terms, apparently encompassing much of the Orange Free State and other lands "fraudulently taken during the wars". It was reported in *The Times* on June 2, 1977, that Chief Jonathan had again restated his country's claims and expressed his intention of bringing the matter before the International Court of Justice. South Africa responded by reiterating a proposal first made in 1968 for the appointment of a joint border commission.

Cross-Border Tensions 1978-93

Lesotho's tempestuous internal politics were to result in continuously tense border relationships with South

Africa from the late 1970s. South Africa had originally enjoyed cooperative relationships with the ruling conservative BNP after independence, as the opposition BCP was the historical vehicle of radical anti-colonialism. South Africa therefore gave crucial covert support to Prime Minister Jonathan when he suspended the constitution after he realized that the BCP had won a narrow victory in the general election of 1970. However, the combination of Lesotho's acute dependence on South Africa and Jonathan's close relationship with Pretoria had long since meant that the international community, and most notably independent African countries to the north, had dismissed the tiny country as little more than one of South Africa's "bantustans".

This was to change after the BNP crushed an attempted coup by the BCP in 1974, forcing the more radical leadership elements of the latter into exile. First, Jonathan began to shed his image as a South African stooge by adopting increasingly radical anti-apartheid rhetoric in order to attract aid and sympathy from the international community. Second, he gravely alarmed Pretoria by establishing diplomatic relations with Yugoslavia (1977), Cuba (1979) and the Soviet Union (1980). Third, and most importantly, following the popular upheavals which erupted in South Africa in the wake of the students' revolt in Soweto in 1976, Lesotho became host to an increasing flow of South African refugees and moved into a close relationship with Pretoria's principal domestic opponent, the African National Congress (ANC). This then set the scene, ironically, for a relationship of convenience between South Africa and the BCP, which following its move into exile had launched the Lesotho Liberation Army (LLA) to wage armed struggle against the BNP.

Based (unofficially) in Botswana, with the objective of launching attacks upon the Jonathan regime from the Basotho QwaQwa homeland (which adjoined Lesotho's northern border) and Transkei, the LLA required the covert assistance of the South African security services to cross South Africa and establish bases in the two homelands. Evidence put to the South African Truth and Reconciliation Commission after 1994 subsequently established that BCP leader Ntsu Mokhehle had made visits to farms used by South African security to train "third force" operatives, that the South African Defence Force (SADF) provided arms and training to the LLA, and that the SADF saw the LLA as an instrument for the pursuit of its policy of destabilization of hostile neighbouring states. As part of this strategy, the LLA was also to take part in several raids launched by the SADF, South African Police, and the Transkei Defence Force against border posts in 1983.

During the period 1979-82, some thirty-odd attacks by the LLA—guerrilla assaults, bombings, assassinations and arson—were made against Lesotho government property and persons, as well as against international organizations, and investors deemed to be supporting the regime. Lesotho repeatedly alleged that these attacks were facilitated and directly assisted by the South African government, which by this time was becoming increasingly alarmed by the ANC's use of Lesotho as a springboard for what it termed "acts of terrorism". These anxieties were to culminate in a commando raid by the SADF upon Maseru in December 1982 in which some 43 people, mostly ANC supporters, were killed. Lesotho thereafter became subject to increased South African pressure in the form of non-payment of customs dues and the holding up of imports and weapons and military equipment before it succumbed to a pact, forged in June 1983, whereby both governments agreed to clamp down on each other's insurgents. Batches of ANC supporters were thereafter airlifted to Mozambique and Tanzania.

A Lesotho government announcement of Oct. 1, 1984, that the ANC had agreed to withdraw completely from Lesotho thereafter led to better relations and a resumption of feasibility studies for the Highlands development scheme, which would provide water to South Africa and hydroelectric power for Lesotho. Critically, the number of raids by the LLA declined sharply, as South Africa switched its principal support to a conservative Basotho Democratic Alliance, which it sponsored. Then, following the rise of a radical faction within the BNP favouring closer relations with the ANC, there was an increase in South African "warnings" about the continued presence of ANC guerrillas. A denouement was reached when, following raids (allegedly by the LLA) on Maseru on Dec. 20, 1985, South Africa imposed a de facto blockade of Lesotho, by means of strict controls and checks at border crossing points. Having forged close relationships with both BNP conservatives and Major-General Justin Lekhanya, the commander of the Lesotho Paramilitary Force, South Africa precipitated a bloodless coup to overthrow Jonathan on Jan. 20, 1986.

The new regime rapidly established good relations with South Africa, marked by the lifting of the South African border controls, an agreement on mutual security, and the signature on Oct. 24, 1986, of a treaty on commencement of work on the Highlands water project.

On April 30, 1987, the two countries signed an agreement to establish trade missions in their respective countries: a South African mission in Maseru and a number of Lesotho missions in places where Basotho were concentrated in the Republic. The agreement was seen as a positive advance for the Lesotho Highland Water Project. A general amnesty, enabling all Basotho exiles to return home without fear of prosecution, was declared in 1987 with the intention of undermining the support base of the BCP and LLA. After assessing the situation, Mokhehle negotiated a return to Lesotho for himself and his followers, although he himself was not to return to the country until 1990.

Feeling that they had been betrayed, four rebel members of the LLA then sought to take their revenge on the occasion of a visit to Lesotho by Pope John Paul II. This visit had already turned into a major embarrassment for the regime, for a mysterious failure of radio equipment at Maseru airport had compelled the

Pope to land at Jan Smuts airport in Johannesburg. South Africa, apparently well prepared, used the occasion for propaganda purposes. A motorcade and police escorts drove the Pope to Maseru and entered Lesotho without paying any attention to its border controls as though the country were even less independent than a Bantustan. In the meantime, the four LLA rebels had hijacked a busload of pilgrims, holding them hostage outside the British High Commission in Maseru. The delivery of the Pope to Maseru by South African security forces was then followed by a bloody end to the hijack drama, when South African commandos played the leading role in flushing out the rebels.

Cooperation and Conflict after 1994

Transition processes which led to democratic elections in Lesotho—won by the BCP in 1993—and in South Africa—won by the ANC in 1994—removed cross-border disputes caused by apartheid but brought with them their own complications. These revolved around the ANC's distrust of the BCP and the latter's inheritance of security forces which, despite the coup of 1986, were aligned closely with the BNP.

Factional struggles between opposing elements of the Royal Lesotho Defence Force (LDF) in January 1994, precipitated by the BCP government's rejection of a claim for a pay rise, initiated a plea from Prime Minister Mokhehle for international assistance to resolve the crisis. The response was the dispatch by the Southern African Development Community (SADC), of which Lesotho was a member, of a tripartite Task Force, comprising representatives of South Africa, Botswana and Zimbabwe, who mediated an agreement whereby the soldiers would return to barracks in return for the government reconsidering their claims. This was followed by a report, submitted by Presidents Masire of Botswana and Mugabe of Zimbabwe, in which they recommended the appointment of commissions of inquiry into the military and the monarchy (an institution in crisis following Lekhanya's replacement in 1990 of King Moshoeshoe II by his son, who became a reluctant monarch as Letsie III).

Slow progress by the Lesotho government in attending to the army's demands, alongside rumours that it was to be rationalized and combined with the LLA, brought new disturbances and the assassination of the Deputy Prime Minister in April 1994 and the flight of some six ministers to South Africa. Warnings by SADC that no government brought to power by a coup would be recognized, and the eventual concession by the government of a substantial pay rise, brought the crisis to a temporary end. However, following the installation of the ANC in power in South Africa at the end of April, and Mokhehle's announcement of the appointment of the two commissions of inquiry, the army supported King Letsie's dismissal of the government in August 1994, citing the need for new elections.

The King's coup, whilst buttressed by the BNP, aroused hostility on the streets and internationally,

provoking suspension of aid by key donor countries and institutions and a warning from the new South African President, Nelson Mandela, that South Africa might be forced to intervene militarily if the situation was not brought under control. Subsequently, strong diplomatic pressure by Mandela, Masire and Mugabe was to result in the restoration of the BCP to power on Sept. 14, 1994.

These events were simply a prelude to more dramatic developments in 1998. In 1993, the BCP had won all 65 seats in parliament under the British-style first-past-the-post electoral system, even though the opposition parties had won some 25% of the vote. Nonetheless, by 1997, the ageing and ill Mokhehle was facing a succession struggle, and had lost control of his party machinery. Even so, he retained the support of a majority of BCP members of parliament. Accordingly he dished his opponents by forming a new party, the Lesotho Congress for Democracy (LCD), which overnight became the ruling party, leaving a rump BCP in opposition. Subsequently, in April 1998, the LCD proceeded to a another landslide victory in the second general election following the restoration of democracy, winning 79 out of the by now 80 constituency seats.

Ironically, the rump BCP now joined hands with its erstwhile bitter rival, the BNP, in repudiating the election. Together, albeit led by the BNP, they called upon their supporters to mass in Maseru, and called upon the King to suspend the government and declare another election. The "troika" was again called in to mediate, and Pius Langa, a South African judge, headed a commission to investigate the fairness of the recent election (eventually concluding that he could find no adequate reason to dispute its outcome). However, by mid-September, with the police force declining to enforce civil order and the army increasingly indicating its support for the opposition, the government had lost the capacity to govern and faced what it termed a "creeping coup". Consequently, Pakalitha Mosisili (anointed by Mokhehle as Prime Minister and leader of the LCD) called for external assistance from SADC.

The outcome was an armed intervention by the South African National Defence Force (SANDF) and the Botswana Defence Force (BDF), which formally acted on behalf of SADC on Sept. 22. Initially poorly planned and executed, this precipitated angry reaction from opposition supporters, most notably from the BNP Youth League, many of whom spread to the streets of Maseru and proceeded to burn down numerous buildings of the government and firms with South African associations. However, after spirited resistance by the LDF was put down by the SANDF, order was restored, although SADC efforts to lay the foundations for political stability were thereafter to meet with numerous difficulties.

Albeit slowly, progress followed after a compromise agreement between the political parties whereby the LCD retained its status as the government whilst an Interim Political Authority, composed of 2 representatives of all 12 political parties which had contested the 1988 election, was charged with devising a new electoral system which would produce a more balanced outcome and facilitate parliamentary representation of the opposition. Although this latter body thereafter engaged in many skirmishes with the government and thoroughly overran its timetable, it eventually recommended replacement of the first-past-the-post electoral system with a Mixed Member Proportional System featuring retention of the existing 80 constituency seats alongside 40 seats elected by a national list system of proportional representation. This provided the basis for a further general election in May 2002. The LCD again won a handsome majority, winning fully 79 out of the 80 constituency seats. However, under MMP, all the 40 national list seats were awarded to the opposition parties, notably the BNP, all of which accepted the election result after only token protests.

The ANC, which had formed a close relationship with the BNP during the 1970s and 1980s, had remained deeply suspicious of the BCP (which, historically, had supported its rival the Pan-Africanist Congress), despite its overwhelming victory in the 1993 general election. However, although initially suspicious that the LCD may have rigged the 1998 election, the retirement of Mokhehle had already paved the way for a more constructive relationship with Mosisili, not least because South Africa had rapidly tired of Lesotho's politics as a cause of disturbance in the heart of its own territory. The SANDF presence in Lesotho, although steadily withdrawn over the coming months, hence provided a crucial opportunity for the reform of the army, and the cutting of its umbilical link to the BNP.

Lesotho: A New Protectorate?

Following the defeat of apartheid and the restoration of democracy in Lesotho, there were calls from some quarters for Lesotho to forego its independence and to join up with a democratic South Africa in the form of a tenth province. However, the debate that followed rapidly established that, whilst Basotho recognized their country's acute economic dependence upon South Africa, the majority retained a strong sense of separate identity, this revolving around the institution of the monarchy. Nonetheless, whilst remaining committed to independence from South Africa, Basotho have endorsed a strengthening of de facto relations with their more powerful neighbour. This has been underlined by South Africa's decision, in October 1995, to offer permanent residence to migrant mineworkers who had entered South Africa before June 13, 1986, and/or who were ordinarily resident before that date. This offer was subsequently broadened to extend the offer of permanent residence to all citizens of SADC countries who could demonstrate continuous residence since July 1, 1991, and who were in productive economic employment, or who had a South African partner or children born in, or lawfully

residing in, South Africa.

Good relations have also been strengthened by joint activities, conducted by the two countries' police forces, along the Eastern and Southern borders of Lesotho to crack down on livestock smuggling. However, South Africa's military intervention in 1998, although apparently conducive to greatly improved conditions of political stability in Lesotho, have in effect reduced the latter country to the status of an informal protectorate, mirroring the relationship between the Cape of Good Hope and Basutoland following the early wars of the nineteenth century.

Roger Southall

1.13 Malawi - Tanzania

In 1967 the government of Tanzania formally stated that in its view Tanzania's border with Malawi lay not along the eastern shore of Lake Nyasa (or Lake Malawi), as shown on current maps, but along the median line of the lake (see Map 7, p. 496). This assertion implied the right of Tanzanians to enjoy access to the waters of the lake and the use of its resources.

Origins of the Dispute over the
Lake Nyasa/Malawi Border

In Article I of an agreement concluded in 1890 between Britain and Germany the alignment of the western border of what had, in 1885, become German East Africa was described as running along the (eastern) shore of Lake Nyasa and to be subject to modification by agreement and demarcation (as provided for in Article VI of the 1890 agreement). In 1891 the British government proclaimed a protectorate over the Nyasaland region (later known as the British Central African Protectorate and renamed, in 1907, the Nyasaland Protectorate). A second Anglo-German agreement (of 1901) merely gave formal approval to the conclusions of a joint boundary commission which had been surveying the frontiers of the two territories for the purpose of demarcation.

In practice, however, German sovereignty extended to the median line of Lake Nyasa until 1922, when most of German East Africa became the Mandated Territory of Tanganyika administered by Britain under the League of Nations. Official British sources for the period 1916-34 showed the western border of the territory as being the median line through Lake Nyasa (e.g. in a map attached to Britain's report for 1923 to the Council of the League of Nations, and in subsequent reports for 1924 to 1939, which referred to the western extent of the Tanganyika Territory as "the centre line of Lake Nyasa to a point due west of the Rovuma river", which constitutes the border between Tanzania and Mozambique).

After World War II Tanganyika was declared a United Nations trust territory, with the British government being answerable for its administration to the UN Trusteeship Council, and with Britain being responsible for bringing the territory intact to independence. However, British reports issued between 1947 and 1961 for Tanganyika and Nyasaland generally abandoned the median-line alignment and showed the boundary between the two territories as being the eastern shore of Lake Nyasa in accordance with the 1890 Anglo-German agreement. This change was apparently reaffirmed with the proclamation of the Central African Federation of Rhodesia and Nyasaland in 1953.

The government of Tanzania—since 1961 the successor to British authority in what is now mainland Tanzania—has rejected this change on the ground that no arbitrary change of boundaries by the administering authority of a UN trust territory could have any legal justification in view of the territory's UN trust status. In addition it has declared itself bound by the July 1964 resolution of the Assembly of Heads of State and Government of the Organization of African Unity (OAU) which stated that the borders of African states, as on the day of their independence, constituted "a tangible reality" and that all member states pledged themselves "to respect the borders existing on their achievement of independence".

Tanzanian Initiative of 1967 and Malawi Claims of 1968

The Tanzanian government raised the question of this border in a note to the government of Malawi in January 1967, stating inter alia: "The government of Tanzania has noted that maps produced in recent years give the impression that the international boundary between Malawi and Tanzania follows the eastern and northern shore of Lake Nyasa. It has also noted that certain actions of the Malawi government appear to give [support to this impression]. The government of Tanzania does not want an international issue to arise between countries sharing the waters of Lake Nyasa. Accordingly it wishes to inform the government of Malawi that Tanzania has no claim over the waters of Lake Nyasa beyond a median line running through the lake and that it is this line alone which is recognized by the government of Tanzania as both the legal and the just delineation between Malawi and Tanzania".

The Malawi government, in replying to this note, stated that the matter would receive consideration. At a Malawi Congress Party meeting in September 1968 President Banda of Malawi declared in regard to what he considered to be Malawi's territory: "The real boundaries [of Malawi] are 100 miles [160 kilometres] north of the Songwe river [Malawi's present northern boundary with Tanzania]. To the south it is the Zambezi river [in Mozambique]. To the west it is the Luangwa river [in Zambia], and to the east it is the Indian Ocean". He based these claims on the ancient Maravi empire shown on early Portuguese maps. In his

speech he also stated that Lake Nyasa had always belonged to Malawi and that he had every right to change its name to Lake Malawi.

At a meeting at Mbeya (Tanzania) on Sept. 27, 1968, Presidents Nyerere of Tanzania and Kaunda of Zambia discussed inter alia a common stand against President Banda's claims. The government of Tanzania subsequently dismissed them as having "absolutely no substance whatever" and not deserving any reply.

Subsequent Developments

The border delineation question has remained an unresolved, albeit dormant, issue between the two countries. Not until May 1985 were diplomatic relations established between Malawi and Tanzania, which the following April signed an agreement designed to give the former improved access to the Tanzanian port of Dar es Salaam via a road link through northern Malawi to the Tazara railway running from Zambia to the Tanzanian coast.

In April 1994 talks were held between President Mwinyi of Tanzania and the outgoing President Banda to discuss improving economic and social cooperation. It was proposed that the joint commission on cooperation which last met in 1989 should be re-established. These talks were followed later in the year by a symbolically important first visit to Malawi by former President Nyerere. In April 1996 an agreement was signed between President Benjamin Mkapa of Tanzania and President Bakili Muluzi of Malawi formalizing cross-border trade. However, the dispute over the Lake Nyasa/Malawi border continues to surface at bilateral meetings. The issue emerged at a meeting between Mkapa and Muluzi in July 2003. President Muluzi noted that: "it is not as controversial as you put it…it affects our people but I think we can talk about it". From the Tanzanian perspective, President Mkapa stated the belief that further integration of the two countries' economies, including water utilization, would make the issue redundant. The two leaders also discussed the question of the boundary along the River Songwe. The river has changed course over the past decade and the demarcation of the border has become confused. To this end the two leaders agreed to cooperate on a river stabilization project. Although a final communiqué played down both border disputes, it was apparent that they remain live issues.

Simon Massey

1.14 Malawi - Zambia

Since achieving independence in 1964, Malawi has from time to time asserted a claim to a substantial area of present-day Zambia (and also of other neighbouring states), basing its case on the extent of the pre-colonial Maravi empire. (Map 7 on p. 496 shows the territorial relationship of Malawi and Zambia.)

Addressing a meeting of the ruling Malawi Congress Party in September 1968, President Hastings Banda declared that Malawi's "real" boundary in the west (i.e. with Zambia) was at the Luangwa river, which runs from north to south about 100 miles (160 kilometres) to the west of the present-day Malawi-Zambia border. He based this assertion on the presumed territory of the ancient Maravi empire as shown on early Portuguese maps (which were also adduced as grounds for claims on substantial areas of Mozambique and Tanzania—see Section 1.13). However, Malawi's claim was not taken seriously by Zambia, which declined to make any official response.

Although the broader Malawian claim has not been reasserted in recent years, a more limited dispute arose in August 1981 over an area on Zambia's Eastern province border with Malawi. In a statement to the Zambian Parliament on Aug. 11, 1981, Minister of State Fitzpatrick Chuula said that an official dispute had been declared over the area, adding that discussions were in progress between the two sides with a view to resolving the issue. Subsequently, a spokesman for the Zambian Foreign Ministry confirmed on Jan. 11, 1982, that 10 Zambian nationals were being held in Malawi for allegedly straying into Malawi and that a protest had been lodged with the Malawi high commissioner in Lusaka in an effort to secure their release.

In February 1982 President Kaunda of Zambia paid his first official visit to Malawi since the two former British colonies became independent in 1964, and received a warm welcome in Lilongwe. Nevertheless, a year later Lusaka radio reported (on Feb. 7, 1983) that villagers at the Kanyara border post, some 50 miles east of Nakonde, had complained of harassment by Malawian police and young pioneers, it being alleged that some Malawians had started cultivating crops on Zambian territory. A joint commission was subsequently established to resolve the dispute, and in August 1986 a Zambian government minister informed Parliament in Lusaka that the commission had recommended that the Zambian government should withdraw its claim to the disputed land.

In September 1993 a meeting in Lusaka between the two governments agreed to continue to work together to solve border issues affecting the two countries. The following year, in the run-up to multi-party elections in Malawi, there were reports in the press that one opposition leader, Chakufwa Chihana, proposed to seek a redefinition of the border if he were elected. Chihana denied the reports, stating that they were part of a strategy by the Banda government to discredit him. In August 1994 the new Malawian government of President Bakili Muluzi began a joint survey with the Zambian government of President Frederick Chiluba to demarcate the border in the Mwanu and Mchinji area. The two governments also agreed to co-ordinate efforts to curb cross-border poaching and drug trafficking.

However, the issue of trans-border intrusion continued to cause friction between the two countries. In June 2003 the District Administrator from Chama complained that Malawians were slowly opening more land for tobacco estates on the Zambian side of the border from Chadiza to Kanyelele near Isoka. In response the Permanent Secretary for Eastern Province, General Peter Tembo, described encroachment by Malawians on Zambian territory as "a serious matter".

Simon Massey

1. 15 Mauritius - United Kingdom (Diego Garcia)

A dispute concerning the island of Diego Garcia —the principal island of the Chagos Archipelago, situated in the Indian Ocean some 1,200 miles (1,900 kilometres) to the north-east of Mauritius and forming part of the British Indian Ocean Territory—came into the open in 1980 when the government of Mauritius demanded that the island should revert to Mauritius, of which it had been a dependency until 1965 (when Mauritius was still a British Crown Colony). The grounds for the claim were in part that, in the view of the government of Mauritius, the British government had violated an undertaking allegedly given in 1967 to the effect that the island of Diego Garcia would not be used as a base for military purposes. However, the UK government has repeatedly denied having given such an undertaking. (Map 3, p. 494 illustrates this dispute.)

Historical and Geographical Background

During the 18th century the Indian Ocean and its African, Arabian and Indian coasts became an area of rivalry between British, French and Dutch companies seeking dominance over the spice trade and routes to India and the Far East. Having colonized Réunion in the mid-17th century, France claimed Mauritius in 1715 and subsequently took possession of the Seychelles island group and the Chagos Archipelago (the latter having strategic rather than commercial importance). During the Napoleonic Wars Britain captured Mauritius and Réunion from the French, who under the 1814 Treaty of Paris recovered Réunion but were obliged to cede Mauritius and its dependencies (the Seychelles and various other islands, including the Chagos Archipelago) to Britain. All these dependencies were administered from Mauritius until in 1903 the Seychelles group was detached to form a separate Crown Colony, the Chagos Archipelago continuing to be administered from the Crown Colony of Mauritius.

British official sources describe the connection

between Mauritius and the Chagos islands (and the Seychelles until 1903) as one of administrative convenience, following pre-1814 French practice, in that (i) there was little actual contact between them and Mauritius given the great distance between the two territories, and (ii) the islands had no economic relevance to Mauritius other than as a supplier of copra oil and as employer of contract labour for the copra plantations.

The British Indian Ocean Territory (BIOT) was established under an Order in Council of Nov. 8, 1965, and originally consisted of (i) the Chagos Archipelago and (ii) the islands of Aldabra, Farquhar and Des Roches (until then administered from the Seychelles, then still a Crown Colony): however, the latter islands were eventually returned to the Seychelles on its achievement of independence in June 1976. Thereafter the BIOT covered some 21,000 square miles (54,400 sq km) of ocean, the Chagos islands themselves (an archipelago of six main island groups on the Great Chagos Bank) having a land area of only 23 square miles (60 sq km). Diego Garcia, the most southerly of the Chagos islands, has a land area of about 17 square miles (44 sq km) and consists of a V-shaped sand cay almost enclosing a large deep-water lagoon.

Anglo-US Co-operation in the Development of a Communications Centre on Diego Garcia, 1965-76

When the creation of the BIOT was announced in the UK House of Commons on Nov. 10, 1965, it was explained that the arrangement had been made in agreement with the Mauritian and Seychelles governments; that the BIOT would be "available for the construction of defence facilities by the British and US governments"; and that "appropriate compensation" would be paid to the Mauritian and Seychelles governments, the amount involved being mentioned as £3,000,000, partly for resettlement of some 1,000 people from the Chagos Archipelago in Mauritius.

In Mauritius the transfer of the islands to Britain was opposed by the *Parti Mauricien social-démocrate*, then the second largest political party, which withdrew from the existing government coalition and whose leader, Gaëtan Duval, said on Nov. 7, 1965, that the party would not accept an Anglo-American base on Diego Garcia or the other islands unless Britain and the United States agreed "to buy all our sugar at a preferential price and to accept Mauritian immigrants".

An agreement concluded between the United Kingdom and the United States on Dec. 30, 1966, provided that the BIOT should remain under British sovereignty but be available to meet the defence needs of both countries. On Dec. 15, 1970, it was jointly announced in London and Washington that work planned under the 1966 agreement would begin in March 1971 on the construction of an Anglo-US naval communications facility consisting of "communications and minimum necessary support facilities, including an airstrip" on Diego Garcia.

On March 23, 1971, the United States opened a military communications station on Diego Garcia for the purpose of controlling the movements of US submarines, vessels and aircraft in the area, the station becoming fully operational in 1973. On Jan. 21, 1974, US Defence Department officials were reported to have confirmed plans for the expansion of the naval station into a base for the support of naval operations as the reopening of the Suez Canal was expected to lead to increased Soviet naval activity in the Indian Ocean. The UK Foreign and Commonwealth Office disclosed on Feb. 5, 1974, that "in response to a US proposal and in accordance with the 1966 Anglo-American agreement" the UK government had agreed in principle to expansion of the facilities on Diego Garcia (which would accommodate aircraft carriers and also KC-135 tanker planes used to refuel B-52 strategic bombers). This agreement was formalized in an exchange of notes on June 22 and 25, 1976, which amended the 1966 agreements.

The high commissioner of Mauritius in New Delhi (India) stated on April 7, 1974, that if the United States were allowed a base on Diego Garcia, Britain would be violating an undertaking given in 1967. The British government, however, denied having given any such undertaking. In a statement made on Dec. 3, 1974, by the UK (Labour) government's Secretary of State for Defence, it was confirmed that the British government had agreed to US proposals "for a relatively modest expansion of the facilities on the island of Diego Garcia", but it was added that the US use of the facilities other than for routine purposes would be a matter for joint decision of the two governments. The proposed expansion of the US naval facilities on the island was finally approved by the US Congress on July 28, 1975, and as a result the US Navy was enabled to proceed with the construction on Diego Garcia of a 12,000-foot runway and refuelling facilities for a carrier task force, involving an increase in US military personnel from 430 to about 600 men.

The matter was apparently not raised in talks which Sir Seewoosagur Ramgoolam, then Prime Minister of Mauritius, had in London with the UK Minister of State for Foreign and Commonwealth Affairs on Sept. 24, 1975, when a Mauritian request for British assistance towards an acceptable resettlement scheme was discussed. It emerged that the British government had paid £650,000 to Mauritius for the purpose of resettling 34 Chagos islander families consisting of 1,151 people (according to Mauritian government records) who had been transferred from the entire Chagos Archipelago between 1965 and 1973, including 359 taken from Diego Garcia when the copra plantations on that island were closed down in 1971. It was later reported that the money had not been paid to these people until 1978, when most of them were living in destitution in Mauritius. In that year the British government offered a further £500,000 but this offer was rejected by a representative committee of the islanders. In mid-1979 a new British offer was made, amounting to £1,250,000 or about £1,000 per person, payable on condition that the islanders undertook that neither they nor their children would ever return to the Chagos Archipelago. By January 1980 it appeared that this offer had been widely accepted by the evacuees.

On Oct. 13, 1975, the UK Secretary of State for Defence confirmed that under the 1966 agreement with the United States the latter had agreed to contribute half the total cost of setting up the BIOT (up to a limit of £5,000,000) by an offset arrangement against surcharges arising out of the British purchase of the US Polaris missile system.

Establishment of US Naval Base on Diego Garcia

It was announced in Washington on Jan. 4, 1980, that as a result of the crises in Afghanistan and Iran the US government had decided to maintain a permanent US naval presence on Diego Garcia, and on Jan. 12 the US government accordingly informed the British government of its intention to reinforce its military facilities on the island. In a summary of the US military position at the end of March 1980, submitted to the House of Representatives foreign affairs committee on April 2, 1980, the US Under-Secretary of Defence for Policy stated inter alia: "The network which we have developed for the region [of the Arabian Sea] is centred around Diego Garcia, where we expect to expand our facilities greatly in consultation with the United Kingdom".

The British Foreign and Commonwealth Office stated on May 29, 1980, that six or seven US cargo ships would be sent to Diego Garcia, and the UK Foreign and Commonwealth Secretary said on June 16 that the United States had a long-term programme for strengthening its military capability in the Indian Ocean. He said in particular: "This programme includes the pre-positioning of equipment to be available for use by forces deployed rapidly to the region in an emergency. At Diego Garcia such equipment will be held in converted merchant ships which will periodically be rotated within the Indian Ocean area. They do not constitute a naval task force. HM government were fully consulted over the proposal to send these ships to Diego Garcia in accordance with the provisions of the 1976 exchange of notes". It had been reported on May 11 that, as soon as adequate facilities were built, up to 4,500 US and other military personnel would be permanently established on Diego Garcia.

Opposition to the Militarization of Diego Garcia

Opposition to the establishment of US military facilities in the Indian Ocean area was registered by many of the states bordering the Indian Ocean (and also by the Soviet Union) and was expressed in repeated international calls for declaring the Indian Ocean a zone of peace.

On a proposal by Sri Lanka (then Ceylon), the General Assembly of the United Nations adopted, on Dec. 16, 1971 (in Resolution 2832/XXVI), a Declaration of the Indian Ocean as a Zone of Peace—the voting being 61 in favour to none against with 55 abstentions (which included those of all major powers

except China and Japan, which voted in favour). In this resolution it was solemnly declared that "the Indian Ocean, within limits to be determined, together with the airspace above and all the ocean floor subjacent thereto, is hereby designated for all time as a zone of peace". The great powers were called upon "to enter into immediate consultations with the littoral states of the Indian Ocean with a view to (a) halting the further escalation and expansion of their military presence in the Indian Ocean [and] (b) eliminating from the Indian Ocean all bases, military installations, logistical supply facilities, the disposition of nuclear weapons and weapons of mass destruction and any manifestation of great power military presence in the Indian Ocean conceived in the context of great power rivalry".

The declaration also called on the littoral and hinterland states of the Indian Ocean, the permanent members of the UN Security Council and other maritime users of the Indian Ocean to enter into consultations with a view to implementing the declaration. They were asked specifically to ensure that warships and military aircraft should not use the Indian Ocean for any threat or use of force against the sovereignty, territorial integrity and independence of any littoral or hinterland state; that the right to free and unimpeded use of the zone by vessels of all nations was unaffected; and that arrangements should be made to give effect to any international agreement which might ultimately be reached for the maintenance of the Indian Ocean as a zone of peace.

The Declaration of the Indian Ocean as a Zone of Peace subsequently was the subject of supporting resolutions adopted at regular sessions of the UN General Assembly, and also at its first and second special sessions on disarmament (held in May-July 1978 and June-July 1982 respectively). However, various initiatives to achieve the implementation of its provisions have made no substantive progress to date.

The Mauritian Claim to Diego Garcia

In Mauritius the claim to sovereignty over Diego Garcia was officially made with greater emphasis during 1980. Thus Sir Satcam Boolell, the Mauritian Minister of Agriculture, Natural Resources and the Environment, said in January 1980 that the US plans to improve the naval base on Diego Garcia might "increase tension in this part of the world and constitute a potential danger to Indian Ocean countries and to Mauritius in particular".

By early June 1980 the return of Diego Garcia to Mauritius was called for by the leaders of all political parties in Mauritius. Sir Seewoosagur Ramgoolam (then Prime Minister and leader of the Labour Party) was quoted on June 17 as saying that he had originally been forced to cede Diego Garcia because Britain "would have been able to take it away"; that he had understood that Britain would use the island as a communications centre; that he had not been told of plans to let it be used by the United States; and that, as Britain was not using the island for the purpose for which it was ceded, he had let it be known that Mauritius wanted it to be returned.

Paul Bérenger, the founder of the (leftist) Mauritian Militant Movement (the largest party in Parliament from 1976 to 1983) said at the same time that his party's fight was "political and diplomatic" for the return of Diego Garcia, which he called "part and parcel of Mauritian territory".

The British Foreign and Commonwealth Office, however, stated on June 24, 1980, that Mauritius had "at no stage" demanded the return of the island and that the matter had not been raised during a recent visit to Mauritius by the UK Minister of State at the Foreign and Commonwealth Office (Richard Luce).

On June 26, 1980, a bipartisan majority (of 48 out of the 70 members) of the Mauritian Parliament formally urged the government to demand the return of Diego Garcia to Mauritius, and Sir Seewoosagur stated on the following day that he would make the claim in London in 10 days' time; at the same time he did not rule out the possibility of taking the matter to the International Court of Justice in The Hague. The Mauritian Parliament subsequently passed an all-party motion calling for the return of Diego Garcia, and Sir Seewoosagur formally lodged the claim in talks which he had with the British Prime Minister (Margaret Thatcher) in London on July 7, 1980.

Following his return to Mauritius, he said on July 16, 1980, that he had pointed out to the British Prime Minister that it had been agreed that Diego Garcia would be returned to Mauritius without compensation when it was no longer needed; he denied that he had received "a polite refusal"; and he added that he would rally world opinion around Mauritius's claim. Earlier, the Assembly of Heads of State and Government of the Organization of African Unity (OAU) had on July 4, 1980, called for the demilitarization of Diego Garcia and for its unconditional return to Mauritius.

Under an agreement signed on July 7, 1982, the United Kingdom undertook to pay Mauritius £4 million in further resettlement assistance for families moved in 1965-73 from the Chagos Archipelago (i.e. the British Indian Ocean Territory). The Mauritian government, however, continued to claim that the Diego Garcia atoll had been wrongfully detached from the territory in 1965 and Mauritius maintains its claim to the entire Chagos Archipelago, which has since also been claimed by the Seychelles.

The case of Diego Garcia was next highlighted in 1989 by an accident. On Nov. 6, 1989, there were protests at the US Embassy in Port Louis and calls for the withdrawal of foreign military presences from the Indian Ocean since these were seen as a threat to the safety of island inhabitants in the Ocean. The protests were in reaction to an incident of Oct. 30, 1989, when a bomb from a US F-18 fighter aircraft was accidentally dropped on the *USS Reeves* off Diego Garcia (five sailors were injured). Mauritius reasserted its sovereignty over Diego Garcia. Following the protests, the US Assistant Secretary of State for African Affairs, Herman Cohen, visited Mauritius

from Nov. 9-11 when he reaffirmed the US intention of maintaining a military presence in the Indian Ocean as long as this was seen to be necessary by Washington.

During the 1991 Gulf War the base was extensively used by US forces to launch air attacks on southern Iraq. It became even more significant in the 2001 war in Afghanistan and was indispensable in the second Gulf War of 2003, when the US government was unable to secure enough bases in the immediate vicinity of Iraq. From the point of view of its critics, indeed, Diego Garcia had become a platform indispensable for US plans for the military control and domination of the whole of the Middle East and for the first time of Central Asia.

Meanwhile the US government maintained its veto on the return of former inhabitants to the archipelago on security grounds. The islanders pursued their case for restitution in the British courts. In 2001 they were granted UK citizenship. However, in October 2003 the High Court in London ruled that the claimants had "no reasonable prospects" of persuading a court that an action for damages should be allowed to proceed, and that any title any of them might have had to property on the islands had been extinguished.

Peter Calvert

1.16 Morocco - Spain

Since achieving independence in 1956 Morocco has actively pursued a claim to four small enclaves of land and three small islands on the north Moroccan coast, all under Spanish sovereignty and now comprising the only remaining European possessions on the African continent. The enclaves, over which Spanish rule dates from the 15th and 16th centuries, are the towns of Ceuta and Melilla and the Peñones (Rocks) of Alhucemas and Vélez de la Gomera; the islands, which were acquired by Spain in the 19th century, are the nearby Chafarinas (see Map 8, p. 496).

Of Spain's former colonial possessions in north-west Africa, the enclave of Ifni on the south-west Moroccan coast was returned to Morocco in 1969 and Spanish (Western) Sahara was effectively ceded to Morocco and Mauritania in 1979 (see Section 1.20). The Moroccan government has demanded that this decolonization process should be completed by the cession of the northern coast enclaves, but Spain has continued to insist that for historical and demographic reasons they are part of Spanish territory rather than colonial possessions.

Morocco also claims the Canary Islands (Islas Canarias), which lie off its Atlantic coast, but has not actively pursued this claim. However, Morocco officially rejected Spain's unilateral designation of a median line from the Canary Islands in 2002 to set limits to its undersea resource exploration and refugee interdiction in the area, although it had been willing previously to allow Spanish fishermen to fish temporarily off the coast of Western Sahara after Spanish fishing grounds had been contaminated by oil.

Ceuta, situated near Tangier and opposite Gibraltar, has a land area of 19 square kilometres, 20 kilometres of sea coast and eight kilometres of land boundaries; it has a predominantly Spanish population of about 67,000. Melilla, situated to the east of Ceuta, close to the town of Nador, has a land area of 12 square kilometres, 3.9 kilometres of sea coast and 10 kilometres of land boundaries; its population, also predominantly Spanish, numbers 65,000. Spain maintains military garrisons in both Ceuta and Melilla.

The Peñones de Alhucemas are made up of three small islands facing Alhucemas (near Ajdir) and, like Peñones de Vélez de la Gomera, are situated between Ceuta and Melilla. The Chafarinas Islands, 27 sea miles east of Melilla, face Kebdana cape. The Peñones have a civilian-military population of less than 100 each, and the Chafarinas of about 200.

Of the five territories, only Ceuta and Melilla are of economic importance, Ceuta being mainly a port for petroleum products and passenger traffic and Melilla a port for the export of iron ore as well as a fishing port. Ceuta, Melilla and the Chafarinas became free port areas in 1863, while the Peñones achieved this status in 1872. Their economic progress proved harmful to traditional Moroccan ports such as Tetouan, particularly when the Rif tribes abandoned the latter in favour of contraband trade with the free ports.

Spain bases its claim to continued possession of the enclaves (known as the Presidios, or military frontier districts, formerly also used as penal colonies, up to the early 20th century) on its conquest of them in the past, on its lengthy occupation of the areas over several centuries, on bilateral treaties concluded with the sultans of Morocco, and on their largely Spanish population. It also points out that the enclaves were acquired before Morocco became an independent nation. The new Spanish constitution which entered into force on Dec. 29, 1978, described Ceuta and Melilla as Spanish cities and provided for them to be represented in the Spanish Cortes by one deputy and two senators each.

Morocco, on the other hand, has consistently claimed the territories as being within the "natural boundaries" of its kingdom, together with the former Spanish Sahara. It adds that, because it has no access to Ceuta and Melilla, it has had to equip ports such as Nador and Tangier for passenger traffic and trade; that the territorial waters around the enclaves interfere with fishing rights; and that Spain has used the same arguments in favour of retaining the enclaves as Britain has used in defence of its possession of Gibraltar against Spain's wishes (for Gibraltar dispute, see Section 4.17).

Historical Background to the Dispute

Ceuta was conquered by the Portuguese in 1415 and became an important town with a military and economic role. When Portugal became attached to Spain in 1580 after the death of King Sebastian of Portugal without an heir, all Portuguese settlements on the north Moroccan coast—Ceuta, Tangier and Mazagan—became Spanish possessions. The union of Spain and Portugal ended in 1640 (when Lisbon rose against Philip IV), and Portugal claimed back its former territories. However, Ceuta proclaimed its allegiance to Spain and was later definitely reincorporated into the kingdom of Castille in 1668.

Of the other enclaves, Melilla was taken by the Spanish in 1497; Peñon de Vélez de la Gomera was occupied in 1508, Spanish sovereignty being confirmed in 1509 by the Treaty of Sintra (although the Spanish lost control of the Peñon from 1522 to 1564); and the Peñones de Alhucemas were occupied in 1673 and then ceded to Charles II by the Sultan of Morocco, on condition that Spain prevented the Turks from seizing strongholds on the Mediterranean coast. The Chafarinas Islands were occupied by Spain in 1848, allegedly to forestall a French occupation of the area; Spain named them Congreso, Isabel II and Isla del Rey (King's Island), although a French study team had previously named them Buckland, Busch and Brongniart.

In the 17th and 18th centuries there were repeated Moroccan attempts to oust the Spanish from the enclaves. Ceuta in particular came under persistent siege from 1694 to 1720, in 1727-28, in 1732 and again in 1790-91 for a 14-month period. Melilla was besieged in 1694-96 and for 100 days in 1774-75. The Peñon de Vélez de la Gomera was besieged in 1687 and its fort was razed to the ground in 1702, although the Peñon itself remained in Spanish hands and was besieged again in 1774 at the same time as Melilla. However, although such attacks (mounted largely by undisciplined tribesmen) continued into the 19th century, the sultans of Morocco meanwhile entered into a series of treaties recognizing the sovereignty of Spain over the Presidios and also dealing with their borders.

In May 1767 a peace and trade treaty was concluded between Charles III of Spain and Sidi Mohamed ben Abdallah (Mohammed III) guaranteeing the safety of any "Christian or renegade" who took refuge in the Presidios and rejecting any request by Spain for an extension of the limits of the Presidios. It stated that "ever since these places have been occupied by Spain, their Imperial Majesties have set their limits according to the opinion of their tolbas and ulemas and have promised not to change anything".

In March 1799, following a siege of Melilla by the same Sidi Mohamed ben Abdallah, a treaty of peace, friendship, navigation, trade and fishing was signed between Charles IV and Moulay Slimane. It renewed the 1767 treaty, confirmed a 1782 agreement on "the boundaries of the camp of Ceuta", and gave Spain the authority to use heavy guns against the Moors of Melilla, Alhucemas and Peñon de Vélez if they continued to cause trouble. This treaty was confirmed by the May 1845 Larache Convention (signed after further tribal incidents) which dealt with the boundaries of Ceuta. Melilla's boundaries were laid down in an August 1859 agreement and were confirmed in an 1862 boundary convention.

In August 1859 the Convention of Tetouan was signed between representatives of Isabella II and Moulay Abderrahman, allowing an extension of Melilla's borders to facilitate its defence. The convention agreed to "cede to her Catholic Majesty the possession and full jurisdiction over territory near the Spanish place known as Melilla as far as necessary for the defence and tranquillity of this Presidio". The limits of the Presidio were to be established as being equivalent to "the range of an old-model 24 cannon shot", and the demarcation took place later the same year when a cannon ball was fired from the top of Melilla's fortress and landed on a southern beach of the town 2,900 metres away, the boundary being then traced in detail from that point. An act delimiting the territory of Melilla was signed in Tangier in June 1862.

Under the Convention of Tetouan the Sultan also promised to place soldiers at Melilla's frontier to suppress any unrest among the Rif tribesmen that might compromise good relations, and troops were also to be placed in the vicinity of the Peñones "to enforce respect for Spain's rights and effectively to ensure free entry into these towns of the necessary foodstuffs and supplies for its garrisons". A neutral area was designated between Spanish and Moroccan territory.

In the meantime hostilities took place between Spain and Morocco in 1859-60 (over reparations for damage caused when tribesmen laid siege to Ceuta). A peace and friendship treaty signed in April 1860 (also in Tetouan) ended the war and prescribed the extent of Ceuta's territory "as far as necessary for the safety and complete defence of the garrison". It also set out full details of reference points necessary to define a zone "ceded in full possession and sovereignty" to Spain in conformity with the results of a study which had been agreed in detail by Spanish and Moroccan commissioners in April 1860. A neutral area was declared around Ceuta as in the case of Melilla. Other agreements specifying the status of the Presidios were signed up to 1911, all of which confirmed the existing frontiers as well as dealing with the day-to-day aspects of life in the enclaves. The only Spanish "jurisdictional territory" in North Africa which did not have a status decreed by convention between Spain and Morocco was the Chafarinas Islands.

Agreements among the great powers of the day recognizing Spain's presence in the Presidios were also signed in the early 20th century, although the major content of the treaties dealt with the delimitation of the borders of Spanish Sahara. Among these, the Franco-British Declaration of April 1904 affirmed Britain's freedom of action in Egypt in return for a British guarantee of France's freedom of action in Morocco, while at the same time it took into consideration "the interests of [Spain] by reason of its possessions on the Moroccan coast of the Mediterranean". Moreover, the Franco-Spanish Convention of October 1904, which was designed to secure Spanish co-operation regarding the April 1904 agreement, recognized the "extent of Spain's rights to guarantee its interest...as the result of having these possessions on the Moroccan coast".

The Franco-Moroccan Treaty of Fez of March 1912 established the French Protectorate in Morocco but specified also that the French government should "come to agreement with the Spanish government with respect to the interest that the latter has as a result of its geographical position and its territorial possessions on the Moroccan coast". The Franco-Spanish Agreement of November 1912 was drawn up "to clarify the respective situations of the two countries with respect to the Cherifien empire" and was largely concerned with Spanish Sahara and Ifni.

After Spain had extended its presence around Melilla in 1908, hostilities broke out in July 1909 when Rif tribesmen hostile to the idea of Spanish mineral prospecting in the region attacked the site of a proposed railway connecting the mines with Melilla. Violent battles that month marked the beginning of years of hostilities between Spain and the Rifs, and by 1920 Spain retained only its enclaves, Larache and Tetouan on the north African coast. The last major battle of the war was at Alhucemas in 1925, which was decisive for the Spaniards and put an end to all but isolated skirmishes.

Moroccan Claims to Enclaves since Independence

Since its independence in 1956 Morocco has strongly reaffirmed its claims to the Presidios before international organizations and in Non-Aligned and Arab forums. In 1961 Morocco called on the UN General Assembly to recognize its rights over the enclaves and began a diplomatic offensive, whereupon Spain reinforced the borders of the enclaves and Morocco imposed transit restrictions. On June 29, 1962, Morocco reasserted its claim to Ceuta and Melilla and on the following day extended its territorial waters from six to 12 miles; this affected the operations of Spanish fishing boats in the waters off the enclaves and resulted in Spain sending warships to escort its fishing vessels in the area, and also in the reinforcement of the military garrisons in the enclaves. Over the next few years, however, the attention of Spain and Morocco was diverted to other questions such as the status of Gibraltar, Spanish Sahara and Ifni. A meeting in July 1963 between Gen. Franco and King Hassan II at Madrid airport marked the beginning of a rapprochement between the two countries, and King Hassan visited Spain in 1965.

In the mid-1970s, as trouble blew up over the question of Spanish Sahara, Morocco again began to press its claims to the enclaves. On Jan. 27, 1975, it formally requested the UN Decolonization Committee to place on its agenda the question of the remaining Spanish enclaves on or close to the Moroccan coast and alluded to UN Resolution 1514/XV of Dec. 14, 1960, condemning colonialism. Spain, however, condemned the Moroccan move as a "threat to Spain's national unity and territorial integrity" and warned that it would use all necessary legitimate means to defend the enclaves, communicating these views to the United Nations on Feb. 12, 1975. The Spanish government maintained that although the Presidios were "geographically separate" from Spain they were not "ethnically or culturally distinct" since their "true indigenous population was of Spanish origin, nationality and language as are their feelings, customs and culture"; it added that this was what differentiated them from Gibraltar, whose population had been driven out when the British entered. Spain also claimed that since the enclaves were "sovereign territories", and not "non-autonomous territories", they did not come within the competence of the Decolonization Committee.

Later the same year three people were killed in bomb explosions in Ceuta and Melilla in June, and about 400 Moroccans were subsequently reported to have been arrested in Ceuta. Spanish and Moroccan troops later confronted each other on the borders of Melilla. These incidents led Morocco to protest in a letter to the UN Secretary-General on June 30, 1975, at the "violations of human rights committed by the Spanish authorities" in Ceuta and to warn that, "if such practices continue, the Moroccan government will be constrained to take the measures necessary to protect the rights and interests of its nationals".

Attention was diverted from the question of the enclaves to the Spanish Sahara with the signature of the Madrid agreement in November 1975 under which Spain withdrew from the latter territory. However, after King Juan Carlos ascended the Spanish throne on the death of Gen. Franco in November 1975 and reaffirmed Spain's aim of re-establishing sovereignty over Gibraltar, King Hassan asserted at a press conference the same month that if Spain came into possession of Gibraltar, Morocco would retrieve Ceuta and Melilla because "no power can permit Spain to possess both keys to the same straits".

Developments in the 1980s

Following the conclusion in August 1984 of a Moroccan-Libyan treaty of federation, Spanish officials privately expressed fears that this could lead to active Libyan support for Morocco's claims. The matter was raised in talks between Col. Moamer al Kadhafi, the Libyan leader, and Felipe González, the Spanish Prime Minister, in December of that year. Some tension between the two countries ensued from a statement made by Kadhafi at a press conference after the talks when he referred to Ceuta and Melilla as "Arab cities". In an interview on Spanish television on Feb. 8, 1985, King Hassan again argued that the enclaves could not remain in Spanish possession following the return of Gibraltar to Spanish sovereignty. In subsequent months, Moroccan officials frequently portrayed the issues as linked, suggesting that both were anachronistic anomalies of colonialism.

The question of the enclaves came to a head in July 1985 with the passage in Spain of the Organic Law on the Rights and Liberties of Foreigners, under which all foreigners residing in Spain were required to reapply for residence permits and those whose documents were not in order would face expulsion. The law caused particular resentment among the Muslim residents of Ceuta and Melilla, who (in contrast to certain other long-standing minority groups in Spain) were not granted special status excepting them from the law's provisions. According to Spanish government figures, fewer than 3,000 of Melilla's 17,000 Muslims currently held Spanish nationality.

Muslim opposition in Melilla crystallized around the "Terra Omnium" organization, led by Aomar Mohamedi Dudu, which organized a mass demonstration in November 1985. The Spanish government subsequently promised that the law would be interpreted "generously" with regard to the enclaves, and that virtually all Muslims who applied could count on obtaining legal residence permits guaranteeing them Spanish citizenship within 10 years if all conditions were fulfilled. This assurance was rejected as inadequate by Dudu and his supporters, who continued to press for a moratorium on the application of the law to the enclaves. Further demonstrations, some of them violent, occurred in Melilla over the next two months, and there were also demonstrations in support of the legislation by European residents.

Growing tension between the European and Muslim communities in Melilla was reflected in the return to the Spanish Parliament in the June 1986 general election of three *Coalicíon Popular* (conservative) deputies, the enclave having previously returned Socialist representatives. A "parallel election" for the majority of Muslims who did not enjoy Spanish nationality (and were thus deprived of the right to vote) was organized by Dudu. A number of violent communal clashes broke out around the time of the election, and included fighting between European demonstrators and Spanish riot police, after which one of the newly-elected deputies was arrested. In an effort to defuse the tension, the government agreed to an 18-month schedule for the granting of residence permits, and in September 1986 appointed Dudu as special adviser to the Minister of the Interior to represent Muslim communities in Spain. Soon after taking up the post, however, Dudu antagonized the government by visiting Morocco for talks with Driss Basri, the Interior Minister, with whom he agreed on the "Arab and Muslim" character of the enclaves.

In November 1986, the Muslim community in Melilla staged a four-day general strike in support of demands for the immediate granting of Spanish citizenship, and violent clashes between Europeans and Muslims erupted at the end of January 1987, in which one Muslim died of gunshot wounds. Arrest warrants were issued for a number of leading Muslims, including Dudu, who had fled into Morocco, on charges of inciting subversive movements. A planned rally by European residents requesting assistance from the United Kingdom, in the absence of sufficient support for their cause from the Spanish government, was banned by security police at the beginning of February.

In a move to defuse the inter-communal tension, Felipe González confirmed in a state of the nation address to the Spanish Parliament on Feb. 24, 1987, that Spanish nationality would normally be granted to Muslim residents of the enclaves. On the other hand, the Spanish government had meanwhile rejected a Moroccan proposal made in January that a joint commission should be set up to discuss the enclaves question at inter-governmental level. Nonetheless, Spain placed high priority on relations with Morocco while the latter was willing to wait for a negotiated settlement.

On Jan. 22, 1989, King Hassan of Morocco released a statement describing as "provocative" a series of legal and administrative measures taken by Spain in relation to the status of Ceuta and Melilla. This led to the immediate postponement of a visit by Spain's Foreign Minister, Francisco Fernández Ordóñez, to Morocco, although it was made on Feb. 3. Later in the year (Sept. 25-27) Hassan visited Spain; he avoided mention of Ceuta and Melilla.

On July 4, 1991, King Juan Carlos of Spain made a state visit to Morocco and a treaty of "friendship, good neighbourliness and co-operation" between the two countries was signed in Rabat by Spain's Prime Minister, Felipe González, and Morocco's Prime Minister, Azzedine Laraki. The treaty guaranteed the peaceful settlement of disputes between the two countries (which related especially to Ceuta and Melilla). On July 6, Morocco's Interior and Information Minister, Driss Basri, and the Emigration Minister, Rafile Haddaoui, visited Ceuta and Melilla at the invitation of the Spanish Interior Minister, José Luis Corcuera. The visit was strongly criticized by the Moroccan opposition newspaper of the Socialist Union of Popular Forces.

In 1997, the five hundredth anniversary of the capture of Melilla, Spain issued a coin showing it as a Spanish province.

The Conflict of 2002

Relations between Morocco and Spain became increasingly tense when in October 2001 the new King of Morocco, Mohammed VI, who had succeeded his father in 1999, withdrew Morocco's ambassador to Madrid. Apart from Spanish support for the Polisario Front in Western Sahara, matters in dispute had included fishing, farming, immigration and drug-smuggling.

Early in July 2002 the Spanish ambassador in Rabat was summoned to the Foreign Ministry to receive a complaint that Spain had, without the advance warning that had previously been normal in such cases, deployed warships to the Peñones de Alhucemas,

which lie within Moroccan territorial waters only 600 metres from the Moroccan port of El-Hoceima (Alhucemas). On July 11, while Moroccans were celebrating the wedding of King Mohammed VI, a small group of Moroccan frontier guards occupied the uninhabited islet of Leila (known in Spain as the Isla del Perejil, or Parsley Island), raised the Moroccan flag and established an encampment. A Civil Guard detachment from the Spanish enclave of Ceuta was driven off at gunpoint.

The Spanish government sent three small patrol vessels to the area and reinforced garrisons in the Chafarinas Islands, where a Moroccan patrol boat had also been sighted. On July 17, twenty-eight Spanish special forces were landed by helicopter and stormed Perejil, capturing six Moroccan soldiers. The captives were taken by launch to Ceuta, from where they were returned to Morocco across the land frontier. Although the Moroccans described this as "a declaration of war", the Spanish Foreign Minister, Ana Palacio, told the Cortés that the intention was not to impose a solution by force but simply to restore the status quo; Spain had no intention of permanently garrisoning the island, though it had raised its flag there. On July 22, Palacio and the Moroccan Foreign Minister, Mohamed Benaissa, ratified an agreement, brokered by US Secretary of State Colin Powell, under which Spain withdrew its troops from Perejil and Morocco agreed to leave it uninhabited, while continuing to assert Moroccan sovereignty.

Peter Calvert

1.17 Namibia - Botswana (Caprivi Strip)

Following Namibian independence from South Africa in 1990, presidential visits were exchanged by Namibia and Botswana and mechanisms established to ensure bilateral co-operation between the two governments. A dispute soon arose, however, over rival territorial claims on Botswana's northern border with Namibia over a narrow piece of Namibian territory called the Caprivi Strip (for position, see Map 9, p. 497). About 100,000 people currently live in Caprivi and the territorial issue was complicated in the late 1990s by the secessionist aspirations of the Caprivi Liberation Front.

Historical Background

The area is a colonial anachronism. The Caprivi Strip extends eastwards from northeastern Namibia as far as the Zambesi and has borders with Zimbabwe, Zambia and Angola, as well as Botswana. Historically the land was part of Barotseland under the jurisdiction of the

Lozi kings, when it was known as Itenge, and these cultural links remain. In the late nineteenth century it fell under the administration of the British Protectorate of Bechuanaland (now called Botswana). The area then became subject to a territorial deal between Britain and Germany. Under the terms of the 1890 Anglo-German treaty the territory was acquired by Germany to give German Southwest Africa access to the Zambesi; it became known in English as the Caprivi Strip after the then German Chancellor and Foreign Minister, Graf Georg Leo von Caprivi de Caprera de Montecuccioli.

After World War I the area returned to British rule, South Africa assuming the Southwest Africa mandate in 1920. The Bechuanaland High Commission administered the area until 1929 when control shifted to Pretoria. In 1966 South Africa's legal right to the mandate was revoked by the UN and the administration of Caprivi returned to Windhoek (the Namibian capital), although South Africa remained in occupation of Namibia. Throughout the 1970s and 1980s South Africa maintained a military presence in the area as part of its campaign against the Namibian liberation movement, the Southwest Africa People's Organization (SWAPO).

Dispute over Kasikili/Sedudu—Other Border Tensions

In October 1992 it was reported in the media that members of the Botswana Defence Force (BDF) had deployed on a small island in the Chobe river called Kasikili in Namibia and Sedudu in Botswana, and confiscated nets from Namibian fishermen. The island is 3.5 sq km in area. The Chobe river divides around Kasikili/Sedudu and the island is flooded for part of the year following the seasonal rains. The Namibian government announced that high-level meetings between officials from both countries had determined that the dispute should be settled amicably. A Namibia-Botswana Commission of Defence and Security was established. However, a Joint Team of Technical Experts convened to determine the boundary around the disputed island could not reach a consensus, citing historical and technical disagreements. At a meeting held in Harare in February 1995, Presidents Ketumile Masire of Botswana and Sam Nujoma of Namibia agreed to submit the dispute to the International Court of Justice (ICJ) for a "final and binding determination". This intention was given legal authority by a Special Agreement signed in February 1996 that came into force in May 1996.

The agreement to take the dispute to the ICJ coincided with Namibia voicing concern over Botswana's wider ambitions, in particular the activities of the BDF near Kasikili/Sedudu. General Seretse Ian Khama, Botswana's Minister of Defence, announced that the deployment of the army was to enforce a government campaign to eradicate cattle infected with bovine lung disease, although the outbreak was several hundred miles away from the disputed island, and as an anti-poaching measure. In response Namibia's Minister of Foreign Affairs, Theo-Ben Gurirab, stated that the Ministry of Defence would attempt to ascertain whether these were the real reasons for the troop build-up, adding that if Botswana was aiming to entrench its presence on the island, there would be very serious consequences. Namibia was also concerned about Botswana's extensive arms procurement programme and general military build up. In 1996-97 Botswana acquired sophisticated F-5 fighter aircraft from Canada and battle tanks from Austria; in addition, the construction of a new airbase at Molepolole was in the process of completion. In an interview with *The Namibian* Botswana's high commissioner in Windhoek, Edwin Matenge, sought to allay Namibian anxieties, stressing that the enhancement of Botswana's military capacity was not linked to the Kasikili/Sedudu dispute. A further issue of contention between the countries was the construction by Botswana of an electric fence along the boundary. The fence was apparently built as another measure to control bovine lung disease. However, the project was undertaken without an environmental assessment, and Namibia was concerned at the impact on wildlife and the concomitant effect on tourism. In October 1997 the Botswanan government agreed to take down part of the fence. By November 1998 the entire fence had been dismantled.

Meanwhile cross-border tension had increased. The BDF had sent troops to islands in Caprivi's Linyanti river to eject Namibian farmers whom they claimed were in Botswanan territory. Namibian villagers had long cultivated land on the Situngu marshlands which they called Singobeka. The heavily-armed BDF soldiers told them to abandon their fields. On Oct. 7 delegations from the two sides met at Situngu. It was decided to refer the matter to the local traditional leaders, again on both sides of the border, to resolve. A further meeting between government officials from both sides was held at the Caprivi capital of Katimo Mulilo in November. As an interim measure it was decided to allow farmers who had already begun cultivating to continue until the dispute was settled.

The continued presence of Botswanan troops on Situngu—officially deployed to prevent poaching—inflamed the dispute. There were reports of BDF harassment of the Namibian farmers. President Nujoma sought the support of regional leaders, visiting President Robert Mugabe of Zimbabwe and President Nelson Mandela of South Africa. In January 1998 at a meeting of the Namibia-Botswana Commission of Defence and Security, Botswana's Minister for Presidential Affairs and Public Administration, Ponatshego Kedikilwe, invited members of the Namibian delegation to visit Situngu. Although the delegation declined, an independent Namibian MP accompanied by members of the Namibian army visited the area, where they were confronted by BDF soldiers and asked to leave. In response the Namiban Minister of Defence, Errikki Nghimtina, accused Botswana of "provoking the situation". The meeting, nonetheless, agreed to establish a Joint Technical Commission, firstly to demarcate the boundary around Situngu, and secondly to demarcate the boundary along the "Kwando-Linyanti-Chobe river system". In May 1998 representatives from the two governments initialled an accord binding them to a diplomatic solution. However, Botswana kept a military presence in the area.

Flight of Caprivians to Botswana in 1998

In October 1998 unrest within Caprivi spilled over the border. About 2,500 Caprivians, mainly from the Mafwe and Kxoe ethnic groups, fled to Botswana. They included the leadership of the Caprivi Liberation Front (CLF). This group, led by Mishake Muyongo, sees itself as a liberation movement but is regarded as a secessionist movement by the government in Windhoek. The exodus was the result of operations carried out as part of a crackdown on the CLF by the Namibian security forces in which Caprivi civilians were abused.

Despite Namibia's calls for their extradition, Botswana granted political asylum to 14 CLF leaders. An agreement was reached whereby the leaders were resettled in Denmark and Finland and mechanisms were put in place in tandem with the UN High Commissioner for Refugees (UNHCR) for the repatriation of the other refugees. However, early 1999 saw renewed security sweeps by the Namibian security forces in Caprivi, resulting in widespread damage to infrastructure and internal displacement of persons. As a result the repatriation process was halted. The majority of the refugees were moved to Dukwe camp in eastern Botswana and around half of the 2,500 refugees agreed to be repatriated over the next four years. However, by March 2004, there remained a core of about 1,200 refugees, mainly from the Mafwe ethnic group most associated with the CLF, who refused to return whilst Caprivi remained under Namibian administration.

ICJ Ruling on Kasikili/Sedudu

On Dec. 13, 1999, the ICJ issued its ruling on the disputed island of Kasikili/Sedudu. The decision turned on Article III, paragraph 2 of the Anglo-German treaty of 1890. The passage translated from German to English reads: "a line runs eastward along that parallel until it reaches the River Chobe; and descends the centre of the main channel of that river to its junction with the Zambesi, where it terminates". Botswana argued that there were different shades of meaning between the English word "channel" and the original German word "thalweg"—the latter more accurately translating as "the way downward", which may be the deepest but not necessarily the main channel of a river. Botswana maintained that, in order to establish the line of the boundary around Kasikili/Sedudu island, it was suffi-

cient to determine the thalweg of the Chobe, which would identify the main channel of the river. Namibia, however, argued that the task of the Court was first to identify the main channel of the Chobe around Kasikili/Sedudu, and then to determine where the centre of that channel lay. Botswana contended that the channel running to the north of the island was the thalweg, whilst Namibia contended that the channel to the south of the island was the main channel.

The Court also considered Namibian claims that local Caprivians had periodically occupied Kasikili/Sedudu, depending on seasonal circumstances and flooding. However, the Court ruled that such occupation was not based on the functional act of state authority, even though Namibia regarded this use as the basis for claims for historical occupation of the island. The Court also found that the supposed occupation of the island by local Caprivians was with the knowledge and acceptance of the Botswana authorities and its predecessors.

The final ruling was given in favour of Botswana by 11 votes to four. The northern channel around Sedudu/Kasikili would be taken as the main channel and, thus, the formal boundary between Namibia and Botswana would be located in the northern channel of the Chobe river. The Court also unanimously ruled that river vessels from both countries should "enjoy equal national treatment".

Agreement on Demarcation of Kwando-Linyanti-Chobe River System

In March 2003 President Festus Mogae of Botswana met his Namibian counterpart, President Nujoma, to discuss the report of the Joint Technical Commission established to delimit and demarcate the boundary along the "Kwando-Linyanti-Chobe river system". The detailed report followed the decision of ICJ in the Kasikili/Sedudu case and concluded that the deeper side of the Chobe, Linyanti, and Kwando rivers was Botswanan territory. This was accepted by both governments and recommended to the respective parliaments. Namibian Defence Minister Nghimtina commended both governments for reaching an amicable solution to the dispute and called on other African countries that face boundary problems to follow the example set by Namibia and Botswana.

Relations between the two countries now seem cordial. In December 2003, in a change of policy, the Botswana authorities handed over seven members of the Caprivi Liberation Army accused of treason to the Namibian authorities. However, the issue of riparian rights along the Okavango river has the potential to develop into a source of conflict. Botswana has signalled concerns over the effect Namibian plans to construct a hydroelectric dam at the Popa Falls in Caprivi will have on its own stretch of the river.

Simon Massey

1.18 Namibia - South Africa

The southern border between Namibia (which as South West Africa was administered by South Africa from 1915 to 1990) and South Africa itself runs for a continuous length of 600 miles (965 kilometres). The alignment of the border was agreed in 1890 by the then relevant colonial authorities, Britain and Germany; it runs along the Orange (also known as Gariep) River, and recently there has been a dispute between Namibia and South Africa as to whether the border runs down the centre of the river, or—as the South African government claims—on its northern bank. This has important implications for diamond prospecting in particular, and the dispute intensified in 2001 as Namibia tried to assert its authority over mineral and water rights along its borders (it failed in asserting similar claims in rivers that formed part of its border with Botswana). New gas and diamond deposits were discovered off the mouth of the Orange River, and the demarcation of the boundary out to sea had potentially important economic consequences. The South African government argued that it was complying with the Organization of African Unity (now African Union) policy of not redrawing colonial boundaries, but in late 2003 the issue remained an area of contention between the two countries.

Walvis Bay Issue

Earlier, the main dispute between the two countries had related to Walvis Bay (for position, see Map 9, page 497). South Africa had claimed that Walvis Bay constituted an enclave within the territory of Namibia, and from 1977 the enclave was administered by South Africa as an integral part of its territory. A number of small islands off the Namibian coast, known collectively as the Penguin Islands, were also regarded by South Africa as forming an integral part of its own territory. These disputes were resolved after the independence of Namibia in 1990, and Walvis Bay and the Islands were formally incorporated into Namibia at the end of February 1994.

South Africa had claimed that Walvis Bay and the Penguin Islands became British possessions in the latter half of the 19th century. They were then annexed by Britain to the British Cape Colony. The whole of Cape Colony became part of the Union of South Africa, established in 1910. Namibia, on the other hand, had come under German colonial rule in 1884 with the establishment of the German protectorate of South West Africa. The former German colony became a League of Nations mandated territory and was entrusted by the League to South African administration in 1920. After the League was dissolved, the United Nations as its post-war successor organization took over responsibility for the mandated territories (designating them as UN trust territories), but the South African government refused to conclude a UN trusteeship agreement and continued to administer the territory, even framing its own abortive constitutional and independence initiative in the mid-1970s. Meanwhile, the UN General Assembly in 1966 declared the South African mandate terminated and in 1967 set up a UN Council to administer the territory, which it resolved in 1968 should be known as Namibia. The illegality of the South African presence in Namibia was confirmed by the UN Security Council in 1969 and in an advisory opinion of the International Court of Justice in 1971.

From 1977, protracted negotiations took place to arrange for a transition to independence in Namibia in a form which would be accepted by the people of the territory as well as by the UN and South Africa. The nationalist South West Africa People's Organization (SWAPO) was recognized by the UN General Assembly from 1973 as the authentic representative, and from 1976 as the sole and authentic representative, of the Namibian people.

It was in the context of moves towards a future independent Namibia that the territorial status of Walvis Bay became an active dispute. Having found it convenient from 1920 to 1977 to administer Walvis Bay as if it were part of the territory of South West Africa under their administration, the South Africans in 1977 announced that Walvis Bay would be administered as an integral part of Cape Province, to which it had technically belonged all the time. This was declared by SWAPO to be an act of illegal annexation, their contention being that Walvis Bay, the only deep-water port along the Namibian coast, was an integral part of Namibia. This position was endorsed by the UN General Assembly and the UN Council for Namibia, but the Western Contact Group, the main mediators in the Namibian conflict, agreed that the issue should be resolved after Namibia's independence.

Territorial Divisions by the Colonial Powers

British annexation of the Penguin Islands. The Penguin Islands are situated a few miles off the Namibian coast in a line running from Hollandsbird or Hallamsbird island (about 100 miles south of Walvis Bay) southward over a distance of some 250 miles (400 kilometres), the most southerly being Roastbeef Island. The group includes the islands called Mercury, Ichaboe, Seal, Penguin, Halifax, Long, Possession, Albatross Rock, Panama and Plumpudding.

A short-lived Dutch occupation of Halifax Island in 1793 was followed by the visit of a British ship in 1795 to a number of bays which were declared British possessions. However, it was not until the 1860s that clear action was taken by the British with regard to the islands, which had become valuable as sources of guano (the guano deposits having been declared by the British governor of Cape Colony in 1845 to be the property of Her Majesty). In 1861 the British took formal possession of Ichaboe Island, and on August 12 of that year the governor of Cape Colony declared British sovereignty over all 12 islands and rocks. This proclamation was disallowed in 1864 but restored in 1866, when on May 5 the captain of a British ship took possession of Penguin Island and declared British sovereignty and dominion over the others. On July 16, 1866, the governor of Cape Colony proclaimed the islands annexed to and part of the colony, this action being authorized in the Royal Letters Patent of February 1867.

The British claim to the islands was recognized by the German colonial authorities in 1886 and 1890 (i.e. after the establishment of the German mainland protectorate), and the islands continued to be regarded as part of the Cape Colony, passing as such from British rule in 1910 and coming thereafter under the administration of the Union (later the Republic) of South Africa.

British annexation of Walvis Bay. Walvis Bay, where a small whaling settlement was established in the 18th century, was one of the bays claimed first by the Dutch in 1793 and then by the British two years later. However, it was not until the 1870s that the British took formal steps towards the annexation of Walvis Bay, after perceiving a possible threat to their interests in south-west Africa if Boer trekkers were to establish themselves north of the Orange River.

The government of the British Cape Colony appointed in March 1876 a commissioner extraordinary for Namaland and Damaraland (the Nama and Damara being tribes indigenous to what is now Namibia), whose report in 1877 recommended the annexation of Walvis Bay (then known as Walfish Bay) and surrounding territory. The captain of a British ship accordingly landed at Walvis Bay and marked out an area which was annexed as British territory on March 12, 1878. His proclamation was ratified by Letters Patent of Dec. 14, 1878, in which it was provided that Walvis Bay and adjacent territory could be annexed to the Cape Colony if the Cape government were to enact legislation to that effect. This was done on July 25, 1884, in the Walfish Bay and St John's River Territories Annexation Act, and the annexation was formalized by the Cape governor's proclamation published on Aug. 8, 1884. The proclamation set out what were the limits of "the port or settlement of Walfish Bay and certain territory surrounding the same" which with effect from Aug. 7, 1884 "shall under the name, designation and title of Walfish Bay become and be part of the Colony of the Cape of Good Hope, and subject to the laws in force therein".

German annexation of South West Africa. The establishment of the German protectorate followed purchases of land along the coast by a German merchant, F. Luderitz, beginning on May 1, 1883, with the bay of Angra Pequena (renamed Luderitzbucht). British and German naval vessels were sent to the area to protect their respective trading interests, and on April 24, 1884, the German consul at the Cape informed the British that Luderitz's possessions along the coast would henceforward come under German protection. A formal declaration of the German protectorate was proclaimed on Aug. 16, 1884, covering the area north of the Orange River as far as the 26th parallel, and extending some 20 miles inland. On Sept. 8, 1884, the German protectorate was extended northward to Cape Fria with the exception of Walvis Bay.

The protectorate's expansion westward was accomplished in the succeeding years by land acquisitions from the tribes of the interior, while its northern border with Portuguese possessions was settled in 1886. The British recognized South West Africa as a German sphere of influence in an agreement of July 1, 1890, in which the Germans also recognized the British title to Walvis Bay subject to the delimitation of the enclave's southern boundary, which was then in some dispute.

Colonial Boundaries of Walvis Bay

The Walvis Bay territory as annexed to the Cape Colony in 1884 was defined in the original description of 1878 as bounded "on the south by a line from a point on the coast 15 miles [24 kilometres] south of Pelican Point to Scheppmansdorf; on the east a line from Scheppmansdorf to the Rooibank, including the plateau, and thence to 10 miles inland from the mouth of the Swakop river; on the north by the last 10 miles of the course of the said Swakop river". However, when this definition was considered by an Anglo-German joint commission in 1885 it was found to contain certain ambiguities with regard to the southern sector, and a degree of vagueness as to what was the "plateau" and whether the distance southward from Pelican Point should be measured in statute or nautical miles.

A unilateral survey by a surveyor from Cape Town, Philip Wrey, was conducted for the Cape government in 1885, in which the southern limit of Walvis Bay was taken as running from 15 nautical miles south of Pelican Point, and the eastern boundary was extended past Scheppmansdorf to Ururas, taking in an area regarded by Wrey as corresponding to the "plateau" of the 1878 description. Wrey's demarcation was disputed by the Germans (with respect only to the southern sector), a second joint commission failing to resolve the dispute in 1888. Under a provision for the matter to be taken to arbitration, set out in Article III of the 1890 Anglo-German agreement, the King of Spain was asked to appoint an arbitrator in 1909, after a third Anglo-German joint commission in 1904 had been unable to reach agreement. The Spanish arbitrator studied the issue and reported in May 1911, his award following Wrey's demarcation. This settled in international law the boundaries of Walvis Bay as an enclave territory.

International Dispute over Walvis Bay

In 1922 South Africa found it convenient for obvious geographical reasons to commence administering Walvis Bay as if it were part of the mandated territory of South West Africa. The South African government made applicable to Walvis Bay as well as to the mandated territory the terms of its South West Africa

Affairs Act of 1922, validated by Proclamation No.145 of the governor-general, dated Sept. 11, 1922. Section I of the act provided that acts of the South African Parliament or proclamations by the governor-general relating to South West Africa would also apply to Walvis Bay unless otherwise stipulated, and that the port and settlement would be regarded as part of South West Africa for judicial purposes. However, the proclamation of the administrator of Walvis Bay (No. 30 of Oct. 1, 1922) confirming this measure referred explicitly to "the port and settlement of Walvis Bay, which forms part of the province of the Cape of Good Hope" being henceforth administered "as if it were" part of the mandated territory.

The convenience of this arrangement, from the South African point of view, ceased to apply when administrative provision in Namibia had to take into account the prospect of the territory's eventual transition to independent status. Unless Walvis Bay were to be part of an independent Namibia, there was little alternative but to resume administering it as part of Cape Province, and it was this latter course that the South African government decided to pursue. The then Prime Minister, B. J. Vorster, declared in the House of Assembly in Cape Town on April 23, 1976, that there should be no misunderstanding about the status of the port of Walvis Bay, which formed part of the Republic of South Africa. In August 1977 (two months after the passing of the South Africa Constitution Amendment Act), two separate South African government proclamations were issued, providing respectively for the administration of South West Africa (Namibia) and Walvis Bay. The Walvis Bay Administrative Proclamation (No. R202 of Aug. 31, 1977, taking effect from Sept. 1) stated that "Walvis Bay shall cease to be administered as if it were part of the territory [Namibia] and as if inhabitants thereof were inhabitants of the territory and shall again be administered as part of the [Cape] province". In terms of Section 5 of the proclamation, Walvis Bay ceased to be part of the electoral division of Omaruru (a division of Namibia) and later became part of the electoral division of Green Point, Cape Province. South African Defence Headquarters announced on Oct. 27 that the "'dormant naval command and control facilities which already exist at Walvis Bay" would be reactivated as from Nov. 1, 1977.

Reactions from the five Western nations party to the Namibia independence negotiations (the United States, Canada, Britain, France and West Germany) reflected the perception that this development was likely to make the negotiations more difficult. A UN spokesman speaking on Sept. 1, 1977, on behalf of Dr. Kurt Waldheim, then UN Secretary-General, also described the move as "unfortunate" and as a "unilateral act" at a time when concerted efforts were being made "to find a peaceful solution to the whole problem of Namibia". Although the question of Walvis Bay had not hitherto been prominent, the possibility that South Africa would press its territorial claim had already resulted in explicit references by Namibian nationalists to the territorial integrity of Namibia *including* Walvis Bay. SWAPO's draft constitutional proposals for the territory, published in 1976, had emphasized this point, and in May 1977, at the International Conference in Support of the Peoples of Zimbabwe and Namibia, held in Maputo, Mozambique, the conference declaration referred to Walvis Bay as an integral part of Namibia and the conference programme of action called upon governments to reject all attempts by South Africa to dismember the territory of Namibia and especially its design to annex Walvis Bay.

It was in similar terms that SWAPO spokesmen, and the UN Council for Namibia, denounced what they described as South Africa's annexation of Walvis Bay in statements issued in September 1977. Daniel Tjongarero, the SWAPO deputy chairman, said on Sept. 1 that Namibians could not be bound by colonial treaties of the 1880s and that South Africa's claim to Walvis Bay was "an expansionist venture and it could be used for possible aggression against Namibia" in the future. Moses Garoeb, the SWAPO administrative secretary, said in Lusaka on Sept. 8 that South Africa's claims to Walvis Bay were wild and baseless, and that he was not aware of any "colonial arrangements" which would give South Africa title over the port, which he described as "part of our country". Peter Katjavivi, the SWAPO information secretary, said in London that South. Africa's historical claim to Walvis Bay was legally invalid and that "Walvis Bay is an integral part of Namibia and as our only port it will be of crucial importance to an independent Namibia". South African moves to hold on to the port were described by Katjavivi as an attempt to sabotage the economic future of Namibia. SWAPO later announced (on Oct. 15) that it would not accept any settlement plan for Namibia which did not include the retention of Walvis Bay as part of its territory.

Dirk Mudge, who was then the chairman of the Turnhalle Constitution Committee (and who was emerging as the most prominent politician working within the framework of the South African administration in Namibia), did not challenge South Africa's claim to Walvis Bay in legal terms, but he did express the hope on Sept. 9, 1977, that South Africa might at some later date feel in a position to hand Walvis Bay over to an independent Namibia.

A statement issued on Sept. 7, 1977, by the UN Council for Namibia, condemned "in the strongest possible terms this unilateral attempt by South Africa to destroy the territorial integrity and unity of Namibia". The Council stated that Walvis Bay had always been an integral part of Namibia and that South Africa had no right to change its status, and described as illegal the South African appropriation of the port as part of its territory. Walvis Bay, the statement said, was "inextricably linked by geographical, historical, cultural, and ethnic bonds" to Namibia, and without the port the independence of Namibia could not be complete. The Council called on the UN Security Council to take measures to maintain the status of Walvis Bay as part of the international territory of Namibia. The UN General Assembly, in its Resolution 32/9D of Nov. 4, 1977, also condemned South Africa's decision to annex Walvis Bay as illegal, null and void and an act of colonial expansion in violation of the Charter of the UN and of the UN Declaration on Decolonization. (The United States, Canada, Britain, France and West Germany, i.e. the five Western nations then attempting to mediate Namibia independence, abstained on Resolution 32/9D, having expressed their view that "all aspects of the question of Walvis Bay" should be discussed between South Africa and an elected government in Namibia.)

In its Resolution No. 432 of 1978, adopted unanimously, the UN Security Council declared that Namibia's territorial integrity and unity must be assured by the reintegration of Walvis Bay within its territory and that, pending attainment of this objective, South Africa must not use Walvis Bay, in any manner prejudicial to the independence of Namibia or the viability of its economy. It decided to lend its full support to the initiation of steps necessary to ensure early reintegration of Walvis Bay into Namibia.

In the Algiers Declaration and Programme of Action on Namibia, adopted by the UN Council for Namibia on June 1, 1980, the Council called upon the UN Security Council to declare categorically that Walvis Bay was an integral part of Namibia and that the question should not be left as a matter for negotiation between an independent Namibia and South Africa.

South African policy remained that the status of the enclave could not be discussed in the context of Namibian independence talks. South Africa transferred various services in the territory from South African control to the transitional government which it set up by proclamation on June 17, 1985. In doing so, however, it excluded those services covering Walvis Bay. This applied notably to railway lines and harbour and other facilities in Walvis Bay, when the financial and operational control of the railways in Namibia was transferred from the South African Transport Services in May 1985, just before the transitional government was brought into being. Assets and control of the South West African Water and Electricity Corporation were transferred to the transitional government from the Industrial Development Corporation of South Africa, hitherto the sole shareholder, in October 1986.

Resolution of Walvis Bay Dispute

Following developments in Angola during 1987-88, as well as the new climate of co-operation between the USA and the USSR resulting from the Soviet policy of perestroika initiated by President Gorbachev, Namibian independence suddenly became an imminent possibility in 1989. Thus, on Jan. 27, 1989, the SADF Chief of Staff, Gen. Jannie Geldenhuys, gave a timetable for the withdrawal of South African troops from Namibia in advance of the November 1989 elections which had been scheduled by the UN. Gen.

Geldenhuys said that during this transition phase South Africa would not increase the number of troops stationed at Walvis Bay, which South Africa regarded as part of its own territory. Walvis Bay was not covered by the Namibia independence agreement.

The elections were held from Nov. 7-11 1989, and gave SWAPO 41 out of 72 seats, allowing it to form a government. On Nov. 22 South Africa's remaining troops were withdrawn from northern Namibia and Namibia became independent on March 21, 1990. Sam Nujoma, the exiled leader of SWAPO who became the first President of Namibia, made it clear that SWAPO would never recognize South African claims to Walvis Bay and that its return to Namibia would be the next item on the agenda after independence.

On Sept. 20, 1991, Namibia and South Africa agreed to a joint administration for Walvis Bay and the Penguin Islands pending a final solution to the dispute. Under this agreement a joint committee would advise both governments on the appropriate structures for a joint administration and a similar committee was agreed to investigate and report on Namibia's southern boundary with South Africa on the Orange River.

On Oct. 29, 1991, President Sam Nujoma announced that Namibia was to open an interests office in South Africa. The joint administration worked well, and Namibia took advantage of the multi-party negotiations over a new South African constitution to press its case that the enclave should be handed over entirely to Namibia. The National Party government in South Africa was by then concerned only with South Africa's future, and it was agreed that there should be a transfer of administration to Namibia from the end of February 1994. That brought the long-standing dispute to an end, though there remained issues of property rights to resolve after the hand-over took place.

Christopher Saunders

1.19 South Africa - Swaziland

In 1982 the apartheid-era South African government made proposals to accede to territorial aspirations harboured by Swaziland by transferring to the latter the KaNgwane black homeland and also the Ingwavuma district of the KwaZulu homeland—both areas being predominantly inhabited by Swazis. However, both homeland governments strongly resisted the proposals, which were subsequently shelved in 1984 pending future agreement on the transfers between Swaziland and the two homelands concerned. After the fall of the apartheid government in South Africa, the government of Swaziland renewed its claim to these areas but to date has been disappointed. (Map 6, page 495, shows Swaziland, KaNgwane and KwaZulu.)

Proposed Territorial Transfers to Swaziland

Negotiations between the governments of South Africa and Swaziland on the cession to Swaziland of the (South African) black homeland of KaNgwane and the KwaZulu homeland's Ingwavuma district (bordering on Swaziland) were begun in 1981. The Chief Minister of KaNgwane, Enos Mabuza, claimed on Dec. 16,1981, that in these negotiations the South African government's real aim was to deprive South Africa's 750,000 Swazis (of whom some 220,000 lived in KaNgwane) of their South African citizenship and to deny them access to South Africa's wealth.

As a first step towards the proposed cession, the South African government issued, on June 18, 1982, a proclamation dissolving the KaNgwane Legislative Assembly and placing that homeland, together with the Ingwavuma district, under the direct control of the (South African) Department of Co-operation and Development. The proposed border adjustment was defended by Dr Piet Koornhof (then South African Minister for Co-operation and Development) as a step towards the fulfilment of the "long-cherished ideal of the Swazi people, who have for long been deprived of Swazi citizenship by an accident of history, to be united under one king in one country".

However, Western commentators suggested that the South African government was seeking to use Swaziland's territorial aspirations as a lever to persuade its government to adopt a firmer attitude towards African National Congress (ANC) guerrillas, who in some instances operated from or through Swaziland. It was subsequently disclosed (in March 1984) that South Africa and Swaziland had signed a non-aggression pact in February 1982, under which each side undertook to combat terrorism, to respect the other's sovereignty and territorial integrity, and to prevent any activity within its boundaries which might threaten the integrity of the other.

The proclamation was opposed by the great majority of the members of the KaNgwane Legislative Assembly and of KaNgwane's Swazi chiefs. It was also opposed by most members of the Organization of African Unity (OAU) on the grounds that it violated the OAU principles on the maintenance of existing boundaries in Africa and that it was based on citizenship principles which had accompanied the birth of South Africa's "independent" homelands.

The Swaziland government, on the other hand, claimed on July 12, 1982, that there had been a favourable response from OAU members to a Swaziland mission sent to explain the border negotiations. It also argued that its territorial claims preceded the establishment of black homelands and that it was merely seeking to correct an historical injustice at the expense of South Africa. (It was reported in the Western press that most Swaziland ministers had been opposed to the deal but had been overruled by two strongly royalist ministers.)

Inside South Africa, the Natal Provincial Council (dominated by the opposition New Republic Party) on June 30, 1982, passed a motion calling on the government to hold a referendum among those affected by the proposed land deal. However, P. W. Botha, the South African Prime Minister, claimed in late June that most South African-born Swazis supported the move, declaring that the government had evidence, "obtained from petitions and reports by different experts", that the people of Swazi origin in South Africa "would generally welcome a border adjustment if their resident rights, work opportunities and general living standards are not prejudiced".

Court Actions taken by KwaZulu Authorities— Establishment of Rumpff Commission

Dr Oscar Dhlomo, the KwaZulu Minister of Education and Culture, on June 23, 1982, filed an application that the proclamation be set aside, and on June 25 Justice D. L. Shearer of the Natal Supreme Court ruled that the Ingwavuma district should revert to KwaZulu control since consultation had not taken place, pending a court action challenging the South African government's decision to take over the administration of the area. However, the government on June 28 issued a retroactive proclamation (this time under the 1927 Administration Act, which empowered the State President to alter the borders of South Africa's native areas without consultation), repealing the original proclamation but again removing the Ingwavuma district from KwaZulu control. The new proclamation further stated that the chiefs appointed by the Ingwavuma regional authority should cease to be members of the KwaZulu Legislative Assembly and that no members of the Assembly should be elected from those areas concerned.

Nevertheless the Natal Supreme Court in Pietermaritzburg on June 30, 1982, nullified the government's second proclamation and again returned control of the Ingwavuma district to KwaZulu. Government lawyers lodged an appeal with the Appeal Court in Bloemfontein and contended on July 1 that the latter proclamation remained valid until the appeal was heard, arguing that the government's administration of Ingwavuma was therefore legal. Christopher Albertyn, representing the KwaZulu Executive Council, maintained on the other hand that the Supreme Court's decision meant that the Department of Co-operation and Development must relinquish administrative control over Ingwavuma, as Justice Shearer had originally ruled. On July 2, 1982, the KwaZulu magistrate in Ingwavuma refused to hand over the administration of the district to the commissioner for black affairs in Nelspruit (Transvaal), who had been appointed by the South African government to administer both KaNgwane and the Ingwavuma district.

The Natal Supreme Court, sitting in Pietermaritzburg on July 5, 1982, allowed an interdict ordering the government and the Department of Co-operation and Development and their officials not to interfere in the administration of the Ingwavuma district until the case had been finally decided by the Appeal Court. The state counsel immediately gave notice of intention to appeal against the interdiction, but leave to appeal was refused and the government was ordered to pay costs.

The Appeal Court in Bloemfontein ruled on Sept. 30, 1982, that the presidential proclamation issued in June purporting to restore Ingwavuma to South African jurisdiction was null and void since the State President had acted ultra vires. The Appeal Court's decision rested on two factors: (i) the right of KwaZulu to seek legal redress against the state, and (ii) the failure of the State President to consult the KwaZulu government as required under the 1971 National States Constitution Act.

It was also announced on the same day that a commission under the chairmanship of Frans Rumpff, a former South African Chief Justice, would be appointed to investigate and report on the conflicting claims between KaNgwane, KwaZulu and Swaziland.

Further Opposition from KaNgwane Authorities — Subsequent Out-of-Court Settlement

Enos Mabuza declared on June 22, 1982, that the KaNgwane Legislative Assembly would defy the June 18 proclamation. The KaNgwane authorities' opposition to the proposed border adjustment was backed by popular demonstrations of support, including a strike by black civil servants in late June and a number of rallies in July; at one of these rallies Mabuza declared on July 25 that his people "would rather the ground opened up and swallowed us than be ruled by Swaziland".

An application brought on behalf of the KaNgwane Executive Council contesting the validity of the proclamation dissolving the KaNgwane Legislative Assembly—on the grounds (i) that the South African government had not consulted the Assembly and (ii) that it had dissolved the Assembly by proclamation, not by statute as required by law—was on July 22, 1982, referred to the full bench of the Transvaal Supreme Court.

However, Dr Koornhof subsequently announced on Nov. 25, 1982, that the South African government had agreed to withdraw the proclamation dissolving the KaNgwane Legislative Assembly within 14 days or at a mutually agreed date. Consequently, Mabuza withdrew the application to the Supreme Court in Pretoria, which was due to be heard that day, for the return of the administration of KaNgwane to the tribal authorities (it being subsequently decided that the KaNgwane government would be re-established on Dec. 9). In addition, costs were awarded against the South African government. Both parties agreed that the issue of whether KaNgwane should be included in the border adjustment should be referred to the Rumpff Commission, to which the KaNgwane government was allowed to appoint three members (the South African government having already appointed five and the KwaZulu authorities three). Mabuza declared on Nov. 27 that the agreement represented a "positive basis for future co-operation" and that the most important outcome was that "the people of KaNgwane would not be incorporated into Swaziland against their will".

Shelving of Territorial Transfer Proposals

The South African government on June 19, 1984, announced the dissolution of the Rumpff Commission and stated that there would be no unilateral incorporation of KaNgwane and Ingwavuma into Swaziland. In its report the commission had recommended that the territorial transfers should not go ahead without the majority support of the people involved, but the South African government took the view that the threat of intimidation made it impossible to hold plebiscites to determine the wishes of the homeland residents.

In dissolving the commission, the South African government recommended that the leaders of Swaziland and the two homelands concerned "should deliberate amongst themselves" on the matter, adding that any proposals made jointly and unanimously would be considered sympathetically. Subsequently, in August 1984, "self-government" status was restored to KaNgwane, while in March 1987 an agreement was reached between the two sides under which the KaNgwane government was to assume responsibility for economic development, administration and township management as soon as possible after April 1, 1987.

Revival of Territorial Transfer Proposals after 1993

Relations between South Africa and Swaziland improved following the demise of the apartheid system and the introduction of majority rule. In late 1993 formal diplomatic relations were established. On April 27, 1994, KaNgwane, along with the other homelands, was reincorporated into the Republic of South Africa, becoming part of the new province of Mpumalanga. Ingwavuma became a district of the new KwaZulu-Natal province. However, Swaziland did not drop its claims to the territories. In February 1994, during an address to parliament, King Mswati III announced that he intended to continue to use all peaceful means to pursue Swaziland's territorial claims against the new South African government. Both countries formed Border Adjustment Committees. A key issue was the nature of the Swazi state: South Africa's President, Nelson Mandela, made several calls for certain countries to live up to the regional ideal, and in the context of Swaziland, this was understood to be a demand that King Mswati increase the pace of democratic change. The implication was that a person of Swazi ethnicity living in the newly democratic Mpumalanga or KwaZulu-Natal would be taking a step backward if these territories were transferred to quasi-feudal Swaziland.

On April 28, 1996, South Africa's Deputy President, Thabo Mbeki, conveyed a message to King Mswati rejecting the territorial claims. The Premier of

Mpumalanga province, Mathews Phosa, noted that Swaziland's territorial claims were at odds with the Organization of African Unity's fundamental principle that colonial borders inherited at the time of independence are inviolable. He urged Swaziland to drop the border adjustment issue. Nonetheless, the claim apparently resurfaced in December 1997 during a meeting between President Mandela and King Mswati. In September 2001 the mandate of the Swazi Border Adjustment Committee was renewed, emphasizing the continued determination of King Mswati to press the claims. In June 2003 the chair of the committee, Prince Khuzulwandle, stated that the disputed territories are "Swaziland, historically and culturally", adding that "we have had commitments in the past from South African governments, most notably Nelson Mandela, that the matter will be resolved, but since Thabo Mbeki took office, there has been silence from Pretoria". South Africa currently shows no indication that it is willing to reappraise its policy concerning Swaziland's territorial claims.

Simon Massey

1.20 The Western Sahara Question

Since Morocco became independent in 1956 it has pressed a claim to sovereignty over the large expanse of desert to its south known as Western Sahara. In 1975, Spain, which had controlled the territory since the 19th century, announced its intention to withdraw and an opinion from the International Court of Justice (ICJ) held that its inhabitants were entitled to exercise the right of self-determination. Instead, both Morocco and Mauritania took advantage of a tripartite agreement of November 1975 with Spain to partition the territory between them. This act was opposed by the Polisario Front, which in 1976 proclaimed an independent Saharan Arab Democratic Republic (SADR) and with the backing of Algeria intensified hostilities against both countries. This led to a large-scale military conflict which placed a heavy burden on the Moroccan and Mauritanian economies. In 1979 Mauritania concluded a peace agreement with Polisario, declared its neutrality in the conflict and withdrew from the southern sector. Morocco immediately occupied the area, an action strongly resisted by Polisario guerrillas.

By 1981, 50 states had recognized the SADR as the legitimate government of Western Sahara, but Morocco, backed by conservative Arab states and the US government, opposed Organization of African Unity (OAU) attempts to mediate and flooded the area with troops. The United Nations subsequently sought to achieve a diplomatic res-

olution, and by 1991 it appeared that agreement had been reached in principle to hold a referendum in the disputed area—procedures for a referendum to take place, under UN auspices, being established in UN Security Council Resolution 691. A UN-administered ceasefire has been in effect since September 1991, but efforts to hold a referendum have stalled and the parties have rejected all compromise proposals.

Geography and Population

The Western Sahara covers an area of approximately 125,000 square miles (325,000 sq km) within boundaries defined by the colonial powers. Since the colonial era its northern section had been named after the Saguia el Hamra river and its southern section after the Rio de Oro; however, on occupation by Mauritania, Rio de Oro was renamed Tiris el Gharbia and later, under Morocco, Oued Eddahab (the Arabic for Rio de Oro).

The Sahrawis of Western Sahara are nomadic livestock-herding Moors (*beidan*) of Berber stock whose migratory area extended from the Oued Draa in southern Morocco to the Senegal river valley in southern Mauritania. They became arabicized after invasions by the (Bedouin) Maqil from the 13th century onwards and came to speak the Hassaniya Arab dialect instead of Berber. They remained largely autonomous within the Western Sahara area and ruled themselves by councils known as *yemaâ*. The major Sahrawi tribes are the Reguibat (the largest), Izarguien, Oulad Delim, Ait Lahsen, Oulad Tidrarin and Arosien.

The Polisario Front (*Frente Popular para la Liberación de Saguia el Hamra y Río de Oro*, or Popular Front for the Liberation of Saguia el Hamra and Rio de Oro) is believed to have drawn many of its recruits from the Sahrawi population outside Western Sahara—in Morocco, Mauritania and Algeria—where their numbers are estimated to be as great as the numbers in Western Sahara itself; many Sahrawis fled to Morocco in 1958 after a joint Franco-Spanish operation crushed the Army of Liberation which fought against Spanish rule in the region, and others were forced into exile in neighbouring countries after the Movement for the Liberation of Saguia el Hamra and Oued Eddahab (MLS)—Polisario's forerunner in Western Sahara—was crushed in 1970. In addition, many Sahrawis have in recent years become sedentary, due to factors such as the rural exodus and droughts which have reduced herds, and have settled all over the region. These factors are thought to be the basis for Polisario's consistent claim that the population of Western Sahara is far greater than the 74,000 accounted for in the Spanish census of 1974. (Map 10, page 497, illustrates this dispute.)

Historical Background to the Dispute

Morocco's ties with the region south of the Oued Draa (including Western Sahara) and also to other areas in north-west Africa including present-day Mauritania (to whose territory Morocco harboured claims as part of a proposed "Greater Morocco" until 1969) date back centuries. However, the pattern of nomadic life in the desert regions meant that Moroccan rulers in the north enjoyed only limited political control over the tribes whose leaders swore allegiance to them, since the area occupied by specific tribes was constantly changing. For this reason also no reliable maps showing the territorial limits of Morocco's old empire existed prior to the 19th century.

Spain, which claimed "historic rights" in southern Morocco because of its early presence north of Cape Yubi (in what later became the Spanish enclave of Ifni) from 1476 to 1524, was drawn to the Western Sahara region by a trading centre at Cape Yubi and established claims to areas south of the Cape, opposite the (Spanish) Canary Islands. It concluded treaties of protection with tribal leaders south of the Cape, and in 1884 it took possession of Rio de Oro—the area of Western Sahara between Cape Bojador and Cape Blanc, then arbitrarily considered to stretch 150 miles (240 kilometres) inland—as the "Spanish Protectorate of the African Coast". It confirmed its rights to Rio de Oro in 1886 under the Treaty of Idjil, concluded with the Emir of Adrar, and the territory was attached to the General Office of the Captain of the Canary Islands by a royal decree of April 1887. Sultan Moulay Hassan of Morocco, however, refused to confirm Spanish rights there.

By the late 19th century, with Spain in control of Rio de Oro, Morocco in the eyes of the colonial powers was exercising control only as far south as the Draa region, along the coastal strip as far as Cape Yubi and, inland, around Tindouf (now in Algeria). Moulay Hassan, however, regarded his empire as extending to the Senegal river and, inland, up to Timbuktu (Mali) and southern Algeria. Morocco later consolidated its influence over tribes south of the Oued Draa (in what became Saguia el Hamra), and in 1895 Moroccan rights to the area between the Oued Draa and Cape Bojador, including Saguia el Hamra and Cape Yubi, were established under an Anglo-Moroccan agreement. However, Saguia el Hamra was subsequently allocated to Spain under a Franco-Spanish convention of 1904, title to the territory being confirmed in an agreement of November 1912. Spain was at the same time granted a protectorate in the Tarfaya region from the northern border of Saguia el Hamra to the Oued Draa, and this zone (Spanish Southern Morocco) was not transferred back to Morocco until 1958.

At the beginning of the 20th century France defined in conjunction with Spain (but without the collaboration of Morocco) the borders of its influence in northwest Africa and the respective zones of influence of the two countries in Morocco. In June 1900 an "agreement on the delimitation of French and Spanish possessions on the coast of the Sahara and on the coast of the Gulf of Guinea" was signed in Paris, establishing the southern and eastern (but not the northern) borders of the Spanish Sahara. The agreement specified that France should be allocated the salt mines of the Idjil region—which accounts for the curve in Rio de Oro's eastern border immediately south of the Tropic of Cancer—and demarcated the frontier on Cape Blanc "in such a way that the western portion of the peninsula including the western bay be given to Spain, and Cape Blanc proper plus the eastern portion of the same peninsula remain in France's possession".

The main purpose of the Franco-Spanish Convention of October 1904 was to secure Spanish co-operation regarding the April 1904 Franco-British declaration (affirming British and French freedom of action in Egypt and Morocco respectively) in return for recognition of a Spanish zone of influence in northern Morocco. At the same time, the convention completed the delimitation of the French and Spanish zones of influence, taking the eastern border of Western Sahara up as far as the Oued Draa. Article 6 of the agreement stated that Spain had "complete freedom of action over the region (i.e. Saguia el Hamra) included between 26° and 27°40′ latitude north and the meridian 11°, which is outside Moroccan territory", but recognized as Moroccan territory everything north of the present-day border between Saguia el Hamra and Morocco.

Consequent upon the Franco-Moroccan agreement of March 1912 setting up a French protectorate of Morocco, an "agreement drawn up to clarify the respective situations of the two countries with respect to the cherifien empire" was signed in Madrid in November 1912. This agreement reduced Spain's control in the north of Morocco but stated that south of parallel 27°40′ the above provisions of the 1904 agreement remained applicable.

Impact of Decolonization Process on Western Sahara Issue

Spain assumed full possession of its Saharan territories and Ifni only in the 1930s. In 1946 it established Spanish West Africa, in which Spanish Sahara and Ifni were distinct entities, and in January 1958 the province of Spanish Sahara was created by the merger of Rio de Oro and Saguia el Hamra, ruled by a governor-general and returning deputies to the Cortes. In May 1967 a *Yemaâ* was installed by Spain to govern the province in line with the "traditional institutions of the Sahrawi people".

With Morocco a French protectorate and with France also controlling south-west Algeria, the central Sahara and Mauritania, the territorial issue remained dormant until after Morocco's independence in 1956. After Algeria's subsequent independence in 1962 a Moroccan claim to Algerian territory south of the Oued Draa (containing the Gara Djebilet iron ore deposits) erupted into a brief armed conflict in 1963, and relations between these two countries were not finally regulated until the Treaty of Ifrane was signed in 1969, followed by agreements in 1972 whereby Morocco renounced claims to the Algerian Sahara and Tindouf and recognized the Oued Draa as the frontier. In return,

Algeria agreed to give diplomatic support to Morocco's claim to Spanish Sahara. Also in 1969 Morocco acquired de jure sovereignty over Ifni from Spain.

Against a background of unrest in Spanish Sahara and the emergence of liberation movements committed to ending Spanish rule in north-west Africa, representatives of Morocco, Mauritania and Algeria agreed at a meeting in Nouadhibou (Mauritania) in September 1970 to collaborate closely on the Spanish Sahara issue and to act in conformity with United Nations resolutions (which since 1965 had called for the holding of a referendum in the territory under UN auspices with a view to granting Spanish Sahara self-determination). The three countries themselves also in 1970 sponsored a UN resolution inviting Spain to organize a referendum among the Sahrawis to determine the territory's future. However, relations subsequently deteriorated between Morocco and Algeria, and in July 1974 King Hassan II of Morocco began a diplomatic campaign to assert the Moroccan claim to the Sahara.

In line with a number of UN resolutions—including 2983/XXVII of Dec. 14, 1972, which called for the independence of Spanish Sahara and urged the Spanish government to consult with the Moroccan and Mauritanian governments to organize a referendum in the territory to this end—Spain finally announced on Aug. 21, 1974, that a referendum was to be held in Spanish Sahara in the first half of 1975 to determine the future status of the territory.

This followed (i) the announcement by the Spanish leader, Gen. Francisco Franco, in September 1973 of a programme of "progressive participation" by the Sahrawis in preparation for their eventual self-determination; and (ii) his announcement in July 1974 that Spanish Sahara would soon be granted internal autonomy (this being opposed by King Hassan II, who warned Franco against unilateral action regarding Spanish Sahara).

The announcement of the proposed referendum was also followed by a deterioration in relations between Mauritania and Morocco, the latter accusing the former of making trouble by maintaining its own claim to Spanish Sahara (in support of which Mauritania mounted its own diplomatic campaign in August 1974).

Submission of Dispute to ICJ for Advisory Ruling

The UN General Assembly on Dec. 13, 1974, approved a resolution (3292/XXIX) sponsored by Morocco and Mauritania urging that an advisory opinion should be sought from the International Court of Justice (ICJ) on two questions, namely (i) whether the Spanish Sahara was vacant territory (res nullius) at the time of its colonization by Spain, and (ii) if it was not, what "legal ties" existed between the territory and the Kingdom of Morocco and the "Mauritanian entity". The UN transmitted the request to the ICJ on Dec. 21, and the proposed referendum in Spanish Sahara was postponed while the ICJ considered the issue.

In the ensuing period, before the ICJ published its ruling on Oct. 16, 1975, there was a series of major developments concerning the Spanish Sahara. Against a background of diplomatic and military tension as Morocco pressed its claim to Spain's African possessions, violent guerrilla activity and disturbances erupted both in Spanish Sahara and the enclaves. Amid UN efforts to find a solution to the Spanish problem Spain announced on May 23, 1975, that it was ready to grant independence to the territory "in the shortest period possible" and made moves to open negotiations with Morocco, Mauritania and Algeria as well as with Polisario, which had by now emerged as the main formation claiming independence for the territory.

Before the emergence in 1975 of Polisario as the main guerrilla formation opposing the Spanish presence in the territory, several other liberation movements had also been prominent. They included the Moroccan-backed Liberation and Unity Front (FLU); the Sahrawi National Union Party (PUNS), a moderate indigenous autonomist movement sponsored by Spain in order to secure an orderly transfer of sovereignty in which its own interest would be protected; and Morehob (the *Mouvement de résistance des hommes bleus* —referring to the Reguibat or "blue people" of Spanish Sahara), which, however, had little influence. The Polisario Front itself emerged from among Sahrawi students at Rabat University in Morocco. Its original aim was to reorganize the opposition to Spanish rule and drive the Spaniards out of Western Sahara; it adopted the aim of independence for the territory only later after it had failed to receive practical assistance from Morocco. Polisario at first based itself in Mauritania but subsequently moved to Algeria, where it received support from the Algerian government.

At the time of the violent upsurge of guerrilla activity, a fact-finding mission of the UN Decolonization Committee visited Spanish Sahara in May 1975 and also held talks with Spain, Morocco and Mauritania. It found evidence of widespread support for Polisario among the people but little following for the Spanish-backed PUNS, and stated that almost all the people it had met in the territory were "categorically for independence and against the territorial claims of Morocco and Mauritania". In its report, published on Oct. 14, 1975, it recommended that the people of Spanish Sahara should be enabled to determine their own future "in complete freedom and in an atmosphere of peace and security".

Spanish Decision to grant Independence

After a meeting of the Spanish Council of Ministers presided over by Franco on May 23, 1975, the government announced that due to the "progressive deterioration" of the situation and the clear desire for independence in the territory, it was ready to "transfer the sovereignty of the Spanish Sahara in the shortest period possible" after the ICJ had delivered its opinion and the United Nations had taken an appropriate decision. It subsequently announced that it would seek to convene a quadripartite conference with Morocco, Mauritania and Algeria to discuss the future of the territory.

Morocco strongly opposed the Spanish decision, accusing Spain of creating an "equivocal situation and a climate of confusion". Mauritania for its part expressed satisfaction at the Spanish intention and recorded its wish that the decolonization should take place within a UN framework; however, at the same time President Ould Daddah of Mauritania said in an interview that Mauritania would take "all appropriate measures to preserve its legitimate rights over the Sahara, which it considers as forming part of its territory".

It became known at this stage (in mid-1975) that Morocco and Mauritania had reached a secret agreement at the end of the previous year on a plan to partition Spanish Sahara between them after the withdrawal of Spain, whereby Morocco would obtain the northern Saguia el Hamra sector and Mauritania the southern Rio de Oro sector, while the phosphate deposits at Bou Craâ would be jointly exploited.

Publication of ICJ Advisory Opinion

On Oct. 16, 1975, the ICJ published the advisory opinion that while certain "legal ties of allegiance" existed between Western Sahara and both the Kingdom of Morocco and the "Mauritanian entity" at the time of colonization by Spain in 1884, these did not in either case support a claim of territorial sovereignty, nor did they affect the application of the principle of "self-determination through the free and genuine expression of the will of the peoples of the territory", as enunciated in the 1960 UN declaration on the granting of independence to colonial countries and peoples.

It went on: "The materials and information presented to the Court show the existence at the time of Spanish colonization of legal ties of allegiance between the Sultan of Morocco and some of the tribes living in the territory of Western Sahara. They equally show the existence of rights, including some rights relating to the land, which constituted legal ties between the Mauritanian entity…and the territory of Western Sahara. On the other hand, the Court's conclusion is that the materials and information presented to it do not establish any tie of territorial sovereignty between the territory of Western Sahara and the Kingdom of Morocco or the Mauritanian entity".

The first question. The Court ruled that, according to state practice at the time of Spain's colonization of Western Sahara in 1884, territories inhabited by tribes or peoples having a social and political organization were not regarded as *terrae nullius*; in their case, sovereignty was not generally considered as effected through simple occupation but through agreements concluded with local rulers. Information furnished to the court showed that at the time of colonization Western Sahara was inhabited by peoples which, although nomadic, were socially and politically organized in tribes and under chiefs competent to represent them. Furthermore, it showed that Spain did not proceed upon the basis that it was establishing its sovereignty over *terrae nullius*—the King of Spain having proclaimed in his royal decree of 1884 that he was taking Rio de Oro under his protection on the basis of agreements entered into with the chiefs of local tribes.

Legal ties. The Court ruled that "legal ties" must be understood as referring to such legal ties as might affect the policy to be followed in the decolonization of Western Sahara and rejected the view that the ties in question could be limited to ties established directly with the territory and without reference to the people in it. The Court found "that at the time of its colonization the territory had a sparse population consisting for the most part of nomadic tribes of the Islamic faith, whose members traversed the desert on more or less regular routes, sometimes reaching as far as southern Morocco or regions of present-day Mauritania, Algeria or other states".

Moroccan claims. Morocco had claimed "ties of sovereignty" over Western Sahara on the grounds of "alleged immemorial possession" of the territory. It had cited in support of its claim (i) the special historical structure of the Moroccan state, namely that it was founded on the common religious bond of Islam and on the allegiance of various tribes to the Sultan through their caids or sheikhs rather than on the notion of territory; (ii) evidence said to show the allegiance of Saharan caids to the Sultan; and (iii) certain treaties dating from the 18th to the early 20th century said to constitute recognition by other states of Moroccan sovereignty over the whole or part of Western Sahara.

The Court found that none of the internal or international acts relied upon by Morocco indicated the existence at the relevant period of either the existence or the international recognition of legal ties of territorial sovereignty between the Western Sahara and the Moroccan state. They did, however, provide indications that a legal tie of allegiance existed between the Sultan and some of the nomadic peoples of the territory and that the Sultan was recognized by other states to possess some authority or influence with respect to these tribes.

Claims of "Mauritanian entity". The court noted that the term "Mauritanian entity" had been used to denote the cultural, geographical and social entity within which the Islamic Republic of Mauritania was later to be created. According to Mauritania, at the relevant period that entity—the Bilad Shinguitti or Shinguitti country—was a distinct human unit, characterized by a common language, way of life, religion and system of laws, with political authority emanating from emirates and tribal groups. While recognizing that the latter did not constitute a state, Mauritania had suggested that the concepts of "nation" and "people" would be more appropriate to explain the position of the Shinguitti people at the time of colonization. At that period, Mauritania said, the Mauritanian entity extended from the Senegal river to the Oued Saguia el Hamra, so that the territory at present under Spanish administration and the Islamic Republic of Mauritania together constituted indissoluble parts of a single entity and had legal ties with one another.

The Court found, however, that while these various links existed, the emirates and many of the tribes in the entity were independent in relation to one another and had no common institution or organs; the entity therefore did not have the character of a personality or corporate entity distinct from the several emirates or tribes which comprised it. On the other hand, the nomadic peoples of the Shinguitti possessed rights, including rights to the lands through which they migrated; these rights constituted legal ties between Western Sahara and the Mauritanian entity which knew no frontier between the territories and were vital to the maintenance of life in the region.

Overlapping Moroccan and Mauritanian claims. The Court noted (i) that Morocco and Mauritania had both laid stress on the overlapping character of the respective legal ties which they claimed Western Sahara had had with them at the time of colonization; and (ii) that, although their views appeared to have evolved considerably in that respect, they both asserted at the end of the proceedings that there was a north appertaining to Morocco and a south appertaining to Mauritania without any geographical void in between, but with some overlapping as the result of the intersection of nomadic routes.

On this aspect the Court confined itself to noting that this geographical overlapping indicated the difficulty of disentangling the various relationships existing in the Western Sahara at the time of colonization.

Moroccan "Green March" and November 1975 Tripartite Agreement

Immediately upon the delivery of the ICJ ruling, King Hassan on Oct. 16, 1975, declared his intention to stage a "green [i.e. peaceful] march" of 350,000 unarmed Moroccans into Spanish Sahara to claim the territory symbolically for Morocco. Despite Spanish and Algerian warnings to Morocco and the convening of the UN Security Council by Spain (which itself was experiencing a political crisis with Franco in the last stages of a fatal illness), the march went ahead on Nov. 6. The marchers penetrated about six miles (10 kilometres) into the north of Western Sahara, kneeling to pray as they crossed the border for the return of "the land of our forefathers, after 90 years of separation". All Spanish troops in Western Sahara had withdrawn behind a mined "dissuasion line" about seven miles inside the Western Sahara frontier on the Tarfaya-El Aaiún road, and the area in between this line and the frontier formed a no-man's-land into which the marchers were allowed to penetrate without reprisals; however, Spanish destroyers, aircraft and troops waited on the alert in the Canary Islands, and Moroccan and Algerian troops were reported to be facing each other within striking distance near their borders. Finally, at the instigation of the United Nations, King Hassan on Nov. 9 ordered the marchers to withdraw to Tarfaya.

Shortly after the march ended it was announced from Madrid on Nov. 14, 1975, that Spain, Morocco and Mauritania had reached an agreement satisfactory to all three parties on the withdrawal of Spain from Western Sahara. After the publication in Spain of a decolonization bill, the terms of the agreement were revealed on Nov. 21.

They provided for the immediate establishment by Spain of a provisional administration in the territory "with the participation of Morocco and Mauritania and with the co-operation of the *Yemaâ* [the Spanish Sahara General Assembly]" and for Spain to hand over to it "the responsibilities and powers which it has discharged in the territory in its capacity as administering power". Two assistant governors would be appointed respectively by Morocco and Mauritania to assist the governor-general of the territory in his duties, and the Spanish presence would come to an end in Spanish Sahara on Feb. 28, 1976.

The agreement was strongly opposed by Algeria and by Polisario, which said that the implementation of the tripartite agreement would open the way for "a bloody war with disastrous consequences for the entire region".

Moroccan and Mauritanian Occupation of Western Sahara

Although according to the agreement a Spanish presence was to be maintained in Western Sahara until Feb. 28, 1976, Morocco asserted its influence over the territory and during December 1975 and January 1976 occupied the main towns of northern Spanish Sahara, including the capital, El Aaiún (Al Ayoun). In the meantime, the UN General Assembly on Dec. 10, 1975, adopted two contrasting resolutions on the future of Western Sahara. The first (3458A), known as the "Algerian resolution", made no mention of the tripartite agreement, requested Spain to take immediate steps to enable "all Saharans originating in the territory" to exercise their "inalienable rights to self-determination" under UN supervision, and appealed to all parties to refrain from unilateral or other action. The second (3485B, known as the "Moroccan resolution"), noted the tripartite agreement and requested the interim administration to take all necessary steps to ensure that "all the Saharan populations originating in the territory" were able to exercise their "inalienable right to self-determination" through free consultations organized with the help of a UN representative.

The last Spanish troops left Western Sahara on Jan. 12, 1976, and the Spanish presence in the territory terminated on Feb. 26, two days before the date laid down in the agreement. On the same day the *Yemaâ* (meeting in El Aaiún with only two-thirds of its full contingent) unanimously voted to ratify the Madrid agreement. The Polisario Front thereupon on Feb. 27-28 proclaimed the Western Sahara as a free, independent and sovereign state known as the Saharan Arab Democratic Republic (SADR), and formed a government which was recognized by Algeria (causing Morocco and Mauritania to break off diplomatic relations with the latter).

Under a convention signed in Rabat on April 14, 1976, Morocco and Mauritania agreed on the delimitation of their border in Western Sahara. This was to run eastwards from a point on the Atlantic coast, north of Dakhla (formerly Villa Cisneros), leaving Bir Enzaran in the Moroccan sector as a border post, and then south-east in the direction of Zouerate (Mauritania). Mauritania received less than one-third of the territory, which became known as Tiris el Gharbia. The Moroccan sector was divided into the administrative provinces of El Aaiún, Smara and Bojador, and the Bou Craâ phosphate mines remained in this sector, a majority share in the Spanish Sahara phosphate company, Fosbucraâ, being in February 1976 transferred to Morocco.

Mauritanian Withdrawal from Conflict

Over the ensuing years the Polisario Front intensified its hostilities in Western Sahara against both Morocco and Mauritania. Mauritania's involvement in the conflict resulted in over 9,000 Mauritanian troops being stationed in the country itself, particularly after Polisario attacks on Nouakchott (the capital) in 1976 and 1977, and Mauritania was forced to expand its own army to 12,000 men and to devote 60 per cent of its budget to defence, with disastrous effects on the economy and on development projects.

In July 1978, however, the government of President Ould Daddah was overthrown by the armed forces, who said that they had seized power because the country was on the verge of bankruptcy and who vowed to co-operate with Morocco in seeking a solution to the war. The Polisario Front immediately ordered a cease-fire in Mauritania and the Mauritanian government began diplomatic initiatives to bring about peace in Western Sahara; later in 1978 Mauritania commenced negotiations with Polisario, which in September extended its ceasefire indefinitely and concentrated its hostilities against the Moroccan sector of Western Sahara. Mauritania also sought closer relations with Algeria following the death in December 1978 of President Houari Boumedienne of Algeria.

In May 1979 there were further changes of orientation in the Mauritanian leadership, the outcome being the recognition by Mauritania on July 17, 1979, of the right to self-determination of the Tiris el Gharbia sector; the conclusion by Mauritania and Polisario of a peace agreement on Aug. 5, 1979; and the withdrawal of Mauritania from Tiris el Gharbia during that month. The first section of the August 1979 agreement stated that "considering the urgent need to find a definitive global solution to the conflict between the two parties which will guarantee the Sahrawi people their full national rights, and the region peace and stability", Mauritania relinquished all present and future claims to Western Sahara and resolved to "extricate itself definitively from the unjust war over Western Sahara". Polisario declared that "it neither has nor will make any territorial claims on Mauritania" and resolved, in the name of the Sahrawi people, to sign a definitive

peace agreement with Mauritania. A second section of the agreement, apparently referring to the application of "agreed principles", remained secret.

The Mauritanian Prime Minister, Lt.-Col. Haydalla, visited Morocco for talks on Aug. 10, 1979, and before leaving later that day, he read out a statement to the press which said (i) that Mauritania had "renounced all claims to Tiris el Gharbia and considers itself definitively disengaged from this conflict", (ii) that Morocco, "noting this new situation, intends to ensure the defence of its rights, its territorial integrity, its security and the stability of the region", and (iii) that Morocco and Mauritania had undertaken not do do "anything which might damage the reciprocal security of the two countries".

Morocco immediately afterwards took control of the Mauritanian sector of Western Sahara, renamed it Oued Eddahab and allocated seats in the Moroccan parliament to the new "province". Lt.-Col. Haydalla described the occupation as an aggression against Mauritania, but he received no response to his demand for the withdrawal of Morocco's troops. Mauritania and Algeria on Aug. 13, 1979, re-established diplomatic relations, and later in August, after the withdrawal of its own troops, Mauritania declared its "total neutrality" in the Western Sahara conflict.

Military and Diplomatic Developments 1979-85— The OAU as Mediator

During the remainder of 1979 and throughout 1980 the Polisario Front concentrated its hostilities in southern Morocco proper as well as continuing to attack positions mainly in the north of Western Sahara. The Front became better armed and organized, and proved a strong adversary for the Moroccan Army. Morocco now had a land border with Algeria and Mauritania of some 2,000 miles (3,200 kilometres) to defend and was obliged to spend one-quarter of its annual budget on the war.

Over this period a "committee of wise men", which had been established at the 1978 OAU Summit to mediate in the conflict and which comprised a number of African heads of state, held meetings and the OAU itself passed a number of resolutions on the Western Sahara issue. At the organization's Council of Ministers' meeting in Freetown (Sierra Leone) in June 1980 the SADR submitted an application for OAU membership. In the event 26 of the 50 OAU members favoured the admission of the SADR, but Morocco (supported by a number of other states) claimed that the SADR was not a sovereign state, maintained that according to some interpretations the OAU Charter required a two-thirds majority for the admission of new members, and threatened to leave the OAU if the SADR was admitted.

The question of admission was put in abeyance and a compromise was eventually reached whereby the committee of wise men was charged with organizing a meeting of all interested parties within three months. This accordingly took place in Freetown in September

1980, attended by the Presidents of Guinea, Mali and Nigeria; representatives of Sudan and Tanzania; and, as "interested parties", the Presidents of Algeria and Mauritania and delegations from Morocco, Polisario and other guerrilla organizations such as the FLS, the FLU, PUNS and Morehob. The meeting formulated a six-point plan for a UN-supervised ceasefire and an OAU-organized referendum, which it said should be implemented from December 1980. The plan was reportedly welcomed by Mauritania and Polisario but was described by Morocco as "nothing new".

In the first half of 1981 Morocco consolidated its position in Western Sahara by completing the first stage of what was to become, with later extensions, a comprehensive line of fortifications across the desert; this defensive wall was intended to protect important towns and installations to its west and became a major target of Polisario attacks. During this period Morocco continued to receive moral and material support from the conservative Arab states and also, following the inauguration of President Reagan in January 1981, from the United States. The SADR, on the other hand, had by mid-1981 been recognized by at least 50 states, in eight of which it had ambassadors and three of which (Mexico, Cuba and Nicaragua) had in March 1981 become the first countries to accredit ambassadors to the SADR.

In a speech on March 3, 1981, on the 20th anniversary of his accession to the throne, King Hassan called on Algeria to hold a summit meeting to "end the spilling of blood in the region"; at the same time he asserted that any agreement to end the conflict should not be "detrimental to an integral part of our national territory". Amid a renewed Moroccan diplomatic offensive in May 1981 directed in particular against Libya for its support of Polisario, the latter accused Morocco of using Libya as a scapegoat for its own failure to end the war and of refusing to submit to the decisions of international bodies.

However, when the Western Sahara issue was discussed at the 18th annual summit of the OAU held in Nairobi on June 24-28, 1981, proceedings were dominated by rapprochement between Morocco and Libya and by a proposal by King Hassan that a referendum should be held in the territory. Addressing the assembled heads of state and government, King Hassan said that to avoid the OAU being "torn apart" on the Western Sahara issue, Morocco envisaged a procedure for a "controlled referendum" which would "simultaneously respect" the objectives of the latest recommendations of the committee of wise men and "the conviction which Morocco has of its legitimate rights".

Earlier, at a press conference in Rabat on June 1, 1981, King Hassan had asserted that the OAU Charter was clear and free of ambiguity in stating that "only countries legally and internationally recognized within recognized frontiers established on the human and geophysical foundation necessary for entering into a regional grouping" could be members of the OAU. He had also warned that Morocco and other states would leave the OAU if the SADR were

admitted to membership.

A resolution adopted by the Nairobi OAU summit recorded its decision to set up an implementation committee in respect of the Moroccan referendum proposal, it being specified that the committee would have full powers and would consist of Guinea, Kenya, Mali, Nigeria, Sierra Leone, Sudan and Tanzania. The same resolution (i) invited the parties to the conflict to observe an immediate ceasefire; (ii) requested the implementation committee to meet before the end of August 1981 to work out, in collaboration with the parties to the conflict, the modalities and all the details relating to the establishment of a ceasefire as well as to the organization and the holding of a referendum; (iii) requested the United Nations to furnish, in collaboration with the OAU, a peacekeeping force to be stationed in Western Sahara to maintain peace and security during the referendum and subsequent elections; and (iv) instructed the implementation committee to take, with the participation of the United Nations, all necessary measures to guarantee the holding of a general and regular referendum on self-determination for the people of Western Sahara.

The resolution contained no reference to the Polisario Front or to its demand for the withdrawal of Moroccan forces and administration from the territory, even though such a concession had been urged on Morocco by a number of OAU member states and was included in a series of conditions laid down in July by Polisario for the holding of a referendum. The other major conditions were (i) that direct negotiations should be held between Morocco and Polisario to agree on steps to bring about a ceasefire and create favourable conditions for the referendum; (ii) that a provisional international administration of the United Nations and the OAU should be established in co-ordination with the SADR to ensure the necessary conditions and security; and (iii) that all Sahrawis should return to their towns and villages.

Little progress was subsequently made towards holding a referendum in Western Sahara, the major problem facing the OAU implementation committee being the refusal of Morocco to engage in direct negotiations with the Polisario Front. Moreover, the military conflict acquired a new dimension in late 1981 when Polisario began to deploy sophisticated new weaponry, including tanks and anti-aircraft missiles, in its operations against Moroccan forces. Within the OAU, a deep rift developed after the SADR was given an OAU seat for the first time at the 38th regular session of the Council of Ministers held in Addis Ababa on Feb. 22-28, 1982.

In protest against this step—which was taken at the instigation of the OAU Secretary-General, Edem Kodjo, on the grounds that 26 of the 50 member states had recognized the SADR—the representatives of a third of OAU members (including Morocco) walked out of the conference. Subsequently, another OAU conference (of Information Ministers) was indefinitely adjourned in Dakar (Senegal) on March 15 after 14 of the 27 participating countries withdrew in protest against Senegal's refusal to admit SADR delegates.

Polisario's military operations were hampered during 1982 by the extension of the Moroccan defensive wall as far as Bojador on the Western Sahara coast. The wall, constructed of sand and stone, was between three and four metres high, and had command posts every four kilometres, equipped with US-supplied electronic monitoring equipment, reportedly capable of detecting movement up to 20 kilometres distant. The phosphate mines at Bou Craâ, which had previously been the target of Polisario attacks, re-opened in July 1982.

In the diplomatic sphere, Polisario continued to demand direct negotiations as a basis for any settlement, claiming that clandestine contacts had already taken place. The guerrillas continued to receive financial and logistical support from Algeria and Libya; Mauritania denied Moroccan accusations that it was allowing arms supplies for the Polisario to pass through its territory. The first "President of the Saharan Republic" was named as Mohammed Abdelazziz, the Polisario secretary-general, at the movement's fifth congress in October 1982.

At the 19th Assembly of Heads of State and Government of the OAU in June 1983, the SADR agreed "voluntarily and temporarily" to refrain from taking its seat, so as to allow the summit to take place. After a report by the implementation committee, the Assembly adopted by consensus a resolution calling for "direct talks" (without specifying the parties to be involved) as a precursor to a referendum to be held in December 1983 under UN and OAU auspices. The resolution also called for the installation of an international peacekeeping force in the Western Sahara. Despite Morocco's repeated undertakings that it would be bound by the result of a referendum, King Hassan warned on July 8, 1983, that whatever the outcome he would not "hand the Sahara on a silver platter to a rabble of mercenaries".

A series of Polisario attacks in July 1983 marked the end of a one-year unilateral ceasefire, adopted by the Front in an effort to encourage a peaceful solution. The guerrillas' freedom of movement was limited by the extension of the defensive perimeter from Zag (in Morocco proper), past Mabhès and Farsia, to Amgala, in June 1984. In the same month, Moroccan officials took journalists on a tour of Haouza, which had formerly been claimed by Polisario to be "the capital of the liberated territories".

Despite these military reverses, the SADR received diplomatic support from a growing number of states. Ecuador, Venezuela and Upper Volta (Burkina Faso) were among those announcing official recognition in late 1983 and early 1984. In February 1984 Mauritania carried out its threat to recognize the SADR if Morocco failed to take steps towards implementing relevant OAU resolutions. Chad, Yugoslavia and Nigeria announced their recognition of the SADR later in the year. At the 20th OAU summit, held in November 1984, both Morocco and Zaire withdrew from the organization after the SADR delegation was allowed to take its seats. Three days before the summit opened, Dr Abdel Latif Filali (the Moroccan Foreign Minister) had expressed a willingness "to sit at the same conference table as the so-called Polisario", adding that Morocco was ready to participate in a referendum in the territory, to be held under the auspices of the UN and OAU. Libyan support for Polisario was withdrawn following the conclusion of a treaty of federation with Morocco in August 1984. In December the same year, a military coup in Mauritania resulted in a new government headed by President Taya, who criticized the Haydalla regime for allegedly supporting Polisario. President Taya undertook to maintain strict neutrality in the conflict. Diplomatic relations with Morocco, which had been severed in 1981, were restored.

Polisario continued to claim significant military victories against Morocco, although independent observers treated these claims with considerable scepticism, bearing in mind the logistical and numerical superiority of the Moroccan forces. An important factor was the apparent effectiveness of the defensive wall, which largely prevented major incursions by Polisario into the populated areas of the territory, although the guerrillas were able to stage harassing attacks along much of the perimeter and to penetrate the wall in small numbers on foot. Many of the more successful Polisario attacks were carried out in the vicinity of Zag (i.e. inside Morocco proper).

During early 1985, Morocco repeatedly denied Polisario claims that there had been direct contacts between the two sides. In particular, Polisario asserted that talks had been held in Madrid in January 1985 with the then Moroccan Interior Minister, Driss Basri, who had rejected an Algerian suggestion that the Western Sahara be granted autonomy, under Polisario control, within the framework of a Moroccan dominion arrangement. King Hassan confirmed in March 1985, however, that there had recently been a series of talks on the Western Sahara question between Moroccan and Algerian officials. The King repeated that Morocco was ready to participate in a referendum, which he said should be conducted by the UN, "without, of course, discarding the OAU from the process". A resolution supporting the referendum proposal was passed unanimously by the Moroccan National Assembly later the same month, the government's policy on the Western Sahara being endorsed by all legal political parties in Morocco.

There was some speculation at this time that Morocco would propose ceding to the Polisario the southern, relatively unpopulated and inhospitable portion of the territory, known as the Tiris el Gharbia (Oued Eddahab, or Rio de Oro). In January 1985, the government had announced plans for the creation of a new province of the Moroccan Sahara, which would encapsulate all of the Western Sahara as well as some of southern Morocco, with its capital at Goulimine (inside Morocco itself).

On the ground, Morocco succeeded in completing further extensions to the defensive perimeter. The first, completed in January 1985, took the wall south from the Ouarkziz hills, tracing a line to the east of Mabhès and the 1984 extension before joining up with the existing fortifications at Amgala. A second extension, completed in 1985, ran west from Amgala along the Mauritanian frontier before turning south through Guelta Zemmour and thence running southwest to the coast of Dakhla. Moreover, the completion in April 1987 of a further extension running due south to the Mauritanian border and then westward to the coast, meant that fortifications now extended the length of the Western Sahara frontier, added to which the walls completed earlier to the north and west of the frontier defences provided additional internal security capability. The number of Moroccan forces permanently stationed in Western Sahara was put at some 100,000 in May 1987, the annual cost being estimated at about US$1,000 million. Polisario, meanwhile, made increasing use of SAM-missiles to bring down foreign light aircraft flying over its declared "war-zone", while ships in Saharan "territorial waters" also came under guerrilla attack. After a Spanish trawler had been sunk in September 1985, Polisario information offices in Spain were closed and its representatives expelled.

The United Nations as Mediator, 1985-91

The UN Decolonization Committee in November 1985 voted by 91 to six, with 43 abstentions (including most Western countries), in favour of "direct negotiations" between Morocco and the Polisario. In response, Dr Filali declared that the situation was now one of "total impasse", and that Morocco would no longer regard itself as bound by UN resolutions or participate in UN discussions on the issue. He added, however, that Morocco would remain open to personal initiatives from the UN Secretary-General, Javier Pérez de Cuellar. A series of "proximity talks", arranged by Pérez de Cuellar, were held in April 1986, but failed to make any progress.

Towards the end of 1986, however, some diplomatic movement became apparent when on Dec. 2 the UN General Assembly's customary resolution reaffirming that Western Sahara was "a question of decolonization which remains to be completed on the basis of the exercise by the people of Western Sahara of their inalienable right to self-determination and independence" was not, as in previous years, specifically opposed by Morocco (which was absent from the vote) and was thus adopted by 98 votes to none with 44 abstentions. Subsequently, on the initiative of King Fahd of Saudi Arabia, King Hassan had talks with President Chadli of Algeria on May 4, 1987—the meeting taking place in the border town of Akid Lufti. A joint communiqué gave no details of their discussions on the Western Sahara question, but recorded that they had agreed to "continue meetings between the two brother countries to resolve outstanding problems".

A new Polisario offensive was carried out over the period from June 1987 to April 1988 but though groups scaled or captured parts of the Moroccan defensive walls, no significant incursions were made into Moroccan-held territory. On Oct. 28, 1987, the UN approved a resolution proposing direct talks between Morocco and the SADR by 93-0 with 53 abstentions. Then, on Nov. 24, Polisaro announced a unilateral ceasefire to coincide with the visit of a UN mission "to guarantee the security of the UN technical mission during their stay in both the occupied zones and in the liberated territories". The UN/OAU technical mission visited Morocco, Sahara, Mauritania and Tindouf in Algeria. Both sides agreed to a proposed referendum. Once the UN mission had departed, Polisario resumed its attacks: there were 122 in December 1987 in which, it claimed, 110 Moroccan troops were killed, 175 wounded and 11 taken prisoner.

During 1987 and 1988 King Hassan of Morocco embarked upon a series of diplomatic initiatives to secure support for Morocco's claim. Thus, in August 1987, the EC renewed the 1983 fishing agreement which recognized Morocco's sovereignty over Western Sahara's territorial waters. However, on Dec. 26, 1987, Albania became the 70th country to recognize the SADR. More important to both sides was the re-establishment of diplomatic relations between Morocco and Algeria (May 16, 1988) which threatened to deprive Polisario of its most crucial ally.

During Jan. 4-5, 1989, King Hassan held talks with senior Polisario officials in Marrakech; this was the first publicly acknowledged meeting between the two sides. They had accepted a UN peace plan advanced the previous August to settle the conflict. The 7th Polisario congress, held at Smara refugee camp in Western Sahara (April 28-May 1, 1989), approved a "national action plan" and sent a message to King Hassan calling for a resumption of the dialogue opened the previous January. On June 22, 1989, UN Secretary-General Javier Pérez de Cuellar visited Polisario refugee camps near Smara.

The heaviest fighting in a year broke out in October 1989 because of Polisario impatience at the slow pace of the UN-sponsored peace negotiations. At the 44th session of the UN General Assembly (Dec. 11, 1989), by consensus, a resolution was passed recognizing the joint efforts of the UN and OAU to achieve a peaceful solution of the conflict. However, by June 1990 disagreement between the two sides came into the open over the question of whether 100,000 Moroccan soldiers and civilians should remain in Western Sahara during the referendum—Polisario called for their withdrawal; Morocco said it would confine them to their camps. Polisario also claimed that the number of Sahrawis had swollen from the 74,000 registered in 1976 to 207,000 in 1987.

On July 8, 1990, the Moroccan Foreign Minister, Abdel Latif Filali, resisted pressure from the UN Secretary-General to hold direct talks with the Polisario; on July 9 UN-sponsored talks were held in Geneva about arrangements for a referendum to resolve the dispute.

On April 22, 1991, the Secretary-General reported details of the proposed referendum: (i) a budget of $200,000,000; (ii) a sum of $34 million to repatriate the estimated tens of thousands of refugees to take part in the referendum, to be covered by voluntary contributions; (iii) an allowance, when the budget was approved, of 16 weeks to arrange a ceasefire; (iv) then a further 11 weeks during which two-thirds of Morocco's troops should be withdrawn from the territory; and (v) the UN Mission for the Referendum in Western Sahara (MINURSO) to be supported by 2,900 civilian, police and military personnel to oversee the referendum—registration of voters, political campaigning and voting—which was scheduled for January 1992. UN Security Council Resolution 690 (to this effect) was passed unanimously on April 29, 1991.

On Aug. 4-5, 1991, a week before UN staff were due in Western Sahara to begin the referendum arrangements, Moroccan aircraft strafed the Oasis of Tfariti in the north-east near the Mauritanian border and Polisario claimed to have shot down a Moroccan plane. More attacks that August ended the 21-month lull in fighting and jeopardized the UN-proposed ceasefire due to take effect on Sept. 6. On Aug. 10, meanwhile, the Moroccans refused to allow the UN official in charge of the referendum, Johannes Manz, to enter the country while on Aug. 27 Polisario claimed that Morocco had massed 200,000 troops round the Tfariti Oasis.

On Aug. 20, 1991, King Hassan called on the UN to postpone the referendum by four months: he disputed the UN consolidated list of 74,000 Sahrawis entitled to vote and objected to Manz's rejection of a Moroccan list of 120,000 people whom he claimed were Western Saharan refugees entitled to vote. Nonetheless, the Sept. 6 ceasefire came into effect, by which time some 240 UN observers were in place.

Armed UN units began to take up positions on both sides of the sand walls which had been constructed by Morocco since 1981; they were under the command of a Canadian, Maj.-Gen. Armand Roy, and the referendum was then still scheduled to take place on Jan. 26, 1992. The UN representative, J. Manz, arrived in El Aaiún on Sept. 21, 1991. A week later, Algerian Radio claimed that 30,000 Moroccans had crossed the border into Western Sahara (unnoticed by foreign observers) to register as voters in El Aaiún.

Repeated Postponement of Referendum—Baker Plan

A report of November 1991 revealed that a UN official sympathetic to Morocco had provided that government with information contained on confidential computer diskettes compiled by the Polisario Front. By January 1992 the referendum had still not taken place and, according to a report of the US Senate Foreign Relations Committee, the UN peacekeeping operation was in jeopardy because of both mismanagement and possible financial irregularities. The report condemned the UN for failing to respond to ceasefire vio-

lations and threats by Moroccan forces to fire on unarmed British, US and Canadian officers (and others) acting as UN military observers. Although by the end of January 1992 MINURSO had reported dozens of ceasefire violations by both sides, including improper troop movements and overflights by Moroccan aircraft, the UN had failed to raise these with either Morocco or the Polisario. The Senate report warned that a failure of the UN mission could lead to renewed fighting between the two sides.

Thereafter the UN continued to extend the mission of MINURSO at regular intervals; it remains in place as of 2004. The referendum that was re-scheduled to take place at the end of 1993 was further postponed because UN-sponsored indirect peace talks between the two parties were consistently inconclusive. In 1995 the former US military representative to MINURSO warned the UN General Assembly that unless a settlement was reached, there could be renewed conflict—it was estimated that Morocco was spending US$1 million a day to occupy Western Sahara; moreover resumption of armed action by Polisario against the 120,000 remaining Moroccan troops could lead to the spread of conflict throughout the region, especially given the fragile political situation in nearby Algeria, the government of which had continually backed the Polisario.

On March 17, 1997, UN Secretary-General Kofi Annan appointed former US Secretary of State James Baker as his personal envoy to break the diplomatic deadlock in the Western Sahara dispute. Both parties expressed to Baker their willingness fully to implement a ceasefire and peace plan. In talks held in London on June 11-12, between Baker and each of the parties separately, in which Algeria and Mauritania served as observers, Baker announced that a UN peace plan could not be implemented before direct negotiations between Morocco and the Polisario took place. Although Bill Richardson, the US representative to the UN, stated that the United States would withdraw support for MINURSO if there was no breakthrough in negotiations, when the UN Security Council once more extended MINURSO's mandate, the United States reiterated its commitment to the holding of a referendum for the self-determination of the Sahrawi people in accordance with a peace settlement adopted by both parties. The Polisario, too, declared that the only way to avert further hostilities and make progress on peace talks was to hold a referendum.

With no signs of progress in the negotiations, plans to reschedule the referendum for February 1999 were shelved. Further talks were held in London in June 2000. However, in February 2001 Secretary-General Annan admitted that relations between the parties to the dispute were deteriorating, and there had been no progress in implementing the settlement plan. In his report to the United Nations Security Council, Annan said that a climate of increased mistrust and bitterness had set between the government of Morocco and Polisario and this was undermining the agreed ceasefire regime. He added that the UN was still unsure whether or not Morocco was prepared to offer or support some devolution of authority to all inhabitants and former inhabitants of the territory.

In 2001 Baker brought forward a compromise plan, providing for a period of several years of autonomy for the Western Sahara under provisional Moroccan sovereignty, followed by a referendum in which the bulk of the Moroccan settlers introduced since 1975 would vote alongside the UN-authenticated Sahrawis. The choice would be between integration with Morocco or independence, with the possibility of a third option, mostly likely continued autonomy, being added—but either way the arithmetic would be weighted in Morocco's favour. The Baker Plan was much less advantageous to the Sahrawis than the former UN Settlement Plan, drawn up in 1988 and approved by the Security Council in 1991. That document had proposed a referendum offering a straight choice between independence and integration, and the electorate would have been limited to the Sahrawi population as identified in the Spanish census of 1974.

In January 2002 the Secretary-General sent Baker to Morocco, to "inform the Moroccan authorities of the rejection by Algeria and Polisario of the draft framework agreement". However, in his report in February, the Secretary-General noted that Algeria and the Polisario, while not accepting the Baker Plan as such, seemed prepared to discuss or negotiate a division of the territory. Meanwhile a complicating factor had emerged in the negotiations—the discovery of petroleum off the coast of Western Sahara by exploration companies licensed by Morocco.

In May 2003 the formal replies to the Baker Plan were finally published. Both sides had rejected it. Morocco remained wholly opposed to any hint of autonomy and evidently only supported continuing UN negotiations because it could no longer simply refuse to accept that a problem existed. The Polisario accepted the principle of Moroccan withdrawal and a referendum, but had not accepted any detailed proposals for implementation. However, talks continued and in October 2003 the Secretary-General could report that the situation on the ground remained calm. The Polisario had in September, as a gesture of goodwill, released 243 prisoners of war, these having been held captive at desert locations across the Algerian border near Tindouf since the 1970s. However, the International Committee of the Red Cross stated that 914 Moroccan soldiers were still being held.

In January 2004, the Secretary-General proposed that the mandate for MINURSO be extended until the end of April in order to give Morocco more time to respond to a revised peace plan recommended by James Baker. The revised peace plan, which had already been accepted by the Polisario but initially rejected by Morocco, would allow for more autonomy to the Western Sahara than Morocco had previously been willing to concede.

Peter Calvert

1.21 Zambia - Democratic Republic of Congo

Relations between Zambia and the Democratic Republic of Congo (DRC, known as Zaïre from 1971-97) became troubled in the 1980s as the result of a border dispute centring principally on the area around Lake Mweru on Zambia's northern border. (Map 7, page 496, shows the DRC-Zambia border.)

History of the Dispute

Although Presidents Mobutu of Zaïre and Kaunda of Zambia joined with President dos Santos of Angola in October 1979 in signing a tripartite non-aggression pact, bilateral relations between Zaïre and Zambia were strained in August 1980 over Zambian claims that Zaïre had set up border posts some 30 kilometres inside Zambian territory in the Kaputa district of Zambia's Northern province. In June 1981 the Zambian Prime Minister announced that the Kaputa border dispute, which also involved the nearby Lake Mweru border area, might be referred to the Organization of African Unity (OAU) and that Zambia was confident of the OAU finding in its favour on the basis of the OAU's 1964 declaration that boundaries drawn up by the former colonial powers should be respected.

Tensions escalated in 1982 amid a series of incidents and skirmishes in various sections of the border area. Thousands of Zambians were reported to have fled from villages along the border near Mufulira (in Zambia's Copperbelt province), following an exchange of fire on Feb. 28, 1982, and the alleged seizure by Zaïreans of Zambian soldiers, two buses and a lorry. The Zaïrean authorities on March 2 closed the border between the two countries in the Sakania area (in southern Shaba province) and claimed that three of their soldiers had been killed by Zambian forces on Zaïrean territory the previous month. Diplomatic sources in Lusaka (the Zambian capital) attributed much of the tension to shortages of food and other essentials in Zaïre's Shaba province and to a recent tightening of customs and immigration regulations in an effort to halt smuggling.

A meeting of the Zaïre-Zambia permanent joint commission in April 1982 agreed on a reciprocal release of prisoners (involving 55 Zaïreans held by Zambia and 25 Zambians held by Zaïre). However, in June 1982 Lusaka radio claimed that Zaïre had established border posts at Mutambala and Musasa, some 18 and 12 miles respectively inside Zambian territory.

After three days of talks in Zaïre, Presidents Mobutu and Kaunda on Aug. 30, 1982, issued a communiqué pledging the two countries to continue negotiations to find a permanent solution to the border dispute. Nevertheless, Lusaka radio subsequently claimed that three Zambians and two tourists on a hunting safari had been abducted in the Kaputa area on Sept. 5. An emergency meeting of the Zaïre-Zambia joint commission on Sept. 16, 1982, in the Zaïrean border town of Kasumbalesa considered Zambian accusations of Zaïrean violations of its territory and resulted in Zaïre agreeing to remove its soldiers from a border village in Luapula province some 10 miles inside Zambia.

In September 1983 Zambian troops were deployed along the border with Zaïre following an incident on Sept. 21 in which two Zambian workers were killed and two wounded in an ambush by Zaïreans near the border town of Mufulira. In announcing the move, President Kaunda said that, in view of an escalation of crimes of banditry and smuggling by Zaïrean nationals in the border area, troops and increased police resources were needed to bring the situation under control. Further strain was caused by a Zambian decision of July 17, 1984, to deport over 2,500 Zaïrean and other African nationals, whereupon Zaïre the following month said that a similar number of illegal residents were to be expelled from Shaba province, most of them Zambians. Although the order against the Zambians was later revoked, some 2,000 Zambian workers had by that time fled from the country.

Relations between Zaïre and Zambia continued to be strained in 1985 with tensions being aggravated by an influx into Zambia of Zaïrean refugees from disturbances in Shaba province in November 1984. On Oct. 4-5, 1986, Presidents Mobutu and Kaunda met for talks at Gbadolite (northern Zaïre) and succeeded in bringing about an improvement in their countries' relations, although the causes of the border tensions of recent years remained unresolved. On June 26, 1987, however, President Kaunda announced that a formula for resolving the Kaputa dispute had been worked out by the two governments and that accordingly the issue would be settled by the end of the year.

During March and April 1989 Zaïre and Zambia held talks on bilateral relations and co-operation. Agreement was reached over the delineation of their common border. This agreement included the restoration of frontier security and the regulation of cross-border trade in the expectation of bringing to an end a decade of tensions over cross-border smuggling and other activities.

On Feb. 21, 1990, however, a Zambian fisherman was shot dead and two others wounded by Zaïrean soldiers while they were fishing in the Luapula river, which forms a common border between the two countries. Zaïre claimed that the fishermen had strayed into its territory. In March 1990 a Zambian minister said that the demarcation of the frontier along the Luapula was not yet complete although "considerable progress" in resolving the border dispute between the two countries had been made.

Developments since mid-1990s

The issue of the location of Zaïrean military camps on Zambian territory or proximate to the border resurfaced in April 1994 when Zambia lodged an official protest at the construction of a camp at Kasumbalesa, only ten metres from the border. The following year "large numbers" of Zaïreans entered the Zambian border town of Chililabombwe through Kasumbalesa. The Copperbelt Deputy Minister noted that the illegal entry of so many people posed a possible security risk. These anxieties were addressed in July 1996 with the signing of an accord promoting joint efforts to address cross-border crime. Shortly after this agreement increased rebel activity in Zaïre led to Zambia reinforcing the border. In mid-April security at the Kasumbelesa border crossing collapsed following fighting between fleeing Zaïrean government troops and Zambian border officers. In May 1997 the Mobutu regime fell to Laurent Kabila's rebel forces. Zaïre was renamed the Democratic Republic of Congo (DRC).

In January 1998 the two countries issued a joint communiqué announcing an agreement to redefine the border. It was recommended that the DRC-Zambia permanent joint commission, dormant since 1989, reconvene to consider "outstanding issues" relating to the demarcation of the border. Discussions in April were reported to be "working out ways of defining borders between the two countries", as well as addressing border security. However, these efforts were suspended following renewed conflict in the DRC. In mid-1998 fighting resumed in the DRC involving numerous rebel groups as well as other national armies. Zambia was not involved in the fighting and sought to mediate the conflict. After talks in June 1999, the Lusaka Agreement between the combatants was signed on July 10. Fighting nonetheless continued.

The Zambian border area suffered from the civil war in the DRC. In June 1999 Congolese rebels attacked Kaputa killing three people, as well as looting and committing arson. Flows of refugees from the DRC, including government soldiers, fled to Zambia in increasing numbers. From mid-November 2000, an intensification of fighting in south-eastern DRC led to an influx of about 30,000 refugees into Zambia. These numbers included between 3,500 and 7,000 soldiers fighting for the DRC government, among them troops from Zimbabwe and former Rwandan and Burundian militia. Zambian troops attempted to disarm the fleeing soldiers, whilst diplomats sought their speedy repatriation. On Jan. 4, 2001, Zambia's President, Frederick Chiluba, met President Kabila in the Copperbelt town of Ndola to discuss the crisis. By Jan. 9, all but a hundred troops had been repatriated.

Simon Massey

AMERICAS

AND ANTARCTICA

2.1 Argentina - Chile

A major dispute between Argentina and Chile over the Beagle Channel (off Tierra del Fuego and north of Cape Horn) and the ownership of three small islands at the eastern entrance of the channel, which had brought the two countries close to conflict in the late 1970s and early 1980s, was settled through papal mediation leading to the Treaty of Peace and Friendship in 1984. This left only one relatively minor border question (the Southern Glaciers question) to be resolved by arbitration in 1999.

History of the Dispute

When Argentina and Chile attained independence from Spain in the early 19th century, their respective territories ran west of the Andes for Chile and east of the Andes for Argentina. However, disputes arose in the latter part of the century over the delimitation of boundaries in the southern part of their respective territories. On July 23, 1881, the two countries signed a treaty in Buenos Aires establishing the frontier along the watershed of the Andes. Disagreement still arose, however, over the precise delimitation of boundaries, particularly in some of the high and inhospitable sections of the Andes where the terrain was so broken that the line of the watershed did not exist.

As a result, a treaty of May 28, 1902 (renewable every 10 years) made the British Crown responsible for arbitrating future territorial disputes. In 1972 Argentina announced that it did not intend to renew the treaty and accordingly a new treaty was signed on April 5, 1972, making the International Court of Justice (ICJ) responsible for assessing disputes that could not be solved by direct negotiation. As the dispute over the Beagle Channel had been referred to Britain in 1971 before the treaty, Britain agreed to submit it to five former judges of the ICJ to determine on behalf of the Crown. An award was made public on May 2, 1977, but on Jan. 25, 1978, the military government of Argentina formally declared it null and void. The Act of Puerto Montt of 1978 set up a joint negotiating commission, but after no progress had been made both countries agreed in December 1979 to accept an offer of mediation from the Vatican. The treaty for submitting disputes to the ICJ was terminated by Argentina in 1982.

The dispute over the Beagle Channel was finally settled at the second attempt at papal mediation in 1984, leading to a Treaty of Peace and Friendship signed in the Vatican on Nov. 29, 1984. In addition to providing an award in the dispute, the treaty, under articles 1-6 and an annex of 41 articles, provided procedures on conciliation and arbitration for other disputes, including both the Southern Glaciers issue and the overlapping claims of Chile and Argentina in the Antarctic (see section on Antarctica).

The provisions of this treaty were used to negotiate a final settlement of the countries' claims in the southern regions. The restoration of civilian government in Chile in 1989 assisted in improving relations between the two countries and on Aug. 1-3, 1989, President Patricio Aylwin Azócar of Chile visited Buenos Aires to sign an agreement with President Carlos Saúl Menem of Argentina. Under the terms of the agreement, 1,079 sq km of disputed territory was awarded to Chile and 1,083 sq km to Argentina. The agreement settled all of the 23 points under dispute apart from one over the Laguna del Desierto in southern Patagonia, comprising some 520 sq km (see Map 11, page 498). This was to be submitted to a panel of five independent jurists under the auspices of the Organization of American States (OAS), who were to reach a decision within a year. The agreement provoked isolated protests within Argentina from ultra right-wing nationalists and from inhabitants in the southern province of Santa Cruz.

In the event the jurists took much longer than had been hoped, but before leaving office President Menem and President Eduardo Frei Ruiz-Tagle of Chile were able to sign a new agreement on the Southern Glaciers question in Buenos Aires on Dec. 15, 1998. With its ratification on June 3, 1999, by the Argentine Senate the last remaining boundary dispute with Chile was officially settled.

Peter Calvert

2.2 Argentina - Paraguay

A dispute has existed since the 19th century over the exact position of the north-eastern part of the border between Argentina and Paraguay, theoretically constituted by the course of the Pilcomayo river (which has its source in Bolivia). The dispute has centred on the fact that the course of the river has from time to time changed by up to 1.5 kilometres towards either side. A supplementary boundary treaty between the Argentine Republic and the Republic of Paraguay on the River Pilcomayo was signed at Buenos Aires on June 1, 1945, but issues arising from it have continued to be the subject of negotiation. (Map 12 on page 498 illustrates this dispute.)

History of the Dispute

In 1974 Argentina and Paraguay signed an agreement to conduct studies on how the Pilcomayo's flood waters could best be exploited. Argentina subsequently carried out certain works designed to control the movement of the river and to lessen flood damage. Early in November 1980 the Paraguayan government alleged that Argentina was unilaterally using water from a portion of the Pilcomayo river shared with Paraguay. Elpidio Acevedo, Paraguay's Deputy

Minister of Foreign Affairs, stated in Buenos Aires that his government had proof that over the past two years Argentina had deliberately been altering the course of the river and that this action was contrary both to the principles of international law and to agreements entered into by the two governments.

This allegation was rejected in a statement issued by the Argentine Foreign Ministry on Nov. 9, 1980, declaring inter alia: "The portion [of the river] shared with Paraguay is changing course as a result of the very special geological formation of the area and the sediment carried by the river. As a result the waters have drained into Argentine and Paraguayan territories at three different points. The situation has been duly studied by the Argentine and Paraguayan governments and agreement has been reached to implement the appropriate measures to dam up the above-mentioned drainage so that the waters can return to their normal course as soon as possible. Seeking an effective and equitable use of the waters of the Pilcomayo river, the Argentine, Bolivian and Paraguayan governments are conducting a joint study with the co-operation of the Organization of American States within a framework of a project for multiple use of the Pilcomayo".

In Argentina fears were expressed that the timing of the revival of the dispute by Paraguay might lead to delays in the construction of a proposed joint Argentine-Paraguayan hydroelectric project at Yacyretá on the Paraná river, on which Argentina and Paraguay had signed an agreement on Aug. 30, 1979.

Under an agreement signed on Aug. 22, 1985, it was decided to expedite demarcation of the boundary where it followed the Pilcomayo river. Argentina also proposed the demarcation of clear boundaries in the Paraná and Paraguay rivers and the determination of sovereignty over islands which would be permanently above water because of the effect on the river level of the hydroelectric projects. Meanwhile resources were finally made available to commence the Yacyretá project and building commenced. On Feb. 9, 1995, the two countries signed an agreement to constitute the National Commission for the Development of the Riverbed Rio Pilcomayo.

Peter Calvert

2.3 Argentina - United Kingdom (Falklands, South Georgia and South Sandwich Islands)

British sovereignty over the Falkland Islands in the South Atlantic has been consistently disputed by Argentina ever since they became a British possession in 1833. Argentina's claim to the islands (which it calls Las Malvinas) is based on earlier Spanish claims, their proximity to its coast, Argentine possession of them for several years in the early 19th century and what it regards as the colonial nature of their acquisition and continued possession by Britain. The British claim is based on prior settlement, reinforced by formal claims in the name of the Crown and completed by "open, continuous, effective and peaceful possession, occupation and administration of the islands since 1833". Britain also lays stress on the fact that the exercise of UK sovereignty has been in accordance with the express wish of the islanders, in which connection UK governments have cited the fundamental principles of the self-determination of peoples enshrined in the UN Charter and other international covenants.

After several years of inconclusive negotiations between the two governments on the question of sovereignty and other issues, the military regime then in power in Argentina launched a surprise invasion of the Falklands on April 2, 1982, its forces overwhelming a small garrison of Royal Marines and installing an Argentine military governor. Britain responded by dispatching a powerful naval task force to the South Atlantic, where a fierce conflict ensued, resulting in the recapture of the islands by British troops by mid-June 1982 and the restoration of British administration. Notwithstanding its military defeat (which led directly to the restoration of civilian government in Buenos Aires), Argentina has continued to assert its claim to sovereignty over the Falklands/Malvinas. However, the British government, while seeking a normalization of relations with Argentina, has refused to enter into negotiations involving the question of sovereignty and has maintained a substantial British military presence in and around the Falkland Islands.

British sovereignty over South Georgia and the South Sandwich Islands was first proclaimed by Captain Cook in 1775. From 1908 to 1985 they were administered as dependencies of the Falkland Islands; since then as British dependencies in their own right. Argentina also claims these South Atlantic islands within the framework of its claims to the Falklands themselves and to certain islands of the British Antarctic Territory. In the 1982 conflict South Georgia was occupied by Argentine forces. When subsequently repossessed by the British a clandestine Argentine naval presence which had been established in Southern Thule in 1976 was also removed. (Map 13 on page 499 illustrates this dispute.)

Geographical, Political and Historical Background

The Falklands/Malvinas lie some 300 miles (480 km) to the east of Argentina, almost opposite the Isla de los Estados (Staten Island) and the eastern entrance to the Magellan Strait. They have a land surface area of

4,618 square miles (12,000 sq km) and a civilian population, largely of British descent, of about 2,200 (which was declining before 1982 but has since risen). Executive power is vested in a Crown-appointed Governor acting with an Executive Council, the latter elected from among its members by a Legislative Council itself elected by universal adult suffrage.

South Georgia, an island of about 1,450 square miles (3,750 sq km), is situated some 800 miles (1,285 km) east-south-east of the Falklands and houses a British scientific base. The South Sandwich Islands lie about 470 miles (750 km) to the south-east of South Georgia and are uninhabited. Having until 1985 been dependencies of the Falklands, South Georgia (together with the nearby Shag Rocks) and the South Sandwich Islands now form a separate British dependency, although the Governor of the Falklands acts as their Commissioner (and is also High Commissioner of the British Antarctic Territory).

Although navigators of several countries have been credited with the discovery of the then uninhabited Falkland Islands (the Argentines claim Magellan in 1504 and the British a Captain Davis of the *Desire* in 1592), the first conclusively authenticated sighting was made by the Dutch sailor Sebald van Weert in 1600. The first recorded landing was made in 1690 by Captain Strong of the English ship *Welfare*, who named the islands after the then Navy Treasurer, Viscount Falkland. French sealers landed at various times after 1704 and named the islands "Les Malouines" (after their home town of St Malo), from which the Argentine name Las Malvinas is derived, but the first permanent settlement was made by the French in 1764.

The French settlers relinquished their rights to Spain in 1766 and received compensation for the settlement. However no formal transfer of sovereignty took place, as Spain claimed that the islands lay within the zone allocated to it in 1494. Meanwhile, in ignorance of the French move, a British settlement was established in West Falkland in 1766. In 1770 the Spanish governor of Buenos Aires sent ships to expel the British. This action brought the two countries to the brink of war but in 1771 Spain, while reserving its claim of sovereignty, recognized the British settlement. The British settlement was withdrawn in 1774, officially on grounds of economy, but according to Argentina because of a secret understanding made in 1771 of which no documentary evidence has been found. However, the British left a plaque declaring that the Falklands were the "sole right and property" of King George III.

Spain withdrew its garrison in 1811 for military reasons, leaving a plaque claiming the islands in the name of Ferdinand VII. At the time of Argentine independence in 1816 (as the United Provinces of the River Plate) the islands were uninhabited. The islands meanwhile became a base for the British and US sealing and whaling industries, and temporary settlements sprang up there. In 1820 the islands were claimed for the Buenos Aires government by a ship which did not

thereafter return to the United Provinces. It was not until 1826 that the government of the United Provinces proclaimed its sovereignty as successor to the colonial power, and in 1828 commissioned Luis Vernet as Governor. In 1829 the British Minister in Buenos Aires formally objected to this, but before any action could be taken, after complaints from sealers about interference with their trading, an American warship expelled the Argentine garrison in 1831. Meanwhile the Admiralty in London had decided to reassert British sovereignty over the islands, which was done by HMS *Clio* on Jan. 3, 1833. A protest was soon after lodged by the government of Buenos Aires, and thereafter at irregular intervals throughout the nineteenth century. In 1844 the government of Buenos Aires offered to sell the islands to Britain; this offer was rejected on the grounds that Britain already owned them.

The approach of the centenary of 1833 aroused a new interest in the islands in Argentina. With the election of General Juan Domingo Perón in 1946, however, they became a major nationalist issue. Fears of a possible military attack led Britain to send HMS *Coventry* to the islands in 1949, and agitation for their "return" continued after Perón's fall in 1955.

The first recorded landing on South Georgia was made by Captain James Cook in 1775 (although it had been sighted at least twice during the previous 100 years), and the South Sandwich Islands were discovered during the same voyage. Argentina first made formal claim to South Georgia in 1927 and to the South Sandwich Islands in 1948. A British offer to submit the question of the Dependencies to arbitration was turned down by Argentina in 1949.

Inconclusive Negotiations between Argentina and Britain, 1966-80

In December 1965 the UN General Assembly approved a general resolution (Resolution 2065/XX) calling for the speedy decolonization of all remaining colonial possessions, and at Argentina's request approved a further resolution noting the existence of a dispute over the Falklands/Malvinas and inviting the two countries to enter into negotiations "with a view to finding a peaceful solution to the problem", bearing in mind the interests of the islanders.

The islanders were solidly opposed to colonization by Argentina, but the British government of the day hoped they might change their minds if closer contact could be established. An agreement was reached therefore to improve communications between the islands and the Argentine mainland. However it had hardly begun before the Argentine government in 1973 (on the return to power of Gen. Juan Perón) again brought up the question of sovereignty over the Falkland Islands. In a note to the UN Secretary-General (Dr Kurt Waldheim) on Nov. 5, 1973, Argentina called for an end to the "colonial situation", accused Britain of "paralysing" talks on sovereignty, and said that Britain's "anxiety to respect the right of self-determination of the inhabitants of the islands would be more praiseworthy and legitimate" if the population had been consulted when the islands were annexed in the 19th century. The UN General Assembly subsequently in December 1973 adopted a resolution (3160/XXVI-II) calling on both countries to "arrive at a peaceful solution of the conflict of sovereignty between them" in order to "put an end to the colonial situation".

The following year, amid reports that the British government was considering granting oil exploration rights off the Falkland Islands to a Canadian company, there were calls from certain political and press sectors in Argentina for an invasion of the islands and for the severance of trade and communications links. In January 1975 Argentina extended its control over air travel to the Falkland Islands (which was operated solely by the Argentine Air Force from Argentina) by making it obligatory for all travellers to obtain clearance from the Argentine Foreign Ministry, in contravention of a July 1971 communications agreement between Britain and Argentina which stated that only Argentines travelling to the Falklands needed a special tourist card.

In October 1975 the Argentine ambassador was recalled from London after Argentina objected to the dispatch of a British mission to the islands, headed by Lord Shackleton, to carry out an "economic and fiscal" survey at the request of the Falkland Islands Executive Council and to assess prospects and make recommendations on developments in "oil, minerals, fisheries and alginates" as well as to advise on capital expenditure needs over the next five years. Argentina warned that both sides had agreed in 1964 to "abstain from unilateral innovations in fundamental aspects of the question" and that the exploitation of natural resources would not be possible, since they belonged to Argentina.

The Shackleton mission nevertheless arrived in Port Stanley (the Falklands capital) aboard the Royal Navy ice patrol ship *Endurance* in January 1976, travelling from an undisclosed Latin American country because the Argentine government had refused to let the team members use the normal air route via Buenos Aires. The Argentine Foreign Ministry then expressed the opinion that the UK ambassador to Buenos Aires should be withdrawn in view of (i) the presence of the mission in the Falklands, (ii) the refusal of the British government to resume negotiations on the sovereignty issue, and (iii) a note from the UK Foreign and Commonwealth Secretary on Jan. 12, 1976, to the effect that the sovereignty dispute was "sterile" and calling for talks on economic co-operation. The ambassador accordingly left for London on Jan. 19, 1976.

During February 1976 another British ship engaged in scientific research in the South Atlantic (the *Shackleton*) was intercepted by an Argentine destroyer which fired shots across its bows and tried to effect an arrest; however, the *Shackleton* (on the orders of the Falklands Governor) ignored the attempt and sailed directly to Port Stanley, with the destroyer following

closely. Argentina claimed in a letter to the UN Security Council on Feb. 11, 1976, that the ship was searching for oil when challenged, while Britain protested to the Security Council at the "provocative" action of Argentina and urged the latter to stop harassing peaceful vessels in contravention of international law. The *Shackleton* left Port Stanley to continue its research on Feb. 17 after talks had been held in New York between British and Argentine government representatives on ways of resuming negotiations and normalizing relations. However on March 23, 1976, a right-wing military government seized power in Buenos Aires and over the next three years killed more than 15,000 of its own citizens in a purge of suspected communists.

In accordance with UN Resolution 31/49 of Dec. 1, 1976—which urged Britain and Argentina to "expedite the negotiations concerning the dispute over sovereignty" in line with Resolutions 2065/XX and 3160/XXVI-II and called on both parties to refrain from taking decisions which implied the introduction of unilateral modifications in the situation—the UK Foreign Office Minister of State in the then Labour government, Edward Rowlands, visited Buenos Aires in February 1977 with a view to seeking formal talks. Prior to the visit, Rowlands went to the Falklands "to hear from the islanders at first hand how they view their future". On his way back to Buenos Aires Rowlands said in a statement that his delegation would attempt to work out terms of reference with Argentina for subsequent formal negotiations on political relations and economic co-operation, and that such talks would have to take into account "the broad issues affecting the future of the islands, including sovereignty"; he maintained that Britain's intention to seek a basis for negotiation had the approval of the Falkland Islands Councils. At the same time, the Argentine Foreign Ministry issued a statement to the effect that the intention of Argentina in the forthcoming talks remained the recovery of the Falklands, and that discussions about the economy remained subordinate to this.

The Rowlands talks took place on Feb. 22-23, 1977, a joint communiqué stating afterwards that they had been held "in a constructive spirit" and that the two delegations now needed to consult with their governments over certain points. It described the talks as considering "all aspects of the future of the Falkland Islands, the South Georgias and the South Sandwich Islands and Anglo-Argentine co-operation in the south-west Atlantic area, and to explore the possibility of establishing terms of reference for subsequent negotiations".

Further rounds of talks were held in 1977 in Rome and New York, and after the latter round the two sides agreed to set up two working groups "on political relations, including sovereignty, and on economic co-operation". A third round was held in Lima (Peru) in February 1978.

Full diplomatic relations were resumed between Argentina and Britain (now under a Conservative government) in late 1979. The new Minister of State at the

Foreign and Commonwealth Office, Nicholas Ridley, had talks in New York in April 1980 with Air-Commodore Carlos Cavandoli (the Argentine Under-Secretary of State for Foreign Relations) and also with a representative of the Falklands Legislative Council, Adrian Monk. Later in that year (Nov. 22-29) Ridley visited the Falklands for talks with the islanders on how best to approach the dispute with Argentina over status; en route he also paid a courtesy call on Air-Commodore Cavandoli in Buenos Aires. While the visit was in progress the Falkland Islands Office in London asserted publicly that one of several options being put to the islanders by the British minister was that of a transfer of sovereignty to Argentina coupled with a lease-back of the islands (this, according to the Office, being the option most favoured by Whitehall). Lord Carrington, the UK Foreign and Commonwealth Secretary, stressed on Nov. 26, however, that there was no question of Britain's acting against the wishes of the islanders.

Argentine Occupation and British Repossession of the Islands

In January 1981 the Falkland Islands Legislative Council passed a resolution stating that, although it was not pleased with any of the ideas presented by Nicholas Ridley regarding the sovereignty issue, it agreed that the British government should continue talks with Argentina and that the Legislative Council should be represented; furthermore, it urged that the British delegation should try to reach an understanding to freeze the dispute for an indefinite period. An Argentine Foreign Ministry spokesman replied that Argentina would negotiate only with Britain on the islands and that the resolution (a copy of which had been presented by the British ambassador) was therefore of no concern to it.

Representatives of the islands' Legislative Council took part in the next three rounds of talks, which were held in New York in April 1980, February 1981 and February 1982. A joint communiqué issued after the February 1982 talks—the first to take place under the new Argentine military government of Gen. Leopoldo Galtieri, which had taken office on Dec. 22, 1981—said that they had been held in a "cordial and positive spirit" and that the two sides had reaffirmed their resolve to find a solution to the dispute. Nevertheless, the Argentine Foreign Ministry issued a statement only two days later (on March 1) warning that, unless a speedy negotiated settlement was reached, Argentina would "put an end" to negotiations, "seek other means" of resolving the dispute, and feel free to choose "the procedure which best corresponds to its interests". In fact, as part of the bargain by which Galtieri gained power, plans were already being prepared for the taking of the islands by force.

Tension between Britain and Argentina escalated sharply soon afterwards, when a party of about 60 Argentine "scrap merchants" landed on South Georgia on March 19, 1982, with an apparently valid commer-

cial contract to dismantle disused whaling installations. The British Antarctic Survey team on South Georgia ordered them to leave and to seek permission from the British authorities if they wished to continue their work, following which most of the party subsequently departed on March 21, lowering the Argentine flag which they had raised. However, the Galtieri government, which claimed to have no prior knowledge of the landing, refused a British request that it should make arrangements for the removal of the remaining dozen men, to whom supplies were delivered by an Argentine naval vessel on March 25. The British Ministry of Defence confirmed on March 24 that the *Endurance* was in the area and was ready to give assistance if required; the presence of Argentine warships and naval vessels was reported in the area soon afterwards.

Despite a UN Security Council meeting on April 1, 1982, and last-minute diplomatic efforts, Argentine troops invaded the Falklands on April 2, on which day the Argentine military junta announced the "recovery of the Malvinas, the Georgias and the South Sandwich Islands for the nation". The small detachments of Royal Marines on the Falklands and South Georgia were overwhelmed, and the British Governor was deported and replaced by an Argentine military governor, Maj.-Gen. Mario Benjamin Menéndez. In an address to the nation on April 2, President Galtieri claimed that the decision to recover the islands "was prompted by the need to put an end to the interminable succession of evasive and dilatory tactics used by Britain to perpetuate its dominion over the islands and their zone of influence". There were no British casualties in this phase of the conflict.

The UN Security Council on April 3, 1982, adopted by 10 votes to one (Panama) with four abstentions (China, Poland, Spain and the Soviet Union) a resolution (502) demanding the immediate cessation of hostilities and an immediate withdrawal of all Argentine forces from the Falklands, and calling on the Argentine and British governments to seek a diplomatic solution and to respect fully the UN Charter.

The British government reacted to the Argentine invasion by dispatching a large naval task force to the South Atlantic, the main body of which had arrived in Falklands waters by late April 1982. During the approximately three weeks taken by the British warships to complete the 8,000-mile journey to the South Atlantic, intensive diplomatic exchanges took place, with the US Secretary of State, General Alexander Haig, acting as principal intermediary, in an effort to resolve the dispute by negotiation. However, the Argentine government refused to yield on its fundamental claim to sovereignty over the islands (which it garrisoned with some 12,000 troops), while Britain insisted on an Argentine military withdrawal as the basic requirement for a peaceful resolution of the immediate crisis. Unsuccessful mediation attempts were also made by the Peruvian government and by the UN Secretary-General.

As the task force sailed for the South Atlantic, international reactions to the escalating conflict included the adoption by a special Foreign Ministers' meeting of the Organization of American States (OAS) in Washington on April 26-28, 1982, of a resolution recognizing Argentine sovereignty over the Falklands/Malvinas and calling on Britain to cease hostilities in the South Atlantic; the voting was 17 to none with four abstentions (Chile, Colombia, Trinidad and Tobago, and the United States). The European Community member states, however, showed solidarity with Britain by unanimously imposing a one-month ban on Argentine imports from April 16 (although the following month Ireland and Italy refused to continue the sanctions, which were eventually lifted on June 22, 1982).

In the South Atlantic theatre, British forces recaptured South Georgia on April 25, 1982, causing the Argentine Foreign Minister to declare that his country was now "technically at war" with Britain (although no such formal declaration was ever made by either side). In the first, and most controversial, naval engagement of the conflict, the Argentine battle-cruiser *General Belgrano* was torpedoed and sunk by a British submarine on May 2 although some 30 miles outside the "total exclusion zone" (TEZ) earlier proclaimed by the UK government. The government had reserved its right to conduct operations outside the zone and claimed that the warship and her escorts had "posed a major threat" to British ships. Two days later, on May 4, the destroyer HMS *Sheffield* became the first Royal Navy loss in the conflict when it was struck by an Exocet missile launched from an Argentine warplane. Other British warships and auxiliaries were sunk or disabled by the Argentine Air Force during and after a landing of British troops in force at Port San Carlos on East Falkland on May 21. Nevertheless, in subsequent heavy land fighting, during which the British established further bridgeheads, the Argentine forces were pushed back to Port Stanley (the capital of the Falklands), where an unconditional Argentine surrender was secured with effect from midnight on June 14-15, 1982.

The UK government subsequently announced, on June 20, 1982, the surrender the previous day of a small group of Argentines stationed on Southern Thule (in the South Sandwich Islands), where Argentina had established a base in December 1976 without British authorization. Whereas Argentina had described the base as a scientific station, the Argentines who surrendered were all found to be military personnel.

During the later stages of the fighting, Britain and the United States on June 4, 1982, had vetoed a UN Security Council resolution, which, like the so-called "Peruvian peace plan" before it, called on both sides to institute a ceasefire. The UK government pointed out that a ceasefire at that stage would have left Argentina in military possession of key areas of the Falklands, including the capital. Nine Security Council members voted in favour of the resolution and four abstained (France, Guyana, Jordan and Togo). It was later stated by Jeane Kirkpatrick, the US Ambassador to the UN, that the US vote against the resolution should have been an abstention but that instructions to that effect had been received too late.

British fatal casualties in the Falklands conflict included 255 task force personnel (237 service and 18 civilian) and three islanders. Argentine fatalities amounted to 646, of whom some 370 were lost in the *General Belgrano*.

Aftermath of 1982 Hostilities

In Argentina the Falklands defeat resulted in the fall of the Galtieri government on June 17, 1982, and the assumption of the presidency by Gen. Reynaldo Bignone. The new government indicated its acceptance that military hostilities had ended de facto (thus allowing Britain to repatriate some 12,000 Argentine prisoners of war). It refused, however, to issue an unconditional declaration of cessation of hostilities.

Britain lifted the TEZ and coastal blockade of Argentina on July 22, 1982, but maintained a 150-mile (240 km) exclusion zone around the islands for Argentine warships and military aircraft. Argentine civil aircraft and shipping were requested not to enter the zone without prior permission. Most of the ships and troops making up the British task force were withdrawn during June-August 1982, but a sizeable garrison of some 4,000 soldiers was retained on the islands, together with a significant naval presence. It was confirmed in June 1983 that a new strategic airfield would be constructed on the Falklands to enable the garrison to be reinforced by air in emergency and this airfield, Mount Pleasant, was subsequently opened in May 1985.

In December 1982 the UK government announced a £31 million programme for economic development of the islands over a six-year period. On March 28, 1983, the British Nationality (Falkland Islands) Amendment Bill was enacted, conferring British nationality on about 400 islanders who had not acquired it under the 1981 British Nationality Act. The UK Prime Minister, Margaret Thatcher, paid a five-day visit to the Falklands on Jan. 8-12, 1983, this being described by the Argentine government as "an act of provocation and arrogance".

UN General Assembly Resolutions, 1982-86

The Bignone government sought to reverse the verdict of war by using the UN General Assembly to exert pressure on the British government to resume negotiations on the sovereignty question. To it Argentina formally resubmitted the Falklands-Malvinas question on Aug. 16, 1982. The subsequent 37th Assembly session adopted by 90 votes (including the United States) to 12 (Britain, 10 Commonwealth states and Oman), with 53 abstentions, a resolution, tabled by Argentina and other Latin American countries, requesting Britain and Argentina to resume negotiations in order to find as soon as possible a peaceful solution to the sovereignty dispute and also asking the UN Secretary-General to undertake a renewed mission of good offices to assist the parties. The UK representative stated that the resolution was unacceptable because it placed no obligation on Argentina to affirm that the hostilities which it had initiated were finished or to renounce the use or threat of force in the future; nor did it acknowledge that the Falkland islanders were the most important party to the dispute. In response, the Argentine Foreign Minister asserted that the dispute was about territorial integrity rather than self-determination, in that the islanders did not have legitimate ties with the territory and therefore did not possess the right to self-determination; maintaining that Britain and Argentina were the sole parties to the dispute, he added that Argentina would never cede its right to sovereignty over the islands.

Similar resolutions were adopted on Nov. 16, 1983, and Nov. 1, 1984, while other resolutions not mentioning the word sovereignty were adopted on Nov. 27, 1985 and Nov. 25, 1986, with a greater number of countries voting for and only four countries (including Britain) voting against.

Developments following Return to Civilian Rule in Argentina

With the inauguration on Dec. 10, 1983, of a civilian Argentine government under President Raúl Alfonsín, the UK government indicated its willingness to enter into talks without a formal declaration of cessation of hostilities having been made by Argentina. However, in his first major policy statement on the Falklands/Malvinas, President Alfonsín on Jan. 3, 1984, remained intransigent. He described the British military presence on the islands as "illegal and forcible" and stressed what he called the "permanent will of the Argentine people to reverse that situation and to obtain restitution of the Malvinas, South Georgia and the South Sandwich Islands". He called on the UK government to negotiate the peaceful transfer of the islands to Argentine sovereignty, offering in return a "special statute" under which Argentina would guarantee the "interests" of the islanders.

The UK government replied on Jan. 4, 1984, that it was ready for immediate negotiations on the restoration of normal relations, particularly economic and commercial links, but that there could be no discussions on sovereignty.

The UK Foreign and Commonwealth Office disclosed on Feb. 2, 1984, that secret UK-Argentine contacts had been in progress since December 1983 through the Swiss Embassy (representing British interests in Buenos Aires) and the Brazilian embassy (representing Argentine interests in London). It further disclosed on Feb. 17, 1984, that Argentina had replied officially to a British proposal (advanced on Jan. 26) for the normalization of diplomatic, economic and cultural relations, the return of the bodies of Argentine soldiers buried on the Falklands and the restoration of air links between the islands and Argentina and between Argentina and the United Kingdom.

The Argentine reply was made in the form of counter-proposals, namely (i) that Argentina would not end

hostilities before negotiations started; (ii) that Argentina would not negotiate on the return of the bodies of war dead, although a humanitarian gesture would be accepted; (iii) that the British garrison on the islands should be replaced by a UN peace-keeping force; (iv) that the protection zone should be lifted before a declaration of an end to hostilities; and (v) that talks should be held without preconditions set by either side and on the basis of an open agenda. The Argentine Foreign Minister said that as "the maximum concession possible" the sovereignty issue could be left until the second round of talks, although the question of the British military presence would be raised at the first round.

A meeting between senior Argentine and British diplomats, arranged by the Swiss Foreign Ministry, was held in Berne (Switzerland) on July 18, 1984. The two sides had originally agreed to hold a two-day meeting on the understanding that Argentina would raise the sovereignty issue, the UK side would refuse to discuss it and then Argentina would then be free to raise any issue it chose. However, the understanding broke down and the talks ended abruptly.

The introduction in 1985 of a new Falkland Islands constitution, containing in its preamble an explicit reference to the islanders' right to self-determination, drew strong criticism from Argentina on the grounds that it implied disregard for UN resolutions calling on both sides to refrain from unilateral actions which modified the existing situation. A statement by the Argentine Foreign Ministry on Feb. 16, 1985, added that the new constitution blocked efforts to find a peaceful solution to the sovereignty dispute by enshrining the right to self-determination, thus in effect giving the islanders the power of veto over parliamentary decisions and enabling them to extend the "colonial status" of the islands indefinitely.

Under the new constitution the title of Governor of the Falklands was restored in place of that of High Commissioner (introduced after the 1982 conflict). The new arrangements also provided (i) for the establishment of South Georgia and the South Sandwich Islands (hitherto dependencies of the Falklands) as separate dependencies of the United Kingdom (although for the time being the Governor of the Falklands would also be Commissioner of South Georgia and the South Sandwich Islands); and (ii) that the Falkland islanders would have consultative rights as regards decisions concerning these islands.

Partial Normalization of UK-Argentine Trade Relations

With effect from midnight on July 8-9, 1985, the UK government lifted the ban on Argentine imports imposed in the wake of the April 1982 invasion, asserting at the same time its desire for a restoration of normal commercial and economic relations between the two countries. The Argentine Foreign Minister responded that the British decision had no real bearing on the question of a normalization of relations but (in a statement on July 10, 1985) offered to declare a formal end to hostilities if Britain agreed to resume bilateral talks, including the sovereignty issue, within 60 days. This offer was, however, rejected by the UK Foreign Secretary, who said on July 12 that Argentina's continued insistence on discussing sovereignty was "neither realistic nor constructive".

Although no official announcement was made by Argentina on the lifting of its reciprocal ban on British imports, UK-Argentine trade relations were subsequently reported to have become "near normal" by April 1986. In an earlier development, the Argentine government had stated on Jan. 2, 1985, that it would refuse to recognize any oil exploration permits granted by Britain in the Falklands area. This announcement followed confirmation being given that an oil exploration contract had been signed between the Falklands administration and a US company in July 1984.

During 1985-86 various contacts took place between British and Argentine political representatives at non-governmental level, notably within the framework of the Inter-Parliamentary Union. Moreover two British opposition leaders, Neil Kinnock of the Labour Party and David Steel of the Liberal Party, had talks with President Alfonsín in Buenos Aires in September and October 1985 respectively, during which both agreed on the need for direct UK-Argentine negotiations from which the question of the sovereignty of the Falklands should not be excluded. At the government level, however, the two sides remained at an impasse, as was demonstrated by the failure of a mediation attempt in April-May 1986 by the UN Secretary-General, who was told by President Alfonsín that the sovereignty question must be included on the agenda of any negotiations and by Prime Minister Thatcher that sovereignty was not negotiable.

A further divide in UK-Argentine relations opened on Oct. 29, 1986, when the British Foreign Secretary announced the creation as from Feb. 1, 1987, of a new 150-mile fisheries protection zone around the Falkland Islands (i.e. conterminous with the existing naval protection zone). Described as an "interim conservation and management zone", the new arrangement was intended to curtail what the British and Falklands governments regarded as the development of serious overfishing in the area, notably by factory ships from Japan, Spain, the Soviet Union and other Soviet bloc countries. As from Feb. 1, 1987, all foreign ships wishing to fish in the zone would require licences, the aim being to reduce the number of such vessels to about 250 as compared with over 600 in the 1986 season.

The UK Foreign Secretary stated that the new zone would be policed by two Royal Navy fisheries protection vessels based in the Falklands and made it clear that other forces remained available "to deter Argentine aggression and maintain the integrity of the protection zone". He also gave notice of "the entitlement of the Falklands, under international law, to a fisheries limit of 200 miles, subject to delimitation with Argentina"—with whose own 200-mile limit a 200-mile Falklands limit would overlap—and asserted "our rights to jurisdiction over the continental shelf up to the limits prescribed by the rules of international law".

President Alfonsín responded by convening an emergency meeting of ministers and military leaders on Oct. 29, 1986, following which all military leave was cancelled. A government statement condemned the British move as "juridically and politically unacceptable since it is asserted over maritime areas in respect of which the Argentine Republic exercises rights of sovereignty and jurisdiction". The statement added that the British decision "will be the cause of very serious tensions and conflicts with still unpredictable consequences, which may even affect the interests of third states". International support subsequently given to Argentina included the unanimous adoption by a special meeting of OAS states (including the United States) in Guatemala City on Nov. 9 of a resolution criticizing Britain for introducing a "new element of tension and potential conflict".

In the course of November 1986 Argentina launched a new diplomatic initiative to gain US and West European support for its case on the Falklands/Malvinas. On Nov. 18, coinciding with a visit to Washington by President Alfonsín, Argentina offered to make a formal declaration of a cessation of hostilities with Britain in return for the lifting of the Falklands protection zone, without making British agreement to sovereignty negotiations as such a precondition for such action. However, this new proposal was dismissed by the UK government as "an exercise in megaphone diplomacy" and as representing no real change in the established Argentine position that direct negotiations must include the sovereignty issue.

During a visit to the Falklands in early January 1987 the UK Defence Secretary reiterated Britain's commitment to the effective defence of the islands. He said that the current British troop strength of some 4,000 would be reduced by about half by the end of 1987, but pointed out that the new Mount Pleasant military airfield gave the local military commander a rapid reinforcement capacity in time of emergency. On Feb. 1, 1987, the new Falklands fisheries protection zone came into effect without incident, some 230 licences having been issued to foreign ships for the forthcoming fishing season.

On Nov. 17, 1987, the UN General Assembly passed another resolution calling for a peaceful solution to the dispute. The voting was 114 countries in favour, and five against (including the UK), with 37 abstentions.

Large-scale military manoeuvres by British forces in the Falklands region in March 1988 were strongly condemned by President Alfonsín and several other Latin American governments, but the informal diplomatic contacts between British and Argentine officials, which had been in progress since 1987, through the mediation of the USA and the UN, continued.

Formal Cessation of Hostilities—Resumption of Full Diplomatic Relations

In May 1989 presidential elections in Argentina were won by Carlos Saúl Menem, the candidate of the

Peronist Justicialist Party. Menem, although outwardly maintaining the rhetoric of Argentina's right to sovereignty, in private expressed a greater willingness to improve relations between the two countries. In talks held in Madrid on Oct. 17-19, 1989, between Sir Crispin Tickell, the UK representative at the UN, and Lucio García del Solar, the personal representative of President Menem, an agreement was reached to end hostilities formally and to reopen diplomatic relations at consular level. Other measures agreed were the creation of a working party to provide information on military activities that might affect the area, the entry of Argentine vessels inside the 150-mile exclusion zone and the resumption of direct air, sea and trade links.

This improvement in relations was followed by a further meeting in Madrid on Feb. 14-15, 1990, at which it was agreed to restore full diplomatic relations and exchange ambassadors while keeping the issue of sovereignty, in President Menem's words "under an umbrella". The UK Foreign Secretary, Douglas Hurd, claimed that the agreement involved "no sacrifice of sovereignty", while President Menem stated that Argentina's claim to sovereignty had not been dropped, but that the agreement eliminated the possibility of armed conflict. Other measures reached included the replacement of the exclusion zone by a security arrangement between the military commanders to give advance warning of military manoeuvres. Argentine warships and aircraft were to be allowed to within 70 and 50 miles of the Falklands respectively. There was to be co-operation on air and sea rescue, navigation, investment and possible joint ventures in the area, anti-drug trafficking measures, and visits by Argentines to war graves in the Falklands under the auspices of the International Red Cross. The Argentines remained excluded from fishing within the Falklands exclusive fishing zone. Negotiations on this point resulted on Nov. 28 in an agreement to create a 200-mile joint Anglo-Argentine co-operation area intended to prevent new fishing by the fishing fleets of other nations. The western part of the new zone was to be patrolled by Argentina where it overlapped with its own 200-mile limit.

On Sept. 25, 1991, the two governments signed further accords reducing the notice of military manoeuvres within 80 miles of the coastline of the Falklands, its dependencies or the Argentine mainland to 14 days; and reducing the notice period to 42 hours for naval vessels to approach within 15 miles of either coast.

On Nov. 21, the Falkland Islands Legislative Council passed a bill allowing surveys for oil in the area. Both the UK and Argentina asserted their claim to mineral deposits in the area around the islands. On Dec. 5-6 officials of both governments met in London and agreed to extend the commercial fishing ban around the islands until the end of 1992. In January 1992, the Foreign and Commonwealth Office Minister of State, Tristan Garel-Jones, visited Buenos Aires to discuss bilateral issues. The issue of sovereignty was not raised, despite earlier comments by President Menem suggesting that the dispute should be placed in arbitration similar to that for disputes between Argentina and Chile, and relations between the two countries continued to improve thereafter.

In 1995 President Menem was re-elected, and when inaugurated on July 8, 1995, reaffirmed his goal of recovering the Falkland Islands by the year 2000 by peaceful negotiation. In the meanwhile, however, the issue of sovereignty was kept "under an umbrella" and talks in London in June, though initially unsuccessful, led to an agreement signed in New York on Sept. 27 on joint exploitation of the Malvinas Basin oil deposits, which enabled oil companies to bid for licences in the disputed area without incurring penalties.

Steadily improving relations between Britain and Argentina were symbolized by the visit to Buenos Aires in January 1996 of the British Chancellor of the Exchequer, Kenneth Clarke, accompanied by a large trade delegation. Despite a dispute in March about the issuing of fishing licences in the disputed waters around the Falkland Islands, on April 13 Malcolm Rifkind, the new British Foreign Secretary, reached agreement with the Foreign Minister, Guido di Tella, in a meeting at Puerto Iguazú, on a conservation regime for the waters around South Georgia. On May 29, *Clarín* published an interview with di Tella in which he stated that Argentina would "never consent" to independence as a possible future for the islands; this suggestion, however, had not been made by either the UK or the islanders.

On Jan. 3, 1997, President Menem, in a communiqué marking the 164th anniversary of Britain's resumption of sovereignty over the islands, reasserted both Argentina's claim to the islands and his policy of seeking a peaceful resolution to the dispute. To this end he sought the assistance of US President Bill Clinton, and on June 12, following the election of a Labour government in the UK, he reiterated his intention of securing his goal by "peaceful means and dialogue". On Nov. 4 the UK government extended President Menem an invitation to visit Britain in 1998. During his official visit to Argentina on Oct.15-19 President Clinton commended Argentina's role in recent UN peacekeeping operations and announced that he would seek non-NATO ally status for it, allowing it to receive a wider range of US weapons. Brazil and Chile both reacted to the suggestion with concern.

In the months leading up to the official visit of President Menem to the United Kingdom in October 1998 relations remained good, though on April 22 the Argentine Senate had approved a bill imposing sanctions on companies drilling in the waters around the Falkland Islands without Argentine permission. In November, in a so-called "charm offensive" proposed by Di Tella, President Menem wrote a conciliatory letter to each of the islands' inhabitants. News on Dec. 17 that the UK was to lift its arms embargo was greeted as an important step in improved relations.

In 1999 the Radical Fernando de la Rúa Bruno was elected President of Argentina and one of the

President-elect's first statements after his election confirmed his intention to maintain existing policy on the Falklands. In mid-January, the outgoing Foreign Minister, Guido di Tella, had offered to freeze his country's claims to sovereignty, in return for a number of symbolic concessions, which once again the islanders were not prepared to concede. During an official visit from March 9-11 HRH Prince Charles, having earlier laid a wreath on the monument to the Argentine dead who fell in the 1982 war, referred to the islanders' right to self-determination. Though this provoked criticism, it did not appear to surprise his hosts, and, during his visit to London in May, the Foreign Minister held talks for the first time with members of the Falkland Islands legislature, at their initiative. On July 14, the UK and Argentine governments concluded an agreement ending restrictions on travel to the islands by Argentine citizens and re-establishing direct air links between the islands and the mainland from Oct. 16. On Nov. 1 the British and Argentine navies began their first joint exercises since 1982 while the armed forces of the two countries jointly patrolled the "green line" in Cyprus.

A serious and prolonged economic crisis in Argentina forced President de la Rúa to resign in December 2001. Five presidents occupied the presidential chair in the next two weeks before the Peronist former Vice President Eduardo Duhalde was chosen as President by Congress. On the day the country formally defaulted on its debt (Jan. 3, 2002), the new Foreign Minister, Carlos Ruckauf, repeated his country's claim to the Falkland Islands, calling on Britain to open negotiations about their future. At a parade in Ushuaia, held on April 2 to commemorate the twentieth anniversary of the Argentine occupation of the Falkland Islands, President Duhalde reaffirmed his country's determination to recover the islands, but only by peaceful means.

In elections held in May 2003, Nestor Kirchner, the Peronist governor of the southern Argentine state of Santa Cruz, was elected President for the period 2003-07. Initial statements made by the new administration confirmed that the previous policy towards the islands remained unchanged and that the issue of sovereignty remained "under an umbrella".

Peter Calvert

2.4 Belize - Guatemala

The British Crown Colony of Belize (formerly British Honduras) became independent in September 1981, notwithstanding the existence of an unresolved Guatemalan claim to its territory dating back to 1859. Under the Guatemalan constitution of 1945 Belize was regarded as the 23rd department of that country, and Guatemala thus claimed that the granting of self-determina-

tion to Belize would disrupt its own national unity and territorial integrity.

While the British government had been ready to grant full independence to the colony much earlier, Belize feared that in the event of a British withdrawal, without adequate defence guarantees, Guatemala would invade to implement its claim. However, following an overwhelming vote at the United Nations in November 1980 in favour of the independence of Belize, the British government decided to proceed with granting independence and convened a constitutional conference followed by tripartite negotiations in which the basis for Guatemalan acceptance of Belize's independence appeared to have been established. Although it later transpired that Guatemala had not substantially modified its position, Belize nevertheless proceeded to full independence on Sept. 21, 1981, with British troops continuing to be stationed there for an indefinite period. Since then Guatemala has maintained a territorial claim against Belize, while indicating since 1983 a willingness to accept a compromise settlement giving it improved access to the Caribbean Sea.

Mexico also has a dormant claim to the northern half of Belize and had previously stated that it would reactivate this claim "in the event of any change in the colony's status which is not in accordance with the right of its inhabitants to self-determination". Map 14, page 499, illustrates this entry.

History of the Dispute

Extending over an area of 8,866 square miles (23,000 sq km), British Honduras was granted internal self-government in 1964 and changed its name to Belize on June 1, 1973. It had become a Crown Colony in 1871, having been a British colony since 1862 and under British sovereignty since 1798. The first settlers were English timber-cutters and their black slaves in the mid-17th century. Under the 1670 Treaty of Madrid, Spain conceded certain rights to the timber-cutters who, over the previous 30 years, had established themselves on the uninhabited shores of the Belize river. The British government did not, however, lay claim to the territory officially. Over the next 130 years the territory was subjected to repeated attacks by Spain, which claimed sovereignty over it. Finally, a Spanish naval flotilla was defeated by a small Belizean boat fleet at the Battle of St George's Caye on Sept. 10, 1798, and British sovereignty over Belize was explicitly recognized by the Peace of Amiens in 1802.

When Mexico and Guatemala became independent in 1821 they both claimed sovereignty over Belize as successors to the Spanish Crown in the region. Their claims were rejected by Britain, however, in view of the fact that British settlers had by this time already established themselves as far south as the Sarstoon river (the present southern boundary). Mexico recognized British Honduras in 1826 and renounced claims to it in 1893 by treaty. The United States recognized it in 1850 (together with British Guiana) as exceptions to the Monroe Doctrine. However, Guatemala continued to regard Belize as part of its territory.

In 1859 Britain tried to settle the territorial dispute between Guatemala and British Honduras by means of a frontier convention, one of whose articles provided for the joint construction of a means of communication between Guatemala and the Caribbean across Belize. This article was never implemented and has remained a bone of contention. A supplementary convention was signed in 1863 under which the British government undertook to pay a substantial amount towards the cost of a road, although this never came to fruition, despite the later renewal of the offer by Britain.

Guatemala on Sept. 24, 1945, conveyed to the British government the text of a draft decree declaring the 1859 convention null and void and inserting into its own constitution a clause laying claim to the whole of British Honduras as Guatemalan territory. Its claim was based on the contention that, as the 1859 convention on communications had never been implemented, the whole convention was null and void and that Guatemala therefore had a claim to the whole of British Honduras, or at least to the southern part. The claim was wholly rejected by Britain, which said that even had the convention lapsed this would be no reason why any part of the territory should belong to Guatemala, since Britain had been in possession for 150 years (i.e. since before the convention was signed or Guatemala became independent). In January 1946 Britain invited Guatemala to submit the dispute to the International Court of Justice (ICJ), and repeated the invitation on subsequent occasions, but Guatemala never took it up.

British Honduras achieved internal self-government on Jan. 1, 1964, following a constitutional conference in London on July 10-22, 1963, at which only British Honduras and Britain were represented. Guatemala (ruled at that time by Col. Enrique Peralta Azurdia) broke off diplomatic relations with Britain on the last day of the conference, claiming that the British government's decision to move towards the independence of British Honduras was "a unilateral action which is a flagrant violation of the inalienable and sovereign rights of Guatemala". Prior to this, President Miguel Ydigoras Fuentes of Guatemala had raised the issue of sovereignty in December 1961 and talks on the issue had taken place in Puerto Rico in April 1962 at the instigation of Britain. Among matters agreed on this occasion were the creation of mixed committees of representatives of Guatemala, Britain and British Honduras on mutual relations, and on economic and social development.

In July 1965 Britain and Guatemala requested the United States to mediate in their dispute. Accordingly, President Lyndon Johnson commissioned a report from a New York lawyer, Bethuel M. Webster, who on April 18, 1968, proposed that Britain and Guatemala should conclude a treaty, and that the former should endeavour to persuade British Honduras to accede to it on becoming independent. It was proposed that the treaty should contain the following conditions: (i) that British Honduras should attain independence by Dec. 31, 1970, with the probable name of Belize; (ii) that there should be unrestricted trade, travel and other contacts between Guatemala and British Honduras; and (iii) that a road should be constructed between the two countries.

George Price, the Prime Minister of British Honduras, declared on May 9, 1968, that his government rejected Webster's proposals because they failed to recognize the colony's right to sovereignty. Britain thus responded on May 20 that since the British Honduras government, with the endorsement of its House of Representatives, had asked Britain not to accede to such a treaty with Guatemala, and since the dispute with Guatemala could only be settled in accordance with the wish of the British Honduras people, it could not endorse the mediator's proposals.

Developments in the 1970s

In 1971 Guatemalan troop movements in the border area gave rise to fears of a Guatemalan invasion of British Honduras. Guatemala subsequently protested over a British military training exercise held there in February 1972 to coincide with British naval manoeuvres in the Caribbean, and the outcome was that Guatemala, in March 1972, broke off informal talks on the Belize issue. At the end of the troop exercise Britain decided to increase the size of its permanent garrison in Belize from one to two companies (i.e. to about 700 men), giving rise to another protest from Guatemala. The presence of an increased number of troops proved a stumbling block to further talks, which did not resume until February 1975. On their resumption, Britain rejected Guatemalan proposals envisaging the cession of the southern quarter of Belize (south of latitude 16°30′), including an area thought to contain oil deposits, in return for the renunciation by Guatemala of its claim to the rest of the colony. The talks broke down in July 1975.

Reports of increased Guatemalan military activity in the border areas in October 1975 led Britain, in November 1975, to send reinforcements to its garrison in Belize at George Price's request. By Nov. 8 British military strength in the colony had been increased to over 1,000 men, supported by six Hawker Harrier vertical takeoff aircraft and a frigate, which patrolled offshore with a detachment of Marines aboard. The UK Foreign and Commonwealth Secretary in the then Labour government, James Callaghan, told the House of Commons in a statement on Nov. 6 that the British garrison in Belize had been strengthened because of the increased Guatemalan military activity on the border and because of "statements by Guatemalan ministers of their intention to incorporate Belize in Guatemala". He said that he had informed Guatemala in September that "if there were an invasion of a

British colony which is seeking to become independent and whose independence is denied only by the Guatemalan claim, we would fulfil our responsibilities to that colony". Despite Guatemalan opposition to the reinforcement of the British military presence in Belize, no further action was taken by Guatemala, and at the end of November 1975 Britain and Guatemala agreed to hold fresh talks, with Belizean participation, early the following year.

The UN General Assembly on Dec. 8, 1975, adopted a resolution on Belize (3432/XXX)—with Mexico abstaining and Guatemala not participating—which had already been adopted by the UN Trusteeship Committee on Nov. 21. This resolution (i) reaffirmed the "inalienable right of the people of Belize to self-determination and independence"; (ii) declared that the "inviolability and territorial integrity of Belize must be preserved"; (iii) called upon all states to respect the right of the people of Belize to self-determination, independence and territorial integrity and to facilitate the attainment by them of their goal of a secure independence; (iv) called upon Britain as the administering power, acting in close consultation with the government of Belize, and on Guatemala, to "pursue urgently their negotiations for the earliest possible resolution of their differences of opinion concerning the future of Belize in order to remove such obstacles as have hitherto prevented the people of Belize from exercising freely and without fear their inalienable right to self-determination and independence"; and (v) declared that "any proposals for the resolution of these differences of opinion that may emerge from negotiations between the administering power and the government of Guatemala must be in accordance with paragraphs (i) and (ii) above".

A similar resolution (31/50) was adopted by the General Assembly on Dec. 1, 1976, urging all states to refrain from any action threatening the territorial integrity of Belize, on which Mexico again abstained. Panama, which had previously supported Guatemala's claim, voted in favour of Resolution 31/50, causing Guatemala to sever diplomatic relations with Panama in May 1977.

Meanwhile, George Price's People's United Party (PUP), which was returned to power in Belize in the October 1974 general elections after calling for early independence, tried during 1975 to internationalize the sovereignty issue, winning the support of the Non-Aligned Movement and being backed by various independent Caribbean states including Jamaica, Cuba, Guyana, and Trinidad and Tobago. The Belize government also decided to seek UN support for its cause, and invited the opposition United Democratic Party (UDP) to join the PUP in formulating a case. The UDP accepted, after agreeing to a formula which affirmed its own commitment to Belize's right to self-determination while reserving its position on the timing of independence (to which it adopted a more gradualist approach).

Talks recommenced between the three parties in April 1976, being followed in October by the first ever bilateral meeting between Belizean and Guatemalan officials (in Honduras). At this stage (the end of 1976) Guatemala was said to have agreed to certain economic co-operation proposals including the use of free-port facilities in Belize City, but it still refused to abandon its claim to that part of Belize south of latitude 16°30′. No progress was made on the fundamental issue of Belizean territorial integrity.

In July 1977 the British military presence in Belize was again strengthened because of tension between the colony and Guatemala; the latter's troops were reported to be massing on the border, and Guatemalan leaders spoke of the possibility of an armed conflict with Britain. A Royal Navy frigate took up position off Belize, British forces were moved to within two miles of the border, and the Hawker Harrier detachment (which had been withdrawn just before the April 1976 talks) was again deployed in the colony. Despite the military tension, however, further tripartite talks were held in July 1977 in Washington.

While in Washington, the British and Guatemalan delegates also had separate talks on the Belize issue with Cyrus Vance, the US Secretary of State in the Carter administration. George Price said on July 8 that he would welcome a US endorsement of Belize's right to "complete independence" and he called for a US defence guarantee after independence if Britain continued to decline to undertake such a commitment.

Negotiations leading to Independence of Belize

Over the next two years (i.e. until the end of 1979) no substantial progress was made towards a settlement, although the parties concerned had numerous contacts and negotiations. The United States assumed an active role, and an increasing number of countries of the region came to support Belize's position.

Following talks in London involving Dr David Owen (then UK Foreign and Commonwealth Secretary), Edward Rowlands and George Price, Dr Owen told the House of Commons on Jan. 25, 1978, that "various proposals including the possibility of territorial adjustments" had recently been discussed between Britain and Guatemala. Price himself emphasized at a press conference later on Jan. 25 that no Belizean territory could be ceded. He revealed for the first time that during the past six months the British government had been considering various proposals for the cession to Guatemala of an area of Belize's southern territory which had been progressively reduced in size over that period, ranging from about 2,000 square miles (comprising land south of Monkey river plus seabed) to about 1,000 square miles (land south of the Moho river plus seabed between the Moho river and Ranguana caye, where oil prospecting was in progress); this latest proposal would give Guatemala sovereignty over an alternative access route (by sea) to its Caribbean port of Puerto Barrios. Price's own view was that the cession of land would create and not solve problems and, since the latest London talks had failed to produce an acceptable basis for settlement, Belize would now seek security guarantees from Caribbean countries.

Belize's aim at this stage appeared to be the stationing of a security force in Belize which would be strong enough to allow Belize to attain independence without having to negotiate a settlement with Guatemala first. However, the Guatemalan government indicated in mid-May 1978 (while a further round of Anglo-Guatemalan talks was in progress) that it was maintaining its demand for a territorial concession and was also demanding in the current talks the formation of a joint Guatemala-Belize military staff and joint consultations on Belize's external relations.

Subsequently, at a meeting in New York in June 1978, Dr Owen, Price and Dean Lindo (the UDP leader) drew up a "memorandum of understanding" whereby (i) Britain undertook to invite the Belize government and opposition to participate in all future talks with Guatemala, (ii) Britain agreed to submit any agreement reached at such talks to a national referendum in Belize and (iii) Price and Lindo agreed to "put the issue of the Anglo-Guatemalan dispute above party politics and treat the search for a solution as a national objective".

After Maj.-Gen. Fernando Romeo Lucas García became President of Guatemala on July 1, 1978, fresh talks involving representatives of the new government opened in September in New York. In December, however, Guatemala rejected British settlement proposals whereby Belize would after independence have refrained (i) from introducing measures regarding its offshore jurisdiction in the Bay of Amatique which would block Guatemala's sea access to its Caribbean ports, and (ii) from entering into any pacts with third countries without Guatemalan agreement. Guatemala would for its part have been granted preferential customs treatment for trade through the port of Belize City, and Britain would have financed the construction of a new road from Guatemala through Belize to the Caribbean. The UN General Assembly on Dec. 13, 1978, adopted a resolution (33/36) urging a settlement to the dispute on the basis of Belize's "right to self-determination, independence and territorial integrity"; the resolution was supported by 128 states, this time including Costa Rica and Colombia (which had voted against a previous resolution on Nov. 27, 1977). On a further resolution (34/38) adopted on Nov. 21, 1979, referring to the inviolability and territorial integrity of Belize, Latin American countries voting for the first time in favour of Belize's right to self-determination included Brazil, the Dominican Republic, Ecuador and Nicaragua.

Tripartite talks opened in May 1980 at which Britain was reported to have taken the line that if a mutually acceptable agreement could not be reached, Britain would unilaterally move the territory towards independence. Guatemala's position in 1980 was considerably weaker than it had been hitherto due to the deterioration of Guatemala's internal security situation, which led the United States and also Mexico to wish to seek a stable solution to the Belize issue in the

interests of regional security. Washington was also anxious at this stage that Britain should continue to exercise its defence commitment to Belize after eventual independence.

On Nov. 11, 1980, the UN General Assembly adopted by 139 votes (including the United States) to none, with seven abstentions and with Guatemala absent, a resolution (35/20) to the effect that Belize should be granted independence by the end of 1981; calling upon Britain to convene a constitutional conference to prepare for Belizean independence; and urging Britain to "continue to ensure the security and territorial integrity of Belize". It also called on Guatemala and independent Belize to "work out arrangements for postindependence co-operation on matters of mutual concern". The British government accordingly announced on Dec. 2, 1980, that it intended to convene a constitutional conference in the near future.

At a round of talks involving Britain, Guatemala and a Belizean delegation in London beginning on March 5, 1981, all three delegations accepted 16 heads of agreement, whose text was formally signed on March 16 by ministerial representatives of the three countries as follows:

"The United Kingdom and Guatemala, in order to settle the controversy between them over the territory of Belize, have reached agreement on the following points:

(1) The United Kingdom and Guatemala shall recognize the independent state of Belize as an integral part of Central America, and respect its sovereignty and territorial integrity in accordance with its existing and traditional frontiers, subject, in the case of Guatemala, to the completion of the treaty or treaties necessary to give effect to these heads of agreement.

(2) Guatemala shall be accorded such territorial seas as shall ensure permanent and unimpeded access to the high seas, together with rights over the seabed thereunder.

(3) Guatemala shall have the use and enjoyment of the Ranguana and Sapodilla [Zapotillo] cayes, and rights in those areas of the sea adjacent to the cayes, as may be agreed.

(4) Guatemala shall be entitled to free port facilities in Belize City and Punta Gorda.

(5) The road from Belize City to the Guatemalan frontier shall be improved; a road from Punta Gorda to the Guatemalan frontier shall be completed. Guatemala shall have freedom of transit on these roads.

(6) Belize shall facilitate the construction of oil pipelines between Guatemala and Belize City, Dangriga and Punta Gorda.

(7) In areas to be agreed, an agreement shall be concluded between Belize and Guatemala for purposes concerned with the control of pollution, navigation and fishing.

(8) There shall be areas of the seabed and the continental shelf to be agreed for the joint exploration and exploitation of minerals and hydrocarbons.

(9) Belize and Guatemala shall agree upon certain

developmental projects of mutual benefit.

(10) Belize shall be entitled to any free port facilities in Guatemala to match similar facilities provided to Guatemala in Belize.

(11) Belize and Guatemala shall sign a treaty of co-operation in matters of security of mutual concern, and neither shall permit its territory to be used to support subversion against the other.

(12) Except as foreseen in these heads of agreement, nothing in these provisions shall prejudice any rights or interests of Belize or of the Belizean people.

(13) The United Kingdom and Guatemala shall enter into agreements designed to re-establish full and normal relations between them.

(14) The United Kingdom and Guatemala shall take the necessary action to sponsor the membership of Belize in the United Nations, the Organization of American States, Central American organizations and other international organizations.

(15) A joint commission shall be established between Belize, Guatemala and the United Kingdom to work out details to give effect to the above provisions. It will prepare a treaty or treaties for signature by the signatories to these heads of agreement.

(16) The controversy between the United Kingdom and Guatemala over the territory of Belize shall therefore be honourably and finally terminated".

George Price said in a broadcast on March 17, 1981, that "Belize has gained its overwhelming objectives while protecting the basic rights of the Belizean people and adhering fully to the UN resolutions that protect our sovereignty and territorial integrity". In Guatemala, the government presented the heads of agreement as an honourable means of settling the dispute in the face of strong international pressure.

The Mexican government was reported to be happy with the agreement and to have no intention of pressing its dormant claim, but the Honduran government made an official protest to Britain over the status of the Sapodilla cayes, to which it had a long-standing dormant claim. Honduras also claimed a right to participate in the proposed negotiations on the grounds that "the delimitation of sea areas could lead to situations of conflict to the detriment of Honduras' legitimate rights".

The British government formally announced on March 20, 1981, that a constitutional conference would begin in London on April 6. However, the UDP continued to oppose the heads of agreement as a sell-out of Belizean interests, and mounted an anti-government campaign which developed into public disorder and led to the declaration of a state of emergency in Belize from April 2-24. In view of the emergency, George Price did not attend the London constitutional conference, the Belize delegation being led by Carl Rogers, the deputy leader of the PUP. The UDP boycotted the conference.

Negotiations on a treaty to give formal effect to the heads of agreement were held in New York from May 20 to 28, 1981, by a tripartite commission of British, Guatemalan and Belizean government representatives.

A further round held in New York on July 6-10 became deadlocked after Guatemala reportedly insisted that its interpretation of the heads of agreement would allow the establishment of naval facilities on Ranguana and Sapodilla cayes, this being rejected by Britain and Belize.

In the absence of agreement on a treaty, and following Belize-UK talks in London on July 19-23, 1981, it was announced on July 26 that independence would be granted to Belize notwithstanding on Sept. 21 and that British troops would continue to be stationed there for "an appropriate period" thereafter. Guatemala responded by restating its intention to "reserve its legal and historic rights" over Belize, although it made it clear that no attempt would be made to occupy Belizean territory by force after independence. On Sept. 7 Guatemala broke off all remaining diplomatic links with Britain, severed commercial ties, and closed its border with Belize.

Independence Day on Sept. 21, 1981, was declared a day of national mourning in Guatemala, and the ceremony in Belize was boycotted by the UDP. At the request of George Price (who became the first Prime Minister of independent Belize), the ceremonial lowering of the British flag took place in total darkness to symbolize the fact that Britain was not wholly relinquishing its responsibilities towards Belize.

A schedule to the Belize constitution defined the territories of the new independent country with reference to (i) the Guatemalan frontier prescribed by the UK-Guatemala treaty of 1859, and (ii) the Mexican frontier prescribed by the UK-Mexico treaty of 1893. Belize's offshore reefs, islands and islets were listed, together with "their adjacent waters as far as the outer limits of the territorial seas appertaining to them".

Continuation of Dispute in Post-Independence Period

Belize was admitted to the United Nations on Sept. 25, 1981, its application being sponsored by Mexico, which subsequently became the first non-Commonwealth country to establish diplomatic relations with Belize. The Guatemalan government stated (on Sept. 25), that it would "continue to struggle, in a peaceful manner, to defend its rights by diplomatic means and international law". In December 1985, apparently in response to local economic pressures, Guatemala reopened one border crossing to Belize.

A statement by the Price government that Belize would apply for full membership of the Non-Aligned Movement was welcomed by the movement's then chairman, President Castro of Cuba, who urged all member countries to "offer their rapid recognition" of the new state. As regards the Organization of American States (OAS), Belize submitted a formal application in October 1981 but stated that it did not wish to be considered for membership immediately (its admission being effectively blocked under the OAS rule requiring the exclusion of applicant states currently involved in territorial disputes with existing members). Nevertheless, Belize was invited to send observer delegations to subsequent OAS conferences. Belize's first post-independence bilateral friendship agreement was concluded with Costa Rica in November 1981.

Following the accession to power in Guatemala of Gen. Efraín Ríos Montt in March 1982, a new attempt was mounted to solve the territorial issue. Although the new regime maintained Guatemala's refusal to recognize the independence of Belize, the Guatemalan Foreign Minister formally proposed in July 1982 (via the Swiss embassy, which was then representing British interests in Guatemala) that Britain and Guatemala should resume negotiations, it being subsequently announced that tripartite talks would open in New York in January 1983. Initially Guatemala had proposed bilateral talks with Britain, which had objected on the grounds that Belize was now an independent country and should therefore be fully represented.

Prior to the new talks, President Ríos Montt announced on Jan. 13, 1983, that whereas Guatemala had previously claimed the whole territory of Belize "now the Guatemalan position has changed: we want the district of Toledo to form part of our territory". He said that the Guatemalan claim to this area—about one-fifth of the total area of Belize and including the southern port of Punta Gorda—was based on considerations of cultural traditions, geography and national security, adding that if the claim were met Guatemala would recognize the independence of Belize. However, this Guatemalan offer (which was reported to have been encouraged by the US government) was immediately rejected by the Belize government.

The tripartite negotiations opened in New York on Jan. 24, 1983, but broke down after only one day. Belize refused to make any territorial concessions, while Guatemala rejected counter-proposals under which it would have gained a sector of Belize's territorial waters, transit rights through the south of Belize and participation in a joint development zone on either side of the Sarstoon river to a width of five kilometres.

After a further Guatemalan military coup in August 1983, the new regime reverted to claiming the whole of Belize, thus apparently withdrawing the Ríos Montt compromise proposal of January 1983. Meanwhile, a contingent of some 1,800 British troops remained in Belize, their presence being regarded as even more essential by the Belize government in the light of the Argentine invasion of the Falkland Islands in April 1982. In the Belize general elections of December 1984 (which resulted in a defeat for Price's PUP and the formation of a UDP government led by Manuel Esquivel) both major parties supported the retention of the British troops and also rejected suggestions—emanating from the UK government—that US troops might replace them.

The UDP government was represented at a further round of talks in New York in February 1985, when the Guatemalan side was reported to have again indicated a willingness to accept a compromise territorial settlement. In May 1985 the Guatemalan Constituent Assembly, in drawing up a new civilian constitution, approved an article empowering the government to take appropriate action to resolve the dispute "in conformity with national interests", thus effectively dropping the previous constitution's assertion that Belize was part of Guatemala. On Dec. 17, 1985, the new civilian President-elect of Guatemala, Vinicio Cerezo, publicly advanced the possibility of Guatemala extending recognition to Belize in return for territorial concessions which would improve Guatemalan access to the Caribbean Sea.

In August 1985 Manuel Esquivel visited London in an attempt to secure a commitment that British troops would remain in Belize until the territorial dispute with Guatemala had been finally resolved. He later stated that the UK government had reiterated its pledge to retain its forces for "as long as necessary" though it had declined to give an indefinite commitment to the defence of Belize. It was agreed, however, that Britain would assist in the training and expansion of the 600-strong Belize Defence Force and would provide aid for economic and infrastructure development.

Having resumed consular relations on Aug. 19, 1986, Britain and Guatemala resumed full diplomatic relations on Dec. 29, 1986, a development which was welcomed by the Esquivel government as potentially facilitating Guatemala's recognition of the independence of Belize. The existence of a civilian government in Guatemala also assisted bilateral relations between Guatemala and Belize. On Oct. 19, 1986, restrictions on trade with Belize imposed by the Guatemalan authorities were lifted.

The first direct talks on the issue between Belize and Guatemala at foreign minister level were held on April 29-30, 1987, in Miami, with a delegation from the UK acting as observers. The talks were described as "cordial", but failed to make any real progress after a reiteration of Guatemalan demands for sizeable territorial concessions. The following year a meeting between the then Belizean Foreign Minister, Dean Barrow, and the Guatemalan Vice President, Roberto Carpio Nicolle, on April 24-25, 1988, led to a further meeting in Miami on May 30-31, at which it was agreed to set up a joint commission of Belizean and Guatemalan officials to meet regularly and discuss the issues further.

Guatemala's Diplomatic Recognition of Belize— Negotiations on Maritime Boundaries

Meetings of the joint Guatemalan-Belizean commission continued through 1989, together with informal contacts between Guatemalan and Belizean ministers and officials. Progress was made gradually, but no definitive draft treaty was reached. A general election in Belize in September 1989 led to the return of George Price and the PUP to power. On assuming office Price promised to continue the talks. Price subsequently met President Cerezo on the Honduran island of Roatán on Dec. 15, 1989, and another round of talks was held on Roatán on July 9. In both cases the Belizean delegation was bipartisan, including representatives of the government and the opposition UDP. The maritime boundaries were agreed in principle, while other areas of co-operation were to be discussed by the reconvened joint commission. A further meeting, attended by British officials, was held in Miami in August 1990 to discuss a proposed economic co-operation treaty and the contribution Britain could make by providing funds for development.

A major shift in the Guatemalan attitude was displayed in January 1991 when the newly elected Guatemalan president, Jorge Serrano Elías, made several statements confirming his belief that the dispute could be settled amicably and that Guatemala should accept the fact that Belize existed and was widely recognized internationally. On Jan. 8, Guatemala supported Belize's accession to the Organization of American States (OAS) in accordance with the decision made by the OAS in December 1985 to suspend the article preventing Belize's accession after a five-year period. In July talks between officials of the two countries resumed in Miami.

Settlement of the maritime boundaries in the Bay of Amatique was seen as an important stage in the progress towards a solution of the overall dispute and Guatemala's eventual dropping of its claim. In August, Guatemala and Honduras set up a joint commission to negotiate an agreement on their territorial waters in the Bay of Amatique. This allowed the Belizean government to introduce a Maritime Areas Bill into the National Assembly on Aug. 16, establishing a general territorial waters limit of 12 miles and an exclusive economic zone of up to 200 miles, apart from the area between Ranguana caye and the Sarstoon river where the limit was to be three miles. By limiting the maritime boundary in the south to three miles instead of the median line between the two countries, Belize would allow Guatemala access to the high seas from the port of Puerto Barrios through deep water. Guatemala had claimed a 12-mile limit since 1939, and the extension of Belize's former three-mile limit to the median line between the two countries would have closed off this traditional route of access enjoyed by Guatemala.

On Sept. 5, 1991, Serrano announced that Guatemala in effect recognized Belize and would continue to seek a definitive solution of the dispute, although he stated that Guatemala's claim had not been formally withdrawn. On Sept. 11, full diplomatic relations between the two countries were established and ambassadors exchanged. The announcement was made without the Guatemalan Cabinet being consulted and the Foreign Minister, Alvaro Arzú Irogoyen, later resigned in protest stating that the constitution had been disregarded.

On Sept. 16, however, a Belizean delegation visited Guatemala City for talks. In the joint communiqué issued as a result of the meeting, Guatemala acknowledged that its claim was not "an obstacle to the recog-

nition of the right of the people of Belize to self-determination" and both governments agreed to "continue to negotiate a definitive agreement to end their differences", with such an agreement subject to approval in referendums in both countries. A bilateral commission was to be established to reach co-operation agreements in the following areas:

(1) Joint exploration of defined areas of Belize's exclusive economic zone (EEZ) for mutual benefit;

(2) Permanent access for Guatemala to the Caribbean from El Petén department and the reciprocal use of port facilities;

(3) Cultural and educational exchanges;

(4) Tourism co-operation, particularly in the Mundo Maya project;

(5) Co-operation in combating the illegal drugs trade;

(6) Development of commerce and investment between the two countries.

In support of its promise to provide funds for development if a successful agreement could be reached to end the dispute, the British government offered £22.5 million after the establishment of diplomatic relations as a contribution to renewing road links between the two countries, thus in a way fulfilling its obligations under the 1859 treaty.

The Belizean government set up a national bipartisan commission to publicize the proposed Maritime Areas Bill prior to discussion in the National Assembly. Concerns by Belizean fishermen in the south that the new boundaries would limit their activities were raised during discussions between Serrano and Price at the end of October. Serrano assured the Belizeans that traditional fishing and navigational rights would be respected. The Maritime Areas Bill was duly passed by the House of Representatives on Jan. 17, 1992, by 16 votes to 12, although the issue caused dissension within the UDP, leading to a number of resignations and expulsions from the party. Belize's improved relations with Guatemala helped improve other relationships in Central America, reflected in an invitation at the presidential summit in December to join the Central American Community, and the joint hosting of a meeting of Central American and CARICOM foreign ministers in Honduras in January 1992.

Further Claims, Tension and Resolution: 1994 Onwards

Despite the apparent resolution of the dispute, or at least easing of tensions, voices within Guatemala had been opposed to the recognition of Belize and in 1994 a new Guatemalan government restated its claim and in 1998 issued a new position claiming more than half of Belize's territory.

This aggressive new policy and posture was backed up on Feb. 24, 2000, when Guatemalan armed forces entered Belizean territory and kidnapped four members of the Belize security forces. They were not released and returned to Belize until March 3. Following this incident, meetings were arranged to be held in Washington in July at the headquarters of the OAS. Both delegations agreed to terms of reference for a Panel of Facilitators and a Mixed Commission to consider and implement confidence-building measures aimed at promoting permanent friendly relations and co-operation between the two nations. They also agreed a mechanism to establish military-to-military contacts and co-operation between the two countries, and to that effect to hold a high-level defence policy meeting presided over by the Ministers of Defence of the two countries on or before Aug. 15, 2000. The meeting and related events were held at the Coral Sand Centre-Belize Yacht Club in San Pedro Town, Ambergris caye, on Aug. 11-12, 2000. Agreements arising from the discussion included the exchange of military attachés by Oct.15, 2000, clear lines of communication between the two Defence Ministers, high level military-to-military meetings every six months and other military confidence-building measures.

After the positive turn represented by these events, relations again suffered a downturn after Belize sought to evict what it believed to be illegal Guatemalan settlers from its territory in a number of settlements at Rio Blanco, Machaquila and Valentin Camp. Once these situations had been resolved, further incidents between Guatemalan forest clearers several kilometres inside Belize and the Belizean Defence Force again kept tensions high in early 2001. Another incident involving a Guatemalan citizen, Lenin García Yoc, further inflamed tensions; his body was recovered from the Mopan river (near the Belize-Guatemala border) into which he had allegedly fled from a Belizean Border Management Agency Patrol.

Throughout, the Panel of Facilitators sought to keep the two sides talking and the Mixed (Joint) Commission oversaw the removal and compensation of illegal settlers.

The Facilitators finally produced their recommendations in September 2002 after extensive consultations with not only both governments, but with the Secretary-General of the OAS, the Inter-American Development Bank, the United Nations and with interested governments, in particular Honduras. The recommendations, amounting to some forty pages, covered land, sea and a "Development Trust Fund". In essence, Guatemala would recognize a land boundary with Belize based on the 1859 treaty lines. The areas east of the line would continue to belong to Belize and those west of the line to Guatemala.

At sea, proposals suggested the creation of (i) an Economic Zone for Guatemala along the Belize/Honduras border, and (ii) an area of approximately 2,000 square nautical miles to be used for all three countries to establish a marine park, including the coastal areas of Guatemala and Honduras and southern cayes of Belize. Belize and Honduras would retain full fishing rights and 50% of the mineral rights in the seabed. The park would be dedicated to conservation and eco-tourism and managed by a trilateral commission. The suggested Development Trust Fund was to be established in the amount of $200 million,

monitored by the Inter-American Development Bank and used to alleviate poverty in both countries. The proposal was to be made available to all residents of Belize and Guatemala with referenda to be held simultaneously within 75 days. Acceptance (a yes vote) would lead to the road of formal treaty. The 75 days was extended due to practical difficulties including Belizean elections in March 2003.

Confidence building measures were agreed with the OAS in February 2003 and reaffirmed in October with an OAS office being set up in the adjacency zone. However, Guatemala proved reluctant to initiate a referendum on the Facilitators' proposals, while Belize, although itself prepared to carry out a referendum, recognized that the two referenda must take place simultaneously. Guatemala has not withdrawn its territorial claims and recent official statements have suggested the view that the Facilitators' proposals run counter to the Guatemalan constitution so that they may not be submitted to a referendum.

Lloyd Pettiford

2.5 Bolivia - Chile (Lauca River Waters)

A dispute over the use of the waters of the River Lauca (which has its source in Chile and flows on to the Andean plateau of Bolivia), which had existed for several years, reached a critical point in 1962 after Bolivia had warned Chile on March 22 of that year that the diversion of water from the river by Chile would be regarded as an act of aggression, as such a diversion could not legally be undertaken without the agreement of both countries. (For an illustration of this dispute, see Map 15, page 500; for the separate dispute between Bolivia, Chile and Peru over the question of Bolivian access to the sea, see Section 2.6.)

History of the Dispute

Despite the Bolivian warning, the Chilean President on April 14, 1962, ordered that the sluice gates of a new dam on the Lauca river should be opened to supply an irrigation scheme and a new hydroelectric project in Chile. Bolivia in turn contended that this action reduced the flow of the Lauca river waters into Bolivia and broke off its diplomatic relations with Chile on April 16.

The Bolivian government also appealed to the Council of the Organization of American States (OAS) to find a solution to the dispute. The Council unanimously decided on May 24, 1962, to call on Bolivia and Chile to come to an agreement by making use of any of the peaceful means for settling disputes contained in the 1947 Inter-American Treaty for

Reciprocal Assistance (the Rio Pact). Bolivia and Chile, however, failed to agree on such means, with Bolivia favouring mediation by five Latin American states and Chile wishing to call for arbitration by the International Court of Justice, on the grounds that the issue was a legal and not a political matter.

On Sept. 3, 1962, however, the Bolivian government temporarily withdrew from participation in the activities of the OAS, stating that it had acted "in strict accordance with the terms of the [OAS] resolution of May 24", whereas the Chilean government appeared not to intend to contribute to the reaching of an immediate solution because it was "the beneficiary of the present illegal situation". Bolivia also claimed that the humidity in the area had already been reduced, that the salinity of Lake Coipasa (into which the Lauca river flows) had been raised, that difficulties had been created in agriculture and cattle-raising in three provinces, and that Chile was also attempting to divert waters from the Caquena river (which like the Lauca rises in Chile and flows into Bolivia).

After the OAS had studied the question for over a year without reaching a solution, the Bolivian government announced on June 12, 1963, that it would withdraw permanently from the OAS, which it called "an incompetent organ" as it had failed to solve the dispute. However, this decision was not carried out and a few months later Bolivia resumed its participation in the work of the OAS.

The first dialogue between Bolivia and Chile for 12 years was held by Presidents Hugo Bánzer Suárez of Bolivia and Augusto Pinochet Ugarte of Chile in Brasilia (in the presence of President Ernesto Geisel of Brazil) on March 16, 1974. President Pinochet stated afterwards that Chile was ready to resolve the dispute. The two Presidents met again on Feb. 8, 1975, in a railway car north-east of Arica on the Bolivia-Chile border. To the surprise of many observers, the Act of Charaña issued at the end of these talks brought about the immediate resumption of the diplomatic relations that had been broken in 1962 when Chile had moved unilaterally to divert the headwaters of the Lauca river.

In 1976 the Chilean government came forward with a comprehensive proposal. This, while providing for an exchange of territory whereby Bolivia would acquire a corridor to the sea, also contained a clause under which Bolivia was to grant Chile the use of the Lauca river waters. Although President Bánzer at first accepted these proposals as "a global basis for negotiation", they were generally rejected in Bolivia.

On March 17, 1978—by which date no progress had been made in negotiations concerning Bolivia's access to the sea—the Bolivian government again broke off diplomatic relations with Chile. In 1983, a new government took advantage of the bicentenary of the birth of Simón Bolívar to demonstrate its willingness to reconsider all outstanding issues in the wider context of Andean solidarity, but with General Pinochet still in power in Chile no further progress was made.

The return of democratic government to Chile was followed by a statement in early 1993 that President Patricio Aylwin had instructed his foreign minister to resolve all outstanding border disputes before the end of the year. Expectations that this announcement might signal a breakthrough in negotiations with Bolivia were soon dashed, however, when Chile clarified its position with an additional statement that it had no outstanding border disputes with either Bolivia or Peru. Throughout the 1990s Chile continued to be cool towards its neighbour.

In February 2000, with diplomatic relations still broken, the Foreign Ministers of Bolivia and Chile met during the joint European Union-Rio Group summit to discuss an agenda for future negotiations. They agreed to begin a dialogue centred on six topics, but the Lauca river waters dispute was not among them, and the issue remains unresolved.

Another dispute concerning the use of the Silala river waters was discussed for the first time at meetings which took place between President Hugo Bánzer Suárez and Chilean President Ricardo Lagos in Brasilia in September 2000 and in Panama later the same year. Unlike the Lauca, the Silala rises in Bolivia and flows through Chile to the sea. Chile claims that it is an international waterway which it is entitled to use but Bolivia argues that since all the sources are in Bolivia the use of its waters is a matter for Bolivia alone.

Peter Calvert

2.6 Bolivia - Chile - Peru

Bolivia has been landlocked since losing its coastal territory in the Pacific War of 1879-84, when Chile seized the then Bolivian port of Antofagasta and the surrounding coastline. Peru, which joined the war in support of Bolivia, lost its own southern provinces of Tacna and Arica to Chile but retrieved Tacna in 1929 under the second Treaty of Ancón. Bolivia's efforts to regain an outlet to the Pacific Ocean have since been hampered by a provision in the Treaty of Ancón to the effect that no Chilean territory formerly belonging to Peru could be surrendered to a third country without the consent of Peru. Bolivia also failed, in the Chaco War of the early 1930s, to obtain proper access to the Atlantic Ocean via the Paraguay river. Bolivia has as a national policy aim the regaining of access to the Pacific and in April 1987 put forward new proposals to that end involving the cession of territory by Chile. However, no real progress has been made towards a solution. (For this dispute, see Map 15, page 500.)

History of the Dispute

The exact border between Chile and Bolivia was not defined when the two countries became independent from the (Spanish) Viceroyaltv of Peru—independence being accomplished by Chile in 1810 and by Bolivia (which was formerly encompassed by the Audiencia of Charcas) in 1824. In 1866 the two countries reached an agreement setting their boundary along the 24°S parallel of latitude to the south of Antofagasta (in the Atacama desert) but providing that the proceeds from nitrate and guano deposits extracted from a common zone between the 23rd and 25th parallels should be equally divided.

After Bolivia had broken an agreement signed with Chile at Sucre in 1874 by placing fresh taxes on Chilean firms already exploiting nitrates in the common zone, a Chilean expeditionary force in February 1879 took possession of Antofagasta and Mejillones (on the coast) and Caracoles (inland). Chile called on Peru to proclaim its neutrality in the conflict and, when the latter refused, declared war on both Peru and Bolivia. Peru thereupon joined forces with Bolivia under a treaty concluded secretly in February 1873, but a joint Peruvian-Bolivian army was defeated at Tarapacá in November 1879 and the Peruvians retreated to Tacna, losing the whole of the Tarapacá nitrate area to Chile. After this Bolivia played little further part in the Pacific War, although Peru fought on, with the result that Lima and Callao were occupied by Chilean troops in 1881.

Chilean forces remained in Lima in strength until 1883, when General Miguel Iglesias was elected President of Peru with Chilean backing and then proceeded to sign the (first) Treaty of Ancón on Oct. 20, 1883. The treaty ceded to Chile in perpetuity and unconditionally the province of Tarapacá and provided that the provinces of Tacna and Arica would remain in Chilean possession and subject to Chilean administration for 10 years, at the end of which time a plebiscite would be held to decide whether the territories should remain in Chilean hands or revert to Peru. The last Chilean forces withdrew from Lima in August 1884. That same year (in April) a separate truce was signed between Chile and Bolivia, terminating the state of war between them and providing that, while the truce remained in force, Chile was to administer the territory from the 23rd parallel to the south of the Loa river on the Pacific. This meant that Bolivia lost not only its seaports but also its nitrate territory.

In October 1904 a treaty was signed in implementation of the 1884 truce agreement, re-establishing peace between Chile and Bolivia, confirming the absolute and perpetual sovereignty of Chile over the former Bolivian territory occupied since the Pacific War, and demarcating the Bolivian-Chilean border from north to south through 96 points.

Article 3 of the 1904 treaty established that the port of Arica would be linked with the plateau above La Paz (Bolivia) by means of a railway which was to be built at Chile's expense, while in Article 6 Chile recognized in perpetuity Bolivia's free and full right of commercial transit through Chilean territory and ports on the Pacific seaboard. In return, under a supplementary protocol of November 1904, Bolivia recognized Chile's absolute and perpetual dominion over the territory between the 23rd and 24th parallels from the Pacific to the Argentinian border. By 1913 the railway was completed and Bolivia was due to come into ownership of its own section in 1928 under the terms of the 1904 treaty. The Peruvian government protested at the bilateral treaty between Chile and Bolivia and warned that such a treaty did not diminish its own rights to the provinces of Tacna and Arica.

In 1918 Bolivia demanded an outlet to the sea by means of a port in either Tacna or Arica provinces, to which it asserted that neither Peru nor Chile had a conclusive right. It stated its preference for Arica on the grounds of geographical proximity, economic considerations and the fact that Arica (as well as Tacna) had been part of the Charcas Audiencia before independence. Furthermore, in 1920 Bolivia called on the League of Nations to obtain a revision of the 1904 treaty on the grounds that it had been imposed by force, that Chile was not carrying out some of its fundamental provisions, that a permanent threat of war existed in the current situation, and that it had no access to the sea. The League ruled, however, that a treaty could only be modified by the parties to it.

Meanwhile, on expiry of the 10-year period stipulated under the Treaty of Ancón, no attempt was made by Chile to hold a plebiscite in Tacna and Arica. By the early 1920s, when the USA was asked to intervene, the areas had already become Chileanized. When registration of voters was eventually carried out in preparation for the holding of a plebiscite, it was found that most Peruvians had failed to enrol, so that the plan to hold a plebiscite was abandoned.

Peru and Chile in 1929 resumed diplomatic relations, which they had broken off some 20 years earlier, and on June 3, 1929, a new agreement, called the (second) Treaty of Ancón, was signed in Lima, returning the territory of Tacna to Peru and leaving Arica in Chilean hands. A complementary protocol of the same date stated that neither government could without the consent of the other cede to any third party any or all of the territory previously in dispute, or build new international railways across it.

Tacna was handed back to Peru at a ceremony on Aug. 28, 1929, and the following year Arica was incorporated by Chile into the province of Tarapacá, its northern boundary forming the frontier with Peru.

The Chaco War

From the late 1870s Bolivia sought the settlement of an old claim to part of the vast and largely uninhabited Chaco territory, including an area between the Pilcomayo and Verde rivers awarded to Paraguay as against Argentina in November 1878. Aspiring partly to gain an outlet to the Atlantic, Bolivia based its claim on the proposition that the Audiencia of Charcas had always exercised jurisdiction as far east as the Paraguay river. A number of agreements on delimitation of territory in the Chaco were signed but not ratified between Bolivia and Paraguay over the next few years, including the Soler-Pinilla protocol of Jan. 12, 1907.

In 1928 the two sides attacked each other's outposts in the Chaco and, despite attempts at arbitration by other South American countries, fighting took place sporadically in 1930-31, breaking out in earnest in 1932. The Bolivian forces were greater in number and better equipped than the Paraguayans, but many of them were Indians accustomed to high altitudes and they died in large numbers on the lower hot plains of the Chaco. Paraguay, on the other hand, was fighting on familiar ground; its forces under Col. José Félix Estigarribia advanced steadily and by the end of 1934 had captured thousands of square miles of territory beyond Bolivia's line of outposts. After some 100,000 men had died, a truce entered into force in 1935 and peace talks were held in Buenos Aires. A final boundary was established in 1938, whereby most of the territory was ceded to Paraguay, and Bolivia was granted the right of rail access to the Paraguay river.

Renewed Bolivian Claims for Access to Sea

In 1962 Bolivia broke off diplomatic relations with Chile after the latter was accused of reducing the flow of the Lauca river waters into Bolivia (see Section 2.5), and relations were not resumed until 1975. In the 1970s, with General Hugo Bánzer in office in Bolivia and General Augusto Pinochet in power in Chile, the question of access to the sea was elevated to a major nationalistic issue in Bolivia, and in 1974 Bolivia and Chile initiated high-level contacts for the first time in 12 years.

In December 1975 Chile put forward a series of proposals aimed at resolving Bolivia's sea access problem. These proposals required, however, that Bolivia should (i) relinquish an equal amount of its own territory (reportedly the mineral-rich area of Los Lipez in Potosí department in south-west Bolivia) in exchange for a corridor to the sea; (ii) purchase from Chile the Chilean sector of the Arica-La Paz railway; (iii) allow Chile full use of the Lauca river waters; (iv) undertake to keep any land corridor demilitarized; and (v) pay compensation for the use of port facilities. President Bánzer accepted the proposals as a basis for negotiation but they were generally ill-received in Bolivia.

Chile itself later declined to consider a set of Peruvian proposals put forward in November 1976 according to which (i) Bolivia would be granted a corridor of land 8½ miles (13½ kilometres) wide along the Chilean-Peruvian frontier, two miles north of the Arica-La Paz railway; (ii) an international zone would be set up under the joint control of Chile, Peru and Bolivia where the corridor reached the coast; (iii) port facilities at Arica would be administered by all three countries; (iv) Bolivia would be allowed to establish a port under its sole sovereignty in the international zone; and (v) the sea area around the zone would be Bolivia's territorial waters.

Thereafter, relations between Peru and Chile continued to be strained over the question of Bolivian access to the sea. Moreover, in March 1978 President Bánzer of Bolivia again broke off relations with Chile

on the grounds that it was not showing sufficient flexibility over the issue. The centenary of the outbreak of the Pacific War (in 1979) was marked in Bolivia by emotional demonstrations in support of the regaining of access to the Pacific Ocean.

In the 1980s the prospects of movement on the Bolivia-Chile-Peru territorial issue appeared to become linked with the Argentina-Chile territorial dispute in their southern border region, and with the Argentina-UK dispute over the Falklands/Malvinas (see Sections 2.1 and 2.3, respectively). Following its defeat in the 1982 South Atlantic war with Britain, Argentina sought to secure Chilean diplomatic support on the Falklands by finally accepting Chile's claims in the Beagle Channel. Further, Argentina reportedly sought to ensure Bolivian and Peruvian support by making its concessions to Chile conditional upon the latter making concessions on the access to the sea question. In the event, however, Chile denied that any such linkage existed under the 1984 treaty with Argentina confirming Chilean sovereignty over the disputed Beagle Channel islands.

Nevertheless, Chile thereafter responded to Bolivian attempts at a diplomatic rapprochement by accepting the appointment of a Bolivian consul in Santiago in February 1986 and by entering into direct talks in New York at foreign minister level. These resulted in the signature on Sept. 30, 1986, of a 30-point agreement on the development of socio-economic and political relations, although the impact of the agreement was somewhat diminished by the simultaneous announcement by Chilean National Railways that it had suspended the Arica-La Paz service because of Bolivia's outstanding debts.

Thereafter, further talks on the access to the sea question took place in various American capitals, culminating in a meeting of foreign ministers in Montevideo (Uruguay) on April 21, 1987, at which the Bolivian side formally presented detailed proposals envisaging that Chile would cede either (i) a narrow strip of territory on its northern border with Peru, north of Arica and stretching eastwards to the current Bolivian border, or (ii) one of three identified coastal enclaves further south, with assured communications to Bolivia proper. It was further proposed that under any of these alternative scenarios Bolivia would make appropriate compensation and that Bolivia and Chile, together with Peru where appropriate, would establish an institutional framework for the economic development of their border regions.

The first of these alternatives envisaged that Bolivia would have full sovereignty, ownership and use in perpetuity of a demarcated strip of territory on the present Chile-Peru border, with full maritime rights off the coast of the ceded territory. Bolivia would also have various permanent rights of access to adjacent communications facilities which would remain in Chilean or Peruvian territory, with Bolivia undertaking to respect all existing private rights in the territory ceded. The three coastal enclaves identified in the alternative Bolivian proposals were a 42-kilometre area north of

Pisagua (totalling 1,068 sq km), a 47-kilometre segment north of Tocopilia (1,238 sq km) and a 50-kilometre stretch north of Mejillones (1,500 sq km). An essential Bolivian requirement was that any such enclave ceded by Chile should contain a serviceable port.

The Bolivian proposals met with a negative response from the ruling military junta in Chile, among whose members the Navy Commander, Admiral José Toribio Merino Castro, publicly rejected any arrangement involving the cession of Chilean territory to Bolivia. It was also pointed out in Chilean ruling circles that any modification of the 1904 treaty with Bolivia would require legislative enactment and might also need to be endorsed in a national plebiscite. A Chilean Foreign Ministry spokesman said on June 9, 1987, that his government was willing to continue exploratory talks with Bolivia on possible solutions to the territorial issue but stressed that any further Bolivian proposals should "not alter the Chilean territory". The following day the Bolivian consul was withdrawn from Santiago and the Bolivian government announced that it was considering suspending trade relations with Chile.

Relations had improved by 1989, however, leading to the reappointment of a consul to Santiago on March 19. In January 1990 Chile stated that the problems between the two countries could be solved independently of the sea outlet issue. Earlier, at a meeting between Presidents Jaime Paz Zamora of Bolivia and Alan García of Peru on Lake Titicaca in October 1989, Peru had stated that it would no longer object to Chile giving Bolivia a corridor to the sea through former Peruvian territory. A meeting by a joint Chilean-Bolivian commission was held in Santiago on March 18-22, 1991, to discuss the precise demarcation of their border.

Agreements and Continued Negotiations on Access to Sea

Bolivia's access to the sea was somewhat improved when on July 1, 1993, President Jaime Paz Zamora stepped into the Pacific at Ilo, where Peru had leased Bolivia a 162-hectare zone for a duty-free port and industrial park, together with a 5-km strip of coast for recreational purposes. In return Bolivia conceded Peru free-port facilities at Puerto Suárez on the Paraguay river adjoining Brazil.

Meanwhile the Peruvian government had continued negotiations with Chile over the right of free passage on the Tacna-Arica Railway to the pier to be assigned to Peru at Arica under the 1929 Treaty, and in May 1993 concluded the so-called Lima Conventions which appeared to resolve all the outstanding issues.

On July 16 the Bolivian President signed four co-operation treaties with Chile on the occasion of the third Ibero-American Summit in Brazil, having reached agreement on April 7 on a ten-year programme of mutual tariff cuts and a feasibility study on the supply of gas to northern Chile. However as a result of his statement on July 22 that Chile was "regrettably in the Stone Age" and "retrograde where Bolivia's maritime situation is concerned", Chile withdrew from further talks. The Chilean position hardened further when the new Bolivian Foreign Minister, Antonio Aranibar Quiroga, raised the issue of access to the sea in June 1994 at the twenty-fourth General Assembly of the Organization of American States (OAS); the Chilean Foreign Minister, José Miguel Insulza, said that the issue of a Bolivian seaport on the Pacific had been ended in 1904. Over the next three years he was to reiterate the official Chilean position that there were no outstanding territorial questions to be settled between Chile and Bolivia.

In the interim, in 1995 the Chilean and Peruvian Foreign Ministers jointly agreed that the Lima Conventions should be set aside and the sudden crisis in the Ecuador-Peru boundary dispute (see Section 2.11) meant that no further progress was made in their joint talks until 1998. Both sides then agreed to make a determined effort to solve their outstanding differences. In November 1999 Foreign Ministers Juan Gabriel Valdés of Chile and Fernando de Trazegnies of Peru signed an Act of Execution (Acta de Ejecución), a package of documents finally implementing the 1929 Treaty and Additional Protocol. The effect of the Act was to ensure for Peru the absolute right of free passage of persons, merchandise and armaments to and from Peruvian territory to a railway station, customs house and wharf at Arica.

The Bolivian administration of Gonzalo Sánchez de Lozada (1994-98) had continued confidential talks with the Chileans with a view to obtaining as an interim measure a free trade agreement that would give Bolivia port facilities at Arica similar to those granted by Peru at Ilo. The hope was that the issue could be taken up as part of a wider programme of mutual co-operation. With the election in 1998 of Hugo Bánzer Suárez to the presidency he had previously held as a military dictator, Foreign Minister Javier Murillo de la Rocha took the Bolivian case to the UN General Assembly in September 1998, but without success. The Bolivian government therefore took the opportunity afforded by the agreement between Peru and Chile to congratulate both parties and to express the hope that Bolivia's access problem might also be addressed. This it now seemed might best be achieved by a broader, trilateral agreement, centring on a pole of development (*polo de desarrollo*) where the three countries' boundaries met.

Early in 2000, therefore, a new round of bilateral talks was opened by Foreign Ministers Valdés of Chile and Murillo of Bolivia, and President Bánzer met with his Chilean counterpart, Ricardo Lagos, in Brasilia in September, in Panama later in the year and in Quebec in April 2001. Though Bolivia made no move to re-establish diplomatic relations, and President Bánzer had to admit he saw no immediate hope of resolving the maritime issue, there were some small practical gains. Then, having been diagnosed with terminal cancer, he resigned on Aug. 8, and the main task of the interim administration was to hold elections in June 2002.

The elections were inconclusive and, under pressure from the US government, on Aug. 4 the Bolivian Congress chose the millionaire businessman and ex-President Gonzalo Sánchez de Lozada to serve for the term 2002-06. However, when in September 2003 he announced a proposal to export gas to the USA and Mexico by way of a pipeline through Chilean territory, the decision sparked riots. Though there was some objection to the route chosen, the riots, which claimed as many as 65 lives, were mainly motivated by the administration's US-backed anti-coca growing policies, which had deprived thousands of farmers of their livelihood. Sánchez de Lozada temporarily suspended the gas export plan, but the demonstrations calling for his resignation continued and eventually he gave way and fled to the USA.

Peter Calvert

2.7 Colombia - Nicaragua

A dispute over the Colombian islands of San Andrés and Providencia, as well as the cayes of Roncador, Quitasueño and Serrana, erupted after Nicaragua unilaterally declared null and void a 1928 treaty recognizing Colombian sovereignty over the islands on Feb. 4, 1980. The islands had been administered as Colombian territory since the early 19th century. (Map 16 on page 500 illustrates this dispute.)

History of the Dispute

San Andrés and Providencia, and the three cayes, are all situated within 200 miles (320 kilometres) of Nicaragua on the Nicaragua Rise (an undersea bank between Nicaragua and Jamaica). Their distance to Colombia is considerably further, although they are somewhat nearer to Panama, which was a province of Colombia prior to its independence in 1903. Panama has a dormant claim to the islands. Since 1953 San Andrés has been developed as a thriving free port, and also possesses a Colombian naval and air force base.

Colombia bases its claim to the islands and cayes on a royal order of 1803 assigning the defence of San Andrés and Providencia and the Mosquito coast against pirates to the Viceroyalty of Nueva Granada (based at Bogotá). Nicaragua, on the other hand, claims that the 1803 order was purely military and points out that under a further royal order of 1806 responsibility for the defence of the areas was restored to the Captaincy-General of Guatemala (under which Nicaragua was administered at the time). Nicaragua also cites bilateral treaties of the 19th and early 20th century establishing Nicaraguan sovereignty over its coast and the adjacent islands. These included the Corn Islands, or Islas del Maíz, which lie some 70 kilometres east of Bluefields on the Atlantic coast of Nicaragua.

Nicaragua was a focus of interest for the colonial powers in the 19th century because of the possibility of constructing an inter-oceanic canal across its territory. In the 18th century Britain had established a protectorate on the Mosquito coast (including part of present-day Honduras), known as the Miskito "kingdom", and its presence in the area was not finally ended until 1894. The 1905 Altamirano-Harrison treaty between Britain and Nicaragua subsequently recognized full Nicaraguan sovereignty over the coast.

The United States intervened militarily in 1912-25 and again in 1926-33. It first proposed to Nicaragua that a treaty should be concluded recognizing Colombian sovereignty over San Andrés and Providencia in 1925 (apparently as recompense to Colombia for the loss of Panama, whose independence in 1903 the USA had supported). However, it was not until the second term of office of President Adolfo Diaz of Nicaragua (1926-28) that the Bárcenas Meneses-Esguerra treaty was signed with Colombia on March 24, 1928. The treaty stated that Colombia recognized Nicaraguan sovereignty over the Mosquito coast in exchange for Nicaraguan recognition of Colombian sovereignty over San Andrés and Providencia (but expressly excepted Roncador, Quitasueño and Serrana). It was not ratified until March 6, 1930, however, when President Moncada of the Liberal Party was in power in Nicaragua.

Just after the signature of the treaty, the USA and Colombia on April 10, 1928, came to an agreement regulating the juridical status of Roncador, Quitasueño and Serrana—the USA having earlier taken possession of the cayes (in 1919) under the US Guano Act, whereby islands considered by the USA as *terrae nullius* became its property if guano was discovered there. The agreement (in the form of an exchange of notes) laid down that in view of the claims of both countries over the islands the status quo should be maintained. Colombia should continue to fish around the islands and the USA should maintain navigational aids in the area.

A treaty between Colombia and the USA (the Vasquez-Saccio treaty), formally recognizing Colombian sovereignty over the three cayes, was signed in Bogotá on Sept. 8, 1972, although it was not ratified by the US Senate until July 31, 1981.

The new Sandinista regime in Nicaragua (installed in July 1979 after the overthrow of President Anastasio Somoza) reopened the question of the islands' sovereignty soon after assuming power by claiming in December 1979 that the islands and cayes were part of its 200-mile continental shelf. On Feb. 4, 1980, it rejected the Bárcenas Meneses-Esguerra treaty, claiming that it had been agreed while Nicaragua was under foreign control. Nicaragua stressed that its action was not intended as a sign of aggression against a neighbouring nation, nor was it claiming part of Colombia's continental shelf, but rather territory which was geographically, historically and juridically an integral part of Nicaragua. It claimed that Nicaragua's history since 1909 had prevented it from defending its right to the continental shelf, the jurisdictional waters and island territories, and that treaties disadvantageous to Nicaragua such as the

Bárcenas Meneses-Esguerra treaty and the earlier Chamorro-Bryan agreement of 1914 were signed under duress and therefore lacked legal validity.

In response to Nicaragua's action the Colombian government reinforced its air, naval and marine presence on San Andrés and recalled its ambassador for consultations. Some clashes over the presence of Nicaraguan fishing boats in the area were reported.

The ratification of the Vasquez-Saccio treaty by the US Senate nine years after it was signed was cited by the Nicaraguan government as a US attempt to intimidate it. The importance of the area was increased by the possible presence of petroleum deposits. Colombia had granted a US company a licence to prospect in the area. Nicaragua and Colombia agreed to hold talks and Colombia also referred its case to the UN Law of the Sea conference. On Oct. 23, 1986, the Colombian Senate approved a maritime delimitation treaty with Honduras (signed on Aug. 2) which endorsed Colombia's sovereignty over the areas in dispute with Nicaragua.

Thereafter the issue appeared to have decreased in importance as it seemed unlikely that the status quo would be overturned. However, on Dec. 12, 2001, Nicaragua instituted proceedings against Colombia at the International Court of Justice (ICJ) concerning title to territory and maritime delimitation in the western Caribbean. Nicaragua claimed that the current situation imperils the lives of Nicaraguans, especially off the Caribbean coast, and suggests that the Colombian Navy has intercepted Nicaraguan boats just 70 kilometres from its coastline. Nicaragua maintained that diplomatic negotiations had failed and reserved the right to claim compensation. On March 1, 2002, the ICJ put fixed time limits on pleadings in the case, with Nicaragua having until April 29, 2003, and Colombia a further year from that date to make any counter arguments.

The granting of oil exploration permits by Nicaragua in 2003 briefly increased tensions, with the Colombians immediately asserting their military preparedness. However, Nicaragua has issued statements that its exploration permits are all in areas where sovereignty is not under dispute.

Related Dispute between Honduras and Nicaragua

A dispute between Honduras and Nicaragua has come to the fore because of developments relating to the dispute between Nicaragua and Colombia.

In November 1999, the Honduran legislature ratified the López-Ramírez Treaty with Colombia, signed in 1986 (see above), that set the maritime boundary between the two nations in the Caribbean. The Nicaraguan government claimed that the treaty deprived Nicaragua of a large portion of national territory along the continental shelf. On Dec. 8, 1999, Nicaragua filed an application before the ICJ instituting proceedings against Honduras in respect of the delimitation of the maritime zones in the Caribbean Sea. Nicaragua argued that it had long "maintained the position that its maritime Caribbean border with Honduras has not been determined", but that

Honduras believed that "there in fact exists a delimitation line that runs straight easterly on the parallel of latitude from the point fixed [in an Arbitral Award of Dec. 23, 1906, made by the King of Spain concerning the land boundary between Nicaragua and Honduras, which was found valid and binding by the International Court of Justice on Nov. 18, 1960] on the mouth of the Coco river".

According to Nicaragua, "the position adopted by Honduras...has brought repeated confrontations and mutual capture of vessels of both nations in and around the general border area". Nicaragua further stated that "diplomatic negotiations have failed". Nicaragua therefore requested the Court "to determine the course of the single maritime boundary between areas of territorial sea, continental shelf and exclusive economic zone appertaining respectively to Nicaragua and Honduras, in accordance with equitable principles and relevant circumstances recognized by general international law as applicable to such a delimitation of a single maritime boundary".

Nicaragua further indicated that it "reserves the right to claim compensation for interference with fishing vessels of Nicaraguan nationality or vessels licensed by Nicaragua, found to the north of the parallel of latitude 14°59′08″ claimed by Honduras to be the course of the delimitation line". It also reserved "the right to claim compensation for any natural resources that may have been extracted or may be extracted in the future to the south of the line of delimitation that will be fixed by the Judgment of the Court". As a basis for the Court's jurisdiction, Nicaragua invoked Article XXXI of the American Treaty on Pacific Settlement (known as the "Pact of Bogotá"), signed on April 30, 1948, to which both Nicaragua and Honduras are parties, as well as the declarations under Article 36, paragraph 2, of the Statute of the Court, by which both States have accepted the compulsory jurisdiction of the Court.

A decision in the case before the ICJ is still pending. Separately the case has been before the Central American Court of Justice; on June 25, 2003, this Court ruled that both parties had acted against regional integration, but both parties accepted this ruling only in so far as it applied to the other. A potential resolution of the dispute will therefore require a ruling from the ICJ.

Lloyd Pettiford

2.8 Colombia - Venezuela

The land boundary between Colombia and Venezuela—originally based on the 1810 boundary between the Spanish captaincies-general of Venezuela and New Granada—was not properly determined until 1932. The two countries had in 1916 decided to submit their long-standing dispute for arbitration by the Swiss Federal Council. Its award was made on March 24, 1922, though it took ten years to achieve its final implementation. Notwithstanding this land border settlement, the two countries have in recent years been at issue over the delimitation of their respective sovereignties in the Gulf of Venezuela and the area around the Los Monjes islands to the north-east of the Goajirá Peninsula (see Map 17, page 501). General tensions between the two countries on border issues and the possible potential for petroleum deposits in the disputed maritime area have hindered a rapid solution to the dispute.

Historical Background

In 1891 the Queen Regent of Spain, acting for the King, awarded the Goajirá Peninsula to Colombia, but under a treaty signed in Bogotá (the capital of Colombia) on April 24, 1894, but not subsequently ratified, Colombia ceded to Venezuela certain territories, including settlements on the east coast of the Goajirá Peninsula.

A new dispute, however, arose in the 1920s over the question of sovereignty over the waters and resources of the Gulf of Venezuela and the area around the islands of Los Monjes in connection with the discovery of oil resources in the area. Los Monjes are small rocky islets, uninhabited, often submerged and without vegetation, which lie some 35 kilometres north-east of the tip of the Goajirá Peninsula. In 1944 Colombia unilaterally declared its sovereignty over Los Monjes, but Venezuela objected and in February 1952 annexed the islands. On Nov. 11, 1952, the Colombian Foreign Minister, Juán Uribe Holguín, renounced his country's claims.

In December 1965 it was alleged in Venezuela that Colombia had granted certain US oil companies concessions for prospecting for oil in Venezuelan territory. The two governments nevertheless agreed in that year to engage in talks on the "delimitation of marine and submarine areas" between their two countries. In 1968 the Venezuelan Foreign Minister defined his government's position as follows: "The submarine areas of the Gulf of Venezuela south of the parallel through Castilletes and Punta Salinas [i.e. roughly 12°N] in their entirety form part of Venezuelan territory [and] are in no case the object of negotiations, and therefore we recognize no kind of concessions in this area". In 1971 Colombia contested the validity of its renunciation of its claim to Los Monjes. In April 1973 Colombia further claimed that Los Monjes did not have their own continental shelf and in the same month talks were broken off.

On July 20, 1975, President López Michelsen of Colombia declared that the Gulf of Venezuela was "a historic bay, a condominium of two riparian states", as the Gulf was not exclusively surrounded by Venezuelan territory.

On Jan. 28, 1976, it was reported that the Colombian government would not submit its claim regarding the Los Monjes islands area to the International Court of Justice (ICJ) but was ready to discuss it in direct talks with Venezuela on the delimitation of marine and submarine areas. At the same time, the Venezuelan Foreign Minister was reported to have stated that Venezuela's sovereignty over Los Monjes was unquestionable.

Draft Treaty on Demarcation of Gulf of Venezuela

Talks over the issue were held during 1978, initially in secret, leading to the creation of a commission to negotiate on the demarcation of the Gulf of Venezuela. The talks continued until it was announced in a broadcast on Oct. 21, 1980, that agreement had been reached on a draft treaty designated the Hypothesis of Caraballeda, to deal with the delimitation of marine areas including "internal waters" and "exclusive economic zones". The draft treaty provided inter alia for the "innocent passage" of all merchant vessels using the ports of the two countries and that of warships and non-commercial state-owned vessels. It reaffirmed that the Los Monjes were part of Venezuela, but recognized limited Colombian rights in the Gulf. On the question of oil production, the draft treaty laid down that any deposits straddling the boundary line would be exploited by each party in its own area and each would receive one-half of the hydrocarbons extracted but would also bear one-half of the cost.

The draft treaty was strongly opposed by certain circles in both countries, but particularly among the armed forces in Venezuela. Widespread hostility in Venezuela towards Colombians, thousands of whom had entered Venezuela in search of work, was exacerbated by the economic downturn and this strengthened the hand of those opposing the treaty. The Venezuelan President, Luis Herrera Campins, stated that the treaty would not be signed if there was no clear consensus on its terms. At the same time the Venezuelan Minister of Energy assured Colombia that Venezuela would not drill for oil in the disputed area until the issue was settled. Further talks between representatives of the two countries were suspended by Venezuela in November 1980.

At a new meeting held on June 14, 1985, the two countries' Presidents expressed their determination to find a peaceful solution to the dispute. However, President Jaime Lusinchi of Venezuela adopted a more intransigent position in the dispute by refusing Colombian requests for direct negotiations. During the course of 1987 tensions increased substantially. The presence of Colombian guerrillas fighting against the Colombian government, drug traffickers and general lawlessness in the border regions contributed to the tensions between the two countries. Colombian guerrillas were involved in attacks on Venezuelan oil-drilling facilities in "reprisal" for the alleged exploitation of Colombian immigrant workers, and kidnapped a number of border farmers. In June guerrillas belonging to the Colombian guerrilla group, the National Liberation Army (Ejército de Liberación Nacional— ELN), attacked a Venezuelan border patrol, killing eight National Guardsmen and an officer.

The decision of President Barco of Colombia to invoke the 1939 bilateral Treaty of Non-Aggression followed the rejection by President Lusinchi of an offer for direct negotiations on the two countries' conflicting claims in the Gulf of Venezuela, thus leaving Colombia without a remedy in the marine boundary dispute. An attack by ELN guerrillas from Colombia on a National Guard patrol in June further exacerbated feeling, and also led to the dismissals of the Minister of Defence and of the chief of staff of the armed forces. On Aug. 13, Venezuela protested at the incursion of a Colombian naval vessel, the corvette *Caldas*, into the disputed maritime area. The Colombian government protested its innocence at the alleged violation, claiming that it was due to the poorly delineated boundary. Both sides reinforced their military presence on the border, with several Venezuelan frigates and gunboats and a further Colombian navy corvette, *Independencia*. Though the intention was clear, to use Venezuela's superior force to back its disputed claims, the Venezuelan refusal to accept mediation brought condemnation from the Organization of American States, where the Permanent Council called for restraint. The Venezuelan Foreign Minister, Simon Alberto Consalvi, brushed aside Colombian proposals for mediation. On Aug. 18 all the Colombian ships were withdrawn. In September Colombia alleged that Venezuelan military jets had violated Colombian airspace.

On Jan. 21, 1988, the two countries' Interior Ministers, José Angel Ciliberto and César Gaviria Trujillo, met at San Antonio del Táchira to discuss border issues and agreed to co-operate in countering drug trafficking and guerrilla activity. After the election of Carlos Andrés Pérez as President of Venezuela, relations between the two countries improved, with a renewed determination by Pérez to solve the dispute. On Feb. 3, 1989, Presidents Barco and Pérez agreed to form commissions to discuss the dispute. This was confirmed at a meeting between the two Presidents on the border bridge at Ureña on Feb. 28, together with Adolfo Suárez Gómez, the former Spanish Prime Minister, who had agreed to chair the conciliation council which was to find a way of demarcating the maritime boundary. Two other commissions were also set up to discuss problems concerning the border regions.

Border Tensions since 1992

On Feb. 4, 1992, there was an attempted military coup in Venezuela led by middle-ranking officers. Paratroops under Lt.-Col. Hugo Chávez attacked the Miraflores presidential palace in the capital, Caracas, while other units attempted to seize other key government buildings and military bases in other parts of the country. Troops loyal to President Pérez succeeded in quelling the insurrection. The rebel leaders, identified as members of an extreme nationalist group within the armed forces, had justified their actions as defending Venezuela's territorial integrity against possible concessions to Colombia in the commission's negotiations.

Meanwhile attacks by Colombian guerrillas in the border areas, meant that additional forces were deployed to the frontier zone and on Nov. 22, 1994, Venezuela and Colombia signed an agreement on joint operations. In February 1995 the ELN mounted a cross-border raid into Venezuela, killing eight Venezuelan marines and wounding four. The Venezuelan government responded on March 15 by sending 5,000 troops to round up and deport illegal Colombian immigrants in the frontier zone and the Colombian government responded by mobilizing some 6,000 troops on the Venezuelan border; the President stating that he would gladly co-operate with the Venezuela government but would not recognize their claim to a right of "hot pursuit", which a later incident in October suggested they were exercising regardless.

In 1998 Hugo Chávez was elected President of Venezuela by a substantial majority, and relations between the two countries became noticeably tenser. In February 2000 President Chávez met Colombian President Andres Pastrana on the Venezuelan side of their joint border. This was followed by a five-hour meeting between the two leaders on May 4 at the Quinta de San Pedro Alejandrino, Santa Marta, Colombia, scene of the death of the Liberator, Simón Bolívar, in 1830. At this historic place the two leaders agreed to reactivate the joint commission to address the series of border problems which continued to plague relations between the two countries. The meeting had been preceded by sessions between the Foreign Ministers of the two countries, some including also the Ministers of Defence and Interior. According to the Venezuelan Foreign Minister, José Vicente Rangel, the reconstituted commission would be charged with the "drawing of marine and submarine limits", as well as matters concerning watersheds, international waterways, boundary monuments, integration, and population density along the borders of the two countries. The border commission was to hold its first meeting in June 2000 and was scheduled to convene at least four times during the next 12 months.

There was evident hope that relations between the two countries would no longer be plagued by the maritime boundary issue. However, the presence of more than a million Colombians in Venezuela, coupled with the problems of drug smuggling and guerrilla incursions, conspired to frustrate the best intentions of both countries. Reports that Venezuelan forces had crossed the frontier on Oct. 13, 2000, and burnt houses and coca plantations near Tres Bocas, Norte de Santander, were denied by the Venezuelan government. However, on Nov. 25 Colombia recalled its ambassador to Venezuela because representatives of another Colombian guerrilla group, the Colombian Revolutionary Armed Forces (*Fuerzas Armadas Revolucionarias de Colombia*— FARC) had been invited to a conference in Caracas. Meanwhile the maritime boundary issue, though not of immediate importance, remains unresolved.

Peter Calvert

2.9 Costa Rica - Nicaragua

In 2000, the two countries settled a legal dispute over navigational rights on the San Juan river (Río San Juan) the southern (Costa Rican) bank of which forms their common border. Though Nicaragua holds absolute sovereignty over the river, bilateral accords grant Costa Rica the right to free navigation on the waterway. However, in 1999, Nicaragua's newly-elected President Arnoldo Alemán prohibited Costa Rican police from travelling armed on the San Juan waterway, a decision that triggered a diplomatic incident.

In 2003 Nicaragua was planning to spend $40-50 million to open a shallow-draft barge canal extending from a point near the Pacific coast to the shipping routes of the Atlantic. It would utilize the naturally existing waterways of Lake Nicaragua and the San Juan river, to form an "ecological" canal 360 km long which would connect the city of Granada, located at the end of Lake Nicaragua near the Pacific and just 45 km south of Managua (the capital), with the Caribbean Sea, and thus the Atlantic. The San Juan river is 200 to 300 metres wide, but the plan approved by the Nicaraguan Congress limits the navigational route to 25 metres from each bank.

This route was a main crossing point on the isthmus between 1540 and 1890, but was virtually abandoned on the opening of the Panama Canal in 1914.

Lloyd Pettiford

2.10 Cuba - United States

The US base at Guantánamo Bay in Cuba was in the latter stages of the Cold War the only US base in the world on communist territory. It was leased to the United States for a nominal rent in 1903 as a naval and coaling base by the newly formed Republic of Cuba, the United States being granted full jurisdiction and control over the territory containing the base in return for recognizing Cuban sovereignty over the area. The agreement on the lease was confirmed by a treaty of 1934. In 1960, following a deterioration in US-Cuban relations after Fidel Castro came to power, President Dwight D. Eisenhower issued a statement to the effect that the agreement could only be modified or abrogated with the consent of both parties, and that the USA had no intention of taking any such step. Diplomatic relations between the two countries were severed in January of the following year, and in 1964 the United States made the base self-sufficient after Cuba cut off fresh water supplies on Feb. 6 of that year. Cuba regards the base as being illegally occupied and has not cashed any of the rent payment cheques since 1960.

The Guantánamo base is located on the southern coast of the eastern end of the island of Cuba, at the foot of the Sierra Maestra mountains, in an area of 117 square miles (300 sq km), one-third of which is taken up by Guantánamo Bay (see Map 18, page 501). The bay, the third largest in Cuba, is a deep, sheltered inlet in a strategic location, which was considered at the time of its acquisition as fundamental to the maintenance of US interests in the Caribbean, South America and Central America, as well as for control of the Panama Canal.

Historical Background

Cuba was a Spanish colony from the 15th century until 1898, except for a brief period of British occupation in 1762-63. Cuban rebels fought to achieve the island's independence in the latter half of the 19th century, and the latest of these independence revolts (in 1895) led to the intervention three years later of the United States, which had shown interest in the island from the beginning of the century. A brief war ensued, after which Spanish dominion over Cuba was transferred to the USA with the signature on Dec. 10, 1898, of the Treaty of Paris.

Before the United States declared war on Spain, a joint resolution was passed by the US Congress in April 1898, authorizing intervention. The resolution declared that "the United States hereby disclaims any disposition or intention to exercise sovereignty, jurisdiction or control over said island except for the pacification thereof, and asserts its determination, when that is accomplished, to leave the government and control of the island to its people". It also stated that "the people of the island of Cuba are, and of right ought to be, free and independent" and that "it is the duty of the United States to demand, and the government of the United States does hereby demand, that the government of Spain at once relinquish its authority and government in the island of Cuba and withdraw its land and naval forces from Cuba and Cuban waters".

Cuba remained under US military jurisdiction from 1898 to 1902, when the government of Cuba was handed over to the island's first President under the terms of the Platt Amendment (named after a Connecticut senator, Orville H. Platt, who presented it to the US Senate, although its text was drawn up by the Secretary of War, Elihu Root). The amendment authorized the US President to relinquish the government and control of the island of Cuba to its people "as soon as a government shall have been established in said island under a constitution which, either as a part thereof or in an ordinance appended thereto, shall define the future relations of the United States with Cuba".

The amendment also stated, however, "that the government of Cuba consents that the United States may exercise the right to intervene for the preservation of Cuban independence, the maintenance of a government adequate for the protection of life, property and individual liberty, and for discharging the obligations with respect to Cuba imposed by the Treaty of Paris on the United States, now to be assumed and undertaken by the government of Cuba". Furthermore, Article VII stated that "to enable the United States to maintain the independence of Cuba, and to protect the people thereof, as well as for its own defence, the government of Cuba will sell or lease to the United States the lands necessary for coaling or naval stations at certain specified points to be agreed upon with the President of the United States".

The Platt Amendment was approved by the Cuban constitutional convention by a narrow majority on June 12, 1901, notwithstanding the earlier failure of the Cuban side to have certain qualifications attached to it and in the face of the US threat to continue to occupy the island if it was rejected. The amendment was attached to the new 1901 constitution, but Cuba has regarded it ever since as contradicting the 1898 joint resolution, which committed the USA to respect for Cuban independence.

In line with Article VIII of the Platt Amendment, which said that the provisions of Article VII would be embodied in a treaty with the USA, a Permanent Treaty was signed on May 22, 1903, between Cuba and the United States, providing for the perpetual lease of lands for coaling and naval stations. It became operative through an agreement signed by Cuba on Feb. 16, 1903, and by the USA on Feb. 23 of that year, which stated that Cuba and the USA were desirous to "execute fully Article VII of the Platt Amendment" and that they had thus reached agreement as follows:

"Article I. The Republic of Cuba hereby leases to the United States, for the time required for the purposes of coaling and naval stations, the following described areas of land and water situated in the island of Cuba: (i) in Guantánamo…and (ii) in north-western Cuba in Bahía Honda…

Article II. The grant of the foregoing article shall include the right to use and occupy the waters adjacent to said areas of land and water, and to improve and deepen the entrances thereto and the anchorages therein, and generally to do any and all things necessary to fit the premises for use as coaling or naval stations only, and for no other purpose. Vessels engaged in the Cuban trade shall have free passage through the waters included within this grant.

Article III. While on the one hand the United States recognizes the continuance of the ultimate sovereignty of the Republic of Cuba over the above described areas of land and water, on the other hand the Republic of Cuba consents that during the period of the occupation by the United States of said areas under the terms of this agreement the USA shall exercise complete jurisdiction and control over and within said areas with the right to acquire (under conditions to be hereafter agreed upon by the two governments) for the public purposes of the United States any land or other property therein by purchase or by exercise of eminent domain with full compensation to the owners thereof".

On Dec. 10, 1903, the USA took possession of the land and sea areas leased for the establishment of the base at Guantánamo at a price of US$2,000 a year in gold throughout the period it occupied and used the areas.

On May 29, 1934, Cuba and the USA signed a Treaty on Relations which abrogated the 1903 treaty and the Platt Amendment, although Article II of the new treaty provided the following: "Until the two contracting parties agree to the modification or abrogation of the stipulations of the agreement in regard to the lease to the USA of lands for coaling and naval stations signed…in 1903…the stipulations of that agreement with regard to the naval station of Guantánamo shall continue in effect…So long as the USA shall not abandon the said naval station of Guantánamo or the two governments shall not agree to a modification of its present limits, the station shall continue to have the territorial area that it now has, with the limits that it has on the date of the signature of the present treaty".

Developments after 1959

After the advent of Fidel Castro to power in 1959, the sharp deterioration in relations between Cuba and the USA elevated the US presence at Guantánamo to a major subject of contention. At the UN General Assembly on Sept. 26, 1960, Dr Castro described the US presence on the island as "the most tragic case in the entire history of the bases now scattered over the world" and the base as being "forcibly placed in what is undeniably our territory, a good distance from the coasts of the United States, against Cuba and against the people, imposed by force and constituting a threat to and concern for our people". In a speech on July 26, 1962, the Cuban leader said that the naval base was "a dagger stuck in the heart of Cuba" and a piece of land which Cuba would not reclaim by force but would never renounce.

President Eisenhower, however, stated on Nov. 1, 1960: "Our rights in Guantánamo are based on international agreements with Cuba and include the exercise by the United States of complete jurisdiction and control over the area. These agreements with Cuba can be modified or abrogated only by agreement between the two parties…Our government has no intention of agreeing to the modification or abrogation of these agreements and will take whatever steps may be appropriate to defend the base. The people of the United States, and all of the peoples of the world, can be assured that the United States' presence in Guantánamo and the use of the base pose no threat whatever to the sovereignty of Cuba, to the peace and security of its people, or to the independence of any of the American countries. Because of its importance to the defence of the entire hemisphere, particularly in the light of the intimate relations which now exist between the present government of Cuba and the Sino-

Soviet bloc, it is essential that our position in Guantánamo be clearly understood".

The US government broke off relations with Cuba on Jan. 3, 1961, after Cuba demanded a substantial reduction in the number of US personnel at the US embassy in Havana. Other major crises erupted (i) in April 1961, when a small force of anti-Castro exiles financed by the US Central Intelligence Agency (CIA) landed in the Bay of Pigs in an abortive attempt to overthrow the regime; and (ii) in October 1962, when the presence of Soviet missile bases was discovered in Cuba. Dr Castro in February 1961 said that relations between the USA and Cuba could only be normalized if a number of conditions were met by the former, one of these being the withdrawal of the USA from the Guantánamo base. However, the tacit agreement between the United States and the USSR which concluded the 1962 Missile Crisis implicitly recognized the right of the USA to retain the base provided that it was not used to launch an attack on Cuba.

Cuba has based its demand for the withdrawal of the USA from Guantánamo not only on historical considerations but also on UN General Assembly resolutions, notably (i) Resolution 2105/XX of Dec. 20, 1965, which calls on colonial powers to dismantle military bases in the colonial territories and to refrain from setting up new ones; and (ii) Resolution 2344/XXII of Dec. 19, 1967, which calls on the UN Disarmament Committee to renew its study of the means of eliminating foreign military bases in the Asian, African and Latin American countries in line with Resolution 2105/XX. The Cuban position has also been supported in resolutions approved at conferences of the Non-Aligned Movement.

In 1976 Cuba adopted by referendum a new constitution, Article X of which states: "The Republic of Cuba rejects and considers illegal and null and void all treaties, pacts and concessions which were signed in conditions of inequality or which disregard or diminish its sovereignty over any part of the national territory".

In 1979 press reports that a Soviet brigade was stationed in Cuba prompted President Jimmy Carter to order the US Marine Corps to carry out a landing exercise at Guantánamo Bay, to demonstrate that the base could easily be reinforced in the event of crisis. The 1,800 Marines of the 38th marine Amphibious Unit landed on Oct. 17 and stayed for a month. Reporters covering the exercise found the base decrepit and run-down, but the Cubans complained that the exercise proved that it constituted a threat to them.

Use of Guantánamo for Detention of "Unlawful Combatants"

In 2002 the USA opened a new chapter in the dispute by establishing a camp, "Camp X-Ray", at Guantánamo for more than 650 prisoners captured in the war in Afghanistan (the camp later coming also to house persons arrested elsewhere in the world). Since this activity was not necessary to a naval base, it faced criticism as being contrary to Article I of the Permanent Treaty of 1903 as confirmed by the 1934 treaty (see above).

The US government refused, moreover, to accord the detainees the status of prisoners of war, designating them instead as "unlawful combatants", a status not recognized by the International Committee of the Red Cross, which has responsibility in the application of the Geneva Conventions (to which the USA is a party). Hence on the conclusion of the war in Afghanistan prisoners were not repatriated, as would be required under the Geneva Conventions.

The use of Guantánamo Bay is held by the US government to have removed the prisoners from the jurisdiction of the US courts in that although the USA has jurisdiction at Guantánamo Bay it is not "sovereign territory". Thus those detained at Guantánamo have been deprived of both the protection of the Geneva Conventions and of due process in the US courts. In March 2003 a US appeals court held that the US courts had no jurisdiction as the detainees were foreign nationals held outside US territory, a decision condemned by the UN Commissioner on Human Rights as leaving the detainees in a legal limbo. The issue has yet to be decided by the US Supreme Court.

Peter Calvert

2.11 Ecuador - Peru

From the first half of the nineteenth century, a large area of the Amazon Basin in what is now the north Peruvian department of Loreto was claimed by Ecuador. The dispute over the area evolved after the various territorial reorganizations under Spanish colonial rule. Ecuador regarded the area as part of the Audiencia of Quito, from which Ecuador derived its territorial jurisdiction on independence in 1822, and complained that Peru had deprived the country of access to either the Amazon river or to the region's other main waterway, the Marañón, thus leaving it without direct access to the Atlantic.

After engaging in hostilities over the issue in 1941, the two sides signed an internationally agreed protocol in Rio de Janeiro in January 1942 (the Rio Protocol) under which the whole of the disputed territory was allocated to Peru. Successive Ecuadorian governments felt, however, that the settlement had been unfairly imposed on them in the interests of hemispheric solidarity following Pearl Harbor. The border remained unmarked and the Protocol was unilaterally declared null and void in 1960 by the Ecuadorian government of the day. From then on, successive governments reaffirmed Ecuador's rights over the Amazon Basin. Peru, on the other hand, regarded the border problem as having been settled by the Rio Protocol.

In 1981 the dispute flared up again with a five-day war between the two countries over an undemarcated section of frontier, and only when an even more severe conflict broke out in 1995 was sufficient diplomatic effort engaged to resolve it. A definitive agreement was signed in 1998.

The area remaining in dispute after 1942 covered 125,000 square miles (325,000 sq km) and included both the Amazon and Marañón rivers. It contained Iquitos, a fast-developing city on the west bank of the Amazon, and also Peru's main inland oil-producing region (in territory between the Tigre and Corrientes rivers in the north). Ecuador claims to have discovered the Amazon, maintaining that the expedition led by Francisco de Orellana set out from Quito in 1542 (although this is disputed by Peru).

Map 19 on page 502 illustrates this dispute.

Origins of the Dispute

The main area of contention between Ecuador and Peru comprised the provinces of Maynas, Tumbes and Jaén. Under Spanish rule these provinces were part of the Audiencia of Quito under the Viceroyalty of Peru. The Audiencia's southern boundary (according to a Spanish royal decree of 1740) ran along the Marañón and Amazon from Tumbes on the Pacific coast, to the borders of the Portuguese territories (Brazil). In 1739 the Audiencia of Quito was attached to the Viceroyalty of Nueva Granada, centred on Bogotá.

In further administrative changes under a Spanish Royal Decree of 1802, the government and commandancy-general of Maynas were separated from Nueva Granada and reattached to the Viceroyalty of Peru, together with the government of Quijos province. In the 1802 decree the frontiers of the Maynas commandancy-general were described as extending along the Marañón to the frontier of the Portuguese territories and also along all the other rivers which entered the Marañón on its northern and southern banks, and other small streams, up to where those rivers ceased to be navigable because of falls or rapids.

Peru thus contended that at the time of its own independence in 1821 Maynas was administered by the Viceroyalty of Peru, pointing out that Ecuador did not exist as such (being part of the Gran Colombia federation until 1830). Ecuador, on the other hand, maintained that the 1802 decree separated only certain military and ecclesiastical aspects of Maynas province from the administration of Nueva Granada at that time, and that Maynas was thus still part of the Viceroyalty of Nueva Granada. Ecuador based its claim to the disputed area largely on (i) an 1829 peace and border treaty, signed between Peru and Gran Colombia, and (ii) an 1830 protocol to this treaty, whose existence is disputed by Peru. The 1829 Guayaquil Treaty was concluded in an effort to settle the territorial conflict which had erupted into a crisis in 1828 after Peru reasserted a claim to Jaén province and also to the whole of Maynas by convening elections there in

1826. Gran Colombia opposed the Peruvian claim to Jaén at this stage on the grounds that Jaén had requested to be reincorporated into the Gran Colombia federation in 1824 despite having earlier become independent; as for Maynas, Peru had previously restricted itself to convening elections in the southern part of that province. On expiry of an ultimatum to Peru to relinquish Jaén and south Maynas, Gran Colombia declared war on Peru in July 1828, and in September of that year Peru blockaded Gran Colombia's ports. The Peruvian Navy captured Guayaquil in 1829 and its army occupied the Colombian province of Loja, but was eventually defeated. The immediate conflict ended with a Colombian victory over Peru at Tarqui in February 1829 and a preliminary peace agreement was concluded. Following a change of government in Peru in June 1829, a truce was signed at Piura in July and talks took place, resulting in the signature of the Guayaquil treaty on Sept. 22, 1829, which stated that both parties recognized as their territorial limits "those of the old viceroyalties".

Peru later regarded this treaty as null and void because it had been concluded with Gran Colombia, and claimed that it was superseded by a later treaty of alliance and friendship signed with Ecuador in 1832 in Lima, which stated that the existing boundaries should be recognized until a boundary convention was negotiated. Ecuador claimed, in contrast, that as a successor state to Gran Colombia, it assumed the rights and duties concerning the area that became Ecuador and that the 1832 treaty was never formally ratified.

On Aug. 11, 1830, just before Ecuador emerged as a separate state, Gran Colombia and Peru signed the Mosquero-Pedemonte protocol, supplementary to the Treaty of Guayaquil, establishing guidelines for the delimitation of their borders. It stated that the Marañón, the Macara and the Tumbes rivers were to be the definitive borders and recognized the full sovereignty of Gran Colombia over all territory on the left bank of the Marañón, and that of Peru over all the territory on the right bank. Peru claimed that the original of this protocol was never exhibited by Ecuador.

Efforts to negotiate a boundary treaty and Peru's recognition of the 1829 treaty during the 1840s failed. In November 1853 Ecuador passed a law establishing free international navigation on rivers such as the Chinchipe, Santiago, Morona, Pastuza, Tigre, Curaray, Napo, Putumayo and other Amazon tributaries and on the section of the Amazon claimed by Ecuador. This provoked a protest from Peru that the rivers came within the limits established by the 1802 decree and were therefore part of Peru. In 1857 Peru broke off relations with Ecuador after Ecuador had decided to pay off certain debts to British creditors in the form of land, including part of Quijos and Canelos provinces over which Peru claimed sovereignty. Preparations were made for war, but only a blockade of Ecuador's ports was decreed in 1858 by President Ramón Castilla of Peru, this not being lifted until August 1859. Peru subsequently claimed that these hostilities were another reason for the invalidation of the Guayaquil treaty, but

Ecuador denied that a proper war had taken place and asserted that the treaty remained in force.

In 1860, during a period of confused government inside Ecuador, the Mapasingue Convention was signed, annulling Ecuador's transfer of land to British creditors and establishing the 1802 decree as a provisional basis for the delimitation of territory. This convention was, however, rejected by the Peruvian Congress and by the newly-established constitutional government of Ecuador.

In 1887 the two sides signed the Espinosa-Bonifaz Treaty, which established that they wished to solve amicably any border questions and that any such issues should be submitted to the King of Spain for arbitration. On the basis of this treaty, arbitration began in 1904, but both countries later refused to accept any award against their interest and the arbitration was suspended. Negotiations recommenced in 1936, but proved fruitless and were adjourned after two years.

The 1941 War and the 1942 Protocol of Rio de Janeiro

On July 5, 1941, despite efforts by Argentina, Brazil and the United States to forestall a conflict, hostilities broke out between Peru and Ecuador, the immediate cause being the stationing of garrisons in the disputed border areas. Stronger military forces allowed Peru to gain the upper hand, as Peruvian forces occupied parts of the disputed territory and the coastal Ecuadorian province of El Rio del Oro, but on Oct. 2, through the efforts of the mediatory nations, the two countries signed the Act of Talará which established a ceasefire and a demilitarized zone along the most advanced positions of the two armies. On Oct. 4, the mediatory nations, through a memorandum, called on the two sides to withdraw their troops to positions 15 kilometres behind the 1936 status quo line as a prior condition to negotiating a settlement.

A Protocol of Peace, Friendship and Boundaries (the Protocol of Rio de Janeiro) was concluded on Jan. 29, 1942, between Peru and Ecuador with the participation of the mediatory nations after negotiations which began on Jan. 13. It was ratified by the Congresses of both Peru and Ecuador on Feb. 26, 1942. Its main provisions were as follows:

"*Article 1*. The governments of Peru and Ecuador solemnly affirm their determined intention to maintain between the two peoples relations of peace and friendship, understanding and goodwill and to abstain each in respect of the other from any act capable of disrupting these relations.

"*Article 2*. The government of Peru will within 15 days withdraw its military forces to the line described in Article 8 of this protocol.

"*Article 3*. The United States, Argentina, Brazil and Chile will co-operate by means of military observers in order to adjust to the circumstances the evacuation and withdrawal of troops under the terms of the previous article.

"*Article 4*. The military forces of the two countries will remain in their positions until the definitive demarcation of the frontier line. Until then, Ecuador shall have civil jurisdiction only in the zones which Peru shall evacuate, which remain in the same state as was the demilitarized zone of the Act of Talará.

"*Article 5*. The negotiation of the USA, Argentina, Brazil and Chile shall continue until the frontiers between Ecuador and Peru have been definitively demarcated, and this protocol and its execution shall remain under the guarantee of [these] four countries.

"*Article 6*. Ecuador shall enjoy the same concessions for navigation on the Amazon and its northern tributaries as Brazil and Colombia, beyond those which are agreed in a treaty on commerce and navigation designed to facilitate navigation on these rivers.

"*Article 7*. Any doubt or disagreement which may arise over the execution of this protocol shall be resolved by the parties with the collaboration of the representatives of the USA, Argentina, Brazil and Chile within the shortest possible time".

Article 8 established the border line with reference to named points.

"*Article 9*. It is understood that the line described above shall be accepted by Ecuador and Peru for the establishment by technicians in that field of the frontier between the two countries. The parties shall nevertheless, in proceeding with their plan of terrain, be able to grant each other reciprocal concessions which they consider proper in order to adjust to the geographical reality. Such rectifications shall be carried out with the collaboration of representatives of the USA, Argentina, Brazil and Chile".

Considerable problems of demarcation ensued, notably in the southern sector, where the Rio Protocol specified that the border should follow the line of the watershed between the Zamora and Santiago rivers (running to the north-west and east respectively of the Cordillera del Cóndor, or Condor mountains). Matters were complicated by the discovery in 1947 (by US aerial photographers) of a new river system, the Cenepa, running north-south into the Marañón between the Zamora and Santiago rivers and separated from each by a natural watershed. In the view of Ecuador, this discovery invalidated the relevant clause of the protocol—which was now shown to have referred to a non-existent single watershed—and entitled Ecuador to additional territory to the south and east of the line of the Cordillera del Cóndor ridge which Peru regarded as the proper boundary. This view was strongly asserted by President Galo Plaza Lasso in a message to the Ecuadorian Congress in August 1951, when he said that his government could only accept a border in this sector which recognized "the inalienable Amazonian right of Ecuador" and allocated it "a proper and sovereign right to the Marañón river".

Demarcation of the frontier then stopped, leaving a 50-mile (80-kilometre) stretch in the southern sector uncharted, and with the line adopted by Peru strongly disputed by Ecuador. Ecuadorian proposals that a special mixed commission should study the geography of the area were rejected by Peru, as was a mediation offer made at Ecuador's request by the four guarantor states. In consequence, in 1960 President José Velasco Ibarra of Ecuador declared the entire Rio Protocol null and void, arguing that acquisition of territorial rights by force was proscribed under the 1933 Montevideo Convention on the Rights and Duties of States, and that Ecuador had been coerced into signing the protocol against its wishes while areas of its territory had been occupied by force. Nevertheless, on Dec. 7, 1960, Ecuador's repudiation of the protocol was declared invalid by the four guarantor powers.

The 1981 Hostilities and Subsequent Developments

Over the two decades following Ecuador's repudiation of the Rio Protocol, co-operative relations between the two countries developed within the framework of various multilateral regional agreements, notably the Andean Pact (created in 1969; now the Andean Community–ANCOM) and the Amazon Co-operation Treaty (signed in 1978). Nevertheless, Ecuador continued to assert its claim to territorial rights in the Amazon Basin, showing the area as belonging to Ecuador in official maps and documents.

Early in 1981 the situation deteriorated sharply in the Condor mountains sector when on Jan. 23, 1981, a Peruvian military helicopter was said by Ecuador to have violated its airspace and to have fired on one of its border posts, and by Peru to have been fired on by Ecuadorian soldiers while on a routine flight. Five days later, on Jan. 28, fighting erupted on the ground as Peruvian forces engaged Ecuadorian troops who had apparently occupied three military posts—Paquisha, Mayayco and Machinaza—several kilometres east of the Condor ridge line which Peru regarded as the international frontier in this sector. The border between the two countries was immediately closed, both sides declared states of emergency and large numbers of troops were mobilized by both sides. After five days of hostilities, a ceasefire came into force on Feb. 2, by which time Peru claimed to have driven the Ecuadorian forces out of the three border posts.

The ceasefire was established in response to a call by representatives of the four guarantors of the Rio Protocol (the United States, Argentina, Brazil and Chile), meeting in Brasília on Feb. 1, 1981, when it was also agreed in consultation with Ecuador and Peru that a military commission of the four countries would supervise the disrupted area. A further serious incident occurred on Feb. 20, when a Peruvian helicopter was shot down in the border area, causing Peru's President to issue a warning on Feb. 22 that "any new infiltration" by Ecuador would be "regarded as an act of war". However, the four guarantor countries announced on Feb. 26 that Ecuador and Peru had agreed to pull their troops 15 kilometres back on either side of the disputed border and to enter into discussions on "a formula for assuring harmony and opening the way to broader agreements". These talks began immediately and resulted in a firm agreement on March 5 on the withdrawal of forces; at the same time, the two sides undertook to maintain peaceful relations and also requested the guarantor countries to propose a solution to their underlying dispute. No such solution was found in the succeeding years, however, and tensions surfaced periodically between the two countries, notably in January 1984 when an Ecuadorian soldier was killed in a clash with Peruvian border guards at a frontier post on the Corrientes river about 400 kilometres south-east of Quito.

Tensions again increased during 1991, culminating in Peruvian allegations in August 1991 of an alleged "invasion" by Ecuadorian troops. (This claim was admitted to have been false by the Peruvian defence minister in October.) The background to the incident was reported to be Ecuador's attempts to persuade Peru to remove a newly established military outpost within a demarcated area. When the Peruvians failed to comply, Ecuador set up its own outpost nearby. After diplomatic exchanges both countries agreed on Aug. 27 to withdraw their troops in the area, but the Peruvian troops were not withdrawn and withdrawal was made conditional on the removal of a long-established Ecuadorian post. On Sept. 15 the four guarantor countries of the Rio Protocol called for a solution to the conflict without bloodshed and tensions gradually reduced, with troops on both sides being pulled back from close proximity in the area during October.

Moves towards reconciliation occurred on Nov. 24, 1991, when President Alberto Keinya Fujimori of Peru proposed a framework that involved (i) completing the demarcation of the border in the Cordillera del Cóndor using the good offices of the Rio Protocol guarantor countries, (ii) joint economic development projects, and (iii) navigation rights for Ecuador on the Peruvian Amazon and tributaries, without which any land that Ecuador might hold would be of little value. The President of Ecuador, Rodrigo Borja Cevallos, responded positively to the proposals, but stressed Ecuador's rejection of the Rio Protocol. The two Presidents met to discuss the issue during a Group of Rio heads of government meeting in Cartagena, Colombia, on Dec. 2-3. On Jan. 9, 1992, Fujimori started a three-day visit to Ecuador, the first official visit by a Peruvian head of state since the 1941 war. Fujimori agreed to Borja's request for papal mediation in the dispute, but only through a joint appeal to the Vatican by the two countries, and for the four guarantor countries of the Rio Protocol to appoint an expert to arbitrate on the disputed border.

The 1998 Settlement

War broke out again in late January 1995 along the 78-km long undemarcated frontier zone of the Cordillera del Cóndor. It resumed in early February after diplomatic intervention by the four guarantor powers of the 1942 Protocol of Rio de Janeiro had failed to secure agreement. Fighting between thousands of soldiers on both sides was fiercest around the headwaters of the disputed Cenepa River, which not only afforded Ecuador some access to the Amazon, but was also persistently reported to hold previously unknown oil reserves.

Peru's President Alberto Fujimori visited the region on Feb. 15 after declaring a unilateral ceasefire. Ecuadorian officials, however, disputed the claim made by him that Peruvian troops had captured the Ecuadorian bases of Cueva de los Tayos, Base Sur and Tiwintza. Two days later the ceasefire was formally "confirmed" by the two sides at a conference attended by the representative of the guarantor powers at the Itamaraty Palace, Brasília, but was almost immediately broken by an alleged Peruvian attack on Tiwintza. Fighting formally ended on Feb. 28, with a fresh meeting between the Foreign Ministers and the guarantor powers in Montevideo, when both sides accepted the immediate deployment of observers. However, skirmishing continued and when the monitored separation of forces began on March 30 some 500 men had been killed and several thousand wounded. The first proposals for demilitarization were rejected by Ecuador in May as unworkable, and it was not until July 25 that agreement was reached with Peru at Williamsburg in the USA for both sides to withdraw all military personnel from the disputed zone, the process to be monitored by an Ecuador-Peru Military Observer Mission (MOMEP).

On Sept. 3 Peru formally re-opened the frontier to trade; on Oct. 6 both sides agreed to talks on the dispute in January 1996; and on Oct. 25 the state of emergency was lifted. Relations between the two countries remained uneasy, though, until following talks in both Quito and Lima, a memorandum of understanding was signed on March 4, 1996, by the commanders of the armed forces on both sides, this establishing confidence-building measures and a framework for further talks. Meanwhile the mandate of MOMEP continued to be extended until a definitive settlement could be achieved. Seven Ecuadorian soldiers, allegedly captured on May 13, 1997, planting mines on land disputed by Peru, were repatriated two days later.

Talks continued and the first breakthrough came in Brasília on Nov. 24-28, 1997, when both sides formally agreed to make peace and to settle their common land border. In January 1998 they agreed on a framework by which four commissions would be set up to deal with all outstanding issues. The commission on the demarcation of the border, however, failed to reach agreement by the deadline of May 30. Following a flare-up in military tension a new agreement on Aug. 13 committed both parties to pull back their troops "temporarily" from the disputed territory, creating a temporary demilitarized zone to the south of the first, also under the supervision of MOMEP. From this point on President Fujimori and the newly elected President of Ecuador, Jamil Mahuad Witt, kept in close personal touch by telephone and meetings to overcome remaining points of difference.

On Sept. 27-28, 1998, agreement was reached on a trade and navigation treaty, which was a necessary corollary to a boundary agreement. Arrangements were also agreed for the clearance of minefields in the dis-

puted frontier zone of the Corderilla del Cóndor. The two Presidents then jointly requested a boundary determination from the four guarantor powers. Following congressional agreement in each case, the two Presidents then signed a formal agreement in Brasília on Oct. 26, accepting the boundary determination given at their request by the four guarantor states and providing for its future administration, thus bringing this long-running dispute to a satisfactory conclusion. This treaty, the Presidential Act of Brasília, was ratified by the Ecuadorian Congress on Nov. 20, and in February 1999 the Presidents of Ecuador and Peru jointly attended the placing in the Lagartococha area of the first of the 27 markers which were to delimit the common frontier thus finally agreed.

Article 1 of the Presidential Act affirms the decision of both nations to resolve their differences.

Article 2: "They state that with the binding determination issued by the Heads of State of the Guarantor Powers, in their letter of October 23, 1998, which forms an integral part of this document, the frontier disputes between the two countries have been definitively resolved. On this basis, the firm and unalterable will of the respective Governments has been registered to complete, in the shortest possible time, the delimitation of the common land frontier".

Article 3 incorporates a list of agreements between the two countries which are to be submitted to domestic procedures to bring them into force as soon as possible.

Article 4 "solemnly reaffirms the renunciation of the threat or use of force in relations between Peru and Ecuador, or any act which could affect the peace and friendship between the two nations".

Article 5 thanks the guarantor powers for their good offices.

Peter Calvert

2.12 El Salvador - Honduras

The dispute between El Salvador and Honduras has been one of the most protracted in Central America, dating back to the 19th century and flaring up into brief hostilities in 1969 (the "Football" or "Soccer" War). A major step towards the resolution of this dispute was the signing of a peace treaty between the two countries in 1980 demarcating two-thirds of the common frontier. The outstanding issues were submitted in 1986 to the International Court of Justice, which in 1992 gave its judgement dividing the contested territory. Detailed demarcation of the border is still underway. (See Map 20, page 502.)

Efforts to Resolve Border Issue in 19th Century

Both El Salvador and Honduras belonged to a federation of Central American states until this was dissolved in 1838. According to Honduras' first political constitution, decreed on Dec. 11, 1825, the country's territorial area corresponded to that covered under Spanish rule by the "Bishopric of Honduras", while El Salvador's first two constitutions (1824 and 1841) specified that its own territorial area corresponded to certain Spanish administrative areas and established its frontiers broadly as the River Paz (in the west), the inlet of Conchagua (in the east), the province of Chiquimula (in the north) and the Pacific Ocean to the south.

A number of local border disputes had already emerged by 1884, and on April 10 of that year the two sides signed a border convention in San Miguel (El Salvador). In the light of the data available to them on territorial claims, this convention fixed land and sea limits from the Gulf of Fonseca (in the Pacific) to the Guatemalan frontier. However, Honduras regarded the convention as prejudicing the rights of Hondurans because it had not taken into account the claims of certain localities on the frontier. Consequently the Honduran Congress on Feb. 7, 1885, abrogated the convention, although it agreed the following month to take all the necessary measures to arrive at a permanent solution to the border problem.

To this end, representatives of the two governments met on Sept. 28, 1886, in Tegucigalpa (Honduras) and decided to set up commissions to determine the delimitation of the border by mutual agreement, it being agreed (i) that both governments would respect the outcome; (ii) that if no agreement was reached the dispute would be submitted to a friendly nation for arbitration; and (iii) that, while the new border line was being drawn, the 1884 line, regarded as the status quo, would be respected.

The two commissions set to work in late 1888 but could only reach agreement on the section of the frontier "constituted by the Goascorán river, from its mouth in La Unión bay (Gulf of Fonseca) upriver to where it flows into the Guajiniquil river", this section being declared "undisputed and indisputable". The commissions were then dissolved without further agreement being reached, and although the two governments agreed in San José (Costa Rica) on Jan. 3, 1889, to put the dispute to the President of Costa Rica for arbitration, no such step was taken.

On Jan. 19, 1895, the Bonilla-Velasco border convention was signed in San Salvador, under the terms of which representatives of the two countries met on Nov. 13, 1897, to work out the delimitation of the frontier between Opatoro and Santa Ana (Honduras) and Lislique and Poloros (El Salvador). The treaty bore little fruit, however, since it was ratified by neither country, and there were few further developments during the period of the treaty's subsequent extension up to 1916. Moreover, no significant progress towards solving the border issue was made over the next 50 years.

The 1969 Football War and its Aftermath

Although the immediate cause of the 1969 war was a series of incidents and violence following World Cup qualifying matches between the two countries' national teams, the major underlying cause was a deep-rooted conflict over Salvadoran immigration to, and settlement in, Honduras. From the 1920s onwards thousands of Salvadorans left their densely populated country and took over pieces of land in Honduras for cultivation. Although a bilateral migration agreement was signed in 1965 giving them the opportunity to regularize their position in Honduras, the latter country estimated that fewer than one per cent of the migrants took advantage of this facility.

In January 1969 the Honduran government applied an agrarian reform which meant that thousands of Salvadorans were expelled from the land on which they had lived. Some 300,000 faced deportation, and the homeward exodus of Salvadorans placed increasing strains on the Salvadoran political and economic systems. As a result, El Salvador's military government broke off diplomatic relations with Honduras following the football incidents, and full-scale fighting began on July 14 after a series of border incidents in the preceding two weeks. The Salvadoran armed forces occupied an area of Honduran territory and bombarded towns and border areas before hostilities ceased on July 18 under a truce negotiated by the Organization of American States (OAS).

The OAS on Oct. 27, 1969, passed seven resolutions regarding bilateral relations between El Salvador and Honduras, covering (i) peace and treaties, (ii) free transit, (iii) diplomatic and consular relations, (iv) border questions, (v) the Central American Common Market, (vi) claims and differences and (vii) human and family rights. These were to form the basis of the general peace treaty signed in October 1980. In the meantime, however, a bilateral working group with a Uruguayan moderator was set up to work towards solving their differences, and met throughout 1970 and 1971.

On June 4, 1970, a "Plan for the Establishment of a Zone of Security with a View to Pacification" was signed in San José, Costa Rica, creating a three-kilometre-wide demilitarized zone on each side of the traditional border; measures were adopted to put this into effect not only on land but also at sea and in the airspace above the demilitarized zone. OAS military observers were designated to supervise the execution of the plan, and Guatemala, Nicaragua and Costa Rica became its guarantors. However, although the plan was designed to allow the inhabitants of both countries to return to the frontier area in safety, its content was stated to have no bearing on any border claim.

Contacts between representatives of the two countries continued over the next few years and work progressed towards the elaboration of a treaty on the basis of the seven OAS resolutions. In July 1976 there were fresh military incidents on the border which led to meetings between the Foreign Ministers of the guarantor nations of the San José plan, and subsequently to the signature on Aug. 9, 1976, of the Act and Protocol of Managua, which placed OAS military observers on the frontier itself. The protocol specified the areas where incidents had frequently occurred as Dolores, Sabanetas, Sazalapa and Las Pilas (in Honduras) and Sazalapa and Monteca (in El Salvador).

The 1980 Lima Peace Treaty

After four years of negotiation under the mediation of Dr José Luis Bustamante y Rivero (a former President of Peru and also of the International Court of Justice in The Hague), a general peace treaty was signed in Lima (Peru) on Oct. 30, 1980, by the Salvadoran and Honduran Foreign Ministers, respectively Fidel Chávez Mena and Col. César Elvir Sierra. Instruments of ratification were subsequently exchanged on Dec. 10, 1980, at a ceremony in Tegucigalpa.

Section IV of the treaty, covering border questions, described the delimitation of the 225 kilometres of border over which there was no controversy (Article 16) and stated that the border was "invariable in perpetuity". The demarcation of this section of the border, the delimitation of that in the disputed areas and the determination of the juridical situation with regard to islands and maritime areas were referred to a mixed border commission set up on May 1, 1980, which was to complete its task within five years (Articles 18-19).

To delimit the border in the disputed areas (among which were parts of the Chalatenango and La Unión provinces of El Salvador and the Goascorán river delta), the mixed commission was authorized to use as a basis documents issued by the Spanish Crown or by any other Spanish secular or ecclesiastical authority during the colonial epoch which dealt with jurisdictional areas or territorial limits; other evidence would be taken into account of a legal, historical or human nature, or of a kind recognized under international law (Article 26). Each new delimitation required the approval of both governments in the form of additional protocols to the treaty (Article 27), and if there was a disagreement within the border commission itself the case would be referred to both governments for a pronouncement to be made within 60 days (Article 28). It was further established that if no agreement was reached on the areas in dispute within the five years laid down, the case would be submitted to the International Court of Justice (Article 31).

Until the frontier had been fully delimited, the two parties undertook not to alter the status quo which existed in the disputed areas prior to July 14, 1969, and to re-establish the status quo in so far as it had been modified, in order to guarantee peace in the areas in question (Article 37). During the five-year period of work of the border commission neither side could unilaterally have recourse to other peaceful means of solving the conflict or place it before international bodies (Article 38), with the proviso that if both sides agreed it could be submitted to the International Court of Justice within the five years (Article 39).

The other major provisions of the treaty were that both sides agreed to maintain "firm and lasting peace, solid fraternity and permanent constructive co-operation" (Article 2); that they would allow free transit across their territory of each other's goods and nationals (Articles 7-9); that they would restore diplomatic relations fully without further formalities (Articles 10-14); that they would contribute to the restructuring of the Central American Common Market (Articles 40-41); that they would not claim compensation for damages incurred in or just before July 1969 (Article 42); and that they would respect the rights of each other's nationals and allow them to reside freely in their countries (Articles 44-45).

The border between El Salvador and Honduras was reopened on Dec. 11, 1980, and thereafter relations between the two countries improved as Honduras gave increasing support to the Salvadoran government in its struggle against left-wing insurgents, and both countries backed US-sponsored actions against the left-wing Sandinista regime in Nicaragua. Talks on the demarcation of the disputed border areas were resumed by a joint border commission on July 20, 1982, and on Aug. 23 of that year an agreement was signed providing for the restoration of trade links from Sept. 1 in accordance with Article 41 of the 1980 Lima treaty. It was stated that both countries were committed to the policy objectives of the new Central American Democratic Community (CDC) established in January 1982 (and also including Costa Rica).

Submission of Dispute to International Court of Justice

Notwithstanding regular meetings of the joint border commission (and talks between the Salvadoran and Honduran Presidents in October 1984 and July 1985), it was apparent by the end of the five-year period specified in the 1980 agreement that most key issues remained to be resolved. Accordingly, Presidents Duarte of El Salvador and Azcona of Honduras signed an agreement on May 24, 1986 (during a Central American summit meeting in Guatemala), providing for the submission of the dispute to the International Court of Justice (ICJ). This agreement entered into force on Oct. 1, 1986, and on Dec. 11 of that year the two governments formally notified the ICJ of their decision.

During talks in El Salvador on July 30-31, 1986, the Salvadoran and Honduran Presidents undertook to implement fully the ICJ's eventual ruling. They also agreed on the advisability of creating a special commission to study and propose solutions to the human, civil and economic problems that might arise once the border dispute had been resolved.

The submission of the border dispute to the ICJ did not, however, eliminate all of the tensions between the two countries. The presence in border regions of guerrillas belonging to the Farabundo Martí National Liberation Front (FMLN) fighting the government of El Salvador, led to a number of clashes between Salvadoran and Honduran troops as Salvadoran troops engaged in "hot pursuit" counter-insurgency operations, particularly since the guerrillas tended to be based in the disputed areas. On May 30, 1989, Honduras complained officially over an attack on a

Honduran patrol in Honduran waters on May 23 and a violation of airspace on May 29. It was anticipated that the peace agreement reached between the FMLN and the Salvadoran government in late 1991, and implemented at the end of January 1992, would assist in the reduction of tensions in the disputed areas.

The ICJ constituted a chamber to consider the case on May 8, 1987, consisting of five judges, including one each appointed by El Salvador and Honduras. Each party in the dispute then engaged in presenting their case and replying to the other's presentation, extending the length of the case.

Intervention of Nicaragua

On Nov. 17, 1989, Nicaragua applied for permission to intervene in the case, stating that it did not want to interfere in the land boundary dispute, but that it wished to protect its legal rights in the Gulf of Fonseca. The demarcation of the maritime boundaries in the Gulf of Fonseca had long been a matter of contention between the three countries. The Gulf provides Honduras's only access to the Pacific and also access to El Salvador's important port of La Unión. Nicaragua wanted to ensure that any agreement on the boundaries, including the division of the small islets in the Gulf, would not impinge on its rights of navigation in the Gulf. All three countries regarded the Gulf as a "historic bay" following the judgement of the Central American Court of Justice on March 9, 1917, which had heard a complaint by El Salvador against Nicaragua. This agreement, however, had not included any precise delimitation of territorial waters, islands or undersea soil in the Gulf, nor rights of jurisdiction or co-ownership.

On Feb. 28, 1990, the chamber considered whether the chamber or the full Court should consider Nicaragua's application to intervene. On Sept. 13 it agreed that Nicaragua had a legal interest in the waters of the Gulf of Fonseca and was allowed to intervene in the case, but strictly only in matters concerning that area. On Sept. 5, 1990, it was announced that Honduras and Nicaragua had established a mixed commission for maritime affairs to deal with mutual problems, such as fishing rights.

ICJ Ruling

The chamber of the ICJ held hearings on each of the six sections of land frontier under dispute: Nahuaterique, Polorós (Dolores), Tepangüisir, Montaña de Cayaguanca (or Las Pilas), Arcatao (or Zazalapa) and the Goascorán river delta, plus the islands in the Gulf of Fonseca (principally Meanguera and Meanguerita) and the Gulf itself.

The dispute was believed resolved by the judgement of the ICJ handed down on Sept. 11, 1992. Under it Honduras was to receive approximately two-thirds of the mainland territory under dispute, and the island of El Tigre in the Gulf of Fonseca, which was in future to be shared with Nicaragua.

The Honduras-El Salvador Border Protocol, ratified by Honduras in 1999, then established a framework for border demarcation. The situation was somewhat complicated in 2002 by the discovery of an antique map which allowed El Salvador to appeal against the original decision within the 10-year timespan allowed. However, most of the original decision is unaffected, with El Salvador claiming just a small area around the Goascorán river, and Honduras has indicated its flexibility should the discovery be authenticated. In response to this new hitch, the Presidents of both countries resolved to speed up the work of border demarcation and the OAS appointed John Gates as a technical assistant to speed the process. He is assisting the two sides on engineering matters, for instance where the original ICJ judgement appears to conflict with geographical features on the ground.

Lloyd Pettiford

2.13 France (French Guiana) - Suriname

There is a dispute between Suriname (a Dutch possession until 1975) and France on behalf of the French overseas department of French Guiana (Guyane) over the sovereignty of a triangular area of land totalling some 5,000 sq km and lying between two upper tributaries of the Maroni river. (See Map 21, page 503.) Earlier disputes over the course of the lower reaches of the river have been settled at various times in the past, but disagreement about the upper course of the river, and hence over the sovereignty of the land concerned, have not been settled. The area is heavily forested, mountainous and sparsely inhabited, while the economic potential of the area remains uncertain.

Historical Background

France and the Netherlands, as the colonial powers controlling the area, first reached an agreement in 1688 specifying that the Maroni river should form the boundary between their respective colonies. At this stage, however, neither country attached great importance to the largely uncharted interior of the territory, preferring to concentrate on the more accessible coastal lands and on the Maroni estuary, which is navigable for a distance of some 40 kilometres. The lower 160 kilometres of the Maroni had thereafter always been respected as the boundary between the two colonies. Differences arose, however, in the early 19th century as to whether the boundary further inland should follow the Tapanahoni river (originating in the south-west of what is now Suriname) or the Awa (or Lawa) river (flowing from the south), these two rivers being of comparable length (although the Awa is wider at the confluence).

Dutch colonists had by this time begun the exploration and settlement of the areas between the Tapanahoni and the Awa, although there was also a limited French presence in the area. The boundary question remained vague for many years, but acquired a new currency in 1815 when France and Portugal reached an agreement at the Congress of Vienna to specify the boundaries of French Guiana with Brazil. A subsequent convention, signed by France and Portugal on Aug. 28, 1817, also defined French Guiana's western boundary as following the Maroni and Tapanahoni rivers. This agreement was reached without the consultation of the Netherlands, which protested against the decision.

On Nov. 9, 1836, the colonial governors of Cayenne and Suriname reached a formal agreement that the western boundary of French Guiana should be the right bank of the Maroni river from its source. This did not define whether it regarded the Tapanahoni or Awa as the source and was subsequently declared by the Dutch in 1849 not to be a definite settlement of the question. A mixed commission was therefore set up by the two colonial governors in 1861, but it failed to reach a conclusive decision.

Renewed efforts to resolve the dispute led on Nov. 29, 1888, to the signature in Paris of an undertaking to put the dispute before an independent arbitrator. Tsar Alexander III of Russia was eventually chosen, but he accepted only on condition that he could choose, if he wished, a middle course between the two rivers rather than one of the two rivers themselves. Although the Netherlands initially objected, this was accepted by both parties. The arbitration body, sitting on May 13-25, 1891, found that the Dutch had maintained military outposts on the Awa since 1700, that the French government had recognized the jurisdiction of the Dutch over "negroes" in the disputed area and that both parties had agreed that the Maroni from its source should be the boundary. It was therefore decided that the Awa should be considered the upper course of the Maroni and the boundary between the two colonies.

The development of the Awa region soon led to further uncertainties as to which of the Awa's tributaries—the Itany (Litani), flowing from the south-west, or the Marouini (Marowijni), flowing from the south-east—ought to considered as its main course. It is this dispute which is still current. At the same time a number of disputes arose over the use of the Maroni estuary. A conference was therefore called at The Hague on April 25-May 13, 1905, to discuss these problems. At the conference it was agreed that the Itany should be regarded as forming the boundary and that the Thalweg principle (defining the border as following the deepest channel) should apply to the estuary. A further agreement was signed by France and the Netherlands in Paris on Sept. 30, 1915, which replaced the Thalweg decision (disputed by the Netherlands) with another which declared that the boundary in the estuary should be the median line at ordinary water level, with sovereignty of the islands in the estuary determined according to whether the greater part of its area lay on the Suriname or French Guianese side.

Developments since the Independence of Suriname

Despite the 1905 recommendations, however, the area between the Marouini and the Itany continued to be claimed by the Netherlands, and discussions since then have reached no positive result on the issue. Suriname assumed the claim to the disputed territory when it attained independence from the Netherlands in 1975. Negotiations conducted in November 1975 and February 1977 resulted in the formulation of a treaty between France and Suriname whereby the latter would recognize French sovereignty over most of the area still in dispute in return for French development aid totalling some 500,000,000 francs for the joint development of any resources in the area. The treaty was initialled on Aug. 15, 1977, but it was not subsequently signed or ratified.

The relationship between the two countries deteriorated in the 1980s, initially as a consequence of the military coup in Suriname that unseated the administration of Prime Minister Henck Arron, and particularly after the mid-1980s and the start of the campaign in eastern Suriname by the Jungle Commando. The Jungle Commando, led by Ronnie Brunswijk, a former bodyguard of the Surinamese military commander and effective ruler, Lt.-Col. Desi Bouterse, mobilized discontent among the "bush negroes" of eastern Suriname and by 1987 was estimated to be in control of much of the interior of the country. Bouterse alleged that Brunswijk received support from across the border in French Guiana and that Jungle Commando supporters were using French Guiana as a conduit for arms, money and communications. The conflict led to an estimated 12,000 displaced Surinamese refugees fleeing across the border. By mid-1990, however, the Surinamese military had gained the upper hand against the Jungle Commando, capturing their base at Langetabbetje, an island in the middle of the Maroni river, in September, and a peace agreement was signed between Bouterse and Brunswijk at the end of March 1991.

Since that time the territorial dispute has been largely in abeyance but it has yet to be definitively settled.

Lloyd Pettiford

2.14 Guyana - Suriname

Relations between Guyana (formerly British Guiana) and Suriname (formerly under Dutch colonial administration) have been periodically strained by a dispute dating from the late 19th century over the sovereignty of a triangular area of land lying within the territory currently administered by Guyana. The area in dispute, comprising some 6,000 square miles (15,000 sq km), is situated between the two tributaries of the Corentyne (Corentijn) River and is bordered on the third and southern side by the watershed which marks the boundary shared by Guyana and Suriname with Brazil. Numerous attempts to reach a peaceful bilateral settlement of the issue have taken place since 1966, but the dispute remains unresolved, although relations between the two countries have improved greatly in recent years (Map 21, page 503 refers).

The origins of the dispute lay largely in the extreme inaccessibility of the terrain in the foothills of the Guiana Highlands, and in consequent confusion over the true course of certain tributaries of the Corentyne River. Whereas a boundary agreement signed between two Dutch colonial governors in 1800 had referred only to the main course of the Corentyne, subsequent investigations established in 1871 that its longest course was not, as hitherto believed, along the Cutari and Curuni rivers running down from central southern Suriname, but rather along the so-called New River, which rises in Guyana well to the west of the Cutari/Curuni, joining the lower reaches of the Corentyne between the third and fourth parallels. Guyana adheres to the original (i.e. Cutari/Curuni) interpretation of the main course, while Suriname maintains that the New River (which it has unilaterally designated the Upper Corentyne) represents its true western boundary, and claims the New River Triangle as its sovereign territory.

At present the disputed area has little economic importance, since no significant mineral deposits have yet been located (bauxite mining being the major source of export revenue for both countries); however, the many freely flowing rivers in the area offer considerable scope for hydroelectric development, and balata (a form of ersatz rubber) is extracted from trees in the area below the high southern savannah.

Early Agreements and Explorations

The first recorded disputes between Suriname and Berbice (now the easternmost county of Guyana) over the ownership of land west of the Corentyne took place in the late 18th century in the form of a domestic conflict (in that both Suriname and Berbice had been Dutch possessions since the mid-17th century). The land then at issue was coastal territory largely comprising fertile cotton plantations, and the metropolitan government in Amsterdam ruled in 1794 that the territory of Berbice extended as far as the west bank of the Corentyne River.

By 1799 both Berbice and Suriname had been acquired by the British, but the Dutch governors of the two colonies (A.I. van Imbyse van Battenburg and J.F. Frederici respectively) were retained in office. The two men sought agreement on the confirmation of the west bank as the eastern boundary of Berbice, and a proclamation to this effect was published by the Governor and Councils of Berbice on Feb. 7, 1800. Guyana has since claimed that, although bilaterally agreed, the proclamation did not in itself constitute a boundary

agreement; for its part Suriname has maintained that the agreement was subsequently confirmed by the 1815 Peace of Paris. Suriname also claims, contrary to Guyana's assertions, that the Peace of Paris made a definite ruling on the sovereignty of the river itself, giving the entire width of the river up to but not including the west bank, as well as all islands, to Suriname. Meanwhile, the Dutch had regained control of both colonies in 1802, although the following year the British recaptured Berbice and in 1831 the colonies of Berbice, Essequibo and British Demerara were united to form British Guiana.

In 1841 the government commissioned Robert Schomburgk, an explorer, to investigate the boundaries of British Guiana; the Suriname authorities were invited to send a commissioner with him on his exploration of the (hitherto uncharted) Corentyne but explained that they had no authority from the Netherlands to do so. Schomburgk reported on his return that the Curuni and Cutari rivers were the main tributaries of the Corentyne, and mapped these rivers as constituting the boundary between Suriname and British Guiana. This interpretation formed the basis of all British and most Dutch maps for the remainder of the century, despite the discovery made in 1871 by a British geologist, Barrington Brown, that the New River was in fact larger than the Curuni/Cutari. Barrington Brown expressed the view that the Curuni/Cutari might in fact be only a tributary but, like Schomburgk, he mapped it as the source of the Corentyne.

Dutch claims to the New River as the source of the Corentyne arose at the time of an 1899 arbitral tribunal investigating British Guiana's border with Venezuela (see Section 2.15 for the Guyana-Venezuela territorial dispute). The British government reacted by describing the Cutari as "a definite and always easily ascertainable boundary...[which] should not be upset by geographical discoveries made long subsequent to the original adoption of the boundary and by theories so uncertain as those which are held to determine the true source of a river".

Dutch Moves towards Settlement of the Border Dispute

The controversy over the New River subsided somewhat over the next 30 years as the Netherlands government adopted a more conciliatory attitude to the dispute. A prominent Dutch geographer, Dr Yzerman, told the Dutch Royal Geographical Society in 1924 that his opinion was that the Cutari river basin was considerably larger than that of the New River, and his arguments were in 1925 and 1926 repeatedly cited by Dutch government ministers resisting Dutch claims to the disputed land on the grounds that no adequate information justifying such claims was available.

In 1926 the British government concluded a treaty with Brazil for the demarcation of the latter's common border with British Guiana. The treaty avoided exact reference to the area in dispute between Suriname and

British Guiana by means of the following formulation: "The British Guiana/Brazil frontier shall lie along the watershed between the Amazon basin and the basins of the Essequibo and Corentyne rivers as far as the point of junction or convergence of the frontier of the two countries with Dutch Guiana".

The Dutch government suggested to the United Kingdom in 1929 that a treaty should be formulated establishing the Suriname/British Guiana border, and on Aug. 4, 1930, offered to settle on the definition of the border as "the left bank of the Corentyne and the Cutari up to its source, which rivers are Netherland territory". This firm Dutch claim to the whole width of the Corentyne and Curuni/Cutari contrasted with the de facto situation in that, in the absence of a universally accepted border treaty, the actual boundary had normally been treated by both countries as following the middle of the river. Nonetheless, Britain declared its willingness to negotiate on this basis, and a final draft of a border treaty was formulated; however, it was never signed because of the outbreak of World War II in 1939. More successful was the fixing in 1936 of a tri-junction point (as provided for in the treaty with Brazil mentioned above), which was established in accordance with the Netherlands' suggestion that a boundary line should be drawn from the source of the Cutari, leading over a particular named rock, and that the tri-junction point should be the intersection of such a line with the Brazilian watershed. A definitive map was drawn up and was signed by Brazil, the United Kingdom and the Netherlands.

Revival of Dutch and Surinamese Claims to the New River Triangle

After World War II the Dutch attitude hardened considerably, and in 1962 the Netherlands presented a revised draft border definition which discarded the Curuni/Cutari line and revived the claim to the New River Triangle. British Guiana was offered the sovereignty of the Corentyne and New rivers up to midstream, and Suriname designated the New River as the Upper Corentyne, a step currently described by Guyana as having no significance in international law. The United Kingdom rejected the Dutch proposals and Suriname, in anticipation of Guyana's achievement of independence (which finally took place in May 1966), called on the British government in April 1966 to place on record that the boundary of Suriname and Guyana was in dispute.

Representatives of Guyana and Suriname met in London in June 1966 to discuss the dispute, but subsequently presented widely varying accounts of the meeting. Suriname described it as one between "good friends and neighbours" (May 1968), but the then Guyanese Minister of State for Foreign Affairs, S.S. Ramphal QC, reported in February 1968 that there had been a "free and frank exchange of views during which Guyana asserted its rights to the New river area and sought to demonstrate how utterly indefensible

was the Suriname contention that the boundary could be otherwise than on the Cutari".

The situation deteriorated markedly in December 1967, when Guyana expelled from the disputed area a group of Surinamese who were thought to be involved in surveys for a new hydroelectric dam. (Suriname later received the support of the World Bank for a hydroelectric project situated outside the disputed area but dependent on water whose origin is in dispute.) Suriname described the expulsion as an inadmissible use of force, and prolonged diplomatic exchanges followed during which Suriname was alleged to have threatened the expulsion of all 2,000 Guyanese workers from its territory. S.S. Ramphal replied on Feb. 2, 1968, that Guyana would not surrender its sovereignty over the New River Triangle, but offered to re-open negotiations with Suriname, and in 1970 new discussions took place, leading to an agreement on economic, social and cultural co-operation and on the demilitarization of the Upper Corentyne. Although a joint standing commission was established the following November to examine the issue and to enforce the demilitarization, it quickly became apparent that neither side intended to make concessions.

A serious incident developed in August 1969, when Guyana alleged that armed Surinamese workers had been driven from the New River Triangle while attempting to set up a landing strip and military camp. Suriname dismissed the report, claiming instead that Guyanese troops had landed at the Tigri aerodrome in Suriname and occupied it, adding later that Guyanese forces had illegally occupied a frontier post in the disputed area.

Suriname maintained its claim to the New River Triangle after its attainment of independence from the Netherlands in November 1975, and a series of minor incidents continued to trouble relations between the two countries despite renewed efforts to reach agreement. In September 1977 the Guyanese authorities confiscated four trawlers, one of which was part-owned by the Suriname government, alleging that they had been fishing in Guyana's exclusive 200-mile fisheries zone without payment of the appropriate fee. Suriname retaliated on Jan. 1, 1978, by withdrawing fishing licences from about 100 Guyanese who had traditionally worked the Corentyne River, and was said to have used gunboats to harass loggers on the river. Talks were opened in February 1978 in Paramaribo, the capital of Suriname, leading in mid-1978 to the settlement of the fisheries dispute and to the return of the Surinamese trawler.

Forbes Burnham, Prime Minister (later President) of Guyana, and Henck Arron, then Prime Minister of Suriname, held talks in Barbados in April 1979, during which the two countries signed a fishing agreement and agreed to reopen negotiations on the border dispute. The Arron government was subsequently overthrown on Feb. 25, 1980, by a military coup, but the new regime continued Suriname's contacts with Guyana through a civilian government installed on

March 15, 1980. Nevertheless, Suriname's growing internal security and economic problems (which it blamed Guyana for exacerbating in various ways) led to a deterioration of relations in the 1980s.

The death of Forbes Burnham in 1985 was followed by an improvement in Guyana-Suriname relations under his successor, Desmond Hoyte, who adopted a generally more pragmatic approach to current issues. President Ramsewak Shankar of Suriname visited Guyana on March 20-21, 1989, at the end of which a joint communiqué was issued stating that a bilateral commission would be established to discuss the border dispute. Hoyte visited Suriname on Aug. 23-25, 1989, when the two governments agreed various economic co-operation agreements. The border between the two countries continued to provide problems, however, mostly caused by smuggling, refugees and, after mid-1989, by the activities of Amerindian guerrillas in western Suriname. In October 1990 the Guyanese government complained over the harassment of traffic on the Corentyne River by members of the Amerindian Tucayana guerrilla group.

Guyana made no formal protest over the overthrow of the civilian government in Suriname on Dec. 24, 1990, and in February 1991 Hoyte was thanked by President Kraag of Suriname at a meeting between the two presidents at the Guyanese border town of Skeldon. At the same meeting, the presidents agreed that petroleum resources in the "Area of Overlap" could be exploited for the benefit of both countries pending a resolution of the border dispute. This agreement was embodied in a Memorandum of Understanding agreed upon by the two countries and signed by Dr Cedric Grant, Ambassador and Special Adviser to the President of Guyana, and Dr John Kolader, Ambassador of Suriname to Guyana; this agreement, however, has yet to be ratified by the Surinamese Parliament.

During a state visit to Suriname in 1994 by President Cheddi Jagan, the two governments agreed that the meetings of the National Border Commissions and the Guyana/Suriname Cooperation Council, which had earlier been established, would be resuscitated to establish a basis for resolution of the dispute. Meetings of the Commissions have not been held, but when in 1995 Suriname was admitted as a full member of the Caribbean Community (CARICOM), the country's application for membership was firmly supported by Guyana. As a further sign of improving relations, a Guyana-Suriname Ferry, funded by the European Union and jointly operated by both countries, began operation in 1998.

However on June 3, 2000, two Suriname gunboats forced the CGX oil rig and its crew to remove from an area of Guyana's exclusive economic zone on the Atlantic continental shelf near to the Suriname maritime border as it was about to commence drilling operations. The Suriname government claimed that the oil rig was in Surinamese territorial waters. Despite meetings in Port of Spain, Georgetown and Paramaribo during June 2000 and also at the CARI-

COM Heads of Government meeting in St. Lucia in early July 2000, efforts to settle this new dispute have not so far been successful.

Lloyd Pettiford

2.15 Guyana - Venezuela

During the 19th century Venezuela and Guyana (then British Guiana) claimed overlapping areas of territory covering about 50,000 square miles (130,000 sq km), consisting mainly of dense tropical rain forest which had discouraged early colonization and development. Despite an 1899 ruling by an international court of arbitration which awarded much of the disputed territory to British Guiana, Venezuela in the 1960s reasserted its claim to Guyana's present territory west of the Essequibo river. In 1970 Venezuela and Guyana signed a protocol declaring a 12-year moratorium on the border issue, but on its expiry in 1982 renewed border tensions became apparent. The following year the UN Secretary-General was requested to mediate by the two governments, which subsequently developed closer economic relations with the aim of creating the basis for a peaceful settlement of the territorial issue. (Map 21, page 503 illustrates this dispute.)

The colony of British Guiana (incorporating former Dutch possessions) was established in 1831; it obtained internal self-government in 1961; and became fully independent, as Guyana, on May 26, 1966. It has an area of 83,000 square miles (215,000 sq km) in its present boundaries. Venezuela, with a present land area of 352,000 square miles (910,000 sq km), declared itself an independent republic in 1811 after three centuries of Spanish rule and separated from the Gran Colombia federation in 1830.

Historical Background to Dispute

The British claim prior to 1899 was to the drainage basin of the Cuyuni river (in the eastern part of what is now Bolivar state, Venezuela) up to within a few miles of the Orinoco and Caroni rivers. The Venezuelan claim was, and remains, to all territory west of the Essequibo river (i.e. about two-thirds of present-day Guyana).

The major issue at the centre of the claim reasserted in the 1960s was the degree of control exercised by the Dutch in the area west of the Essequibo prior to British rule, which Guyana claimed was extensive. It said that the Dutch settlement of Kykoveral (established in 1616) had controlled the Essequibo; that the Dutch had controlled trade as well as the indigenous population by means of trading posts established on the upper Essequibo as well as on the Pomeroon, Barima and Cuyuni rivers; and that the provinces of Essequibo and Berbice had been recognized as Dutch possessions under the 1648 Treaty of Münster (Westphalia) which ended the Spanish-Dutch wars.

Venezuela said in support of its own claim that the Essequibo formed the most natural eastern frontier for Venezuela and pointed to the geographical unity of the land between the Orinoco and the Essequibo. It claimed that Spain had first discovered, explored and settled the British Guiana region and had exercised political control over it, and it produced evidence of the activity of Spanish missions in the area (which Guyana disputed).

The boundaries of British Guiana were established in the mid-19th century on the basis of explorations carried out by Robert Schomburgk, a surveyor and botanist engaged by the British government for that purpose. Starting in 1841, Schomburgk surveyed most of the colony's territory in the disputed and other areas, preparing as he went maps on which he marked the boundary line he had established. According to the Schomburgk line, the boundary between British Guiana and Venezuela began at the mouth of the Amacuro river, followed it to its source in the Imataca mountains, ran along the crest of the ridge to the sources of the Acarabisi creek, then to the junction of the Cuyuni river with the Venamo (Wenamu), and finally to the Venamo's source in the Mount Roraima.

Further surveys were later carried out by two British geologists, James Sawkins and Barrington Brown, from 1867 to 1871. They travelled over the present North-West district of Guyana, as well as the Demarara and Essequibo rivers, the Rupununi and Mahu savannas, and the Takatu and Kwitaro rivers. Brown alone explored the whole of the southern district, discovering the Kaieteur Fall in 1870, and the two men surveyed the Corentyne, Berbice and Mazaruni rivers together, before leaving the colony in 1871.

In the early 1880s the boundary issue was raised after the British government discovered that the Venezuelan government had made two grants of land in the Amacuro region within the Schomburgk line. The whole area granted (including part of Venezuela proper, islands at the mouth of the Orinoco, the whole of the coastal district between the Orinoco and Pomeroon, and the area between all that section and the Essequibo) was destined to be part of a new federal territory. Britain immediately took steps to reassert British claims and in 1886 declared the boundaries of British Guiana officially, also issuing a map showing the Schomburgk line.

After Britain had proclaimed the borders of its colony, it took further steps to pre-empt Venezuelan claims to the Barima and Amacuro areas, where British colonists had already settled, by proclaiming the region the North-West district of British Guiana. Gold was discovered there in the 1890s, much of the activity centring on the Barima and Arakaka.

After an incident in 1895, in which two inspectors of the British Guiana police were seized by Venezuelan police from a station on a tributary of the Cuyuni river, President Grover Cleveland of the USA (who was supporting Venezuela in its territorial claim) warned Britain that any unilateral action by Britain would constitute an infringement of the Monroe Doctrine (under which the USA regarded any attempt by European powers to reassert or extend their influence in the Americas as dangerous to its peace and security); to avert such a possibility, he demanded that the dispute should be submitted to arbitration. After a period of strained relations between Britain and the United States, Britain agreed, and an arbitration treaty was signed in 1897 with Venezuela, both countries agreeing to accept the tribunal's award as a "full, perfect and final settlement". The tribunal which was appointed consisted of two Americans, two British members and a Russian president.

The ruling of the court of arbitration, announced in 1899, awarded to British Guiana most of the territory within the Schomburgk line and to Venezuela a valuable portion at the mouth of Orinoco river. British Guiana lost some land in the North-West district and much of the Cuyuni basin, the loss amounting to about 5,000 square miles (13,000 sq km). A mixed border commission appointed by the two governments met and demarcated the border, an agreement recording the demarcation line being signed in 1905. In the meantime, the King of Italy had been asked to arbitrate on British Guiana's border dispute with Brazil. His pronouncement in 1901 again followed the Schomburgk line, although British Guiana lost some territory.

Reopening of the Border Issue—1966 Geneva Agreement

In 1951 Venezuela questioned the validity of the 1899 ruling and demanded the reopening of the border issue on the basis of the posthumous publication of a memorandum by Sevro Mallet-Prevost, an American consul, which alleged that the award had been an illegal compromise and that international political pressures had been used to obtain it. This was denied by the British government, but Venezuela raised the issue at the 17th session of the UN General Assembly in 1962, stating that it could no longer accept the arbitral award and wished to put it on record before British Guiana became independent that Venezuela did not accept that the border issue was settled. Accordingly, Britain agreed to engage in talks with Venezuela and British Guiana to re-examine all the documentary evidence on the border question, but stressed that this did not constitute an offer to engage in substantive talks about a revision of the frontier.

The talks led to the signature on Feb. 17, 1966, of the Geneva Agreement between Britain and Venezuela, establishing procedures for the settlement of their dispute. Article 1 provided for the setting up of a mixed commission to seek satisfactory solutions for the practical settlement of the controversy; Article 2 provided that within two months of the entry into force of the agreement each country would appoint two representatives to the commission; Article 3 required the commission to present six-monthly reports on progress; and Article 4 said that if full agreement had not been reached within four years from the date of the agreement, any outstanding questions would be referred to the respective governments, which would then "without delay choose one of the means of peaceful settlement provided in Article 33 of the UN Charter". Article 5 provided that no new or enlarged claim might be asserted while the agreement was in force, except within the mixed commission.

The work of the mixed commission was repeatedly interrupted by border incidents. In October 1966 Forbes Burnham, then Prime Minister of Guyana, said that about 100 Venezuelans had entered the Guyanese section of Ankoko island (on the Venamo river) and had begun mining operations; and in July 1968 Venezuela published a decree declaring territorial rights over waters nine miles beyond Guyana's three-mile limit—i.e. affecting waters to the west of the mouth of the Essequibo. This decree was immediately declared null and void by the Guyana Parliament, while the British government informed the Venezuelan ambassador in London of its concern over the decree. Finally, in February 1970 Guyana protested to Venezuela over "military attacks against Guyanese territory", whereupon Venezuela denied that its troops had opened fire near the disputed Ankoko island and said that Guyanese units had provoked the incidents.

1970 Port of Spain Protocol

After receiving in June 1970 the final report of the mixed commission, which had failed to settle the dispute, the governments of Britain, Guyana and Venezuela on June 18, 1970, signed the Protocol of Port of Spain. This protocol, which was supplementary to the Geneva Agreement (Article 4 of which was suspended while the protocol was in force), placed a 12-year moratorium on the territorial dispute.

Article 1 stated that "so long as this protocol remains in force and subject to the following provisions, the government of Guyana and the government of Venezuela shall explore all possibilities of better understanding between them and their peoples and in particular shall undertake periodical reviews, through normal diplomatic channels, of their relations with a view to promoting their improvement and with the aim of producing a constructive advancement of the same".

Article 2 stated that as long as the protocol remained in force "no claim whatever arising out of the contention referred to in Article 1 of the Geneva Agreement shall be asserted by Venezuela to territorial sovereignty in the territories of Guyana or by Guyana to territorial sovereignty in the territories of Venezuela". *Article 5* stated that the protocol would remain in force for an initial period of 12 years which would be renewable thereafter for successive 12-year periods.

In October 1978 President Carlos Andrés Pérez became the first Venezuelan head of state to visit Guyana; he and Forbes Burnham afterwards indicated only that they had established "an intelligent understanding on the border dispute". However, after an official visit to Venezuela early in April 1981, Burnham (who had been installed as the first executive President of Guyana in January 1981) said that his country would "not cede an inch" of the Essequibo region to Venezuela, whereas President Luis Herrera Campins of Venezuela reiterated his country's claim to the region and denied reports of a proposed extension of the 12-year moratorium under the Protocol of Port of Spain, due to expire in June 1982.

On June 2, 1981, the Venezuelan President disclosed that he had told President Burnham that the Venezuelan government was committed to "keeping alive the historic claim to the Essequibo territory"; that there was, for the time being, no possibility of continuing to implement the Port of Spain Protocol; and that Venezuela had "to continue to study the Geneva Agreement [of 1966] for a way to reach a satisfactory solution which would permit a practical settlement of the issue". He claimed that the Geneva Agreement was not only "the law of the Republic" (of Venezuela) but had also been signed by the governments of Great Britain, Guyana and Venezuela, who were "committed to comply with it". Venezuela notified Britain on Dec. 11, 1981, that it would not extend the Port of Spain moratorium when it expired.

Developments in the 1980s-1990s—Improving Relations

Tensions over the Essequibo dispute increased over an alleged border incursion by Venezuelan soldiers on May 10, 1982, following which Guyana lodged a formal protest with the UN Security Council. Two more protests were made in September 1982, when Guyana claimed that on Sept. 3 a Venezuelan helicopter carrying military personnel had tried to land at an airstrip 70 kilometres inside the Guyanese border, and that on Sept. 5 Venezuelan troops had tried to enter Guyanese territory at Eteringbang on the western bank of the Essequibo river. The following month Guyana appeared to be preparing for a possible armed conflict with Venezuela, by signing a substantial arms supply agreement with Brazil and agreeing that some Guyanese troops should receive military training in Brazil.

Against this background, the Guyanese Foreign Minister, Rashleigh Jackson, proposed to the UN General Assembly on Oct. 12, 1982, that either the Assembly or the International Court of Justice should be asked to select a procedure for resolving the dispute, to which his Venezuelan counterpart, José Alberto Zambrano Velazco, responded with a counter-proposal that the UN Secretary-General should be asked to act as a mediator. The Venezuelan proposal was eventually accepted by Guyana on March 28, 1983, but no immediate progress was made towards an accommodation.

Following the accession to the Venezuelan presidency of Dr Jaime Lusinchi in February 1984, Venezuela adopted a more conciliatory approach to the Essequibo dispute. A new Venezuelan Foreign Minister, Dr Isidro Morales Paúl, visited Guyana on Feb. 6-9, 1985, and agreed with Rashleigh Jackson that a "new spirit of friendship and co-operation" now infused relations between the two countries, and also that the UN Secretary-General should be invited to send a special envoy to both capitals to mediate. This special envoy, Diego Cordóvez, duly visited Caracas and Georgetown in March 1985 and announced afterwards that the groundwork for resolving the dispute had been laid.

Two years later, President Desmond Hoyte of Guyana paid a visit to Caracas on March 24-27, 1987, during which he agreed with President Lusinchi that their respective governments would continue bilateral contacts in order "to assist the work of the UN Secretary-General" in seeking a solution to the Essequibo dispute. Various economic and other co-operation agreements were concluded during the visit, these being described as potentially creating the climate for an eventual resolution of the dispute. Nevertheless, President Hoyte warned that "no-one should feel that we will, by sleight of hand, settle in a few days a problem that is rooted in the remote colonial past". On Nov. 16-18, 1987, Lusinchi paid a return visit to Georgetown.

The election of Carlos Andrés Pérez for a second term as President of Venezuela in 1988 led to a further improvement in relations. Pérez's policy of improving Venezuela's external relations within the region led to increased contacts and agreements over economic co-operation between the two countries on matters of trade, raw materials, and cultural and training links. Among these was the intention to link Guyana's electricity grid to output from Venezuela's planned Guri hydroelectric project. During a visit by Hoyte to Venezuela on Nov. 8, 1989, Pérez agreed to accept Alister McIntyre, vice-chancellor of the University of the West Indies, as "good officer" in the dispute on behalf of the UN Secretary-General. His role was to liaise between the two parties and suggest procedures for resolving disputes. The Venezuelan Foreign Minister, Reinaldo Figueredo Planchart, visiting Georgetown on Feb. 10-11, 1990, confirmed McIntyre's appointment and signed agreements on greater economic co-operation.

Thereafter UN mediation continued and helped keep the dispute under control. In late October 1990 the Chief of Staff of the Guyana Defence Force, Brig. Joe Singh, announced that the force was being restructured and scaled down, partly in response to improved relations with Venezuela and Suriname.

Revival of Tensions Following Election of Chávez

Concern rose again in Guyana, however, after the election in 1998 of the former coup leader and populist Hugo Chávez as President of Venezuela. It was not long before Guyanese suspicions were confirmed. In October 1999 Venezuela commemorated the 100th anniversary of the contested agreement, calling it "null" and charging that Venezuela had been "illegally stripped" of the Essequibo region as a result of the 1899 decision. Guyana brushed aside the renewed claim, saying the Essequibo was an integral part of the territory of Guyana. In response to Guyanese claims that Venezuelan troops crossed the frontier on Oct. 5, the Venezuelan Foreign Ministry issued a statement saying: "The Venezuelan National Guard was carrying out routine operations against illicit drug trafficking last Tuesday, without intentions to make an incursion into the Essequibo region. In no way should (the mobilization) be interpreted as an unfriendly act by the Government of Venezuela".

The dispute was, however, exacerbated in the same year when Guyana sold 100,000 acres in Essequibo to US-based Beal Aerospace Technologies, which planned to build a satellite launch pad there. President Chávez insisted that the US government was providing security for the launching site, and could use it as a military base. The US Embassy in Caracas stated that the United States had no role in the project except for granting export licenses.

In July 2001 the Venezuelan Foreign Minister, José Vicente Rangel, raised the stakes by announcing that his government proposed to issue licences to private companies to drill for oil in the Essequibo territory. He added that Venezuela had already contacted prospective oil companies.

Lloyd Pettiford

2.16 Haiti - United States (Navassa Island)

A long-standing dispute exists between Haiti and the United States over the sovereignty of Navassa Island, a small uninhabited outcrop of rock situated in the Jamaica Channel about 32 miles (50 km) west of Haiti. The US claim to the island has been periodically contested by Haiti, although the issue has never been formally submitted to arbitration. Dormant for many years, the dispute resurfaced in mid-1981, when the island was briefly symbolically "occupied" by a group of Haitian nationals with official backing. (For the location of Navassa Island, see Map 18, page 501.)

History of the Dispute

Navassa Island, with an area of about two square miles (5 sq km), was claimed by the United States under the "Guano Island C Act" of 1857, one of a series proclaiming sovereignty over various uninhabited islands in the Caribbean and Pacific with a view to exploiting their deposits of guano (seabird droppings), a valuable source of nitrogen fertilizer. Mining took place between 1865 and 1898. Following the cessation of mining on the island, the US claim under the original Act formally lapsed but occupation continued.

The US claim was challenged by Haiti in 1859. Haiti did not mention the island by name in its territorial claims before then, but its early constitutions claimed all adjacent islands. In 1872 the Haitian government presented the US State Department with documentary evidence that Navassa had been discovered by Christopher Columbus in 1493 and so had been included in the treaty of 1697, by which Spain ceded the western part of the island of Hispaniola to Paris, as well as in the Ordinance of 1825, by which France recognized the independence of Haiti. US Secretary of State Hamilton Fish rejected Haitian assertions of ownership, on the grounds that no instance had been given of "occupation of the Island previous to its possession and occupation by citizens of the United States in 1857" or of any attempt to enforce Haitian laws there.

In the 1950s Haiti built a church on the island for use by passing fishermen (although the island is difficult to land on by boat). On July 18, 1981, a group of six Haitian radio "hams" (i.e. amateur enthusiasts) landed on Navassa by helicopter with the intention of transmitting from the island under its rarely-used call prefix (as had been achieved two years previously by a group of US hams). Although the permission of the US Coastguard was normally required to land on the island, the Haitian hams declined to seek such approval on the grounds that Navassa belonged to Haiti, depicting their action as a symbolic occupation of the island. Official government approval of the landing was indicated by the fact that the then President of Haiti, Jean-Claude Duvalier, made three helicopters available to the group, who were accompanied by a camera crew from the Haitian national television station. At the same time the Haitian Communications Authority allocated a Haitian radio call prefix to the island, hitherto identified by an American prefix. On landing on the island, the Haitian party was greeted by a detachment of six US Marines, who took down the names and addresses of the hams before returning by helicopter to a nearby US Navy vessel. The camera crew then recorded a ceremonial raising of the Haitian flag on the island.

Navassa Island Light, a 46-metre-tall lighthouse on the southern side of the island, built in 1917, was shut down in September 1996, when administration of Navassa Island was transferred from the US Coast Guard to the Department of the Interior. A 1998 scientific expedition to the island described it as a unique preserve of Caribbean biodiversity and the following year it was proclaimed a National Wildlife Refuge.

Peter Calvert

2.17 Paraguay - Brazil

A short section of the boundary between Brazil and Paraguay, just west of Salto das Sete Quedas (Salto de Guaíra) on the Río Paraná, has been in dispute for many years.

History of the Dispute

As far as Brazil is concerned, its entire boundary with Paraguay was fixed by the Treaty of 1872 which ended the War of the Triple Alliance. This generally follows the line of major rivers, in the case of the Paraná upstream as far as the Falls of the Salto de Guairá (Sete Quedas). From there it follows the watershed of the Sierra de Maracayú westward until it comes to the peak of the same name. Under a Complementary Treaty (Tratado Complementar) of 1927 a joint Commission, the Comisión Mixta de Limites y de Caracterización de la Frontera Paraguay-Brasil, was appointed in 1930 to demarcate the agreed boundary. However, this still left some uncertainty where—as in the vicinity of the Falls themselves—there was more than one channel, and in 1962 the Brazilian government sent troops into part of the disputed area, with a view to securing the upper hand in negotiations for the construction of the proposed Itaipú dam.

In 1973 the two countries reached an agreement on the construction, operation and sharing of the power generated by the dam, embodied in the Treaty Between the Federative Republic of Brazil and the Republic of Paraguay Concerning the Hydroelectric Utilization of the Water Resources of the Paraná River Owned in Condominium by the Two Countries, From and Including the Salto Grande de Sete Quedas or Salto del Guaira, to the Mouth of the Iguassu River (also known as the Treaty of Asunción). The Treaty contains a reservation by which the creation of the impoundment behind the dam will not alter the agreed frontier, but it does not clarify the route of the frontier immediately west of the Falls where the line of the watershed is unclear.

Peter Calvert

2.18 Uruguay - Argentina

The Uruguay River and the Río de la Plata have been considered to form the boundary between Argentina and Uruguay since the preliminary Peace Convention of August 27, 1828.

The Treaty between the Argentine Republic and the Eastern Republic of Uruguay concerning the boundary constituted by the River Uruguay, signed at Montevideo, on April 7, 1961, allocated the islands from Brasilera Island downstream on the Uruguay River to the parallel of Punta Gorda, between Argentina and Uruguay. The treaty, however, specifically states that Isla Martín García is under the jurisdiction of Argentina although the boundary places it on the Uruguayan side of the line.

On Nov. 19, 1973, the Treaty of the Río de la Plata and its Maritime Limit delimited a boundary in the Río de la Plata from the parallel of Punta Gorda to the line of the declaration of Jan. 30, 1961, between Punta del Este and Punta Rasa, a point immediately south of Isla Martín García, which is the seat of an administrative commission for the Río de la Plata. A short section of the frontier remains in dispute.

Peter Calvert

2.19 Uruguay - Brazil

In 1934 Uruguay raised a question on the delimitation of its frontier with Brazil in the region of the "Rincón de Artigas". Currently two short sections of boundary are in dispute, one concerning the Arroio Invernada (Arroyo de la Invernada) area of the Rio Quarai (Rio Cuareim) and the other islands at the confluence of the Rio Quarai and the Uruguay River.

The Boundary Treaty (Tratado de Límites) of 1851, which is still in effect, fixed the western end of the boundary between the Empire of Brazil and the Eastern Republic of Uruguay on the River Quarai (Río Cuareim), a tributary of the River Uruguay. When the commission came to fix the point at which the land frontier intersected the valley of the Quarai, however, there was uncertainty as to which of two tributaries was intended by the treaty, and a similar problem arose in the region of the modern towns of Livramento and Rivera. An Amendment Treaty (Tratado de Permuta) was therefore agreed in September 1857 but not ratified by the Uruguayan Congress.

In 1933 Uruguayan officials raised doubts about the correct positioning of Marker 49. Hence by a Note of Aug. 10, 1934, the Uruguayan Foreign Minister asked his Brazilian counterpart for a "scientific determination" of the course of the Arroyo de la Invernada. Brazil's reply, on Oct. 26, 1934, was that the phase of demarcation was long since over (the treaty having been in force for 78 years), and that there was no evidence it was incorrect. A desultory correspondence followed until the most recent Uruguayan Note, on Aug. 17, 1988, with two annexes giving evidence for its claims, and the Brazilian reply, Note 272 of Dec. 4, 1989, left the issue unresolved.

Peter Calvert

2.20 Venezuela - Eastern Caribbean (Aves Island)

Isla de Aves, or Bird(s') Island, is the most lonely island in the Caribbean Sea. It is located at 15°40′N and 63°36′W, more than 500 km from the mainland, 700 km NE of Caracas and 230 km west of Dominica. Aves is a low bank of sand and coral, some 4.5 metres high. Before a hurricane in 1979 it measured some 1,000 metres north to south and 400 metres east to west, but it is reported since to have broken into two. Because of the island's position and height it has always been a threat to navigation and several valuable treasure ships were sunk on its reefs. There is a big iron light tower on it, 18 metres high, a radar-base and a Venezuelan coast guard station erected in 1979.

History of the Dispute

The island was first reported in 1587 by the Spaniard Avaro Sanzze and named by him Isla de Aves on account of the numerous species of birds for which the island is celebrated. At various times it was controlled by England, Spain, Portugal and the Netherlands, but not settled until 1878 when the American Guano & Copra Company built some wooden houses on the island for its workers and then mined guano until 1912 when the supply ran out. Since then it has had no immediate economic value though the sea around it is said by some to be potentially rich in oil. The island had been regarded as part of Venezuela since independence in 1821, but remained unused until formally established as a military base. It is a celebrated bird sanctuary and was declared a nature reserve in 1972. Any landing or stay on the island needs special permission from the government in Caracas and is restricted to Venezuelans.

Its diplomatic significance stems from the fact that the island is slowly disappearing. If it were to disappear, Venezuela, which claims that its ownership of Aves Island creates a Venezuelan exclusive economic zone (EEZ) extending over a large portion of the Caribbean Sea, would be unable to make such a claim. Meanwhile not only Dominica, but the independent island states of Saint Kitts and Nevis, Saint Lucia, and Saint Vincent and the Grenadines all contest the Venezuelan claim and resent the fact that it has been recognized by the United States, France and the Netherlands.

There has been much discussion over the years in Dominica about its claim or lack thereof to Aves, which it terms Birds' Island, and which lies well within the 200-mile (320 km) seaward limit normally recognized in the region. Former Prime Ministers Patrick John and Roosevelt Douglas both expressed interest in the island. Speculation was heightened in 2001 when the Caribbean Community (CARICOM) heads of government indicated that they might be willing to back up Dominica's claim. However, to date the government of Dominica has not indicated whether it will lodge a claim.

Peter Calvert

2.21 Antarctica

World maps offer uncertain guidance about Antarctica's territories and boundaries. Frequently, this vast ice-covered continent, though amounting to circa 14 million square kilometres (5.4 million square miles) and exceeding the combined extent of, say, China and India, is depicted by only a token section of coastline, or even omitted altogether. Nor are matters necessarily much clearer when the whole continent is shown on maps claiming to record the boundaries of such territories as Antártida Argentina, Australian Antarctic Territory, British Antarctic Territory, or French Adélie Land. Such cartographic certainties are undermined by the varying, even conflicting, answers to the question of "Who owns Antarctica?", although these maps highlight the fact that the Antarctic sector between 90°W-150°W constitutes one of the few unappropriated areas left on earth—see Map 22, page 503.

History of the Claims

The first formal claim to Antarctica was advanced in 1908 and 1917 by the British government, which included Graham Land, the South Shetland Islands and South Orkneys in the Falkland Islands Dependencies (FID). In 1962 the territories south of 60°S therein were separated from South Georgia and the South Sandwich Islands to make British Antarctic Territory, which covers circa 1.7 million square kilometres (0.66 million square miles). After the First World War, Argentina, Australia, Chile, France, New Zealand and Norway followed Britain in announcing claims (see Figure 1 on page 125), so that by the early 1940s seven governments claimed circa 80%-90% of the continent and adjacent islands. Only one relatively inaccessible sector remained unclaimed.

Initial disagreements about boundaries between France on the one hand and Australia and Britain on the other, as well as between Norway and Britain, were resolved by the late 1930s. More seriously, a large proportion of the Argentine, British and Chilean claims overlap. Thus, the whole of Antártida Argentina is in dispute, while only small sections of the FID and Territorio Chileno Antártico remain undisputed. During the 1940s and 1950s, the frequent exchanges of diplomatic notes between Buenos Aires, London and Santiago, abortive British efforts to involve the International Court of Justice, fears of a naval confrontation, and occasional incidents highlighted the dispute's potential for causing conflict. Perhaps the most serious case occurred in February 1952, when Argentine military personnel fired shots over the heads of British scientists at Hope Bay. In 1953 an Argentine hut on Deception Island was torn down by the British, while two Argentines were arrested and returned to Argentina for being present "illegally" in British territory.

Territorial rivalries were aggravated by legal controversies about the most appropriate method (e.g. prior discovery, formal taking of possession, legislative measures, sector principle, effective occupation) of supporting claims in a region unsuitable for permanent human settlement. In particular, controversy centred upon the question of how far, if at all, individual claimants satisfied the key criterion of "effective occupation". Indeed, could "effective occupation" ever be established in a hostile polar environment unsuitable for permanent settlement? Alternatively, was a lower standard of effectiveness acceptable as compared with elsewhere?

The Antarctic issue was further complicated by the fact that the USA, which became increasingly active in the region after the late 1920s, failed either to make a claim or to recognize existing claims on the grounds of the alleged impossibility of perfecting legal title through effective occupation under Antarctic conditions. Instead, the US government merely reserved its "rights" in Antarctica based upon prior discovery, exploration, scientific activities and the occupation of base stations. As the US government reaffirmed in a note sent to the UN on May 29, 1984, "the United States does not recognize any claims to territorial sovereignty in Antarctica and does not assert any claims of its own, although it reserves its basis of claim". A similar stance was taken by the Soviet Union, which began to take a closer interest in Antarctica during the late 1940s. Thus, as stressed in a note sent to the US government on June 2, 1958, "the Soviet Union reserves for itself all of the rights based on the discoveries and explorations of Russian navigators and scientists, including the right to make corresponding territorial claims in Antarctica". Other governments, most notably those of Brazil, Peru and Uruguay, have placed on record both their respective legal "rights" in Antarctica and their refusal to recognize existing claims. In the meantime, both claimants and non-claimants sought to protect their respective legal positions. Thus, claimants enacted laws, issued postage stamps and performed symbolic acts to establish the effectiveness of their sovereignty, while non-claimants ensured that nothing was done implying either recognition of any government's sovereignty—for instance, the US government instructed its nationals to refrain from requesting permission to enter and undertake exploration within any claimant's territory—or any diminution of their own rights.

The Antarctic Treaty and Antarctic Treaty System

Against this background, during the late 1950s alarm that a Hope Bay-type incident might escalate into a serious conflict, alongside fears about the possible spread of the Cold War and nuclear weapons to Antarctica, led interested governments to search for a solution of the ownership dispute. In the event, it proved impossible to reach a consensus about Antarctica's territorial status and boundaries. Instead, on Dec. 1, 1959, the twelve governments represented at Washington DC—Argentina, Australia, Belgium, Chile, France, Japan, New Zealand, Norway, South Africa, the Soviet Union, United Kingdom, and the USA—signed the Antarctic Treaty, which provided a framework designed to contain and manage the unresolved sovereignty problem. By keeping the lid closed upon a veritable Pandora's box, it preserved regional peace and stability, while enabling interested governments to continue the scientific collaboration developed during International Geophysical Year (1957-58).

The Antarctic Treaty became effective in June 1961. Henceforth, Antarctica, defined as "the area south of 60°S latitude, including all ice shelves", was dedicated to peace, international co-operation, and scientific research through articles providing for its non-militarization (article I), the peaceful settlement of disputes (article XI), the prohibition of nuclear explosions and disposal of nuclear waste (article V), freedom of scientific research (article II), and confidence-building measures, like the free exchange of scientific information (article III) and the right of inspection (article VII). Semantic ingenuity enabled article IV to accommodate simultaneously the contrasting positions of claimants and non-claimants. This article, stating that claims and rights could not be improved or weakened during the lifetime of the treaty, provided a modus vivendi according to which claims were neither renounced, diminished, nor prejudiced, but merely set aside, that is placed "on ice", for the duration of the treaty. Lacking any time limit—the preamble even includes the word "forever"—the treaty may last indefinitely. In turn, this non-solution of the territorial problem enabled the parties to move on from an issue capable of thwarting both the treaty negotiations and future multilateral co-operation on scientific and other matters.

The Antarctic Treaty became the nucleus for the "Antarctic Treaty System" (ATS), a term describing the multilateral arrangements used by the Antarctic Treaty parties (ATPs) to "govern" Antarctica by consensus through annual (formerly biennial) Consultative Meetings (ATCMs) held by rotation in member states. More recently, in 2001 ATPs agreed to establish a permanent secretariat located at Buenos Aires. During its 40-year plus lifetime the ATS has been characterized by three main trends: a growth in membership from the initial twelve treaty signatories to 45 ATPs (January 2004); the regime's continuing evolution (see Figure 2 on page 125), particularly in the sphere of marine resource management and conservation, resulting in the declaration of Antarctica by the Protocol on Environmental Protection as "a natural reserve, devoted to peace and science" in which ATPs accepted an indefinite ban on mining subject to review after 50 years; and the emerging interest of the international community, acting through the UN, in Antarctic affairs, especially following the discovery of the ozone hole in the mid-1980s and the more recent growth of fishing and tourism.

More than forty years on from the signature of the Antarctic Treaty, territorial claims have not disappeared. Maps continue to record individual territories, even if ATPs, not excluding claimants, now interpret the ATS as the most appropriate framework for the pursuit of their respective national interests in Antarctica. Indeed, for some commentators, growing collaboration in managing the affairs of Antarctica has been interpreted as diluting sovereignty, perhaps resulting in a shared jurisdiction over Antarctic territory as a whole. Of course, claimants view things differently, and continue to "govern" their Antarctic "territories". For example, British Antarctic Territory (BAT), which is administered as a British Overseas Dependent Territory, has its own legal system and issues postage stamps. Even so, ATPs have refrained from pushing their respective legal positions too far, thereby enabling the regime development characteristic of recent decades. Thus, the Commission for the Conservation of Antarctic Marine Living Resources (CCAMLR) regime, established under a Convention signed in 1980 and whose northern boundary extends to the Antarctic Convergence, was negotiated notwithstanding the varying views of ATPs about maritime boundaries. Likewise, in 1982 the Antarctic Treaty insulated the region from the sovereignty issues underlying the Anglo-Argentine War over the nearby Falkland Islands (for which see Section 2.3).

During the early 1980s the "Question of Antarctica" became an annual agenda item at the UN. Significantly, most ATPs, whether or not claimants, found common cause in opposing the efforts of treaty outsiders led by Malaysia to replace the ATS with an allegedly less exclusive and more transparent regime. Attacking the anachronistic, neo-colonial nature of existing claims, the critics sought to make Antarctica, like the deep seabed, the common heritage of mankind. Although the UN is still seized of the "Question of Antarctica", the critical lobby has lost much of its momentum, as evidenced by the fact that the topic is now only placed on the UN agenda on a triennial basis. The next UN reference is scheduled for 2005. The ATPs, though prepared to provide information about Antarctic developments to the wider international community, oppose external UN interference in the region's affairs. For them, Antarctica is subject to legal rights and claims predating the UN's establishment. More importantly, they argue that the region is managed by a valid and comprehensive legal regime embedded in the framework of international politics and law and open to accession by any UN member.

ATPs, claiming between them to represent more than 80% of the world's population, point to the way in which the ATS benefits the wider international community through the preservation of regional peace and stability as well as the responsible management of a polar environment of global significance. Indeed, hitherto, the successful development of the ATS, based upon the preparedness of ATPs to push aside the sovereignty issue, has increasingly obscured the continuing lack of agreement between both ATPs and treaty outsiders about the ownership and boundaries of a continent accounting for some 10% of the world's land surface.

Peter Beck

Fig. 1 Antarctic Territorial Claims

Claimant	Date of Claim	Title of the Territory	Definition	Approximate Extent
Argentina	1943	Antártida Argentina	25°W-74°W, south of 60°S	1.4 million sq kms
Australia	1933	Australian Antarctic Territory	45°E-136°E & 142°E-160°E, south of 60°S	6.1 million sq kms
Chile	1940	Territorio Chileno Antárctico	53°W-90°W, no northern limit defined	1.3 million sq kms
France	1924	Adélie Land	136°E-142°E, south of 60°S	0.4 million sq kms
New Zealand	1923	Ross Dependency	160°E-150°W, south of 60°S	0.45 million sq kms
Norway	1939	Dronning Maud Land	20°W-45°E, undefined northern and southern limits	problematic due to lack of definition
United Kingdom	1908, 1917	British Antarctic Territory (formerly part of Falkland Islands Dependencies)	20°W-80°W, south of 60°S	1.7 million sq kms

Fig. 2 The Development of the Antarctic Treaty System

Antarctic Treaty – signed: 1 December 1959; in force: 23 June 1961.

Agreed Measure for the Conservation of Antarctic Fauna and Flora – adopted: 1964; in force: 1983.

Convention for the Conservation of Antarctic Seals (CCAS) – adopted: 1972; in force: 1978.

Convention on the Conservation of the Antarctic Marine Living Resources (CCAMLR) – adopted: 1980; in force: 1982.

Convention on the Regulation of the Antarctic Mineral Resource Activities (CRAMRA) – adopted: 1988; superceded by the Protocol and hence unlikely to become effective.

Protocol on Environmental Protection to the Antarctic Treaty – adopted 1991; in force: 1998.

Note: Normally, the impact of any lengthy gap between a measure being adopted and coming into force has been qualified by the fact that, following adoption, ATPs treated the measure as in effect being in force.

ASIA
AND THE PACIFIC

3.1 Afghanistan - Pakistan

An unresolved dispute exists between Afghanistan and Pakistan over areas on the eastern side of their common border inhabited by Pathan or Pashtun (or Pushtu, or Pakhtoon) tribes, whose members are partly settled and partly nomads (i.e. seasonal migrants and also raiders or refugees crossing the border). The dispute came into the open through Afghanistan's refusal to accept the internationally recognized border between the two countries and Afghan demands for integration of all Pathans either in Afghanistan or in an autonomous or perhaps an independent Pakhtoonistan. In some instances Afghan claims have included the transfer to Afghanistan of the Pakistani province of Baluchistan (which would give Afghanistan access to the Indian Ocean). (See Map 23, p. 504.)

The Pathan tribes are broadly of the same culture—Sunni Muslim in religion, Pushtu or Pakhtoon in speech—but they are politically divided into the settled tribes of the administered districts of Pakistan's North-West Frontier Province (NWFP), those of tribal agencies in that province and those of Afghanistan.

The border between the two countries was delimited, by means of a map, under an agreement between Afghanistan and British India in 1893 after the so-called Second Afghan War (of 1878-80). Both sides recognized the area between this line and British India as "free tribal territory". Although under British sovereignty, the inhabitants of this territory were not British subjects and retained their tribal autonomy. The line was drawn as part of an agreement signed on Nov. 12, 1893, between the then ruler of Afghanistan, Abdur Rahman Shah, and Sir Mortimer Durand, the foreign secretary of the colonial government of India. It was delineated in 1894-95 and became generally known as the Durand line. The agreement was confirmed by further treaties concluded in 1905, 1921 and 1930, and its effect was to divide the Pathans in such a way that some 2,400,000 remained in British territory.

The Afghan Claim

It was the partition of India in 1947, when an apparently weak Pakistan replaced the British Raj as a sovereign neighbour of Afghanistan, which induced the latter to declare its claim. Arguments adduced by Afghanistan for its claim were legal, historical and ethnic.

It was asserted in Afghanistan that the 1893 agreement was not legally binding because Afghanistan had signed it under duress; that in any case the tribal territories between Afghanistan and the administered areas of the British sphere formed independent territories; and that Pakistan could not inherit the rights of an "extinguished person" (i.e. the British in India). It was also argued that historically Afghanistan had controlled much of India, and certainly the area of what was currently western Pakistan. Finally it was pointed out that the Pathans in Afghanistan and Pakistan formed a single ethnic unit which should be united in one state.

On the other hand, it has been argued that the eastern Pathans had enjoyed close economic and political ties with major states of the Indus valley and had developed linguistic differences with the western Pathans. Moreover, in its widest extent the area claimed for Pakhtoonistan, stretching from the Pamir to the Arabic Sea and bounded in the west by Afghanistan and Iran and in the east by the Indus river, included large areas where there were few Pathans—such as Chitral, Gilgit, Baltistan and Baluchistan.

Pathan Aspirations at time of Achievement of Independence by Pakistan

In 1946 a British proposal that under the constitution of an independent India the North-West Frontier Province should, for the purpose of drafting provincial constitutions, be grouped with the Punjab, met with strong objections from NWFP political leaders. Khan Abdul Ghaffar Khan (a member of the Indian Congress working committee and leader of the autonomist Redshirt movement) said on Dec. 6, 1946, that the question of whether or not the province should join any group should be left to the free will of the province itself. Dr Khan Saheb, the Premier of the NWFP, said on Dec. 20: "The Frontier people do not bother themselves about sections or groups. They will have their independence and nobody can force them to join anybody else".

Nawabzada Allah Nawaz Khan, the Speaker of the NWFP Legislative Assembly, stated on Dec. 16: "The Pathans and the Punjabis are two major nations by any definition or test of nationality, and the very thought of grouping the NWFP with the Punjab is revolting to the Pathan mind. We frontier Pathans are a nation of 3,000,000, with our own distinctive culture, civilization, language, literature, names and nomenclature, legal codes, customs and calendar, history and traditions, aptitudes and ambitions. By all canons of international law, a Pathan is quite a separate entity from a Punjabi".

On the other hand, Mohammed Ali Jinnah, leader of the Muslim League, declared on April 30, 1947: "The question of a division of India, as proposed by the Muslim League, is based on the fundamental fact that there are two nation—Hindus and Muslims. We want a national state in our homelands which are predominantly Muslim and comprise six units—the Punjab, the NWFP, Sind, Baluchistan, Bengal and Assam".

Under a British plan announced on June 3, 1947, for the immediate transfer of British power to India, it was laid down that a referendum was to be held in the NWFP to choose between joining the Pakistan or the Hindustan Constituent Assembly. Khan Abdul Ghaffar

Khan, however, urged that the electorate of the NWFP should be given the opportunity of voting for an independent state in the province under the name of Pathanistan. Both the Indian Congress and the Muslim League nevertheless accepted the British plan and its proposal to confine the vote in the NWFP to a straight decision on the issue of union with Pakistan or otherwise. Khan Ghaffar Khan reiterated his demand on June 24 (while admitting that Jinnah was opposed to the idea of a separate Pathan state) and declared on June 25 that the Redshirt movement would boycott the referendum.

On July 3, 1947, it was announced in London and New Delhi that the government of Afghanistan had presented notes to the British and Indian governments concerning the future of the tribal areas of the NWFP and drawing attention to an alleged desire of the tribesmen in these areas to dissociate themselves from India. The Afghan notes were said to have asked that the inhabitants of the NWFP and also of Baluchistan should have the right to decide whether their future should lie with Afghanistan or India or be based on complete independence. However, the British governor of the NWFP (Sir George Cunningham) subsequently toured the tribal territories and heard all the jirgas (tribal assemblies) of the leading tribes stating that they were part of Pakistan and wished to retain the same relations with Pakistan as they had with the British.

The referendum, held from July 6, 1947, onwards (after many Hindus and Sikhs had left the NWFP during June), resulted, as announced on July 20, in 289,244 votes for union with Pakistan and only 2,874 for union with India (in a 50.99 per cent poll).

The newly-established government of Pakistan assured the Wazir and Mahsud tribal jirgas in the NWFP that it desired to eliminate all suspicion among Muslims and to abandon the military control of their areas established by the British India government. The jirgas thereupon made pledges of full loyalty to Pakistan, and between Dec. 6 and 27, 1947, all Pakistani troops were withdrawn from Waziristan (in the NWFP), important frontier posts were abandoned and control of the areas reverted to civil armed forces recruited from the local tribesmen.

Nevertheless, there remained in the NWFP autonomist movements led by Khan Abdul Ghaffar Khan and the Fakir of Ipi, a rebellious tribal leader in Waziristan. On March 8, 1948, the former issued a manifesto announcing the formation of a Pakistan People's Party aspiring to autonomy for "cultural and linguistic units" in Pakistan and to the establishment of a "union of free socialist republics" in Pakistan. However, on June 15 he was arrested on suspicion of complicity with the Fakir of Ipi in the planning of disturbances, and on June 16 he was sentenced to three years' rigorous imprisonment. There followed arrests of some of his followers (including Dr Khan Saheb) and also of adherents of the Fakir of Ipi between June 28 and July 6, 1948, following which the Redshirt organization was banned on Sept. 16.

The 1949-50 Afghan Campaign for an Independent Pakhtoonistan

In March 1949 the Kabul press and radio launched a campaign against Pakistan, demanding that the area between the Durand line and the Indus, comprising the NWFP and the tribal territory, should be recognized as an independent Pakhtoonistan and given the right of self-determination.

Afghan spokesmen claimed that the 1893 agreement establishing the Durand line had been "brought about by economic force" because the tribesmen drew from the British, and continued to draw from Pakistan, subsidies amounting to over £3,750,000 a year. They also claimed that the referendum by which the NWFP had entered Pakistan was unsatisfactory because it did not offer the Pathans (whom the Afghans considered as racially akin to themselves) the alternative of joining Afghanistan (where there were an estimated 3,000,000 Pathans out of a total population of 11,000,000, while there were 2,500,000 Pathans in the tribal territory and 3,000,000 in the NWFP).

A statement made by Khwaja Nazimuddin, then governor-general of Pakistan, to the effect that the tribal territory formed an integral part of Pakistan, was strongly criticized by the Afghan government in a communiqué issued on March 24, 1949, describing that statement as contrary to pledges allegedly given by Jinnah in 1948. Moreover, addressing a demonstration in Kabul on April 27, Shah Mahmud Khan, then Prime Minister of Afghanistan, said that his government would "rescue our brother Afghans" from alleged atrocities by Pakistani forces, if possible by negotiation but if not "by other means". In June 1949 the Afghan Parliament formally rejected the Durand line and since that time no Afghan government has accepted it as the boundary. In Pakistan, however, Sir Muhammad Zafrulla Khan (then Foreign Minister) stated on July 11, 1949, that neither the Durand line agreement nor any subsequent treaty relating to the frontier was open to question but that Pakistan would welcome discussions with Afghanistan on matters of economic co-operation.

During June 1949 Afghan territory was, apparently inadvertently, bombed by a Pakistani aircraft which was said to have been fired upon by followers of the Fakir of Ipi and by Afghans. At the same time Afghanistan accused Pakistan of having assisted Agha Amin Jan (half-brother of ex-King Amanullah of Afghanistan, who had abdicated in January 1929) in an unsuccessful attempt to seize the throne of Afghanistan (after he had for some months been living among the Mahsud tribe of Waziristan), but this was strongly denied by Pakistan, which claimed that the authorities of the tribal territories had dispersed Amin Jan's forces and had informed the Afghan government of his activities. Pakistan in turn alleged that Afghan officials had welcomed the Fakir of Ipi when he had entered Afghanistan in June and were planning to proclaim him King of "Pathanistan".

In Britain the Secretary for Commonwealth

Relations (Philip Noel-Baker) said in the House of Commons on June 30, 1949, that Pakistan was in international law the inheritor of the rights and duties of the former government of India and of the UK government in the territories on the North-West Frontier, and that the Durand line was the international frontier. He added that the British government had been in continuous consultation with Pakistan, was convinced that there was no outstanding question between Pakistan and Afghanistan that could not be settled by peaceful means, and was confident that there could be no question of armed aggression by Afghanistan.

The Afghan ambassador in London, however, stated on Aug. 4, 1949, that his government could not accept the British view that Pakistan had inherited the rights and duties of the former government of India in the tribal areas and that, if negotiations with Pakistan for a settlement failed, Afghanistan would appeal to the United Nations.

As part of an intensified Afghan campaign against Pakistan from December 1949, the Afghan ambassador to India alleged on Dec. 20 that the government of Pakistan was refusing to "apply the UN Charter to an oppressed nation" and expressed regret that attempts which had been made by the Afghan government to settle the matter with the governments of Pakistan and Britain had achieved no result. He said in particular that the arrangements whereby the "Pakhtoons" (Pathans) had "found themselves debited to Pakistan's account as a mute transferable commodity" had aroused resentment among "the whole Pakhtoon nation" and that only the influence of the Afghan government had restrained them from taking up arms. He further alleged that the flag of "Pakhtoonistan" had been hoisted throughout the tribal territory; that "national assemblies" had been set up in Tirah and the Khyber; and that the Pakistan government had sent troops against the tribesmen, causing "immense loss of life", had bombed the Waziristan areas from the air, had enforced an economic blockade of the tribal territory and had imprisoned popular leaders from all over the NWFP and Baluchistan.

A number of border incidents which occurred in 1950 included, according to a Pakistan government statement of Oct. 4 of that year, an invasion of Pakistan on Sept. 30 by "a large body of Afghan tribesmen and regular troops" commanded by a brigadier of the Afghan Army, who were driven back on Oct. 5 by Pakistani troops supported by aircraft. The Afghan government, however, denied that any Afghan troops had been involved in the clashes and claimed that the detachment concerned had consisted entirely of tribesmen from the Pakistani side of the border who supported the "Pakhtoonistan" movement.

Dispute Dormant following 1951 NWFP Elections

In elections held in the NWFP between Nov. 26 and Dec. 12, 1951 (the first to be held on an adult franchise, including that of women), the banned pro-Pakhtoonistan Redshirt movement nominated a number of candidates standing as independents; however, after the election all elected independent Muslims applied for Muslim League membership (as a result of which the Muslim League eventually held 80 of the 85 seats in the NWFP Legislative Assembly). The provincial Minister of Education observed that the result had "buried the myth of Pathanistan for all time" and that the fact that the Muslim League had captured all seven seats in the Charsadda sub-division (a former stronghold of the Redshirts) was significant of the scant "respect" which Pathans had for those hostile to Pakistan or to the existing government. During the next few years the Pakhtoonistan issue remained dormant.

On Jan. 5, 1954, it was announced that Khan Abdul Ghaffar Khan, the former Redshirt leader who, after serving his three-year sentence, had been detained under security regulations, would be released. At the same time 45 other detainees were released unconditionally under a general amnesty, with their confiscated property being restored to them, and restrictions imposed on Dr Khan Saheb were lifted.

Afghanistan's Foreign Minister (then Sardar Mohammed Naim) asserted in a press statement during a visit to Karachi on Nov. 7, 1954, that the basic differences between Pakistan and Afghanistan did not involve any territorial adjustment, but he also said that the people of "Pushtoonistan" should be given opportunities to express themselves on "their status and their way of living". He emphasized that the two countries' national interests were similar and that there were good possibilities of close economic cooperation.

Revival of the Dispute after the Integration of West Pakistan

On Nov. 25, 1954, the NWFP Legislative Assembly unanimously approved a government proposal for the integration of West Pakistan into a single administrative unit. A subsequent proposal by the government of Pakistan to incorporate the tribal territory of the NWFP in the unified Province of West Pakistan was met by protests (on March 29, 1955) by Sardar Mohammed Daud Khan, who had become Prime Minister and Minister of the Interior of Afghanistan on Sept. 7, 1953, and who was known to be a strong advocate of Afghan support for the tribal elements in the NWFP. On March 30, 1954, a formal Afghan note was presented in Karachi, protesting against the proposed merger of territory of "occupied and free Pakhtoonistan" in the new province—but the protest was rejected by the Pakistan government on the ground that the unification of West Pakistan was a purely internal matter.

There followed large-scale demonstrations, leading to riots, before the Pakistan embassy in Kabul and also at Pakistan consulates elsewhere in Afghanistan. These incidents led to counter-demonstrations in Pakistan and to mutual recriminations, and on May 4, 1954, to the proclamation of a state of emergency in Afghanistan and a call-up of men between 25 and 32 years of age who had performed military service. The Pakistan Minister for States and Frontier Regions (Maj.-Gen. Iskander Mirza) said after a tour of the North-West Frontier areas on May 11: "We regard the Afghan government's claim to sponsor the 'Pakhtoonistan' stunt as an interference in Pakistan's internal affairs, and we shall fight for the maintenance of the Durand line as our national boundary with Afghanistan. There can be no compromise on this issue".

Eventually the Afghan government agreed on Sept. 9, 1955, to make amends for insults to the Pakistani flag during the Kabul riots earlier in the year, and both governments undertook not to conduct propaganda calculated to arouse hatred and to incite violence against each other. A proposed meeting between the prime ministers of the two countries was, however, put off by the Afghan government after it had been advised on Oct. 12, 1955, that Pakistan would not accede to Afghanistan's request for a postponement of the One-Unit Act setting up a unitary West Pakistan.

On Oct. 13, 1955, the Afghan government, in a further note to the government of Pakistan, expressed its concern at the incorporation of "Pushtunistan" in the new province of West Pakistan and asserted that this was against the wishes of the Pathans (Pushtus), but it still proposed a high-level meeting to settle "all outstanding differences". This proposal was rejected by Pakistan, which reiterated that all territories lying to the east of the Durand line were an integral part of Pakistan and completely outside the jurisdiction of the Afghan government. Nevertheless, the Pakistan government still expressed its willingness to have a meeting of ministers provided that matters purely of Pakistan's own concern were excluded from the discussions. The Afghan minister in Karachi and the Pakistan ambassador in Kabul were recalled in October 1955, as a result of which diplomatic relations between the two countries were in fact suspended.

After the Soviet Union had indicated that it supported Afghanistan in this dispute, the Council of the South-East Asia Treaty Organization (SEATO)—consisting of the foreign ministers of the organization's then eight member countries (Australia, France, New Zealand, Pakistan, the Philippines, Thailand, the United Kingdom and the United States)—declared on March 8, 1956, inter alia: "Insofar as those [Soviet] statements referred to 'Pushtunistan', the members of the Council severally declared that their governments recognized that the sovereignty of Pakistan extends up to the Durand line, the international boundary between Pakistan and Afghanistan".

A marked improvement in relations between the two countries from August 1956 (when the then President of Pakistan, Gen. Mirza, paid a state visit to Afghanistan) culminated in an agreement on June 10, 1957 (during a visit to Kabul by Hussein Shaheed Suhrawardy, then Prime Minister of Pakistan), to restore full diplomatic relations between the two countries, to co-operate in international affairs, to resolve their differences through friendly negotiations and to

consolidate the existing basis for permanent friendship. However, the contentious Pathan issue came to the fore again after the proclamation of martial law and the abrogation of the constitution of 1956 in Pakistan in October 1958.

Under martial law the leaders of the left-wing National Awami Party (NAP) were arrested, among them Khan Abdul Ghaffar Khan (who, after all remaining restrictions on his movements had been lifted in July 1955, had reportedly opposed the one-unit plan for West Pakistan and proposed a referendum to be held on this issue) and Abdus Samad Khan Achakzai (known as "the Baluchi Gandhi") as leaders of the movement for an autonomous Pathan province of "Pakhtoonistan" inside West Pakistan.

Further Deterioration in Afghan-Pakistani Relations from 1960—Soviet Support for Afghanistan's Position

From 1960 onwards relations between Afghanistan and Pakistan deteriorated rapidly, partly because of strong Soviet support for Afghanistan on the "Pakhtoonistan" issue. In a joint communiqué issued in Kabul at the end of a visit by Nikita Khrushchev, then Prime Minister of the Soviet Union, it was stated inter alia on March 4, 1960, that the two sides had "exchanged views on the destiny of the Pushtu people and expressed their agreement that the application of the principle of self-determination on the basis of the UN Charter for settling this issue would be a reasonable way of easing tension and ensuring peace in the Middle East". On his return to Moscow the Soviet Prime Minister asserted on March 5 that "historically" Pakhtoonistan had "always been part of Afghanistan".

In response to this development the Pakistan Foreign Minister, Manzoor Qadir, said on March 6 that it was "regrettable that the Soviet Union deemed it fit to interfere in this country's internal affairs", and on March 7 he challenged the Afghan government to hold a referendum in order to discover whether the Pathans of Afghanistan wished to join Pakistan. He said that he had made this proposal to the Afghan Foreign Minister, Sardar Mohammed Naim, during talks in Rawalpindi in January 1960, but that the latter had replied that he had "not come to negotiate". Manzoor Qadir explained his proposal as follows: "It is reasonable to assume that Pakhtoons (Pathans), whether they live in Pakistan or in Afghanistan, want to be together and under the same flag. That flag can be the flag of either Pakistan or Afghanistan...Since a referendum has already been held among the Pakhtoons of Pakistan [in 1947], who by an overwhelming majority decided to be in Pakistan, it is only logical that we should now ask the Pakhtoons in Afghanistan what their wishes are. In all probability their verdict will be in favour of Pakistan. In the unlikely event of Pakhtoons in Afghanistan choosing freely not to join Pakistan, any further steps to be taken can be considered".

The Pakistani suggestion of a referendum was,

however, rejected by the Afghan Foreign Minister, and the Afghan government subsequently refused to renew visas for Pakistanis living in Afghanistan. The Pakistan Foreign Minister stated on Aug. 4, 1960, that Pakistan had sent a number of notes protesting against alleged maltreatment of Pakistanis in Afghanistan, and in September 1960 and March 1961 mutual accusations were made about fighting in the border area.

On the latter occasion (i.e. in March 1961) it was alleged in Afghanistan that Pakistani forces were carrying out repressive measures against the Pathans, while *Pravda* (the official organ of the Soviet Communist Party) asserted on April 3, 1961, that eight Pakistani divisions supported by tanks and aircraft were active in the Pathan areas, bombing villages and causing substantial casualties; the paper reaffirmed Soviet support for the Afghan demand for Pathan self-determination and declared: "The situation emerging in the direct proximity of our frontier is not a matter of indifference to us". The government of Pakistan admitted on April 6 that bombing operations had taken place in the Bajaur area early in March when, it claimed, a house had been used as headquarters and an ammunition dump by an Afghan agent for the distribution of arms, ammunition and money among the tribesmen of Bajaur.

Further fighting in the Bajaur area was reported in May 1961, when the Pakistan Minister for States and Frontier Regions stated that Afghan forces had attacked Pakistani border posts and had infiltrated the Bajaur area but had been repulsed, and that 20 Afghan agents had been arrested and had confessed that they had been commissioned by the Afghan government to start terrorist activities in Pakistan. President Ayub Khan of Pakistan said on May 21 that, whereas in the past there had been raids by irregulars from Afghanistan, the Afghan government had now for the first time used army troops in a border incident, and on May 23 he said that Afghanistan had recently received large quantities of Soviet arms; that the border situation was becoming serious as the great powers were showing interest; and that the people of the areas concerned did not want the setting-up of any "Pakhtoonistan"; but he admitted that trouble was being fomented among "the disgruntled and the poor".

Temporary Severance of Diplomatic and Trade Relations ended by Tehran Agreement of 1963

Further concentrations of Afghan troops along the Durand line were reported by Pakistan military sources in June 1961, and in September of that year diplomatic and trade relations between the two countries were broken off, and the common border was closed (although as an exceptional measure the frontier was temporarily reopened on Jan. 29, 1962, to allow for the delivery of goods destined for Afghanistan under US aid schemes). The closure of the border also resulted in the exclusion from Pakistan of large numbers of Pathan tribal nomads (powindahs), who were Afghan nationals who had normally crossed

the border for winter employment in Pakistan.

Various mediation efforts failed to result in the reopening of the border until, after a change of government in Afghanistan, agreement was reached in Tehran (Iran) on May 23, 1963, when the governments of Afghanistan and Pakistan agreed (i) to restore diplomatic, consular and trade relations with each other; (ii) to see to it that the duties and conduct of their representatives would be in accordance with the recognized principles of international law, usage and practice, and would be confined to the discharge of their official functions; and (iii) to endeavour to create an atmosphere of goodwill, friendship and mutual trust.

However, the leader of the Afghan delegation (Sayyid Qasim Rashtiya, the Afghan Minister of Information and Broadcasting) was said to have stated in Tehran on May 29, 1963, that Afghanistan had never recognized the Durand line as his country's international boundary with Pakistan and that "Pakhtoonistan" continued to be the main issue dividing the two countries. Zulfiqar Ali Bhutto, Pakistan's Prime Minister, however, said on the same day that "Pakhtoonistan" was "a closed issue" and that his government would continue to refuse Afghan nomads access to Pakistan.

The Tehran agreement was implemented on July 20, 1963, when the border between Afghanistan and Pakistan was reopened.

The "Pakhtoonistan" issue was again raised in Afghanistan on Sept. 19, 1964, when the *Loya Jirga* (Grand Assembly of Afghanistan, a body which had been summoned only five times during 40 years to consider major questions of policy and which had in 1955 supported the Afghan government's commitment to "Pakhtoonistan") approved, after adopting a new constitution, a government-sponsored resolution referring to "the religious, national and historical duty" of the Afghans to support the rights of the Pathan people of Pakistan to self-determination and stating that Afghanistan was "waiting for the day when the issue of Pakhtoonistan will be settled on the basis of the true aspirations of the people and leaders of Pakhtoonistan".

Effect of Constitutional Changes in Pakistan, 1970-73

In Pakistan new constitutional proposals published on March 29, 1970, and a presidential order issued in April of that year provided that the one-unit structure in West Pakistan was to be dissolved and the four former provinces restored—among them the NWFP and Baluchistan (including Las Bela).

After the Supreme Court of Pakistan had, on April 20, 1972, declared illegal the proclamation of martial law (on March 25, 1969), martial law was ended and Zulfiqar Ali Bhutto (who had become President of Pakistan on Dec. 20, 1971) was sworn in as President under the new constitution on April 21, 1972. New provincial governments were thereupon formed, those of the NWFP (under Maulana Mufti Mahmood) and in

Baluchistan (under Sardar Ataullah Mengal) being both based on coalitions of the (pro-Soviet) NAP and the *Jamiat-i-Ulema-i-Pakistan* (of left-wing mullahs).

In the new constitution adopted by the Pakistan National Assembly on April 9, 1973, the territory of the Islamic Republic of Pakistan was defined as consisting of Baluchistan, the NWFP, the Punjab, Sind, the federally-administered tribal areas and such states or territories as were or might be included in Pakistan, whether by accession or otherwise.

Revival of the Pakhtoonistan Issue by the Republican Regime in Afghanistan

Afghanistan's claim to the areas of Pakistan inhabited by Pathans was revived by the republican regime that came to power in Afghanistan on July 17, 1973, under Lt.-Gen. Sardar Mohammed Daud Khan, who had, as Prime Minister in 1953-63, expressed his support for the cause of "Pakhtoonistan". After a public rally in support of Afghanistan's claim had been held in Kabul on July 21, President Bhutto declared on July 26 that his country would scrupulously adhere to the good relations which it had enjoyed with Afghanistan, but he added that Pakistan was "quite capable" of defending itself against possible Afghan claims to the NWFP.

In an interview published in *Le Monde* on Feb. 3-4, 1974, President Daud said: "We support in every way the right of our brothers in Pakhtoonistan to self-determination". He added: "When bombs are falling on our brothers, when they are being murdered, if they ask for our aid we shall not remain indifferent". Although expressing the hope that the problem would be solved "in a friendly and peaceful way", he claimed that the NWFP and Baluchistan had "always formed an integral part of Afghanistan", from which they had been separated by "unequal and unjust treaties".

Uprising in the Pakistani Province of Baluchistan

In the Pakistani province of Baluchistan it appeared that the overwhelming majority of the population had endorsed the province's adherence to Pakistan, but from 1963 onwards there was widespread unrest and armed opposition to the federal government, which sent in troops to restore order. At a *jirga* held on June 29, 1947, all the tribal chiefs of what was then British Baluchistan had decided by a unanimous vote to join Pakistan (although Kalat, the largest Indian state in Baluchistan, was not represented at the *jirga,* which was attended only by representatives of the British part of the territory).

On April 12, 1952, the government of Pakistan announced that, on the basis of a recommendation by a committee on constitutional and administrative reforms in Baluchistan, the rulers of the Baluchistan states of Kalat, Las Bela, Makran and Kharan had agreed to integrate their territories in a single Union with a common executive, legislature and judiciary. On June 16, 1954, the Pakistan government decided to merge the resultant Baluchistan States Union with the rest of Baluchistan under one central administration. Moreover, the *Shahi Jirga* of Baluchistan approved, on Nov. 29, 1954, the government proposal for the integration of West Pakistan in a single administrative unit, and an agreement was signed on Jan. 3, 1955, by the rulers of the states forming the Baluchistan States Union for the merger of all these states in a unified West Pakistan.

In provincial elections held on Dec. 17, 1970, one seat in the Provincial Assembly was gained by a Pakhtoonkwa National Awami Party (PNAP), which had been formed by Abdus Samad Khan Achakzai (who had been a close associate of Mahatma Gandhi in the Indian independence movement, had opposed the formation of Pakistan, had after partition been imprisoned for many years for advocating the creation of an independent Pakhtoonistan, had later joined the NAP but had broken with it to form his own party, and had then been regarded as a supporter of Zulfiqar Ali Bhutto). The PNAP leader was assassinated in Quetta (the capital of Baluchistan) on Dec. 3, 1973, however, and his death was followed by riots which were subdued with the aid of troops.

The existence of a Baluchistan Liberation Front (BLF) had been reported in February 1973. It was said to have an office in Iraq and a clandestine radio operating from that country, and to be supplied with finance and guerrilla training for separatist activities in Baluchistan. On Feb. 10, 1973, the Pakistani authorities seized some 300 submachine-guns, 60,000 rounds of ammunition, 40 incendiary grenades and other military equipment at the Iraqi embassy in Islamabad, but it was not clear whether these arms were intended for the BLF or for a similar movement in the south-east of Iran. The government of Iraq subsequently emphasized its respect for Pakistan's sovereignty and territorial integrity.

In connection with this arms find at the Iraqi embassy, Sardar Akbar Bugti (leader of the Bugti tribe) alleged on Feb. 10, 1973, that NAP leaders had plotted the secession of Baluchistan with the help of foreign weapons. Sardar Bugti had himself led a tribal rising in 1963, for which he had been condemned to death and later pardoned by President Ayub Khan; he had become the treasurer of the NAP but had resigned from it after the appointment of Ghaus Bakhsh Bizenjo as governor of Baluchistan as the nominee of the NAP on April 29, 1972. Although G. B. Bizenjo had on Feb. 13 categorically denied that the arms were meant for use in Baluchistan and had demanded a judicial inquiry, he was dismissed as governor by President Bhutto on Feb. 15 and replaced by Sardar Bugti, while the government of Sardar Ataullah Mengal was also dismissed for failing to check "large-scale disturbances" and President's rule was imposed in Baluchistan.

Khan Abdul Wali Khan, the president of the NAP, and G. B. Bizenjo alleged on Feb. 20, 1973, that Sardar Bugti had, while abroad, sought foreign assistance (in Moscow, Baghdad, Kabul and London) for a plan for an independent Baluchistan, and they suggested that he was connected with the arms seized at the Iraqi embassy.

A new provincial government, of which Jam Ghulam Qadir of the Qayyum Muslim League was sworn in as Chief Minister on April 27, 1973, was opposed as illegal by Sardar Mengal, who declared on the same day that he and his followers in the NAP would "defeat it in the Assembly or if necessary in the streets". There followed widespread unrest and G. B. Bizenjo said on Aug. 13 that unless the government's military intervention were ended quickly the situation in Baluchistan would become uncontrollable and sections of the NAP might be tempted to seek aid from abroad. He was thereupon arrested on Aug. 15, together with Sardar Mengal as well as the president of the Baluchistan NAP and the commander of the party's militia.

Sardar Bugti tendered his resignation as governor on Oct. 13, 1973, because he disagreed with the federal government's handling of affairs in Baluchistan. (He was said to have advised the Prime Minister to restore the NAP government and to withdraw the troops from Baluchistan.) He was on Jan. 3, 1974, replaced as governor by the Khan of Kalat (the overlord of the Baluchi sardars or tribal chieftains). On April 14 Bhutto announced that military operations in Baluchistan would cease from May 15 and that an amnesty would be granted to all persons detained in the province except those accused of serious criminal offences. Guerrilla warfare nevertheless continued and the opposition leaders alleged in the National Assembly on June 24 that 800 people had been killed by Air Force bombing a week earlier (but this was denied by the federal Minister of Law).

The government of Pakistan repeatedly accused the Afghan government of supporting the uprising in Baluchistan and of being responsible for bomb explosions in other provinces and alleged that the NAP connived with the Kabul regime. On June 19, 1974, it was asserted by Bhutto (who had ceased to be President and had become Prime Minister again on Aug. 13, 1973) that a professional assassin had been hired in Afghanistan to kill him in February 1973, and that a former general secretary of the NAP (Ajmal Khattak), who had lived in exile in Kabul since March 1973, had been involved in the plot. On Aug. 12 Radio Pakistan referred to another attempt by three Afghan guerrillas to kill Bhutto during a recent tour of Baluchistan.

On Oct. 1, 1974, the Pakistan Prime Minister stated in a note to the UN Secretary-General (Dr Kurt Waldheim) that he possessed "irrefutable evidence that the present Afghan government is systematically organizing, aiding and abetting the commission of acts of sabotage and terrorism through hired elements within our territory". The Afghan Deputy Foreign Minister (Waheed Abdullah) thereupon declared in the UN General Assembly on Oct. 7 that "the use of force, oppression and imprisonment of those who demand their human rights" in Pakistan would "adversely affect the maintenance of peace and stability in our region", and he proposed that Pakistan and Afghanistan should negotiate a peaceful solution of the Pathan and Baluchi questions.

At the end of an official visit to Moscow by Bhutto in October 1974, it was stated in a joint communiqué that the two sides had "expressed the hope that differences between Pakistan and Afghanistan will be settled by peaceful means through negotiations on the basis of the principles of peaceful coexistence". There followed a brief period of improvement in relations between the two countries.

However, after two Pakistani military posts had been temporarily overrun by Pathan tribesmen near the Khyber Pass and hundreds of refugees from Baluchistan had fled to Afghanistan, Bhutto sent a second note to the UN Secretary-General which as published on Jan. 24, 1975, again accused Afghanistan of "actively encouraging and assisting subversive activities and acts of terrorism and sabotage within Pakistan".

Pakistan Government Measures to curb Unrest in the North-West Frontier Province

On Feb. 8, 1975, Hayat Mohammad Khan Sherpao, Home Minister of the NWFP (and previously a member of the federal government), was killed by a bomb at Peshawar. Over 60 leading members of the NAP were thereupon arrested in the NWFP, the Punjab and Sind; the NAP was banned on Feb. 10 and its property and funds were confiscated; and over 300 more party members were arrested during the next three days. On Feb. 10 the National Assembly granted the government full powers, in particular to extend the state of emergency beyond six months without parliamentary approval. The NWFP government was dissolved on Feb. 17 and the province was for three months placed under the rule of the governor because "a neighbouring foreign power is actively involved in disturbing normal life in the province and there can be no doubt that this is a situation which is beyond the power of the provincial government to control". Numerous bomb explosions took place in Peshawar during the next two months, and a new NWFP government (under a Chief Minister from the ruling Pakistan People's Party) was sworn in on May 3, 1975.

The ban on the NAP was on Oct. 30, 1975, upheld by the Pakistan Supreme Court, which ruled that the party had never reconciled itself to the existence and ideology of Pakistan; had attempted to bring about the secession of the NWFP and Baluchistan through insurrection, terrorism and sabotage; had, in order to destroy the idea of a single Muslim nation, promoted the concept that the Punjabis, Pathans, Baluchis and Sindhis constituted separate nations, each of which had the right of self-determination; and had attempted to propagate hatred of the Punjab in the other provinces.

Abdul Wali Khan and 30 other NAP officials were on April 21, 1975, charged with sabotage and causing bomb explosions. Isfayandar Wali (the son of the party's president) and two other men were on Aug. 2

sentenced to 10 years' rigorous imprisonment after having allegedly confessed to causing the explosion which killed H.M. Khan Sherpao, while Isfayandar Wali was sentenced to a further seven years under the Defence of Pakistan rules.

Renewed Tension between Afghanistan and Pakistan, 1975-76

President Daud of Afghanistan renewed his government's campaign against Pakistan on March 2, 1975, when he declared in a letter to the UN Secretary-General: "Afghanistan has, since the time the British divided our land by force of arms and...annexed part of our territory to their empire, supported the lawful rights of these people [i.e. the Pathans and the Baluchis] and will continue to do so until they are fully restored". He protested against the dissolution of the NAP and the detention of its leaders in Pakistan; suggested that a UN fact-finding mission should investigate the situation in Baluchistan; and appealed for UN aid to refugees who had entered Afghanistan from Baluchistan and the NWFP.

On the other hand, for the Pakistan government Prime Minister Bhutto stated in a letter to the UN Secretary-General published on April 12, 1975, that President Daud's letter betrayed "Afghanistan's expansionist design". He reiterated that the frontier of Afghanistan had been delimited almost 100 years earlier by agreement between the Afghan and British Indian governments, and that the areas inhabited by Pathan and Baluchi tribes on the Pakistani side of the frontier constituted integral parts of Pakistan's national territory. He denied that there had been an influx of refugees from Pakistan into Afghanistan and declared: "The Afghan agents provocateurs and a handful of sympathizers who, because of their commission or instigation of unlawful acts, have become unwelcome among the tribal people of Baluchistan have made their way into Afghanistan as fugitives from justice". Some of the so-called refugees, he stated, wished to return but had been forcibly detained in Afghanistan, and thousands of Afghans who traditionally migrated to Pakistan in the winter months were refusing to return to Afghanistan because of the "terror and oppression" which awaited them. He described President Daud's suggestion for a UN fact-finding mission as "a clear attempt to secure UN cover for [Afghanistan's] interference in Pakistan's internal affairs" and he asserted that Afghanistan's "provocative and aggressive posture, accompanied by continuous exhortations from Radio Kabul to its agents to commit acts of murder, sabotage and destruction in Pakistan" had been responsible for the assassination of H.M. Khan Sherpao. The Pakistan Prime Minister nevertheless repeated that Pakistan remained ready to enter into a dialogue with Afghanistan and was committed to a peaceful settlement of the differences between them in conformity with the principles of respect for territorial integrity and sovereignty, and non-interference in each other's domestic affairs.

The Pakistan Minister of State for Defence and Foreign Affairs (Aziz Ahmed) protested in a separate letter to the UN Secretary-General against steps taken by the latter to ascertain what could be done to help Pakistani refugees in Afghanistan and alleged that as a result of the "reign of terror" in Afghanistan over 170,000 refugees had entered Pakistan.

President Daud, in a further letter to the UN Secretary-General on Oct. 10, 1975, denied that Afghanistan entertained expansionist designs against Pakistan; stated that many of the Baluchis entering Afghanistan were women, children and elderly men; and repeated his request for a UN fact-finding mission as "the only way by which the international community could be informed correctly about the truth of the matter and about the real identity of the Baluchi refugees". In an interview with an Indian newspaper (*Blitz*) on March 8, 1975, the Afghan President had stated that Pakistan was directly involved in espionage, arms smuggling and other incidents inside Afghanistan and was strengthening its fortifications on the frontier.

With reference to an incident in the Panjshir district of Afghanistan on July 22, 1975, Kabul radio alleged that "reactionary troublemakers" had engaged in robbery and subversion and had confessed after their arrest that they had been armed and incited by the Pakistan government. Pakistan radio, on the other hand, asserted that a revolt by some 700 tribesmen had been crushed by the Afghan army, with over 600 people being killed.

There followed, during the next six months, further Pakistani radio allegations about revolts, riots, acts of sabotage and "barbaric repression" by the police in Afghanistan. However, following the renewal for a further 10 years of a 1931 Soviet-Afghan treaty of neutrality and mutual non-aggression (which had been extended for a further 10 years in 1965) during a state visit to Kabul by President Podgorny of the Soviet Union on Dec. 9-10, 1975, the tension between Afghanistan and Pakistan abated during 1976. In a joint communiqué issued at the end of the Soviet President's visit it was stated that the two sides were "firmly convinced that the outstanding problems that exist in the South Asian sub-continent should be resolved through talks without any interference from outside" and "expressed the hope that political discord between Afghanistan and Pakistan will be settled by peaceful means by way of talks".

At the invitation of President Daud, Prime Minister Bhutto visited Kabul on June 7-11, 1976, when the two leaders "exchanged views with the aim of solving their political and other differences on the basis of the five principles of peaceful coexistence" and agreed to refrain for the time being from hostile press and radio propaganda against each other. Moreover, a visit to Pakistan by President Daud took place on Aug. 20-24, 1976, as part of "a continuing dialogue" to find an honourable solution to the political and other differences between the two countries. Nevertheless a "Pakhtoonistan national day" was celebrated in

Afghanistan on Aug. 31, with members of the Cabinet taking part in the ceremonies.

Meanwhile although large numbers of rebels surrendered to government forces during the first half of 1975, guerrilla activities continued in Baluchistan. The Chief Minister (Jam Ghulam Qadir) stated on March 4, 1975, that 44 people arrested had confessed that they had been given training in guerrilla warfare by Afghan army officers. On May 19 it was officially announced that a store of light machine-guns with Afghan markings had been discovered, together with an instruction manual issued by the Afghan War Ministry, although Kabul radio described the announcement as "a blatant lie".

On Dec. 31, 1975, the federal government suspended the Baluchistan administration and Provincial Assembly and placed the province under governor's rule, inter alia because the provincial government had "failed to make good use of the sizeable allocations made by the federal government for the development of Baluchistan".

On April 8, 1976, the Pakistan Prime Minister announced that the sardari system in Baluchistan and the NWFP had been abolished with immediate effect. Under this system the sardars (tribal chieftains) had held great power in the two provinces, had controlled private armies, administered justice, and collected taxes and other dues, including one-sixth of their tribesmen's crops. On April 10 the Prime Minister said that the former sardars must release all prisoners in their private jails, failing which the jail buildings would be demolished.

In the Iranian province of Baluchistan and Sistan (contiguous with the Baluchistan province in Pakistan), where about 550,000 Baluchis constituted the majority of the population and were predominantly Sunni Muslims (whereas the majority of Iranians are Shia Muslims), there existed a Baluchi movement campaigning for autonomy within Iran, economic assistance and cultural equality with the (Shia) Sistans of the province. However, this movement did not advocate union with Baluchis outside Iran.

Position adopted by Government of Gen. Zia ul-Haq

A change in the situation inside Pakistan took place with the assumption of power by Gen. Mohammed Zia ul-Haq on July 5, 1977, after protest demonstrations, strikes and riots had followed general elections held on March 7, 1977, and had led to the death of about 350 people. The change of regime involved the dissolution of the National Assembly and of all Provincial Assemblies, and it was followed by clemency measures affecting political opponents of the former government of Zulfiqar Ali Bhutto.

On Aug. 15, 1977, it was announced that Gen. Zia ul-Haq had appealed to the Marri tribesmen who had fled Baluchistan in 1973-74 to return to their homes, promising that no action would be taken against them and that they would be rehabilitated. Sardar Mengal,

the former Chief Minister of Baluchistan (who had been on trial with other former NAP leaders), was released on bail on Aug. 19. On Dec. 9 Abdul Wali Khan and 15 other men, all facing trial on conspiracy charges, were also released on bail, and on Jan. 1, 1978, Gen. Zia announced that the charges against them had been withdrawn and that the special court set up to try them had been dissolved as the charges were "99 per cent politically motivated"—but that the ban on the NAP would remain in force. It was officially announced in Quetta on March 21 that over 900 people detained during the rebellion in Baluchistan had been released.

The Issue of Afghan Muslim Rebel Refugees in Pakistan

The (Communist) Revolutionary Council which took power in Afghanistan in April 1978 appeared to maintain the attitude of previous Afghan governments on the issue of "Pakhtoonistan", but a new factor affecting relations between Afghanistan and Pakistan was the massive influx of Afghan Muslim rebels who fled Afghanistan, more especially after the Soviet intervention in that country which began in December 1979.

On July 27, 1978, the Deputy Prime Minister and Minister of Foreign Affairs of Afghanistan, Hafizullah Amin, expressed the hope that "the only political difference between Afghanistan and Pakistan regarding self-determination for the Pushtu [or Pathan] and Baluchi people" would be "solved through cordial and realistic talks". The government of Pakistan stated in response on July 30: "The national destiny of the Pushtu and Baluchi population of Pakistan as of the rest of the people was determined by them freely and jointly when they decided to establish the sovereign state of Pakistan. The Afghan statement, by calling into question Pakistan's territorial integrity, constituted a serious violation of the principles of the UN Charter, of peaceful coexistence and of the Non-Aligned Movement".

During 1978-79 various Muslim organizations waging guerrilla war against the pro-Soviet Afghan government set up headquarters in Peshawar (NWFP). The number of Afghan Muslim refugees in Pakistan reached about 30,000 by Jan. 16, 1979, but rose to over 1,000,000 in 1980. The Pakistan government stated officially on Jan. 31, 1979, that it had accepted the Afghan refugees on purely humanitarian grounds; that it did not allow them to train as guerrillas near Peshawar; and that its policy towards Afghanistan was one of "good-neighbourliness and respect for the principles of non-interference in its internal affairs". According to an estimate made on June 22, 1981, by the UN High Commissioner for Refugees, the number of Afghan refugees in Pakistan had by then reached more than 2,000,000.

In Moscow, however, *Pravda* stated on March 19, 1979, that "Afghan reactionaries" were "relying on support from certain circles in Pakistan, China and some Western countries" and continued: "Everything indicates that it was not without the knowledge of the official Pakistan authorities that the activities of the rebels developed". On June 1, 1979, it was stated in *Pravda*: "The attacks on the sovereignty of the young democratic republic [of Afghanistan], the intrusion of armed gangs on its territory from Pakistan and the attempts to create a crisis in the region cannot leave the USSR indifferent". In response to such assertions, the Pakistan government repeatedly denied that it was backing the rebel Muslims in Afghanistan and that its army was planning to conduct raids into that country.

Following the Soviet intervention in Afghanistan in December 1979, more than 100,000 Pushtu refugees from Afghanistan were on Sept.1, 1980, reported to have set up camps near Pishan in Baluchistan (with more than 700,000 head of livestock brought in by them competing with the Baluchis' sheep for scarce grazing land).

Proposals for a peace settlement, made by the Afghan government on May 14, 1980, called for "a guaranteed ending of incursions into Afghanistan by bandit detachments from the territories of the neighbouring states, in the first place Pakistan". The proposals were, however, rejected by Pakistan on June 11 on the ground that they did "not offer an acceptable basis for a settlement of the crisis".

The decade of the 1980s was dominated by the armed conflict between the Muslim rebels (mujaheddin) on the one hand and the Afghan and Soviet government forces on the other. As a result the Afghan territorial claim against Pakistan was not raised officially during this period, although the fighting involved numerous border violations. These included Afghan and Soviet air attacks on targets in Pakistan from which the mujaheddin received arms and supplies. Pakistan claimed that such attacks were directed against villages and refugee camps but the Afghan and Soviet authorities claimed that the targets were rebel bases or supply routes.

The main object of the government of Pakistan through the war was to achieve a solution which would enable the millions of Afghan refugees in Pakistan to return home. By the end of 1986, for example, official Pakistani figures suggested that over 3,000,000 Afghans had sought refuge in Pakistan, and that more than a quarter of Afghanistan's population had fled their country since the 1979 Soviet invasion. They included up to 50,000 Pushtu-speaking people (as were the bulk of the inhabitants of Pakistan's North-West Frontier Province). In Peshawar, the province's capital, there were half-a-million refugees, practically the same number as the population of the city, and this led to frequent strife and acts of violence directed against refugees. On March 21, 1982, it was claimed by the *Hizb-e-Islami* (Muslim rebel organization) in Quetta (Pakistan) that groups of Baluchis in Afghanistan who rejected the 1947 incorporation of much of Baluchistan in Pakistan [see above] were betraying the whereabouts of Muslim rebels to the Soviet and Afghan authorities.

The government of Pakistan refused to enter into direct negotiations with the Afghan government, and so from June 1982 "proximity talks" were conducted by Diego Cordovez, special envoy of the UN Secretary-General, respectively with the Foreign Ministers of Afghanistan and Pakistan. Following such talks held on June 20-24 and Aug. 29-30, 1985, Cordovez announced that Afghanistan and Pakistan had agreed to invite the Soviet Union and the United States to act as guarantors of a future agreement. Further proximity talks were held on Dec. 16-19, 1985, and on May 5-23, 1986, but no agreement was reached on a timetable for the withdrawal of Soviet troops from Afghanistan.

The newly appointed Afghan leader, Dr Muhammad Najibullah (who succeeded Babrak Karmal), on Jan. 2, 1987, announced a ceasefire, to become effective on Jan. 15. The ceasefire was designed to pave the way for the return of the refugees and for the creation of a government of national reconciliation. This was rejected by the seven major mujaheddin organizations, and the fighting continued. Pakistan did not recognize the new Soviet-backed government of Najibullah and so talks between the two sides continued to be conducted through the UN special envoy Diego Cordovez in an attempt to find a solution to the seven-year old war. On Nov. 30, 1987, Najibullah was elected President (being the sole candidate).

Two bombs which exploded in Karachi in July 1987 and killed 75 and wounded 300 were blamed on Khad, the Afghan secret police, and were seen as part of a campaign to discredit the Afghan refugees. The bomb outrages were followed by anti-refugee demonstrations.

On Jan. 20, 1988, Khan Abdul Ghaffer Khan, who had long campaigned for an autonomous state for the Pathans or Pashtuns in the North-West Frontier Province of Pakistan and had been known as the "frontier Gandhi", died aged 98. His death led to the first visit in 28 years to Pakistan by an Indian Prime Minister (Rajiv Gandhi). Ghaffer Khan had opposed the partition of India but when this appeared certain he campaigned for a separate Pakhtoonistan. On Jan. 22 two car bombs were detonated at Ghaffer Khan's funeral in Jalalabad where almost the entire Afghan leadership was in attendance.

On Feb. 8, 1988, President Gorbachev announced that Soviet troops would start a 10-month withdrawal from Afghanistan as of May 15. On April 14, 1988, the USA, USSR, Afghanistan and Pakistan signed an agreement in Geneva under which Afghanistan and Pakistan pledged they would not interfere in each other's affairs and would work for a voluntary and safe return of refugees. Then, on May 15, the USSR began the withdrawal of its 115,000 troops. On May 19, however, Afghanistan accused Pakistan of violating the Geneva accords by supplying the mujaheddin guerrillas in Pakistan with fresh arms. In November 1988 the USSR halted the withdrawal of its troops and began to supply the Afghan army with powerful additional weapons, claiming that increased guerrilla action in

Afghanistan was supported by Pakistan. Both Afghanistan and Pakistan accused each other (during the latter half of 1988) of violating the April Geneva accords.

Despite these setbacks all the Soviet troops had been withdrawn by Feb. 15, 1989, according to schedule (after nine years of intervention at a cost of 15,000 Soviet dead). By this time some five million Afghans had become refugees in Iran and Pakistan. The withdrawal of the Soviet troops did not bring an end to the fighting and Najibullah did not fall from power (as predicted in the West) until 1992 (see below). The rebels, therefore, established an interim government in Pakistan but though an assembly of 440 members was set up no agreement could be reached between the Pakistan-based rebels (who were Sunnis) and the Iran-based rebels (who were Shi'ites), the latter claiming that they were not being given adequate representation.

Relations following Soviet Withdrawal from Afghanistan

Relations between Afghanistan and Pakistan deteriorated further during 1989 and although Pakistan did not ban any refugees from its territory, they imposed a great strain upon the economy. Following the Soviet withdrawal, on the other hand, Pakistan was able to try to implement the concept of "strategic depth", a doctrine first articulated by the army chief General Mirza Aslam Beg and tried out in 1989-90 in the Zarb-I-Momin military exercise. The aim was to disperse Pakistan's military assets in Afghanistan beyond the Durand line and well beyond the current offensive capabilities of Indian forces. This in turn implied that there should not only be neutral areas around the Durand line but Pakistani-dominated areas well within Afghanistan.

The civil war in Afghanistan continued through 1990 but quarrels in the ranks of the government-in-exile in Pakistan made it ineffective against the Najibullah government in Kabul. The main rebel offensive of 1990 was led by the fundamentalist Gulbuddin Hekmatyar, who had been supported by Pakistan for most of the war. Under Pakistan's new Prime Minister, Benazir Bhutto, support for the mujaheddin was reduced. Following her downfall (Aug. 6, 1990), however, Pakistan support for the mujaheddin guerrillas was increased once more.

After the fall of Najibullah in April 1992 there was every indication that the different guerrilla factions would continue fighting each other for ultimate power. However, on May 25 the new Defence Minister, Ahmad Shah Massoud, and the fundamentalist guerrilla chief, Gulbuddin Hekmatyar, met and agreed a peaceful settlement and to hold elections within six months. It was also understood that the interim President, Sibghattullah Mojaddedi, who had replaced Najibullah (then in hiding), should not remain in office longer than two months, when he was scheduled to hand over to Burhanuddin Rabbani.

The Rise of the Taleban

In November 1993 a new problem developed in the long-running boundary dispute. Although successive Afghan governments had not accepted the 1893 Agreement, they had also argued that it had been made for one hundred years only. It therefore lapsed at some time between 1993 and 1995. However, in the meanwhile the country had slid back into civil war as mujaheddin commanders who had been armed by the West against the Soviet Union emerged as regional warlords. In these circumstances there was no hope of renegotiating the Agreement and for the time being no progress was made.

A group of mujaheddin, calling themselves Taleban (seekers of knowledge), who had coalesced behind the leadership of Mullah Mohammad Omar, previously village mullah of Singesar, Kandahar province, emerged as a new force early in 1994. The Taleban was based in Pashtun territory and many of the young Pashtun men who made up its rank and file had studied religious fundamentalism in Pakistani madrasas. By October 1994 the government of Pakistan had begun to support the new movement, seeing in it a way to establish a government friendly to its interests, while Pakistani traders seeking access to Central Asia gave it financial backing. Meanwhile the capture of Kandahar itself had given the movement access to a large supply of heavy weapons; the capture had been aided by the siezure of the border crossing at Chaman through which, with the connivance of the Pakistani authorities, a large number of theological students returned to fight for the Taleban. At the same time the Saudi dissident Osama bin Laden offered them the support of his terrorist network, *Al-Qaeda*, in return for bases to train militants ostensibly to support Pakistan in Kashmir.

Over the next two years the Taleban expanded its control; first to the west, where its capture of Shindand and Herat in September 1995 cut off its fundamentalist rival *Jamiat-e-Islam* from its links with Iran, and then to the north, seizing first Jalalabad and then Kabul itself by the end of September 1996. When fighting resumed in 1997, General Rashid Dostum, who had maintained a mini-state of five provinces centred on Mazar-i-Sharif in the north, lost control when his chief deputy defected to the Taleban on May 19, 1997. The Pakistani government not only lost no time in recognizing the Taleban as the legal government of Afghanistan on May 23: it also strongly supported it, allowing large numbers of Pakistani fighters to cross the border in support of the Taleban *jihad* against the Northern Alliance of non-Pashtun peoples led by former Defence Minister Gen. Ahmad Shah Massoud of *Jamiat-e-Islam*. In a temporary reversal in May 1997 the Alliance had been able to recapture Mazar-i-Sharif, but at the third attempt, in August 1998, Taleban forces took back the city.

In the same month, the United States government, which through its Central Intelligence Agency (CIA), had initially supported the rise of the Taleban, launched air strikes against the training camps alleged to be situated in the disputed zone near the Pakistani border. Among these was said to be the headquarters of Osama bin Laden, whose terrorist network, *Al-Qaeda* had recently been linked with successful bomb attacks on US embassies in Nairobi (Kenya) and Dar-es-Salaam (Tanzania). At Tashkent, in July 1999, an attempt was made to broker peace talks. The attempt was unsuccessful, and was followed within days by a Taleban offensive against the Alliance in which thousands died. In October Taleban aircraft bombed Taloqan and the United Nations, which had withdrawn its mission from Kabul in August 1998, imposed sanctions on Afghanistan by freezing its assets abroad and cutting air links with the outside world. The effect of these was at least to some extent offset by *Al-Qaeda* giving financial support to the Taleban and its leaders, and on Sept. 5, 2000, the Taleban recaptured Taloqan, massacring more than two thousand of its inhabitants.

By mid-2001 Alliance forces had again regrouped and, despite a severe drought that caused great hardship in the north, launched a series of guerrilla attacks on government troops. Then on Sept. 9, 2001, the Alliance suffered a critical setback when two *Al-Qaeda* suicide bombers disguised as Arab reporters fatally injured Gen. Massoud—an attack designed to remove permanently the one leader who, because of his excellent war record against the former USSR, might have displaced them.

Developments affecting Dispute since Sept. 11

Two days later there followed the terrorist attacks in the USA, of which Bin Laden and *Al-Qaeda* were judged the perpetrators. When US demands for the Taleban to hand over Bin Laden and his associates failed, the USA launched military operations in Afghanistan in conjunction with the Northern Alliance and other international allies, principally the UK, on Oct. 7. This led to the fall of Kabul by Nov. 13 and the rout of the Taleban throughout the country over the following few weeks. Neither Mullah Omar nor Bin Laden was captured, however, and some Taleban and *Al-Qaeda* forces dispersed into remote parts of the country as well as Pakistan's North-West Frontier Province.

An international conference held near Bonn in December 2001 laid the basis for the future administration of Afghanistan. Those who did not participate included Rabbani (who was forced to resign from his nominal position as President of Afghanistan) and Hekmatyar. The conference agreed the establishment of an interim administration led by Hamid Karzai (a Pashtun), with members of the National Alliance taking the majority of other key positions. The Bonn agreement provided for the interim administration to pave the way for the creation of a transitional government by a *loya jirga* of tribal and other leaders within six months. The resultant *loya jirga*, held in June 2002 under UN auspices, named Karzai as head (President) of the transitional government, while other posts in the

government were distributed to take account of the various ethnic groups, but with ethnic Tajiks of the Northern Alliance retaining control of most posts relating to foreign affairs, defence and national security.

Although the Pakistani military government of Gen. Pervez Musharraf (who had deposed the elected civilian government of Nawaz Sharif in October 1999) had given unconditional support to the US campaign in Afghanistan, there were substantial elements in Pakistan who were unhappy about it, either on religious or on strategic grounds, particularly in the NWFP. There also remained some question as to whether the Pakistani armed forces were operating to some degree independently of their government. At the beginning of 2003, Pakistani troops were reported to have crossed the border at Chaman, shifting some Pakistani border posts into nominally Afghan territory. Some Western analysts believed that Islamabad was seeking to take advantage of the undemarcated border to extend its territorial gains. One Western diplomat even went so far as to call it a "thinly veiled land grab".

Later in the year the Pakistanis openly crossed the border at the Mohmand Tribal Agency into Afghanistan's Nangarhar province. Ostensibly they were, under the doctrine of "hot pursuit", conducting a joint operation in search of *Al-Qaeda* operatives on their side of the border, while US troops carried out parallel raids on the Afghan side. Instead, according to international news reports from the area, Pakistani soldiers dug themselves into shelters on the ridge above the indisputably Afghan village of Tutkai—some 40 km within what had previously been regarded as Afghan territory—and surrounded the forward Afghan post at Yaqoubai. An exchange of mortar fire followed, but the Pakistani forces did not retreat.

In June 2003 a Tripartite Commission was formed to resolve the security issues between its member states—the United States, Pakistan and Afghanistan. In its first two meetings, the border issue dominated the proceedings as the Karzai government was critical of Pakistan for alleged incursions into its territory during military operations in Mohmand Agency, an allegation termed baseless by Pakistan. Officials of the Commission were called in to verify the situation on the ground.

The Afghan government has also asked that the Tripartite Commission be empowered to resolve the border dispute in line with Afghanistan's demand to re-demarcate the Durand line. This was strongly opposed by Pakistan on the grounds that the Afghan government was merely an interim government and as such had no authority to deal with such a significant matter. Hence the Tripartite Commission meeting held on Aug. 12, 2003, in Bagram, failed to come up with any agreed recommendations on the border issue, which was remitted to future meetings, beginning with one in Rawalpindi in September.

Taleban cadres have continued to operate from sanctuaries in Pakistan, raiding into southern and eastern Afghanistan in order to demoralize the newly-raised army, police and personnel of the Karzai government in the hope of thereby inducing large-scale desertions. They have avoided direct confrontations with US forces, lest they pursue them into Pakistani territory. As a result, while there were nearly 400 fatal casualties among Afghan government officials and civilians between August 2002 and September 2003, only four Americans were killed. The fundamentalist *Hizb-e-Islami* of Gulbuddin Hekmatyar has also been operating in Afghanistan, apparently in conjunction with the revived Taleban out of Pakistani sanctuaries.

Peter Calvert

3.2 Bangladesh - India

A dispute developed between India and Bangladesh in 1979 over a new island in the Bay of Bengal, which is called New Moore Island by India and South Talpatty Island by Bangladesh and which both governments claim as part of their national territory.

History of the Dispute

The island lies in the estuary of the River Hariabhanga, the mid-stream of the main channel of which forms the western border between Bangladesh and India, and of the Raimangal, an internal river of Bangladesh. Indian official statements maintain that it is 5.2 kilometres from the Indian coast and 7.2 kilometres from the nearest point in Bangladesh, and that the main channel of the Hariabhanga flows to the east of it, whereas Bangladesh claims that the main channel flows to the west. Its area varies between 12 sq km at low tide and 2 sq km at high tide.

The island—which is believed to have been formed after a cyclone and tidal wave in 1970—was discovered in the following year by India, which laid claim to it, named it New Moore Island and notified the British Admiralty of its location. The Bangladesh government first laid claim to it at the end of 1978, and subsequently maintained that during a visit to Dhaka in April 1979 Morarji Desai (then the Indian Prime Minister) had agreed to a joint survey to determine its location and ownership. A joint statement issued on Aug. 18, 1980, after a visit to Dhaka by the Indian External Affairs Minister, P. V. Narasimha Rao, merely said that "the two sides agreed that after study of the additional information exchanged between the two governments further discussion would take place with a view to settling it peacefully at an early date", no reference being made to a joint survey.

In May 1981, after an Indian naval survey ship had anchored off the island and landed personnel, Bangladeshi gunboats entered the area, whereupon an Indian frigate (INS *Andaman*) came to the survey ship's assistance. In a subsequent exchange of notes

each government accused the other of acting in a provocative manner and of sending warships into its territorial waters. Bangladesh again proposed a joint survey in a note of May 18, but India rejected the proposal two days later.

A joint statement issued on Sept. 13, 1981, after talks in New Delhi between P. V. Narasimha Rao and the Bangladesh Foreign Minister, Prof. Mohammad Shamsul Huq, said that they had agreed to seek an early and peaceful resolution of all unresolved problems, and that the two countries' Foreign Secretaries would hold early talks to examine all available data on the New Moore-South Talpatty Island dispute. The Bangladesh Foreign Ministry stated on Oct. 6, 1981, that India had withdrawn its presence from the island, and had removed the remaining Indian ships from the area.

Eric Gonsalves and Humayun Rasheed Choudhury, Foreign Secretaries of India and Bangladesh respectively, met in New Delhi on Jan. 13-15, 1982, for discussions on the island. A joint communiqué issued on Oct. 7, 1982, after discussions in New Delhi between Lt.-Gen. Hossain Mohammad Ershad, the Chief Martial Law Administrator of Bangladesh, and Indira Gandhi, the Indian Prime Minister, said that talks at Foreign Secretary level on the status of the disputed island would continue.

After an Indian minister of state had told the Indian Parliament in early April 1987 that the island was "essentially part of India", a spokesman of the Bangladesh Foreign Ministry on April 12 expressed surprise over this assertion and disclosed that his country's high commissioner in New Delhi had been instructed to take the matter up with the Indian government. He added that the ownership of the island had been under discussion between the two countries for several years, and that it had been agreed that the matter would be settled amicably through exchange of data and, if necessary, a joint survey.

Other Border Issues

By the early 1990s the 4,143 km border between the states was still to be demarcated on a 6.5 km stretch and border marking posts, or pillars, were in a state of disrepair in a number of areas. While such issues were not as significant as the problems with Indian borders adjoining Pakistan and China, the ambiguity did give rise to periodic bouts of tension and minor hostilities in the border regions.

Border issues related to trans-border crime, illegal immigration, water sharing and water rights, and the impact of terrorism on India. An India-Bangladesh conference (Aug. 27-29, 1991) between Brigadier Abdullah Al-Hussein (Bangladesh) and G. K. Rajagonpandam (India) considered many of these issues, together with the maintenance of border markers between the two states. Following this meeting it was reported that the Tin Bigha corridor would be returned to Bangladesh by the end of the year, and representatives of both India and Bangladesh agreed on Feb. 26, 1992, to a leasing arrangement to enable Bangladesh to link with its enclaves of Dahagren and Angorpota. The start date for the lease was June, but tensions between the local populations led to clashes with police on June 14-15, 1992, although inter-governmental relations remained calm.

An agreement for annual meetings of the Home Secretaries of each state and biannual meetings of the border security forces to allow discussions on bilateral border issues and resolve any problems emerged in October 1993. However, reports in January 1994 referred to an "exchange of fire" between the border security forces in the township of Belonia, in the Char area, although under an agreement on Jan. 15 India signalled its adherence to the 1974 and 1975 border guidelines. Difficulties and "exchanges of fire" were reported for a few days beyond the apparent agreement.

Renewed exchanges of fire in mid-January 1996 followed Indian attempts to rebuild a customs office at the Tambil point section of the border, even though later reports claimed that Indian officials suspected that the tensions were "artificial" and linked to the Feb. 15 general election in Bangladesh. During 1996 agreements on water-sharing from the River Ganges and concerns in both India and Bangladesh about insurgents crossing their mutual borders helped create a move to resolve a number of minor border dispute-related issues. The threat of insurgents led to calls for renewed efforts on fencing off the border in particular areas, and the State government of West Bengal aimed to complete fencing off 900 km of its shared 1,600 km with Bangladesh border by the end of 1999. Formal talks between the Bangladeshi and Indian border security forces on Oct. 26, after 22 Bangladeshis had been killed in the preceding months, were marginally successful.

The most significant breakthrough was reported in early January 2000 when an accord was struck over the Feni-Belonia boundary with a report indicating that a senior Bangladeshi official viewed the accord as "a major development in removing long-standing border irritants between two neighbours". The accord did not resolve the dispute, but a political agreement was expected to emerge from it.

Following the Sept. 11, 2001, attacks in the USA and the Dec. 13, 2001, terrorist attack on the Indian federal parliament in which 14 people died, Indian authorities stepped up their efforts to police all their borders but skirmishes and exchanges of fire along the Bangladesh-India border continue to date.

Jez Littlewood

3.3 Bhutan - China

Bhutan and China did not have a common border at all until China invaded Tibet in 1950, after which Bhutan found itself with a 570-kilometre boundary with China. The border has never been formally delimited, but a traditional customary boundary has long marked the extent of each government's jurisdiction. Bhutan maintains that it has no dispute with China, as the border is well defined by geographical features, and that the question at issue relates merely to demarcation of the boundary. China holds, however, that there are discrepancies in the delineation of certain small areas on the two countries' maps on which agreement needs to be reached. Bhutan and China do not have formal diplomatic relations, but have conducted a series of talks to resolve border issues. (For the territorial relationship of Bhutan and China, see Map 24, p. 504.)

Background

A treaty between Bhutan and the Dominion of India signed in 1949, which replaced a treaty of 1910 between Bhutan and the government of British India, provided that Bhutan would seek the advice of the government of India on its external relations, but remained free to decide whether or not to accept it. India's claim to speak for Bhutan on the question of its border with China was never recognized by China. Following the rebellion in Tibet against Chinese rule in March 1959, Jigme Dorje (the Prime Minister of Bhutan) visited New Delhi in August 1959, when he declared that about 1,000 sq km of Bhutanese territory were shown on Chinese maps as belonging to China, and received an assurance from Jawaharlal Nehru (the Indian Prime Minister) that India would defend Bhutan against any intrusion by a foreign power.

Since 1971, when Bhutan was admitted to the United Nations, it has increasingly asserted its status as an independent sovereign state. When India protested to China in 1979 against alleged Chinese incursions into Bhutan, China ignored the protest, but informed the Bhutanese government that it was always ready to discuss the demarcation of the border. Bhutan thereupon decided to enter into direct negotiations with China without Indian participation, and India tacitly accepted the decision. Although India has traditionally guided Bhutan's external relations, over the question of borders Bhutan has distanced itself from Delhi and undertaken negotiations with Beijing on a bilateral basis, the exclusion of India from these talks being regarded by Beijing as a prerequisite for any progress on the matter.

Border Negotiations 1984-2002

Discussions between Bhutanese and Chinese officials opened in Beijing in April 1984, and were followed by further rounds of talks in Thimphu (the capital of Bhutan) in April 1985 and in Beijing in June 1986. Although no final agreement was reached, both sides affirmed their desire to maintain "a peaceful and friendly border" while seeking an early settlement. A fourth round of talks was held in 1987 in Thimphu at which the discussion of principles and procedures advanced to substantive negotiations. On May 10-14, 1988, the fifth round of bilateral boundary talks were held in Beijing but though no agreement was reached the talks were cordial and a joint communiqué, issued on May 14, outlined the principles guiding the negotiations which included not using force to resolve the dispute.

These talks have continued on an annual basis, with the two sides taking turns to host discussions. Substantial progress towards a resolution of border disputes began to emerge between 1996 and 1998. At the tenth round of talks, held in November 1996, China proposed an exchange of territory: Beijing would hand over 495 sq km of its territory on Bhutan's northern border in exchange for 269 sq km of land in north-west Bhutan. Bhutan reportedly accepted this arrangement in principle, although it has yet to be formalized. The agreement is not without wider strategic impact, because part of the Bhutanese territory that would be handed to China shares a border with India, with which China has an uneasy relationship.

The eleventh round of talks the following year did not produce any further progress on the exchange of territory, but the twelfth round on Dec. 12, 1998, saw the signature of an agreement on "The Maintenance of Peace and Tranquillity Along the Sino-Bhutanese Border Areas". The agreement noted that the two sides had "reached consensus on the guiding principles of the settlement of the boundary issues" and stated that both would not resort to unilateral action to alter the status quo of the border. Two years later, at the fourteenth round in November 2000, Bhutan extended its claim beyond that which China had offered in 1996, and despite continuation of talks since then, a breakthrough has not yet been achieved. In 2002, it was reported that Bhutan had urged China to be "generous" in resolving border disputes with its small neighbouring state, a clear reference to the Bhutanese extension of its claim. This was met with a Chinese response that China bordered 26 states and could not afford to be generous with one neighbour in particular.

Mark Smith

3.4 Central Asian Republics

What used to be referred to as Soviet Central Asia now consists of the five sovereign republics of Kazakhstan, Uzbekistan, Turkmenistan, Tajikistan and Kyrgyzstan, located to the south of the Russian Federation. Strictly speaking, Kazakhstan, by far the largest of the five, is geographically somewhat distinct from the other four. But it shares their history in having been part of the Muslim lands conquered by Tsarist Russia in the 19th century. In the disintegration of the Soviet Union at the end of 1991, all five republics became independent and joined the Commonwealth of Independent States (CIS). With the exception of Tajikistan, the governments of these countries continue to be run by the leaders who had held power under Soviet hegemony, although the demise of the Soviet Communist Party obliged the ruling parties in the Central Asian republics to change their names.

One consequence of the end of central Communist rule was a general revival of Muslim religious adherence and the emergence of Islamic fundamentalist movements. The ruling elites have responded by gravitating towards Turkey, which they hope will provide an alternative model for their populations. Turkey has responded positively to these overtures. Its interest in the republics derives in part from the fact that their peoples, with the exception of the Persian-speaking Tajiks, are mainly Turkic in ethnic composition and language and, like the Turks, mainly Sunni Muslims.

Geography and Population

In total, the five Central Asian ex-Soviet republics cover an area of some 4,000,000 sq km, extending from the Caspian Sea to the Pamir mountains bordering Afghanistan and to the Tien Shan range between the ex-Soviet Union and the Xianjiang (Sinkiang) province of China (see Map 25, p. 505).

Kazakhstan has an area of 2,717,300 sq km and a population that the 1999 census showed as being 14.9 million, with Kazakhs (53.4 per cent) and Russians (30 per cent) as its largest components, followed by ethnic Germans (5.8 per cent) and Ukrainians (5.4 per cent). As with all of the Central Asian republics, since independence there has been a large outward migration of Russians and other nationalities. For example, the 1989 Soviet census estimated that Russians constituted 37.8 per cent and Kazakhs 39.7 per cent of the total population, which at that time numbered 16.5 million.

Turkmenistan covers 491,210 sq km and its population of 5,200,000 (2000 census) is mainly Turkmen (81 per cent), with Uzbeks constituting 9.7 per cent and Russians 4.3 per cent of the population (9.5 per cent in 1989).

Uzbekistan extends to 447,400 sq km and in 2000 had a population of 24.4 million in which Uzbeks (80 per cent) predominated, followed by Russians, constituting 5.5 per cent (8.4 per cent in 1989), Tajiks (5 per cent) and Kazakhs (3 per cent).

Kyrgyzstan has an area of 198,500 sq km and, according to the 2000 census, its population was 4.9 million, composed mainly of Kyrgyz (65.7 per cent), Russians (11.7 per cent, down from 21.5 per cent in 1989) and Uzbeks (13.9 per cent).

Tajikistan, the smallest of the five, amounts to 143,100 sq km and, according to the 1999 UNDP report, the population now numbers 6.3 million. Tajiks are the dominant population group (67 per cent), followed by Uzbeks (23.5 per cent) and Russians (3 per cent, down from 7.6 per cent in 1989).

At independence Uzbekistan contained within its borders the Kara-Kalpak Autonomous Republic, covering 165,000 sq km at the north-western end of the republic around the Aral Sea. It was created to provide a political entity for the distinct Kara-Kalpak people, although they form only about 31 per cent of its population of 1,100,000, of which Uzbeks make up 30 per cent and Kazakhs 27 per cent. The Kara-Kalpaks constitute only 2.5% of the Republic's population overall. The only other autonomy in the region was the Gorno-Badakhshan Autonomous Region in southern Tajikistan, consisting of 64,000 sq km of territory in the Pamir mountains. Its population of some 150,000 is 83 per cent Tajik (and 11 per cent Kyrgyz) but is distinct by virtue of being predominantly of the Ismali Muslim sect.

Historical Background—Creation of Central Asian Republics

Imperial Russia began to penetrate south-east of the Urals into what was then called Turkestan in the late 18th century and by 1825 had conquered what is now eastern Kazakhstan on the northern and eastern littoral of the Caspian Sea. Most of the rest of Kazakhstan was added under Tsar Nicholas I (r. 1825-55) and defensive fortifications hundreds of miles long were constructed to keep out the Muslim tribes of southern Turkestan. Much of what is now Uzbekistan and Kyrgyzstan became Russian territory under Alexander II (r.1855-81), whose armies captured Tashkent in 1866, Samarkand in 1868 and Kokand in 1876 (following an anti-Russian revolt). The khanate of Kokand was then abolished, whereas the ancient emirate of Bukhara and the khanate of Khiva, along the Oxus river, retained sovereignty under Russian protection until after World War I.

Under Alexander III (r. 1881-94) Russian rule was extended to what is now Turkmenistan, while to the east of the Bukhara khanate Tsarist forces penetrated to the Pamir mountains in the late 1890s. In 1907 northern Persia (Iran) became a Russian sphere of influence, so that the old Tsarist aim that the Caspian Sea should be a "Russian lake" was realized, albeit only temporarily. After World War I, at the insistence of Britain, northern Persia ceased to be a Russian sphere in 1921.

The Bolshevik regime which seized power in Russia in late 1917 established its authority in Turkestan in 1919-20. The khan of Khiva and the emir of Bukhara were both deposed in 1920 and their lands became people's republics. In April 1921 the former governorship of Russian Turkestan, covering the rest of the region, was proclaimed an autonomous soviet socialist republic (ASSR) within the Russian Soviet Federated Socialist Republic (RSFSR). By late 1924 the new Bolshevik authorities were ready to make more definitive territorial dispositions on the basis of ethnic/national composition. Turkmenistan and Uzbekistan were both established (in October 1924) as full soviet socialist republics (SSRs), while what are

now Kazakhstan and Kyrgyzstan became ASSRs within the RSFSR and Tajikistan became an ASSR within Uzbekistan. In further changes, Tajikistan became a full SSR in December 1929, as did Kyrgyzstan and Kazakhstan in December 1936.

The new boundaries varied greatly from the old ones and in part traced ethnic demarcations with circuitous complexity, especially where Uzbekistan bordered on Kyrgyzstan and Tajikistan in the Fergana valley. The former territory of the Khiva khanate was divided between Uzbekistan, the Kara-Kalpak ASSR, Kazakhstan and Turkmenistan. The Bukhara emirate was divided between Uzbekistan, Turkmenistan and Tajikistan. And the Kokand khanate was apportioned between Uzbekistan, Tajikistan, Kyrgyzstan and Kazakhstan.

Of the main ethnic groups accommodated by the Soviet boundary-drawing in Central Asia, the Persian-speaking Tajiks and related Badakhshan people are descended from the original inhabitants of the region. In contrast, the Turkic-speaking Kazakh, Kyrgyz, Turkmen and Kara-Kalpak peoples are descended from nomadic tribes which penetrated the region in the 6th and 7th centuries AD. As for the Uzbeks, they are a mixture of the indigenous Sarts of the Fergana valley and other oases, incoming nomads whose Turkic language displaced the Sarts' original Persian, and a later admixture of Mongol Tatars. The ethnic term Uzbek is in fact derived from the Uzbek-Khan epoch of the Tatar Golden Horde (14th century), although the Tatars did not conquer Central Asia until the early 16th century. Thereafter Uzbeks formed the elite of the Khiva khanate and the Bukhara emirate until the advent of Soviet rule. At that point the formerly subject Sarts also became known as Uzbeks, but there remain basic differences between Uzbeks of nomadic/Tatar origin and those who are really Sarts.

Rise of Inter-Ethnic Strife in 1980s—Autonomy Demands

Under Soviet rule the five Central Asian republics were always regarded as distinct from the rest of the Soviet Union. Despite the official discouragement of religious belief, they remained part of the Islamic world and of the "backward south" in the eyes of European Russia. In economic terms they became important for the Soviet Union, particularly as agricultural producers but also as sources of raw materials such as oil and gas, non-ferrous metals, gold and uranium. During and after World War II (1939-45) large numbers of people of other nationalities were deported to Soviet Central Asia, notably from the Caucasus and Ukraine. This enforced population movement in part reflected Stalin's enthusiasm for clearer boundaries between the European and Asian nationalities under Moscow's rule. At the same time, the government sponsored a major post-war influx of ethnic Russians into the Central Asian republics, where they mostly became pillars of Soviet rule and came to form a large component of the population of Kazakhstan in particular.

Through the decades of Soviet hegemony, one-party authoritarian rule enabled the local Communist leaderships to maintain the fiction that inter-ethnic conflict had been eradicated in Central Asia. When central discipline began to be relaxed in the late 1980s such conflict re-emerged with an intensity that was perhaps all the greater for having been suppressed for so long. In June 1989 over 100 people were killed in fighting between Uzbeks and Meskhetian Turks in the Fergana valley of Uzbekistan. Then numbering some 160,000 in Uzbekistan, the Meskhetian Turks had been deported from Georgia to Central Asia in 1944 as punishment for their alleged collaboration with the Germans. Also in June 1989 there were fatalities in clashes between Kazakhs and immigrant Caucasians in the Kazakhstan oil town of Novy Uzen, while in February 1990 anti-Armenian riots erupted in Dushanbe (the capital of Tajikistan). The worst violence of this period occurred in June-July 1990 in Kyrgyzstan, where over 300 people were killed in fighting between Kyrgyz and Uzbeks in the border district of Osh.

In May 1992, Tajikistan descended into a five-year civil war with an estimated loss of life ranging from 20,000 up to 50,000 inhabitants. During the civil war, various factions divided along regional lines with the Khodzhent and Kulyab regions pitted against the Kurgan-Tyube, Gharmi and Gorno-Badakhshan regions. The former two factions dominated the political structures of the Republic during the Soviet period. Although the events surrounding the beginning of the war are extremely complicated, broadly speaking the descent into violent conflict can be understood as a failure of the various political/regional parties to reach agreement on a post-Soviet political arrangement that would accommodate the interests of all of the regions concerned.

These and other outbreaks of inter-ethnic conflict in the twilight of the Soviet era were often indirectly connected to territorial claims. When the Soviet Union finally disintegrated, therefore, such territorially based ethnic unrest was ready to surface into actual political demands, often involving aspirations to territorial autonomy where minorities were concerned. Both of the existing autonomies—the Kara-Kalpak republic in Uzbekistan and the Gorno-Badakhshan region in Tajikistan—declared their desire for sovereignty; and the latter in April 1992 unilaterally converted itself into the Pamirs-Badakhshan Autonomous Republic, against the opposition of the Tajikistan government. Other claims to autonomy made by early 1992 included those of the Uigurs in Kazakhstan, the ethnic Germans of Kazakhstan and Kyrgyzstan, the Uzbeks in Tajikistan and Kyrgyzstan, the Kurds in Turkmenistan, the Koreans in Uzbekistan and Kazakhstan, and the Russians in northern Kazakhstan.

Territorial Issues

To the extent that the political frontiers established in Soviet Central Asia often departed from old ethnic and cultural boundaries, it was inevitable that territorial issues would emerge following the five republics' transition to independence in 1991. Even though all the governments in power declared their support for the maintenance of existing borders, in each republic movements developed with the aspiration to territorial change prominent in their agendas. Throughout the 1990s, the monitoring and control of borders became an important issue as a result of increasing illegal migration, drug trafficking and terrorist activity. It has now risen to the top of the political agenda in the aftermath of the Sept. 11, 2001, attacks in the USA.

In February 1999, an attempt was made to assassinate President Islam Karimov of Uzbekistan in Tashkent. Believing this to be the work of the Islamic Movement of Uzbekistan led by Juma Namangani (Jumabai Khojiev), which has bases in the mountainous regions of Uzbekistan's neighbours, the President ordered the planting of mines along its common border with Kyrgyzstan and Tajikistan and began the construction of fencing along its border with Kazakhstan. In a similar move, Turkmenistan constructed a 1,700 km-long fence along its borders with Uzbekistan and Kazakhstan.

In such an atmosphere, negotiations delimiting the borders between these states have become highly charged. An illustration of the sensitivity surrounding such territorial issues can be found in the redrawing of the 900-km border between Kyrgyzstan and China. Although an agreement reached in 1999 was ratified by the Kyrgyz legislature in May 2002, it involved ceding a swathe of territory in the Uzgeni-Kush river basin. This, combined with the arrest of a leading figure in the political opposition, Azimbek Beknazarov, who had strongly criticized the border agreement, led to widespread demonstrations culminating in the forced resignation of the Kyrgyz cabinet.

After the dissolution of the Soviet Union, major outstanding territorial issues between Kazakhstan and the Russian Federation still remained, not only over the threat of secession implicit in the autonomy aim of the ethnic Russians of northern Kazakhstan but also over the existing borders between the RSFSR and Kazakhstan, which were seen by many in the latter as having been established at the behest of the central authorities in Moscow. Conversely, concern in Kazakhstan that the Russian Federation aimed at border changes mounted when President Boris Yeltsin stated on Aug. 26, 1991, that the Russian Federation "reserves the right to raise the issue of a revision of borders" with all contiguous republics except the Baltic states.

Specifically, nationalists in Kazakhstan maintained that the republic's natural western frontier with the Russian Federation was the Volga river and that on geographical and historical grounds Kazakhstan had a legitimate claim to Astrakhan, Volgograd and Orenburg district. In the north, moreover, they advanced Kazakhstan's claim to a swathe of Russian territory from Kurgan and Omsk to the Altay mountain territory in the north-east. For their part, Russian nationalists responded by laying claim to substantial areas of Kazakhstan, principally on the grounds of predominant ethnic Russian composition. The areas specified included (i) the Aktyubinsk and Uralsk districts of north-western Kazakhstan; (ii) a large slice of northern Kazakhstan, including the towns of Kustanany, Kotchetav and Tselinograd; (iii) the region east of the Irtysh river; and (iv) the mountainous area of West Siberia lying east of Semipalatinsk.

Although much progress has been made during the border delimitation talks between the two countries, by the end of 2001 agreement had been reached on only half of the 7,000 km border.

As regards its Muslim neighbours to the south, Kazakhstan had, in the view of many Kazakhs, territorial claims on two of them. In the case of Uzbekistan, the Kara-Kalpak autonomous republic (which itself claimed wider borders) was seen as more properly a territory of Kazakhstan, which gave unofficial backing to its efforts to achieve sovereignty. A complication here was that some Kara-Kalpak activists favoured eventual transfer to the non-contiguous Russian Federation. In addition, Kazakhstan laid claim to the Tashkent regions as part of the territory of the Great Horde. At the same time, in Uzbekistan there were aspirations to the southern part of Kazakhstan's Chimkent region, to the west of Tashkent between the Syrdarya and Arys rivers.

An initial agreement delineating the borders between these two countries was drawn up in the autumn of 2001, but this left unresolved the rather thorny issue of the border villages of Bagys and Turkestan just over the border in Uzbekistan and the Arnasay Dam region, all of which have large majorities of ethnic Kazakhs. In December 2001, tension between the two sides increased due to one of the villages declaring itself as an independent Bagys Kazakh Republic, resulting in the Uzbek Army enforcing a curfew within the region. However, by September of the following year a final agreement was reached covering all of the 2,440-km border between the two countries. It was agreed that Arnasay and Bagys would go to Kazakhstan whilst Turkestan and three villages (Nsan 1, Nsan 2 and Baymurat) in the Karalkalpak District of Kyzyl-Orda region would be ceded to Uzbekistan.

Within Kyrgyzstan, the districts north of Lake Issyk-Kul were claimed by some Kazakh nationalists. In Kyrgyzstan some saw the southern districts of the Alma-Ata and Taldy-Kurgan regions of Kazakhstan, forming the northern slopes of the Kungey Alatou and Transily Atalau mountains, as legitimate targets for territorial revision in Kyrgyzstan's favour. A conference on border delimitation was first convened in 1996 and progress was rather slow. However, in July 2001 Presidents Nazarbayev of Kazakhstan and Akayev of Kyrgyzstan signed an agreement delimiting the 1,000-km border between their two countries.

Apart from the Kara-Kalpak and Chimkent problems with Kazakhstan, independent Uzbekistan also faced territorial complications with all three of its other neighbours. In the case of Turkmenistan, Uzbek nationalists claim (i) the strip of territory south-east of Chardzhou between the existing border and the Oxus river; and (ii) part of the Tashauz region of northern Turkmenistan (where the existing border already runs to the west of the Oxus). The response in some Turkmen circles has been to lay claim to the region of Uzbekistan south of Bukhara and even to that ancient city itself, as well as to Khiva where their ancient capital of Khwarazm is based. In Turkmenistan a claim was also mooted to part of Kazakhstan's Mangyshlak region on the Caspian Sea littoral. These disputes have since been settled and, in summer 2000, agreement was reached between Uzbekistan and Kazakhstan on the delimitation of their border. Similarly, in July 2001 Presidents Niyazov of Turkmenistan and Nazarbaev of Kazakhstan signed a treaty delimiting their countries' 450-km common border.

As regards Kyrgyzstan, one element of potential dispute concerns the eastern end of the tongue of Uzbek territory extending into the Fergana valley. According to Uzbek nationalists, part of the region of Kyrgyzstan surrounding the border town of Osh (where the brutal Uzbek-Kyrgyz clashes of mid-1990 occurred) should rightfully be part of Uzbekistan. These disputes are further complicated by the existence of the Uzbek enclave of Sokh within the territory of southern Kyrgyzstan. Residents within this enclave are seeking land corridors providing unhindered access to Uzbekistan. In addition, the borders around this region continue to be disputed by both sides. The issue is complicated by the fact that, during the Soviet period, two agreements were made—one when these republics were created and the other in the 1950s. Uzbekistan interprets the border according to the original delineation whilst Kyrgyzstan insists upon the 1950s agreement that created an Uzbek enclave within the territory of Kyrgyzstan. In the winter of early 2003, Uzbekistan cut off its gas supply to southern Kyrgyzstan, possibly to apply political leverage in the ongoing border talks. Such complications are slowing progress on any agreement delineating the borders of these two countries.

Uzbekistan's most complex territorial problems arise from its close geographical relationship with Tajikistan. For many Tajiks the inclusion in Uzbekistan of Samarkand, Bukhara and other historic Tajik-populated cities of the Zeravshan valley was a great injustice on the part of the Soviet boundary-drawers of the 1920s, since it deprived them of many important cultural and religious sites. Some Tajiks also lay claim to the Surkhan-Darya region west of the existing border to the south-west of Dushanbe. For their part, the Uzbeks recall that Fergana valley towns such as Khodjent (called Leninabad from 1932 to 1990), Isfara and Kanibadam had been excluded from the Tajikistan ASSR created in 1924 and had only been included in Tajikistan on its elevation to full republican status in 1929. Many Uzbeks still reside within the Khodjent region. This combination has led to calls for the integration of at least part of Khodjent into a greater Uzbekistan Their aspirations to the "recovery" of such areas reflects the long Uzbek ascendancy in the region under the old Bukhara emirate.

Under Soviet rule the inclusion of many Samarkand and Bukhara Tajiks in the Uzbekistan hierarchy helped to keep Tajik discontent in check. However, after independence had given a boost to nationalism, Uzbeks began to replace Tajiks in state bodies, with the result that the growing Tajik national movement had its own consciousness raised. A Tajik national-cultural society called "Samarkand", active in Uzbekistan since the late 1980s, had to face increasing official persecution after independence on the grounds that it was separatist and in league with irredentist forces in Tajikistan. Claiming that Tajiks predominated in the main urban centres, Samarkand activists complained about the lack of schools and media facilities available to Tajiks in Uzbekistan. They also protested against the post-independence reversion to old Uzbek street names in Samarkand and Bukhara, in place of the "socialist" appellations familiar in the Soviet era.

Tajikistan also has potential territorial claims against Kyrgyzstan, specifically to (i) the Batken district of the tongue of Kyrgyz territory extending south-west of Osh up to the narrow corridor of Tajik territory linking the main area of Tajikistan with the Fergana valley; and (ii) the northern slopes of the Alay and Zaalayskiy mountains. Conversely, Kyrgyz nationalists have laid claim to various stretches of Tajikistan's present territory, including (i) the southern slopes of the Alay and Zaalayskiy mountains; (ii) the northern area of the Gorno-Badakhshan (Pamirs-Badakhshan) region in the Pamir mountains; and (iii) the upper reaches of the Surkhob river valley. There are also two Tajik enclaves, Warukh and western Qalacha, within the territory of southern Kyrgyzstan close to the Isfara Valley. As in the case of Uzbekistan, the Tajik residents of these enclaves are demanding land corridors providing unhindered access to Tajikistan. At the beginning of 2003, riots erupted in the region pitting Kyrgyz against Tajiks. Although accounts of what sparked these disturbances varied, the common element appeared to be the intensification of border controls within the region by both authorities. A complicating factor in these issues is that the substantial Uzbek minorities in both Tajikistan and Kyrgyzstan have their own territorial ambitions deriving from the historical dominance of Uzbeks in the pre-Soviet Muslim polities of the region. However, delimitation talks between Kyrgyzstan and Tajikistan resumed in December 2002 aimed at finally resolving the forty disputed areas along their 940-km border.

China and the Central Asian Republics

Historically, the borders between China and the Central Asian republics of Kazakhstan, Kyrgyzstan and Tajikistan have also been disputed. As is described in Section 3.7 on China and Russia/Soviet Union, in the 17th century China had established its suzerainty over Xinjiang and controlled much of the area of what is now known as the three Central Asian republics. The Russian military advance into Central Asia in the mid-19th century resulted in two Sino-Russian treaties in the 1860s recognizing Russia's claim to vast swathes of Central Asian territory. China has viewed these as "unequal treaties" that were signed under duress and which are not therefore recognized as legitimate documents. The borders between the Soviet Union and China were thus a heated point of contestation between these two countries throughout the twentieth century.

The dissolution of the Soviet Union in 1991 created an opportunity for renewed talks on the border issue. In 1993 a commission was set up which included China, Russia, Kazakhstan, Kyrgyzstan and Tajikistan to examine, amongst other things, the demarcation of the border between China and the other countries. In 1996 these five states signed the Shanghai Accord establishing the "Shanghai Five" as a forum for resolving their border disputes. This later evolved into the Shanghai Co-operation Organization in June 2001 and at the same time expanded to include Uzbekistan.

The five-state commission provided a useful forum for the initiation of border talks between China and the three newly independent Central Asian states. A major border agreement was signed by China and Kazakhstan in April 1994 and several supplementary agreements were signed in September 1997 and July 1998. Finally, in March 1999, Kazakhstan ratified a treaty between itself and China establishing the border between them. The disputed area encompassed some 944 sq km, of which 56.9 per cent was allocated to Kazakhstan.

A border agreement between Kyrgyzstan and China was initially signed by Presidents Askar Akayev and Jiang Zemin in July 1996, a further supplement to this being agreed in 1999. China made claim to much of the disputed territory (96 per cent) but finally settled for about one-third of the area being negotiated. However, this meant that in total Kyrgyzstan had to cede about 1,250 sq km of land— 300 sq km in the 1996 agreement and 950 sq km in the 1999 agreement. As mentioned earlier, the later settlement of 1999, ceding a swathe of territory in the Uzgeni-Kush basin, proved to be highly controversial in Kyrgyzstan and led to widespread demonstrations against the treaty. Although initially the treaty failed to get past the upper chamber of the Kyrgyz parliament on May 14, 2002, it was ratified on a second reading later that month.

China also made claims to large areas of present day Tajikistan, totaling 28,000 sq km. During a state visit to China in August 1999, Tajikistan's President, Imomali Rakhmonov, signed an agreement demarcating some of the border areas between the two countries. However, several disputed border sections in the Gorno-Badakhshan region remained unresolved. In May 2002 a final agreement was reached whereby Tajikistan agreed to cede in total 1,000 sq km of territory in the Pamir Mountains.

The Caspian Sea

The Caspian Sea should represent a considerable source of energy in the future with an estimated 150 billion barrels of oil and vast quantities of gas. However, since the dissolution of the Soviet Union the Caspian Sea has become one of the main regions of territorial dispute with all five littoral states (Russia, Kazakhstan, Turkmenistan, Iran and Azerbaijan) contesting ownership of the area.

In July 2001 this contestation erupted into open hostility when a British Petroleum vessel conducting research in the Araz-Alov-Sharg field on behalf of Azerbaijan was threatened by Iranian gunboats. Both Iran and Turkmenistan declared that Azerbaijan's claim to certain fields had no basis in law as the delineation of territorial rights in the Caspian Sea was still unresolved. Prior to this, tensions had been exacerbated by the purchase of naval hardware by several of these littoral states. It is believed that shortly before this clash, Turkmenistan had obtained several gunboats from both Russia and Ukraine, Azerbaijan had obtained gunboats from the United States, and Turkey had agreed to supply Kazakhstan with similar equipment. Despite such procurements, Russian and Iran continue to possess the largest naval presence. Possibly as a reminder of this fact, Russia flexed its muscles by holding a series of naval war games in the area in August 2002.

The main obstacle to a speedy and equitable resolution to this dispute is the different ideas of what principles should guide such an agreement. Kazakhstan, Russia and Azerbaijan seek to share the waters in common whilst dividing the seabed along international boundary lines using a variant of the median-line principle. This entails allocating territory according to the length of each state's coastline with each state's border finishing at a median line drawn down the middle of the sea between neighbouring states. This would in effect give the greatest amount of seabed to those with the longest shorelines. On this basis bilateral treaties were signed between Russia and Kazakhstan in March 2002 and between Azerbaijan and Russia in September 2002. Russia and Kazakhstan agreed to joint exploitation of three fields: Kurmangazy, Central and Khvalynskoye. As a result of these bilateral treaties, Kazakhstan gained 29 per cent of the seabed while both Azerbaijan and Russia received approximately 19 per cent.

Unsurprisingly, given its smaller coastline, Iran has argued that the resources ahould be divided equally so that each receives a fifth of the overall mineral wealth. If the median-line principle were to be followed, Iran would only receive a 13 per cent share of the seabed. Meanwhile, Turkmenistan has sought to strike a compromise by advocating that each state be allocated a national coastal zone that extends fifteen to twenty miles into the sea with the remaining area being shared. The situation is complicated, however, by the fact that both Turkmenistan and Azerbaijan lay claim to the Serdar/Kyapaz oil field, which is believed to contain 2.3 billion tons of oil.

Talks were convened between all five states in Almaty in May 2003, but the sticking point continued to be the different interpretations of how to divide the spoils.

John Glenn

3.5 China - India

The Sino-Indian frontier, which is some 2,500 miles (4,000 kilometres) long, falls into three sections: (i) the eastern section, about 700 miles long, where Tibet borders on Arunachal Pradesh (formerly the North-East Frontier Agency); (ii) the central section, where Tibet borders on the independent kingdom of Bhutan, Sikkim (since 1975 a state of the Indian Union), the kingdom of Nepal and the Indian states of Uttar Pradesh and Himachal Pradesh; and (iii) the western section (including the Ladakh frontier), where Kashmir borders on Tibet and Xinjiang (Sinkiang) to the east and Xinjiang to the north. Since 1959 the eastern and western sections of the frontier have been the subject of major territorial disputes between India and China. (See Map 24, p. 504.)

Eastern Section during British rule in India

The frontier problem in the eastern section arises from the mountainous terrain and the limited control formerly exercised by the British over the tribal peoples living in the foothills of the Himalayas and by the Chinese over Tibet. Chinese suzerainty over Tibet was nominally established in 1720, but in practice Tibet continued to be ruled by the priestly caste headed by the Dalai Lama. After the annexation of Assam by the British in 1838, British control was gradually extended into the tribal areas, which were placed under the jurisdiction either of political agents or of the deputy commissioners of the adjoining districts of Assam. To regulate the entry of lowlanders into the tribal areas an "inner line" running along the foot of the hills was defined in 1873; this was purely an administrative device, however, the international boundary remaining undefined. During the same period Nepal, Sikkim and Bhutan increasingly fell within the British rather than the Chinese sphere of influence.

Following violations of the Sikkim border by the Tibetans, a British expeditionary force invaded Tibet in 1903-04, and in 1906 an Anglo-Chinese convention recognized Chinese suzerainty over Tibet. Chinese troops invaded the country in 1910, deposed the Dalai Lama, who fled to India, and proclaimed Chinese sovereignty (as opposed to suzerainty) over Tibet. After the Chinese revolution of 1911, however, the Chinese garrison in Tibet mutinied, and in the following year the

Dalai Lama returned and declared Tibet independent.

To achieve a settlement of the controversy over Tibet's status a conference was held at Simla in 1913-14 at which Britain, China and Tibet were represented. A convention which was initialled by representatives of all three countries recognized that Tibet formed part of Chinese territory, whilst China undertook not to convert it into a Chinese province. Tibet was divided into an inner zone under direct Chinese control and an autonomous outer zone; the Chinese government would not interfere in the administration of the latter, send troops into it or provide for its representation in any future Chinese parliament. The convention was subsequently signed by the British and Tibetan representatives, but the Chinese government repudiated its representative's action in initialling the document, as it objected to the proposed boundaries of the outer and inner zones.

Sir Henry McMahon, the head of the British delegation, took the opportunity presented by the Simla conference to negotiate the frontier between Tibet and India by means of an exchange of letters with the Tibetan delegation, which formed an appendix to the convention. The proposed border, which followed the watershed of the Himalayas north of the tribal territories, stood back about 100 miles from the plains of Assam, and as the intervening country consisted of difficult hills and valleys it constituted a strong barrier against invasion.

The validity of this agreement remains a subject of controversy. The Indian government maintains that it was valid as it was approved by the Tibetan government, which at that time was considered competent to enter into direct dealings concerning its borders. China claims that it was an "unequal treaty" imposed upon Tibet without China's consent, and therefore had no legal force. British and Indian scholars have suggested that McMahon acted on his own initiative, and was not supported by his superiors because the agreement was in breach of treaties which Britain had concluded with China and Russia; hence it was not mentioned in John MacMurray's standard work *Treaties and Agreements with and concerning China* (1921) or in volume XIV of *Aitchison's Treaties, Engagements and Sanads,* the official record of all treaties entered into by the government of India, which appeared in 1929.

In 1935 Olaf Caroe, deputy secretary of the Foreign and Political Department of the Government of India, "unearthed" (in his own phrase) the 1914 agreement, which had remained a dead letter, and persuaded the government of India that the "McMahon Line" should be regarded as the boundary. This line appeared as the frontier on official Survey of India maps for the first time in 1938, although it was still shown as undemarcated until 1954, and to support the new policy the 1929 edition of volume XIV of *Aitchison's Treaties* was withdrawn in 1938 and replaced by a new volume, still bearing the date 1929, which included the 1914 agreement. This policy was criticized by Sir Henry Twynam, the Acting Governor of Assam, who suggested in a letter to the Viceroy in 1939 that the government was not on "absolutely firm ground juridically", as the letters exchanged between McMahon and the Tibetan delegation were "lacking in the formalities associated with a treaty", and that the fact that the government of India had taken no steps to implement the agreement from 1914 to 1938 must adversely affect its position in international law.

However, the Balipara Frontier tract (of which Tawang was a part) came under the direct administration of the Governor of Assam from April 1, 1937, and a letter of the Governor to the government of India in May 1937 referred to the fact that Tawang had been "ceded to India" in 1914. The first British officer to go on an official mission to Tawang was Captain G. A. Nevill in 1914. In 1938 the Governor of Assam (Sir Robert Reid) made a plea to the government of India for the despatch of the Lightfoot Expedition to Tawang in that year. In September 1938 the Acting Governor of Assam, Sir Gilbert Hogg, forwarded the proposals of Captain Lightfoot to the government of India and recommended the declaration of a "control area" for Tawang.

At this time the government of India also looked at the Sadiya Frontier Tract, which included the Lohit and Siang areas of Arunachal Pradesh. Regular tours were undertaken in the area and the government of India sanctioned the extension of the "control area" (of the Political Officer of the Sadiya Frontier Tract) up to the McMahon Line in the Siang Valley (in May 1941). The Governor of Assam visited the region in December 1941.

From 1944 onwards, British control over the tribal territories was extended up to the McMahon line, and it was then discovered that some areas south of the line were still under Tibetan administration and the population were paying taxes to the Tibetan authorities.

Eastern Section after Indian Independence

After India became independent in 1947 the new government brought the tribal areas of the North-East Frontier Agency under the direct administrative control of the Governor of Assam. (In 1972 they became a union territory separate from Assam under the name of Arunachal Pradesh.)

Although successive Chinese governments continued to assert their claim to sovereignty over Tibet, internal strife and the war with Japan prevented them from enforcing it until after the Communist victory in the civil war. In 1950 Chinese troops occupied Tibet, and in the following year an agreement was signed whereby the Dalai Lama accepted Chinese suzerainty and China guaranteed Tibet's internal autonomy. This change in Tibet's status did not immediately affect relations between India and China, which remained friendly. Under an agreement signed in 1954 the two countries agreed to base their relations on the "five principles" of respect for each other's territorial integrity and sovereignty, non-aggression, non-interference in each other's internal affairs, equality and mutual benefit, and peaceful coexistence, whilst India renounced all extra-territorial rights in Tibet in return for concessions for Indians visiting trade centres and places of pilgrimage.

When his attention was drawn in 1950 to Chinese maps showing Tibet's southern boundary as extending to the Brahmaputra River in Assam, Jawaharlal Nehru, the Indian Prime Minister, declared that the McMahon line "is our frontier, and we will not allow anyone to cross it". The reference in the 1954 agreement to mutual respect for territorial integrity was interpreted in India as an implicit guarantee that China would accept the existing frontier. During a visit to India in 1956 Zhou Enlai (the Chinese Premier) told Nehru that although the Chinese government thought the McMahon line unfair, because it was an accomplished fact and because of their friendly relations with India they were of the opinion that they should recognize it, but that they must consult the Tibetan authorities first. Chinese maps continued to show a frontier far south of the McMahon line, however, and a number of minor border incidents occurred in the next three years, none of which involved any clashes between Chinese and Indian troops.

Relations seriously deteriorated after the Tibetan uprising of March 1959 and the flight of the Dalai Lama to India, which gave rise to Chinese allegations of Indian interference in Chinese affairs. In August 1959 a Chinese force occupied the Indian frontier post of Longju after expelling the small garrison. In a letter to Nehru published on Sept. 8 of that year Zhou Enlai stated that "the Chinese government absolutely does not recognize the so-called McMahon line", and maintained that Indian troops had unlawfully occupied Longju, which he claimed was north of the McMahon line and in Chinese territory. The Indian government declared in a note of Sept. 10 that it "stands firmly" on the McMahon line, though it was prepared to "discuss the exact alignment of the line at places where it departs from the geographical features marking the international boundary". Two days later Nehru told the Indian Parliament that the government was prepared to consider minor rectifications of "a mile here or a mile there", but not "to hand over the Himalayas". A map depicting China's territorial claims, compiled from official Chinese maps and published by the Indian External Affairs Ministry, showed that China claimed about 32,000 square miles (83,000 sq km) of territory south of the McMahon line, including three of the four political divisions of the North-East Frontier Agency (Kameng, Subansiri and Siang) and part of the fourth (Lohit).

Eastern Section—Developments 1960s-1980s

Zhou Enlai visited New Delhi in April 1960 for talks with Nehru, at the conclusion of which they announced that as they had not succeeded in resolving the differences that had arisen, officials of the two governments would meet to examine all relevant documents. At a press conference on April 25, 1960, Zhou suggested that the following six points could form the basis for a settlement: "(i) There exist disputes with regard to the boundary between the two sides. (ii) There exists between the two countries a line of actual control up to which each side exercises administrative jurisdiction. (iii) In determining the boundary between the two countries, certain geographical principles, such as watersheds, river valleys and mountain passes, should be equally applicable to all sectors of the boundary. (iv) A settlement of the boundary question between the two countries should take into account the national feelings of the two peoples towards the Himalayas and the Karakoram mountains. (v) Pending a solution of the boundary question through discussions, both sides should keep to the line of actual control and should not put forward territorial claims as preconditions, but individual adjustments may be made. (vi) In order to ensure tranquillity on the border and thereby facilitate discussions, both sides should continue to refrain from patrolling along all sectors of the boundary". Points (iii) and (iv) were interpreted as a suggestion that China was prepared to accept the McMahon line as the border in the eastern section if India accepted the Chinese claim that the watershed of the Karakoram mountains formed the border in the western section (see below). The proposed talks between officials produced no result.

The eastern section of the border remained quiet for three years after the Longju incident, but on Sept. 20 and Oct. 10, 1962, two clashes occurred in the area of the trijunction of the Bhutanese, Indian and Tibetan borders, with some loss of life on both sides. In a subsequent exchange of notes each side claimed to have acted in self-defence and accused the other of crossing the McMahon line.

On Oct. 20, 1962, the Chinese army launched an offensive at the western end of the McMahon line, which was followed by a similar offensive at the eastern end. During the next month the Chinese troops advanced over 100 miles south of the McMahon line at the western end and 25 to 30 miles south at the eastern end, threatening the plains of Assam. On Nov. 21, however, the Chinese government announced that its troops would observe a ceasefire and would withdraw to positions 20 kilometres (12 miles) north of the McMahon line, and that it would set up checkpoints on its side of the line of actual control existing on Nov. 7, 1959. The Chinese subsequently withdrew, but established checkpoints at Dhola and Longju, at the western end and in the central sector of the McMahon line respectively.

At the proposal of Sirimavo Bandaranaike, the Prime Minister of Ceylon, representatives of six Asian and African non-aligned countries—Burma, Ceylon, Ghana, Indonesia, Cambodia, and the United Arab Republic—met in Colombo on Dec. 10-12, 1962, to discuss means of bringing India and China together. The following proposals were put forward: (i) In the western section the Chinese should withdraw their military posts by 20 kilometres, as they had proposed on Nov. 21, and the Indian forces should keep their existing positions. The area vacated by the Chinese would be a demilitarized zone, to be administered by civilian posts of both sides. (ii) In the eastern section the line of actual control should serve as a ceasefire line. (iii) These proposals once implemented should pave the way for discussions on solving problems entailed in the ceasefire position. Although both India and China announced their acceptance of the proposals, they differed in their interpretation of them, and in consequence they remained ineffective.

Occasional border incidents thereafter occurred in the eastern section, in the most serious of which four Indian soldiers were killed in October 1975. The Indian government alleged in a note of June 26, 1986, that about 40 Chinese personnel had intruded into the Sumdorong Chu valley on June 16 to a point 2.3 kilometres south of the McMahon line. A Chinese Foreign Ministry spokesman said on July 16 that they had been north of the line of actual control and hence in Chinese territory. K. R. Narayanan, the Indian Minister of State for External Affairs, said on Aug. 6 that information had been received suggesting that Chinese personnel had constructed a helicopter landing area in the Sumdorong Chu valley. The official New China News Agency accused Indian military personnel and aircraft on Aug. 22 of persistently crossing the line of control in the eastern border region in an attempt to "nibble further at Chinese territory and to create more disputed territory".

The legal status of Arunachal Pradesh caused controversy on a number of occasions. An Indian parliamentary delegation cancelled a proposed visit to China in October 1981 after the Chinese authorities refused to issue a visa to a delegate from Arunachal Pradesh; a compromise was reached, however, whereby all the delegates were given visas, not on their Indian passports, but on separate sheets of paper. The participation of dancers from Arunachal Pradesh in the closing ceremony of the ninth Asian Games in New Delhi in December 1982 was strongly criticized by the New China News Agency, which described it as "a deliberate step to propagate India's sovereignty over the state and legalize it".

The constitutional status of the union territory of Arunachal Pradesh was raised to that of a state of the Indian Union under a bill passed by the Indian Parliament on Dec. 9, 1986. A Chinese Foreign Ministry spokesman said on Dec. 11 that this measure had "seriously violated China's territorial integrity and sovereignty"; an Indian official spokesman subsequently described the Chinese protest as "clear inference" in Indian affairs.

The Central Section

Only minor disagreements have arisen concerning the status of a number of mountain passes and other relatively small areas in this sector, and no serious border incidents have occurred. When in 1954 an agreement on trade and travel between India and Tibet was being negotiated the Chinese draft stated that the Chinese government agreed to open six mountain passes. This

wording was challenged by the Indian delegation, which maintained that the passes were Indian. In its final form the agreement referred to them as border passes open to nationals of both countries.

A Chinese note of Dec. 26, 1959, stated that "according to Indian maps…the boundary line in the middle sector is relatively close to the delineation of the Chinese maps, but still a number of areas which have always belonged to China are included in India". The note based the Chinese claims to these areas on the fact that their population was of Tibetan origin. In reply, an Indian note of Feb. 12, 1960, recalled that Zhou Enlai had said in 1957 that the Sino-Burmese boundary line "is often found dividing into two parts a nationality living in compact communities on the borders" and had continued: "This is the result of historical development…When we solve the question of the undefined boundary line between China and Burma, we must realize beforehand that it will be hard to avoid separating the nationalities concerned".

The Ladakh Frontier

Ladakh, formerly an independent state, came under the suzerainty of the Moghul Emperors in 1664. When the Tibetans invaded Ladakh in 1681-83 the Ladakhis defeated them with Moghul assistance, and a peace treaty signed in 1684 stated that "the boundaries fixed in the beginning…shall still be maintained". After the decline of the Moghul empire, Ladakh was conquered in 1834 by the Raja of Jammu, who in 1846 received the title of Maharaja of Jammu and Kashmir. A new war with Tibet in 1841-42 was concluded by a peace treaty signed by representatives of the Raja of Jammu, the Dalai Lama and the Chinese Emperor. Under this agreement Tibet recognized the Raja as the political overlord of Ladakh, although the Ladakhi Buddhists continued to regard the Dalai Lama as their spiritual overlord, and each side undertook to respect "the old-established frontiers". The accession of Jammu and Kashmir to the Indian Union in 1947 and the Chinese occupation of Tibet in 1950 brought the governments in New Delhi and Beijing into direct contact in this area.

The border area was described by Nehru in 1959 as "a barren and uninhabited region, 17,000 feet high and without a vestige of grass", and by Sir H. A. F. Rumbold (a former senior India Office official) in 1977 as a "frozen, uninhabitable wilderness". Neither the treaty of 1684 nor that of 1842 defined where the boundary was, and the region was not even surveyed until 1864. Although the British authorities in India proposed on a number of occasions down to 1899 that the boundary should be delimited, they received no response from the Chinese government, and the official *Aitchison's Treaties*, volume XII (1931), described the northern and eastern frontier of Jammu and Kashmir as "undefined".

Many British official maps, including that attached to the Simon Commission's report of 1930 and that submitted by the general staff of the Indian Army to the British Cabinet Mission in 1946, showed the boundary as following approximately the crest of the Karakoram mountains, although other British maps showed either a firm line or a colour wash right up to the Kuenlun mountains, about 80 miles to the north-east. Suggestions which were put forward by Sir John Ardagh in 1897 that the boundary should be extended to the crest of the Kuenlun range were rejected by the general staff, on the ground that the new frontier would be difficult to defend and strategically useless, and were never officially accepted. In July 1954, however, the Indian government published a new official map which showed a boundary line following the crest of the Kuenlun mountains, and for the first time included the whole of the Aksai Chin plateau (an area of about 14,000 square miles or 36,000 sq km) within Indian territory, although since 1950 this area had been under Chinese control.

Strategically the Aksai Chin is of great importance to China, as it forms the link between Tibet and Xinjiang (Sinkiang), and in 1956-57 the Chinese built a road across it connecting the two regions. As India asserted its claim to sovereignty over the area only by sending occasional patrols, the Indian government remained unaware of the road's existence until its attention was drawn to a Chinese press report. Two reconnaissance parties were sent in 1958 to investigate, one of which was captured by Chinese troops, whilst the other confirmed that the road ran through territory claimed by India. In response to Indian representations the Chinese government released the arrested men, but maintained that the road ran only through Chinese territory.

In a letter of March 22, 1959, to Zhou Enlai, Nehru based India's claim to the Aksai Chin partly on the treaty of 1842 and partly on evidence of actual occupation and administration, such as detailed surveys, explorations, hunting rights, travellers' accounts, use of pastures, collection of salt, construction of trade routes and sending of patrols. In his reply, published on Sept. 8, 1959, Zhou Enlai pointed out that the 1842 treaty "only mentioned in general terms that Ladakh and Tibet would each abide by their borders, and did not contain any specific provisions regarding the location of this section of the boundary". He continued: "This section of the boundary has never been delimited. Between China and Ladakh there does, however, exist a customary line derived from historical traditions, and Chinese maps have always drawn the boundary between China and Ladakh in accordance with this line".

A clash between an Indian police patrol and Chinese troops, in which nine of the former were killed, occurred on Oct. 21, 1959, in the Chang Chenmo valley, west of the Lanak La pass, which lies on the borderline claimed by India. In a subsequent exchange of notes each government alleged that the incident had taken place on its own territory and had been caused by an intrusion by the other's forces. According to an Indian External Affairs Ministry statement of Nov. 27, 1962, Chinese troops occupied 6,000 square miles (15,000 sq km) of territory in the disputed area during 1959-62, establishing check posts and constructing roads connecting them with their bases.

Three encounters between Chinese and Indian troops occurred in July 1962 in the Galwan river valley, near Pangong lake and in the Chip Chap valley, the only casualties being two Indian soldiers wounded in the last incident. On Oct. 20, 1962, the Chinese Army opened an offensive in the Aksai Chin at the same time as that on the McMahon line (see above). Fighting took place in three areas: immediately south of the Karakoram pass, around Pangong lake, 100 miles to the south-east, and around Damchok, in the extreme south-east of the disputed territory. During the fighting the Chinese occupied all the Indian outposts east of the boundary claimed by China, but made no attempt to occupy an Indian post two miles west of this line, which had been evacuated by its garrison. As on the eastern front, China declared a ceasefire on Nov. 21, and announced that its troops would withdraw to positions 20 kilometres behind the line of actual control existing on Nov. 7, 1959.

Since 1962 the situation in the Aksai Chin has generally remained peaceful, apart from an incident in September 1965 (when India was at war with Pakistan) in which three Indian policemen were killed.

Demarcation of China-Pakistan Border

Pakistan and China announced on May 3, 1962, that they had agreed to demarcate their common border, i.e. the border of Xinjiang and the area of Kashmir under Pakistani control. An Indian note to Pakistan of May 10 of that year contended that Pakistan and China had no common boundary, as Kashmir formed "an integral part of the Indian Union"; that India would not be bound by the results of any bilateral discussions between Pakistan and China; and that the border of Kashmir west of the Karakoram pass followed well-known natural features and did not require fresh delimitation.

An agreement between China and Pakistan delimiting the boundary was signed in Beijing on March 2, 1963. A Pakistani Foreign Ministry spokesman stated that out of 3,400 square miles (8,800 sq km) in dispute, Pakistan had obtained 1,350 square miles under the agreement, including 750 square miles which were actually in Chinese possession, and China had obtained 2,050 square miles. Pakistan also abandoned her claim to over 13,000 square miles of Xinjiang territory, which had previously been shown as part of Kashmir on Pakistani but not on Indian maps.

After the delimitation of the border China and Pakistan co-operated in the construction of two all-weather highways linking the Pakistani-controlled area of Kashmir with Xinjiang, one of which, running through the Mintaka pass, was opened in 1968, whilst the other (the Karakoram highway), running through the Khunjerab pass, was opened in 1978. Strong protests against both projects were lodged by India.

Sino-Indian Negotiations on Border Dispute 1978-1990

A goodwill mission led by Wang Bingnan, president of the Chinese People's Association for Friendship with Foreign Countries, which visited India on March 7-23, 1978, met Morarji Desai and A. B. Vajpayee (Prime Minister and External Affairs Minister respectively in the Janata Party government then in power), and on behalf of the Chinese government extended an invitation to Vajpayee to visit China, which was accepted. Desai told Parliament on March 16, however, that he had made it clear to the Chinese mission that "full normalization of relations, of course, cannot be attained till the main outstanding issue—the border question—is resolved to our mutual satisfaction by negotiations".

Vajpayee arrived in Beijing on Feb. 12, 1979, for his visit, the first by an Indian minister for over 20 years, and had talks with Huang Hua (the Chinese Foreign Minister), whom he invited to visit India to continue the dialogue, before returning to New Delhi on Feb. 18. Reporting to Parliament on Feb. 21, he said that he had emphasized the fundamental importance of the boundary question, which "must be satisfactorily settled if relations of mutual confidence are to be established". He had also informed the Chinese leaders that the attitude towards the Kashmir question adopted by China in the past 15 years had been "an additional and unnecessary complication to the prospects of Sino-Indian relations", and reiterated India's concern at the construction of the Karakoram highway across territory forming part of the state of Jammu and Kashmir.

Eric Gonsalves, the Indian External Affairs Secretary, visited Beijing for discussions on June 20-23, 1980, and delivered a new invitation to Huang Hua to visit India. In an interview with an Indian journalist on June 21, Deng Xiaoping (then the senior Chinese Deputy Premier) said: "So long as both sides are sincere, respect the present state of the border and are tolerant towards each other, the Sino-Indian boundary question can be solved through peaceful negotiations. As a matter of fact, ever since negotiations on boundary questions began China has never asked for the return of all the territory illegally incorporated into India by the old colonialists. Instead, China suggested that both countries should make concessions, China in the eastern sector and India in the western sector, on the basis of the actually controlled border line so as to solve the Sino-Indian boundary question in a package plan, thus fully demonstrating the spirit of mutual understanding and concessions". Indian sources pointed out that this proposal, which was repeated in a New China News Agency commentary on June 25, 1980, was merely a "feeler" which had not been officially put forward during the talks with Gonsalves.

Huang Hua paid a visit to New Delhi (the first by a Chinese minister since Zhou Enlai's visit in 1960) on June 26-29, 1981, and after he had met the Prime Minister, Indira Gandhi, she announced that it had been agreed to hold talks to resolve the border issue, three rounds of talks then taking place in 1981-83. Although no details of the negotiations were published officially, China was reported to favour a package deal along the lines suggested by Zhou Enlai in 1960 and by Deng Xiaoping in 1980, i.e. a border settlement along the existing lines of control, whereby China would accept the McMahon line as the frontier in the eastern section and India would accept China's claim to the Aksai Chin. The Indian delegation, on the other hand, proposed at the first round (i) that the two sides should accept the proposal of the Colombo Conference for demilitarization of the territory occupied by China in 1962, and (ii) that they should hold separate and simultaneous discussions on each section of the border, as a prelude to a comprehensive settlement. The next two rounds were devoted to debate on which approach should be adopted.

An advance was achieved at the fourth round, held in New Delhi on Oct. 25-30, 1983, when the Chinese accepted the Indian proposal for a sector-by-sector review of the border, and both sides agreed to take into account the relevance of historical evidence, custom and tradition to the position in each sector. After the fifth round, held in Beijing on Sept. 17-22, 1984, Indian officials said that principles had been formulated upon which the dispute would be negotiated sector by sector, and the New China News Agency reported that the two sides had "made efforts to narrow differences and expand common points". The sixth round, held in New Delhi on Nov. 9-11, 1985, was devoted to matters relating to the eastern sector of the border. At the seventh, held in Beijing on July 21-24, 1986, no substantial progress was made.

In the absence of further negotiations, Sino-Indian tensions increased in mid-April 1987 when the Chinese Foreign Ministry claimed that its Indian counterpart had "totally confounded black and white" in its latest report on alleged Chinese territorial violations. Later the same month Deng Xiaoping told a visiting Indian Communist Party leader (on April 20) that the Sino-Indian border dispute should be settled in a spirit of mutual understanding and accommodation. However, tension again flared in early May 1987 when the Chinese claimed that Indian troops had encroached on Chinese territory and also attributed airspace violations and troop concentrations to the Indians. The Indian Foreign Ministry responded that India did not want a confrontation with China and expressed a willingness to resume talks at any time.

The Indian Foreign Minister, Narain Dutt Tiwari, had talks on the latest crisis in Beijing on June 15-16, 1987, during which he agreed with Chinese leaders that "peace and stability" should be maintained, and "provocations" avoided, along the Sino-Indian border, pending a negotiated settlement of the dispute.

On Oct. 9, 1987, demonstrations in New Delhi were held outside the Chinese Embassy and the UN

Office to protest at Chinese actions in Tibet, following a series of demonstrations for independence which met with severe Chinese repression. The demonstrators in Delhi also expressed their disappointment at the Indian government's stand on Tibet since it had closed its border with that country on Oct. 7 to prevent an influx of Tibetan refugees. Nine Tibetan Youth Congress members were arrested during the demonstrations in Delhi. A further anti-Chinese demonstration by Tibetans took place in Delhi on Nov. 16.

Indo-Chinese relations improved following the visit to Beijing (Dec. 19-23, 1988) of Rajiv Gandhi (the first by an Indian Prime Minister in 34 years) and as a result of the visit a joint working party to resolve border disputes between the two countries was created. Linked to this both states agreed to hold annual diplomatic consultations between foreign ministers.

However, on March 7, 1989, China imposed martial law in Lhasa and tensions between India and China did not noticeably subside. The first meeting of the Sino-Indian working party was held in Beijing from June 30 to July 4, 1989. On Oct. 11, 1989, the Chinese Vice-Premier, Wu Xueqian, visited Delhi to discuss bilateral matters under the annual meeting, which was significant since he was the highest ranking Chinese minister to visit India since 1962. The two sides described the prospects of settling the border issue as "good". Both sides subsequently scaled down the number of troops along their respective borders.

Sino-Indian Dialogue on Border Dispute, 1991-2003

Between December 1988 and June 1993 six rounds of talks were held by the Indian-Chinese Joint Working Group (JWG) on the border, and while some positive progress was made the developments were subject to wider political issues throughout the 1990s. Further Chinese clampdowns in Tibet took place in March 1991 and on May 23, 1991 (the 40th anniversary of the Chinese "liberation" of Tibet) large numbers of Chinese troops were stationed in Lhasa to prevent demonstrations.

The third meeting of the Sino-Indian JWG on the border issue (the second meeting having been held in Delhi Aug. 30-Sept. 1, 1990, without achieving noticeable progress) was held in Beijing on May 13, 1991. The Chinese delegation was led by the Vice-Minister of Foreign Affairs, Xu Dunxin, while the Indian delegation was led by the Foreign Secretary, Muchkund Dubey. According to the Xinhua Chinese news agency (May 13) the talks "further promoted mutual understanding" while the Indian Press Trust reported that the two sides had agreed to finalize arrangements for establishing consulates-general in Mumbai (Bombay) and Shanghai—these being opened in December 1992.

Over Dec. 11-16, 1991, China's Premier, Li Peng, visited Delhi for talks with the Indian government (the first visit by a Chinese Premier in 31 years) and the visit, which was a success, was seen as a further thaw in Sino-Indian relations. But though the visit led to a number of agreements in other areas, the two sides failed to resolve their outstanding border problems. Hopes for such a settlement had been raised a week before Li's visit when he had said China would seek "mutual accommodation" and "pending a resolution of the border issue, both sides should abide by the border lines under actual control". This, effectively, meant an acceptance of the status quo. A communiqué of Dec. 16, 1991, stressed that both sides would continue to work towards "a mutually acceptable solution to the boundary question", using the joint working party established for this purpose in 1988. All India Radio reported Prime Minister Rao as saying "there has not been much progress on the border issue with China". In addition, India reaffirmed that "Tibet is an autonomous region of China".

Significant changes began to occur in 1993, even though the sixth round of talks in New Delhi (June 26-27, 1993) did not result in the expected agreement on troop numbers along the border. Prior to the meeting there was a widespread expectation that an agreement to reduce troop numbers would be reached, but the issue of parity in reductions in troop numbers and how to verify such reductions blocked final agreement.

On Sept. 7, 1993, Tang Jiaxuan (Vice Foreign Minister, China) and R.L. Bhatia (Minister of State for External Affairs, India) signed an "Agreement on the Maintenance of Peace and Tranquillity along the Line of Actual Control in the India-China Border Areas". Under this it was agreed inter alia: (i) That the boundary question(s) would be "resolved through peaceful and friendly consultations" and neither India nor China would resort to the use, or threat of use, of force to resolve the disputes; in the absence of a solution both sides would "strictly respect and observe the line of actual control [LAC]"; (ii) Military forces on either side of the LAC would be kept to the minimum level and the two sides agreed to reduce their forces along the LAC "in conformity with the requirements of the principle of mutual consultations between the two countries", although the nature, extent, depth and timing of such reductions—which would take place in stages by geographical sectors—had yet to be agreed; (iii) To "work out…effective [confidence-building measures]" and prior notification of military exercises along the LAC; (iv) "Contingencies or other problems" in the areas along the LAC would be dealt with through meetings and consultations between border personnel; (v) To take measures to avoid air incursions and consult on possible restrictions on air exercises near the LAC; (vi) Effective verification measures and supervision of force reductions would be agreed; and (vii) Diplomatic and military experts would be appointed to the India-China Joint Working Group on the boundary question to advise on the resolution of differences and supervision of the agreement.

Talks in February 1994 did not yield further progress on the above agreement, but in July 1994 both states agreed, and reiterated, that border problems would be resolved peacefully through "mutual understanding and concessions." The gradual warming of relations continued through 1994 and 1995 with both sides reportedly "seriously engaged" in defining the LAC and resolving the border disputes in Beijing in July 1995.

On Nov. 29, 1996, a 12 article "Agreement Between the Government of the Republic of India and the Government of the People's Republic of China on Confidence-Building Measures in the Military Field Along the Line of Actual Control in the India-China Border Areas" was signed. As the preamble stated, this agreement was "pursuant to" the 1993 agreement and indicated the (relative) success of the negotiations and dialogue of the previous decade.

Putting the substance of the 1993 and 1996 agreements into operation proved a lengthy process, but the Joint Working Group established in 1988 was making steady progress in reducing tensions between the two states. However, the eleventh annual meeting scheduled for 1998 in Beijing was not convened by China, following the protests over the Pokhran II nuclear explosions by India in May 1998, which disrupted the relationship and led to a renewed chill in Sino-Indian relations. In part this was due to sabre rattling by the Indian Defence Minister, George Fernandes, who prior to the tests had accused China of intruding into India's state of Arunachal and referred to China as "a bigger potential threat" than Pakistan. In addition, a letter from Prime Minister Atal Bahari Vajpayee to US President Bill Clinton cited China's threat to India as a partial rationale for the nuclear weapons tests and development.

By February 1999 a thaw in relations was apparent with the first round of consultations on bilateral, regional and international issues taking place. The eleventh meeting of the JWG was convened on April 26-27, 1999, in Beijing. This was followed in June by a two-day visit of India's External Affairs Minister, Jaswant Singh, to China at the invitation of the Chinese Foreign Minster, Tang Jiaxuan, when the two states decided to celebrate jointly on April 1, 2000, the 50th anniversary of the establishment of diplomatic relations between China and India. Singh stated that the meeting was "very cordial, comprehensive, friendly and very productive" in terms of dialogue and undid some of the tension by declaring that China was "not a security threat to India".

During the 50th anniversary celebrations Indian and Chinese army personnel held a commemorative border meeting at the Nathu La pass along the LAC in Kashmir, even though relations were still wary. India was reportedly worried about the increase in the number of incursions along border areas— approximately 200 since 1997 and 100 in 1999 alone. President K. R. Narayanan of India, a former Ambassador to Beijing, made a week-long state visit to China (May 28-June 3, 2000), which contributed to the continued warming of relations between the two states. (The twelfth JWG on border issues had met in New Delhi in April and the inaugural round of the China-India Security Dialogue had been held in March.) This was followed by a state visit of Tang Jiaxuan to India (July 21-22, 2000).

The thirteenth meeting of the JWG was held on July 31, 2001, but progress on putting the 1993 and 1996 agreements remained slow, not least in actually defining where the LAC was according to both India and China, with an Indian official spokesperson stating that, "such matters needed time and patience and that there was no fixed time-frame for resolving such issues". More significant progress was made in 2002, helped in part by the huge growth in trade between the two states since the mid 1990s. (The first direct air link between China and India was established by China Eastern Airlines in March 2002.) The fourteenth JWG on the boundary question convened in New Delhi (Nov. 21) and was described as "positive" and "good and forward looking", with Indian Foreign Secretary Kanwal Sibal informing the media that India and China have "reached a reasonable understanding on how to deal with…[boundary clarification]…and on how to move forward". A later response (February 2003) to a question in the Indian Parliament by Shri Digvijay Singh, Minster of State in the Ministry of External Affairs, stated that a "process of clarification of the LAC has started within existing mechanisms. Maps of the LAC in the Middle Sector have been exchanged. Discussions have commenced on clarification of the LAC in the Western Sector of the India-China boundary".

Progress remained slow, however, and a scheduled meeting of experts in January 2003 did not take place. As *The Hindu* reported on May 22, 2003: "Fifteen years after India and China began discussing their boundary dispute, tranquillity and the absence of incident are to be welcomed. But the two countries appear to be far away from reconciling their differences and in approaching a final settlement". Prime Minister Vajpayee visited China (June 22-27, 2003) and the summit produced no dramatic breakthroughs, even though a new border crossing point for trade between Tibet and Sikkim was agreed. The significance of this is that it is viewed by observers as tacit recognition by China of India's claim to Sikkim, no doubt assisted by the recognition by India during the summit of Tibet as the "Tibet Autonomous Region" of China, which is the official name of Tibet according to China. It later emerged, however, that during the visit an Indian patrol was detained by Chinese troops in the Arunachal Pradesh region. Nevertheless, progress in the last decade, however slow and pragmatic, is unmistakable.

Jez Littlewood

3.6 China - Japan - Taiwan (Senkaku/Diaoyu Islands)

The Senkaku Islands, as they are called in Japan, are known as the Diaoyu Tai in China and the Tiao-yu T'ai in Taiwan. They are situated about 320 km west of Okinawa and about 160 km north-east of Taiwan (see Map 26 on page 505). They became the subject of a dispute between the People's Republic of China, Taiwan and Japan following the signing of the San Francisco peace treaty between the Western Allies and Japan in September 1951. The issue lay largely dormant until the 1970s, since when it has been the subject of sporadic, occasionally surreal incidents.

Origins of the Dispute

There are a total of eight islands, none of which is more then 3 km long, and three of which barely qualify under the term "island" at all. They appear to have been known to Chinese shipping from the fourteenth century onwards, and may have been used as navigational aids. The current dispute has its roots in the events of 1895, when Japan annexed the Okinawa chain of islands and incorporated the Senkaku/Diaoyu Islands into that administration. Later the same year, after China's defeat in the 1894-95 Sino-Japanese war, Japan also took over the Chinese territories of Taiwan and the Pescadores Islands under the Treaty of Shimonoseki. Japan has always claimed that the Senkaku/Diaoyu Islands were part of the Okinawa annexation, whereas China claims that in fact the islands are part of Taiwan's islands and therefore were transferred to Japan under the Treaty of Shimonoseki.

This apparently sterile distinction is in fact highly relevant, because under the post-World War II settlement the Shimonoseki Treaty became null and void, while the Okinawa chain was placed under temporary US administration. This meant that Japan considered the islands to have been under US control along with the rest of the Okinawa chain, whilst China and Taiwan (both of which claimed to be the legitimate Chinese governments) regarded the islands as having been returned to them along with the rest of the former Japanese-occupied Chinese territory. This also produced the bizarre situation in which the islands had three claimants but only two claims: the claim that they are part of Okinawa was put by Tokyo, whilst the claim that they are part of the Taiwanese chain was put by both Beijing and Taipei, both of which laid claim to be the sole legitimate governments of China.

The dispute was dormant until 1971, when two events gave the issue an increased significance. The first event was a 1968 announcement that oil reserves might lie in the vicinity of the islands. The announcement, made by the UN Economic Commission for Asia and the Far East, gave the islands significance

beyond the merely symbolic, and both Taiwan and Japan registered rival bids with US oil exploration companies to carry out surveys of the vicinity. In July 1970, Japan protested to the Taiwanese administration that its bid was invalid; the following September, Taiwanese protesters responded by planting a Taiwanese flag on one of the islands, and members of the Taiwanese National Assembly made a public visit to the disputed territory.

The second event, which arose the following year, was the return of Okinawa to Japanese control. Under the 1951 San Francisco peace treaty, the Senkaku/Diaoyu Islands were included in the Okinawa Islands and accordingly placed under US administration. Having already denounced the treaty as "illegal" and its provisions as "null and void", the Beijing government also protested when, under a US-Japan treaty of June 17, 1971, all the islands were declared to have reverted to Japan on May 14, 1972. In a statement issued on Dec. 30, 1971, China declared that the Senkaku/Diaoyu Islands appertained to the island of Taiwan and had, like the latter, been "an inalienable part of Chinese territory since ancient times". (For an account of China-Taiwan territorial issues, see Section 3.8.)

The Taiwan government, having also laid claim to the islands on June 11, 1971, announced their incorporation into Taiwan in February 1972. The Japanese government protested on Feb. 17, 1972, and later issued a document maintaining that the Senkaku (together with Taiwan and the Pescadores) had only been incorporated into Japan in 1895 after it had been established that the rule of the Chinese empire had not extended to them.

Events since the early 1970s

The USA has kept a low profile in respect of this dispute since 1971, but this came after some initial tilting towards the Japanese claim, followed by actions that seemed almost calculated to make matters worse. The 1971 agreement returning the Okinawa chain to Japanese administration clearly included the Senkaku/Diaoyu chain within the terms delineating the islands to be handed back, but during the ratification process in Washington the US Senate stated that, in fact, the agreement did not affect the determination of the Senkaku/Diaoyu dispute. Since then, US policy has been to avoid taking a position on this issue.

During negotiations in February 1975 on a possible treaty of peace and friendship between China and Japan (which was eventually signed on Aug. 12, 1978), it was believed in Japan that China would shelve the issue of these islands. This was corroborated by the Chinese government's attitude to an incident that occurred in April 1978, when a fleet of Chinese fishing vessels began to operate in the territorial waters of the Senkaku/Diaoyu Islands, which the fishermen claimed to be Chinese waters. Following Japanese representations to the Chinese government, a Chinese

Deputy Premier stated on April 15 that the incident was not intentional but "an accidental affair", and on the following day the Chinese vessels withdrew from the vicinity of the islands. Liao Cheng-chi, a vice-chairman of the Standing Committee of the National People's Congress of China, said on April 27 that the government would make all-out efforts to avoid any conflicts over the islands.

After the signing of the treaty between China and Japan, a spokesman of Japan's ruling Liberal Democratic Party stated that China had effectively recognized Japan's control over the islands, and that Deng Xiaoping (then a Chinese Deputy Premier) had emphasized that no further incidents would take place in the area. Nevertheless, the Beijing government maintained its claim that legally the islands were part of Chinese territory.

Japan and China were unwilling to relinquish their respective claims, but were nonetheless reluctant to let the dispute cloud their relationship unnecessarily. Consequently, incidents tended to be either a result of policies on other issues, or the result of the actions of activists. An example of the former arose in 1996, when both China and Japan ratified the UN Convention on the Law of the Sea on June 7 and 20 respectively. The significance of this was that Articles 55-75 of the Convention allow a signatory to declare an Exclusive Economic Zone (EEZ) up to 200 nautical miles beyond its territorial waters, in which that state has sovereign rights over exploration and exploitation of natural resources. Japan and China both declared their EEZs, but the zones inevitably overlapped in places, compelling them under the Convention to reach some form of agreement. Japan deliberately exempted the Senkaku/Diaoyu Islands from its fishing EEZ, and by August 1997 had agreed a jointly-controlled fishing zone around the islands with China. In other words, the two governments got around the problems posed by EEZs by shelving the matter and agreeing that they would both maintain their current fishing in the vicinity of the islands. Both were nonetheless at pains to point out that they still claimed the territory as their own.

Nationalist Protests

However, the emotive attraction of the dispute drew activist groups to the islands. This was seen in 1990, when Japan decided to permit the renovation of a lighthouse that had been built on one of the islands by *Nihon Seinensha* (Japan Youth Federation), an ultra-nationalist right-wing political organization. The Taiwanese response to this included, bizarrely, the dispatch of an athletics team to plant an Olympic torch on the islands. This action seemed to have been undertaken by the mayor of a Taiwanese city without his government's consent, and was repelled by the Japanese coastguard.

Nihon Seinensha returned in 1996 to build another lighthouse, and the Japanese coast guard again intervened to turn away a boat carrying Taiwanese journalists who had come to report on the story. To Chinese protests, another Japanese group, the Senkaku Islands Defence Association, planted a Japanese flag next to the lighthouse, and *Nihon Seinensha* returned for a second time that year after a typhoon had damaged the lighthouse. The Japanese coast guard turned away protesters, and events took a tragic turn on Sept. 26 when one of the demonstrators drowned after his boat was blocked and he tried to swim to the island instead. The following year, an attempt by Taiwanese activists to parachute onto the islands failed when their plane caught fire, and two attempts to land protesters by boat were repelled. On April 20, 2000, *Nihon Seinensha* returned to build a shrine on the islands, again to angry protests from China and Taiwan, and a Japanese assertion that the islands were Japanese territory.

In 2003, Japan announced that three of the islands, which it said were privately owned, would be leased to the Japanese government. It was claimed that a year after the 1895 annexation of Okinawa, a Japanese businessman named Koga Tatsujiro had leased the islands from the Japanese government for 30 years. When the lease was up, he had then purchased the islands outright in 1930. Ownership later passed to his son, Koga Yoshitsugu, who in turn leased the islands back to the Japanese government for $183,000 per year, in order to prevent any further landings.

A further incident occurred in January 2004, when Chinese activists sailed two boats close to the islands, flying banners saying "Chinese territory—Japanese get out". The Japanese coastguard responded by using water cannon on the boats, injuring one of the 20 on board.

Mark Smith

3.7 China - Russia (Soviet Union)

This Section deals with the border disputes between (i) China and the former Soviet Union, and (ii) China and the Russian Federation, in relation to the Russian section of the former Soviet border—China's border issues with the newly independent former Soviet Central Asian Republics are considered in Section 3.4.

The boundaries between China and the old Soviet Union were laid down by 19th-century treaties between the Chinese Emperors and the Russian Tsars, and were a subject of controversy from 1963 onwards. The frontier fell into two sections, divided by the buffer state of Outer Mongolia (now Mongolia): the Far Eastern Boundary, adjoining the Russian Soviet Federated Socialist Republic (RSFSR) and the Central Asian Boundary, adjoining Kazakhstan, Kyrgyzstan and Tajikistan.

Origin of the Soviet Far Eastern Boundary

The Far Eastern Boundary divided Manchuria from Eastern Siberia. In the seventeenth century, the wastelands north of the River Amur and east of the River Ussuri were sparsely populated by hunting and fishing tribes, which paid tribute to the Manchu kings. After the Manchu conquest of China in 1644-62 they came under the suzerainty of the Chinese empire, but they were never settled or effectively controlled by either the Manchus or the Chinese. Meanwhile, Russian colonization of Siberia, which had begun in the late sixteenth century, had been pushed rapidly eastward, and in 1644 a Russian military expedition reached the mouth of the Amur. Further expeditions followed, and in 1665 a Russian outpost was established on the Amur. Russian encroachment met with armed resistance from the Manchus. After nearly forty years of sporadic fighting the Treaty of Nerchinsk, signed in 1689, fixed the boundary between the Russian and Chinese empires north of the Amur along the line of the Stanovoi Mountains.

Russian troops and colonists again occupied the territory north of the Amur in the mid-nineteenth century, while the Opium Wars weakened China. The Chinese commander on the Amur was forced in 1858 to sign the Treaty of Aigun, which gave Russia sovereignty over 480,000 sq km (185,000 square miles) of territory north of the Amur and placed 336,698 sq km between the Ussuri (the Amur's principal tributary) and the Pacific under joint Sino-Russian sovereignty pending a future decision on the matter. The Treaty of Tianjin (Tientsin) confirmed this arrangement later in the same year, and in subsequent negotiations in 1860 the Tsar demanded the area east of the Ussuri (the Maritime Territory) as his reward for remaining neutral in the Second Opium War and using his good offices to negotiate a peace settlement. The Chinese granted his claim by the Treaty of Peking (Beijing), which also defined the Sino-Russian border in Central Asia (see below). In their newly acquired territories the Russians founded the city of Khabarovsk on the Amur in 1858, and the port and naval base of Vladivostok in the Maritime Territory in 1860.

Origin of the Soviet Central Asian Boundary

The Central Asian boundary divides the Chinese region of Xinjiang from the former Soviet Republics of Kazakhstan, Kyrgyzstan and Tajikistan. Although earlier dynasties had temporarily imposed their suzerainty upon Xinjiang ("New Frontier"), Chinese supremacy was not finally established there until the late 17th century. The population consisted of Kazakhs, Tajiks, Kyrgyz, Uighurs and Uzbeks—Turkic in race and Muslim in religion—and there was little Chinese settlement, apart from the military garrisons and political exiles. The garrisons consisted of "permanent pickets" close to the towns and "movable pickets" set up in the frontier areas to prevent the nomadic population from driving their flocks and herds into Chinese territory. Although Chinese rule was exercised indirectly through local chieftains, it was bitterly resented by the native population, and armed uprisings occurred in 1825-26, 1827, 1830 and 1857.

From about 1840 onwards the Russians gradually extended their control of Central Asia into the Kazakh and Kyrgyz steppes, which were nominally under Chinese suzerainty. The Treaty of Peking (Beijing) in 1860 fixed the boundary between the Chinese and Russian empires as "following the mountains, great rivers and the present line of Chinese permanent pickets", and provided for a joint survey of the areas in dispute from the foothills of the Altai in the north to the Pamirs in the south. The survey was protracted for four years, as the Russians contended that under the treaty the boundary should follow the hills where the Chinese maintained permanent pickets, whilst the Chinese also claimed the territory farther west occupied by their movable pickets. The Treaty of Chuguchak (or Tarbagatai), signed in 1864, accepted the Russian claim to 900,000 sq km of territory which had not been under effective Chinese control, but in which Chinese movable pickets had operated.

In the same year (1864) the whole of Xinjiang revolted against Chinese rule and established its independence under the leadership of a local chieftain, Yakub Beg. To prevent the revolt from spreading into his own Central Asian territories, the Tsar sent troops in 1871, who occupied the Ili river valley as far as the town of Kulja. Although the Chinese reconquered Xinjiang with Russian assistance in 1877, the Russians continued to occupy Kulja and the Upper Ili valley until 1881, when by the Treaty of St Petersburg they agreed to evacuate the area.

The Russian Revolution and the "Unequal Treaties"

After the overthrow of the Chinese empire in 1911, the new republican regime headed by Dr Sun Yat-sen demanded the abrogation of all "unequal treaties" and the restoration of China's "traditional" frontiers—the term "unequal treaties" being applied to all agreements by which in the 19th and early 20th centuries China had been compelled to surrender territory or to grant extra-territorial rights to the Western powers, Russia and Japan. This concept met with considerable sympathy from the Russian Bolsheviks after their seizure of power in 1917. By the Karakhan Declaration of July 25, 1919, the Soviet government stated that it "declares null and void all the treaties concluded with China by the former governments of Russia, renounces all seizure of Chinese territory and all Russian concessions in China, and restores to China, without any compensation and forever, all that has been predatorily seized from her by the Tsar's government and the Russian bourgeoisie".

The declaration specifically annulled treaties dealing with spheres of influence in China, with rights of extra-territoriality and consular jurisdiction, concessions on Chinese territory, and the Russian share of the indemnities imposed on China after the suppression of the Boxer Rising of 1900. It did not mention the treaties of Aigun, Peking and Chuguchak, however, and on territorial questions it stated: "The Soviet government has renounced the conquests made by the Tsarist government which deprived China of Manchuria and other areas. Let the people living in those areas themselves decide within the frontiers of which state they may wish to dwell, and what form of government they wish to establish in their own countries".

An agreement between China and the Soviet Union signed on May 31, 1924, provided that at a future conference they were to "annul all conventions, treaties, agreements, protocols, contracts, etc., concluded between the government of China and the Tsarist government and to replace them with new treaties, agreements, etc., on the basis of equality, reciprocity and justice...to re-demarcate their national boundaries...and pending such re-demarcation to maintain the present boundaries". Talks were held in 1926 to discuss the re-demarcation of the border and the conclusion of a new treaty, but no agreement was reached.

Thereafter the border question remained in abeyance, as China was preoccupied for over 20 years with the civil war between the Kuomintang and the Communists, the Japanese invasion and the renewed civil war that followed the defeat of the Japanese. It was still regarded as unsettled by the Chinese, however, and maps of Central Asia published by the Kuomintang government laid claim to large areas of territory then under Soviet control.

During this period of confusion Xinjiang remained virtually independent of central government control, and the Soviet Union was able to bring Xinjiang within its sphere of influence by supplying military aid to the provincial governors, who controlled both its internal and its external policies. The extent of Soviet influence was demonstrated in 1944, when an a governor who adopted an anti-Soviet policy was expelled by a Soviet-inspired Muslim uprising, and an "East Turkestan Republic" was established in the Ili valley with its capital at Kulja, in the region occupied by the Russians in 1871-81.

Communist China and the Soviet Union, 1949-60

For some years after the victory of the Chinese Communists in 1949, relations between China and the Soviet Union remained apparently friendly. The "East Turkestan Republic" was reintegrated into China. The Common Programme summarizing the new Chinese government's policies said that it would examine all treaties and agreements with foreign powers concluded by the Kuomintang government and either recognize, abrogate, revise or renegotiate them, but did not mention treaties concluded by earlier Chinese governments.

Chairman Mao Zedong, the new head of state, said on Dec. 16, 1949, that "the Soviet Union was the first to denounce unequal treaties and concluded with China new equal agreements", suggesting that China did not regard the boundary treaties as "unequal". The 30-year treaty of friendship, alliance and mutual assistance between China and the Soviet Union signed in 1950 contained no reference to boundary questions, apart from an undertaking by each side to respect the other's territorial integrity. As late as April 28, 1960, Zhou Enlai, the Chinese Prime Minister, described the differences on border questions between China and the Soviet Union as "insignificant divergences on the maps" which could "easily be peacefully resolved".

There were nevertheless indications that China did not regard the boundary question as settled. Up to 1953 official Chinese maps showed the boundary between Xinjiang and Soviet Tajikistan in the Pamirs plateau several hundred kilometres to the west of its present position, and later maps marked the frontier in this area as "undefined". A map in *A Short History of Modern China*, published in Beijing in 1954, included among "Chinese territories taken by imperialism" the Far Eastern territories ceded in 1858 and 1860 and parts of Soviet Kazakhstan, Kyrgyzstan and Tajikistan as far west as Lake Balkhash. It also included Nepal, Sikkim, Bhutan, Assam, Burma, Malaya, Thailand, Cambodia, Vietnam, Laos, Korea and Sakhalin, and showed Outer Mongolia as an integral part of China.

Deterioration of Sino-Soviet Relations in 1960s

The boundary question, far from being resolved, was therefore smothered by ideological considerations, and quickly resurfaced when Sino-Soviet relations deteriorated from 1960 onwards. Although no publicity was given to border incidents at the time, later statements from both Soviet and Chinese sources revealed that border incidents began in July of that year.

Chinese and Soviet statements issued in September 1964 indicated that a tense situation already existed on the Xinjiang border. The Beijing *People's Daily* alleged on Sept. 6 that Soviet agencies and personnel had carried out "large-scale subversive activities in the Ili region of Xinjiang and incited and coerced several tens of thousands of Chinese citizens into going to the Soviet Union". This statement appeared to confirm reports from Moscow that riots had occurred in Xinjiang among the Muslim Kazakhs, Uighurs and other nationalities, who resented mass Chinese settlement in the region and attempts to suppress their religion and languages, and that between the middle of 1962 and September 1963 about 50,000 Kazakhs and other tribesmen had fled into the Soviet Union. In response, a Soviet statement issued on Sept. 21, 1964, declared: "since 1960 Chinese servicemen and civilians have been systematically violating the Soviet border. Attempts are also being made to 'develop' some parts of Soviet territory without permission".

Boundary negotiations began in Beijing on Feb. 25, 1964, but were suspended in May without any progress having been achieved. According to Soviet sources, the Soviet delegation put forward proposals for the "clarification" of certain sections of the border, but the Chinese delegation laid claim to over 1,500,000 sq km of Soviet territory, while stating that China would not press her claims for the present. According to the Chinese version, the Chinese delegation, while regarding the Treaties of Aigun and Peking as "unequal treaties", offered to take them as a basis for determining the entire alignment of the boundary, subject to "necessary readjustments" at individual places on the boundary by both sides, but the Soviet delegation refused to accept these proposals. Although it was agreed in principle to resume the talks in Moscow at a later date, no further negotiations took place until 1969.

The tension on the borders greatly increased with the beginning of the Cultural Revolution in China in the summer of 1966. It was reported from Moscow on Oct. 2, 1966, that an estimated 2,000,000 Chinese had taken part in mass demonstrations on the Soviet frontier, especially in the Far Eastern sector, in support of China's territorial claims, and that Chinese troops had opened fire several times on Soviet ships on the Amur. The situation became particularly tense in January and February 1967, when howling mobs besieged the Soviet embassy in Beijing for over a fortnight. Beijing radio asserted on Feb. 2 that a plot by the "Soviet revisionists and US and Japanese imperialists" to attack China through Manchuria had been smashed, and on Feb. 11 all Chinese frontier troops were placed on the alert. Western sources estimated the number of troops on the frontier at this time at nearly 40 Soviet divisions, many of which had recently been transferred there from Eastern Europe, and between 50 and 60 Chinese divisions, or more than 600,000 men. The tension relaxed after Feb. 12, 1967, however, when the siege of the Soviet embassy was lifted, and on Feb. 21 it was reported from Moscow that except for frontier guards all Chinese troops had been withdrawn about 160 km from the Soviet and Mongolian borders.

Many minor border incidents were believed to have taken place in the later months of 1967 and in 1968, but neither side gave them any publicity at the time. According to later Chinese and Soviet statements, fighting took place on several occasions around a small uninhabited island in the River Ussuri, known to the Russians as Damansky Island and to the Chinese as Zhenbao Island, lying about 177 km south of Khabarovsk and 400 km north of Vladivostok.

The status of the island under the Treaties of Aigun and Peking is disputed. The Soviet Union maintained that a map approved by both governments in 1861 showed the Chinese bank of the Ussuri as the boundary line in this area. The Chinese Foreign Ministry, on the other hand, contended that the map had been drawn unilaterally by the Russian authorities; that the island was situated on the Chinese side of the central line of the river's main channel, which under international law formed the boundary line; and that it had formed part of the bank on the Chinese side until eroded by the river, had always been under Chinese jurisdiction and had been admitted to be Chinese by the Soviet delegation at the 1964 boundary negotiations. The problem was complicated by the fact that after the breaking up of the ice in spring the Ussuri regularly floods its banks and frequently shifts its channel.

Armed clashes between Soviet and Chinese frontier guards, of which the two sides gave contradictory accounts, occurred on the island in March 1969, causing considerable loss of life. According to the Soviet version, about 300 Chinese soldiers crossed the frozen river to the island during the night of March 1-2, opened fire in the morning on Soviet frontier guards, and were expelled only after a two-hour battle in which the Soviet troops lost 31 killed. Chinese official statements, however, declared that a large Soviet force had opened fire on Chinese frontier guards on normal patrol duty, killing and wounding many of them.

Fighting on a much larger scale broke out on March 15, 1969, and continued for several hours, causing heavy casualties; Soviet press reports mentioned by name 12 officers and NCOs, including a colonel, who had been killed, suggesting that a full regiment of frontier guards and reserves had been engaged on the Soviet side. Sporadic incidents continued on the islands in the Ussuri and the Amur throughout the spring and summer, and caused a few casualties on each side.

Meanwhile a series of incidents on the Central Asian border, for which each side held the other responsible, had begun in April 1969 and continued throughout the next three months, culminating in fighting on Aug. 13 which resulted in casualties on both sides. Tension reached such a height that on Aug. 23 the Chinese Communist Party issued a statement declaring that war might break out at any time. The situation was transformed, however, by the death on Sept. 3, 1969, of President Ho Chi Minh of North Vietnam and by the publication of his political testament, in which he appealed for "the restoration of unity among the fraternal parties". After attending Ho Chi Minh's funeral, the Soviet Prime Minister, Alexei Kosygin, flew to Beijing where he met Zhou Enlai. As a result of this meeting the two sides agreed to reopen border talks.

Inconclusive Talks in 1970s

Negotiations on the border opened at Deputy Foreign Minister level in Beijing on Oct. 20, 1969, and continued with a number of breaks until June 1978. No progress was made, as the Soviet delegation rejected the Chinese demand for the withdrawal of troops from disputed areas, on the ground that the border line shown on Chinese maps did not coincide with that defined by the treaty documents.

On April 3, 1979, China gave notice of its intention not to extend the 1950 Sino-Soviet Treaty of Alliance when it expired a year later, but proposed that negotiations should be held for the solution of outstanding issues and the improvement of relations between the two countries. Talks formally opened in Moscow on Oct. 17, 1979, and continued until Nov. 30. According to unofficial reports, the Chinese delegation repeated its demand for the withdrawal of troops from disputed areas, and also called for the reduction of the strength of the Soviet troops on the frontier and their withdrawal from Outer Mongolia. Following the Soviet intervention in Afghanistan, the Chinese government stated on Jan. 19, 1980, that it would be "inappropriate" to hold the second round of talks at that time. On April 3, 1980, the 1950 treaty therefore expired.

Chinese Condemnation of 1981 Soviet-Afghan Border Treaty

A new source of friction in Sino-Soviet relations arose in June 1981 when the Soviet Union signed a border treaty with Afghanistan that recognized as Soviet territory an area to the northeast of Afghanistan to which China laid claim. The signature of the treaty, on June 16, 1981, coincided with Soviet military occupation of the strategically important Wakhan salient (the narrow strip of Afghan territory running eastwards to the Chinese border between Soviet territory to the north and Pakistan to the south) and gave rise to suspicions in China and the West that the treaty provided for Soviet annexation of the salient.

Although no exact details of the treaty were published either by the Soviet Union or Afghanistan, official comments from both sides indicated that it provided only for the legal delimitation and affirmation of the existing boundary between the two countries. Nevertheless, the Chinese Foreign Ministry on July 22 declared the treaty "illegal and invalid", arguing that the Soviet Union had no right to conclude a border treaty with a third country involving this line, since the territory immediately to the north had been in dispute between Beijing and Moscow for some 90 years. At the same time China stressed that it had no outstanding territorial disputes with Afghanistan itself, with which it had signed an agreement in November 1963 regulating the 70-kilometre Chinese-Afghan border at the eastern end of the Wakhan salient.

China's case against the Soviet Union rested on an 1884 protocol "concerning the Chinese-Russian border in the region of Kashgar" (officially described by China as the "Sino-Russian Kashgar boundary treaty"). This agreement, which had been reached after a long period of Russian penetration into central Asia, had specified that from the Uz-Bel Mountain pass in the Pamirs "the Russian boundary turns to the southwest and the Chinese boundary runs due south". According to Chinese accounts, the Russians had nevertheless in the 1890s proceeded to occupy some 20,000 sq km of Chinese territory by armed force and had subsequently attempted to legitimize this encroachment by describing a Chinese-Soviet exchange of notes in 1894 as a border treaty regulating the issue. According to China, however, the 1894 exchange of notes showed that the two sides had agreed to differ over the sovereignty of the area in question and had decided to maintain the status quo pending a permanent settlement.

The Soviet news agency Tass responded to the Chinese assertions on Aug. 11, 1981, by stating that the new Soviet-Afghan border treaty was a bilateral matter involving no third countries and by accusing China of "falsifying history" in order to invent a dispute over a question which had been finally settled in 1894. There was "no other line" than that determined in 1894, continued Tass, as demonstrated by the fact that the border in question was shown on Chinese maps exactly as on Soviet maps. This claim was in turn rejected by China on Aug. 31 as a "deliberate misrepresentation", in that the Chinese government had consistently made known its view that the frontier in the Pamirs was not finally delineated and that a dispute existed which had yet to be settled.

Talks on Normalization of Relations

The Soviet Union made several attempts to re-open talks with China during 1981 and 1982. Chinese spokesmen during this period repeatedly identified the three major obstacles to improved Sino-Soviet relations as (i) the deployment of large numbers of Soviet troops on the Chinese border and in Mongolia, (ii) the Soviet intervention in Afghanistan and (iii) Soviet support for the Vietnamese occupation of Cambodia. Talks at Deputy Foreign Minister level on normalization of relations took place in Beijing in October 1982, and both sides agreed to continue the consultations alternately in Moscow and Beijing.

A second round of talks took place in Moscow on March 1-15, 1983. According to Chinese sources, the Soviet delegation proposed the signing of a non-aggression pact and measures to restore confidence on the frontier, but refused to discuss Afghanistan or Cambodia on the ground that these questions involved third countries. The Chinese delegation, on the other hand, held that the signing of such a pact would have little meaning unless the three main obstacles to normal relations were all removed. Before the third round of talks, which was held in Beijing on Oct. 6-30, 1983, a Chinese Foreign Ministry spokesman stated on Oct. 5 that the deployment by the Soviet Union of SS-20 missiles along the border should be included within "the three obstacles", as China hoped that the Soviet Union would reduce its troops along the border, including both conventional and nuclear weapons. Wu Xueqian, Huang Hua's successor as Foreign Minister, said on December 7 that the talks had made no headway because of Moscow's refusal to discuss "the three obstacles". No progress was achieved on these issues at the next three rounds, held in Beijing on Oct. 6-30, Moscow on March 12-27, 1984, and Beijing between Oct. 18 and Nov. 3, 1984.

In March 1985, the new Soviet leader, Mikhail Gorbachev, stated that the Soviet Union would seek "a serious improvement in relations with China". The sixth, seventh and eighth rounds of talks, however, produced no significant progress, and matters took a turn for the worse on July 12, when a Chinese was killed in a clash between Soviet and Chinese border guards on the Xinjiang-Kazakhstan frontier. This represented the first serious border incident since 1980, and the Soviet government made a verbal protest on July 14, alleging that a Chinese patrol had entered Soviet territory and opened fire. The Chinese Foreign Ministry denied this three days later. After the incident had been reported for the first time by a Japanese newspaper on Aug. 22, the Chinese Foreign Ministry confirmed on the following day that "an isolated incident" had occurred, whilst a Soviet Foreign Ministry spokesman said that everything was now quiet on the border. The fact that both governments attempted to minimize the incident was regarded as evidence of their desire to improve relations.

Resumption of Border Talks

In a speech in Vladivostok on July 28, 1986, Gorbachev said that "the Soviet Union is prepared, at any time and at any level, to discuss with China additional measures for creating a good-neighbourly atmosphere". On specific points he stated that the Soviet Union was ready to discuss troop reductions with China; that the number of Soviet SS-20 missiles in Asia would not be increased, and that SS-20s removed from Europe would be liquidated and not transferred elsewhere; that "the question of withdrawing a substantial part of the Soviet troops from Mongolia is being examined jointly with the Mongolian leadership"; that six Soviet regiments would be withdrawn from Afghanistan before the end of the year; and that all the Soviet troops would be withdrawn once a political settlement had been reached.

Gorbachev also made an important concession on the Far Eastern border question in his Vladivostok speech, stating that the official border on the Amur and the Ussuri "might pass along the main ship channel". Elaborating on this point, Mikhail Kapitsa (a Soviet Deputy Foreign Minister) said on Aug. 7, 1986, that this meant that "a number of islands that in 1860 were considered Russian would be beyond the line of the main channel and therefore in the future be transferred to China". According to unofficial reports, the Soviet government had agreed to make this concession, which would involve acceptance of the Chinese claim to Damansky/Zhenbao Island, at earlier border talks, but only as part of a settlement of the whole border issue.

China welcomed Gorbachev's initiative, but said that it nonetheless fell far short of removing the three major obstacles. He had evaded in particular the question of withdrawing Vietnamese troops from Cambodia, an issue about which China was most concerned. The Soviet and Chinese Foreign Ministers, Eduard Shevardnadze and Wu Xueqian, held extensive discussions on normalizing relations and on international issues at the United Nations on Sept. 25, 1986, at which it was agreed to resume talks on border disputes at Deputy Foreign Minister level in 1987. This agreement was generally believed to have resulted from Gorbachev's initiative in his Vladivostok speech. The ninth round of talks on normalizing relations was held in Beijing in October 1986. A communiqué

issued at the end of the talks announced that it had been agreed to resume the boundary negotiations in Moscow in February 1987.

Although a clear thaw in Sino-Soviet relations occurred in 1987 with Beijing watching the Gorbachev reforms carefully, China still insisted that any real improvement in relations must depend upon the removal of "the three obstacles". Bilateral talks in August witnessed some progress towards solving differences along the eastern sector of their joint border and expert groups were formed to adjudicate disputes. Between April and June 1987 the USSR withdrew 20 per cent of its 65,000 troops from the Mongolian border with China, a reduction that was welcomed by China although it was regarded as too small to be significant.

A further round of border talks were held in Beijing on Aug. 7-18, 1987, at which both sides agreed in principle to redraw their disputed eastern river boundary. In a Soviet communiqué of Aug. 21, 1987, Gorbachev repeated that the official border on the Amur and Ussuri rivers "might pass along the main ship channel" (i.e. be accepted according to the Thalweg principle) as opposed to passing along the Chinese banks.

1988 was a good year in Sino-Soviet relations though there was disagreement over islands at the confluence of the Amur and Ussuri rivers because of Soviet military installations on the island. The proposed Soviet withdrawal from Afghanistan (to be completed by February 1989) was a major reason for improved relations since it met one of China's "three obstacles". At the same time the partial withdrawal of Soviet troops from the border regions as well as increased efforts to resolve the Cambodia conflict further contributed to the thaw in relations, as did a large increase in trade between the two countries.

At the beginning of February 1989 the Soviet Foreign Minister, Eduard Shevardnadze, visited China for talks with Deng Xiaoping, when it was agreed that a Sino-Soviet summit would be held the following May in Beijing. During the meeting a wide measure of agreement was reached on Cambodia including the withdrawal of Vietnamese troops, although there were differences about the form of a transitional government. Shevardnadze claimed that the USSR intended to reduce its troops along the Soviet eastern and southern borders with China by 200,000 and 60,000 respectively. On March 12, 1989, the USSR announced the withdrawal of 75 per cent of its troops in Mongolia.

Gorbachev's May 1989 visit to Beijing for the summit was disrupted by the demonstrations in Tiananmen Square and the schedules had to be altered. In a speech of May 17 Gorbachev included details of military cutbacks: 200,000 troops in the eastern Soviet Union by the end of 1990 including 120,000 in the Far East. He said the USSR was prepared to work with China to demilitarize their common frontier and to transform it into a border of "peace and good neighbourliness". The summit (May 15-18, 1989) marked an end of Sino-Soviet estrangement and the two sides pledged themselves to a further expansion of trade and reiterated their respect for each other's sovereignty.

Developments Since 1991

The disintegration of the Soviet Union at the end of 1991 and the subsequent emergence of its former republics as independent states meant that as from January 1992 China would have to deal with four independent states over border issues as opposed to only the USSR up to that date. Thus, questions relating to the Far Eastern border (east of Mongolia) now became a matter between China and Russia, although the problems here had—it was hoped—largely been covered by the agreement of May 16, 1991 (see below). However, outstanding questions relating to what had been the Sino-Soviet Central Asian border to the west of Mongolia (running from Mongolia to Afghanistan) would have to be resolved in separate agreements between China and Kazakhstan, Kyrgyzstan and Tajikistan—see Section 3.4.

The earliest efforts to resolve the eastern boundary issue are in the 1988 agreement on general principles, where it was reported that the two sides had agreed that where rivers marked the border, the boundary would lie along the channel of navigable rivers and the middle of unnavigable ones. This was a mutually satisfactory arrangement, but the issue of islands in the rivers appears to have been fudged. The outstanding areas were two islands in the Amur River, called Tarabarovskiy and Bolshoy Ussuriyskiy, and one in the Argun River, called Bolshoy Island, all of which were claimed by China. The agreement putting the border as running along the median channel of the river left the status of the islands as ambiguous, although Russia had de facto jurisdiction over the islands.

Reportedly, Gorbachev and Shevardnadze both favoured resolving the issue by recognizing China's claim, apparently on the grounds that this was a price worth paying in order to obtain a comprehensive resolution of the boundary dispute. Others in the then-Soviet government resisted them in this, especially the Prime Minister and the Defence Minister. Consequently, in May 1989 Gorbachev and Deng Xiaoping seem to have agreed that the islands' issue should not be allowed to stymie the whole agreement and should therefore be shelved for the time being. This was pivotal in facilitating the Agreement on the Eastern Sector of the National Boundaries, signed by the Chinese and Soviet Foreign Ministers, Qian Qichen and Alexander Bessmertnyhk, on May 16, 1991. Under the agreement, 700 islands and 1,500 hectares of land along the eastern border were handed back to China. This provoked furious local protests. Nevertheless, following the collapse of the Soviet Union, the Russian Federation ratified the agreement on Feb.13, 1992, and China followed suit on Feb. 24.

As the Russian Ambassador to China noted, this meant that about 98 per cent of the Sino-Russian border was settled. It was further agreed that the border demarcation process should be completed by 1997.

Negotiations continued within the framework of the new Commonwealth of Independent States. With the great bulk of the Sino-Russian border issue solved, progress was sufficiently rapid for the new Russian President, Boris Yeltsin, to be able to agree a Memorandum on Guiding Principles for the Mutual Reduction of Armed Forces and the Strengthening of Trust in the Border Region in Beijing, December 1992. This included a package of confidence-building measures, including joint demarcation of borders and reductions in armed forces in border regions.

In April 1993, a five-state commission comprising China, Russia, Kazakhstan, Tajikistan and Kyrgyzstan met in Beijing to discuss implementation of the agreement. This commission met regularly and established two technical-level working groups on border demarcation and force reductions in addition to the high-level political discussions. The disputed islands in the East, however, remained under de facto Russian jurisdiction. On May 6, 1994, a joint China-Russia study on border demarcation was established and concluded on May 18 with the signing of a protocol clarifying the direction of the border but apparently avoiding the issue of the islands.

The problems over the islands were not allowed to obstruct progress elsewhere. At a Foreign Ministers' meeting in Moscow on Sept. 3, 1994, a joint agreement was signed on the short length of Sino-Russian border in the Western Territory. This 55-km stretch of the frontier appeared when Kazakhstan became an independent state. Russian officials claimed that the Sino-Russian border dispute was now "99% solved", and the Chinese official news agency concurred with an announcement that "the overwhelming part" of the border was now delineated.

Two years later, the five-state commission signed the Shanghai Accord on April 26, 1996. Under the accord, limits were placed on military exercises within 100 km either side of the border, and efforts proceeded on the establishment of a demilitarized zone along the boundaries.

The boundary demarcation process was largely complete by November 1997, when a Sino-Russian summit made an announcement to that effect. A total of 1,182 border pillars and 24 buoys had been planted along the border, the first time that the boundary had been clearly marked at ground level. However, it was also announced that an agreement on national and joint ownership of the islands in the river would be negotiated separately. Once again, it seemed, the dispute over the islands would not be allowed to stand in the way of overall agreement.

The negotiations were completed in April 1999, when it was announced that, of the 2,444 islands on the border rivers, 1,163 were handed to Russia and 1,281 to China.

Principal Areas of Contention

Controversy in relation to the disputes on the Sino-Russian border since 1991 has focused on three areas:

(i) The Maritime Territories

Under the 1991 agreement, three territories were to be given to China. These were 3 sq km in Khasan near the Sea of Japan; 9 sq km in Ussuriisk; and 3 sq km at Lake Khanka. They were occupied during the 1930s when the Soviet Union was fighting the Japanese in Manchuria, but it appeared to be generally accepted by the national leadership that the occupation by the Soviet Union was a violation under its existing treaty obligations with China.

Khasan was the most controversial of the Maritime Territories' land to be handed to China, especially as the land included the graves of Russian dead from the Battle of Khasan, a particularly bloody battle against Japan fought on Aug. 6, 1938. Economics also played a part: the agreement gave China a narrow strip of land along the Tumen River, giving it access to the Sea of Japan, and local Russian people feared that China would use the access to build a river port and undercut Russian ports, particularly those of Posyet and Zarubino.

The Russian governor of the Maritime Territories, Yevgenii Nazdratenko, organized strong local resistance to the planned handover, including disruption of the boundary demarcation process and exploitation of public hostility to Chinese immigration in the region. Despite this, the demarcation process was completed in 1997, and the Nov. 9 agreement included the transfer of the three strips of land to Chinese ownership. Local feelings were recognized, however, in the Khasan case, where Russia was able to retain the land containing the graves of its soldiers, while China took the remaining land and made a pledge not to construct a river port there.

(ii) Islands on the Amur and Ussuri Rivers

These islands are near the Russian city of Khabarovsk, which tends to regard them as a strategically important shield between it and China. Bolshoy Ussuriyskiy, the largest island, is 36 km long and 9 km wide, and the total disputed area is about 175 sq km. The "main channel" principle agreed in 1991 would put the islands entirely in Chinese territory, but Russia has, with the exception of Gorbachev and Shevardnadze in 1989, consistently rejected that principle. Consequently the agreement left the issue of the islands to be resolved on the principle of "justice and rationality", although it did permit China free navigation along the disputed border.

The dispute was unresolved in 1997 and remains so at the time of writing. In July 2000, the governor of Khabarovsk, Viktor Ishayev, announced plans to increase economic activity on the islands, doubtless in order to strengthen the status quo that favours Russia, and also stated that he was looking into dredging the strait between Bolshoy Ussuriyskiy and the Chinese side of the river. The strait had been silting up and the resultant sandbanks threatened to join the island with the Chinese mainland.

(iii) Bolshoy Island

This island is located on the Argun River near the point where the Hailar and Hulum rivers meet. Under an agreement signed between Tsarist Russia and Imperial China, it was stated that this island, along with 17 others in the Argun River, belonged to Russia even though the river channel had shifted to China's advantage. That arrangement was dissolved after the Russian Revolution, but Bolshoy Island continued to be a heated topic in the late 1980s. It was not included in the 1991 agreement, although the other islands in the Argun River all went to China.

Mark Smith

3.8 China - Taiwan

Taiwan, otherwise known as Formosa and officially the Republic of China (ROC), is an island some 150-200 km off the south-east Chinese mainland coast. Together with certain small islands controlled by the Republic, it has a total land area of 36,000 sq km and a population of some 23 million. After December 1949 Taiwan became the seat of the Kuomintang (KMT) government, which fled from mainland China following the Communists' victory in the civil war, and both regimes thereafter claimed to be the only legitimate government of all China. In 1991 Taiwan effectively withdrew its claim to be the government of the mainland, but the Beijing government continues to define Taiwan as a "province" and its government as illegitimate. (Map 26, p. 505, shows the territorial relationship of China and Taiwan.)

Early and Post-War History

The island of Taiwan was occupied in 1624 by the Dutch, who encouraged immigration from China in order to develop its agricultural resources. Supporters of the Ming dynasty, which had been overthrown by the Manchu invaders in 1644, expelled the Dutch in 1661 and used the island as a base for operations against the mainland until 1683, when it was conquered by the Manchus and incorporated into the Chinese empire. Immigration continued throughout the 18th century, and by 1800 the Chinese population far outnumbered the aboriginal inhabitants.

After the Sino-Japanese War of 1894-5 Japan annexed Taiwan and the Pescadores (also known as the Penghu Islands), a group of 48 small islands 30 miles (48 km) west of Taiwan, which had been under Chinese rule since 1281. The 1943 Cairo Declaration issued by Britain, the United States and China laid down that the territories taken from China by Japan should be restored to Chinese sovereignty after the defeat of Japan, and in 1945 the Chinese government took over the administration of Taiwan and the Pescadores pending the conclusion of a peace treaty. Although this change was initially welcomed in

Taiwan, the corruption of the new administration led to a serious revolt in 1947.

On the mainland the civil war between the ruling KMT and the Communists culminated in the proclamation of the People's Republic of China in Beijing on Oct. 1, 1949. The KMT government fled on Dec. 8 from Chengdu, to which it had transferred its capital, to Taiwan, where it established its new capital at Taipei. Over 1,500,000 refugees, including about 750,000 members of the armed forces, followed it. Thereafter the two regimes both claimed to be the only legitimate Chinese government: the People's Republic of China, controlling the mainland, and the Republic of China, controlling Taiwan and a number of offshore islands.

Although Hainan, the largest of the islands, was occupied by the Communists in April 1950, the KMT retained control of (i) the Pescadores; (ii) Quemoy, an island 12 miles (19 km) across, lying about four miles off the mainland port of Xiamen (Amoy), and three smaller islands nearby; (iii) Matsu, off Fuzhou (Foochow); (iv) the Nanchi Islands, about 130 miles (210 km) north of Taiwan; and (v) the Tachen Islands, off the coast of Zhejiang (Chekiang) province, about 200 miles (320 km) north of Taiwan. The Taiwan government also maintained a garrison on Itu Aba, one of the Spratly Islands, in the South China Sea (see Section 3.18). Gen. Chiang Kai-shek, who had headed the KMT government of China since the late 1920s, became President of Taiwan and retained this post until his death in April 1975.

The People's Republic of China was immediately recognized by the Communist countries, and by January 1950 had also been recognized by 11 other European and Asian countries, including Britain. The process of international recognition, however, was delayed by the outbreak of the Korean War and China's intervention in it. Resolutions in favour of the admission of the People's Republic to the United Nations were submitted annually to the General Assembly from 1950 onwards, but were regularly defeated until 1969. In consequence, China continued to be represented in the United Nations by the Taipei government, which held the status of a permanent member of the Security Council, with the right to veto any decision.

Under the peace treaty signed at San Francisco in September 1951, Japan renounced all claims to Taiwan and the Pescadores. However, the treaty did not define to which Chinese government they belonged, and was denounced by both Chinese governments, neither of which had been invited to the San Francisco conference. In 1952, however, Japan signed a separate peace treaty with the Taiwan government, a document that recognized all residents of Taiwan and the Pescadores who were of Chinese nationality as "nationals of the Republic of China".

The KMT government announced in June 1949 a blockade of all that part of the Chinese coast and territorial waters then under Communist control, which after its withdrawal to Taiwan it extended to the whole coast of mainland China. The blockade led to a num- ber of attacks by KMT warships and aircraft on British and US shipping. On June 27, 1950, two days after the outbreak of the Korean War, President Truman announced that he had ordered the US Seventh Fleet to prevent any attack on Taiwan; that he was calling upon the Taiwan government to cease all air and sea operations against the mainland; and that "the Seventh Fleet will see that this is done". His successor, President Eisenhower, however, announced on Feb. 2, 1953, in his first State of the Union message to Congress, that he had issued instructions that "the Seventh Fleet shall no longer be employed to shield Communist China".

Zhou Enlai, the Prime Minister of the People's Republic, stated on Aug. 11, 1954, that the "liberation" of Taiwan was an affair that concerned the Chinese people only, and that any attempt by foreign powers to resist it would constitute an infringement of China's sovereignty. John Foster Dulles, the US Secretary of State, declared on Aug. 24 that the Seventh Fleet would protect Taiwan against any attack from the mainland, as well as other islands the defence of which was intimately connected with that of Taiwan. In defiance of this warning, the Chinese army began a heavy bombardment of Quemoy on Sept. 3, 1954, to which KMT warships and aircraft replied by attacking military targets on the mainland. A mutual security treaty between the United States and the Taiwan government was signed on Dec. 1, 1954, under which the United States undertook to defend Taiwan, the Pescadores and "such other territories as may be determined by mutual agreement" against any armed attack. The Taiwan government gave an undertaking on Dec. 10 that it would not attack the mainland without prior consultation with the government of the United States.

The small island of Yikiangshan, situated eight miles (13 km) north of the Tachen Islands, was captured by Communist forces on Jan.18, 1955, and after heavy air attacks from the mainland, KMT forces evacuated the Tachen and Nanchi Islands in February of that year. At President Eisenhower's request, a resolution authorizing him to employ the armed forces to protect Taiwan and the Pescadores, as well as "such related positions and territories of that area now in friendly hands" as he judged to be appropriate, was adopted by the US House of Representatives on Jan. 25 and by the Senate three days later.

The bombardment of the Quemoy group of islands was resumed after a long interval on Aug. 23, 1958. A declaration issued by the government of the People's Republic on Sept. 4 of that year extended the limit of China's territorial waters from three to 12 nautical miles, and stated that no foreign warships or aircraft might enter Chinese territorial waters and the airspace above them without permission from Beijing. Although the effect of the declaration was to bring Quemoy and Matsu within the new 12-mile limit, US warships were used from Sept. 7 to escort supply convoys to Quemoy. The Chinese government suspended the bombardment on Oct. 6, and announced that supplies might be sent to Quemoy on condition that there was no US escort, but resumed the shelling on Oct. 20 on the ground that this condition had not been observed. From Oct. 25, however, shelling was confined to odd dates, to allow supplies to be brought in on alternate days.

Sporadic shelling continued over the next 20 years, although during the latter part of this period the shells largely contained propaganda leaflets. Communist leaders continued to announce their determination to "liberate" Taiwan, and KMT leaders their determination to "liberate" the mainland, but neither side made any serious attempt to carry out its threats. Occasional clashes occurred, however, including periodic raids on the coast by KMT commandos and a naval engagement in the Taiwan Strait in 1965 in which each side claimed to have inflicted serious damage on the other. The People's Republic gradually emerged from its isolation, despite its strained relations with the Soviet bloc after 1960 and the damage to its international reputation caused by attacks on foreign embassies during the Cultural Revolution. During the later 1950s and the 1960s it was recognized by an increasing number of countries, including Egypt in 1956, France in 1964 and Italy in 1970. The 1970 session of the General Assembly voted in favour of the admission of the People's Republic to the United Nations by 51 votes to 49, with 25 abstentions, but the resolution remained inoperative, as the Assembly had previously passed a resolution declaring the Chinese representation issue an "important question" requiring a two-thirds majority for its adoption.

Improvement of Relations between China and USA

The dramatic improvement in relations between the People's Republic and the United States from 1971 onwards, transformed relations between the People's Republic and Taiwan and between both and the outside world. After it had been announced on July 15, 1971, that President Nixon had accepted an invitation to visit the People's Republic, William Rogers (then Secretary of State) said on Aug. 2 that the United States would support the admission of the People's Republic to the United Nations, while opposing "any action to expel the Republic of China or otherwise deprive it of representation in the United Nations". The General Assembly, however, rejected on Oct. 25, 1971, a US "important question" resolution, and adopted an Albanian resolution recognizing the representatives of the People's Republic as "the only lawful representatives of China to the United Nations" by 76 votes to 35, with 17 abstentions. The People's Republic in consequence immediately replaced the Republic of China (Taiwan) in the General Assembly and the Security Council and Taiwan ceased to be a member of the UN.

President Nixon paid an official visit to China on Feb. 21-27, 1972, at the conclusion of which he and Zhou Enlai issued a long communiqué in Shanghai. On the Taiwan question this stated: "The Chinese side reaffirmed its position: the Taiwan question is the cru-

cial question obstructing the normalization of relations between China and the United States; the government of the People's Republic of China is the sole legal government of China; Taiwan is a province of China which has long been returned to the motherland; the liberation of Taiwan is China's internal affair in which no other country has the right to interfere; and all US forces and military installations must be withdrawn from Taiwan. The Chinese government firmly opposes any activities which aim at the creation of 'one China, one Taiwan', 'one China, two governments', 'two Chinas' and 'independent Taiwan', or advocate that 'the status of Taiwan remains to be determined'. The US side declared: The United States acknowledges that all Chinese on either side of the Taiwan Strait maintain that there is but one China and that Taiwan is a part of China. The US government does not challenge that position. It reaffirms its interest in a peaceful settlement of the Taiwan question by the Chinese themselves. With this prospect in mind, it affirms the ultimate objective of the withdrawal of all US forces and military installations from Taiwan. In the meantime, it will progressively reduce its forces and military installations on Taiwan as the tension in the area diminishes".

President Nixon's visit was followed by the recognition of the People's Republic by various other states, including Japan, West Germany, Australia, New Zealand and Spain. During a visit to Beijing in September 1972 the Japanese Prime Minister, Kakuei Tanaka, signed a joint statement with Zhou Enlai recognizing the government of the People's Republic as the sole legal government of China, and stating that the Japanese government "fully understands and respects" the Chinese government's stand that "Taiwan is an inalienable part of the territory of the People's Republic of China". By July 1974 the People's Republic was recognized by 95 countries and Taiwan by only 33.

The United States and the People's Republic agreed in 1973 to establish liaison offices in each other's capitals. The movement towards normalization of relations, which developed slowly during the next four years, made rapid progress in 1978, and coincided with a slight softening in the Chinese government's attitude towards Taiwan. In a speech to the National People's Congress on Feb. 26, 1978, Hua Guofeng, the Prime Minister, declared that "the Chinese People's Liberation Army must make all the preparations necessary for the liberation of Taiwan", but also stated that "it has been our consistent policy that 'all patriots belong to one big family, whether they come over early or late'".

A senior Chinese official assured a visiting US Congressman in July 1978 that Beijing did not rule out a negotiated settlement with the Taiwan regime, as the Communist Party and the KMT had worked together in 1924-27 and again during the war with Japan. Deng Xiaoping, then the senior Deputy Premier, told *The New York Times* on Nov. 29 that China would seek a negotiated settlement which took into account the fact that Taiwan's political system differed from that of the mainland, although it would not enter into any pledge to abstain from the use of force, as such a pledge would make the Taiwan authorities refuse to negotiate.

US Recognition of People's Republic of China

It was announced on Dec. 15, 1978, that the People's Republic and the United States had agreed to recognize each other and to establish diplomatic relations from Jan. 1, 1979. The joint communiqué said: "The USA recognizes the government of the People's Republic of China as the sole legal government of China. Within this context, the people of the USA will maintain cultural, commercial and other unofficial relations with the people of Taiwan...The government of the USA acknowledges the Chinese position that there is but one China and Taiwan is part of China".

The two governments at the same time issued statements defining their respective positions on the Taiwan question. The US statement, after announcing that the mutual defence treaty of 1954 would be terminated and that the remaining US military personnel would be withdrawn from Taiwan within four months, emphasized that "the USA continues to have an interest in the peaceful resolution of the Taiwan issue, and expects that the Taiwan issue will be settled peacefully by the Chinese themselves".

The Chinese statement said: "The question of Taiwan was the crucial issue obstructing the normalization of relations between China and the USA. It has now been resolved between the two countries in the spirit of the Shanghai communiqué...As for the way of bringing Taiwan back to the embrace of the motherland and reunifying the country, it is entirely China's internal affair". President Chiang Ching-kuo of Taiwan commented on Dec. 16, 1978: "Under whatever circumstances, the Republic of China will neither negotiate with the Chinese Communist regime nor compromise with communism, and she will never give up her sacred tasks of recovering the mainland and delivering the compatriots there".

The shelling of Quemoy and Matsu was officially terminated on Jan. 1, 1979, when the Standing Committee of the National People's Congress proposed that the military confrontation between the People's Republic and Taiwan should be "ended through discussion". President Chiang, however, declared on the same day that "our anti-Communist struggle will never cease until the Chinese Communist regime has been destroyed".

The American Institute in Taiwan was incorporated on Jan. 16, 1979, to enable the US and Taiwanese peoples to maintain commercial, cultural and other relations without official government representation or diplomatic relations, and on Feb. 15 the Taiwan government announced the establishment of the Taiwan Co-ordination Council for North American Affairs to act as a liaison office in Washington. An agreement between the two organizations signed on Oct. 2, 1980, provided that they and their staffs would enjoy full diplomatic privileges and immunities. The People's Republic protested against the agreement in a note to Washington of Oct. 15.

Although no progress towards reunification was made during 1979-80, the leaders of the People's Republic continued to refer to the question in conciliatory terms, and ceased to speak of the "liberation" of Taiwan. In contrast to his speech of Feb. 26, 1978, Hua Guofeng merely said when addressing the National People's Congress on Sept. 7, 1980, that "we shall work energetically for the return of Taiwan to the motherland, fulfilling our lofty aim of unifying our homeland at an early date".

The People's Republic announced on April 4, 1980, that it had decided to abolish all customs duties on imports and exports between the mainland and Taiwan, on the ground that Taiwan was part of China. Although in theory exporting goods from Taiwan to China was punishable by severe penalties, trade between Taiwan and the mainland, conducted mainly through Hong Kong, Singapore or Japan, had greatly increased since 1978. According to Hong Kong government figures, the value of Taiwan's exports to China through the colony rose from US$41,000 in 1978 to US$22,000,000 in 1979 and US$222,000,000 in 1980.

The Taiwan Independence Movement

After the flight of the KMT government to Taiwan in 1949 the Legislative Yuan (the Chinese parliament established under the 1946 constitution) was established on the island as its supreme legislative body. As this body supposedly represented the whole of China, the members elected in 1948 to represent mainland constituencies continued to hold their seats, in theory until new elections could be organized on the mainland. This in practice meant for life, and only in the Taiwan constituencies were elections held periodically. A similar situation existed in the National Assembly, a body with limited functions, including the election of the President and Vice-President and the adoption of amendments to the constitution.

The political domination of Taiwan by immigrants from the mainland, although they constituted only 13 per cent of the population, led to demands both for the democratization of the regime and for recognition of Taiwan as a state independent of China. An underground Taiwan Independence Movement, which called for self-determination for the island and rejected "all forms of dictatorship—Chinese, Communist or KMT", was responsible for a number of bomb explosions between 1970 and 1976. Although it was effectively suppressed in Taiwan, many of its members being imprisoned as "rebels", it was reported in 1978 to be supported by many Taiwanese in Japan, where it had nearly 10,000 members, and in the United States. The American section of the movement, United Formosans for Independence, was believed to be responsible for a series of bomb explosions in 1979 at offices of Taiwan government institutions in American cities.

As opposition political parties were forbidden under the martial law code in force since 1949, opponents of the KMT regime established during the 1970s a series of magazines which formed a rallying centre for their activities. A number of opposition leaders, including democrats and socialists as well as advocates of Taiwanese independence, founded in August 1979 the monthly *Formosa,* which pressed for a representative parliament, a free press, an amnesty for political prisoners and the ending of martial law, and within two months reached a circulation of over 100,000. After a demonstration organized by *Formosa* on Dec. 10, 1979, in the port of Kaohsiung to celebrate Human Rights Day developed into a riot (the seriousness of which, according to foreign observers, was deliberately exaggerated by the authorities), the magazine was banned. Eight leading dissidents associated with *Formosa* were found guilty on April 18, 1980, of having attempted to seize power and collaborated with exiled advocates of Taiwanese independence, and received sentences ranging from 12 years to life imprisonment.

During the next four years little was heard of the separatist movement, but on April 5, 1984, the Taiwan government declared the League of Formosan Independence a seditious organization, and stated that any activities in collusion with it would be regarded as illegal. The central standing committee of the KMT approved on Oct. 15, 1986, a proposal by President Chiang Ching-kuo to lift martial law, but stipulated that new parties which advocated Taiwanese independence should not be permitted.

1981 Chinese Proposals for Reunification

In a major new development in late 1981, Marshal Ye Jianying (Chairman of the Standing Committee of the Chinese National People's Congress, a post equivalent to head of state) put forward detailed proposals for the peaceful reunification of China and Taiwan. Although the Chinese government had previously suggested that within a reunited China, Taiwan might retain full autonomy as well as its own armed forces and economic system, Marshal Ye's proposal was the first in which the Chinese Communist Party had officially offered to share power with the KMT.

Marshal Ye's nine-point plan, which he put forward in an interview with the New China News Agency on Sept. 30, 1981, was formulated as follows: "(i) In order to bring an end to the unfortunate separation of the Chinese nation as early as possible, we propose that talks be held between the Communist Party of China and the KMT of China on a reciprocal basis so that the two parties will co-operate for the third time to accomplish the great cause of national reunification. The two sides may first send people to meet for an exhaustive exchange of views. (ii) It is the urgent desire of the people of all nationalities on both sides of the straits to communicate with each other, reunite with their families and relatives, develop trade and increase mutual understanding. We propose that the two sides make arrangements to facilitate the exchange of mails, trade, air and shipping services, family reunions and visits by relatives and tourists, as well as academic, cultural and sports exchanges, and reach an agreement thereon. (iii) After the country is reunified Taiwan can enjoy a high degree of autonomy as a special administrative region, and can retain its armed forces. The central government will not interfere with local affairs on Taiwan. (iv) Taiwan's current socio-economic system will remain unchanged, as will its way of life and its economic and cultural relations with foreign countries. There will be no encroachment on the proprietary rights and lawful right of inheritance over private property, houses, land and enterprises, or on foreign investments. (v) People in authority and representative personages of various circles in Taiwan may take up posts of leadership in national political bodies and participate in running the state. (vi) When Taiwan's local finance is in difficulty, the central government may subsidize it as is fit for the circumstances. (vii) For people of all nationalities and public figures of various circles in Taiwan who wish to come and settle on the mainland, it is guaranteed that proper arrangements may be made for them, and there will be no discrimination against them, and that they will have freedom of entry and exit. (viii) Industrialists and businessmen in Taiwan are welcome to invest and engage in various economic undertakings on the mainland, and their legal rights, interests and profits are guaranteed. (ix) The reunification of the motherland is the responsibility of all Chinese. We sincerely welcome people of all nationalities, public figures of all circles and all mass organizations in Taiwan to make proposals and suggestions regarding affairs of state through various channels and in various ways".

Responding to Marshal Ye's proposals, Sun Yun-suan (Taiwan's Prime Minister) said in the Legislative Yuan on Oct. 2, 1981: "The nine-point overture of the Chinese Communists...has not gone to the heart of the problem, which is whether China should adopt a free and democratic system or a totalitarian and dictatorial one...We implement benevolent rule, whereas the Chinese Communists enforce a tyrannical one, so there is no room for compromise". President Chiang Ching-kuo declared at a meeting of the central standing committee of the KMT on Oct. 7: "We shall never negotiate with the Chinese Communists...I want to tell our compatriots on the Chinese mainland that we are resolved to remove the yoke that the Communists have imposed upon them".

Despite these rebuffs, Chinese spokesmen continued to elaborate on Marshal Ye's proposals. Peng Deqing, the Minister of Communications, said on Oct. 3, 1981, that his ministry was ready to establish regular passenger and cargo services with Taiwan by sea and air at any time. Zhen Tuobin, Minister of Foreign Trade, on Oct. 7 suggested measures for the expansion of trade between China and Taiwan whereby each would supply the other's needs: China, for example, could supply Taiwan with coal, oil and herbal medicines at preferential prices. Chang Yanqing, vice-president of the Bank of China, proposed on Oct. 10 that exchange transactions and settlement of accounts should be conducted through bank representatives in Hong Kong until direct transactions could be established, and stated that the bank was ready to open savings accounts for Chinese in Taiwan and to guarantee freedom to deposit and withdraw money.

Hu Yaobang, who had succeeded Hua Guofeng as Chairman of the Chinese Communist Party in June 1981, repeated the proposal for co-operation between the KMT and the Communist Party on Oct. 9, in a speech to commemorate the 70th anniversary of the revolution of 1911, which overthrew the Ching dynasty and established the Chinese Republic. Chairman Hu said that the three great tasks confronting China were to modernize agriculture, industry, national defence, and science and technology, to defend world peace, and "to ensure Taiwan's return to the motherland". "The question of Taiwan is entirely China's internal affair", he continued. "It should be settled by the leaders and people on both sides of the strait. The KMT and the Communist Party co-operated twice in history, to complete the northern expedition [in 1926-27] and conduct the war against Japanese aggression. This gave a strong impetus to our nation's progress. Why can we not have a third period of co-operation between the KMT and the Communist Party to build a unified state? It is true that neither of the previous co-operations lasted long, but fair-minded people all admit that the two unfortunate splits were not caused by the Communist Party. We do not wish to settle old accounts here. Let bygones be bygones! Let the past lessons help us to co-operate better in the future!".

He continued: "There is nothing in our present proposal which is unfair or should cause anxiety to the Taiwan side. If the Taiwan side is still worried about something, it may raise questions for study and settlement in the course of negotiations. It is understandable for a certain distrust to exist as a result of long-term separation. But if we do not come into contact and talk things over, how can we remove the barriers and build up mutual trust?" In conclusion, he suggested that the late President Chiang Kai-shek's remains should be brought back to China for burial in his family cemetery, which had been kept in good repair, and invited President Chiang Ching-kuo, Sun Yun-suan and other KMT leaders to visit the mainland, even if they did not wish to enter into talks for the time being. A Taiwan government spokesman described this invitation on the same day as "another joke".

KMT Proposals for Reunification

At the 12th congress of the KMT, held in April 1981, no reference was made to the reconquest of the mainland. Instead, the slogan put forward was "Unify China in accordance with the Three Principles of the People", i.e. nationalism, democracy and "the people's livelihood", the three principles laid down by Dr Sun Yat-sen, the founder of the KMT and first President of the Republic of China.

Sun Yun-suan elaborated on this slogan and replied to the Chinese government's reunification proposals in a speech of June 10, 1982, in which he suggested that peaceful reunification might become possible as a result of internal changes in Communist China. "The Chinese Communists' peace talks proposals", he said, "have two accompanying preconditions: (i) the government of the Republic of China is to be considered a 'provincial Government' under the jurisdiction of the Chinese Communist regime; (ii) the invasion of Taiwan by force is not ruled out if peace talks fail. In other words, this so-called peace proposal is actually an attempt to annex the Republic of China".

"Even the leadership of the Chinese Communist regime has been compelled to admit openly that mainland China cannot catch up with Taiwan economically", he went on. "The Chinese Communists have tacitly followed the successful experience of the Republic of China in seeking national development. They have imitated our free export processing zones by opening so-called 'special economic zones'. They have introduced foreign capital to help enlarge exports, and readjusted the order of economic construction by giving first priority to agriculture. They recently tried again to adjust the economic structure. While continuing to recognize 'ownership by the whole people' and 'collective ownership', they began in a small way to accept the 'individual economy' of urban and rural workers. All these changes are signs that the consistently dogmatic Chinese Communist regime has been compelled to bow to reality and make an about-face after a series of setbacks".

"In advocating the reunification of China on the basis of the Three Principles of the People we are not trying to embarrass the Chinese Communist regime", Sun declared. "As early as September 1937, soon after the outbreak of the Sino-Japanese War, the Chinese Communists announced: 'Dr Sun Yat-sen's Three Principles of the People are needed today in China, and this party is willing to help carry them out'. In recent years the Chinese Communists have often expressed their respect for Dr Sun Yat-sen. They have thus recognized the superiority of the Three Principles of the People. All freedom-loving Chinese sincerely hope that the Chinese Communists will truly return to and identify with Dr Sun Yat-sen's Three Principles of the People, and that they will take earnest action to implement the Three Principles...We believe that Chinese reunification should be based on the free will of the Chinese people as a whole...If the political, economic, social and cultural gaps between the Chinese mainland and free China continue to narrow, the conditions for peaceful reunification can gradually mature. The obstacles to reunification will be reduced naturally with the passage of time".

Adoption of New Chinese Constitution

A new Chinese constitution adopted by the National People's Congress (NPC) on Dec. 4, 1982, contained a number of passages intended to facilitate the reunification of China and Taiwan on the basis of autonomy for Taiwan. The preamble to the previous constitution, adopted in 1978, had declared: "Taiwan is China's sacred territory. We are determined to liberate Taiwan and accomplish the great cause of unifying our motherland". The corresponding passage of the new constitution, however, stated: "Taiwan is part of the sacred territory of the PRC [People's Republic of China]. It is the lofty duty of the entire Chinese people, including our compatriots in Taiwan, to accomplish the great task of reunifying the motherland". The phrase "liberate Taiwan" was thus omitted, and the possibility of reunifying China in co-operation with "our compatriots in Taiwan" recognized. Whereas the preamble to the 1978 constitution had referred only in general terms to the period of "more than a century of heroic struggle" preceding the Communist revolution of 1949, the 1982 constitution specifically mentioned that "the revolution of 1911, led by Dr Sun Yat-sen, abolished the feudal monarchy and gave birth to the Republic of China".

A completely new article in the constitution (Article 31) stated: "The state may establish special administrative regions when necessary. The systems to be instituted in special administrative regions shall be prescribed by law enacted by the NPC in the light of the specific conditions". Reporting on the work of the committee for the revision of the constitution to the NPC on Nov. 26, 1982, Peng Zhen, vice-chairman of the committee, said that Article 31 would allow Taiwan's current economic and social systems, way of life and economic and cultural relations with foreign countries to remain unchanged after peaceful reunification with the People's Republic.

The Hong Kong Agreement and the Reunification Question

The Chinese government's views on the form that a future reunification with Taiwan might take were reflected in an agreement with the British government on the future status of Hong Kong, which was initialled on Sept. 26, 1984, after two years of negotiations. After receiving the approval of the Standing Committee of the NPC, the British Parliament and the Hong Kong Legislative Council, it was signed by the Chinese and British Prime Ministers in Beijing on Dec. 19, 1984.

Hong Kong Island, which together with adjacent islets has an area of 30.3 square miles (78.4 sq km), was ceded to Britain by China in perpetuity in 1842 by the Treaty of Nanking, signed after the First Opium War. Kowloon, on the mainland opposite, and Stonecutters Island, which together total 4.4 square miles (11.3 sq km), were ceded under the Treaty of Peking (Beijing) in 1860 after the Second Opium War. The Chinese Communist government, like the KMT government before it, had consistently repudiated the treaties of Nanking and Peking as "unequal treaties" imposed upon China by force. The New Territories, comprising the hinterland of the Kowloon peninsula

and 235 islands, with an area of 375.9 square miles (973.8 sq km), were leased to Britain for 99 years under the Convention of Peking in 1898. China regarded this agreement as having been signed under duress, and before World War II consistently rejected British proposals for the cession of the territories. The lease was due to expire on June 30, 1997, when the New Territories (without which the economy of Hong Kong Island and Kowloon would not be viable) were due to revert to China.

The 1984 agreement provided that the Chinese government would resume the exercise of sovereignty over Hong Kong from July 1, 1997, and in accordance with Article 31 of the constitution would establish a Hong Kong Special Administrative Region (HKSAR). This would be directly under the authority of the Chinese government but would enjoy a high degree of autonomy, except in foreign and defence affairs, which were the Chinese government's responsibility. It would be vested with executive, legislative and independent judicial power, including that of final adjudication, and the laws currently in force in Hong Kong would remain basically unchanged. The government of Hong Kong would be composed of local inhabitants. "'The current social and economic systems in Hong Kong will remain unchanged, and so will the lifestyle", the agreement continued. "Rights and freedoms, including those of the person, of speech, of the press, of assembly, of association, of travel, of movement, of correspondence, of strike, of choice of occupation, of academic research and of religious belief will be ensured by law in the Hong Kong Special Administrative Region. Private property, ownership of enterprises, legitimate right of inheritance and foreign investment will be protected by law".

Hong Kong would retain the status of a free port, a separate customs territory and an international financial centre; its markets for foreign exchange would continue; there would be free flow of capital; and the Hong Kong dollar would continue to circulate and remain freely convertible. Hong Kong would have independent finances, and the Chinese government would not levy taxes there. Hong Kong might maintain and develop economic and cultural relations and conclude relevant agreements with states, regions and relevant international organizations. The Hong Kong government might issue travel documents, and would be responsible for public order in the region. An annex to the agreement stated that the Basic Law of the HKSAR, to be promulgated on July 1, 1997, would stipulate that "the socialist system and socialist policies shall not be practised" and that "Hong Kong's previous capitalist system and lifestyle shall remain unchanged for 50 years".

Zhao Ziyang, the Chinese Prime Minister, said on Sept. 30, 1984, that China was ready to open consultations with Taiwan on reunification, and announced that the "one country, two systems" strategy, which guaranteed the continuation of Hong Kong's economic system, would be applied to Taiwan. President Chiang Ching-kuo, however, described the Hong Kong agreement as "nothing but a fraud", and declared that "the Chinese Communists have no right to represent the Chinese people, and any accord bearing their signature is invalid".

The first official contact between Taiwan and China since 1949 occurred as a result of the defection to China on May 3, 1986, of the pilot of an aircraft of Taiwan's state-run China Air Line (CAL). Although CAL initially rejected a Chinese invitation to negotiate on the return of the aircraft and the two other members of its crew, Chinese and CAL officials finally held talks in Hong Kong on May 17-20, following which the aircraft and crew members were returned to Taiwan.

Taiwan's Claim to Mongolia

In a statement issued on Jan. 28, 1987, the Taipei government reiterated its claim, as in its view the legitimate government of China, to sovereignty over the People's Republic of Mongolia (formerly the Chinese province of Outer Mongolia). The statement recalled that the post-World War II Sino-Soviet agreement confirming the independence of the People's Republic of Mongolia had been abrogated by Taiwan in 1953.

Developing Thaw, 1987-91

Despite the above statement by the Taipei government relating to Mongolia, 1987 saw the beginning of a new thaw and growing realism in relations between China and Taiwan. In September two Taiwanese journalists visited Beijing in defiance of Taipei; they were the first in 37 years. A month later (Oct. 14, 1987) a KMT spokesman said that Taiwanese residents (apart from civil servants and members of the military) would be allowed to visit relatives "by blood or marriage" in China. The death of Gen. Chiang Ching-kuo (Chiang Kai-shek's son) on Jan. 13, 1988, removed the last close link with the Generalissimo, and made the process of reconciliation potentially easier. His successor, the Vice-President Lee Teng-hui, was the first native-born Taiwanese to become President. China's reaction to Chiang's death was "sympathetic". The Chinese Communist Party general-secretary, Zhao Ziyang, said, "at this time, when the leadership of the KMT is being replaced, we reaffirm that our party's principles and policy of peaceful reunification of the motherland will not change".

During 1988 there was a softening of Taiwan's approach to mainland China. Thus, in October Prime Minister Ya Kuo Lua said that reunification was a long-term goal and that it could best be achieved by ensuring that those on the mainland knew of Taiwan's achievements. This followed a change of policy on both sides the previous month (September) when Taiwan reduced the monetary rewards on offer for hijacking planes from the mainland by 64.6% while China abolished rewards for members of the military defecting to the mainland. A Taiwan bill of Dec. 24, 1988, to govern relations with the mainland included

60 articles covering legal aspects of visits to both sides. This period saw a sharp increase in trade between Taiwan and mainland China.

On May 4-6, 1989, Shirley Kuo (Taiwan's Minister of Finance) became the first senior Taiwanese official to visit Beijing since 1949. She led a 12-member Taiwanese delegation to the 22nd annual meeting of the Board of Governors of the Asian Development Bank (ADB). However, Taiwan's Foreign Minister, Lien Chan, said Kuo's visit had "nothing to do with our policy towards the Chinese communist regime" which would continue to be based on the "three no's": no negotiation, no compromise, no contact. Nonetheless, 1989 and 1990 saw the growth of closer relations between Taiwan and China although the suppression of the pro-democracy movement in Tiananmen Square (May 1989) presented Taipei with a major propaganda weapon. In December 1989 an unofficial China-Taiwan "trade mediation" group was set up in Hong Kong. In February 1990 Taiwan lifted a ban on its entertainers performing in mainland China and eased restrictions on academic exchanges.

On May 20, 1990, Lee Teng-hui was sworn in as chairman of the KMT; in his acceptance speech he offered the possibility of "full academic, cultural, economic, trade, scientific and technological exchanges between the two countries" leading to the possibility of future reunification. However, the offer depended upon China adopting "democratic politics and the free economic system" and renouncing its commitment to reconquer Taiwan by force. China should also refrain from "obstructing our development of foreign relations". This drew a response from the official New China News Agency on May 22 criticizing Lee's "impossible preconditions" and restating Beijing's claim to be "the sole legitimate government representing all Chinese people".

On Oct. 18, 1990, a Mainland Affairs Council was created in Taiwan. This was followed (Nov. 1) by the Taiwan cabinet approving a draft statute on relations with the Chinese mainland that legalized civilian contacts. Then, on Nov. 21 a privately funded Foundation for Exchange Across the Taiwan Strait was set up. These moves reflected a new policy in Taipei that aimed at a gradual easing of relations with the mainland.

An End to the Civil War, 1991

On March 14, 1991, the Taiwanese Cabinet adopted the Guidelines for National Unification, which stated that "a democratic, free and equitably prosperous China" should be based on the principle that "both the mainland and Taiwan areas are parts of Chinese territory". Unification was to be pursued in three stages. A short-term phase of "exchanges and reciprocity" was to include respecting "the other's existence as a political entity", and an end to the state of hostility. A medium-term phase of "mutual trust and cooperation" would see the re-establishment of official communication channels such as postal and transport links, and the long-term phase would see "a consultative organization for unification...through which both sides, in accordance with the will of the people in both the mainland and Taiwan areas...jointly discuss the grand task of unification and map out a constitutional system to establish a democratic, free and equitably prosperous China".

On April 24, 1991, China announced an end to its "loudspeaker war" with Taiwan although Taiwan insisted it would continue its loudspeaker broadcasts to the mainland to inform the people of free world developments. Meanwhile, on April 28, 1991, the first formal Taiwanese delegation consisting of 14 members of the Straits Exchange Foundation (SEF) visited Beijing and met with officials from the Chinese State Council's Taiwan Affairs Office (TAO) for talks. Prior to the visit the Mainland Affairs Council of Taiwan authorised the SEF to handle "cross strait disputes" over illegal immigrants, smuggling, piracy, travel and trade issues.

On April 30, 1991, President Lee Teng-hui of Taiwan signed a document declaring an end to the "Period of Mobilization for the Suppression of the Communist Rebellion". This officially brought to an end four decades of "civil war" between the KMT government and the People's Republic of China. At a news conference President Lee acknowledged: "We must face the fact that the mainland area is now controlled by the Chinese communist regime". This did not mean, however, that Taiwan had abandoned its one-China policy. President Lee also announced the termination of the "Temporary Provisions" which had been in existence since 1948 and effectively rendered the constitution inoperative and gave to the President enormous overriding powers. In future, elections would be based solely upon Taiwanese constituencies. The ending of the "Period of Communist Rebellion" removed a major obstacle to closer ties with China.

The SEF visit to Beijing ended after two series of talks with the Chinese State Council's Taiwan Affairs Office (TAO) on May 5 and two days later Taiwan lifted martial law on Quemoy and Matsu. SEF's leader, Chen Chang-wen, said that the tasks of the visit had been fulfilled but that "repeated efforts will be required to handle the many details in the future". Taiwan's Defence Ministry announced on May 2 that it had cancelled measures designed to encourage Chinese soldiers to defect from the mainland.

On July 29, 1991, the Mainland Affairs Committee approved new rules to permit some local banks to provide foreign exchange for Taiwan individuals to send remittances to individuals in China. Two mainland journalists arrived in Taiwan on Aug. 12, 1991, to cover the trial of a group of Chinese fishermen arrested off Taiwan in July and accused of theft and piracy. The journalists were the first from the mainland since 1949.

These improvements in relations received a setback in October 1991 when the main Taiwan opposition party, the Democratic Progressive Party (DPP), published a draft manifesto with a clause pledging "to build a Taiwanese republic with independent sovereignty". China expressed "grave concern" at the DPP commitment to independence for Taiwan and on Oct. 9 China's President, Yang Shangkun, warned: "Those who play with fire will be burnt to ashes".

An SEF delegation visited Beijing on Nov. 4-7, 1991, for talks with TAO and reached initial agreement on fighting piracy and smuggling in Taiwan Strait. The two sides also agreed that early in 1992, after China had set up an equivalent body to SEF, formal talks would be held on the principle of "one China". The talks covered co-operation over judicial disputes. China's Vice-President, Wu Xueqian, told SEF's secretary-general, Chen Chang-wen, on Nov. 7 that the SEF visit was a "good beginning" for achieving reunification.

Developments from 1992

On Dec. 16, 1991, China established a non-governmental Association for Relations Across the Taiwan Straits (ARATS), an equivalent body to Taiwan's SEF, to promote exchanges and co-operation with Taiwan. Chen Jung-chieh (SEF's deputy secretary-general) sent a message of congratulation to Wang Daohan, the president of ARATS. Discussions between the two associations, led by Wang for ARATS and Koo Chen-fu for SEF, appeared to produce results when in November 1992 they came up with what became known as the "1992 consensus". This is the subject of some controversy, since it was a purely oral understanding, but the consensus appears to have been that both sides adhered to the principle that there was only one China whilst still accepting that there were differing interpretations of what China was. This "1992 consensus" played a key role in making cross-Strait negotiations possible, since it delicately traced a path between the two positions.

SEF had been negotiating from a position of strength in 1992, as the KMT had won a resounding victory in the Second National Assembly elections on Dec. 21, 1991. The KMT election ticket, based on gradual expansion of Taiwan's democratization and a negotiated framework with mainland China, contrasted sharply with that of the DPP, which advocated a Republic of Taiwan. The result of the election was that the DPP gained only 20% of the vote, as against 78% for the KMT.

The 1991 electoral mandate and the "1992 consensus" paved the way for the first official meeting between ARATS and SEF, held in Singapore on April 27-30, 1993. Annual meetings, sometimes referred to as the Koo-Wang talks, were held in 1993, 1994 and 1995, and three meetings at the vice-chairman level in 1994-5. They discussed functional issues in the slowly-developing cross-Strait dialogue: fishing rights, repatriation of illegal immigrants and co-operation on crime control.

Meanwhile, in 1993, Taiwan applied to join the United Nations. In August 1993, however, China published an official White paper on its position regarding

Taiwan: "To settle the Taiwan question and achieve national reunification: this is a sacrosanct mission of the entire Chinese people. The Chinese Government has persistently worked towards this end since the founding of the People's Republic. Its basic position on this question is: peaceful reunification; one country, two systems". Following Chinese pressure, Taiwan's UN application was rejected.

Setback in Relations, 1995-96

The development of something approaching rapprochement was broken in 1995-96, however, by a crisis in US-Chinese-Taiwan relations. The year 1995 began well, with the Chinese leader Jiang Zemin announcing an eight-point proposal for ending hostility with Taiwan, which including the establishment of the "three direct links"—trade, transport, communications—that currently did not exist across the Straits.

However, in May the Taiwanese President, Lee Teng-hui, was given permission to enter the USA (with which Taiwan had no official relations), after votes in the Senate (97-1 in favour) and House (360-0). President Clinton agreed to this on May 22, even though only the previous month Warren Christopher (the Secretary of State) had told the Chinese Foreign Secretary that allowing a visit would be "inconsistent" with US policy. Clinton had in fact already raised the protocol level for US treatment of Taiwanese officials in 1994. The Chinese Foreign Ministry responded by saying that this was the latest step in Lee's efforts to create "one China and one Taiwan", i.e. Taiwanese independence, and cancelled the planned and imminent visit of its Defence Minister, Chi Haotian, to Washington. On June 16, ARATS informed SEF that it was suspending their talks: "As a result of a series of actions by Taiwan that are destructive to cross-Strait relations, the atmosphere for conducting the next round of Koo-Wang talks and associated preparatory consultations has been seriously affected. We have no choice but to postpone those preparatory consultations and talks". Despite regular appeals from SEF, it would be 1998 before talks were resumed.

Lee's visit to the USA went ahead from July 7-12, 1995, and included a visit to Cornell University. He had been back less than a week when China announced that it would be conducting missile tests and naval and air exercises in the Straits from July 21 to 28. The tests ended only a few days before Warren Christopher and the Chinese Foreign Minister, Qian Qichen, met for talks in Brunei. As well as Taiwan, they discussed arms proliferation, trade and human rights. Christopher gave Qian a confidential letter from Clinton stating that the USA opposed Taiwanese independence, opposed a two-China policy, opposed one China and one Taiwan, and did not support Taiwanese entry into the UN. This was a restatement of US policy since 1972. Qian retorted that "the true value of a promise is shown in real action", and the Chinese Prime Minister echoed this: "It is not enough to make oral statements".

From Aug. 15-25, 1995, a second round of Chinese missile tests and naval exercises took place near Taiwan. The day they concluded, the US Under-Secretary of State, Peter Tarnoff, visited China. He reiterated Christopher's assurances on independence and UN membership. China wanted to produce a joint communiqué, committing the United States to opposing Taiwanese independence and ruling out further visits to the USA by Taiwanese leaders, but this did not happen. On Nov. 15, China conducted the third round of exercises that year, this time including a mock invasion of Taiwan. Official sources said that this was to demonstrate "determination to firmly oppose and contain Taiwanese independence". In Taiwanese elections two weeks later, Lee's KMT had its majority cut to two seats.

The following year, 1996, the USA granted another visa, this time for Taiwan's Vice-President, Li Yuan-zu, to transit through the USA on his way to Guatemala and Haiti. This was followed in March by a heavy Chinese troop build-up in Fujian province opposite Taiwan: 100,000 took part in exercises, followed by another round of Chinese missile tests off the coast of Taiwan from March 8-18. The sense of "weapons diplomacy" was heightened on March 10, when the USA decided to deploy two carrier battle groups (the *Independence* and the *Nimitz*) to the vicinity of Taiwan. China continued with its own signals: air and naval exercises off the coast of Taiwan from March 12-20, a missile test on March 13, and joint air, ground and naval exercises near Taiwan on March 18-25.

Fluctuating Relations, 1997-2000

This round of tit-for-tat signalling represented the low-point in cross-Strait relations in recent times. Signs of a thaw did not emerge until September 1997, when the National Congress of the Chinese Communist Party called for talks with Taiwan on "procedural affairs for political negotiations", and shifted its previous insistence that negotiations must take place on the "One China" principle narrowly defined (i.e. "one country, two systems", or the Hong Kong model). The following month, on Oct. 29, President Clinton met with Jiang Zemin and stated at a press conference: "I told President Jiang that we hope the People's Republic and Taiwan would resume a constructive cross-Strait dialogue and expand cross-Strait exchanges. Ultimately, the relationship between the PRC and Taiwan is for the Chinese themselves to determine peacefully".

These efforts began to bear fruit in April 1998, when ARATS invited the Deputy Secretary-General of SEF, Jan Jyh-horng, to Beijing. This was not a resumption of the technical talks, which had been suspended since Lee's visit to the USA in 1995, but simply a visit. The Koo-Wang talks were finally resumed in October, when Koo Chen-fu of SEF visited the mainland to recommence high-level cross-Straits dialogue. In June, Clinton himself visited China, where he gave his support to the "three no's" principles: "I had a chance to reiterate our Taiwan policy, which is that we don't support independence for Taiwan, or two Chinas, or one Taiwan-one China. And we don't believe that Taiwan should be a member in any organization for which statehood is a requirement".

Relations took another turn for the worse in 1999. The Chinese missile build-up near Taiwan had continued. Chinese Prime Minister Zhu Rongji said in March that the missiles were not targeted at "our brothers and sisters in Taiwan", although he still refused to rule out the use of force. Working-level talks between ARATS and SEF continued, however, and in June they agreed that Wang Doahan would visit Taiwan in September or October, following on from Koo's visit to Beijing in October 1998.

This visit was, however, shelved in view of developments in July. On July 9, President Lee was interviewed on a German radio station. He said that the 1991 amendments to Taiwan's constitution "recognize the legitimacy of the rule of the PRC on the mainland", but that the amendments also meant that Taiwan and China now had "a state-to-state relationship or at least a special state-to-state relationship". This was a change from his previous characterization of the relationship as being between "two equal political entities". The Chinese Foreign Ministry instantly responded that Lee "should not underestimate the firm resolve of the Chinese government to safeguard state sovereignty, dignity and territorial integrity". Jiang Zemin met President Clinton on Sept. 1, and said "China will never commit itself to abandoning the use of force in order to safeguard its national sovereignty and territorial integrity". China had also warned the USA not to aid Taiwan with a missile defence system, after the Taiwanese Executive Yuan (cabinet) decided on Aug. 19 that such a system should be pursued.

It appeared that even a natural disaster held the scope to worsen relations. On Sept. 21, 1999, a large earthquake hit Taiwan and left 2,100 dead and 8,700 wounded. The following day, the Chinese Foreign Minister, Tang Jiaxuan, spoke at the UN General Assembly, and expressed thanks to the international community for their offers of help to "the Taiwan province of China". Taiwan responded furiously by accusing the Minister of exploiting the earthquake for political gain.

China released another White Paper on "The One-China Principle and the Taiwan Issue" on Feb. 21, 2000, in which it noted that, despite the existence of the 1993 White Paper (see above), "we deem it necessary to further explain to the international community the Chinese government's position and policy on the One-China Principle". It explained this principle thus: "China established the basic principle of 'peaceful reunification, and one country, two systems'. The key points of this basic principle and the relevant policies are: China will do its best to achieve peaceful reunification, but will not commit itself to ruling out the use of force; will actively promote people-to-people contacts and economic and cultural exchanges between the two sides of the Taiwan Straits, and start direct trade, postal, air and shipping services as soon as possible;

achieve reunification through peaceful negotiations and, on the premise of the One-China Principle, any matter can be negotiated. After reunification, the policy of 'one country, two systems' will be practised, with the main body of China (Chinese mainland) continuing with its socialist system, and Taiwan maintaining its capitalist system for a long period of time to come. After reunification, Taiwan will enjoy a high degree of autonomy, and the Central Government will not send troops or administrative personnel to be stationed in Taiwan. Resolution of the Taiwan issue is an internal affair of China, which should be achieved by the Chinese themselves, and there is no call for aid by foreign forces". On a more ominous, if familiar, note, the paper also stated that China "cannot allow the resolution of the Taiwan issue to be postponed indefinitely".

Consequences of Election of DPP President of Taiwan

The following month (March 2000) saw a seismic shift in the political life of Taiwan. In the presidential elections, Chen Shui-bian of the DPP defeated the KMT candidate (Lee Teng-hui being barred from standing for a further term) to become President of Taiwan. This was the first-ever electoral defeat for the KMT, although (following legislative elections in 1998) the KMT retained a majority in the Legislative Yuan (parliament). Chen was generally known as an advocate of Taiwanese independence and his election produced intense concern in Beijing.

In his inaugural address on May 20, 2000, President Chen established a "Five No's" policy on cross-strait relations. He pledged that, unless the Chinese Communists used military force against Taiwan, he would not: (1) declare Taiwan independent; (2) change the name of the nation; (3) push for the inclusion of former president Lee Teng-hui's "special state-to-state relationship" in the Constitution; (4) hold a referendum to change the status quo on the question of independence or unification; or (5) move to abolish either the Guidelines for National Unification or the National Unification Council. However, the following month he rejected a call for talks from China, and firmly stated that talks could only take place if the "One China" principle highlighted in China's White paper was a topic for negotiation: acceptance of the principle could not be a precondition for talks as China insisted.

China responded to Chen's election by courting other Taiwanese political parties and business leaders: representatives of the KMT and two other opposition parties visited China, and in total over a third of parliament's members went to the mainland. In October, Beijing issued a policy document entitled "China's National Defence in 2000", in which it described cross-Strait relations as "complicated and grim", and said China was determined to keep its territorial integrity if Taiwan should be separated from China, invaded by a foreign country, or if "Taiwan authorities refuse indefinitely the peaceful settlement of cross-Straits reunification through negotiations".

Dialogue was not resumed in 2001. The "three small links" (post, travel, and trade for specified areas) were implemented in some small Taiwanese islands, but elsewhere relations remained poor. The Dalai Lama visited Taiwan in April, to strong protests from China. President Bush of the USA stated that "whatever it takes, we will defend Taiwan if it is attacked, as long as it does not declare independence". In May, President Chen made a visit to the USA, where he met with a group of congressmen, and also the Mayor of New York, Rudy Giuliani. Before leaving, Chen remarked: "Taiwan is a sovereign, independent country".

The political fall-out from the presidential elections continued in Taiwan. In August 2001, KMT members loyal to Lee Teng-hui decided to form a breakaway party called the Taiwan Solidarity Union (TSU). This was the first time a political party had included the name Taiwan in its title. Lee did not leave the KMT but publicly supported the TSU and was stripped of KMT membership. The TSU's stated aim was to "mobilize those who favour stability and a middle course", by forming an alliance with the DPP. Twenty former KMT members stood for the TSU in the Legislative Yuan elections scheduled for Dec. 1, and Chen and Lee both said they were trying to form cross-party alliances. In the elections, the KMT lost its parliamentary majority for the first time ever. The DPP won 87 seats (up from 68), the KMT 68 (down from 115), the TSU 13, and the People's First Party (PFP) 46. Chen invited the PFP and KMT to join a coalition government, but they refused.

Taiwan entered the World Trade Organization in January 2002, only a few weeks after China did so. Unlike China, Taiwan did not join as a country, but as a separate customs territory. Later that month, President Chen bluntly rejected the "one country, two systems" model, and also approved plans for Taiwanese passports to have the word "Taiwan", along with the ROC title. China's protests at this were followed on Jan. 30 by invitations for DPP members to visit Beijing, but it was pointedly stressed that the invitation was not extended to include Chen or his Vice-President, Annette Lu.

Proposal of Referendum on Status of Taiwan

On Aug. 3, 2002, Chen caused a furore when he made a speech to the World Federation of Taiwanese Associations and seemed to raise the prospect of a referendum on Taiwanese independence. He stated that: "Taiwan is not a part of someone else, not someone else's local government, and not someone else's province…it must be clearly distinguished that both Taiwan and China are a country on either side of the strait". He went on to say that "China's so-called 'one China principle' or 'one country, two systems' is to change the status quo in Taiwan. It is impossible for us to accept this because whether Taiwan's future and the status quo should be changed is an issue not to be decided by any country, government, party, or individual. Only the great 23 million people of Taiwan have

the right to decide on Taiwan's future, destiny, and status quo. How do we make a decision when necessary? [A] referendum…is the ideal and goal we have been pursuing over a long period of time and the common idea of everyone. [A] referendum is a basic human right and the 23 million people of Taiwan have this basic human right, which should not be deprived or restricted".

China responded on Aug. 4 with a Foreign Ministry statement that China "would never tolerate" an independent Taiwan. Taiwan's Mainland Affairs Council moved hastily to repair the breach on Aug. 8, in a statement that there were no plans for a referendum, and that one would not be held unless China forced the issue.

On Sept. 12, 2002, China blocked Taiwan's tenth annual bid to join the UN, when the general committee to the General Assembly voted not to put the matter to the Assembly itself. By this time, only 27 states accorded diplomatic recognition to Taiwan, most of them small and poor, and all of them in the Pacific, Africa and Latin America and the Caribbean. No significant power accords recognition to Taiwan, although it informally maintains representative offices in many countries.

Chen continued to press his point concerning a possible referendum. Speaking on the second anniversary of the Sept. 11, 2001, terrorist attacks on the USA, he claimed that "the terror and threat posed to Taiwan's people has virtually exceeded those brought by any terrorist attacks", a statement followed only weeks later by a pledge that Taiwan's constitution would be revised in 2006 (the twentieth anniversary of the founding of his party). He did not specify what these changes entailed, but the statement brought a warning from the US State Department to the effect that Chen's August 2000 pledges were still taken "very seriously" in Washington.

That Chen was serious rather than playing to the gallery ahead of the March 2004 elections was demonstrated in November 2003 when a highly controversial referendum bill was put to the Taiwanese legislature. The bill made provision for referenda on constitutional issues, but was significantly watered down by the KMT, which successfully added a clause preventing the government calling referenda on changes to Taiwan's name, flag or territorial status. Instead, in peacetime such referenda could only be called by the legislature under the review of a cross-party supervisory committee, or by the public by a petition signed by at least 5% of the electorate.

This appeared to rule out the possibility of a referendum on independence in 2004, but within days Chen had begun to try another tack. The law did allow the government to call a "defensive referendum" on "issues of national security concern", provided that a foreign threat to the island was imminent. In December Chen released details of what he called "the ongoing threat towards Taiwan"—the 500 or so Chinese ballistic missiles deployed within range of the island—and announced that he would hold a defensive referendum on whether Taiwan ought to call on China to remove them. The referendum was scheduled for March 20, 2004, the date of the Taiwanese presidential elections.

A US State Department spokesman immediately responded that "we don't want a referendum", adding that this would merely "confirm the obvious"—that the Taiwanese people almost universally wanted the missiles removed. Lien Chan (the leader of the KMT) danced nimbly along the line by arguing that "the missiles deployed by the Chinese communists pose a serious threat, but they don't put Taiwan's sovereignty and the status quo in immediate danger". The legislature was, however, unable to maintain a united front on the referendum, and a parliamentary resolution aimed at heading off the possibility ended with two resolutions: one from the DPP asking China to remove its missiles and respect Taiwanese sovereignty, and one from the KMT and PFP expressing a hope that no more missiles would be deployed and the existing ones removed.

During a visit to Washington in December by the Chinese Premier, President Bush remarked that "the comments and actions made by the leader of Taiwan indicate that he may be willing to make decisions unilaterally to change the status quo, which we oppose". This was followed the next month by similar comments by President Chirac of France on a visit to China, who called the referendum "a grave mistake". The latter remarks were greeted with public repudiation by Chen.

Despite the clear opposition from the USA, Chen in January 2004 published details of the referendum, which he said would contain two questions:

"If China does not remove missiles pointed at Taiwan, and does not renounce force against Taiwan, do you agree that the government should set up more anti-missile defences, in order to strengthen Taiwan's defensive capability?

"Do you agree that the government should open negotiations with China and establish a peaceful and stable framework for interaction, to seek consensus and well-being?"

This was an innocuously-worded referendum, and it was suggested that pressure from Washington may have forced Chen to water down his questions to avoid any explicit mention of the "red lines" that would trigger serious action from Beijing: Taiwan's name, flag, and territorial status.

In the March 20 presidential elections, President Chen secured a narrow victory, by fewer than 30,000 votes, over his KMT challenger Lien Chan, with the narrowness of the vote and allegations of electoral fraud leading to KMT demands for a recount and the issue being taken to the courts. In the referendum vote, Chen's position had majority support, but the total turnout of 45% (against 80% for the presidential election) was not enough for the proposals to be passed.

Mark Smith

3.9 China - Vietnam

Major disputes between China and Vietnam developed in the 1970s over four territorial and boundary questions: (i) their common land frontier; (ii) territorial waters in the Gulf of Tonkin; (iii) the Paracel Islands; and (iv) the Spratly Islands (for which see Section 3.18). In 1979 China and Vietnam fought a brief but fierce war in the border area. Throughout the early and mid-1980s there were periodic border clashes between the two sides. However, tension diminished in the late 1980s, and in 1991 relations between the two countries were normalized. This paved the way for the eventual signing of agreements on the land border in 1999 and the Gulf of Tonkin in 2000, although the Paracel Islands dispute has not been resolved. (Map 28, p. 506, illustrates these disputes.)

The Land Border Dispute

The land frontier was the scene of the worst clashes in the China-Vietnam border disputes—far more bloody than the disputes over the Paracel Islands, the Gulf of Tonkin, or the Spratly Islands. Paradoxically, it was this dispute that saw the most significant progress after normalization of relations in 1991, and a land border treaty had been signed and ratified by the close of the decade, taking effect on July 9, 2000.

(i) The Background to the Dispute

The Sino-Vietnamese frontier, 1,200 kilometres long, was defined by a convention between the French Republic, which then exercised a protectorate over Tonkin, and the Chinese empire, signed in Peking (Beijing) in 1887. This was slightly modified by a second convention signed in 1895, stones being erected to mark the frontier. Under the conventions the frontier was not clearly delineated at certain points, where the population living on either side traditionally crossed it freely.

Vietnam was partitioned in 1954 into a Communist state in the North, with its capital at Hanoi, and a pro-Western state in the South, with Saigon as its capital. Until the reunification of the country in 1975, North Vietnam was preoccupied with its relations with its southern neighbour, and in the undeclared war that developed between them it was largely dependent on China for military aid. In these circumstances, North Vietnam was in no position to press its territorial claims against China.

In November 1957 the Vietnamese Communist Party proposed that the two countries should maintain the status quo and should settle any border disputes through negotiations, this proposal being accepted by the Chinese Communist Party in April 1958. Vietnamese statements issued in 1979, however, alleged that after 1954 the Chinese government had taken advantage of the situation to carry out a large number of encroachments by sending Chinese to settle on Vietnamese territory, moving the border stones, building roads on Vietnamese territory, altering the border line on maps printed in China for the Vietnamese government, and sending troops to occupy border areas. In particular, it was alleged that during repairs to the international railway line between China and Vietnam in 1955 the Chinese had deliberately moved the junction point more than 300 metres into Vietnamese territory.

(ii) Border Clashes 1974-1991

Clashes on the border began in 1974. Although no details were published by either side at the time, later Vietnamese statements alleged that the Chinese had been responsible for 179 border incidents and encroachments on Vietnamese territory in that year, whilst Chinese statements accused North Vietnam of making 121 "provocative attacks on the Chinese border" in 1974. The Chinese government proposed on March 18, 1975, that negotiations should take place on the border question, but the North Vietnamese government, while agreeing in principle, suggested on April 12 that talks should be postponed, as it was preoccupied with the war in South Vietnam, then approaching its end. According to Chinese sources, the Chinese government repeated its proposal in 1976 and again early in 1977, on both occasions without result.

During a visit to Beijing by Pham Van Dong (the Vietnamese Prime Minister), Li Xiannian, a Chinese Deputy Premier, handed him a memorandum on June 10, 1977, in which he said that although "no big dispute" over the border had arisen before 1974, since that year Vietnam had "continually provoked disputes", and that some shooting incidents had occurred. Admitting that "some of these incidents were caused by violations of our policies by our local personnel", he gave an assurance that measures would be taken to prevent them from crossing the border, and again proposed that negotiations be held, to which Pham Van Dong agreed.

Negotiations between the two countries' Deputy Foreign Ministers opened in Beijing on Oct. 7, 1977. According to Chinese reports, the Chinese side put forward the following proposals for a settlement: (i) the two sides should recheck the alignment of the entire boundary and settle all disputes on the basis of the Sino-French conventions; (ii) areas under either side's jurisdiction which lay beyond the boundary line should be returned to the other side unconditionally; (iii) the two sides should settle any differences on the alignment of the boundary through friendly consultations; and (iv) they should then conclude a new boundary treaty, delimit the boundary and erect new boundary markers.

The negotiations failed to reach agreement and were broken off in the summer of 1978. Relations between China and Vietnam rapidly deteriorated during 1978 as a result of Chinese support for Cambodia in its border war with Vietnam, the mass exodus of the Chinese community from Vietnam from April onwards, the admission of Vietnam to the Soviet-led Council for Mutual Economic Assistance (Comecon) in June 1978, the ending of Chinese economic aid to Vietnam in July, and the conclusion of a treaty of friendship and co-operation between Vietnam and the Soviet Union in November. According to diplomatic sources in Hanoi, serious fighting occurred on the border in April 1978, and from September onwards both Vietnam and China frequently reported incidents on the border, a number of which were said to have led to fatal casualties.

The situation reached crisis point after Vietnamese troops invaded Cambodia on Dec. 25, 1978, drove the Chinese-supported government from the capital, Phnom-Penh, and installed a Vietnamese-sponsored government on Jan. 8, 1979. Clashes on the Sino-Vietnamese border increased both in number and in scale during January and the first half of February 1979; the Vietnamese Foreign Ministry said on Feb. 14 that whereas there had been 583 Chinese armed encroachments on Vietnamese territory in 1978, since the beginning of 1979 there had already been 230, in which over 40 people had been killed, hundreds wounded and over 20 abducted to China.

Chinese troops invaded Vietnam along the entire length of the frontier on Feb. 17, 1979, and after a fortnight of heavy fighting entered Lang Son, 18 km south of the border. On March 1, China proposed that the two governments should open negotiations, but Vietnam refused to negotiate until the Chinese had withdrawn to "the other side of the historic borderline". The Chinese government accordingly announced on March 5 that its troops were withdrawing and on March 16 that their withdrawal had been completed. The Vietnamese government, however, alleged on March 27 that Chinese troops were still occupying Vietnamese territory.

Negotiations opened in Hanoi on April 18, 1979, when the Vietnamese side proposed that both sides should establish a demilitarized zone by withdrawing their armed forces to a distance of three to five kilometres from the line of actual control prior to Feb. 17, 1979, and that border problems should be settled on the basis of respect for the borderline laid down in the conventions of 1887 and 1895. The Chinese side put forward as a basis for a settlement an eight-point statement of principles covering the whole field of Sino-Vietnamese relations, which included a proposal that, pending a settlement of border disputes on the basis of the Sino-French conventions, each side should strictly maintain the status quo as it existed in 1957-58. The talks were adjourned on May 18, resumed in Beijing on June 28, and continued until Dec. 19, 1979, without any progress being made.

After 1979 the two sides continued to accuse each other of causing border incidents. A Vietnamese statement of Dec. 29, 1980, alleged that during that year the Chinese forces had carried out over 2,500 armed provocations, made repeated raids deep into Vietnamese territory, regularly shelled centres of population, occupied many hilltop positions along the border and killed or wounded hundreds of Vietnamese border guards and civilians. A Chinese Note of May 5, 1981, asserted that since the beginning of the year Vietnamese troops had made 241 attacks on Chinese territory, killing over 60 people, and had fired on Chinese territory almost every day. The Vietnamese reply, sent on the following day, rejected the Chinese "slanders", and alleged that since the beginning of the year the Chinese had shelled or made armed incursions into Vietnamese territory on over 700 occasions.

The more intense clashes on the border appeared to coincide with Vietnamese offensives in Cambodia in support of the Heng Samrin government against the Chinese-backed *Khmer Rouge* guerrillas. In April 1983 the Chinese launched a major shelling campaign, allegedly in retaliation after Vietnamese artillery attacks, at a time when Vietnamese troops were conducting a dry-season offensive against the guerrillas. A year later China launched a new cross-border shelling campaign on April 21, 1984, to coincide with a Vietnamese offensive in the Thai border area of Cambodia that had led to clashes between Vietnamese and Thai troops. A Vietnamese spokesman alleged on May 3 that an offensive by three Chinese regiments against Ha Tuyen province had been repelled with more than 100 Chinese troops killed or wounded, and, on May 9, that since April 2 China had fired 50,000 shells at over 100 points situated within 26 of the 28 districts in the six northern provinces. Major clashes continued until July, culminating in a 10-hour battle on July 12 on the border of Ha Tuyen.

After a lull in the fighting, the Chinese renewed their shelling campaign on Nov. 21, 1984, three days after the Vietnamese army had opened its dry-season offensive in Cambodia, and clashes continued until the end of May 1985. Sporadic shelling and incursions by troops of both sides were reported on a number of occasions between September 1985 and February 1986, although there was no dry-season offensive in Cambodia during this period. Heavy fighting was reported in October 1986, in which Vietnam claimed on Oct. 20 that 250 Chinese had been "put out of action".

Fighting believed to be the most serious since the Chinese invasion of 1979 occurred on Jan. 5-7, 1987. According to Vietnamese reports, Chinese infantry in divisional strength made repeated attacks on hill positions in Ha Tuyen, all of which were repulsed, nearly 1,500 Chinese being killed. Chinese sources, on the other hand, stated that their forces had counterattacked in response to Vietnamese incursions, and estimated the number killed at about 500 Vietnamese and "a few dozen" Chinese. (See below for later developments in the land border dispute.)

The Gulf of Tonkin Dispute

The Gulf of Tonkin (known to the Vietnamese as the Bac Bo Gulf and to the Chinese as Beibu Wan) lies between Vietnam to the west, the Chinese mainland to the north, and the Luichow Peninsula and the island of Hainan (both Chinese) to the east, and at its greatest

extent is 170 nautical miles wide. It has two outlets to the South China Sea, one to the south, which is 125 nautical miles wide at its narrowest point, and another to the east through the Hainan Strait.

The Franco-Chinese convention of 1887 stated that islands in the Gulf lying to the east of longitude 105°43′E of the Paris meridian (or 108°03′13E″ of the Greenwich meridian) belonged to China, and islands to the west of this meridian belonged to Vietnam. The Vietnamese maintained that this meridian marks the boundary between the two countries' territorial waters across the entire Gulf. The Chinese, however, contended that both the wording of the convention and the attached map make plain that this article refers only to the offshore islands and does not lay down a sea boundary line.

A statement of the Chinese case published on Dec. 2, 1980, put forward the following additional arguments: (i) If the line were extended southward to take in the entire Gulf it would be more than 130 nautical miles east of the Vietnamese coast and only about 30 west of Hainan, and would give Vietnam two-thirds of the area of the Gulf; (ii) No expert on international law had ever mentioned that the Gulf belonged to Vietnam and China; (iii) Under international law the sea area within a territorial bay was regarded as inland waters (through which ships could pass only with a special permit), but since 1887 neither France nor Vietnam had ever treated foreign ships sailing across the Gulf as ships passing through inland waters; (iv) A French decree on the fishery area in Indo-China laid down that territorial waters extended 20 kilometres from the shore, and made no special provision for the Gulf of Tonkin; (v) Vietnam announced in 1964 that its territorial waters extended 12 nautical miles from the shore, and this had been accepted in the latest fishery agreement between China and Vietnam.

The North Vietnamese Foreign Ministry informed the Chinese government on Dec. 26, 1973, of North Vietnam's intention to prospect for oil in the Gulf of Tonkin, and proposed that, as the sea boundary had not been delimited, negotiations should be held on the subject. The Chinese Foreign Ministry accepted this proposal on Jan. 18, 1974, but stipulated that prospecting should not take place in the area between the 18th and 20th parallels and the 107th and 108th meridians, and that third countries should not be involved in the exploration and exploitation of the Gulf. When negotiations opened in Beijing on Aug. 15, 1974, the Vietnamese delegation maintained that the boundary had already been delineated in the 1887 convention, and proposed that it should be officially delineated. As the Chinese refused to accept this contention, the talks were suspended at the end of November 1974 without agreement being reached.

At the negotiations on the land and sea boundaries, which began on Oct. 7, 1977, the Chinese refused to discuss the land border unless the Vietnamese gave up their claim that a sea boundary already existed. As a compromise, the Vietnamese suggested that the land border should first be discussed and that each side should maintain its own views on the Gulf of Tonkin, which would be discussed later. As no agreement was reached on the land border, the question of the sea boundary also remained unsettled. A Vietnamese Foreign Ministry statement of Dec. 13, 1979, protested against reports that China had signed contracts with foreign firms to explore for oil in the Gulf of Tonkin as a breach of the convention of 1887. (See below for later developments regarding Gulf of Tonkin.)

The Paracel Islands

The Paracel Islands, known to the Chinese as the Xisha (Western Sands) Islands and to the Vietnamese as Hoang Sa, consist of about 130 barren and waterless islands, none larger than a square mile (1.6 sq km) in area, lying about 265 km southeast of the Chinese island of Hainan and 360 km east of the Vietnamese coast. They are divided into two main groups, the Crescent group to the west and the Amphitrite group to the east. The Western name "Paracel" is derived from the Portuguese word for reef.

(i) The Background to the Dispute
A Chinese Foreign Ministry document of Jan. 30, 1980, claimed that the islands were discovered by Chinese mariners and were described in Chinese geographical works of the third century AD; that the Chinese Emperor exercised jurisdiction over them in the 11th century; and that they were shown as Chinese territory in official maps of the 18th and early 19th centuries. A Chinese fleet which visited the islands in 1909 set up stone tablets and hoisted the Chinese flag, and two years later they were placed under the administration of Hainan island. The document therefore claimed that "consecutive jurisdiction was exercised over them by successive Chinese governments for more than a thousand years".

A Vietnamese White Book of Sept. 28, 1979, on the other hand, maintained that "the Vietnamese feudal state was the first in history to occupy, claim ownership of, exercise sovereignty over and exploit" the islands, and in support of this claim quoted Vietnamese geographical works of the 17th and 18th centuries. The Emperor of Annam ordered the occupation of the islands in 1816, and his successor in 1836 commanded a survey of them to be carried out and markers to be erected.

The French government, which then exercised sovereignty over Cochin China and a protectorate over Annam and Tonkin, claimed in a note to China in 1931 that the Empire of Annam had a prior title to the islands, and in 1938 the Emperor Bao Dai annexed them to the territory of Thua Thien province. In the following year, however, the Japanese occupied them. Japan renounced its claim to them by the peace treaty signed in San Francisco in 1951, but the treaty did not state to whom they belonged. A Chinese official statement commenting on the draft treaty claimed that they had "always been China's territory". At the San Francisco conference, the Vietnamese delegate formally affirmed Vietnam's claim to the islands, whilst in the absence of China, which was not represented, the Soviet delegate described them as China's "inalienable territory".

After Vietnam was divided in 1954 into two states, the South Vietnamese government continued to assert its claim to the Paracels, whereas the North Vietnamese government temporarily accepted China's claim to them. According to the Chinese Foreign Ministry document cited above, North Vietnamese official statements in 1958 and 1965 referred to the islands as Chinese territory, and they were shown and referred to as such in maps and textbooks issued by the North Vietnamese government down to 1974. Both China and South Vietnam exercised control over some of the islands during the period from 1954 to 1974; the Chinese occupied Woody Island, the main island in the Amphitrite group, whilst South Vietnam maintained a small garrison on Pattle Island, the largest of the Crescent group, to man a radio and meteorological station.

After the South Vietnamese government had announced its intention of carrying out surveys for oil off its coast opposite the Paracels, the Chinese Foreign Ministry issued a statement on Jan. 11, 1974, affirming its claim to the islands, this claim being rejected by South Vietnam on the following day. South Vietnamese warships that were sent to the islands withdrew after an engagement with Chinese warships on Jan. 19, and on the following day Chinese troops occupied the three islands still under South Vietnamese control. A North Vietnamese spokesman commented in a non-committal statement on Jan. 21 that "disputes handed down by history, often very complex ones" should be settled through negotiations. Both the United States and the Soviet Union adopted a strictly neutral attitude towards the dispute, and a request by the South Vietnamese government for a meeting of the UN Security Council failed to secure the necessary support for placing the question on the Council's agenda.

(ii) The Paracels Dispute Before Normalization
Following the overthrow of the Saigon regime in 1975 and the reunification of Vietnam in the following year, the Hanoi government openly laid claim to the Paracels. The Vietnamese White Book of 1979 stated that the question had been discussed between the Vietnamese and Chinese governments in September 1975, and that the latter had admitted that a dispute existed. An official Vietnamese map issued in 1976 showed the Paracels as Vietnamese territory. A government statement of May 20, 1977, said that Vietnamese territorial waters were 12 miles wide and that its exclusive economic zone extended to 200 nautical miles from the coast, and referred to "the islands and archipelagos belonging to Vietnamese territory and situated outside the territorial waters mentioned" without specifying the islands and archipelagos in question. In the memorandum that Li Xiannian handed to Pham Van Dong on June 10, 1977 (see above), he

accused Vietnam of making the Paracels, "over which there was never any issue", a major subject of dispute. According to Chinese sources, Pham Van Dong replied that "in the war of resistance we of course had to place resistance to US imperialism above everything else", and that earlier Vietnamese statements on the subject must be understood "in the context of the historical circumstances of the time".

Both sides issued a series of statements in 1979 and 1980 reaffirming their claims to the Paracels. At the negotiations held in Hanoi in April and May 1979, the Chinese delegation demanded that Vietnam should recognize China's sovereignty over the islands, this demand being rejected by Vietnam. Following reports that China had signed contracts with foreign companies to prospect for oil around the Paracels, the Vietnamese Foreign Ministry gave warning on Dec. 13, 1979, that companies which conducted exploration in this area without Vietnam's consent "must bear all consequences of their wrongdoings".

Hanoi radio announced on March 3, 1982, that 40 armed Chinese vessels had entered Vietnamese waters to conduct espionage and obstruct fishing and that, after a Vietnamese fishing boat had been damaged, "militiamen on board Vietnamese fishing vessels" had set fire to three of the intruders and captured another. The Chinese version of the incident was that Vietnamese gunboats had attacked Chinese fishing boats on the high seas, destroying one, damaging another and capturing a third. In another incident on the following day the Chinese captured what was described as "a Vietnamese reconnaissance boat intruding into China's territorial waters" with its crew of 10, who were released in an exchange of captured intruders on June 21.

Vietnamese proposals for talks were consistently rejected by China. A Chinese statement of Sept. 3, 1981, rejected one such offer on the grounds that Vietnam had "intensified its hostile policy of aggression and expansionism", and that there was no real basis for discussing the normalization of relations. The Vietnamese government renewed its proposal on Jan. 30, 1982, and on the following day welcomed an offer of mediation from Javier Pérez de Cuéllar, the UN Secretary-General. The Chinese Foreign Ministry rejected on April 9, 1984, an offer by Nguyen Co Thach, the Vietnamese Foreign Minister, for talks "at any level and anywhere" on easing the border tension, describing it as "hypocritical and wrought with ulterior motives".

Wu Xuenqian, the Chinese Foreign Minister, declared on Jan. 29, 1985, that China might have to "teach Vietnam a second lesson" if Vietnamese forces continued their operations in the Thai-Cambodian border area, and Hu Yaobang, then general secretary of the Chinese Communist Party, said in February that the elimination of "the Vietnamese threat to China" was a major Chinese policy decision. A Chinese Foreign Ministry spokesman denied on Sept. 11, 1985, reports that China and Vietnam were engaged in secret negotiations, stating that there was no chance of an improvement in relations until all Vietnamese troops were withdrawn from Cambodia.

The official communiqué issued after a meeting on Aug. 17-18, 1986, of the Foreign Ministers of Vietnam, Cambodia and Laos reaffirmed Vietnam's readiness to enter into talks with China "at any level and anywhere whatsoever". China rejected the offer on Aug. 20, however, on the ground that it could not enter into normalization talks until all Vietnamese forces were withdrawn from Cambodia. Truong Chinh, then general secretary of the Vietnamese Communist Party, proposed to negotiate an unconditional settlement with China, but the offer was immediately rejected.

Normalization of Relations

During the late 1980s and early 1990s relations between Vietnam and China improved greatly. The improvement largely reflected changes in the wider international sphere that served to draw the two countries together. The progressive collapse of communism in the Soviet Union had a major impact on both countries and the final disintegration of the USSR in 1991 left China isolated as the main bastion of communist orthodoxy. Vietnam, for its part, was left without its sole economic and political patron. Inevitably, the changing international climate brought the two communist neighbours closer together.

However, the transformation was far from sudden, as events in the late 1980s had already encouraged Sino-Vietnamese rapprochement. Vietnam's *doi moi* (renovation) campaign, launched in 1987, had mirrored the Deng Xiaoping, as opposed to Gorbachev, reform model, concentrating on economic rather than political restructuring. Most importantly, however, by the late 1980s both Vietnam and China had agreed on the necessity to solve the Cambodian conflict, the one issue that had kept the two sides apart. Hence, the signing of the Cambodian peace agreement in October 1991 opened the way for full normalization in November.

A breakthrough in Sino-Vietnamese relations had occurred in January 1989 when Dinh Nho Liem, a Vietnamese Deputy Foreign Minister, paid an unofficial visit to China for talks with, amongst others, Qian Qichen, the Chinese Foreign Minister. The talks focused on Cambodia and occurred at a period of accelerated diplomatic manoeuvring on the conflict. Liem's visit was the first direct contact between the two countries since 1979. The meeting provided a first indication that the long-standing enmity between the two countries was showing some signs of easing.

A vital step towards normalization occurred in September 1989 when Vietnam withdrew the last of its remaining troops from Cambodia. In January 1990 Vietnamese Foreign Minister Nguyen Co Thach and Qian Qichen exchanged greetings "on the occasion of the 40th anniversary of the establishment of diplomatic relations between the two countries". Relations with China improved markedly during 1990. In June Chinese Deputy Foreign Minister Xu Dunxin visited

Hanoi, the highest-level visit since 1979. The pace of normalization quickened in September 1990 with the holding of a secret Sino-Vietnamese summit in China. Discussions centred on the Cambodian problem, the issue that still threatened to block full normalization. After the meeting there were signs that relations between the two countries had improved dramatically. In mid-September the Chinese government opened their southern border with Vietnam at the "Friendship Pass" in order to allow Vietnamese athletes to travel to the Asian Games in Beijing.

A further important step towards normalization occurred at the CPV's seventh congress in June 1991 when Foreign Minister Nguyen Co Thach, an arch-opponent of a pro-Chinese foreign policy direction, was removed from the politburo. Nguyen Manh Cam, the new Vietnamese Foreign Minister, visited China in September for talks with Chinese leaders. Do Muoi, the Communist Party general secretary, and Vo Van Kiet, the Vietnamese Premier, finally normalized relations in November following a visit to Beijing. The Vietnamese leaders' visit ended with the signing of a trade agreement and a "provisional agreement" on the handling of border affairs.

The process by which agreement was reached on the issues of the land border and the Gulf of Tonkin began in February 1992, with a visit to Vietnam by the Chinese Foreign Minister, Qian Qichen. Here it was agreed to establish working groups to discuss territorial issues. Talks at the expert and government levels continued, and after a government meeting from Aug. 23-30 it was announced that agreement on "fundamental principles" for resolving disputes had been reached. A formal agreement to that effect was signed at another round of talks from Oct. 18-21, 1993, and the working groups began to meet the following year: Feb. 22-25 for the Land Border Working Group, and March 22-25 for the Gulf of Tonkin Working Group.

Agreement on Land Border

In step with the process of normalization, a total of 21 sites for border gates was agreed upon. A Vietnamese announcement of March 27, 1991, issued a directive to that effect, and opened the first gate at Lang San. In fact, all border gates in the region had been temporarily opened on the occasion of the New Year on Feb. 6, but the March announcement marked the beginning of a permanent opening. The following year, three more border gates were opened: Lao Cai Bridge on March 18, Thanh Thug on June 20, and Ta Lung-Shui Kou on Dec. 1. Progress was hampered by the fact that the 1300-km border region was heavily mined, but on April 7, 1993, China began a clearing operation.

The Land Border Working Group was established under the Agreement on the Fundamental Principles to Settle Issues Relating to the Border and Territorial Issue, and met a total of 17 times before agreement was reached in 2000. The first round of talks took place from Feb. 22-25, 1994, in an atmosphere officially described as "friendly". The same year, only one

border gate opened, the Bacluong Bridge on April 18, but mine clearing was progressing well. By September, the official Chinese news agency reported that nearly 300,000 landmines had been cleared from the border area. The border gates, it should be noted, were the sites for re-establishing trade links; there were over 150 border passages opened by 1995. That November, progress was sufficiently good to allow agreement on the resumption of cross border rail links and freight. Rail travel between Hanoi and Beijing was resumed on Feb. 12, 1996.

In the Land Boundary Working Group, meetings continued, although few details were made public apart from bland statements that almost invariably described the talks as "frank", "friendly", or "pragmatic". The group reported to higher-level negotiations on land and sea disputes, and in July 1997 the Chinese and Vietnamese Foreign Ministers felt able to up the pace by announcing that negotiations on land border and Gulf issues would be speeded up to allow resolution "at an early date". On Aug. 11, 1999, one of the major practical obstacles to border demarcation was removed when China announced that the last landmines had been cleared from the border: in total, over 2.2 million mines had been disposed of. This was swiftly followed on Dec. 3 by a joint statement that said: "Problems concerning the land border between China and Vietnam have all been resolved, and relevant substantive talks have ended. According to a common understanding reached between the secretaries general of the parties of China and Vietnam, in the next step, the two sides should concentrate efforts on drafting a land border agreement and strive to formally sign a land border agreement by the end of the year".

The agreement was duly signed on Dec. 30, 1999. It was ratified by China on April 29, 2000, and by Vietnam on June 9, 2000. The treaty officially entered into force on July 6, 2000, the day that instruments of ratification were exchanged. This was a real achievement, but subsequent developments revealed some tricky aspects. The border demarcation process post-dated the treaty, and when the process began in December 2001 it quickly became clear that local people in border regions had not been consulted or informed of the exact location of the boundary. There were protests that some Vietnamese villages at the border had discovered that they were now in China when the demarcation process began. A public outcry subsequently forced the government to publish the text of the agreement on the website of the state news agency Nhan Dan in August 2002.

The treaty was subsequently removed from the website after an angry public reaction to what some Vietnamese saw as a case of their government handing territory over to China in a highly unequal deal. However, an unofficial translation reveals that the treaty has a total of eight articles, the longest of which by far is Article Two, which describes the boundary. The article lists 62 boundary points and their positions, and then describes where the border runs between each point. Much of the border follows geographical features: mostly rivers, streams, mountain ridges and ravines. In some it refers to "the red lines on the map attached to the land treaty", which delimit sandbanks and stretches of land on both sides of rivers and streams. Presumably there were also regions where geography was either insufficient, inappropriate or unacceptable as a basis for drawing a border. Article Six establishes a Vietnam-China Joint Committee for Border Delineation and Border-Marker Placement. It was the beginning of this committee's work that originally caused the public protests.

Agreement on Gulf of Tonkin

The Gulf of Tonkin Working Group met a total of 14 times. The Gulf dispute proved more difficult to resolve, due to the fact that it was linked with the wider multinational dispute over the South China Sea. Economic issues, and in particular fishing rights, also intruded to an extent that was not the case with the land border.

Negotiations continued through the 1990s. An early Vietnamese argument was that the Gulf ought to be divided along a north-south line as it had been in the Sino-French Treaty of 1887. This maritime boundary began where the Sino-Vietnamese land boundary met the sea, and continued in a straight line south from there. This position was abandoned, and international law became the basis for negotiations. This inevitably meant following the UN Convention on the Law of the Sea and established international norms regarding territorial sovereign waters.

Vietnam ratified the UN Convention on the Law of the Sea on July 25, 1994, and almost immediately protested about what it saw as Chinese encroachment into its waters. Chinese fishing vessels, especially from Hainan Island, were considerably more active in the Gulf of Tonkin, and the Vietnamese coastguard was regularly deployed to repel and sometimes detain Chinese boats. Within a year of the 1993 agreement on fundamental principles, for example, Vietnam intercepted and detained three Chinese fishing boats, to loud protests from the Chinese Foreign Minister. China's case was that the Gulf waters were traditionally and historically used by China, and that the Convention on the Law of the Sea stated that 12 nautical miles from the continental shelf was public water. This position was rejected by Vietnam, which claimed that there were no public waters in the Gulf.

The most practical way to resolve the dispute was to apply the principle of equidistance under Article 15 of the UN Convention. This was used when two neighbouring states faced each other across seas, and stated that the maritime boundary should be drawn at an equidistant point between the national territorial waters. This raised the issue of how to treat islands in the Gulf—should an island be given full weight as a part of national territory and thus a basepoint for drawing the equidistant line; no weight at all, and thus not taken into account when drawing the line; or a partial

weight? This was an important question, since if islands were given full or partial weight, then that would confer larger territorial waters for the state that owned the islands. This issue was especially pertinent in the case of Bach Long Vi island in the Gulf, which had been given to Vietnam by China in the 1950s. The island lay very close to a geographical median line in the Gulf, and consequently the issue of whether to count it as an island proper under the UN Convention was significant for drawing the equidistant line. To put it prosaically, the question was whether the equidistant line ought to have a bump around Bach Long Vi or not.

Negotiations in the Working Group continued through the 1990s. As with the Land Border Working Group, the Gulf group talks were held in private and there was little information in the public realm beyond ritual promises to resolve the matter through negotiations and international law. Occasionally, incidents would give the matter public prominence, such as Vietnamese actions against Chinese fishing boats. The potentially rich natural resources of the Gulf, particularly oil and natural gas, also provoked tension. China had drilled for oil in a disputed region of the Gulf in September 1992, and Vietnam attempted to invite tenders for development of the Gulf from foreign investors in October 1994. Similar developments in the South China Sea, especially the Spratly Islands, also produced protests, although the Spratly issue does not appear to have significantly affected negotiations in the land border or Gulf working groups.

Signs that progress would be made in the Gulf Working Group came in 1996-97, when a succession of meetings indicated a consensus that the pace of negotiations in both groups should be quickened. Government-level talks in September 1996 discussed how to speed up negotiations, and the following July the Chinese Communist Party leader, Jiang Zemin, met with his Vietnamese opposite number in Beijing to agree that things should proceed more quickly.

The Gulf Working Group, which had met eight times at that point, then met a further nine times in the following three years. On July 16-18, 1997, it discussed the application of international law in resolving the dispute and, on March 30, 1998, agreed to set a deadline of the end of 2000 for resolving the dispute. The group was successful in that goal, but it was a close-run thing: the Agreement on the Demarcation of Waters, Exclusive Economic Zones and Continental Shelves in the Gulf of Tonkin was signed on Dec. 25, 2000.

Unlike the Land Border Agreement, the Gulf treaty contains a set of map coordinates defining where the boundary lies, and thus demarcation questions do not arise as they have on the land border. The agreement has not been made public, but the coordinates appear to have been leaked. The boundary appears to run some distance west of the line of equidistance, and thus Bach Long Vi does not seem to be fully incorporated as a basepoint. It has been calculated that China gains about 3,200 square nautical miles on top of what it would have if a strict equidistant line were applied, although a Vietnamese analysis claims that Bach Long Vi has been accorded some impact. (For a map based on the leaked coordinates, see Ramses Amer, "The Sino-Vietnamese Approach to Managing Border Disputes", IBRU *Maritime Briefing*, vol. 3, no. 5.)

The agreement on the Gulf also requires further agreement on fishing rights to be concluded. An Agreement on Fishing Cooperation in the Gulf of Tonkin had been signed on the same day as the demarcation treaty, but a set of supplementary protocols had not been finalized. Consequently, the Gulf agreements were unratified at the time of writing, and the prickliness of the issue is illustrated by the continued seizure of Chinese fishing boats by Vietnam. Nonetheless, the annual governmental meeting between the two sides in January 2004, with Chinese Deputy Foreign Minister Wang Yi and his Vietnamese opposite number Le Cong Phung leading their delegations, produced a pledge to resolve the outstanding technical issues within the next six months.

The Paracels Dispute since Normalization

The progress on the land border and Gulf of Tonkin issues has not been paralleled in the case of the Paracel Islands. As well as the problem of the islands' potential natural resources, strategic factors also impact on the Paracels dispute. The islands are located about 600 km from the disputed Spratly Islands, and China has used its possession of the Paracels to enhance its military capabilities in the South China Sea. In 1993 it emerged that China had constructed an airstrip and military barracks on Woody Island on the Paracels a few years previously, a story that was given added impact by reports on Philippines radio (denied by Beijing) that 25 Chinese military aircraft were stationed in the Paracels. Less in dispute are the Chinese satellite relay station on the Paracels, and the intelligence gathering facility on one of the islands (Rocky Island, also known as Shin-tao), which reportedly made a significant improvement to China's intelligence coverage of the Spratly Islands region. By the mid-1990s, China had around 1,000 troops deployed on the islands.

Nonetheless, a working group on "sea issues" met in Beijing from July 2-7, 1996, and announced agreement that international law, including the UN Convention on the Law of the Sea, would be used to resolve the Paracels issue. This was in spite of China's ratification of the Convention on May 16, in which Beijing announced that the Paracels would have "quasi-archipelagic" status, which would allow China to use the islands as a baseline for setting maritime zones.

It also can hardly be a coincidence that on the very day the sea issues working group concluded the July meeting, Chinese state television reported that archaeologists had discovered Chinese relics on the Paracels dating from the Tang and Qing dynasties (which ruled from 618-907 and 1644-1911 respectively). A stone tablet was planted, announcing "Historical Site under the Protection of Hainan Province". By November 1997, Chinese media reported that 1,300 "cultural relics" had been discovered, and claimed that this discovery had "irrefutably proven that the Xisha Islands have been China's sacred territory since ancient times". The following year, in April 1998, China announced that it would be scaling down its military presence in the Paracels in order to allow visitors and tourists to visit the islands. This plan, which reportedly involved conversion of the barracks into a hotel, was not implemented.

The Paracels issue is further complicated by the fact that Taiwan has pursued a parallel claim to the islands, based on its claim to be the legitimate government of China. On May 21, 1992, Taiwan passed a law on territorial waters that included the Spratlys, and in April 1994 it also laid claim to the Paracels.

The Paracels issue remains unresolved at the time of writing. There has been no increased pace of negotiations, as had been the case with the land border or the Gulf of Tonkin disputes. However, it also appeared that neither side was prepared to countenance the use of force in order to resolve the dispute, and public rhetoric appeared to be toned down towards the close of the 1990s. One possible way forward was the emergence of Codes of Conduct over disputed territory. In August 1995, China signed a Code of Conduct with the Philippines in which the two committed themselves to resolving their competing claims over the Spratly Islands through peaceful means. Vietnam signed a similar Code with the Philippines the following November.

These agreements seem to have laid a path for a multilateral Code of Conduct on the South China Sea, signed on Nov. 5, 2002, by China and the ten member states of the Association of South East Asian Nations (ASEAN—comprising Brunei, Cambodia, Indonesia, Laos, Malaysia, Myanmar, Philippines, Singapore, Thailand and Vietnam). The text of the agreement contained a pledge to "exercise self-restraint in the conduct of activities that would complicate or escalate disputes and affect peace and stability including, among others, refraining from action of inhabiting on the presently uninhabited islands, reefs, shoals, cays, and other features and to handle differences in a constructive manner". The Code of Conduct did not specify any particular territory, referring only to the South China Sea. Early drafts had avoided mentioning territory by name, but the Code did need to have a geographical area of application in the text. The ASEAN states initially used the term "the disputed area", but China refused to accept even that, on the grounds that the wording would imply recognition of claims other than its own. Vietnam had lobbied strongly for the Paracels to be covered by the Code, but again China's refusal led to the idea being dropped.

Mark Smith

3.10 India - Pakistan

The dispute between India and Pakistan over the state of Jammu and Kashmir arose from the circumstances in which British India was partitioned in 1947. The accession of the princely states to either India or Pakistan took place smoothly, except in three states in which the religion of the ruler differed from that of the majority of his subjects. After the Muslim ruler of the overwhelmingly Hindu state of Junagadh had announced its accession to Pakistan, with which his territory was nowhere contiguous, the state was occupied by Indian troops and was incorporated into India after a plebiscite, despite Pakistani protests. The Muslim Nizam of Hyderabad, which was entirely surrounded by Indian territory, announced that he wished to maintain its independence, but when order threatened to break down Indian troops moved in and the Nizam agreed to accede to India. The third state was Jammu and Kashmir, generally referred to as Kashmir. (Map 23, p. 504, shows the division of Kashmir.)

Kashmir before 1947

The state was founded by Gulab Singh, a Hindu military adventurer who in return for his services was created Raja of Jammu by the Sikh ruler Ranjit Singh in 1820, and who conquered Ladakh in 1834. After the defeat of the Sikhs by the British in 1846, Gulab Singh undertook to pay the indemnity of 75,000 rupees demanded by the British from the Sikhs, on condition that he was given Kashmir, then under Sikh rule. This arrangement was confirmed by the Treaty of Amritsar and Gulab Singh was recognized by the British as Maharaja of Jammu and Kashmir.

Jammu and Kashmir has an area of 84,471 square miles (about 220,000 sq km), and borders on India to the south, Pakistan to the west, Afghanistan to the north-west and China to the north and east. According to a census conducted in 1941, it then had a population of 4,023,180, of whom 77.1 per cent were Muslims, 20.1 per cent Hindus, and 2.08 per cent Sikhs, Buddhists and others. The Valley of Kashmir is overwhelmingly Muslim; Hindus constitute the great majority of the population of Jammu, in the south, and also form a considerable part of the population of Srinagar, the capital of the state; the Sikhs are also found mainly in Jammu and Srinagar; and the Buddhists are confined to Ladakh, in the north. Economically, Kashmir is linked with Pakistan by its river system, as its three main rivers, the Indus, the Chenab and the Jhelum, all flow into Pakistan, which is largely dependent on them for its irrigation.

Strong opposition to the autocratic rule of the then Maharaja, Sir Hari Singh, developed before World War II under the leadership of Sheikh Mohammed Abdullah, who in 1930 founded the Muslim Conference to agitate for reforms. He broke away from it in 1938, however, to form the Kashmir National Conference, a non-communal organization which maintained close links with the Indian National Congress. He launched an agitation demanding constitutional government in 1945, and was subsequently imprisoned.

The Accession of Kashmir to India

When India and Pakistan became independent on Aug. 15, 1947, it was generally assumed that Kashmir, as a contiguous state with a predominantly Muslim population, would accede to Pakistan. The Maharaja, however, hesitated whether to accede to Pakistan or to India or to seek to maintain Kashmir's independence, and accordingly proposed to both India and Pakistan that both should enter into a standstill agreement with Kashmir. The Indian government asked for further discussions; Pakistan accepted the proposal, but as a means of pressure began an economic blockade of Kashmir, rail and road traffic being discontinued and supplies of food and petrol cut off. Early in October 1947 an armed revolt of the Muslim peasantry in Poonch province, south-west of Srinagar, was joined by many deserters from the Kashmir state forces and by thousands of tribesmen from Pakistan armed with modern weapons supplied by the Pakistan army, and on Oct. 27 the invaders captured Baramula, only 30 miles north-west of Srinagar.

In a letter to Lord Mountbatten, then Governor-General of India, the Maharaja stated: "With the conditions obtaining at present in my state, and the emergency of the situation, I have no option but to ask for help from the Indian Dominion. Naturally they cannot send the help asked for by me without my state acceding to India. I have accordingly decided to do so, and attach the Instrument of Accession". In his reply accepting Kashmir's accession, Lord Mountbatten wrote: "In consistence with their policy that, in the case of any state where the issue of accession has been the subject of dispute, the question should be decided in accordance with the wishes of the people of the state, it is the government's wish that, as soon as law and order have been restored in Kashmir and her soil cleared of the invader, the question of the state's accession should be settled by reference to the people".

The accession of Kashmir to India was officially announced on Oct. 27, 1947. At the same time Indian troops were flown to the Srinagar front to reinforce the Maharaja's forces, and by the end of the month the invaders, who had advanced to within 18 miles (29 kilometres) of the state capital, had been driven back several miles. Sheikh Abdullah, who had recently been released from prison, was sworn in as Prime Minister on Oct. 31. The rebels meanwhile set up their own "provisional government of Azad (Free) Kashmir", headed by Sardar Mohammad Ibrahim, president of the Muslim Conference.

On Oct. 28, 1947, Jawaharlal Nehru, the Indian Prime Minister, invited the Prime Minister of Pakistan, Liaquat Ali Khan, to meet him in Delhi to discuss the

Kashmir question, and proposed that Pakistan should co-operate in preventing the raiders from entering Kashmir. He also gave an assurance that India had no desire to intervene in Kashmir's affairs once the state had been cleared of the raiders, and regarded the question of accession as one solely for the decision of the Kashmiri people. The Pakistan government, however, declared on Oct. 30 that "the accession of Kashmir to India is based on fraud and violence, and as such cannot be recognized". Nehru repeated in a broadcast on Nov. 2 that "we are prepared, when peace, law and order have been established, to have a referendum held under international auspices like the United Nations".

Indian Complaint to the United Nations

On Dec. 22, 1947, the Indian government requested Pakistan to deny to the invading tribesmen all use of its territory for operations against Kashmir, all military and other supplies, and all other aid that might prolong the struggle. As no reply was received, the Indian government made a formal complaint to the UN Security Council on Jan. 1, 1948, stating that the invaders, who included Pakistani nationals, were using Pakistani territory as a base for operations, drew much of their military equipment, transport and supplies from Pakistan, and were being trained and guided by Pakistani officers. Nehru stated on Jan. 2 that in addition to the 50,000 raiders already in Kashmir, another 100,000 were being trained and equipped in Pakistan by the Pakistan army.

After both sides had put their case before the Security Council, it was agreed on Jan. 20, 1948, that a commission of three members should visit India and Pakistan to investigate the facts and report to the Security Council. Differences arose, however, over two issues. Whereas Pakistan demanded the immediate establishment of an "impartial" administration in Kashmir and the withdrawal of the Indian forces under the commission's supervision, India insisted that Sheikh Abdullah's government should hold a plebiscite under the commission's aegis, and that the Indian forces must stay to ensure external and internal security so long as Kashmir remained acceded to India. The Security Council accordingly adopted on April 21, 1948, a resolution containing the following proposals for the settlement of the dispute.

(1) The commission, whose membership would be increased to five, would place itself at the two governments' disposal to facilitate measures for the restoration of peace and the holding of a plebiscite.

(2) Pakistan would withdraw all its nationals who had entered Kashmir to take part in the fighting, prevent such persons from entering Kashmir and refuse them all aid.

(3) When the commission was satisfied that the tribesmen were withdrawing and an effective ceasefire was in force, India would reduce its forces in Kashmir to the minimum required for the maintenance of order.

(4) The plebiscite would be conducted by a Plebiscite Administration headed by a Plebiscite Administrator appointed by the UN Secretary-General. During the plebiscite the Kashmir state forces and police would be under the supervision of the Plebiscite Administration.

(5) To ensure that the plebiscite was completely impartial, the Kashmir government would be enlarged to include representatives of the major political groups in the state, and the Indian government would undertake to ensure freedom of speech, assembly and movement, the release of all political prisoners, and guarantees against intimidation and victimization.

Both India and Pakistan informed the Security Council that although they were prepared to lend the commission all assistance in their power, they could not commit themselves to accept all the resolution's recommendations. India objected to the proposals for the withdrawal of Indian troops, the control of the state forces by the Plebiscite Administration and the inclusion of members of other parties in the state government, while Pakistan demanded the withdrawal of all Indian troops and maintained that a government headed by Sheikh Abdullah would be unlikely to permit a free plebiscite.

The Ceasefire in Kashmir

The Indian troops meanwhile had cleared the Kashmir Valley of the invaders in November 1947, but in the following month the tribesmen opened a new front in south-west Kashmir, where heavy fighting continued until March 1948. Regular Pakistani troops entered Kashmir early in May to reinforce the tribesmen, and took a major part in a new offensive in north-west and north Kashmir which began in August 1948.

The UN Kashmir Commission, consisting of representatives of Argentina, Belgium, Colombia, Czechoslovakia and the United States, visited India and Pakistan in July, and put forward the following proposals on Aug. 13, 1948:

(1) India and Pakistan would simultaneously issue a ceasefire order, would not augment the military potential of the forces under their control, and would create and maintain an atmosphere favourable to the promotion of further negotiations. The commission would appoint military observers to supervise the observance of the ceasefire.

(2) The Pakistani troops, whose presence constituted "a material change in the situation", the tribesmen and "Pakistani nationals not normally resident therein who have entered the state for the purpose of fighting" would be withdrawn. Pending a final solution, the territory evacuated by Pakistani troops would be administered by the local authority under the commission's surveillance. When the tribesmen had withdrawn and the Pakistani troops were being withdrawn, the Indian government would begin to withdraw the bulk of its forces in stages to be agreed with the commission. India would maintain within the lines existing at the ceasefire those troops which the commission considered necessary for the maintenance of order.

(3) India and Pakistan would enter into consulta-

tions with the commission to determine fair and equitable conditions whereby free expression of the will of the people would be ensured.

India accepted the proposals, but Pakistan maintained that only the Azad Kashmir government could issue ceasefire orders. It also demanded that the Azad Kashmir government should continue to administer the territories under its control, that the Azad Kashmir forces should remain intact and that all Indian troops should be withdrawn. As a result the fighting continued until, following further mediation efforts by the UN Commission, a ceasefire was agreed upon on Dec. 31, 1948, and came into force on the following day. Agreement was reached on July 27,1949, on the ceasefire line, which ran from Manawar on the Pakistan frontier north to Keran, and thence east to the glacier area. Under the agreement troops would remain at least 500 yards from the ceasefire line (to be supervised by a UN observer team), and neither side would introduce fresh troops into Kashmir.

UN Commission's Resolution on Plebiscite

A resolution on the holding of a plebiscite was adopted by the UN Commission on Jan. 5, 1949, and accepted by India and Pakistan, its provisions being as follows:

(1) The accession of Kashmir would be decided through a free and impartial plebiscite, which would be held when the commission found that the ceasefire and truce arrangements set forth in Parts 1 and 2 of the resolution of Aug. 13, 1948, had been carried out and arrangements for a plebiscite completed.

(2) The UN Secretary-General would nominate a Plebiscite Administrator, who would be formally appointed by the Kashmir government.

(3) After Parts 1 and 2 of the resolution of Aug. 13, 1948, had been implemented and the commission was satisfied that peaceful conditions had been restored, the commission and the Plebiscite Administrator would determine in consultation with India the final disposal of the Indian and state armed forces, and in consultation with the local authorities the final disposal of other armed forces.

(4) All Kashmir citizens who had left the state on account of the disturbances would be free to return.

(5) All persons who had entered Kashmir since 1947 for other than lawful purposes would be required to leave.

(6) All authorities in Kashmir would undertake to ensure that there was no intimidation or bribery of voters in the plebiscite, that no restrictions were placed on legitimate political activity, that all political prisoners were released and that minorities were afforded adequate protection.

By agreement with the governments of India and Pakistan, Fleet-Admiral Chester Nimitz, the US naval commander in the Pacific during World War II, was appointed Plebiscite Administrator on March 21, 1949.

As no agreement had been reached on the imple-

mentation of the truce, the UN Commission proposed on Aug. 9, 1949, that a joint meeting at ministerial level should discuss the withdrawal of the Pakistani forces, the tribesmen and the bulk of the Indian forces. The Indian government in reply suggested the inclusion of three other items in the agenda: clarification of the phrase "local authority" in the resolution of Aug. 13, 1948, disbanding and disarming of the Azad Kashmir forces, and the administration and defence of the mountainous and sparsely populated regions of northern Kashmir. As the Pakistan government objected to these items, the meeting did not take place. A proposal by the commission that Admiral Nimitz should arbitrate on the differences between them was accepted by Pakistan but rejected by India, on the ground that the disbanding and disarming of the Azad Kashmir forces was "no more a matter for arbitration than the complete withdrawal of Pakistani forces".

Failure of Mediation Attempts

In its third and final report, submitted on Dec. 9, 1949, the commission recommended the appointment of a single person to endeavour to bring India and Pakistan together on all unresolved issues. A resolution adopted by the UN Security Council on March 14, 1950, provided for the dissolution of the commission and the appointment of a mediator, who would supervise a jointly-agreed programme of demilitarization and decide when it had gone far enough to enable a plebiscite to be held. Sir Owen Dixon, an Australian high court judge, was appointed mediator on April 12, 1950.

During talks with both governments in the spring and summer he proposed that a plebiscite should be held only in those areas where the people's desires were uncertain, notably in the Valley of Kashmir, and that those areas where the inhabitants' desires were known should be partitioned between India and Pakistan. This proposal was accepted by India but rejected by Pakistan. A suggestion for a partition of Kashmir without a plebiscite proved impracticable, as it became evident that both parties would in that event insist upon having the Valley of Kashmir.

Following the failure of Sir Owen Dixon's mission, the Security Council adopted a resolution on March 30, 1951, providing for the appointment of a UN Representative for India and Pakistan, who would effect the demilitarization of Kashmir on the basis of the UN commission's resolution. Dr Frank P. Graham, president of the University of North Carolina, was appointed to the post of UN Representative on April 30. After prolonged negotiations with the Indian and Pakistan governments, he reported to the Security Council on March 27, 1953, that substantial differences still existed on the number of the armed forces which should remain on either side of the ceasefire line, and suggested that India and Pakistan should negotiate directly instead of through a UN mediator as hitherto. Subsequent negotiations and correspondence between Nehru and Mohammed Ali, the Prime

Minister of Pakistan, produced no result, and in a final letter of Sept. 21, 1954, the latter declared that as there was no scope left for further direct negotiations the issue should revert to the Security Council.

Constitutional Developments in Kashmir

The question had meanwhile been complicated by constitutional developments in Indian Kashmir. Like all the princely states, Kashmir had acceded to India with regard to defence, communications and foreign policy only, but whereas the other states had since integrated themselves fully with the Indian Union, Article 370 of the Indian constitution, adopted in 1949, limited the Union Parliament's power to legislate for Kashmir to those three subjects and such other matters as the President might by order specify, with the concurrence of the state government.

Despite Pakistani protests, a Kashmir Constituent Assembly was elected in September 1951 and National Conference candidates were returned unopposed in all but two of the constituencies, in which they defeated independent candidates. An agreement between the Indian and Kashmir governments concluded in July 1952 provided that the head of the state would be elected by the State Legislature; that the Indian national flag would have the same position in Kashmir as in other parts of India, but the Kashmir state flag would be retained; and that although citizenship would be common, the existing law preventing non-residents from acquiring immovable property in Kashmir would remain. Hereditary monarchy was subsequently abolished, and Yuvraj Karan Singh, the son of the former Maharaja, who had been acting as regent since his father left Kashmir in 1949, was elected *Sadr-i-Riyasat* (head of state) by the Constituent Assembly.

The degree to which Kashmir should be integrated with India gave rise to violent controversy inside the state, and the *Praja Parishad*, a Hindu communalist organization, launched an agitation in Jammu demanding the complete accession of Kashmir to India. This was strongly opposed by Sheikh Abdullah (the Prime Minister), who emphasized in his public statements that Kashmir must enjoy complete internal autonomy. After a split in the Cabinet, in which he was opposed by three of his four ministers, he was dismissed by Yuvraj Karan Singh on Aug. 9, 1953, and was arrested later the same day.

The Constituent Assembly finally ratified Kashmir's accession to India on Feb. 15, 1954, and the Indian President issued an order on May 14 greatly extending the application of the Indian constitution to Kashmir. The Indian government was empowered to legislate for Kashmir on the majority of the subjects included in the Union List (i.e. the list of subjects on which only the central government might legislate), but the Concurrent List of subjects on which both the central and the state governments might legislate would not apply to Kashmir, these subjects being reserved for the state government.

Indian Protests against Pakistani Military Alliances

Mohammed Ali announced on Feb. 22, 1954, that Pakistan had asked the United States for military aid, and on Feb. 25 President Eisenhower stated that the United States would comply with this request. In a letter to the Indian Prime Minister, President Eisenhower gave an assurance that this decision was not directed against India, and offered similar assistance to the Indian government, which declined the offer. Nehru said in the Indian Parliament on March 1 that the Kashmir issue "has to be considered from an entirely different point of view, when across the border large additional forces are being placed at the disposal of Pakistan", and called for the withdrawal of the American observers attached to the UN team on either side of the ceasefire line, as they could "no longer be treated by us as neutrals". The American observers were subsequently withdrawn. Admiral Nimitz had previously resigned on Sept. 3, 1953, after Nehru had suggested that the Plebiscite Administrator should be chosen from one of the smaller countries.

In a letter of March 5, 1954, to Mohammed Ali, Nehru said that the granting of US military aid to Pakistan had changed "the whole extent of the Kashmir issue", and continued: "If two countries have actually been conducting military operations against each other in the past, and are in a state of truce, military aid given to either of them is an act unfriendly to the other...What was said at a previous stage about the quantum of forces has little relevance. We can take no risks now, as we were prepared to take previously, and we must retain full liberty to keep such forces and military equipment in Kashmir as we may consider necessary in view of this new threat to us". Although in reply Mohammed Ali denied that Pakistan intended to seek a military solution in Kashmir, Nehru continued to uphold his view that US military aid to Pakistan had radically altered the situation.

Indian suspicions were increased by Pakistan's entry into a network of military alliances. On May 19, 1954, a Mutual Defence Assistance Agreement between Pakistan and the United States was signed. At the Manila conference, in which India had refused to take part, Pakistan on Sept. 8, 1954, became a founder member of the South-East Asia Treaty Organization (SEATO), together with the United States, the United Kingdom, France, Australia, New Zealand, the Philippines and Thailand. On June 30, 1955, Pakistan joined the Baghdad Pact alliance, of which the United Kingdom, Turkey and Iraq were already members, and which was subsequently joined by Iran.

A communiqué issued by the SEATO Council on March 8, 1956, called for "an early settlement of the Kashmir question through the United Nations or by direct negotiations". In a speech on March 20 Nehru commented: "How the question of Kashmir could come within the scope of the SEATO Council is not clear to us. Its reference to Kashmir could only mean that military alliance is backing Pakistan in its disputes with India". Despite this protest, the Council of the Baghdad Pact on April 19 issued a similar call for "an early settlement" of the Kashmir dispute.

Indian Attitude to Plebiscite Plan

The Indian Home Minister, G. B. Pant, said on July 9, 1955, that the conditions for a settlement in Kashmir had been transformed by changes in the situation, including the military alliance between Pakistan and the United States and the "definite decision" taken by the Kashmir Constituent Assembly. In reply to Pakistani protests against this statement, Nehru pointed out on Aug. 22 that at the time of the accession of Kashmir India had made a unilateral declaration that the people of the state would be consulted, no mention being made of a plebiscite. Two years later the UN commission had adopted a resolution (which had been accepted first by India and later by Pakistan) recommending the holding of a plebiscite, provided that certain conditions were fulfilled. There had since been many discussions on the fulfilment of these conditions that had not led to any settlement, and meanwhile there had been developments which would "be taken into consideration".

Following the SEATO Council's pronouncement on Kashmir, Nehru said in the Indian Parliament on March 29, 1956, that the holding of a plebiscite could not be considered until Pakistan had withdrawn all her forces, which still remained in Kashmir eight years after the Security Council had categorically demanded their withdrawal. US military aid to Pakistan had created "not only a new military situation but a new political situation", and that situation had become progressively worse because of the conclusion of the SEATO and Baghdad pacts, which "tend to encircle us". Asked at a press conference on April 2 whether he was no longer in favour of a plebiscite, he said that that inference was "largely correct". He announced on April 13 that he had suggested to the Pakistan government the holding of discussions to settle the question by a demarcation of the border on the basis of the ceasefire line. Chaudhri Mohammad Ali, who had succeeded Mohammed Ali as Prime Minister of Pakistan in 1955, dismissed this proposal on the following day as "preposterous".

The Constituent Assembly adopted on Nov. 17, 1956, a constitution declaring that Kashmir was "an integral part of the Union of India", and that its territories comprised "all territories which on Aug. 15, 1947, were under the sovereignty or suzerainty of the ruler of the state" (i.e. including Azad Kashmir). All sovereignty rested with the state, which had executive and legislative powers in all matters "except those in which [the Indian] Parliament has power to make laws for the state under the provisions of the constitution of India".

In response H. S. Suhrawardy (Chaudhri Mohammad Ali's successor as Prime Minister of Pakistan) declared on Nov. 17, 1956, that Pakistan would never recognize "the right of this or any other such body to represent and legislate on behalf of the people of Jammu and Kashmir", and that by an international agreement, which could not be repudiated by one party to suit its own ends, the question of accession would remain open until it was decided by a free and impartial plebiscite.

Unsuccessful Negotiations, 1957-63

At Pakistan's request, the UN Security Council resumed consideration of the Kashmir question on Jan. 16, 1957. The Pakistani Foreign Minister, F. K. Noon, maintained that the accession to India by the "puppet Constituent Assembly" was "wholly devoid of any legal effect", as the Assembly did not represent Azad Kashmir, its members had been returned unopposed because the population had boycotted the elections, and it had not voted in favour of accession until after Sheikh Abdullah had been imprisoned. He therefore proposed that all Indian and Pakistani forces should be withdrawn from Kashmir, the local forces disbanded and a UN force introduced in preparation for a plebiscite.

The Indian representative, Krishna Menon, maintained in reply that the only problem confronting the Security Council was the Indian complaint about Pakistani aggression. Denying that India was under any legal commitment to hold a plebiscite, he said that the conditions for a truce agreement laid down in the resolution of Aug. 13, 1948, had not been fulfilled by Pakistan, which had not withdrawn its troops, and the Indian government therefore did not consider itself bound by the resolution.

The Security Council adopted on Jan. 24, 1957, a resolution reaffirming the principle that the final disposition of Kashmir would be made through a plebiscite conducted under UN auspices, and declaring that any action taken by the Constituent Assembly would not constitute a disposition of the state in accordance with this principle. At the Council's request the Swedish representative, Gunnar Jarring, visited India and Pakistan in March and April for discussions with the two governments. The Indian government maintained that, as Part 1 of the resolution of Aug. 13, 1948, had not been implemented by Pakistan, it was premature to discuss the implementation of Parts 2 and 3 or of the resolution of Jan. 5, 1949. The Pakistan government, on the other hand, maintained that it had fully implemented Part 1 of the 1948 resolution, and that the time had come to proceed to the implementation of Part 2.

After considering Jarring's report, the Security Council adopted on Dec. 2, 1957, a resolution directing Dr Graham to visit India and Pakistan and to make recommendations to the two governments for furthering implementation of the UN commission's resolutions. Dr Graham accordingly submitted the following plan to them on Feb. 15, 1958: (i) The two governments would undertake to refrain from statements and actions which would aggravate the situation. (ii) They would reaffirm that they would respect the ceasefire line. (iii) Following the withdrawal of the Pakistani army from Kashmir, a UN force would be stationed on the Pakistan side of the Kashmir border. (iv) The UN representative would hold discussions with the two governments on the possibility of a plebiscite. (v) A conference of the two Prime Ministers on these questions would be held at the earliest practicable date. These recommendations were accepted in principle by Pakistan, but were rejected by India on the grounds that they bypassed the question of Pakistan's failure to implement the resolution of Aug. 13, 1948, and would "place the aggressor and the aggressed on the same footing".

No major developments in the dispute then took place until Jan. 11, 1962, when Pakistan asked for a meeting of the UN Security Council on the question. When the Council met on April 27 (the meeting having been postponed because of the Indian general elections), Sir Muhammad Zafrulla Khan offered on behalf of Pakistan to submit the question to arbitration or to the International Court of Justice, and rejected the Indian claim that a plebiscite was no longer needed as the people of Kashmir had expressed their will in the elections to the Srinagar Assembly. In reply Krishna Menon contended that whatever Lord Mountbatten had written or Nehru had said did not necessarily mean a plebiscite, and pointed out that whereas Pakistan had had no elections in 15 years, there had been three elections in Kashmir since partition (to the Constituent Assembly in 1951 and to the Legislative Assembly in 1957 and 1962). He maintained that the only basis for a plebiscite was the resolution of Jan. 5, 1949, and that the conditions for a plebiscite no longer existed. An Irish resolution reminding the two parties of the principles contained in the commission's resolutions and urging them to enter into negotiations with a view to a settlement was vetoed by the Soviet delegate.

As a result of an Anglo-American initiative, a series of talks were held at ministerial level between Dec. 26, 1962, and May 16, 1963, in preparation for direct talks between Nehru and President Ayub Khan of Pakistan. After India had refused to consider a plebiscite, the two delegations discussed proposals for the partition of Kashmir, but no agreement was reached, as neither side was prepared to abandon its claim to the Kashmir Valley. India offered to transfer to Pakistan about 3,000 square miles (7,750 sq km) west and north of the valley, in addition to those parts of Kashmir already held by Pakistan, totalling about 34,000 square miles (88,000 sq km) out of a total area of 84,471 square miles (220,000 sq km). Pakistan, on the other hand, was prepared to cede to India only about 3,000 square miles in the extreme south of Jammu. In consequence the proposal for talks between Nehru and President Ayub automatically lapsed.

The integration of Kashmir with India was carried a stage further in 1964, when the provisions of the Indian constitution enabling President's rule to be proclaimed if the constitutional machinery broke down and empowering the Indian Parliament to legislate for a state where President's rule was in force were extended to Kashmir by presidential order. An amendment to the Kashmir constitution adopted by the State Assembly in March 1965 provided that, as in the other Indian states, the *Sadr-i-Riyasat* should be known as the governor, that instead of being elected by the Assembly he should be appointed by the President of India, and that the Prime Minister should be known as the Chief Minister.

The War of 1965 and the 1966 Tashkent Declaration

A major crisis was precipitated when on Aug. 5, 1965, armed infiltrators from Azad Kashmir began entering Indian Kashmir in an unsuccessful attempt to foment a revolt. In order to prevent further raiders from crossing the ceasefire line, Indian troops occupied a number of points on the Pakistani side of the line from Aug. 16 onwards. The Pakistan Army launched an offensive into Jammu on Sept. 1, whereupon the Indian Army invaded Pakistan in three sectors during Sept. 6-8, 1965. Fighting continued until Sept. 23, when a ceasefire came into force at the demand of the UN Security Council.

At the Soviet government's invitation, Lal Bahadur Shastri (who had succeeded Nehru as Prime Minister on the latter's death in 1964) met President Ayub Khan in Tashkent (Uzbekistan) for talks on Jan. 4-10, 1966. In a joint declaration they affirmed their intention to settle their disputes by peaceful means, and stated that they had discussed the Kashmir question against this background. They also agreed that all armed personnel of the two countries should be withdrawn to the positions which they had held before Aug. 5, 1965, and that the two sides would continue meetings "at the highest and other levels on matters of direct concern to both countries".

In accordance with the Tashkent Declaration, talks took place in Rawalpindi on March 1-2, 1966, between Swaran Singh and Zulfiqar Ali Bhutto, the Indian and Pakistani Foreign Ministers respectively. Diplomatic exchanges on the possibility of holding further talks continued throughout the spring and summer, but led to no result, as Pakistan maintained that the most important issue to be discussed was that of Kashmir, whereas the Indian government continued to uphold its view that Kashmir was an integral part of India.

The War of 1971 and the Simla Agreement

During the Indo-Pakistan war of Dec. 3-17, 1971, caused by the civil war in East Pakistan (now Bangladesh), both sides crossed the ceasefire line in Kashmir. Pakistani troops occupied 52 square miles (135 sq km) east of the line in the Chhamb sector, west of Jammu, whilst the Indian forces occupied 480 square miles (1,240 sq km) west and north of the line in the Poonch, Tithwal and Kargil sectors.

At talks in Simla between Indira Gandhi, who had become Indian Prime Minister in 1966, and the new President of Pakistan, Zulfiqar Ali Bhutto, it was agreed on July 2, 1972, that "the line of control resulting from the ceasefire of Dec. 17, 1971, shall be respected by both sides without prejudice to the recognized position of either side", and that talks should continue on arrangements for the establishment of a durable peace, including a final settlement of the Kashmir question. Gandhi said on July 12 that although India continued to regard the Pakistani-held areas of Kashmir as Indian territory, it was prepared to consider any proposal for converting the ceasefire line into a permanent border.

After the Simla talks the Indian government sent a memorandum to the United Nations requesting the withdrawal of the UN observers, on the ground that the former ceasefire line no longer existed. Pakistan asked that they should be retained, however, as the line was still intact except in a few pockets and the issue had not been withdrawn from the United Nations.

Constitutional Status of Indian Kashmir and Azad Kashmir

The constitutional status of Indian Kashmir was defined as follows by an agreement concluded in 1974 between the Indian government and Sheikh Abdullah, who was subsequently reinstated as Chief Minister:

(1) Relations between Kashmir and the Indian Union would continue to be governed by Article 370 of the Indian constitution.

(2) The residuary powers of legislation would remain with the state of Kashmir, although the Union Parliament would continue to have powers to make laws relating to the prevention of activities directed towards the secession of a part of Indian territory from the Union.

(3) Where any provision of the Indian constitution had been applied to Kashmir with adaptations and modifications, these might be altered or replaced by presidential order, but the provisions already applied without modification were unalterable.

(4) The state government might review laws made by Parliament or extended to the state after 1953 on any matter on the Concurrent List, and might decide which of them needed amendment or repeal. The state government would be consulted on the application to Kashmir of laws made by Parliament in future on matters on the Concurrent List.

(5) The President's assent would be necessary for any amendment to the Kashmir constitution passed by the State Legislature relating to the appointment and powers of the Governor, elections and the composition of the Legislative Council (the Upper House of the State Legislature).

The constitutional status of Azad Kashmir is anomalous, as Pakistan in theory still regards the whole state as disputed territory. The Pakistani constitution of 1956 said that if the people of Kashmir decided to accede to Pakistan, the relationship between Kashmir and Pakistan would be determined by the people of the state, and this wording was imitated in the subsequent constitutions of 1962 and 1973. Azad Kashmir in consequence has never been represented in the Pakistan Assembly, although until 1974 the Pakistan Cabinet regularly included a Minister for Kashmir Affairs.

Until 1960 the President of Azad Kashmir was elected by the Muslim Conference, but in that year a system of indirect election similar to that then in force in Pakistan was introduced, whereby the President and a State Council of eight members were elected by 1,200 elected members of "basic democracies" in Azad Kashmir and 1,200 elected representatives of Kashmiris settled in Pakistan. This system was abolished by the Azad Kashmir Government Act of 1964, which provided that the President of Azad Kashmir should be appointed by the Pakistani Ministry of Kashmir Affairs and should be responsible to its Joint Secretary. In 1968 it was announced that the President would be elected by the State Council, which was enlarged by the adoption of four nominated members, from among its own members.

Following an agitation in Azad Kashmir against "Pakistani domination", a constitution was introduced in 1970 whereby the President and a 25-member Legislative Assembly were elected by adult franchise. This was replaced in 1974 by a new constitution, which established an Azad Kashmir Council consisting of the Prime Minister of Pakistan as chairman, five Pakistani ministers or members of Parliament nominated by him, and seven members elected by the Azad Kashmir Assembly. The Council would lay down policy and exercise full legislative and executive powers to deal with matters not reserved exclusively for the Pakistan government or the Azad Kashmir Assembly, the Pakistani Ministry of Kashmir Affairs being abolished. The President of Azad Kashmir would be elected by popular vote, and the Prime Minister by the Assembly. After the coup in Pakistan led by Gen. Mohammad Zia ul-Haq in 1977, the Azad Kashmir Assembly was dissolved, like the National and Provincial Assemblies in Pakistan, and in 1978 Gen. Zia, who had assumed the presidency of Pakistan, dismissed the President of Azad Kashmir, replacing him with his own nominee. An agitation in support of demands for a return to democratic rule was suppressed in the later months of 1982, a number of prominent local figures being arrested.

President Zia announced on April 3, 1982, the appointment of observers from the Northern Territories (Gilgit, Hunza and Skardu) to sit in the Federal Advisory Council, which had been established as an interim parliament pending elections to a National Assembly. According to the magazine *India Today*, he said in an interview that these territories were integral parts of Pakistan, and that their representation in the Council was of no relevance to the Kashmir question. The Indian ambassador in Islamabad lodged a protest on April 16, however, pointing out that the territories had not been named as part of Pakistan in the constitution of 1973 or its predecessors, and concern was also expressed in both sectors of Kashmir. Three political leaders in Azad Kashmir warned President Zia in a letter of May 3,

1982, that this development was "tantamount to a division of the state of Jammu and Kashmir" and would reduce its population by 500,000, to the benefit of "the government of India, which wishes to dominate all Kashmiris". A White Paper issued by the Kashmir state government on May 29 maintained that the Northern Territories were historically an inalienable part of Jammu and Kashmir, and that an arrangement whereby the Maharaja had leased Gilgit to the British in 1935 had not constituted a derogation of his sovereignty over the area.

Developments in Indo-Pakistan Relations, 1980-90

The Soviet intervention in Afghanistan at the end of 1979 led to a temporary improvement in relations between India and Pakistan, notwithstanding each side's suspicion that arms acquisitions by the other indicated an attempt to obtain military superiority. After talks in Islamabad on April 10-14, 1980, between Swaran Singh (by then ex-Foreign Minister of India) and Agha Shahi (who later became Foreign Minister of Pakistan), the latter stated publicly that he had given assurances that "acquisition of arms by Pakistan would be purely for self-defence in view of the new situation [i.e. in Afghanistan] that has arisen", while the former said that both sides should have no difficulty in discussing the Kashmir issue in accordance with the Simla agreement. Moreover, President Zia met Indira Gandhi for talks in Harare on April 18, 1980, during Zimbabwe's independence celebrations, and the Indian Prime Minister said afterwards that she had withdrawn her objections to Pakistan receiving military aid.

However, relations between the two countries again deteriorated during the summer of 1980, principally because both sides took major steps to strengthen their armed forces, but also because of continuing tensions over the Kashmir issue. A statement issued by the Indian External Affairs Ministry on July 4, 1980, deplored the fact that President Zia had raised the Kashmir question at recent Islamic Conference meetings and described this action as "inconsistent with the spirit of the Simla Agreement". Nevertheless, President Zia again raised the matter in an address to the UN General Assembly on Oct. 1, 1980, when he said that the process of normalizing Indo-Pakistan relations "can and will be further accelerated with a peaceful settlement of the question", and referred to the UN's inability to "redeem its promise to the people of Jammu and Kashmir to enable them to decide their future in accordance with its relevant resolutions".

President Zia publicly suggested on Sept. 15, 1981, that Pakistan and India should enter into negotiations on the conclusion of a non-aggression pact, and this proposal was formally communicated to the Indian government on Nov. 11. India at first reacted with considerable scepticism, as Pakistan had repeatedly refused in the past to discuss Indian offers of a non-aggression pact unless the Kashmir dispute was settled first, and President Zia had made his offer when

announcing Pakistan's acceptance of a package of US military aid, including advanced F-16 military aircraft. At the same time, clashes on the Kashmir ceasefire line were reported to have reached their highest level for several years; Indira Gandhi stated on Nov. 26, 1981, that there had been 55 firing incidents and two minor incursions by Pakistani armed personnel across the line of control in the past three months. The Indian government nevertheless agreed on Dec. 24 to take part in preliminary discussions.

Talks took place in New Delhi on Jan. 29-Feb. 1, 1982, at which it was agreed to hold a second round in Islamabad. On Feb. 19, however, the Pakistani representative at the UN Human Rights Commission made a statement in which he compared Indian-controlled Kashmir to Palestine or Namibia as a region "under foreign military occupation". The Indian government, which held that raising the Kashmir issue in an international forum in a contentious manner was a violation of the spirit of the Simla Agreement, announced on Feb. 25 that in view of these "objectionable statements" the resumption of talks was being postponed indefinitely.

After an emissary from Prime Minister Gandhi had delivered a letter from her to President Zia, it was announced on June 1, 1982, that discussions would be resumed, and a second round of talks was held at Foreign Secretary level in Islamabad on Aug. 11-12, 1982. Three draft documents were placed before the meeting: (i) a Pakistani draft of a non-aggression pact, (ii) Indian proposals for the establishment of a permanent joint commission and (iii) an Indian draft of a treaty of friendship and co-operation. The Indian draft treaty was reported to include a restriction on the acquisition of weapons beyond limits fixed to correspond to either country's "legitimate defence requirements". This point reflected India's concern that Pakistan was developing a nuclear weapons capability and that its US-made F-16 aircraft would be so advanced as to upset the military balance in the subcontinent.

The two countries' Foreign Ministers signed an agreement in New Delhi on March 10, 1983, establishing a joint commission to promote co-operation in a range of areas, with the exception of political and military questions. No progress was made, however, on the proposals for a non-aggression pact and a treaty of friendship and co-operation. In particular, Pakistan rejected Indian proposals that all disputes should be solved on a bilateral basis without recourse to international forums such as the United Nations, and that both sides should promise not to provide military facilities for third countries. Indo-Pakistani relations seriously deteriorated in 1984 because of Indian suspicions that Pakistan was assisting a terrorist campaign by Sikh separatists in the Indian state of Punjab, and negotiations between the two countries' Foreign Secretaries and meetings of the joint commission were suspended.

During this period a new outbreak of fighting occurred in Kashmir in the Siachen Glacier region, an area near the Chinese border at an altitude of about 6,000 metres, about 160 miles (250 kilometres) north-east of Srinagar. Neither the 1949 ceasefire line nor the 1971 line of control had demarcated the border in this region, as no fighting had taken place there, and the area was so inhospitable that neither side had thought it likely to become a matter of contention; both agreements merely said that "the line continues northwards" into the glacier region from the last demarcated point just north of the Shyok river. Pakistan claimed that its control over the area was internationally recognized, as was shown by the facts that foreign mountaineering expeditions had obtained the Pakistan government's permission before going there and that reputable map publishers showed the line of control running north-east from the Shyok river to the Karakoram Pass (i.e. with the whole of the Siachen Glacier area under Pakistani control). The Pakistan-China border agreement of 1963 fixed the north-eastern terminus of the line of control at the Karakoram Pass, east of the Siachen Glacier; this agreement was not recognized by the Indian government, however, which maintained that Pakistan was "illegally" in control of the area.

Starting in the late 1970s, small units from the Indian High Altitude Warfare School were sent onto the 75 kilometre-long glacier from the Nubra river valley to the south, and early in 1984 a force of 100 Indian troops occupied its northern end. Pakistani troops made unsuccessful attempts to dislodge this force in June 1984 and again in June and September 1985.

Following the assassination of Indira Gandhi by Sikh separatists on Oct. 31, 1984, President Zia appealed for an improvement in Indo-Pakistani relations. The talks at Foreign Secretary level were subsequently resumed in Islamabad on April 4-5, 1985, and after another meeting in New Delhi on July 30-Aug 1, at which the proposals for a non-aggression pact and a treaty of friendship and co-operation were discussed, it was announced that both sides had agreed to "continue efforts aimed at the conclusion of a comprehensive treaty".

At a meeting between President Zia and the new Indian Prime Minister, Rajiv Gandhi, in New Delhi on Dec. 17, 1985, it was agreed that the two countries' Defence Secretaries should meet to find a peaceful solution of the Siachen Glacier issue. The Defence Secretaries subsequently held two meetings, but their discussions remained inconclusive. Five Pakistani soldiers were reported killed in June 1986 in an artillery exchange on the glacier. President Zia told a press conference on Nov. 12, 1986, that the situation there had reached a stalemate, and that this state of affairs would continue until India came to an agreement with Pakistan on the issue.

A tense situation developed on the border after India began winter manoeuvres involving about 200,000 troops in late October 1986, and in December Pakistan began military exercises on a similar scale. The Indian government closed the Punjab frontier on

Jan. 23, 1987, accusing Pakistan of preparing to attack, whereupon the Pakistan government proposed immediate talks to reduce tension. Although talks between senior diplomats and army officers opened in New Delhi on Jan. 31, the centre of tension shifted from the Punjab border to Kashmir, where according to Indian sources the army evacuated 100 villages after Pakistani troops shelled part of the area on Feb. 1-2. An agreement was signed on Feb. 4 whereby India and Pakistan would withdraw their troops from the border in stages, beginning with about 50,000 men on each side in Kashmir.

In June 1988 protests at electricity price rises in Srinagar led to demonstrations followed by bomb attacks in October and November launched by militant groups leading to the arrest of 80 people (Nov. 21) who were charged with subversion. On Jan. 26, 1989 (Republic Day), there were anti-Indian demonstrations in Kashmir which were to last off and on throughout the year. On April 23 the Kashmir Liberation Front mounted a three-day protest against police actions. Three militant groups—the Pakistan-based Kashmir Liberation Front, the People's League and the Islamic Students' League—formed a united front. India accused Pakistan of arming and training Kashmiri militants, although the People's League under Shabir Shah, while admitting that Pakistan military intelligence had provided such assistance in the past, now insisted that Benazir Bhutto's government had suspended these operations.

Clashes between Indian and Pakistani forces in the Siachen Glacier region occurred in May 1989 leading to casualties on both sides. A fifth round of talks was held between India and Pakistan at Rawalpindi (June 14-17, 1989) to find a comprehensive settlement of the Siachen Glacier dispute in north-east Kashmir, at which it was agreed that the actions of both sides were to be "based on redeployment of forces to reduce the chances of conflict, avoidance of the use of force and the determination of future positions on the ground so as to conform to the Simla agreement and to ensure durable peace in the Siachen area".

Pro-Pakistan secessionists exploded a series of bombs in Srinagar on Aug. 15, 1989 (India's Independence Day), in which 15 people were injured. By December 1989 the mounting campaign for secession led by the Kashmir Liberation Front (KLF) had made Srinagar (the summer capital) virtually ungovernable. The Kashmir Valley was paralysed by KLF-sponsored strikes or by the resulting government curfews. The Indian response was to send large reinforcements of Hindu troops to the Kashmir Valley.

On Jan. 16, 1990, New Delhi imposed Jagmohan as state governor of Jammu and Kashmir causing the Chief Minister, Farooq Abdullah, to resign in protest. Jagmohan at once imposed Governor's (or emergency) rule. Four days later (Jan. 20) new riots erupted in Srinagar following the arrest of extremists and the next day 35 people were killed when troops fired on crowds in the city. On Jan. 25, following the shooting of four Indian Air Force officers, large numbers of Indian troops were brought into Srinagar and the Indian government imposed a news blackout.

These troubles led to deteriorating relations between India and Pakistan. Already, on Jan. 14, a Pakistan government spokesman had expressed "deep concern over the deteriorating situation in the Indian-occupied Kashmir". This drew a response from the Indian External Affairs Minister describing the Pakistani statement as "wanton, unwarranted and unacceptable interference" in India's internal affairs.

On Jan. 21 the Pakistan Foreign Minister, Yaqub Khan, visited Delhi for three days of talks, but once back in Pakistan he said he had reaffirmed Pakistan's long-established position that Kashmir was disputed territory and he denied that his country was providing weapons and training for Kashmiri insurgents. His statement drew a sharp response from India and the Indian Army Chief of Staff, Gen. V. N. Sharma, said his troops were fully prepared to protect Kashmir's border "at any cost".

On Feb. 12, 1990, an inspector of the Indian Intelligence Bureau was shot dead in Srinagar and the following day the head of state television, Lasa Koul, was also assassinated. On Feb. 19 Governor Jagmohan dissolved the State Assembly. On Feb. 23 an estimated 400,000 people took part in a peaceful demonstration in Srinagar to deliver letters to the UN Military Observers' group calling for a UN-supervised plebiscite on the future of Kashmir. It was reported at this time that US officials had persuaded the Pakistan Army not to intervene in Kashmir and Indian Army HQ contacted their Pakistani counterparts to dissuade them from manning forward defences in Jammu and Kashmir. Other disturbances followed and political leaders in Azad Kashmir (including its President Sardar Abdul Oayyum Khan) threatened to send 10,000 people over the line of control in support of Kashmiri self-determination.

On April 6, 1990, students of the Kashmir Liberation Front seized and later killed three hostages in an effort to get three militants released. In response to the kidnapping, the militant Hindu Bharatiya Janata Party (BJP) called on the Indian government to engage in "hot pursuit" of terrorists and strike at training camps in Pakistan. On April 11 the Indian Prime Minister, V. P. Singh, told the Lok Sabha (lower house): "Our message to Pakistan is that you cannot get away with taking Kashmir without a war". On April 13 the two sides exchanged fire and by April 15 the Indian Home Minister, Mufti Mohammed Sayeed, was reported to hold the view that a war with Pakistan would be justified if it broke "the stranglehold of the secessionists". By the middle of April there were widespread fears that the mounting crisis would produce a full-scale war between India and Pakistan and the governments of the USSR, Iran and the USA expressed their concern and called for a peaceful solution. Eight political groups in Kashmir were banned including the Kashmir Liberation Front and the People's League; three newspapers were closed down while proceedings against other newspapers were

instituted on the grounds that they had "incited violence". At the UN in New York (April 25) the Indian External Affairs Minister, I. K. Gujiral, and his Pakistan counterpart, Yaqub Khan, called for continuing contact between their respective military establishments.

There was continuing unrest through May and then on the 21st of the month Maulvi Mohammad Farooq, the Kashmiri senior Muslim cleric and leader of the Awami Action Committee, was shot dead in his Srinagar home. He had campaigned peacefully for an independent Kashmir. His death led to a heightening of the crisis and major troop movements by both sides. At the end of the month Jagmohan resigned as governor of Kashmir and was replaced by Girish Chandra Saxena. In June, the two sides withdrew their troops from the immediate border area so as to defuse the crisis and agreed to hold talks in July. Then, on June 18, Amanullah Khan, the chairman of the KLF, announced the formation of a provisional government to represent Kashmiris living under Indian occupation.

On July 19, 1990, New Delhi imposed President's rule on Kashmir (earlier, on July 5, Governor Girish Chandra Saxena had declared the whole Kashmir Valley and the 20-kilometre border belt in the Punch and Rajaori districts a "disturbed area"), thus greatly increasing the powers of the security forces. The two sides held talks in July at Islamabad (July 18-19) but without obvious results. By that time India had an estimated 350,000 troops along its north-eastern border with Pakistan in Punjab and Kashmir. At least 1,000 deaths were reported from the Kashmir Valley alone during 1990, following the Indian crackdown on the separatist campaign, and despite claims and counter-claims about attacks across the military control line, New Delhi admitted that its forces had increased their vigilance along the border "to prevent infiltration of Kashmiri militants into Indian-ruled Kashmir".

Continued Tension and Unrest, 1991-97

Disputes along the Line of Control (LoC) continued into early 1991 and after this period of abnormal strain, India and Pakistan held talks in New Delhi on April 4-6, 1991, in order to agree confidence-building measures. The two sides agreed on measures to prevent violation of each other's airspace by military aircraft and to give advance notification of military exercises and troop movements, while also agreeing "in principle" to resume their dialogue on Siachen. Prior to these talks (March 26), leading officials from the two sides had settled upon an early demarcation of the Sir Creek area in the Great Rann of Kutch.

Clashes between Indian and Pakistani forces continued nonetheless and, after the death of 68 Kashmiri militants in May, Pakistan stated that India must be forced to end its "reign of repression" in Kashmir by the rest of the world. In late August, a Chinese delegation on a visit to Pakistan supported Pakistan's claim on Kashmir and its leader, Song Ping, said the Kashmir issue could be solved peacefully but only with patience. Along the LoC during August 1991 there was some cross-line shelling by Pakistan, although on Aug. 27 a Pakistan government spokesman confirmed that India and Pakistan had decided to "take effective steps to prevent escalation of tension" along the border and a general cease fire along the Line of Control in Kashmir came into effect during September.

Early in February 1992 the Pakistan High Commissioner was summoned to the Indian Foreign Office and informed that any attempt to cross the LoC would result in firm action from New Delhi, although the reported involvement of the ambassadors of the five permanent members of the UN Security Council by India in February 1992 for consultations indicated a potential shift in Indian policy, which had previously rejected any attempt at an international solution to a "bilateral" issue. As reports of troop build-ups emerged, Pakistani security forces stated they would intervene to prevent a march by approximately 7,000 supporters of the KLF who intended to deliberately cross the LoC on Feb. 11, 1992. Sixteen deaths and 350 injuries were reported as KLF supporters and Pakistani security forces clashed, although no militants were reported to have crossed the LoC. India had earlier reinforced the LoC and intimated that crossing the LoC would "invite decisive retaliation". Similar, or follow-up, marches were arranged in March-April and were also prevented from fulfilling the same objectives.

At the end of March 1993, during a visit to the UK, the Prime Minister of Pakistan made a statement to the press that the "Kashmir issue must be resolved on the basis of United Nations Resolutions", which India comprehensively rejected in May, after US exploration of a West Asia solution to the India-Pakistan border dispute. Renewed troop build-ups, sporadic exchanges of fire and continued verbal clashes between Indian and Pakistani troops and government officials continued through June, July and August, with reported deaths in mid-August following the Independence Day celebrations in both states only serving to heighten tensions. Such tensions fluctuated throughout the remainder of the year and on Nov. 1, 1993, the Indian Prime Minister, Narasimha Rao, stated that "no force on earth" could take Kashmir away from India.

Overtures to both India and Pakistan by the USA encouraged further dialogue and on Jan. 1, 1994, new talks on the disputed territory were opened. They collapsed without agreement after two days, although one point common to both India and Pakistan was that neither supported independence for Kashmir. Sporadic violence continued throughout the next few months, with a UN report confirming that in the first three months of 1994, 39 people had been killed and 120 wounded in the Azad Kashmir sector. In May, Sardar Leghavi, then President of Kashmir, ruled out the possibility of using the Line of Control as an international border through simple conversion of it; the dispute, according to Leghavi, would only be resolved by reference to the desires of the Kashmiri people themselves. Tensions in the region as a whole, including

Afghanistan and Tajikistan, ensured the war of words between India and Pakistan continued, but by October 1994, with India pushing for elections in Kashmir and Pakistan claiming that such elections were not wanted by Kashmiris, the dispute seemed frozen.

In mid-May 1995 India reportedly offered greater autonomy within India to Kashmir in an attempt to entice opposition groups to more meaningful discussions. This was followed in July with news agencies reporting that India had offered talks without preconditions to separatists in Kashmir. Later in the year, on Dec. 7, Pakistan called for third-party mediation on Kashmir, this being rejected by India on Dec. 18.

In 1996, tensions escalated despite the welcome extended by India's External Affairs Minister to the proposal from Prime Minister Benazir Bhutto for the resumption of talks at prime ministerial level. However, the requirement for Pakistan to attend the talks without attaching any preconditions to any discussions, the arming of village militias by the Indian police forces in the Doda district and continued cross-border exchanges of fire and artillery all reduced the likelihood of any meaningful dialogue taking place. The government in Pakistan had assured its Parliament in January that Pakistan would "continue to extend moral, political and diplomatic support to the Kashmiris [until] the realization of their right to self-determination". Violence at the end of January and calls for a general strike in opposition to Indian plans to build a permanent 240 km fence along the Line of Control to prevent insurgents from the Azad Kashmir region maintained high levels of tension.

Border clashes continued throughout the remainder of 1996 and much of 1997 and Foreign Minister discussions in June and September 1997 were inconclusive in their attempts to resolve the long-standing dispute.

Declaration of Pakistan and India as Nuclear Powers, 1998

While 1998 remained as violent, a dramatic development took place in Indo-Pakistani relations in that year as a result of nuclear tests by both states in May and the official admission for the first time that both had nuclear weapons. The dangers posed by a nuclear confrontation over Kashmir turned world attention to the region briefly, but both India and Pakistan retained their long-standing positions on the issues. Atal Bihari Vajpayee, the Indian Prime Minister, informed Parliament on June 8, 1998, that there was "simply no question of India ever agreeing" to internationalization of the dispute. For India, it remained a bilateral issue, whereas for Pakistan third-party mediation would be encouraged and welcomed. The call in November 1998 by Farooq Abdullah, Chief Minister of Jammu and Kashmir, for India to "give Pakistan permanent ownership of Occupied Kashmir in return for peace" and the conversion of the Line of Control into an international border, was rejected swiftly by India and Pakistan. Later discussions on other border issues, such as the Sir Creek area and the Siachen Glacier, were also inconclusive. Under the UN Convention on the Law of the Sea, the boundary in the Sir Creek area, a tidal creek between Gujarat, India and Sindh, Pakistan, must be submitted to UN mediation if the issue is not resolved by 2004.

Modest hope of progress did, however, emerge in early 1999 with the Lahore declaration of Feb. 21. This followed the visit of Prime Minister Vajpayee to Pakistan, symbolically crossing the border on a bus. The respective Prime Ministers signalled and recognized that Kashmir was the main obstacle to peace between the two states, and reaffirmed the 1972 Simla agreement, as well as some confidence-building measures on nuclear weapons and other military matters. The two governments agreed inter alia to intensify their efforts to resolve the issue of Jammu and Kashmir and to refrain from intervention and interference in each other's internal affairs.

Intensification of Conflict in 1999

Hope, such as it sprang from this declaration and apparent warming of relations between the two states, was soon replaced by renewed conflict in Kashmir. In May 1999 up to 600 militants crossed the Line of Control from Pakistan and dug themselves in at Kargil, approximately 6 km inside the Indian border overlooking the main Srinager-Leh road between Jammu and Kashmir and Ladakh. India claimed the insurgents were members of Pakistan's regular armed forces, or had received extensive support from Pakistan in order to infiltrate the mountainous region and re-supply themselves. Pakistan rejected such claims and stated they were simply freedom fighters from Kashmir.

Major fighting in the Kargil area in late May resulted in air strikes against the insurgents and the loss of two Indian planes. While India reiterated it intended to strike at the insurgents only from its side of the LoC, tensions still rose and international pressure on Pakistan to use its influence on the insurgents increased through June. Indian forces made slow but continued progress in winning back the area and on July 4 the key Tiger Hill peak was retaken and the insurgents were being driven back.

After US pressure to resolve the dispute and appeals to Pakistan to rein in the Kashmiri militants, the Kargil battle effectively came to an end on July 11 when the insurgents agreed to withdraw. Although both India and Pakistan claimed victory, the restraint of India in attacking only from its side of the LoC and avoiding escalating a more protracted conflict with Pakistan's military forces won more plaudits among international observers. Militarily, the insurgency may have been a success because of the agreement to withdraw rather than outright defeat of the forces which had occupied Kargil, but diplomatically Pakistan was viewed by many as the aggressor in the conflict, tacitly accepting an attempt to change the Line of Control by force. Significantly, India also viewed the conflict as a "betrayal of trust" after the hopes invested in the Lahore declaration.

The reverberations this diplomatic setback had in Pakistan were unsettling for Prime Minister Nawaz Sharif, and in October 1999 he was deposed by a military coup led by General Pervez Musharraf, who became the new head of government. For a brief period border tensions were reduced, but by early November regular cross-border skirmishes were being reported. Indian concerns about terrorism were heightened by the hijack to Afghanistan on Dec. 24 of an Indian Airlines flight with approximately 190 hostages on board. One week later, India released three prisoners from jail and the hostages were released.

Developments in 2000-01

Clashes in January 2000 intensified, with up to 1,000 lives being lost in a series of border skirmishes accompanied by heightened rhetoric from both Pakistan and India. On Feb. 4 Gen. Musharraf stated on Pakistani television that Pakistan was ready for dialogue, but only on the issue of Kashmir "as it is the main problem", whereas on Feb. 6 Prime Minister Vajpayee ruled out such discussions. Meanwhile, militants in Kashmir threatened to launch an all-out "final offensive" and tensions increased prior to the planned visit of the US President, Bill Clinton, to India. On Feb. 17 India rejected President Clinton's offer to broker a solution to the Kashmir problem. The publication of the Indian government sponsored report on possible autonomy for Indian-controlled Kashmir, led to a debate and in July 2000 Farooq Abdullah demanded immediate autonomy for the region, which was quickly rejected by the Indian cabinet on July 4. On July 24 *Hizbul Mujahideen*, possibly the largest of the many groups operating in the Kashmiri region (and a group, favouring the integration of Jammu and Kashmir with Pakistan, sometimes alleged to have links with Pakistan's Inter-Services Intelligence agency) announced a unilateral ceasefire and invited talks with the Indian government. But after an initial flurry of promising words, the ceasefire collapsed on Aug. 8 when India rejected any possibility of tripartite discussions involving Pakistan, following a particularly violent period on Aug. 1-2 when more than 100 people were killed.

The leaders of both India and Pakistan used their 2000 Independence Day speeches to reassert their respective hard-line positions. General Musharraf stated that: "Pakistan stands united with its Kashmiri brothers and sisters in their just cause and will continue to extend all moral, diplomatic and political support to their indigenous struggle against state-sponsored terrorism". Prime Minister Vajpayee stated that Kashmir would always remain part of India. In an attempt to break the deadlock General Musharraf called for UN Security Council intervention in early September on the basis that the Security Council can decide to act if one party to a dispute remains intransigent to peaceful means of resolution, but India maintained that it would not discuss issues with Pakistan until what it claimed was military support to Kashmiri forces was halted.

In a surprise move India called a unilateral ceasefire on Nov. 19 for the period of Ramadan, which began on Nov. 27-28, the truce in fact lasting for six months, until being called off in May 2001. Despite the fact that over 400 civilians and 200 security force personnel were killed during the period between November 2000 and May 2001, the ceasefire was something of a success and contributed to better relations between India and Pakistan. Between July 14-16, 2001, a summit in Agra, India, began well with General Musharaff stating that there was "no military solution" to the Kashmir dispute and the possibility of annual meetings of India and Pakistan and six-monthly meetings of Foreign Ministers, as well as a number of confidence-building measures, on offer. However, the summit collapsed without agreement after disputes over language about the place and importance of Kashmir.

Crisis of December 2001-May 2002—Subsequent Easing of Tensions

The global context of India-Pakistan relations changed after the terrorist attacks in the USA on Sept. 11, 2001, and the commencement on Oct. 7 of the US-led military invasion of Afghanistan to overthrow the Taleban regime. Pakistan was regarded as the principal external supporter of the Taleban and faced considerable criticism from US circles for its role in backing the Taleban and, in particular, for the reputedly close links between the Inter-Services Intelligence agency (ISI), the Taleban and groups associated with it, including *Al-Qaeda*. Gen. Musharraf responded to this dangerous situation by declaring unequivocal support for US action, and the warm welcome given to this by the USA appeared to cause India concern that the USA might tilt in Pakistan's direction over the Kashmir issue by seeking to internationalize the dispute rather than allowing it to remain—as was India's wish—a bilateral matter.

In October 2001 Indo-Pakistani relations saw a marked increase in tension after India began shelling across the Line of Control after nearly a year of restraint. The situation was exacerbated by a series of terrorist incidents in India. An attack on the Kashmiri assembly left 38 dead. Then, on Dec. 13, terrorists struck at the Indian Parliament in New Delhi on Dec. 13, leaving 14 dead. India blamed Pakistan for sponsoring the groups blamed for both attacks.

Following the attack on the Parliament, both countries withdrew their high commissioners and cut transport links. A massive military build-up produced a state of high tension lasting for several months in which a million armed men faced each other across the international border and the Line of Control.

As a gesture to de-escalate the stand off, Musharraf banned a number of Islamic militant groups in January 2002 and pledged to clamp down on Islamic extremism within Pakistan, though this was viewed with undisguised scepticism by India. He repeatedly countered charges that the ISI continued to help infiltrate militants into Kashmir with the claim that Pakistan gave only moral, not material, support to the cause of Kashmiri "self-determination". Through the early months of 2002 there were intense diplomatic efforts by the world's leading powers to keep the two sides from war, although much of the bellicose rhetoric from both India and Pakistan seemed to be for domestic consumption rather than indicating serious intent to commence hostilities. Such rhetoric reached a climax on May 22 when Vajpayee, addressing troops in the immediate aftermath of the assassination of Abdul Gani Lone, a leading moderate Kashmiri political figure, warned that the time had come for a "decisive fight" to stop cross-border terrorism, stating "we tried all kinds of peace efforts with our neighbours but nothing worked". India's practical military options against Pakistan were nonetheless limited. Even an offensive confined to militant training camps in Azad Kashmir had the potential to escalate to a general war in which both sides might be tempted to use nuclear weapons. Furthermore, Pakistan's official policy (unlike that of India, with its far greater conventional military strength) provided for "first use" of nuclear weapons in the event of attack.

Tensions began to ease in June 2002 despite continuing separatist violence within Kashmir itself, after Musharraf gave renewed pledges to the USA to ensure that a suspension of cross-border infiltration was made "permanent and irreversible". This development was welcomed by India, which nonetheless emphasized the need to bring about the dismantling of terrorist infrastructure within Pakistan. On June 10 India ordered the withdrawal of battleships from the Arabian Sea and ended a five-month old ban on direct flights to Pakistan. Full diplomatic relations were restored later that month. In October 2002, the Indian government announced a phased withdrawal of 700,000 troops stationed on the border with Pakistan, although full mobilization of forces would be maintained along the Line of Control.

According to the Indian government, by the end of 2002 around 40,000 people had been killed in Kashmir since the beginning of the intensified conflict in 1989. Kashmiri separatists and international human rights groups produced higher estimates, some being as high as 80,000 dead.

In February 2003, a setback occurred when India expelled the Pakistan acting high commissioner, Jalil Jilani, accusing him of financing separatist groups in Kashmir, with Pakistan retaliating by expelling the acting Indian high commissioner from Islamabad. On Feb. 9 Vajpayee stated that "Pakistan does not appear to be interested in establishing tension-free and good-neighbourly relations with India by ending its proxy war against our country".

On April 18, 2003, however, Vajpayee told a public meeting in Srinagar that "open dialogue" was the only way to bring peace to Kashmir and that "guns can never solve problems". The restoration of full diplomatic relations, together with transport links, between the two countries was announced on May 6, 2003. Later in May Vajpayee publicly acknowledged that Pakistan did not have control over all the separatist groups operating in Kashmir. By this time India had dropped its demand for a complete end to terrorist violence as a precondition of discussions with Pakistan and Pakistan had continued with reciprocal gestures to demonstrate its commitment to curbing hardline groups.

On Nov. 25, 2003, India and Pakistan began an official ceasefire across the Line of Control, following an unconditional ceasefire offer by Pakistan announced on Nov. 23, although India said that the ceasefire could only be maintained if terrorist infiltration into Indian-controlled Kashmir was halted. Developments in the relationship were, however, more positive than at any time since the failed Agra summit of July 2001. On Dec. 19, 2003, India and Pakistan signed a three-year agreement to restore direct rail links, and air links and a bus service were to be restored. Even though, at the end of 2003, there were some 450,000 Indian military personnel in Kashmir, positive moves by both India and Pakistan meant that by the end of January 2004 Amitabh Mattoo, a leading Indian expert on the Kashmir region was reporting that, "for the first time in years you can see the light at the end of the tunnel". In the last week of January 2004 India and Pakistan agreed to meet for the first round of talks on Feb. 16-18, 2004.

Jez Littlewood

3.11 Japan - South Korea (Tokto/Takeshima/ Liancourt Rocks)

Since the 1950s a dispute has persisted between Japan and South Korea over the rightful ownership of an outcrop of rocks in the Sea of Japan known collectively as Tokto by the South Koreans, Takeshima by the Japanese and internationally as the Liancourt Rocks. Whereas South Korea asserted its jurisdiction over the islets in 1952, Japan has consistently claimed that they form part of its historic national territory. (The location of the islets is shown in Map 29, p. 507)

Geographical and Historical Background

The disputed rocks are situated in the Sea of Japan (known as the East Sea in Korea) some 200 kilometres east of the central South Korean mainland and about 200 kilometres north by north-west of the main Japanese island of Honshu. There are 34 islets in the group, including the two main islets which rise about 150 metres above sea level and have a combined area of 23 hectares (less than a tenth of a square mile). The islets have substantial phosphate (guano) deposits which have never been developed. There is no safe

anchorage and access can only be achieved by small boat in calm weather conditions. The islets had no permanent inhabitants until the South Koreans established a Coast Guard presence on them in 1954. Fertile fishing grounds surround the rocky islets and as a result, exploitation rights have often driven the competing claims for sovereignty over Tokto/Takeshima.

Japan cites various extant documents and maps which it claims show inter alia that Japanese families exercised title to the islets in the early 17th century (when they were known in Japan as Matsushima) and that subsequently they were consistently regarded as part of Japanese territory. It also points out that in 1905 (the year in which Japan established a protectorate over Korea, prior to outright annexation in 1910) the Japanese government specifically announced the incorporation of the islets into Honshu's Shimane prefecture and that from then until World War II the Japanese authorities regularly issued licences for sea-lion hunting on the islands.

For its part, South Korea claims that the islets have been Korean national territory throughout history and that any early attempts by Japan to exercise authority over them had no legal validity. It regards Japan's incorporation of the islets into Shimane prefecture in 1905 as an act of imperialism characteristic of Japanese policy at that time and essentially as illegal under present-day international law as the subsequent annexation of Korea itself.

Conflicting Views of 1945-47 Territorial Dispositions—1952 Proclamation of South Korean Jurisdiction

South Korea supports its claim to historic sovereignty over the islets with the additional contention that after Japan's defeat in World War II, Korean jurisdiction was confirmed by the wartime allies in their dispositions relating to Japanese-held territory. Texts cited by the South Korean side include: (i) the declaration issued by the United States and Britain at Potsdam on July 26, 1945, that post-war Japanese sovereignty "shall be limited to the islands of Honshu, Hokkaido, Kyushu and Shikoku [the four main Japanese islands] and such minor islands as we shall determine"; (ii) a memorandum (SCAPIN No. 677) issued on Jan. 29, 1946, by the Supreme Allied Commander in Japan, Gen. Douglas MacArthur, defining Japan as including "the four main islands...and the approximately 1,000 smaller adjacent islands" and decreeing the cessation of Japanese administration over various non-adjacent territory, including the Liancourt Rocks (i.e. Tokto/Takeshima); and (iii) the peace treaty signed in San Francisco in September 1951 between Japan and the Western allies, under which Japan renounced in perpetuity its formal imperial possessions, including Korea. (These texts are also central to the Japan-Russia dispute over a number of islands off northern Japan, for which see Section 3.12.)

Japan, on the other hand, contends that none of these texts, nor any other internationally valid post-war instrument, amounted to a definitive territorial settlement requiring the surrender of its claim to sovereignty over the islets. It maintains in particular that SCAPIN No. 677 was expressly concerned with administrative functions and not with sovereignty, pointing out that the memorandum itself recorded that its content did not indicate allied policy as to the "ultimate determination" of islands being excluded from Japanese administration. Japan also lays stress on the fact that the "MacArthur line" established under SCAPIN No. 677 was abolished by the allies on April 25, 1952 (three days before the entry into force of the San Francisco peace treaty), claiming that at that point the islets legally reverted to Japanese sovereignty as part of Shimane prefecture.

Three months before the Japanese peace treaty came into force and while the Korean war was still in progress (see Section 3.13 for an account of the Korean question), President Syngman Rhee of South Korea on Jan.18, 1952, proclaimed Korean jurisdiction over waters within a line running an average of 60 nautical miles (and up to 170 miles) from the Korean coast. Aimed principally at excluding Japanese and other fishermen from some of the richest fishing grounds in the Sea of Japan, this so-called "Syngman Rhee line" ran beyond the Tokto/Takeshima islets, which were therefore expressly included within Korean territory. The Japanese government responded on Jan. 28, 1952, by officially protesting against what it described as South Korea's unilateral proclamation of jurisdiction over the high seas and also declaring its non-recognition of the South Korean assumption of rights to the islets, which were described as being "without question Japanese territory".

The South Korean government replied on Feb. 12, 1952, with a Note Verbale recording that it "does not feel inclined to enter into full arguments...over the owership of the Liancourt Rocks, known as Tokto in Korea through long centuries, and merely wishes to remind the Japanese government that SCAPIN No. 677 dated Jan. 29, 1946, explicitly excluded the islets from the territorial possessions of Japan and that, further, the same islets were left on the Korean side of the MacArthur line—facts which endorse and confirm the Korean claim to them, which is beyond dispute". This argument was in turn rejected on April 25, 1952, by Japan, which reiterated its contention that, since SCAPIN No. 677 had only directed that Japan should "cease exercising, or attempting to exercise, government or administrative authority over the Liancourt Rocks", it had not decreed the exclusion of the islands from Japanese sovereignty.

1953-54 Incidents—Establishment of South Korean Presence

Following what it regarded as the reversion of the islets to Japanese sovereignty in April 1952, the Japanese government laid plans for the re-establishment of actual control, but was precluded from doing so immediately by the fact that the area in question had been des-ignated a US bombing practice zone. (The physical dangers arising from this status had already been demonstrated by an incident near Tokto/Takeshima in June 1948 when 16 Korean fishermen had been killed and four of their boats destroyed by US Air Force planes engaged in bombing practice.)

When the designation was eventually lifted by a joint US-Japanese decision of March 19, 1953, the Shimane prefectural authorities began consideration of the issue of licences for fishing and sea-lion hunting at the islets; however, on May 28, 1953, the Japanese marine investigation vessel *Shimane-maru* discovered about 30 Korean fishermen on the islets engaged in collecting seaweed and shellfish. Accordingly, the Japanese government on June 22, 1953, protested to South Korea against "these illegal acts of invasion into Japan's territory committed by Korean nationals" and requested that "adequate and effective measures be taken to prevent the recurrence of a similar case in the future".

The following month, on July 12, 1953, a Japanese patrol boat which ordered the Koreans to leave the islets was fired on by "armed Korean officials" protecting the fishermen. Moreover, a series of notices subsequently erected on the islets by the Japanese, warning against unauthorized fishing activities, were quickly taken down by the Koreans.

In June 1954 the South Korean Interior Ministry announced that the Korean Coast Guard had established a permanent presence on the islets "to protect them from Japanese aggression", following which a Korean-constructed lighthouse came into operation on Aug. 10. In a further incident on Aug. 23, another Japanese patrol boat was fired at by South Korean personnel stationed on the islets, where according to Japanese accounts they subsequently established various facilities including radio communications, unloading derricks and several buildings.

In view of the tensions around the islets, the Japanese government on Sept. 25, 1954, proposed to South Korea that the sovereignty dispute should be submitted to the International Court of Justice (ICJ), stating that it would accept whatever decision the Court made and also proposing that in the interim the two sides should consult on steps to prevent any further aggravation of the situation. This proposal was, however, rejected by the South Korean government on Oct. 28, 1954.

Maintenance of Japanese Claim post-Normalization

Although Japan and South Korea normalized their diplomatic relations in 1960, the territorial issue was left unresolved, and Japan has regularly reiterated its claim to Tokto/Takeshima. Since 1986 both countries have participated in annual Foreign Ministers' talks which have addressed both the territorial dispute and other contentious issues such as the size of the South Korean trade deficit with Japan, the treatment of the large Korean minority within Japan, and the question of the demarcation of fishing zones.

Although no tangible progress was made on the Tokto/Takeshima question, relations between the two countries generally improved in the late 1980s. Japan relaxed the restrictions upon its Korean population, and during South Korean President Roh Tae Woo's state visit to Japan in May 1990, Emperor Akihito apologized for his country's past treatment of Korea. During the visit Roh became the first South Korean President ever to address the Japanese Diet. In his speech he called for a breaking of "the shackles of the past", and for the development of closer bilateral relations. In January 1991 the Japanese Prime Minister, Toshiki Kaifu, visited Seoul in a move which coincided with a further relaxation of measures against the Korean population within Japan. Kaifu also promised to make further efforts to reduce Japan's large trade surplus with South Korea.

Japanese Prime Minister Kiichi Miyazawa visited South Korea in January 1992. The trade deficit ($8,800 million in 1991, a figure which constituted 90 per cent of the total South Korean deficit) was once again a major source of discussion. A further source of controversy was provided by the revelation that, during its wartime occupation of Korea, the Japanese authorities had forced as many as 200,000 Korean women to become "sex slaves" of the Japanese armed forces fighting in China and south-east Asia. The revelation that the forcible recruitment of these "comfort women" had been an official policy led to South Korean demands that Japan should provide compensation. Roh ordered a full inquiry into the issue, and on Jan. 21 the South Korean government formally petitioned for compensation. The Japanese response was unclear. Initially Miyazawa suggested that, whilst it was a matter for the courts, Japan should provide some compensation to demonstrate its remorse. However, others suggested that all matters relating to wartime reparations had been dealt with by the 1955 normalization treaty between the two countries. In a speech to the Diet on Jan. 24, Miyazawa made a general public apology to "the people of the Asia-Pacific region" who had "endured unbearable suffering and sorrow as a result of Japanese actions".

This emotive issue continued to embroil the two states; compensation claims to former "comfort women" remained unsettled and in 1994 two Japanese cabinet ministers were forced to resign after making comments which were criticized for whitewashing Japan's past militaristic activity. In the Japanese Diet, there were protracted internal wranglings over the apology for Japan's wartime actions. A group of over 150 Liberal Democratic Party politicians lobbied against a formal apology for the war, and the deep division of opinion amongst the Diet members over the precise wording of the apology resulted in an insipid resolution that simply expressed "deep remorse". Such lengthy debate had given the impression that the sentiment was not genuine and it fell far short of the apology sought by many. Japanese Prime Minister Tomiichi Murayama offered a landmark personal apol-

ogy for Japan's wartime actions during his speech on the anniversary of Japan's surrender in World War II but, despite this effort, Japan's relations with its neighbour were again strained when Murayama expressed support for the legal validity of Japan's 1910 annexation of Korea. In the same year, Japanese cabinet minister Takami Eto was forced to resign after he claimed that Japanese colonialism had resulted in significant benefits for subjugated states and he accused South Korea and China of whipping up anti-Japanese sentiment for political gain. It was against this backdrop of strained relations between Japan and South Korea that the territorial dispute again erupted in 1996.

Renewal of the Dispute in 1996

On Feb. 8, 1996, Japan formally requested that South Korea cancel its proposed plans for the construction of a wharf on the easternmost island of Tokto/Takeshima. South Korea dismissed the request as "absurd", stating that it was legitimately exercising sovereignty over the islets, and a war of words ensued. On Feb. 10, the South Korean President, Kim Yong-sam, cancelled a meeting with Japanese policy makers in protest at Japan's renewed claim to ownership of the islets. After strengthening the island garrison, the Korean President made a number of highly publicised telephone calls to the garrison guards instructing them to defend Korean territory and national pride. The issue dominated headlines and anti-Japanese protests sprang up all over South Korea.

On Feb. 15, South Korea began military manoeuvres in the sea surrounding the islands. This quarterly exercise had originally been cancelled to avoid further aggravating relations between the two countries. Following the revival of the territorial dispute, however, this decision was reversed and the South Korean Defence Ministry announced that the exercise had been rescheduled in order to "display the nation's sovereign power over the islet in the face of Japan's claim to it". Some commentators remarked that it was no coincidence that the South Korean premier had chosen to adopt such a tough stance in the run up to key legislative elections.

Tokto/Takeshima continued to dominate bilateral discussions as both parties sought to mark out their exclusive economic zones (EEZ). In the early months of 1996, both Japan and South Korea announced their intentions to declare 200 nautical mile (one nautical mile = 1,852 metres) EEZs around their coastlines in accordance with the UN Convention on the Law of the Sea, which came into force in 1994. According to this treaty, a state has exclusive rights to exploit resources, including fish stocks, within its EEZ. However, because Japan and South Korea are less than 400 nautical miles apart, there are overlapping areas which are claimed by both parties. The sovereignty dispute over the Tokto/Takeshima islets (these being somewhat more than 100 nautical miles almost equidistant from the Korean and Japanese mainland) complicated the issue further as both states wished to include the islets in their own EEZ and therefore, claim exclusive rights to fish in the surrounding waters.

Despite heated feelings on both sides, the Japanese Prime Minister, Ryutaro Hashimoto, and the Korean President, Kim Yong-sam, meeting at the Asia-Europe Meeting (ASEM) in Bangkok in March 1996, agreed to separate the fishing dispute from the territorial question. Both parties agreed to prioritise the negotiation of a new fishing pact (to replace a 1965 treaty which demarcated territorial waters around Tokto/Takeshima) and the establishment of a jointly controlled fishing area around the islets as well as conducting negotiations on EEZ boundaries. Reaching an acceptable compromise, however, proved difficult as officials from both states were under pressure to negotiate the best deal for their fishing industries and—despite agreeing to separate the territorial dispute from the fishing negotiations, in order to sustain friendly and co-operative bilateral relations—both parties continued to publicly assert their claim over the islets.

In September 1998, after months of negotiation, Japan and South Korea reached a basic agreement on a new fisheries pact. The agreement, signed by both states in November 1998, established a "provisional fishing zone" around Tokto/Takeshima (at 35 nautical miles from the shores of both countries) and set out arrangements by which vessels from Japan and Korea could fish in each other's EEZs.

Recent Developments

Whilst progress has been made in the fishing dispute, the territorial dispute is no closer to resolution. The issue of Tokto/Takeshima's sovereignty remains unsettled and continues to provoke sporadic displays of patriotic fervour on both sides. In recent years, a number of incidents have brought the dispute back into the headlines and renewed disagreement. In 1999, for example, the Japanese authorities accepted an application by a group of Japanese nationals to register their permanent addresses on the islets. This move caused consternation in South Korea, where the authorities reacted by granting their own citizens the same right.

In 2000, the sovereignty issue was again in the spotlight when Japan renewed its claim over the Liancourt rocks by highlighting the issue in its annual "Blue Book" diplomatic report for the first time in three years. Although the Japanese ministry claimed that there was no particular motive for including the issue in the 2000 version, South Korea reacted by reiterating its own claim to the island chain. Tensions again ran high after the North Kyongsang Province of South Korea on March 6, 2001, halted all exchanges with its Japanese sister prefecture of Shimane, in protest at remarks by the prefecture's governor that South Korea was illegally occupying Takeshima.

Whilst the issue of Tokto/Takeshima does not usually dominate relations between the two states, periodically it becomes an issue which can inflame diplomatic relations. It is an emotive issue of principle for some groups in both states who are critical that their governments do not do more to assert their claims for territorial jurisdiction. In South Korea, activity by civic groups seeking exclusive Korean control of the islets demonstrates the particularly strong feeling generated by the sovereignty issue in sectors of the domestic population. An example of this came in March 2001 when the territorial dispute triggered a silent "cyber-war". The territorial conflict had already been established in cyberspace with many pro-Korean Tokto web-boards and websites in existence and reported incidents of Korean internet-users hacking into Japanese webservers hosting pro-Japanese Takeshima websites. However, when it became known that the two internet domains of tokdo.net and takeshima.net would be released for new ownership, an active on-line campaign was launched by Korean "netizens" to secure South Korean control. On March 14, 2001, at 8.30pm, the competition for the domains began and it took just 13 minutes for South Korea to win control of both. One of the two successful parties, a Korean domain-service provider, pledged to donate their domain name to the Tokdo Guardian Party, a civil organization which promotes South Korean ownership of the islets. Most of the domain names related to Tokto/Takeshima now have Korean ownership and a South Korean victory in cyberspace has been declared by Korean activists.

Tokto/Takeshima may now be virtual Korean territory but in the real world, the sovereignty issue is very much unresolved and proves to be a perennial source of disagreement for the two states. One of the most recent developments in the long-running dispute is the Korean announcement that it plans to designate an area of approximately 300 square kilometres around the islands of Ulleung and Tokto/Takeshima as a national park in 2004. The Korean Environment Ministry said that the plan was intended to preserve the natural environment of the islands, but some observers have remarked that it is a deliberate move on the part of South Korea to stake out its claim to the islets. It remains to be seen how Japan will respond to this move.

Jez Littlewood

3.12 Japan - Russia (Soviet Union)

The unresolved dispute over what in Japan are known as the "Northern Territories" and in Russia as the "southern Kurile Islands" continues to be a source of friction between the two countries. (For this dispute, see Map 30, p. 507.)

Following the end of World War II in 1945, relations between Japan and the Soviet Union were overshadowed by a territorial dispute over a number of islands off the north-east coast of

Japan which were occupied by the Soviet Union in the closing stages of the war. The islands in question are the Habomai group together with Shikotan, Kunashiri and Etorofu, all of which are regarded by Japan as integral parts of its national territory. Although the two countries normalized their diplomatic relations in 1956, the unresolved dispute over the northern islands proved the main stumbling-block to the conclusion of a formal peace treaty between Japan and the Soviet Union. Indeed, with the passage of time the dispute became more intractable. Whereas the Soviet Union appeared to be willing in the mid-1950s to return the Habomai islands and Shikotan to Japan, provided the latter signed a peace treaty which recognized Soviet sovereignty over Kunashiri and Etorofu, in later years the Soviet Union insisted that the territorial issue between the two countries was closed.

During the period of Mikhail Gorbachev's leadership of the Soviet Union (1985-91), there appeared to be renewed hope that the dispute could be settled. However, although the period since the dissolution of the Soviet Union in 1991 (when Russia became the successor state to the USSR in respect of this dispute) has seen an improvement in relations between the two countries, expectations of a solution have not come to fruition.

The Disputed Islands

The disputed islands are the Habomai group (i.e. Suisho, Shibotsu, Yuri Akiyiri and Taraku) as well as Shikotan, Kunashiri and Etorofu—all situated off the north-east coast of Hokkaido, the northernmost of Japan's four main islands. They comprise a total land area of 4,996 sq km, of which Etorofu accounts for 3,139 sq km, Kunashiri 1,500 sq km, Shikotan 225 sq km, and the Habomais 102 sq km. In terms of distance, Suisho island in the Habomais is only five kilometres from the nearest point of Nemuro peninsula on the north-east tip of Hokkaido.

Etorofu and Kunashiri are the two most southerly islands in the chain of 20 main islands running south from the Kamchatka peninsula. Whereas Soviet (and subsequently Russian) sovereignty over the 18 Kurile islands stretching from Uruppu island northwards is not in dispute, Japan has consistently maintained that Etorofu and Kunashiri are distinct from the Kurile islands and that together with the Habomai group and Shikotan they are historically part of Japan in that until 1945 Russian influence had at no time extended south of Uruppu island. Japan also claims that as regards flora and fauna all the disputed islands are Japanese in botanical character and have a mild climate, whereas the islands from Uruppu to the north are sub-arctic. For its part, the Soviet Union (and Russia, as its successor) contested Japanese versions of the history of the disputed islands and in any case consistently maintained that its sovereignty over them was clearly estab-

lished under agreements between the allied powers concluded towards the end of World War II. It also officially described the disputed islands as the southern Kuriles.

The disputed islands occupy an important strategic position in the seas around them and contain several deep-water, ice-free natural harbours as well as large tracts of open land suitable for military bases. Moreover, the waters around the islands are a rich fisheries area traditionally exploited by Japanese fishermen.

Japanese and Russian accounts of the early history of the disputed islands differ as to which side was the first to become the dominant influence in the area in question. They also express conflicting views as to the validity and significance of certain treaties signed by Japan and Tsarist Russia in the 19th and early 20th centuries. Japan maintains in particular that the Treaty of Commerce, Navigation and Delimitation (also known as the Shimoda treaty) signed with Russia in 1855—and also the 1875 Russo-Japanese treaty under which Japan conceded Russian sovereignty over Sakhalin island in exchange for the Kurile islands—both confirmed Japanese sovereignty over the disputed islands. On the other hand, Russia contends that these treaties have no present-day significance, arguing that Russian territorial concessions to Japan in this period were exacted under duress and specifically that the Japanese aggression against Russia in 1904 nullified all agreements between the two sides.

Soviet Occupation of Disputed Islands in 1945

Over the next four decades the territories ceded to Japan under the 1905 and other treaties remained part of the Japanese empire, which in the 1930s embarked upon a course of massive territorial expansion by military conquest. As regards its relations with the Communist government which came to power in Moscow in 1917, Japan signed the Anti-Comintern Pact with Germany in November 1936 (Italy joining a year later) and following the outbreak of full-scale war between Japan and China in 1937 Japanese forces on several occasions clashed with Soviet troops on the Soviet-Mongolian border, notably in the Nomonhan region in mid-1939. However, as Hitler launched his invasion of the Soviet Union in April 1941 the Tokyo and Moscow governments signed a neutrality pact which was to survive until the very last days of World War II. Not until five days before the unconditional Japanese surrender on Aug. 14, 1945, did the Soviet Union enter the war against Japan, whereupon Soviet forces occupied Sakhalin and the islands south of Kamchatka right down to the northern coast of Hokkaido (meeting no resistance from the now surrendered Japanese). Japanese accounts of this operation show that the Soviet occupation of the islands was not completed until Sept. 3, 1945, i.e. the day after the Japanese surrender instrument was signed on USS *Missouri* in Tokyo Bay.

The Soviet Union's declaration of war on Japan was

made on the evening of Aug. 8, 1945 (48 hours after the atomic bomb attack on Hiroshima), and came into effect the following day. The war declaration referred to a "request by the Japanese government to the Soviet government to mediate in the war in the Far East" but rejected this proposal in view of Japan's refusal to capitulate unconditionally. It therefore associated the Soviet Union with the proclamation issued at Potsdam the previous month by the United States and Britain (and approved by the Republic of China) calling upon the Japanese to surrender and reaffirming the stipulations regarding Japanese-held territories contained in the earlier Cairo declaration issued by the United States, Britain and China following a summit conference in the Egyptian capital on Nov. 22-26, 1943. It is these documents, together with the agreements reached between the United States, Britain and the Soviet Union at Yalta in February 1945, which are at the centre of the continuing dispute between Japan and Russia over the northern islands.

World War II Agreements and Declarations Relevant to Dispute

The November 1943 Cairo conference brought together President Roosevelt of the United States, Winston Churchill (the British Prime Minister) and Gen. Chiang Kai-shek of China. Their joint declaration recorded that they had "agreed upon future military operations against Japan" and had resolved "to bring unrelenting pressure against their brutal enemies by sea, land and air". It continued: "The three great allies are fighting this war to restrain and punish the aggression of Japan. They covet no gain for themselves and have no thought of territorial expansion. It is their purpose that Japan shall be stripped of all the islands in the Pacific which she has seized or occupied since the beginning of World War I in 1914, and that all the territories that Japan has stolen from the Chinese, such as Manchuria, Formosa and the Pescadores, shall be restored to the Republic of China. Japan will also be expelled from all other territories which she has taken by violence or greed. The aforesaid three great powers, mindful of the enslavement of the people of Korea, are determined that in due course Korea shall become free and independent".

At the Yalta conference of Feb. 4-11, 1945, Roosevelt, Churchill and Stalin agreed in a protocol —which remained secret at the time but which was eventually published in Washington, London and Moscow on Feb. 11, 1946—that "in two or three months after Germany has surrendered and the war in Europe has terminated the Soviet Union shall enter into the war against Japan on the side of the allies". Among the specified conditions for this action were (i) that "the status quo in Outer Mongolia shall be preserved" [i.e. its independence would be recognized]; (ii) that "the former rights of Russia violated by the treacherous attack of Japan in 1904 shall be restored", under which heading it was stipulated that "the southern part of Sakhalin, as well as the islands adjacent to

it, shall be returned to the Soviet Union"; and (iii) that "the Kurile islands shall be handed over to the Soviet Union". The protocol also recorded that the three leaders "have agreed that these claims of the Soviet Union shall be unquestionably fulfilled after Japan has been defeated".

During the US-UK-Soviet Potsdam conference of July 17-Aug. 2, 1945, the United States and Britain on July 26 issued a proclamation to the Japanese people calling for surrender to avoid the total destruction of Japan. Article 8 of this proclamation (which was approved by radio by Gen. Chiang Kai-shek) specified: "The terms of the Cairo declaration shall be carried out and Japanese sovereignty shall be limited to the islands of Honshu, Hokkaido, Kyushu, Shikoku, and such minor islands as we determine".

In the Soviet view the above agreements between the wartime allies, and particularly the Yalta secret protocol, restored the "historical status quo" in the Far East and confirmed Soviet sovereignty over all the northern islands occupied by Soviet forces at the end of World War II. The sentiments underlying this attitude received forceful articulation from Stalin himself when he broadcast to the Soviet people on Sept. 2, 1945, to announce the Japanese surrender and the Soviet occupation of Sakhalin and the Kuriles. In this broadcast the Soviet leader said: "The Japanese invaders inflicted damage not only on our allies— China, the USA and Great Britain—but also most serious damage on our country. Therefore we have a special account of our own to settle with Japan. In February 1904, while negotiations between Japan and Russia were still in progress, Japan took advantage of the weakness of the Tsarist government and treacherously, without declaring war, attacked our country and assaulted a Russian squadron at Port Arthur in order to disable Russian warships and thus to place her own navy in a position of advantage. Characteristically, 37 years later, Japan repeated exactly the same treacherous device against the USA at Pearl Harbor".

Stalin continued: "Russia suffered defeat in the war with Japan, and Japan took advantage of Tsarist Russia's defeat to wrest southern Sakhalin from Russia, to strengthen her hold over the Kurile islands, and in this way to close for our country in the east all outlets to the ocean. But the defeat of 1904 left painful memories in the minds of our people. Our people trusted, waiting for the day to come when Japan would be routed and the stain wiped out. For 40 years we, men of the older generation, have waited for this day. And now it has come. Japan has acknowledged her defeat and signed the act of unconditional surrender. This means that southern Sakhalin and the Kurile islands will pass to the Soviet Union, and from now on will not serve as a means for isolating the Soviet Union from the ocean and as a base for Japanese attack on our Far East, but as a means of direct communication for the USSR with the ocean and a base for the defence of our country against Japanese aggression".

On the other hand, Japan has consistently maintained that none of the allied agreements towards the end of World War II specifically mentioned the Habomais, Shikotan, Kunashiri and Etorofu and that therefore they were never intended to confirm Soviet sovereignty over these islands. As regards the 1943 Cairo declaration, Japan argues (in its Foreign Ministry document) that since the Kuriles were ceded to Japan by Russia by "peaceful negotiations" surrounding the 1875 treaty, these islands "can in no way be considered as territories which Japan took 'by violence and greed'". Moreover, Japan argues, "it is clear that the northern territories, which are distinct from the Kurile islands and are inherent territories of Japan, were not included in the areas thus designated".

As regards the Yalta agreement, the Japanese Foreign Ministry document again stresses that "the names of the islands to be included in the term 'Kurile islands' were not specified", and continues: "From a legal point of view the Yalta agreement was only a declaration of common objectives made by the leaders of Great Britain, the United States and the Soviet Union. On this point, the United States government, one of the participants in this agreement, said in an aide-mémoire to Japan dated Sept. 7, 1956 [see below], that it 'regards the so-called Yalta agreement as simply a statement of common purposes by the then heads of the participating powers and not as a final determination by those powers or of any legal effect in transferring territories'. Furthermore, Japan is not a party to the Yalta agreement nor is there any mention of the Yalta agreement in the Potsdam declaration which Japan accepted. Therefore, Japan is not legally bound by it. Likewise, the Soviet Union cannot claim any rights against Japan on the basis of this agreement, which is not binding upon Japan".

On the Potsdam proclamation, the same document makes the following observations: "The final disposition of territories as a result of war is to be made by a peace treaty, and in that sense the stipulations of the Potsdam declaration cannot have any legal effect, as distinguished from that of a peace treaty, with regard to the final disposition of territories. Besides, the declaration merely states 'such minor islands as we determine' and does not specify the names of any islands. Nor can it be interpreted as the expression of a principle which runs counter to the principle of no territorial expansion as contained in the Cairo declaration. As clearly stated in Article 8, the Potsdam declaration is the successor to the Cairo declaration, and Japan accepted it as such at the time of surrender. Further, Soviet participation in the Potsdam declaration can be taken as proof that it admitted the principle of no territorial expansion contained in the Cairo declaration".

A further document of this period which has been cited in the dispute is the memorandum issued on Jan. 29, 1946, by the Supreme Allied Commander in Japan, Gen. Douglas MacArthur, under the title "Governmental and administrative separation of certain outlying areas from Japan". This memorandum (SCAPIN No. 677) stipulated that "for the purposes of this directive Japan is defined to include the four main islands of Japan and the approximately 1,000 smaller adjacent islands...and excluding inter alia the Kurile (Chishima) islands, the Habomai island group and Shikotan island". It also stated that "nothing in this directive shall be construed as an indication of allied policy relating to the ultimate determination of the minor islands referred to in Article 8 of the Potsdam declaration".

The MacArthur memorandum thus excluded not only Kunashiri and Etorofu (as covered by the term "Kurile islands") but also the more southerly Habomais and Shikotan from the territorial scope of the allied military administration; for this reason it has been cited by the Soviet Union as further evidence of the intention of the wartime allies that the islands should become Soviet territory. Japan, on the other hand, argues that the memorandum was "an expedient measure to facilitate the administrative functions of the occupation" and had "nothing to do with the final determination of the territorial issue", as shown by its reference to Article 8 of the Potsdam declaration.

1951 San Francisco Peace Treaty and Related Developments

At the conclusion of a conference held in San Francisco in September 1951, a peace treaty with Japan was signed on Sept. 8, 1951, by 48 of the 51 wartime allies or associated states represented; the three countries which participated but did not sign were the Soviet Union, Czechoslovakia and Poland (while Burma, India and Yugoslavia did not attend and neither Communist nor Nationalist China was invited to participate). The treaty, which came into force on April 28, 1952, committed Japan inter alia to recognizing the independence of Korea and renouncing all claims to (i) Korea, Formosa (Taiwan) and the Pescadores, (ii) the Kurile islands and "that portion of Sakhalin and the islands adjacent to it over which Japan acquired sovereignty as a consequence of the Treaty of Portsmouth of Sept. 5, 1905", (iii) the Pacific islands formerly mandated to Japan by the League of Nations, (iv) any territory in Antarctica, and (v) the Spratly and Paracel islands. Under the treaty Japan also agreed to place under UN trusteeship, with the United States as the sole administering authority, the Ryukyu Islands south of 29° N (including Okinawa), the Bonin islands, the Volcano islands, Marcus island and some smaller islands.

During the lengthy drafting negotiations associated with the San Francisco treaty, the Soviet Union had repeatedly objected to the procedure being followed and also to certain of the terms generally agreed by the non-communist countries involved. In particular, it had demanded that the treaty should be drawn up by the four major wartime allies (i.e. Britain, China, the USA and the USSR) rather than by the 12-nation Far Eastern Commission, as favoured by the United States and Britain. Soviet spokesmen also, before and after the treaty's signature, criticized its provisions as containing insufficient safeguards against a revival of Japanese militarism and as a US device to convert Japan into a military bridgehead in the Far East.

At the same time, these broad divergences were accompanied by the surfacing of disputation over the particular question of the northern islands. Already, in a speech delivered in Los Angeles on March 31, 1951, John Foster Dulles (President Truman's foreign affairs adviser) had noted that "South Sakhalin and the Kurile islands were allotted to Russia at Yalta" but had added: "Any peace treaty validation of Russia's title should, we suggest, be dependent on Russia's becoming a party to that treaty". At the San Francisco conference itself, as it transpired that the Soviet Union would not sign the treaty with Japan, Dulles made it clear that the only definition of peace terms binding on Japan and the allies were those contained in the Potsdam declaration and that private understandings among some of the allied powers were not binding upon either Japan or the allies.

In Japan itself the territorial question had become an important issue in the debate over the proposed peace treaty terms. Against a background of demands from opposition deputies in the Diet that the northern islands (as well as the Ryukyu and Bonin islands) should be returned to Japan under the peace treaty, the government submitted materials to the United States intended to show that the Habomais and Shikotan were part of Hokkaido and that Kunashiri and Etorofu had never belonged to a foreign country. Moreover, at the peace conference the Japanese Prime Minister, Shigeru Yoshida, called the attention of the participants to Japan's view that the Soviet-held northern islands were integral parts of Japan proper.

As regards the actual terms of the peace treaty, the Japanese government has consistently pointed out that Japan's renunciation of South Sakhalin and the Kuriles was not accompanied by any stipulation that they should belong to another country and that "unilateral measures" by the Soviet Union to absorb these territories "have no legal effect in transferring title". It has also stressed that in any case the geographical limits of the term "Kurile islands" were again not clearly defined and that therefore "it is quite natural for Japan to consider that the Habomais, Shikotan, Kunashiri and Etorofu are not included in the term".

Following the entry into force of the San Francisco peace treaty on April 28, 1952, the Allied Council for Japan (consisting of representatives of the United States, the British Commonwealth, the Soviet Union and China) was dissolved, whereupon the Japanese government informed the Soviet mission in Tokyo that it no longer had any raison d' être. On June 20 the head of the Soviet mission was recalled to Moscow, and since there had been no formal termination of the state of war between Japan and Soviet Union it followed that there could be no diplomatic relations between the two countries.

On the same day as the signing of the San Francisco peace treaty, Japan and the United States entered into a bilateral defence pact under which the Japanese government agreed to the indefinite retention of US forces "in and about Japan" so as to deter any armed aggression against the latter country. Eight years later this pact was replaced by a treaty of mutual co-operation and security (signed on Jan. 19, 1960, and in force from June 23, 1960) under which Japan was no longer treated as the weaker partner but was placed on an equal footing with the United States. The new treaty was clarified by an exchange of notes, in one of which the treaty area was defined as the territory under Japanese rule at any time therefrom, while the parties also agreed to consult together in the event of an armed attack or threat of attack against the islands over which Japan claimed residual sovereignty.

Unsuccessful Japanese-Soviet Peace Treaty Negotiations

In view of the Soviet Union's non-signature of the 1951 peace treaty with Japan, the two sides subsequently entered into discussions on the conclusion of a separate peace treaty, on which formal negotiations eventually opened in London on June 1, 1955. Over the following 14 months the issue of the northern islands became central to these negotiations, and although both sides made concessions on their initial positions it eventually caused the breakdown of the talks in August 1956. On the other hand, agreement was reached on the termination of the state of war between Japan and the Soviet Union and the resumption of diplomatic relations, as set out in a joint declaration signed by the two sides in October 1956.

The opening Soviet conditions put forward in the first round of talks in June-September 1955 included the territorial stipulation that Japan should relinquish all claims to South Sakhalin, the Kurile islands, the Habomais and Shikotan, whereas the Japanese side initially demanded the return of these same territories. When the second round of negotiations began in January 1956 (also in London) the Soviet Union indicated its willingness to return the Habomais and Shikotan to Japanese sovereignty but continued to uphold its claim to South Sakhalin and the Kuriles on the grounds (i) that Japan had renounced all right, claim and title to these territories under the San Francisco peace treaty; and (ii) that the allies had agreed to their cession to the USSR at the Yalta conference. Japan on the other hand maintained (i) that the San Francisco treaty did not determine the ultimate ownership of South Sakhalin and the Kuriles; (ii) that Etorofu and Kunashiri were an integral part of Japanese territory over which Japanese sovereignty had been recognized by the San Francisco treaty, which had not defined the term "Kuriles"; and (iii) that the Soviet Union could not claim title to these territories by virtue of a treaty which it had not signed. The Japanese government therefore proposed that the southern Kuriles should be returned to Japan and that the future of South Sakhalin should be decided by a conference of the signatories of the San Francisco treaty and the Soviet Union.

The London talks were suspended on March 20, 1956, but negotiations resumed in Moscow on July 31, when the Japanese side immediately announced that

Japan had renounced its claim to South Sakhalin and the northern Kuriles but could not relinquish Etorofu and Kunashiri. At the second round of talks on Aug. 3 the Soviet side reaffirmed its view that Etorofu and Kunashiri formed part of the Kuriles, the future of which had been decided at Yalta and San Francisco. Japan responded that it could not be bound by the Yalta agreement, to which it was not a party, and that under the Potsdam and Cairo declarations the Soviet Union had renounced territorial aggrandizement as a war aim. With both sides adhering to their positions, the talks remained deadlocked and were eventually suspended on Aug. 13, 1956, on which date the Japanese Foreign Minister expressed the view at a Moscow press conference that it was advisable for Japan to conclude a peace treaty even on the Soviet terms. But an emergency meeting of the Japanese Cabinet on the same day sent him instructions not to sign the treaty at that stage.

Amid considerable criticism of the proposed terms of the treaty within Japan, the Japanese Prime Minister, Ichiro Hatoyama, sent a personal message to his Soviet counterpart, Nikolai Bulganin, in which he proposed that the territorial question should be temporarily shelved and that negotiations should be resumed on the basis of a five-point plan covering the ending of the state of war between the two countries, the exchange of ambassadors, the repatriation of Japanese war criminals held in the Soviet Union, the conclusion of a 10-year fisheries agreement and Soviet support for the admission of Japan to membership of the United Nations. After talks between Hatoyama and Bulganin in Moscow, a formal agreement was reached on Sept. 29, 1956, that "the negotiations for the conclusion of a peace treaty between the two countries, including the territorial issue, will continue after normal diplomatic relations have been restored between the two countries".

1956 Joint Declaration

On the basis of these preliminaries, the Japanese and Soviet Prime Ministers proceeded to the signature in the Kremlin on Oct. 19, 1956, of a joint declaration providing for the termination of the state of war between the two countries and the re-establishment of diplomatic relations and also regulating other aspects of their bilateral relations. This declaration, Paragraph 9 of which referred to the territorial issue, was worded as follows:

"(1) The state of war between the USSR and Japan ends on the day the present declaration comes into force, and peace and good-neighbourly relations are established between them.

"(2) Diplomatic and consular relations between the USSR and Japan are reestablished, and the two states will exchange ambassadors without delay. The question of the opening of consulates in the Soviet Union and Japan will be settled through diplomatic channels.

"(3) The USSR and Japan confirm that they will be guided by the principles of the UN Charter in their mutual relations, and in particular by the following principles in Article 2 of the Charter: *(a)* to settle their international disputes by peaceful means in such a manner as not to endanger international peace, security, and justice; *(b)* to refrain in their international relations from using the threat of force, or its use, against the territorial integrity or political independence of any state, or from acting in any other manner incompatible with the aims of the United Nations; *(c)* the USSR and Japan confirm that, in accordance with Article 51 of the UN Charter, each of the states enjoys the inalienable right of individual or collective defence; *(d)* the USSR and Japan mutually undertake not to interfere directly or indirectly in each other's internal affairs, whether out of economic, political, or ideological motives.

"(4) The Soviet Union will support Japan's application for membership of the United Nations.

"(5) All Japanese citizens sentenced in the Soviet Union will be freed and repatriated as soon as the joint declaration enters into force. As regards those Japanese whose fate is unknown, the USSR, at Japan's request, will continue to attempt to investigate their fate.

"(6) The Soviet Union waives all claims to reparations against Japan. The USSR and Japan mutually waive all claims for war damages on behalf of the state, its organizations and citizens, against the other state, its organizations and citizens, which may have arisen since Aug. 9, 1945.

"(7) The Soviet Union and Japan agree to start negotiations as soon as possible for the purpose of concluding treaties or agreements with a view to placing their trade, shipping and other business relations on a stable and friendly basis.

"(8) The Convention on Fishing in the Open Seas of the North-West Pacific, and the agreement between the Soviet Union and Japan on mutual co-operation in sea-rescue operations signed in Moscow on May 14, 1956, enter into force simultaneously with the present joint declaration. Taking into consideration the interest of both the Soviet Union and Japan in the preservation and rational utilization of natural fishing resources and other marine biological resources, the two countries will take measures, in a spirit of co-operation, to preserve and develop the fishing resources and to regulate and limit catches in the open sea.

"(9) The USSR and Japan agree to continue, after the re-establishment of diplomatic relations between them, negotiations on the conclusion of a peace treaty. In this connection, the USSR, meeting the wishes of Japan and taking into account the interests of the Japanese state, agrees to hand over to Japan the Habomai and Shikotan islands, with the reservation that the actual transfer of these islands to Japan is to take place after the conclusion of a peace treaty between the Soviet Union and Japan.

"(10) The present joint declaration is subject to ratification and comes into force when instruments of ratification are exchanged. Exchange of instruments of ratification will take place as soon as possible in Tokyo".

In later years the Japanese government consistently cited Paragraph 9 of the 1956 joint declaration to refute the Soviet contention that there is no territorial issue between the two countries. It argues that the negotiations referred to were clearly intended to concern the territorial question, since the major problems normally covered by a peace treaty had been resolved by the joint declaration, and specifically the problem of Kunashiri and Etorofu, since it had already been agreed that the Habomais and Shikotan would revert to Japan on the conclusion of a peace treaty.

Shortly before the signature of the joint declaration a significant development occurred when the United States defined its view on the Japan-Soviet peace treaty negotiations and in particular on the territorial question. An aide-mémoire issued by the US State Department on Sept. 7, 1956, contained the following passages: "The United States regards the so-called Yalta agreement as simply a statement of common purposes by the then heads of the participating powers, and not as a final determination by those powers or of any legal effect in transferring territories. The San Francisco peace treaty (which conferred no rights upon the Soviet Union because it refused to sign) did not determine the sovereignty of the territories renounced by Japan, leaving that question, as was stated by the US delegate at San Francisco, to 'international solvents other than this treaty'. It is the considered opinion of the United States that, by virtue of the San Francisco peace treaty, Japan does not have the right to transfer sovereignty over the territories renounced by it therein. In the opinion of the USA, the signatories of the San Francisco treaty would not be bound to accept any action of this character, and they would presumably reserve all their rights thereunder. The USA has reached the conclusion, after careful examination of the historical facts, that the islands of Etorofu and Kunashiri (along with the Habomai islands and Shikotan, which are part of Hokkaido) have always been part of Japan proper, and should in justice be acknowledged as under Japanese sovereignty. The USA would regard Soviet agreement to this effect as a positive contribution to the reduction of tension in the Far East".

The October 1956 Japanese-Soviet joint declaration and related conventions came into force on Dec. 12, 1956, when instruments of ratification were exchanged between the two governments in Tokyo. During the debate on the agreements in the Japanese Lower House the previous month, 58 deputies of the ruling Liberal-Democratic Party absented themselves from the proceedings in protest against the omission of any specific provision in the joint declaration for continued negotiations on Japan's claim to Etorofu and Kunashiri .

Consequent upon the formal ending of the state of war between Japan and the Soviet Union and the restoration of full diplomatic relations between the two countries, a Japanese application for membership of the United Nations was unanimously approved by the Security Council on Dec. 12 and by the General Assembly on Dec. 18, 1956.

1960 Japan-US Security Treaty—Hardening of Soviet position

Within a few years of the signing of the 1956 joint declaration, the conclusion in January 1960 of the new Japan-US mutual co-operation and security treaty referred to above brought about a hardening of the Soviet stance on the northern islands—any territorial concession on which it now specifically linked with a withdrawal of all foreign (i.e. US) troops from Japanese territory as well as the conclusion of a formal peace treaty.

In a memorandum of Jan. 27, 1960, protesting against the new Japan-US treaty, the Soviet government stated that it "perpetuates the actual occupation of Japan, places her territory at the disposal of a foreign power…and its provisions inevitably lead to the military, economic and political subordination of Japan". In this "new situation" and in view of the fact that the treaty was "directed against the Soviet Union and also against the Chinese People's Republic", the Soviet government could not "allow itself to contribute to an extension of the territory used by foreign armed forces" by handing over the Habomai islands and Shikotan, which would be transferred to Japan "only on condition that all foreign troops are withdrawn from the territory of Japan and a peace treaty is concluded between the USSR and Japan".

The Japanese government responded on Jan. 28, 1960, by accusing the Soviet Union of "interference in Japan's domestic affairs" and of wishing to impose an additional condition on the Soviet undertaking of 1956, thereby revealing "the Soviet attitude of contempt for international pledges". A week later, on Feb. 5, the Japanese government formally rejected the Soviet demand for the withdrawal of foreign troops.

During the latter half of 1961 the US-Japan security treaty and the territorial question formed the subject of correspondence between the Soviet and Japanese Prime Ministers. The exchange opened with a message from Nikita Khrushchev to Nasanosuke Ikeda (delivered by the Soviet First Deputy Prime Minister, Anastas Mikoyan, during a visit to Tokyo in August 1961) in which the Soviet leader appealed to Japan to close "foreign military bases" and end its alliance with the United States, since these two factors did "not help in deepening mutual trust and normalizing relations between Japan and the Soviet Union". In his reply Prime Minister Ikeda rejected Khrushchev's assertions and called on the Soviet Union to restore good relations by settling territorial differences between the two countries and signing a peace treaty. Replying on Sept. 25, Khrushchev categorically refuted Japanese territorial claims, asserting specifically that the status of Kunashiri and Etorofu had been permanently settled "through various international agreements".

In a further letter to Khrushchev on Nov. 15, 1961, the Japanese Prime Minister described the Soviet leader's arguments as "contrary to fact and lacking adequate grounds", adding that Japan could "not remain indifferent" to the fact that the Soviet government was sending more and more Soviet citizens to Kunashiri and Etorofu, whose final status could only be settled in a peace treaty. After saying that the international agreements cited by Khrushchev were "presumably" the Yalta agreement and the 1951 San Francisco peace treaty, Ikeda maintained that the Yalta accord did not determine legally to whom the Kurile islands should belong, even though it contained a statement of common purpose towards them; moreover, Japan had not been a party to the Yalta agreement, while the Potsdam declaration, which Japan had accepted, contained no reference to Yalta. In these circumstances, he continued, Japan was not bound legally or politically by the Yalta decisions, which the Soviet government could therefore not invoke in this question. While accepting that under the San Francisco peace treaty Japan had renounced all rights to South Sakhalin and the main Kurile group, Ikeda pointed out that the treaty had not laid down the final ownership of these territories and that since the Soviet Union had refused to sign the treaty it could not cite its provisions to support the Soviet case. He also reiterated that Japan had never renounced its claims to Kunashiri and Etorofu, having always contended that the Japanese renunciation had applied to the 18 islands of the main Kurile group, and that the two southernmost islands formed part of Japan proper.

In his reply to Ikeda, which was published on Dec. 12, 1961, Khrushchev again rejected the Japanese arguments. He declared that the Soviet Union would not transfer to Japan its rights over South Sakhalin and the Kuriles, maintaining that they had been acquired under the Yalta agreement, and asserted that Japan was attempting to evade obligations undertaken in international agreements after its unconditional surrender in August 1945.

Developments in Soviet-Japanese Relations in 1960s and 1970s

Over the following decade there were no significant diplomatic developments relating to the basic Japanese-Soviet territorial dispute, but economic relations between the two countries flourished to the extent that the Soviet Union became one of Japan's main trading and economic co-operation partners. In July 1966 Andrei Gromyko became the first Soviet Foreign Minister to pay an official visit to Japan and a joint communiqué issued on that occasion announced that a bilateral consular convention had been signed and that the two countries had agreed to hold regular consultations "both on questions of bilateral Soviet-Japanese relations and on international problems in the solution of which both countries are interested". Without specifically referring to the territorial issue, the communiqué also said that both sides had agreed that it was "possible further to develop relations between Japan and the USSR in all spheres in the spirit of the Soviet-Japanese declaration of 1956" and that the "development of friendly and good-neighbourly relations between Japan and the Soviet Union will

greatly contribute to the safeguarding of peace and security in Asia and to the cause of world peace".

Gromyko paid a further visit to Tokyo in January 1972 during which he had extensive talks with his Japanese counterpart, Takeo Fukuda, and also with the Japanese Prime Minister, Eisaku Sato. The principal result of the talks, as recorded in an official communiqué, was a decision to hold further Soviet-Japanese talks later in the year with a view to the conclusion of a peace treaty. Although the communiqué made no specific reference to the question, it was understood that the Japanese side had again raised the issue of the northern islands in relation to a possible peace treaty. When the specified talks took place in Moscow at the level of Foreign Ministers in October 1972, they ended inconclusively amid continued deadlock on the territorial issue. Meanwhile, Japan had on June 26, 1968, secured the reversion of the Bonin and Volcano island groups together with certain smaller islands (under an agreement signed with the United States on April 5, 1968), while on June 17, 1971, a further Japan-US agreement provided for the return to Japanese jurisdiction of the Ryukyu islands (including Okinawa)— the latter agreement being subsequently implemented on May 14, 1972.

In March 1973 the new Japanese Prime Minister, Kakuei Tanaka, sent a letter to the General Secretary of the Soviet Communist Party, Leonid Brezhnev, stressing that the conclusion of a peace treaty was indispensable for the establishment of good-neighbourly relations with the Soviet Union and proposing that further discussion on a peace treaty should be held within the year. After the Soviet leader had responded favourably, Tanaka paid a four-day visit to Moscow on Oct. 7-10, 1973—the first Japanese Prime Minister to do so since Hatoyama's visit in 1956. In a joint communiqué issued after Tanaka's talks with Brezhnev and other Soviet leaders there was again no specific reference to the territorial question, the document containing the following passage: "The two sides recognized that to conclude a peace treaty by resolving the yet unresolved problems remaining since World War II would contribute to the establishment of truly good-neighbourly relations between the two countries and conducted negotiations on matters concerning the content of such a peace treaty. The two sides agreed to continue negotiations for the conclusion of a peace treaty between the two countries at an appropriate time during 1974".

According to the Japanese version of the Tanaka visit to Moscow in October 1973, the question of the northern islands formed the main topic in four meetings between the Japanese Prime Minister and Brezhnev, during which the former twice secured the concurrence of the latter that the territorial issue constituted one of the unsettled post-war issues between the two countries. In the Japanese view, therefore, the talks produced a confirmation that the territorial question, as an unsettled post-war issue, should form the subject of negotiations between the two countries for ultimate resolution in the context of a Japan-Soviet peace treaty.

The next round of talks did not in fact take place until January 1975, when Kiichi Miyazawa (Japanese Foreign Minister) visited Moscow to urge the Soviet government to resume formal negotiations on a peace treaty. On this occasion Gromyko proposed that the two countries should postpone the conclusion of a peace treaty and sign instead a treaty of good-neighbourliness and co-operation, but this suggestion was rejected as inappropriate by Miyazawa. In response to Gromyko's request that Japan should take a "realistic attitude", the Japanese Foreign Minister insisted that if the Soviet Union wished genuinely to establish friendly relations with Japan a truly realistic attitude would be to resolve the territorial issue under a peace treaty. A communiqué issued after Miyazawa's visit repeated the formulation used in the October 1973 text, making no reference to the territorial question as such, but the Japanese Foreign Minister stated that Japan would continue to press its claim.

The new Soviet proposal was repeated in a personal letter from Brezhnev to the Japanese Prime Minister, Takeo Miki, which as delivered on Feb. 13, 1975, suggested that the two sides could conclude a friendship treaty "while continuing negotiations for a peace treaty". This proposal was immediately rejected by the Japanese government, however, on the grounds that a peace treaty was the first requirement and also that the prior conclusion of a friendship treaty would represent a virtual shelving of the northern islands question. An important factor in these new exchanges was the improvement in Sino-Japanese relations which had been underway since the early 1970s and the negotiations then in progress between Japan and China on a bilateral treaty of peace and friendship. The Soviet government repeatedly warned Japan that it would regard the conclusion of such a treaty as an unfriendly act and directed particular criticism at the proposed inclusion of an "anti-hegemony" clause as propounded by China (whose use of this term was generally seen as referring in particular to the Soviet Union). When the China-Japan peace and friendship treaty was eventually signed in Beijing on Aug. 17, 1978—containing in Article 2 a specification that neither side "should seek hegemony in the Asia-Pacific region or in any other region" and that each "is opposed to efforts by any other country or group of countries to establish such hegemony"—the Soviet government delivered a formal protest to the Japanese government and official Soviet sources claimed that Japan had yielded to Beijing's "diktat" by deciding to sign the treaty on China's terms.

Meanwhile, Andrei Gromyko had paid a further visit to Tokyo in January 1976 during which he was reported to have indicated the Soviet Union's willingness to return the Habomais and Shikotan to Japan if the latter agreed to sign a treaty of goodneighbourliness and co-operation with the Soviet Union. However, it was understood that the Japanese government had again rejected this proposal and emphasized Japan's insistence on the return of all the islands in dispute. At the end of the Gromyko visit the Japanese Foreign Minister said that he had made no progress in discussions on the territorial issue, asserting that the Soviet Union appeared to be "obsessed" with the proposed Sino-Japanese treaty and disclosing that Gromyko had not accepted his explanation that the controversial "anti-hegemony" clause in such a treaty would not be directed against the Soviet Union but rather had universal application.

Tensions in Japanese-Soviet Relations, 1976-80

Japanese accounts of the territorial question suggest that from about 1975 the Soviet Union began to take a harder line, in particular by maintaining that the Japanese claim for the return of the northern islands was a "baseless and unwarranted demand made by a small segment of people" and that it was "instigated directly from outside". Such assertions were consistently rejected through diplomatic channels by the Japanese government, which in 1976 also protested when the Soviet Union imposed a requirement that Japanese citizens wishing to visit the graves of relatives on the northern islands should have valid Japanese passports and Soviet visas. Tensions also developed in Japanese-Soviet relations in late 1976 when a Soviet pilot landed a supersonic MiG-25 warplane in Hokkaido on Sept. 7 and was subsequently granted political asylum in the United States; despite Soviet demands for its immediate return, the aircraft was retained for examination by Japanese and US military experts and not returned until mid-November, causing the Soviet Union to take a number of diplomatic and other measures which were interpreted as indicating its displeasure.

Moreover, in December 1976 the territorial issue became directly entangled with questions of fishery rights when on Dec. 10 the Soviet Union proclaimed a 200-mile fishing zone around its coasts and announced that fishing operations could be undertaken by foreigners in this zone only on the basis of agreements or other forms of understanding reached with the Soviet government. The Japanese government responded on Jan. 26, 1977, by extending Japan's territorial waters limit from three to 12 nautical miles (with the exclusion of the three international straits of the region), specifying that the new 12-mile limit would encompass the disputed northern islands. On Feb. 24 the Soviet government announced that it would enforce the 200-mile fishing zone from March 1 and made it clear that the zone would incorporate the waters around the northern islands—this being described by the Japanese government on Feb. 25 as "an unfriendly and regrettable act" and as unacceptable to Japan. However, during talks in Moscow on Feb. 28 between the Japanese Agriculture Minister and the Soviet Fisheries Minister it was agreed that for the time being the Soviet Union would "not apply coercive measures" against Japanese fishing vessels within the zone.

Later in 1977, on May 27, an interim Soviet-Japanese fisheries agreement was signed in Moscow providing for Japanese fishing operations during the rest of the year in seven limited areas within the Soviet 200-mile zone. Moreover, after Japan had itself implemented a 200-mile fishing zone from July 1, 1977, it signed a further interim agreement with the Soviet Union on Aug. 4 granting reciprocal rights to Soviet fishermen within the Japanese zone (this agreement containing a stipulation that nothing in it would impair the positions of either side on any outstanding bilateral or multilateral problem). Negotiations conducted in Moscow between Sept. 29 and Oct. 20, 1977, resulted in the extension for a further year—until the end of 1978—of the two interim Japanese-Soviet fisheries agreements; but as a result of Japan's decision to proceed with the signature of a peace and friendship treaty with China in August 1978 [see above], the Soviet government announced an indefinite postponement of negotiations on a longer-term fisheries agreement with Japan. From the Japanese point of view, this breakdown of co-operation with the Soviet Union over fishing rights was significant not only because of the traditional importance of Japanese fishing operations in waters now within the Soviet economic zone but also because of the relationship between the fisheries and the territorial issues—the failure to resolve the latter being an important underlying factor in tensions over the former. According to official Japanese figures issued in 1977, more than 1,500 Japanese fishing vessels had been seized by the Soviet authorities over the three post-war decades and nearly 13,000 Japanese fishermen had undergone the experience of detention.

During the dispute over fisheries the Japanese and Soviet governments continued diplomatic contacts on the basic peace treaty question, but according to Japanese accounts of these further exchanges the Soviet side from late 1976 took the line that no territorial dispute existed between the two countries. After talks between Sunao Sonoda (Japanese Foreign Minister) and Soviet leaders in Moscow in February 1978 had ended without a communiqué being issued, Sonoda reported on his return to Tokyo that the Soviet side had again denied the existence of a territorial problem and claimed that this was a "unilateral negation" of the undertaking given in the 1973 Tanaka-Brezhnev communiqué. Later in the month the Soviet newspaper *New Times* asserted that a peace treaty could be based "only on a recognition by both sides of the realities that have emerged as a result of World War II".

On Feb. 11, 1978, the Soviet ambassador to Japan, Dmitry Polyansky, presented the Japanese government with a draft treaty of good-neighbourly relations and co-operation between the two countries, but this was immediately rejected by the Japanese Prime Minister (Takeo Fukuda) principally on the grounds that it failed to mention the territorial issue and that such a treaty could not precede a formal peace treaty. This attitude came under strong attack in the official Soviet media, notably in *Pravda,* which on March 3 carried an article claiming that the Japanese government was "closing its eyes to reality" and arousing "revanchist illusions" among the Japanese people.

Soviet Military Build-up on the Islands

Throughout the period 1979-80 the Japanese government repeatedly drew attention to what it claimed was a significant build-up of Soviet forces on the northern islands, including the stationing of some 2,000 troops on Shikotan (which had not been militarized since 1960). By May 1980 Soviet military strength in the northern islands was estimated by Japan at some 13,000 troops, compared with about 1,000 in 1976, and Japan also claimed that direct command communications had been established between Kunashiri, Etorofu and Vladivostok (the base of the Soviet Pacific fleet). On Oct. 6, 1979, the Japanese government announced its intention to begin aerial reconnaissance over Shikotan as part of its periodic inspections of the northern islands, this step being condemned as "wild interference" by the Soviet Union.

In a newspaper interview published on March 7, 1980, Dmitry Polyansky said that the Soviet Union would under no circumstances reopen the territorial question. His remarks coincided with the adoption of a resolution by the Japanese House of Representatives calling for an early return of the northern islands and the withdrawal of all Soviet military facilities from them. The resolution, the third of its kind since 1973, called for efforts to consolidate peaceful and friendly relations with the Soviet Union and for the conclusion of a peace treaty. In response to the Soviet claim that the territorial question was now closed, the Japanese Foreign Minister stressed that this was a unilateral decision with which Japan could not agree since in Japan's view the matter had been left as an unresolved issue in the 1956 joint declaration and later communiqués.

On May 7, 1980, Polyansky defended the Soviet military build-up in the region on the grounds that it "should not be considered in isolation from the military and political situation in that area". He said that the Soviet Union could not neglect such factors as the anti-Soviet co-operation of Japan and the United States, the strengthening of US-Chinese relations and the instability of the Korean peninsula and Indo-China. On Aug. 19, a Moscow radio broadcast claimed that Japan's "illegal and groundless" claim to the northern islands was largely responsible for what it described as the "stagnant" state of Soviet-Japanese relations, while on Sept. 2 the Soviet news agency Novosti marked the 35th anniversary of Japan's formal surrender at the end of World War II by publishing a strongly-worded article accusing Japan and the United States of falsifying the history of that period and also referring to Japan's "dangerous alliance with American and Chinese hegemonists on the basis of nationalism and anti-Sovietism".

Japanese-Soviet relations deteriorated sharply in early 1980 as a result of the Soviet military intervention in Afghanistan, in protest against which Japan participated in Western sanctions against the Soviet Union and also joined the United States and about 30 other countries in boycotting the 1980 Olympic Games in Moscow. Further aggravation of tensions developed in late 1980 when a Japanese salvage company began operations to raise the contents of a former Tsarist naval vessel (*Admiral Nakhimov*) which had sunk off the Japanese coast in 1905 with a cargo of gold, platinum and other precious metals whose current value was variously estimated at between US$3,800 million and US$40,000 million. The vessel had been seized by the Japanese during the Russo-Japanese war and had subsequently been sunk outside the former three-mile Japanese territorial waters limit but inside the 12-mile limit introduced in 1977. On Oct. 3, 1980, the Soviet Union claimed proprietary rights over the ship, to which the Japanese government responded (on Oct. 10) that no precedent existed for the return of a ship submerged for so long and (on Oct. 20) that the vessel was rightfully the property of the Japanese government. This in turn brought an angry reaction from the salvage company, which claimed the ship as its own property and which caused some annoyance in Japanese government circles by directly offering the vessel to the Soviet Union in exchange for the return to Japan of the northern islands.

Developments in the 1980s—Resumption of Foreign Ministers' Meetings

In January 1981 the Japanese government announced that Feb. 7 (the anniversary of the signature of the 1855 Shimoda treaty—see above) had been designated as "Day of the Northern Territories" and would henceforth be the occasion of a national demonstration over the Soviet Union's refusal to recognize the Japanese claim and also over its militarization of the islands. At the same time Japan requested the other countries which had signed the 1951 San Francisco peace treaty not to mark the disputed northern islands as Soviet territory on maps published by them.

Addressing a rally in Tokyo on Feb. 7, 1981, the Japanese Prime Minister, Zenko Suzuki, said that it was "to be deeply regretted, for the sake of promoting peaceful and friendly relations", that the islands had not yet been returned to Japan, and he reiterated the Japanese view that a peace treaty with the Soviet Union could be concluded only on the basis of their return. Following the Japanese government's announcement, the Soviet Foreign Ministry had on Jan. 20 called in the Japanese ambassador in Moscow to protest at the designation of Feb. 7 and had warned him that Japan was thereby undermining the positive achievements of Soviet-Japanese relations. Moreover, a statement from the Soviet news agency Tass on this occasion repeated the Soviet view that no outstanding territorial issue existed with Japan and asserted that Japan was "working to stir up artificially the non-existent territorial issue".

Further forceful expression of the Soviet position was given in an article by the Tokyo correspondent of *Izvestia* published in mid-June 1981 as follows: "The 'territorial problem', which is an invention from beginning to end, is in fact an open infringement of the sovereignty and territorial integrity of the Soviet Union which has been raised to the status of state policy. In the whipping up of barefaced hostility towards a neighbouring state which has always supported good-neighbourliness, peace and equality in mutual relations, it is impossible not to see the revival of a completely different 'tradition'. This tradition was decisively stopped in 1945: by putting their signature to the act of unconditional surrender the then leaders of Japan promised in the name of the Emperor, the government and their ancestors to fulfil the conditions of the Potsdam declaration.

"The shameless campaign of encroachment on Soviet territory which is being carried out at present shows that these obligations are being thrown aside by Tokyo. In fact, not one of the 'arguments' used by the present authorities and their propaganda apparatus to whip up nationalist hysteria around non-existent problems holds water. Least persuasive of all is the assertion that the Kurile islands are supposedly 'age-old Japanese territory'. The USSR's primordial rights to the Kurile islands were acknowledged by its allies long before the defeat of Japanese militarism in World War II. Japan's pledges irrevocably stem from the act signed by its authorized representatives of unconditional surrender in which the validity of the Potsdam declaration, and before it of the Crimea [i.e. Yalta] conference, were recognized. If Tokyo after the event is claiming the role of an unexpectedly far-sighted interpreter of the Yalta decisions, then such attempts can only be interpreted as a desire to revise the results of World War II and to take a kind of propaganda revenge for the defeat of Japanese militarism in 1945.

"In its encroachments on Soviet territories, Japanese ruling circles often receive support from the USA. There are many examples of this, but only one conclusion can be drawn: Washington's repudiation of the war-time understandings on a post-war settlement goes back to the 'cold war' era, when the Truman administration began to throw overboard the legacy of Roosevelt and the USA's pledges of the first post-war years. However, Tokyo's vain attempts to recarve the map of the Far East in alliance with Washington and Beijing are senseless. No matter how hard the enthusiasts of revanchism and their interested benefactors try to turn back the wheel of history, their efforts are doomed to failure".

Despite this and other indications of Soviet displeasure with the attitude of the Japanese government, Zenko Suzuki and members of his Cabinet embarked on what was officially described as a "tour of inspection" of the northern islands on Sept. 9, 1981, visiting the Nemuro peninsula on the north-eastern tip of Hokkaido and flying by helicopter along the Japanese coast. This action was described as "absurd" and "provocative" by official Soviet sources, which again accused Japanese ruling circles of fanning anti-Sovietism over a non-existent territorial question.

The official Soviet view that no territorial dispute existed with Japan was reiterated by the Soviet Prime Minister, Nikolai Tikhonov, in an interview with

Japanese journalists given in Moscow and issued by Tass on Feb. 13, 1982. In answer to a question on the state of Soviet-Japanese relations and the prospects for a peace treaty, Tikhonov said inter alia: "The Soviet Union has been and remains in favour of placing Soviet-Japanese relations on the firm basis of a treaty. It is not our fault that a peace treaty has not been concluded to this day. You know well the reason for its absence. It is the unrealistic stand of the Japanese side. We have declared many times, including at the highest level, that there is no such subject in our relations as the allegedly unsettled 'territorial issue'. Meanwhile, the Japanese side is making attempts to interpret unilaterally in a distorted way certain provisions of the Soviet-Japanese statement of Oct. 10, 1973. That statement...registered agreement to continue talks on the conclusion of a peace treaty. To assert that the Soviet Union has admitted the existence of the invented 'territorial issue' means deliberately distorting our stand and misleading the Japanese public. These actions of the Japanese side do nothing to bring closer the prospects of reaching agreement on a peace treaty".

Soviet-Japanese relations continued to be strained by various factors over the next three years, including the shooting down of a South Korean airliner by a Soviet fighter over Sakhalin island in September 1983 and a series of expulsions of alleged spies of the other country. Moreover, Japan continued to criticize what it regarded as a Soviet military build-up in the region, while the Soviet side attacked what it described as "nuclear co-operation" between Japan and the United States. There were also regular protests by Japan against alleged violations of Japanese airspace by Soviet military aircraft, unannounced firing practice by Soviet naval vessels and the unilateral closure of sea areas, including part of Japan's 200-mile fishery zone, for Soviet missile tests.

As regards economic relations, the effect of the Afghanistan-inspired Japanese economic sanctions against the Soviet Union and their partial reactivation in February 1982 over the Polish crisis was to reduce Japan from first to sixth rank among Moscow's capitalist trading partners by 1984. Although bilateral trade increased in 1985 over 1984, its value remained well below the levels of the late 1970s. On the other hand, the two countries signed a new fisheries agreement on May 12, 1985 (the first between two governments under the 1982 UN Law of the Sea Convention), governing the fishing operations of each country in the other's economic zones and territorial waters.

On the diplomatic front, the Japanese Foreign Minister, Shintaro Abe, visited Moscow for the funeral of Yury Andropov in February 1984 and had talks with Andrei Gromyko in which the two sides agreed on a resumption of dialogue with a view to improving relations. However, not until the accession to the Soviet leadership of Mikhail Gorbachev in March 1985 was there significant movement, leading to an official visit to Japan on Jan. 15-19, 1986, by the new Soviet Foreign Minister, Eduard Shevardnadze. The latter began the visit (the first by a Soviet Foreign Minister to Japan since the Gromyko visit of 1976) by declaring that he hoped that a "wind of change" would now produce an improvement in relations between the Soviet Union and Japan and that the two countries would become good neighbours.

The January 1986 talks between Abe and Shevardnadze covered arms control and defence matters as well as prospects for an expansion of trade and economic co-operation. The two ministers also discussed the territorial issue at an unscheduled meeting on Jan. 17, although the matter was not specifically mentioned in the joint communiqué issued on Jan. 19. The main points of this document were (i) that regular consultative meetings of Foreign Ministers would be held alternately in Moscow and Tokyo at least once a year; (ii) that negotiations on the conclusion of a peace treaty would be continued at the next meeting, on the basis of the 1973 Brezhnev-Tanaka statement; and (iii) that bilateral trade and economic relations would be expanded on the basis of mutual benefit. After the talks, Abe said that Japan was determined to negotiate patiently on the territorial issue, using the new communiqué as a starting point.

In an address to the Japanese Diet on Feb. 10, 1986, Prime Minister Nakasone asserted that the continued Soviet "occupation of the northern territories" meant that no formal peace treaty could be signed between Japan and the Soviet Union in the foreseeable future; he also indicated that he would be unwilling to accept the Soviet Union's invitation to visit Moscow (delivered by Shevardnadze the previous month) until "major progress" had been made towards resolving the dispute.

The next Foreign Ministers' meeting took place in Moscow on May 29-31, 1987, during which Abe had talks with Gorbachev as well as with his Soviet counterpart. There was no movement on the Soviet side in respect of the territorial issue, although the visit led to an agreement (which was formalized on July 2, 1986) that Japanese citizens would again be allowed to visit family graves on the northern islands without visas, although they would have to carry identification papers issued by the Japanese government. Arrangements for reciprocal visits to graves on the Soviet and Japanese mainlands were also eased under the agreement.

On July 22, Gorbachev reiterated the established Soviet position that Japan had closed the matter in the mid-1950s when it had rejected the offered return of Shikotan and the Habomai group. Nevertheless, relations between Japan and the Soviet Union during the Gorbachev years were marked by continued improvement. Resurgent nationalist sentiment in many regions of the Soviet Union suggested that a redefinition of the existing Soviet borders was becoming more of a possibility than at any time since 1945. This trend was accentuated by the Soviet Union's increasing need for aid from the capitalist world as Gorbachev struggled to achieve fundamental economic reforms. The possibility of concluding a peace treaty with Japan and, thereby, opening the way for Japanese assistance, provided a powerful dynamic for the Soviet government to seek a resolution to the dispute.

Shevardnadze made an official visit to Japan on Dec. 18-21, 1986. The resulting talks were positive in tone and, although no substantive progress was made on the territorial issue, the two sides agreed to establish a body at deputy ministerial level to keep the question under review. The Shevardnadze visit was also seen as preparing the ground for a later visit by Gorbachev himself, and there was speculation that the Soviet leader might use the occasion to offer to resolve the dispute by making significant concessions. Abe visited Moscow in January 1990, during which he discussed the issue with Gorbachev and attempted unsuccessfully to extract the concession that Japan had the right to make a claim upon the disputed islands.

On Sept. 4-7, 1990, Shevardnadze once again visited Tokyo. Prior to his visit, during the last week of August, the Soviet authorities brought their policy regarding Etorofu—the largest and militarily the most sensitive of the islands—into line with the other territories by permitting parties of Japanese to visit family graves on the island. Nevertheless, on the eve of Shevardnadze's arrival, the Japanese Prime Minister, Toshiki Kaifu, had stated unequivocally that there could be no significant improvement in relations between the two countries until significant progress was made over the territorial dispute. Shevardnadze's visit was cordial, and the Soviet Foreign Minister did appear to hint at possible concessions when he told journalists that whilst his country regarded its frontiers with Japan as fixed in international law, there could be scope for "amendment" through "negotiations based on rational dialogue".

Visit to Japan by Gorbachev

Hopes that there would be progress prior to the visit of the Soviet President were dashed by Shevardnadze's resignation in December 1990. Nevertheless, in early 1991 there was an unprecedented degree of diplomatic activity between the two countries, culminating in a visit by Ichiro Ozawa, the secretary-general of Japan's ruling Liberal Democratic Party, to Moscow in late March. It was rumoured that Japan had offered the Soviet Union a US$26,000 million package of loans, cash and aid in exchange for the return of the islands. The rejection of the deal was indicative of Gorbachev's limited room for manoeuvre on the issue. He was constrained not merely by the long-standing opposition of the high command of the Soviet military forces towards giving up the islands, but also by the growing nationalism and autonomy of the Russian Republic, within whose territory the islands were included. The President of Russia, Boris Yeltsin, declared in Moscow on Feb. 8 that his government would oppose returning the islands, or any other steps that would threaten the territorial integrity of Russia.

Thus, although Gorbachev made his historic visit to Japan on April 16-19, 1991, it was not accompanied by any breakthrough on the territorial issue, despite sev-

eral unscheduled sessions of talks between the Soviet leader and Kaifu. The two leaders signed a dozen minor political and economic accords, and agreed a final communiqué which committed both sides to work towards signing a peace treaty based upon "all positive developments" made since the 1956 joint declaration. This ambiguously worded statement was the farthest that Gorbachev was prepared to go towards reaffirming the 1956 accord, Japan's original minimum objective for the summit. During the course of his visit Gorbachev did, however, depart from recent Soviet policy by acknowledging the nature of the dispute, and also promising to reduce Soviet forces based on the islands and to ease Japanese access by allowing visa-free travel between the islands and Japan. It was reported on May 14 that the troop reduction was under way in all four of the islands.

Transfer of Dispute from Soviet Union to Russia

The growing power of the individual republics at the expense of the central state structure of the Soviet Union accelerated during 1991 following the failed coup attempt in August. Thereafter, in the latter part of the year it was unclear as to where the authority for negotiations lay. Gradually, however, it became evident that the position of Boris Yeltsin's Russian government was of greater significance to the dispute than that of Gorbachev and the Union government. In early September Ruslan Khasbulatov, acting president of the Russian parliament, visited Japan and delivered a letter from Yeltsin to Kaifu in which the former expressed his firm resolve to settle the territorial dispute. During the course of his visit Khasbulatov stated that Russia wished to "realize the long cherished dreams" of the Japanese people over the matter, and suggested that forthcoming Japanese aid could have an important effect in decreasing the existing objections of Soviet public opinion towards the return of any of the disputed territory. He also emphasized that it was the Russian government rather than the government of the Union that was in charge of foreign relations.

The confusion arising from the dual power structure in the Soviet Union was heightened when, on Sept. 9, Georgy Yavlinsky, vice-chairman of the Union's interim Cabinet, appeared to reverse the long-held position of the Soviet central government. His opinion, given as a written reply to a question posed by Kyodo News Service, stated that under the terms of the Russo-Japanese 1855 Treaty of Commerce, Navigation and Delimitation, the islands of Shikotan, Etorofu, Kunashiri and the Habomai group should be returned to Japan. As the treaty was freely entered into, claimed Yavlinsky, it should be respected by all parties. During his visit to Japan, however, Khasbulatov dismissed Yavlinsky as a "boy", and distanced the Russian government from his remarks.

Nevertheless, in early October Yavlinsky's view was supported by a senior Soviet Foreign Ministry official. Oleg Ivanov, deputy chief of the ministry's Pacific and Southeast Asia bureau, pointed to newly-discovered documents which showed that in 1853 Tsar Nicholas I acknowledged Japanese sovereignty over the four disputed territories, thereby adding weight to Japan's claim that historically the islands had been Japanese.

At the end of September a delegation led by Russia's Deputy Foreign Minister, Georgiy Kunadze, visited the Kuriles and suggested that the Yeltsin government was ready to implement the 1956 joint agreement. The visit touched off a series of protests led by Valentin Fyodorov, the governor of Sakhalin island, who claimed that the visit was part of a campaign to brainwash the Soviet public into sanctioning a return of the territories. In addition to organizing demonstrations against any concessions on the issue, Fyodorov threatened to lead a campaign of secession by Sakhalin if the Kuriles were returned to Japan. Although of limited significance, the campaign highlighted one of the greatest impediments to a settlement: the nature of the changes which had occurred within the islands since 1945. Under Soviet occupation some 17,000 Japanese residents were removed and replaced by a current population of 25,000 Soviet citizens, excluding military personnel. In a referendum on the issue of the islands' future, held on March 17, 1991, slightly over 81 per cent of voters on Etorofu and more than 70 per cent of voters on the other islands had recorded their opposition to a return of the territories to Japan.

The Japanese Foreign Minister, Taro Nakayama, visited Moscow in mid-October 1991 for talks with both the Soviet central government and the government of the Russian Republic. The atmosphere of the visit was sweetened by the announcement on Oct. 8 of a $2,500 million package of assistance to the Soviet Union, one of the largest to be granted by Japan to any country. On Oct. 14 the two sides agreed upon the details of visa-free visits for former Japanese and current Russian residents of the territories, as promised by Gorbachev in April. On the following day the Soviet President stated that any solution to the territorial dispute should be within the context of the 1956 joint declaration but also in accordance with Soviet public opinion which was believed to be heavily opposed to returning the islands.

In an open letter on Nov. 14, President Yeltsin stated to the people of Russia that it was the absolute duty of the new Russian leadership to search for ways of solving all of the problems inherited from policies of the past. He emphasized the importance of concluding a peace treaty with Japan and recognized the legacy of the territorial dispute in impeding this. He stated that his government would "respond to the norms of civilized international dealings and make legality, justice and unswerving observance of international law the main criteria of our policy". He also gave assurances that the interests and dignity of the peoples of Russia, particularly those resident in the Kuriles, would be respected. On the following day the Japanese Foreign Minister, Michio Watenabe, praised Yeltsin's "forward-looking" position and his emphasis on abiding by international law.

The final dismantling of the Soviet Union at the end of 1991 represented a significant break with the past and appeared, thereby, to offer the possibility of accelerating the process of arriving at a solution to the territorial dispute. Certainly the demolition of the Soviet state reduced the significance of some of the factors which had militated against concessions in the past. Considerations such as the strategic importance of the territories in safeguarding the Soviet fleet's access to the Pacific, or the impact of the precedent of redrawing the Soviet Union's post-1945 boundaries upon national minorities seeking independence, were of significantly less importance to Russia than they had been to the global superpower from which it had emerged.

Japan extended diplomatic recognition to Russia on Dec. 27 and once again called for a return of the four disputed islands. In January 1992, the new Japanese Prime Minister, Kiichi Miyazawa, met Yeltsin at the UN headquarters in New York. At the meeting it was confirmed that Yeltsin would make a visit to Japan in September 1992, and Yeltsin was reported to have stated that Russia would honour the 1956 agreement between Japan and the Soviet Union. Miyazawa described the meeting as having produced an "opening" for progress on the dispute.

In February 1992 the Japanese Deputy Foreign Minister, Kunihiko Saito, visited Moscow for the first working-level negotiations on the dispute since the collapse of the Soviet Union. On Feb. 11 he restated the belief that Japanese public opinion would prevent the extension of economic assistance to Russia whilst the territorial dispute remained outstanding. He also stated, however, that the two days of talks had been fruitful and that the Russian government was "much more positive, much more serious" about negotiating a treaty with Japan than had been its Soviet predecessor.

Developments since 1993

Since 1993 relations between Russia and Japan have become increasingly cordial. Aspects of this growing cordiality have included co-operation in the fight against international terrorism, Russian support for Japan's pursuit of a permanent seat on the UN Security Council, Japan's avoidance of criticism of Russian policy in Chechnya, the establishment of a joint committee for the conclusion of a peace treaty, and numerous declarations on the need to reach a consensus on the Kurile Islands/Northern Territories question.

Nonetheless it does seem that while the nature of, and attitude towards the need for, dialogue has changed, the debate continues to revolve around many of the same issues. In the case of Russia the continuing belief in the merits and righteousness of its position, a position inherited from the days of the USSR, prevails. For Japan, the primary determining factor is that the Soviet occupation of the Northern Territory, days before Japan's official surrender, represented a form of territorial expansion which was contrary to the principles of the Cairo declaration and the Potsdam proclamation. Japan remains keen to stress that the term "Kurile Islands" as contained within the San Francisco Peace Treaty "does not include and was not intended to include the Habomai islands, or Shikotan, or the islands of Kunashiri and Etorofu which have always been part of Japan proper and should, therefore, in justice be acknowledged as under Japanese sovereignty".

However, recognition that the collapse of the Soviet Union offered new opportunities has brought about a much more nuanced and multi-layered approach from the Japanese Foreign Ministry. In June 1992, for example, the Foreign Ministry issued a pamphlet entitled "Japanese Northern Territory" which sought a flexible and negotiated settlement. It stated: "Japan will not demand an immediate return of all four islands, and is ready to discuss the formula of the return in a flexible manner, if the sovereignty of Japan over the four islands is recognized by the Russian government; Japan strives for the return of the islands not from a revanchist viewpoint but for the sake of law and justice, the common norms of the international community that the new Russia has just joined enable both nations to embark on frank, long-term cooperation; the Japanese government and people support democracy and free economy in Russia and will continue to render assistance". At the same time, despite Japan facing more pressing regional security concerns, the Northern Territories continue to evoke a great deal of public concern and are never far from the top of the agenda. Keeping the issue alive is reportedly part of the mission statement of over one hundred organizations (especially on the northern island of Hokkaido) that lobby for the return of the Islands. This culminates on a yearly basis on Feb. 7 with "Northern Territories Day" thereby ensuring that the issue remains at the forefront of the political agenda.

In Russia, however, the territorial issue remains bound to questions of national frontiers and the wider regional and security context. The fear that ceding national sovereignty could open the floodgates for other territorial claims is a powerful inhibitor.

Russian-Japanese Summits and Declarations since 1993

The 1990s and early 2000s have proved to be a period of increasing diplomatic manoeuvrings, media events and high-profile summits.

The October 1993 summit between President Yeltsin and the Japanese Prime Minister, Morihiro Hosokawa, resulted in the "Tokyo Declaration". This set out a roadmap whereby the two countries would work towards a solution of the problem on the basis of "legal principles and justice".

The 1997 Krasnoyarsk Agreement arose from what was dubbed the "no-necktie" summit in Krasnoyarsk. On this occasion President Yeltsin and the Japanese Prime Minister, Ryutaro Hashimoto, promised to resolve relations by 2000. Though they failed to do so, many observers believe that resolution of the issue will ultimately be decided by economics. This line of reasoning has gained increasing momentum since the 1997 Japanese government decision to end its policy of linking economic assistance and the Northern Territories question. Today the need for Japanese technical and financial assistance in the economic development of the Russian Far East provides Japan with a strong hand. Concomitantly, the Japanese desire to reduce their dependence on oil from the Middle East gives the Russians an important bargaining chip.

In the 1998 Japan-Russia summit talks, Prime Minister Hashimoto introduced a conciliatory proposal that came to be known as the "Kawana Plan". The plan sought agreement on a commonly recognized border, likely to be established between Etorofu and Uruppu islands. In addition, the administrative rights over Kunashiri and Etorofu islands would remain with Russia. Such a plan, which would enable Japan to take back Habomai and Shikotan, would provide the basis upon which a peace treaty could be concluded.

In 1998 the Japanese Foreign Ministry opened its first local office in Yuzhnosakhalinsk. This, according to Kimie Hara, "virtually constitutes Japanese recognition of Russia's sovereignty over southern Sakhalin, also seized by the USSR in 1945, reversing a long-standing position that sovereignty over it is undecided in terms of international law".

In November 1999, Keizo Obuchi became the first Japanese Prime Minister in 25 years to make an official visit to Russia. He and President Yeltsin signed the Moscow Declaration on Establishing a Creative Partnership between Japan and the Russian Federation. Building upon the Tokyo Declaration and the Krasnoyarsk and Kawana Agreements, the Declaration highlighted the need to continue developing trust between the two nations as the basis upon which any sort of agreement could be forged. Agreement was reached on the establishing of subcommittees on border demarcation and joint economic activities within the framework of the Japanese-Russian Joint Committee on the Conclusion of a Peace Treaty, and on implementation of so-called free visits to the disputed islands by former residents and their families.

The momentum generated by these developments during the Yeltsin era has continued with his successor Vladimir Putin. After becoming President of the Russian Federation, he and the Japanese Prime Minister, Junichiro Koizumi, jointly issued the Irkutsk Statement on March 25, 2001. In a further meeting on Jan. 10, 2003, they issued a joint statement that called for a "new horizon for broad Japan-Russia partnership, by ultimately overcoming difficult legacies from the past between the two countries, and affirming their determination to conclude a peace treaty as soon as possible through the solution of the issue of where the islands of Etorofu, Kunashiri, Shikotan and Habomai belong and therefore accomplish complete normalization of Japan-Russia relations..." The statement also reaffirmed the continuation of the long upheld approach of overcoming national fears and stereotypes through the promotion of mutual understanding and cultural awareness. It also recognized Japan's contribution to the economic development of the Russian Federation.

Dominating the agenda in 2003 was the proposed development of the Siberian oil fields and whether a pipeline should carry the oil to China or to Nakhodka (near Vladivostok) from where it could be shipped to Japan. It may well be the case that the fate of this pipeline is destined to provide many of the answers vis-à-vis the true nature of relations between the two nations. Japanese Foreign Minister Yoriko Kawaguchi was quoted as saying that "if the project materializes, it will become one of the solid pillars of mutual trust". It remains to be seen if the Russians seek Japanese or Chinese partnership. Japan's only option is to continue its efforts to convince Putin, other key Kremlin officials and the Russian people that signing a peace treaty will benefit Russia's interests in the long run.

Japan sent the warmest of congratulations following Putin's presidential election victory in March 2004. A month later former Prime Minister Mori represented Japan at the inaugural meeting of the "eminent persons group" that is seeking to formulate a basis upon which a peace treaty can finally be signed between the two nations.

Stephen Day

3.13 The Korean Question

The present boundary between the Democratic People's Republic of Korea (North Korea) and the Republic of Korea (South Korea) is a provisional line established adjacent to the 38°N parallel under the 1953 armistice which brought to an end three years of armed conflict between the Communist North and the US-backed South. (See Map 29, p. 507.) Since then both North and South Korea have continued to claim legitimate jurisdiction over all Korea.

Although technically the two sides remain at war as no peace treaty has ever been concluded, there have been periodic initiatives towards the reunification of Korea. Such initiatives made little substantial progress until late 1991 when, in the context of the dramatic alteration in international relations wrought by the collapse of the Soviet Union, the two Koreas agreed to a non-aggression accord and a treaty to prohibit nuclear weapons from the Korean peninsula. In the years that have followed, however, North-South relations have veered between periods of high tension and periods of détente and the Korean peninsula has twice fallen under the shadow of nuclear crisis. Whilst the "Agreed Framework" of 1994 and an historic and productive inter-Korean summit in 2000 fostered some hope for reconciliation between the two sides, heightened controversy since 2002 over North Korea's nuclear pro-

gramme has renewed tensions between the North and South. Future progress on this issue now hinges on the peaceful resolution of the nuclear issue and the success of the inter-Korean political process.

Korea and World War II—Korean War

During World War II the Allies agreed that, after the defeat of Japan, Korea would become independent (a nominally independent Korea having existed until the defeat of Russia by Japan in 1904-05, after which time Korea had become a Japanese protectorate and had been annexed by Japan in 1910). Under this agreement there was to be a temporary period of Allied control when the Soviet Union would take charge of the zone north of the 38°N parallel and the United States would take charge of the zone to the south of it. In addition, a mixed US-Soviet commission would set up a provisional Korean government representing all "democratic" parties and mass organizations.

In the event, however, post-war dispositions were made rather differently. In the northern zone, a provisional Communist government was set up in February 1946 under the authority of the Soviet occupation forces. In the South, unsuccessful negotiations concerning a possible unified government (in 1946-47) were followed by the establishment of a provisional Legislative Assembly dominated by the Representative Democratic Council (a right-wing nationalist coalition led by Dr Syngman Rhee). Following an initiative by the United States in 1947, the UN General Assembly resolved, against Soviet objections, that elections should be held under UN supervision throughout Korea. However, the UN supervision commission that was subsequently appointed was refused permission to enter North Korea in 1948. As a result, separate elections were held (under UN supervision) in the South only in May 1948, and the independent Republic of Korea (ROK) was established in August of that year.

Soviet forces withdrew from North Korea in December 1948 and US forces from South Korea in mid-1949. In June 1950, Soviet-equipped North Korean forces crossed the 38°N line in an attempt to conquer the South (which received US naval and air support) and almost succeeded in doing so. An appeal by the UN Security Council for the withdrawal of North Korea's forces was ignored, and the Security Council thereupon recommended (in the absence of the Soviet Union, which was then boycotting the Council) that UN member states should assist South Korea. As a result, 16 UN member states sent contingents to form a UN Command (UNC) under General Douglas MacArthur of the United States. The UN and South Korean forces, repelling those of North Korea, crossed the 38th parallel in September 1950. The People's Republic of China had earlier issued a warning that it would cross its boundary with North Korea (i.e. the Yalu river) if UN forces moved into North Korea so when, despite this warning, General MacArthur ordered a "final" offensive against the

North, China entered the war in October 1950 and drove the UN forces back into the South.

The war continued until 1953, when an armistice was concluded and a provisional boundary was agreed along a demilitarized zone (DMZ) mainly to the north of the 38th parallel, to be supervised by UN forces. This armistice line has remained the effective boundary between North and South Korea ever since. A joint Military Armistice Commission (MAC) consisting of representatives of the North Korean and the United Nations forces (the latter headed by a US officer) was established and thereafter held regular meetings in Panmunjom.

The armistice delineated the Military Demarcation Line (MDL) on land but there was disagreement over the location of a sea border. As a result, a sea border, the Northern Limit Line (NLL), was unilaterally demarcated by the UNC one month after the 1953 armistice and a buffer zone was created south of it to avoid armed clashes. North Korea has since claimed that it has never recognized this de facto border but the South argues that North Korea has demonstrated tacit recognition of the maritime demarcation line (e.g. by including a map marking the NLL in an annual published in 1959) despite repeatedly violating it.

Unsuccessful Proposals for Reunification, 1971-81

Proposals for talks on reunification were made by North Korea on April 12, 1971, but were rejected by South Korea. However, on July 4, 1972, it was announced that agreement had been reached that "peaceful unification of the fatherland" should be achieved "as early as possible"; that mutual hostile propaganda and armed provocation should cease; and that a North-South co-ordinating committee should be set up. Representatives of the two sides first met at Panmunjom on Oct. 12, 1972, and in November of that year they agreed to establish the proposed North-South co-ordinating committee, which held its first meeting on Nov. 30-Dec. 1, 1972. Further talks were, however, suspended in August 1973.

On June 23, 1973, the South Korean government issued a special foreign policy statement in which it said that it would not object to North Korea becoming a member of international organizations (jointly with South Korea) pending eventual unification. In a statement on Jan. 18, 1974, President Park Chung Hee of South Korea proposed the conclusion of a non-aggression pact between the two governments. At the same time he rejected earlier North Korean proposals for the withdrawal of foreign troops from all of Korea (in effect of the 40,000 US troops still remaining in South Korea), the reduction of each side's armed forces to 100,000 men, a ban on the introduction of foreign military equipment and the abolition of the armistice agreement. His proposal concerning a non-aggression pact, however, was rejected by North Korea on Jan. 26, 1974.

On Aug. 15, 1974, the South Korean government declared three basic principles for peaceful unification: (i) peace should be firmly established on the Korean peninsula; (ii) the two sides should open their doors to each other through constructive dialogue, exchanges and co-operation; and (iii) unification should be achieved through free general elections under fair management and in direct proportion to the indigenous population.

During 1974-75 a number of naval incidents occurred in which gunboats and fishing vessels of both sides were sunk; it was also found that North Korean forces had dug tunnels beneath the demilitarized zone. In an incident in the joint security zone around Panmunjom, two US officers were killed in fighting with North Korean soldiers on Aug. 5, 1976. Under an agreement reached on Sept. 6 of that year the joint security area was divided into two parts by the Military Demarcation Line (MDL), and guards were required to remain on their own side of the line.

On Jan. 12, 1977, President Park again proposed the conclusion of a non-aggression pact. His proposal was rejected by North Korea on Jan. 25, when North Korea demanded the unconditional withdrawal of US forces. On Jan. 1, 1979, President Park called for a resumption of talks between North and South Korea: three meetings were subsequently held between representatives of the two sides in February and March 1979 but revealed fundamental differences over the level at which talks should be held. A joint US-South Korean proposal for tripartite talks was rejected by North Korea on July 10, 1979.

On Jan. 12, 1980, the North Korean government, for the first time, acknowledged the South Korean government (which it had previously regarded as a "US puppet"). A new effort to revive talks between the two sides was begun in March 1980 and a number of meetings of representatives of both sides took place at Panmunjom. However, relations between North and South Korea then deteriorated sharply as a result of a number of incidents involving the infiltration of North Korean agents into the South and the sinking of naval vessels, leading to the placing on alert of the armies of both North and South Korea by June 25. Early in September 1980 the North Korean Army began to transmit broadcasts calling on the South Korean forces to overthrow President Chun Doo Hwan (who had succeeded President Park after the latter's assassination on Oct. 26, 1979).

On Aug. 11, 1980, it had been reported that North Korea had declared itself ready for peace talks with the United States (which had always refused to negotiate with North Korea without South Korean participation) without prior withdrawal of US troops. On Sept. 14 of that year President Kim Il Sung of North Korea stated that, if the US agreed to sign a peace treaty with North Korea, the latter would repudiate its military alliances with China and the Soviet Union and would not seek reunification with the South by military means. South Korea again proposed a renewal of the unification talks on Oct. 7, 1980.

President Kim Il Sung declared on Oct. 10, 1980, that the situation in Korea was so strained that there was "a constant danger of war breaking out at any moment" and that this danger could be removed only if the 1953 armistice agreement were replaced by a peace treaty with the United States. He proposed that the North and the South should be reunited as a confederal state in which each side would exercise regional autonomy and would retain its own ideology and social system without trying to impose them on the other. To this end, a "supreme national confederal assembly" should be formed, in which the North and the South would have an equal number of representatives, and should appoint a "confederal standing committee", which would decide on political affairs, defence, foreign affairs and other questions of common concern. Under this proposal, economic co-operation and exchanges between North and South would take place on the basis of a mutual recognition of differing economic systems; however, the northern and southern armies would be combined into a single national army.

These North Korean proposals were officially rejected by the South Korean government on Oct. 15, 1980. In a New Year broadcast published on Jan. 12, 1981, the South Korean President invited President Kim Il Sung to visit the South Korean capital "without any condition attached and free of any burden", adding that he was prepared to visit North Korea if invited; he also said that it was South Korea's paramount task to reunify the homeland into an independent and democratic state. In North Korea, however, the invitation was rejected on Jan. 19.

1982 Proposal for Reunification Conference— North Korean Rejection

In a New Year policy speech on Jan. 22, 1982, President Chun of South Korea put forward detailed proposals for reunification through a conference of representatives of both the South and the North, which would draw up a draft constitution. The South Korean National Assembly unanimously approved President Chun's proposals on Jan. 23, 1982, and adopted a resolution appealing to the North Korean government to respond favourably to this initiative and to third countries to support the proposals. North Korea rejected the proposals on Jan. 26, however, declaring that the only way of solving the reunification question was by the establishment of a confederal republic. Despite this hostile North Korean reaction, the South Korean Minister of National Unification, Sohn Jae Shik, put forward on Feb. 1, 1982, a list of projects for co-operation between the South and the North. These included the opening of a highway between Seoul and Pyongyang (the respective capitals of South and North Korea); permission for separated families to exchange mail and to meet; establishment of joint fishery and tourist zones; free travel through Panmunjom for overseas Koreans and foreigners; promotion of free trade; ending of "slanderous" broadcasts and jamming; encouragement of sports, cultural and economic exchanges; freedom for journalists to collect material; joint historical and scientific research; joint develop-

ment and use of natural resources; removal of all military facilities from the demilitarized zone; and establishment of a direct telephone link between the military authorities on each side.

The North Korean Committee for the Peaceful Reunification of the Fatherland put forward alternative proposals on Feb. 10, 1982, for a conference of 50 political figures from the North and 50 from the South, which would discuss all possible proposals for reunification. It also published a list of the proposed participants in the conference—the 50 from the South included well-known opposition figures, but no representatives of any existing parties. The proposal was summarily rejected by the South.

During the above exchanges between North and South Korea, numerous incidents continued to occur in the border region and at sea. These incidents included the shooting of alleged Northern infiltrators in South Korea, the sinking of alleged South Korean spy ships, and the seizure of South Korean fishing boats by North Korean patrol boats. (In 1982 South Korean sources stated that since 1953 a total of 453 South Korean fishing boats and 3,554 fishermen had been abducted, although most of these had later been returned.)

1983 Rangoon Bomb Episode—North Korean Reunification Proposals of 1984

Relations between North and South Korea deteriorated seriously as a result of a bomb explosion in Rangoon (Burma) on Oct. 9, 1983, when 21 people were killed, including four visiting South Korean government ministers. It was widely believed that the intention had been to kill President Chun Doo Hwan of South Korea, who arrived on the scene several minutes later. The Burmese government announced on Nov. 4 that the bomb had been planted by North Korean army captains, and that Burma was breaking off its diplomatic relations with North Korea. On Dec. 9, 1983, two North Korean army officers were condemned to death in Rangoon for their part in the bombing.

Notwithstanding the Rangoon episode, the North Korean government renewed its appeal for the "peaceful reunification" of the Korean peninsula when a joint session of the Supreme People's Assembly and the Central People's Committee in Pyongyang approved proposals on Jan. 10, 1984, for "tripartite talks" on this issue with the United States and South Korea, to be held at Panmunjom or in a mutually acceptable third country. The North Korean government asserted that its proposals were a response to the mounting danger of nuclear war on the Korean peninsula, for which it blamed the United States and South Korea, claiming that their aggressive military policies had incited a "war atmosphere" in which "South Korea had become a US powder keg for nuclear war and a nuclear-attack base aimed at the northern half of the Republic". The statement alleged that the USA had already stationed about 1,000 nuclear weapons in South Korea and that in addition it intended to deploy Pershing II and cruise missiles as well as neutron bombs.

The South Korean government demanded an acknowledgement and apology for the Rangoon incident. It renewed its call for bipartite talks between the "highest authorities" of South and North Korea, but also said that the South Korean government would be interested in an "enlarged meeting" at some future date. The South Korean government subsequently offered (on Feb. 9, 1984) to meet North Korean representatives directly to present its official reply to the North's proposals for tripartite talks. This meeting took place at the level of officials, on Feb. 14 at Panmunjom, when a letter was delivered from the South Korean Prime Minister to his North Korean counterpart. The letter proposed a summit between North and South Korea which could later be expanded to include the United States, China, the Soviet Union and Japan. During the eight-minute exchange the South Korean representatives proposed the resumption of the telephone "hot line" between Seoul and Pyongyang, but the North Korean officials refused to discuss the issue at that meeting. (The telephone "hot line" had been reopened on Feb. 6, 1980, after a three-year break, but had been cut off by the North Koreans on Sept. 25, 1980.)

Talks on possible economic co-operation held by North and South Korean delegations between May 17 and Nov. 20, 1985, remained inconclusive. Inter-parliamentary talks between the two sides, held between July 23 and Sept. 25, 1985, on the formation of a consultative body to discuss the reunification of Korea led to no agreement on procedure, with the North Koreans proposing the drafting of a constitution for a united Korea, and the South Koreans insisting that a non-aggression pact should be the first step.

Red Cross Negotiations—Sports Meetings

A delegation of the North Korean Red Cross Society had visited Seoul between Aug. 30, 1972, and July 13, 1973, when it was agreed (i) to seek to ascertain the whereabouts and fate of dispersed Korean people (estimated at about 10,000,000); (ii) to facilitate free mutual meetings and visits; (iii) to facilitate free postal exchanges; (iv) to facilitate the reunion of dispersed people according to their wishes; and (v) to discuss other humanitarian issues. However, further Red Cross talks on the reunification of families separated in the war, held in December 1977, had failed to lead to any agreement.

The first new Red Cross meeting was held on Sept. 18, 1984, and discussed details of a flood relief offer made to South Korea by North Korea's Red Cross Society. Such operations were subsequently completed by Oct. 7, 1984. The North Koreans thereupon suggested the reopening of talks on the reunion of separated families, and at a meeting at Panmunjom held on Nov. 20, 1984, it was agreed to adopt the five-point agenda of 1972-73 [see above]. However, the proposed talks were postponed indefinitely on Jan. 9, 1985, following controversy over a South Korean announcement that annual military exercises of South Korean and US forces would begin on Feb. 1, 1985.

A further visit to Seoul was nevertheless paid by a North Korean Red Cross delegation on May 28-30, 1985, when it was agreed in principle with the South Korean Red Cross Society that there would be an exchange of groups of family members, reciprocal cultural visits and (on a North Korean proposal) "free travel across the demilitarized zone". Detailed agreements in these fields were reached at Panmunjom on July 15 and Aug. 22, 1985. Further discussions followed when a South Korean Red Cross delegation visited Pyongyang between Aug. 27 and Sept. 22, 1985. However, later talks held in Seoul on Dec. 3-4, 1985, ended in disagreement when the South Koreans rejected a North Korean suggestion of free border crossings for people in search of family members (on the ground that this would lead to attempts to "infiltrate trained political agents" into the South), while the North Koreans would not agree to an exchange of letters between family members.

From October 1985 talks were held between representatives of North and South Korea and the International Olympic Committee (IOC) in Switzerland to discuss the question of North Korea's participation in the 24th Olympic Games to be held in Seoul in 1988 and in particular its demand that the events be co-hosted between Pyongyang and Seoul. Whereas South Korea initially took the view that such a division would be a violation of the Olympic Charter, the IOC subsequently put forward proposals for a limited number of events to be held in the North. The 10th Asian Games held in Seoul in September-October 1986 were boycotted by the North because of their alleged "impure political aims".

Deterioration of Relations in 1986—New Initiative by the North

On Jan. 20, 1986, North Korea announced that it was suspending all negotiations with the South, in protest against the South Korean announcement, on Jan. 18, that the annual "Team Spirit" joint military exercises with US forces would go ahead the following month. On April 24, 1986, the North said negotiations would only be resumed if the South indicated a change in its attitude towards future military exercises and displayed greater tolerance of its internal dissidents. On the same day a South Korean warship sank a North Korean vessel which had allegedly opened fire when challenged but which the North claimed was an unarmed trawler.

A further source of tension during 1986 was the proposed construction of the Kumgangsan hydroelectric dam on a northern tributary of the Han river about 10 kilometres north of the demilitarized zone. On Nov. 6, 1986, the South Korean Defence Minister warned that his country would be forced to take "self-defence measures" unless work on the dam ceased immediately, claiming that it would have a storage capacity of up to 20,000 million tonnes of water which, if released, would submerge much of Korea, including Seoul. The South Korean figures and analysis were subsequently contested by the North, but the South announced on Nov. 26 that work was to begin immediately on a dam of equal size to protect Seoul against the possibility of flooding from the North.

Addressing the North Korean Supreme People's Assembly on Dec. 29, 1986, President Kim Il Sung asserted that the "peaceful reunification of the country" constituted "the most urgent task" currently facing his government. He went on to call for the "founding of a confederal state which would make neither side the conqueror or the conquered" as the long-term solution to the division of the country, and proposed that a joint conference should be established to facilitate "a national dialogue" between the ruling parties and other representative organizations of the North and the South. In January 1987 North Korean ministers followed up the President's initiative by proposing that high-level political and military negotiations should begin forthwith in an effort "to achieve a breakthrough for peace and peaceful reunification".

In response, the South Korean government on Jan. 12, 1987, reiterated its position of rejecting the creation of new channels of communication while those previously set up remained inoperative. President Chun did, however, indicate that he was prepared to have a summit meeting with President Kim in the course of 1987.

Any possibility of such a meeting disappeared, however, when a South Korean airliner was destroyed over Burma in November 1987 by a bomb planted by two North Korean agents. All 115 passengers and crew were killed and—although the North Korean government denied all prior knowledge of the attack—one of the saboteurs, Kim Hyon Hui, was captured and confessed to having planted the bomb on the orders of Kim Il Sung's son, Kim Jong Il. Kim Hyon Hui's public confession and subsequent trial in South Korea inflamed public opinion in a manner reminiscent of the period following the Rangoon bombing. Relations remained frozen in the run-up to the Olympic Games in Seoul in September 1988, the freeze destroying any prospect of the North sharing some aspects of the Games, or of participation by a joint Korean team.

Resumption of Dialogue

The freeze on all official channels of communication ended on Aug. 19, 1988, just before the opening of the Games, when delegations from the legislatures of the North and the South met in Panmunjom to discuss the proposed inter-parliamentary meeting. Although the talks made no progress and North Korea boycotted the Games, the symbolic importance of the meeting in marking a resumption of dialogue was considerable. The dynamic for this resumption came in large measure from the new South Korean President, Roh Tae

Woo, who had been inaugurated in February 1988. Not merely was Roh more imaginative and flexible than his predecessors, he was also under increasing pressure to wrest the initiative in the sphere of North-South relations away from student radicals who, still flushed from their success in bringing down the Fifth Republic, were keen to force a reconciliation with North Korea. Upon becoming president, one of Roh's first acts was to remove responsibility for the formulation of policy towards North Korea away from the Agency for National Security Planning (formerly the Korean Central Intelligence Agency) to a newly-created presidential think-tank.

During 1988, despite the freeze in relations and the legacy of ill will stemming from the bombing of the airliner, Roh held open the possibility of joint Korean participation in the Olympics. On July 7, he made a major policy speech in which he reiterated the importance of achieving Korean reunification and outlined a six-point plan to achieve this. The plan included (i) the encouragement of exchange visits between the two states; (ii) the facilitation of greater contact by members of families divided within the Korean peninsula; (iii) the removal of obstacles to inter-Korean trade; (iv) the ending of South Korea's opposition to the North establishing trading relations with South Korea's allies; (v) the ending of diplomatic rivalry, and the initiation of attempts to reduce the North's level of international isolation; and (vi) the improvement of the South's relationship with the Soviet Union and China, and the improvement of the North's relationship with the USA and Japan. On Aug. 15 he also suggested holding a summit between himself and Kim Il Sung, an initiative which received a positive but guarded response from the veteran communist leader.

Nevertheless, the Roh government continued to use force to prevent the students from taking matters into their own hands. A planned rendezvous of Northern and Southern students at Panmunjom on Aug. 15 was prevented by the mobilization of massive South Korean security forces and the arrest of at least 1,200 students in the week preceding the planned meeting.

Following the resumption of dialogue on Aug. 19, there were six further rounds of preparatory inter-parliamentary talks before the end of the year, but the process appeared to be unlikely to bear fruit. In January 1989, Roh renewed his call for a summit meeting with Kim. In the same month the two sides agreed to hold talks at premier level, alternating between Seoul and Pyongyang. Preparatory talks to agree upon the details of the Premiers' talks began in February, but became immediately stalled because of the South's refusal to cancel the Team Spirit exercise. In March the Olympic committees of the two states also agreed to begin negotiations on the creation of a joint Korean team for the Asian Games in Beijing in 1990.

The holding of Team Spirit, together with the trial in Seoul of saboteur Kim Hyon Hui, and the prosecution of the Rev Moon Ik Hwan—a Presbyterian minister who had made an unauthorized trip to North Korea for which he received a 10-year prison sentence—all served to sour relations between the two states. Tension was also caused by the South's prohibition on its citizens attending the 13th World Youth and Student Festival, in Pyongyang, on July 1-9. Although the festivities were attended by 15,000 representatives from 180 countries, including a 91-member delegation from the USA, the South Korean government once again used massive force to prevent attempts by students to attend the event.

The six-month freeze in relations thawed in September when Roh outlined a proposal for a Korean commonwealth—based upon self-determination, peace, democracy, and joint North-South state structures—which was designed to serve as a transition towards full reunification. Roh also repeated his call for a presidential summit in order to "open an era of fully fledged inter-Korean co-operation and unification". Kim Il Sung responded to the initiative by claiming that Roh's plan would perpetuate the current division of the Korean peninsula. Instead, Kim called for a bilateral consultative conference to discuss the 1980 suggestion of a confederal state. This was dismissed by the South as containing nothing new.

This exchange of proposals marked the beginning of an improvement in relations between the two Korean states. Although several channels of communication were reopened during October, little progress was achieved. The preliminary negotiations to prepare for the Premiers' talks, postponed since March, were resumed on Oct. 12. The negotiations continued until the end of the year but made little progress. Also, a preparatory meeting between North and South Korean Red Cross officials on Oct. 16 agreed in principle to allow an exchange visit by members of families divided between the two Korean states. The planned visit, scheduled for Dec. 8, promised only the second such exchange since the end of the Korean War. Although agreement was reached over the criteria for selecting the family members, the talks collapsed in November over peripheral details.

North-South sports talks, designed to create a joint Korean sports team to compete in the 11th Asian games, resumed on Oct. 20 after almost seven months. The delegates reached agreement on the colour of the team's flag, but not the name under which the team should compete. They continued until the end of the year, but progress remained intangible. The talks regarding the establishment of a joint legislative meeting were also resumed on Oct. 25 after a 10-month suspension. Familiar obstacles, however, including the North's condemnation of the Team Spirit military exercises and South Korean judicial action against dissidents making unauthorised visits to the North, meant that little progress was achieved, although they continued until the end of the year.

A further aspect of Roh's strategy of dealing with the North began to emerge in 1989 with the improvement in relations between South Korea and communist countries which had hitherto been clearly aligned with the North. Trade agreements and aid packages bore immediate fruit with the establishment of full diplomatic relations with both Hungary and Poland. A series of similar successes were recorded in 1990, including the establishment of full diplomatic relations with the Soviet Union.

Progress During 1990

Kim Il Sung called in his 1990 New Year national address for freedom of movement between the two Korean states. To this end he proposed that representatives from the two states hold "top-level" talks on dismantling the barriers within the heavily fortified Demilitarized Zone (DMZ). Roh "welcomed" Kim's proposals and repeated an earlier invitation for the two leaders to meet "as quickly as possible". He also revealed that, as a gesture of goodwill, the annual Team Spirit military exercises between South Korea and the USA would be reduced in size and duration and would be accompanied by invitations to North Korea, China and the Soviet Union to send military observers. Roh also suggested that, as a first step towards free movement, the two countries should allow exchanges of letters and telephone calls by displaced persons and divided families, and should immediately allow visits by those over 60 years old.

Notwithstanding these initiatives by the two Presidents, there was no progress during January 1990 within any of the established channels of inter-Korean communication. The approach of the 1990 Team Spirit exercise, and South Korea's refusal to accede to the North's demands that it be cancelled, once again had the effect of freezing all contact. However, the enormous changes in Eastern Europe, together with the continuing success of Roh's policy of reconciliation with communist and former communist states, increased North Korea's international isolation and had the effect of pushing the North towards an early resumption of dialogue with the South. An initiative from the North in late June led to the arrangement of a seventh round of preliminary talks to organize a joint Premiers' meeting and a further round of talks over the proposed inter-parliamentary meeting. Although the legislative talks were cancelled by the North before taking place, the Premiers' talks began to bear fruit. After further contacts it was agreed at the eighth preliminary meeting, on July 26, that the Premiers should meet on Sept. 4-7, with a further session of talks to be held in Pyongyang from Oct. 16-19.

A further unexpected Northern initiative occurred on July 5, when it was announced that the northern side of the border at Panmunjom would be opened from Aug. 15 in an attempt to encourage contacts between the two countries. Initially the South responded cautiously to the Northern invitation to reciprocate. Nevertheless, President Roh welcomed the recent progress in relations between the two states and, on July 6, suggested that he expected to see Korean reunification achieved within five years. During a televised national address on July 20, Roh announced that his government would open the border at Panmunjom for five days from Aug. 13 and allow unrestricted crossings, although a government spokesman later suggested that the country's leading dissidents would not be permitted to travel to the North. The response of the North was to suggest that Roh's gesture would be considered sincere only if it was accompanied by the removal of certain border defences and the abolition of the National Security Law (which prohibited unauthorized visits to the North). Further proposals and counter-proposals failed to produce any agreement on the border-opening issue.

In early August more than 61,000 South Korean citizens, many of whom had relatives in North Korea, applied for permission to visit the North during the period that the border was to be open. The South Korean authorities insisted that the North Korean government should accept the full list of names and guarantee the safe return of all who made the trip. The North stated that it would only accept the list of visitors if the South met three preconditions. These were (i) the abolition of the draconian National Security Law relating to sedition and espionage; (ii) admission of a North Korean "consolation" delegation to visit three South Korean dissidents jailed under the National Security Law for having made unauthorized visits to the North; and (iii) the authorization of South Korean dissidents to attend a pro-unification rally due to be held in Panmunjom on Aug. 15. A South Korean government spokesman described the preconditions as "absolutely preposterous and unacceptable".

South Korea made an eleventh-hour concession on Aug. 12 by suggesting that the North might be permitted to select only those whom it wished to receive from the 61,000 names on the list. Nevertheless, on Aug. 13 the North Koreans failed to attend a meeting arranged by the South to hand over the list. Therefore, although the South established "an international port of entry" on the southern bank of the Injim river—complete with immigration control and currency exchange facilities—not a single person was permitted to cross the border in either direction during the entire five-day period.

Meeting of North and South Korean Premiers

The border-opening debacle, and the wave of mutual recrimination which it engendered, appeared to threaten the tentative agreement to hold the first ever summit between the premiers of the two Korean states in Seoul on Sept. 4-7. On Aug. 30, however, a meeting in Panmunjom agreed the final procedural details and the Premiers' talks went ahead as scheduled. Yon Hyong Muk led a delegation of seven senior North Korean officials for the unprecedented three-day official visit to South Korea on Sept. 4-7. It was the highest level of direct contact between the two Korean states since their formation, and was the first official border crossing since December 1985. During the course of the visit the group had several sessions of talks with seven senior South Koreans, including Kang Young Hoon, the South Korean Prime Minister.

Whilst each side recognized the growing demand of the Korean people for reunification, the means through which this was to be achieved remained elusive. However, during the two days of talks the Prime Ministers each presented proposals for easing political and military tensions within the Korean peninsula. Kang restated the South's belief in securing a gradual improvement in bilateral relations through the promotion of confidence-building measures including multi-level exchanges and various forms of co-operation between the two states. These included the fostering of economic co-operation through agreements which would encourage freer travel (particularly for members of divided families), communications and trade, and through the establishment of a joint economic co-operation organization. Political confidence would be instilled through each side ceasing its propaganda efforts and undertaking to recognize and respect the political and social systems of the other until such time as reunification was achieved. In the military sphere, Kang suggested the exchange of military personnel and information, the notification of significant troop movements and the establishment of a "hot-line" telecommunications link between the Defence Ministers of the two states.

The North's proposals concentrated upon reducing military and political confrontation as a prerequisite to achieving improvements in the economic, cultural or social spheres. Yon reiterated the proposal for an arms control agreement between the two states which would involve a three-phased troop reduction programme based upon the cutting of the standing army of each side to fewer than 10,000 men within three or four years. The agreement would also involve the withdrawal of the 43,000 US forces stationed in South Korea and the removal of nuclear weapons from the Korean peninsula. The North Korean Premier also proposed the installation of a communications link between the two sides' military commands, the formation of a joint military group to discuss border disputes and the provision for on-site inspections to ensure that the arms agreement was observed. The North's willingness to accept a phased withdrawal of US troops from the South marked an apparent departure from its previous insistence upon their immediate removal. Nevertheless, Yon reiterated his government's oft-stated demand for negotiations with the USA alone in order to replace the current armistice agreement with a full peace treaty to end the Korean War. This demand remained a precondition for the North agreeing to a non-aggression declaration with the South.

Furthermore, Yon outlined three preconditions for the successful pursuit of inter-Korean dialogue. These were the release of South Korean dissidents imprisoned for making unauthorized visits to the North; a termination of the annual South Korean-US Team Spirit military exercises; and an end to the South's attempts to achieve unilateral entry to the United Nations. Although the South did not make an official response to the preconditions—all of which it had rejected in the past—it did agree to suspend its pursuit of membership of the United Nations until the two

Korean states had discussed the issue further. A meeting duly took place on Sept. 18 at Panmunjom, at which the North put forward its advocacy of a single UN seat in order to avoid cementing the country's temporary division. The South Korean negotiators dubbed this proposal "unrealistic and unworkable" and reiterated their call for simultaneous entry to the UN by both Korean states.

Although no agreement was reached, the Prime Ministers agreed to proceed with the second round of scheduled discussions in Pyongyang on Oct. 16-19. This too produced little tangible progress, with the Southern delegation again demanding the agreement of inter-Korean reconciliation measures, including telephone and mail links, freer travel and economic exchanges and co-operation, whilst the Northern delegation insisted upon a joint non-aggression declaration and a commitment to disarmament. The question of UN membership also continued to be divisive. The talks ended without agreement upon a joint statement, with each side adhering to its previously outlined position. Nevertheless, it was agreed to hold a further session of talks in Seoul on Dec. 11-14.

During the course of his visit to the North, Yon had a meeting with Kim Il Sung, who suggested that he wished to hold an early meeting with Roh, but that this would be dependent upon the Premiers' talks yielding "visible results". A presidential summit, claimed Kim, "should be an encounter that produces good results; if there is no outcome it will disappoint the people".

The third round of talks in Seoul, on Dec. 11-14, was held in an atmosphere that was more markedly hostile than at the previous two meetings. Yon proposed signing a 10-point Declaration of Non-aggression and Reconciliation, which incorporated the North's previous insistence upon a non-aggression agreement with the South's demand for confidence-building measures such as freedom of travel between the two Koreas, the restoration of communications and co-operation in economic and technical spheres. Yon also reiterated the North's demand for the suspension of the annual South Korean-US Team Spirit military exercise, the release of those imprisoned for making unauthorized visits to North Korea, and the abandonment of South Korea's aspirations for separate membership of the UN. Kang rejected the draft document, proposing instead the acceptance of a 10-point Basic Agreement on Inter-Korean Relations—which concentrated upon the achievement of basic confidence-building measures— as a prelude to the negotiation of a non-aggression agreement. The mood of the meeting was also adversely affected by President Roh's forthcoming trip to the Soviet Union, and by a series of confrontations involving journalists in the Northern delegation who made unauthorized visits to several of Seoul's universities where they met with student radicals.

Deterioration of Relations in early 1991

Relations between the two countries deteriorated in early 1991 against the background of the Gulf War and the approach of the 1991 Team Spirit exercise. On Feb. 4, Roh placed South Korea's armed forces on maximum alert, stating that the preoccupation of the USA with the Gulf War meant that "the possibility of North Korean provocation is higher than ever before". Roh alleged that North Korea had positioned Scud missiles along the Demilitarized Zone. On Feb. 26 the Supreme Command of the North Korean army ordered a full mobilization of its forces as "a legitimate step to cope with the new war provocation moves of the United States and the South Korean authorities". The move was interpreted more as a mechanism for displaying the North's disapproval of the decision to proceed with Team Spirit, than as a direct response to South Korea's military alert.

The 1991 exercise, which was due to involve 140,000 troops and to last for 10 days starting on March 11, was the smallest ever to have been held. Nevertheless, the North claimed that it rendered the climate for the talks unsuitable, and on Feb. 18 suspended the fourth round of the Premiers' talks scheduled for Pyongyang on Feb. 25-28.

The dialogue was resumed following a statement by the South Korean Foreign Ministry on July 1 which departed from its previous position by announcing that it was willing to discuss nuclear non-proliferation with the North. Whilst reiterating that the demand for international inspections of North Korea's nuclear facilities could not be linked to other issues, the government stated its willingness to discuss the nuclear issue "for the purposes of reducing tension and building confidence". There followed, on July 11, an invitation from the North to resume the suspended Premiers' talks in Pyongyang on Aug. 27. (It was again postponed by the North, ostensibly on the grounds of a cholera outbreak in the South, but eventually went ahead in October.) The invitation was one of several encouraging initiatives during July.

On July 12, Roh reiterated previous calls for the negotiation of a non-aggression declaration and a peace treaty between the two states. As a prelude to eventual reunification, he also proposed increased social and cultural contacts including the exchange of radio and television broadcasts. On July 15 both countries issued specific proposals designed to increase cultural contacts. A further sign of improving relations was apparent in July when a South Korean ship laden with 5,000 tonnes of rice left the port of Mokpo on July 27 en route to the North Korean port of Najin, which marked the first direct trading contact between the two Korean states since the Korean War.

Both Koreas Join the United Nations

In early July 1991 North Korea also made a volte face by applying for membership of the UN. The North's policy revision, announced in May, followed a visit to North Korea by Chinese Premier Li Peng, and was widely interpreted as having been motivated by Li's insistence that China would not use its Security Council veto to block South Korea's application for membership. In early August South Korea made a similar application. Both states were admitted at the start of the General Assembly session in New York on Sept. 17.

Signing of Non-Aggression Accord

At the fourth round of Premiers' talks on Oct. 22-25, 1991, the two Prime Ministers agreed in principle to draw up an agreement which would contain a non-aggression declaration, together with measures for reconciliation and the promotion of exchanges and economic co-operation. The details of the accord were agreed at the fifth round of talks in Seoul, on Dec. 10-13, and the "Agreement on Reconciliation, Non-aggression, and Exchanges and Co-operation between the South and the North", was signed on Dec. 13, 1991, by South Korean Prime Minister Chung Won Shik and his Northern counterpart Yon Hyong Muk. The accord represented the most dramatic improvement in relations between North and South since the end of the Korean War, for although the two states remained technically in a state of war, the agreement laid a realistic foundation for the negotiation of a full peace treaty.

The accord contained 25 articles arranged under the following sub-headings:

North-South reconciliation: each state agreed to recognize and respect the other, including their respective political and social systems. Each pledged to desist from slander, vilification and acts of sabotage. Both countries agreed to work towards a peace treaty to replace the 1953 armistice agreement. It was also agreed to establish a North-South Liaison Office at Panmunjom within three months.

North-South non-aggression: both countries committed themselves not to attack or invade the other, and to resolve disputes through a process of dialogue. It was agreed to create a joint military committee and establish a direct telephone hotline between the two military commands. Amongst the confidence-building measures to be discussed and promoted by the joint committee were the exchange of military information, prior notification of major troop movements, and arms reduction, including the removal of weapons of mass destruction.

North-South Co-operation and Exchange: both sides agreed to encourage economic discussion, including the joint development of resources, and participation in joint industrial and commercial ventures. It was agreed to exchange information in various fields including science, culture, news and sport. Both sides undertook to promote reunification measures including allowing inter-Korean travel, postal and telecommunications contacts.

Negotiation of Nuclear Weapons Ban— Developments in 1992

The main omission from the non-aggression accord concerned the issue of nuclear weapons. Although these were obliquely referred to under the article dealing with confidence-building measures, the longstanding Northern demand that the South renounce the US nuclear weapons based on its soil was not addressed, nor was the more recent Western demand that North Korea allow international inspection of its nuclear facilities. Shortly before signing the non-aggression accord, however, the two sides announced that they would hold a meeting at Panmunjom on Dec. 26, in order to discuss the issue of nuclear weapons on the Korean peninsula.

The climate for an agreement on nuclear weapons had been improved by a number of developments in the three months prior to December. US President George Bush had authorized the removal of US nuclear artillery shells and bombs in late September and mid-October respectively, although the timing of the withdrawal remained unclear. This was followed by an announcement on Nov. 8 from Roh renouncing the manufacture, possession and use of nuclear or chemical weapons. Roh called on North Korea to follow a similar course. Pressure on North Korea was increased when it was announced in mid-November that concern over the North's nuclear programme was such that the ongoing process of the reduction of US troops based in South Korea was to be halted indefinitely. On Nov. 25, the North Korean government declared that it would sign an agreement permitting international inspection of its nuclear facilities once the United States had begun withdrawing its nuclear weapons. (Although North Korea had signed the Nuclear Non-Proliferation Treaty in 1985, it had failed in its obligation to sign an inspection accord within the following 18 months.)

Prime Minister Chung announced on Dec. 11 that all US atomic weapons had been removed from South Korean soil, and offered to open US military bases to inspection by the North on condition that the North permitted simultaneous inspection of its own nuclear facilities. Following the signing of the non-aggression accord, Roh stated in a televised speech that "there do not exist any nuclear weapons whatsoever anywhere in the Republic of Korea". He called upon the North to close its nuclear reprocessing and enrichment facilities and to submit its nuclear programme to international inspection.

Against this background, the Panmunjom talks began on Dec. 26, and on Dec. 31 the two sides agreed a six-article document under which both countries committed themselves not to "test, manufacture, produce, accept, possess, store, deploy or use nuclear weapons". Both also banned the development of nuclear reprocessing and uranium enrichment facilities. A joint committee was empowered to draw up a plan for mutual inspections.

During the fifth Premiers' talks there were also strong rumours that arrangements had been discussed for a summit meeting between Presidents Roh and Kim in 1992. The rumours were reinforced in mid-December when Roh suggested that, as "a basic framework on inter-Korean relations had been set", then "summit talks will be held earlier than had been expected".

The thaw continued in early 1992 and the North Korean government finally chose to sign an International Atomic Energy Agency (IAEA) nuclear Safeguards Accord, which allowed international inspection of its nuclear facilities, on Jan. 30. The agreement was signed at the IAEA headquarters in Vienna by Hong Sun Pyo, North Korea's Deputy Nuclear Energy Minister, and Hans Blix, the IAEA director general, and it was ratified by North Korea on April 9, 1992.

Initial co-operation with the IAEA by North Korea in April 1992 raised a number of questions about the North's nuclear installations when a report from Pyongyang detailing its nuclear installations disclosed previously unsuspected sites. Although IAEA delegations were received by the North throughout the year, officials did not co-operate fully with the agency and inspectors were given only limited access to a small number of sites, drawing particular criticism from Japan and the USA. The nuclear issue was a significant stumbling block for inter-Korean relations and the dialogue, begun in 1991, which had generated some hope for progress between the two powers came to a halt in late 1992.

A seventh round of Prime Ministers' talks was held in May 1992 and the two parties reached basic agreement over the establishment of liaison offices at Panmunjom, the establishment of three joint commissions to carry out the reconciliation act and an exchange of visits between citizens over 50 to mark National Liberation Day on Aug. 15. However, further progress was hindered by disagreement over the details of these plans and the issue of nuclear inspections overshadowed proceedings. In the June rounds of North-South Red Cross working delegates, the parties attempted to reach agreement over numbers of participants and the duration of reunion exchange visits for separated families. (Later the South's Vice Unification Minister, Yim Tong-won, was to urge North Korea to withdraw various attached prerequisites to a home-town visitors exchange programme, dubbing them "unreasonable" demands and asking that the North show a "sincere humanitarian posture" towards family reunions.) The talks stalled as South Korea continued to pressure the North to accept mutual inspection of nuclear capabilities intimating that any further delay might hinder progress in relations between the two countries. The South accused the North of delaying tactics and in return the North made it clear that further co-operation between the two sides would be contingent on a change of attitude by the South over the nuclear issue.

Despite the ever-present tension over the nuclear issue, talks between the two states over the summer of 1992 yielded agreement in some sectors. Prime Minister Chong Wonsik of South Korea suggested a joint ecological survey of the DMZ, in close collaboration with the UN Environment Programme (UNEP), and the North responded positively. The two sides also agreed on chapter one of the proposed auxiliary agreement, "Economic Exchanges and Co-operation". This covered guarantees of free economic activities for each side in one another's territory; protection of the other side's patent and trade mark rights; linking of railways and roads; and promotion of measures for joint efforts abroad in the economic area. The September prime ministerial talks were also relatively successful and a number of minor agreements were signed.

By the end of the year, however, the North-South dialogue had all but ceased. In October 1992, the South Korean Agency for National Security arrested 62 people—some of whom were said to have links with South Korean opposition groups—for spying offences. South Korea cancelled a planned visit to the North by its Deputy Prime Minister and the North cancelled the ninth round of Premiers' talks scheduled for December. In protest at North Korea's non-agreement over mutual inspection, the USA and South Korea announced that they would resume the Team Spirit military exercise in 1993. This move was denounced by North Korea as "nuclear blackmail" and the 12th meeting of the Joint Nuclear Control Committee in Panmunjom was dominated by discussion of this decision. In early 1993, the situation on the Korean peninsula was to worsen further.

1993-94: Nuclear Crisis on the Korean Peninsula

In January 1993, North Korea refused an IAEA request to inspect certain sealed sites at Yongbyon, arguing that the sites were military installations and not nuclear sites. This refusal fuelled speculation that the North had hidden some parts of its nuclear programme. The North denied that it had been or was developing nuclear weapons and reacted to the IAEA demands by announcing its withdrawal from the Nuclear Non-Proliferation Treaty (NPT) on March 12 (to be effective on June 12). This dramatic action dealt a further blow to North-South relations and prompted the USA to initiate direct talks with North Korea. A series of meetings took place between US Assistant Secretary of State Robert Galluci and the North Korean Vice-Foreign Minister, Kang Sok Chu, and resulted in last minute agreement in June when North Korea agreed to suspend its withdrawal from the NPT in return for further talks with the USA.

Strained relations between North and South Korea were put under further pressure by a number of incidents in the DMZ in May-June 1993. The United Nations Military Armistice Commission (MAC) sent a team to investigate two incidents of North Korean gunfire into the DMZ. North Korea also reported two occasions over the same period when South Korea was said to have fired on a North Korean civil police post inside the DMZ. North Korea accused South Korea of a naval incursion by three warships into North Korean waters with the intention of seizing Northern fishing boats, deeming it an act of "military provocation".

By December 1993, the USA had succeeded in getting the North to agree to allow the resumption of some IAEA nuclear inspections and to the reopening of contacts with South Korea, in return for the cancellation of the Team Spirit exercises and the continuation of talks with the USA. This agreement was not to last, however, as by March 1994 North Korea was refusing to allow the IAEA full access to its nuclear sites and this led the agency to declare the North in non-compliance with its NPT obligations. The situation on the Korean peninsula deteriorated further when, on June 14, North Korea informed the UN Security Council that it was withdrawing from the IAEA.

As the nuclear crisis continued, North-South relations worsened. North Korea responded to threats of sanctions by claiming that their application would be tantamount to an act of war, and that it would reduce Seoul to a "sea of flames". North Korea continued to push for a peace treaty with the United States to replace the 1953 armistice agreement and in May 1994 announced its withdrawal from the Military Armistice Commission. This prompted concern in the South but the USA insisted that the MAC was still in existence and sent assurances to the South that the USA would continue to deal with Pyongyang through this machinery only. A series of US diplomatic interventions, including talks between former US President Jimmy Carter and Kim Il Sung, defused the situation and an historic presidential summit between the leaders of North and South Korea was planned for July 25-27.

Talks were under way to arrange the details of the auspicious meeting when Kim Il Sung died. When the South failed to send condolences to the North this was condemned by North Korea and the discussions collapsed.

The 1994 "Agreed Framework"—Developments 1995-96

In spite of the North-South freeze, North Korea continued its discussions with the USA throughout 1994, these resulting in the "Agreed Framework" of Oct. 21, 1994. This set out that the North Koreans were to receive two light-water reactors (LWRs), assistance with other energy supplies, and normalization of relations with the USA. In return, North Korea agreed to rejoin the IAEA, freeze all work on its current nuclear programme, dismantle its existing reactors, open all its nuclear facilities to inspection after several years, and engage in North-South dialogue. An international body, the Korean Energy Development Organization (KEDO), was to be set up to arrange the financing and supply of the new technology to North Korea.

Early implementation of the agreed package was successful but stalled when North Korea refused to accept that the LWRs would come from South Korea. US and North Korean negotiators met for three weeks in Kuala Lumpur, Malaysia, and on June 12, 1995, finally reached an accord resolving this issue. On Dec. 15, 1995, KEDO and North Korea signed the Light Water Reactor Supply Agreement.

Reunification efforts moved no further forward in 1995-96. North Korea continued to undermine the 1953 armistice agreement and in February 1995, the Polish Neutral Nations Supervisory Commission (NNSC) delegation, part of the MAC machinery, withdrew from Panmunjom after North Korean coercion. There were some minor proposals for co-operative activity between the two sides in 1995, including the creation of a joint university campus near the DMZ between universities from the North and South and the construction of a railway which would link the Koreas via China and Russia to Rotterdam in Europe. However, the general relationship between the two sides remained strained and North Korean allegations of South Korean naval incursions into its waters and South Korean protestations at the apparent military build-up in the North led to strong verbal exchanges between Seoul and Pyongyang.

The following year, in February 1996, North Korea proposed a revision of the armistice, suggesting instead that a "tentative agreement" should be signed between the North and the USA to "deter armed conflict" and maintain the armistice. This was to include systems to manage the Military Demarcation Line (MDL) and DMZ, "ways to resolve armed conflict and accidents" and a joint military commission, similar to the joint Korean body already functioning. The North also suggested replacing the MAC in Panmunjom with a new body and proposed that the new agreement would replace the present one until a permanent peace deal could be reached. This proposal, however, was dismissed by South Korea as containing nothing new. On April 4, 1996, the North Korean representative office at Panmunjom announced it would renounce its duty of maintaining and managing the DMZ.

North-South relations were further damaged following an incident on Sept. 18, 1996, when a North Korean submarine ran aground on South Korea's east coast near Kangnung. South Korea claimed it was an infiltration mission and mounted a hunt for the 26 crew members that had come ashore. In the days that followed all but two of the crew were either killed by South Korean forces or were found apparently having committed suicide or been executed, possibly to avoid capture. There were also a number of South Korean military and civilian casualties and the incident caused uproar in the South. Seoul demanded an apology from the North and hinted that it was prepared to take military action if it did not receive an apology and an undertaking that there would be no repetition of the event. Pyongyang in turn denounced the South's "reckless provocation" in bringing the Korean peninsula "to the brink of war" by "brutally" killing its soldiers who, it argued, had no choice but to go ashore following an accident in routine training. The North demanded the return of the submarine and the remains of the crew. Both sides traded bellicose insults and stepped up measures to reinforce their military defences. After pressure from the USA, North Korea issued an apology and an undertaking not to repeat the incursion.

Kim Dae Jung's "Sunshine Policy"

The North-South relationship remained tense but stable throughout 1997 and in December four-party talks between North and South Korea, China and the USA, proposed by President Clinton and South Korean President Kim Young Sam in 1996, took place. Although the outcome of the talks was little more than an agreement to meet again, the meeting in itself was an achievement. 1998 brought little real progress towards reunification although there were greater efforts towards rapprochement on both sides. Just before the inauguration of South Korea's new President, Kim Dae Jung, North Korea approached the South, through the Red Cross, requesting dialogue between the two sides. The South too was keen to engage the North, and Kim Dae Jung unveiled his "sunshine policy" designed to further North-South reconciliation.

This policy departed from earlier South Korean policies of containment and instead stressed inter-Korean peaceful co-operation through direct social and economic interaction. "Reunification" was dropped from policy rhetoric and the Premier explicitly ruled out "absorbing" North Korea as a foreign policy aim, talking instead of "flexible reciprocity". The policy advocated the separation of economic and political relations, which was particularly important as the two sides were in the midst of economic and financial crisis. The policy also encouraged the resolution of political and military tensions through multilateral frameworks including the four-party talks and KEDO.

These measures bore some fruit and there was greater discussion between North and South Korea despite little in the way of actual agreement. In March 1995, the North had proposed US-North Korean general officer-level talks to replace the MAC. However, the UN Command (UNC) and South Korea argued that there was a need to keep a reliable negotiation channel open for crisis management under the armistice framework and in February 1998, proposed general officer-level talks between the UNC and the North Korean People's Army (KPA) instead. This offer was accepted by the North and eleven rounds of talks were held from June 1998 to September 1999. Notable too was the first formal bilateral meeting between the North and South in four years, held on April 11-14, 1998— although it ended without success when the two parties failed to reach agreement over agricultural aid to the North and reunion visits between divided families.

At the second plenary of four-party talks, held on March 16-20, 1998, North Korea insisted that US troop withdrawals from the South and the negotiation of a bilateral treaty between North Korea and the USA should top the agenda, and the talks broke down. However, the third plenary, on Oct. 21, 1998, was more successful as the parties agreed to establish two sub-committees to work on "the establishment of a peace regime on the Korean Peninsula and tension reduction there". Whilst there had been little inter-governmental agreement over the year, non-governmental economic relations improved markedly. Tourist links were also established between the two sides and South Korean tourists visited the North for the first time since the Korean War.

The Northern Limit Line (NLL) and the 1999 Naval Clash in the Yellow Sea

The year 1999 did not bring the progress in Korean relations that some had hoped for and there were a number of tense naval stand-offs between the two sides that threatened the co-operative talks. The clashes occurred in the Yellow Sea (or West Sea) in March and June in the waters along the disputed sea border, the Northern Limit Line (NLL) established by the UNC in 1953 (see above).

The NLL is equidistant between five South Korean islands (Paengnyong, Twechong, Sochong, Yongpyong and Woo) and the North Korean coastline. The north-western islands are geographically closer to North Korea, which argues that it has never recognized the "illegal line" running close to the south-western coast in the North's 12-mile territorial waters. In December 1973, the North suddenly rejected the NLL, unilaterally drawing up a new sea border that brought the islands within North Korean territorial waters. At that time, the North stated that although it accepted that the islands were under UNC control as stipulated in the ceasefire agreement, the waters surrounding the islets belonged to the North and that, therefore, South Korean vessels required Northern approval to pass through them. Since then, each side has periodically accused the other of violating the border. The disputed waters are fertile and popular with fishermen particularly because of the lucrative blue crab beds around the islands. Fishermen from both sides routinely fish in the waters, accompanied by military vessels, occasionally resulting in naval confrontation. Fishing activity (and therefore, the potential for military clashes) intensifies in the crab-fishing season of June.

In early June 1999 there was a series of incidents in which each side accused the other of illegally crossing the maritime demarcation line, provoking "cat and mouse" confrontations between naval vessels from the North and South. In one incident, on June 9, vessels from the North and South collided with each other and both sustained damage. South Korea accused North Korean fishing boats of attempting to expand the crab-fishing grounds near Yongpyong island, and North Korean naval patrol boats of protecting them. The North, however, responded by deeming the incidents to constitute a "grave military provocation" and claimed that South Korea had "illegally infiltrated a group of warships into our territorial waters on the West Sea" as a "pretext for war".

On June 13, North Korea was reported to have accepted an invitation to talks by the UNC. However, half an hour before the sixth round of general officer-level talks were due to begin, on June 15, South Korean warships sank a North Korean torpedo boat in another confrontation. The South Korean Defence Ministry stated that 20 North Korean fishing boats and four patrol boats crossed the Military Demarcation Line (MDL) into the "South Korean" buffer zone, and were rammed by the South Korean navy in an attempt to force them back. There was an exchange of fire and a number of North Korean sailors were injured in the battle, which constituted the most serious armed clash between the two sides since the ceasefire in 1953. The scheduled talks between the two sides took place, but made little progress.

Further general officer-level meetings were held in an attempt to find ways of reducing naval tension between the two states. Following the eleventh round of talks, however, North Korea announced, on Sept. 2, that it no longer recognized the NLL and would defend a new border by "various means and methods". The new maritime demarcation line, announced by North Korea in March 2000, brought the five islands under South Korean control into North Korean territory. The North also announced a six-point charter stipulating that vessels would be allowed to and from the islands only through designated sea routes, and that if vessels strayed from the designated passages it would be regarded as a violation of the North's territorial waters. The South and the UNC, however, reaffirmed that the NLL was the de facto sea border and that it would be maintained until a new maritime demarcation line could be established through the Joint Military Commission on the Armistice Agreement. Commentators speculated that the North's actions may have been intended to provoke negotiations that would lead to a peace treaty with the USA. The South made it clear, however, that it intended to press ahead with the "sunshine" policy and would not be drawn into any attempt by the North to use the issue to promote the idea of a peace treaty between Pyongyang and Washington. As events in 2000 unfolded, this policy appeared to be bringing success.

Inter-Korean Summit, 2000

On June 13, 2000, the North Korean leader Kim Jong Il (who had succeeded his father in 1994) and the South Korean President, Kim Dae Jung, met in Pyongyang at the first ever summit between the two states. This historic meeting began with a rare public appearance by Kim Jong Il, who greeted the South Korean President in a lavish ceremony at Pyongyang airport. At the summit, both sides agreed to work together for reconciliation, co-operation and unification. The leaders discussed a variety of measures to improve relations including the opening of road and railway lines across the border and setting up a telephone hotline between the leaders so that discussions could continue. It was agreed that the border liaison offices would be reopened on Aug. 8. Kim Dae Jung announced that "unification is the ultimate goal for this era", adding "if both sides join forces, Korea could become a first-class nation".

Internationally, the summit was heralded as an encouraging development and an important step in inter-Korean relations. In the six months that followed the summit, the two states held four sets of ministerial-level talks and in September defence chiefs from North and South met for the first time ever, on the island of Cheju, in an attempt to reduce military tension on the Korean peninsula, promote confidence-building measures and discuss the eventual formation of a military commission. There was further progress in relations as North Korea ceased its loudspeaker broadcasts across the DMZ and the South began work on repairing pre-war rail links and clearing mines in the DMZ in preparation for the restoration of road and rail links. A rail link was proposed that would run from Seoul to Pyongyang and on to Shinuiji on the northern border with China. Seoul also planned to spend about 55 billion won on laying a 12-km rail track from Munsan to the border, and a further 100 billion won to extend a four-lane highway alongside the rail track. Liaison offices re-opened at Panmunjom on Aug. 8, on the first day of what was dubbed "Reconciliation Week"—in which events culminated in a joint Korean commemoration of the anniversary of Korea's liberation from Japanese rule. The first of three rounds of reunion exchange visits between separated families began in August 2000 and the South Korean environment ministry announced plans for environmental conservation to prevent over-development in the DMZ in the wake of rapprochement between North and South Korea.

Internationally, there were greater efforts to normalize relations between North Korea and Japan, moves toward North Korean-Russian co-operation, and North Korea entered into diplomatic relations with several Western states. In October 2000, the North Korean Foreign Minister, Paek Nam Sun, and the US Secretary of State, Madeleine Albright, met in Bangkok. The US administration of President Bill Clinton was keen to negotiate a deal which would secure North Korean agreement not to build or test long-range missiles or export missile-related technology. Although Pyongyang had agreed to a moratorium on further long-range missile tests in exchange for an end to US economic sanctions, no comprehensive agreement was reached on this issue before Clinton's term in office ended.

Renewal of Tension in 2001

This period of détente between North and South Korea appeared at an end, however, when North Korea cancelled the fifth ministerial meeting scheduled for March 2001 and postponed further discussion concerning family reunion visits. A six-month diplomatic impasse followed. In the autumn, discussions were renewed and the fifth ministerial talks were held in September. Reunion exchanges were scheduled for October 2001 but days before they were due to take place the North postponed the meetings, citing security concerns in the wake of the Sept. 11 terrorist attacks in the USA. The sixth ministerial meeting between North and South Korean ministers failed to make progress but, following a series of secret meetings between the two sides, there was an announcement on March 25, 2002, that in an attempt to reinvigorate dialogue between the two sides, the North and South would exchange high level envoys.

Deteriorating relations between North and South Korea mirrored the worsening relations between North Korea and the USA. The administration of George W. Bush, which came to office in January 2001, cancelled the talks that the Clinton administration had been having with North Korea and began a review of US Asian policy. The review, completed in June 2001, concluded that talks involving the parties should resume but with no preconditions. Washington wanted to focus on improvements in the implementation of the Agreed Framework; the adoption of verifiable constraints on missile development; and a ban on missile exports and "a less threatening conventional military posture".

North Korea responded formally to these proposals on June 18 and made it clear that before the North would discuss arms control measures, the USA would have to withdraw its troops from South Korea and provide security assurances. Instead, the North wished to discuss compensation for the delay in constructing the light-water reactors (due to have been completed by 2003 but by now running several years behind schedule). The two sides clearly had very different priorities in terms of a discussion agenda and the events over the following months only served to galvanize their opposing positions, causing deadlock. The Bush administration's classified "Nuclear Posture Review" made reference to North Korea as a state against which the USA should be prepared to use nuclear weapons in the event of a nuclear confrontation. North Korea was incensed by this and by remarks in President Bush's State of the Union address on Jan. 29, 2002, that North Korea, together with Iraq and Iran, constituted an "axis of evil". Such rhetoric served to fuel Pyongyang's fears of a pre-emptive nuclear strike by the USA and hardened its demands for assurances of US non-aggression before there could be any discussion of North Korean disarmament. Washington, however, continued to press the case for North Korean disarmament and the need for new verification measures that would provide assurances that the North was not cheating on its current obligations. Neither side was willing to back down.

As tensions on the Korean peninsula were ratcheted up, there was a further blow to reconciliation efforts between North and South Korea when vessels from the two sides clashed once again at the disputed NLL in June 2002. The battle was the most serious maritime clash since the incident in the Yellow Sea in June 1999. Five South Korean soldiers lost their lives and 20 were wounded. North Korea also admitted to having sustained losses but declined to reveal the exact numbers. Officials from the South claimed that Northern vessels had crossed the NLL and fired on its boats, provoking a gun battle. North Korea maintained that the South had committed a "grave provocation" by opening fire on its vessels, which were on "routine coastal guard duty". As a result of this serious incident, the USA postponed its talks with North Korea. When representatives from Washington and Pyongyang finally met in October 2002 to discuss the security issue, the situation spiralled from diplomatic impasse to crisis.

2002-03: The Second Nuclear Crisis on the Korean Peninsula

From Oct. 3-5, 2002, Pyongyang played host to delegations from the USA and North Korea who met to discuss the emerging security crisis. At the first meeting, James Kelly, US Assistant Secretary of State for East Asian and Pacific Affairs, informed the North Korean delegation that the USA had obtained intelligence evidence which confirmed that North Korea was pursuing a clandestine nuclear weapons policy and that, as a consequence, it was in breach of the 1994 Agreed Framework. The North Korean delegation denied this charge maintaining, however, that they were "entitled" to acquire a nuclear weapons capability as the USA had made threatening overtures towards them and had failed to deliver on its own obligations under the Agreed Framework (by delaying completion of the promised reactors and failing to provide assurances that it would not use nuclear weapons against the North). The USA subsequently claimed that in a surprising development at the second meeting, Pyongyang privately admitted that it did in fact have a nuclear weapons programme. Publicly, however, this claim was strenuously denied by North Korean officials, who nevertheless continued to reiterate that North Korea had a right to self-defence as long as the USA refused to sign a non-aggression pact.

On Dec. 13, 2002, North Korea announced that it was immediately reactivating the Yongbyon nuclear facility that had been frozen by the 1994 agreement. The North claimed that this was in reaction to the US suspension of oil shipments to North Korea, part of the Agreed Framework, one month before. Less than a week after the announcement, the North removed the seals at all frozen facilities, removed IAEA monitoring cameras and announced the expulsion of IAEA inspectors. From this point onwards, the crisis escalated. North Korea withdrew from the NPT (on Jan. 10, 2003), restarted its plutonium-based nuclear facilities and has periodically reported advances in its nuclear weapon capabilities since then.

Despite efforts towards defusing the nuclear crisis, the US-North Korean stalemate has continued. Multilateral talks were held between North Korea, China and the USA in April 2003 and in August they were joined at the negotiating table by South Korea, Japan, and Russia. These talks, however, have so far failed to yield agreement and whilst Washington has been keen to reach agreement through this multilateral forum, North Korea is continuing to press for the conclusion of a bilateral non-aggression pact with the USA, an option that President Bush dismissed as "off the table" in October 2003. Meanwhile, Pyongyang continues its nuclear programme, announcing on Oct. 2 that it had finished reprocessing 8,000 nuclear fuel rods (thereby obtaining enough material to make up to six nuclear bombs).

In the current climate of unease, North-South relations, which had been boosted by the events of 2000, have come under considerable strain. Throughout the 2002 US-North Korean stand-off, North and South Korea had continued to work on rebuilding the North-South rail link and the South Korean President, Roh Moo Hyun (who succeeded Kim Dae Jung on Dec.19, 2002), expressed his intention to continue the course of constructive engagement with North Korea set by his predecessor through what he dubbed a "peace and prosperity policy". However, on March 22, 2003, North Korea suspended economic talks with the South that were to have covered completion of the North-South road and rail links and shipping and fishing arrangements, arguing that the talks would be impossible due to the heightened military alert and South Korean participation in military exercises with the USA. Three days later, the North announced that it would no longer send liaison officers to conduct routine border consultations with the UNC.

As far as the future is concerned, the outcome of both the North Korean nuclear issue and the inter-Korean political process will ultimately determine the stability (or instability) of the Korean peninsula and the prospects for reconciliation and reunification between North and South. In January 2004 North Korea clarified earlier suggestions that it would refrain from the testing and production of nuclear weapons and even cease the operation of nuclear power plants for peaceful purposes, in exchange for a lifting of political and economic sanctions by the US. This move was described as "a positive step" by US Secretary of State Colin Powell. South Korea has reiterated that inter-Korean progress and co-operation in tourism and industrial projects will depend on the easing of nuclear tensions.

Alexandra McLeod

3.14 Laos - Thailand

The 1,754-kilometre Laos-Thailand border (which follows the watershed between the Mae Nam Nan and Mekong river systems before looping eastwards and then southwards along the Mekong river itself for some 800 kilometres—see Map 31, p. 508) has been the scene of periodic border incidents, often involving shooting exchanges across the Mekong. In 1984 a serious territorial dispute arose over three villages on the northern section of the border (west of the Mekong), over which both countries claimed sovereignty. Another dispute arose in late 1987 and the two countries fought a brief but bloody war. Following the signing of a ceasefire agreement in early 1988 relations between the two countries improved, and in 1996 demarcation of the land frontier began and was largely complete by end-2002 although significant areas remained in dispute.

Historical Background—Laos-Thailand Relations, 1975-82

Siam (the name by which Thailand was known until 1939) invaded the first Lao kingdom (Lan Xang) in 1535, but it was not until 1791 that the three Lao provinces of Vientiane, Luang Prabang and Champassak came under Siamese suzerainty. In 1893 Siam ceded to France Lao-populated territory east of the Mekong, including the islands in the river itself, thereby consolidating French control of Indo-China. A series of treaties and conventions signed by France and Siam in 1902, 1904 and 1907 extended the border of French-controlled Laos to the west of the northern Mekong to include the province of Sayaboury (whose border is at the centre of the later "three villages" dispute). Under the 1907 treaty approximately 1,100 km of the common frontier is formed by the Mekong and other rivers and a Franco-Siamese Treaty of 1926 governing these has given rise to different interpretations. More than 700 km of land frontier remained undemarcated when Laos achieved independence from France in 1949.

Throughout the Vietnam War in the 1960s and early 1970s, Thailand committed itself to the anti-communist camp and units of Thai irregular soldiers operated in Laos against the pro-communist Pathet Lao (the controlling force in the northern regions following the de facto partition of the country in 1965). Relations between the two countries after the Pathet Lao gained full control of Laos in May 1975 tended to reflect this previous alignment and the fact that Thailand remained in a defence treaty relationship with the United States. The emigration of Lao right-wing forces and politicians to Thailand after the communist victory became a particular source of tension, with Laos consistently accusing successive Thai governments of supporting insurgents based along the border, while Thailand made similar accusations concerning Lao support for communist *Phak Mai* (New Party) guerrillas.

In the months prior to the overthrow of the monarchy and the formation of the Lao People's Democratic Republic (LPDR) in December 1975, clashes across and on the Mekong, particularly in the vicinity of Vientiane (the Laotian capital), resulted in Thailand closing the border to Lao imports and exports, thereby necessitating the airlifting of essential goods to Laos from Vietnam. Nevertheless, Thailand's initial response to the communist victory in Indo-China was essentially conciliatory and resulted in a visit to Vientiane by the Thai Foreign Minister, Pichai Rattakul, on July 31-Aug. 3, 1976. On that occasion a joint statement asserted that bilateral relations should be based on the principles of peaceful co-existence and non-intervention in each other's affairs; it was further agreed to reopen a number of border points and to create a mechanism to hold local meetings in the event of a border incident.

However, a militantly anti-communist regime under Thanin Kraivichien came to power in Thailand in October 1976 (as the result of a military coup) and throughout the following year a series of border incidents led Thailand to re-impose a partial economic blockade. Lao sources claimed that during April 1977 Thai forces attacked three Lao islands in the Mekong; namely Sang Khi, Con Tam and Singsou. However, a new Thai government which came to power in November 1977, with Gen. Kriangsak Chamanan as Prime Minister, attempted to improve relations with Laos by immediately lifting the partial economic blockade. In March 1978 the Lao Minister of Foreign Affairs, Phoune Sipaseuth, visited Bangkok (the capital of Thailand) and reaffirmed the principles of peaceful co-existence and non-intervention agreed in August 1976. The number of border incidents decreased in 1978, but in December of that year a major skirmish occurred on the Mekong, resulting in the sinking of four military vessels and the deaths of a number of Thai and Lao military personnel.

Gen. Kriangsak visited Vientiane on Jan. 4-6, 1979, following which Kaysone Phomvihane (General Secretary of the ruling Lao People's Revolutionary Party and Chairman of the Council of Ministers) paid a return visit to Bangkok on April 1-4. In a joint communiqué issued at the end of Kaysone's visit, the two leaders described the Mekong as a "river of genuine peace, friendship and mutual benefit" and stated that both countries would adopt 44 "necessary and effective measures to prevent and smash all movements of terrorists using the border areas as hiding places". A Memorandum of Understanding, providing for the establishment of a border liaison committee, the reduction of armed patrols on the Mekong and the opening of a fifth official passage across the Mekong, was signed during the visit of a Thai government delegation to Vientiane in August 1979.

Relations again deteriorated after Gen. Prem Tinsulanond succeeded Gen. Kriangsak as Prime Minister of Thailand in March 1980. On June 15 of that year Lao troops fired on a Thai patrol boat operating in the Lao half of the Mekong, killing a naval officer. Thailand responded by closing the frontier for most of July, thereby causing serious food shortages in Vientiane. Another period of tension began on Jan. 20, 1981, when Thai troops reportedly fired on a Lao civilian vessel travelling on the Mekong, killing one crew member; seven days later another Lao boat was attacked and two of its crew were killed. A series of clashes took place in the last week of January and the first three weeks of February 1981, around the small Lao island of Don Sangkhi, in the Mekong near Vientiane. In response, Thai officials closed three points of entry on the border.

During 1981 and 1982 there were reciprocal ministerial visits. However, shooting incidents across the Mekong recurred in October and November 1981 and in April and June 1982. In the June 1982 incident Thailand alleged that (on June 16) Lao troops stationed on Don Sangkhi island fired on a Thai village, and that the following day Lao forces had shelled Thai patrol boats operating near the island.

The "Three Villages" Dispute

A dispute over the sovereignty of three villages, situated near the land border where the western Lao province of Sayaboury meets the northern Thai province of Uttaradit, began in March 1984. The disputed villages—Ban Mai, Ban Klang and Ban Sawang—cover an area of some 19 square kilometres and had a combined population of approximately 1,800 Lao-speaking people.

According to Thai sources, Lao troops occupied the three villages in April 1984, having intruded four miles into Uttaradit province during the previous month in an attempt to disrupt Thai construction of a road. This road, described initially by the Thai military as a "strategic" road but later as "developmental", was originally planned to pass near to the three villages but subsequently diverted from the area. Prior to the occupation of the three villages, Lao forces had on April 15 clashed with Thai border patrol police and paramilitary Rangers. After another clash in late May, Thai military officials publicized the dispute and on June 6, 1984, Thai troops of the first Cavalry Division took control of the three villages, with little apparent Lao opposition.

The first Lao response to the establishment of Thai military control in the three villages consisted of a series of radio broadcasts blaming the "encroachment" on "ultra-rightist reactionaries in the Thai ruling circles". The same broadcasts linked the latest episode to Thailand's support of the exiled Coalition Government of Democratic Kampuchea (CGDK) as well as to alleged Chinese incursions into Vietnam's northern provinces during April 1984. (For Sino-Vietnamese territorial issues, see Section 3.9.) Lao broadcasts further contended that a direct link existed between Thailand's military occupation of the three villages and a visit to China in May 1984 by Gen. Arthit Kamlang-Ek, the Supreme Commander of the Thai Armed Forces. Thailand in turn accused Vietnam of playing a role in aggravating and internationalizing the dispute, with the aim of distracting world attention from the Kampuchea issue. Prasong Soonsiri, the Secretary-General of Thailand's National Security Council, told a press conference on June 22 that "Vietnam's involvement proves beyond doubt that the leaders of the Lao government are being used as a tool".

A Lao delegation visited Bangkok for talks with Thai officials on July 21-24, 1984, and again on Aug. 7-15, but no agreement was reached on the withdrawal of Thai troops from the disputed area, the two sides produced conflicting maps of the area in support of their claims to sovereignty. The Lao map had originally been produced as an addendum to the 1907 border treaty between France and Siam; in addition, the Lao delegation cited the precedent of the Preah Vihear temple dispute between Thailand and Cambodia in 1962, when the International Court of Justice (ICJ) had based its ruling on the 1907 Franco-Siamese border treaty. The Thai delegation cited a map published in 1978 (and drawn largely from US aerial reconnaissance photographs), claiming that it showed the three villages to be in Thai territory—i.e. in an area to the west of the Mae Nam Nan-Mekong watershed line (which both countries agreed should form the line of the border). The talks were broken off by Thailand on Aug. 15 after the Lao delegation refused to accept a Thai proposal for a joint technical team to visit the disputed area in order to determine the border.

After Lao troops had in September 1984 killed two border policemen and a mechanic near the disputed area, Air Chief Marshal Siddhi Savetsila (the Thai Foreign Minister) threatened to lodge a complaint at the United Nations. However, in a subsequent address to the UN General Assembly on Oct. 2 he stated that Thai troops were to be withdrawn from the three villages. A Thai Foreign Ministry spokesman announced on Oct. 15 that the withdrawal had been completed, but warned that this step should not be seen as a renunciation of a Thai claim on the three villages. Addressing the same session of the UN Security Council in October 1984, Phoune Sipaseuth described Air Chief Marshal Siddhi's statement as an "attempt to mislead Thai and international public opinion". He also criticized the Thai Foreign Minister's failure to address the questions of Lao villagers allegedly captured by Thai soldiers and of compensation for the "human and material losses suffered by the population".

Lao officials confirmed in late October 1984 that Thai forces had withdrawn from the three villages, but claimed that they continued to occupy strategically important high ground in the vicinity. Lao calls for talks on the dispute in November and December 1984 were rejected by Thailand, which claimed that with the withdrawal of Thai troops the problem had been solved. Talks on the three villages dispute figured prominently during a visit to Vientiane by a Thai delegation on July 29-Aug. 3, 1985. The discussions ended in disagreement, however, with the Lao side insisting on further negotiations at a national level and the Thai delegation maintaining that the issue should be settled at a local level. The Hong Kong-based *Far Eastern Economic Review* reported on Aug. 22, 1985, that officials in the Thai Foreign Ministry had recently confirmed the existence of a number of previously undisclosed territorial disputes with Laos along their common border. Reports in August 1985 indicated an increase in border hostilities and on Aug. 10 an incident resulted in the death of a Thai border patrol policeman.

On June 14, 1986, Thai government officials announced that 40 Lao troops had crossed the northern land border and launched an attack on a makeshift encampment of illegal Lao immigrants, near the town of Chiang Kham, killing 35 and seriously wounding a number of others. A formal Thai protest to the United Nations was rejected by Laos as a "pretext for creating tension" along the border. Thereafter, relations between the two countries appeared to improve, beginning in early August 1986, when Kaysone sent a letter

of congratulations to Gen. Prem on his reappointment as Thailand's Prime Minister, expressing a wish for better relations. On Sept. 24, 1986, Laos delivered a memorandum to the Thai ambassador in Vientiane proposing that both countries should appoint high-level working groups to prepare for future ministerial talks, this being agreed the following day during talks at the United Nations in New York.

A senior Thai delegation led by Arun Panupong (a Foreign Ministry adviser) visited Vientiane on Nov. 27-29, 1986, and during talks both sides reportedly agreed to stop propaganda attacks against each other. Talks at governmental level continued on March 24-28, 1987, when a Lao delegation led by the deputy Foreign Minister, Souban Salitthilat, paid a visit to Bangkok. Prior to these talks, on Feb. 18, the Thai Foreign Trade Department had issued an order reducing the number of "strategic goods" banned for export to Laos from 273 to 61.

The Ban Rom Klao Dispute

Further armed clashes were reported on the border in May and June 1987, but fighting which broke out in late 1987 was both unexpected and more serious than anything previously seen. Events leading up to the outbreak of hostilities began in May when Laos accused Thailand of massing troops in the Ban Rom Klao region near the northern land border (where the western Lao province of Sayaboury met the northern Thai province of Phitsanuloke) to protect illegal logging activities. The territory under dispute covered some 80 sq km and was made up mostly of forest-covered hills. In mid-December Thai fighter planes began combing the area with the aim of clearing the region of Lao troops. From this point on, fighting between Lao and Thai forces opened in earnest, and according to some reports as many as 700 soldiers died battling for the territory. Lao soldiers were still positioned in the disputed region when a ceasefire agreement was signed by the Lao andThai army chiefs in mid-February, and the Lao government claimed that they had been victorious.

Developments since 1988—Border Demarcation Agreement, 1996

The ceasefire along the Sayaboury-Phitsanuloke border held during 1988 and at the end of the year a joint border committee was created. Relations began to improve the following year and in October joint co-operation committees were formed, headed by the two countries' army chiefs. A report on Vientiane domestic radio on Oct. 6, 1989, described the formation of the committees as an "important basis for promoting and expanding co-operation in the economic, trade, cultural, scientific and technical fields between the two countries". The following month the Thai Cabinet agreed to lift the ban on "strategic goods" exports to Laos, in order to help "boost relations". It was hoped that the decision, which would allow exports of certain chemicals, "non-lethal" military hardware and electronic goods, would also reduce smuggling across the joint borders. The joint border committee convened in Vientiane in January 1990 to discuss the results of a survey and inspection of the disputed Ban Rom Klao region, carried out by a technical group appointed by the committee in April 1989. The two sides "informed each other of the border situation" and discussed means whereby the "problem could be settled". The technical group was to continue the study of legal aspects of the disputed region and report back.

Relations continued to improve in the early 1990s. In November 1990 the Thai Prime Minister, Gen. Chatichai Choonhaven, visited Laos. The following March, Gen. Suchinda Kraprayoon, the Thai Army commander and leader of the military junta which had toppled Chatichai in February 1991, visited Laos where he signed an agreement on the withdrawal of troops from disputed border areas. In June the two countries agreed on a plan under which Lao refugees living in Thailand would be repatriated or resettled by the end of 1994. In August a security and co-operation agreement was signed. President Kaysone Phomvihane of Laos paid an official visit to Thailand in January 1992 where he held talks with, amongst others, King Bhumibol Adulyadej and Prime Minister Anand Panyarachun. However, the repatriation proceeded slowly, as many of the Laotian refugees, many of them hill tribe Hmong, feared for their safety if they were to return. The repatriation mission, managed by the two governments in conjunction with the UN High Commissioner for Refugees, remained in abeyance for several years.

In 1996, with the Ban Rom Klao issue still unresolved, the two governments reached a general agreement on the demarcation of the 1,800 km-long common boundary. At a meeting between Foreign Ministers Amnuay Veeravan of Thailand and Somsavat of Laos, the two ministers signed a memorandum of understanding agreeing on the 1907 treaty as the basis for the process, though Laos continued to deny the applicability of the attached maps. In 1997 Gen. Sisavath, who had been Laotian chief of staff at the time of the 1988 clash, became Premier of Laos. With his strong support, the first marker was set in position and over the next few years the process went ahead quickly with only a minor interruption by Thailand in 1998.

During a visit by the Thai Foreign Minister, Surin Pitsuwan, to Vientiane in June 1998 both sides signed a joint declaration of intent to complete the process by 2003. The Laotian refusal to accept the validity of the 1907 maps remained an obstacle to agreement on 39 areas—including Ban Rom Klao in Phitsanuloke, the three villages in Uttaradit, Chong Mek in Ubon Ratchathani, Khang Pha Dai, Phu Chi Fa and Doi Phatang in Chiang Rai, and Doi Kui Kha, Phu Sam Sao, Huay Sa Thang and Huay Khone in Nan province— but over the rest of the line the work continued until by December 2002, 619 km of the approximately 702 km land border had been demarcated. It was agreed that on the conclusion of the process, pos-

sibly by the end of 2003, work would begin on the settlement of the water boundary, where the maps were disputed and in any case parts of the Mekong watershed had changed. In August 2003 it was agreed for the first time that for this purpose, under the 1926 treaty, technical teams from both countries should jointly determine the source of the Hueng river as a key boundary marker.

Peter Calvert

3.15 Malaysia - Philippines (Sabah)

The Philippines' claim to Sabah—a territory of some 76,000 sq km situated in the northeast corner of the island of Borneo, 18 nautical miles from the southernmost part of the Philippines (see Map 32 on p. 508)—emerged in 1961, in the context of British and Malayan government proposals for the creation of a Federation of Malaysia, comprising Malaya, Singapore, Sarawak and Sabah. The origins of the dispute over the status of Sabah may be traced back to the latter part of the nineteenth century, when the British government acquired interests in North Borneo, including areas of Sabah previously under the jurisdiction of the Sultan of Sulu in what is now the Republic of the Philippines. Since the late 1960s the Philippines has not actively pursued the claim to Sabah, but it has not unequivocally denounced it, mainly perhaps because the claim of the Sultan of Sulu has become an element in the tensions which have characterized relations between the Philippine government and its minority Muslim population.

The Origins of the Dispute

In 1704, much of present-day Sabah was ceded by the Sultan of Brunei to the Sultan of Sulu as payment for the latter's assistance in putting down a rebellion, though the Sulu sultanate's interests were largely limited to the coastal areas of the northeast. European interest in the area began in the eighteenth century, and by the 1860s the British had acquired the offshore island of Labuan and had leased land from the Sultan of Sulu to establish a coastal trading settlement at Sandakan on the east coast. In 1878 the Sultan of Sulu transferred his rights in North Borneo, "for ever and in perpetuity", to a British syndicate, in return for a guaranteed annual payment. (An annual amount of 5,300 ringgit is still paid by the Malaysian government to the Sultan of Sulu.) From 1881 to 1941 Sabah was governed as a British protectorate by the North Borneo Chartered Company. The ceding of rights to "the government of British North Borneo" was confirmed in a deed signed by the Sultan of Sulu in 1903. Following the wartime Japanese occupation of 1941-45, Sabah became the crown colony of British North Borneo. The proposal to grant the colony independence through merger with Malaysia in 1963 received widespread support within Sabah.

The Philippine government's claim to Sabah was based on the argument that the Sultan of Sulu had no legal right to cede territory, since Spain, as the colonial power in the Philippines, had sovereignty in the Sulu archipelago, and by extension North Borneo. It cited treaties between Spain and the Sultan of Sulu in 1836, 1851 and 1864. Supporters of the Philippine claim have also argued that the intention of the Sultan in the nineteenth century was to lease Sabah to the British, not to cede it outright.

Initially Britain did not recognize the treaties between Spain and the Sultan of Sulu, on the grounds that Spanish authority had not been established in the southern islands. However, in 1885 the two countries signed a treaty accepting Spanish sovereignty in the Sulu archipelago and British sovereignty over "the territories on the continent of Borneo formerly belonging to the Sultan of Sulu". Following the Spanish-American War of 1898, sovereignty over the Philippine islands was transferred from Spain to the USA, and in 1930 an Anglo-American boundary convention acknowledged the British protectorate in North Borneo; this was noted in 1946 when the independence of the Philippine Republic was proclaimed. Somewhat ironically in view of the previous argument, however, the Philippines has argued that it cannot be bound by agreements undertaken by a colonial power.

In opposing the Philippine claim, Malaysian sources also point out that in 1915 Sultan Mohammad Jamalul Kiram II agreed to recognize the sovereignty of the USA, except in spiritual matters, and on his death in 1936 the sultanate was effectively abolished, "disappearing as an entity of any kind". The institution was revived under the Marcos administration, but has been contested by rival claimants to the title.

Activating the Philippine Claim

In 1950 Philippine Congressmen Diosdado Macapagal, Arsenio Lacson and Arturo Tolentino filed a congressional resolution calling on the government to pursue the Philippine claim over Sabah. Twelve years later, on April 30, 1962, the Philippine House of Representatives unanimously resolved that: "The claim of the Philippine Republic upon a certain portion of the island of Borneo and adjacent islands is valid" and requested then President Macapagal to take the necessary steps consistent with international law and procedures to recover the territory. Subsequently President Macapagal argued that North Borneo was essential to the Philippines' national security, given the communist threat in Southeast Asia. In June 1962 the Philippine government sought talks with the British government on the North Borneo issue; the British agreed to talks, but reiterated the view that the status

of North Borneo was not in dispute. Talks were held in London in January-February 1963, and it was agreed to exchange documents concerning the two countries' positions, but no agreement was reached.

In a statement in January 1963, President Macapagal argued that while his government claimed sovereignty over British North Borneo, it also upheld the principle of self-determination and believed that the people of North Borneo should be consulted on their future status—independent, as part of the Philippines, or "placed under another state"—perhaps through a UN-sponsored referendum. However, in September 1962 the North Borneo Legislative Assembly had unanimously endorsed entry to the proposed Federation of Malaysia, and in elections in 1962 and 1963 supporters of incorporation gained a substantial victory. A UN mission to observe these elections concluded that the voters of North Borneo had demonstrated their support for federation with Malaysia.

Notwithstanding this, when the Federation of Malaysia was formally established in September 1963, the Philippines in protest downgraded its embassy in Kuala Lumpur to a consulate. Malaysia's Prime Minister, Tunku Abdul Rahman, retaliated by withdrawing Malaysia's diplomatic staff from Manila. (Indonesia, which also disputed Malaysia's sovereignty in North Borneo, refused to recognize the new Federation, beginning a period of confrontation with Malaysia.) The following year, meetings took place between Tunku Abdul Rahman and President Macapagal, which were described as having cleared the air and paved the way for a resumption of diplomatic relations: the two governments would consider the best way to settle the Philippine claim to Sabah, including the possibility of referral to the International Court of Justice (ICJ). Consular relations were restored in May 1964 and full diplomatic relations in June 1966 (following the end of Indonesia's confrontation with Malaysia). But two years later the Philippine claim to Sabah was revived during a meeting of officials in Bangkok, when the Philippine chief delegate demanded that the Sabah dispute be referred to the ICJ. The Malaysian chief delegate rejected the demand, on the grounds that the Philippine claim was neither legally nor politically valid, and left the meeting. The Philippine government responded by withdrawing its ambassador in Malaysia.

In August 1968 the Philippine House of Representatives legislated to include Sabah within the national boundaries of the Philippines, the bill being signed by President Marcos the following month. Tunku Abdul Rahman denounced the bill as a violation of Malaysia's sovereignty and territorial integrity, "a highly provocative act tantamount to aggression", and again suspended diplomatic relations. In October the Philippine Foreign Secretary reiterated the demand for the Sabah dispute to be referred to the ICJ, and said that until the issue was settled the Philippine government would not recognize the authority of the Malaysian government to represent the people and territory of Sabah. The following month, their diplomatic status having been revoked by Malaysia, the Philippines' entire diplomatic staff was withdrawn from Kuala Lumpur. This marked the nadir in Philippine-Malaysian relations.

The Sabah Issue in Philippine Politics

In the 1960s, there were growing tensions in the southern islands of the Philippines—Mindanao and the islands of the Sulu archipelago—as "inmigration" (internal migration) of Christian Filipino settlers from the north encroached on the traditional homelands, and political power, of Philippine Muslims. Sabah became part of this story. In 1968 tempers flared when a number of young Muslim recruits to the Armed Forces of the Philippines (AFP) were killed in an alleged mutiny on Corregidor Island (the so-called Jabidah massacre). It was rumoured that the soldiers were being secretly trained for an invasion of Sabah. Whatever the true circumstances of the Corregidor incident, reports of the planned invasion enraged Tunku Abdul Rahman. Soon after, a group of Philippine Muslim political activists, who became the core of the separatist Moro National Liberation Front (MNLF), left for Malaysia to undertake guerrilla training. They received support from the then chief minister of Sabah, Tun Mustapha. Subsequently, during the 1970s, as fighting between the MNLF and the AFP escalated, large numbers of people displaced by the conflict took refuge in nearby Sabah; by the early 1980s there were estimated to be around 200,000 Filipinos (mostly Muslims) in Sabah. Among the Muslim nationalists, the failure of the Philippine government to pursue the claim to Sabah on behalf of the Sultan of Sulu represented a further sell-out of Philippine Muslims' rights.

Following the formation of the Association of South-East Asian Nations (ASEAN) in 1967, Malaysia and the Philippines resumed diplomatic relations, and the claim to Sabah was put aside (though in 1973 a new constitution referred to the Philippines' "historic right and legal title"). In August 1977, at an ASEAN meeting in Kuala Lumpur, President Marcos announced that as a contribution to the unity of ASEAN the Philippines intended to renounce its claim to Sabah. Subsequently, the two countries commenced joint border patrols between Sabah and the Philippines to counter piracy, smuggling and drug trafficking, and also to cut off support from Malaysia to the MNLF. No formal renunciation ever eventuated, however. Marcos probably decided that the cost of alienating Philippine Muslims was greater than the benefits from placating Malaysia.

When the Marcos regime was brought down in the "People Power Revolution" of 1986, and a new constitution was drafted, the question of the Philippines' claim to Sabah was raised briefly in the context of defining the Philippines' national boundaries, and discussions were initiated between Foreign Ministry officials of the two countries. But despite early reports that the officials had reached an understanding, and Philippine assurances that the government did not intend to re-activate the claim, there was again no formal renunciation, and although the constitutional provisions on National Territory modified the wording of the 1973 constitution, the constitution of 1986 left scope for the Philippines to pursue its claim to Sabah. In August 1988 Philippines Foreign Secretary Raul Manglapus agreed to a proposal to waive the claim as a precondition for joint discussions with Malaysia, but the matter was not resolved.

In 2001 the Philippines requested intervention in a case before the ICJ concerning a territorial dispute between Malaysia and Indonesia over the islands of Sipadan and Ligatan, off the coast of Borneo, on the grounds that the ICJ's decision in this case could affect the interests of the Philippines in respect of its claim over Sabah. The Court refused the request but ruled that the Philippines' claim would not be affected by the dispute between Malaysia and Indonesia. At the time, Philippine Foreign Affairs Undersecretary Magallona referred to "our historic title to Sabah" and noted that, in appearing before the ICJ, "we have put on record a territorial claim to North Borneo".

For some years, the large number of people displaced by the fighting in the southern Philippines and taking up residence in Sabah has been a source of concern in Malaysia. Not only has the movement of people across the border substantially changed the ethnic and religious composition of Sabah, Filipino refugees have also been accused of contributing to a growing crime rate. In 2002 authorities in Sabah launched a campaign to send some 80,000 Filipinos back to the Philippines. This caused a strong backlash in the Philippines, with calls for the government to revive its claim to Sabah and Sulu Sultan Jamalul Kiram III saying that he would seek to take the claim to the Organization of Islamic Conference. President Macapagal-Arroyo set up a panel of the Legislative-Executive Development Advisory Council, headed by a presidential adviser on special concerns, to look into the issue. However, the government of President Macapagal-Arroyo (whose father it was who raised the claim back in 1950 and carried it forward in 1962-63) seems content to maintain the status quo, by not reviving the claim, but not renouncing it either.

R. J. May

3.16 Myanmar - Thailand

Thailand and Myanmar (Burma) have a long and highly contentious border which has been the cause of much of the tension in bilateral relations. Of the 2,400-kilometre border, only 48 kilometres have been formally demarcated to both countries' agreement. There are now five main points of disagreement on demarcation. These disputes are exacerbated by the enduring problems of civil conflict in Myanmar, which generates tens of thousands of refugees, fuels large scale drug smuggling into Thailand, and causes regular armed exchanges between the two countries.

Historical Background—Agreements on the Border

The first demarcation of the border was the Burney Treaty signed in 1826 after the first Anglo-Burmese War. A convention between the British and the Siamese king was reached in September 1868, although only for the territory of the lower Salween river to the Andaman Sea. In 1883 a treaty was signed for trade and anti-crime co-operation in the central border area near Chiang Mai. In 1894, a set of maps resulting from five years of survey was exchanged between the Kingdom of Siam and the British, resulting in a protocol providing for the use of the maps for future demarcation.

In 1967 a Joint Border Committee was created to address the growing problems created by internal conflict in both countries, which was fuelling smuggling and illegal migration along the frontier. The isolationist policies of socialist Burma rendered this committee largely ineffective. It was not until the early 1990s that development along both sides of the frontier, particularly in Thailand, gave government agencies easy access to the borderlands. Following large scale logging by Thai companies, especially in Thailand's Tak province adjacent to Myanmar's Karen state, trade agendas dominated attempts to solve boundary issues, particularly after Myanmar legalized border trade with China in 1988.

Myanmar and Thailand signed a Memorandum of Understanding relating to the Fixed Boundary on the Mae Sai-Nam Ruak Rivers Sector in 1991, to quell disputes over the demarcation line. This is the only formal demarcation agreement that exists. In January 1993, a Thailand-Myanmar Joint Border Commission was created to oversee economic and political matters, leaving military concerns to the moribund Regional Border Commission. Both countries also maintain five Township Border Committees to encourage trade and cultural links.

Efforts to solve border disputes were increased in 1994 when the two countries agreed to formalize border-crossing points. In May 1997, they signed an Agreement on Border Crossing. There are now three legal border crossings—Mae Sai-Tachilek in the far north, Mae Sot-Myawaddy in the central borderline, and Ranong-Kawthaung (Victoria Point) in the south. Plans were announced in January 2004 to open a point near Mae Hong Son for trade, although there is no town of comparable size on the Myanmar side.

In May 1997, the Joint Boundary Committee agreed to demarcate the entire border. This is made problematic because the sides disagree on which maps are more accurate, Thailand using a 1994 version, and Myanmar an earlier 1989 map.

Current Major Points of Dispute

There are currently five major points of dispute. The first is Hillock E-7 located on the edge of Thailand's Chiang Rai province close to Mae Sai, which provides a haven for the anti-Myanmar-government insurgent group the Shan State Army (SSA). Though it appears to be inside Myanmar, the Thai government claims the hill as Thai territory. The Myanmar government accuses the Thai military of helping the SSA occupy the hill.

The second point of disagreement is Hill 491, located in Thailand's southern Chumphon province and the scene of bitter dispute in February 1992 when Myanmar troops occupied the hill and refused to withdraw. The hill has been declared off limits to both countries until a joint survey and formal demarcation can be undertaken.

Third, and the most contentious, are islands in the Moei river in Tak province agreed upon in the 1868 treaty. The changing flow of the river also causes dispute. In mid-1998 the countries were in disagreement over the natural redirection of the river due to flooding, and the resultant land dispute. Unilateral development efforts in 1997 and 1998 increased tensions, and the Myanmar government accused Thailand of attempting to steal land though its development activities.

Fourth, there are islands in the mouth of the Pakchan river near Ranong, including Lam island, Kan island, and Khee Nok island. When the two states agreed formally to delimit their sea boundaries, the islands' issue was excluded as being too contentious.

The fifth point of dispute is over a strategic hill near the town of Pilok in Thailand. This is the point where the Yadana gas pipeline crosses the border from Myanmar into Thailand. The hill is currently jointly occupied by Myanmar and Thai soldiers.

Cross-Border Crime and Insurgency

Issues which exacerbate border disputes include the flow of drugs from Myanmar, refugees, and claims that anti-government insurgents use Thai territory as safe havens. Thailand has charged the Myanmar government with doing little to stem the flow of heroin and amphetamine-like stimulants (ATS) produced in border laboratories by pro-government ethnic militias like the United Wa State Army (UWSA). In June 2003 there were 143,474 registered refugees in camps along the border, although tens of thousands of illegal migrants also compound the difficulties in bilateral relations. The number of internally displaced Shan people spilling over the border is also increasing, although these people have no formal refugee camps and are not supported by the Thai government.

Tensions also arise because the borderline is a haven for anti-government insurgent armies, particularly those of the Karen National Union (KNU), Karenni National Progressive Party (KNPP) and the SSA, which maintain more that a dozen bases. Often these groups maintain offices and train personnel in Thai border towns. Frequent requests by Myanmar officials to permit their soldiers to traverse Thai territory in order to assault anti-government forces are always turned down. Myanmar's troops instead often cross the border illegally either in military operations or raiding parties in support of their ethnic militia allies, such as the Democratic Karen Buddhist Army (DKBA), who staged numerous raids on refugee camps on Thai territory between 1995 and 1999.

Spillover from fighting between the Myanmar army and the SSA drew a vigorous Thai response, and the two countries exchanged artillery fire over alleged incursions by Myanmar troops during February 2001. Myanmar closed the border in protest. In May 2002, heavy fighting between the Myanmar army and SSA insurgents again spilled over the border, leading to further exchanges with Thai forces. Myanmar again closed all three legal crossings, leading to a massive loss in trade for both countries until the border reopened in October 2002.

In June 2003, the Royal Thai Army forced a unit of UWSA militia back over the border after they had set up a tax station on a road inside Thailand. In October, the Thai army relocated a SSA base back across the border at Doi Kham in Chiang Mai's Chiang Dao district, with the co-operation of the insurgent group. A village of displaced Shan civilians was also relocated during the operation. To ease tensions further, it was announced in December 2003 that the tidal islands in the Moei river near Mae Sot will be developed into a recreation zone which both Thai and Myanmar citizens can utilize.

David Scott Mathieson

3.17 Pacific Island States

The Pacific is perhaps the least volatile area of the world when it comes to international border conflict. The reason is fundamentally because the island states are so small and isolated and separated by thousands of square kilometres of ocean. Unlike landlocked countries where borders are physically identifiable, Pacific island state borders are more or less "virtual" in nature. They are lines drawn on the map based largely on the rule establishing a 200-mile (320 km) wide exclusive economic zone (EEZ) around each country.

The only Pacific country with a land border is Papua New Guinea, while the rest are largely "watery continents" where the ocean area far exceeds the land area by a factor of more than a hundred to one. In general, the only potential border dispute is in relation to how the 200-mile EEZ is shared, but even this is very rare.

However, two disputes have occurred over the last two decades involving land issues, those involving France (for New Caledonia) and Vanuatu, and Fiji and Tonga.

France-Vanuatu (Matthew and Hunter Islands)

A dispute arose in 1982 over two uninhabited South Pacific islands known as Matthew and Hunter, when the Republic of Vanuatu (the former Anglo-French Condominium of the New Hebrides) declared them to be part of its sovereign territory (and renamed them Umaenupnae and Umaeneag respectively), whereas the French government maintained that they formed part of the French overseas territory of New Caledonia.

The two islands are barren volcanic rocks situated about 350 kilometres south-east of the island of Anatom in Vanuatu and about 450 kilometres due east of the mainland of New Caledonia. The importance of the islands lay principally in the fact that the state exercising sovereignty over them would, under the 200-mile exclusive economic zone system envisaged in the UN Law of the Sea Convention (opened for signature in 1982, and coming into force in 1994), be entitled to exploitation of some 150,000 square miles (about 390,000 sq km) of the surrounding ocean in respect of fishery, mineral and other resources.

It appeared that no country had ever formally claimed the islands until the 1960s, although maps of the area, including those prepared by the French authorities, had generally shown them as part of the New Hebrides. Following an inconclusive attempt by an Englishman and Frenchman (resident in the New Hebrides and New Caledonia respectively) to claim them jointly as their private property, France laid formal claim in 1975 when a landing party set up a plaque on Matthew Island. In December 1976 a French law declared that they were part of New Caledonia, and a memorandum to that effect was given to the Vanuatu authorities by France and Britain when the Condominium was dissolved prior to independence in July 1980.

The independent government of Vanuatu refused to recognize the French claim, however, and obtained support for its case from pro-independence groups in New Caledonia itself. When it appeared subsequently that a maritime boundary agreement between France and Fiji implied recognition of the French claim, protests from Vanuatu drew assurances from Fiji that the agreement was without prejudice to the Vanuatu claim. In March 1983 a Vanuatu landing party removed the French plaque from Matthew Island and erected a replacement claiming the islands for Vanuatu. French helicopters and ships were reported to be present in the area shortly afterwards, but no confrontation occurred. In May 1983 Vanuatu issued postage stamps depicting Umaenupnae and Umaeneag as part of its territory and gave notice that it intended to pursue its claim in international organizations.

Commenting on Vanuatu's erection of a plaque on Matthew Island, the French Minister for External Relations, Claude Cheysson, told the defence and armed services committee of the French Senate on May 27, 1983, that this action had "absolutely no effect whatsoever on France's legally indisputable and recognized national sovereignty over those islands". It was reported in March 1985 that France had established a military garrison on Matthew Island.

Criticism of French policy in New Caledonia was a feature of Vanuatu's relations with France during 1987, culminating in the expulsion of the French Ambassador, Henri Crépin-Leblond, on Oct. 1 (the third such expulsion since 1980) for interference in the country's domestic affairs. France retaliated by cutting the level of its aid to Vanuatu and so (Nov. 2) Vanuatu expelled two more French diplomats and removed France from the list of countries not requiring visas for visits to Vanuatu. After a lull, however, relations between the two countries improved, following the signing on June 26, 1988, of the Matignon Accord between France and New Caledonia, and in November 1989 Vanuatu's Foreign Minister, Donald Kalpokas, made an official visit to Paris where a process of rapprochement was initiated.

The case had implications for the two territories' exclusive economic zones (EEZs), based as they were in their claims to their respective territorial boundaries. After the Law of the Sea Convention came into effect, its provision relating to the 200-mile EEZ established sea boundaries generally at 200 miles away from the furthest land point, but where two EEZs intersect, as in the case of Vanuatu and New Caledonia, the area of intersection is equally divided.

Fiji-Tonga

The only other significant territorial dispute involving both land and water is that between Fiji and Tonga. Tonga's territorial claims were first promulgated in 1887, when "all the islands, rocks, reefs, foreshores, and waters lying between 15° and 23°30′South latitude, and between 177° and 173° West longitude" were designated Tongan territory. These have come to be known as Tonga's historic claims. They were reaffirmed in 1968 when oil exploration began in this general area. Fiji and Tonga would then already have had a substantial overlap of their respective EEZs if Tonga were to declare the limits of its historic claims as the base from which its EEZ was to be measured.

However, both island states were quick to take advantage of circumstances to expand their boundaries within the rules of the 200-mile EEZ. In 1972, Tonga formally laid claim to the Minerva Reefs (or Teleki Tonga and Teleki Tokelau), two volcanic formations a few miles apart situated 23°83′S and 179°00′E, some 180 miles south-west of the nearest island in the main Tongan group. North and South Minerva Reefs are about 18 nautical miles apart and more than 165 nautical miles from the nearest Tongan island.

This claim followed an attempt by Michael J. Oliver to create a microstate on the reefs, by having sand heaped on them to create a land mass. Their acquisition significantly increased Tonga's share of the maritime zone, though a complication was that at that time a 200-mile Tongan EEZ around the Minerva Reefs would also have overlapped with New Zealand's EEZ around the Kermadec Islands (a New Zealand dependency). Although Fiji acknowledged Tonga's claim to these reefs (as noted on its Chart 81/3), the EEZ claimed by Fiji still enclosed the reefs. The Tongan government has since built an artificial island and installed navigation beacons on each reef.

Meanwhile in 1965 Fiji had laid claim to the Conway Reef—today more often known by its Fijian name, Ceva-i-Ra. Ceva-i-Ra is a sand cay located 21°44′S and 174°38′E, some 300 miles south-west of Kadavu, the nearest island within the Fijian archipelago, and because it is naturally above water at high tide, it seemed indisputable that it would be entitled to a territorial sea, a contiguous zone, and hence an EEZ. The baseline for Ceva-i-Ra is the low-water line of the drying reefs that surround the island. The island itself measures only about 100 metres by 325 metres (some 6.5 acres), and the internal waters enclosed by the claimed baselines are approximately 2.5 sq km. A Fijian EEZ for Ceva-i-Ra would, however, overlap with the EEZ of either France (in respect of New Caledonia) or Vanuatu, depending on which finally succeeded in establishing sovereignty over Matthew and Hunter islands (see above). In 1983 Fiji formally annexed Ceva-i-Ra following underwater volcanic activity in the area. The "annexation" ceremony was carried out by the Governor General himself, who visited the island on a naval ship.

A crisis was narrowly averted when in 1993 King Taufa'ahau Tupou IV of Tonga claimed that Tonga's sovereign border needed to be extended westwards to incorporate the eastern Lau group of islands, where many of the inhabitants have Tongan ancestry. The Tongan king justified this on the grounds that in the nineteenth century one of his ancestors had invaded and ruled over much of eastern Fiji. However, this would have had the effect of transferring half of Fiji to Tonga. Fiji's reaction to this claim was prompt but restrained. It sent a high-powered delegation to Tonga to cool down a potentially tense and embarrassing situation. Given the very close traditional and cultural links between Fiji and Tonga it is not thought that this claim will be revived in the immediate future.

Since the UN Convention on the Law of the Sea came into effect in 1994 its provision relating to the 200-mile EEZ has established that sea boundaries are drawn 200 miles away from the furthest land point in each case and where two EEZs intersect, as in the case of Fiji and Tonga, the area of intersection is equally divided. Apart from the above, there have been no other cases of border disputes in the Pacific region and there seem unlikely to be more in the future.

Steven Ratuva

3.18 The Spratly Islands

The Spratly Islands (known to the Chinese as the Nansha Islands, to the Vietnamese as the Truong Sa and to the Philippines as Kalayaan) are a group of islets, coral reefs and sandbars in the South China Sea dispersed over 600 miles (965 kilometres). They are claimed, either in whole or in part, by the People's Republic of China, the Republic of China (Taiwan), Vietnam, the Philippines and Malaysia. (Map 32, p. 508, shows the location of the Spratly Islands.)

Importance of the Islands

The Spratly Islands lie nearly 300 miles (480 kilometres) west of the Philippine island of Palawan, slightly over 300 miles east of Vietnam and about 650 miles (about 1,050 kilometres) south of Hainan, the nearest Chinese territory. All the islands are very small—the largest, Itu Aba (known to the Chinese as Taiping), has an area of only 90 acres (36 hectares). Despite their small size these islands are important for both resource and strategic reasons. The resources in question are both non-renewable (oil and gas) and renewable (fish). The strategic significance arises from the fact that they command the sea passage—or sea lines of communication—from Japan to Singapore.

The economic development of many Asian states, most notably China and the "tiger economies" of the region's newly industrialized countries (NICs), has increased the Asian states' demand for oil and gas. Thus despite substantial oil reserves China became a net importer of oil in 1993, and although it has increased oil production since the early 1990s, its oil consumption has risen at a greater rate. China is now one of the world's ten largest oil importers. Likewise, China's natural gas consumption has also risen and this, unsurprisingly, has led to considerable interest in the availability of hydrocarbons in the South China Sea.

The scale of such resources is uncertain. In 1989 China's Geology and Mineral Resources Ministry estimated that the area around the Spratlys contained some 130 billion barrels of oil as well as natural gas reserves, but independent sources have put the figure much lower. One reason for these differing estimates is simply a lack of data, although governments have an interest in making bold statements to attract international interest and investment, while oil companies talk down the figures to secure more commercially favourable contracts. Nevertheless, despite questions over the amount of oil and gas available, it appears quantities are sufficient for commercial exploitation, especially in the Vanguard Bank and to a lesser extent the Reed Bank.

In addition to oil and gas deposits, the South China Sea has a considerable stock of renewable resources, of which fish are particularly important. The Sea provides the 500 million people who live on its coast with their main source of protein. Of the total Asian fish catch, the fisheries of Southeast Asia account for 23 per cent. The South China Sea is thus of great importance to the welfare of the region's populations, and it is coming under increasing threat from human activity; the most direct problem is over-fishing in the region. The reduction in fish numbers is encouraging fishermen to either fish illegally in other states' maritime zones, or fish in those areas that are subject to competing claims. This (illegal) fishing has led to a number of clashes between the fishing fleets of one state and the naval patrol vessels of another, which helps to explain why fish are central to understanding the Spratlys dispute.

In addition to resource issues, the Spratly Islands are important for strategic reasons—their potential use to disrupt transportation. It is estimated that more than 41,000 ships a year pass through the South China Sea, more than double the number that pass through the Suez Canal and nearly three times the total for the Panama Canal. To the south, the Strait of Malacca connects the South China Sea to the Indian Ocean, while to the north the Taiwan Strait connects the South China Sea to the Pacific Ocean. Freedom of movement along these sea lines of communication (SLOC) is crucial to the economic survival and prosperity of a number of Asian states, including Japan. For Japan unfettered access to the SLOC are vital for its oil imports from the Middle East and its exports of manufactured goods to Asia and Europe. The freedom of navigation is thus of critical importance for Japan. It is also an important military issue for the USA, since the "freedom of navigation" principle implies that US warships have the right of "innocent passage" through the South China Sea. That is, they do not need to inform governments of countries bordering the ocean of their warships' passage. Should, for example, the Spratly Islands therefore fall under the control of China the fear is that this will interfere with the SLOC and extend the dispute beyond Southeast Asia and draw in such external powers as Japan and the USA.

The Rival Claims

Beijing and Taipei both claim that the islands were discovered by Chinese navigators, were used by Chinese fishermen for centuries and came under Chinese administration in the 15th century, and that China's sovereignty over them was never disputed until the 1930s. They also claim that the Spratlys form a continuation of the Paracel Islands, which are claimed by both China and Vietnam (see Section 3.9). Vietnam maintains that the Spratlys became part of the Empire of Annam in the early 19th century, and that they had not previously been under the administration of any country. The Philippines bases its claim on proximity and administrative control, but has laid no claim to Spratly Island itself, which lies over 200 miles (320 kilometres) south-west of the main group of islands. For its part, Malaysia published an official map in December 1979 showing a southern portion of the Spratly archipelago as part of its continental shelf. Brunei's claim is based upon the exclusive economic zone (EEZ) that it was granted under the 1982 United Nations Law of the Sea Convention.

The above are the present states that lay claim to all or part of the Spratly Islands. In addition to these claimants the Spratlys have in the past been claimed in part or whole by Britain, France and Japan. The Japanese even established a submarine base on Itu Aba and used it in 1942 as one of the vantage points for the Japanese invasion of the Philippines. This fact has been used in more recent times by Manila to support their claim the Spratlys have a strategic importance for their security.

The reason why the Spratly Islands dispute has drawn attention is because of the surge of claims that began in the 1970s due to the concurrence of two factors. First, although British and US oil companies had been interested in exploiting oil in the area since the 1950s, it was only in 1969, after a geological survey had been published revealing oil in the South China Sea, that control of the oil resources of the area became an issue. Second, the third United Nations Conference on the Law of the Sea (UNCLOS III), which met between 1973 and 1982, resulted in adoption of the 1982 Convention on the Law of the Sea (finally in force from 1994). This established the principle that every coastal state could claim a continental shelf (out to a maximum of 350 nautical miles if the shelf was naturally prolonged that far) and an exclusive economic zone (EEZ) of 200 nautical miles. The EEZ not only applied to resources in the sea (fish, for example) but those of the seabed as well.

With oil to exploit and the possible extension of continental shelf claims, the states around the South China Sea began to position themselves to take advantage of this new legal regime. The Philippines in 1974 awarded a concession for a consortium of oil companies to explore for oil in the Reed Bank where the Philippines occupied eight islets. In 1973 South Vietnam awarded a number of oil exploration contracts to US companies. When in 1974 China attacked and drove out the South Vietnamese from the western Paracels (since 1974 China has been in sole control of the Paracels), Saigon used these troops to occupy several islands in the Spratlys. With the reunification of Vietnam, Hanoi took command of these garrisons and has since steadily expanded its control. Vietnam occupies more reefs and islands than any other claimant. With Sabah and Sarawak joining Malaya to form the Malaysian Federation in 1963, this enabled Kuala Lumpur to lay claim to those areas of the South China Sea near Borneo. In 1979 it published a map showing an extensive continental shelf claim north of Borneo, and in 1983 and 1986 sent troops to occupy islands on the continental shelf. By the mid-1980s the Philippines, Malaysia, Vietnam and Taiwan (which occupies Itu Aba) had occupied virtually all the features in the Spratlys that were above the sea at high tide—the latter being the legal requirement for a feature to be recognized as an island.

Chinese Assertiveness

In the late 1980s, China became the last claimant to enter the scramble for features in the Spratlys. With Vietnam issuing oil concessions to areas that China claimed, it became imperative to Beijing that China had a presence there. The opportunity presented itself when Hanoi's ally, the Soviet Union, began, as part of Mikhail Gorbachev's reforms, to scale back its deployments in the area. In 1988 the Chinese began to occupy several reefs including Fiery Cross Reef. In the vicinity were Vietnamese forces and in March a naval exchange occurred near Johnson Reef. Although Chinese forces did not attempt to dislodge Vietnamese forces from their garrisons, the naval clash saw three Vietnamese vessels sunk and 77 sailors lose their lives. Despite some recent minor skirmishes, the 1974 and 1988 incidents remain the most serious examples of force being used over rival claims in the Spratlys.

These assertive actions by China led, in the 1990s, to concern over Chinese intentions in the South China Sea. The adoption by China on Feb. 25, 1992, of the Law on the Territorial Waters and their Contiguous Areas, through which Beijing essentially claimed suzerainty over the whole of the South China Sea, appeared to confirm the view that the claimant with the greatest military power was embarking upon an aggressive policy to fortify its claim. Then, in 1995, the Philippines discovered that China had been constructing structures on one of the reefs it claims, the aptly named Mischief Reef. The structures appeared to be guard posts with satellite antennas and a helipad. There were also three Chinese naval vessels with five support boats. The Chinese claim, that the structures were shelters for their fishermen, was widely regarded as duplicitous and only confirmed worst-case thinking about Chinese intentions. The Mischief Reef structures, coupled to the airbase discovered in 1990 that the Chinese constructed on Woody Island in the Paracels, appeared to be another stepping stone in the Chinese goal of achieving military dominance in the South China Sea.

China's claims to the Spratly Islands were initially driven by its desire to recover the "lost territories" allegedly taken during the 19th century by the colonial powers. The Spratly Islands were thus of great national importance and were regarded by Liu Huaqing (appointed China's naval commander in 1982 and a member of the Central Military Commission until 1997) as akin to recovering Hong Kong and Taiwan. This helps to explain the controversial territorial law passed in 1992 in which China treated the South China Sea as internal waters. It also helps to explain the naval expansion the Chinese have embarked upon since the early 1990s. In March 1989 China established a South China Sea frontline headquarters, naval patrols in the

South China Sea were increased and new naval vessels such as the *Luhu*-class guided missile destroyer and the *Jiangwei*-class guided missile frigate were procured. It is widely anticipated that China will acquire an aircraft carrier and in April 2000 the Chinese successfully carried out mid-flight refuelling, an essential capability for achieving power projection in the South China Sea.

These improving military capabilities coincided with China's propensity to threaten to use force to fulfil its objectives. In 1995-96 Beijing held provocative military exercises close to Taiwan during the island's presidential elections and began the construction of structures on the Philippine-claimed Mischief Reef. These structures were completed in 1999 and regarded by the then Philippines Defence Secretary as "a dagger at our underbelly". The facilities on Mischief Reef make it a staging post for oil exploration and it also provides support for the Chinese fishermen who persistently clash with the Philippine authorities. The political message is clear: China can and will challenge the other claimants. While Beijing is not yet capable of resolving the South China Sea dispute through military force it is the only claimant that could pursue this solution in the foreseeable future. The failure throughout the 1990s of China to agree to a code of conduct on the South China Sea and to compromise in negotiations with the other claimants, creates the perception that China is merely biding its time until its military capability enables it to impose its own solution.

Diverse Approaches of Claimants in 1990s— ASEAN Dimension

With the exception of Taiwan, all the claimants other than China are members of the Association of Southeast Asian Nations (ASEAN). In response to China's new territorial law, ASEAN on July 22, 1992, issued a Declaration on the South China Sea, which included a provision for negotiating with China a code of conduct. However, while the Chinese Foreign Minister, Qian Qichen, agreed that a peaceful settlement to the dispute was desirable, progress in resolving the dispute would, he said, occur "when the conditions are ripe"; when these conditions would be ripe was not specified.

Although the Chinese assertion of sovereignty over the Spratlys can be understood as recovering "lost territory", as an explanation for Chinese behaviour this became less important during the 1990s. An alternative explanation lies in Beijing's desire to extract the renewable and non-renewable resources located in and around the Spratlys. However, China also wishes to create a propitious environment for its growing economy to strengthen further by establishing stable relations with its neighbours. In order to exploit the Spratlys oil, gas and fish resources it has been in Beijing's interest to resolve the dispute, but China has indicated that it is not prepared to negotiate over the question of ownership. Instead, Beijing's interest has

lain in negotiating bilateral joint development projects with the other claimants. These proposals date back to 1992 and illustrate China's preference for reaching bilateral as opposed to multilateral agreements. In addition to exploiting the resources, China's economic growth requires a stable region in order to maintain and enhance its economic prosperity. This need for co-operative economic relations was given tangible form by the creation of the ASEAN Plus Three (APT) process in December 1997 in response to the economic and financial crisis that wreaked havoc in East Asia.

Throughout the 1990s ASEAN sought a solution to the Spratlys dispute through the adoption of a multilateral code of conduct that created norms to regulate the behaviour of the claimants. The key provisions were to refrain from the use or threat of force and to halt the construction of new structures in the South China Sea. The emphasis on a multilateral rather than bilateral solution ensured a lukewarm response from China and the best achieved by 1995 was a bilateral code of conduct between the Philippines and China that ASEAN endorsed in July 1996 as laying "the foundation [for] long term stability". The ASEAN claimants were, however, struggling to reach agreement amongst themselves over the terms of a code of conduct. Vietnam wanted to include the Paracels as well as the Spratlys, while the Philippines was only interested in the latter. The Philippines wanted a code that adopted the language of a formal treaty while Malaysian and Indonesian officials preferred a political rather than a legal document. The Philippines also wanted a provision committing the signatories to refrain from occupying new islands, reefs or shoals, which garnered little support from Malaysia and Vietnam.

The failure to achieve progress towards a code of conduct coupled to the Chinese construction of buildings on Mischief Reef and other infringements of the bilateral code of conduct between Beijing and Manila, resulted in Malaysia and the Philippines adopting two different approaches to resolving the Spratlys dispute. Malaysia sought to bandwagon with China, while the Philippines sought to balance China.

The Philippines signed a new Visiting Forces Agreement (VFA) with the USA on Feb. 10, 1998. US forces had previously been asked to leave the Philippines and had completed their withdrawal in 1992 with the closure of the naval facilities at Subic Bay. The VFA allowed US forces to access Philippine facilities again and engage in military exercises with Philippine troops. While there is some ambiguity as to whether the VFA, or indeed the 1951 US-Philippine Mutual Defence Treaty, extends to assisting the Philippines defend territory in the Spratlys, in February-March 2000 US-Philippine military exercises were conducted off Palawan in the South China Sea. The message to Beijing was clear—as with Taiwan, if China sought to resolve the Spratlys dispute through force, it would need to consider the possibility of US intervention.

By contrast the Malaysian approach was to try to resolve the dispute by agreeing to China's proposals for bilateral agreements and joint development, and thereby obligate China to act within the commitments it agreed with Malaysia. In May 1999 Malaysia and China issued a joint statement calling for bilateral negotiations; Malaysia occupied an additional two reefs, and the Malaysian Prime Minister, Mahathir Mohammad, publicly emphasized that the United States should be excluded and the dispute should be resolved by the claimants themselves. The Philippine Foreign Ministry accused Malaysia of breaking ranks with ASEAN and colluding with the Chinese.

By the end of the 1990s a peaceful settlement of the dispute based upon a multilateral code of conduct looked unlikely. The ASEAN claimants were in disagreement with one another, and China's proposals not only remained fixed on bilateral solutions but China was now urging all parties to refrain from actions that would "complicate or magnify the disputes", which was seen as a reference to the US-Philippine VFA. In 2000 and 2001 the ASEAN claimants continued their discussions over the geographical scope of a code of conduct and whether a ban should be placed on new structures.

Declaration on the Conduct of Parties in the South China Sea, 2002

In July 2002 Malaysia proposed signing a declaration on a code of conduct rather than a code itself; that is, something less binding than a code of conduct. This was acceptable to the Chinese, since a declaration would be a mechanism for resolving the dispute but it would leave unsaid what that mechanism would be. The Chinese were also able to gain Philippine agreement to Article 5 of the declaration that called for sig-natories to "refrain from action of inhabiting uninhabited islands, reefs, shoals" rather than banning the erection of new structures on reefs already inhabited. The Chinese were additionally able to insert in Article 10 that their obligation to work towards a code of conduct would be achieved "on the basis of consensus". The resultant Declaration on the Conduct of Parties in the South China Sea was signed at the 8th ASEAN summit at Phnom Penh in November 2002. The ASEAN claimants were delighted to have gained Chinese acquiescence to a multilateral agreement, albeit one that fell short of a code of conduct with a legal status.

Although the 2002 declaration calls for continued negotiation to create a proper code of conduct on the South China Sea this seems very unlikely. Instead, the declaration represents the end of the attempt adopted ten years previously to achieve a peaceful resolution by this means. With increasing energy demands leading to claimants awarding concessions to oil and gas companies to exploit the resources in contested areas, plus the frequent seizure of vessels caught fishing in contested waters, the Spratlys dispute is likely to remained unresolved for a long time. Yet, the use of force to resolve this dispute is perhaps less likely than it was. The improving relations between China and the ASEAN claimants is not only epitomized by the 2002 declaration but is also reflected in their wider relations. In addition to the APT process, China and ASEAN agreed in November 2001 to implement a free trade area by 2010, and perhaps most significantly, in October 2003 China became the first state outside Southeast Asia to accede to ASEAN's Treaty of Amity and Co-operation.

Alan Collins

EUROPE

4.1 Albania - Greece (Northern Epirus)

A dispute between Greece and Albania over the southern part of Albania inhabited by ethnic Greeks has been referred to in Greece as "the northern Epirus question", implying that the disputed area should be regarded as part of the Greek region of Epirus on both historical and ethnic grounds. Any residual official Greek aspiration to territorial change was implicitly abandoned when the Athens government, in August 1987, formally acknowledged that it was no longer in a state of war with Albania. Nevertheless, the existence of an ethnic Greek minority in Albania remained a complicating factor in relations between the two states. This was demonstrated graphically when the collapse of Communist rule in Albania in 1990-91 precipitated a mass exodus of ethnic Greeks seeking a better life in Greece, and similar complaints were raised in Albania about the position of ethnic Albanians on the Greek side of the frontier. Tensions over the status of minorities on both sides of the frontier peaked in 1994, however, and with much improved relations evident the border issue may now be regarded as settled. (Map 33, p. 509, illustrates the area.)

History of the Dispute

Ancient Epirus traditionally consisted of the mountainous region of the Adriatic coast and hinterland opposite the island of Corfu, extending southwards from the Vijose river in modern Albania into what is now north-western Greece. Having been on the fringes of classical Greek civilization, the kingdom of Epirus achieved some prominence in the post-classical Hellenistic world. It reached its zenith in the early third century BC under King Pyrrhus, who won costly ("Pyrrhic") victories over the Romans, but eventually became part of the Roman province of Macedonia (146 BC). As part of the Eastern Roman (Byzantine) Empire, Epirus was largely unaffected by the Slavic penetration of the Balkan peninsula from c.600 AD, its population remaining a mixture of ethnic Greeks and Albanians (descendants of the ancient Illyrians). As Byzantine authority declined, a semi-independent despotate of Albania and Epirus emerged in the early 13th century. In the 14th century the whole area became part of the short-lived Serbian empire, before falling, with the rest of the Balkans, to the all-conquering Ottoman Turks in the 15th century. Under Turkish rule, most Albanians, including those of Epirus, were forcibly converted to Islam, whereas the Greeks mostly retained their Orthodox Christian faith.

In the long decline of Ottoman power Epirus became a focus of contending Greek and Albanian national aspirations. In 1798 Albania achieved a measure of autonomy, within ill-defined borders, but was to remain under Turkish sovereignty throughout the 19th century. In contrast, an independent Greek kingdom had been established by 1829. It was confined at first to Livadia, the Peloponnese and the western Aegean islands but later expanded northwards, acquiring Corfu and the other Ionian islands in 1863 (from Britain) and Thessaly in 1881 (from the Turks). Further Greek ambitions in the Turkish-ruled north then centred on the ancient province of Macedonia, the Greek claim to which encompassed not only the whole of Epirus but also much of present-day Albania. Such aims were pursued in the Balkan Wars of 1912-13, during which the Turks lost all their remaining territory in Europe (apart from Eastern Thrace) and Macedonia was partitioned between Greece, Serbia and Bulgaria. However, schemes that Serbia and Montenegro would divide up Albania and that Greece would obtain the whole of Epirus were thwarted by the proclamation on Nov. 12, 1912, during the First Balkan War, of an independent principality of Albania.

The new Albanian state was recognized by a conference of European powers held in London in December 1912, although the precise delimitation of its frontiers was reserved for a future decision. Agreement in principle on Albania's borders was subsequently reached at an ambassadors' conference in London in mid-1913, while the Second Balkan War was in progress. Under the Treaty of Bucharest of Aug. 10, 1913, Albanian independence was internationally recognized within virtually its present-day borders, meaning that Albania included the northern part of Epirus, where Albanians outnumbered ethnic Greeks. For its part, Greece obtained the mainly Greek-populated southern region of Epirus as part of its acquisition of Aegean Macedonia. For Albania, the inclusion of northern Epirus in its territory was some compensation for the acquisition by Serbia and Montenegro of Albanian-majority areas in the north and east. However, for the dominant "greater Greece" school in Athens, northern Epirus became one of a number of outstanding issues in the quest to extend the borders of modern Greece to all areas regarded as historically part of the Greek/Hellenistic world.

During World War I Greece occupied northern Epirus in October 1914 (while northern and central Albania was occupied by Austro-Hungarian troops in 1915). In the secret Treaty of London of 1915, designed to bring Italy into the war on the side of the Allies, Italy was promised a protectorate over the greater part of Albania, with the north going to Serbia and the south to Greece. This was rejected by the Albanians, who again declared their own independent state in 1920. After armed Albanians had attacked an Italian-held port, Italy withdrew from Albania in August 1920 and recognized Albania's independence and territorial integrity. Following Albania's admission to the League of Nations on Dec. 17, 1920, a boundary commission composed of Britain, France and Italy delimited Albania's frontiers and completed its work in 1926. A final demarcation act was signed by the above powers and also Greece and Yugoslavia in Paris on July 30, 1926. Under its terms, northern Epirus was confirmed as belonging to Albania.

After the advent of the Fascist regime in Italy and the conclusion of a treaty of friendship and security between Italy and Albania in November 1926, Italian influence increased greatly in Albania, culminating in the occupation of the latter by Italian forces as from April 17, 1939. From Albanian soil Italian forces attacked Greece in October 1940, but they were defeated by the Greeks, who subsequently took over about half of Albania and declared northern Epirus to be liberated. However, in April 1941 Hitler's forces overran both Greece and Yugoslavia, and Italy again obtained control over all of Albania.

During the period of resistance by the Albanians against the Italian (and later German) occupation forces, there emerged a National Front formed by Albanian Communists and nationalists. The provisional government set up by the Front under the leadership of Col. Enver Hoxha was recognized by the Allies towards the end of 1945, but the Greek government protested against the Allies' recognition on Nov. 10, 1945, and at the demand of all Greek political parties except the Communists declared its claim "for the union of northern Epirus with the Greek motherland". This Greek claim was supported by the US Senate, which in July 1946 passed the "Pepper resolution" in favour of northern Epirus being ceded to Greece. However, when the Greek claim was raised at a Paris meeting of Allied Foreign Ministers in August-September 1946, it was removed from the agenda by James Byrne (the US Secretary of State) after Hoxha, representing Albania, had declared that "neither the Paris conference nor the conference of the Big Four nor any other gathering can review the frontiers of my country, which has no foreign territory of any kind under its jurisdiction". The Allies thus de facto reaffirmed Albania's 1913 (1926) frontiers.

Rapprochement between Albania and Greece

No mention of the Greek claim was made when the Foreign Ministers of Greece, Turkey and Yugoslavia (then members of a tripartite grouping which became the Balkan Pact) met in Athens on July 7-11, 1953, and agreed that "the independence of Albania constitutes an important element of peace and stability in the Balkans". On July 2, 1958, the Albanian government expressed its desire to establish "normal and good-neighbourly relations" with Greece, but at the same time it rejected a Greek statement to the effect that there was still a state of war between the two countries resulting from Albanian participation in Italy's attack on Greece in 1940. The Greek response to Albania's proposal was said to have included a reiteration of Greece's claim to "northern Epirus" but also an offer to seek a settlement of this problem through normal channels. The Albanian side rejected the Greek reply on Aug. 14, 1958, denying again that there was a state of war between the two countries and rebutting the

Greek territorial claim on the ground that "the question of northern Epirus does not exist, as this is Albanian territory".

On Jan. 9, 1962, the Albanian government again expressed its readiness to establish diplomatic relations with Greece, provided the Greek government abandoned its "baseless" claim to part of southern Albania. A first trade agreement between the two countries at non-government level was concluded on June 2, 1970. It was followed by the establishment of diplomatic relations on May 6, 1971, this step being understood to imply Greek recognition of Albania's existing borders. Further trade agreements or protocols were signed in later years, and on March 28, 1978, a direct air link was set up.

The question of Greek-Albanian relations was again raised when a map was published in Yugoslavia in May 1981, purporting to show that the Communist government of Albania had claims to a "greater Albania" incorporating territories currently parts of Yugoslavia and of Greece; it was found, however, that this map had been produced by Albanian exiles in the West in 1971. George Rallis, then Greek Prime Minister, stated in mid-1981 that the Greek government was opposed to "any attempt to disturb the status quo in the area", while in an eight-page document issued by the Albanian embassy in Athens it was emphasized that Albania desired the continuation of good relations between the two countries, to which was added: "The healthy sections of Greek public opinion know that the so-called northern Epirus issue is long dead and has no future".

During a visit to Albania (the first by a Greek minister since World War II) by Karolos Papoulias, the Greek Alternate Minister of Foreign Affairs, on Dec. 3-6, 1984, agreements were signed on transport, postal services, telecommunications, cultural relations and scientific exchanges. Papoulias, who was himself born in Albania, also met representatives of the Greek community in Albania. The border crossing at Kakavia, which had been closed since 1940, was reopened on Jan. 12, 1985, although mainly for official traffic only. An economic co-operation agreement was signed on Jan. 25, 1985, and a cultural exchange programme on March 8, 1985. In July of that year a protocol was signed on the restoration of border markers and procedures for the settlement of border disputes and violations.

In a move to facilitate full normalization of relations with Albania, the then Greek government of the Pan-Hellenic Socialist Movement (PASOK) declared on Aug. 23, 1985, its intention of officially terminating the state of war with Albania which in the Greek view had existed since October 1940. A formal Greek cabinet decision to this effect was subsequently announced on Aug. 28, 1987, when a government spokesman said that the return to peaceful status would contribute to the further strengthening of bilateral relations. He added that the decision would be of particular benefit for the Greek minority community in northern Epirus, whose situation would continue to have the full attention of the Greek government. Widely seen as effectively a formal annulment of the Greek territorial claim to northern Epirus, the move was warmly welcomed by Albania but strongly contested by the political right in Greece. Thus the leader of the conservative opposition, Konstantinos Mitsotakis, described it as "an inadmissible act, constitutionally, politically and nationally", which failed to safeguard "the basic human rights of the Greeks of northern Epirus". Nevertheless, on coming to power in April 1990, Mitsotakis and his conservative government made no move to rescind the August 1987 decision.

Situation of Greek Minority in Albania

The ethnic Greek community in Albania, the country's largest minority, is concentrated in the southern districts of Korce and Gjirokaster. Before World War II it was estimated (by Greek consular authorities) to number some 300,000, or about 20 per cent of Albania's total population. During and immediately after the war many Greeks left Albania, mainly for Greece, but the extent of this exodus and the numbers remaining have been matters of dispute, aggravated by the refusal of the post-war Communist regime in Tirana to publish statistics on ethnic minorities. According to Greek data published in 1981, 62 of Albania's 250 parliamentary deputies were then of Greek origin or Greek-speaking, including three cabinet ministers, two under-secretaries and one deputy speaker of parliament. Two years later, in 1983, the then Albanian leader, Enver Hoxha, maintained that there were only 28,000 ethnic Greeks in Albania, whereas nationalist circles in Greece at that time were claiming that the real figure was as high as 400,000. More recent Western estimates have usually opted for a probable total of 200,000, although the 1989 Albanian census recorded 59,000 people as declaring themselves to be ethnic Greeks.

In a speech on March 23, 1978, Hoxha gave assurances that the Greek minority in Albania would continue to be allowed to speak and study the Greek language and to maintain its Greek culture. This official policy of recognition of ethnic Greek rights was reflected in the existence, in the early 1980s, of a twice-weekly Greek newspaper (the only one published by any minority in Albania) and the regular publication of books in Greek. There were also Greek schools (in strictly defined areas) and an academy for the training of ethnic Greek teachers. However, to the extent that ethnic Greeks derived their identity from adherence to the Orthodox Christian Church, they suffered from the official atheism of the Communist regime (as did other religious groups). Following the declaration of Albania as "the first atheist state in the world" (in 1967), some 630 major Orthodox churches were razed to the ground and an equal number converted to other uses. Moreover, ethnic Greeks were particular targets of the official prohibition (in 1975) of "foreign" or religious personal and place names. There were also periodic reports of government action to disperse ethnic Greeks and to settle ethnic Albanians in Greek areas, and also of semi-official discouragement of the speaking of Greek in public places.

Although the closed nature of Communist Albania meant that firm evidence of the situation of ethnic Greeks was often elusive, Greek nationalist circles had no doubt that they were subjected to persistent official persecution. The Northern Epirus Society (led by Xenophon Kountouris) and the Pan-Epirus Federation of America and Canada (led by Menelaos Tzelios) repeatedly claimed that many thousands of ethnic Greeks were being held in Albanian prisons and concentration camps and that the Albanian regime was systematically denying ethnic Greeks access to their relatives in Greece. In 1983 a Committee for the Protection of the Rights of the Greek Minority in Northern Epirus claimed that up to 25,000 ethnic Greeks had been imprisoned in Albania. Following a hunger strike by two Greek refugees from Albania, detained by the Greek police in Athens, the Greek Prime Minister declared on Feb. 21, 1984, that his government would not tolerate "the violation of human rights of Greeks in Albania" (although he added that Greece had no territorial claim).

After Hoxha's death in April 1985, the succeeding regime of Ramiz Alia appeared to adopt a less harsh line on minority and religious questions, and relations with Greece improved markedly. In response, the Athens government in August 1987 finally acknowledged that it was no longer in a state of war with Albania (see above). In 1988 visitors to Albania reported extensive restoration of churches (and mosques) as cultural relics, while the number of Greek nationals allowed to visit relatives in Albania increased steadily, as did visits in the other direction. Nevertheless, the continued potential of the minority question for aggravating Greek-Albanian relations was demonstrated in late 1989 when Greek public opinion was outraged by Yugoslav reports that four ethnic Greek brothers had been tortured and killed for trying to flee Albania. When the Albanian Deputy Foreign Minister, Sokrat Plaka, visited Athens in January 1990 in an attempt to defuse this particular crisis, he was pelted with eggs and tomatoes by demonstrating crowds.

Exodus of Ethnic Greeks from post-Communist Albania

Albania's retreat from, and eventual abandonment of, one-party Communist rule in 1990-91 appeared to bring with it a more relaxed official attitude towards the country's Greek minority. In June 1990 the Albanian government eased entry and exit restrictions for visits in both directions across the Greek-Albanian border. At the same time, Albania declared its wish to become a party to the various instruments of the Conference on Security and Co-operation in Europe (CSCE), including those dealing with human rights and protection of minorities. However, Albania's political transformation resulted, from late 1990, in a dramatic acceleration in the flow of escapees across the Greek border, most of them young unskilled males.

Albanian border guards were reportedly no longer shooting on sight at people attempting to cross the heavily fortified frontier, so that by December 1990 the numbers leaving daily—up to 600—had risen to the level recorded for the whole of the three years 1987-89. A sudden upsurge to 3,500 a day at the turn of the year was apparently prompted by a rumour that the Greek authorities were going to close the border. On Jan. 2, 1991, Greek officials said that this rumour had been put about by the Albanian authorities with the aim of ridding the country of ethnic Greeks.

During a visit to Tirana on Jan. 13-14, 1991, the Greek Prime Minister appealed to ethnic Greeks to remain in Albania and received a promise from the Albanian government that the refugees could return to Albania without fear of punishment. His visit did nothing to stem the exodus. On Jan. 20 the Greek authorities declared that no Albanian nationals would be allowed to enter Greece without a passport and visa. By this time, the number of ethnic Greek refugees arriving since Dec. 30 stood at over 11,000. Over 5,000 were repatriated in the following week, but by late February 1991 the total of ethnic Greeks from Albania seeking asylum in Greece was reported to have reached 17,000. Many of them found their only refuge on the streets of Athens, so that Greek sympathy for the plight of ethnic Greeks in northern Epirus came to be qualified by the perceived negative impact of their arrival in Greece (and there were doubts whether all the refugees were in fact Greeks).

In this situation, the Greek government maintained its position that the solution to the problem must lie in better treatment for ethnic Greeks within Albania and that there was no territorial issue between the two countries. Nevertheless, as post-Communist Albania descended into economic and social chaos, voices were increasingly heard on the Greek nationalist right to the effect that the "northern Epirus question" should be reopened with a view to seeking a revision of the existing border. In early 1992 such sentiments were strengthened by an escalation of violence against ethnic Greeks in southern Albania and of cross-border incidents involving incursions by Albanian marauders. The violence in southern Albania included the burning down of Greek shops in the port of Sarande and the vandalizing of the offices of Omonia, the political party of ethnic Greeks. In the March-April 1991 Albanian elections Omonia had taken five of the 200 Assembly seats but had subsequently found itself covered by a ban, enacted in January 1992, on parties of an ethnic minority character. Because of the ban, support for Omonia in the general election of March 1992 was channeled to a new Human Rights Union.

Meanwhile, concern was rising in Albania over the treatment of ethnic Albanians in the north-west corner of Greece. The area—known in Albania as southern Cameria—was inhabited, according to various estimates, by between 90,000 and over one million Cams. However, Athens had not considered these ethnic Albanians to be a separate ethnic group; they had not been entitled to any special minority rights and complained that had been prevented from establishing any educational, cultural, or political associations inside Greece. Hence after the establishment of representative government in Albania in early 1991, the Albanian Cams had organized as a pressure group within Albania on behalf of their co-ethnics in Greece. In March 1991, the first national conference of the Cameria Political Association (CPA) was held in Tirana with many of its activists drawn from the Albanian community who had been expelled from Greece after the war. The CPA intended to bring to international attention the neglected linguistic, cultural, and educational rights of Orthodox Albanian Cams who, they claimed, had been subjected to a Greek policy of assimilation. The group has also launched campaigns on behalf of Cam exiles in Albania. It has encouraged the expansion of contacts with compatriots in Greece, the return of exiles to their family areas, and the payment of compensation for property and land that was illegally taken from them during their expulsion.

The crisis in Greek-Albanian relations reached a peak in the summer of 1994, when an Albanian court sentenced five members (a sixth member was added later) of Omonia to prison terms on charges of undermining the Albanian state. Greece responded by imposing its veto on all EU aid to Albania and deporting tens of thousands of illegal Albanians. In May 1994 the Greek government spokesman, Evangelos Venizelos, said his government was firmly committed to safeguarding human rights for the 400,000-strong ethnic Greek community in Albania. "The rights of the Greek minority are not negotiable. They are defined by international law, and it would be proper for the Albanian government and public authorities to respect them". He reiterated that good relations between the two countries hinged on Albania's respect for the human rights of the Greek ethnic minority.

Commenting on recent accusations by Albanian President Sali Berisha against Greece, Venizelos said that "too many and too intense statements do not help cultivating good relations between the two countries". President Berisha had accused Greece of irredentist designs against his country, because it had not ratified the Florence Treaty setting the borders between the two countries. "Ratifying the treaty would be comparable to ending the warring situation between the two countries". In December 1994, however, Greece began to permit limited EU aid to Albania, while Albania released two of the Omonia defendants and reduced the sentences of the remaining four. Over the next few years relations between the two countries improved substantially. Occasional ethnic tensions have been evident, but there is now no serious challenge to the status quo, and Greece is one of Albania's three largest trade partners. It has been a strong proponent of Albania's eventual integration into the EU and NATO and at the Albanian government's request, about 250 Greek military personnel are stationed in Albania to assist with training and restructuring its armed forces.

Peter Calvert

4.2 Armenia - Azerbaijan (Nagorno-Karabakh)

The conflict over Nagorno-Karabakh stands out as the most intractable in the South Caucasus as it embodies a combination of separatism and irredentism and has exacerbated the relations between two neighbouring countries—Armenia and Azerbaijan—whose geopolitical orientation, subject to cross-cutting regional and external interests and influences, is still in the balance. Nagorno-Karabakh is also the first major conflict in which the Organization for Security and Co-operation in Europe (OSCE) has been centrally involved as a mediator and peacekeeper. In 1992-93, the conflict escalated into a full-blown war leaving the death toll at 25,000 and the number of displaced people and refugees on both sides at over one million. Although a ceasefire has been in effect since May 1994, a state of "neither peace nor war" prevails and the region of Nagorno-Karabakh is de facto, if not de jure, independent and outside of the jurisdiction of Azerbaijan. (For this dispute, see Map 34, p. 509.)

Landlocked Armenia (29,800 sq km in area, with Yerevan as its capital) is bounded by Georgia in the north, Turkey in the west, Iran in the south and Azerbaijan in the south and east. Azerbaijan (86,600 sq km in area, with Baku as its capital) borders the Caspian Sea to the east, Iran to the south, Armenia to the west, Georgia to the north-west and the Russian Federation to the north. Within Azerbaijan the autonomous Armenian-majority oblast (district) of Nagorno-Karabakh (meaning "mountainous black garden"), with Stepanakert as its capital, covers 4,400 sq km of mountainous terrain in the south-western part of the country and shares no border with Armenia. Azerbaijan also includes the Azeri-dominated autonomous republic of Nakhichevan, covering 5,500 sq km and separated from Azerbaijan proper by a 50-kilometre-wide strip of Armenian territory. To complicate matters further, there are three tiny Azeri enclaves within Armenia's borders (two in the north-east and one in the south-west close to Nakhichevan) and a tiny Armenian enclave on the Azerbaijani side of the border.

According to the January 1989 Soviet census, Armenia's population was 3,304,776, of whom 93.3 per cent were Armenians and 2.6 per cent Azeris. The same census gave the population of Azerbaijan as 7,021,178, of whom 82.7 per cent were Azeris, 5.6 per cent Armenians and 5.6 per cent Russians. In 1989, the population of Nagorno-Karabakh was approximately 75 per cent ethnic Armenian (145,000) and 25 per cent ethnic Azeri (40,688).

Early Historical Background

Armenians trace the origins of their settlement in eastern Anatolia and the Caucasus back to the eighth century BC. They attach particular importance to the fact that under Roman rule the semi-autonomous Armenian kingdom became, in 301 AD, the first state to adopt Christianity as its official religion. In 387 Armenia was partitioned between the Eastern Roman (Byzantine) and Persian empires. The former recognized the independence of the Armenian Catholic Church; the latter's Zoroastrian rulers sought to extirpate Armenian Christianity. Amid a great flowering of Armenian letters, Byzantine Armenia achieved autonomy in 886. In the 11th century it was divided into two separate kingdoms (Greater Armenia in eastern Anatolia and Cilicia on the eastern Mediterranean littoral) by the encroaching Seljuk Turks, following their victory over the Byzantines at the Battle of Manzikert in 1071.

Devastations by Mongol hordes in the 13th and 14th centuries preceded the conquest of both Cilicia and Greater Armenia by the Ottoman Turks, who by the mid-16th century had extended their eastern frontier at Persia's expense to encompass most of ancient Armenia. In 1590 loose Turkish suzerainty was also established over Azerbaijan and other lands south of the Caucasus and west of the Caspian Sea. But the Turkish presence was regularly contested by the Persians, who in 1730 recovered suzerainty over Azerbaijan and other regions east of the present-day Turkish border, including Armenian-populated Yerevan province. Whereas the Turks were Sunni Muslims, the long-established Azeri tribes, although Turkic-speaking, shared the Persians' adherence to the Shia version of Islam.

From the early 18th century historic Turkish-Persian rivalry in Transcaucasia was transcended by the southward expansion of imperial Russia, assisted by the advent of Russian naval power. Although Russia's acquisition of the southern littoral of the Caspian Sea proved to be brief (1723-32), it consolidated its control of the western littoral, before absorbing the khanates of the hinterland in the early 19th century in a series of wars with Persia and the Ottomans. Under the 1813 Treaty of Gulistan, Persian Azerbaijan north of the River Araks was ceded to Russia, which under the 1828 Treaty of Turkamanchai also acquired Nakhichevan and Yerevan provinces from Persia. These changes were recognized by the Turks in the 1829 Treaty of Adrianople, under which Russia also obtained Turkish territories further north. They set the borders between Russia, Turkey and Persia at roughly their post-1945 position, but there was much turmoil to come, most of it related to the fact that the bulk of the Christian Armenians remained under Muslim Turkish rule.

Early Armenian claims to nationhood were rebuffed by the European powers at the 1878 Congress of Berlin, at which Russia was awarded part of Turkish Armenia (Kars and Ardahan). Thereafter Armenian aspirations came increasingly into conflict with a Turkish regime determined to preserve its Asia Minor heartland from the sort of disintegration being experienced by the Ottoman empire in the west. An armed uprising by Armenian nationalists in the mid-1890s was crushed with great bloodshed by Kurdish irregulars brought in by the Turks. This first Armenian massacre of modern times elicited only moral disapproval from the powers, mainly because of Russia's fears of stirring up unrest among its own Armenian subjects. Instead, Russia concentrated on quelling the rising incidence of clashes between Armenians and Azeris under its rule and on schemes for further expansion southwards at the expense of Persia.

World War I and its Aftermath—Brief Armenian Independence

World War I (1914-18) unlocked the door to nationhood for many subject European peoples but brought disaster to the Armenians. Allied with the Central powers, Turkey saw its Armenian population as a fifth column ready to assist the Entente (Russia, Britain and France) in the hope of post-war reward. Having repulsed a British invasion attempt at Gallipoli on the Dardanelles, Turkey in 1915 took action against its Armenian minority. The nature and extent of this action has been the subject of bitter dispute ever since. According to Armenian spokesmen (and many independent historians), the Turkish solution of the "Armenian question" involved wholesale massacre, deportation and death from disease and starvation, amounting to at least 1,000,000 fatalities. The Turkish authorities have always denied that there was any systematic massacre of Armenians, claiming that any brutalities which occurred were a tragic consequence of wartime circumstances.

Prospects of an Armenian state rose in the latter stages of World War I. Following the Bolshevik Revolution in Russia in late 1917, the new regime withdrew from the conflict and, under the Brest-Litovsk treaty of March 1918, accepted German terms which included withdrawal from Transcaucasia. In May 1918 Russian Armenia became an independent republic under German tutelage, as did Azerbaijan (including part of Persian Azerbaijan). The eventual defeat of the Central powers in November 1918 gave even more hope to the Armenians, in that the victorious powers were committed to the principle of self-determination among the peoples of the vanquished empires. An independent Greater Armenia was declared, uniting the Turkish and Russian regions, and British forces occupied Transcaucasia to ensure post-war stability. Under the Treaty of Sèvres, signed between the victorious powers and the Turkish Sultan on Aug. 10, 1920, the new Greater Armenian state secured international recognition, subject to US arbitration as to the precise delimitation of its border with Turkey.

Even as the Sèvres treaty was being signed, however, events were moving rapidly against the new Armenian state. British troops had been withdrawn from Transcaucasia in mid-1919, amid bloody conflict between Armenians and Azeris over what was to become the familiar issue of control of the Nagorno-Karabakh enclave. Before departing, the British had awarded the enclave to Azerbaijan, but this decision was not accepted by the Armenians. More ominously, the Sèvres terms were rejected by the new Turkish provisional government proclaimed in Ankara in April 1920 by Kemal Ataturk (as he later became known). Calling for Turkey's national regeneration, Ataturk formed an alliance with the Russian Bolsheviks aimed at restoring the pre-war status quo in Transcaucasia. By the autumn of 1920 the Armenians had been crushed and Armenia was again divided into Turkish-ruled and Russian-ruled areas. In the process, the Armenians again suffered great brutalities at the hands of the Turks and were virtually eliminated from Turkey. Those who escaped the killing fled to Russian Armenia or were dispersed around the world.

The alliance with Turkey enabled the Bolsheviks to establish Soviet rule not only in Russian Armenia but also in Azerbaijan up to the River Araks, both areas being proclaimed soviet socialist republics in the course of 1920. Under the Soviet-Turkish Treaty of Kars (October 1921), Turkey's eastern border was restored to its pre-1878 position (i.e. it regained Kars and Ardahan), which remains its location today. As history records, Ataturk then succeeded in re-establishing Turkish rule throughout Anatolia and in Eastern Thrace, effectively consigning the Sèvres terms to oblivion. The last hope for the Armenians of Turkey—that they might survive under French protection in Cilicia—disappeared when French forces were withdrawn in 1921. On July 24, 1923, the Sèvres treaty was formally superseded by the Treaty of Lausanne, under which Turkey secured international recognition within its present-day borders.

Transfer of Nagorno-Karabakh to Azerbaijan under Soviet rule

In late 1920 the new Communist leadership of the Azerbaijan Soviet Socialist Republic (SSR), in a fraternal gesture, ceded Nagorno-Karabakh to the Armenian SSR. However, the persistence of ethnic strife, combined with pressure from Turkey, persuaded Joseph Stalin, then Soviet Commissar of Nationalities, to return the enclave to Azerbaijan in July 1923. In that it was impossible to draw lines which made the historic lands of the Armenians and Azeris co-terminous, the solution adopted was that Nagorno-Karabakh became an autonomous region (oblast) within Azerbaijan. In February 1924, moreover, Azeri-populated Nakhichevan became an autonomous republic attached, constitutionally not geographically, to Azerbaijan (this step having been approved by Turkey under the 1921 Kars treaty, which gave it a say in any change in Nakhichevan's status). From 1922 Soviet Armenia and Azerbaijan were constituent administrative divisions of the Transcaucasian Soviet Federal Socialist Republic. Under the 1936 Soviet constitution, however, they became fully-fledged republics of the USSR.

Having brought the Armenian-Azeri problem under some sort of control, the Soviet government also kept a wary eye on continuing aspirations to unity among Azeris north and south of the Soviet Persian border. Here the growing importance of the Baku oilfields for Stalin's inter-war industrialization programme strengthened Moscow's determination to retain firm control of Soviet Azerbaijan. During World War II (1939-45) Soviet forces occupied northern Persia (and British forces occupied the south), withdrawing in 1946 only with some reluctance. They left behind an autonomous regime in Persian Azerbaijan, but this was quickly suppressed by the government of Iran (as Persia now called itself). Thereafter, Moscow gave some support to Azeri separatists in Iran against the Shah's pro-Western regime. But there was little enthusiasm among Iranian Azeris for unity schemes which involved rule from Moscow.

Soviet demands in 1945 that Turkey should retrocede the Armenian border provinces of Kars and Ardahan were successfully resisted by the Western Allies, with whom Turkey became closely allied with the onset of the Cold War in the late 1940s. Over the succeeding four decades the rigidities of Communist rule and the East-West stalemate placed an effective freeze on ethnic and territorial issues in the region. Moreover, the Soviet authorities had some success in defusing the national question by allowing local autonomy (albeit Communist-controlled) under which the Armenian and Azeri languages and cultures secured recognition. Nevertheless, the emergence in the 1970s of militant nationalist groups among Armenian exiles, especially in Lebanon, demonstrated that historic grievances had not been forgotten. Such groups concentrated their terrorist actions on Turkish targets, on the grounds that Turkey had committed genocide against the Armenian people. But their demand for the restoration of an Armenian state within historic borders had clear implications for the status of Soviet Armenia.

Among Azeris the event which marked a major turning-point was the 1979 Islamic revolution in Iran and the rise of a brand of fundamentalism that was anti-communist and anti-Western in about equal measure. As seen from Moscow, the new phenomenon posed a particular threat to the stability of Azerbaijan, because of the historic cross border links of the Azeri people. The new regime in Tehran was if anything more hostile to Azeri separatism than the Shah had been, but this only served to promote the development of a pan-Azeri nationalism increasingly fundamentalist in orientation. To add to its problems, the Soviet Union launched a massive military invasion of Afghanistan in December 1979. Intended to shore up the pro-Moscow regime in Kabul, this intervention was seen in much of the Muslim world as a latter-day continuation of the historic expansion of imperial Russia at the expense of the

Islamic south. In the long, ultimately unsuccessful, Soviet campaign in Afghanistan, Azeri nationalists were prominent in their support for the anti-government Afghan guerrillas (*mujaheddin*).

Post-1988 Upsurge of Violence over Nagorno-Karabakh

As early as 1987, the status of the autonomous oblast of Nagorno-Karabakh posed a significant dilemma for Mikhail Gorbachev, who had become Soviet leader in 1985, and demonstrated the seriousness of the nationalities problem in the Soviet Union. Against the background of glasnost and perestroika, it was the call for remedying the injustices inflicted upon the ethnic groups during Communist rule, which primarily galvanized the opposition political forces in the Caucasus. Nagorno-Karabakh was also the most persuasive example of the inconsistency of Moscow's nationalities policy, which in its turn alienated the nations and ethnic groups from the centre and invigorated their national aspirations and demands.

The events in Armenia and Azerbaijan in the period preceding the dissolution of the Soviet Union in 1991 represent a cycle of action and counter-action, with a spiral of increasing ethnic tension and strife. Demands for Nagorno-Karabakh's unification with Armenia first emerged in 1987. On Feb. 20, 1988, the Nagorno-Karabakh regional soviet voted in favour of a transfer to Armenia, the vote being accompanied by large-scale demonstrations and strikes. The first widely publicized bloodshed was an incident in the Azerbaijani town of Sumgait on Feb. 28-29. Official figures put the death toll at 33, of whom 26 were Armenians, and Soviet sources for the first time used the word "pogrom".

In March 1988, demonstrations in favour of the transfer of Nagorno-Karabakh spread to Moscow, as the Azerbaijani authorities categorically rejected any change in borders. The Nagorno-Karabakh regional soviet again voted in favour of a change in status on March 13, and on March 17 was supported by the local Communist Party leadership. A week later regular Soviet troops appeared on the streets of Yerevan and the authorities in both Armenia and Azerbaijan were instructed to restore order. The result was a series of general strikes in Armenia punctuated by mass demonstrations of a million or more people in Yerevan. Similar demonstrations occurred in Baku. Leading activists on both sides of the ethnic divide were arrested or deported, as the authorities strove unsuccessfully to curb the mounting disturbances. The Communist Party leaders of Armenia and Azerbaijan were both replaced on May 21, 1988.

On June 15, 1988, the Armenian Supreme Soviet called unanimously for a direct approach to the Azerbaijan and USSR Supreme Soviets with a view to securing the transfer of Nagorno-Karabakh. But this proposal was opposed by the Azerbaijan Supreme Soviet on June 17, on the grounds that it contravened the provision of Article 78 of the Soviet constitution that "the territory of a Union republic may not be altered without its consent". Addressing an extraordinary party congress in Moscow on June 28, Gorbachev appeared to rule out a change in Nagorno-Karabakh's status, saying that "collisions" between national groups must be resolved "within the existing state structure". The response of the enclave's soviet on July 12 was to vote for immediate secession from Azerbaijan and incorporation into Armenia under its ancient name of Artsakh, but this demand was rejected the same day by the Azerbaijan Supreme Soviet and by the Presidium of the USSR Supreme Soviet on July 18, 1988.

Tensions remained high in both republics for the rest of 1988. On Sept. 21, 1988, the Soviet government imposed "special status" on Nagorno-Karabakh amid renewed strikes, demonstrations and ethnic clashes. The declaration prompted renewed mass protests in Yerevan, where troops and tanks were deployed on Sept. 22 to enforce a ban on street gatherings. Further serious inter-communal violence occurred in late November 1988 when Azeri nationalists attacked Armenians in several Azerbaijan cities after a Moscow court had passed the death sentence on an Azeri convicted of seven of the Sumgait murders in February. The major earthquake which devastated northern Soviet Armenia in early December 1988, did little to cool mounting national passions, especially when Armenian spokesmen accused Azerbaijan of blocking the distribution of aid. On Dec. 10 police arrested seven members of the "Karabakh Committee" responsible for organizing the Armenian campaign on Nagorno-Karabakh; this was followed at the end of the month by a crackdown against Azeri nationalists.

Official figures released in February 1989 gave the death toll since the onset of the ethnic unrest 12 months earlier as 87 civilians and four soldiers, while about 1,650 people had been injured. It was also stated that as a result of the November 1988 upsurge of ethnic strife some 150,000 Armenians had fled from their homes in Azerbaijan and that about 140,000 Azeris had moved the other way.

Imposition of Direct Moscow Rule in Nagorno-Karabakh

Against the background of the escalation of hostilities, in January 1989 the USSR Supreme Soviet established a "special form of administration" in Nagorno-Karabakh under the leadership of a special committee with full legislative and executive powers, removing the autonomous oblast from the Azerbaijan jurisdiction and placing it under central control. A senior central party official, Arkady Volsky, became chairman of a special administrative committee charged with responsibility for Nagorno-Karabakh. This step was accompanied by wholesale dismissals and replacements of ministers and party officials in both Armenia and Azerbaijan.

Direct rule kept the peace for a few months, but

violence returned in May 1989 amid mass rallies in Armenia calling for the release of the "Karabakh Committee" members (which was ordered on May 31). A major flare-up occurred in and around Stepanakert in July 1989, as rival bands of Armenians and Azeris set up road blocks, disrupted road and rail communications and engaged in looting and arson attacks. By mid-August 1989 official Soviet sources were describing the situation in Nagorno-Karabakh as bordering on anarchy. In Azerbaijan proper, meanwhile, huge demonstrations were being mounted by the newly formed Azerbaijan Popular Front, which demanded economic and political autonomy from Moscow and assurances that Nagorno-Karabakh would remain part of the republic. Such manifestations intensified in late August 1989 in protest against the formation by Nagorno-Karabakh Armenians of a "National Council" to run the enclave "until constitutional forms of government are restored". A general strike called by the Popular Front from Sept. 4 brought economic life in Azerbaijan to a virtual halt and developed into a full-scale blockade of road and rail links with Armenia.

At the urging of Front leaders, the Azerbaijan Supreme Soviet on Sept. 18, 1989, called for an end to Moscow's direct rule over Nagorno-Karabakh. Four days later, on Sept. 22, the Armenian Supreme Soviet appealed to Moscow for help against the Azeri blockade. In an address to the USSR Supreme Soviet on Sept. 25, Gorbachev warned the leaders of Armenia and Azerbaijan that they must negotiate a solution within two days or face emergency measures. This ultimatum brought about some relaxation of the blockade from Sept. 27, but Azeri militants continued to prevent food and fuel from reaching Armenia by rail. Accordingly, the USSR Supreme Soviet on Oct. 3 authorized the Soviet army to take over the running of the railways in Azerbaijan. In Nagorno-Karabakh itself, ethnic clashes continued to be an almost daily occurrence.

On the political front, the Azerbaijan Supreme Soviet on Sept. 23, 1989, adopted a new sovereignty law which marked a major shift by the Communist establishment towards the positions of the Popular Front, not least by declaring Azeri to be the state language of the republic. The law asserted (i) Azerbaijan's sovereignty over Nagorno-Karabakh and the inviolability of the republic's frontiers; (ii) Azerbaijan's right to secede from the Soviet Union; (iii) the right of the Azerbaijan Supreme Soviet to veto any legislation proposed by Moscow; and (iv) the republic's full control over its natural resources. On Oct. 5, 1989, the Popular Front was permitted to register as an official organization in Azerbaijan.

In a parallel development, the Armenian Pan-National Movement (APNM) held its founding congress in Yerevan on Nov. 4-7, 1989, having been granted official registration by the government authorities. Linking various groups from Soviet Armenia, Nagorno-Karabakh and the Armenian diaspora, the new formation called for "genuine sovereignty" for the

Armenian people, economic independence and a political solution to the Nagorno-Karabakh question. Speakers at the founding congress included the first secretary of the Armenian Communist Party.

Ending of Direct Rule and the January 1990 Crisis in Azerbaijan

In a decision taken in Moscow on Nov. 28, 1989, the USSR Supreme Soviet voted to end direct rule over Nagorno-Karabakh and to return the region to the jurisdiction of Azerbaijan's authorities. The latter were given two months to enact new legislation guaranteeing "full and real autonomy" for the enclave, including the creation of new government bodies. The 5,000 Soviet troops deployed in the region were to remain, under the supervision of a new "observation commission". Armenian and Nagorno-Karabakh deputies stormed out of the Supreme Soviet chamber prior to the vote, claiming that it represented a surrender to radical Azeri demands. Prior to the decision, the Azerbaijan Popular Front had organized strikes and demonstrations in Baku calling for the return of Nagorno-Karabakh.

Predictably, the Armenian Supreme Soviet, at a joint sitting with the Nagorno-Karabakh National Council on Dec. 1, 1989, opposed the USSR Supreme Soviet's decision by declaring that the disputed enclave was part of the "unified Armenian republic" and that its legal government was the National Council. On Dec. 4, on the other hand, a majority of the Armenian deputies refused to back radical proposals for the abolition of the Communist Party's "leading role", the dropping of "Soviet Socialist" from Armenia's official name and an Armenian right of veto over legislation and appointments decided in Moscow. This refusal provoked a siege of the Supreme Soviet building by 40,000 angry demonstrators supporting the radicals, whose demands reflected the pro-democracy wave sweeping through the Soviet empire as a result of the fall of the Berlin Wall the previous month and the attendant crumbling of Communist regimes.

In January 1990 simmering unrest in Azerbaijan erupted into a major challenge to the existing order, in which the local Communist authorities had little option but to associate themselves with the demands of the Popular Front. With Soviet rule appearing to collapse for a while, the crisis involved an explosion of ethnic violence across the republic and on the Armenian border. It began in early January 1990 when Azeri rioters destroyed barriers on the border between Nakhichevan and Iran, demanding freer access to fellow Azeris in northern Iran. Such actions, which later spread to the border between Azerbaijan proper and Iran, were condemned by the authorities as the work of Azeri extremists seeking to create a unified state with Iranian Azerbaijan. On Jan. 8 mass demonstrations began again in Baku, focusing on Azeri nationalists' objections to Moscow's retention of responsibility for security in Nagorno-Karabakh

after the end of direct rule. Further Azeri anger was provoked on Jan. 10-11 when the Armenian Supreme Soviet voted to extend the provisions of the republican budget and electoral laws to Nagorno-Karabakh and to grant itself the right of veto over USSR laws. The latter decision appeared to be in response to a USSR decree of the previous day ruling that the declaration of a "unified Armenian republic" on Dec. 1, 1989, was unconstitutional.

On Jan. 13, 1990, Azeri anger escalated sharply into an anti-Armenian pogrom in Baku, after reports had spread that Armenians had themselves committed atrocities. Over the next three days up to 60 people were killed, most of them Armenians. Inside Nagorno-Karabakh, and in the nearby districts of Shaumyan and Khanlar, a bitter guerrilla war developed between heavily armed Azeri and Armenian irregulars. The USSR authorities responded on Jan. 15 by ordering the despatch of an additional 11,000 troops to Azerbaijan, to join the 6,000 already deployed there. A state of emergency declared in Nagorno-Karabakh and the various border areas on Jan. 15 was extended to Baku four days later. On Jan. 19-24 Soviet forces launched an assault to regain control of Baku and its port area (which had been blockaded by nationalists). The death toll in the resultant fighting was 83 according to official sources at the time, although a parliamentary inquiry in Azerbaijan later concluded that 131 people had been killed and 744 injured in what was described as "a criminal act" by Soviet forces. The Soviet military action provoked a mass burning of Communist Party membership cards by Azeris and was followed by a clamp-down on the Popular Front and the allied National Defence Council. In Nakhichevan nationalist elements on Jan. 19 declared the enclave's secession from the Soviet Union.

Hopes of a resolution of Azeri-Armenian conflict were raised in early February 1990 when both sides agreed to attend peace talks in Riga sponsored by the Latvian Popular Front. However, the agreement reached at these talks, on Feb. 3, broke down almost immediately, with the Armenian side claiming that Azeris were attempting the "forced deportation" of Armenians in parts of Azerbaijan. The situation in the two republics was discussed by a closed session of the USSR Supreme Soviet on Feb. 19, 1990, but no new ideas were forthcoming. Azeri deputies staged a walkout during a speech by the Soviet Defence Minister, as did Armenian deputies when Gorbachev stressed the inviolability of Azerbaijan's borders. A further closed session of the USSR Supreme Soviet on March 5 resolved that Armenia and Azerbaijan should "enter into talks immediately to conclude an inter-republic treaty on restoring trust and accord between peoples, proceeding from the principles of equality of rights and the sovereignty and territorial integrity of both republics".

Following the January 1990 crisis in Azerbaijan, events in the Caucasian republics tended to be overshadowed by the push for full independence in the Baltic states and by the rapid pace of political change in Moscow itself. Nevertheless, the Armenian-Azeri conflict over Nagorno-Karabakh and other issues simmered on, erupting into further violence at regular intervals throughout 1990. There were particularly bloody clashes in Yerevan in May, coinciding with the anniversary of Armenia's declaration of independence in May 1918. On July 28, 1990, a newly elected Armenian Supreme Soviet voted to suspend the application on Armenian territory of a decree issued by Gorbachev on July 25 ordering that illegal "armed formations" should be disbanded within 15 days and their weapons impounded. Armenian leaders warned that any attempt by Soviet troops to disarm the nationalist militias operating in Armenia and Nagorno-Karabakh could result in a bloodbath.

Declaration of Independence by Armenia

On Aug. 4, 1990, the new Armenian Supreme Soviet elected non-Communists to the republic's presidency and premiership, namely Levon Ter-Petrossian and Vazguen Manukyan, respectively. Both had been among the leaders of the "Karabakh Committee" arrested in December 1988 for campaigning for Armenian control of Nagorno-Karabakh; both had subsequently become leading members of the pro-independence APNM. The new deputies proceeded, on Aug. 23, 1990, to adopt (by 183 votes to two) a declaration of the "independent statehood" of the "Republic of Armenia", whose constitution and laws took precedence over any external instruments. According to the declaration, Armenia would immediately form its own army and police (and the government's permission would be needed for the deployment of "foreign troops" on its territory) and would have full control over its natural resources, economy, financial institutions and foreign policy. The declaration asserted that Armenia's "inviolable" borders included the Nagorno-Karabakh region.

Ter-Petrossian averted an immediate confrontation with the Soviet authorities by securing a two-month extension of the Gorbachev decree of July 25 ordering the disbandment of unofficial militias. In Armenia the largest such group was the Armenian National Army (ANA), which on Aug. 29, 1990, murdered an Armenian deputy trying to persuade the group to subordinate itself to the APNM. The government responded by declaring a state of emergency and using the APNM's paramilitary wing to enforce the surrender and dissolution of the ANA. It then awaited the outcome of elections in Azerbaijan, which were held on Sept. 30 and Oct. 14, 1990, just as the USSR Supreme Soviet was passing a law formally legalizing multi-party politics. In the event, the Azerbaijan Communist Party scored a clear victory, defeating a challenge by an opposition alliance including the Popular Front. While favouring continued membership of the Soviet Union, the Communists ruled out any compromise on the status of Nagorno-Karabakh. They also advocated adoption of the name "Republic of Azerbaijan" (dropping "Soviet Socialist"), this change being later imple-

mented in a decree issued by the President of Azerbaijan, Ayaz Mutalibov.

Armenian-Azeri clashes flared up again in December 1990, but the early months of 1991 were relatively free of violence. In the all-union referendum called by Gorbachev on March 17 (on the question "Do you consider it necessary to preserve the USSR as a renewed federation of equal, sovereign republics in which human rights and the freedoms of all nationalities will be fully guaranteed?"), there was a "yes" vote of 93.3 per cent in Azerbaijan, on a turnout of 75.1 per cent. Armenia was one of six republics which officially boycotted the referendum. After Azerbaijan had endorsed Gorbachev's proposed new union treaty on April 23, 1991, Armenia accused the Soviet authorities of openly siding with Azerbaijan in a new upsurge of violence from April 30, when troops stormed two Armenian villages just to the north of Nagorno-Karabakh. The villages were reportedly believed to harbour Armenian guerrillas who had not complied with the July 1990 decree on paramilitary groups. Armenian sources claimed that at least 17 villagers were killed in the assault, which sparked off fierce fighting all along the Armenia-Azerbaijan border.

Meeting in emergency session as soon as news of the attack reached Yerevan, the Armenian Supreme Soviet passed a resolution accusing Gorbachev of permitting Azerbaijan to commit "state terrorism" and of "drawing Armenia into war". After talks with the Soviet leader in Moscow on May 3, 1991, President Ter-Petrossian announced that he had received assurances that the wounded would be evacuated from the villages and that the Soviet authorities would intervene to stop Armenians being deported from communities in the border area. He nevertheless continued to accuse the Soviet leadership of colluding with Azerbaijan against Armenia and of seeking to bolster the flagging support of the Communist regime in Baku. The USSR Interior and Defence Ministries responded with a joint statement on May 4 placing the blame for the latest violence solely on the Armenian leadership because of its support for paramilitary groups. On May 7 the Foreign Ministry in Baku claimed that Armenia was waging an undeclared war against Azerbaijan, detailing over 300 cross-border attacks since the beginning of 1991, in which 61 Azeris had been killed.

Such exchanges were accompanied by further assaults on Armenian border villages by Azerbaijan and Soviet troops using tanks, heavy artillery and helicopters. By mid-May 1991 several had been razed to the ground to prevent their being used by militia groups, heavy casualties and further deportations being reported. Further such operations were mounted in July 1991, apparently by Azerbaijan forces acting alone, after Gorbachev had accepted Mutalibov's promise to ensure the safety of local people. That the Armenian paramilitaries remained in business, however, was demonstrated in mid-August 1991 when a group in Nagorno-Karabakh seized a detachment of Soviet troops and bartered them for the release of detained Armenian guerrillas.

Moscow Coup Attempt—Abortive Zheleznovodsk Accord

The Nagorno-Karabakh dispute was transformed by the abortive Moscow coup launched on Aug. 19, 1991, as was much else in the Soviet Union. Whereas the Armenian government kept its counsel on events in the Soviet capital, the Azerbaijan leadership immediately came out in support of the hardliners' seizure of power and in consequence faced mass protests from Popular Front supporters. Following the collapse of the coup on Aug. 21, Azerbaijan's leadership sought to retrieve its position by declaring the republic's independence on Aug. 30, while the local Communist Party severed its links with the Soviet party. In direct elections in Azerbaijan on Sept. 8, Mutalibov was duly re-elected President as the only candidate, the turnout being officially 83.7 per cent. But this figure and the legitimacy of the process were hotly disputed by the Popular Front, which attracted widespread support for anti-government protests. In Nakhichevan, moreover, the autonomous republic's leadership refused to allow the election to take place and declared its support for the Popular Front.

In Armenia the abortive Moscow coup accelerated the push for full independence. In a referendum held on Sept. 21, 1991, 94.4 per cent of those voting (in a turnout of 95.5 per cent) favoured secession from the Soviet Union. Two days later, on Sept. 23, the republic was declared an independent state, its territory being deemed to include Nagorno-Karabakh. The latter had on Sept. 2 declared itself a republic separate from Azerbaijan, within borders encompassing the adjoining Shaumyan district, which had not previously been part of the enclave. It was made clear by President Ter-Petrossian that Armenia would not observe the five-year transitional period laid down in Soviet legislation on secession. In a presidential election on Oct. 16, 1991, Ter-Petrossian was returned to office with 83 per cent of the vote, defeating five other candidates.

In the aftermath of the abortive coup and the ascendancy of Boris Yeltsin, there was a new opening for Moscow to take a hand in the dispute over Nagorno-Karabakh (where the estimated death toll since February 1988 had risen to about 800 by mid-September 1991). Together with President Nursultan Nazarbayev of Kazakhstan, Yeltsin had separate meetings with the Armenian and Azerbaijan leaderships on Sept. 21-22, 1991, before bringing together the two Presidents and the Nagorno-Karabakh leadership in the southern Russian town of Zheleznovodsk. There a ceasefire agreement was signed on Sept. 24, on the basis that Nagorno-Karabakh would remain part of Azerbaijan but would enjoy substantial self-government (which was to be restored by January 1992). The accord provided for the withdrawal and disarming of all armed groups by the end of 1991 (except for Soviet troops); in addition, hostages were to be freed, weapons of mass destruction banned and deportees returned to their villages. To implement the agreement, Armenia and Azerbaijan were to enter into talks "on a permanent basis" on Oct. 1, with the Russian Federation and Kazakhstan acting as brokers and guarantors.

The Zheleznovodsk agreement quickly became a dead letter, however, not least because the accelerating collapse of the USSR itself meant that Soviet forces could not be committed to its enforcement. On Oct. 18, 1991, moreover, the Azerbaijan Supreme Soviet adopted a law confirming the republic's declaration of independence and envisaging the creation of military forces to defend "the interests, sovereignty, territorial integrity and independence" of the republic. The following month the situation deteriorated when Azerbaijan cut off gas supplies to Armenia (on Nov. 5) and when a helicopter crash (on Nov. 20), in which 21 people died, was attributed to Armenian forces by Azerbaijan. On Nov. 26 the Azerbaijan deputies voted to annul the autonomous status of Nagorno-Karabakh, which was henceforth to be governed by a "National Unity Council". The Soviet State Council in Moscow responded on Nov. 27 by urging both sides to "abrogate all acts which change Nagorno-Karabakh's legal status". Both Armenia and Azerbaijan accepted the resolution but rejected a proposal by Gorbachev that a 10-kilometre buffer zone should be established between the two sides.

This was virtually the last initiative of the beleaguered Soviet President, who resigned on Dec. 25, 1991, following the creation of the Commonwealth of Independent States (CIS) in succession to the USSR. Both Armenia and Azerbaijan became members of the CIS, the founding Minsk and Alma-Ata declarations of which (adopted in December 1991) asserted the inviolability of existing republican borders. Nevertheless, the issue of Nagorno-Karabakh remained a festering sore in relations between Armenia and Azerbaijan. In accordance with its declared independence, Nagorno-Karabakh applied for membership of the CIS in its own right and on Dec. 28 held elections to a new parliament, as a result of which Artur Mkrtchyan became the enclave's president. President Mutalibov of Azerbaijan responded on Jan. 2, 1992, by placing Nagorno-Karabakh under direct presidential rule and appointing Salam Mahmedov to head the region's administration. On Jan. 3 the Armenian Supreme Soviet supported Nagorno-Karabakh's assertion of independence, but it appeared that the Armenian authorities were either unwilling or unable to control the enclave's militia groups.

Escalation of Conflict in 1992

The Nagorno-Karabakh conflict erupted in a full-scale war in 1992 as weapons poured into the region and mercenaries joined the fighting on both sides.

In January 1992, Stepanakert was bombarded by surrounding Azerbaijani forces, while Armenian forces attacked the mainly Azeri town of Shusha. There were reports of fuel cuts and a breakdown of water and sewage systems in the Nagorno-Karabakh capital. Some 40 people died when an Azerbaijani civilian helicopter was shot down near Shusha on Jan. 28, this prompting a major Azerbaijani offensive against Stepanakert on Jan. 31. Fighting intensified in the following weeks, as Azerbaijani forces began shelling the Nagorno-Karabakh capital and attacking Armenian villages in the north-east of the region. Armenian forces responded on Feb. 26-27 by taking the Azeri-majority town of Khojali, to the north of Stepanakert. Azerbaijani claims that over 1,000 Azeris were killed in this episode were rejected by Armenian spokesmen; Western accounts put the number killed at between 100 and 450. At the end of February the CIS commander-in-chief ordered the withdrawal of all remaining CIS troops from the region, as Azerbaijani forces massed on the borders of Nagorno-Karabakh.

Matters were complicated when on March 6, 1992, Mutalibov was forced to resign as Azerbaijan's President, having been accused of failing to protect Azeri lives in Nagorno-Karabakh. He was replaced by Yagub Mamedov, who on March 15 sanctioned a cease-fire agreement signed in Tehran under Iranian auspices. By early April, however, fighting had resumed, with Azerbaijani forces mounting a sustained bombardment of Stepanakert, while the Armenians sought to extend their area of control. The divide between the two sides deepened when the Nagorno-Karabakh president, Artur Mkrtchyan, was shot dead in Yerevan on April 14, in unclear circumstances. Although a further ceasefire was agreed by Presidents Ter-Petrossian and Mamedov in Tehran on May 8, Armenian forces simultaneously launched a new offensive on Shusha. This last remaining Azerbaijani stronghold in Nagorno-Karabakh was captured on May 9, when Armenian forces were in overall control of the enclave for the first time. By May 17, moreover, the Armenians had also taken the town of Lachin and thus established a corridor of Armenian-controlled territory between Armenia and Nagorno-Karabakh. These setbacks resulted in a further power struggle in Azerbaijan, where Mutalibov was reinstated on May 14 but again deposed and replaced on May 18 by Isa Kambarov of the Popular Front, pending new elections.

The danger of the Nagorno-Karabakh conflict taking on a wider dimension increased from May 18, 1992, when Armenian forces launched an assault on hills surrounding the town of Sadarak in Nakhichevan. Recalling that under the 1921 Kars treaty Turkey was a joint guarantor of the status of this enclave, the Turkish Foreign Minister, Hikmet Cetin, warned on May 19 that, if Armenia persisted with its "aggression", it would face serious consequences. Also on May 19, President Turgut Ozal of Turkey called for Turkish troops to be sent to Nakhichevan and for Lachin and Shusha to be returned to Azerbaijani control. The prospect of Turkish involvement against Armenia in support of Azerbaijan, pitting Turkey against Russia, prompted the CIS commander-in-chief, Marshal Yevgeny Shaposhnikov, to warn on May 20 that the crisis "could lead to World War III". On the same day, however, the Turkish Prime Minister,

Suleyman Demirel, ruled out direct Turkish military intervention.

Presidential elections in Azerbaijan on June 7, 1992, resulted in victory for the Popular Front leader, Adulfaz Elchibey, who declared the recovery of Nagorno-Karabakh to be his main priority (and also maintained that Azerbaijan was not legally a CIS member because the decision to join had not obtained parliamentary approval in Baku). More aligned with Turkey that his predecessors, Elchibey denounced Iran's mediation as designed "to help Armenia, not Azerbaijan", and expressed a public preference for a negotiated solution through the UN and Conference on Security and Co-operation in Europe (CSCE) channels. Prospects of an accommodation appeared to increase when Presidents Elchibey and Ter-Petrossian both attended the inaugural meeting in Ankara on June 22-23 of the Turkish-initiated "Black Sea zone of economic co-operation", linking 11 countries of the region.

However, subsequent ceasefire negotiations in Rome were undermined by an Azerbaijani military offensive launched in June 1992 against Armenian positions in the Geramboi (Shaumyan) region of Azerbaijan and the Mardakert province in Nagorno-Karabakh. As a result of this offensive, the Azeri army captured nearly 80 per cent of the Mardakert province, leading to the flight of nearly 40,000 ethnic Armenian refugees.

Continued Conflict in 1993-94—Ceasefire Agreement

In February 1993, a large-scale Karabakh Armenian offensive in the Mardakert region recaptured numerous villages as well as the Sarsang reservoir, severing the Terter-Kelbajar road and cutting off the Kelbajar province from the rest of Azerbaijan. In a short military offensive from March 27 to April 5, the Karabakh Armenian forces, allegedly supported by Russian and Armenian forces, seized Kelbajar, with 60,000 people fleeing. On April 30 the United Nations Security Council adopted Resolution 822, which called for a ceasefire, the withdrawal of "all occupying forces" from the Kelbajar region, the resumption of negotiations and open access for humanitarian efforts. This resolution provided the impetus for a Russian-Turkish-US peace initiative that called for withdrawal of forces, a 60-day ceasefire, the end of the energy blockade of Armenia, and continued peace talks. Both Azerbaijan and Armenia accepted the plan, while the Karabakh Armenians rejected it. On May 24 Azerbaijan declared a unilateral ceasefire.

The peace plan was modified to include additional guarantees for Karabakh's civilian population and five hundred CSCE military observers were to monitor its implementation. Under pressure from Armenia's President, Ter-Petrossian, the Karabakh Armenians accepted the new plan on June 14, but asked for one month's deferral of its implementation. In the meantime, the series of military defeats set off a political crisis in Azerbaijan, leading to the ouster of the elected Popular Front President Elchibey in June 1993 by the popular army commander Surat Husseinov, bringing back to power Heidar Aliev, the former chairman of the Azerbajiani Communist Party. In the following months Heidar Aliev sought to consolidate his hold on power and received 98.8 percent of the vote in the presidential elections of Oct. 3, 1993.

A week after Husseinov's coup, Karabakh Armenian forces launched an offensive towards Agdam—situated in Azerbaijan about six kilometres from Nagorno-Karabakh's eastern border—and seized the town on July 23. On July 25, Karabakh Armenian authorities and the Azerbaijani government announced a ceasefire. Four days later, the UN Security Council passed Resolution 853 which condemned the seizure of Agdam, called on all parties to cease the supply of weapons, and called on the Armenian government to use its influence with the Karabakh Armenian authorities towards compliance with UN resolutions.

The period of August-October 1993 saw a dramatic increase in military offensives against four Azerbaijani provinces—Qubatli, Jebryail, Fizuli and Zangelan— located south of Nagorno-Karabakh bordering on the Araks river. On Aug. 18, the UN Security Council issued a statement condemning the attack on the Fizuli region from Nagorno-Karabakh. Russian mediation efforts resulted in a shaky ceasefire announced on Aug. 31. At the first bilateral Azerbaijani-Karabakh talks, held on Sept. 13 in Moscow under the aegis of the Russian Foreign Ministry, the ceasefire was extended until Oct. 5. With its end, both Azerbaijan and the Karabakh Armenians agreed to extend the ceasefire for another month, until Nov. 5.

On Oct. 9, just four days after agreement on a ceasefire extension, fighting broke out again in the area, leading to a third UN Security Council resolution on the issue on Oct. 14. Resolution 874 condemned the fighting and called on all sides to accept the CSCE "Adjusted Timetable of Urgent Steps". Armenia accepted the proposal, the Karabakh authorities deferred a clear position, while Azerbaijan rejected the plan as it linked the withdrawal of Karabakh forces from Azerbaijani territory with the lifting of Azerbaijan's embargo of Armenia.

A large-scale Azerbaijani offensive was launched in late December 1993, this lasting until mid-February 1994, when Karabakh Armenian forces pulled back. Another Russian-brokered ceasefire was signed on Feb. 16, 1994. In mid-April, however, heavy fighting broke out near Agdam and Mardakert.

In May 1994 a further ceasefire agreement was worked out through the mediation efforts of the Russian Defence Minister, Pavel Grachev. On July 27, the Defence Ministers of Armenia and Azerbaijan and the head of Karabakh's armed forces signed another ceasefire agreement giving legal status to the May accord. The ceasefire has now been largely observed for 10 years.

International Mediation

As newly sovereign states, both Armenia and Azerbaijan were admitted to the Conference on Security and Co-operation in Europe (renamed the Organization for Security and Co-operation in Europe, OSCE, with effect from Jan.1, 1995) on Jan. 30, 1992, and both applied for UN membership. In early February spokesmen for Armenia, Nagorno-Karabakh and the Russian Federation all urged that CSCE mediators and UN peacekeeping forces should become involved in the Nagorno-Karabakh dispute. Azerbaijan resisted such moves to "internationalize" the conflict, and on Feb. 5 specifically vetoed the deployment of UN peacekeeping forces. On the other hand, a CSCE mission was permitted to visit Nagorno-Karabakh on Feb. 12 and both sides subsequently agreed to receive former US Secretary of State Cyrus Vance as Special Representative of the UN Secretary-General, charged with seeking a peaceful resolution of the crisis. Their recommendations included a ceasefire agreement, lifting the economic blockade against Armenia, banning arms transfer to the warring parties, emergency humanitarian assistance, and a CSCE observer mission.

Since 1992, the political settlement of the conflict over Nagorno-Karabakh has been discussed within the framework of the so-called Minsk Group. At a meeting of the CSCE Council of Foreign Ministers held on March 24, 1992, the participating states agreed that a conference under the auspices of the CSCE would provide an ongoing forum for negotiations towards peaceful settlement of the crisis. It was agreed that the conference would be convened in Minsk and would have as participants Armenia, Azerbaijan, Belarus, the Czech and Slovak Federal Republic, France, Germany, Italy, the Russian Federation, Sweden, Turkey and the USA. As for "elected and other representatives of Nagorno-Karabakh", it was agreed that they would be invited to the conference as "interested parties by the Chairman of the conference after consultation with the states participating at the conference". The Minsk Conference, however, was never convened. Instead, in 1992, negotiations were launched within the Minsk Group, which is still the sole forum for holding negotiations on the political settlement of the conflict. In 1994, Russia was designated as co-chair of the Minsk Group alongside the state holding the OSCE presidency, namely Sweden in 1995 and Finland in 1996. In early 1997, following extensive consultations, the OSCE Chairman-in-Office designated France, Russia and the United States as co-chairs of the Minsk Group. In August 1995, the office of Personal Representative of the OSCE Chairman-in-Office was created.

In 1996 at the Lisbon OSCE Summit, after the veto by Armenia of paragraph 20 of the final document, the Chairman-in-Office made a statement outlining three basic principles as a basis for a future political settlement—the territorial integrity of Armenia and Azerbaijan, the highest degree of self-government of Nagorno-Karabakh as part of Azerbaijan, and guaranteed security for Nagorno-Karabakh and its population.

Throughout the negotiations, four key issues have been apparent. These are the status of Nagorno-Karabakh, Armenian withdrawal from Azerbaijani territory, the security of Armenians in Nagorno-Karabakh, and the return of Azerbaijani refugees. Due to the complexity of the issues, the Minsk Group was faced with the dilemma of whether to tackle them concurrently or successively, leaving decisions on the status for Nagorno-Karabakh for a later stage, possibly the Minsk Conference. Two approaches have thus emerged—"package" and "step-by-step".

The first fully-fledged peace plan worked out by the Minsk Group, in July 1997, followed the "package" solution, emphasizing the need to solve certain aspects concurrently. The plan outlined six basic principles for a settlement: full self-government for Nagorno-Karabakh within Azerbaijan; Armenian withdrawal from all of the occupied territories; return of Azerbaijani refugees; an OSCE peacekeeping force to patrol the buffer zone; the lease of Lachin from Azerbaijan to Nagorno-Karabakh; and the lifting of all economic blockades.

Later in 1997, the Minsk Group launched its new strategy with a shift from the "package" to the "phased" or "step-by-step" option. The plan contained some of the same aspects as the previous one—Armenian withdrawal, return of refugees, lifting of blockades—while postponing any decision on the status of Nagorno-Karabakh until the last phase of the peace process. Armenia and Azerbaijan accepted the proposal, but the leadership of Nagorno-Karabakh opposed the postponement of the status question as too risky and failing to take into account their security concerns.

In 1998, the Minsk Group presented a new peace plan to the parties in the conflict based on the concept of a "common state", which would allow non-hierarchical relations between Azerbaijan and a de facto independent Nagorno-Karabakh that would not have the right to unilateral secession. Article 1 of the published peace proposal stipulated that Nagorno-Karabakh and Azerbaijan shall form a common state to be governed by a joint commission comprised of representatives of the two entities. This plan, envisaging the establishment of horizontal rather than vertical relations between Nagorno-Karabakh and Azerbaijan, was rejected by Baku, while embraced by Yerevan and Stepanakert.

The year 2001 saw an increase in diplomatic activity and reinvigoration of the Minsk process. In July 2001, the Presidents of Armenia and Azerbaijan met in Paris to discuss the so-called "Paris principles" for settlement of the conflict, reiterating the "common state" concept, the most essential aspect being the establishment of horizontal relations between Nagorno-Karabakh and Azerbaijan, thus ruling out the possibility of subordination. Under the proposed plan, neither Azerbaijan nor Nagorno-Karabakh could unilaterally change the provisions of the common state and the Nagorno-Karabakh Republic would itself form its own executive, legislative, and judicial branches as well as a national guard and police.

The last round of substantive negotiations within the framework of the Minsk Group was held in Key West, Florida, in April 2001. The peace plan proposed at that time reiterated some of the crucial aspects of earlier plans, including the withdrawal of Armenian troops from six of the seven Azeri districts (the seventh being Lachin, which provides the link between Armenia and Nagorno-Karabakh); effective self-government for Nagorno-Karabakh; and an internationally-patrolled corridor linking Azerbaijan to Nakhichevan through Armenian territory. Though based on some of the elements of the 1998 concept, the reference to "common state" has been abandoned as rejected earlier by Azerbaijan.

Despite the prevailing optimism for a breakthrough throughout 2001, the parties' stands on the issue of Karabakh's status, which is the most crucial point in the negotiations, still appeared to be as far as ever. While Azerbaijan has insisted on its territorial integrity by granting Nagorno-Karabakh an autonomous status, Armenia and the leadership of Nagorno-Karabakh reject any "vertical" subordination of the enclave to Baku. Meanwhile, Nagorno-Karabakh has adopted all the appurtenances of statehood with its own president, parliament, and the normal range of ministries and departments of state. Since independence, there have been three parliamentary elections and two presidential elections, with Arkady Ghukasyan being re-elected as president with 88.4% of the vote on Aug. 11, 2002.

Nadia Milanova

4.3 Austria - Italy (South Tyrol)

Since the end of World War I relations between Italy and Austria have sometimes been strained by the problem of the large proportion of native German speakers living in South Tyrol (i.e. in the province of Bolzano/Bozen, now part of the autonomous Italian region of Trentino-Alto Adige). The region was ceded to Italy by Austria in 1919 following Italy's intervention on the side of the Entente powers in World War I. Austria has not made any territorial claim against Italy since 1946, when the World War II Allies rejected its request for the return of South Tyrol. But thereafter Austria often complained that Italy was not honouring its undertaking of 1946 to grant autonomy to the province and rejected Italy's contention that the creation in 1948 of the broader autonomous region of Trentino-Alto Adige (containing an Italian majority) fulfilled this requirement. Austria accordingly welcomed a framework agreement of 1969 under which South Tyrol itself was to have more autonomy, but later complained about slow implementation of the agreement. In the late 1980s greater regional co-operation between Italy and Austria further defused the South Tyrol issue at governmental level. (Map 35, p.510, illustrates this dispute.)

Regional and Demographic Characteristics

The province of Bolzano/Bozen, also known as Alto Adige or South Tyrol, is 7,400 sq km in area and is delineated in the north by the Italian Alpine border with Austria (including the Brenner Pass), in the south-east by the Dolomites and in the south-west by the Adige river valley; its southernmost point is near Salurn. The province is predominantly agricultural in character, though industry and commerce have been developing rapidly in the towns of Bolzano and Merano. Trento (Trentino) province (6,213 sq km), apart from a strip running north-east along the southern edge of the Dolomites, centres on the middle reaches of the Adige river, to the south of Bolzano province.

In 2001 German speakers in Bolzano province numbered some 290,000, or about 69.3 per cent of the total population of 428,690, as against over 90 per cent in 1900 but only around 62.2 per cent in 1961. Italian speakers in 2001 numbered some 110,000 (26.3 per cent), representing a decline on the 1961 figure of 128,271 (34.3 per cent), the community's post-World War II high watermark. Speakers of Ladin (a Rhaeto-Romanic dialect) numbered some 18,000 (4.3 per cent) in 2001. By contrast, Trento province has always been overwhelmingly Italian-speaking, the proportion in 2001 being 98 per cent in a population of 477,859. The language divide in Bolzano is largely one between the rural (German-speaking) and urban (Italian) areas, some country districts being 95 per cent German-speaking. In 1971 Italian speakers represented only 5 per cent of the agricultural workforce, but they occupied 72 per cent of all posts in the public administration.

Since the early 1980s the region has benefited from preferential treatment deliberately applied by central government, and especially from generous budgetary support. Standards of living are high in comparison with other parts of Italy and the census revealed that the proportion of professional and executive people in the workforce was well above the Italian average. This relative prosperity has helped to defuse some of the worst complaints of the local German-speaking population, whereas some economically disadvantaged Italian speakers are particularly bitter about alleged positive discrimination in favour of the German speakers.

South Tyrol Question to 1946

The Tyrol takes its name from the castle of Tirol (near Merano), whose lords displaced episcopal authority in the area in 1271 but died out in 1363. The Tyrol then passed to Austria, becoming an apanage of a junior Habsburg line. In the Napoleonic era loose Austrian suzerainty over the more southerly bishopric of Trento was consolidated in 1803, but in 1806 the whole of the Tyrol was joined with Bavaria within the French-sponsored Confederation of the Rhine. In 1809-10 the celebrated Tyrolean hero Andreas Hofer led an uprising against Bavarian rule. Under the 1814 Treaty of Paris, the Tyrol (with Trento) reverted to Austria, which also acquired substantial other territory in northern Italy. Although most of these lands were incorporated into the unified Italian state established by 1870, the predominantly Italian-speaking region of Trento remained under Austrian control as part of the Tyrol. Italian irredentist aspirations towards Trento were clearly expressed by many Italians towards the end of the 19th century, supported by numerous nationalist groups in Trento itself. Prominent in pre-1914 Trento politics was Alcide De Gasperi, who was to become Christian Democratic Prime Minister of Italy after World War II but who began his career as a member of the Austrian parliament.

At the outbreak of World War I, Italy declared itself neutral and negotiated briefly with Austria for the acquisition of the *terre irredente* in recognition of its neutrality. However, in a secret treaty signed in London on April 26, 1915, Italy agreed to enter the war on the side of the Allies, in return for which Great Britain, France and Russia offered the cession to Italy not only of Trento but also of southern Tyrol as far north as the Brenner Pass (as well as Trieste, Gorizia and Istria and part of Dalmatia). Consequently, on May 23, 1915, Italy declared war on Austria-Hungary and later also opened hostilities against Germany. An armistice was signed with Austria on Nov. 3, 1918, and in February 1919 the Italian government submitted to the Paris peace conference a memorandum claiming substantially the same territories which had been agreed under the Treaty of London; subsequently, in Article 27 of the Treaty of St Germain, signed on Sept. 10, 1919, Italy received, among other territories, Trento and South Tyrol as far north as the Brenner Pass. One effect of the transfer was to divide Austria's remaining Tyrol territory into two regions.

Austria protested strongly at the Allied failure to apply the principle of self-determination to South Tyrol, but immediately after its annexation by Italy in 1919 both the Italian monarchy and the commander of the army occupying the region gave assurances that the customs and language, the local institutions and the self-administration of South Tyrol would be respected. Nonetheless, the province of Bolzano was immediately united with Trento to form the Italian province of Venezia Tridentina, and although the new province was in 1927 re-divided into Bolzano and Trento, the latter retained numerous lowland areas previously administered from Bolzano.

Particularly decisive in the development of the South Tyrol region was the advent to power of the Italian Fascists under Benito Mussolini in 1922. Mussolini embarked upon an intensive policy of

Italianization of South Tyrol, one feature of which was the establishment of an industrial zone. Teachers and civil servants were drafted in, with the result that the Italian population of Bolzano province (which according to the 1921 census then comprised only 20,000 of the total population of 243,000) grew to one-third of the total. Italian was declared to be the only official language, and those not speaking it were removed from all administrative posts. Thus the German-speaking communal staff in Bolzano province were dismissed and replaced by mayors brought in from other parts of Italy; German-speaking schools were abolished and even private German tuition banned; German ceased to be recognized as a legitimate medium for legal transactions; virtually all place names were changed and many families were obliged to Italianize their surnames; and the active policy of appointing Italians to public service posts was accompanied by an influx of Italian labour brought about by the deliberate installation of industries in the province.

An attempt to resettle the German-speaking South Tyrolese occurred at the beginning of World War II. An agreement was published by Italy and Germany on Oct. 21, 1939, relating to the "return of Germans of the Reich and emigration of ethnic Germans from the Alto Adige". This in effect obliged the Germans and Ladin speakers of the South Tyrol to choose either German nationality, meaning compulsory resettlement in Germany or in Austria (an integral part of Germany since the 1938 Anschluss), or acceptance of Italian nationality (which in itself offered no guarantee of the right to remain in the province). Some 212,000 persons (86 per cent) accepted the first option (although in fact only about 75,000 moved, due to the disturbances caused by the war) and about 34,000 opted for Italy; of the Ladin population, about 45 per cent opted for Italy. Although after the war Italy offered the right of return to the resettled persons, only a third accepted. German troops occupied South Tyrol in late 1943, receiving the general support of much of the population, but no attempt was made by Germany to annex South Tyrol.

The Paris Agreement of 1946

Pressure for the return of South Tyrol to Austria mounted again at the end of World War II. The Austrian Chancellor, Leopold Figl, was presented on April 22, 1946, with a petition bearing the signatures of 158,628 South Tyrolese calling for its return to Austria. Three days later the Austrian government submitted a memorandum to the member states of the United Nations reiterating Austria's claims to South Tyrol. However, on April 30 a conference of Allied Foreign Ministers in Paris decided to make no major changes to the Italian-Austrian border, although it stated that applications for minor adjustments would be considered. An Austrian application was made on May 30 for the return of a border area, but a subsequent Foreign Ministers' conference in Paris rejected this request on June 24, 1946.

Austria's response to the failure of its applications to the Paris conference was to seek a bilateral agreement with Italy whereby it could argue on behalf of South Tyrol for the achievement of autonomy for the region and for the protection of the German-speaking community. Consequently, the Austrian Foreign Minister, Dr Karl Gruber, and the Italian Foreign Minister, Alcide De Gasperi, signed an agreement in Paris on Sept. 5, 1946, relating to the province of Bolzano and to the lowland territories lost to Trento in 1927. The first two articles of the agreement read as follows:

"(1) German-speaking inhabitants of the Bolzano province and of the neighbouring bilingual townships of the Trento province will be assured a complete equality of rights with the Italian-speaking inhabitants within the framework of special provisions to safeguard the ethnic character and the cultural and economic development of the German-speaking element.

"In accordance with legislation already enacted or awaiting enactment, the said German-speaking citizens will be granted in particular: (*a*) elementary and secondary teaching in the mother tongue; (*b*) parification of the German and Italian languages in public offices and official documents as well as in bilingual topographic naming; (*c*) the right to re-establish German family names which were Italianized in recent years; [and] (*d*) equality of rights as regards the entering upon public offices with a view to reaching a more appropriate proportion of employment between the two ethnic groups.

"(2) The populations of the above-mentioned zones will be granted the exercise of autonomous legislative and executive regional power. The frame within which the said provisions of autonomy will apply will be drafted in consultation also with local representative German-speaking elements".

Article 3 of the 1946 agreement contained a pledge by the Italian government to consult with the Austrian government within one year on the revision of the 1939 citizenship options, on the mutual recognition of academic qualifications, and on the facilitation of goods and passenger transit between the two countries, including preferential treatment for the exchange of characteristic products.

The De Gasperi-Gruber agreement became Annex IV of the overall peace treaty signed between the Allies and Italy in Paris on Feb. 10, 1947, and was thus, in accordance with the stipulation of Article 85, to be considered an integral part of the treaty.

However, the Italians noted that the Paris agreement contained no renunciation of South Tyrol by Austria. Worse, the anger in Austria at the failure for the second time to obtain self-determination for the South Tyrolese led to statements that the agreement was only temporary. The result was a restrictive autonomy restrictively applied, with minimum consultation with the South Tyrolese.

1948 Autonomy Statute for Trentino-Alto Adige

On June 27, 1947, the Italian Legislative Assembly decided to place the two provinces of Bolzano and

Trento within the framework of a single region. The autonomy statute for the new region of Trentino-Alto Adige was accordingly approved by the Assembly on Jan. 29, 1948, and came into effect on March 14, 1948. Under the new statute, Bolzano province retrieved the lowland and border territories lost to Trento in 1927. However, most of the primary and secondary legislative and executive powers relating to economic and social affairs lay with the newly-created joint Regional Council (Assembly) for Trentino-Alto Adige which, because of the population ratio, thus had a two-thirds/one-third Italian majority.

The statute also provided for institutionalized power-sharing, the first of its kind. Under the new arrangements the Regional Council, which would be directly elected, would be composed of the members of the Bolzano and Trento Councils, and ministers would have to be appointed according to the ethnic composition of the region, i.e. two-thirds Italian, one-third German. Similarly, the members of the Bolzano Provincial Council would appoint Ministers in the ratio of two-thirds German, one-third Italian. The presidents of the Regional Council and Bolzano Provincial Council would be elected for a term of two years and be alternately an Italian and a German speaker.

Over the next seven years the South Tyrolese, through their main political party, the *Südtiroler Volkspartei* (SVP), raised a number of complaints about the autonomy and the implementation of the Paris agreement. The first related to the status of the German language. Did the fact that it was "parified" with Italian under Art.1(b) mean that it was locally official? If it was not official then there would be no obligation for civil servants and state employees, 75 per cent of whom were Italian, to know German. The Council of State ruled that German was not an official language since the makers of the Paris agreement could have made it so, but did not do so explicitly. It was only necessary therefore for the administrative offices to have someone available who knew German in dealings with the South Tyrolese public rather than have all civil servants and state employees bilingual.

Second, there was the issue of ethnic proportions in public offices. Were they a requirement under Art. 1(d) of the Paris agreement? And what was meant by "public offices"? The Italians were ready to accept them in the provincial administration but adamantly rejected that they should apply to state institutions (ministries, banks, the railways, post office, insurance and housing consortia) operating in the province—the point being that if they were applied to state institutions, then many Italians would have to give up their posts to South Tyrolese. Furthermore, the regional and provincial administrative offices reflected the locus of the legislative powers concerned, and these lay overwhelmingly with the region.

Third, the autonomy statute provided that "normally" the region would exercise its administrative functions by delegating them to the provinces and local public bodies. The South Tyrolese believed "normally" meant "automatically". This was rejected by the Italian-dominated region.

Fourth, government approval had to be given to provincial legislation before it could take effect. This approval usually required the issue of "Executive Measures", cabinet decrees having the force of law, and whose function was to co-ordinate the legislative powers of the state with the regions and provinces. The procedure was cumbersome and lengthy, and in a number of cases the state vetoed the province's legislation. This happened particularly in relation to housing, one of the few areas where the province enjoyed primary legislative competence. Fifth, state legislation could only be contested before the Constitutional Court by the region, not the provinces. And sixth, the provinces had very little money to carry out programmes.

It was not until Austria regained its full independence with the 1955 State Treaty—which, incidentally, confirmed Austria's boundaries as those existing before the 1938 Anschluss and made it clear that changes would be most unlikely to be accepted by the Great Powers—that Vienna was able to come to the support of the South Tyrolese. However, its efforts were dismissed by Rome on the grounds that implementation of the autonomy was an Italian domestic affair.

By 1960 the situation had deteriorated. The key issue was housing. In October 1957 the Italian government announced a programme to build 5,000 houses in the city of Bolzano. This was seen by the South Tyrolese as a means of importing Italian workers to the industrial zone in order to start upsetting the ethnic balance in the province. Coupled with the continued rejection of provincial government legislation on housing, the result was that the SVP withdrew from the regional coalition.

These events were also taking place against an increasing level of violence against infrastructural targets, later extending to Italian service personnel. Begun in the early 1950s by local South Tyrolese, the original aim was to break the grip of the region and have its powers transferred to the province in order to provide for a meaningful autonomy. Later, when stiffened by support from Austrian and pan-German groups, the aim changed to secession of South Tyrol from Italy. The Italian government repeatedly accused the Austrian authorities of aiding and protecting the extremists. On July 11, 1961, following a particularly sharp exchange of notes, Italy introduced a visa requirement on all Austrians visiting Italy in view of Austria's alleged failure to stop the passage of explosives across the border. This requirement, which gave rise to strong protests from Austria, was lifted on Sept. 14, 1962. But Italian attitudes were hardly softened by the decision of an Austrian court in Graz in October 1965 to acquit 27 Austrians and West Germans of attacks in Italy (to which several had freely confessed).

Negotiations leading to 1969 Agreement on South Tyrol

In the period 1959-61 Austria made repeated representations to the United Nations concerning the alleged non-realization of the 1946 Paris agreement. On Oct. 27, 1960, the UN General Assembly unanimously passed a resolution calling on Italy and Austria to seek a solution bilaterally or, failing this, to seek recourse to any peaceful means of their choice, thus ending Italian pretension that fulfillment of the agreement was an Italian domestic affair.

In September 1961 the Italian government appointed a mixed "Commission of 19", comprising experts and politicians—some of whom were SVP deputies in the Italian parliament—to study the problem of the South Tyrol. By 1963 its investigations had reached such a point that Austria and Italy decided to resume bilateral negotiations, and in May 1964, following the final report, the two countries set up a joint committee of experts. The package offered by Italy in December 1964, including extended powers for Bolzano and the creation of a special referee commission (later retracted), was rejected by the SVP and Austria, however. Following prolonged negotiations a new package of legislation, backed up by a "calendar of operations", or fixed sequence of international procedures, was devised and was published in the autumn of 1969. Although they did not fully satisfy the party's demands for full regional autonomy for Bolzano, these measures went sufficiently far to receive the SVP's narrow approval at a party conference held on Nov. 22-23, 1969.

Under the new package of reforms the South Tyrolese largely got what they wanted. Although Bolzano was still to remain a province in the region Trentino-Alto Adige and provincial legislation still needed approval by Rome, most of the important sectoral legislative powers of the region, such as agriculture and tourism, were transferred to it, together with the offices to administer them, so that delegation of administrative powers was no longer a problem. On the basis of the wording of the Paris agreement it was accepted that German should be a local official language although where there was a bilingual text Italian would be the authentic version. The principle of ethnic proportions was extended to apply to all state and semi-state bodies operating in the province except for the Ministry of Defence and the various police forces, to come into effect by the year 2002. But competence in both German and Italian was required, through examination, for entry, promotion and transfer, at every grade from chauffeur or caretaker through to director. Since the question of ethnic identity was very important—governing the school to which children should go, access to public employment and public housing, and even the candidature of those standing for office—everyone in the province was now required to make an official declaration at the time of the national census as to their ethnic group, with parents making the declaration on behalf of their children, and

these declarations could not be contested by the authorities. The province would now be able to contest state laws before the Constitutional Court. The province would receive nine-tenths of taxes raised there as well as a proportionate share of the state health budget and grants from the state's regional development programmes.

The calendar of operations, which specified no fixed time-span but only a fixed sequence, was designed to offer all parties the maximum security in the realization of the package. Its main stages were as follows: (i) agreement on amendments to Article 27 of the European convention on the peaceful settlement of international conflicts and recognition of the rights of jurisdiction of the International Court of Justice in the dispute; (ii) alteration of Italian state regulations to permit inter alia changes in the use of the German and Italian languages; (iii) and (iv) government statements in Austria and Italy; (v) the establishment of an Italian commission to propose formulations for legislative and constitutional amendments; (vi) statements by both countries to the UN General Assembly; (vii)-(ix) the signature of agreement (i) above and its approval, together with constitutional amendments, by the Italian parliament; (x) development by Italy of individual executive laws; (xi) declaration of the executive laws; (xii) publication of a decree on the transfer of powers to Bolzano; (xiii) concluding declaration by Austria within 50 days of the publication of the last executive law and an exchange of documents ratifying (i) above; (xiv)-(xvii) Italian acknowledgement of (xiii) and notifications of the end of the dispute to the United Nations, the International Court of Justice and the Council of Europe; and (xviii) signature of an Austrian-Italian treaty of co-operation.

Implementation of the 1969 Package Agreement

During the next twenty years many of the measures stipulated in the 1969 package were slowly implemented by Rome. However, some items deemed essential to autonomy, such as the effective parity of the German language in police procedure and court proceedings, remained unfulfilled. Also a number of controversies arose from the working of the new autonomy. For example, what should persons not from the three linguistic groups in the province state in the vital declaration as to their ethnic origin? Did not the obligation to give such a declaration violate the equality of rights postulated in Article 3 of the Italian Constitution? What would happen if, for whatever reason, the quota reserved for a linguistic group in a public body failed to be filled? And with the privatization of many public bodies in the 1980s, would the system of ethnic proportions and the linguistic requirements attached to it be allowed to continue? It was also a matter of concern to both South Tyrolese and Italians that Italian families—feeling that job opportunities in the future would be better in the German quota—were declaring their children to be German, something that could not be contested by the authorities but could lead to disruption in German-language schools. The South Tyrolese were also concerned that according to the Constitutional Court the state could carry out its own housing programme in the province if this was considered to be in the "national interest". And a standing source of anger amongst the South Tyrolese was the obligation to maintain bilingualism in regard to the names of places, rivers, mountains etc. It was argued that since the province had primary legislative competence for place names it should be able to approve the versions of names that were part of the historical and ethnic patrimony of the land but that some 8,000 Italian names decreed by the Fascists should be abolished.

By the early 1990s the problems relating to the system of ethnic proportions, the use of German in police and court proceedings and access to schools (but not that of place names) had been settled to the satisfaction of the South Tyrolese. As a result, in 1992 the SVP was able to inform the Austrian government that the package had been implemented to its satisfaction and the latter was able to declare that the dispute with Italy over fulfillment of the Paris agreement was over.

But the early 1990s had seen other momentous events: the collapse of Communism and the end of divided Europe; the establishment of a European Committee of the Regions under the 1992 Maastricht Treaty; the collapse of the traditional party system in Italy; and, in June 1994, the Austrian vote to join the European Union. The South Tyrolese were eager to share their experiences with other central European minorities. Along the lines of the 1980 Madrid Convention on Transfrontier Co-operation, the South Tyrolese argued that in many border areas it was clear that not all problems could, or indeed should, be solved by inter-state foreign policy but by local regional politicians and civil servants. And indeed most regions of Europe had cross-border or trans-frontier agreements. South Tyrol was itself a member of the Arge-Alp group with a number of German, Austrian and Swiss regions.

Since Tyrolese reunification had never been far from the minds of any Tyroler, North or South, in 1994 the South Tyrolese accordingly proposed the creation of an Autonomous European Region Tyrol (AERT), to include North and South Tyrol, Trento and (possibly) Vorarlberg. However this ambitious project was soon slapped down. Quite apart from the need to harmonize the legislative and administrative powers and institutional organization of the areas involved, far-reaching proposals to have the regions transfer their powers to the AERT were vetoed by both Vienna and Rome. The former argued that it would be unconstitutional for North Tyrol to cede its powers to an international authority; the latter rejected the scheme on the grounds that it would seem a loss of national territory and incite a nationalist backlash in Italy.

Indeed, schemes like the AERT, the numerical decline of the Italian community and the feeling among a number of Italians that Rome was failing to stand up for the rights of Italians in the province, if not accepting outright de-Italianization, had led to a rise in the vote in the province of the neo-fascist MSI (*Movimento Sociale Italiano*), later renamed *Allianza Nazionale* (AN), which in 1994 formed part of the national government coalition. Certainly the party in the province wanted the abolition of the autonomy statute, an end to the system of ethnic proportions, and an end to any official status for the German language. In successive elections in the 1990s the party obtained the highest number of votes in the Italian community, thus making it the largest Italian party in the provincial parliament and the Bolzano city council. The danger was clear: since the autonomy statute required power-sharing between the political parties of the two major linguistic groups, should all the Italian deputies come from the AN, how would it be possible for the SVP (or any other German-speaking party) to share power with it?

Indeed, to the Italian community in the province the government in Rome seemed to be giving even more concessions to the South Tyrolese. In 2001 the autonomy statute was revised again. The internationally guaranteed nature of the South Tyrol autonomy was explicitly recognized, so that it could not be diminished or brought into question. Laws adopted by the South Tyrol parliament would no longer need the approval of Rome in order to come into effect. Both provinces of Trento and Bolzano would be able to decide their own form of government and voting system. Finally, since the Ladins formed only 4 per cent of the population of South Tyrol, under the system of ethnic proportions the group would find it practically impossible to fill the highest political posts. Under the revised arrangements a Ladiner could now become Speaker or Vice-President of the South Tyrol parliament. And in 2003 the intention was for further reform to enable the Ladins to be represented in the government of the province and to have their own constituency in the province of Trento.

It is true that a small minority of South Tyrolese still call for unification with Austria (or rather, Tyrol) in order to right the wrong perceived to have been done in 1919. And there still are a number of matters that cause irritation between the linguistic groups. But by and large the so-called "South Tyrol Question" now poses few problems. Various reasons explain this. First, there was the gradual recognition that the protection of cultural minorities is a continual process against a background of changing times, changing values and technological progress, and that therefore autonomies should not be legalistically rigid and static, but dynamic, capable of responding to changing economic and social situations. In the case of South Tyrol, even after the declaration by Vienna that the dispute was over, there was an evident need to establish a mechanism by which Rome and Bolzano should maintain a dialogue. In 1992 a standing committee was established with access to the Italian cabinet to examine problems affecting the cultural, economic and social development of the province's three linguistic groups.

Second, there was the process of European integration. On the one hand, the acceptance of national boundaries meant that threats of secession by violence were severely diminished, and indeed the doctrine of self-determination was itself re-interpreted during the South Tyrol question to mean that a group should have the right to decide freely what legislative and administrative powers it should have in the economic, social and cultural field in order to maintain its separate identity and life-chances. Only if these legitimate demands were rejected by the host state should secession be justified. On the other hand, under the aegis of the Council of Europe, a number of instruments have been agreed relating to the protection of minorities, including the 1992 European Charter for Regional and Minority Languages and the 1994 Framework Convention for the Protection of National Minorities.

Third, a flourishing economic and cultural life and competent administration now exist in South Tyrol. The substantial financial resources flowing in on account of all-the-year-round tourism and the Common Agricultural Policy has led to one of the lowest rates of unemployment in Europe. A free university has been established, and radio and TV programmes are received from Austria, Germany and Switzerland as well as Italy. The province has its own ombudsman and statistical office. Finally, the Italian community of South Tyrol is now in its third, if not fourth, generation, and therefore the province is their homeland too. The autonomy which the South Tyrolese originally believed should be for their benefit, not only guarantees group and individual rights but as a territorial autonomy all those resident in the province benefit from its provisions. This inclusivity has ensured that the three groups have come closer in appreciating that the autonomy is for them all. It is not surprising therefore that a 1994 survey revealed that over 80 per cent of South Tyrolese and nearly 80 per cent of Ladiners identified themselves with their homeland rather than the region, Tyrol as a whole, Italy or Austria, and even 17.7 per cent of Italians did so also.

Antony Alcock

4.4 Baltic States - Russia

The Baltic states of Estonia, Latvia and Lithuania regained their independence as part of the process of the dissolution of the Soviet Union. Relations with Russia have subsequently been complicated by a range of issues, including the Baltic states' pursuit of NATO entry and their admission to the European Union (with effect from May 2004). In the case of Latvia and Estonia, a particular issue has been the status of the Russian minority populations, who account for over one-third of the population. There has also been no success in agreeing a border treaty between Latvia and

Russia. However, the most significant territorial issue has been that regarding the position of the Russian enclave of Kaliningrad, which is surrounded by Lithuania and Poland. (Map 36, p. 510, illustrates the region.)

The desire of the Baltic states to join NATO also has had significant implications for relations with Russia. The signals from Russia under President Vladimir Putin had down to December 2003 been quite relaxed, as long as the new members were prepared to comply with the 1990 Treaty on Conventional Armed Forces in Europe, and NATO to the 1997 Nato-Russia Founding Act. However, the Baltic states attained full membership of NATO on April 2, 2004, without signing the conventional armed forces in Europe treaty controlling troop deployments in signatory states, alarming nationalist opinion in Russia.

Following the accession of the Baltic states to the EU on May 1, 2004, the relationship between the Baltic states and Russia is now bound to the framework of EU foreign policy. On April 27, 2004, an agreement was signed whereby Russia recognized the 10 new EU member states as part of the Partnership and Co-operation Agreement between Russia and the EU.

The Kaliningrad Question

In strategic terms, the territory of the Baltic republics had great value for the Soviet Union in the post-World War II era, especially after the onset of the Cold War in the late 1940s. In the first place, they provided naval and air bases for the Soviet military in the southern Baltic. Secondly, the Lithuanian SSR provided territorial contiguity with the Soviet Union's latest acquisition on the Baltic, namely the northern half of old East Prussia (Königsberg/Kaliningrad). This part of pre-war Germany was annexed by Stalin in 1945 when he restored Soviet rule in the eastern Polish regions annexed in 1939 and, by dint of annexing German territory in the west, shifted Poland some 250 kilometres westward. The Soviet part of East Prussia became a major military centre and was allocated to the Russian Soviet Federated Socialist Republic (RSFSR), from whose main territory it was separated by the Lithuanian SSR.

Following the dissolution of the Soviet Union, there were some in Lithuanian nationalist circles who advocated that Lithuania should press a formal claim to the whole of the Kaliningrad region. Such aspirations received short shrift in Moscow, however, and never became official Lithuanian policy. The Russian intention was that Kaliningrad would be transformed, from being primarily a military base, into a free economic zone and a trade and communications centre for the Russian Federation. Under this plan, Kaliningrad's ice-free port would be developed into the Federation's principal entrepôt for trade with the West, using its extensive road and rail links with Russia proper. To this end, President Yeltsin in late 1991 secured a guarantee from Lithuania of continued overland access to the enclave.

Membership of the European Union means that both Lithuania and Poland come under the Schengen agreement, facilitating free movement for citizens of the EU but calling for a visa regime for non-EU nationals. This has posed significant difficulties in respect of Kaliningrad, which has become a complication in the "Northern Dimension" of the EU. Chris Patten (the EU External Relations Commissioner) and Anna Lindh (the then Swedish Foreign Minister) wrote in the *Financial Times* of Dec. 20, 2000, that: "Kaliningrad suffers from organized crime, environmental pollution and extensive drug and health problems. Not only are such problems mirrored elsewhere in the region, but they have obvious trans-border implications. That is why we are already involved in many projects in the region. These include the modernization of the main border crossing with Lithuania and Poland, institutional support to the Kaliningrad regional development agency, waste and water management and reform of the health system. Russia's troubled environmental inheritance and, in particular, the nuclear waste of north-west Russia must be addressed".

The EU's Northern Dimension, established in June 2000, was very much a reflection of the need for co-ordinated action within a multilateral framework. According to the European Commission's working document *The Second Northern Dimension Action Plan (2004-2006)*, "the responsibility for the development of the Kaliningrad Oblast of Russia lies of course with the Russian Federation. Given its particular geographic situation as a Russian enclave surrounded by the European Union it is however particularly important to enhance dialogue and co-operation between Kaliningrad and neighbouring Northern Dimension partners".

The most controversial issue has been that of visa-free travel, which Kaliningraders have enjoyed with both Lithuania and Poland. EU membership and the need to comply with the Schengen accords—involving free movement within the borders of the EU but increased vigilance at the external borders—necessitated a change of the status quo. A "Joint Statement of the European Union and the Russian Federation on Transit between the Kaliningrad Region and the rest of the Russian Federation" read:

"1. The parties acknowledge the unique situation of the Kaliningrad Region as part of the Russian Federation but separated from the rest of the Federation by other states. With the aim of further developing the strategic partnership between the EU and Russia, the parties therefore agree to make a special effort to accommodate the concerns on both sides related to the future transit of persons and goods between the Kaliningrad Region and other parts of Russia, and to intensify their co-operation to promote the social and economic development of the region as a whole.

"2. On the economic and social development of the oblast, the parties agree to implement a comprehensive package of measures in order to ensure easy passage of borders for legal purposes with a view to facilitate

human contacts and promote the development of the Kaliningrad Region".

The transit issue was finally resolved on Sept. 1, 2003, when terms for the introduction of the "facilitated transit document" (FTD—a sort of multi-entry visa) were drawn up to the satisfaction of all parties. In future a train ticket would be ordered and a request made for a transit document to the Lithuanian authorities; if successful, the train ticket could be issued. The costs of the FTDs will be met by the EU. By this time Lithuania and Russia had also finally ratified the treaty that recognized their common border.

Stephen Day

4.5 The Bessarabia Question

The territorial settlement established between Romania and the Soviet Union after World War II in the peace treaty signed with Romania by the Allies in Paris on Feb. 10, 1947, was intended to be a definitive solution of long-standing Romanian-Russian conflict over the eastern part of Moldavia (Bessarabia). Romania's frontiers with the Soviet Union were defined according to a line which was political, not ethnic. Most of Bessarabia, where two-thirds of the population were Romanian, was incorporated into the Moldavian Soviet Socialist Republic (SSR) in 1940. In the post-war period the Communist government of Romania consistently stressed that it had no territorial dispute with its fellow Warsaw Pact member; yet the "Bessarabia question" remained an important underlying factor in Romanian-Soviet relations. (See Map 37, p. 511, for the location of Bessarabia.)

In the disintegration of the Soviet Union in 1991, the Moldavian SSR first changed its name to the Republic of Moldavia (Moldova) and then, on Aug. 27, 1991, declared its independence, which was immediately recognized by Romania. This development radically transformed the "Bessarabia question" from one of Romanian aspirations towards a territory annexed by the Soviet Union to one of the exercise by the population of the Moldavian Republic of the right of self-determination. In other words, the question became centred on whether Moldavia would remain independent or would decide to unite with Romania, with the additional complication that breakaway "republics" were declared in two mainly non-Romanian areas of Moldavia.

Early Historical Background

The origin of the name Bessarabia can be traced to the emergence of the Romanian principalities. The first of these is considered to have been founded circa 1330 by the ruler Basarab I; it eventually included the territory that was later to be called Wallachia, as well as the southern part of the area between the Prut and the Dniester. The association of the name of the Wallachian dynasty of Basarab with the territory of the first principality was perpetuated in the use by medieval cartographers of the term Bessarabia. This term, however, was employed very loosely, sometimes designating much of present-day Romania, or merely Wallachia or Moldavia. Later it was confined either to the land between the Prut, the Dniester and the Black Sea, or to the southern part of this region—the Budjak.

Moldavia was the name applied to the second principality of Romanians which was established circa 1350, its frontiers being the Dniester in the east and the dominions of Basarab in the south. Moldavia extended its control over the latter area during the early 15th century. The Genoese port of Maurocastro (Akkerman) at the mouth of the Dniester was obliged to pay tribute to Alexander the Good of Moldavia (1400-32) and this same prince even secured the port of Chilia on the Danube for a brief period. Apart from the narrow strips of territory around Chilia and Akkerman, which came under direct Ottoman rule following their capture in 1484 (and to which the Turks sometimes referred as Bessarabia), Moldavia never formed an integral part of the Ottoman empire, although, like Wallachia, it was subject to Turkish suzerainty.

Over the following four centuries Moldavia became increasingly vulnerable to the territorial ambitions of its northern neighbours, as was most graphically demonstrated by the Treaty of Bucharest of May 1812, which concluded the 1806-12 Russo-Turkish war. The principality was partitioned, the Porte ceding all the Moldavian territory between the Dniester and the Prut to Russia in return for the Russian evacuation of the rest of Moldavia and Wallachia. Alexander I incorporated the ceded area into Tsarist Russia, but to distinguish it from the rest of Moldavia he resurrected the name of Bessarabia. The western half of Moldavia remained under Turkish suzerainty until it became part of the independent state of Romania, which received international recognition in 1878. However, under the 1856 Treaty of Paris which ended the Crimean War, the Russians were obliged to restore to Moldavia the south-western districts of Bessarabia bordering on the Danube—Cahul, Bolgrad and Ismail—for strategic rather than ethnic reasons, since Britain and France wished to deny Russia access to the Danube. When the union of Moldavia and Wallachia took place in 1859, these three districts automatically became part of the new United Principality of Romania. In 1878 the Treaty of Berlin returned the three districts to Russia, despite Romania's expectation that it would retain that part of Bessarabia in return for having come to Russia's aid during the Russo-Turkish war of 1877-78 and for having signed in 1877 a pact allowing Russian troops passage against the Turks.

Although the Congress of Berlin awarded Romania most of the Black Sea province of Dobruja (with a mixed population), Romanian dissatisfaction with the 1878 settlement strengthened an irredentist movement for the return of Bessarabia and for the inclusion of other Romanian-populated areas within the country's borders. In Bessarabia, the ethnic composition of the population in the late 19th century still supported the Romanian claim, despite a policy of resettlement by the Tsarist authorities which brought in an influx of Jews, Bulgarians and Germans. The effects of the policy were mirrored in the first Russian census of 1897, which distinguished the population not by nationality but by native language. According to its results, of the total population of 1,936,012, 47.6 per cent (921,441 persons) were Romanian speakers (this was the term used), 19.6 per cent (379,698) Ukrainian, 8.1 per cent (155,774) Russian, and 11.8 per cent (228,168) Yiddish. Mother-tongue Bulgarians and Germans represented 3.4 per cent and 3.1 per cent respectively.

World War I and its Aftermath

Romania entered World War I in August 1916 on the Entente side, its territorial aspirations focusing not only on Bessarabia but also on the Austro-Hungarian provinces of Bukovina and Transylvania (see Sections 4.11 and 4.14). Heavily defeated by the Central powers, Romania was forced to sign the disadvantageous Treaty of Bucharest (May 1918) but re-entered the war in November 1918 just before Germany's defeat. Its reward under the post-war redrawing of the European map was a "greater Romania" which included all the disputed provinces. While the war was still in progress, in April 1918, a National Council of Bessarabia, containing a majority of Romanian representatives, had proclaimed the union of the province with Romania. The victorious Allied powers recognized the union in the Treaty of Paris of October 1920.

The aggrieved party was the new Bolshevik government of the Soviet Union, which refused to sign the treaty, although it did agree to open negotiations with the Romanian government on the question of restoring diplomatic relations between the two countries. A series of preparatory meetings culminated in the Vienna conference of March 1924, the agenda for which was a discussion of territorial and political differences. Romania's demand for Soviet recognition of its acquisition of Bessarabia met with the USSR's insistence that its government still regarded the province as part of its state territory. With both sides refusing to give ground, the conference broke down and relations between the two countries rapidly deteriorated.

Ukrainian authorities after 1918 did not recognize the Romanian border on the Dniester river, proposing a redistribution of territories by ethnographic criteria. The government of Hetman Skoropadskyi claimed for Ukraine the Ismail and Bilgorod-Dnistrovskyi districts, the left bank of the Dniester river, all Khotin (Khotyn) district and Northern Bukovina. The Ukrainian People's Republic (UNR), however, was succeeded by the Ukrainian Soviet Socialist Republic by the end of 1920, this formally joining the USSR in December 1922.

Soviet opposition to Romanian rule in Bessarabia was translated into open hostility on Aug. 4, 1924, when a Romanian frontier post was attacked by a group of men in Russian uniforms. On Sept. 15 of that year the town of Tatar Bunar was seized by a Communist group, which proclaimed the establishment of a Moldavian Soviet Republic in Bessarabia. Although Romanian troops drove the insurgents from the town, Soviet intentions with regard to Bessarabia had now become clear. Since the Tatar Bunar "revolution", as it was termed in Soviet Moldavian historiography, failed to win significant local support, the Soviet government had to use other means to provide the nucleus for a Soviet Moldavia. Hence the announcement on Oct. 12, 1924, by the Kharkiv Council of the Commissioners of the People in the Ukrainian SSR that the Autonomous Moldavian Soviet Socialist Republic (AMSSR) had been created in south-west Ukraine on the left bank of the Dniester. Of the new republic's half-million population, only about 32 per cent were Romanians; the other major populations were Ukrainians (46 per cent) and Russians (10 per cent). Initially the town of Balta was designated its capital but in 1928 the seat of authority was transferred to Tiraspol. Thus a territory which had never before been called Moldavia, nor been part of the medieval principality of Moldavia, was created in an effort to give credibility to the Soviet government's claim to Bessarabia and to provide a catalyst for the "reunification" of the Moldavians on the left bank of the Dniester (in the AMSSR) with those on the right bank (in Bessarabia).

Almost a month before the announcement of the creation of the AMSSR, the politburo of the Communist Party of the Ukraine charged activists assigned to duties in the embryonic republic with the introduction of the Russian Cyrillic alphabet and with the "development of the national Moldavian language". This was the first signal that the Soviet government intended to give to ethnic Romanians under its authority a distinct identity as compared with the inhabitants of the Romanian national state. The imposition of the Cyrillic alphabet for writing Romanian was the most obvious feature of this drive. Its accomplice was the prescriptive use of the obfuscatory adjective "Moldavian". However, in the case of the AMSSR, Moldavian (Romanian) was spoken by a minority. This fact was reflected in the actual language policies pursued, since it was understandably the use of Ukrainian rather than Moldavian which was cultivated in the republic.

Soviet-Romanian relations began to cool after King Carol's dismissal of his Foreign Minister, Nicolae Titulescu, in August 1936. Titulescu's removal dealt a death blow to the Soviet-Romanian Treaty of Mutual Assistance which he had been on the point of signing with his counterpart, Maxim Litvinov. The increasingly pro-German and fascist orientation of successive Romanian governments alarmed the Soviet authorities, which translated their concern into a reminder that the Bessarabia question had still to be resolved. In its issue of Jan. 11, 1938, *Le Journal de Moscou* warned that "the Soviet Union cannot be indifferent to events in a neighbouring country" and that "Romania is the only neighbouring state with which the Soviet Union has not regulated certain fundamental questions". The Soviet Union's displeasure was emphasized by the withdrawal of its ambassador from Bucharest on Feb. 4, 1938.

World War II and the 1940 Soviet Ultimatum

On Aug. 23, 1939, Nazi Germany and the Soviet Union signed their infamous non-aggression pact. Secret clauses of this agreement provided for much of Eastern Europe to be divided into German and Soviet "spheres of influence", Bessarabia being one of the territories "assigned" to the Soviet Union. The German invasion of Poland a week later caused the outbreak of World War II and increasing tensions between Romania and the Soviet Union, which came to a head in mid-1940. Shortly before midnight on June 26 the People's Commissar for Foreign Affairs, V. M. Molotov, summoned the Romanian minister in Moscow to the Kremlin and presented an ultimatum demanding that Romania should cede Bessarabia and Northern Bukovina to the Soviet Union. The Soviet note called for a reply from the Romanian government within 24 hours. The Romanian reply, handed to Molotov on the evening of June 27, indicated that King Carol's government was prepared to discuss the Soviet proposals and requested the Soviet Union to name the time and place for talks. Molotov completely ignored this request and handed the Romanian minister a further note calling for the evacuation by Romanian troops of the two areas by 2 p.m. on June 28. The Romanian cabinet decided to yield in order, as it said, "to avoid the grave consequences of a recourse to force". (For similar reasons, Romania later also yielded to the German-inspired Vienna Award of August 1940, under which Northern Transylvania was returned to Hungary, and also agreed to cede southern Dobruja to Bulgaria in September 1940.)

The total area annexed by the Soviet Union in 1940 covered some 51,000 sq km and contained a population of about 3.8 million, of whom two million were Romanians, 580,000 Ukrainians, 390,000 Russians, 274,000 Jews, 186,000 Bulgarians, 125,000 Germans and 190,000 (six) other nationalities. Northern Bukovina, an area of roughly 6,000 sq km and half-a-million inhabitants, together with the Herla (Gertsa) region, the northern Bessarabian district of Hotin (Khotin), and the southern Bessarabian districts of Cetatea Alba (renamed Belgorod Dniestrovskii) and Ismail—these covering about 15,000 sq km and supporting a population of one million—were incorporated into the Ukrainian Soviet Socialist Republic. On Aug. 2, 1940, by a decision of the Supreme Soviet, the Moldavian Soviet Socialist Republic (MSSR) was created from the union of the rest of Bessarabia with the western part (some 3,400 sq km) of the AMSSR (the areas around Tiraspol, Dubossary and Rebnita). The greater, eastern part of the AMSSR (some 4,900 sq km) was returned to the Ukrainian SSR—a step which demonstrated that its creation in 1924 had been a political stratagem to give credibility to the Soviet claim to Bessarabia. The new Moldavian SSR covered an area of 33,700 sq km with a population of some 2.4 million.

Immediately after the annexation of Bessarabia, the Soviet authorities nationalized the province's land and private enterprises. The process of sovietization was facilitated by the transfer of 13,000 specialists from Russia, the Ukraine and Belorussia. Over 10,000 Romanians were deported from the new republic to Central Asia in order to work in factories and collective farms as replacements for those drafted into the Red Army between 1940 and 1941. The deportations were interrupted by the German attack of June 22, 1941, on the Soviet Union, in which Romania, under General Ion Antonescu, participated with the aim of recovering Bessarabia and Northern Bukovina. These lost provinces were regained by July 27, 1941, in a German-led advance which not only brought Bessarabia back under Romanian rule but also gave Romania territory of the same size to the east of the Dniester river, which was named Transdniestria (Transnistria).

However, the reconquest of Bessarabia was accomplished by the Red Army in August 1944, when the Soviet generals Malinovsky and Tolbukhin successfully launched a massive assault of almost one million troops and 1,500 tanks against the combined German and Romanian forces straddling the Prut. Most of Bessarabia was reincorporated into the Moldavian SSR in its August 1940 frontiers, the former southern Bessarabian districts of Ismail and Cetatea Alba being assimilated into the Odessa oblast of the Ukrainian SSR. These territorial realignments were formalized in the Soviet-Romanian armistice of September 1944 and confirmed by the Paris peace treaty of 1947 between the Allies and Romania (although Romania recovered Northern Transylvania from Hungary).

The fierce rearguard action fought by the German and Romanian armies in Bessarabia caused the virtual destruction of the towns in the province. The capital Chisinau (Kishinev) was reduced to ruins and the damage to roads, railways and bridges posed considerable supply problems for the Soviet authorities. The difficulties faced by the recreated Moldavian SSR, the economy of which was based almost entirely upon agriculture, were exacerbated by the severe droughts of 1946 and 1947, which created a widespread famine. Several thousand party activists were brought from the Ukraine and Russia to supervise the establishment of the republic's organizational infrastructure, thus diluting the Romanian element in the population, which was further weakened by mass deportations to the republics of Central Asia. In 1949 some 36,000 Romanians were resettled and the process continued in the 1950s. Most of the Romanian schools were given over to teaching in Russian, for which teachers were imported from the other Soviet republics. The ubiquity of Russian and Ukrainian activists in the republic's official apparatus provided the Soviet authorities with a justification for the priority given to the use of Russian in the official life of the republic. At the same time, the influx of Russians and Ukrainians acted as a check against potential nationalist agitation amongst the Romanians, who were now officially called Moldavians.

The Post-War Period

Soviet difficulty in winning over native Moldavians in the post-war period was exemplified by the choice of first secretaries of the Moldavian Communist Party (MCP), none of whom were of Romanian origin. The best-known was Leonid Brezhnev, who held the position between 1950 and 1952. Throughout the republic's post-1945 history as part of the Soviet Union, the percentage of Moldavians who were members of the MCP was the lowest amongst any indigenous nationality in a Soviet republic. In 1970 only 1.3 per cent of Moldavians were members of the party, compared with 3.8 per cent of Ukrainians and 7.3 per cent of Russians in the republic.

The process of Russification in the Moldavian SSR was accelerated by enforced socio-economic changes, the most important of which were urbanization and migration. The urban growth rate in the republic after 1944 was among the most rapid in the Soviet Union. Indeed, comparison of the 1959 and 1979 censuses showed that it was the highest of any republic during that period. In this context, it should be borne in mind that before World War II Moldavia (i.e. Bessarabia) was a predominantly agricultural province largely starved of Romanian investment. Its towns were mainly peopled by Russians, Ukrainians and Jews. The demographic changes registered between 1959 and 1979 reflected not only a period of intense urban development but also a shift in the balance between urban and rural populations. The rural population fell from 77.7 per cent of the total in 1959 to 61 per cent in 1979, while the urban population increased from 22.3 per cent in 1959 to 39 per cent in 1979.

A concomitant of Moldavia's urbanization was migration, both within the republic from rural to urban areas and from outside the republic. Between 1959 and 1979 the numbers of Russians in Moldavia jumped dramatically from 290,000 to over 500,000. This influx not only consolidated the use of Russian as the republic's official language but, more significantly for the position of the Moldavian language, led to an increase in the use of Russian by the other peoples of the republic. As language was considered by Moldavians to be the badge of national identity, their fears about assimilation by the Russians grew, as more and more of their number became bilingual in Moldavian and Russian.

As long as the Romanian Communist Party (RCP) remained completely subservient to Moscow, representations from Bucharest over the plight of the Romanians (Moldavians) in the Moldavian SSR could not be expected. A Treaty of Alliance was signed between Romania and the Soviet Union on Feb. 4, 1948, in which each country undertook to show mutual respect for the independence and sovereignty of the other, and to refrain from interference in the other's internal affairs. The treaty was valid for 20 years but the relationship of servility changed before its expiry, leading to a carefully-orchestrated campaign by the RCP to reassert the country's historical right to Bessarabia. In a statement on April 23, 1964, the RCP proclaimed a new autonomous line in economic and foreign policy, and in October of the same year it authorized the publication of Karl Marx's *Notes on the Romanians*. These notes had been discovered by a Polish historian in an archive in Amsterdam and included a contestation by Marx of Russia's annexation of Bessarabia in 1812: "The Porte renounced Bessarabia. Turkey could not give what did not belong to her because the Ottoman Porte never had sovereignty over the Romanian lands".

The RCP's appeal to national sentiments and its defiance of the Soviet Union's supranational pretensions served to increase its popularity in Romania and at the same time offered a signal to the Romanians in the Moldavian SSR that Bessarabia was regarded by Bucharest as unredeemed territory. The Moldavian Communist Party reacted in 1965 when its first secretary, Ivan Bodiul, made a speech on the 40th anniversary of the founding of his party in which he quoted an RCP manifesto of 1940 welcoming the Soviet "liberation" of Bessarabia and Northern Bukovina "from the heavy yoke of Romanian imperialism". The new RCP secretary, Nicolae Ceausescu, replied in the following year in kind. Without mentioning Bessarabia by name, Ceausescu's speech of May 7, 1966, on the occasion of the 45th anniversary of the foundation of the RCP, constituted the strongest and most authoritative claim that Romania made to Bessarabia during the Communist period. He criticized resolutions of the third, fourth, and fifth RCP congresses, held in 1924, 1928, and 1932 respectively, in which "Romania was mistakenly called 'a typical multinational state' formed from 'the occupation of certain foreign territories'". He added that the Romanian party's mistaken stance over territories acquired at the end of World War I was a "consequence of the practices of the Comintern, which laid down directives that ignored the concrete realities of our country, gave tactical orientations and indications which did not accord with the economic, socio-political and national conditions prevailing in Romania".

The sudden and unexpected journey of Leonid Brezhnev to Bucharest only three days after Ceausescu's May 1966 speech was seen as an indication of how seriously the Soviet leader regarded the Romanian assertions. However, the Brezhnev-Ceausescu talks did nothing to stem "tit-for-tat" exchanges, which in fact intensified between the Romanian and Moldavian CPs over the next decade,

particularly concerning the position of Bessarabia and the successor Moldavian SSR. The low-point in these exchanges was reached with the publication in 1974 in Russian of a lengthy polemical work entitled *Moldavian Soviet Statehood and the Bessarabian Question* by A. M. Lazarev, the Russian president of the Moldavian Supreme Soviet. The thrust of Lazarev's book was that the Moldavians were not Romanians but a distinct people with an historical tradition separate from that of the Romanians of Wallachia and Transylvania; and that their aspirations had been only partially fulfilled with the establishment of the Moldavian SSR. The logical extension of Lazarev's argument was that Romanian Moldavia was a legitimate unrecovered part of Soviet Moldavia. Far from deterring Bucharest, Lazarev's book had the opposite effect. In 1975 a new Romanian museum of national history opened with prominently-displayed maps showing Bessarabia and Northern Bukovina as part of Romania. In the following year two members of the RCP's Institute of Historical Studies produced a work on Romanian politics between 1918 and 1921, in which they referred to Bessarabia as "this ancient Romanian territory".

Emergence of Moldavian Nationalism

Soviet-Romanian sparring continued over Bessarabia during the 1980s. However, with the advent to power of Mikhail Gorbachev in the Soviet Union in 1985, and encouragement of glasnost ("openness"), Moldavian intellectuals were able to assert their own Romanian identity more forcibly and to take up the Bessarabian issue. Glasnost brought to the surface previously-repressed dissatisfaction among the Moldavians in the republic about the status of their language and provision for schooling in Moldavian. Pressure for economic and language reform was exerted by a number of newly-created groups, the most notable of which were the Moldavian Democratic Movement in Support of Perestroika and the Alexei Mateevici Cultural Club. However, Semyon Grossu, the MCP leader, not only refused to consider reform but also attempted to persuade the non-Moldavians in the republic to oppose the Moldavian demands. Denied access to the media and the possibility of legal registration, the unofficial Moldavian groups decided in May 1989 to join together to found the Popular Front of Moldavia. The Front set itself the main objectives of acting as an umbrella organization in any dialogue with the republican or Soviet authorities and creating links with other unofficial movements elsewhere in the Soviet Union.

The Front mobilized support for language demands in a series of demonstrations in Chisinau which culminated in a rally attended by half a million people on Aug. 27, 1989, two days before the Moldavian Supreme Soviet was due to consider draft laws making Moldavian the official language of the republic. Opposition to the laws came from Russian-speakers in the republic, 100,000 of whom went on strike on Aug.

29, demanding that Russian also be proclaimed a state language and the language of inter-ethnic communication. In Moldavia's second largest city, Tiraspol, which had a Russian-speaking majority, 30,000 protesters called for the withdrawal of two Moldavian books recently printed in the Latin alphabet from local bookshops. Faced with these conflicting pressures, the Moldavian Supreme Soviet on Sept. 1 approved legislation which (i) made Moldavian the state language of the republic, (ii) reinstituted the use of the Latin alphabet proscribed by Stalin following the annexation of Bessarabia and (iii) designated both Moldavian and Russian as languages of inter-ethnic communication.

Party leader Grossu's opposition to language reform and perestroika finally led to his dismissal on Nov. 16, 1989. He was replaced by Petru Luchinsky (a native of Moldavia and, unlike his predecessor, a fluent speaker of Romanian), who was said to be more in tune with the ideas of Gorbachev. The Moldavian Popular Front responded by promising to avoid a confrontation in order to give the new leader a breathing space. New parliamentary elections were held on Feb. 25, 1990. Although only the Communist Party had official recognition, the most significant political force in the elections was the Moldavian Popular Front. Assuming the role of a patriotic umbrella organization, the Popular Front endorsed Communists who professed to place Moldavian interests first, but did not attempt to validate candidates in predominantly Russian and Ukrainian speaking constituencies. Of the 370 deputies elected to parliament, 85 per cent were Communists and 70 per cent were Moldavians; some 30 per cent of deputies (112) received the backing of the Popular Front, 15 per cent were Russians and about 10 per cent were Ukrainians.

The elections therefore confirmed the growing power of the Popular Front and the waning influence of the Communist Party in Soviet Moldavia. At the same time, they marked a polarization along ethnic lines between the Moldavians and other national groups. In parliament the Front soon flexed its muscles. At the first session, which opened on April 17, 1990, the Front, with the support of other Moldavian deputies, defeated the attempt by Luchinsky to become chairman and instead elected Mircea Snegur, a Popular Front sympathizer but formerly a Communist functionary. (On Sept. 3, 1990, the Supreme Soviet created the office of President of the republic and elected Snegur to the post.) In May 1990 the Communist government led by Petru Pascaru was brought down by a vote of no confidence and replaced by one of reformers under the premiership of Mircea Druc, an economist. Both moves not only signalled the demise of the Communists but also represented a transfer of power to the Moldavian majority.

Assertion of Moldavian Independence— Breakaway "Dniester" and "Gagauz" Republics

Sovereignty was foremost on the parliamentary agenda and symbols of Moldavian Romanian identity were quick to appear. On April 27, 1990, the Romanian flag was adopted as the flag of Moldavia, and on June 5 parliament decided to rename the republic the "Soviet Socialist Republic of Moldova", thus adopting the Romanian name for Moldavia instead of the Russian-sounding (although Latin-based) "Moldaviya". Following the example of other Soviet republics, the Moldavian parliament made a declaration of sovereignty on June 23, 1990.

This acted as an invitation to secession to the predominantly Ukrainian and Russian area of the republic east of the River Dniester. Deputies representing the area, meeting in Tiraspol on Sept. 2, 1990, proclaimed their own autonomous republic, which they named the "Dniester Moldavian Soviet Socialist Republic" (see also Section 4.14). At the time of the declaration the "Dniester Republic" had a population of 760,000, of whom about 60 per cent were non-Romanians (mostly Ukrainians and Russians). Moreover, the previous month representatives of the Gagauz ethnic group of south-western Moldavia, meeting in Komrat, had on Aug. 19 declared the "Gagauz Autonomous Soviet Socialist Republic". Numbering some 150,000, the Gagauz people were of Turkic/Bulgarian ancestry but Christian Orthodox in religion. (This separatist region has been reunited with Moldova as an autonomous region since 1994.)

On Feb. 11-16, 1991, President Snegur of Moldova paid an official visit to Romania, the first by any leader from the republic since the Soviet annexation of Bessarabia in 1940. The visit marked the end of a ban on ties between the Moldovan Republic and Romania imposed by the Soviet Union. Snegur addressed both chambers of the Romanian parliament in a nationwide broadcast and recognized a common Moldovan-Romanian identity. He called for closer economic ties with Romania and announced the opening of a Moldovan consulate in Iasi in northern Romania and a Romanian consulate in Chisinau.

These steps were welcomed by the Moldovan Popular Front, but the Front was strongly critical of Romania's signature on April 5, 1991, of a Treaty of Friendship and Co-operation with the Soviet Union. In the Front's view, the treaty "denies the right of captive peoples in the Soviet empire to national and state independence". This was a clear reference to Moldova's position. An affirmation of the illegality of Moldova's and, by extension, Bessarabia's incorporation into the Soviet Union was provided by a three-day international conference devoted to the "Molotov-Ribbentrop Pact and its consequences for Bessarabia" organized in Chisinau by the Moldovan government and parliament on June 26-28, 1991. In a declaration adopted by the Moldovan parliament on the final day of the conference, the 1939 Molotov-Ribbentrop Pact, which gave the green light for the Soviet annexation of the Baltic republics, Bessarabia and Northern Bukovina, was stated to be "'null and void".

The holding of this conference forced the government and parliament of Romania to take a stand on the issue of Bessarabia (and Northern Bukovina). The

Romanian government had assiduously avoided comment on these matters, an attitude which seemed to irritate Moldovan leaders and the Moldovan people. Indeed, the Romanian-Soviet friendship treaty, which the Romanian President, Ion Iliescu, had hastily negotiated in April 1991, appeared to place the Romanian authorities on the other side of the issue. Critics of the treaty noted its tone of subservience to the interests of the Soviet Union, its specific affirmation that World War II boundaries were not subject to discussion or modification, and the total absence of any reference to Romanian national concerns in the Soviet Union.

The Romanian deputies, faced with the prospect of the Chisinau conference, suddenly became deeply concerned about their kinfolk in the territories annexed by the Soviet Union. On June 24, they unanimously adopted a statement declaring: "The Ribbentrop-Molotov Pact, by which the Soviet Union and Germany established for themselves spheres of influence from the Baltic to the Black Sea, taking it upon themselves to decide the destinies of sovereign states, among them Romania, flagrantly contravenes the fundamental principles and norms of international law. Consequently, in the name of the Romanian people, parliament condemns this pact from the outset as being null and void". This declaration was subsequently presented at the Chisinau conference to guarded applause. Moldovan reserve implied that proof of the bona fides of the Romanian parliament's declaration would be provided by the manner in which it dealt with the ratification of the Iliescu-Gorbachev treaty. In the event, however, the collapse of the Soviet Union rendered the proposed treaty defunct.

The failure of the attempted coup in Moscow in August 1991 signalled the final breakdown of the Soviet Union and the removal of political obstacles to the assertion of a Moldovan independence that went beyond the symbolic stage of new flags and national anthems. President Snegur, on Aug. 19, was one of the first republican leaders to denounce the Moscow coup as unconstitutional. At 11 a.m. on Aug. 19 the commander of the Soviet garrison in Chisinau, together with the military commissar of the republic, sought an audience with Prime Minister Muravschi and requested that the Moldovan capital be placed under Soviet military control. This request was refused. On the following day President Snegur issued two decrees, one nullifying the decisions of the Moscow coup leaders, the other setting up a Supreme Security Council to defend the independence and territorial integrity of Moldova. On the same day 100,000 people attended a rally in Chisinau called by the Moldovan Popular Front at which President Snegur denounced the coup and called for the reinstatement of President Gorbachev. Following the coup's collapse, the Moldovan parliament issued a resolution on Aug. 23, 1991, outlawing the Moldovan Communist Party and confiscating all its funds and property. It also set up a committee to examine the activities of those—including Igor Smirnov and Stefan Topal, the respective leaders of the self-declared Russian Dniester and Turkic Gagauz republics within Moldova—who had declared their support for the attempted coup. Topal was detained on Aug. 23, while Smirnov was arrested by a snatch squad of the Moldovan police in Kiev on Aug. 29 and taken to Chisinau. On Oct. 1, 1991, both men were released in response to a sit-in in Tiraspol, the capital of the Dniester Republic, which blocked the main railway line linking Moldova to the Ukraine for over a month.

On Aug. 27, 1991, the Moldovan parliament adopted a declaration affirming the Republic's sovereignty and independence and requested admission to the United Nations as a full member. Romania recognized Moldova's independence on the same day and on Aug. 30 a protocol was signed by the Foreign Ministers of both countries for an exchange of ambassadors.

Escalation of Conflict over "Dniester Republic"

On Dec. 9, 1991, Mircea Snegur was the sole candidate for the office of President of the Moldovan Republic and was elected with 98 per cent of the votes cast. Polling was disrupted in the Dniester and Gagauz republics, where a week earlier separate elections for their own presidents had been held. Tension in the Dniester Republic then mounted as several hundred Russian Cossacks were invited to the area by the newly-elected "President" Smirnov, in order to act as a local militia. Several police stations manned by Moldovan police were attacked. Attempts by the Chisinau authorities to impose their authority in the breakaway republic failed when, as a result of clashes between the Moldovan police and the armed separatists, several policemen were shot dead at Dubasari on Dec. 13, 1991.

On Dec. 21, 1991, President Snegur committed Moldova to the newly-formed Commonwealth of Independent States (CIS) at the meeting of leaders of the republics held at Alma-Ata. His reasons for doing so were economic, given Moldova's dependence on the resources of the other republics and the continued existence of a common currency. However, Snegur insisted on the right of Moldova to raise its own army and on Dec. 30 this right was agreed at the Minsk summit of the CIS. On Jan. 24, 1992, the Deputy Defence Minister of the CIS agreed that artillery troops based in Moldova should pass under the control of the Moldovan President, while airborne troops should remain under the command of the CIS Minister of Defence.

President Snegur met President Iliescu of Romania at the Moldovan border town of Ungheni on Jan. 25, 1992. Further steps were envisaged in conformity with the concept of "two republics, one nation", expressed both by Snegur (in February 1991) and by the Romanian Foreign Minister, Adrian Nastase (in March 1991). Attempts to develop a cultural confederation, initiated in 1991, were now bolstered by moves to facilitate an economic union. Agreement was reached at Ungheni on creating a free-trade zone in the border area between the two countries, on allowing unrestricted passage of Moldovans and Romanians across the border, and on abolishing customs duties between both countries. It appeared to be the aim of both governments to move towards unification, although such unification was to be gradual. The creation of an economic union was expected to pave the way to de facto unification, which would receive a de jure validation when both governments, and both populations, deemed that to be realistic.

Meanwhile, a critical factor for full Moldovan independence, and for union with Romania, was the question of the control of ex-Soviet troops stationed on Moldovan territory. In this respect, the position of the former Soviet 14th Army, based largely in Tiraspol, was crucial. In the early months of 1992 it was not clear whether this army was obeying orders from Moscow or Kiev (respectively the capitals of the Russian Federation and Ukraine) or indeed any superior authority. In an area where the writ of the Moldovan Republic did not run (i.e. the Dniester Republic), it was likely that the ex-Soviet army would become the arbiter of authority, because it apparently supported the breakaway Dniester Republic. While the army continued to remain in its present strength in the region, it represented a threat not only to the independence of the Republic of Moldova as a whole but also to the security of Moldova's neighbouring states of Ukraine and Romania.

The confrontation between Moldova and the Dniester Republic escalated into serious armed conflict in March 1992, during which there were some 50 reported fatalities and thousands of ethnic Russians and Ukrainians fled into Ukraine. The Romanian government on March 8 denied a Moscow television report that Romanian nationals were involved in the fighting, while on March 17 the Ukrainian government mobilized its border forces and threatened "possible retaliatory measures" against Russian Cossacks seeking to join the forces of the Dniester Republic. On March 19 President Iliescu of Romania contacted the Russian and Ukrainian Presidents to express concern about the deteriorating situation and in particular about the role of Cossack irregulars. Meeting in Helsinki on March 23, the Foreign Ministers of Moldova, the Russian Federation, Ukraine and Romania issued a call for a cessation of hostilities and declared their support for Moldova's territorial integrity. However, a series of ceasefire declarations on the ground proved to be of short-lived effect.

Having become commander-in-chief of the Moldovan armed forces on March 18, 1992, President Snegur on March 28 declared a state of emergency and imposed direct presidential rule throughout Moldova, calling on the people to prepare to "fight for the motherland". The Dniester Supreme Soviet on March 30 condemned Snegur's actions and called on the 14th Army to guarantee the safety of its citizens. In contrast President Iliescu offered "all necessary support to the leadership of Moldova in its efforts to defend the republic's territorial integrity". In early April the Romanian government denied claims by the Dniester

Republic that it was massing forces on the Moldovan border with a view to intervening directly in the conflict. Thereafter, Moldovan, Russian, Ukrainian and Romanian negotiators worked to defuse the crisis, on the basis that the Dniester Republic would become a special economic zone and that the introduction of Romanian as the official language would be delayed. On May 24 the Foreign Ministers of the four republics signed a truce agreement in Lisbon under which the 14th Army would return to barracks and "strictly observe the ceasefire". However, units of the 14th Army became involved on the Dniester side in an escalation of fighting in late May and early June 1992 that turned into a full-scale war. Although the 14th Army was transferred to Russian command under a decree by President Yeltsin in April 1992, up to 70 per cent of its officer corps originated from the Dniester Republic and one way or another was involved in clashes between the Dniester army and the Moldovan forces up until 1994. The armed confrontation cost the two sides over a thousand battle-related dead, with thousands wounded and up to 100,000 refugees, not to mention the destruction of infrastructure and the economy.

Aftermath of War—Conflict Resolution

The inability to bring the breakaway republic under control by military means caused a deep political crisis in Chisinau and a re-evaluation of its policy. The "war party" in the Moldova government lost, resulting in the resignation of Minister of Defence Ionu Kostashu and Minister of National Security Anton Plugary in July 1992. In September 1992, President Snegur signed an agreement allowing the CIS (i.e. Russian peacekeepers) to separate the warring parties in the conflict zone.

From August 1992 Moldova and Russia conducted ten rounds of talks that resulted in an agreement in September 1994 providing for Russian forces to be withdrawn within three years. However, the withdrawal of Russian troops was made conditional on a full political settlement between Chisinau and Tiraspol, with the latter demanding de facto confederation with Moldova and its own membership in the CIS. The Dniester Republic leadership was recognized in Moscow as a de facto equal party for negotiations with Moldova, with high-ranking ministers or diplomats exchanging official visits. When Ukraine joined Russia as guarantor of the peace process in the region under the observation of the OSCE in July 1995, Tiraspol used it to claim international recognition in inter-state relations. The Moscow accord in May 1997 allowed the Transdniestrian leadership to claim the legal right to conduct diplomatic missions and to seek foreign guarantees in the declared process of creating a single Moldovan state of two equal partners: the Transdniestrian Moldavian Republic (PMR) and the Republic of Moldova. Subsequent talks in Kyiv (Kiev) (1999, 2000) and Tiraspol (1999) failed to clarify the principles of the unified Moldovan state.

Since its election in April 2001 the new Moldovan

Communist Party government, led by President Vladimir Voronin, has conducted a series of talks with the Dniester Republic. However, the political process of re-unification between the breakaway republic and Moldova has stalled. In the summer of 2003, President Smirnov of the Dniester Republic accused the Communist leadership of Moldova of betrayal of its electoral promise to settle for confederation and of imposing a de facto economic blockade of Transdniestria. With Chisinau continually accusing the Dniester Republic leadership of covering up corruption, drug-trafficking and illegal arms-trading, against a background of continued economic pressure by Moldova and a refusal to discuss federal arrangements, any political settlement without international mediation seemed unlikely.

The most comprehensive and ambitious plan so far was proposed by President Putin in a memorandum in November 2003. This envisaged a united Moldova as a loose asymmetrical confederation, neutral and demilitarized, with two federal constituencies (Transdniestria and Gagauz), each with its own legislation, executive and judicial bodies, independent budget and tax systems, state emblems etc., but with a single defence force, customs union and currency. Federal executive and legislative bodies would have equal representation for Transdniestrian and Gagauz officials on the one hand and Moldovan officials on the other. The state language would be Moldovan with Russian also being an official language.

The Russian proposal was initially regarded positively in Tiraspol, Chisinau and Kyiv at the level of the political leadership, but mass protests by the united opposition in the Moldovan capital led to the cancellation of Putin's planned official visit on Nov. 25, 2003. The opposition regarded his plan as an attempt to turn Moldova into a Russian protectorate after only 12 years of independence, and secured a "promise" from President Voronin not to sign the memorandum. However, the key factor may have been the negative reaction to the Russian peace plan from both the EU and the USA. Russian Foreign Minister Igor Ivanov made a strong statement at the CIS summit in Kyiv that the memorandum on the Dniester region settlement "was not signed because of the pressure on the Moldovan leadership which was put by certain states and organizations", and warned the national leaderships of the CIS member states that they should draw appropriate conclusions from the example of the recent change of regime in Georgia in order to prevent interference in their internal affairs in the future.

Economic, Social and Political Factors

Moldova is often referred to as a failed state because of its economic and social conditions as well as its democratic return to a Communist government in 2001. Moldovan GDP per capita after a decade of independence was still only one-third of what it used to be before 1991. The registered daily income of 80 per cent of the population was less than $1. The official poverty line is set at around $220 which is below the World Bank's "dollar a day" level. Some estimates show that at least 20 per cent of the population live completely outside the cash economy and an estimated 20-25 per cent of the population has emigrated.

These conditions lay behind the election of a Communist government in relatively free and fair elections in 2001. However, once in power, the Communist government lacked either the will or the capacity to fight corruption and smuggling, so no effective control of the Moldovan Transdniestrian border was established. Transparency International estimates that more than half of state revenues are lost through customs fraud and tax evasion, while 50% of expenditures are lost through inefficient and fraudulent procurement systems. The Moldovan economy is therefore left between rural subsistence and the black market, leaving it with no revenues as well as mounting external debts for imported energy supplies.

International Factors

Moldova has been a member of the CIS since its creation in 1991 and ratified the CIS economic union in April 1994. Moldova has also taken an active part in NATO's Partnership for Peace since March 1994 and was admitted to the Council of Europe in July 1995. In November 1994 Moldova signed a friendship and co-operation treaty with the EU and achieved observer status in the EU's Stability Pact for South-eastern Europe. The evolution of the Moldovan political process—from national communists to popular front and back to having national communists in power—did not influence the formal orientation of Moldova toward integration with the European Union. Despite its CIS membership Moldova also joined the GUAM—a regional organization of Ukraine, Georgia and Azerbaijan that enjoyed the support of the USA and did not include Russia. Moldova joined the WTO in 2001. Despite its Communist leadership Moldova joined the Russian-backed project of the Eurasian Economic Union only as an observer and avoided the even more ambitious project of the Single Economic Space. President Voronin declared in spring 2003 that integration into Europe constituted a priority of state policy with an ultimate goal of EU membership.

Moldova, however, remains outside the club of nations on the path to joining the EU in the near future, unlike neighbouring Romania. Moldovan institutions and economy fall short of European standards. With the majority of Moldovans (around 70 per cent) against re-unification with Romania, Chisinau seems set to be divided from Bucharest by the EU border and visa regime. Only in April 2000 did Moldova and Romania agree a treaty normalizing their relations, and after seven years of difficult negotiations they still have not resolved such contentious issues as the future nature of their relationship, the language issue and border settlements. Romanian elites and society in general seem to agree that the most pressing issue for Romania is to join NATO and the EU.

The Russian military presence became as much part of the problem as it was earlier part of the temporary solution. With Russia, Ukraine and the OSCE acting as mediators it took over a decade to end military confrontation, still with no political settlement in view. Indeed, Transdniestrian and Moldovan forces demilitarized the security zone along the Dniester river only in August 2003, withdrawing altogether 71 armoured vehicles and leaving the Russians in control. Chisinau seems to have completely abandoned the idea of achieving territorial unity with the help of the Russian peacekeepers. It has been considering the offer of a European Union peacekeeping force suggested by the OSCE in July 2003. Without Russian military backing and with the imminent threat of sanctions from the USA and the EU, the Dniester Republic would have little choice but to start meaningful negotiations with Chisinau. Politically, however, President Voronin would find it difficult to accept a Western-led peacekeeping force in Moldova even if it is the only way out of the deadlock.

Russian leaders have promised to withdraw the 14th Army from Moldova since April 1995 despite the opposition of the Dniester Republic, which even held a referendum on the matter in March 1995. Since President Putin has "allowed" Western troops on the territory of the Central Asian republics and Georgia, it would be difficult for Moscow to make an exception of Moldova. At the same time, Russia will inevitably remain the key player in defining Moldova's foreign policy orientation as long as it remains the single source of gas and oil supply and is a guarantor of a settlement with Transdniestria. Some experts believe that Russia has no interest in resolving the Transdniestrian conflict and will attempt to preserve the status quo in its own favour unless Moscow is offered some kind of trade-off by the USA in some other area of Russia's geopolitical interests.

Moldovan-Ukrainian Relations

Ukraine took a relatively neutral position in the conflict between Tiraspol and Chisinau considering that Ukrainians have historically constituted the largest ethnic group on the left bank of the Dniester (Dnistro) and that this territory belonged to the Ukrainian SSR in the inter-war period. The homeland of the Gagauz people is also divided between Moldova and Ukraine, providing them with a choice of ally in case of mass mobilization for national self-determination. However, when independence was established in 1991, Ukraine had too many of its own problems, including an almost million-strong Soviet army on its territory. The prospect of a territorial dispute in Transdniestria was not appealing to the ex-communist elites that have ruled Ukraine since independence. Although Ukrainian leaders from the very beginning established friendly relations with Moldovan governments and even allowed the arrest of the breakaway leader Igor Smirnov in Kyiv, Ukraine did not support an economic blockade against the Transdniestrians. The Tiraspol-

Odessa motorway remains the main connection of the Dniester Republic with the outside world and the Reni sea terminals are the main gates for Transdniestrian exports (mainly steel, but allegedly also armaments). After Kyiv refused to establish Moldovan-Ukrainian (as opposed to Ukrainian-Transdniestrian) checkpoints on the border of Ukraine and Transdniestria in 2002, President Voronin did not hide his frustration, accusing Ukraine of dealing with the "criminal leadership" of the Dniester Republic.

Strategically supporting independent Moldova, Ukrainian leaders do not rule out territorial exchanges between the two countries. In fact, Ukraine and Moldova created a precedent in the successor states of the former USSR by voluntarily exchanging territory in 1999. Moldova received a 100-metre strip on the Danube to build a strategically important oil terminal, while Ukraine got 7.7 km of narrow corridor for the Odessa-Reni highway that used to run through Moldovan territory.

Kyiv would prefer to have Moldova as a buffer against potential Romanian territorial claims. It is clear that if the majority of Moldovans one day vote in favour of a single state with Romania, both Chisinau and Bucharest will be bound to renegotiate territorial arrangements with the Gagauz autonomous region and the Transdniestrian Republic. With Russia geographically far away, both autonomies might want to join Ukraine, giving Kyiv additional leverage in negotiations with Romania. Meanwhile, it is in Kyiv's interests to have friendly relations with both Chisinau and Tiraspol. Indeed, when Communist government in Chisinau was under threat from pro-Romanian demonstrations in 2002, the President of Ukraine despatched his special envoy to demonstrate support for President Voronin.

At the same time, Ukraine does not wish to see the Dniester Republic becoming a stronghold of Russian influence and military power as well as a source of criminal activity. Hence, Ukraine supported in early 2003 the ban proposed by the USA and EU on issuing visas to the Transdniestrian leaders, in order to put pressure on Tiraspol to be more flexible. Being under Russian pressure itself, Kyiv is trying to keep a difficult balance.

Prospects for the Bessarabia Question

The viability of Moldova as an independent state is the key to the Bessarabia question in the near future. With no immediate prospect of reunification with Romania, Moldova so far has shown a poor record of providing its citizens with economic prosperity and national dignity. The country remains divided territorially and politically. However, Moldova is a recognized member of the international community and—whatever the outcome of the Transdniestrian settlement—it will fall to the Moldovan people to decide whether the two states' solution for one Romanian speaking community is no longer suitable, or whether they will remain a separate nation with their own state.

The key international factors in determining the future of Bessarabia are the prospective expansion of the European Union to include Romania, and Moscow's final military withdrawal from the region that the Russian state dominated for the last two centuries. Successful integration of Romania into the EU might influence Moldovan public opinion in favour of unification with Romania in line with the example of German re-unification, while Russian military withdrawal might provide a more favourable political climate for achieving a settlement to a problem in Transdniestria that was never a purely ethnic conflict as such. With Romania and Ukraine aspiring to membership of NATO and the EU, there are no immediate geopolitical obstacles to the mutually beneficial solution of the Bessarabia question or indeed a prosperous and independent Republic of Moldova. In the long term, the Bessarabia question might be fully encompassed within the potential further expansion of the European Union to include Romania, Moldova and Ukraine.

Olexander Hryb

4.6 The Cyprus Question

Cyprus, the third largest island in the Mediterranean after Sardinia and Sicily, is situated in the eastern Mediterranean about 80 miles (130 kilometres) west of Syria, 44 miles (80 kilometres) south of the Turkish coast and some 500 miles (885 kilometres) south-east of the Greek mainland. Having been a Greek island in terms of population and culture since ancient times, Cyprus was captured by the Ottoman Turks in the 1570s and remained under Turkish dominion for more than three centuries. During this period it acquired a significant Muslim Turkish population, which today is estimated to constitute just under 19 per cent of the island's total population of approximately 900,000.

In the modern era the existence of the two distinct communities in the island, the one gravitating towards Greece and the other towards Turkey, has effectively precluded the establishment of agreed political and constitutional arrangements. In consequence the island's status has proved a major source of strain in relations between the Athens and Ankara governments, within a broader context of centuries-long conflict between Greeks and Turks in the eastern Mediterranean region, even though Greece and Turkey both joined the North Atlantic Treaty Organization (NATO) in 1952. (For an account of the Greek-Turkish dispute in the Aegean Sea area, see Section 4.10.) Although Cyprus became an independent republic in 1960 after 82 years of British rule, intractable differences between the two communities led to the effective division of the island into Greek and Turkish areas—a process consolidated by the intervention of Turkish military forces in 1974.

Since then inter-communal talks have been pursued periodically under United Nations auspices; however, although both sides support the principle of preserving Cyprus as one independent state, no resolution has yet been achieved of the complex political, constitutional, territorial and security issues which divide the two communities. In the absence of any such solution, the Turkish Cypriot area declared itself independent in November 1983 as the "Turkish Republic of Northern Cyprus" (TRNC), but received recognition only from Turkey. (See Map 38, p. 511, for the division of Cyprus.)

The period between 1992 and 1995 saw attempts to reach agreement on confidence building measures, but negotiations deadlocked over core issues such as recognition and sovereignty. The issue of Cyprus' prospective EU membership played a major role in negotiations between both sides. Heightened tensions between 1996 and 1998 caused by incidents on Cyprus and elsewhere hindered any meaningful progress in talks. The years 1999-2000 witnessed a series of proximity talks, led by UN Secretary-General Kofi Annan and involving the leaders of both the Greek and Turkish Cypriot communities. However, disagreements over core issues, which had plagued previous negotiations, led to the breakdown of the proximity talks. Direct talks between the two leaders took place in 2002 and this process culminated in Secretary-General Annan presenting a settlement plan on Nov. 11, 2002. After many intensive discussions, there was no agreement and Cyprus, still a divided island, signed the Treaty of Accession to the European Union on April 16, 2003.

The decision to relax travel restrictions made by the Turkish Cypriot authorities in late April 2003 received much praise and worldwide media coverage. The Greek Cypriot authorities reciprocated by announcing measures intended to aid Turkish Cypriots. After the December 2003 elections in the TRNC, which saw opposition forces make large gains, UN sponsored direct talks resumed in February 2004. In March 2004, negotiations between both communities and the governments of Greece and Turkey ended in stalemate. UN Secretary-General Annan finalized a settlement plan on March 31, which was put to simultaneous referenda on April 24. The Greek Cypriot community overwhelmingly rejected the settlement plan, whilst a large majority of Turkish Cypriots voted in favour. As a consequence only the Greek Cypriot-controlled south of Cyprus joined the European Union on May 1, 2004.

Historical Background to the Cyprus Question

The historical existence of the two distinct communities in Cyprus derived from the economic importance of the island, its fertility and its location on eastern Mediterranean trading routes, as well as from its strategic importance as a base for military operations in the Middle East region. These factors explain why Cyprus was ruled by a succession of foreign powers throughout much of recorded history, which in turn exposed the island to a continuous series of cultural influences from outside.

The Greek language is believed to have been brought to Cyprus between 1500 and 1200 BC, when first Mycenaean and then Achaean merchants began to establish themselves. In the fourth century BC Cyprus became part of the empire of Alexander the Great, on whose death it passed to the dominion of the Ptolemaic kings of Egypt. In the first century BC the island was annexed by the Romans and by the fourth century AD it had become part of the Eastern Roman (Byzantine) Empire. Richard I (Coeur de Lion) of England conquered Cyprus during the Crusades in 1191 and used it as a Mediterranean strategic base; it then passed to Guy de Lusignan, the dispossessed King of Jerusalem, whose successors ran it as a feudal monarchy. In the 14th century the kingdom of Cyprus formed an alliance with the Papacy against the Turks, achieving brilliant military successes under Peter I. But his assassination in 1369 ushered in two centuries of instability, during which first the Genoese and then the Venetians, from 1489, enjoyed periods of possession. The Ottoman Turks conquered Cyprus in 1571 and the island then remained under Turkish rule for more than three centuries.

The Muslim Turks were at first relatively generous to the Christians, giving them a wide degree of autonomy and restoring the Greek Orthodox archbishopric. However, as the Ottoman empire declined in the 18th and 19th centuries its rule became increasingly oppressive, and a series of revolts took place among the Greek-speaking population, the most important being that of 1821. At the 1878 Congress of Berlin it was agreed that Britain should take over the administration of Cyprus under continued Turkish sovereignty, in return for a British pledge of support for Turkey against any aggression from Russia. By this time the desire for *enosis* (union with Greece) had become prevalent among the Greek Cypriots, who were encouraged in this aspiration by the "greater Greece" nationalists in Athens.

Britain annexed Cyprus at the outbreak of World War I when Turkey declared war on the Allied powers. In 1915 Greece declined Britain's offer to cede Cyprus in return for a Greek declaration of war on the Allied side—a proposal which was not repeated when Greece eventually became a belligerent in 1917. Under the 1923 Treaty of Lausanne both Greece and Turkey recognized British sovereignty in Cyprus, which became a Crown Colony in 1925. However, a rising tide of anti-British feeling among the supporters of *enosis* led in 1931 to serious rioting in the course of which the British government suspended the constitution, abolished the legislative council and transferred all powers to the British governor. After World War II British efforts to restore democratic rule in Cyprus under continued British sovereignty met with constant opposition from the Greek government (who demanded *enosis*) and from the Greek Orthodox Church in Cyprus, led from 1950 by Archbishop Makarios III; consequently, attempts to devise an acceptable constitution made little headway until the late 1950s. Meanwhile, anti-British violence mounted both in Greece and in Cyprus, in the latter case instigated mainly by guerrillas of the pro-*enosis* EOKA (*Ethniki Organosis Kyprion Agoniston*—National Organization of Cypriot Fighters) led by Gen. George Grivas.

At a tripartite meeting called in London in late August 1955 and attended by representatives from Greece, Turkey and the United Kingdom (as well as members of the Greek and Turkish Cypriot communities), Archbishop Makarios repeated his calls for *enosis*. However, the Turkish Cypriot representative, Dr Fazil Kutchuk, adopted the standpoint that Cyprus was historically Turkish and geographically an extension of the Anatolian peninsula, and that the "so-called Cyprus question" had been invented by Greeks who, he contended, had no right to be consulted. The talks were broken off in early September and two months later, amid mounting anti-British violence, the governor of Cyprus declared a state of emergency (which was not revoked until December 1959). In March 1956 Archbishop Makarios was deported to the Seychelles for "seditious activities" including alleged involvement with EOKA; although allowed to return to Greece in April 1957 (following the declaration of a ceasefire by EOKA the previous month), the Archbishop remained barred from Cyprus until March 1959.

In June 1956 Dr Kutchuk presented his own proposals for a self-governing Cyprus within the British (as it then was) Commonwealth. These envisaged a bicameral system whose lower house would comprise one elected member for every 10,000 of the electorate (giving Greek Cypriots an effective 4-1 majority over Turkish Cypriots) and whose upper house, with powers of veto over lower house decisions, would comprise eight Greek Cypriot and eight Turkish Cypriot members. By mid-1957, however, he had adopted the view of the Turkish government that partition of the island between Greece and Turkey (*taksim*) was the only viable solution to the problem. In June 1958, as Turkish Cypriot riots broke out in Nicosia and Larnaca, some 200,000 people demonstrated in Istanbul for *taksim*. Meanwhile, EOKA had resumed its attacks in the autumn of 1957, while a Turkish Cypriot resistance movement called TMT emerged as the successor to the Volkan underground group.

Formulation of the 1960 Constitution

As the hostilities in Cyprus mounted the United Nations adopted a resolution on Dec. 5, 1958, expressing its confidence that all involved parties would reach "a peaceful, democratic and just solution in accordance with the UN Charter". After Greece and Turkey had on Feb. 11, 1959 concluded the "Zurich Agreement" on the structure of an independent Cyprus, a trilateral conference in London later in the month (also attended by Greek and Turkish Cypriot representatives) resulted in the initialling on Feb. 19, 1959, of an agreement, which formed the basis of the Cypriot constitution of 1960. However, this outcome produced a bitter dispute, never completely resolved, between Archbishop Makarios and Gen. Grivas, the latter accusing the former of making unnecessary and secret verbal concessions to the other parties at the London meeting. The London agreement was ratified on Feb. 28, 1959, by the Greek parliament and on March 4 by the Turkish parliament. There was no direct consultation of either Cypriot community at that stage.

The constitution subsequently drafted came into effect on Aug. 16, 1960—the day on which Cyprus became independent. It stipulated that the Republic of Cyprus would be presided over by a Greek Cypriot President and a Turkish Cypriot Vice-President, each of whom would have certain rights of veto over laws relating to foreign affairs, defence or security. The President would nominate a fixed contingent of seven Greek Cypriot Ministers to the Council of Ministers (the chief executive organ) and the Vice-President three Turkish Cypriot Ministers. In general elections the Greek and Turkish Cypriot communities were to vote separately in divided municipalities, the former electing 35 deputies to the House of Representatives and the latter 15. Any modification of the electoral law, or the adoption of any law pertaining to the separate electoral municipalities or to certain areas of financial legislation, would require the approval of simple majorities of both the Greek and the Turkish Cypriot contingents of the House—a situation which made it difficult to raise the necessary majorities on sensitive issues. The Supreme Constitutional Court and the High Court of Justice were to be presided over by a neutral president, the constitution providing that Turkish Cypriot judges should try cases involving only Turkish Cypriots, that Greek Cypriots should try Greek Cypriot cases and that mixed courts should try cases involving both communities. Although the Turkish Cypriot community at this time constituted only 18 per cent of the population, it was guaranteed 30 per cent of all civil service posts and 40 per cent of army and police force positions.

Under a Treaty of Guarantee initialled in London by Cyprus, Turkey, Greece and the United Kingdom in February 1959, any or all of the three latter parties retained certain rights of political intervention for the purpose of restoring the conditions specified by the London agreement, if they were deemed to be endangered. A Treaty of Alliance, also initialled in London in February 1959 and signed in 1960 by Greece, Turkey and Cyprus, provided for the maintenance of limited contingents of Turkish and Greek troops in Cyprus. The United Kingdom also negotiated its retention of sovereignty—which it still maintains—over two military bases totalling 99 square miles (256

sq km) at Akrotiri (south-western coast) and Dhekelia (south-eastern coast). (Cypriot spokesmen note that Britain's retention of sovereignty in parts of Cyprus is without precedent in the history of decolonization. Although no formal demand has yet been made, there is general agreement in Cypriot government circles that at some future date Britain will be requested to cede the sovereignty of the two base areas.)

On Dec. 13, 1959, Archbishop Makarios was elected as the first President of Cyprus and Dr Kutchuk as Vice-President. Cyprus joined the United Nations on Aug. 24, 1960, and became a member of the Commonwealth on Sept. 20, 1960. The Maronite, Roman Catholic and Armenian communities of Cyprus, which between them comprised some 5 per cent of the population, voted on Nov. 13, 1960, in favour of association with the Greek majority for constitutional purposes.

Constitutional Crises and the Turkish Involvement of 1964

Despite the specific recommendations made by the 1960 constitution in relation to the respective political and cultural rights of the Greek and Turkish Cypriot populations, a series of differences arose during 1961 and 1962 over their interpretation, leading to a constitutional crisis and to full-scale inter-communal hostilities. A claim by the Greek side that regular Turkish troops participated in the fighting was denied by the Turks. The situation was eventually contained by the installation in March 1964 of a United Nations peace-keeping force in Cyprus (UNFICYP).

The first dispute arose in March 1961 over a Greek Cypriot bill, which the Turkish Cypriots feared would erode certain community rights embodied in the tax system; the Turkish Cypriot deputies in the House of Representatives used their veto to block the passage of the bill, and for two years the tax situation remained very uncertain. The second and more significant dispute arose over the maintenance of separate Greek and Turkish Cypriot communities. The government proposed, despite the strong opposition of its Turkish Cypriot members, (i) to replace the segregated National Guard units with mixed ones under a Greek Cypriot commander, (ii) to remove the provision guaranteeing Turkish Cypriots 30 per cent of administrative positions in local government, and (iii) to dissolve the divided municipalities in the five largest towns (Nicosia, Limassol, Larnaca, Famagusta and Paphos), replacing them with "improvement boards" appointed directly by the government under a 1950 law passed under British rule.

In opposition to this third and most controversial proposal, the Turkish Communal Chamber on Dec. 29, 1962, approved a bill to preserve the five divided municipalities and to create one more, whereupon President Makarios rejected the decision as "legally non-existent" and issued a decree abolishing the municipalities as from Jan. 1, 1963. The House of

Representatives (the Turkish members being absent) approved on Jan. 2, 1963, a bill installing the "improvement boards", and although the Supreme Constitutional Court subsequently rejected this move it caused deep resentment among Turkish Cypriots. On Nov. 30, 1963, President Makarios made 13 proposals for constitutional reform aimed especially at the removal of communal distinctions, including the removal of the presidential and vice-presidential veto, changes in the functions of the Vice-President and a reduction in the proportion of administrative positions allocated to Turkish Cypriots. However, the latter, supported by the Turkish government, rejected the proposals on the grounds that they would relegate Turkish Cypriots to minority status, in contravention of the 1960 constitution. In December 1963 the Turkish Cypriot ministers and parliamentary deputies, claiming that their security could not be guaranteed in Greek Cyprus, withdrew from their respective bodies, to which they have never returned. Thereafter, the Turkish Cypriot side consistently maintained that its non-participation in the island's governmental structures meant that no government of "Cyprus" had constitutional legitimacy. The Greek Cypriot side, on the other hand, asserts that constitutional legitimacy remained with the government from which the Turkish Cypriots withdrew (and its successors), as evidenced by the fact that it continued to have UN and general international recognition.

Serious inter-communal fighting broke out in late 1963, and despite the efforts of all sides to establish a permanent ceasefire it continued periodically throughout most of 1964. Turkish naval units were reported to have left Istanbul during December 1963 for the eastern Mediterranean, giving rise to complaints from Greek Cypriots that a Turkish invasion was imminent. Meanwhile, part of the Turkish Army contingent in Cyprus took up a position outside Nicosia, so as to command the strategically important road linking Nicosia with Kyrenia, the only major port on the north coast of Cyprus. After the Greek and Cypriot governments had rejected a UK-US proposal that a NATO peace-keeping force should be installed on the island, on March 4, 1964, the United Nations Security Council decided to establish a UN force (UNFICYP) in Cyprus. Initially introduced for a three-month period, its mandate was thereafter repeatedly renewed. On April 27, 1964, the UN Secretary-General, U Thant, appointed a special representative for Cyprus to oversee and report on the situation.

On the arrival of the UN force in late March 1964, President Makarios asked the Turkish government to withdraw its troops from the Nicosia-Kyrenia road. Turkey replied that its troops were overseeing the restoration of order, whereupon Cyprus unilaterally terminated the 1959 Treaty of Alliance (a step which Turkey refused to recognize). Despite the presence of the UN force the inter-communal fighting continued, and on Aug. 9 Turkish warplanes carried out retaliatory attacks on Greek Cypriot targets in north-western Cyprus. A ceasefire was declared the next day in accordance with a resolution passed by the UN Security Council, to which Turkey protested concerning the alleged reduction of Turkish Cypriots to "ghetto" conditions by the Greek Cypriot imposition of economic sanctions. The sanctions had been applied particularly to the Turkish Cypriot-controlled villages of Kokkina and Mansoura in north-western Cyprus following Greek Cypriot allegations that they were being used for clandestine landings of Turkish troops and equipment, and had led to acute shortages of food in the area. The blockade was eased on Aug. 18, however, following the intervention of UNFICYP and the International Red Cross.

Turkey at this time claimed that Greece was maintaining some 10,000 troops in Cyprus compared with the 950 specified by the Zurich and London agreements, but it was itself believed to have marginally exceeded its own quota of 650. A further confrontation arose in this connection during August 1964, when Cyprus refused to allow the regular rotation of one-third of the Turkish contingent of troops on the island, claiming that it had the right to do so in view of its unilateral abrogation of the Treaty of Alliance. The issue was eventually settled, however, and control of the Nicosia-Kyrenia road was handed over to UNFICYP.

Meanwhile, former US Secretary of State Dean Acheson had proposed in Geneva in July 1964 an arrangement whereby Cyprus was to be allowed union with Greece in return for concessions including (i) the creation of rented areas (amounting to 50 sq km) in north-eastern Cyprus, which were to be used for Turkish military bases and refugee areas; (ii) the cession to Turkey of the small Greek island of Castellorizo, close to the Anatolian coast; (iii) the placing of two of the six districts under Turkish Cypriot administration; and (iv) the creation of a central body under an international commissioner to protect Turkish rights. Despite its demand for ownership, not merely tenancy, of the military areas, the Turkish government indicated its acceptance of these proposals, whereas the Greek Cypriots rejected them as "a betrayal of the whole of Hellenism". Turkey responded to the Greek and Greek Cypriot positions with an escalation of anti-Greek and anti-British feeling, and during 1964 many thousands of Greek citizens resident in Turkey were obliged to leave after the Turkish authorities declined to renew their residence permits.

Establishment of Turkish Cypriot Autonomous Administration

Despite the stabilization of the internal security situation in late 1964, no real progress was achieved over the next six years in bilateral communal talks, which were embarked upon by the two communities. A report by the then UN mediator, Dr Gala Plaza, was published on March 30, 1965, and outlined a solution based on the preservation of Cyprus as one state; but his proposals were immediately rejected by the Turkish government. In June 1965 the Cypriot House of

Representatives (still without its 15 Turkish Cypriot deputies) unanimously passed bills (i) extending for one year the five-year term of President Makarios in view of the alleged impossibility of conducting proper elections (this exercise being repeated annually until 1968); and (ii) abolishing the separate electoral registration of Greek and Turkish Cypriot voters. It was also announced that Dr Kutchuk's post as Vice-President was regarded as having lapsed in view of his continued absence, and that the three Turkish Cypriot ministers (also absent) had been replaced by Greek Cypriots. Turkish and British protests at these moves were rejected by the Makarios government, which told the UN Security Council on Aug. 3-10, 1965, that they represented an interference in its internal affairs. An increasingly bitter power struggle between President Makarios and Gen. Grivas (who had returned to Cyprus in 1964) highlighted the complexities of relations between Athens and Nicosia. Still an *enosis* man at heart, Gen. Grivas now commanded the National Guard and the Greek "volunteer" forces in Cyprus, where he was seen as being aligned with right-wing circles in Greece. Accordingly, his role and that of his followers took on heightened importance after the colonels seized power in Athens in April 1967.

At US and NATO prompting, the new military regime in Greece had top-level talks with Turkey in September 1967, but a Turkish proposal that Cyprus should in effect be partitioned was rejected by the Greek side. An escalation of inter-communal violence in November produced a Turkish government ultimatum to the Greek Cypriots and Athens that all "illegal" Greek forces should be withdrawn from Cyprus and that Gen. Grivas should leave immediately. Urgent US and UN mediation resulted, the following month, in an undertaking by the Greek and Turkish governments to withdraw from Cyprus all troops in excess of the contingents permitted in the 1959 agreements. This withdrawal was said to have been completed by mid-January 1968, but towards the end of that year the deadlock intensified when Turkish Cypriot leaders announced on Dec. 29 the setting up of a "Turkish Cypriot Autonomous Administration" to run Turkish Cypriot affairs "until such time as the provisions of the 1960 constitution have been fully implemented". A set of 19 "basic laws" on executive, judicial and legislative matters received the support of the Turkish government, and Dr Kutchuk was appointed president of the Autonomous Administration and Rauf Denktash as its vice-president. (Denktash, a former president of the Turkish Communal Chamber, had returned to Cyprus in April 1968 following two periods of exile in Turkey dating back to 1964.) The new administration also set up a Legislative Assembly comprising the Turkish deputies of the House of Representatives and the members of the Turkish Communal Chamber, and established a nine-member Executive Council (i.e. cabinet). President Makarios described the new Turkish Cypriot administration as "totally illegal", and warned foreign diplomats against attempting to contact it (though this ban was lifted on Dec. 31, 1968). U

Thant expressed his misgivings that it could harm relations in Cyprus, but Dr Kutchuk claimed that it was non-political, purely administrative and fully constitutional.

Elections for the 35 Greek Cypriot seats to the House of Representatives were held on July 5, 1970 (for the first time since 1960), and passed off quietly; on the same day the Turkish community held elections for its 15 House of Representatives mandates and its 15 Communal Chamber seats. Following the unopposed return of President Makarios as President of the Republic on Feb. 8, 1973, Rauf Denktash was on Feb. 16 declared elected by the Turkish Cypriots as Vice-President in succession to Dr Kutchuk. The two leaders were separately inaugurated on Feb. 28, Denktash at an official ceremony held in the Turkish quarter of Nicosia.

Overthrow of President Makarios—Turkish Invasion of 1974

On July 15, 1974, President Makarios was overthrown by a military coup led by Greek officers seconded to the Cypriot National Guard; he fled to Malta, subsequently arriving in the United Kingdom and the United States. For some years the President had faced growing opposition among Greek Cypriots, not only from Gen. Grivas (until his death in January 1974) but also from the National Guard (accused by him of involvement with the EOKA-B movement). He had, moreover, come into conflict with the three Greek Orthodox bishops of Paphos, Kyrenia and Kirium, who objected to his simultaneous functions as Archbishop and President and who had tried to vote him out of his religious office, only to be defrocked at his instigation in July 1973. The President had also survived a number of assassination attempts by extreme supporters of *enosis* since 1960.

Nicos Sampson, the leader of the Progressive Party and a former EOKA leader, was sworn in on July 15 as the new President of the "Hellenic Republic of Cyprus", and the following day formed a government of *enosis* supporters. He immediately announced that the new government would honour all international agreements, continue to strive for an inter-communal solution to the problems of Cyprus and pursue the goal of independence, adding that there was thus no justification for Turkish intervention. Meanwhile, however, a conference was held in London on July 16 at which the then Turkish Prime Minister, Bulent Ecevit, claimed that the Greek government had landed troops on Cyprus—an action which, he said, was tantamount to an invasion by Greece—and announced that "we cannot tolerate a government which has no legal basis".

At an emergency session of the UN Security Council on July 16, Zenon Rossides (the Cyprus permanent representative to the UN) urged "appropriate measures to protect the independence, sovereignty and territorial integrity of Cyprus", while the Greek permanent representative, Emmanuel Megolokonomos, described the matter as purely internal and denied that his government was involved. On the other hand, Osman Olcay (Turkey) claimed that what he called the Greek intervention violated the agreements guaranteeing the independence of Cyprus, and stressed Turkey's obligations to protect the interests of the Turkish Cypriot population. President Makarios told the Security Council on July 19 that there had been "an invasion which violated the independence and sovereignty of the Republic", and urged the Security Council to "call on the military regime of Greece to withdraw from Cyprus the Greek officers serving in the National Guard and to put an end to the invasion".

In the light of British and Greek reactions to the crisis, the Turkish government concluded that it was entitled to invoke Article 4 of the 1959 Treaty of Guarantee, under which each guarantor power had reserved "the right to take action with the sole aim of restoring the state of affairs created by the present treaty". At dawn on July 20, 1974, Turkish troops landed near Kyrenia and engaged immediately in heavy fighting with the Greek Cypriot National Guard for control of the port of Kyrenia. By July 22, when the first ceasefire was declared on the recommendation of the UN Security Council, Turkey had gained control of the entire region surrounding the Kyrenia-Nicosia road as well as a large part of Nicosia itself, which had been taken by paratroopers dropped into the Turkish Cypriot quarter of the city. Between 30,000 and 40,000 Turkish troops were thought to have been involved in the invasion.

The UN Security Council again held an emergency session on July 20, this time to discuss the Turkish invasion, and adopted on the same day a resolution calling on all states to respect the sovereignty, independence and territorial integrity of Cyprus while also urging (i) the declaration of a ceasefire by all parties, (ii) the immediate cessation of foreign military intervention in the Republic and (iii) the withdrawal of all invasion forces, as well as of 650 Greek officers of the Cypriot National Guard (whom President Makarios had accused of plotting his overthrow). Greece, Turkey and the United Kingdom were urged to begin negotiations for the restoration of peace in the area, and a ceasefire was agreed for July 22.

The peace talks were opened in Geneva on July 25, 1974, under the chairmanship of James Callaghan, the British Foreign and Commonwealth Secretary. By July 30 a ceasefire line was agreed, a security zone proclaimed, an exchange of prisoners provided for, the evacuation of Greek Cypriot or Greek forces from Turkish Cypriot enclaves agreed and the convening of a second round of talks initiated. By Aug. 9, when the ceasefire line agreement was signed, the Turks had extended their area of control to the east and west of the Nicosia-Kyrenia road and had more than doubled the extent of the Turkish-controlled coastline. At the same time, Greek Cypriot forces remained in effective control of Turkish Cypriot enclaves south of the ceasefire line.

Meanwhile, following the fall of the military regime in Greece on July 23, 1974, Nicos Sampson resigned on that day as President of Cyprus and, in the absence of President Makarios, was replaced by Glafcos Clerides, the Speaker of the Cypriot House of Representatives, who had conducted the inter-communal talks with the Turkish Cypriots. On Aug. 8 acting President Clerides appointed a new Cabinet of moderates and liberals.

The second phase of the Geneva talks opened on Aug. 8, 1974, but broke down on Aug. 14 following disagreements between Greece, Turkey and the two sides in Cyprus. No progress could be made on a proposal for a federal system giving a large degree of autonomy to the Turkish Cypriots, with the result that Denktash proposed instead the creation of an autonomous Turkish Cypriot region in the north of the island, occupying about 34 per cent of the total area of Cyprus. Turkey had proposed a compromise plan which gave the Turkish Cypriots half of the northern part of the island as well as pockets of autonomous territory in other parts of the island, but rejected the requests of Greek and Greek Cypriot representatives for time to discuss the proposals with their respective governments. Claiming that the talks had broken down, the Turks launched a new offensive in Cyprus, this being regarded as unprovoked aggression by the Greek Cypriots as well as by external governments. By Aug. 16, when a new ceasefire was declared, Turkey controlled 36.7 per cent of the territory of Cyprus, including most of the northern and eastern coastline. The UN Security Council, which had repeatedly deplored the resumption of hostilities, adopted a resolution of Aug. 16 calling on both sides to resume the Geneva peace talks without delay. The dividing line between the opposing forces, which became known as the Attila line, ran through Nicosia and in a circuitous but broadly east-west line across the breadth of the island, following the northern perimeter of the British sovereign base area of Dhekelia in the east.

Proclamation of the Turkish Federated State of Cyprus

The transitional Turkish Cypriot Autonomous Administration announced on Feb. 13, 1975, that it supported the formation of a "Federal Republic of Cyprus", which was to be a "bi-regional federation" of the two Cypriot communities. It added that, in order to pursue such a federation, it had restructured itself into "a secular and federated state" in the north of the island, to be known as the Turkish Federated State of Cyprus (TFSC). Rauf Denktash was appointed president of the new entity (subsequently being confirmed in this office in elections held on June 20, 1975, in which his National Unity Party won 30 of the 40 seats in the newly-formed Constituent Assembly). On Feb. 13 the Greek side was sent the new administration's proposals for a bi-zonal and bi-regional federated state in which the state itself would be vested "only with the powers necessary for the establishment of the federation, so as to enable the state to function effectively", while "all power" was to be vested in the federated states. The proposals also maintained that the 1959 international treaties of guarantee should remain in force after the formation of the new state.

Archbishop Makarios, who had meanwhile returned in December 1974 to resume the presidency, attempted from 1975 onwards to restart the negotiations with the Turkish Cypriots. Five rounds of talks were held in Vienna between April 1975 and February 1976, but they foundered over the Greek Cypriot insistence that Cyprus should be indivisible and that foreign troops should withdraw without delay. The deadlock started to loosen in January 1977, when Denktash and Makarios met on the proposal of the UN Secretary-General's special representative for Cyprus, agreeing on Jan. 27 to continue the inter-communal talks. The two subsequently announced on Feb. 13 their agreement on a set of guidelines envisaging the formation of an independent, bi-zonal, non-aligned federal republic in which the central government would hold such powers as were required to safeguard the unity of the state. UN Secretary-General Kurt Waldheim, who attended the February talks, applauded the guidelines as a first sign of a willingness to discuss substantive issues such as the size of the areas to be administered by the respective regional bodies.

The new series of talks began in Vienna on March 31, 1977, when the Greek Cypriots published proposals accepting the principle of the bi-communal state, and when they presented a map offering 20 per cent of the total area of Cyprus to the Turkish Cypriots. However, the talks broke down over the issue of Varosha—a largely Greek Cypriot area of Famagusta whose original population (which had largely fled) should, Turkish Cypriots argued, be subject to the administration of the Turkish Cypriot Federated State on their return. The Turkish Cypriots for their part presented proposals based on northern autonomy, and offered a minor reduction of the area to be occupied by Turkish troops. This being unacceptable to the Greek Cypriot side, negotiations remained once again stalled for a period of more than two years.

On May 18-19, 1979, however, President Spyros Kyprianou (who had succeeded President Makarios on the latter's death in August 1977) met Denktash and the two reached agreement on a 10-point programme for the resumption of negotiations which were to give priority to the resettlement of Varosha under UN auspices and to the "constitutional and territorial aspects of a comprehensive settlement". The programme also defined as its basis the Makarios-Denktash guidelines of February 1977, and envisaged the demilitarization of Cyprus. Talks were resumed on June 15-22, 1979, and continued at intervals thereafter, although without result on any of the substantive issues.

Declaration of Turkish Republic of Northern Cyprus

Under the military regime which seized power in Turkey in September 1980, the Ankara government took a harder line on the question of Cyprus—a cue taken by the Turkish Cypriots themselves. Legislative

elections held in June 1981 in the TFSC resulted in the National Unity Party forming a government headed by Mustafa Catagay. On Nov. 15, 1983, the new legislature unanimously approved the formation of a "Turkish Republic of Northern Cyprus" (TRNC). The proclamation of independence "before the world and before history" accused the Greek Cypriots of deliberately blocking the negotiations. Referring to the May 1983 resolution of the UN General Assembly, in which the UN had called for the withdrawal of all foreign troops, it accused Nicosia of "taking the Cyprus problem to international forums where the Turkish Cypriot people had no opportunity of being heard". The proclamation declared the Turkish side's conviction "that these two peoples, who are destined to coexist side by side in the island, can and must find peaceful, just and durable solutions to all the differences between them, through negotiations on the basis of equality". It also stated its expectation that the declaration of independence would "facilitate the re-establishment of the partnership between the two peoples within a federal framework and [would] also facilitate the settlement of the problems between them".

President Kyprianou accused Denktash, however, of attempting to proceed by fait accompli, in order to promote Turkish expansionist plans and to use Turkish troops for introducing an illegal partition. The British government called the decision tantamount to an act of secession; Turkey, the only state to recognize the TRNC, claimed that it would rather have seen a just and lasting solution arrived at through the inter-communal talks, instead of by a declaration of independence. The Turkish Cypriot line at the ensuing UN discussions was that the 1960 treaties had been made unworkable for the north of the island because of years of dilution of Turkish Cypriot rights by Greek Cypriots in Nicosia. Nonetheless, the UN Security Council declared on Nov. 18, 1983, that the declaration of the Turkish Cypriot state was invalid and incompatible with the 1960 treaties of establishment and guarantee.

Denktash meanwhile continued his efforts to obtain wider international recognition of the TRNC, but without success. In the mid-1980s, he regularly accused the United States of pressurizing potential sympathizers among the Muslim states of the Middle East not to recognize his state. Yet even among the many Muslim states and organizations not normally susceptible to such pressure (if it was exerted), Islamic solidarity with the Turkish Cypriot cause could in no case be converted into formal recognition of the TRNC.

Immediately after the proclamation of the TRNC in November 1983, a new Turkish Cypriot government was sworn in under the leadership of Nejat Konuk, the Prime Minister of the TFSC from 1976 to 1978. On Dec. 2 a 70-member Constituent Assembly was formed from the existing 40 parliamentary representatives and 30 other persons, of whom Denktash nominated 10. A draft constitution was accordingly drafted and was published in May 1984, and it was approved by a referendum held in the Turkish zone on May 5, 1985. A presidential election followed on June 9, in which Denktash won 70.5 per cent of the vote, and elections to the new 50-member Parliament produced a coalition government comprising his own National Unity Party and the left-wing Communal Liberation Party (TKP).

Failure of 1985 Summit and Subsequent Talks

The early 1980s were marked on both sides by a hardening of attitudes to the question of the island's future status. In part, this was because the post-1980 military government in Turkey proclaimed that northern Cyprus was "the daughter of our motherland...an integral part of Turkey". Before the 1980 Turkish military coup, the two sides had succeeded in opening discussions on (i) the resettlement of Varosha, (ii) measures to promote goodwill, mutual confidence and a return to normal conditions, and (iii) constitutional and territorial aspects. However, formal inter-communal talks initiated by the UN Secretary-General faltered in 1981 and came to an abrupt halt on the proclamation of the TRNC in November 1983. Thereafter, Greek Cypriot negotiators refused to sit in the same room as their Turkish Cypriot counterparts, on the grounds that to do so would give legitimacy to an illegal regime.

The deadlock in the early 1980s did, however, give increasing credibility on the Greek Cypriot side to the UN Secretary-General's support for a "bi-zonal" solution, in which Cyprus would become a federation of two relatively autonomous states. Assisted by the gradual restoration of democratic rule in Turkey from late 1983, a new initiative was launched in August 1984, in which the Secretary-General started a series of bilateral discussions with each of the two sides in the form of proximity talks. By the third round, the Turkish Cypriots had abandoned their insistence on an alternating Greek Cypriot and Turkish Cypriot presidency for the proposed unified state, and they had offered to reduce their territorial hold to 29-30 per cent. While the proximity talks clearly gave a propaganda advantage to the apparently more flexible Turkish Cypriot side, the resulting summit conference between Presidents Denktash and Kyprianou in New York on Jan. 17-20, 1985, showed that little had changed on either side. Kyprianou refused at once to recognise the UN Secretary-General's draft as implying any kind of draft agreement (a move for which he was then bitterly attacked by other Greek Cypriot bodies), and the talks ended amid mutual recriminations.

A revised version of the UN plan for a bi-zonal federation, presented in July 1985, got a better reception from the Greek Cypriot side, but negotiations eventually broke down over, principally, the timetable for a withdrawal of Turkish troops and the nature of international guarantees for the island's security. In January 1986 the Soviet Union stirred the pot by floating a proposal for the withdrawal of "all foreign troops and bases" from Cyprus—i.e. including Turkish, UN and British forces—and for an UN-sponsored international conference on the question. This intervention served to concentrate the minds of the immediate protago-

nists, who on March 29, 1986, received a "draft framework agreement on Cyprus" from the UN Secretary-General, Javier Pérez de Cuellar. Based on earlier plans, this one proposed a bi-zonal, power-sharing federation in which the Turkish Cypriots would have about 29 per cent of the island's area and an effective veto on any attempt to change the constitution. The following month Denktash gave a "positive reply" to the framework agreement, but President Kyprianou responded on May 8 with counter-proposals, which were described as "not viable" by Pérez de Cuellar.

As submitted on June 10, 1986, Kyprianou's response objected that the framework agreement would bind the Greek Cypriots to unworkable constitutional and other arrangements (including excessive veto powers for the Turkish side) without imposing corresponding obligations on the Turkish Cypriots. He repeated the Greek Cypriot view that a balanced settlement could be achieved only on the basis of (i) the withdrawal of Turkish troops, (ii) the withdrawal of post-1974 settlers in the north, (iii) international guarantees and (iv) acceptance of the "three basic freedoms" (of movement, settlement and property ownership) for all citizens of the island. In the Turkish view, Kyprianou's rejection of the 1985-86 UN proposals was a major lost opportunity, in light of which the US and other Western governments reportedly concluded that no settlement could be achieved while Kyprianou remained President.

Early in 1987 (with attempts to revive talks still blocked), tensions in Cyprus rose amid reports that Turkey had increased its military presence by 25 per cent in 1986 to a total of some 36,000 men and had deployed new offensive weapons in the north of the island. However, Turkish Cypriot spokesmen maintained that there were only 20,000 Turkish troops on the island and that this level was necessary as "a deterrent against upsetting the status quo of peace"; they added that the allegations of increased Turkish forces were a "smokescreen" to divert attention from the recent equipment of the Greek Cypriot National Guard (numbering 10,000) with new anti-tank missiles and armoured troop carriers.

Vassiliou-Denktash Summits, 1988-90—Economic Divergence of Greek and Turkish Areas

Two events early in 1988 appeared to increase the prospects of progress on the Cyprus deadlock. On Jan. 30-31 the Greek Prime Minister, Andreas Papandreou, had talks with his Turkish counterpart, Turgut Ozal, in Davos (Switzerland), which resulted in a joint undertaking to seek solutions to bilateral issues, including the Cyprus problem. The following month Greek Cypriot voters rejected the further presidential candidacy of Spyros Kyprianou, electing instead Georgios Vassiliou, an independent whose backers included the powerful AKEL Communist Party. Regarded as more flexible than his predecessor, President Vassiliou immediately put out peace feelers, which led to both sides accepting a UN proposal for new talks without preconditions. The resultant first summit between Vassiliou and Denktash, held in Geneva on Aug. 24, 1988, was proclaimed a success, although substantive issues were referred to direct negotiations under UN supervision. The target date for a comprehensive settlement was set, ambitiously, at June 1, 1989. Despite three UN-sponsored Vassiliou-Denktash review meetings in New York between September 1988 and June 1989, this could not be achieved, as the two sides found themselves to be still deeply divided on long-standing political and constitutional issues.

The only significant achievement, as the deadline approached, was the implementation in May 1989, under UN supervision, of a "de-confrontation" agreement, whereby each side withdrew its forces from 24 military posts along the sensitive central Nicosia sector of the Attila line. Yet even this modest step backfired when, in July 1989, crowds of Greek Cypriot women took advantage of the lower military presence on the ceasefire line to march into the TRNC in support of their demand for reunification. That several dozen of the demonstrators were promptly arrested by the Turkish Cypriot troops on whom they had verbally vented their frustration did nothing for the delicate condition of inter-communal relations in the island.

At the UN Secretary-General's instigation, a second Vassiliou-Denktash summit was held in New York on Jan. 26-March 2, 1990, but again ended in failure, for which each side blamed the other. The key stumbling block this time was Denktash's demand that Turkish Cypriots should be recognized as a "people" with the right to self-determination in UN terms. For President Vassiliou, this demand smacked of an aspiration to de jure secession and partition. While accepting that the Turkish Cypriots constituted a distinct "community", he condemned the "recognition as a people" demand as running directly counter to the UN's bi-zonal federal concept, which both sides had long accepted in principle. Later in March 1990, the UN Security Council approved a resolution effectively rejecting the Denktash demand and reiterating the UN's view that a bi-zonal federal solution must be found which preserved Cyprus as one sovereign state.

Thus rebuffed, Denktash felt it necessary to call an early election in the TRNC, where voices condemning his alleged negotiating intransigence were increasingly heard. He easily defeated his opponents in the presidential contest on April 22, and the ruling National Unity Party was victorious in parliamentary elections on May 6. Nevertheless, in the latter poll, an opposition alliance secured 44 per cent of the vote on a platform advocating more concessions in the UN negotiations on the future status of Cyprus.

Economic realities in the island were highlighted by the Cypriot government's submission, on July 4, 1990, of a formal application for full membership of the European Community (EC). This move to upgrade the existing association agreement with the EC was not thought likely by observers to bear speedy fruit, but was nevertheless immediately condemned by the TRNC government as a "unilateral" act, which would complicate the search for a political settlement. An additional complication was the fact that Turkey itself had applied for full EC membership in 1987 but had made no progress in that direction, in part because Greece (a full EC member since 1981) secured support for its view that the Cyprus question must be resolved before Turkish membership could be contemplated.

Some commentators detected in the EC membership issue a latter-day conflict between Christian Europe and the Islamic world. Whether or not this was true, in Cyprus the years of effective partition had created a sharp economic divide between the two parts of the island, as the Greek Cypriots had forged ahead of the Turkish-controlled sector. After the 1974 partition, Greek Cypriots had complained bitterly that the most productive parts of the island had come under Turkish control. Figures published by them in 1975 had shown that the Turkish area had accounted for 70 per cent of the island's pre-division gross national product (GNP), mainly because the best tourist and fruit-growing areas were in the north (largely under Greek Cypriot ownership). Over the next decade and a half, however, Greek Cyprus had experienced an economic boom, which had not extended in the same measure to the TRNC. By 1991 the per capita GNP of Greek Cypriots had risen to some $10,000, more than three times greater than the TRNC level.

The TRNC's response to the EC application was to move to even closer economic dependence on Turkey. Agreements signed on Oct. 1, 1990, envisaged the creation of a full customs union between the TRNC and Turkey, the abolition of passport controls and the introduction of a TRNC currency backed by the central bank of Turkey (the Turkish lira having been in general use in the north since 1983). These steps were in turn condemned as "unilateral actions" by the Greek Cypriots, who also took grim satisfaction from the major economic crisis which developed in the TRNC in late 1990 as a result of the collapse of the London-based conglomerate Polly Peck International and the preferment of fraud charges against its Turkish Cypriot chairman, Asil Nadir. Once described by Denktash as the "economic commander" of Turkish Cyprus, Nadir had built a fruit-packaging and tourism empire which was estimated to account for a third of the TRNC's gross domestic product and 60 per cent of its exports. According to the Greek Cypriot authorities, several of his major properties in the north had been expropriated from Greek Cypriots after 1974.

Another Greek Cypriot charge heard in 1989-90 was that the TRNC government was actively preparing, in contravention of UN resolutions, to settle sensitive northern areas such as Varosha with ethnic Turkish refugees from Bulgaria and also with Palestinians. This particular row was the latest round of a broader dispute over refugees and settlement which had rumbled on since 1974. Then, in a migration involving about a third of the island's population, some 180,000 Greeks had fled south and at least 45,000 Turks had moved north (the precise numbers being disputed between the two sides). In subsequent negotiations, the right to return became a central demand of the Greek Cypriot side, which also repeatedly claimed that the demographic character of the north was being changed by an official policy of "colonization" involving the encouragement of migration from Turkey. Numbers were greatly disputed, the Greek Cypriots claiming that about 80,000 mainland Turks had been settled in the TRNC by the early 1990s whereas the Turkish Cypriots put the figure at 18,000. The UN estimate in 1991 was 40,000 to 45,000.

Post-Gulf War Revival of Negotiating Process

The onset of the Gulf crisis in early August 1990 effectively placed the Cyprus question on the international back-burner for the duration, although once the US-led allies had liberated Kuwait in February 1991 optimists felt that a Cyprus settlement might soon follow. US pressure, this school believed, would be exerted on Greece and Turkey to bring the two Cypriot sides to the conference table again, this time ready to make the concessions needed for implementation of the UN plan. Moreover, the rapid collapse of the Soviet Union in 1991 was seen as weakening Turkey's traditional leverage with Washington as a front-line NATO member. Pessimists, on the other hand, noted that Turkey saw its active participation in the war against Iraq as entitling it to concessions to its point of view on Cyprus, which would make agreement with the Greeks even more difficult. They also noted that the Greek Cypriots insisted on drawing parallels between the Iraqi invasion of Kuwait and the Turkish occupation of northern Cyprus since 1974. To this the Turkish response was that any similarity lay rather in the attempted Greek military takeover of Cyprus immediately before the Turkish intervention.

Despite these unpromising attitudes, international diplomatic activity on the Cyprus question intensified in the wake of the Gulf crisis, with the United States now to the fore. In March 1991 the Greek Cypriot Foreign Minister, Georgios Iacovou, had talks in Washington with US Secretary of State James Baker, who the following month also received Denktash, taking care to stress that the latter was recognized as leader of the Turkish Cypriot community, not as TRNC president. In May 1991 President Vassiliou travelled to Washington to meet President Bush and by the end of June the US government was working actively with the UN to convene a negotiating conference on Cyprus. This objective was pursued by Bush during visits to Greece and Turkey in mid-July 1991, when the US President made it clear that the status quo in Cyprus was unacceptable to the US government. Meanwhile, the EC Foreign Ministers had on April 1, 1991, launched the first specifically European initiative on Cyprus, while the newly-institutionalized Conference on Security and Co-operation in Europe (CSCE) was being urged by Greece and the Greek Cypriots to deal with the problems of what President Vassiliou described as "the only European country facing foreign occupation".

These and other endeavours culminated in an announcement by President Bush on Aug. 2, 1991, that the Greek and Turkish Prime Ministers had confirmed to him that they were prepared to attend a UN-sponsored conference in the USA the following month with the aim of ending the partition of Cyprus. Both President Vassiliou and Denktash welcomed the announcement and indicated that they would attend the talks. The envisaged quadripartite framework was seen as being nearer to the Turks' demand than to the stated Greek Cypriot preference for a UN-chaired gathering attended by all five permanent members of the UN Security Council together with the Greek, Turkish and Cypriot governments and representatives of the two Cypriot communities. However, any euphoria generated by the US announcement quickly evaporated when the UN Secretary-General made it clear that the conference would not be convened unless real progress had been made beforehand on outstanding differences. By early September it was clear that such progress was not being made, with the result that the conference was not convened that month. In a report to the UN Security Council on Oct. 8, 1991, the Secretary-General said that in the latest discussions Denktash had stated "that each side possessed a sovereignty which it would retain after the establishment of a federation, including the right of secession", and had sought "extensive changes in the text of the ideas that were discussed". Recalling that the Security Council had "posited a solution based on the existence of one state of Cyprus comprising two communities", he concluded that the introduction of the Denktash concept would "fundamentally alter the nature of the solution" envisaged in previous agreements and in Security Council resolutions.

On Sept. 17, 1991, President Vassiliou gave a television address in which he referred to "the great mobility in the Cyprus problem which became evident this summer", but also criticized Denktash for his "negative position" in the pre-conference negotiations. On the same day the TRNC Assembly called for direct negotiations between the leaders of the two communities and stressed that the TRNC could make no concessions "on the principles of sovereignty, self-determination...[and] the existence of two separate peoples". Such assertions showed that the two sides remained far apart in their conceptions of basic principles, despite their public willingness to negotiate within the framework of the UN draft plan. Also apparent was a wide gulf on the implementation of a bi-zonal solution, notably as regards the amount of territory which the Turks would effectively surrender (i.e. which would not form part of a Turkish Cypriot autonomous area) and the number of Greek Cypriots who would be allowed to return to the area currently under Turkish control.

In a resolution adopted on Oct. 11, 1991, the UN Security Council regretted that it had not yet been possible to convene the high-level conference on Cyprus and requested the Secretary-General to continue his efforts to that end. The Council reaffirmed its view that the "fundamental principles" on which a Cyprus settlement should be based were: "the sovereignty, independence, territorial integrity and non-alignment of the Republic of Cyprus; the exclusion of union in whole or in part with any other country and any form of partition or secession; and the establishment of a new constitutional arrangement for Cyprus that would ensure the well-being and security of the Greek Cypriot and Turkish Cypriot communities in a bi-communal and bi-zonal federation". The resolution also reiterated that the Council's "position on the solution to the Cyprus problem is based on one state of Cyprus comprising two politically equal communities".

On taking office on Jan. 1, 1992, the new UN Secretary-General, Boutros Boutros-Ghali, initiated another attempt to establish the basis for a high-level conference on Cyprus. UN envoys paid visits to Cyprus, Turkey and Greece in February and Boutros-Ghali had meetings in New York with Vassiliou and Denktash on Jan. 20-21 and March 26-30. These efforts appeared to be assisted when the new Turkish Prime Minister, Suleyman Demirel, met his Greek counterpart, Konstaninos Mitsotakis, at another Davos summit on Feb. 1 and agreed to work with him towards a negotiated settlement of the Cyprus question under UN auspices. However, in a report to the UN Security Council on April 7, 1992, the Secretary-General advised that no progress had been made towards resolving basic disagreements and that "there has even been regression". Although there was broad agreement on the shape of a federal government structure, the issues of "territorial adjustment" and displaced persons remained serious problems, reported Boutros-Ghali. On April 10, the Security Council reaffirmed that a settlement "must be based on a state of Cyprus with a single sovereignty and international personality and a single citizenship, with its independence and territorial integrity safeguarded and comprising two politically equal communities". It also instructed the Secretary-General to pursue his efforts to resolve outstanding differences. In addition, Boutros-Ghali included in his April report to the Security Council a "set of ideas" for progress in discussions that had stemmed from consultations with both sides.

1992-95: Fruitless Negotiations and Movement towards EU Membership

A series of further talks between Vassiliou and Denktash took place between July 15 and Aug. 14, 1992, in New York under the chairmanship of Boutros Boutros-Ghali, when the Secretary-General introduced an expanded version of the "set of ideas". However the talks were deadlocked and proved inconclusive. Following the talks, the UN Security Council on Aug. 26, 1992, adopted Resolution 774, which endorsed territorial adjustments for a federal solution and the Secretary-General's expanded "set of ideas".

The next round of meetings occurred in New York between Oct. 26 and Nov. 11, with the Secretary-General codifying the positions of the two sides. These

talks also resulted in deadlock due to lack of agreement on a number of issues, such as territorial division, the powers of each community in a federal structure and the return of refugees. In a report (S/24830) submitted to the Security Council by Boutros-Ghali on Nov. 19, the Secretary-General suggested a number of measures to increase confidence, such as the reduction of Turkish forces, bi-communal projects and the return of Varosha to UN control.

After consideration of Boutros-Ghali's report, the Security Council on Nov. 25, 1992, approved Resolution 789, which noted that the recent joint meetings did not achieve their intended goal, in particular because certain positions adopted by the Turkish Cypriot side were fundamentally at variance with the "set of ideas", and called upon the Turkish Cypriot side to adopt positions more consistent with the "set of ideas". Denktash reacted angrily to the strongly worded Resolution 789 and threatened to resign if forced to sign an agreement based on Security Council lines.

Glafcos Clerides was sworn in as the fourth President of the Republic of Cyprus on Feb. 28, 1993. Clerides' new government gave priority to the resumption of discussions based on UN lines and to Cyprus' entry to the European Union. A new round of UN sponsored discussions started in May 1993, where the Secretary-General presented Clerides and Denktash with documents for the implementation of a package of confidence building measures (CBMs), which Boutros-Ghali believed would increase confidence for progress towards an overall settlement. These included proposals for the placement of the Turkish-occupied town of Varosha and Nicosia International Airport under UN control. Both sides accepted in principle but talks broke down over the details of the CBMs and issues of recognition, amongst others. The Greek Cypriot leadership angrily rejected any measures that might constitute recognition of the TRNC, whilst Denktash protested against the recognition of the Greek Cypriot authorities as the official government of Cyprus and the reduction of territory such as Morphou, which Denktash claimed would create tens of thousands of Turkish Cypriot refugees.

On June 30, 1993, the European Commission presented its opinion on Cyprus' application to join the European Union. It stated that as a European state practicing democracy, with social and economic levels comparable with several other existing Union members, Cyprus was, "in the southern part of the island at least", in all essential respects eligible. The serious obstacle was the northern part of Cyprus or TRNC. The Turkish Cypriot leadership declared the whole EU application process illegal since there was no legitimate government of Cyprus and said the Greek Cypriots had no right to act on behalf of the whole island.

In July 1993, UN envoys visited Athens, Ankara and Nicosia to begin talks on confidence measures. Sovereignty, a rotating presidency and the demilitarization of Cyprus were key issues discussed in the talks. Little progress was made, with Clerides accusing Denktash and Ankara of lacking the political will for a settlement, and Denktash, now strongly advocating confidence building measures, accusing Clerides of being obsessed with EU membership.

In November 1993, consultations between Andreas Papandreou, the Greek Prime Minister and leader of the Pan Hellenic Socialist Movement (PASOK), and Clerides resulted in an agreement that both countries would make joint decisions in future negotiations over Cyprus. Ankara's long running influence in the Cyprus issue had prompted this decision. Closer ties in defence planning were agreed, commonly known as the "defence dogma". Greece promised to defend Greek Cypriot-controlled Cyprus by land, sea and air in the event of attack.

On Feb. 17, 1994, the two sides entered into separate proximity talks in Nicosia, held by the Secretary-General's Special Representative in Cyprus, Joe Clark, and Deputy Special Representative, Gustave Feissel. Both sides had accepted the idea of confidence building measures, but differences were still evident in the content. Draft ideas for implementation of the package of confidence building measures were presented to Clerides and Denktash on March 9. After intensive discussions, the draft was presented again on March 21. Clerides agreed to accept the revised paper, if the Turkish side followed suit. However, agreement was not forthcoming: Clerides again claimed that Denktash did not have the political will to arrive at a settlement, whilst Denktash stated that the final package of CBMs differed from the measures initially agreed upon.

Differences centred upon the contentious issue of Varosha, the arrangements for Nicosia airport and customs issues. Gustave Feissel held further talks in Vienna on May 11-12 with officials from Turkey, the United States and the Turkish Cypriots. On May 31, Denktash said he would accept the CBMs if improvements were made. However, Clerides did not want to negotiate outside the draft presented on March 21, to the extent proposed by Denktash.

Secretary-General Boutros-Ghali presented his report (S/1994/629) to the Security Council on May 30, 1994, expressing his disappointment at the lack of progress and the absence of agreement, which he attributed essentially to a lack of political will on the Turkish Cypriot side. As a result, Boutros-Ghali offered the Security Council five options to study. In June more positive discussions took place between the Turkish Cypriot side and the representatives of the Secretary-General. This culminated in a letter from Boutros-Ghali on June 28 (S/1994/785) informing the Security Council of positive manoeuvres by the Turkish side towards implementation of the confidence building measures. However, questions of sovereignty in an overall settlement were still blighting discussions.

Security Council Resolution 939 on July 29, 1994, welcomed the acceptance by the Greek Cypriot community of the revised draft package of CBMs on March 21, 1994, and welcomed the considerable progress towards agreement made by the leader of the Turkish Cypriots, as described in the Secretary-General's letter on June 28, 1994. The Security Council reaffirmed that a Cyprus settlement must be based upon a State of Cyprus with a single sovereignty and international personality and single citizenship, with its independence and territorial integrity safeguarded, in a bi-communal, bi-zonal, federation.

The Court of Justice of the European Union ruled in July 1994 that exports from the TRNC required certification from the Cyprus government. Exports to EU states from the TRNC without certification could not be accepted. Disagreements over the possible form of a settlement rumbled on, with Turkish Cypriots disputing federation as the sole form of settlement on Cyprus. Informal talks took place between Clerides and Denktash from Oct. 18-30, 1994, in Nicosia to break the deadlock. However no progress was made. In December 1994, Boutros-Ghali instructed his representatives to continue their efforts for the resumption of direct talks.

The United States increased its involvement in the Cyprus problem in early 1995. President Bill Clinton appointed Richard Beattie as his Special Emissary for Cyprus. US Assistant Secretary of State for European Affairs, Richard Holbrooke, accompanied by State Department Special Coordinator for Cyprus, James Williams, had talks in Cyprus. Gustave Feissel led another round of talks in early 1995. Denktash, protesting at the EU's boycott of exports from the TRNC, threatened not to attend; however, he changed his mind and on Jan. 20, 1995, Denktash submitted to Feissel a 14-point plan with ideas for a settlement on Cyprus. However, Clerides rejected Denktash's position that EU membership for Cyprus should progress only after a settlement had been reached.

Having decided at the European Councils in June 1994 and December 1994 that the next EU enlargement should include Cyprus and Malta, the EU Council of Ministers decided on March 6, 1995, that the EU would start negotiations on Cyprus' membership six months after the conclusion of the 1996 Intergovernmental Conference. The Greeks had lifted their veto on a EU-Turkey customs union in return for such a definite timetable. Denktash was re-elected as President of the TRNC on April 22, 1995.

Between May 21-23, 1995, informal talks between representatives of the Greek Cypriots, Turkish Cypriots, the USA and Britain were held in London. However, the momentum towards EU accession talks was gathering pace. In June 1995, the Cyprus-EU Association Council met in Luxembourg and adopted a resolution for structured dialogue towards EU membership. September and October 1995 saw the inauguration of the structured dialogue between the EU and Cyprus, in addition to confirmation that negotiations for full membership of the EU would begin six months after the completion of the 1996 Intergovernmental Conference. In December 1995, Turkey and the Turkish Cypriot leadership reiterated their view that accession negotiations should be initiated with the EU after a comprehensive settlement has been reached and that a federal Cyprus and Turkey should join simultaneously.

Renewed Tensions, 1996-98

Relations between Greece and Turkey took a dramatic turn for the worse in January 1996, in a conflict over a small island in the Aegean named Imia by the Greeks and Kardak by the Turks. However, as a result of rapid intervention by US mediator Richard Holbrooke, direct armed conflict was avoided. New US initiatives to solve the Cyprus problem were put forward in the first half of 1996 and diplomats from the USA and UK and representatives from the UN discussed ways of kick-starting the negotiation process. In July 1996, Madeleine Albright, US Permanent Representative at the UN, with Richard Beattie visited Greece, Turkey and Cyprus.

The worst incident in this time of increased tension began on Aug. 11, 1996, when a highly publicized motor-cycle rally beginning in Berlin, to symbolize the end of the division of the city, announced it was going to attempt to cross the "green line" and ride through to Kyrenia. The Orthodox Church of Cyprus had contributed to the funding of the rally and the occasion received widespread television coverage. The rally provided the opportunity for nationalists on both sides to cause problems. The motorcyclists breached the buffer zone separating the two sides at several points. The worst incident was caused at Dherinia, when Greek Cypriot demonstrators, many apparently unrestrained by the Greek Cypriot authorities, crossed into the buffer zone. In response to the rally, a significant number of members of the "Grey Wolves", a Turkish extreme nationalist group, had arrived from the Turkish mainland. "Grey Wolves" armed with batons clashed with a number of Greek Cypriot demonstrators in the buffer zone, leaving one demonstrator with fatal injuries.

Three days later, after the demonstrator's funeral, the deceased's cousin attempted to scale a flagpole on the Turkish Cypriot side of the buffer zone and pull down a Turkish flag. He was immediately shot dead, rather than arrested. Several UN peacekeepers were injured by further Turkish gunfire and in attempts to control the incited crowd. The incidents received extensive publicity and tensions were especially high for many weeks. As a result, tourism on Cyprus suffered. Further incidents occurred, which included two Turkish soldiers being shot near the British Sovereign base of Dhekelia by unknown persons on Sept. 8 and a Greek Cypriot civilian being killed in the buffer zone on Oct. 13, 1996.

On Jan. 1, 1997, Kofi Annan became the Secretary-General of the United Nations, in succession to Boutros Boutros-Ghali. Tensions increased later in January, when Clerides announced that the Republic of Cyprus had ordered 48 S-300 air defence missiles from Russia. Immediately Turkey threatened to use the Turkish air force and any means possible to prevent installation of the missiles. On Jan. 20, Denktash and Turkish President Demirel signed a joint defence agreement, declaring that any attack on the TRNC would be an attack on Turkey. After much diplomatic pressure on the Clerides government, it was eventually announced in December 1998 that the missiles would be stationed on Crete. Exercises by the Greek and Turkish air forces over Cyprus in May 1997 also increased tensions, but a July 1997 NATO meeting held in Madrid produced a commitment from Greece and Turkey to reduce tensions and respect international law and sovereignty.

Direct talks were held between Clerides and Denktash during July 9-13, 1997, hosted in Troutbeck, New York State, by UN Special Advisor on Cyprus, Diego Cordovez (who had been appointed by Kofi Annan on April 28). As a result of this meeting, Clerides and Denktash met in Nicosia on July 28-31 to discuss humanitarian issues such as missing persons from the 1974 conflict. A second round of talks was held at Glion-sur-Montreux, Switzerland, between Aug. 11-15. Both rounds of talks produced no progress, with a major stumbling block being disagreement over Cyprus' EU accession process. In addition, Denktash argued that progress could not be made without political equality and sovereignty for the Turkish Cypriots.

Moreover, the EU's "Agenda 2000" programme left Turkey off the list of candidates for full membership. In late July-early August 1997, Turkey signed a partial integration agreement with the TRNC and threatened to annex the TRNC if Cyprus joined the EU without a settlement. In September 1997, Clerides and Denktash discussed the issue of security under the chairmanship of Gustave Feissel. Military exercises by Greece and Turkey over Cyprus resumed in October, resulting in complaints from both sides. On Sept. 25, 1997, Greece threatened to veto EU expansion eastwards if Cyprus was not accepted into the EU because of its division. The EU's Luxembourg Summit on Dec. 12-13, however, set March 1998 as the start of negotiations for Cyprus' membership of the EU, while Turkey was not even given a date to begin negotiations. Denktash reacted angrily stating all "intercommunal talks have ended" and that negotiations would only continue between states of equal political status. On Dec. 27, the Turkish Cypriot authorities suspended all bi-communal activities except pilgrimages to religious sites.

Tensions continued into 1998. In January, the military base at Paphos became operational for use by Greek fighter planes—the S-300s ordered by the Clerides government were in part intended to protect the Paphos instillation. The UN peacekeeping force (UNFI-CYP) introduced a package of measures to reduce tensions along the buffer zone. On April 23, Denktash, in collaboration with Turkish President Demirel, reiterated the view that negotiations for a settlement should only take place between states of equal sovereignty. On June 16, Greece sent four F-16 fighter planes and a cargo plane to Paphos. In response to this, Turkey sent six F-16s to northern Cyprus on June 18.

Arguments continued to rage over the system of government in a proposed settlement. On Aug. 31, 1998, Denktash proposed a loose confederation, which included provisions for a special relationship between Turkey and the TRNC and Greece and the Greek Cypriot authorities. However the UN and the US administration reaffirmed the view that a settlement must be based on a bi-zonal, bi-communal federation.

Secretary-General Kofi Annan in his Dec. 14 letter to the President of the Security Council (S/1998/1166) stated that his Deputy Special Representative for Cyprus, Dame Ann Hercus, was continuing talks, concentrating on reducing tensions through humanitarian and goodwill measures, in addition to addressing the core issues. The Secretary-General described a "flexible approach by both sides".

Security Council Resolution 1217, on Dec. 22, 1998, renewed the UN peacekeeping mandate until June 30, 1999. On the same date, Security Council Resolution 1218 expressed appreciation for the spirit of co-operation and constructive approach the two sides had demonstrated thus far in working with the Deputy Special Representative of the Secretary-General. On Dec. 29, 1998, Clerides, under diplomatic pressure, decided not to install the S-300s on Cyprus.

The Turkish general elections in April 1999 resulted in the formation of a new government led by Bulent Ecevit. In May, Greek Foreign Minister George Papandreou met Turkish Foreign Minister Ismail Cem for discussions on bilateral issues. On June 20, at the G-8 summit, the leaders of the major industrialized countries called for further negotiations without preconditions. Kofi Annan, in his report to the Security Council on June 22 (S/1999/707), declared his readiness to invite both leaders to begin negotiations. On June 29, the Security Council passed Resolution 1250, which appreciated the statement by leaders from the G-8 summit that called for comprehensive negotiations in the autumn of 1999 under the auspices of the Secretary-General. Moreover the resolution called for Greek and Turkish Cypriot leaders to commit themselves to the following principles: no preconditions; all issues on the table; commitment in good faith to continue to negotiate until a settlement was reached; full consideration of relevant UN resolutions and treaties.

Security Council Resolution 1251 renewed the UNFICYP mandate and reiterated that a settlement must be based on the establishment of a State of Cyprus with a single sovereignty comprising two politically equal communities in a bi-communal, bi-zonal federation. However, the Turkish Cypriot insistence on recognition of the TRNC as an equal to the Republic of Cyprus and on confederation as a system of government were issues that prevented meaningful negotiations.

1999-2000: Breakdown of Proximity Talks

Relations between Greece and Turkey warmed in August 1999. The Turkish earthquake on Aug. 17, to which Greece responded rapidly with aid and rescue teams, changed somewhat the hostile attitudes held in the press and public opinion. This aid was reciprocated when Athens, too, suffered an earthquake on Sept. 7. The annual Greek-Greek Cypriot military exercises on Oct. 2-7, 1999, were conducted without major incidents or protests. On Nov. 1, Kofi Annan nominated Peruvian diplomat Alvaro de Soto as his Special Advisor on Cyprus. On Nov. 13, under diplomatic pressure from the USA and the UN, Denktash agreed to proximity talks with Clerides in December 1999. Secretary-General Annan and Alvaro de Soto began the first session of proximity talks with Clerides and Denktash in New York from Dec. 3-13. According to UN spokesmen, the talks focused on four core issues, namely distribution of powers under a settlement, security arrangements, property rights and territorial questions. At the request of the Secretary-General, a news blackout was put into place over the detailed content of the talks.

The European Union summit in Helsinki on Dec. 10-11, 1999, made two important decisions, which were to impact on the Cyprus talks. Firstly, a decision was made to grant Turkey the status of an official candidate for EU membership. Secondly, heads of government asserted that a settlement of the Cyprus problem was not a precondition for Cyprus' accession to the EU. The UN Security Council passed Resolution 1283 on Dec. 15, which extended the mandate of UNFICYP for a further period ending June 15, 2000. An addendum to the Secretary-General's Nov. 29 report (S/1999/1203/Add.1) to the Security Council, added on Dec. 15, provoked arguments between both sides. The Turkish Cypriot authorities claimed that the addendum represented an important shift towards the Turkish Cypriot position, in so far that it acknowledged two equal sides on the island. The Greek Cypriot side rejected these claims and sought reassurance from the UN and USA that there was no shift in policy. The issue was raised with the Secretary-General and the Secretary-General's spokesman stated on Dec. 18 that the addendum had been included to report the position of the Turkish Cypriot side and "there was no change in UN policy".

A second round of proximity talks was held in Geneva from Jan. 31-Feb. 8, 2000. A third round took place from July 5 to Aug. 4 and a fourth round followed between Sept. 9-26 in New York. In a press release on Sept. 12 (SG/SM/7546), Secretary-General Annan stated that the "parties share a common desire to bring about, thorough negotiations in which each represents its side—and no one else—as the political equal of the other" and that "I have concluded that the equal status of the parties must and should be recognized explicitly in the comprehensive settlement".

This statement angered the Greek Cypriot authorities and Clerides boycotted the talks until he received assurances that the talks would be based upon UN resolutions for a federal solution. Clerides rejoined the process and, at the end of the talks, Alvaro de Soto stated on Sept. 26 that "it is fair to say, that a qualitative step forward has taken place during the last two weeks, and the two sides had engaged in the substance in a way they have not before". The confederation solution comprising two nations, proposed by the Turkish Cypriots, versus the federal solution proposed by the Greek Cypriots, still dominated discussions.

A fifth round of proximity talks took place in Geneva from Nov. 1-8, 2000. UN Secretary-General Annan presented a paper entitled "Oral Remarks" to both sides on the Nov. 8. This resulted in the breakdown of the proximity talks. The Turkish Cypriot leadership believed that the assessment presented by Annan fundamentally disregarded the existence of two separate states in Cyprus. Denktash met with the Turkish leadership on Nov. 24 and subsequently announced his withdrawal from the negotiations because no progress could be made unless two separate states were recognised. As a consequence planned proximity talks in January 2001 proved fruitless.

2001-03: Direct Talks, the "Annan Plan" and EU Accession Issues

On May 14, 2001, Secretary-General Annan addressed a gathering of European Union Ministers for Foreign Affairs in Brussels. He discussed a number of issues in relation to Cyprus, including the question of how Turkish Cypriot concerns could be met in the context of the accession to the European Union of Cyprus in view of the fact that "given economic and numerical disparities, the unrestricted application of the *acquis communautaire* in the north would be problematic for the Turkish Cypriots, and that special arrangements would be needed for Cyprus". In response, the President of the European Commission visited Cyprus in November 2001 and stated that the European Union would never be an obstacle to finding a settlement in Cyprus and could accommodate arrangements in the context of a political settlement.

Denktash met Annan on Aug. 28, 2001, in Salzburg, Austria. Following this meeting, Alvaro de Soto had contacts in Cyprus with the two parties between Aug. 30 and Sept. 5. On Sept. 5, Annan invited both parties to New York for talks on Sept. 12. Denktash did not accept this offer, but invited Clerides to face-to-face talks on Cyprus without the participation of third parties. Denktash met Clerides on Dec. 4 in the UN buffer zone in Cyprus with Alvaro de Soto present. In the statement made by Alvaro de Soto after the meeting, it was announced that the two leaders had agreed to enter into direct talks in mid-January 2002. According to this, the negotiations would start without preconditions: all issues would be on the table; and talks would continue under the auspices of the UN until a comprehensive settlement was achieved, while nothing would be agreed until everything was agreed. Clerides attended a dinner at Denktash's residence on Dec. 5 and Denktash visited Clerides' private residence on Dec. 29.

On Jan. 16, 2002, Clerides and Denktash met with Alvaro de Soto and agreed to hold negotiations begin-

ning on Jan. 21 in a UN building at Nicosia airport. The aim was to reach a settlement by mid-2002. Under a news blackout, a first round of direct meetings between the two leaders ran from Jan. 16 to Feb. 19. A second round took place from March 1-27 with a third round in April. Kofi Annan visited Nicosia on May 14–16 and met with both leaders, separately and together. A fourth round of direct talks ran from May 7 to July 2. On May 16, Secretary-General Annan reminded everyone: "an historic opportunity exists now to reach a settlement".

Clerides and Denktash had four more face-to-face meetings in June. However, the talks were facing deadlock on the four core issues of governance, security, territory and property. Ideas from the Belgian model and constitution were introduced to the discussion table. A fifth round of talks got underway on July 16, with missing persons a key topic on the agenda. A sixth round took place in Nicosia on Aug. 27.

Secretary-General Annan met with both leaders in Paris on Sept. 6 to add some impetus to the talks. Since talks had resumed in January, no significant progress had been made despite over 51 face to face meetings in six rounds of talks. Disagreements over separate sovereignty were plaguing the talks. Denktash cited the Swiss and Belgian models as offering potential guidelines towards a comprehensive settlement. The Turkish Cypriot side restated their view that it would be unacceptable if a divided Cyprus were admitted into the EU. Clerides and Denktash met in New York on Oct. 3-4 for further talks with Annan amidst growing pressure for a settlement before the expected formal approval in mid-December 2002 of Cyprus' application to join the EU. Annan stated that discussions in Paris "confirm my belief that, though serious differences remain, the elements of a comprehensive settlement that would meet the basic needs of both sides do in fact exist".

Secretary-General Annan introduced the idea of ad hoc bilateral committees to make recommendations on technical issues in relation to a number of the core issues. Denktash underwent open heart surgery on Oct. 7. On Oct. 25, there was an announcement that planned military exercises by Greece, Cyprus and Turkey would be cancelled to consolidate trust and cooperation. Then Turkish elections held on Nov. 3, won by the Turkish Justice and Development Party (AK) led by Recep Tayyip Erdogan, threw the question of Turkish approval into doubt.

On Nov. 11, 2002, Annan submitted his "Basis for Agreement on a Comprehensive Settlement of the Cyprus Problem". The two sides were asked to sign up to the key provisions before the EU summit in Copenhagen on Dec. 12 –13, so that the whole island could be approved for EU membership. On Nov. 18 Clerides agreed to negotiate on the Secretary-General's settlement plan and Denktash followed suit on Nov. 27. The plan envisaged that the common state would consist of two politically equal component states, one Greek Cypriot and the other Turkish Cypriot, each with its own administration and legislature. The common state would have a single international legal personality and sovereignty, with a single citizenship, and would join the EU as such. The common state would have a parliament consisting of a senate and a chamber of deputies, each with 48 members popularly elected for five-year terms. The senate would have an equal number of members from each component state, while the chamber would be composed in proportion to population, with the proviso that neither component state would have less than 12 seats. Executive power in the common state would be vested in a six-member presidential council elected in the senate.

After a three-year transition period, a president and vice president of the common state, who could not be from the same component state, would be drawn from the presidential council, rotating every 10 months, subject to neither component state providing more than two consecutive presidents. Lines of control would change, increasing Greek Cypriot control from 63.3 per cent of territory to 71.4 or 71.5 per cent depending on the option chosen. Cyprus would be demilitarized, but Greece and Turkey, as guarantor powers, would each be entitled to deploy up to 9,999 troops on the island. UN peacekeepers would remain as long as the common state, with agreement from the component states, so decided.

On Dec. 5, Clerides and Denktash both submitted comments. The Greek Cypriot leadership raised concerns over power sharing, the return of refugees and mainland Turkish settlers, amongst other issues. The Turkish Cypriot side's concerns included the loss of territory, sovereignty and the return of Greek Cypriot refugees. On Dec. 10, Annan presented a revised plan. He stated that "Cyprus has a rendezvous with history" and asked the two leaders to give the revision urgent consideration with a view to reaching conclusions so that a reunited Cyprus could join the European Union. The Secretary-General also asked the two sides to be available for talks in Copenhagen, where the European Council would meet.

Spokesman of the UN Secretary-General Fred Eckhard made the following statement after the EU summit: "Alvaro de Soto, the Secretary-General's Special Adviser on Cyprus, has held intensive consultations in Copenhagen on the 12th and 13th of December 2002. Unfortunately, it has not proved possible to achieve a comprehensive settlement. However, the parties' positions have never been closer, and agreement seemed possible up until the last minute". Consequently, Kofi Annan set Feb. 28, 2003, as a deadline for agreement so referenda could be held on March 30, in anticipation of membership of the EU.

In December 2002 and January 2003, mass rallies were held in the Turkish-occupied part of Nicosia, in which thousands of Turkish Cypriots called for the acceptance of the Annan Plan. Face-to-face talks between Clerides and Denktash resumed in Nicosia on Jan. 15, 2003. An agreement was made on Jan. 23 to set up a UN-sponsored competition to find a national flag and anthem for a united Cyprus. In addition two ad hoc committees of representatives from both sides began work on legislation and treaties.

Tassos Papadopoulos of the centre-right Democratic Party (DIKO) replaced Glafcos Clerides as President of the Republic of Cyprus as a result of elections on Feb. 16, 2003. Papadopoulos attracted 51.5 per cent of the vote compared with Clerides' 38.8 per cent. Clerides attended subsequent talks as an advisor to ensure continuity in the discussion process and UN officials maintained the goal of agreement by Feb. 28. Annan, after travelling to Greece and Turkey, arrived in Cyprus on Feb. 26 with a second revision of the settlement plan. Changes included adjustments to territorial control and the reduction of the number of Greek and Turkish troops allowed to be stationed in Cyprus. Moreover, the option of creating a Greek enclave on the Karpass peninsula was dropped in the revised plan. The British offered to cede nearly half of its sovereign base areas (SBA), or 45 sq miles, to the Republic of Cyprus provided an agreement was made on the UN settlement plan. However, both sides said they needed more time to study the revised plan.

On Feb. 28, Papadopoulos and Denktash accepted Secretary-General Annan's invitation to The Hague on March 10 to confirm whether they would submit the settlement plan to referenda at the end of the month. Annan left Cyprus on Feb. 28, calling the revised plan "fair and balanced" and urged all parties to "catch the tide before it turns, perhaps irreversibly".

On March 10, Annan met Papadopoulos and Denktash in The Hague to get their responses to his request of permitting separate and simultaneous referenda on the settlement plan. Papadopoulos had raised concerns and wished to be sure that gaps regarding federal legislation and constituent state constitutions would be filled, in addition to security provisions being fulfilled by the guarantor powers of Greece and Turkey prior to a referendum. Papadopoulos argued more time was needed for a campaign on the referendum. However, Papadopoulos agreed to call a referendum as long as the people knew what they were being asked to vote on, without reopening substantive provisions, if Denktash did likewise.

Denktash, however, was not prepared to agree to put the plan before a referendum. He said he had fundamental objections to the settlement plan on basic points. In addition, he argued that further negotiations were likely to be successful only if they began from a new starting point and if the parties agreed on basic principles. Denktash informed the Secretary-General that Turkey was not in a position to sign the statement requested of the guarantors and Turkey confirmed this. Annan tried to rescue the process and suggested an extended deadline of March 28, in time for referenda on April 6. But after many hours of intensive diplomacy through the night, on March 11, 2003, at 05.30 local time, Annan had to announce that there had been no agreement and declared "we have reached the end of the road". The Secretary-General made it clear that the "plan remained on the table, ready for the Greek

Cypriots and the Turkish Cypriots to pick it up and carry it forward if they could summon the will to do so".

In regard to the settlement plan, Kofi Annan's April 1 report (S/2003/398) said "there have been many missed opportunities over the years in the United Nations good offices on Cyprus. Both sides bear a share of blame for those failures. In the case of the failure of this latest effort, I believe that Mr. Denktash, the Turkish Cypriot leader bears prime responsibility". Security Council Resolution 1475 on April 14, 2003, stated that it "regrets that, as described in the Secretary General's report, due to the negative approach of the Turkish Cypriot leader culminating in the position taken at the 10-11 March 2003 meeting in the Hague, it was not possible to reach agreement to put the plan to simultaneous referenda as suggested by the Secretary General".

At the EU summit held in Brussels on March 20-21, 2003, delegates expressed strong support for the continuation of talks and reaffirmed Cyprus would sign the accession treaty on April 16 and would join the EU on May 1, 2004. On March 28, Turkish Prime Minister Erdogan belatedly proposed a conference on the Cyprus issue, with Turkish Cypriots, Greek Cypriots, Turkey, Greece and Britain. In response, Greece and the Greek Cypriot authorities dismissed the idea, insisting the Cyprus problem must be resolved within the UN framework. In addition, on April 2 Denktash wrote to Papadopoulos proposing six confidence building measures; however Papadopoulos urged Denktash to accept the settlement plan tabled by the Secretary-General as the basis for further negotiations.

On April 16, 2003, in Athens, President Tassos Papadopoulos signed the Treaty of Accession of Cyprus to the European Union. The Protocol on Cyprus, attached to the Treaty of Accession, provides for "the suspension of the application of the *acquis communautaire* in those areas of the Republic of Cyprus in which the government of the Republic of Cyprus does not exercise effective control". It adds that in the event of a settlement of the Cyprus problem, "the Council, acting unanimously on the basis of a proposal from the Commission, shall decide on the adaptations to the terms concerning the accession of Cyprus to the European Union with regard to the Turkish Cypriot community".

On April 21, 2003, the Turkish Cypriot authorities announced they were easing travel restrictions to the northern part of Cyprus to build confidence between the two communities. Thousands of Greek and Turkish Cypriots took the opportunity to see property, land and people inaccessible since the conflict of 1974, sparking many emotional scenes widely covered by the international media. On April 30 a package of measures intended to extend a number of rights and benefits of the Turkish Cypriots was announced by Tassos Papadopoulos. On June 3, the EU Commission proposed a number of measures to facilitate economic development in the north of Cyprus. President George W. Bush made a pledge to Greek Prime Minister Simitis on June 25 in Washington, that the USA would

join the EU in new efforts to revive talks. Denktash tabled new confidence building measures on July 11, such as the reopening of Nicosia airport for both communities.

In July, following Denktash's proposal, both leaders agreed to co-operate with the UN in clearing minefields in the Nicosia area. Turkish Foreign Minister Gul had talks with US Secretary of State Colin Powell in Washington on July 24. On July 30, the Secretary-General, at his mid-year press conference, stated that he would assist the negotiation process if a real and genuine political will existed to achieve a settlement. Turkey and the Turkish Cypriot authorities signed a "Customs Union Framework Agreement" on Aug. 8 in an attempt to boost the Turkish Cypriot economy.

Greek Foreign Minister Papandreou then met with Colin Powell, the US President's National Security Advisor Condoleezza Rice, and the US State Department Special Coordinator for Cyprus, Thomas Weston, in mid-September to discuss a number of issues including the Cyprus problem. The US government reiterated its wish to see a settlement before Cyprus joined the European Union on May 1, 2004, thus allowing a united Cyprus to join the EU.

Papadopoulos addressed the UN General Assembly and met with Secretary-General Annan on Sept. 25. Thomas Weston visited Cyprus on Oct. 23-24 and Nov. 20-22 for talks with Papadopoulos and Turkish Cypriot party leaders. For the second year running military manoeuvres due to take place in October were cancelled following an agreement between the governments of Cyprus, Greece and Turkey. Turkish Prime Minister Recep Tayyip Erdogan's visit to the TRNC to mark the 20th anniversary of the declaration of the TRNC on Nov. 15 drew strong criticism from the Greek Cypriot side, which declared the visit "illegal".

Elections in the TRNC on Dec. 14, 2003, resulted in the Republican Turkish Party (RTP) and the Democratic Party (DP) forming a coalition government on Jan.12, 2004. The Republican Turkish Party, which gained 35.2 % of the vote and 19 of the 50 seats, campaigned on a platform of opposition to TRNC President Denktash's policies regarding the Annan plan and EU accession. The leader of the RTP, Mehmet Ali Talat, became the new Prime Minister of the TRNC. Serdar Denktash, son of Rauf Denktash and leader of the DP, was named as Deputy Prime Minister and Foreign Minister in the new administration, while Rauf Denktash continued his role as chief negotiator in settlement talks.

April 2004 Referenda on UN Settlement Plan

Following talks with Annan in New York on Feb. 10-13, 2004, Papadopoulos and Denktash agreed to a timetable of progress beginning with the resumption of intercommunal talks on Feb. 19 in Nicosia. Under the New York accord, failure to meet agreement by March 22 would result in Greece and Turkey, as guarantor powers, being asked to help resolve any differences; if there was still no agreement by March 29, the UN Secretary-General would use his discretion to produce a final version of his settlement plan to be put to simultaneous referenda on April 24, 2004.

Intercommunal talks began in Nicosia under the chairmanship of Alvaro De Soto on Feb. 19. The main unresolved issues continued to be the structure and powers of the central government; EU accession matters; the number of Greek Cypriot refugees to return to the north; territorial issues; the number of Turkish troops to be stationed in Cyprus; the fate of towns such as Varosha; and compensation for loss of land. The Turkish Cypriot leadership argued for a delay to Cyprus' EU accession until a comprehensive settlement had been reached.

On March 19, Secretary-General Annan invited the Greek Cypriot and Turkish Cypriot leadership, in addition to Greece and Turkey, to Lucerne in Switzerland for the second phase of talks to begin on March 24. Both Greek Prime Minister Costas Karamanlis and Turkish Prime Minister Recep Tayyip Erdogan accepted the invitation, but Rauf Denktash refused to attend the talks, citing continued Greek Cypriot "intransigence" at the negotiating table. As a result, the TRNC Prime Minister, Mehmet Ali Talat, and TRNC Deputy Prime Minister, Serdar Denktash, led the Turkish Cypriot delegation in Switzerland. The Lucerne conference produced no agreement, with the issue of refugees and property rights proving to be the largest stumbling block. Consequently, Annan used his discretionary authority under the New York accord to produce a fifth and final version of his settlement plan, which was presented to the parties on March 31. The UN formally confirmed that the settlement plan would be put to simultaneous referenda on April 24.

After consideration, President Papadopoulos urged the Greek Cypriot community to reject the UN settlement plan. TRNC President Denktash also remained opposed to the plan, whilst TRNC Prime Minister Ali Talat and Turkish Prime Minister Tayyip Erdogan argued for acceptance of the plan. In the period leading towards the referenda, the Greek Cypriot community were largely opposed to the plan in view of revisions to the plan providing for a reduction in the number of of Greek Cypriot refugees to return to the north and the proposed continued presence of Turkish troops on the island. AKEL, the strongest political party in the Republic of Cyprus, eventually argued for rejection of the settlement plan after their proposals to delay the referenda were rejected.

In the referenda of April 24, the Greek Cypriot community overwhelmingly rejected the settlement plan, with 76% voting "No", prompting an angry response from the European Union. In contrast, 65% of the Turkish Cypriot community voted to accept the UN settlement plan, opening the possibility of a partial lifting of EU trade restrictions on the TRNC. As a consequence of the referendum results, the Greek Cypriot controlled south of Cyprus joined the EU on May 1, with Cyprus still divided. It was not immediately clear what the effect of the referenda would be on the Republic of Cyprus' position within the EU and the status of the TRNC in the international community.

Charlie Pericleous

4.7 Finland - Russia (Karelia, Petsamo)

After 500 years of Swedish rule and then another century as a possession of Tsarist Russia, Finland achieved independence at the end of World War I. The borders of the new state were confirmed by the 1920 Treaty of Tartu with the new Soviet Union. Under that treaty Finland included the Finnish-populated parts of Karelia as well as the Petsamo region in the far north. Two decades later Finland was defeated in the 1939-40 Winter War with the Soviet Union. It was obliged to cede the Finnish Karelian territories under the 1940 Treaty of Moscow. In 1941 Finland participated in the German invasion of the Soviet Union. An armistice, which not only reimposed the cession of Finnish Karelia but also gave Petsamo to the Soviet Union, was signed in 1944. These transfers were confirmed in Finland's 1947 peace treaty with the victorious powers. Over the next 40 years they appeared to have been the final settlement of Finnish-Russian territorial issues. However, at the beginning of the 1990s, following the collapse of the Soviet Union, the question of recovery of the ceded areas became a subject of public debate in some circles in Finland. (Map 39 on p. 512 illustrates the area.)

Historical Background—Under Swedish and Russian Rule

An important ancient trade route from the Atlantic via the great Russian rivers passed through the Karelian isthmus between the Gulf of Finland and Lake Ladoga. Sweden, Denmark, traders of the Hanseatic League and of the Great Novgorod of northern Russia (then part of Kievan Rus') had the aim of gaining control of this trade. After a hundred years of conflict between the western and eastern powers, Swedish dominion over the northern banks of the Gulf of Finland was confirmed with the delegates of Novgorod by the 1323 Treaty of Nötheburg (originally in Russian known as Oreshek, the Swedes translated the name in the 17th century to Nötheburg; in the 18th century the town was called Schlüsselburg, in Finnish the name is Pähkinäsaari, and from 1944 it was renamed in Russian as Petrokrepost. All these names appear in historical writings). The border set by the Nötheburg treaty divided the Karelian isthmus in two between the Swedish and Russian sides.

The Finns who settled the Swedish side were converted to the Christianity of the Papal Church during the eleventh and twelfth centuries. Russian Karelia was inhabited mostly by Karelians. They spoke the Finnish-related Karelian language but were converted to the Orthodox faith by the Russians. The Karelian people were also strongly influenced by Russian culture. The Swedish-Russian border of 1323 divided the Finns and Karelian people and Roman Catholic and Orthodox worlds from each other.

During the fourteenth and fifteenth centuries the Finnish and Karelian settlements spread towards the north, to the regions north of Lake Ladoga. Because the Finnish settlement had spread over the border marks in these northern areas there were numerous disputes, and even a war in 1556–58, between the Swedish and Russian Crowns. In 1595 the Teusina Peace Treaty confirmed a new border. The regions inhabited by the Finns were confirmed as Swedish properties. The border separated the Swedish/Finnish province of Savonia from the Russian/Karelian province (*uezd*) of Korela. However, this was a period of disorder in Russia; the Swedes became involved in Russian domestic policies and, when their plans failed, they took the province of Korela under their domination. The Swedes called the annexed *uezd* of Korela the province of Käkisalmi.

In the Stolbovo peace treaty the provinces of Korela and Ingria (between Karelia and Estonia) were annexed to Sweden in 1617. The population of the new Swedish province in Karelia was Karelian and belonged to the Orthodox Church. The Swedes and Finns had divorced from the Roman Church in the 1520s and Sweden was declared as Lutheran. Lutheran Finns began to move to the annexed new province, resulting in many disputes between the newcomers and Orthodox natives. The Karelian people began to migrate away from the region and during the war period in 1656–58 almost all of them did flee to Russia. Only small Karelian settlements in the most fertile plains and in the parishes nearest to the border were left after the war. Soon the Finns inhabited the abandoned areas with the result that the population of the annexed province was changed almost totally.

In rising to Great Power status Sweden had injured the interests of all the neighbouring countries. By taking Ingria Sweden had enclosed the Baltic Sea from the Russians. Russia, Denmark and Poland allied to attack Sweden in 1700. The Great Northern War ended in the Peace Treaty of Uusikaupunki (Swedish, Nystad) in 1721. Extensive regions on the eastern and southern littorals of the Gulf of Finland, including the Karelian isthmus just up to north of the town of Vyborg as well as western Karelia, were ceded to Russia. The Swedes tried to re-gain the lost Finnish and Karelian territories in the "War of the Hats" in the 1740s. However, in the Peace Treaty of Turku (Swedish, Åbo) in 1743 the Russian territory was enlarged up to the Kymi region of Finland and further to the west and north of Vyborg. Only the remotest northern corner of the former province of Käkisalmi

remained Swedish. The Russians called the annexed Karelian territories "Old Finland". This territory was ruled by extraordinary principles. The old possessions, Lutheran religion and Swedish laws (when not contrary to Russian laws) were maintained. So, the territory of "Old Finland" retained a "Finnish" or "Swedish"' identity inside the Russian empire.

Napoleon Bonaparte and Tsar Alexander I agreed in Tilsit in 1807 that Russia had to force Sweden to join the Continental blockade against England. The result was a war between Russia and Sweden. By the Hamina (Swedish, Fredrikshamn) Peace Treaty of 1809 the whole of Finland was annexed to the Russian empire as an autonomous Grand Duchy. Tsarist rule was confirmed by the Congress of Vienna (1815) and was to last for over a century.

In the course of the nineteenth century the Grand Duchy of Finland acquired substantial autonomy within the Russian empire. Finland had its own parliament (Diet), judicial system and monetary arrangements. It also maintained its own customs posts, which levied tolls on goods passing to and from Russia proper. In 1812 the territory of "Old Finland" was annexed to the Finnish Grand Duchy and the Finnish-Russian border was restored to its pre-1721 position. Finland was now deemed to include western Karelia north of Lake Ladoga as well as the Karelian isthmus down to about 30 miles north of St Petersburg. The determining principles were (i) that the border north of Lake Ladoga should follow the ridge dividing the respective watersheds of the Baltic and White seas, and (ii) that only areas wholly Finnish in ethnic composition should be part of Finland (mixed areas being deemed to be part of Russia). This border was marked to the terrain in 1827–33. The Finnish territory was enlarged to the east in the northern parts of the border. In the late 19th century, Finnish representatives secured an undertaking from the Tsar that Russia would transfer the Petsamo (Pechenga) region in the far north (west of Murmansk), to give Finland access to the Arctic Ocean. This pledge was never implemented.

Establishment of Finnish Independence

Seizing the opportunity presented by the fall of the Tsar, the Finnish Diet on Dec. 6, 1917, declared Finland independent. A civil war ensued between pro-Bolshevik Reds and anti-Bolshevik Whites, in which the former received support from the Russians and the latter from the Germans. Withdrawal from Finland was one of the conditions which the Germans imposed on the new Soviet Bolshevik regime under the March 1918 Treaty of Brest-Litovsk. Although Germany accepted defeat in the west in November 1918, in Finland the Whites eventually emerged victorious. Under the Treaty of Tartu (Dorpat) signed with the Soviet Union on Oct. 15, 1920, the new Finnish Republic secured recognition for its independence within borders which included western Karelia north of Lake Ladoga as well as the Karelian isthmus north of St Petersburg (by then called Petrograd, later to be renamed Leningrad). In addition the Petsamo region was included within Finland, which meant that Finnish territory was extended to the Arctic Ocean. Under a 1921 League of Nations convention, the Swedish-populated Åland Islands (in Finnish Ahvenanmaa) in the Gulf of Bothnia, remained under Finnish sovereignty. (See Section 4.8 for the Åland Islands dispute.)

Loss of Karelia in Winter War—Post-World War II Settlement

The Soviet Union had cool, almost chilly, relations with the right-wing governments of Finland during the 1920s and 1930s. After the Nazi-Soviet non-aggression pact of August 1939 had secretly listed the Gulf of Finland as a Soviet sphere of influence, Stalin demanded that Finland should, among other things, withdraw from the area north of Leningrad in return for the cession of parts of eastern Karelia further north. When Finland demurred, Soviet forces launched a surprise attack. In what became known as the Winter War (1939-40), brave Finnish resistance eventually succumbed to the more numerous Soviet forces. Under the Treaty of Moscow signed on March 12, 1940, Finland was compelled to make territorial concessions substantially greater than the original Soviet demands. The areas lost were the Karelian isthmus and an adjoining area to points north and west of Vyborg, Finnish Karelia north of Lake Ladoga and a number of islands in the Gulf of Finland. In other words, Stalin re-established the boundary in the south on the 1721 line secured by Peter the Great. In addition, the Soviet Union obtained the right to lease Hangö peninsula (at the western end of the Gulf) for the purposes of a military base, as well as right of unrestricted transit for people and goods through Petsamo province into Norway. There was also a major border adjustment in the Soviet Union's favour in the area south of Petsamo, around the parish of Kuolajarvi.

Embittered by the Soviet terms and subjected to continued political pressure from Moscow, Finland moved closer to Nazi Germany and in June 1941 participated in the German invasion of the Soviet Union. Finnish historians note that Finland signed no formal alliance with Hitler and that Finnish forces took no active part in the German siege of Leningrad of 1941-44. Instead they concentrated on recovering the territory ceded under the March 1940 treaty and on establishing Finnish rule in eastern Karelia near Lake Onega in Russia. The outcome was a further defeat by the Red Army and an armistice (signed in Moscow on Sept. 19, 1944) under which Finland was obliged to accept Soviet terms even more draconian than those of 1940. Not only were the Moscow treaty's territorial stipulations in the south restored; in addition, Finland was obliged to cede Petsamo province in the north and was thus deprived of access to the Arctic Ocean (while Norway acquired a frontier with the Soviet Union). Moreover, the Soviet Union, while it gave up its right to the Hangö lease, obtained similar rights to establish a military base on Porkkala-Udd peninsula, a few

miles south-west of the Finnish capital, Helsinki. Following the armistice, Finland regained a measure of favour with the Allies by driving German forces out of the country.

The armistice terms were confirmed by the 1947 peace treaty between Finland and the wartime Allies and associated powers. This instrument signed in Paris on Feb. 10, 1947, was ratified by Finland on April 18, 1947, and entered into force on Sept. 10, 1947. The terms meant that Finland lost more than a tenth of its pre-war territory, which had contained 11 per cent of its population. In the event, virtually the entire Finnish population of the ceded regions (about 420,000 people) opted to move to Finland within its new borders. The ceded regions were inhabited by the settlers brought in from various parts of the Soviet Union. The migration of the Karelian inhabitants to Finland placed a great burden on the shattered Finnish economy, which also had to generate $300,000,000 payable in war reparations to the Soviet Union under the Paris treaty. It transpired, moreover, that the ceded Petsamo region contained valuable nickel deposits. Not surprisingly, many Finns reflected on the contrast between their post-war lot and that of Sweden, which had remained neutral in the recent hostilities and become substantially wealthier by trading with both sides (as it had in World War I). As it turned out, however, the Finnish economy recovered relatively quickly, with the result that reparations were paid off by 1952.

In recognition of post-war strategic realities, Finland signed a Treaty of Friendship, Co-operation and Mutual Assistance with the Soviet Union on April 6, 1948. The first article of this treaty, which was renewed in 1970 and 1983, specified that Finland would fight "with all the forces at her disposal" to repel any attack on the Soviet Union launched through Finnish territory by Germany "or any state allied to the latter". In such an eventuality, continued the treaty, "the Soviet Union will render Finland the necessary assistance, in regard to the granting of which the parties will agree between themselves". In return for its accommodation of Soviet strategic interests (a relationship for which the term "Finlandization" was coined by Western observers), post-war Finland was able to preserve its independence and democratic political system and to develop an increasingly prosperous market economy. It also, in 1955, secured the withdrawal of Soviet troops from the Porkkala base. But Finland had always to tread carefully in the succeeding decades, aware that the rulers in Moscow would brook no interference with the territorial and security arrangements which had resulted from World War II.

As regards the administrative status of the territories ceded by Finland, the Soviet authorities made some significant changes in 1946. Before the war, Soviet Karelia had been an autonomous Soviet socialist republic (ASSR) within the Russian Soviet Federated Socialist Republic (RSFSR). Following the signature of the Moscow treaty in March 1940, all the southern territory gained from Finland (except for an area around Leningrad) was added to the Karelian ASSR, which became the Karelo-Finnish Soviet Socialist Republic (SSR) and the twelfth full republic of the USSR. In 1946, however, the southern part of the Karelo-Finnish SSR, including the Karelian isthmus, was transferred to the Leningrad region (oblast) of the RSFSR. The remainder reverted to the status of an ASSR within the RSFSR, with its capital at Petrozavodsk. At the same time, the ceded Petsamo and Kuolajarvi regions in the north became part of the Murmansk oblast of the RSFSR.

Re-emergence of the Finnish-Russian Territorial Question in the 1990s

Finnish-Soviet relations remained set in their post-war mould for over four decades. During this era barely a whisper was heard in Finland about the territories lost to the Soviet Union in 1940 and 1944. All Finnish governments, of whatever political complexion, followed the standard line emanating from Moscow that the border question had been settled once and for all and that there were no territorial issues between the two sides. Both countries, moreover, were keen proponents of the 1975 Helsinki Final Act of the Conference on Security and Co-operation in Europe (CSCE), which included a stipulation that existing European borders should be regarded as inviolable.

However, behind these official declarations of governments there were groups amongst the Finns that tried to press governments and politicians to negotiate with the Soviet leaders about the "Karelian case". Hopes of regaining the ceded regions lived on among the Karelian refugees and some right-wing politicians especially. The post-1989 collapse of Communist rule in Eastern Europe and the accelerating process of disintegration in the Soviet Union itself had major consequences for relations between Helsinki and Moscow. As the nature of these relations changed towards full normalization, to Finland's benefit, the public debate grew in Finland about the ceded lands and about the prospects for securing a revision of the post-war territorial settlement. Highly influential in this respect was the example of the three Baltic republics in regaining their independence in 1991 and thus reversing some of the results of the 1939 Nazi-Soviet pact.

In terms of formal relations, the main change was that the 1948 treaty was replaced by a new instrument which did not have the unequal aspects of the old one. Negotiations on a new text were completed in early November 1991, but before it could be signed the Soviet Union finally expired. Accordingly, a suitably adjusted treaty of good neighbourliness and mutual co-operation was signed by Finland and the Russian Federation on Jan. 20, 1992. Unlike the 1948 text, it contained no military commitments (and did not mention Germany), specifying that future relations between the two countries would be based on international law and the accords of the CSCE. The parties agreed never to use force against each other and to respect the inviolability of their common border. Two other agreements signed at the same time covered reciprocal trade and economic co-operation in the Finnish-Russian border area. In the latter respect, Finland had in December 1991 made an initial allocation of FIM 30,000,000 (over 500,000 euros) to assist reconstruction in the Russian regions of Karelia and St Petersburg (the name to which Leningrad had reverted in September 1991).

The new treaty was ratified by the Russian parliament on May 14, 1992, on which occasion the chairman of its foreign affairs and trade committee, Yevgeni Ambartsumov, made some positive references to Finland's role following the German invasion of the Soviet Union in 1941. Recalling that the Finnish military commander, Marshal (Baron) Mannerheim, had been a Tsarist general before 1917 and spoke fluent Russian, Ambartsumov said that this background had been "decisive for Mannerheim's limited advance over the old border, which in turn prevented the enemy [i.e. the Germans] from taking Leningrad".

It was pointed out in Finnish government circles that the new treaty provisions did not exclude the possibility of border changes being peacefully agreed by negotiation within the CSCE framework. As things stood, however, neither the government nor any of the mainstream parties advocated that a formal territorial claim should be made in the foreseeable future. On the other hand, members of the populist Rural Party began to call for a formal reopening of the territorial issue, while discussion of the question in the Finnish media and in political circles was no longer taboo. By early 1992 opinion polls in Finland were showing that some 60 per cent of respondents believed that the government should take up the question of the ceded territories. In the revival of Finnish interest in the territorial question a prominent role came to be played by a new pressure group called the Tartu Peace Movement, advocating that Finland should seek by negotiation to recover the borders established under the 1920 Tartu treaty. According to the chairman of this movement, Dr Martti Siirala, the 1920 borders reflected the ethnic boundary between Finns and Russians which had existed for a millennium (and which had been recognized by the Russians themselves when Finland was a Tsarist possession).

At the beginning of the twenty-first century a new movement has been established in Finland. The descendants of those who moved from Karelia in the 1940s have begun to demand property rights over the farms and lands their parents and grandparents owned in Karelia before World War II. More than one hundred petitions have been sent to the Russian government calling for restitution of farms and land. The goal of this movement is not to move the border between the states but to amend Russian legislation so that foreign ownership would be permitted and pre-war property rights restored.

According to the official foreign policy of Finland there are no plans to re-open the "Karelian case". Since the dissolution of the Soviet Union the Russian Federation has consistently maintained that border changes are not open for discussion. However, the possibility of granting foreigners the right to own land in Russia in the future has not been absolutely ruled out.

Much has happened on the Finnish-Russian border in the post-Soviet period. New frontier crossing points have been opened and the volume of trade, tourism and all kinds of interaction over the border have increased exponentially. The opportunity for those who left Karelia after World War II, or their descendants, to visit Karelia has helped considerably to ease the traumatic feelings for the lost old home places. The Finnish-Russian border has become the eastern border of European Union, and in the context of European integration borders can no longer be treated purely as internal or national matters.

Kimmo Katajala

4.8 Finland - Sweden (Åland Islands)

Situated at the entrance to the Gulf of Bothnia (between Finland and Sweden), the 6,500 Åland Islands (with a Swedish-speaking population of some 24,000) were part of Sweden until 1809 and have been part of Finland since then. The islands have not been a cause of dispute between the governments of Finland and Sweden since a 1921 League of Nations decision maintained their status quo as part of Finland. However, there was dissatisfaction with this decision among the inhabitants of the islands, of whom a majority decided, both during World War I and at the end of World War II, to ask for the islands' return to Sweden. The issue is of special significance because of the League of Nations decision in favour of the maintenance of the frontiers of an existing state against the expressed wishes of a minority in part of that state. Under legislation adopted by the Finnish parliament in 1991, the Åland Islands' existing autonomy was substantially enhanced. (Map 40 on p. 512 illustrates the position of the islands.)

Historical Background

The Åland Islands (Ahvenanmaa in Finnish) were part of Sweden until 1809, when they were seized by Russia and joined with Finland (which had also been a Swedish territory). Finland then became a partially autonomous Grand Duchy within the Russian Empire, with its own Diet responsible for internal matters, but not for foreign affairs. In 1854 British and French fleets destroyed the islands' fortifications at Bomarsund, and under the 1856 Treaty of Paris, which ended the Crimean War (between the Western powers and Russia), the islands were de-militarized, but

remained with Finland under Russian suzerainty.

During World War I the Finnish Diet on Dec. 6, 1917 (i.e. after the October Revolution in Russia) assumed supreme powers and constituted a Republic with a national government, which was recognized by Russia in January 1918 and later also by other states. The communes of the Åland Islands, however, had in August 1917 informed the King of Sweden that they had, at a meeting at Finström, adopted a resolution expressing their desire to be reunited with Sweden, and in a plebiscite held subsequently an overwhelming majority of the islanders voted in favour of reunion with Sweden. The King of Sweden supported their move and in February 1918 a Swedish military expedition was sent to the islands in order to secure the withdrawal of all Finnish forces—i.e. of the White and Red Guards who were then at war with each other.

The League of Nations Decision

In June 1920 both Finland and Sweden put their cases to the League of Nations Council. As against the islanders' call for self-determination, the Finnish government pointed out that the islands had been part of Finland for over 100 years, and that they were also recognized as part of the independent Finland constituted in 1917, with the result that the destiny of the islands was a purely domestic matter in which the League had no authority to intervene.

The Council appointed a commission of jurists to decide whether or not the Council had a right to intervene, and this commission concluded that the issue involved "a situation of doubt and ambiguity concerned with the break-up of nations" and was therefore "a problem of great concern to the international community and of great importance for the growth of international law", and that the League of Nations Council was competent to adjudicate in the matter. The commission also stated that the principle of self-determination had to be balanced against other principles and that a compromise along the lines of minority guarantees might be the best solution.

The Council thereupon sent a commission of rapporteurs to the area and charged it with making specific recommendations. The commission, in its opinion given in April 1921, concluded that "to detach the islands from Finland would be...an alteration of its status, depriving this country of a part of that which belongs to it". Regarding the principle of self-determination, the commission stated that it was "not, properly speaking, a rule of international law but a general principle expressed in a vague formula", and that it would certainly not apply to "fractions of states" (like the Åland Islands) in the same way as it applied to "a people with a defined national life" (like the Finns). The commission stated explicitly: "To concede to minorities, either of race or of religion, or to any fractions of a population, the right to withdraw from the community to which they belong, because it is their good will or their good pleasure, would be to destroy order and stability within states and to inaugurate anarchy in international life; it would be to uphold a theory incompatible with the very idea of the state as a territorial and political unity".

The commission also recommended, however, that Finland should be obliged to give a number of guarantees to the Ålanders to preserve their national culture and identity, namely the right of pre-emption of land in the Ålands; five years' minimum residence as a qualification for the franchise; the use of Swedish as the teaching language in schools; the assurance that governors would not be appointed against the wish of the people; and the right of recourse to the League of Nations Council. The commission's report was endorsed by the Council in June 1921 and both Finland (which undertook to give the required guarantees) and Sweden subsequently accepted this decision.

The decision was formalized in a Geneva Convention of Oct. 20, 1921, providing for the islands' regional autonomy within the Finnish Republic and their demilitarization and neutralization, with their inhabitants being exempt from Finnish military service. This convention was signed not only by Finland and Sweden but also by Britain, Denmark, Estonia, France, Germany, Italy, Latvia and Poland (but not by the Soviet Union) and it has remained in force for all the signatories.

World War II Developments—Islanders' Unsuccessful Attempt to Rejoin Sweden

When the outbreak of war between Germany and the Soviet Union was considered possible, Finland and Sweden agreed on Jan. 8, 1939, on a plan for limited remilitarization of the islands, including fortification in the south and military service for the inhabitants. The two governments explained their decision in a note addressed to the signatories of the 1921 convention, stating that in case of imminent war in the Baltic, Sweden reserved the right to collaborate, at the request of Finland, in applying measures to safeguard the neutrality of the islands, and that both parties would decline any offer by a belligerent power to "protect" the islands. During April-May 1939 the plan was approved by all the signatories of the convention except Germany. However, the islanders themselves, in a petition bearing 10,800 signatures, protested to the League of Nations Council against the proposed remilitarization.

On a request by Finland and Sweden the League of Nations Council considered the remilitarization plan on May 22-29, 1939, but reached no agreement because the Soviet Union did not consider itself to be in possession of all the information necessary for defining its attitude, although Finland and Sweden claimed that they had supplied the USSR with the same information as had been furnished to all the other powers.

On May 31, 1939, the Soviet Union proposed an effective pact of mutual assistance against aggression to be concluded by Britain, France and the Soviet Union, with the possibility of guarantees against aggression being given to the Baltic states. Sweden thereupon withdrew from the remilitarization plan on June 3, whereas the Finnish Minister of Defence stated on June 5 that his government would proceed with the fortification of some of the Åland Islands. With regard to the guarantees proposed by the Soviet Union, the Finnish Foreign Minister stated on June 6 that Finland could not accept them but would have to treat as an aggressor every state which, on the basis of such an unasked guarantee, intended to give its so-called assistance whenever it considered that the "guaranteed" state required help.

Following the outbreak of war between Finland and the Soviet Union on Nov. 30, 1939, the Finnish government informed the League of Nations on Dec. 4 that it had decided to fortify the Åland Islands. However, after the conclusion of the Finnish-Soviet peace treaty (ratified by the Finnish parliament on March 15, 1940), the Finnish government announced on July 18, 1940, that it had begun to demilitarize the islands, and on Oct. 12 of that year Finland and the Soviet Union ratified an agreement under which Finland undertook to demilitarize the islands and not to place them at the disposal of other states.

At the end of World War II the Landsting (Legislative Assembly) of the Åland Islands unanimously demanded, on Sept. 12, 1945, the islands' reunion with Sweden and the dissolution of the existing union with Finland, and requested an opportunity of putting their case to the Allies in their peace negotiations with Finland. In the Landsting resolution it was recorded that the islands had been compulsorily separated from Sweden under the 1809 peace treaty of Hamina but that their inhabitants had never given up hope of a reunion. It was also claimed that the 1921 convention no longer conformed to the existing situation. In Sweden, however, the Foreign Ministry officially denied on Sept. 13 any Swedish initiative in the islanders' demand for a revision of their islands' status.

In the event, the peace treaty concluded between the Allied powers (including the Soviet Union) and Finland—which was signed in Paris on Feb. 10, 1947, ratified by Finland on April 18 and effective from Sept. 16, 1947—laid down (in Article 5) that the Åland Islands would remain demilitarized as part of Finland. Their status as it had obtained between 1921 and 1939 was thus restored. Under Finnish legislation enacted in 1951, the islands were granted a large measure of local autonomy, exercised by its parliament (Landsting) and an executive council (Landskapsstyrelse). The Ålands also elect one member to the Finnish Diet in Helsinki.

Enlarged Autonomy for Åland Islands

Since 1947 no inter-governmental controversy has arisen over the status of the Åland Islands, as Finland and Sweden have pursued ever-closer co-operation within the Nordic and other frameworks. From time to time statements by Swedish ministers have indicated that the Stockholm government monitors the situation of the islanders, but its conclusion has consistently been that the Finnish authorities are fulfilling their obligations as regards the preservation of Swedish language and culture. During the long era of the Cold War, the islands' military potential represented a sensitive regional factor, in that the Soviet government attached great importance to their remaining demilitarized (and to both Sweden and Finland remaining neutral states).

This background changed dramatically in 1990–91 when the Cold War ended and the Soviet Union disintegrated; but there appeared to be no likelihood that the status of the Åland Islands would be affected. When, in January 1992, Finland's restrictive 1948 friendship and mutual assistance pact with the Soviet Union was replaced by an even-handed good-neighbourliness treaty with the Russian Federation, Finland nevertheless remained bound by the 1947 peace treaty and by its stipulations regarding the Ålands. (For Finnish-Russian territorial issues, see Section 4.7.)

Four decades after the last autonomy measures for the Åland Islands, the Finnish Diet in February 1991 adopted, by a 170 to 8 majority, a major reform of the 1951 legislation intended to strengthen the islanders' right to self-government, especially in the economic sphere. Due to be implemented in 1993, the reform enshrined the islands' autonomous status in the Finnish constitution, which in the Helsinki government's view would provide additional surety that the best international norms would be respected (in the absence of any real international guarantee of autonomy).

The new act established the Ålands, for the first time legally, as a unilingual Swedish-speaking area and introduced more rigorous Swedish-language requirements for those applying for right of domicile in the islands. Other articles provided that the Ålands' parliament and executive council must participate in any international decisions concerning the islands, gave the islanders much greater scope to fly the Ålands' flag, and specified that residents' passports must show them as coming from the Ålands. Other provisions strengthened local legislative, administrative and financial powers, notably by giving the parliament full authority over population, ship and trade registration, banking and credit systems, employment and alcohol legislation. Nonetheless, opinions in favour of the dissolution of the union with Finland and joining Sweden are still heard from the islands.

Finland and Sweden both joined the European Union in 1995 following popular referendums. The Åland islanders also voted for EU membership but Finland negotiated some exceptions for the Ålanders. All the stipulations regarding the islanders' rights to self-government remained in force. In addition to this, the Åland Islands were exempted from EU directives on taxation. Because EU customs regulations do not apply to boats visiting the harbour of Mariehamn, the capital of the Åland Islands, boat passengers between Sweden and Finland are still allowed to buy tax-free goods whereas tax-free shopping elsewhere in the EU

was ended in 2000. The self-governmental status of the Finnish Åland province has proved a blessing for the Finnish and Swedish shipping companies.

Kimmo Katajala

4.9 Germany - Poland

The frontier between Germany and Poland has been subject to many changes over the past millennium. Until the 20th century the pattern was one of gradual German expansion eastwards into lands which, in many cases, became predominantly German in character and population. Germany's defeat in World War I reversed this process, although the 1919 Versailles peace settlement established German frontiers which still encompassed substantial territories to the east of the present border. The Nazi regime's drive to restore and extend the German Reich in the east ended in Germany's defeat in World War II. Principally at the behest of the USSR, in 1945 Germany was deprived of all its former territories east of the Oder (Odra) and western Neisse (Nysa Luzycka) rivers, most of their German inhabitants being expelled. The resultant German-Polish border question was complicated by the post-war division of Germany itself into Western and Soviet occupation zones which became, respectively, the Federal Republic of Germany (FRG) and the German Democratic Republic (GDR). Whereas the Communist GDR recognized the Oder-Neisse line in a treaty with Poland concluded in 1950, not until 1970 did the FRG do likewise, and then subject to the reservation that the existing border remained without international legal foundation pending a formal peace treaty between Germany and the wartime Allies. Although the FRG also signed a treaty with the GDR (in 1972), it maintained its policy of refusing to recognize East Germany as a foreign country and continued to have reunification as its constitutional goal.

This Cold War impasse persisted until the dramatic opening of the Berlin Wall in November 1989 and the attendant collapse of the GDR regime opened the path to reunification. After a rapid sequence of momentous events, this was achieved on Oct. 3, 1990, when the FRG in effect absorbed the East German territory. As a necessary prior step under international law, the two German governments plus the four powers with post-war responsibility for Germany (the USSR, USA, UK and France) on Sept. 12, 1990, signed a "final settlement" treaty, one of the clauses of which specified that unified Germany and Poland would "confirm the existing border between them in a treaty that is binding under international law".

However, not until after reunification was safely accomplished did the FRG, on Nov. 14, 1990, sign a treaty with Poland confirming the Oder-Neisse line as the definitive border between the two countries. In Germany the treaty had the almost unanimous support of the parties represented in the federal parliament, but vociferous opposition to it was expressed by parties of the extreme right. However with the subsequent ratification of the treaty by the parliaments of both Germany and Poland the question is now regarded as definitively settled. (See Map 41, p. 513, for the revision of the Polish-German border consequent upon World War II.)

Early German-Polish Relations—18th-century Partition of Poland

The complex and contentious history of Germany's territorial relationship with Poland dates back well over a thousand years. From the time of their arrival in the lands between the Oder and Vistula rivers (c. 700 AD), the Slav Polanie ("people of the open fields") faced a potential threat from German tribes to the west, given the absence of a natural frontier between the two peoples. Under the Piast dynasty, Poland became a powerful Christian kingdom from the late 10th century, encompassing not only the Polish heartlands but also the Slav province of Silesia in the west and, briefly, Pomerania in the north. But Polish disunity and fragmentation from the early 12th century coincided with the onset of large-scale colonization of Polish and other lands by German settlers from the west, often at the invitation of local rulers. On the Baltic coast, this German penetration eastwards was aided by the formation in 1190 of the Teutonic Knights, a military order which combined the work of Christian conversion with conquest and Germanization. By the mid-14th century the Knights had imposed feudal dominion over much of the southern and eastern Baltic littoral, including Latvia and Estonia, as the Hanseatic League (founded in 1368) began to establish German hegemony over regional trade. Ancient non-Slavic Baltic peoples Germanized by the Knights included the Prussians, who gave their name to a new German state founded in 1255 and centred on the fortress port-city of Königsberg (present-day Kaliningrad).

After nearly two centuries of internal strife, the Polish kingdom was reunified in 1320. Although Silesia was ceded to the kingdom of Bohemia in 1335 (and later passed to the Austrian Habsburgs), Poland itself entered a golden age under the Polish-Lithuanian royal union dating from 1386. In 1410 the combined forces of the dual monarchy won a major victory over the Teutonic Knights at Tannenberg, after which Poland-Lithuania became Europe's largest state, with suzerainty over most German principalities on the Baltic littoral, including Prussia. On the final dissolution of the Knights in 1560, Poland-Lithuania acquired Latvia (and Estonia passed to Sweden). However, even at its greatest extent, Poland-Lithuania's western frontier with the German empire was well to the east of the Oder-Neisse line. By 1500, moreover, the western and northern marches of Poland had been extensively penetrated by land-hungry ethnic Germans, who had established swathes of settlement in and around cities such as Posen (Posnan), Stettin (Szczecin) and Danzig (Gdansk). This process was abetted by the weakness of the Polish state after the Jagiello dynasty died out in 1572 and was complicated by the impact of the Reformation. Whereas the Poles and Lithuanians remained staunchly Catholic, the northern German states embraced Luutheran Protestantism, none more enthusiastically than Prussia, which in 1618 completed a Hohenzollern dynastic union with the German margravate of Brandenburg.

With Berlin as its capital, Brandenburg-Prussia made some territorial gains in the 17th century, notably by acquiring East Pomerania in 1648. But not until the 18th century did the kingdom of Prussia (as it became in 1701) begin its remarkable expansion, often at the expense of the Poles and other Slavs. After gaining most of West Pomerania from Sweden during the Great Northern War (1700-21), Prussia dispossessed the Austrian Habsburgs of Silesia during the War of Austrian Succession (1740-48), after which the Germanization of the province intensified, notably around Breslau (Wroclaw). Under the leadership of Frederick the Great, Prussia then came to the brink of defeat by Austria in the Seven Years' War (1756-63) but emerged victorious and ready to participate, with Austria and Russia, in the dismembering of the weak Polish kingdom. In the first partition of Poland (1772), Prussia took the coastal region east of Pomerania, renaming it West Prussia and thus establishing territorial contiguity with East Prussia (Königsberg). In the second (1793), Danzig and central western Poland came under Prussian rule (the latter territory becoming South Prussia). In the third (1795), Prussia annexed a segment of central Poland, including Warsaw, and renamed it New East Prussia. In these partitions, Austria acquired south-western Poland and Russia the vast eastern steppes, with the result that Poland as a state disappeared from the political map.

Prussia's defeat by Napoleon Bonaparte at Jena in 1806 resulted in the creation of a French-sponsored Grand Duchy of Warsaw the following year. But this partial reversal of the 18th-century Polish partitions was itself reversed on Napoleon's final defeat in 1815, although with the important difference that most of Prussia's gains from the second and third partitions were awarded to Russia by the Congress of Vienna. Russia therefore became ruler of the bulk of the old Polish kingdom, although Prussia retained the whole of the Baltic littoral, the Posen region and Silesia (and Austria retained Galicia and Lodomeria). As compensation for its partial retreat in the Slav east, Prussia was awarded substantial territories in the German west, thus strengthening its credentials to challenge Austria for the leadership of the German Confederation. As history records, by 1870 Hohenzollern Prussia had succeeded in uniting Germany (minus Austria) under its leadership, within borders which excluded the Habsburg domains but included Prussia's extensive territories to the east of the old Confederation frontier. Under the Second German Empire, the former Polish parts of these territories inevitably underwent further Germanization, resulting in part from the rapid growth of German economic power.

Re-establishment of Polish State—World War II

Meanwhile, the rump of old Poland had been fully integrated into Russia in 1831 and Polish national aspirations awaited a change in European power structures. This occurred in World War I (1914-18), in which the German, Austrian and Russian empires fought one another to destruction. Germany quickly avenged the Teutonic Knights' defeat 500 years earlier by routing invading Russian armies at another battle of Tannenberg (August 1914). Further Russian military reverses contributed to the collapse of Tsarist rule in 1917 and the seizure of power by Lenin's Bolsheviks, who sued for peace. Under the Treaty of Brest-Litovsk (March 1918), Russia was stripped not only of Poland but also of Finland, the Baltic provinces, Belorussia, the Ukraine and the Caucasus. But these draconian terms were invalidated by Germany's defeat in the west later in 1918 and by the resultant Versailles peace treaty of June 1919. Seeking to redraw the map of Europe on the principle of national self-determination, the Paris peacemakers recognized the new Polish republic, which had been proclaimed by Marshal Jozef Pilsudski in November 1918. Under the treaty, the Polish-German border was set mostly at the pre-partition line, except that Germany lost a small part of Silesia to Poland (which also regained Galicia from the dismantled Habsburg Empire). Germany therefore retained not only most of Silesia and Pomerania but also old East Prussia (Königsberg), so that the new Weimar Republic was, like pre-1772 Prussia, divided by a "corridor" of Polish territory up to German-populated Danzig, which became a "free city" under the League of Nations.

In the early 1920s it was Poland's eastern border that generated most dispute, as Marshal Pilsudski sought by force of arms to restore the full extent of the former Polish-Lithuanian empire in Belorussia and the Ukraine. The 1921 Treaty of Riga gave him considerably less territory but nevertheless established the Polish-Soviet border well to the east of the Curzon line (named after the then British Foreign Secretary) favoured by the Western powers in the light of ethnic and historical factors. Poland was thereby established as the largest state in Eastern Europe, but with aggrieved parties to both east and west. In Germany, resentment over the Versailles border settlement helped to bring the Nazis to power in 1933, inaugurating the Third German Empire. Although Hitler signed a non-aggression pact with Poland in 1934, his demand for *Lebensraum* ("living space") in the east, coupled with the Nazi belief in the racial superiority of Germans over Slavs, represented a growing threat to

Polish security. Poland's fate was sealed by the Nazi-Soviet non-aggression pact of Aug. 23, 1939, secret clauses of which provided for Poland to be divided into German and Soviet "spheres of influence", more or less on the Curzon line. A week later, on Sept. 1, Germany invaded Poland and, despite fierce Polish resistance, quickly overran it up to the Bug river east of Warsaw. Soviet forces entered Poland on Sept. 17 and occupied the eastern half of the country, meeting virtually no opposition. Although they could offer little practical assistance, Britain and France honoured their guarantees to Poland by declaring war on Germany on Sept. 3.

During World War II (1939-45), Germany annexed western and northern Poland, almost up to the full extent of Prussia's gains from the 18th-century partitions in central Poland and beyond them in the north. The annexations stopped just short of Warsaw, which served as the capital of the German-occupied "General Government of Poland". In the annexed territory the Polish population was either deported to Germany as forced labour or expelled to the General Government area. The Soviet Union likewise annexed its occupation zone and deported large numbers of Poles. However, this tacit German-Soviet co-operation in the dismemberment of Poland ended when Hitler launched his long-planned invasion of the Soviet Union in June 1941. In the first phase of rapid German advances, Nazi territorial dispositions included the extension of the south-east frontier of the Polish General Government to include the south-western Ukraine. But this German attempt to "move Poland eastwards" in compensation for the annexations in the west was thwarted by the eventual victory of the Red Army, which entered Warsaw in January 1945 and then drove the Germans out of western Poland. During the conflict Poland sustained colossal human and material damage, including the extermination by the Nazis of Polish Jewry.

Establishment of post-World War II German and Polish Borders

The Allies' victory over Germany in World War II enabled Stalin to impose a Soviet solution to the age-old question of Poland's territorial relationship with Germany. His solution was in effect to "move Poland westwards" by some 250 kilometres, at Germany's expense and to the Soviet Union's benefit. Pre-war Poland to the east of a slightly adjusted Curzon line (an area of about 178,000 sq km) was annexed by the Soviet Union, which also took the eastern end of Czechoslovakia (Transcarpathia) immediately to the south of the annexed Polish territory. As compensation, Poland's border with Germany was moved westwards to the line of the Oder and western Neisse rivers (in Polish the Odra and Nysa Luzycka respectively), so that Poland obtained some 101,000 sq km of German territory, including Silesia, eastern Brandenburg, Pomerania and southern East Prussia. Northern East Prussia (Königsberg/Kaliningrad), contiguous with what had become the Soviet republic of Lithuania, was annexed by the Soviet Union. Involving the expulsion of millions of Germans from lands acquired by Poland, these territorial dispositions restored the German-Polish border to roughly its position over nine centuries earlier.

The Soviet Union's claim to eastern Poland had been endorsed by the other two major Allied powers (Britain and the United States) at the Tehran conference between Stalin, Churchill and Roosevelt on Nov. 28-Dec. 1, 1943. Moscow's annexation of the territory was therefore not a matter of post-war international dispute, especially after a pro-Soviet Communist government had been installed in Poland in 1947. The Allies were also agreed on the need to extirpate the name of Prussia from the political map (this being formally decreed on March 1, 1947, on the grounds that "from its earliest days [the Prussian state] has been a promoter of militarism and reaction in Germany"). On the other hand, Stalin's redrawing of Germany's eastern borders, particularly the establishment of the Oder-Neisse line as the German-Polish frontier, gave rise to lasting controversy, not least in Germany. It was, moreover, a controversy given additional complexity by the post-war division of Germany itself into Western and Soviet occupation zones and by protracted disputes over the status and mutual relationship of the two German states which emerged in these zones.

Proposals for the frontiers of Germany after World War II had first been agreed upon by a European Advisory Council (constituted by Britain, the Soviet Union and the United States) as laid down in two protocols signed in London on Sept. 12 and Nov. 14, 1944. These proposals were finally agreed to by Britain in December 1944, by the United States on Feb. 1, 1945, and by the Soviet Union on Feb. 6 of that year. The protocol of Sept. 12 provided for the division of Germany (within its frontiers as at Dec. 31, 1937, i.e. before Hitler's annexations) into three occupation zones (British, US and Soviet), with Greater Berlin (as defined by a German law of April 27, 1920) to be occupied in separate sectors by the three Allied powers and to be administered by a joint *Kommandatura*. The protocol of Nov. 14 specified the limits of the Western zones and laid down (in 11 articles) details of the administration by the three military commanders who would form a Control Council. At the Yalta conference, held on Feb. 4-10, 1945, Churchill, Roosevelt and Stalin agreed that France should be invited to occupy a zone of Germany (including a zone of Berlin) and to co-operate in the Control Council as a fourth member.

On the question of Poland's frontiers, it was stated in the Yalta agreement: "The three heads of government consider that the eastern frontier of Poland should follow the Curzon line with digressions from it in some regions of five to eight kilometres in favour of Poland. It is recognized that Poland must receive substantial accessions of territory in the north and west. They feel that the opinion of the new Polish provisional government of national unity should be sought in due course on the extent of these accessions and that the final delimitation of the western frontier of Poland should thereafter await the peace conference".

In a message to the German people Marshal Stalin declared on May 9 that: "The USSR celebrates victory but it has no intention of dismembering or destroying Germany". However, the Soviet Union had on April 21, 1945, in an agreement with the Polish provisional government, specified that German territories to the east of the Oder and the western Neisse should be placed under Polish administration. This agreement did not become known to the Western powers until at least two months later. Although tacit acceptance was forthcoming from the provisional French government, the British government protested against the agreement. Moreover, the US State Department declared on June 29 that the transfer of the territories to Polish control was "an infringement of the Crimea [Yalta] decision and of the general tripartite understanding regarding the disposal of occupied German territory". President Truman, speaking on behalf of the three Western powers, stated in a message to the Polish provisional government on Aug. 1, 1945: "The territorial boundaries have been established. The actual agreement of the three heads of government [of Britain, the Soviet Union and the United States], however, was that the final delimitation of the western frontier of Poland should await the peace settlement and that, pending the final determination of the frontier, Stettin and the area east of the Oder-Neisse line should be under the administration of the Polish state".

In the final communiqué of the Potsdam conference, held by the heads of government of Britain, the Soviet Union and the United States between July 17 and Aug. 2, 1945, it was stated with regard to Poland's western boundaries that their "final delimitation...should await the peace settlement" but that "pending the final determination of Poland's western frontier the former German territories east of a line running from the Baltic Sea immediately west of Swinemünde [Swinoujscie], and thence along the Oder river to the confluence of the western Neisse river, and along the western Neisse to the Czechoslovak frontier, including that portion of East Prussia not placed under the administration of the USSR, and including the area of the former free city of Danzig, shall be under the administration of the Polish state, and for such purposes shall not be considered as part of the Soviet zone of occupation in Germany". In a previous section of the communiqué, it was stated that the conference had "agreed in principle to the proposal of the Soviet government concerning the ultimate transfer to the Soviet Union of the city of Königsberg and the area adjacent to it" and that the President of the United States and the British Prime Minister would "support the proposal of the conference at the forthcoming peace settlement".

Another chapter of the Potsdam agreement, entitled "Orderly Transfer of German Populations", recognized that "the transfer to Germany of German populations, or elements thereof, remaining in Poland, Czechoslovakia and Hungary, will have to be undertaken".

The Polish government, then and now, has consistently regarded the Potsdam decision on Poland's western frontiers as quite unambiguous on the following grounds: (i) that it refers, in an introductory section, to "the western frontier of Poland" and not to any provisional line of demarcation; (ii) that it uses the term "former German territories", thereby indicating that they are no longer regarded as belonging to Germany; (iii) that, as these territories were "not part of the Soviet zone of occupation", they were not part of Germany (the whole of which was placed under Allied occupation), and the "administration" referred to in the agreement had nothing in common with the Allied occupation but meant that the parties to the agreement consented to Polish administration in these territories; and (iv) that the transfer of the German population from the territories confirmed that the words "final delimitation" meant only the formal tracing of the border on the ground, which was also, in the Polish view, confirmed by the statement that the "final delimitation " would await a "peace settlement"—not a peace treaty.

The US State Department announced on Dec. 7, 1945, that since the end of hostilities 6,550,000 Germans had been moved from neighbouring countries to Germany (including 3,500,000 from Poland). According to a West German census of Sept. 13, 1950, almost 8,000,000 German "refugees and expellees" had reached the FRG so far, and it was said that the majority of them had been integrated and assimilated in an expanding economy. Some of the Germans who entered the FRG from the east organized themselves in *Landsmannschaften* (regional expellees' organizations), which were encouraged by some FRG politicians in their hope of returning one day to their region of origin, perhaps simultaneously with the restoration of a German Reich. Although a Charter of German Expellees, adopted on Aug. 5, 1950, expressed the wish of the *Landsmannschaften* to refrain from any act of revenge or the use of force, there existed in the FRG extremist anti-Polish groups which, among other activities, distributed maps showing Germany's frontiers as being those of 1914.

Creation of GDR and FRG

From 1946 onwards developments in the Soviet occupation zone on the one hand and in the Western occupation zones on the other diverged increasingly with the establishment of a Communist regime in the East and the gradual integration of the Western zones into the alliance of Western states—first in the Western European Union and later in the North Atlantic Treaty Organization. Owing to these developments the border between the Soviet and Western occupation zones eventually became a border between states, and the city of Greater Berlin was also divided into two separately administered parts.

West Germany took an important step towards sovereignty when a Grundgesetz (Basic Law or constitution) of the FRG was finally approved by a Parliamentary Council on May 8, 1949. In force from May 24 of that year, the Basic Law was (under its Article 23) to apply, in the first instance, not only in the Länder of the Western occupation zones but also in Greater Berlin. In a preamble to the law it was stated that its authors had "acted also on behalf of those Germans to whom participation was denied" and that "the entire German people is called upon to accomplish by free self-determination the unity and freedom of Germany". The Foreign Ministers of the three Western powers had made it clear, on April 22, 1949, that Berlin should not, at that stage, be included in the FRG as a Land. The chief burgomaster of West Berlin, however, signed the Basic Law on May 23. The FRG was inaugurated on Sept. 7, 1949, when its parliament elected the first Federal President, and on Sept. 14 the Bundestag (federal lower house) elected the first Federal Chancellor (Dr Konrad Adenauer).

The response in East Germany to the inauguration of the FRG was immediate. A new constitution, approved by a German People's Congress in East Berlin on May 30, 1949, declared inter alia: "Germany is an indivisible democratic republic built upon the Länder…There is only one German citizenship". A new state, the German Democratic Republic, was proclaimed on Oct. 7, 1949. It was immediately recognized by the Soviet Union whereas the Western powers and the FRG declared it to be "without legal basis" as its government had not been freely elected. Under the Treaty of Zgorzelec (Görlitz), signed on July 6, 1950, the Oder-Neisse line was declared to be the "frontier of peace and friendship" between the GDR and Poland. An agreement on the final delimitation of this frontier was signed on Jan. 27, 1951. In the FRG, neither of these instruments was regarded as having any validity, on the grounds that Germany's legal borders remained those of end-1937 until and unless they were changed by due process of international law.

Evolution of Separate German States in 1950s

Allied military government in the Western occupation zones was ended on Sept. 21, 1949, with the entry into force of an occupation statute (issued on April 10, 1949), which was "designed to encourage and facilitate the closest integration…of the German people under a democratic federal state within the framework of the European association". The statute laid down inter alia that any amendment of the Basic Law of the federal state would require the express approval of the occupation authorities before becoming effective. The Foreign Ministers of the three Western powers, meeting in New York on Sept. 12-14, 1950, declared that their governments "consider the government of the FRG as the only German government freely and legitimately constituted and therefore entitled to speak for Germany as the representative of the German people in international affairs". In a convention on the relations between the three Western powers and the FRG, signed on May 26, 1952, it was laid down (in Article 2) that, in view of the international situation which had until then prevented the reunification of Germany and the conclusion of a peace treaty, the three powers retained the rights and responsibilities which they exercised or held in respect of Berlin and of Germany as a whole, including the reunification of Germany and a settlement through a peace treaty.

The West Berlin constitution of Sept. 1, 1950, stated in Article 3 that "(i) Berlin is a German Land and at the same time one city; (ii) Berlin is a Land of the FRG; (iii) the Basic Law and laws of the FRG are binding for Berlin". In Article 7 it was stated (without any mention of the division of the city into two sectors) that the Berlin house of representatives (which replaced the city assembly) was entitled to decide, during a transitional period, that a law of the FRG would be applied without modification in Berlin. (Under the 1949 Basic Law, the West Berlin house of representatives appointed 22 delegates to the federal Bundestag, although without a vote on substantive matters; West Berlin also had four seats in the Bundesrat, the federal upper house.)

An anti-Communist rising by workers in East Berlin and other East German cities was crushed in June 1953 with the help of Soviet occupation troops, casualties being officially stated to include 25 persons killed and 378 injured, whereas the government of the FRG believed that 62 persons had been sentenced to death and 25,000 imprisoned. The number of refugees from East Berlin and the GDR was, in 1956, given as 122,000 in 1952, over 300,000 in 1953, over 184,000 in 1954 and over 252,000 in 1955, with the grand total since 1950 exceeding 1,500,000.

Under agreements signed in Moscow on Aug. 20-22, 1953, the Soviet Union waived further reparations payments from the GDR with effect from Jan. 1, 1954 (a similar decision being announced by Poland on Aug. 23, 1953). On March 25, 1954, the Soviet Union recognized the GDR as a sovereign independent state, in which the functions of the Soviet High Commission would be limited to security questions and to liaison with the Western Allies on all-German questions, with Soviet troops remaining in the GDR under the existing four-power agreements. The Bundestag, however, in a resolution adopted unanimously on April 7, 1954, refused to recognize the Soviet Union's right "to create an East German state" and reiterated the previously expressed West German view that the federal government had the sole right to represent the German people.

The FRG became a full and equal member of the Brussels Treaty Organization (later the Western European Union) and the North Atlantic Treaty Organization (NATO), as laid down in declarations embodied in the Final Act of a nine-power conference which ended in London on Oct. 3, 1954, and in agreements signed in Paris on Oct. 23 of that year. All of these texts subsequently entered into force on May 5, 1955, on which date the FRG achieved sovereignty. In a declaration incorporated into the 1954 Paris agreements, the FRG undertook "never to have recourse to force to achieve the reunification of Germany or the modification of the present boundaries of the FRG, and to resolve by peaceful means any disputes which may

arise between the Federal Republic and other states".

In a simultaneous declaration the three Western powers recorded their belief (i) that "a peace settlement for the whole of Germany, freely negotiated between Germany and her former enemies...remains an essential aim of their policy"; (ii) that the "final determination of the boundaries of Germany must await such a settlement"; (iii) that "the achievement through peaceful means of a fully free and unified Germany remains a fundamental goal of their policy"; and (iv) that "the security and welfare of Berlin and the maintenance of the position of the three powers there are regarded by the three powers as essential elements of the peace of the free world" and that "they will treat any attack against Berlin from any quarter as an attack upon their forces and themselves".

On the other side of the Iron Curtain, the GDR became a member of the Warsaw Treaty Organization at the latter's establishment on May 13, 1955. A treaty concluded between the USSR and the GDR on Sept. 20, 1955, stated in its preamble that both sides would respect the obligations undertaken by them under "international agreements relating to Germany as a whole" (and thus recognized by implication the four-power status of Berlin). In Article 1 it was stated that the GDR was henceforth "free to decide questions concerning its internal and foreign policy, including its relations with the FRG as well as its relations with other states". In Article 4 it was stated: "The Soviet forces at present stationed in the GDR under international agreements will continue to be stationed there temporarily with the approval of the government of the GDR and on conditions to be settled by an additional agreement between the two governments". In Article 5 the two sides stated that they would "make the necessary efforts towards a settlement by a peace treaty and towards the restoration of the unity of Germany on a peaceful and democratic basis".

Following the establishment of diplomatic relations between the FRG and the Soviet Union during a visit to Moscow by the Federal Chancellor (Dr Adenauer) on Sept. 9-14, 1955, the Soviet government stated on Sept. 15: "The Soviet government regards the FRG as a part of Germany. The other part of Germany is the GDR...The question of the frontiers of Germany was solved by the Potsdam agreement...The FRG is carrying out its jurisdiction on the territory under its sovereignty". Dr Adenauer, however, had stated at a press conference in Moscow on Sept. 14 that in the FRG's opinion a final settlement of Germany's frontiers must await the conclusion of a peace treaty and the government of the FRG was "the only legitimate government of all Germany".

"Ostpolitik" Treaties of Early 1970s—Provisional German Acceptance of Oder-Neisse Line

The division of Germany appeared to harden in the 1960s, as the FRG consolidated its "economic miracle" of the 1950s and widened the gap between the material conditions of its citizens and those of the

GDR. A member of the European Community (EC) since its creation in 1952, the FRG became an enthusiastic participant in West European integration, while in 1963 Dr Adenauer consummated post-war Franco-German reconciliation by signing a friendship treaty with President de Gaulle. By contrast, although it derived some benefit from the fact that East-West German trade was treated as "internal" under EC tariff rules, the GDR economy became bogged down in the rigidities of central state planning and locked into a Comecon trading system geared essentially to the interests of the Soviet Union. As the economic gulf between East and West Germany deepened, moreover, the Communist (Socialist Unity Party) SED regime in East Berlin increasingly combined hardline repression at home with slavish dedication to the Moscow line abroad. In 1968, for example, East German troops participated in the Soviet-led invasion of Czechoslovakia to crush Alexander Dubcek's "Prague Spring" (as did those of the equally hardline regime in Poland).

With the economic and political division of Germany and Europe having apparently become a permanent fixture of the international scene, FRG foreign policy underwent a significant reorientation in the 1960s, beginning after Dr Adenauer finally left office in October 1963. To many FRG politicians, especially within the Social Democratic Party (SPD), the established policy of rigid non-recognition of the GDR appeared to be dated and unproductive, as did the Adenauer line on the Polish-German border question. On the latter, there remained powerful voices opposed to any move towards recognition of the Oder-Neisse line (and in the mid-1960s the extreme right-wing National Democratic Party had some success in Land elections on a platform which called for the recovery of Germany's lost eastern territories). Nevertheless, the view gathered strength that FRG interests would be better served in the longer run if foreign policy became more geared to the realities of the existence of the GDR and of the Oder-Neisse line, although without abandoning the legal positions implicit in the Basic Law and other instruments.

For the proponents of the new school, the futility of the old line was demonstrated by an exchange towards the end of the Erhard chancellorship. In a note sent by the government of the FRG on March 25, 1966, to all governments with which it had diplomatic relations, and also to East European and Arab states, and containing proposals for peace and disarmament, it was asserted that under the 1945 Potsdam agreements the settlement of Germany's frontiers had been "postponed until the conclusion of a peace treaty with the whole of Germany" and that under international law Germany continued to "exist within its frontiers of Dec. 31, 1937, until such time as a freely elected all-German government recognizes other frontiers". In response to this note the Soviet Union declared on May 17, 1966, that the Oder-Neisse frontier was "final and unalterable"; accusing the FRG of trying "to restore the German Reich with all its pretensions", it pointed out that not a single European state had territorial claims against the FRG.

However, following the election to the federal chancellorship in October 1969 of Willy Brandt (former SPD chief burgomaster of West Berlin and Vice-Chancellor and Foreign Minister in the "grand coalition" of 1966-69), the government of the FRG embarked on a new "Ostpolitik" designed, as the new Chancellor stated on Oct. 28, to "arrive at a modus vivendi [with the GDR] and from there to proceed to co-operation" on the basis of the existing "two states of Germany" which "are not foreign countries to each other". Over the next three years the FRG proceeded to conclude treaties with the Soviet Union, Poland and the GDR respectively and these treaties incorporated various passages relating to the existing German borders.

Article 3 of the treaty of Aug. 12, 1970, with the Soviet Union stated: "The USSR and the FRG share the realization that peace in Europe can only be maintained if no-one disturbs the present frontiers. They undertake to respect the territorial integrity of all states in Europe within their existing frontiers; they declare that they have no territorial claims whatsoever against anybody, and will not assert such claims in the future; they regard as inviolable now and in the future the frontiers of all states in Europe as they are on the date of the signing of this treaty, including the Oder-Neisse line, which forms the western frontier of the Polish People's Republic, and the frontier between the FRG and the GDR". In Article 4 it was stated: "The present treaty between the USSR and the FRG does not affect any bilateral or multilateral treaties and agreements previously concluded by them". In a separate letter the FRG expressly stated: "This treaty does not conflict with the political objective of the FRG to work for a state of peace in Europe in which the German nation will recover its unity in free self-determination".

In the treaty with Poland, published on Nov. 20, 1970, Article 1 specified: "The FRG and the People's Republic of Poland state in mutual agreement that the existing boundary line, the course of which is laid down in Chapter IX of the decisions of the Potsdam conference of Aug. 2, 1945, as running from the Baltic Sea immediately west of Swinemünde, and thence along the Oder river to the confluence of the western Neisse river and along the western Neisse to the Czechoslovak frontier, shall constitute the western state frontier of the People's Republic of Poland. They reaffirm the inviolability of their existing frontiers now and in the future and undertake to respect each other's territorial integrity without restriction. They declare that they have no territorial claims whatsoever against each other and that they will not assert such claims in the future".

Article IV of this treaty stated: "The present treaty shall not affect any bilateral or multilateral international arrangements previously concluded by either contracting party or concerning them".

Article 3 of the Basic Treaty of Dec. 21, 1972, between the FRG and the GDR stated: "[The FRG and the GDR] affirm the inviolability, now and in the future, of the border existing between them, and pledge themselves to unrestricted respect for each other's territorial integrity". The treaty also stated, in Article 6: "The FRG and the GDR proceed from the principle that the sovereign power of each of the two states is confined to its [own] state territory. They respect the independence and sovereignty of each of the two states in its internal and external affairs". Under Article 9 the two sides also "agreed that bilateral and multilateral international treaties and agreements previously concluded by or concerning them are not affected by this treaty". Under a supplementary protocol the two sides agreed to set up a commission to "examine and, so far as is necessary, renew or supplement the demarcation of the border between the two states" and to "compile the necessary documentation on the line of the border".

The treaties with the Soviet Union and Poland entered into force on June 3, 1972. They had not been ratified by the Bundestag until May 17, 1972, and then only with the abstention of the opposition Christian Democratic and Christian Social Union (CDU-CSU) members and after the unopposed adoption of a joint resolution intended to clarify the FRG's position. In this resolution it was stated inter alia that "the treaties proceed from the frontiers as existing today, the unilateral alteration of which they exclude"; that "the treaties do not anticipate a peace settlement for Germany by treaty and do not create any legal basis for the frontiers existing today"; that "'the policy of the FRG, which aims at a peaceful restoration of national unity within the European framework, is not inconsistent with the treaties, which do not prejudice the solution of the German question"; that "the rights and responsibilities of the four powers with regard to Germany as a whole and to Berlin are not affected by the treaties"; and that the Bundestag, "in view of the fact that the final settlement of the German question as a whole is still outstanding, considers as essential the continuance of these rights and responsibilities".

The Basic Treaty between the FRG and the GDR was approved by the Bundestag on May 11, 1973, and by the Volkskammer (East German parliament) on June 13, and it entered into force on June 21, 1973. The Bundestag approved the relevant bill at its second reading by 268 votes to 217 (CDU/CSU). An application by the CSU Land government of Bavaria to the Federal Constitutional Court for a ruling as to whether the treaty was in conflict with the Basic Law (the constitution of the FRG) resulted in a court ruling, given on July 31, 1973, to the effect that the treaty did not conflict with the Basic Law. In this ruling the Court reaffirmed the continued existence in law of the German Reich (a thesis which, in the Court's view, had formed the basis of the 1949 Basic Law, or constitution, of the FRG) and took the view that the FRG was "a state identical with the state of the German Reich". The Court also declared reunification as being "constitutionally imperative" and explicitly referred in its decision to "the borders of the German Reich as at

Dec. 31, 1937" as one of several legal possibilities that might result from reunification. In September 1973 the FRG and the GDR were both admitted to membership of the United Nations.

The Final Act of the Conference on Security and Co-operation in Europe, signed in Helsinki on Aug. 1, 1975, by 35 countries (including all those of Europe except Albania), reaffirmed the inviolability of frontiers and the territorial integrity of states. The relevant passages—in Basket One, (A) I and IV—read as follows: "The participating states regard as inviolable all one another's frontiers as well as the frontiers of all states in Europe and therefore they will refrain now and in the future from assaulting these frontiers. Accordingly they will also refrain from any demand for, or act of, seizure and usurpation of part or all of the territory of any participating state...The participating states will respect the territorial integrity of any of the participating states".

Under a protocol agreed to at the conclusion of the Helsinki Final Act, between 120,000 and 125,000 ethnic Germans were allowed to leave Poland and settle in the FRG during the following four years, with further emigration applications being permitted after the expiry of that period. The protocol was signed on Oct. 9, 1975, and was finally approved on March 15, 1976. In the FRG it was stated that between early 1950 and September 1975 a total of 471,760 ethnic Germans had been allowed to emigrate from Poland to the FRG.

Opening of the Berlin Wall—"Two-plus-Four" Negotiations

For most of the 1980s the division of Germany and the legal impasse on the German-Polish border question appeared to belong in the category of international disputes which were unlikely to be resolved in the foreseeable future. The Cold War had re-intensified towards the end of the 1970s, and in December 1979 NATO decided that a new generation of intermediate-range nuclear forces (INF) would be deployed in the FRG (and certain other NATO countries). In Poland, a flowering of democracy in the first phase of the Solidarity trade union movement had been snuffed out with the imposition of martial law in December 1981. In retrospect, however, it is clear that the history of the East-West divide in Europe entered a radically new phase in March 1985 with the accession to power in the Soviet Union of Mikhail Gorbachev. Committed to restructuring the moribund Soviet economy (perestroika) and to "openness" (glasnost) in the media and cultural spheres, Gorbachev released a surge of pro-democracy feeling throughout the Eastern bloc. The new mood was accentuated by the signature in December 1987 of a Soviet-US treaty providing for the removal of INF missiles from Europe and highlighted by the warmth of the reception given to Gorbachev when he visited the FRG in June 1989.

In the GDR, the late 1980s saw a rising tide of popular demonstrations against the SED regime and against the division of Germany. Large numbers of

GDR citizens showed their discontent by fleeing to other East European countries with the aim of reaching the FRG, in whose embassies thousands took refuge. In September 1989 the FRG Chancellor, Helmut Kohl, secured agreement from the Hungarian authorities that 50,000 GDR refugees currently in Hungary would be allowed to travel to West Germany. Similar agreements were reached in respect of GDR refugees in Poland and Czechoslovakia. In the GDR itself, massive anti-government protests led to the removal of Erich Honecker as SED leader and head of state on Oct. 18, 1989 (after 18 years in power), shortly after a visit to East Berlin by Gorbachev. The following month, as the popular upsurge became irresistible, the GDR authorities on Nov. 9, 1989, surprised the world by announcing the opening of "all border crossings" to the FRG and West Berlin. Amid huge national and international celebration, Germans from each side of the familiar divide were at last free to move to the other. The Berlin Wall and its extensions, hated symbols of the Cold War, were quickly demolished by the German citizenry.

Placing himself at the head of this remarkable turn of events, Chancellor Kohl presented a 10-point plan to the Bundestag on Nov. 28, 1989, proposing the creation of a new German confederation as a framework for eventual reunification. The following month EC heads of government, meeting in Strasbourg on Dec. 8-9, 1989, supported a process of German unification which was "in full respect of the relevant agreements and treaties and of all the principles defined by the [1975] Helsinki Final Act" and embedded in European integration. At that stage, the view in the FRG was that German unity might take several years to achieve—a timescale which was, moreover, the initially preferred scenario of several other Western governments. However, an acceleration in the pace of events in 1990 persuaded FRG ministers that unification was not only achievable within months rather than years but also urgently necessary in light of the threat of economic collapse in the GDR. In the latter respect, concern focused on the economic and social problems arising from the mass exodus of GDR citizens to the FRG. Only speedy unification, it was believed, could arrest this dangerous trend.

A key development was a meeting between Kohl and Gorbachev in Moscow on Feb. 10, 1990, during which the latter accepted the principle that Germans had the right to live within one German state. Three days later, on Feb. 13, the two German governments and the four former Allied powers with post-war responsibility for Germany (the USSR, the United States, the United Kingdom and France) agreed to initiate urgent "two-plus-four" talks on the "external" legal and security aspects of reunification. Meanwhile, the Communist regime in the GDR had collapsed and campaigning had begun for the country's first-ever free elections. Held on March 18, 1990, these were won by an alliance headed by the GDR wing of the Christian Democratic Union, although the resultant GDR coalition government included the SPD and Free

Democrats. On April 19, the new GDR Prime Minister, Lothar de Maizière, declared his government's commitment to German unity. On May 18, in Bonn, GDR and FRG ministers signed a Treaty Establishing a Monetary, Economic and Social Union. This treaty was approved by the Bundestag and the Volkskammer on June 21 and by the Bundesrat on June 23. It entered into force on July 1, 1990.

NATO and Group of Seven summits—held respectively in London on July 5-6 and in Houston (USA) on July 9-11, 1990—both welcomed the prospect of German unification. Kohl then made another important trip to the USSR, where in Stavropol on July 15-16 he secured Gorbachev's agreement that unified Germany would have full sovereignty and be free to join whichever alliance it wished (i.e. it would be able to maintain the FRG's NATO membership). Up until this point, the Soviet government had resisted the idea that a united Germany would be a NATO member, at first advancing the old Soviet concept of a neutral Germany and later suggesting that unified Germany might belong to both NATO and the Warsaw Pact (as successor to the FRG and the GDR respectively). That Gorbachev yielded on this important matter in part reflected the view of other Warsaw Pact states, notably Poland and Czechoslovakia, that a neutral Germany would pose a greater potential threat than one anchored in NATO. Also agreed at the Stavropol talks was a reduction in the FRG's armed forces to a maximum of 370,000 men and the withdrawal of Soviet troops from East Germany over three to four years.

The Stavropol accord cleared the way for the "two-plus-four" talks to reach broad agreement in Paris on July 17, 1990, on the "external" aspects of unification. Since March 1990 the Polish government had been a specially invited participant in these talks insofar as they dealt with the German-Polish border question. Under the formula agreed in Paris, international legality would be bestowed on the reunification of Germany by means of a "treaty of settlement" rather than a peace treaty. The USSR had originally called for a peace treaty, on the precedent of those concluded with other Axis powers of World War II at Paris in 1947, but was eventually persuaded that a treaty of settlement would be more appropriate in 1990.

The Reunification of Germany, October 1990

On Aug. 23, 1990, the GDR Volkskammer resolved that the five newly-restored Länder of East Germany (Mecklenburg-West Pomerania, Brandenburg, Saxony, Saxony-Anhalt and Thuringia) would accede to the FRG on Oct. 3, 1990. On Aug. 31, in Berlin's Crown Prince Palace, the FRG Interior Minister, Wolfgang Schäuble, and the GDR State Secretary to the Prime Minister, Günther Krause, signed a Treaty on the Establishment of Germany Unity. In the FRG, this historic document secured approval by the Bundestag on Sept. 20 by 442 votes to 47; in the GDR, on the same day, the Volkskammer endorsed it by 299 votes to 80. FRG deputies opposed to the treaty included the

Greens and 13 Christian Democrats; in the GDR the Greens likewise voted against but the bulk of the opposition came from the Party of Democratic Socialism (PDS), successor to the SED.

The "two-plus-four" process culminated in the signature in Moscow on Sept. 12, 1990, of a Treaty on the Final Settlement With Respect to Germany. This instrument formally ended the four wartime Allies' rights and responsibilities in relation to Berlin and Germany, the latter being accorded "full sovereignty over its internal and external affairs". Described by the Soviet Foreign Minister, Eduard Shevardnadze, as drawing "the final line under World War II", the treaty confirmed "the final nature" of the existing frontiers of Germany. It also recorded Germany's renunciation of nuclear, biological and chemical weapons, and provided for the withdrawal of Soviet forces from East Germany by the end of 1994. After that date, the only forces permissible in the ex-GDR would be "German units of territorial defence which are not integrated into the alliance structures" to which unified Germany might choose to belong (i.e. NATO). Until the completion of the Soviet withdrawal, US, British and French forces would remain in Berlin "at German request".

As an adjunct to the treaty, the FRG Foreign Minister and the GDR Prime Minister signed a letter dealing with certain matters which the USSR, in particular, had sought to have included in the treaty text itself. The letter specified that memorials to the victims of war and fascism would be maintained and that political parties "intent on impairing or eliminating...freedom and democracy" would be banned in unified Germany. The letter also confirmed that "expropriations carried out on the basis of occupation law and occupation sovereignty (1945-49) [could] no longer be reversed". In a separate bilateral exercise, the FRG and the USSR on Sept. 13, 1990, signed a 20-year friendship and co-operation treaty and three other agreements, one of which covered the FRG's pledge to make a major financial contribution to the maintenance of Soviet troops in East Germany until end-1994 and to their eventual resettlement in the USSR.

Legally the "two-plus-four" treaty could not come into force until it had been ratified by all the signatories. However, in order that unification could take place on Oct. 3 as scheduled, the four wartime Allies on Oct. 1 signed a document in New York suspending their responsibilities and rights for Germany and Berlin pending ratification. The London and Potsdam agreements of 1944-45 and the Quadripartite Agreement on Berlin of 1971 were thereby suspended. This enabled unification to become a fact at midnight on Oct. 2/3, 1990, amid joyous celebrations in Berlin and throughout German territory. At that moment the GDR ceased to exist, as the five East German Länder acceded to the Federal Republic of Germany under Article 23 of the FRG Basic Law.

United Germany had a population of some 78,000,000 (substantially the largest in the European Community) and an area of 357,000 sq km (second

only to France in the EC). Emergency procedures agreed by the EC Council of Ministers on Sept. 12, 1990, provided for the immediate integration of the FRG's new Länder into the Community. All-German general elections were held on Dec. 2, 1990, for a Bundestag enlarged to 662 seats, and gave a modest new majority to the ruling coalition of Christian Democrats and Free Democrats under Helmut Kohl. In June 1991 the Bundestag voted narrowly in favour of Berlin (the official capital of Germany under the unification treaty) becoming the FRG's government and legislative seat, instead of Bonn.

Completion of the "external" legalization of Germany's reunification entailed, first, the submission of the "two-plus-four" treaty to the CSCE summit meeting held in Paris on Nov. 19-21, 1990, at which the Cold War in Europe was officially declared to be over (and notice given of the dissolution of the Warsaw Pact). Second, the treaty required ratification by its signatories. Ratification by the FRG Bundestag and Bundesrat took place on Oct. 5 and 10, 1990, respectively, the latter date also being the occasion of the US Senate giving consent, with the specific qualification that its decision should not be construed as implying US acceptance of the Soviet annexation of Estonia, Latvia and Lithuania in 1940. UK ratification was notified on Nov. 9 and the French National Assembly approved the treaty on Dec. 13. The last, and most crucial, ratification was that of the USSR Supreme Soviet, which was accomplished on March 4, 1991, together with ratification of the FRG-USSR co-operation treaty. The deposit of Soviet instruments of ratification in Bonn on March 15, 1991, was the final piece in the jigsaw, marking the definitive legal achievement of full sovereignty by the unified German state.

Treaty Confirmation of Existing Polish-German Border

During the rapid progress towards German reunification, Chancellor Kohl came under considerable international pressure, especially from the Polish government, to give an unequivocal, legally-binding undertaking that the FRG accepted the post-1945 Oder-Neisse border with Poland. In these exchanges, the FRG position was seen to shift somewhat but in essence held to the established line that any treaty commitment beyond those given in the 1970 treaty with Poland and in the 1975 CSCE Final Act must await reunification and united Germany's achievement of full sovereignty under international law. In November 1989 the FRG Chancellor was on a six-day visit to Poland when the news came through of the opening of the Berlin wall on Nov. 9. He interrupted his visit to go to Bonn and West Berlin on Nov. 10-11, one of his cancelled engagements in Poland being a German-language mass at the Franciscan monastery in Annaberg in Silesia (where in 1921 a Polish uprising against German rule had been put down by forces of the Weimar Republic).

In a statement issued on the eve of the Kohl visit,

the FRG government said that Poland should know that "its rights to live within safe borders will not be called into question by us Germans" and that "the wheel of history will not be turned back". The statement was a response to pressure from Poland to resolve the ambiguity surrounding the fact that the 1970 treaty had guaranteed the inviolability of the Oder-Neisse line without making the border definitive under international law. After being cheered by thousands of ethnic Germans at Krzyzowa in southern Silesia on Nov. 12, Chancellor Kohl the following day told an audience at the Catholic University of Lublin that he appreciated East European fears about German unity and stressed that Germany was now committed to the democratic, Christian values of Europe and to a United States of Europe. "Warsaw, Moscow, Prague, Budapest and Vienna are as much part of Europe", he said, "'as Brussels, London, Paris, Rome and, of course, Berlin". A joint declaration signed on Nov. 14, 1989, by Kohl and the Polish Prime Minister, Tadeusz Mazowiecki, committed the FRG to accepting the fact of the post-1945 frontiers of Poland and gave a reciprocal pledge of respect for minority German and Polish cultural rights. It also provided for consultation and co-operation between the two countries and for substantial FRG financial assistance to Poland.

In February 1990 Chancellor Kohl came under renewed criticism for the FRG's reluctance to give a legally-binding commitment to the Oder-Neisse border. On Feb. 28, 1990, he bowed to pressure from other governments and from within his own coalition by proposing that the Bundestag and the GDR Volkskammer should each make a statement on the border after the forthcoming GDR elections. However, further controversy surrounded a statement from the Chancellor's office on March 2 that a new FRG commitment on the border "would have to make it clear that the Polish government's declaration of Aug. 23, 1953, waiving any claims to reparations from Germany, remains valid and that the rights of Germans as agreed by Chancellor Kohl and Prime Minister Tadeusz Mazowiecki in the joint declaration of Nov. 14, 1989, will be regulated by a treaty". This statement not only unleashed strident criticism from the Polish and other European governments but also strained relations between Kohl and FRG Foreign Minister Hans-Dietrich Genscher, of the Free Democratic Party, the junior coalition partner. Discussions within the FRG government eventually resulted in an agreement on March 6, 1990, that both German parliaments would issue a government-backed declaration after the GDR elections, to the effect that Germany had no territorial claim against Poland and would not link the border question with either reparations or the rights of ethnic Germans in Poland.

After the GDR elections on March 18, 1990, the Volkskammer on April 12 adopted a declaration affirming "the inviolability of the Oder-Neisse frontier" and also accepting joint responsibility for Nazi atrocities in Poland and elsewhere during World War II. During a visit to Poland on May 2-4, 1990, the FRG President, Richard von Weizsäcker, said: "Poland's current western frontier will remain inviolable. Neither today nor in the future do we make any claims whatsoever on territory in Poland or in any other neighbouring country". The following month, on June 21, 1990, the FRG Bundestag and the GDR Volkskammer adopted identically-worded resolutions calling for the existing Polish-German border to be "definitively confirmed by a treaty under international law" and reaffirming the "inviolability of the frontier existing between [Germany and Poland] now and in the future". In the 400-member GDR parliament, the resolution was adopted with only six votes against and 18 abstentions. In the FRG Bundestag, the vote was 486 in favour, 15 against (including the CDU president of the German expellees' organization) and three abstentions.

In a powerful speech urging the Bundestag to adopt the resolution, Chancellor Kohl argued that the understandable attachment of many Germans to historic German territories in the east should be weighed against the greater good of reunification. Declaring that "we must give a clear answer to the question of the Polish western frontier", he continued: "Let no-one be mistaken: today we face an absolutely clear choice. Either we confirm the existing border or we gamble away the chance of German unity". Referring to the past, the Chancellor said: "I am aware that, in view of the 700-year history of the Germans in the regions beyond the Oder and Neisse, it is not easy for a number of colleagues…to vote in favour of this resolution…We look back on a long shared past during which the towns and villages of Silesia, eastern Brandenburg, Pomerania, West and East Prussia and other regions were home to Germans…The 700-year history and culture of the German part of Eastern Europe is and will remain a fundamental part of the German nation's heritage". He also described the post-1945 expulsion of Germans from "their native regions" as "a grave injustice" which still had "no justification, either moral or legal". Coming to contemporary circumstances, the Chancellor said: "Today the territories beyond the Oder and Neisse rivers have become home to Polish families of the second and third generations…The unification of Germany now offers an opportunity to achieve final and lasting reconciliation with the Polish people".

As finally signed on Sept. 12, 1990, the "two-plus-four" treaty settling the "external" aspects of German unification dealt with the border question, in Article 1, as follows: "(i) The united Germany shall comprise the territory of the FRG, the GDR and the whole of Berlin. Its external borders shall be the borders of the FRG and the GDR and shall be definitive from the date on which the present treaty comes into force. The confirmation of the definitive nature of the borders of the united Germany is an essential element in the peaceful order of Europe. (ii) The united Germany and the Republic of Poland shall confirm the existing border between them in a treaty that is binding under international law. (iii) The united Germany has no territorial claim whatsoever against other states and shall not assert any in the future". In the FRG-USSR co-operation treaty signed on Sept. 13, 1990, Article 2 contained a reciprocal undertaking "to respect the territorial integrity of all states in Europe" and a declaration that the FRG and the USSR had no territorial claims against any state and would not make any such claim in the future.

Bilateral German-Polish Border and Friendship Treaties

In accordance with the settlement treaty's stipulation, the FRG government, after unification, proceeded the following month to enter into a formal treaty commitment with Poland that existing borders were definitive. The treaty was signed in Warsaw on Nov. 14, 1990, by Genscher and his Polish counterpart, Krzystof Skubiszewski, and specified that the German-Polish border was as defined in the 1950 GDR-Polish treaty and later implementing agreements and in the 1970 FRG-Polish treaty. Prior to the signing, Chancellor Kohl and Prime Minister Mazowiecki had met at the German-Polish border, first on the German side at Frankfurt an der Oder and then on the Polish side at Slubice. In signing the treaty by which Germany gave up all claim to territory now forming a third of the area of Poland, Genscher described the step as a difficult one for the millions of Germans who had been expelled from these lands, but noted that the treaty surrendered nothing that had not been lost long ago.

German-Polish relations were subsequently consolidated by the signature on June 17, 1991, of a 10-year treaty of good-neighbourliness and friendly co-operation. The treaty included, for the first time, formal Polish recognition of the right of the ethnic German minority in Poland (numbering some 500,000) to their own language, culture, family names and religion. But contrary to the wish of some German Christian Democrats, it did not include a "right of return" for expellees or cover the use of German place names in German-populated areas. Instead, these matters were dealt with in an accompanying exchange of letters, in which the FRG also pledged support for eventual Polish membership of the EC. For its part, Poland declared that the prospect of its joining the EC "will increasingly create opportunities to make it easier" for German citizens to settle in Poland.

The November 1990 border treaty and the June 1990 friendship treaty were both ratified by the German and Polish lower houses of parliament on Oct. 17 and 18, 1991, respectively. During the Bundestag debate, Chancellor Kohl said that the friendship treaty enshrined a formal recognition of the German minority in Poland. In the Polish Sejm, Foreign Minister Skubiszewski said that the implications of the treaties went beyond bilateral relations, in that without German-Polish reconciliation there could be no unified Europe. In the Polish voting only one deputy opposed the border treaty (and six abstained), whereas there were 26 votes against the friendship treaty (and 60 abstentions). In the Bundestag there was near-unanimous approval for the friendship treaty, whereas 25 deputies (all CDU or CSU) voted against the border treaty. Shortly before the ratifications, a bilateral agreement had been signed under which Germany would provide financial compensation for certain Polish victims of Nazi crimes.

Among German parties not represented in the Bundestag, those of the extreme right, including the Republicans and the German People's Union (DVU), condemned the border treaty with Poland as a surrender of historical German territory to which the FRG had a legitimate claim under international law. In 1991 such parties made some electoral progress, notably in the Bremen Land election in September, and Polish migrants in Germany increasingly suffered from neo-fascist violence directed against "foreigners". These developments caused some renewed friction in German-Polish relations, which early in 1992 were also strained by an FRG proposal that a special economic development zone should be created to straddle the Oder-Neisse border. While the post-Communist Polish government welcomed the growing German economic presence in Poland, the zone proposal was seen by some Poles as would-be German "recolonization" of lost territories. On the other hand, the ratification of the Oder-Neisse treaty was generally regarded as having resolved once and for all the long dispute over Poland's western border. Indeed, in 1991 it was Poland's eastern and northern borders that came more into the news, as the Soviet Union disintegrated and the independent successor republics of Lithuania, Belorussia and Ukraine found that their existing borders with Poland, as decreed by the Soviet Union after World War II, were subject to challenge—see Section 4.13.

Recent Developments on Polish-German Border

Since 1994 six new bridges across the border have been opened, and Germany has become Poland's biggest foreign trade partner, in 2001 accounting for more than US $8.25 billion, or 35 per cent, of Polish exports and US $8.45 billion, or 26 per cent, of its imports. Visas were abolished in 1990, and border crossings since then have risen tenfold, although it is fair to say that even in 2004, on the eve of Poland's accession to the European Union, the disparity in incomes between Poland and Germany is still so marked that relations between Poles and Germans remain correct rather than friendly. The German border patrols, which still include former East German Volkspolizei (Vopos) who used to guard the Berlin Wall and the Iron Curtain, have in recent years been kept fully occupied trying to stem the tide of would-be immigrants from Eastern Europe, some of whom still drown trying to cross the fast-flowing waters of the Oder and the Neisse. The desire of the substantial number of German speakers left behind in Poland, particularly in central Silesia, to assert their rights to their own language and cultural traditions has continued to arouse some tension, but has been kept within limits acceptable to the national and local authorities.

Peter Calvert

4.10 Greece - Turkey

Disputes between Greece and Turkey over the Aegean Sea, which lies between the Greek and Turkish mainlands, have for some years been a source of tension between the two countries and have on several occasions given rise not merely to diplomatic measures but also to states of military alert in either or both states. In the present day the only major islands in the Aegean under Turkish sovereignty are Gokceada (Imvros) and Bozcaada (Tenedos) in the northern Aegean close to the mouth of the Dardanelles. Greek sovereignty over most of the others was confirmed by the 1923 Treaty of Lausanne, in the dismemberment of the non-Turkish parts of the Ottoman empire, which followed World War I, while the Dodecanese in the south-eastern Aegean were ceded to Greece by Italy after World War II under the 1947 Treaty of Paris. Since then neither side has officially sought to challenge the respective sovereignties resulting from these territorial adjustments. However, an unresolved and acrimonious dispute over the delimitation of the Aegean Sea in part reflects historical animosities between Greeks and Turks in the eastern Mediterranean and recurrently stimulates sentiment in sections of both populations that existing territorial arrangements are unsatisfactory. An aggravating factor has been the unresolved problem of the island state of Cyprus, which has been effectively partitioned since 1974 into Greek Cypriot and Turkish Cypriot areas (see Section 4.6).

After a deterioration of relations between Greece and Turkey caused by a series of incidents, the most serious being the dispute over Imia/Kardak in 1996, relations between the neighbouring countries have greatly improved since the summer of 1999. Many agreements on mutual issues have been produced, but disputes regarding the Aegean Sea have yet to be resolved. (Map 42 on page 513 illustrates this entry.)

Historical Background

The establishment of Greece's sovereignty over most of the Aegean islands in the 20th century has stemmed from its aspiration to bring within the national territory all those areas with longstanding Greek populations which had previously been excluded for various reasons; moreover, the eastern Aegean islands have major strategic importance for Greece in that they command most of the eastern coastline of Turkish Anatolia (Anatalya). Since 1970, however, attention has been increasingly focused on the mineral potential of the continental shelf in the Aegean itself, and consequently questions of maritime, strategic, economic and purely territorial advantage have become intermixed. The arguments surrounding the sovereignty of the continental shelf between the eastern Aegean islands and the Greek mainland remain problematic, based as they are on complex rulings and conventions, parts of which can be, and frequently are, quoted to the advantage of either party. Cases in point are the UN conventions on the continental shelf (1958) and the law of the sea (1982), which Turkey has declined to ratify while at the same time disputing Greece's interpretation of their application to the Aegean situation. Indeed, in respect of the 1982 convention, Turkey has stated that any unilateral Greek attempt in the eastern Aegean to apply its general provision for a territorial waters limit of 12 nautical miles would be regarded as a *casus belli*.

The Aegean dispute, although currently centring on the law of the sea, is nonetheless relevant to a consideration of the territorial relationships between Greece and Turkey insofar as it has often been the theatre in which other disputes were enacted. It has been particularly important, for example, at various stages of the Cyprus dispute, whether in terms of military strategy or of actual territorial bargaining; moreover, the resentment still felt by many Turks at the Greek possession of the islands can be seen as a significant factor in the general and continuing tension between the two countries. Although Turkey has at present no formal claims for their return, the issue remains politically alive in Turkey and has frequently been exploited as a source of electoral support, particularly by nationalist forces. Greek spokesmen recall that during and after World War II (in which Turkey remained neutral until the final stages) claims to the Aegean islands emanated from various Turkish sources. They also point out that in 1976 the extreme right-wing National Action Party (NAP) leader and then Deputy Prime Minister, Col. Alparslan Turkes, made a series of controversial statements on the alleged Turkish character of the Greek Aegean islands, demanding that all islands within 50 kilometres of the Anatolian coast (including Lesbos and the Dodecanese) should be returned to Turkey.

As far as Greek opinion is concerned, its perception of Turkish intentions remains historically coloured by the disastrous defeat suffered by Greek forces in the 1921-22 war with Turkey. This was initiated by Greece in an attempt to secure the Ottoman territories which it had been awarded under the 1920 Treaty of Sèvres— i.e. most of Thrace west of Constantinople (Istanbul), the islands of Imvros and Tenedos and the Dodecanese (except Rhodes), as well as mandated authority over the Anatolian port of Smyrna (Izmir) and its hinterland. Lacking any support from the European powers, the Greek forces were driven out of Anatolia by Kemal Ataturk in 1922. Under the Treaty of Lausanne of July 24, 1923, Greece recognized Turkish sovereignty over the disputed territories, except that the Dodecanese were formally ceded to Italy (which had occupied them since 1911 and had backed the Turks in the recent war). Although the 1922 disaster effectively marked the end of "greater Greece" aspirations, in many Greek minds the episode is still seen as an avoidable defeat for Christian Europe at the hands of the Muslim East.

In the post-World War II era the exigencies of the international balance of power brought both Greece and Turkey into the North Atlantic Treaty Organization (NATO) and the two countries have also come together under the umbrella of the Council of Europe. Nevertheless, their relations have continued to be adversely affected by underlying historical strains and in particular by Greek suspicions concerning Turkey's military intentions in the area. These strains have from time to time escalated into open diplomatic conflict, notably in connection with the occupation of northern Cyprus by Turkish troops in July 1974, in protest against which Greece withdrew its armed forces from NATO until the 1980s.

Basic Greek and Turkish Positions on the Continental Shelf Issue

The argument adduced by Greece as regards the current Aegean Sea dispute is fundamentally based on the theses (i) that every island is entitled to a full continental shelf; (ii) that under international law and practice (including Turkish practice in the Black Sea and the Mediterranean Sea) Greece has the right in principle to extend its territorial waters in the Aegean, presently set at six nautical miles, to a maximum of 12 miles—a right which Greece says it is not prepared to surrender in the face of Turkish pressure; and (iii) that in accordance with the principles of indivisibility of sovereignty and political unity the national territory of one country cannot be "enclaved" in the continental shelf of another country, as would be the case if Turkish claims to the Aegean shelf west of the Greek islands were to be accepted.

The first-mentioned argument concerning the continental shelf of islands was based in particular on the UN convention on the continental shelf adopted on April 23, 1958, within the framework of the first UN Conference on the Law of the Sea held in Geneva on Feb. 24-April 28, 1958. This convention, which was ratified by Greece but not Turkey, for the first time codified pre-existing rules and practice on continental shelf delimitation. Article 1 defines the shelf as "(a) the seabed and subsoil of the territorial areas adjacent to the coast, but outside the area of the territorial sea, up to a depth of 200 metres or, beyond that limit, to where the depth of the superjacent waters admits of the exploitation of the natural resources of the said areas; (b) the seabed and subsoil of similar submarine areas adjacent to the coasts of islands". Articles 2 and 3 provide inter alia that the coastal state exercises exclusive rights to the exploitation of mineral resources in the shelf, although these rights "do not affect the legal sta-

tus of the superjacent waters as high seas, or that of the airspace above those waters" (implying that international shipping, etc, would normally enjoy free passage over the continental shelf).

The 1958 convention also provided that, in cases where a continental shelf bordered on two or more countries (as, for example, the Aegean borders on Greece and Turkey), the boundary of the shelf was to be determined by mutual agreement; failing that, and unless unusual circumstances justified a different solution, it would, according to Article 6, follow the median line "every part of which is equidistant from the nearest points of the baselines from which the breadth of the territorial sea of each state is measured" (i.e. a line half-way between what could reasonably be described as the broad coastal outlines of the two countries). Failing bilateral agreement, disputes were to be settled by the compulsory jurisdiction of the ICJ (a principle rejected by Turkey as a non-signatory of the convention), or by an independent arbitral tribunal.

On territorial waters, Greece bases its case primarily on the comprehensive law of the sea convention adopted in New York on April 30, 1982, by the third UN conference. Among its provisions, this convention lays down in Article 3 that every state "has the right to establish the breadth of its territorial sea up to a limit not exceeding 12 nautical miles, measured from baselines determined in accordance with this convention". It also provides for boundaries of (i) up to 24 nautical miles for a "contiguous zone" (within which a state would control customs, immigration and other matters), (ii) up to 200 miles for an exclusive economic zone and (iii) 200 miles for a continental shelf boundary (to be extended to up to 350 miles in certain circumstances). Among the 130 countries voting in favour of this convention was Greece, whereas Turkey was one of four that voted against.

The convention finally entered into force only in November 1994, after agreement had been reached on modifications to take account of resistance to its provisions on the exploitation of the resources of the deep seabed. Greece pointed out that resistance to ratification was almost wholly on grounds unrelated to the convention's territorial waters and other boundary provisions which had, Greece argued, become the international norm and were recognized as such by the International Court of Justice. It was, therefore, Greece's position that the starting-point in any negotiations with Turkey must be recognition of the Greek right to a 12-mile territorial limit.

The Turkish argument is based on the claim that the Aegean is a special case. While not at present seriously disputing Greek sovereignty over the Greek Aegean islands, Turkey maintains that in geological terms they represent an extension of the Anatolian peninsula and that they thus fall within the scope of a statement made by the International Court of Justice in a 1969 case concerning the North Sea continental shelf, to the effect that the rights of the coastal state extend over "the areas of the continental shelf which constitutes a natural prolongation of its land territory". Proceeding on this basis, Turkey has claimed what amounts to half of the Aegean, defining the rightful delineation of the continental shelf as that which follows the north-south median line between the Greek and Turkish mainlands. On Nov. 1, 1973, the Turkish *Official Gazette* published a map based on this principle and showing a line which starts from the mouth of the River Evros (Meric) on the Greek/Turkish mainland border and passes to the west of Samothrace, Lemnos, Aghios Efstratios, Lesbos, Psara, Chios and most of the Dodecanese.

Turkey allows each of the Greek islands a six-mile territorial waters limit but rejects the Greek view that a 12-mile limit, having become the international standard, is its legal entitlement in the Aegean. In Turkey's view, Article 3 of the 1982 convention means that 12 miles is the "maximum" limit that a country may set—in the case of the Aegean, it contends, the stipulation of the convention that exercise of the rights given by the convention should not constitute "an abuse of right" clearly applies. According to Turkish figures, the existing six-mile limit gives Greece 43.7 per cent of the area of the Aegean as its territorial waters, while Turkey has only 7.5 per cent and 48.8 per cent are high seas (i.e. international waters); however, if a 12-mile limit were established, 71.5 per cent of the Aegean would become Greek territorial waters, against 8.8 per cent for Turkey and only 19.7 per cent high seas. Turkey has therefore repeatedly warned that even a partial Greek declaration of a 12-mile limit would be regarded as an immediately unacceptable attempt to turn the Aegean into a "Greek lake".

Greece responds to this argument with the claim that Turkish shipping would enjoy the right of innocent passage both through Greek territorial waters and over the Greek continental shelf, although military shipping would be subject to certain restrictions including a ban on manoeuvres.

Confrontations in 1970s over Oil Prospecting and Cyprus

Although the prospects of finding significant oil deposits in the Aegean appear modest at present, the question of Greek and Turkish prospecting rights in the Aegean has prompted the most open manifestations of Greek and Turkish claims in respect of the continental shelf, and has at times led to military tensions and confrontations in the area. Turkey has on the whole treated its regular seismic exploration of the Aegean as part of the process of registering its claim to the sovereignty of the eastern Aegean continental shelf. Greece, on the other hand, describes this kind of practice as an attempt to resolve the dispute by fait accompli, and rejects the legitimacy of the Turkish explorations, although it accepts the right of the Turkish seismic vessels to innocent passage when they are not actually prospecting.

Following the November 1973 publication of the Turkish map claiming half of the continental shelf, the Turkish government offered on Feb. 27, 1974, to negotiate with Greece on the question of jurisdiction over the Aegean outside the two countries' territorial waters. No Greek reply being forthcoming, work was started in April-May 1974 on the seismic exploration by Turkey of 27 sites in the Aegean. Greece offered on May 25 to negotiate with Turkey on the basis of the 1958 Geneva convention, but repeatedly asserted its claim to any oil found under the continental shelf; however, Turkey rejected the Geneva convention as a basis for discussion, and a deadlock ensued which repeated bilateral discussions at ministerial level failed to resolve.

Relations between the Turkish government and what was then the Greek military regime worsened steadily during the following months, and deteriorated markedly on July 20, 1974, when Turkish troops launched an invasion of northern Cyprus. One important consequence of this crisis was the closure of Aegean air space to commercial traffic, as a result of unilateral action by both Turkey and Greece on grounds related to their continental shelf claims. Not until February 1980 were the Aegean air corridors reopened, in a reversion to the pre-1974 status quo which left the basic dispute entirely unresolved.

Turkey resumed its plans to explore the Aegean seabed in January 1975. However, on Jan. 30, the Norwegian vessel *Longva,* which had contracted to undertake the mission, refused to prospect in disputed waters, so that the project was cancelled. It then proved difficult for Turkey to find vessels of other nationalities to undertake research on its behalf. The most serious military confrontation of this period involved the Turkish vessel, *Sismik I* (a converted ship formerly known as the *Hora),* which began in late July 1976 an exploration of the disputed waters between Lemnos and Lesbos despite calls from several countries, including the United States, for a postponement of its activities. Turkey had already on July 15, 1976, threatened that any Greek interference with the mission would be met by force, but when the *Sismik I* sailed on July 23 it was shadowed by the Greek oceanographic research vessel *Naftilos* and by several Greek warships.

Greece protested to Turkey on Aug. 7 at the alleged violation of its continental shelf, although Turkey replied that there was neither a Greek nor a Turkish continental shelf while the issue was in dispute.

On Aug. 10, 1976, the Greek government called for an emergency meeting of the UN Security Council in view of what appeared to be a threat of war. It also, on the same date, petitioned the ICJ on the merits of the case, asking for a temporary injunction banning the Turkish exploration while the case was pending. The Security Council met on Aug. 12 and passed a resolution on Aug. 25 recommending that the two countries should enter into negotiations, keeping in mind the availability of UN dispute-resolution machinery such as the ICJ. On Sept. 11, 1976, the ICJ rejected the Greek application for a temporary injunction on Turkish exploration. A wide range of issues was raised by the two sides in presenting their cases to the UN

Security Council. Turkey referred to the "unwarranted harassment" of the *Sismik I,* accused Greece of attempting to annex Cyprus by the overthrow of Archbishop Makarios on July 15, and complained particularly of what it described as the illegal Greek militarization of the eastern Aegean islands (i.e. in contravention of the 1947 Paris peace treaty between the Allies and Italy, under which the Dodecanese had been ceded to Greece and to which Turkey was not a party).

Since the 1960s—and particularly after the 1974 Turkish intervention in Cyprus—Greece had engaged in the military development of certain of the eastern Dodecanese in view of what was regarded as a direct military threat from Turkey. Turkey had responded in July 1975 by creating a new Fourth Army division, known as the "Aegean Army", comprising all ground and naval units on the Aegean coast, with its headquarters in Izmir.

Unsuccessful Attempts to Find a Settlement, 1975-87

Greece had proposed to Turkey on Jan. 27, 1975, that the Aegean dispute should be placed before the ICJ, and the Turkish government had immediately agreed. It rapidly became clear, however, that opinions within Turkey were divided on the advisability of this course, and Turkey began later that year to insist that the ICJ should be invited to rule only on matters which could not be decided by bilateral negotiation. Greece, while agreeing to have bilateral discussions, nevertheless maintained its application to the ICJ for a ruling on the merits of the case. Following the 1976 confrontation and a period of similar tension in March 1977 over Turkish drillings and military manoeuvres in the Aegean, Greece on July 18, 1977, submitted a memorial of its arguments to the Court (its application to the ICJ being filed under the 1928 General Act on the Peaceful Settlement of International Disputes, to which Turkey is a signatory). Turkey, however, refused to recognize the authority of the Court, which began its examination of the case in late 1977. In a decision of Dec. 19, 1978, the ICJ found that it was incompetent to make a ruling, since in its opinion the case had territorial implications, which had been excluded from its jurisdiction by a Greek reservation at the time of the signature of the General Act.

Meanwhile, in accordance with Turkey's wishes, the two countries engaged from September 1976 onwards in bilateral discussions with the aim of determining a technical basis for the delineation of Aegean seabed rights. The first such discussions took place in New York in September 1976 between the Greek and Turkish Foreign Ministers, and on Nov. 11, 1976, an agreement was signed in Berne providing for the establishment of a joint standing committee of experts to study "inter-state practice and international rules for the determination of sea-bed boundaries" and also containing an undertaking that both sides would refrain from any initiative or action which might have an adverse effect on the negotiations. Although the talks were broken off in 1977 during a period of particular tension over naval manoeuvres in the Aegean, they resumed in March 1978, when it was agreed by both countries to refrain from publishing details of the discussions in order to avoid disturbance by domestic factors on either side.

The military coup in Turkey in September 1980 had the effect of blocking further substantive discussions, which were officially terminated when the Papandreou government came to power in Greece in October 1981. Following the gradual restoration of civilian rule in Turkey from 1983, the authorities in Ankara sought to initiate new talks with Greece on all the issues which divided the two countries. However, preliminary talks in mid-1983 were cut short by Turkey's recognition of the newly-proclaimed Turkish Republic of Northern Cyprus, and the Athens government ruled out any further direct discussions until Turkey undertook to withdraw its troops from Cyprus and to accept what the Greek side termed "the existing legal regime in the Aegean".

Greece also repeatedly raised its complaints against Turkey within the forum of the European Community, which it joined as a full member in 1981. The Greek insistence on this issue was forthright, notwithstanding the European Commission's recommendation at the time of admission that the Community should not be made a party to Greek-Turkish territorial disputes. As a prelude to its application for full membership of the European Community (lodged on April 14, 1987), the Turkish government confirmed in February 1987 that it intended to lift a decree dating from 1964 preventing Greek nationals living in Istanbul (numbering about 7,000) from selling their property. The lifting of this decree had been required by Greece as a condition for accepting the application of the EC-Turkey association agreement on Greek territory. It did not make Greece more amenable to full Turkish membership (Greece being the only Community country to vote against the referral of the Turkish application to the European Commission on April 27). Greek charges of Turkish mistreatment of Greek nationals in Istanbul were regularly countered by Turkish allegations that Turks on the Greek side of the border in Thrace suffered officially-condoned disadvantages.

More serious problems also arose within the context of the North Atlantic Treaty Organization, where Greek-Turkish aerial and naval tensions proved a real obstacle to co-operation in security matters. Conflict surrounded the refusal of NATO to use the Greek army and air force bases at Lemnos, or their reconnaissance facilities, in aerial or naval manoeuvres, on the grounds that this would amount to taking sides on the disputed issue of Greece's right to develop military installations on the island. Greece, on the other hand, argued that the 1923 Lausanne treaty's demilitarization of Lemnos and Samothrace effectively ended with the signature of the 1936 Montreux Convention, which entitled Greece and Turkey to remilitarize Lemnos and the Straits respectively (with adjacent islands). In 1982, 1983 and 1984, Greece cancelled its participation in NATO exercises in northern Greece, largely because of the NATO refusal to incorporate Lemnos into combined manoeuvres in the Aegean. Both sides repeatedly expressed apprehension over NATO proposals for military expansion in one or the other country, with Greece insisting that the United States' fixed ratio of assistance (US$10 to Turkey for every US$7 to Greece) must be maintained at all costs.

December 1986 Military Frictions in Thrace

The area of Thrace between Istanbul and the River Evros (which forms the border between Greece and Turkey) has remained within Turkey's borders since the defeat of Greek forces in the 1921-22 war with Turkey. Although Greece no longer lays any formal claim to any part of the territory, and although relations between the mixed Greek and Turkish elements on either side of the border have been generally peaceful, they have tended to improve or deteriorate in accordance with the climate of bilateral relations. The region's proximity to Samothrace and Imvros has lent a particular local currency to the issues of territorial waters and general Aegean security, and the conflicts over the Aegean, Cyprus and other issues were reflected in the late 1970s and 1980s in considerable tensions which periodically erupted into violence.

One of the worst of these incidents occurred on Dec. 19, 1986, on the Evros border near the Greek town of Ferrai, when a Greek soldier and two Turkish soldiers were killed in what was described by the Greeks as a calculated ambush of one of its patrols. The shooting took place as Greek troops were attempting to prevent Iranian refugees from crossing the border, it being alleged by the Greek side that the Turkish authorities were assisting such illegal entry. Both sides claimed that the other had committed a territorial infringement.

The Turkish Prime Minister, Turgut Ozal, said that the incident proved the need for Greek-Turkish dialogue and renewed an offer made in April 1985 to conclude a treaty of friendship and co-operation with Greece and to guarantee the existing frontiers between the two countries. However, the Greek government rejected the proposal as "a trap".

Further Aegean Tensions, 1986-87

In the Aegean Sea, periodic incidents in the early 1980s developed into further sharp tensions from mid-1986, with each side accusing the other of violations of national airspace by military aircraft and of infringements of territorial waters. On July 29, 1986, the Greek government protested over the alleged violation of its coastal limits by the Turkish scientific research vessel *Piri Reis,* while it was reported the next day that Turkey had complained that Greek aircraft and warships had harassed the vessel in international waters. A further Greek protest was lodged over an incident on Sept. 16, when it was alleged that Turkish warships had fired five volleys close to a

Greek patrol boat in international waters near Lesbos. The Turkish authorities rejected the protest, however.

Further incidents occurred in the Aegean in early March 1987 involving the *Piri Reis,* with the Greek authorities protesting that its course near or around Greek islands was provocative and the Turkish side again complaining of harassment of the vessel. Relations were also strained by the tabling of a government bill in the Greek parliament on March 6 providing for government control of the North Aegean Petroleum Company (NAPC), which exploited the Prinos oilfield off the island of Thasos. The Athens government justified this step on the grounds that the NAPC's stated intention to begin exploratory drillings outside the Greek territorial limit (but within what Greece regarded as its continental shelf) should be a state responsibility in view of the potential international implications. The Turkish government responded that it would take "the necessary measures to safeguard its rights and interests in the Aegean" if the NAPC proceeded with its plans, claiming that any exploration would be in breach of the 1976 Berne agreement, under which the two sides had undertaken not to search for oil outside their respective territorial waters while the continental shelf issue remained unresolved. The Greek side replied that in its view the Berne agreement was no longer valid and asserted that Greece would decide when, where and how to conduct exploration on the "Greek continental shelf".

On March 25, 1987, the Turkish government decided to issue a permit to the state owned Turkish Petroleum Corporation (TPAO) for oil exploration outside Turkish territorial waters, off the Greek islands of Lesbos, Lemnos and Samothrace. On the following day the Athens government warned that if the TPAO research vessel *Sismik I* carried out work "in areas where under conventional and customary law the continental shelf belongs to Greece", Greece would take "the necessary measures to ensure its sovereign rights". Greece also reiterated its long-standing offer to submit the Aegean Sea continental shelf dispute to the arbitration of the ICJ.

The Greek Prime Minister, Andreas Papandreou, stated on March 27, 1987, that the Greek armed forces would "teach the Turks a very hard lesson" if Turkey continued with its "aggressive acts" in the Aegean, and warned that in the event of hostilities breaking out US military bases in Greece would be closed. Amid reports that the armed forces of Greece and Turkey had been placed on alert, strenuous mediation efforts were mounted within the NATO framework and produced an announcement by the Turkish Prime Minister later on March 27 that the *Sismik I* would not commence exploratory operation outside territorial waters unless the Greek side did so first. Although the vessel set sail from the Dardanelles on March 28 accompanied by a naval escort, the Turkish government announced later in the day that the escort had been withdrawn and that the *Sismik I* would not operate in disputed waters. For its part, the Greek government also gave assurances that oil exploration would not be conducted in disputed areas and that NAPC plans in that respect had been frozen. In the period after the March 1987 crisis, the Greek and Turkish Prime Ministers exchanged messages in which the former again urged that the Aegean dispute should be submitted to the ICJ, while the latter repeated his preference for bilateral talks to resolve the matter.

Although the immediate crisis subsided, further incidents in 1987 included alleged violations of Greek airspace in September during the annual US-Turkish military manoeuvres in the Aegean. Moreover, in October 1987 Turkey filed a map with the International Maritime Organization showing the customary Turkish mid-point delimitation of the Aegean and including many Greek islands in the area in which Turkey proposed to provide search and rescue services. The Greek government issued a formal rejection of this map on Jan. 11, 1988, shortly before further strains in Greek-Turkish relations were caused by clashes between ethnic Turks and Greek police in Western Thrace.

1988 Davos Summit—Lack of Real Progress in Resumed Bilateral Talks

Nevertheless, there was an unexpected improvement in bilateral relations at the end of January 1988 as a result of a summit meeting in Davos (Switzerland) between the Greek Prime Minister, Dr Papandreou, and his Turkish counterpart, Turgut Ozal. In their talks (held on Jan. 30-31), the two leaders agreed to hold regular meetings thereafter and to establish a "hotline" link with a view to defusing the sort of crises that had brought the two countries to the brink of war in the past. They also decided to set up joint committees on economic co-operation and on the main areas of political disagreement, including the Aegean dispute, Cyprus, Greek opposition to Turkish membership of the European Community, and the rights of the national minority in the other's country.

On Feb. 6, 1988, the Turkish government formally lifted the 1964 decree freezing the assets of Greek nationals in Istanbul and made it clear that it expected Greece to reciprocate by taking a more accommodating line on Turkey's relations with the European Community. Some difficulties remained, in that Greece argued that the decree must be made retroactive (so that compensation would be payable for losses incurred during the freeze). Nevertheless, after the Turkish Prime Minister had given assurances, at a further meeting with Papandreou in Brussels on March 3-4, 1988, that all discriminatory measures against ethnic Greeks in Turkey would be rescinded, Greece lifted its veto on some aspects of the further development of the Community's existing association agreement with Turkey (although without modifying its basic opposition to full Turkish membership). At the Brussels meeting, which was held in the wake of a NATO summit, the two leaders agreed to "abstain from any action or declaration which would under-

mine the spirit of Davos". Subsequently, senior Greek and Turkish officials met in Athens on March 30-April 1, 1988, to discuss ways of moderating recurrent tensions over air and naval exercises in the Aegean.

On May 23-27, 1988, Mesut Yilmaz undertook what was reported to be the first visit to Greece by a Turkish Foreign Minister since 1952. During the visit the new Greek-Turkish joint committee on political issues reached agreement on the prevention of friction over military exercises in the Aegean (which were to be avoided in the peak tourist season) and on a formula for reciprocal respect of each other's sovereignty in the region. It was also agreed that visa requirements on each other's diplomats would be relaxed and that both sides would expurgate bias on the history of Greek-Turkish relations in their school textbooks. The following month, on June 13-15, 1988, Ozal became the first Turkish premier to visit Greece since 1952, holding talks with Papandreou in what was described as a "constructive spirit".

The new relationship continued with a visit to Ankara on Sept. 5-7, 1988, by the Greek Foreign Minister, Karolos Papoulias, who reached agreement with his Turkish counterpart that both sides would refrain from actions and statements which might adversely affect bilateral confidence. Agreements on co-operation against international terrorism and smuggling were also concluded, while a simultaneous meeting on economic co-operation, held in Athens, made progress on a range of issues. However, an intended visit to Ankara by Papandreou did not take place before he lost power in June 1989, by which time the "spirit of Davos" had all but evaporated. By mid-1989 familiar strains in Greek-Turkish relations had reappeared and the two sides remained far apart on the Aegean delimitation dispute.

Cyprus was the main immediate cause of renewed tension, in that the Greek government regarded the ending of the island's partition as an urgent priority and blamed the Turkish government for the lack of progress in that direction. By the end of 1989, moreover, the Ankara government was blaming Greece for the European Community's effective rejection, at least until 1993, of Turkey's membership application. In its opinion on the application, delivered on Dec. 18, 1989, the European Commission said that workers', citizens' and minority rights in Turkey all fell short of EC norms, despite recent improvements, while Turkish social and economic conditions were such that EC membership would present major difficulties. The Commission added that it "could not overlook the negative effects" of continuing Greek-Turkish differences, especially over Cyprus.

Renewed unrest in Western Thrace caused a further deterioration in Greek-Turkish relations in January 1990. Tension mounted in the area after two leaders of the 120,000-strong local Muslim community had been found guilty on Jan. 26 of "inciting violence and dissension" and of using the word "Turkish" in their political literature (in contravention of a Greek Supreme Court ruling of 1988). Clashes between Greeks and ethnic Turks in Komotini on Jan. 29 resulted in about 20 people being injured and in the Turkish ambassador in Athens being recalled to Ankara on Feb. 1. Two days later the Turkish consul-general in Komotini was expelled by the Greek government for having referred to the local Muslims as "fellow countrymen". Turkey responded immediately by expelling the Greek consul-general in Istanbul.

The delicate situation in Western Thrace was rendered even more fragile by the arrival, starting in 1989, of substantial numbers of Pontian Greeks from the Soviet Union. These immigrants were descended from the inhabitants of the ancient Greek cities of the Black Sea (Euxinos Pontos) and had become dispersed in recent times. Official Greek sources put their number in the Soviet Union at about 500,000, of whom at least 20 per cent were thought likely to take advantage of more lenient travel rules to leave the country. The Greek government's plan to resettle Pontian Greeks in Thrace drew criticism from Turkey that it was intended to alter the region's demography, but Greece dismissed such protests as "unwarranted intervention in Greek domestic affairs".

Impact of Gulf War and of Soviet and Yugoslav Disintegration

The impasse between Greece and Turkey on the Aegean dispute persisted into the 1990s, as each side periodically rehearsed its established positions and devoted substantial effort and resources to presenting its case to the wider world. From August 1990 the onset of the Gulf crisis represented a diversion from bilateral exchanges, in that both Greece and Turkey became active participants in the US-led multinational coalition against Iraq. Once Kuwait had been liberated by the end of February 1991, there was much international expectation that the US government would exert its influence on both Athens and Ankara to promote a negotiated settlement of outstanding issues, beginning with the Cyprus problem. Such expectations were heightened when US President George Bush included both Greece (July 18-19, 1991) and Turkey (July 20-22) on a tour of US allies in the region. However, efforts to bring about a resumption of direct talks between the parties to the Cyprus dispute ran into difficulties in the second half of 1991.

The rapid disintegration of the Soviet Union in 1991 added further complexities to regional power relationships with a bearing on the Greek-Turkish dispute. The end of the Cold War in Europe meant that Turkey's special status as a front-line NATO member facing the menace of communism was reduced in Western eyes. At the same time, Turkish external policy became increasingly focused on the opportunities provided by the predominantly Turkic-populated Islamic republics of the former Soviet Union. In Greek eyes, this Turkish interest in building relations with the newly independent Central Asian republics confirmed what many Greeks had claimed all along—namely that Turkey was an Asian state and not a European one.

Accordingly, Greece hoped that Turkey's new preoccupation with the east would make it easier, if Western opinion were brought to bear, to secure a settlement in the west confirming that the Aegean was essentially a Greek/European sea rather than half Turkish/Asian.

On the other hand, it became clear that, notwithstanding the disappearance of the Soviet threat, Turkey remained a valued ally of the United States. Most immediately, there was the perceived need for continued containment of Iraq to Turkey's south. More broadly, the US government backed Turkey's overtures to the ex-Soviet southern republics, seeing growing Turkish influence there as preferable to penetration by Iran and Islamic fundamentalism. Moreover, Turkey's new easterly interest in no way diminished its perception of itself as a European country or its aim of joining the European Community. For example, pursuit of its "European" vocation was apparent in Turkey's keen interest in the post-1991 disintegration of Yugoslavia, and here too Turkish-Greek differences intruded. Emulating the EC member states, Turkey extended speedy recognition to newly independent Slovenia, Croatia and Bosnia-Herzegovina early in 1992. Unlike the EC states, it also recognized Macedonia, on which EC reservations reflected the fear of the Greek government that an independent Macedonia might have territorial ambitions on Greek Macedonia (see Section 4.19). For the Turkish government, this possibility was not regarded as a reason for withholding recognition.

Notwithstanding the Cyprus and Macedonia complications, the newly elected Turkish Prime Minister, Suleyman Demirel, met his Greek counterpart, Konstantinos Mitsotakis, at another Davos summit on Feb. 1, 1992. They issued a seven-point joint communiqué recording that the two governments were planning to conclude an accord of friendship and co-operation later in the year and were committed to working together towards a negotiated settlement of the Cyprus issue under UN auspices. On the substantive aspects of the Aegean Sea dispute, however, the two leaders made no apparent progress in bridging long-standing differences between the two sides.

Continuing Incidents, 1992-95

The unresolved Cyprus issue placed a constant strain on Greek-Turkish relations post-1991. The Greek-Turkish Aegean dispute posed problems for NATO in 1992, with disagreements over a new command structure in terms of regional command and the deployment of forces. Consultations between Andreas Papandreou, the Greek Prime Minister, and Glafcos Clerides, leader of the Greek Cypriot authorities, in November 1993 resulted in closer ties in defence planning, commonly known as the "defence dogma". The first joint manoeuvres resulting from this, in October 1994, provoked an angry response from Ankara. In addition, Greece continued to claim that Turkey was violating its ten-mile airspace, recorded intrusions increasing from approximately 240 in 1991 to over 700 in 1995. Greece initially vetoed a customs union (in December

1994) between Turkey and the EU, but this veto was subsequently withdrawn when Cyprus was given a definite timetable for EU accession in 1995.

In February 1995, a Turkish F-16 fighter plane crashed near the island of Rhodes while exiting the Athens Flight Information Region. Two Greek Air Force Mirage F-1 planes had intercepted the Turkish fighter plane. The F-16's pilot safely ejected and was later rescued by a Greek search-and-rescue helicopter and repatriated. In May 1995, a Turkish Minister, Yildirim Aktuna, with a delegation of parliamentary committee members and press, made an unofficial visit to the Greek region of Thrace. During the visit, Aktuna complained that ethnic Turks in the area were suffering discrimination at the hands of the Greek government. A violent demonstration in Thessaloniki against the visiting Minister by Greeks, Cypriots, Armenians and Kurds provoked criticism from Turkish Prime Minister Tansu Ciller. Greek government spokesman Evangelos Venizelos denied repeated claims from Turkish sources that Greece was providing military training to Kurdish activists.

In June 1995, the Greek parliament ratified the 1982 UN Convention on the Law of the Sea, which had entered into force the previous November (see above). The issue of whether Greece would or indeed could impose a twelve-mile limit around its Aegean islands instead of the six nautical miles adhered to by Turkey (Turkey has not ratified the convention), provoked fierce arguments from both countries. Ankara repeated the threat that the imposition of a twelve-mile limit would in effect make the Aegean a "Greek lake", which was unacceptable and would be regarded as a *casus belli*. Athens stated that it would not impose a twelve-mile limit, but insisted that under international law, it had the right to do so.

Imia/Kardak Crisis—Further Military Tensions

An incident in December 1995 led Greece and Turkey to the brink of armed conflict. The dispute centred upon the uninhabited islet of Imia (in Greek) or Kardak (in Turkish), which lies approximately 3.8 miles from the Anatolian coast of Turkey and 5.5 miles from the Greek island of Kalimnos. On Dec. 25, 1995, a Turkish freighter, the *Figen Akat*, ran aground on Imia/Kardak rocks. The Greek authorities offered to commence salvage operations on Jan. 20, 1996, but the captain of the freighter refused the offer, stating the vessel was in Turkish territorial waters. The Greek and Turkish media soon both began stirring up the issue of sovereignty on both sides on the Aegean. Greece rejected Turkish claims of sovereignty over the islet and vice versa. The mayor of the nearby Greek island of Kalimnos raised the Greek flag on Imia/Kardak, only for it to be replaced by a Turkish flag by Turkish journalists. Greek and Turkish commandos became involved, in addition to naval vessels from both countries.

At the height of the crisis, a significant number of opposing forces were situated barely a few hundred yards apart. US President Bill Clinton and US diplomats quickly intervened in the dispute and armed conflict was avoided. National flags were removed and armed forces pulled back. Many nationalists from Greece and Turkey were not happy at this compromise. A view repeatedly expressed by Turkey is that the question of Imia/Kardak and many other islands falls into the unresolved problem regarding so-called "grey zones" in the Aegean, in which the status of certain islands, islets or rocks has not been officially determined through international treaties.

Partly in response to this incident, in November 1996 the Greek government announced a ten-year programme to modernize and expand its armed forces at a cost of US$16 billion. Turkey opposed the inclusion of the island of Gavdos in NATO "Dynamic Mix" exercises in 1996 in view of its (in Turkey's view) disputed status. Again, in May 1997, Turkish President Demirel caused outrage in Greece when he questioned the sovereignty of over a hundred islands in the Aegean.

In January 1997, Glafcos Clerides, the Greek Cypriot leader, announced that the Republic of Cyprus had ordered 48 S-300 air defence missiles from Russia, these being intended to protect Greek/Greek Cypriot air and naval bases. Immediately, Turkey threatened to use the Turkish air force and any means possible to prevent installation of the missiles. On Jan. 20, 1997, Rauf Denktash, the Turkish Cypriot leader, and Turkish President Demirel signed a joint defence agreement, declaring any attack on the Turkish Republic of Northern Cyprus (TRNC) would be an attack on Turkey. In May 1997, exercises by the Greek and Turkish air forces over Cyprus threatened to spill over into direct conflict.

Various attempts at easing Greek-Turkish tensions were made in 1997, but with little lasting success. In March 1997, the Turkish Chief of General Staff visited the Greek embassy in Ankara and in April, Greece and Turkey agreed to set up committees of "wise men" to propose ideas to resolve the dispute in the Aegean. In July 1997 at the NATO conference in Madrid, the two sides agreed to implement confidence building measures and respect sovereign boundaries. Greek and Turkish officials reached agreement on six principles to govern their bilateral relations. However, within a few months, the two countries were again in dispute regarding Aegean airspace and sovereignty matters. A deterioration in Turkey-EU relations occurred at the European Union's Luxembourg Summit on Dec. 12-13, 1997, when Greece and other EU countries blocked the inclusion of Turkey in the list of states to be assigned candidate status for the next round of EU enlargement.

In January 1998, the Greek/Greek Cypriot military base at Paphos in Cyprus became operational for use by Greek fighter planes. The S-300s ordered by the Clerides government were in part intended to protect the Paphos installation. The Greek government, noting the Turkish threat to use any means possible to prevent installation of the missiles, stated that any attack on the Paphos airbase would be met with immediate retaliation. On June16, 1998, Greece sent four F-16 fighter planes and C-130 transport planes to Paphos airbase. In response to this, Turkey sent six F-16s to the Gecitkale airbase in northern Cyprus on June 18. The issue was partly resolved after consultations between Greek Cypriot leader Clerides and Greek Prime Minister Simitis and much diplomatic pressure, especially from the USA and UK. It was eventually announced in December 1998, amid considerable Turkish protests, that the S-300 missiles would be stationed on Crete (out of range of the Turkish mainland).

In October 1998, relations were strained once more when Turkish fighter jets "buzzed" the Greek Defence Minister in travelling to and from his duties in Cyprus. The seizure in February 1999 in Kenya by Turkish secret service agents of Abdullah Ocalan, the leader of the Kurdish Workers' Party (PKK) separatist organization in Turkey, after he had been flown into Greece by a retired army officer and then sheltered in the Greek embassy in Nairobi, led to renewed accusations from Turkey that Greece was supporting and giving aid to the PKK.

Greek-Turkish Rapprochement

In the aftermath of the Ocalan affair, three ministers were forced to resign and George Papandreou replaced the more hard-line Theodoros Pangalos as Greek Foreign Minister. Papandreou announced that he had no objection if Greece's Muslim minority referred to themselves as Turks, ignoring the convention that minorities in Greece are described on religious rather than ethnic grounds. This drew widespread criticism from nationalists in Greece and from inside his own party.

Greece and Turkey co-operated in addressing the refugee issue caused by the NATO intervention in Kosovo in March 1999 and agreed to discuss bilateral issues, but two unpredictable events caused the most significant thaw in Greek Turkish relations. On Aug. 17, 1999, an earthquake measuring 7.4 on the Richter scale struck the north-western region of Turkey. The rapid response of Greek rescue teams to help victims and the sympathy shown by the Greek people greatly improved relations between officials and populations on both sides. In addition, Greece lifted its embargo on EU aid for Turkey, which had resulted in part from the dispute over the proposed installation of Russian S-300 missiles on Cyprus. This aid and support was reciprocated when Athens suffered an earthquake measuring 5.9 on the Richter scale on Sept. 7, 1999. The resulting goodwill, aid and improved bilateral relations became known as "earthquake diplomacy".

Moreover, at the Helsinki EU summit in December 1999, Greece did support Turkey's application for candidate status for EU membership. A condition placed by Greece for support was the need to resolve the Aegean disputes by the end of 2004, otherwise the dispute would be referred to the ICJ.

The developing relationship between Greek Foreign Minister Papandreou and his Turkish counterpart, Ismail Cem, led to bilateral agreements and improved relations. In the summer of 1999, Papandreou and Cem agreed to establish bilateral committees to deal with issues of mutual interest such as tourism, culture, crime, maritime transport, environmental protection and economic issues. The issues of so-called "high politics" such as the Aegean dispute were deliberately left off the agenda. In January 2000, Papandreou made the first official visit to Turkey by a Greek Foreign Minister for nearly four decades. A further example of the rapprochement between the two countries was the landing of 150 marines and Turkish fighter jets in Greece during NATO's operation "Dynamic Mix 2000" in May-June 2000. However, another NATO exercise codenamed "Destined Glory 2000" in October of the same year, saw Greece withdraw in protest from the operation and Turkey complain that the Greek Air Force had constantly violated the NATO exercise plan and directives.

A set of confidence building measures agreed by Papandreou and Cem in Budapest in October 2000, sought to establish a climate of trust and co-operation between the two countries. Relations between Greece and Turkey in regard to NATO-EU issues proved more troublesome. In early 2001, Turkey said that it would not allow the EU to use NATO resources for its planned rapid reaction peacekeeping force, fearing that the EU could use the force in Cyprus or in the Aegean dispute. Turkey insisted that the Europeans could only have automatic access to NATO resources if Turkey had the right to veto or at least participate in EU actions. A deal brokered by the USA and Britain was reached in late 2001, allowing Turkey to participate in EU operations and consult with the EU on the deployment of the force. However, in December 2001, Greece rejected the solution, arguing that it would allow both a NATO and non-EU member crucial influence in EU affairs, in addition to giving Turkey a unique status within NATO. After the EU's Seville summit in mid-2002, Greece reached a compromise with the EU over the rapid reaction force, but Turkey rejected the EU's proposal, unhappy at assurances given to Greece. Turkish worries were resolved in December 2002 at the EU Copenhagen summit and the European Union and NATO finalized an agreement. The EU announced thereafter that it was ready to send a peacekeeping force into the former Yugoslav republic of Macedonia and was also willing to deploy soldiers in Bosnia to replace NATO forces.

On bilateral issues, relations improved to the degree that in 2001 Greece and Turkey agreed to submit a joint bid to host the 2008 European Football Championship. Moreover, Greece and Turkey in November 2001 signed a Protocol on the Formation of a Joint Hellenic-Turkish Standby Disaster Response Unit, which will operate in the Mediterranean region in cases of earthquakes, floods and landslide disasters.

In March 2002, Greece and Turkey returned to discussions on resolving the decades-long disagreement over Aegean Sea boundaries. Greek and Turkish officials met in Ankara for preliminary or exploratory talks. Talks continued but with little public disclosure of specific matters. However by the end of 2003, it became clear that not much progress had been made on the crucial issues of maritime borders, disputed islands and the continental shelf under the Aegean. Greece continues to believe that the continental shelf problem should only be resolved at the International Court of Justice, whilst Turkey maintains that the issues should be dealt with bilaterally, not on an international platform, in view of the special nature of the Aegean dispute.

In contrast, agreements on other issues continued to be produced. Agreements on co-operation in agriculture, veterinary protection and between diplomatic academies came into force in 2002 and 2003. Co-operation in the field of energy is also occurring, with agreements on the interconnection of the electric and gas networks. On Sept. 25, 2003, the Foreign Ministers of Greece and Turkey agreed with the Secretary-General of the United Nations to implement the means to ratify the Ottawa Convention banning anti-personnel landmines.

As in 2002, Greek Foreign Minister Papandreou and the Turkish Foreign Minister, Abdullah Gul, agreed at the Mediterranean Forum (FOROMED) in October 2003 to cancel separate military exercises planned in Cyprus and the eastern Mediterranean. Papandreou stated that the agreement was "a significant gesture for peace and security in the region", while Gul stated that "we see this as a sign of improvement in ties between our countries"; in addition, he added, "both sides have the will to solve problems. Talks are going on. We are optimistic".

Confidence building measures were further cemented when Abdullah Gul paid his first official visit to Greece on Oct. 21, 2003, to discuss the Cyprus problem, economic co-operation, Turkey's EU ambitions and arrangements for the 2004 Athens Olympics.

Violations of airspace in the Aegean continue to be reported, especially by the Greek government. However, Turkey and Greece signed an agreement in September 2003 to regulate air traffic over the Aegean. The new accord, which went into effect on Dec. 25, 2003, was designed to accommodate an expected rise in air traffic during the 2004 Olympics hosted by Athens.

Support for a settlement on Cyprus had been growing in late 2003, especially in the TRNC. Elections in Northern Cyprus on Dec.14, 2003, saw the pro-settlement and pro-EU Republican Turkish Party make large gains and become the dominant party in a coalition government with the Democratic Party led by Serdar Denktash, son of TRNC President Rauf Denktash. The leader of the Republican Turkish Party, Mehmet Ali Talat, became the new Prime Minister of the TRNC. In addition, it remains to be seen what impact the victory of Costas Karamanlis' conservative New Democracy Party in the Greek general election on March 7, 2004, will have on Greek-Turkish relations and the Cyprus issue.

Although agreements on so-called "low political" issues and confidence building measures have been successful, agreements on the Aegean dispute have been less forthcoming. In September 2003, the then Greek Prime Minister Costas Simitis called on his Turkish counterpart, Recep Tayyip Erdogan, to deal with any domestic obstacles which stood in the way of solving the Cyprus and Aegean continental shelf issues, warning that the EU's setting a date for Turkish accession talks at its 2004 summit would depend on progress on these two issues. As stated above, one caveat placed by Greece on support for Turkey's entry into the EU, acknowledged by the other EU members, was the need to resolve disputes surrounding the Aegean by the end of 2004. It was agreed that, if no adequate progress were made toward resolution, the dispute would be referred to arbitration by the ICJ. It was clear, at least, that the EU accession process for Turkey and Cyprus, assisted by greatly improved Greek-Turkish relations, was meanwhile providing the catalyst for greater co-operation in the region.

Charlie Pericleous

4.11 Hungary - Romania (Transylvania)

After many centuries of Hungarian rule the ancient province of Transylvania was awarded to Romania in the post-World War I dissolution of the Austro-Hungarian empire, on the grounds that ethnic Romanians formed the substantial majority of its population. In 1940, at the behest of the Axis powers, Romania was forced to cede Northern Transylvania to Hungary, but Romania regained the area at the end of World War II under territorial dispositions dictated by the Soviet Union. Romania's present frontiers were confirmed by the 1947 Paris peace treaty between Romania and the wartime Allies, since when no formal dispute has existed between Hungary and Romania over the sovereignty of Transylvania.

Nevertheless, there have been regular manifestations of official Hungarian concern over the Romanian government's treatment of the Hungarian inhabitants of Transylvania, who constitute the largest national minority group in Europe. There have also been recapitulations by Hungarian historians of Transylvania's important history as a Hungarian-ruled province, to which Romanian spokesmen have responded by accusing Hungary of harbouring revanchist aims. Such exchanges were increasingly prevalent in the long era of Communist rule in both countries, although post-1945 Soviet hegemony in Eastern Europe ensured that they posed no real challenge to existing borders. When both communism and

Soviet hegemony collapsed after 1989, expectations that the Transylvania question would become less of an issue between the new democratic governments of Romania and Hungary were at first disappointed. In the early 1990s inter-communal tensions mounted in the province and many Romanians became increasingly concerned that Hungary aimed at territorial revision. However, since then ethnic tensions have ebbed and in 1996 both countries signed a treaty of reconciliation confirming the existing border and guaranteeing the rights of ethnic Hungarians in Romania. (Map 43, p. 514, illustrates this entry.)

Historical Background

The province of Transylvania is a mountainous plateau located to the west and north of the south-westerly loop of the Carpathian mountains, which divides present-day Romania geographically. The province has been the focus of contending national aspirations for a thousand years, since it serves as a referent of ethnic identity for both Romanians and Hungarians. Most Romanian historians claim a continuous Romanian presence in Transylvania from the time of the Roman colonization of the area (called Dacia) after its conquest by Trajan at the beginning of the 2nd century AD. Hungarian historians discount this theory by arguing that when the Romans abandoned Dacia in the third century AD, and retreated south of the Danube, its inhabitants accompanied them. They also insist that when the Magyars (Hungarians) entered Transylvania during the 10th century, its only inhabitants were Slavonic tribes. The Romanian presence in Transylvania is ascribed by such historians to immigration at the end of the 12th century from the provinces of Moldavia and Wallachia, respectively east and south of the Carpathians. What is not disputed is that Transylvania was conquered by King Stephen of Hungary at the beginning of the 11th century and that the Hungarian crown extended its authority over the region by encouraging Hungarian-speaking Szekler and German colonists to settle during the 12th and 13th centuries. The so-called "union of the three nations" (*unio trium nationum*) was concluded in 1437 between the Magyar nobility, the Saxons and the Szeklers and granted political rights and privileges only to these three recognized peoples, thus excluding the Romanians.

That the Hungarian crown also exercised suzerainty over Moldavia and Wallachia until the 1360s is one of the factors cited in favour of the thesis of the historical unity of these provinces with Transylvania. Hungarian historians stress, however, that the trans-Carpathian provinces were distinct from Transylvania in that their cultural heritage was Byzantine and the religion of their peoples Greek Orthodox, whereas the Magyar rulers, Szekler bondsmen and German settlers of Transylvania were Catholic and looked to the west. These differences were enhanced, according to the Hungarian thesis, by the experience of Ottoman Turkish rule and its aftermath. After a brief period of independence, Wallachia succumbed to the Ottomans in 1393, followed by Moldavia in 1504 (after a century of Polish-Lithuanian rule) and by Hungary itself in 1526 (as a result of the Turkish victory at the Battle of Mohacs). But Transylvania retained exceptional autonomy under Ottoman suzerainty (established in 1541), so that its Magyar nobility was able to ensure the continuity of the Hungarian polity. Moreover, whereas Hungary with Transylvania passed from Turkish to Austrian Habsburg rule under the 1699 Treaty of Carlowitz, Moldavia and Wallachia were to remain under Ottoman rule for a further 160 years. For their part, Romanian historians contend that the long political separation of Transylvania from Moldavia and Wallachia did not destroy the underlying social and cultural unity of the three provinces. In their view, the crucial fact is that through the centuries of Hungarian rule Transylvania's population remained predominantly Romanian in ethnic composition and outlook.

In the first half of the 19th century Transylvania was an important centre of Hungarian efforts to throw off Austrian rule, notably as the scene of much conflict and national assertion during the Hungarian revolt of 1848-49. Regarded by the Hungarians as part of their national territory, Transylvania became part of the Hungarian half of the Austro-Hungarian dual monarchy created by the *Ausgleich* ("compromise") of 1867. But the new independent state of Romania, created from the union of Moldavia and Wallachia (1859) and given international recognition by the Congress of Berlin (1878), inevitably aspired to incorporate into its territory all adjoining lands of predominant Romanian population. The most important of these was Transylvania, in respect of which a powerful Romanian irredentist movement developed in the late 19th century, although Romania's need for defence guarantees from Austria-Hungary against Russia, as provided under a treaty of 1883, precluded the active pursuit of a territorial claim.

Romania's Acquisition, Partial Loss and Recovery of Transylvania, 1918-45

Initially neutral, Romania entered World War I in August 1916 on the side of the Entente powers (Britain, France and Russia) in return for a promise of Transylvania and other Romanian-populated territories. Romania suffered military humiliation at the hands of the Central powers, but on the eventual defeat of the latter in late 1918, and the collapse of the Austro-Hungarian empire, Romanian forces occupied Transylvania. The union of Transylvania with Romania was proclaimed by a Romanian National Assembly meeting in Alba-Iulia on Dec. 1, 1918, and was recognized under the Treaty of Trianon (of June 4, 1920) between the victorious powers and Hungary on the basis that 11 of the province's 15 counties had a clear Romanian majority. Transylvania as ceded to Romania consisted of an area of 102,000 sq km (whose population of 5,700,000 included 1,700,000 Hungarians and 600,000 Germans) and encompassed not only the historic province (57,000 sq km) but also adjoining areas. Thereafter, the whole ceded area was commonly referred to as Transylvania.

In the inter-war period Romania sought to construct alliances which would protect its post-1918 borders. Nevertheless, in the 1930s, as the Versailles treaty system collapsed, its possession of Transylvania came under increasing challenge from the Hungarian regime of Admiral Horthy, which aligned itself with Nazi Germany and Fascist Italy. Following the conclusion of the Nazi-Soviet non-aggression pact of Aug. 23, 1939, and the outbreak of World War II a week later, pressure on Romania intensified, not only from Hungary but also from Moscow. In June 1940 Romania was forced to cede Northern Bukovina and Bessarabia to the Soviet Union—for accounts of the Bessarabia question and of Romania's dispute with Ukraine over Northern Bukovina, see Sections 4.5 and 4.14, respectively. Two months later, after inconclusive direct negotiations with the Horthy regime, Romania was forced to cede the north-eastern half of Transylvania (commonly known as Northern Transylvania) to Hungary. The transfer took place under the Second Vienna Award (or "Diktat") of Aug. 30, 1940, of which Germany and Italy were the "arbitrators". The area ceded by Romania totalled 43,492 sq km and had a population of 2,600,000. According to Romanian sources, 50.3 per cent of its inhabitants were Romanians and 37.1 per cent Hungarians. A Hungarian census of 1941, taken after an exodus of Romanians, gave the Hungarians a slender numerical majority.

Romania's territorial truncation continued when it was forced to cede the Black Sea coastal region of Southern Dobruja to Bulgaria under the Treaty of Craiova of Sept. 7, 1940, again under pressure from the Axis powers. Whereas Romania as recognized by the 1878 Congress of Berlin had included Romanian-majority Northern Dobruja, the smaller southern part, containing a mixed population of Romanians (20 per cent), Bulgars, Greeks, Turks and others, had not become part of Romania until 1913, when it was ceded by Bulgaria under the Treaty of Bucharest which ended the 1912-13 Balkan Wars. Southern Dobruja had been briefly recovered by Bulgaria in May 1918 on Romania's initial defeat by the Central powers in World War I but had been regained by Romania under the post-war Treaty of Neuilly (of Nov. 27, 1919) between the victorious powers and Bulgaria.

Internally, the effect of Romania's enforced cessions in 1940 was to bring to power a pro-Axis regime which placed its hopes of territorial recovery in an alliance with Nazi Germany. In that Hungary was also allied with Germany, with the aim of preserving its gains under the Vienna Award, Romania was obliged to focus on its former eastern lands rather than on Northern Transylvania. In 1941 Romania joined Germany in its invasion of the Soviet Union and succeeded in recovering Bessarabia and Northern

Bukovina. However, in August 1944 the advance by the Red Army on Romanian territory caused Romania to switch sides and join the Allied camp. Its military endeavour alongside the Russians in sweeping the Germans from the west of Romania, Hungary and Czechoslovakia, coupled with Stalin's desire to win popular support for the puppet government installed in Romania in March 1945, prompted the Soviet leader's decision to restore Northern Transylvania to Romania on March 9, 1945. This disposition was enshrined in the 1947 Paris peace treaties signed by the Allies with Hungary and Romania (although the Soviet Union retained Northern Bukovina and Bessarabia, and Bulgaria kept Southern Dobruja).

Post-War Dissension over Minorities Question

During the two-year period between the end of the war and the conclusion of the peace treaty, the Romanian government allowed the Hungarian minority to use their language freely and to retain their schools, although the German minority was completely shorn of its rights. The establishment of Communist rule in 1947 coincided with the beginning of a systematic attack on the separate identity of both the Hungarian and the German minorities, under the pretext of a so-called class struggle against "bourgeois nationalism" and "imperialism and its agents". In 1950 Aron Marton, the Hungarian Catholic bishop of Transylvania, was found guilty of such "offences" in a show trial, along with several other representative Hungarians. The number of schools with Hungarian as the language of instruction was steadily reduced, private travel between Romania and Hungary ceased, and the links of Transylvanian Hungarian culture with Hungary were cut. The conditions for a "Marxist-Leninist solution to the national question" and "realization of complete equality for workers of all national affiliations" were considered to have been provided by the maintenance of Hungarian schools in wholly Hungarian areas and the inclusion in the party and state leadership of individuals whose mother tongue was Hungarian or who were of Hungarian origin. All independent cultural initiatives qualified as "nationalism" and were strongly repressed by the agencies of state security.

It should be noted that in the first post-war decade the widespread use of police terror, and the dislocation caused by rapid industrialization, affected Romanians and Hungarians alike in many respects. The Hungarian Revolution of 1956 was supported not only by large numbers of Hungarians in Transylvania but also by Romanian students, who participated in joint Hungarian-Romanian demonstrations in Cluj (Transylvania) in 1957 in protest against the suppression of the revolution by Soviet forces. However, the withdrawal of Soviet troops from Romania in 1958 marked a turning-point which had particular consequences for the Hungarian minority. The withdrawal was accompanied by a second wave of police arrests to counter any conceivable threat to the Communist regime, which was now devoid of an immediate Soviet military buttress. At the same time, the Romanian Communist Party (RCP) sought to identify itself with the national interest, in an effort to win greater support from the Romanian population. Romanian national cohesion became a major goal of the regime and the policy towards the Hungarian minority was subordinated to this end. In 1959 the Romanian government decided to destroy the separate identity of most of the Hungarian educational system in Transylvania by merging the Hungarian Bolyai University of Cluj with its Romanian counterpart (this being accomplished at a meeting presided over by a young RCP central committee secretary called Nicolae Ceausescu). At the same time, Hungarian secondary schools were joined with Romanian ones and Hungarian-language sections created within the new schools.

Until the late 1960s the situation of the Hungarian minority in Romania caused few overt problems between the two governments, because the equally dictatorial regime in Budapest took the line that it was an internal Romanian matter, and broader Hungarian society was unable to express any dissentient opinion. Moreover, it appeared initially that Nicolae Ceausescu (who became RCP leader in 1965 and President in 1967) was committed to a more enlightened line on minorities than his predecessor. However, the growing political divergence of the two regimes from 1968 onwards was accompanied by increasing readiness on the part of Hungary to raise the question of the minority in Transylvania, as it became clear that Ceausescu's approach was little different from what had gone before. In that year the Romanian authorities split the Mures autonomous province, embracing many of the Hungarians of Transylvania, into three counties (Harghita, Covasna and Mures), thereby diluting the separate identity of the Hungarian population of the region. Harghita and Covasna became the only two Transylvanian counties with Hungarian majorities (84.5 per cent and 78 per cent respectively) and as such the focus of particular attention on the part of Hungary (although neither is contiguous with Hungarian territory).

From the late 1960s the Hungarian government of Janos Kadar combined a foreign policy of complete loyalty to the Soviet Union with a degree of political and economic liberalization internally (so-called "goulash communism"). In contrast, Romania distanced itself from the Soviet Union (refusing to participate in the Soviet-led invasion of Czechoslovakia in 1968) but fiercely resisted any idea of internal political change. As a substitute for domestic reform, moreover, the Ceausescu regime resorted to official reinforcement of nationalism and warnings against "outside threats", with inevitable adverse consequences for minorities, especially the Hungarians of Transylvania. Against this background, Hungarian spokesmen increasingly took the opportunity to raise the minority question under the camouflage of complaints about Romania's departure from Moscow-line orthodoxy. Thus in August 1971 a member of the Hungarian polit-

buro, Zoltan Komocsin, said that Hungarian Communists were "fundamentally interested that the people of both our countries—including the Hungarians living in Romania—should come to understand that the fate and destiny of our peoples are inseparable from socialism". This remark brought a retort from a Romanian politburo member, Paul Nicolescu-Mizil, that "no-one can set himself up as an arbiter or judge of the progress of socialism in one country or another", especially not those who in 1956 were "unable to cope with the task of governing their own party and people and registered lamentable political failures".

Such exchanges did not prevent Hungary and Romania from renewing (on Feb. 24, 1972) their 1948 treaty of friendship, co-operation and assistance for a further 20 years. Moreover, in mid-1977 President Ceausescu had talks with the Hungarian party leader, Janos Kadar, in Debrecen (Hungary) on June 15 and in Oradea (Romanian Transylvania) on June 16, during which it was agreed that the minorities question was a "domestic affair" of each individual host country and that the existence of Hungarians in Romania and of Romanians in Hungary was "the result of the development of history and several centuries of neighbourhood". (Romanian statistics at that time gave the number of Hungarians in Romania as 1,700,000, whereas Hungary put the total at 2,000,000; the number of Romanians living within Hungary's borders was estimated at 20,000.) Nevertheless, such attempts to defuse the Transylvania question at inter-governmental level were accompanied by further indications of unrest among the Hungarian minority in Romania and by the appearance in various Hungarian and Romanian publications of polemical articles on the issue.

Allegations of government repression of the Hungarian minority in Romania were made in an open letter sent in December 1977 to the leadership of the RCP by Carol Kiraly, a former high-ranking party official of Hungarian extraction, who maintained in particular that Hungarians living in Romania were subject to discrimination in employment and education. The Romanian government responded by branding Kiraly a traitor, threatening to expel him from the party and denying all allegations that minorities were being repressed—this last contention being quickly endorsed by meetings in Bucharest of both the Hungarian and the German national councils of Romania. Nevertheless, it was reported on April 24, 1978, that three prominent members of the Hungarian community who held leading positions in the RCP—namely Janos Fazekas (a Deputy Premier), Prof. Lajos Takacs (a former chancellor of the University of Cluj) and Andras Suto (a well-known writer)—had sent separate appeals to the Romanian leadership protesting against the government's alleged discriminatory policies towards its minority groups and demanding a number of improvements.

Although the Hungarian government made no official comment on these developments, its continuing interest in the Transylvania question was indicated by the appearance during this period of articles by individuals expressing dissatisfaction with Romania's treatment of its Hungarian minority. Moreover, in December 1977 the Budapest newspaper *Magyar Hirlap* published comments by a Hungarian historian who called into question official Romanian theories on the origins of the Romanian people and their continued presence in Transylvania. The Romanian authorities responded with their own articles denying allegations of anti-minority discrimination and criticizing Hungary for permitting the publication of material "hostile" to Romania. At the same time (i.e. early May 1978) the official Romanian news agency Agerpres republished in full an article by the Romanian historian Dr Ion Spalatelu dealing in depth with the atrocities perpetrated by Hungary under Admiral Horthy during its occupation of Northern Transylvania in 1940-44. This article concluded with the assertion that, although the overwhelming majority of Hungarian nationals lived in complete harmony and shared equal rights with Romanian citizens, they still had to fight against "fascist and Horthyist elements in various parts of the world" who were attempting "to revive the chauvinistic, irredentist policy which caused so much suffering to broad masses of citizens".

Continued Tensions over Transylvania in the 1980s

From 1982 Hungarian-Romanian relations became increasingly strained over the Transylvania question, as further allegations were made in Hungary of official Romanian discrimination against the Hungarian population of the region. Although the Foreign Ministers of the two countries agreed in March 1983 that the minority issue must be solved by diplomatic means, during that year polemics developed between newspapers and journals of the two countries, particularly over what was viewed by the Hungarian side as the overtly nationalist tone of Romanian celebrations of the 65th anniversary of the original union of Transylvania with Romania. In September 1984 an official Romanian delegation to Hungary, including three members of the RCP secretariat, was reportedly presented with a 12-page document suggesting ways in which the position of the Transylvanian Hungarians could be improved. However, all allegations of discrimination against the minority were rejected by Romanian officials. Later the same month (September 1984), the parliamentary assembly of the Council of Europe (then consisting only of West European states) adopted a report on the position of minorities in Romania and called on the Romanian government to ensure respect for their rights.

In December 1984 the Romanian news agency Agerpress twice carried articles from *Romania Literara* (the organ of the Union of Writers) strongly criticizing the Hungarian journal *Kritika* for publishing historical documents which supported Hungary's claim to the Hungarian-inhabited areas of Transylvania. In the same month the central committee of the ruling Hungarian Socialist Workers' Party

(HSWP) issued guiding policy principles which raised the issue of Hungarian minorities abroad, apparently for the first time in such a context. The documents stated that it was "natural to demand that citizens of Hungarian nationality in neighbouring countries should be permitted to develop fully their national culture and to use their mother tongue". At the end of the month, President Ceausescu responded by defending his government's record on minorities at a joint meeting of the Council of Working People of Hungarian Nationality and its German counterpart, voicing strong opposition to the belief that "the national question in one country…should be dealt with by parties or governments in other countries".

Official Hungarian concern for the Transylvanian minority did not extend to giving any support to dissident intellectuals who called for more vigorous action vis-à-vis the Romanian government. In fact, restrictive measures were taken against several intellectuals who had once lived in Transylvania, notably Gaspar Miklos Tamas, who in mid-1984 had written to *The Times* of London requesting help from "Western media and elected bodies" for the Hungarian minority and drawing attention to the cases of four Transylvanian Hungarians who had been detained by the Romanian authorities since late 1982 on "apparently absurd grounds". For their part, the Romanian authorities were reported in October 1985 to have searched the homes of a number of Romanians and ethnic Hungarians living in Transylvania and to have confiscated copies of a memorandum protesting about the position of the Hungarian minority. It was understood that the memorandum had been submitted to the European Cultural Forum held in Budapest in October-November 1985 within the framework of the Conference on Security and Co-operation in Europe (CSCE), while a year later Hungary was a joint sponsor with Canada of a resolution on the protection of national minorities submitted to the third CSCE follow-up meeting which opened in Vienna in November 1986.

The issue flared up again in February 1987, when President Ceausescu publicly condemned a three-volume history of Transylvania published in November 1986 by the Hungarian Academy of Science, which apparently challenged the view that the region had been occupied first by ethnic Romanians and only later by Magyars (i.e. Hungarians). Speaking to representatives of Romania's ethnic minorities, the President described the work as reviving "Horthyist, fascist, chauvinist and even racist ideas" and asked: "Whom does this science serve, except the most reactionary imperialist circles?". He added that, in his view, such ideas "by no means serve the cause of friendship and collaboration, or the cause of socialism". In what was seen as a retaliatory measure, the Romanian authorities proceeded to impose a ban on the use of Hungarian place-names within Romanian territory.

On March 3, 1988, Ceausescu announced plans to complete by the year 2000 the urbanization or "systematization" of half of Romania's 13,000 villages by moving the country's peasants into "agro-industrial" complexes consisting of small blocks of flats. The Hungarian government was particularly alarmed because members of the Hungarian minority in Transylvania believed that the programme was designed to lead to their assimilation through the destruction of their homes and cultural heritage. The plan was criticized by leading members of the HSWP, and on June 27 a protest rally was held in Budapest drawing about 50,000 demonstrators. Ceausescu retaliated by closing the Hungarian consulate in Cluj in Transylvania. In an attempt to improve relations, the Hungarian Prime Minister, Karoly Grosz, met Ceausescu in the Romanian border town of Arad at the end of August, but in November 1988 each country expelled one of the other's diplomats. Throughout 1989 Hungary gave much publicity to the plight of several thousand refugees, mostly Hungarians from Transylvania, who fled Romania because of chronic food shortages.

Fall of Ceausescu—Subsequent Violence in Transylvania

It was not without significance that the overthrow of Nicolae Ceausescu (in December 1989) was sparked off by a protest of ethnic solidarity by Hungarians and Romanians in the western Transylvanian city of Timisoara against the expulsion of a Hungarian pastor, Laszlo Tokes, of the Protestant Reformed Church. Access to Hungarian and Yugoslav television had made the population of the region fully aware of the collapse of Communist regimes elsewhere in Eastern Europe and had fuelled the confidence of those willing to resist the iniquities of the Ceausescu regime. The protest against Tokes's expulsion turned into a mass demonstration against the regime on Dec. 16, 1989, and spread to Bucharest on Dec. 21. On the following day Ceausescu and his wife fled the capital and were later captured and executed. But whereas opposition to Ceausescu temporarily united Romanians and Hungarians, the events following the revolution divided them. Mistrust of Hungarian motives, fear of Hungarian revanchism, concern about an erosion of Romanian dominance in Transylvania, general unease about the economic future—all contributed to create a climate of heightened inter-ethnic tension in Transylvania.

Romanian suspicion of Hungarian intentions was aroused by the rapidity and efficiency with which the Hungarian community in Transylvania organized and asserted itself after the overthrow of Ceausescu. An association called the Hungarian Democratic Union of Romania (HDUR) was established in Cluj on Dec. 21, 1989, and issued an appeal to "our dear Romanian friends to unite in putting an end to evil". Two days later the HDUR issued a statement of its aims which included the following demands: the immediate development of an educational system which guaranteed the opportunity for minority language instruction at every level; the re-establishment of the independent Hungarian university in Kolozsvar (Cluj); the introduction of mandatory bilingualism in Transylvania, with administrative and judicial proceedings conducted in the Romanian and Hungarian languages; and the establishment of a Ministry of Nationalities. Pastor Tokes became honorary president of the HDUR (and was, in March 1990, elected Bishop of Oradea in place of the disgraced Laszlo Papp).

The provisional government of the National Salvation Front (NSF) soon took steps to restore Hungarian-language radio broadcasts, while four hours of national TV time were allocated for programmes in Hungarian. A Transylvanian Hungarian, Attila Palfalvi, was appointed Deputy Minister of Education in charge of minority schools, and on Jan. 15, 1990, he announced that the Hungarian Bolyai University of Cluj (which had been compulsorily merged with the Romanian Babes University in 1959) would reopen and would take under its aegis the Hungarian Medical Institute in Tirgu Mures. Five days later the Ministry of Education announced that it had begun to reorganize primary and secondary schools with a view to assuring education in their native tongue for the minorities. However, the speed and manner of this reorganization attracted a chorus of criticism from Romanians in Transylvania and elsewhere. As a result, Palfalvi was dismissed on Jan. 27 for "taking decisions on his own in such a manner that contributed to creating tension between the Magyar population and the Romanian population in some Transylvanian settlements" (Rompres, Jan. 27, 1990), and replaced by a Hungarian historian, Lajos Demeny. Four days later, the Education Minister, Mihail Sora, stated that agreements on the separation of exclusively Hungarian and Romanian schools which had been made "in a spontaneous way in Transylvania" would be implemented. However, in what was clearly an attempt to forestall further agitation, he announced that where local agreements had yet to be reached the question of separation would wait until the beginning of the academic year.

Postponement of the process of reorganization angered the Hungarian population, which staged demonstrations in the major towns of Transylvania calling for the separation of schools. Romanians opposed to these demands held counter-protests and in Cluj several people were injured after clashes between rival groups on Feb. 8, 1990. Two days later an estimated 40,000 Hungarians marched peacefully through the centre of Tirgu Mures (a city of mixed Hungarian-Romanian population) in support of separate schools. It was against this background that a nationalist group calling itself *Uniunea Vatra Romaneasca* (Romanian Hearth Union) emerged as the self-proclaimed champion of Romanian rights in Transylvania. Linked to the *Fratia Romaneasca* (Romanian Brotherhood) cultural organization, *Vatra* accused the Bucharest government of weakness in having made concessions to the Hungarians' demand for separate schools.

For the HDUR, on the other hand, the government

had gone back on its initial promise to introduce Hungarian schools by postponing implementation until September 1990. Education Minister Sora's announcement to this effect prompted a series of peaceful demonstrations by Hungarians in Tirgu Mures but tension increased after celebrations on March 15, 1990, of Hungary's National Day. Several thousand Hungarians from Hungary joined relatives in Transylvania to celebrate this event, draping buildings with both Hungarian and Romanian flags as a sign of communal solidarity. In Tirgu Mures, however, the celebrations of the 1848 proclamation of Transylvania's union with Hungary were deemed by many Romanians to be overtly provocative. A series of demonstrations and counter-demonstrations deteriorated into serious inter-communal clashes on March 19-20, when thousands of Romanian nationalists, many of them brought in from surrounding villages, stormed the HDUR headquarters in Tirgu Mures and attacked other Hungarian targets. Eight people died in the violence and over 300 were injured, most of the casualties being Hungarians. A state of emergency was declared in Tirgu Mures on March 20 and the Romanian army was sent in with tanks to separate the two sides.

Hungary's Prime Minister, Miklos Nemeth, reacted to the Tirgu Mures violence by sending a letter of protest to the Romanian government and appealing to the United Nations to intervene. On the evening of March 20, 1990, an estimated 70,000 ethnic Hungarians demonstrated in Bucharest in protest against the government's alleged failure to curb Romanian nationalist excesses in Transylvania. In expressing his regret at the violence, the Romanian Prime Minister, Petre Roman, pleaded for understanding of the feelings of Transylvanian Romanians, recalling that they had suffered greatly under Hungarian rule during World War II. Amid criticism that the government's reactions to the clashes had been dilatory and biased, the HDUR and *Vatra* held government-sponsored conciliation talks on March 22-24. These produced a joint appeal for respect for the rights of both nationalists and minorities and for the right to education in a mother tongue. HDUR representatives declared that the Hungarian community were loyal supporters of Romania as a sovereign and unitary state.

Romania's first free elections since 1937, held on May 20, 1990, brought a further polarization of ethnic differences. While President Iliescu's NSF won a commanding majority, the HDUR emerged as the joint second-largest party in the lower house, with 7.2 per cent of the national vote and 29 seats (out of 400) .The Party for the National Unity of Romanians (PUNR), which espoused "the socio-cultural principles" of *Vatra*, received 2.1 per cent and nine seats in the lower house. Thereafter both the PUNR and *Vatra*, together with extreme right-wing publications such as the weekly *Romania Mare*, intensified their anti-Hungarian propaganda, with consequential negative effects on inter-communal relations in Transylvania.

A particular theme of the nationalists' campaign was the situation of the Romanian minority in the two Hungarian-majority Transylvanian counties of Harghita and Covasna. In October 1991 the Romanian parliament received a committee report which claimed that some 4,000 Romanians had been driven from the counties since the December 1989 revolution (although the two HDUR deputies on the committee refused to endorse the report). In the same month a wave of Romanian nationalist protests greeted a proposal by some Hungarians in Harghita and Covasna that an autonomy referendum should be held in the counties. However, the HDUR dissociated itself from the initiative, which was shelved.

Since then the 1.6 million Hungarians in Transylvania have consistently voted solidly for their ethnic party, the HDUR, this taking around 7 per cent of the total seats in parliament. The HDUR, for its part, has attempted to accommodate all political positions ranging from strong nationalism to moderate collaborative inter-ethnic politics. This means that it has been able to satisfy the demands of the majority of its constituency. In the 1996 elections the Democratic Convention, incorporating the HDUR, was successful in achieving power, and as members of the coalition the Hungarian minority party entered the new government already prepared to engage in the complex negotiations necessary to build a consociational democracy.

Reactions in Hungary to Post-Ceausescu Events in Transylvania

Developments in Transylvania following the fall of Ceausescu were closely monitored by the government of Hungary (where Communist rule was also thrown off in late 1989 and early 1990). An immediate cause of concern was the increasing flow of ethnic Hungarian refugees from Romania as a result of inter-communal tensions and other factors. Because of this exodus, the Budapest government in February 1990 unilaterally abrogated a 1979 treaty with Romania which specified that neither country would grant dual citizenship to nationals of the other. Explaining this decision (which meant that ethnic Hungarians who were Romanian citizens could also be granted Hungarian citizenship), the Hungarian Foreign Ministry said that it was prompted by the Romanian government's "negative" attitude and by the unsettled status of thousands of refugees from Transylvania and other parts of Romania. According to official Hungarian figures, from January 1988 to April 1991 a total of 49,788 people fled from Romania to Hungary, of whom 77 per cent were ethnic Hungarians.

The 70th anniversary of the Treaty of Trianon was marked by nationalist speeches and statements in both capitals. Speaking at a rally in Budapest on June 1, 1990, the new Hungarian Prime Minister, Jozsef Antall, said that he condemned the treaty "historically speaking" but noted that Hungary had signed the 1975 Helsinki Final Act of the CSCE guaranteeing existing borders in Europe. The day before, on May 31, 1990, the parliamentary groups of the main Hungarian parties issued a joint declaration saying that the Treaty of Trianon had "signified the partition of historical Hungary" and that "European politicians and writers and millions of people declared it to be unjust". While reaffirming Hungary's commitment to existing borders, the declaration continued that "this country expects the individual and collective minority rights of the Hungarian community beyond our borders to be fully guaranteed".

In a statement issued on Aug. 22, 1990, the Hungarian government expressed concern at reports that "certain extremist Romanian groups intend to utilize the 50th anniversary of the so-called Second Vienna Award signed on Aug. 30, 1940 (in which Hungary was awarded the smaller, northern part of Transylvania, which had been annexed to Romania under the Treaty of Trianon), in order to hold provocative demonstrations, principally in parts of Transylvania where the majority of the population is Hungarian". The statement expressed the view that "it is particularly undesirable for the relations between the new Central and Eastern European democracies to be burdened by scholarly and journalistic debates" on historical events. Asserting that Hungary "does not aspire to a forcible change in the borders or an infringement of peace by military or any other means", the statement added: "There is no cause or legal ground for anyone to interpret as an irredentist, hostile endeavour the sense of responsibility felt for the fate of the three-and-a-half million Hungarians who live as minorities in the countries neighbouring Hungary as a result of the peace treaties of 1920 and 1947".

Despite such disclaimers, "Hungarian irredentism" was precisely how Hungary's interest in Transylvania was depicted by Romanian nationalist movements such as *Vatra*. Moreover, the Romanian government itself remained watchful for any move on Hungary's part which might be interpreted as an actual or potential threat to Romanian territorial sovereignty. On Sept. 11, 1991, for example, President Iliescu publicly condemned a proposal by a joint Hungarian-Polish-Czechoslovak working group on economic co-operation that Transylvania should be included in an "economic space" to be created by the three countries. Earlier in the year, President Iliescu had come under attack in Romania for signing a friendship treaty with the Soviet Union (on April 5) stipulating mutual respect for existing borders. On that occasion he had sought to deflect criticism that Romania had thereby endorsed Soviet possession of former Romanian territory (Bessarabia and Northern Bukovina) by stressing the importance of having Moscow's support against any Hungarian claim to Transylvania.

Further strains between Budapest and Bucharest were apparent in the reaction of the Hungarian government to the new Romanian constitution adopted by national referendum on Dec. 8, 1991. Whereas the Romanian view was that this document enshrined full guarantees of minority rights, in Budapest it was assessed as containing fewer rights than the previous text. Hungarian spokesmen pointed out in particular that it declared Romania to be a "national state" and established Romanian as the sole official language at national level. They also noted that in the parliamentary debate on the text, in November 1991, nationalist deputies had sought, unsuccessfully, to delete the word "territorial" from a clause defining as unconstitutional any attempt to promote territorial separatism. In Hungary's view, this attempt was aimed specifically at the rights of the Hungarian minority in the social and cultural fields. Moreover, concern mounted in Budapest when an ethnic Hungarian candidate was disqualified from standing in local elections in Tirgu Mures in February 1992, on what appeared to be dubious legal grounds.

The Hungarian government, in the latter part of 1991, expressed regret that Romania had failed to respond to its proposal for a bilateral treaty or declaration on the mutual protection of minorities. It also regretted that any Hungarian proposal concerning the status of the Hungarian minority in Romania was automatically perceived by the Romanian government as masking designs of territorial revision in Transylvania and that the Romanian authorities had still not at that stage allowed Hungary to reopen its consulate in Cluj.

On a more positive note, the Hungarian government expressed the hope that the process of European integration would in the course of time bring about a solution to the Transylvania question. This has since happened. Both Romania and Hungary are now bound by the human rights convention of the Council of Europe, of which Hungary had become a member in November 1990. Despite the expectation at that time that the differing rates of progress of Hungary and Romania towards full democracy and respect for the rule of law made it likely that Transylvania and the status of its Hungarian minority would remain a fraught issue between the two countries for the foreseeable future, ethnic rivalries have remained subdued. Instead in Romania, attention has been focused on how to achieve a stable, secure and democratic environment, with a view to gaining entry into NATO and the EU. This has necessitated co-operation not only among the numerous ethnic groups within Romania, but with Romania's neighbours. Hence Romania and Hungary were forced to work together in their quest for entry into the Euro-Atlantic institutions and improving ethnic relations became a priority for both nations.

1996 Treaty—Hungarian Renunciation of Territorial Claims

A breakthrough came in 1995, when the Prime Ministers of the two countries met several times, and Hungary's chief diplomat, Laszlo Kovacs, was received by Romanian President Ion Iliescu. In August, Iliescu proposed a formal Romanian-Hungarian reconciliation along the lines of France and Germany. An official draft of the proposed agreement was sent to Hungary the following month and, on Dec. 29, the Romanian Foreign Ministry received the

Hungarian reply, confirming their acceptance of the Romanian proposal for a historical reconciliation. Consultations began in January on the details of the bilateral basic treaty, the proposal for reconciliation and other aspects of the relations between the two countries, and progressed quickly.

In September 1996 the two governments signed the definitive Treaty on Understanding, Co-operation and Good Neighbourhood, under which Hungary formally renounced all claims to Transylvania while the Romanian government guaranteed the rights of the ethnic Hungarian population to their own language and culture. The two key articles were Articles 4 and 14. Article 4 of the Treaty reads: "The Contracting Parties confirm that, in accordance with the principles and norms of international law and the principles of the Helsinki Final Act, they shall respect the inviolability of their common border and the territorial integrity of the other Party. They further confirm that they have no territorial claims on each other and that they shall not raise any such claims in the future". Article 14 states: "The Contracting Parties shall promote the climate of tolerance and understanding among their citizens of different ethnic, religious, cultural and linguistic origin. They condemn xenophobia and all kind of manifestations based on racial, ethnic or religious hatred, discrimination and prejudice and will take effective measures in order to prevent any such manifestation".

Inevitably some of the details have yet to be worked out. In 2003 Hungary had yet to amend its law extending special social and cultural benefits to ethnic Hungarians in Romania, who objected to being singled out in this fashion, confirming that ethnicity is becoming less and less important for both Hungarians and Romanians in Transylvania. However, the border issue can now be regarded as definitively settled.

Peter Calvert

4.12 The Northern Ireland Question

The partition of Ireland in 1920 has been the source of serious dispute and conflict ever since. The following year, 1921, the Anglo-Irish Treaty granted Dominion status to the (overwhelmingly Catholic) twenty-six counties of the Irish Free State (since 1949 the independent Republic of Ireland) and allowed the (mainly Protestant) six counties of Northern Ireland to opt for Home Rule within the United Kingdom. (Map 44, p. 514, illustrates the division of Ireland.) In the twenty-six counties partition has always been regarded as artificial and temporary and successive governments have remained committed to reunification as a basic objective; recent ones

have, however, recognized that this should be achieved only with the consent of a majority of the people in the North. In Northern Ireland the overwhelming majority of the Protestant community (and a substantial majority of the whole population) have consistently voted to remain part of the United Kingdom and opposed union with the Republic.

In 1949 the UK government confirmed the principle that no change should be made in Northern Ireland's status without the consent of its parliament. From 1969, however, the fundamental political deadlock in the North was challenged by a serious escalation of violence. This took the form both of armed conflict between militant pro-unification terrorist movements and security forces on both sides of the border and of sectarian conflict between the Protestant (Loyalist or Unionist) and Catholic (Nationalist or Republican) communities in Northern Ireland itself. Successive UK governments have accordingly felt it necessary at various times since the early 1970s to impose direct rule over the province, suspending elective institutions. The 1985 Anglo-Irish Agreement represented a new departure at governmental level in that, in return for obtaining a consultative role in Northern Irish affairs, the Dublin government formally accepted that Irish reunification could only be achieved with the consent of the Northern majority. However, the agreement was strongly opposed not only by Protestant Unionists in the North but also by the militant Irish nationalist groups.

Since the early 1990s a "peace process" has become established. In 1991 the UK government initiated the latest in a long line of attempts to bring the Northern Ireland parties to a political agreement based on power-sharing. These talks were suspended in early 1992 amid an upsurge of violence in Ireland and major bomb incidents in London. They were then resumed after the April 1992 UK general elections, leading to the Downing Street Declaration of 1993, in which the UK government confirmed that it had no selfish interest in retaining Northern Ireland against its will. Further protracted discussions led to the Good Friday Agreement of April 1998 and to a general ceasefire which still held as of March 2004.

Constitutional and Demographic Position

The existing boundary between the Republic of Ireland and Northern Ireland (a province of the United Kingdom of Great Britain and Northern Ireland) was confirmed in 1925, after the establishment of the Irish Free State as a self-governing Dominion under an Anglo-Irish treaty signed on Dec. 6, 1921, which came into force in 1922. Under this treaty the Irish Free State became a co-equal member of the Commonwealth with full internal self-government, but its high commissioners and ambassadors were accredited by the British King, who was represented in the Irish Free State by a governor-general; moreover, members of the Irish parliament (Dáil Eireann) were required to swear an oath of allegiance to the Crown.

The conclusion of the treaty followed the passage at Westminster of the Government of Ireland Act, which became law on Dec. 23, 1920, and came into operation in June 1921. This act provided for a federal structure of Home Rule in Ireland. In practice this meant that it enabled the Protestant Unionists in the north to retain control of six of the nine counties of the Irish province of Ulster—i.e. Antrim, Armagh, Down, Fermanagh, Londonderry and Tyrone, but not Cavan, Donegal and Monaghan—and reflected their belief (as stated in a report to a cabinet committee) that the inclusion of the latter counties in a separate political entity in the north would "provide such an access of strength to the Roman Catholic party that the supremacy of the Unionists would be seriously threatened". Under the 1921 treaty the six counties were given the option of retaining their status under the 1920 act, and they exercised this option immediately, so that the partition of Ireland became a fact in 1922, with Cavan, Donegal and Monaghan becoming part of a 26-county Irish Free State.

The 1920 act also gave Northern Ireland its own government and parliament (for which a new building was completed at Stormont, Belfast, in 1932). The act also created a Council of Ireland, which was intended to link the two parts of Ireland in a confederation, but after the settlement of the boundary in 1925 this Council was formally dissolved in 1926. Those parts of the act referring to the Irish Free State were repealed by the British parliament in 1927. In 1936 the Irish Free State, by its External Relations Act, took advantage of the Abdication crisis to cut its links with the Crown. A new constitution was adopted in 1937, providing for an elected President in place of the Crown. Articles 2 and 3 of this constitution defined "the national territory" as "the whole island of Ireland" (in Irish, 'Eire') but provided that "pending the reintegration of the national territory" the constitution would apply only in the 26 counties. In 1938 the UK government voluntarily relinquished the right to use naval bases in the South, a decision which was subsequently to lead to much unnecessary loss of Allied life during the Second World War.

Under a 1948 Act Eire formally became a republic on Easter Sunday 1949, on which day it left the Commonwealth. The Unionist government in the North called a general election, which returned it to power with an overwhelming majority. The UK government thereupon passed the Ireland Act 1949, which guaranteed Northern Ireland's constitutional position, stating in particular: "It is hereby declared that Northern Ireland remains part of His Majesty's dominions and of the United Kingdom, and it is hereby affirmed that in no event will Northern Ireland or any part thereof cease to be part of His Majesty's dominions and of the United Kingdom without the consent of the parliament of Northern Ireland".

Northern Ireland has a land area of only 5,452 square miles (14,121 sq km) and its total population is about 1.5 million, compared with about 4 million in the Republic. The conflict over the separation of the six counties from the rest of Ireland has run parallel with the conflict within the six counties themselves, where area boundaries exist (from village to village, or between parts of villages and between one street and another in towns and cities) between Protestants and Roman Catholics. An important influence on the course of the conflict has been the changing demography of Northern Ireland as a formally considerable Protestant majority has steadily dwindled in the face of a higher Catholic birth rate. By the time of the 2001 Census the Protestant population had declined to a comparatively narrow majority of some 53.13% per cent of the total population, while the Roman Catholic minority stood at 43.76%, compared with only 37% when the "Troubles" began in the late 1960s. However, the falling Catholic birth rate in very recent years has called into question the assumption in some circles in the 1990s that demographic factors alone would lead to a Catholic majority in the North favouring a united Ireland in the coming decades. The west and south of the province are increasingly Catholic in composition, the Protestants concentrating increasingly in the east: Belfast itself is 49% Protestant and 46% Catholic.

The total length of the border between Northern Ireland and the Republic is 280 miles (450 km). In many places the border runs through comparatively remote and thinly populated areas, often with a mainly Catholic population with Republican sympathies, and at the height of the Troubles in the 1970s and 1980s these factors contributed to the border being fairly easily crossed by Republicans moving to and from the North for operational purposes.

Early Historical Background

At the time of the Roman empire the Celtic inhabitants of Ireland had a common Gaelic language, a flourishing culture and a common (Brehon) law, but little political unity. The advent of Christianity is traditionally dated from the arrival of St Patrick in 432. Both before and after that time the many lesser kingdoms of Ireland gave only sporadic allegiance to a high king at Tara until the collapse of the central monarchy in 563. At the end of the eighth century Norsemen founded settlements which later became many of the main towns of Ireland, including Dublin itself. In c.1000 most of the Irish tribes were formally united under Brian Boru, who defeated the Norsemen at the Battle of Clontarf (1014) but was killed in the battle.

More disunity ensued, so that Ireland was easy prey for the Norman invaders who arrived by way of England and Wales after 1167. By 1172 the various kings of Ireland had been forced to acknowledge the overlordship of Henry II of England. Henry, whose Angevin empire already stretched as far south as the Pyrenees, had secured authorization to subjugate independent Irish Christianity to the Church of Rome from Pope Adrian IV (so far the only English-born cleric to become Supreme Pontiff). Over the following two centuries the Anglo-Norman conquerors embraced Irish ways and wives with enthusiasm, becoming so assimilated that in 1366, by the Statutes of Kilkenny, intermarriage between English and Irish was forbidden and the Irish language officially outlawed. Thereafter, English overlordship of Ireland was secure only within "the Pale", extending about 50 miles (80 kilometres) in an arc to the west of Dublin. Beyond the Pale, assimilated Anglo-Irish barons of uncertain allegiance held sway amid hostile Irish tribes. Residual Irish self-rule continued until Sir Edward Poynings, sent to Dublin by Henry VII, enacted Poynings' Law (1494) to the effect that no Irish parliament could make laws without the consent of the King and Council in England.

The power of the Norman feudal lords was broken by Henry VIII, who in 1541 adopted the title of King of Ireland. However, his doctrine of ecclesiastical superiority received little support in Ireland, and the Reformation, although carried out with much bloodshed, was largely ineffective as regards the Irish people, who conformed only outwardly with the reformed doctrines. Under Elizabeth I Roman Catholics in Ireland were persecuted, and Irish nationalism and Catholic religion combined to inspire resistance to English rule. During the Counter-Reformation insurrections took place (including the Geraldine rebellion of 1579-83, supported by the Spanish and the Italians, and the O'Neill, Earl of Tyrone, rebellion of 1595) but were crushed. Under King James VI & I, beginning in 1607, confiscated Irish lands in Ulster were apportioned to Scottish settlers, mainly Presbyterians. After the Battle of Drogheda (1649) and the suppression of another Irish rebellion by the troops of Cromwell and Ireton, more land was distributed among Cromwellian soldiers and London merchants. The Catholic religion was suppressed until the Restoration in 1660, when it was given a degree of toleration. However, newly imposed trade restrictions again alienated the Irish people.

The Catholic Irish supported King James II in his fight against William of Orange but were defeated both in the north (at the Battle of the Boyne in 1690) and in the south, where the fighting was concluded by the Treaty of Limerick (1691), which allowed the remnants of the Irish fighting force to go into exile. A new penal code denied Catholics any rights of citizenship or ownership of property, and the government of Ireland passed into the hands of an Irish Protestant oligarchy. Thousands of Irish people emigrated and many served in the armies of France and Spain.

The American War of Independence caused the British government to make some concessions to the Irish, the principal results being the granting of an independent parliament and the repeal (in 1782) of Poynings' Law. The outbreak of the French Revolution brought about the establishment in 1791 of the Society of United Irishmen by Wolfe Tone (a Protestant) as a

revolutionary organization (which later became separatist). A planned invasion by a French revolutionary force in support of the United Irishmen failed in 1796, and a subsequent rebellion, aimed at achieving Catholic emancipation, parliamentary reform and separation from Great Britain, was crushed with considerable loss of life.

The political solution applied by the British Prime Minister, William Pitt the Younger, was the Act of Union (passed in 1800 and in force from 1801) which created the United Kingdom of Great Britain and Ireland. The Irish parliament was dissolved and Ireland was to be represented in the UK parliament by 28 peers and four bishops (elected to the House of Lords for life by the Irish peerage) and by 100 members in the House of Commons. Pitt had intended the act to be accompanied by a measure of Catholic emancipation but King George III opposed this and Pitt resigned in 1801. Hence Roman Catholics were unable to sit in the House of Commons until 1829, when the Roman Catholic Emancipation Act finally allowed them to do so.

During the middle of the 19th century the Irish people suffered the greatest human and economic setback in their history. Blight brought the failure of the potato crop across Europe in 1845-47, but Ireland was uniquely dependent upon it for cheap food. Competition from the United States in the grain market and Britain's adoption of free trade (whereby Ireland lost protection for its wheat) brought about famine, a state of general misery and mass emigration, mainly to the Americas. Of Ireland's then total estimated population of 8,000,000, over 1,000,000 died as a direct consequence of the famine and 1,250,000 left the country (250,000 of them for Britain). Between 1864 and 1914 Ireland changed from being a land of tillage to being mainly one of pasture.

Following the failure of British Liberal governments to secure adoption of Irish Home Rule bills in 1886 and 1893, another Home Rule bill received the royal assent in 1914 but its implementation was suspended owing to the outbreak of World War I. Meanwhile the Irish Land Act began the process of converting tenant farmers into landowners at the expense of the British Government.

The Protestant Domination of Northern Ireland

The evolution, in parts of Ulster, of a society different in certain fundamental respects from that in the rest of Ireland began with what has been called "the Plantation of Ulster", i.e. the settlement in northern Ireland, dating from 1607, of some 170,000 people from Britain—150,000 of them Presbyterians from the lowlands of Scotland. This settlement followed the flight of the last of the Irish earls. The Plantation was resisted by the original inhabitants, who in 1641 murdered thousands of settlers and expelled others from their lands but were themselves ultimately put down, in particular by Cromwell's troops. The success of the Plantation was finally secured by the Battle of the

Boyne in 1690, when Protestant forces of William of Orange defeated Catholics led by James II. (The anniversary of this battle, July 12, is a public holiday celebrated by many of Northern Ireland's Protestants to this day.) By 1703 the remaining Catholics in Ulster owned less than 14 per cent of the land.

The Presbyterians were responsible for rapid capital accumulation and the development of industry in Ulster in the 19th century, and this further distinguished Ulster from the rest of Ireland. Nevertheless, the Catholic and Protestant communities in Northern Ireland were not always in opposite camps and the Protestants themselves were divided. Some Ulster Protestants were hostile to British government even in the 17th century, and a number of them emigrated to America at the time of the American War of Independence and fought against the Crown's forces. Presbyterians, dissenters and Catholics alike had to pay tithes to the established (Episcopalian) Church but were deprived of effective participation in political life. There was a temporary alliance between them in the United Irishmen formed in Belfast in 1791 (largely by Protestants) with the object of uniting "the whole people of Ireland" and "to abolish the memory of all past dissensions and to substitute the common cause of Irishmen in place of the denominations of Protestant, Catholic and dissenter". Both communities contributed to the passing of the 1793 Catholic Relief Act which gave parliamentary franchise to Catholics on equal terms with Protestants (but without allowing them to sit in parliament). This alliance was ended in 1798, however, when an Irish rebellion received virtually no support from either community in the north.

By the end of the 19th century, the basis of Belfast's prosperity was (in the estimation of the Unionist Thomas Sinclair) its "economic link with Britain", for which reason it was "not prepared to come under the rule of a Dublin parliament dominated by impoverished small farmers from Munster and Connaught". Both employers and workers among the Protestants feared that Home Rule for all Ireland (as proposed by the British government) might sever the commercial ties which bound them to Britain; the Protestant tenant farmers had not suffered from extortionate landlords as had the farmers in the south; and they all feared Catholic domination and perhaps oppression.

These arguments were exploited by British Conservatives, notably Lord Randolph Churchill, who in 1886 expressed the view that the British parliament should not leave the Protestants of Ireland in the lurch and that, if necessary, Ulster should "resort to the supreme arbitrament of force", adding: "Ulster will fight [against Home Rule or separation], Ulster will be right".

This precedent was remembered in 1912 when the Liberal government of H.H. Asquith introduced the third Home Rule bill. Sir Edward Carson (later Lord Carson), a Protestant Dublin lawyer who stood for the maintenance of the Union of 1800, read out in Belfast what became known as the Ulster Covenant, which was said to have been signed by 471,414 people who undertook to use "all means which may be found necessary to defeat the present conspiracy to set up a Home Rule parliament in Ireland" and, if it were set up, to "refuse to recognize its authority". Also in 1912 an Ulster Volunteer Force was recruited from among Protestants and was armed with rifles and ammunition smuggled in from the continent of Europe. Its formation was backed by the Ulster Unionist Council (founded in 1905), which regarded itself as a provisional government and was led by Carson. The formation of the Volunteer Force was also encouraged by the Conservatives in Britain, whose leader (Bonar Law) was the son of an Ulster Presbyterian minister and believed that a parliament in Dublin would mean the destruction of the Protestant north. When, early in 1914, the authorities took precautionary steps to protect military supplies from possible Volunteer Force raids, some of the officers responsible for such protection were prepared to resign rather than carry out orders. This "Curragh Mutiny" was supported by Sir Henry Wilson, head of military operations at the War Office, with the result that it became clear that the Army could not be relied upon to enforce Home Rule.

For most of the 20th century the political mouthpiece of the Protestant community in Northern Ireland was the Unionist Party, founded in 1898 and the predominant force in the province's politics until the 1970s, since when it has been challenged by other "Loyalist" formations and has itself split into different groupings. The Unionist Party has been permeated by the spirit of the Orange Order, which was founded in 1795 as an Episcopalian peasant self-defence group which did not officially admit Presbyterians until 1834, since when it has served to weaken confessional antagonisms within the Protestant community but strengthen its political leverage. In the 19th century one of the Order's leaders defined as its enemy "popery...a religio-political system for the enslavement of the body and soul of man [which] cannot be met by any mere religious system or by any mere political system" and must be opposed "by such a combination as the Orange Society, based upon religion and carrying over religion into the politics of the day". Every Prime Minister of Northern Ireland (i.e. up to the establishment of direct rule in the early 1970s) belonged to the Orange Order, which had also provided 95 per cent of all Unionist MPs at Westminster.

Northern Ireland's major Protestant denominations were united in the Irish Council of Churches (which first met in 1923), all of them being united in their aim to maintain the existing border and to resist "Rome rule". An Ancient Order of Hibernians, which had adopted this title in 1938 and formed a Roman Catholic counterpart to the Orange Order, stood for loyalty to the Pope, the principle of a united Ireland, support for the Irish language, and anti-communism. However, it never attracted more than a small percentage of Northern Ireland's Catholic population into membership.

The Rise of Militant Irish Republican Movements

The famine of 1845-48 accelerated the rise of new Irish nationalist movements. First was the Young Ireland movement, whose leaders were sentenced to transportation to a penal colony before they could carry out a rebellion planned for 1848. It was followed by the Fenians (named after a legendary band of Irish warriors), the core of whom was constituted by the Irish Republican Brotherhood (IRB), founded in 1858 as a conspiratorial revolutionary organization responsible for many acts of violence both inside and outside Ireland. It carried its "war of independence" to England in 1867 by bombing Clerkenwell prison in London and shooting a police officer in Manchester in attempts to rescue Fenian prisoners. Members of the "Invincibles", an offshoot of the IRB, murdered the (Liberal) Chief Secretary for Ireland, Sir Frederick Cavendish, in Dublin's Phoenix Park in 1882, whereupon the British government introduced a drastic Coercive Act.

The effect of this act was that at the 1885 general elections the Irish nationalists, standing for Home Rule and led by Charles Stewart Parnell, won every seat in the three provinces of Connaught, Leinster and Munster and even a small majority in Ulster, thus gaining the balance of power between Liberals and Conservatives in the House of Commons. However, an attempt by the Liberal Prime Minister (Gladstone) to give Ireland Home Rule was defeated by the defection of a number of Liberals led by Joseph Chamberlain. In a fresh election in 1886 the Conservatives and Chamberlain's Liberal Unionists obtained a majority large enough to make any Home Rule legislation impossible at that stage. A second attempt in 1893 was also unsuccessful.

In support of the third Home Rule bill and in response to the formation of the (Protestant) Ulster Volunteer Force, a National Volunteer Force was recruited in the south in 1913 (at the suggestion of Eóin MacNeill) and was soon infiltrated by the IRB. However, when this latter force was, in 1914, called upon (by the Irish Home Rule party) to fight on the side of the Allies in World War I in order to prove Ireland's right to full nationhood, it became divided. A minority, which regarded the proposal as a betrayal of Irish nationalism, was supported by the IRB, *Sinn Féin* (a group founded as a political party in 1905 by Arthur Griffith as a purely nationalist movement) and the infant Irish labour movement. This determined and well-disciplined minority formed, with a Labour Citizen Army, the group which carried out the 1916 Easter Rising in Dublin, which had been prepared by the IRB. The original plans for this rising were not fully implemented, and in the event it was only a relatively small force of 1,500 men that occupied the General Post Office in Dublin, where their leader, Padraic Pearse, proclaimed the Irish Republic. Within less than a week the rising was crushed and some 1,000 people had lost their lives. Several of the rebel leaders were executed, while others were given life sentences but were released under a general amnesty in 1917. These included Eamonn de Valera (later the Irish Prime Minister), who although he had commanded a key strongpoint in the Easter Rising, was not executed because he could claim US nationality.

The effect of the executions was to strengthen the nationalist movement and in particular *Sinn Féin* which, although most of its leaders were under arrest, gained 73 of the 105 Irish seats in the House of Commons in the 1918 general elections, standing on an outright Republican programme. *Sinn Féin* had campaigned on an abstentionist platform and thus did not take its seats in the UK parliament, forming instead a Constituent Assembly (Dáil Eireann) in Dublin. However, when this Assembly met in January 1919, only 28 members attended, the Ulster Unionists staying away and half the *Sinn Féin* members being in prison.

Under the leadership of Michael Collins, *Sinn Féin* embarked on guerrilla warfare against the British government, which decided to reinforce the country's constabulary by an additional security force, which became known as the Black and Tans because it was kitted out in a mixture of army and police uniform. This force became immensely unpopular on all sides because of its indiscriminate raids on nationalists and unionists alike. *Sinn Féin*, meanwhile, obtained control of much of the machinery of government in the island, and in 1921 the British Prime Minister (David Lloyd George) began negotiations with Eamonn de Valera, president of the Irish provisional government, which led to the conclusion of the Anglo-Irish treaty in December of that year.

The 1921 treaty, however, divided *Sinn Féin*. One wing led by Arthur Griffith (who died in August 1922) and Michael Collins (who was assassinated, also in August 1922) regarded the treaty as a first step towards independence, but a section led by Eamonn de Valera, who had given Griffith and Collins full authority to negotiate it, rejected the settlement because it abandoned the principle of an all-Ireland republic. The settlement was endorsed by a small majority of the Dáil and by a decisive majority at the ensuing general election. The anti-treaty wing of *Sinn Féin* began a civil war which lasted until 1923, and in 1926 de Valera formed the Republican Party (*Fianna Fáil*) and brought his followers into the Dáil, taking the oath of allegiance but disregarding it as "an empty formula". In 1932 *Fianna Fáil* formed the Free State's first government under de Valera's leadership and remained in power until 1948.

During the civil war the Volunteer Force had adopted the name of Irish Republican Army (IRA), which at a meeting in Dublin in July 1923 broke with the IRB. It later decided, in April 1924, to support the *Sinn Féin* party, but its influence subsequently declined. In 1936 the Dublin government declared it an illegal organization and its leaders were imprisoned. During World War II some of its members were pro-German and were responsible for bomb explosions in England in 1940. In 1956-62 the IRA re-emerged in Northern Ireland, but the authorities were able to confine its bombing campaign to the border areas.

Provisional IRA Campaign in Northern Ireland
1969-1991

The political scene in Northern Ireland changed with the establishment in Belfast in February 1967 of the Northern Ireland Civil Rights Association by non-political liberals who wished to co-ordinate the activities of local associations aiming at improving the status of Catholics. The Association soon came under the influence of members of People's Democracy, a group founded in 1968 by the (Trotskyist) International Socialists at Queen's University, Belfast, but after People's Democracy had broken away from the Association in 1970 its leadership was gradually taken over by the Official IRA, the Marxist rump of the original IRA. The Provisional IRA (the "Provos") broke away from the Officials in 1969 and in October of that year launched a terrorist campaign with the aim of making Northern Ireland ungovernable and forcing the UK government to withdraw its armed forces from the province and to relinquish all responsibility for it.

While both the Official and Provisional IRA were later declared illegal in both North and South, their respective political wings have remained legal organizations—(i) Official (Marxist) *Sinn Féin*, which later became the Workers' Party, with the aim of uniting the working class and rejecting sectarianism because it "killed workers", and (ii) Provisional *Sinn Féin*, which later dropped the description "Provisional" from its title.

An Irish Republican Socialist Party broke away from the Official IRA in December 1974 and became a legal party in the Republic, with the aim of "ending British rule in Ireland" and establishing "a united democratic socialist republic". The military wing of this party, the Irish National Liberation Army (INLA), emerged in 1975 with the object of conducting armed warfare to bring about a British military withdrawal from Northern Ireland, which was to be united with the Republic on the basis of "socialist" principles. The INLA was proscribed in the UK in July 1979.

The sectarian conflict in Northern Ireland took on a violent complexion after the Civil Rights Association had, in a march on Oct. 5, 1968, defied a police ban designed to keep it out of a traditionally Unionist area in Derry/Londonderry, and had thus clashed with the police. William Craig, then Northern Ireland Minister of Home Affairs, said afterwards that the Association was "definitely a Republican front" and "clearly unacceptable to the loyalist community". Further marches and clashes took place in the ensuing months, and early in 1969 the UK government agreed to make troops available to protect key installations against attacks, especially by militant Protestants. Disturbances nevertheless spread and reached a climax in Belfast in August 1969, when troops moved in to prevent Protestants from invading the Catholic Falls Road area and to create a "peace line".

In October 1969 the Provisional IRA began a campaign of sniping at soldiers and bombing property; by September 1971 the IRA was using rocket launchers,

and in April 1973 letter bombs appeared, to be followed by parcel bombs sent to senior civil servants. In August 1971 the authorities introduced internment without trial of suspects, which remained in force for four years despite a civil disobedience campaign called by the Catholic opposition parties in Northern Ireland. In circumstances which are still to be fully elucidated, British troops fired on and killed 13 persons in Derry/Londonderry on Jan. 30, 1972, and in a reprisal action for this so called "Bloody Sunday" the British embassy in Dublin was attacked and destroyed by local protesters. The front was now clearly drawn between, on the one hand, the Provisional IRA and, on the other, the British Army, the locally-recruited Ulster Defence Regiment (UDR) and the Royal Ulster Constabulary (RUC, the Northern Ireland police), while members of paramilitary Protestant organizations such as the Ulster Defence Association were held responsible for numerous deaths (not all of them of Catholics).

In 1972 the Northern Ireland parliament was suspended and direct rule from Westminster briefly imposed. A 78-member representative Assembly was formed in 1973 but Unionists rejected the proposed power-sharing Executive. A Constitutional Convention elected in 1975 was unable to agree on a workable system of government for the province. A third attempt was made to form a representative Assembly and elections held in 1982, but nationalist members refused to take their seats. Throughout this whole period, the elections that continued to be held for representatives in the UK parliament continued to return a substantial Unionist majority.

For most of the 1970s the sequence of violence was unremitting, although from the late 1970s a gradual reduction was apparent, as the security forces succeeded in reducing the effectiveness of the paramilitary groups and the latter themselves concentrated more on specific targets rather than on indiscriminate attacks. The incidence of violence continued on a downward trend until the mid-1980s, but then showed an upturn, although to nothing like the scale of the period 1971-76. Official British statistics for the period 1969-91 showed that over those 23 years the total number of people killed in Northern Ireland as a result of the Troubles was 2,942, of whom 2,028 were civilians (including many suspected members of paramilitary organizations), 630 Army or UDR personnel and 284 RUC members or reservists. Having averaged 275 a year in 1971-76, the average annual death toll fell to 96 in 1977-81 and to 70 in 1982-86, but then moved back up to 84 in 1987-91. Over the same period (1969-91) the violence resulted in injuries to 33,956 persons, of whom 23,371 were civilians and 10,585 security personnel.

Security force levels in Northern Ireland reached a peak in 1972, during which there were 21,800 British Army troops deployed in the province for a particular operation, in addition to 9,000 UDR and 6,300 RUC personnel. Having averaged some 15,000 in the late 1970s, the British Army presence was scaled down to around 10,000 through the 1980s (and the UDR was reduced to about 6,300), whereas the RUC (including reservists) increased its strength to 12,600.

Within Ireland the most prominent victim of the Provisional IRA in this period was Earl Mountbatten of Burma, who was killed by a bomb explosion on his fishing boat at Mullaghmore (County Sligo, in the Republic) on Aug. 27, 1979, together with members of his family and a boat boy. Major actions undertaken by the Provisional IRA in Great Britain included a series of public house bombings in Guildford, Woolwich and Birmingham in November 1974 in which 28 people died and which resulted in the introduction of emergency Prevention of Terrorism legislation. A bomb explosion on Oct. 12, 1984, at the Brighton hotel where the Prime Minister, Margaret Thatcher, and other government members were staying for the Conservative Party conference, resulted in five people being killed.

The Provisional IRA made use of its international contacts to obtain arms supplies or financial support from European countries (some Soviet-bloc weapons having been intercepted) and from radical Arab states, notably Libya. It also continued to receive substantial financial contributions from members of the large Irish community in the United States (clandestine arms shipments from this country having also been intercepted), despite efforts by both the British and the Irish governments to dissuade Irish Americans from giving such support.

During the 1970s and 1980s, at the height of the IRA's military campaign, *Sinn Féin* was only a modest electoral force in the North. Although, in the UK general election of June 1983, the *Sinn Féin* leader Gerry Adams was elected in the Belfast West constituency (and was re-elected in 1987), *Sinn Féin* typically polled only between nine and 13 per cent of the province-wide vote in elections in the 1980s, and came a poor second to the moderate nationalist Social Democratic Labour Party (SDLP) in its share of the Catholic vote. It was even less of a force in the Republic. In the Republic's general election of June 1981 two Provisional IRA members, both of them on hunger strike in the Maze prison in the North, were elected (one of them dying on Aug. 2). However, no Provisionals were elected in either of the two 1982 general elections or in the 1987 election (when *Sinn Féin* secured less than 2 per cent of the vote). In November 1986 *Sinn Féin* decided to end its ban on its members taking up seats in the Dáil if elected and was officially registered as a political party in the Republic shortly before the 1987 elections. In the June 1989 general election, however, *Sinn Féin* candidates polled only 1.2 per cent overall, none being elected.

In an effort to deprive the terrorists of the "oxygen of publicity", *Sinn Féin* was one of 11 Ulster groups (Catholic and Protestant) covered by a ban imposed by the UK government in October 1988 on the broadcasting of the spoken views of those supporting or condoning terrorism. Eight of the 11 groups listed were already proscribed but *Sinn Féin*, Republican *Sinn Féin* and the UDA were not. It was not clear how this ban (which was relaxed during pre-election periods) affected the performance of *Sinn Féin* at subsequent electoral contests and it soon became a considerable embarrassment to the UK government. The broadcasting restrictions were ultimately lifted in September 1994 in the context of the emerging peace process.

The Search for a Political Solution, 1965-81

Northern Ireland's relations with the South were in a state of "cold war" during the rule of Eamonn de Valera, who regarded the ending of partition as the over-riding goal of the Irish government. The division between North and South was further exacerbated by provisions of the 1937 Constitution of Ireland (Eire), which not only (as stated above) implied a territorial claim to the whole of Ireland and made the Irish language compulsory as the country's first official language, but also included certain other provisions reflecting Catholic social doctrine which exacerbated Protestant suspicions in the North. In particular, the constitution prohibited divorce and accorded the Roman Catholic Church a "special position" as "guardian of the faith professed by the great majority of the citizens". Under this general provision the Irish government imposed prior censorship of books and other printed material. Ireland was neutral in the Second World War though (as in the First) many of its young men contributed to the Allied war effort as volunteers in the British Army.

The situation changed with the advent of Seán Lemass as Prime Minister of the Republic in 1959. State-aided industrialization replaced traditional agrarianism and in 1961 Lemass announced that the Dublin government intended to join the European Economic Community (EEC) whether the UK did so or not. In 1965 Lemass went to Belfast to meet the Northern Ireland Prime Minister (Capt. Terence O'Neill), this being the first meeting of the heads of the two Irish governments for 40 years, and a return visit took place a few weeks later. However, these meetings and his attempts to introduce some reforms in favour of the Catholics led to the downfall of Capt. O'Neill, not only owing to Loyalist agitation against him led by the Rev. Ian Paisley but also because of opposition from within the Unionist Party led by the Finance Minister Brian Faulkner. O'Neill was replaced as Prime Minister on May 1, 1969, by Maj. James Chichester-Clark, who was himself replaced by Faulkner in March 1971.

In the wake of the January 1972 "Bloody Sunday" incident, the Northern Ireland Catholics withdrew all co-operation with the Stormont government, and talks between that administration and the British government broke down on March 23, 1972, over the question of which of the two was to control security. The British government thereupon invoked powers granted under the 1920 act to prorogue the Northern Ireland parliament on March 30, 1972, and imposed direct rule over the province by the UK parliament and government for an initial period of one year (which was extended for another year in March 1973). For this purpose a new UK office of Secretary of State for Northern Ireland was created, William Whitelaw being appointed as its first incumbent.

The imposition of direct rule was initially welcomed by the Dublin government as a contribution to solving "the remaining problems in Anglo-Irish relations". In a speech to the Dáil on April 20, 1972, the *Fianna Fáil* Prime Minister, Jack Lynch, said that the prospects were opening for a real and lasting solution to Ireland's troubles in a way which would bring peace and unity to the island. Significance was also attached in Dublin to the fact that both Britain and Ireland had finally in January 1972 signed accession treaties to join the European Community (from Jan. 1, 1973), it being anticipated that joint EC membership would over time reduce the importance of the border with the North. As a contribution to easing the path to Irish unity, the Lynch government on Dec. 8, 1972, secured overwhelming referendum approval for the deletion from the Irish constitution of the clause guaranteeing the "special position" of the Catholic Church.

A year after the imposition of direct rule, a referendum was held in Northern Ireland on March 8, 1973, to ascertain the views of the population on any possible change in the province's status. However, this so-called "border poll" was boycotted by the nationalist community with the result that only 58.6 per cent of the eligible electorate went to the polls. The results showed that 591,820 people (57.4 per cent of the total electorate of 1,030,084) had voted in favour of Northern Ireland remaining as part of the United Kingdom and 6,463 (0.63 per cent) for Northern Ireland to be joined with the Irish Republic outside the United Kingdom, while 5,973 (0.58 per cent) spoiled their ballot papers.

The British government thereupon enacted the 1973 Northern Ireland Constitution Act, which confirmed the status of Northern Ireland as part of the United Kingdom for as long as a majority wished it to be so, but abolished the Westminster-style Stormont parliament and put in its place a Northern Ireland Assembly, to be elected by the single transferable vote method of proportional representation (as used in the Republic of Ireland but not in Britain), and an executive based on the principle of power-sharing between the Protestant and Catholic communities.

This act, however, led to disagreement within the Unionist movement, where it was opposed by the Orange Order, Paisley's Democratic Unionist Party and the Vanguard Unionist Party (VUP)—the last newly founded in March 1973 by William Craig. In the Assembly elected under the act in June 1973, the 78 seats were distributed as follows: Unionist followers of Brian Faulkner in favour of power-sharing 22, Official Unionists opposed to power-sharing 13, Paisley supporters 8, Craig supporters 7, SDLP 19, the Alliance Party (formed in 1970 "to cross the sectarian divide in Northern Ireland") 8, Northern Ireland Labour Party (NILP) 1.

The principle of power-sharing was endorsed at a conference held in December 1973 at Sunningdale (Berkshire) between members of the British government (led by Prime Minister Edward Heath), of the Irish Cabinet (led by Prime Minister Liam Cosgrave) and of the Northern Ireland Executive-designate (set up by Faulkner with SDLP and Alliance participation). At the same time agreement was reached on the formation of a Council of Ireland consisting of representatives of Northern Ireland and the Republic to develop North-South relations. At the conference the Irish government "fully accepted and solemnly declared" that there could be no change in Northern Ireland's status until a majority in the province so wished, while the UK government reaffirmed that its policy remained to support the wishes of the majority of the people of Northern Ireland and that if in the future such a majority "should indicate a wish to become part of a united Ireland the British government would support that wish".

Direct rule was ended under a Northern Ireland Constitution (Devolution) Order which (effective Jan. 1, 1974) implemented an amendment to the Northern Ireland Constitution Act by allowing for the appointment of an 11-member Executive and a 15-member Administration in Belfast. However, on Jan. 4, 1974, the Ulster Unionist Council, the policy-making body of Faulkner's party, rejected the Sunningdale proposals by 427 votes to 374, and the first meeting of the Assembly on Jan. 22 had to be suspended when Faulkner's opponents prevented members of the Executive from taking their seats. On the following day the Official Unionists led by Harry West and also the Paisley and Craig parties withdrew from the Assembly. In elections to the UK House of Commons on Feb. 28, 1974 (held under the traditional first-past-the-post system), the 12 Northern Ireland constituencies returned 11 candidates opposed to the Sunningdale agreement.

The anti-Faulkner Unionists were supported by two paramilitary organizations, namely (i) the Ulster Volunteer Force (UVF), originally formed in 1912 (see above) and reconstituted in 1966, and (ii) the Ulster Defence Association (UDA), formed in 1972 to defend Protestant areas from IRA incursions and estimated to have recruited 50,000 members within three months. These groups in turn supported a general strike called in May 1974 and widely endorsed in the Protestant community. The new British (Labour) government led by Harold Wilson declared a state of emergency in the province on May 19 and sent in more troops to maintain civil order. The Executive resigned on May 28, the Assembly was prorogued on May 29 and the UK government again assumed direct authority in Northern Ireland.

On May 1, 1975, elections were held to a Constitutional Convention, which was to report on the establishment of a future government of Northern Ireland commanding the support of the whole community. The result of these elections was not very different from that of the elections for the Assembly of June

1973, seats being gained as follows: the anti-power-sharing United Ulster Unionist Council (UUUC) 46, Unionist Party of Northern Ireland (UPNI, supporting Faulkner) 5, SDLP 17, Alliance Party 8, NILP 1, Independent Loyalist 1. The UUUC was divided into 19 Official Unionists (led by West), 14 VUP members, 12 Paisley supporters and an independent with UUUC support. However, all UUUC members of the Convention except Craig stated during September 1975 that they were opposed to any coalition with the SDLP. The Convention ceased to meet on Nov. 7 of that year and was formally dissolved on March 5, 1976, having failed to agree on a government system based on partnership between Protestants and Catholics.

Also on March 5, 1976, the British and Irish Prime Ministers (respectively Harold Wilson and Liam Cosgrave) met and agreed that "'an acceptable form of government for Northern Ireland could be established only by both communities agreeing on a system of government providing for partnership and participation" and that, pending such an agreement, a period of direct rule (by Westminster) and stability was necessary.

A new call for a general strike was made in May 1977 by a United Unionist Action Council, which included the Paisley formation and the UDA, with the aim of forcing the British government to carry out the Unionist demand for a virtual return to the 1920 act, but was called off on May 13 for lack of support. It led, however, to the foundation in October 1977 of two new parties—the Irish Independence Party and the Ulster Independence Party—to promote the idea of an ultimate declaration of independence by Northern Ireland from the United Kingdom. (William Craig's VUP was dissolved in February 1978, when he joined the Official Unionist Party.)

In the Republic Lynch had meanwhile become Prime Minister again and, on Jan. 8, 1978, called for a British declaration of intent to withdraw from Northern Ireland and stated in particular that he would like to see a start in "bringing Irish people together"; that the British government should indicate "in a general way" that they did "not wish to continue subsidizing a small corner of Ireland to the extent that they have been doing over the past 50 years"; and that the British people themselves had "no stomach for that kind of subsidization which involves taxation on them" (in fact the subsidies paid to Northern Ireland by the rest of the UK formed a very minor part of the national budget, and few voters in Great Britain even knew that they existed). He added that "the people of Northern Ireland would be realistic enough to know that there should be, and ought to be, accommodation found between the [nationalist] minority and themselves in the first instance, and between them and us in the long term".

In May 1979 Margaret Thatcher became Prime Minster of the UK at the head of a Conservative Government. Lynch's successor, Charles Haughey, called on Feb. 16, 1980, for a joint initiative on Northern Ireland by the United Kingdom and Irish governments.

He found the picture in Northern Ireland "'a depressing one" as its agriculture and industry were producing less than in the early 1970s and the population had remained static. While emphasizing that in the Republic the rule of law would be firmly upheld and democracy defended, he said that for over 60 years the situation in Northern Ireland had been a source of instability because "the very entity [of Northern Ireland] itself is artificial and has been artificially sustained". The reality, he claimed, was that Northern Ireland as a political entity had failed and that a new beginning was needed. He added that it would be his concern to ensure that the place of Protestants in the Ireland of the future would be secure and that their traditions were honoured and respected. He looked forward to "some free and open arrangement in which Irish men and women on their own, without a British presence but with active British goodwill, will manage the affairs of the whole of Ireland in a constructive partnership with the European Community". Unionists, however, considered that as they were themselves British in the sense of being citizens of the UK, the question of "a British presence" in Northern Ireland was not negotiable.

A constitutional conference held in Belfast from Jan. 7 to March 24, 1980, but not attended by the Official Unionist Party, was adjourned after it had failed to reach agreement by the parties represented on the role of the Catholic minority in a devolved government of the province. After the publication in July 1980 of further British proposals on Northern Ireland, Humphrey Atkins, then British Secretary of State for Northern Ireland, announced in the House of Commons on Nov. 27, 1980, that there was not sufficient agreement among the parties to justify bringing forward proposals for setting up a devolved administration at that stage, and that new ways would have to be explored.

On the other hand, Charles Haughey and Margaret Thatcher, meeting in London on May 21, 1980, were able to agree that "they wished to develop a new and closer political co-operation between the two governments" and to hold regular meetings. At a further meeting (held in Dublin on Dec. 8, 1980), the two Prime Ministers agreed inter alia that the economic, social and political interests of their peoples were "inextricably linked" but that the full development of these links had been "put under strain by division and dissent in Northern Ireland" and that peace, reconciliation and stability must be achieved there.

The Anglo-Irish meetings at prime ministerial level were particularly strongly opposed by Paisley, who on Feb. 19, 1981, signed in Belfast, with other members of his party, a covenant similar to that of 1912 in which the signatories pledged themselves to use all means necessary "to defeat the present conspiracy...to edge Northern Ireland out of the United Kingdom and to establish an ongoing process of all-Ireland integration".

Notwithstanding both this and more moderate Unionist opposition, a further UK-Irish summit meeting was held in London on Nov. 6, 1981, at which Thatcher agreed with Dr Garret FitzGerald (who had succeeded Haughey in June 1981 at the head of a *Fine*

Gael-Labour coalition) to set up an Anglo-Irish Inter-Governmental Council (AIIC). It was stated that this body would meet regularly at ministerial and official levels to discuss matters of common concern, in which context the London meeting received a report on joint studies (commissioned by the previous session in Dublin) covering possible new institutional structures to link the two countries, citizenship rights, economic co-operation, measures to encourage mutual understanding and co-operation on security matters. A communiqué said that the two Prime Ministers had "agreed on the need for efforts to diminish the divisions between the two sections of the community in Northern Ireland and to reconcile the two major traditions that exist in the two parts of Ireland"; that FitzGerald had "affirmed that it was the wish of the Irish government and, he believed, of the great majority of the people of the island of Ireland to secure the unity of Ireland by agreement and in peace"; and that both Prime Ministers took the view that "any change in the constitutional status of Northern Ireland would require the consent of the majority of the people of Northern Ireland".

Before meeting Thatcher, FitzGerald had stated in a radio interview on Sept. 27, 1981, that he favoured changes in the Irish constitution to make the reunification of Ireland more attractive to Northern Protestants, including amendments to the definition (in Articles 2 and 3) of the national territory as being the whole of Ireland. Maintaining that the Republic had "slipped into a partitionist attitude with institutions which…could never be the basis to enter discussions with Unionists in Northern Ireland", Dr FitzGerald continued: "What I want to do is to lead a crusade—a Republican crusade—to make this a genuine Republic on the principles of Tone and Davis [i.e. Wolfe Tone and Thomas Davis, two early Irish patriots who were both Protestants], and if I can bring the people of this country on that path and get them to agree down here to the type of state that Tone and Davis looked for, I believe we could have the basis then on which many Protestants in Northern Ireland would be willing to consider a relationship with us".

Dr FitzGerald lost office as a result of the February 1982 Irish elections, however, and was succeeded by Haughey, who had made it clear that his *Fianna Fáil* party was still opposed to any piecemeal abandonment of the national ideals and aspirations enshrined in the constitution. There followed a sharp deterioration in UK-Irish relations, notably over the Haughey government's attitude to the UK-Argentine conflict over the Falklands (see Section 2.3), which was described in Dublin as being one of neutrality but which was seen in London as pro-Argentine.

Failure of 1982 Devolution Proposals and Northern Ireland Assembly

After consultations with interested parties, the UK government secured the approval on July 23, 1982, of a new Northern Ireland Act providing principally for the eventual resumption of legislative and executive functions by an elected Assembly in Northern Ireland, in succession to the Assembly which had been dissolved in 1974 with the reintroduction of direct rule from Westminster.

The legislation specified (i) that a 78-member unicameral Assembly would be elected by the single transferable vote method of proportional representation from multi-member constituencies which would be co-terminous with House of Commons constituencies, then numbering 12 (but increased to 17 from the 1983 UK general election onwards); (ii) that the Assembly's functions, pending devolution of powers, would be consultative and deliberative, including scrutiny of draft legislation and making reports and recommendations to the Secretary of State for Northern Ireland, who would lay them before parliament; (iii) that prior to devolution the Assembly would have departmental committees, whose membership, chairmen and vice-chairmen would, in their party affiliation, reflect the distribution of seats in the Assembly (i.e. minority parties would be represented); (iv) that the Assembly could proceed to full devolution of powers either directly or via partial devolution, the essential criterion being that representatives of both communities should agree on how executive powers should be discharged; (v) that the support of at least 70 per cent of the total membership of the Assembly would normally be required for any devolution of powers to be activated (although the Secretary of State could pursue specific proposals to that end if they had the support of a majority of the total membership and if he believed that they were acceptable to both sides of the community); (vi) that under full devolution the Northern Ireland Executive would consist of not more than 13 members, who would be replaced following consultation with the parties; and (vii) that as under the 1973 Northern Ireland Constitution Act certain "excepted" matters (e.g. Crown affairs, foreign policy and defence) would remain the permanent responsibility of Westminster and certain "reserved" matters (principally law and order) could not be devolved immediately, while "transferred" matters (i.e. those which could be devolved) would include responsibility for agriculture, commerce, education, environment, finance and personnel, health and social services, and manpower services.

Adopted with the tacit consent of the opposition Labour Party, the 1982 Northern Ireland Bill was vigorously opposed by the Unionist representatives at Westminster, who were supported by a small group of Conservative backbench MPs. The main thrust of the Unionist opposition was that, while the prospect of a restored Northern Ireland administration was welcomed, the proposals were unworkable because they would effectively enable a minority of 31 per cent of the new Assembly's members to block progress towards devolution of powers. In their subsequent manifestos for the Assembly elections, both the Official Unionist Party (OUP) and Paisley's Democratic Unionist Party (DUP) pledged themselves to resist any power-sharing in the new body and to seek to change the 70 per cent requirement for the activation of devolution steps.

On the Republican side, both the SDLP and *Sinn Féin* also condemned the new Assembly, the former proposing an alternative plan for a "Council for a New Ireland" to consist of members of the Dublin parliament and those elected to the Assembly; both formations in addition pledged that their successful candidates would refuse to take their seats in the new body. Only the small Alliance Party expressed positive support for the Assembly, although with the qualification that it would not enter into any partnership arrangement for devolving power until the Unionist parties agreed in principle that any major party which recognized the present institutions of the state, whatever its ultimate aspirations, had the right to share in that arrangement.

The results of the elections, held on Oct. 20, 1982, gave the OUP 26 seats, the DUP 21, the SDLP 14, the Alliance Party 10, *Sinn Féin* 5, and one seat each to an Independent Unionist and the Ulster Popular Unionist Party (UPUP). There was a valid turnout of 632,664 voters (60.3 per cent) among an electorate of 1,048,807. One of the successful SDLP candidates, Seamus Mallon (the party's deputy leader), was subsequently disqualified because of his membership of the Irish Senate; the SDLP did not contest the consequent by-election on April 20, 1983, which was won by the OUP, whose representation was thus increased to 27.

At the first meeting of the Assembly on Nov. 11, 1982, in the main chamber of Stormont Castle, James Kilfedder (UPUP) was elected presiding officer (combining the functions of Speaker with the task of appointing departmental committee chairmen) by 31 votes (DUP and Alliance) to 25 (OUP). Both the SDLP and *Sinn Féin* carried out their threat to boycott the Assembly, which was thereby effectively reduced to 59 members (60 after the April 1983 by-election) of whom 55 would be required to support any devolution proposal to meet the 70 per cent requirement.

The Assembly failed to make any substantive progress in the directions envisaged by the British government. The OUP boycotted its proceedings from November 1983 to May 1984 and in November 1985 the OUP and the DUP combined to suspend Assembly business in protest against the signing of the Anglo-Irish Agreement (see below). Against this background, both Houses of the UK parliament on June 19, 1986, approved an Order dissolving the Assembly, although this measure did not abolish the legal basis of the Assembly and left open the date for possible new elections (which had been due in October 1986).

Unionist perceptions of the Irish Republic as a society dominated by Catholic dogma were strengthened by the outcome of two constitutional referenda held south of the border in the mid-1980s. In the first, Irish voters on Sept. 7, 1983, opted by margin of two to one in favour of the existing legal ban on abortion being enshrined in the constitution. In the second, on June 26, 1986, a proposal to lift the existing constitutional ban on divorce was defeated by a similar margin.

Developments leading to 1985 Anglo-Irish Agreement

Dr FitzGerald's return to office in Dublin in December 1982 brought about an improvement in UK-Irish relations and the resumption of direct ministerial contacts within the framework of the AIIC. Meetings at the level of Prime Ministers were resumed at Chequers on Nov. 7, 1983, and continued with a further session, also at Chequers, on Nov. 18-19, 1984. After the latter meeting some tension developed over Margaret Thatcher's categoric dismissal of all three options for the future of Northern Ireland identified in May 1984 by the New Ireland Forum initiative (set up in early 1983 by the Irish government on the proposal of the SDLP and consisting of representatives of the SDLP and the three main parties in the Republic)—namely a unitary Irish state (the Forum's preference), a federal or confederal arrangement between North and South, and joint UK-Irish authority over Northern Ireland—all of which the British Prime Minister said were "out".

However, the next summit, held at Hillsborough Castle (the former residence of Northern Ireland governors) on Nov. 15, 1985, was the occasion of the signature by Thatcher and FitzGerald of a major new agreement establishing, within the framework of the AIIC, an Inter-Governmental Conference (IGC) concerned with Northern Ireland and with relations between the two parts of Ireland. This Anglo-Irish Agreement, or Hillsborough Accord, specified in particular that the IGC would deal on a regular basis with political matters, with security and related questions (including the administration of justice) and with the promotion of cross-border co-operation.

Article 1 of the agreement was worded as follows: "The two governments (a) affirm that any change in the status of Northern Ireland would only come about with the consent of a majority of the people of Northern Ireland; (b) recognize that the present wish of the majority of the people of Northern Ireland is for no change in the status of Northern Ireland; (c) declare that, if in the future a majority of the people of Northern Ireland clearly wish for and formally consent to the establishment of a united Ireland, they will introduce and support in the respective parliaments legislation to give effect to that wish". Article 2, after providing for the establishment of the IGC, continued: "The UK government accept that the Irish government will put forward views and proposals on matters relating to Northern Ireland within the field of activity of the Conference in so far as those matters are not the responsibility of a devolved administration in Northern Ireland...The Conference will be mainly concerned with Northern Ireland, but some of the matters under consideration will involve co-operative action in both parts of the island of Ireland, and possibly also in Great Britain. Some of the proposals considered in respect of Northern Ireland may also be found to have application by the Irish government. There is no derogation from the sovereignty of either the UK government or the Irish government, and each retains responsibility for the decisions and administration of government within its own jurisdiction".

Article 3 dealt with the structure and modalities of the IGC, specifying that meetings at ministerial level would be chaired jointly by the UK Secretary of State for Northern Ireland and an Irish minister designated as the Permanent Irish Ministerial Representative. Article 4 stated inter alia that the IGC "'shall be a framework within which the Irish government may put forward views and proposals on the modalities of bringing about devolution in Northern Ireland, insofar as they relate to the interests of the minority community". Article 5 included a clause that "if it should prove impossible to achieve and sustain devolution on a basis which secures widespread acceptance in Northern Ireland, the Conference shall be a framework within which the Irish government may, where the interests of the minority community are significantly or especially affected, put forward views on proposals for major legislation and on major policy issues which are within the purview of the Northern Ireland departments and which remain the responsibility of the Secretary of State for Northern Ireland".

Article 6 provided that the Irish government "may put forward views and proposals on the role and composition of bodies appointed by the Secretary of State for Northern Ireland or by departments subject to his direction and control, including the Standing Advisory Commission on Human Rights, the Fair Employment Agency, the Equal Opportunities Commission, the Police Authority for Northern Ireland and the Police Complaints Board". Article 7 covered the IGC's consideration of security policy, relations between the security forces and the community, and prisons policy; Article 8 set out how the IGC would deal with legal matters, including the administration of justice; Articles 9 and 10 dealt with cross-border co-operation on security, economic, social and cultural matters; Article 11 specified that the working of the IGC would be reviewed three years from signature of the agreement, or earlier if requested by either government; Article 12 stated that "'it will be for parliamentary decision in Westminster and in Dublin whether to establish an Anglo Irish parliamentary body"; and Article 13 specified that the agreement would enter into force on exchange of notifications of acceptance by the two governments.

The Anglo-Irish Agreement was approved by the Dáil on Nov. 21, 1985, by 88 votes to 75 (mainly *Fianna Fáil* deputies) and by the Irish Senate on Nov. 28 by 37 votes to 16. In the UK parliament it was approved in the House of Lords on Nov. 26 and in the House of Commons on Nov. 27; the Commons vote was 473 in favour (most Conservative and Labour members, Liberals, Social Democratic Party and John Hume, leader of the SDLP) with 47 against (20 Conservatives, 13 Labour members and 14 Ulster Unionists). The agreement came formally into force on Nov. 29 following the exchange of notifications of acceptance in Dublin, and the inaugural meeting of the IGC was held in Belfast on Dec. 11, 1985.

Reactions to Anglo-Irish Agreement—Unionist Opposition

In the Republic, Fianna Fáil's opposition to the Anglo-Irish Agreement derived principally from the party's view that Article 1 gave a treaty guarantee to the Northern Unionist position, in contravention of the national aspirations enshrined in the Irish constitution. As opposition leader, Charles Haughey in the course of 1986 said that a *Fianna Fáil* government would seek to renegotiate the agreement, which he claimed brought no real benefits to Northern Catholics. However, after regaining the premiership as a result of the February 1987 Irish elections, Haughey said that his government would "fulfil and operate" the agreement and accepted that Article 1 was "an integral part of a binding international agreement" and that the mutual agreement required to change it "would not emerge".

At the same time, the Haughey government indicated that it would review new extradition legislation, associated with the parliamentary ratification in the last days of the FitzGerald government of the 1976 European Convention on the Suppression of Terrorism (Ireland's early accession to which had been envisaged under the Hillsborough Accord). Adopted against the opposition of *Fianna Fáil*, the legislation was intended to facilitate the extradition of political terrorists and was due to come into force in December 1987, to allow time for the administration of justice in the North to be made more acceptable to the minority community. Particular areas of concern to the Dublin government were the continued use of single-judge, non-jury ("Diplock") courts to try suspected terrorists and also of uncorroborated informer evidence in so-called "super-grass" trials, as well as the reliability of the English judicial process where Irish terrorist offences were concerned. In addition to sharing these concerns, *Fianna Fáil* had called during the Irish election campaign for the addition to the legislation of a requirement that an authority requesting extradition should make a prima facie case in support of each application. Following Fianna Fáil's return to power, such an amendment was approved by the Irish government on Nov. 24, 1987, enabling the European convention to be ratified by the Republic on Dec. 1. However, cases continued to occur thereafter of Irish courts refusing to extradite suspects to the United Kingdom, to the chagrin of the British government.

Within Northern Ireland, the Unionist parties declared a policy of total opposition to the Anglo-Irish Agreement, which they regarded as giving a foreign government the right to intervene in the sovereign affairs of the United Kingdom. At a special meeting of the Northern Ireland Assembly in Belfast on Nov. 16, 1985, a Unionist resolution calling for a referendum on the agreement in Northern Ireland was carried by 44 votes to 10 (the Alliance Party opposing the resolution). Following the rejection of this proposal by the UK government, the Unionist majority suspended Assembly business indefinitely (having also announced the withdrawal of Unionists from all government advisory boards and authorities in the province). Moreover, the UK parliament's approval of the agreement on Nov. 26-27 provoked the resignation from their House of Commons seats of all 15 Unionists MPs (11 OUP, three DUP and one UPUP) and the calling of by-elections in which the Unionists sought to demonstrate the extent of opposition to the agreement.

In the event, the contests (on Jan. 23, 1986) resulted in the OUP losing one seat to the SDLP and the other 14 Unionists being re-elected. The Unionist candidates increased their aggregate vote slightly as compared with the 1983 general election, polling 418,230 votes in a lower turnout, but fell short of what was generally considered to be their target of 500,000 votes.

Other actions taken to demonstrate Unionist opposition to the agreement included a one-day "Loyalist strike" on March 3, 1986, and an instruction given by Unionist leaders on Nov. 15, 1986 (the first anniversary of the signature of the agreement), that all Unionist local councillors should resign their seats, the aim being to make Northern Ireland ungovernable until the Anglo-Irish Agreement was revoked. The agreement was also denounced by the Provisional IRA as perpetuating the "British occupation" of Northern Ireland.

Progress of Anglo-Irish Inter-Governmental Conference

Despite unbending Unionist opposition, the Anglo-Irish Inter-Governmental Conference became a regular fixture of relations between London and Dublin insofar as the Northern Ireland question was concerned. In addition to considering longer-term institutional and other aspects, the IGC was also used as a forum for seeking to defuse crises which arose from time to time over, for example, British security policy in Northern Ireland or the resistance of the Irish courts to extraditing suspected IRA terrorists to British jurisdiction.

In accordance with the Hillsborough Accord, a review of the working of the IGC was conducted at what was its 27th meeting, held in Belfast on May 24, 1989, with the Unionist parties declining to participate. In the published account of that review, both sides reaffirmed their commitment to the Anglo-Irish Agreement and announced an extension of the scope of future IGC meetings. Henceforth the IGC would be attended by more ministers, would meet even more regularly and would have a wider range of issues on its agenda. It was also stated that the Irish government supported the British government's objective of encouraging "progress towards the devolution of responsibility for certain powers to elected representatives in Northern Ireland". Both sides recognized that "the achievement of devolution depends on the co-operation of constitutional representatives of both traditions within Northern Ireland". It had been revealed in February 1989 that the four main "constitutional" parties of Northern Ireland (the OUP, DUP, SDLP and

Alliance) had conducted secret talks the previous October in the German city of Duisberg, and had continued this contact on "home ground" subsequently, although without reaching agreement.

In the review both governments emphasized their determination to continue to cooperate against terrorism. Further measures were promised to instil in the Catholic community in Northern Ireland greater confidence in the security forces, including monitoring of the nature, pattern and handling of complaints by the public about the conduct of the army and police. The review stressed the "central importance...of measures to accommodate the rights and identities of the two traditions in Northern Ireland, to protect human rights and prevent discrimination". In this context, the Irish government welcomed a number of positive measures implemented by the British government since the signature of the Hillsborough Accord. These included the repeal of the Flags and Emblems Act (a Stormont act which had made flying the Irish tricolour illegal in Northern Ireland), the enfranchisement of certain previously disqualified voters, the enhancement of police powers to control potentially provocative marches, and the passage of the Fair Employment (Northern Ireland) Act (which received the royal assent on July 27, 1989). On the other hand, the review recorded that the British side was "not at present persuaded" of the merits of Dublin's proposal that "Diplock" (i.e. single-judge, non-jury) courts for terrorist cases in Northern Ireland should be replaced by three-judge courts reflecting the communal balance.

The IGC review noted that in September 1986 the two governments had created an International Fund for Ireland (IFI), with financial support from the United States, Canada and New Zealand (and later from the EC). The IFI had to date committed over £50,000,000 to projects in Northern Ireland and the border counties of the Republic, creating "a significant number of new jobs". The two sides also welcomed "the progress which has been made towards the establishment of a British Irish inter-parliamentary body...which would provide a valuable independent forum for inter-parliamentary contacts". The review concluded by stressing that the Anglo-Irish Agreement "does not represent a threat to either tradition in Northern Ireland" but rather "provides a framework which respects the essential interests of both sides of the community and their right to pursue their aspirations by peaceful means".

Further meetings of the IGC were held in September and October 1989, by which time Peter Brooke had been appointed UK Secretary of State for Northern Ireland (on July 24, 1989). At these sessions, Irish ministers pressed for a reassessment, and possible curtailment, of the role of the UDR in Northern Ireland. This stance followed allegations that UDR members had leaked information about IRA suspects to Protestant paramilitary groups and the UK government's confirmation that the UDR had been issued with plastic bullets (previously used only by the British Army). On the former controversy, a government-commissioned inquiry by the deputy chief constable of Cambridgeshire, John Stevens, was published on May 17, 1990. It concluded that information had been passed on a limited scale and recommended procedural and technical changes to prevent a recurrence. Such matters coloured the IGC sessions held in London in March and April 1990, as did the continuing British dismay over refusals by Irish courts to grant extradition of terrorist suspects. Unionist opposition to the IGC process was not reduced by a visit to Northern Ireland on April 11, 1990, by Haughey in his capacity as the Prime Minister of the country then holding the EC Presidency, even though he pledged full co-operation in combating terrorism. This was the first public appearance of an Irish Prime Minister in Northern Ireland for 25 years.

The inaugural meeting of what was designated the British-Irish Parliamentary Body took place in London on Feb. 26, 1990. It was supposed to be attended by 25 members of the Dáil and 25 from the UK parliament. However, the two UK seats allocated to the Northern Ireland Unionists were not taken up because of their opposition to the Hillsborough Accord and consequent initiatives.

Brooke Devolution Talks, 1991-92—Upsurge of Violence

A further IGC meeting in Belfast on July 17, 1990, ended in some disarray over the timetable for UK devolution talks with the "constitutional" parties of Northern Ireland, as desired by Brooke and envisaged in the 1989 review of the IGC process. The problem at this stage was the Irish government's insistence on being involved in the talks at an early stage, whereas the Unionists were reluctant to allow Dublin to take part until substantial progress had been made towards a new form of devolved government. The Unionists also pressed their view that the 1985 Anglo-Irish Agreement should be scrapped altogether but the UK government refused to consider doing so. In November 1990, after a prolonged political crisis in London, Margaret Thatcher was forced to resign as Prime Minister and replaced by John Major. Hence not until March 26, 1991, was Brooke able to announce that sufficient preliminary agreement had been reached for all-party talks on the constitutional future of Northern Ireland—the first since 1975—to commence at the end of April 1991.

Brooke explained in his announcement that there would be three phases of talks lasting about 10 weeks in all, during which the operation of the Anglo-Irish Agreement would be suspended. First, the Secretary of State would chair discussions between the "constitutional" parties of Northern Ireland (the OUP, DUP, SDLP and Alliance), focusing on devolution and power-sharing. Second, there would be "North-South" talks between the Northern Ireland parties and the Irish government, under a chairman to be agreed by the interested parties. Third, there would be "East-West" talks between the London and Dublin govern-

ments. Brooke said that the Unionists would be able to participate in the second phase as part of a UK delegation. Any agreed outcome of the process would be put to referendums in both Northern Ireland and the Republic. In accordance with Brooke's announcement, the IGC on April 26 decided that it would not convene again until July 16, 1991.

Although preliminary first-phase talks opened on schedule on April 30, 1991, the Brooke initiative quickly ran into all the traditional procedural and political obstacles. The planned opening of the first phase proper on May 7 was postponed amid a dispute over the venue of the second phase, for which the OUP and DUP preferred London, while the SDLP and the Irish government wished it to alternate between Belfast and Dublin. After an unexpected meeting in London on May 15 between the UK Prime Minister, John Major, and the OUP and DUP leaders (respectively James Molyneaux and Paisley), a compromise was announced under which the second phase would open in London, move to Belfast for its substantive work and conclude in Dublin. Argument then focused on who was to chair the second phase, so that the delayed opening of the first phase, rescheduled for May 28, was again postponed. On May 30 the Unionist parties rejected the suggested appointment as second-phase chairman of Lord Carrington (the former UK Foreign Secretary and former NATO secretary-general), alleging that he had a "deplorable" record on Northern Ireland. Eventually, on June 15, an agreement was announced that the second phase would be chaired by Sir Ninian Stephen, a retired Australian judge and former Governor-General of Australia.

With the procedural problems apparently resolved, the first inter-party talks in Northern Ireland for 16 years opened in Belfast on June 17, 1991. The first session lasted three days and a further session took place on June 24, during which period the Northern Ireland situation was among matters discussed by Major and Haughey at a meeting in London on June 21. However, it quickly became apparent that Brooke had greatly overestimated the willingness of the parties to look for common ground. The immediate cause of breakdown was the demand of the OUP and DUP that the IGC meeting scheduled for July 16 should be postponed, which Brooke rejected. More fundamentally, the Unionist parties remained resolutely opposed to any proposal or formula that appeared to give the Dublin government a role in Northern Ireland's affairs. In announcing on July 3 that the talks had been brought to an end (without getting beyond the first phase), Brooke expressed the view that the "commitment and seriousness of purpose" shown by all the parties was a source of encouragement for the future. He added that he hoped that bilateral discussions could be resumed later in the year with a view to establishing a new basis for formal talks.

The IGC convened as scheduled in Dublin on July 16, 1991, on which occasion Paisley presented a letter of protest to the Irish government. Having blamed Dublin for the breakdown of the talks, the DUP leader asserted that "if there are going to be talks, they will have to be on a different foundation and the Anglo-Irish Agreement will have to be suspended for the whole period of the talks". At the next IGC session, in Belfast on Sept. 13, ministers were pessimistic about a speedy revival of formal talks. Brooke had exploratory talks with Dr Paisley and Molyneaux in Belfast on Sept. 20, with the result that the next session of the IGC, held in Dublin on Nov. 20, was able to note some limited progress. However, on Jan. 27, 1992, Brooke announced the suspension of the talks process, saying that his efforts to revive them had not produced agreement between the parties on a suitable framework. In an agreed statement, the four Northern Ireland parties stressed the "great potential" of political dialogue but admitted that it was "not possible in present circumstances to proceed to launch fresh substantive talks on the lines envisaged". Unwilling to allow his initiative to expire, Brooke convened a further round of talks on March 9, principally to convey the assurance of both the ruling Conservatives and the opposition Labour Party that talks would be pursued whatever the outcome of the imminent UK general elections.

The January 1992 suspension of the Brooke initiative occurred amid an upsurge of political and sectarian violence in Northern Ireland and a series of IRA bomb attacks in London. Accordingly, the UK authorities on Jan. 19, 1992, deployed an additional army battalion in Northern Ireland, bringing the number of regular British troops in the province to 11,000. Predictably, increased IRA activity was accompanied by an escalation of attacks on Catholic targets by Protestant paramilitaries of the UVF and the Ulster Freedom Fighters (UFF) .

In prime ministerial talks in Dublin on Dec. 4, 1991, Major and Haughey had agreed to hold further such meetings every six months, alternately in Britain and Ireland. Two months later, on Feb. 11, 1992, Haughey was replaced as Irish Prime Minister by Albert Reynolds, who had been elected leader of *Fianna Fáil* on Feb. 6. Both he and his new Foreign Minister, David Andrews, represented a more moderate nationalist tradition than their predecessors. In the UK the Conservative Party was returned for a fourth successive term in the UK elections held on April 9, on a platform which included a commitment to continuing the Anglo-Irish Agreement process. In a post-election cabinet reshuffle, Brooke was replaced as Northern Ireland Secretary by Sir Patrick Mayhew, who on April 17 announced his intention to resume devolution talks with the four "constitutional" parties.

In the elections the 17 Northern Ireland constituencies returned 12 Unionist MPs (nine OUP and three DUP), four from the SDLP (which won 22.7 per cent of the popular vote) and one independent Unionist. A notable result was the defeat in West Belfast of the *Sinn Féin* leader, Gerry Adams, who lost to the SDLP and saw his party's share of the vote fall to 10.3 per cent. Immediately after the elections, on the night of April 10-11, the IRA exploded two huge car bombs in London, killing three people and injuring over 20.

Detonated at the Baltic Exchange in the City financial district and at an important motorway junction in north London, the two bombs were the biggest so far planted by the IRA outside the island of Ireland and caused damage estimated to be well in excess of £1,000 million.

Start of Peace Process—Downing Street Declaration

What was to become known simply as "the peace process" is widely accepted to have begun as early as Jan. 11, 1988, with the first of a series of meetings between John Hume, leader of the SDLP, and Gerry Adams, then president of *Sinn Féin*. The process consists of a series of negotiations to achieve sufficient agreement on political institutions to enable the military conflict in Northern Ireland to come to an end, and throughout it has been evident that it has been strongly supported by the vast majority of the ordinary citizens of the province. The initial series of talks broke down and were not resumed until after it had been disclosed in 1992 that the Major government had itself, despite its formal policy of not doing so, been engaged in contacts with *Sinn Féin* for some time previously. In 1993, the dialogue between the nationalist leaders resulted in a document known as the "Hume-Adams initiative" which was conveyed to both the United Kingdom and Irish governments.

Discussion at their regular inter-governmental meetings, resulted in December 1993 in an agreement between John Major, as Prime Minister of the United Kingdom, and Albert Reynolds, as Irish Prime Minister, embodied in a document known as the "Downing Street Declaration". In it, the British government stated explicitly that it had "no selfish interest" in retaining control over Northern Ireland, and the Irish government agreed to amend its constitution to withdraw its territorial claim to the Six Counties. There was general agreement that the future of Northern Ireland was a matter for its own citizens to decide.

On Aug. 31, 1994, following a meeting between the *Sinn Féin* leaders, Gerry Adams and Martin McGuinness, and the British government, the IRA Army Council announced a "complete cessation" of military action. In October a similar cessation of Loyalist hostilities was announced by the Combined Loyalist Military Command.

In December 1995 the US President, Bill Clinton, visited Northern Ireland to lend his support to the process, appointing former US senator George Mitchell as his special representative. However there was no agreement on how to proceed, and John Hume, the SDLP leader, accused Major of wasting the preceding 17 months. On Feb. 9, 1996, the IRA Army Council announced a resumption of hostilities and an hour later a massive bomb exploded at the Canary Wharf office complex in east London, killing two people. A few days later a bomb exploded prematurely on a bus in central London, killing the would-be bomber and eight others. The UK government then agreed to the Irish government's proposal to resume proximity talks leading up to an election to a 110-member "Forum".

In April, the British government reiterated that the IRA must restore its ceasefire and *Sinn Féin* must accept the six "Mitchell principles" (as laid down by Senator George Mitchell in January 1996, and involving the concept of decommissioning in parallel with talks, rather than before or after) before it could join the talks. All-party talks began in June 1996 with *Sinn Féin* excluded, the IRA responding by detonating a massive bomb in Manchester on June 15 that destroyed the Arndale shopping centre, although with no fatalities. An Anglo-Irish summit in Dublin on Dec. 9 confirmed that the UK government was not prepared to readmit *Sinn Féin* to talks until the ceasefire had been resumed and had held for a significant time.

New UK Government—Sinn Féin Join All-Party Talks

The election of a Labour Government in the UK in May 1997 began a new stage in the peace process. In Northern Ireland itself the Catholic electorate showed a marked increase in support for *Sinn Féin* and the combined Republican and nationalist vote, some 40 per cent of the total, was the largest ever recorded to that time. The new Prime Minister, Tony Blair, and the new Secretary of State for Northern Ireland, Marjorie ("Mo") Mowlem, with strong backing by the Clinton administration, immediately took an active role in a new attempt to seek an agreement to end the "Troubles". The immediate response from the IRA was encouraging: on July 19 it announced the "unequivocal restoration" from the following day of the 1994 ceasefire.

The response of David Trimble, the leader (since September 1995) of the Ulster Unionist Party (UUP, as the Official Unionist Party had become) when he met Blair, however, had already been to reject draft proposals on the grounds that they only required the IRA to make "due progress" towards decommissioning their arms, and Paisley declared the talks "dead in the water". At this point, George Mitchell was finally accepted by the Unionists as an acceptable neutral to chair the peace talks. In August 1997, having met directly with Gerry Adams, Mowlem announced that *Sinn Féin* would be admitted to the talks. The following month (Sept. 9) *Sinn Féin* publicly proclaimed its acceptance of the so-called Mitchell principles of democracy and non-violence, including the total disarmament of all paramilitary organizations and the end of the punishment killings and beatings by which the IRA had been able so successfully to maintain their hold over the nationalist community. As a result, for the first time, representatives of all groups met in October, and in December a *Sinn Féin* delegation headed by Gerry Adams met Prime Minister Blair at 10 Downing Street. Meanwhile serious dissension among the Loyalist paramilitaries led to the killing at

the Maze Prison of one of their most feared leaders, Billy Adams, and so to a series of violent incidents over Christmas and the New Year. On Jan. 8, 1998, therefore, to avert the collapse of the peace talks, Mowlem went personally to the Maze prison near Belfast and met with Loyalist prisoners, who announced their continuing support for the peace process. On Jan. 12, the British and Irish governments jointly presented all parties with a document proposing a balanced package of constitutional change north and south of the border. Over the next two months tensions remained high, with first the Loyalist UUP and then *Sinn Féin* being suspended for brief periods from the talks chaired by Mitchell.

The Good Friday Agreement, 1998

The talks culminated with an agreement reached on April 10, 1998, which, being Good Friday, had a special significance for many of those concerned. The purpose of the Belfast agreement, more commonly known as the "Good Friday agreement", was to set up a new power-sharing administration in Northern Ireland which would be fully representative of all currents of opinion.

The agreement consisted of a Declaration of Support for an inter-governmental agreement on constitutional issues, together with a number of annexes spelling out detailed arrangements. The key sentence in the Declaration of Support stated: "It is accepted that all of the institutional and constitutional arrangements—an Assembly in Northern Ireland, a North/South Ministerial Council, implementation bodies, a British-Irish Council and a British-Irish Intergovernmental Conference and any amendments to British Acts of Parliament and the Constitution of Ireland—are interlocking and interdependent and that in particular the functioning of the Assembly and the North/South Council are so closely inter-related that the success of each depends on that of the other".

The inter-governmental agreement read in full:

"The participants endorse the commitment made by the British and Irish Governments that, in a new British-Irish Agreement replacing the Anglo-Irish Agreement, they will:

"(i) recognise the legitimacy of whatever choice is freely exercised by a majority of the people of Northern Ireland with regard to its status, whether they prefer to continue to support the Union with Great Britain or a sovereign united Ireland;

"(ii) recognise that it is for the people of the island of Ireland alone, by agreement between the two parts respectively and without external impediment, to exercise their right of self-determination on the basis of consent, freely and concurrently given, North and South, to bring about a united Ireland, if that is their wish, accepting that this right must be achieved and exercised with and subject to the agreement and consent of a majority of the people of Northern Ireland;

"(iii) acknowledge that while a substantial section of the people in Northern Ireland share the legitimate wish of a majority of the people of the island of Ireland for a united Ireland, the present wish of a majority of the people of Northern Ireland, freely exercised and legitimate, is to maintain the Union and, accordingly, that Northern Ireland's status as part of the United Kingdom reflects and relies upon that wish; and that it would be wrong to make any change in the status of Northern Ireland save with the consent of a majority of its people;

"(iv) affirm that if, in the future, the people of the island of Ireland exercise their right of self-determination on the basis set out in sections (i) and (ii) above to bring about a united Ireland, it will be a binding obligation on both Governments to introduce and support in their respective Parliaments legislation to give effect to that wish;

"(v) affirm that whatever choice is freely exercised by a majority of the people of Northern Ireland, the power of the sovereign government with jurisdiction there shall be exercised with rigorous impartiality on behalf of all the people in the diversity of their identities and traditions and shall be founded on the principles of full respect for, and equality of, civil, political, social and cultural rights, of freedom from discrimination for all citizens, and of parity of esteem and of just and equal treatment for the identity, ethos, and aspirations of both communities;

"(vi) recognise the birthright of all the people of Northern Ireland to identify themselves and be accepted as Irish or British, or both, as they may so choose, and accordingly confirm that their right to hold both British and Irish citizenship is accepted by both Governments and would not be affected by any future change in the status of Northern Ireland.

"2. The participants also note that the two Governments have accordingly undertaken in the context of this comprehensive political agreement, to propose and support changes in, respectively, the Constitution of Ireland and in British legislation relating to the constitutional status of Northern Ireland".

The Good Friday agreement was put to a referendum in both Northern Ireland and the Irish Republic on the same day, May 22, 1998, and achieved overwhelming support in each. In Northern Ireland—where the agreement was endorsed by both *Sinn Féin* and the SDLP but rejected by various formations on the Loyalist side, most notably by the DUP—71.1% (676,966) voted "Yes" and only 28.9% (274,879) "No", while in the Republic the agreement was endorsed by 94.4% of those who voted. However, by that date it was clear that the peace process was already running into trouble. The problem stemmed from the way in which the annex to the agreement dealing with the decommissioning of paramilitary weapons had been drafted. The relevant paragraph simply stated:

"All participants accordingly reaffirm their commitment to the total disarmament of all paramilitary organisations. They also confirm their intention to continue to work constructively and in good faith with the Independent Commission, and to use any influence they may have, to achieve the decommissioning of all paramilitary arms within two years following endorse-

ment in referendums North and South of the agreement and in the context of the implementation of the overall settlement".

Tony Blair had on May 20 issued five hand-written assurances to reassure Unionist voters. The UUP (whose leadership backed the Good Friday agreement) claimed that these assurances meant that the Provisional IRA would lay down its arms within days, even though this was not explicitly stated in the agreement itself.

Establishment of Northern Ireland Assembly— Stalling of Peace Process

Elections were held on June 25, 1998, for the new Northern Ireland Assembly established by the Good Friday agreement in succession to the Northern Ireland Forum, which was wound up on April 24. The elections gave pro-agreement candidates 75% of the votes and 80 seats and anti-agreement candidates 25% of the votes and 28 seats, divided as follows: UUP 28 seats, SDLP 24, DUP 20, *Sinn Féin* 18, Alliance Party 6, United Kingdom Unionist Party (UKUP) 5, independent Unionists 3, Northern Ireland Women's Coalition (NIWC) 2 and Progressive Unionists (PUP) 2. Every party that had obtained enough votes, in order of the number of votes cast, was entitled to claim a post (or posts) in the devolved government. The Assembly therefore met for the first time on July 1 to elect David Trimble (UUP) as First Minister and the Deputy Leader of the SDLP, Seamus Mallon, as Deputy Chief Minister. The Northern Ireland Act, giving a legal basis for the agreement in the UK, became law on Nov. 19, 1998.

On July 28, 1998, the Secretary of State for Northern Ireland had declared the IRA, the Ulster Defence Association (UDA) and the Ulster Volunteer Force (UVF) "inactive", so that prisoners who were members of these organizations could benefit from the early release provisions of the Good Friday agreement. However, dissident Republican violence continued, this including the worst single incident in thirty years of conflict when on Aug. 15 a bomb placed in the main square of Omagh, Co. Tyrone (Northern Ireland) by a faction calling itself the Real IRA resulted in 29 deaths. The hostile reaction to this atrocity among the Catholic community led the Real IRA to announce a "complete cessation" of its campaign on Sept. 7.

When the Assembly resumed its sittings on Sept. 14, the two main issues were the formation of the new Executive and the decommissioning of weapons. The Unionists claimed they had been promised early decommissioning and refused to establish institutions of devolved government until the IRA had disarmed. The IRA said that no other organization had a right to determine when and how it might decommission and *Sinn Féin* for its part maintained it had no authority over the IRA. Meanwhile communal violence and so-called "punishment beatings", often involving serious physical injury, continued, which implied that the paramilitaries were continuing to control their own communities from behind the scenes, regardless of the formal political agreement. In fact the level of violence had actually increased, causing 55 terrorist or terrorism-related deaths in the course of the year. However, on Oct. 17, 1998, the award of the Nobel Peace Prize jointly to David Trimble and John Hume was announced.

Disputes over decommissioning, policing and other issues continued through much of 1999. Elections for the European Parliament on June 10 strengthened the rejectionist position by giving the DUP the largest share of Unionist votes. Part of the problem was Unionist suspicion of Dr Mowlem, who was seen by them as being too sympathetic to nationalist and Republican opinion. On June 22, David Trimble had said in a lobby briefing that he hoped she would be replaced by Peter Mandelson, who had been forced to resign from the Trade and Industry portfolio and from the Cabinet some months previously. In a cabinet reshuffle on Oct. 14 Mowlem was moved to another post and Mandelson was appointed Northern Ireland Secretary. After talks had been moved to the US ambassador's residence in London, agreement was finally arrived at on a series of choreographed moves by which (i) the Ulster Unionists reluctantly agreed to enter into the power-sharing Executive with *Sinn Féin* before actual decommissioning had taken place, (ii) the IRA agreed to deal with the independent body appointed to oversee decommissioning, and (iii) the Irish government promulgated the agreed changes to the Irish Constitution abandoning its historic claim to Northern Ireland. On Dec. 2, 1999, powers were finally devolved to the Executive by Westminster.

Efforts to save the Good Friday Agreement

Since 1999 there has been complete agreement between the UK and Irish governments that the only practicable constitutional arrangements for the foreseeable future are those promulgated in the Good Friday agreement. In the first two months of 2000, however, the Provisional IRA took no further action towards decommissioning, and the Ulster Unionist members of the Executive notified London that they proposed to resign if such action was not forthcoming. On Feb. 2 Prime Minister Blair refused to publish the report by Gen. John de Chastelain, the Canadian General appointed to verify the decommissioning process. Peter Mandelson wrote to the IRA to ask its intentions, but a reply was not received until after the deadline he had set, and at midnight on Feb. 3, 2000, the devolved government was again suspended and direct rule from Westminster reinstated, although *Sinn Féin* objected that there was no provision for such a procedure in the agreement.

On March 16, 2000, First Minister David Trimble broke the deadlock by conceding that it was possible to have a return to power-sharing before the decommissioning of weapons. A new phrase entered the dialogue, the idea that weapons should not be decommissioned but placed "beyond use". With the full backing

of the UK and Irish governments, a series of steps was then agreed by which the Executive was restored on May 30. The following month, on June 26, an IRA statement confirmed that contact had been restored with Gen. de Chastelain, who had carried out an inspection of a number of arms dumps. It was confirmed by two independent monitors, Cyril Ramaphosa of the African National Congress and Martti Ahtisaari, former President of Finland, that the weapons they had inspected could no longer be used without detection.

Unfortunately, towards the end of the summer "marching season", on Aug. 19, an incident on the Shankill Road, Belfast, sparked off an internal Loyalist feud, which by the time it was ended, on Dec. 16, had cost twelve lives, forced some 200 families to flee their homes, brought troops back onto the streets of Belfast and demonstrated the Executive's evident lack of power to keep order. Meanwhile, in September, a planned reduction of troop levels in the border area and the closure of UK military bases in Fermanagh gave ammunition to Trimble's critics, though he successfully survived a vote of confidence at his party's conference in October. The proposals made by a commission chaired by the former British Governor of Hong Kong, Chris Patten, for a new Northern Ireland Police Service, to replace the RUC, passed the House of Lords on Nov. 21, but in an attenuated form which led both *Sinn Féin* and the SDLP to withdraw their support for them. The Disqualification Act, passed on Nov. 30, allowed members of the Dáil to sit in the UK House of Commons or the Northern Ireland Assembly, if they wished to do so.

As Secretary of State, Peter Mandelson had in fact been quite outspoken in pointing out that Unionists could not expect to continue to receive government support if they did not accept power sharing. However, on Jan. 24, 2001, Mandelson was unexpectedly forced to resign for a second time from the Blair government, for reasons unrelated to Northern Ireland. The new Secretary of State for Northern Ireland, John Reid, was the first Catholic to hold the office and retained his post after the UK general election in June 2001, which saw the Labour government retained to power with an undiminished majority. His first problem was to obtain support for the new policing proposals; these won the support of the SDLP on Aug. 20, only after the Northern Catholic bishops and the Irish government had already approved them, though *Sinn Féin* still refused to accept them. On Nov. 17 the Gaelic Athletic Association, which over the years had done so much to maintain the separation of the two communities, abolished Rule 21, barring from membership members of the UK security forces.

Meanwhile Trimble found it difficult to continue as First Minister as long as there was no further progress on arms decommissioning. In the face of constant attack from the rejectionist DUP he resigned his post and on Oct. 17, 2001, withdrew the Ulster Unionist ministers from the Executive. The IRA now found itself in a very unwelcome position, against the background of heightened international co-operation post-Sept. 11 against terrorist groups: even before the Sept. 11 attacks in the USA, the Bush administration in Washington had regarded the IRA with suspicion, on account of the arrest in Colombia in August 2001 of three alleged IRA operatives accused of training guerrillas opposed to the US-supported government. On Oct. 20, in response to a public request from Gerry Adams, the IRA in accordance with the agreed procedures and under the personal supervision of Gen. de Chastelain, put a significant quantity of weapons "beyond use". Ominously, however, both the DUP and significant elements of Trimble's own party refused to accept the assurances they were given, owing to IRA insistence on secrecy about the details, and the First Minister was only re-elected after the Alliance Party and the Women's Party had agreed to be categorized as "unionists" to achieve the majority required.

The Executive resumed its work and, on a day to day basis, functioned satisfactorily into the early part of 2002, though a series of Loyalist outrages was a reminder of the underlying tensions, and Catholics failed to take up the places designated for them in the new Police Service of Northern Ireland. On April 8 the independent commission was able to report that it had witnessed the IRA put another consignment of arms beyond use. The IRA also on July 16 formally apologized for "all the deaths and injuries of non-combatants" it had caused. However, distrust of the IRA's true intentions continued to erode support for the Good Friday agreement within the UUP. Matters again came to head when in October police raided a number of Sinn Féin offices, including those at Stormont. The documents seized, which included copies of confidential correspondence between Secretary of State John Reid and Tony Blair, appeared to confirm Unionist fears that an IRA "spy ring" had been operating within Stormont. In response David Trimble resigned as First Minister, but before the resignation could take effect, both the Assembly and the Executive were again suspended on Oct. 14 and for the fourth time in less than three years direct rule was restored. At the same time Blair moved John Reid to the chairmanship of the Labour Party and appointed Paul Murphy as the new Secretary of State.

The original plan was to hold fresh elections for a new Assembly early in 2003. However, as it became increasingly clear that support for the agreement was unravelling, with the probability that the new Assembly would be even more polarized, the elections were twice postponed, on March 5 and May 1, 2003. After further talks in London on May 20, and a meeting between the British and Irish Prime Ministers in Greece on Oct. 21, a further act of IRA decommissioning was reported and elections fixed for Nov. 26. However, at the last minute Trimble declined to support the package which had been minutely agreed behind the scenes by the two governments.

The result of the election, therefore, was fully as disastrous as could have been predicted. It was true that some 70 per cent of the voters voted for officially pro-agreement parties. However, Ian Paisley's DUP, with 30 seats, emerged as the largest party in the new Assembly at the expense of Trimble's badly divided UUP, which took 27 seats, and it was implacably opposed to sharing power with Sinn Féin. Sinn Féin, in turn, in winning 24 seats displaced the moderate nationalist SDLP (18 seats) to become the largest party representing the Catholic community. The results created an impasse which made formation of a power-sharing Executive impossible in the immediate term and direct rule from Westminster remained in place. Thus, while the positions of the British and Irish governments in dealing with the Northern Ireland question had historically never been closer, the sectarian division within Northern Ireland itself, notwithstanding the general decline of violence in recent years, remained as pronounced as ever.

Peter Calvert

4.13 Poland's Eastern Borders

Partitioned between Russia, Prussia and Austria in the 18th century and placed largely under Russian rule in 1815, the ancient state of Poland regained its independence in 1918 at the end of World War I within eastern borders which, under the 1921 Treaty of Riga, encompassed what are now the western regions of Ukraine and Belarus as well as the present-day Vilnius region of Lithuania. Under the 1939 Nazi-Soviet non-aggression pact Poland was invaded and partitioned between Germany and the Soviet Union, as a result of which former eastern Poland was allocated to the Ukrainian and Belorussian Soviet Socialist Republics and the Vilnius region to what became Soviet Lithuania.

These territorial dispositions were for the most part reimposed by Stalin at the end of World War II, in compensation for which Poland was awarded substantial former German territories in the west. In the long post-war era of Communist hegemony in Eastern Europe they came to acquire an aura of permanence. Following the post-1989 collapse of Communist rule in Poland and the eventual emergence of Lithuania, Ukraine and Belarus as sovereign independent states, the question of Poland's eastern borders resurfaced as a controversial factor in regional relations. However, once the question of its country's western border with unified Germany had been settled (for which see Section 4.9), the post-Communist Polish government moved quickly to sign border treaties with its eastern neighbours, and now considers that it has no remaining territorial or boundary disputes. (For the changes to Poland's borders consequent upon World War II, see Map 45, p. 515.)

Early Historical Background—18th-Century Partition of Poland

Converted to Christianity in the mid-10th century, the Priast dynasty of Poland created a powerful kingdom based on the Polish heartlands but extending westwards to Slav-populated provinces such as Silesia and, briefly, Bohemia and Moravia. In the east, the 11th-century Polish kingdom included part of present-day Belarus, although its border with the westernmost extent of Kievan Rus' was imprecise and disputed. Polish disunity from the early 12th century coincided with the onset of large-scale colonization of Polish and other East European lands by German settlers from the west. From the east, the Mongol/Tatar hordes not only destroyed Kievan Rus' in the early 13th century but also devastated southern Poland, after routing a combined Polish/German army at Legnica in 1241.

Recovery began with the reunification of Poland in 1320-70. Although Silesia was ceded to Bohemia in 1335 (and later became an Austrian Habsburg province), Poland in 1386 entered into a dynastic union with Lithuania which heralded the golden age of Polish history. Under the Jagiello dynasty, Poland/Lithuania decisively defeated the Teutonic Knights at Tannenberg in 1410 and became Europe's largest state, extending from the Baltic in the north to the Black Sea in the south. In the west, Poland/Lithuania's border with the German empire settled down well to the east of the present-day Oder-Neisse line. But in the east the dual monarchy's dominions included the Ruthene-populated lands of what are now Belarus and Ukraine, while in the north the dissolution of the Teutonic Knights in 1560 resulted in Latvia and southern Estonia coming under Polish/Lithuanian rule.

Under the 1569 Union of Lublin, Lithuania became a principality of the unified Polish kingdom/republic, but the end of the Jagiello dynasty in 1572 marked the beginning of the end of the golden age. There were further conquests in the east in the early 17th century, including Smolensk, which extended the Polish border to within 100 miles of Moscow. However, military defeat in the Northern War of 1621-29 obliged Poland to cede southern Estonia and northern Latvia (i.e. Livonia) to Sweden, the dominant power in the Baltic in the 17th century. Thereafter, Poland's growing predilection for internal strife made it a soft target for the expansionist Tsars of Muscovy in their self-proclaimed role as the heirs of the old Kievan Rus'. Kiev itself fell to the Russians in 1654, together with north-eastern and central Ukraine, following an anti-Polish revolt by the Ukrainian Cossacks. Further north, Russia had, by the end of the 17th century, gained the Smolensk and adjoining regions from Poland although its western border remained to the east of the present eastern frontier of Belarus.

To give legitimacy to their territorial expansion, the Tsars "of all the Russias" designated the Ukrainians as "Little Russians" and the Belorussians as "White Russians". In fact, both peoples were part of the Ruthene branch of the East Slavs and ethnically distinct from the so-called "Great Russians" of Muscovy and Novgorod. In the Great Schism of 1054 the Ruthenes had opted for the Greek Orthodox camp and had thus been co-religionists of the Russians. However, in the 1594 Union of Brest-Litovsk the Ruthenian Church, while preserving the Slavonic/Greek rite, had changed to the Roman allegiance of the Polish rulers, becoming the Uniate Catholic Church. Those Ruthenes who remained faithful to Greek Orthodoxy had then migrated eastwards to the steppes of eastern Ukraine and established semi-autonomous Cossack warrior communities. When these were brought under Russian rule in the 17th and 18th centuries, the border between Russian-ruled and Polish-ruled Ukraine corresponded in part to the line of religious division.

Poland's last effective ruler was John III Sobieski (r. 1674-96), who led the Polish/German armies which lifted the Turkish siege of Vienna in 1683. By dint of its alliance with the Austrian Habsburgs, Poland recovered the southern province of Podolia (south-western Ukraine) from the Turks under the 1699 Treaty of Carlowitz. However, the endemic weakness of the elective Polish monarchy made it increasingly vulnerable to the territorial ambitions of its powerful neighbours. Of these, Peter the Great's Russia emerged from the Great Northern War (1700-21) as the dominant power in the eastern Baltic, where its gains from Sweden included Estonia and northern Latvia. To Poland's west, Prussia was also a rising power, aspiring to establish territorial contiguity, at Poland's expense, between its eastern and western parts. And to the south-west, the Habsburg Empire saw the acquisition of Polish territory as compensation for its loss of Silesia to Prussia in 1745. The result was the complete dismemberment of Poland by these three powers.

In the first Polish partition (1772) Russia annexed a relatively small area north-east and south of Smolensk, while Austria took Galicia and Lodomeria, and Prussia the coastal lands between Pomerania and East Prussia. In the second partition (1793) Russia gained Podolia and most of Belorussia, while Prussia took Danzig (Gdansk), Poznan (Posen) and central western Poland. In the third partition (1795) Russia annexed southern Latvia, Lithuania and the rest of Belorussia, while Prussia took Warsaw and the territory adjoining East Prussia, and Austria annexed West Galicia. Meanwhile, Russia had also annexed the Tatar khanate of the Crimea (1783) and neighbouring Jedisan (1792), so that, on the completion of the Polish partitions, the whole of modern Ukraine had been brought under Russian rule.

Prussia's defeat by the French at Jena in 1806 enabled Napoleon Bonaparte to set up the Grand Duchy of Warsaw in part of the former Polish territory. However, on Napoleon's final defeat in 1815 Poland again disappeared from the political map, although with the important difference that at the

Congress of Vienna Prussia ceded most of its gains from the second and third partitions to Russia in return for being awarded substantial territory in Germany. At the same time, Austria agreed to withdraw from West Galicia in Russia's favour, while retaining Galicia and Lodomeria to the south. Russia therefore became the ruler of the bulk of the old Polish kingdom, although Prussia retained the whole of the Baltic littoral, Poznan and Silesia, while Austria retained what became known as East Galicia. Under Russian rule the Tsar became king of "Congress Poland", which was accorded an autonomous government. However, the separate kingdom arrangement was ended by the Russians in the wake of the Polish revolt of 1830, while Poland's autonomy was withdrawn in the wake of the revolt of 1863-64.

Poland's Recovery of Independence in 1918— Polish-Soviet War of 1920

Poland's opportunity to reassert its historic independence came in World War I (1914-18), during which both the Entente and the Central powers courted Polish nationalist groups. The key development was the overthrow of the Tsar in 1917 and the decision of the new Bolshevik regime to withdraw from the war. First the Central powers, on Feb. 8, 1918, signed the separate "Peace of Bread" with a newly declared independent government of Ukraine. Then, on March 3, 1918, they secured the signature of the Treaty of Brest-Litovsk, under which the Russians surrendered sovereignty in Poland, Ukraine, Belorussia, the Baltic provinces, Finland and Transcaucasia. With most of these territories being under the military occupation of the Central powers, the Brest-Litovsk treaty seemed to presage German hegemony in place of Russian rule. However, its terms were invalidated by the Central powers' acceptance of defeat in the west on Nov. 11, 1918. On the same day as the armistice the various Polish nationalist groups united under Marshal Jozef Pilsudski to declare Poland's independence.

Poland's independence was recognized by the victorious powers at the Paris peace conference, but major problems arose in applying the principle of national self-determination to the drawing of its eastern borders. The Treaty of Versailles of June 28, 1919, between the victors and Germany, established the German-Polish border mostly at the pre-partition line, so that the new Weimar Republic was, like pre-1772 Prussia, divided by a "corridor" of Polish territory up to German-populated Danzig, which became a "free city" under the League of Nations. Moreover, under the Treaty of St Germain of Sept. 10, 1919, between the victors and Austria, the latter surrendered what had been Habsburg-ruled East Galicia (now called simply Galicia). However, under these treaties the precise demarcation of Poland's eastern borders was to be determined at a later date, having regard to ethnographic, religious and historical factors. The task of investigating these factors fell to the British Foreign Secretary, Lord Curzon, who published his findings in

December 1919. They envisaged that Poland's eastern borders should be drawn on a line which excluded not only Lithuania and Belorussia but also the eastern two-thirds of former Austrian Galicia (present-day western Ukraine).

What became known as the Curzon line was not well received in Poland. Among Polish nationalists there was a vociferous demand for the full restoration of the 1772 borders. Some even aspired to the re-establishment of the medieval Polish/Lithuanian empire. More diplomatically, Marshal Pilsudski called for a Polish-Lithuanian-Belorussian-Ukrainian "confederation" under the leadership of Poland. In part his caution derived from wariness about Russian intentions, in that neither the Bolsheviks nor their White opponents regarded themselves as under any obligation to abandon Russia's pre-war empire. However, by April 1920 Pilsudski believed that Russia was so weakened by its civil war (and by the emerging Bolshevik victory therein) that it was time to act. Having concluded an alliance with the anti-Bolshevik Ukrainian "government", Poland proceeded to occupy Ukraine up to and including Kiev, which Polish troops entered on May 6, 1920. Further north, Polish forces at that stage also held most of Belorussia, including Minsk.

The Polish occupation of Kiev lasted only five weeks, after which Russian Bolshevik forces drove the Poles back across the Curzon line. By late July 1920 the Russians were on the Vistula and threatening to take Warsaw, to the great consternation of the Western allies (and also of Germany). There followed the so-called "miracle of the Vistula", in which regrouped Polish forces, supported by French military advisers, launched a counter-attack which routed the Russians and drove them into headlong retreat. According to some contemporary accounts, this Polish victory was as crucial for European civilization as the relief of the Turkish siege of Vienna had been in 1683. By the time an armistice was signed, at Riga in October 1920, Polish forces had not only driven the Russians back across the Curzon line but had also recaptured eastern Galicia and Belorussia up to the Pripet Marshes. The Polish military campaign was notable for having featured the last successful cavalry charges in European warfare.

Meanwhile, the new Soviet Union had cut its losses in the Baltic provinces by signing treaties recognizing the independence of Estonia, Lithuania and Latvia, in February, July and August 1920 respectively. Under the second of these instruments, the city of Vilnius was acknowledged as being part of Lithuania (having been captured by the Russians from the Poles, who had held it since early 1919). The problem was that its inhabitants were mainly non-Lithuanian (Jews forming the largest group, followed by Poles) and that Polish nationalists regarded it as part of Poland's historic territory.

Although born near Vilnius himself, Pilsudski appeared at first to be ready to accept its loss. Indeed, under the Treaty of Suwalki signed with Lithuania on Oct. 7, 1920, Poland formally renounced Vilnius. However, three days later, irregular Polish forces under the command of Gen. Zeligowski seized the city and its surrounding region, it transpiring later that the Polish government had approved of the planned action. Two days after that, on Oct. 12, 1920, the Polish-Russian armistice was signed, with Poland effectively in possession not only of eastern Galicia (western Ukraine) and western Belorussia but also of what the Lithuanians regarded as their historic capital.

These territorial outcomes were confirmed by the formal Treaty of Riga signed on March 18, 1921. Although some Polish nationalists evinced disappointment, Poland became substantially the largest state in Eastern Europe, with an eastern border some 250 kilometres east of the ethnic frontier between Poles and non-Poles. In the west, moreover, Poland added to its gains from Germany when in March 1921 it obtained the industrial and coal-mining region of Upper Silesia (Katowice), despite a plebiscite which showed that 60 per cent of its population wished to remain German. A plebiscite was also held in the Vilnius region early in 1922—this one, organized by the Poles, showing a majority in favour of Polish rule. Called Wilno by the Poles, the territory was formally annexed by Poland on March 4, 1922, and Polish possession was eventually recognized by the Western powers on March 15, 1923. Nevertheless, Lithuania maintained its claim to Vilnius and demonstrated its chagrin over the issue by refusing to establish diplomatic relations with Poland and by closing its border to all traffic between the two countries. The "temporary" Lithuanian capital was established at Kaunas (Kovno), to the west of Vilnius.

Taking a leaf out of the Polish book, Lithuanian irregular troops in January 1923 took control of the small former German territory of Memel (Klaipeda) on the Baltic coast. The Versailles treaty had placed this German-populated enclave under the League of Nations pending a decision on its future and French troops had been in occupation since February 1920. The League gave its conditional approval to the Lithuanian takeover, subject to the territory being granted autonomy, which was duly implemented in May 1924 under the Memel Convention.

Onset of World War II—German-Soviet Partition of Poland

Marshal Pilsudski resigned as President in December 1922, but a deepening political crisis persuaded him to seize power again in May 1926, after which he remained virtual dictator of an authoritarian regime until his death in May 1935. Aware sooner than many of the implications of Hitler's accession to power in 1933, Pilsudski took Poland into a non-aggression pact with Nazi Germany in 1934, having signed a similar treaty with the Soviet Union in 1932. But neither he nor his successors were under any illusions as to the extent of German and Soviet resentment over, respectively, the Versailles and Riga territorial settlements. In

the case of the Soviet Union, soviet socialist republics (SSRs) had by then become established in the Belorussian and Ukrainian territories under Moscow's rule. Despite the existence of the Polish-Soviet non-aggression pact, it was the manifest, if as yet unspoken, aim of the Soviet government that sooner or later each should incorporate the millions of ethnic Belorussians and Ukrainians living under Polish rule.

Before the major drama broke in 1939, Poland used its own relative regional strength in 1938 to resolve outstanding territorial issues with two smaller neighbours. Following a serious border incident, the Polish government on March 18, 1938, sent an ultimatum to Lithuania threatening military action unless relations between the two countries were normalized. The Lithuanian government was obliged to accept the Polish terms, which included the establishment of normal diplomatic relations and the reopening of communications between the two states. While the Poles also ruled out any discussion on the question of Vilnius, Lithuania notified the League of Nations that it had not juridically abandoned its claim to the city.

This successful Polish démarche against Lithuania was followed up in September 1938 by another, against Czechoslovakia, which was forced to cede part of the disputed border region of Teschen (Cieszym) to Poland. Once part of the Bohemian kingdom, the duchy of Teschen had been under Austrian Habsburg rule from 1772 until the end of World War I, by which time it had become a major industrial region. Claimed by both Poland and the new state of Czechoslovakia, it had been divided between the two countries by decision of the victorious powers in July 1920. But Poland—distracted at the time by its war with Russia—had always regarded the division as unfair, because Czechoslovakia had got the coal-rich part, even though its population was predominantly Polish. The Polish ultimatum for the cession of the disputed territory was presented on Sept. 21, 1938—i.e. a few days after the Munich agreement by which Britain and France agreed to Germany's occupation of the Sudetenland of Czechoslovakia. The Prague government accepted the Polish demands on Oct. 1, after which the Polish occupation of the territory was completed by Oct. 10, 1938.

Less than a year later it was Poland's turn to receive an ultimatum from a stronger neighbour. Under secret clauses of their non-aggression pact of Aug. 23, 1939, Germany and the Soviet Union agreed that Poland should be partitioned into "spheres of influence" (and Moscow received a free hand territorially in other adjoining lands). On Aug. 31 Germany broadcast a 16-point "settlement plan", demanding the immediate cession of Danzig and the granting of territorial rights in the Polish "corridor" pending the holding of a plebiscite there on a return to German sovereignty. Nine hours later, on Sept. 1, Germany invaded Poland, it being claimed by Hitler that the Warsaw government had refused to negotiate. Despite stout Polish resistance, German forces quickly overran northern and western Poland up to the Bug river east of Warsaw. Although powerless to affect the outcome, Britain and France honoured their treaty guarantees to Poland by declaring war on Germany on Sept. 3, 1939. Asserting that events had "revealed the internal insolvency and obvious impotence of the Polish state", the Soviet Union invaded Poland on Sept. 17 and rapidly occupied the eastern half of the country. Ahead of the Soviet troops, leaflets were dropped declaring that they were coming to liberate Ukrainians and Belorussians from "the yoke of Polish rule".

With their occupation completed, Germany and the Soviet Union on Sept. 28, 1939, signed a treaty in Moscow providing formally for the partition of Poland and for "relations of friendship" between the two countries. An attached map partitioned Poland almost exactly on the Curzon line in the southern and central sectors and about 150 kilometres to the west of that line in the north; however, a secret treaty protocol gave Germany a larger area in the north (and also transferred Lithuania from the German to the Soviet sphere). As regards the area taken by Germany, on Oct. 8, 1939, Hitler signed an order annexing western and northern Poland almost up to the extent of Prussia's gains from the 18th-century partitions. In the south the whole of the Teschen region was detached from Poland and assigned to the German protectorate of Bohemia-Moravia (created on the final collapse of Czechoslovakia in March 1939, in which month Germany had also compelled Lithuania to cede Memel). The German annexations stopped just short of Warsaw, which became the capital of the German-occupied "General Government of Poland". In Soviet-occupied western Belorussia and western Ukraine, single-list elections on Oct. 22, 1939, produced Assemblies which voted unanimously, on Oct. 26 and 28, for incorporation into the Soviet Union. Their annexation was formally decreed by the USSR Supreme Soviet on Nov. 1-2, 1939.

The fourth partition of Poland coincided with Soviet diplomatic action against the three Baltic republics, which had been designated as a Soviet "sphere of influence" under the agreements with Germany. In the course of October 1939 the Soviet government demanded and obtained extra-territorial rights in all three states, which were compelled to sign mutual assistance treaties with Moscow and to accept Soviet military bases. In Lithuania's case, the compensation was substantial, in that its treaty with the Soviet Union (signed in Moscow on Oct. 10, 1939) provided for its acquisition of the Vilnius and Suwalki regions of Soviet-occupied eastern Poland. The cited grounds for the cession of Vilnius were the terms of the July 1920 Moscow treaty between Lithuania and the Soviet Union, as well as the October 1920 Suwalki treaty between Lithuania and Poland. However, the Polish government-in-exile protested strongly against these transfers, claiming that they had no validity under international law.

As it turned out, Lithuania, Latvia and Estonia were soon to follow eastern Poland into the Soviet empire.

Soviet ultimata delivered in June 1940 forced the installation of pro-Soviet governments in each republic. Single-list elections the following month produced new parliaments which each voted unanimously in favour of incorporation into the Soviet Union. On the approval of the necessary legislation by the USSR Supreme Soviet on Aug. 6, 1940, Lithuania, Latvia and Estonia became soviet socialist republics (SSRs).

Territorial Outcome of World War II—Poland's New Borders

Nazi-Soviet "friendship" ended abruptly when German forces launched Hitler's long-planned invasion of the Soviet Union in June 1941 and rapidly advanced deep into Soviet territory. By mid-1942 Germany was in occupation not only of the Baltic lands up to the outskirts of Leningrad but also of Belorussia, western Russia and the whole of Ukraine. Its territorial dispositions in these vast regions included the annexation to the Reich of part of northern Belorussia centred on Bialystok (south-east of old East Prussia) and the extension of the border of the "General Government of Poland" to incorporate western Ukraine. In addition, the "Reichskommisariat of Ostland" included not only Lithuania, Latvia and Estonia but also Belorussian territory up to just east of Minsk, while the "Reichskommisariat of Ukraine" covered much of the rest of Ukrainian territory. As history records, however, such schemes to "move Poland eastwards" and to give Germans *Lebensraum* ("living space") in the east were to be dashed by the eventual victory of the Red Army. By early 1945 Soviet and allied forces had driven the German armies from all of the occupied lands. By April 1945 Berlin itself had fallen to the Russians.

Germany's unconditional surrender on May 7, 1945, created the circumstances for the Soviet Union to impose a territorial settlement in Eastern Europe which was partly a restoration and partly new. The new elements arose mainly from the fact that Germany was divested of not only its post-1938 gains but also East Prussia (Königsberg) and the German territory to the east of the Oder-Neisse line (Pomerania, Poznan/Posen and Silesia). Of these regions, the area between the old Polish border and the Oder-Neisse line was allocated to Poland, as was the southern portion of East Prussia, while the northern part was annexed by the Soviet Union itself. Poland's western border was thus moved some 250 kilometres to the west, in partial compensation for the fact that in the east Stalin reinstated most of his 1939 annexation of pre-war eastern Poland, even closer to the Curzon line than before. As compared with the 1939 partition, the changes in the east were that Poland was allocated an additional strip of territory in the south, as well as the Bialystok and Suwalki regions in the north. The remainder of former eastern Poland was restored to the Belorussian and Ukrainian SSRs, while the Lithuanian SSR retained Vilnius and regained Memel/Klaipeda. Stalin also decreed the reinstatement of the 1920 division of Teschen between

Poland and Czechoslovakia, thus in part compensating the latter for the transfer of Transcarpathia to Soviet rule as part of the Ukrainian SSR (see Section 4.18 for the Transcarpathia question).

Whereas the post-war German-Polish border remained a contentious issue until 1990, the eastern Polish borders as determined by the Soviet Union were much less controversial in the East-West arena. In part they had been agreed by the major Western powers (Britain and the United States) as early as the Tehran conference between Stalin, Churchill and Roosevelt on Nov. 28-Dec. 1, 1943. At the subsequent Yalta and Potsdam conferences (held on Feb. 4-10 and July 17-Aug. 2, 1945, respectively) there was further agreement on Soviet territorial dispositions in the east, with which the new provisional government of Poland also concurred. Their effect was that Poland lost some 178,000 sq km of its pre-war territory in the east, but gained about 101,000 sq km of former German territory in the west and north. The changes involved the expulsion of millions of ethnic Germans from what was now Polish territory. By 1947 Poland had a fully Communist government which made it an article of faith that territorial issues as between Poland and the Soviet Union had been finally resolved.

Post-Communist Re-emergence of Territorial Issues

During the long period of Soviet/Communist hegemony in Eastern Europe the post-war territorial settlements appeared to be immutable. When that hegemony collapsed in the late 1980s it was inevitable that the move to political democracy and to genuine national sovereignty would be accompanied by an upsurge of public interest in the way in which borders had been drawn by Soviet diktat after World War II. Poland was no exception. As it progressed from one-party rule to political pluralism in 1989-91 one consequence was that the question of its eastern borders began to feature in public debate, in a way that had not been possible under the old regime. Among intellectuals and historians, for example, there was a determination to uncover the full circumstances of the 1939 Nazi-Soviet agreements under which Poland had been invaded and partitioned. On the nationalist right, claims began to be voiced that Poland should aim at the restoration of its pre-war borders with Ukraine, Belorussia and Lithuania, focusing on the long Polish history of ancient cities such as Lvov/Lemberg (in western Ukraine) and Vilnius.

Another complication was that some Ukrainian nationalists articulated a claim to a stretch of adjoining Belorussian territory, namely part of the Gomel region in southeastern Belorussia. Conversely, some Belorussian nationalists laid claim to the border area of Ukraine north of Zhitomir, to the west of Kiev.

At the government level post-Communist Poland emphasized that it had no territorial claims against any other country and stressed its commitment to the

1975 Helsinki Final Act of the Conference on Security and Co-operation in Europe (CSCE), which had enjoined the inviolability of existing European frontiers. In taking this line its prime motivation was the perceived overriding need to secure a final legal settlement of the western Polish border with Germany. But even when this objective was at last attained in November 1990, following the reunification of Germany, there was no change in the official stance that the post-war territorial settlement must be respected. Indeed, once Lithuania, Belarus and Ukraine had all achieved full independence in the course of 1991 (and become full parties to the CSCE), Poland proceeded to sign treaties or agreements with each country explicitly recognizing the existing borders. Nevertheless, elements of territorial dissension, actual and potential, continued to cloud Poland's relations with its eastern neighbours.

Poland-Ukraine

In late 1990, Poland and Ukraine, which was already nominally independent of the Soviet Union in foreign affairs, signed a declaration of friendship and co-operation, renouncing all territorial claims against one another and guaranteeing the rights of national minorities on their territories. As soon as the results of the referendum on Ukrainian independence were announced in December 1991, Poland became the first country to grant it diplomatic recognition. A new treaty of friendship and co-operation was signed on May 18, 1992, during the state visit to Warsaw of Ukraine's President, Leonid Kravchuk. The treaty agreed to respect the existing frontier, reaffirmed the rights of the substantial minorities on each side of the common frontier, and provided for annual consultations between the countries' Foreign Ministers and co-operation in economic, cultural, scientific, and environmental affairs.

During Polish President Lech Walesa's visit to Moscow later in May 1992 he observed that the concept of a Warsaw-Moscow-Kiev alliance, raised in his talks with President Yeltsin, would depend most heavily on peaceful relations between Russia and Ukraine, and reaffirmed Poland's neutrality in ongoing Russian-Ukrainian disagreements over the ownership of the Black Sea Fleet, Crimea, and other territories. Meanwhile, however, nationalist groups in both Poland and Ukraine maintained positions in favour of territorial changes, and demanded that their respective governments should negotiate such changes through the mechanisms of the CSCE.

The Polish minority is widely dispersed in Ukraine, though the city of Lvov—which was in Austria-Hungary before 1914 and in Poland before its annexation by Hitler, being known as Lemberg in the German Reich until 1945—has a long history as a Polish city. Sentiments in Poland for its return were matched by a reciprocal aspiration in the re-emergent Ukrainian nationalist movement, within which some groups maintained that part of Ukraine's national territory remained under Polish rule. Such elements, notably the ultra-nationalist State Independence Organization, focused in particular on the area of south-eastern Poland, around the city of Przemysl, which had been annexed by Stalin in 1939 (because it lay to the east of the Curzon line) but had been restored to Poland in 1945. By December 1991 such claims had become so vociferous that the Ukrainian representative in Warsaw found it necessary to issue a public statement that Ukrainian nationalist groups which laid claim to Polish territory "are not a political force of any importance". A complicating factor was the development in western Ukraine of a campaign for the re-legalization of the Uniate Catholic Church (which had been banned on Stalin's orders in 1946 and forcibly merged with the Russian Orthodox Church). For some Polish nationalists this was evidence that western Ukraine belonged, spiritually at least, to Catholic Poland, although it was by no means clear that Ukrainian Catholics shared this view.

Poland-Belarus

By contrast, Polish overtures towards the Belorussian Republic (as it was known before independence) were treated with great caution and in late 1990 the Belorussians refused to sign a declaration of friendship and co-operation, although Russia and Ukraine had already signed similar agreements. Minsk specifically objected to wording about its borders with Poland and to the treatment of the approximately 300,000 ethnic Belorussians in Poland. However, relations evolved rapidly once Belarus had declared its independence in August 1991. In a declaration of friendship and co-operation, signed in October 1991, each party renounced territorial claims against the other and promised to respect minority rights. In December 1991, Poland extended diplomatic recognition to Belarus. Commercial ties between the two countries were encouraged and a treaty of co-operation in security, environmental, economic, and other matters was signed in 1992.

There was still dissatisfaction in both Polish and Belarusian nationalist circles with the existing border between the two countries, in the former case because it was well to the west of the pre-war frontier, in the latter case because it was well to the east of the Curzon line. Poland has an historic claim to the region around Bialystok, which is largely inhabited by ethnic Belarusians. However, since 1991 Poland has maintained that it has no terrritorial disagreement with Belarus and both the Polish and the Belarusian governments seem to have agreed to keep this issue out of the political arena.

Nonetheless, it took almost two years of hard bargaining for Poland and Belarus to reach agreement on arrangements for cross-border travel on the Poland-Belarus frontier, not least because these also involved simultaneous negotiation with the Russian government. The cost of travelling into and out of Poland was the chief sticking point in the negotiations with both

Minsk and Moscow. Poland preferred a lower visa fee, while Russia preferred a high one, initially proposing a fee of up to 40 euros for a single-entry visa. The sides compromised on 10 euros for a single-entry visa, 16 euros for a two-entry visa and 50 euros for a multiple-entry visa. Similar tariffs were to apply on the border between Russia and Belarus.

Poland-Lithuania

Poland's relations with newly independent Lithuania, on the other hand, have been strained not only by the claim in some Lithuanian circles that the Suwalki area should be restored to Lithuania but also by a revival of the vexed inter-war question of Vilnius, with the familiar additional ingredient of allegations of improper treatment of a national minority, in this case the 300,000-strong ethnic Polish minority in Lithuania.

The strains in relations with Lithuania began to develop before that republic regained independence. In September 1989 the local soviets (councils) of the Vilnius and Salcininkai districts in south-eastern Lithuania, both with Polish majorities, declared themselves to be "self-governing Polish national territorial districts". Unimpressed by the local Poles' claim that recent republican laws had infringed the rights of minorities, the Lithuanian parliament annulled both declarations. When Lithuania unilaterally declared independence from the Soviet Union in March 1990, the reaction in Poland was noticeably unenthusiastic. It became even less so when, on the eve of obtaining final Soviet recognition in September 1991, the Lithuanian parliament on Sept. 5 dissolved the two Polish councils (and another in an ethnic Russian district) and imposed direct rule from the centre. The move provoked widespread protests but was justified by the Lithuanians on the grounds that the councils had backed the August 1991 coup attempt by hardliners in Moscow.

At independence, ethnic Poles and Russians were estimated to make up 7.2 and 9.4 per cent respectively of Lithuania's population of 2,700,000, which was 80 per cent ethnic Lithuanian in composition. In the Lithuanian independence referendum held on Feb. 9, 1991, most ethnic Poles and Russians did not participate. Like Estonia and Latvia, Lithuania proceeded to adopt a new citizenship law (on Dec. 5, 1991) which was alleged to discriminate against ethnic minorities. The legislation drew criticism from official Polish spokesmen, as did a subsequent Lithuanian government decision to ban all school textbooks printed abroad. In a protest delivered on March 9, 1992, the Polish Foreign Ministry complained that ethnic Poles in Lithuania would no longer be able to use history books printed in Poland and threatened to take the issue to the Council of Europe. Another protest followed when on March 18 the Lithuanian parliament approved a six-month extension of direct rule over Vilnius and Salcininkai and postponed the fixing of a date for elections in the two districts. However in a meeting in Helsinki between the Polish and Lithuanian Foreign Ministers on March 25, 1992, the two ministers signed a ten point declaration of friendship and a consular convention. In the declaration, each country renounced all territorial claims against the other and pledged to adhere to European standards in respecting the rights of its minorities, including native-language education rights.

Lithuanian government spokesmen subsequently characterized the activities of ethnic Poles in Lithuania as "unconstitutional" and complained that both Poland and the Russian Federation were promoting an international search for human rights violations in Lithuania as part of "a new phenomenon of political rhetoric". For his part, President Lech Walesa of Poland on April 18, 1992, expressed criticism of the maintenance of direct rule in Vilnius and Salcininkai, saying that it deprived people of their democratic rights. At the same time, he stressed that Poland had no territorial claims against Lithuania and added, in allusion to the Polish seizure of Vilnius in October 1920, that he was "not another Zeligowski".

With a much less nationalistic government in power in Lithuania, there has been a substantial improvement in Polish-Lithuanian relations. Military co-operation, involving joint exercises as well as Polish assistance to Lithuania, has developed to the point that a joint Lithuanian-Polish battalion was formed in 1999, to be deployed in peace support operations. Meanwhile economic relations have continued to develop and the Polish minority in and around Vilnius seems to have come to accept the existing state of affairs.

Poland-Russia (Kaliningrad)

Although neither side was prepared to argue for change in the Soviet-era frontier between Poland and the Russian Federation enclave of Kaliningrad, the continued high level of the Russian garrison in Kaliningrad after the collapse of the Soviet Union was regarded by the Polish authorities with understandable concern. Maintaining a large garrison in Kaliningrad served a useful purpose for President Yeltsin's government in helping keep down unemployment and reassuring his supporters, as well as providing necessary support for the Russian Baltic fleet stationed there.

Poland and Russia were able to agree on a relatively liberal regime for travel across Poland's land border with the Kaliningrad enclave, with the intention of keeping the extensive cross-border trade there going. Visas were to be free of charge and no invitations will be required. This arrangement marked a definite weakening of Russia's initial proposals, which included running an "extra-territorial corridor" from Belarus to Kaliningrad, an idea which, because reminiscent of the inter-war "Danzig corridor," was strongly condemned by the Polish authorities. (For further details on Kaliningrad, see Section 4.4.)

Peter Calvert

4.14 Romania - Ukraine (Northern Bukovina, Serpents' Island)

Having been part of Romania in 1918-40, Northern Bukovina was confirmed as a possession of the USSR under the 1947 Paris peace treaty between the World War II Allies and Romania, as were the small adjacent Moldavian district of Herta (Gertsa) and a portion of the Bessarabian county of Hotin (Khotyn). The three areas were incorporated into the Ukrainian Soviet Socialist Republic as the Chernivtsi region (oblast) and became integral territory of the independent Republic of Ukraine proclaimed in 1991. (Map 46, p. 515, illustrates this dispute.)

According to the Soviet census of 1989, the Chernivtsi region had a population of 940,000, of whom more than 70 per cent were Ukrainians and 20 per cent Romanians. Nevertheless, post-Communist Romanian aspirations to restore pre-war borders included a revival in certain circles of the claim to Northern Bukovina, to the detriment of relations with independent Ukraine.

A separate territorial issue between the two countries concerns Serpents' Island (Insula Serpilor in Romanian, Ostriv Zmiinyi in Ukrainian) to the east of the Danube delta. This island was used as a communications facility by the former Soviet Black Sea fleet but its possession by the USSR was never ratified by an internationally recognized legal instrument.

Historical Background

Bukovina was the name given by the Habsburg authorities to a province created from the northern part of the principality of Moldavia which the Ottoman Turks, as suzerain power, ceded to the Habsburg empire in 1775. The Habsburg government initially called the ceded territory "Austrian Moldavia", but renamed it Bukovina after the beech forests (*bucov* means "beech tree" in Slavonic) which characterized the region in order to distinguish it from the rest of Moldavia. Bukovina, with an area of 10,442 sq km, was a region of upland pastures and plains, peopled principally by Romanians, who according to Austrian figures compiled in 1775 represented 85 per cent of the population of 75,000. Under Habsburg rule the settlement of Uniate Catholic Ukrainians from neighbouring Galicia was encouraged and this had the effect of diluting the Romanian Orthodox population. The demographic configuration of the province was further altered by the arrival of several thousand German colonists and by Jews from the Pale and Russia. According to the 1910 census conducted in the Austro-Hungarian Empire, Bukovina had a population of 795,000, of whom 34.4 per cent were Romanians.

In November 1918, at the end of World War I, representatives of the Romanians proclaimed the province's union with Romania, a decision which was recognized by the victorious powers at the Paris conference and enshrined in the Treaty of St Germain of Sept. 10, 1919. Bukovina's population in 1930, according to the Romanian census, was 853,000, of whom 379,691 (44.5 per cent) were Romanians, 236,130 (27.6 per cent) Ukrainians, 92,492 (10.8 per cent) Jews, 75,533 (8.8 per cent) Germans, 30,580 (3.5 per cent) Poles and 8,000 Russians. Cession of the northern part of Bukovina and the province of Bessarabia was demanded in an ultimatum presented by the Soviet government to Romania on June 26, 1940 (see Section 4.5). Despite the fact that Northern Bukovina had never formed part of the Russian Empire, the Soviet Union was able to base its claim to that part of Bukovina "where the predominant majority of the population is connected with the Soviet Ukraine by common historical destinies", as the ultimatum put it, on demographic evidence. Estimates of the Ukrainian population in the northern part of the province demanded by the Soviet Union vary between 167,000 and 200,000, while the number of Romanians is usually given as 136,500.

The rapacity of the Soviet government was indicated by the delineation of the proposed new frontier on the map accompanying the ultimatum of June 1940. Marked with a thick red pencil line on a small map on the scale of 1:1,800,000, the frontier as drawn represented a seven-mile band of territory throughout its course, thus causing confusion over which localities fell on the Soviet side. Even worse, the crudeness of the pencil stroke cut across the north-eastern corner of the Romanian province of Moldavia, which included the town of Herta with its almost exclusively Romanian population. Despite Romanian protests that this area was not mentioned in the ultimatum, the Soviet representatives on the joint Romanian-Soviet commission, charged with implementing the ultimatum, insisted that Herta be included in the ceded territories.

Thus Northern Bukovina, an area of roughly 6,000 sq km and some 475,000 inhabitants, and the district of Herta (Gertsa), neither of which had ever been under Russian or Ukrainian rule, were annexed by the Soviet Union and incorporated into the Chernivtsi region (oblast) of the Ukrainian Soviet Socialist Republic (SSR), together with part of the county of Hotin (Khotyn) in Bessarabia. At the same time, the two southern Bessarabian counties of Cetatea Alba (Bilgorod Dnistrovskii) and Ismail were incorporated into the Odessa oblast of the Ukrainian SSR. The new Chernivtsi oblast covered an area of 8,100 sq km. Its frontiers with the newly created Moldavian SSR, formed from the annexed territory of Bessarabia which was also ceded by Romania to the Soviet Union in June 1940, were approved by the Moldavian and Ukrainian leaders on Aug. 22, 1940. In June 1941, on the eve of the German invasion of the Soviet Union, 13,000 Romanians were deported from Northern

Bukovina to Siberia. Those that survived were allowed to return in 1959.

The recovery of Northern Bukovina and Bessarabia was the principal motive for Romania's involvement in the German invasion of the Soviet Union on June 22, 1941, and was achieved by July 27 at the cost of 10,486 Romanian dead. In the winter of 1941-42 there were massive deportations of Jews and Gypsies from the whole of Bukovina to camps in Transnistria, an area in the Ukraine between the Dniester and the Bug rivers which was administered by Romania. Many thousands died of starvation or were shot by German and Romanian units. Bukovina was overrun by the Red Army in the early autumn of 1944, after which Northern Bukovina, together with the district of Herta and a part of the Bessarabian county of Khotyn, were restored to the Chernivtsi oblast of the Ukrainian SSR. The restoration was confirmed by the Paris peace treaty with Romania signed on Feb. 10, 1947.

Re-emergence of Romanian Claim to Territories Lost in 1940

An officially-expressed Romanian interest in Northern Bukovina and in the other territories annexed by the Soviet Union in June 1940 was implicit in Romanian-Soviet verbal sparring over Bessarabia which began in the mid-1960s. Conducted in the context of strained ideological relations, such exchanges often took the form, on the Romanian side, of assertions of the illegality of the August 1939 German-Soviet non-aggression treaty (the Molotov-Ribbentrop Pact), secret clauses of which had countenanced the Soviet annexations. In the Communist era a restraining factor on Romania was its concern that, if it pressed territorial issues with the Soviet Union, the latter could retaliate by backing Hungarian claims on Transylvania (see Section 4.11). Following the overthrow of Ceausescu in December 1989, the new government of the National Salvation Front (NSF) also took the "Transylvania factor" into account in its dealings with Moscow, but in broader circles resurgent Romanian nationalism came increasingly to focus on the idea of restoring the country's pre-1940 borders.

Romanian interest in the territories annexed in 1940 intensified amid the fragmentation of the Soviet Union in 1991, the two key developments being the transformation of the Moldavian SSR into the independent Republic of Moldavia (Moldova), containing a majority of Romanians, and the assertion of independence by Ukraine. As regards the former, an important catalyst was an initiative by Moldova to declare the Molotov-Ribbentrop Pact "null and void". A declaration to that effect was made at the end of an international conference devoted to "the Molotov-Ribbentrop Pact and its consequences for Bessarabia" organized in the Moldovan capital of Chisinau (Kishinev) by the Moldovan government and parliament on June 26-28, 1991. A direct impact of this conference was to force the government and parliament of Romania to take a stand on the issue of Bessarabia and Northern

Bukovina. The Romanian government had assiduously avoided comment on this matter, an attitude which irritated Moldovan leaders and the Moldovan people. Indeed, the new Romanian-Soviet treaty of friendship and co-operation, which President Ion Iliescu of Romania hastily negotiated with President Gorbachev in April 1991, appeared to place the Romanian authorities on the other side of the issue, with its tone of subservience to the interests of the Soviet Union and specific affirmation that World War II boundaries were not subject to discussion or modification.

The Romanian parliament, under the pressure of the forthcoming Chisinau conference, on June 24, 1991, unanimously adopted a statement declaring: "The Molotov-Ribbentrop Pact, by which the Soviet Union and Germany established for themselves spheres of influence from the Baltic to the Black Sea, taking it upon themselves to decide the destinies of sovereign states, among them Romania, flagrantly contravenes the fundamental principles and norms of international law. Consequently, in the name of the Romanian people, parliament condemns this pact from the outset as being null and void". This declaration was subsequently presented at the Chisinau conference to guarded applause, Moldovan reserve implying that proof of the bona fides of the Romanian parliament's declaration would be provided by the manner in which it dealt with the ratification of the Iliescu-Gorbachev treaty. In the event, the collapse of the Soviet Union rendered the proposed treaty defunct.

The parliament of the then Ukrainian SSR responded to the declaration of the Romanian parliament with a statement which treated it as a territorial claim against Ukraine. The Ukrainian parliamentarians termed Northern Bukovina and Southern Bessarabia "ancient Ukrainian lands" that Ukraine "had helped to liberate from foreign rule". Following the Soviet diplomatic tradition, the parliament claimed that the Ukrainian-Romanian border was a result of the post-war settlement and not of the Molotov-Ribbentrop Pact.

The break-up of the Soviet Union and the affirmation of Ukraine's independence following the referendum in that republic on Dec. 1, 1991, transformed the issue of the territories lost to the Soviet Union into a matter of contention between Romania and Ukraine. Indeed, on Nov. 28 the Romanian parliament passed a strongly worded statement on the organization of the referendum in which it declared: "Bearing in mind that this referendum is due to take place on Romanian territories…the Romanian parliament solemnly declares that these territories were torn from the country's body", continuing that "this referendum cannot be valid as regards the Romanian territories which were abusively annexed by the former Soviet Union, territories which have never belonged to Ukraine and which are of right Romania's…The Romanian parliament solemnly declares that the referendum organized by the Kiev authorities in the Romanian territories forcibly incorporated in the former Soviet Union, namely Northern Bukovina, the district of Herta, the district of Hotin and the counties in southern

Bessarabia, is null and void, as are the consequences of this referendum".

The Romanian parliament's declaration appeared to have been timed to coincide with a visit by the Ukrainian Foreign Minister to Bucharest on Nov. 29, 1991. The Foreign Minister promptly cancelled his visit and the Romanian government felt obliged to make conciliatory noises. It formally recognized the independence of Ukraine on Nov. 29, although it took no immediate steps to establish diplomatic relations. Romania's position towards Ukraine was explained by Foreign Minister Adrian Nastase at a meeting between the Prime Ministers of Romania and Moldova held in Bucharest on Dec. 28-29, 1991. He pointed out that Romania had no territorial claims on Ukraine and had recognized all the former republics of the USSR. Through the declaration of Nov. 28 Romania had wanted only to register its position of principle regarding the Molotov-Ribbentrop Pact and its desire to remove its consequences, including those affecting the territories seized by the Soviet Union during World War II and assigned to the Ukraine. Romania, Nastase went on, did not make the resolution of this problem a condition of establishing diplomatic relations with Ukraine; at the same time, the government could not ignore it and wished, at a suitable time, to open discussions in the spirit of the Helsinki Final Act and the Charter of Paris for a New Europe (of the Conference on Security and Co-operation in Europe).

Subsequent discussions between Romania and Ukraine were complicated by the territorial claims of two breakaway republics in areas of Moldova with non-Romanian majorities. The "Moldavian Dnestr Soviet Socialist Republic" was declared in Tiraspol on Sept. 2, 1990, by representatives of the area east of the Dniester (Dnestr) river opposed to Moldova's assertion of independence. Over half of its population of 546,000 were non-Romanian (27 per cent Ukrainian and 25 per cent Russian, although 40 per cent were Romanian at the time of its declaration). The "Gagauz Autonomous Soviet Socialist Republic" was declared in Komrat on Aug. 19, 1990, by representatives of the Gagauz ethnic group (of Turkic/Bulgarian origin but Christian Orthodox in religious faith), numbering some 150,000 and located in south-west Moldova. Both republics were regarded as illegal by the Moldovan authorities, a perception which was enhanced when both declared their support for the attempted coup by hardliners in Moscow in August 1991.

As regards the "Dnestr republic", one possible scenario was that, on a union of Moldova with Romania, the territory of that breakaway republic would be ceded to Ukraine in return for concessions to Romania in respect of Northern Bukovina and/or the former southern Bessarabian counties now part of Ukraine. This would be advantageous to Romania in two respects. Finally, the union of these areas with Romania would mitigate the economic loss of the Dnestr republic, which contained over 40 per cent of Moldova's industrial capacity. Secondly, such a cession would mean that Romania/Moldova did not have to cope with large Ukrainian and Russian minorities within its borders (although such minorities would remain of significant numbers). (See section 4.5 for details of the development of hostilities over the Dnestr republic.)

With time it became clear that the problem of the Dnestr republic would not be solved quickly owing to the geopolitical interests of Russia, which kept its troops there, and the Romanian government decided to press Kyiv harder on other territorial issues. Foreign Minister Teodor Melescanu stated at a press conference in December 1995 that Romania would demand a review of the 1948 protocol that made Serpents' Island a part of the USSR.

History and Present Status of Serpents' Island

Serpents' Island was taken by the Ottoman Turks at the end of the 15th century and remained under their control until it was annexed, together with the Danube delta, by Russia under the terms of the Treaty of Adrianople signed at the end of the 1828-29 Russo-Turkish War. Under the Treaty of Paris of 1856 and an additional protocol, Turkey regained possession of the delta and the island (which had been originally omitted from the maps used at Paris), but under the Treaty of Berlin of 1878, concluded at the end of the Russo-Turkish War of 1877-78, both the delta and the island were awarded to Romania in partial compensation for Romania's loss to Russia of three southern Bessarabian counties contiguous to the delta. Romania remained in possession of Serpents' Island from this date until the late 1940s. The Paris peace treaty of 1947 did not mention the island when it established the frontier between Romania and the Soviet Union as that "fixed in accordance with the Soviet-Romanian agreement of June 28, 1940"—i.e. following the Romanian cession of Bessarabia and Northern Bukovina, which itself had left the island in Romanian hands.

How the island passed into Soviet control is unclear. However, some light was shed on the matter by a Romanian Foreign Ministry spokesman on Nov. 23, 1990, when he revealed that a protocol handing over Serpents' Island to the Soviet Union had been signed on Feb. 4, 1948, by Soviet Foreign Minister Molotov and the Romanian Prime Minister, Petru Groza. This spokesman claimed that control of the island had subsequently been restored to Romania, but that it had been reoccupied later by the Soviet Union, although precise details were lacking. The status of the island was raised at a press conference given by President Ion Iliescu on April 5, 1991, during his visit to Moscow to negotiate the Romanian-Soviet friendship treaty. Iliescu explained that, when the territorial waters of Romania and the Soviet Union had been delineated according to a protocol signed in 1948, Serpents' Island had fallen within Soviet waters and had therefore been handed over. Iliescu said that he had "presented the issue" of the island to President Gorbachev, who had responded that "he was not familiar with the issue, would inform himself and would consider the claim in a spirit of good-

will". The Romanian President added: "The issue is therefore open".

The question of sovereignty over the island took on a new complexion following Ukraine's declaration of independence in December 1991 and was complicated by the subsequent Russian-Ukrainian dispute over control of the Black Sea fleet (see Section 4.15). It would appear that the transfer of the island to the Soviet Union was in breach of the Paris peace treaty, whose other signatories did not give their agreement, so that any control exercised by Ukraine would be de facto and not de jure. By this time the island did not just play a strategic role: it also had considerable economic importance, since it lies in an area of gas and oil deposits. By 1990 there were 11 Romanian drilling rigs in Romanian territorial waters in the Black Sea and 20 more underwater oil deposits had been identified. Both Ukraine and Romania proved reticent about the areas of seabed around and belonging to Serpents' Island to which they lay claim.

Gorbachev's sympathetic statements about the island were perhaps uttered in order to make the Romanian-Soviet friendship treaty more palatable to the Romanian public. However, when the Soviet Union finally collapsed at the end of 1991, the treaty became defunct. Any concession to Romanian claims by the successor power, Ukraine, would be regarded as setting a precedent for the wider Romanian-Ukrainian territorial disputes involving Northern Bukovina and the southern Bessarabian counties.

Ukrainian-Romanian Treaty on Good-Neighbourliness and Co-operation

The territorial dispute became entrenched in historical debates that could lead nowhere. The more the Romanians insisted on condemnation by Kyiv of the Molotov-Ribbentrop Pact, the more the Ukrainians would demand that Bucharest condemn Romania's seizure of Ukrainian lands in 1918 and the Hitler-Antonescu agreement—it was, after all, Romania that had occupied Ukrainian lands as a part of the Nazi invading force and established its rule in the Southern Ukraine. No party wished to make territorial concessions, and the Ukrainian position was lent support by the fact that the Helsinki Final Act recognized the existing boundaries between European countries as inviolable. Romania was prepared to formally renounce any territorial claims to Ukraine but insisted on mutual agreement to reconsider the delimitation of borders.

A breakthrough came with the final stages of Romania's negotiations to join the EU and NATO in mid-1997. A few weeks before the NATO Madrid summit, the government formed after Emil Constantinescu's presidential victory faced the risk of being left without an invitation to join NATO, as NATO would not accept states with outstanding territorial disputes. Bucharest accepted most of the Ukrainian demands and the two Presidents, Leonid Kuchma of Ukraine and Constantinescu, signed a bilateral treaty in Constanta in June 2, 1997.

This Treaty on Good Neighbourliness and Co-operation recognized that the two states respect each other's territorial integrity. The preamble does not mention specifically the Molotov-Ribbentrop Pact or the Hitler-Antonescu agreement but generally holds "as unjust the acts of totalitarian and military-dictatorial regimes that have in the past had a negative effect on relations between the Ukrainian and Romanian peoples". The 1997 accord also included Article 13 where the contracting parties pledged to create equal conditions for learning their native language for the national minorities in both countries, recognizing the rights of Ukrainians in Romania and Romanians in Ukraine to receive education in their own languages. This clause entailed more responsibility on the part of the Romanian government, as all Ukrainian schools in Romania had been closed in the Ceausescu era, while in Ukraine there was an existing state-run education network of schools where children are taught in Romanian.

Implicitly Romania agreed to acknowledge Serpents' Island as Ukrainian territory, Ukraine subsequently demilitarizing the island as a gesture of good will. Bucharest, however, insisted on continuing negotiations on the delimitation of the continental shelf and the two states' exclusive economic zones in the Black Sea, threatening to take this issue to the International Court of Justice if no agreement could be reached. The Romanians insisted that Serpents' Island is a rock, rather than an island that would affect the division of the territorial waters between Romania and Ukraine. Ukraine insisted on "island" status and consequently considered an area extending for 12 nautical miles around Serpents' Island to be its own territorial waters. The obvious issue of contention is the potential division of oil and gas that could be extracted in future from the continental shelf.

To prove the point that Serpents' Island is inhabited Ukrainian territory, some private Ukrainian companies started to build infrastructure there such as a post office, a shop and a new sea terminal. The island—once populated by Ancient Greek colonists who built there a temple devoted to the legendary warrior Achilles—seems likely to remain the Achilles heel of Ukrainian-Romanian relations for the foreseeable future.

The overall prospects for Ukrainian-Romanian relations are framed by the declared strategic goals of the two countries to join both NATO and the European Union. The 1997 treaty proclaimed that both countries "shall support each other in their efforts directed towards integration into European and Euro-Atlantic structures". A month after the signing of the bilateral treaty, the Presidents of Ukraine, Romania and Moldova met in Izmail and signed a trilateral protocol on the creation of the Lower Danube Euroregion and a free economic zone that included Ukrainian Reni, Romanian Galata and Moldovan Giurgiulesti. Both Kyiv and Bucharest were keen to show their Western allies that the two countries could be regional leaders and champions of a united Europe.

Olexander Hryb

4.15 Russia - Ukraine (Crimea)

The Crimea was annexed by imperial Russia in 1783 and was made an autonomous Soviet republic by the newly established Bolshevik regime in 1921, in recognition of its distinctive Muslim Tatar heritage. Unjustly accused of general collaboration with the German invaders in World War II, the Crimean Tatars were deported en masse to Central Asia in 1944-45, whereupon the Crimea became a region of the Russian Federation and received an inflow of ethnic Russians. In 1954 it was transferred to Ukrainian jurisdiction and in the 1960s became the focus of agitation for permission to return by the Crimean Tatars, who were officially rehabilitated in 1967. Following Gorbachev's assumption of power in 1985, restrictions on Tatar resettlement were lifted but they remained a tiny proportion of the Crimean population in 1991, when the Ukrainian authorities granted the Crimea autonomy within Ukraine.

However, on the demise of the Soviet Union in December 1991, the Russian Federation reopened the question of the Crimea's status, indicating that it did not rule out territorial claims on adjoining areas of other ex-Soviet republics which contained an ethnic Russian majority. The Russian parliament revoked in May 1992 the 1954 decree transferring the Crimea to Ukraine and approved a resolution in June 1993 to assert the "Russian federal status" of Sevastopol. Although a Ukrainian–Russian treaty of friendship and co-operation in 1997 proclaimed mutual respect for each state's territorial integrity, Russia tried to avoid delimitation of land and sea borders. Lack of agreement on what should constitute territorial waters for Russia and Ukraine around Crimea in the Sea of Azov and the Kerch strait erupted into open confrontation in November 2003 over Tuzla island, after the Krasnodar territorial authorities had built a 5 km causeway with the evident intention of linking Tuzla to the Russian mainland. The possession of Tuzla island ensured Ukrainian control of the Kerch strait and it appeared the Kremlin may have perceived this as a strategic threat following the Ukrainian application to join NATO. Despite an ambitious Russian initiative (the Single Economic Space) to create a new union with Ukraine, launched early in 2003, Moscow has refused to admit that Tuzla belongs to Ukraine and the issue remained unresolved by the end of the year. Work on the causeway was halted when it was only 100 metres away from the Ukrainian border and only after Kyiv conducted a number of military exercises in the area and deployed troops on the island. (Map 47, p. 516, shows Crimea and the Russian-Ukrainian border.)

Geographical and Historical Background

The Crimea (Krym) autonomous republic within Ukraine has a total area of 25,900 sq km and forms a peninsula bounded to the south and west by the Black Sea and to the east by the Sea of Azov. It is linked to the Ukrainian mainland by the Perekop isthmus and separated from the Russian Federation to the east by the Kerch strait. Its capital is Simferopol and other major cities include Sevastopol (the base of the ex-Soviet Black Sea fleet), Kerch and Yalta (the main holiday resort of what used to be called the "Soviet Riviera"). Northern Crimea is semi-arid steppe, supporting wheat, corn and cotton crops, whereas south of the Crimean mountains the Black Sea littoral is sub-tropical. The peninsula is rich in minerals and has much heavy industry, including ironworks and chemicals plants. The population of the Crimean region was estimated at about 2,500,000 in mid-1991—68% were ethnic Russians, most of the rest Ukrainians and only 2% Crimean Tatars. By 2001, however, the population had decreased to just 2,024,000 with 58% Russians, 24% Ukrainians and 12% Tatars.

Inhabited in ancient times by a Cimmerian people called the Tauri, the Crimea experienced Greek coastal colonization from the seventh century BC and later came under Roman influence. From the third to the eighth centuries AD successive waves of conquerors included the Goths, Huns and Khazars. By 600 AD Christianity was well-established in south-eastern Crimea, which in the early 11th century became part of the Byzantine empire, shortly after the Norse-founded Kievan Rus', centred on the historic capital of Ukraine, had also embraced the Christian faith. Mongol-Tatar invasions from the 13th century overran the early Russian principalities as well as the Crimea, where an independent Muslim Tatar khanate was established in the 15th century, extending to a large area of the hinterland.

Ottoman Turkish suzerainty was recognized by the Crimean khanate from the early 16th century, as the Tsars of Muscovy began the inexorable expansion of their territories. In 1654 Kiev and a region to its east fell to Tsar Alexis, after which Peter the Great (r. 1696-1725) crowned his northern conquests by giving the name Russia to Muscovy and establishing St Petersburg as its capital. Under Catherine the Great (r. 1763-96), huge Russian advances in the west and south included the annexation of the Crimea (in 1783) and of most of modern Ukraine in the second partition of Poland in 1793. During Catherine's reign the northern Crimea was one of the Russian regions to which German free peasant settlers were invited with the aim of bringing virgin land into use.

In the 19th century the peninsula was the battleground of the Crimean War (1853-56) between Russia on the one hand and Britain, France, Turkey and Sardinia on the other. The Crimea was also the scene of much conflict during World War I and the Russian civil war which followed the Bolshevik Revolution of 1917. It formed part of the short-lived Republic of Taurida declared by anti-Bolsheviks in 1918, but was brought under Bolshevik rule by 1921, becoming an autonomous soviet socialist republic (ASSR) in October of that year. Similarly, a newly-declared independent Ukraine eventually succumbed to Soviet and Polish arms, the Soviet part becoming a soviet socialist republic (SSR) in July 1923.

Although the Muslim Tatars made up only 25 per cent of the Crimean ASSR's population, they enjoyed something of a golden age in the early Soviet period, serving as an example of the cultural autonomy and economic progress available to national minorities under Bolshevik rule. However, together with many other groups, the Tatars later suffered from the forcible collectivization programme and political purges of "bourgeois nationalists" instituted by Stalin in the 1930s.

Catastrophe overtook the Crimean Tatars during the Second World War (1939-45). Invading German forces occupied the Crimea in late 1941 and were welcomed as liberators by some fifth-column elements. On the return of the Red Army in 1943-44, Stalin exacted a stern punishment for this alleged collaboration (as he did on other "suspect" national groups). In May 1944 the Soviet authorities began the forcible deportation of the entire Crimean Tatar population to Soviet Central Asia, an operation which resulted in an estimated 100,000 deaths (about 22 per cent of those deported). Many Tatars died in transit, many from famine in the largely barren areas where they were settled and some from hostile action by the local inhabitants.

East European territorial changes in 1945 included the cession to the Soviet Union of pre-war eastern Poland, the southern part of which (East Galicia) was joined to the Ukrainian SSR, as was what had been Czechoslovak Transcarpathia (see Sections 4.13 and 4.18). Ukraine became a founder member of the United Nations in its own right, together with Belorussia, as a concession by the Western Allies to Stalin's wish that the Soviet Union should have some automatic voting support in the new world organization. In post-war changes to the Soviet structure, the Crimea lost its autonomous status and became an administrative region (oblast) of the Russian Soviet Federated Socialist Republic (RSFSR). At the same time, many Crimean towns previously with Tatar names were given Russian versions, reflecting the fact that the deported Tatars were replaced mostly by ethnic Russian settlers.

1954 Transfer of Crimea to Ukraine— Rehabilitation of Tatars

Following Stalin's death in March 1953, the deportation policy was reviewed and then denounced by Nikita Khrushchev in 1956. But the Crimean Tatars were among the national groups still not allowed to move back to their original homeland, on the grounds that they had "taken root" in the Central Asian Soviet republics of Uzbekistan, Kazakhstan and Tajikistan. Meanwhile, in a partial relaxation of Moscow's grip, the oblast of Crimea had been transferred from the

RSFSR to the Ukrainian SSR on Feb. 19, 1954, under a decree signed by Marshal Klimenti Voroshilov, then Chairman of the Presidium of the USSR Supreme Soviet (i.e. head of state). The official Soviet announcement said that the transfer had been agreed between the two republics because of Crimea's "common economic interests, territorial proximity and cultural ties" with Ukraine. Other sources explained that the intention was to demonstrate, on the 300th anniversary of Russia's acquisition of Kiev, that Ukraine was now an integral part of the Soviet Union.

Under two decrees signed by President Nikolai Podgorny on Sept. 5, 1967, the Crimean Tatars were officially rehabilitated by the Soviet government. The first asserted that the fact that "a certain section" of them had actively collaborated with the Nazis during World War II "was unjustifiably used to blame the entire Tatar population". It continued: "These indiscriminate accusations…should be withdrawn, especially since a new generation of people have entered the work and political life of the country". The second decree said that the Tatars were free to live anywhere in the Soviet Union and to return to the Crimea if they wished.

However, of some 6,000 Tatars who thereupon travelled to the Crimea, only a few were allowed to settle there. The result was increased agitation by Tatars in Central Asia, where clashes with security forces occurred in Tashkent (Uzbekistan) in April 1968, and periodic protests in Moscow. Over the following decade, numerous Tatar activists received prison sentences for "anti-Soviet propaganda" and other alleged offences. The situation eased somewhat in the late 1970s, to the extent that by late 1978 about 16,000 Tatars had been allowed to return to the Crimea from Central Asia. However, arrests and deportations of Tatar protesters continued into the 1980s, as the authorities continued to resist the idea of wholesale return.

Following Mikhail Gorbachev's assumption of power in Moscow in March 1985, Tatars took advantage of the new *glasnost* freedoms to stage a week-long protest in Moscow in July 1987. Their demands included not only an unrestricted right of return but also the restoration of the autonomy which the Crimea had enjoyed in the pre-war period. On July 27, 1987, their representatives met President Andrei Gromyko, who had just been appointed to chair a state commission charged with examining Tatar grievances, but expressed themselves to be dissatisfied with the results of the meeting. Further demonstrations by Tatars in the Tashkent area were broken up by police in August 1987, while in October 1987 an attempted Tatar march on the Crimean capital (to coincide with the 66th anniversary of the creation of the Crimean ASSR) was halted by the authorities.

The findings of the Gromyko commission, as released by the official news agency Tass on June 9, 1988, were that all impediments had been removed to the resettlement of Tatars in the Crimea and that there were "no grounds for re-establishing Crimean autonomy". The commission noted that "the relevant authorities have lifted all restrictions on the rights of Crimean Tatars…and guarantee their complete equality with other citizens in all matters, including the choice of place of residence, work and study". The Tass account of the committee's report continued that in the previous year some 2,500 Crimean Tatars had been granted residence permits and had found work in the Crimea, and that new opportunities had been created for the study of the Crimean Tatar language and culture, especially in Uzbekistan but also in the Crimea itself and in the neighbouring Krasnodar territory (kray). It also accused "individual Tatar groups" of hindering a positive resolution of Crimean Tatar grievances by insisting on the restoration of the Crimean ASSR and noted that Tatars formed only 2 per cent of the Crimea's population at the time.

Restoration of Crimea's Autonomy within Ukraine —Russian Claims

From mid-1990 the Crimean Tatar question was eclipsed by larger political developments, as Russia, Ukraine and other Soviet republics moved to assert their individual sovereignty. Following the election of Boris Yeltsin to its presidency on May 29, 1990, the RSFSR was declared a sovereign state by its newly constituted Congress of People's Deputies on June 12, 1990. Under pressure from the pro-independence opposition *Rukh* movement, the Ukrainian Supreme Soviet followed suit on July 16, 1990, although, unlike the Russian parliament, it did not assert a right to secede from the Soviet Union.

Changes in Ukraine's Communist hierarchy elevated Leonid Kravchuk to the presidency of the republic on July 23, 1990. The caution subsequently displayed by Kravchuk as regards Yeltsin's calls for radical reform in Soviet structures in part derived from his life-long dedication to Communist orthodoxy. But it also reflected a growing awareness that a break-up of the Soviet system could expose Ukraine to Russian territorial claims on Ukrainian regions where ethnic Russians formed the majority. Such fears persisted even though the Russian Federation and Ukraine signed a treaty on Nov. 19, 1990, guaranteeing existing borders.

Aware that the Crimea was a Russian-majority region, the Ukrainian authorities did not prevent the holding of a referendum in the oblast on Jan. 20, 1991, on whether autonomous status should be restored, even though the proposition was that the Crimea should be independent of Ukraine. Organized by the regional soviet, the referendum drew participation from over 81 per cent of eligible voters, of whom 93.3 per cent voted in favour of Crimean autonomy. Representatives of the Crimean Tatars opposed the referendum on the grounds that they were the indigenous people and should have been the only ones allowed to vote. There was also a call for a boycott by the *Rukh* national-democrats, on the grounds that Ukraine's territorial integrity was being threatened.

In light of the outcome of the referendum, the Ukrainian Supreme Soviet on Feb. 12, 1991, made the best of a bad job by approving the restoration of the

Crimean ASSR, but still within Ukraine in terms of sovereignty. It was unclear at that stage whether the change would be recognized by the USSR or Russian authorities, neither having been directly consulted. The situation was complicated in late June 1991 when the first national congress (*kurultay*) of the Crimean Tatars met in Simferopol and proclaimed the Crimea to be "the national territory of the Crimean Tatar nation, on which it alone has the right to self-determination". On June 29 the congress elected a 31-member representative body (*majlis*), of which Mustafa Dzhemilev, of the Crimean Tatar National Movement, was elected chairman.

The attempted hardline coup in Moscow in August 1991 hastened the disintegration of the Soviet Union, and exposed the underlying tensions in Russian-Ukrainian relations. The attempted coup was denounced by the Ukrainian leadership, and on Aug. 24 the Supreme Soviet in Kiev voted in favour of full independence subject to a popular referendum. This was held on Dec. 1, 1991, and resulted in a 90 per cent vote in favour of independence on a turnout of 84 per cent of eligible voters. In simultaneous presidential elections, Kravchuk was confirmed in office, defeating six other candidates. A feature of the referendum result was that predominantly Russian areas such as the Crimea recorded majorities for independence. By that time, however, rumbles of territorial dispute between Ukraine and the Russian Federation had already been heard.

As the first President of a Soviet republic to be popularly elected (on June 12, 1991), Yeltsin had emerged from the abortive coup dominant over the discredited Gorbachev. In a statement on Aug. 26, 1991, he said that the Russian Federation "reserves the right to raise the issue of a revision of borders" with all contiguous republics except the Baltic states. Observers noted that, apart from the Crimea, the Russians also had a potential territorial claim on the Donbass coal-mining region of eastern Ukraine, where ethnic Russians formed a significant 45 per cent of population. Conversely, they also noted that Ukraine could make claim to part of the Rostov region of the Russian Federation, to the east of the Sea of Azov.

Yeltsin's statement provoked angry reactions from the leaderships of both Kazakhstan and Ukraine. After a propitiatory visit by a Russian delegation, the RSFSR and Ukraine agreed on Aug. 29, 1991, to abide by their November 1990 treaty guaranteeing existing borders and to work for increased economic co-operation. However, Ukrainian doubts about Russian intentions revived when on Nov. 28, 1991, the RSFSR Supreme Soviet adopted a law granting citizenship to Russians living outside the borders of the Russian Federation where they had not taken local citizenship. It was estimated that Russians covered by this law numbered some 26,000,000, including a large proportion of the Russian contingent of 22 per cent in Ukraine's population of 51,400,000.

Black Sea Fleet Issue

On the demise of the Soviet Union in December 1991, the Commonwealth of Independent States (CIS) appeared at first to enshrine a determination on the part of the participating ex-Soviet republics to adhere to existing borders. The founding Minsk declaration of Dec. 8, 1991, signed by the Russian Federation, Ukraine and Belarus (the three Slav republics), specifically enjoined respect for the existing territorial configuration, as did the Alma-Ata declaration of Dec. 21, when Armenia, Azerbaijan, Kazakhstan, Kyrgyzstan, Moldova, Tajikistan, Turkmenistan and Uzbekistan all joined the CIS. Moreover, on Jan. 30, 1992, the CIS states were admitted to membership of the Conference on Security and Co-operation in Europe (CSCE), a key text of which was the 1975 Helsinki Final Act specifying that adherent states should refrain from making territorial claims against one another.

Nevertheless, the Russian Supreme Soviet passed a resolution on Jan. 23, 1992, to the effect that its legislative, international affairs and external economic relations committees would all examine the constitutionality of the 1954 decree by which the Crimea was transferred to Ukraine. The clear implication was that there were doubts about whether the transfer had been done in a constitutional way. Moreover, the same session resolved that sailors of the ex-Soviet Black Sea fleet, based at Sevastopol in the Crimea, should be required to take the military oath of allegiance agreed by the CIS heads of government at a meeting in Moscow on Jan. 16, 1992.

The Russian parliament's Black Sea fleet decision followed the development of a controversy with Ukraine over whether the 45 warships and 300 smaller vessels (and their crews) should be deemed to be part of the Russian-commanded CIS forces, as desired by the Russian Federation. Ukraine's position hardened after President Yeltsin declared on Jan. 9 that "the Black Sea fleet was, is and will continue to be Russian, and no-one will take it away from Russia, including Kravchuk". Talks between Russia and Ukraine in Kyiv (Kiev) on Jan. 11, 1992, resulted in agreement that "the sides acknowledge that the armed forces stationed in Ukraine comprise a grouping of CIS strategic forces, excluding a section of the Black Sea fleet which will form part of the Ukrainian armed forces". In further talks, however, the number of ships to be assigned to Ukraine came under dispute, and was not resolved at CIS ministerial meetings in February 1992.

On the Crimea issue, a delegation of the Ukrainian Supreme Soviet held talks with the newly established Crimean Supreme Soviet on Feb. 5, 1992, and reached agreement on the need to demarcate powers between the two bodies. On the following day Ukrainian deputies approved a statement asserting that the Russian decision to re-examine the 1954 transfer of the Crimea to Ukraine ran counter to a number of treaties, including those creating the CIS and the 1975 Final Act of the CSCE. Also on Feb. 6, the Russian Supreme Soviet decided to set up a state commission "to study all the circumstances of the legal grounds of the decision taken in 1954". Under a resolution adopted on Feb. 26 the Crimean Supreme Soviet decided that the name of the autonomous republic should henceforth be "Crimea Republic" (Respublika Krym).

A law confirming the Crimea's autonomy within Ukraine was passed by the parliament of independent Ukraine on April 22, 1992. The measure named Ukraine as the guarantor of the Crimea's sovereignty and stated that the republic could not be transferred to another sovereignty without the agreement of its people. It also recorded that both Ukraine and the Crimea recognized the rights of the Crimean Tatars. At about the same time, Vice-President Alexander Rutskoi of the Russian Federation caused further unease in Kyiv by publicly questioning whether Ukraine possessed territorial viability within its existing frontiers. Ukrainian deputies responded by passing a resolution saying that "such actions of the Russian leadership are aimed at ruining Ukrainian-Russian relations and destabilizing the situation in Ukraine". The resolution added that if Ukraine wished to follow the Russian example it could legitimately "claim territories where Ukrainians live", whereas it neither advanced territorial claims on others nor was prepared to entertain them on itself.

Further complications ensued on May 5, 1992, when, in direct defiance of the Ukrainian authorities, the Crimean parliament passed a resolution in favour of separate independence for the region, subject to approval in a referendum in August 1992. Taken together with the Russian Federation's decision to re-examine the transfer of the Crimea to Ukraine in 1954, the Crimean deputies' decision was widely seen as a step in the direction of reunification with Russia. This was certainly how it was seen in Kyiv, where President Kravchuk condemned the Crimean vote as illegal and where the Ukrainian parliament on May 13 voted to annul the declaration as being contrary to the republic's constitution. On the previous day, moreover, the Crimean Tatars' *majlis* denounced the Crimean parliament's vote and also criticized the granting of autonomy to the Crimea by Ukraine, on the grounds that all existing structures excluded the Tatar people from their rightful position. Apparently succumbing to Ukrainian pressure, the Crimean parliament on May 20, 1992, voted to rescind its independence declaration.

However, the dispute escalated on May 21, 1992, when the Russian parliament, meeting in closed session, voted to rescind the 1954 decree under which the Crimea had been transferred to Ukraine. Its cited grounds were that the transfer had been carried out in contravention of the Russian constitution. The Ukrainian response, as conveyed in a Foreign Ministry statement of May 25, was that "the status of the Crimea is an internal Ukrainian matter which cannot be the subject of negotiations with another state". Nevertheless, pro-independence activists in the Crimea continued to solicit signatures in support of an independence referendum, and were reported to have collected over 200,000 by the end of June. At that point the Ukrainian parliament, in an attempt to appease Crimean opinion, adopted a new autonomy law for the republic granting it wide-ranging powers of self-rule in the economic, social and cultural spheres and also specifying that Ukrainian armed forces could be deployed in the Crimea only with the agreement of its government. Approved by 264 votes to four (but with the *Rukh* fraction abstaining in protest), the measure stated that the Crimean republic "is an autonomous composite part of Ukraine" and left responsibility for foreign policy, defence, customs and monetary affairs in the hands of the Kyiv government.

As regards the Black Sea fleet, further negotiations in April and May 1992 failed to resolve the question of its division and were complicated by the demand of Georgia (not a CIS member at the time) that it should receive some of the ships on the strength of its status as an ex-Soviet republic on the Black Sea coast. In a statement on the issue on May 26, the CIS commander-in-chief, Marshal Yevgeny Shaposhnikov, said that the entire fleet would be removed from the CIS command and would not henceforth form part of CIS strategic forces.

Crimean Autonomy within Ukraine

The first regional constitution of Crimea was adopted in May 1992 on a wave of Russian nationalist rhetoric that swamped the peninsula when the Crimean parliament felt encouraged by the politicians from the Russian Duma. The Republic of Crimea was proclaimed a "state" with sovereign rights over its resources and territory. The right to control law enforcement structures and conduct foreign relations was proclaimed as well; however, these claims were denied as illegitimate by the Ukrainian Verkhovna Rada (parliament). The Kyiv authorities imposed a moratorium in order to conduct a referendum on the status of Crimea and a new version of the Crimean constitution approved on Sept. 25, 1992, defined the republic as a state "within" Ukraine comprising the "multi-ethnic people of Crimea".

Russian ethno-national mobilization in Crimea coincided with a large-scale return of Crimean Tatars from Central Asia. Whereas in 1989 Crimean Tatars accounted for 1.9 per cent of the peninsula's population, by the time of the 2001 census their population had increased to 12 per cent of the total. The return of the Tatars, who allied themselves politically with the Ukrainian *Rukh*, inevitably contributed to tensions with those Russian settlers who had been moved in by the Soviet authorities since the 1950s and settled on the land and property of evicted Tatars.

After the Ukrainian and Russian Presidents announced a preliminary decision to split the Black Sea fleet in June 1993, the Russian parliament unanimously adopted a resolution to assert the Russian federal status of Sevastopol. The Ukrainian Verkhovna Rada responded by labelling the Russian resolution as "an aggressive political act" and appealed to the UN Security Council to condemn it. The Russian movement (Republican Movement of Crimea) was a central force behind the election of the first and the last Crimean President, Yuri Meshkov, in January 1994. Meshkov called for a boycott of the elections to the Ukrainian Verkhovna Rada and managed to win a narrow majority for his block "Russia" in the Crimean parliament.

The UN Security Council criticized the Russian parliament for its inconsistency in not following the UN Charter and the Russian-Ukrainian treaty of November 1990, and expressed the UN's "commitment to the territorial integrity of Ukraine". Despite that, and with Russian support, Sevastopol City Council declared the port to be Russian territory in August 1994. The same month, the CSCE initiated a mediating mission to Crimea aiming at conflict prevention and management between Kyiv and Simferopol.

The Ukrainian Verkhovna Rada rescinded the Sevastopol City Council's decision on Sept. 15, 1994, and President Meshkov could do little about it as the Crimean parliament simultaneously voted out his government on the grounds of incompetence and corruption. With the decline of Meshkov's popularity and power, the new Ukrainian President, Leonid Kuchma, managed to convince the Crimean parliament to approve his son-in-law, Anatolii Franchuk, as prime minister of Crimea in October 1994. By the end of 1994 the Russian separatist movement had failed to deliver on socio-economic issues and had become deeply divided, allowing President Kuchma to condemn "Crimean separatism" and to abolish the Crimean presidency in March 1995.

The Verkhovna Rada insisted that Crimean legislation should be firmly located within the Ukrainian framework. Negotiations between the parliaments partly succeeded, with an incomplete Crimean constitution being adopted in April 1996 that postponed decisions on a separate Crimean citizenship, Crimean state symbols and power-sharing. A new Ukrainian state constitution ratified in June 1997 allowed for an "Autonomous Republic of Crimea" and negotiations continued until the end of 1998. Finally, on Dec. 23, 1998, the Ukrainian Verkhovna Rada ratified a revised Crimean constitution that defined the Crimean assembly merely as a "representative organ" with the right to pass normative acts rather then laws. It also reaffirmed Crimea's status within Ukraine and Kyiv's control over Crimean politics and law-enforcement bodies. Elite bargaining, however, largely left the Crimean Tatars out of the negotiation process, since the new Crimean Assembly was elected in 1998 without the national quota used between 1994 and 1998 to allocate Crimean Tatars 14 out of 98 seats. This situation, however, improved after elections in 2002 when Crimean Tatars received seven places in the Crimean parliament and three in the Ukrainian Verkhovna Rada. Altogether 957 Crimean Tatars were elected as local, city or regional councillors in Crimea, exceeding even the expectations of their *majlis*.

Division of Black Sea Fleet—Status of Russian Navy Base in Sevastopol

The dispute over Crimea and the Black Sea was the primary reason why Russia and Ukraine signed their main friendship and co-operation treaty only on May 30, 1997, when President Yeltsin, after a number of cancellations, finally visited Kyiv. Two days before that, the Prime Ministers of both countries had signed an agreement to divide the fleet of 525 naval vessels, allocating Ukraine 254 and Russia 271. Russia also agreed to rent port facilities at Sevastopol for 20 years with an annual payment of $100 million. An important part of the deal was that Ukraine would hand over 118 ships from its own share to compensate for the writing off of half a billion dollars of state debt for Russian oil and gas. In practice, therefore, Ukraine retained only 18 per cent of the Black Sea fleet and rented out its most crucial naval infrastructure. Sevastopol as a city remained under Ukrainian civil administration, but Sevastopol bay remained the main Russian military base in Crimea and the Black Sea. Division of the fleet became possible as a result of a compromise when Ukraine gave away military assets but retained sovereignty over territory disputed by Moscow, while Russia acquired most of the Navy and control of the naval base. Sacrifices on both sides made the agreement unpopular on both sides with nationalists in Russia and Ukraine denouncing it as treason.

In the long term, the compromise has proved to be problematic. Russia faces prohibitively high costs if it wishes to develop an alternative naval base in Novorossiysk. President Putin has already attempted unsuccessfully in 2002 to extend the lease of Sevastopol, by exploiting the vulnerable position of the Ukrainian President after "Kuchmagate"—the major political crisis that overshadowed Kuchma's second term in office. The Ukrainian constitution does not envisage a foreign military presence on its territory and subsequent Ukrainian Presidents will have to address this issue. Ukrainian attempts to join NATO will inevitably lead to questioning of the Russian military presence on Ukraine's soil. Finally, the Ukrainian Navy is left without vital naval infrastructure: when Ukraine's only submarine was repaired in 2003, the Russians refused to let it enter the only bay where it could be stationed or to use relevant servicing facilities.

The Tuzla Conflict and the Territorial Waters Issue

The Russian military presence in Crimea emerged as a clear threat to Ukrainian strategic interests during the confrontation over Tuzla island that reached its peak in October 2003. Effectively, the Russian government openly challenged Ukrainian territorial integrity and sovereignty for the first time since 1991, claiming the island to be a "disputed" territory and building a causeway to link it with the Taman peninsula. After a number of failed appeals from the Ukrainian authorities at all levels, Moscow finally stopped the rapid construction of the causeway just 100 metres from the administrative border and promised to consider "the disputed" island as part of a package with the delimitation of the Sea of Azov and Kerch strait.

Tuzla is an island in the middle of the Kerch strait that used to be connected with the Russian mainland before 1925, when storms washed away the spit that joined it to the Taman peninsula. The distance to the Crimean coast is around 4 km while the distance to the Russian mainland is 5.5 km. The island is approximately 6 km long and 0.5 km wide. It has a population of a few fishing families and seasonal staff working at two private resorts belonging to Crimean enterprises. The Ukrainian authorities opened permanent border outposts on the island on Dec. 2, 2003, with buildings and facilities for 50 servicemen and their families permanently stationed there.

Tuzla island was transferred from the jurisdiction of Russian Krasnodar kray to the then Russian Crimean oblast in 1941 and then from the jurisdiction of the RSFSR to the Ukrainian SSR together with the Crimea in 1954. The administrative border between the Soviet Ukraine and Russian Federation by sea, however, was legally confirmed only in 1973 when the Kerch strait was delimited and Tuzla was assigned to the Crimean city of Kerch. In practice, the two regional governors drew the administrative border between the two regions, the Ukrainian SSR and the RSFSR, and signed relevant documents marking the boundary on the map east of Tuzla island. Since then all administration and development of the island's infrastructure as well as the conduct of elections to the Supreme Soviet by residents of Tuzla, have been conducted by the Crimean authorities. However, despite the agreement between the Ukrainian SSR and the RSFSR in 1990, as well as that between independent Ukraine and the Russian Federation in 1997, to recognize Soviet administrative borders as state borders, Moscow up to now has not committed itself to delimit those borders either on land or at sea. The issue of borders has proved so sensitive for public opinion in both Ukraine and Russia, that Presidents Kuchma and Putin negotiated an agreement on the Ukrainian-Russian border almost secretly and signed it in February 2003 without disclosing details to the public. However, even their secret deal could not resolve the differences in their positions on delimitation of borders on water and the seabed and this aspect was left for further negotiations that erupted into conflict over Tuzla in October 2003.

The extent of the Kremlin's dissatisfaction became evident when, in the middle of the Tuzla confrontation, the head of Putin's presidential administration, Aleksandr Voloshyn, declared to Ukrainian journalists on Oct. 20, 2003, that: "Russia will never leave the Kerch strait for Ukraine. It is bad enough that Crimea is Ukrainian already and we can hardly calm people down on this issue today. It is enough for our humiliation. If need be we will do everything possible and impossible to defend our position. If necessary we will throw a bomb there". The Kremlin later dismissed that statement as a "joke" and a few weeks later Voloshyn was himself dismissed. However, the official Russian position on Tuzla, Kerch strait and the Sea of Azov remained the same. Hence the Ukrainian parliament passed a resolution on Oct. 23, 2003, on "removing the threat of violation of the Ukrainian territorial integrity that appeared as a result of causeway construction in the Kerch strait by the Russian Federation", calling on the governments of both countries to resolve the conflict through negotiations.

Facing flag-waving Cossack troops from the Russian mainland a hundred metres from Tuzla, and complete silence from the Kremlin, Kyiv deployed troops and special police forces to the island. Meanwhile it had also become clear to the Ukrainian authorities that the Russian Black Sea fleet was an immediate military threat for Ukraine "from within". The military implications were so obvious that they immediately sparked renewed debates within Ukrainian society, raising doubts as to how wise it was to give away its nuclear arsenal in return only for guarantees from the nuclear armed countries, including Russia. When NATO, the EU and the USA made clear that they expected Moscow and Kyiv to resolve the conflict over Tuzla in a friendly manner, Ukrainian President Leonid Kuchma declared that: "the closer the causeway to our coast the closer we are to Europe and the West in general in our mood".

For Moscow the stakes were almost as high. If Russia were to lose both the Sevastopol naval base and control over the Kerch strait and Ukraine become a member of NATO, Western warships would be able to pass through and advance as far as Taganrog without Russian permission. Ukraine announced its intention to join NATO in May 2003 and received an encouraging response from NATO. Dmitriy Rogozin, chairman of the Russian State Duma's international affairs committee, stated on Radio Mayak (Oct. 22, 2003) that: "Ukraine may calculate that since it and it alone is in control, US squadrons may be allowed to enter. They will come close to Taganrog, Rostov-on-the-Don. We may not allow this to happen, because of political reasons, because of security reasons, because of economic reasons and also because of ecological reasons".

This is probably why the Kremlin insisted on considering the Sea of Azov and Kerch strait as "internal waters" for both Ukraine and Russia without establishing the maritime boundaries between the two. There are important economic consequences should Ukraine accept such a proposal as the Azov seabed, including Kerch strait, contains substantial reserves of oil and gas. The Russian proposal implied a "joint" use of natural resources as well as fishing stocks. Ukraine insisted instead on a complete delimitation of the maritime border and economic zone because Ukrainian territorial waters in this case would cover two-thirds of the Sea of Azov. Moreover the delimitation of territorial waters to the east of Tuzla island would leave Ukraine in control of the only deep water channel in the Kerch strait, commanded by the city of Kerch.

After a delay the Russian Foreign Ministry officially requested from Kyiv "copies of documents, including maps, on the basis of which the Ukrainian party considers the spit (island) Tuzla as its own". The Russian ambassador to Ukraine, Viktor Chernomyrdin, confirmed in November 2003 that Russia considered Tuzla a "disputed territory" that along with the Kerch strait needed to be considered by the Russian and Ukrainian governments. Preliminary consultations, however, confirmed that Ukraine is not willing to discuss territorial claims on Tuzla and therefore any talks promised to be indefinite. It became clear by December 2003 that a solution of the dispute by force would be politically damaging to Moscow as a champion of the reintegration of the former USSR, because it would place Russia in the unappealing light of a potential aggressor. Even though the troops preparing to take over Tuzla were Cossack irregulars, the Russian government clearly encouraged territorial claims. At a meeting of the Krasnodar Cossacks' Assembly on Nov. 29, 2003, governor Aleksandr Tkachev said: "When we speak about the Tuzla spit, we have a unanimous position and it is indisputable. It is our island, our spit and it will always be ours".

Towards the end of 2003 President Putin "persuaded" Leonid Kuchma to give in to the Russian demands and negotiated secretly a deal on the Azov Sea and Kerch strait of which even the Foreign Ministries of the two countries were not initially aware. Late on Dec. 19, the presidential administrators announced a top-level meeting to be held in Crimea as early as Dec. 24. Leonid Kuchma did not let his Foreign Minister know what documents he had agreed to sign, fearing that his Foreign Ministry would object. In the event, the Presidents of Russia and Ukraine during their meeting in Crimea on Dec. 24 agreed to use the Sea of Azov and the Kerch strait "jointly" as their internal waters. Foreign commercial ships and warships may enter both the sea and the strait but only after obtaining permission from both Ukraine and Russia. President Kuchma also agreed to set up a joint venture between Ukraine and Russia to "manage" the Kerch channel. Although both parties reaffirmed their mutual respect of administrative/state boundaries, their future demarcation as well as the fate of Tuzla were left for future negotiations. Thus the Ukrainian President surrendered to Russia the right to veto the entrance of foreign ships and warships even to the Ukrainian ports in the Sea of Azov. However, this agreement would still require ratification by the Ukrainian parliament.

Although potentially the future extension of Sevastopol bay's lease for the Russian Black Sea fleet could pose a political problem, Kyiv has been actively involving international organizations such as the OSCE, EU and NATO in its dialogue with Russia. The only outstanding issue that has remained unsolved since the collapse of the USSR is the delimitation of maritime borders around Crimea in the Sea of Azov and the Kerch strait. Despite the heightened tension between Kyiv and Moscow over Tuzla island at the end of 2003, the two countries have established a firm foundation for dialogue based on the comprehensive

1997 treaty of friendship and co-operation that recognized the administrative borders of the USSR as the state borders of the Russian Federation and Ukraine. Due to the open fears of the Ukrainian establishment that giving away the Kerch strait and Tuzla island would only fuel the Russian appetite for all of the Crimea, it remained unclear how much effective political pressure Moscow could exercise over Kyiv in future. It was clear, though, that the closer Ukraine moved to NATO the less likely Russia would be to get Kyiv to agree on Tuzla and Kerch strait in its favour.

Olexander Hryb

4.16 South Caucasus

The South Caucasus (Transcaucasia) includes three former republics of the Soviet Union—Armenia, Azerbaijan and Georgia. The geographic term designates a region of distinct political and social processes of transformation that has been the most unstable part of the former Soviet Union in terms of the number, intensity and length of its conflicts. (See Map 48, p. 516, for this region.)

Armenia, Azerbaijan and Georgia gained their independence in December 1991 alongside Byelorussia, Kazakhstan, Kyrgyzstan, Moldova, the Russian Federation, Tajikistan, Turkmenistan, Ukraine, and Uzbekistan. The Baltic republics—Estonia, Latvia and Lithuania—had achieved legal independence in September 1991. On the final demise of the USSR, 11 of the republics joined a new Commonwealth of Independent States (CIS), the non-participants being the three Baltic republics and Georgia. The founding Minsk and Alma-Ata declarations of the CIS, adopted on Dec. 8 and Dec. 21 respectively, committed the member states to observance of existing borders within the former Soviet Union and to the principle of their inviolability by force.

Nevertheless, the dissolution of the Soviet Union had the effect of aggravating or reviving not only a number of border disputes between ex-Soviet republics and external states but also a myriad of territorial issues between and within the ex-Soviet republics themselves. Three violent conflicts on the territory of the former Soviet Union developed in South Caucasus. Two of the conflicts—involving Abkhazia and South Ossetia—took place on the territory of Georgia but have resulted in the creation of de facto independent entities tacitly supported by Russia. The third conflict, over Nagorno Karabakh, involved Armenia and Azerbaijan (and is dealt with separately in Section 4.2). After a sharp increase in violence at the beginning of the 1990s, the conflicts in South Caucasus subsided into a state of "neither peace nor war" and are often referred as "frozen conflicts". Abkhazia, South Ossetia, and Nagorno Karabakh have de facto, if not de jure, independence, while the international community has been trying to find political solutions acceptable to all parties.

Historical and Demographic Background

By the early 18th century the Caucasus mountains formed the natural frontier between Russian dominion and loose Ottoman Turkish and Persian suzerainty south of the mountains. Russian penetration south of the Caucasus began in the 18th century, at first on the Caspian Sea littoral and later inland. In 1801 the ancient Christian kingdom of Georgia accepted Russian rule, which was also imposed on the surrounding khanates in a series of wars with Turkey and Persia in the early 19th century. Under the 1813 Treaty of Gulistan Russia acquired Persian Azerbaijan north of the Araks river, while the 1829 Treaty of Adrianople enshrined Turkish recognition of Russian rule within roughly the post-1945 Soviet borders in Transcaucasus, including what became Soviet Armenia. (See also Section 4.2 for additional historical information on the region.)

Following the 1917 Russian Revolution, Caucasus was one of the regions which the new Bolshevik regime surrendered under the March 1918 Treaty of Brest-Litovsk with the Central powers. But the eventual victory in World War I of the Western powers enabled the Bolsheviks, in alliance with the new nationalist regime in Turkey, to establish their authority in the region. Thus the fledgling independent states of Georgia, Armenia and Azerbaijan were all suppressed by 1921 and converted into soviet socialist republics (SSRs). However, the problem facing the Soviet administrators was that, apart from the Georgians, Armenians and Azeris, the Caucasus contained about 60 other distinct national or ethnic groups, some Muslim, some Christian (of assorted denominations) and belonging to various language groups and families. Dagestan, itself containing some 30 nationalities, was made an autonomous republic (ASSR) within the Russian Soviet Federated Socialist Republic (RSFSR) in January 1921, but an attempt to federate the other mountain peoples in the Gorskaya ASSR was quickly abandoned. From the 1920s right up to the 1950s there were frequent changes in the boundaries and alignments of autonomies in the region. The main Soviet aim was to establish viable economic units, for which purpose a common pattern was the creation of "bi-ethnic" entities grouping two main national groups in one autonomy.

As the Soviet Union came to an end in 1991, the South Caucasus was inevitably the region in which the greatest incidence of territorial conflicts and uncertainty was apparent. Some of the disputes centred on territorial claims by one republic against another, usually at government level notwithstanding the enjoinder of the CIS founding declarations that existing borders

should be respected. Most involved aspirations to change the territorial composition and/or status of the various autonomous republics and regions, or to create entirely new ones. In some cases, aspirations of the latter type implied a challenge to the main republican borders.

Segmenting the territory into formations with different levels of autonomy and dividing the society into titular and non-titular nationalities, the Soviet Union had a strict hierarchical order of ethnic groups, each eligible to varying degrees of statehood, rights and privileges. Given this complex structure, the policies of glasnost and perestroika, pursued by Mikhail Gorbachev from 1985, unleashed claims for independence and for exercise of the right to self-determination, coming from both titular and non-titular nations. Confronted with increased demands for independence and the imminent dissolution of the Soviet Union, Gorbachev tried to deal with the complex nationalities crisis by measures to broaden the rights of smaller state and territorial formations and to enhance the status of their nationalities in the decision-making process to a level that they had not previously enjoyed.

The case of Georgia provides ample evidence as to the complexity of ethnic divisions and the consequences of a policy conceived to exploit these divisions. Within its official borders, Georgia (capital Tbilisi) covers an area of 70,000 sq km. According to the 1989 Soviet census, Georgia had a population of 5,400,841, of which Georgians (who are mainly Orthodox Christian) formed 70.1 per cent. The other main national/ethnic groups were Armenians (8.1 per cent), Russians (6.3 per cent) and Azeris (5.7 per cent). As a Union republic, Georgia included two autonomous republics, Abkhazia (capital Sukhumi) and Ajara (Adzharia, capital Batumi), and one autonomous province (oblast), South Ossetia (capital Tskhinvali).

Abkhazia consists of 8,600 sq km on the Black Sea coast. By 1991, when Georgia became independent, the ethnic Abkhaz (mostly the Muslim part of the population) made up only 18 per cent of the population of the region, or around 94,000 out of a total of 525,000. Georgians accounted for 46 per cent, Russians for 14 per cent, Armenians for 15 per cent and Greeks for 3 per cent. Ajara, amounting to 3,000 sq km in the southwest corner of Georgia, had a population of 380,000, of whom over 80 per cent were (mainly Muslim) Georgians, 10 per cent Russians and 4.6 per cent Armenians. The autonomous province of South Ossetia, covering 3,900 sq km on the Russian border, had a population of 100,000, of which Muslim Ossetians formed 66.5 per cent and Georgians about 30 per cent.

In 1989, the national aspirations of the constituent units broke on several levels. Georgian political activists organized a series of demonstrations in Tbilisi and across the country to demand greater political and economic autonomy and to protest against increasing Russification. A demonstration in Tbilisi on April 9, 1989, known as "Bloody Sunday", was suppressed by the tanks and troops of the Soviet Ministry of the Interior. Concurrently, Abkhazia launched its demands for removal from Georgia and its attachment to the Russian Socialist Federal Soviet Republic (RSFSR). A few months later, the autonomous province of South Ossetia accelerated its campaign for upgrading its status to that of an autonomous republic. This campaign was viewed as a forerunner of the demand for unification with the North Ossetian Autonomous Republic within the RSFSR. The Azeri population of Georgia demanded the establishment of their own autonomous formation.

The spiralling upheaval of ethnic tensions further reinforced the latent hostilities between the different ethnic groups. Following the bloody suppression of the demonstrations in Tbilisi, Georgia strengthened its belief that its national survival depended on its secession, boycotted the all-Union referendum on preserving the Soviet Union, conducted its own referendum and declared Georgia's independence on April 9, 1991. Georgia's alienation from Moscow grew stronger following the declaration "On Sovereignty and Status of South Ossetia". The escalation of hostilities in South Ossetia and the presence of troops of the Soviet Interior Ministry prompted Georgia to take hard measures on its way to independence by cancelling the envisaged transition period of three to four years.

ABKHAZIA

Abkhazia had been a separate Soviet republic in the 1920s, until becoming an autonomous republic of the Georgian SSR in 1931. By 1991, when Georgia became independent, only 18 per cent of the region's population were Muslim Abkhazians, while ethnic Georgians constituted the majority. In the 1930s, the Soviet Georgianization policy in Abkhazia enforced the spread of Georgian language and culture, in part by closing down all native-language schools. In the 1980s, the growth of Georgian nationalism and pro-independence agitation strengthened separatist tendencies among the Abkhazians. Their demands for a return to full republican status triggered a response in Georgia proper, where nationalist demonstrations in Tbilisi on April 9, 1989, were brutally suppressed by Soviet forces, with 20 fatalities. In the Abkhazian capital, Sukhumi, further violence in mid-1989 over the status of the Sukhumi branch of Tbilisi University escalated when on Nov. 19, 1989, the Tbilisi parliament declared Georgia's sovereignty. On Aug. 25, 1990, the Abkhazian parliament voted in favour of secession from Georgia, but this decision was declared illegal by the Georgian government (and was in fact rescinded by the Abkhazians on Aug. 31).

However, separatist sentiment remained strong in Abkhazia, where many came out in favour of eventual accession to the Russian Federation. This mood strengthened when elections in Georgia on Nov. 11, 1990, brought anti-Communist nationalists to power under Zviad Gamsakhurdia, on a platform of independence from the Soviet Union. On March 17, 1991,

unlike Georgia proper, Abkhazians participated in the Gorbachev referendum on the preservation of the Soviet Union, but they boycotted the Georgian referendum held on March 31, in which 99 per cent of the participants voted for independence. Gamsakhurdia threatened to disband the Abkhazian Supreme Soviet and abolish the Abkhazian autonomy.

When the Tbilisi parliament proceeded to declare Georgia's independence on April 9, 1991, Abkhazian leaders urged Moscow to maintain Soviet troops in the republic. The reinforced Russian military presence compelled Gamsakhurdia to make concessions and allow elections to the Abkhazian parliament to proceed on a quota basis: 28 seats to the Abkhazians, 26 to the Georgians, and 11 to all the remaining ethnic groups. The elections were duly held, in two stages, in October-December 1991 and the Abkhazian Supreme Soviet started to function in early 1992.

Following the demise of the Soviet Union, the situation was complicated by the overthrow of Gamsakhurdia in early January 1992 by the radicalized opposition. The deposed leader attempted to make Abkhazia one of his bases for a comeback—one of his proposals, made on Jan. 16 after he returned from exile, being for the creation of a "Mengrel-Abkhazian republic" in western Georgia. The Abkhazian leadership sought to reinforce its political and military position. In early May, Georgian deputies started to boycott the sessions of the Abkhazian parliament. In June they began a campaign of civil disobedience and attempted to set up parallel power structures. On July 23, a partial Abkhazian parliament (with the Georgian deputies abstaining) voted to return to the Abkhazian Constitution of 1925, which gave the region the status of a "Sovereign Republic associated with Georgia". The State Council of Georgia declared the vote invalid.

Soon the conflict between Georgia and Abkhazia took on serious proportions and violence exploded. Following a series of kidnappings of Georgian officials, on Aug. 14 Georgian President Eduard Shevardnadze sent the Defence Minister, Tengiz Kitovani, to Abkhazia to investigate the cases. In defiance of orders, as stated by Shevardnadze during a Russian television interview, Kitovani's tank column entered Sukhumi, joining battle with the Abkhazian forces. The Abkhaz soviet's Supreme Chair, Vladislav Ardzinba, declared war on Georgia and called for a full-scale mobilization. Georgian Prime Minister Tengiz Sigua called for an immediate ceasefire and withdrawal. An agreement was negotiated enabling Abkhazians to retreat to Gudauta in the north of Abkhazia. However, on Aug. 18 Kitovani's forces unexpectedly re-entered Sukhumi, occupied the Abkhazian parliament and captured the town, leaving 2,000 civilians and military killed.

The assault of August 1992 opened a year-long war in which around 10,000 people lost their lives. Almost the entire ethnic Georgian population was driven out of the region, creating more than 200,000 refugees.

The period was also marked by a series of ceasefire agreements brokered by Russia. The first ceasefire agreement was signed on Sept. 3, 1992 as a result of talks between Russian President Boris Yeltsin and Georgian President Shevardnadze, with the participation of the Abkhazian parliamentary Chair, Vladislav Ardzinba. The agreement defined Abkhazia as part of Georgia without any reference to a federal structure. Under pressure from Russia, Ardzinba was compelled to agree to the presence of Georgian troops on Abkhazian territory. The agreement, however, was quickly broken in October, when Abkhazian forces captured Gagra and other territories adjoining the Russian borders.

The second ceasefire agreement was negotiated by Russia and Georgia in Sochi on May 14, 1993. It stipulated the withdrawal of Georgian heavy weaponry from the conflict zone. The Abkhaz claimed that it was Georgia's failure to comply quickly with this injunction that prompted a renewed Abkhazian offensive and assault on Sukhumi at the beginning of June.

On July 27, 1993 in Sochi, the Georgian, Russian and Abkhazian sides signed a new agreement. It provided for a ceasefire, withdrawal of the Georgian army from Abkhazia, staged demilitarization, and installation of a new government in Sukhumi that had to be further agreed on by the two sides. The agreement also provided for the establishment of Georgian-Abkhazian-Russian supervisory groups to monitor compliance with the ceasefire regime. The plan required the Russian troops still deployed in Abkhazia to observe strict neutrality. At the same time it was agreed that a limited number of Russian military observers would be stationed along the Gumitsa river overlooking Sukhumi.

Large sections of the Georgian public were demoralized by the agreement, and this enabled the comeback of Zviad Gamsakhurdia, who proclaimed himself the "saviour" of the country. A third of the Georgian troops withdrawn from Abkhazia went over to Zviadist forces. In July and August, the Zviadist forces captured Senaki, Abashi and Khobi in order to prevent the withdrawal of the Georgian army from Abkhazia. On Sept. 16, the Abkhazian forces launched an all-out attack on Georgian forces, capturing Sukhumi on Sept. 27. Gamsakhurdia chose this moment of defeat of the central Georgian authorities to launch a full-scale march on Tbilisi. Russian support helped Shevardnadze retain his position at the price of Georgia's joining the CIS as well as other concessions, such as a Georgian-Russian agreement on the status of Russian troops in Georgia and the leasing of military bases. The Russian army was called upon to guard strategic roads and communication lines in support of the resistance of the Georgian government to the Zviadist forces, which were finally defeated in November. This episode in the fight over Abkhazia ended with the death of Gamsakhurdia in unclear circumstances in a remote village in Western Georgia on Dec. 31, 1993.

Abkhazia has served as a test case for the international community in responding to violent conflicts in the former Soviet Union. The key issues for interna-tional mediators have been to find a political settle-ment to the conflict, to facilitate the return of 200,000 Georgian refugees to their homes in Abkhazia, pre-dominantly in the Gali district, and to provide peace-keepers.

The precondition for setting up a UN peacekeeping operation in Abkhazia was for the two sides to achieve a certain degree of progress in their talks—however, the Security Council deemed the progress insufficient and did not proceed with a peacekeeping operation. At the request of President Shevardnadze, the UN Secretary-General proposed an immediate deployment of 50 military observers to monitor the first ceasefire agreement of Sept. 3, 1992, and a comprehensive peace plan for the longer term. The sending of the first team of ten military observers and the creation of an 88-strong UN Observer Mission in Georgia (UNOMIG) were approved by the Security Council in August 1993. The violation of the Sochi ceasefire agreement in September 1993 forced the UN to reduce the staffing of its observer mission to five people. The Secretary-General proposed the establishment of either a UN peacekeeping operation or a Russian one. The idea of a UN peacekeeping force had support up until the spring of 1994. The option of Russian peace-keeping was broadly defined in a Security Council res-olution of January 1994. On April 4, 1994 the Abkhazian and Georgian sides, with Russia's media-tion and UN and OSCE participation, signed a "Quadripartite Agreement on the Voluntary Return of Refugees and Displaced Persons". A Quadripartite Commission, composed of Abkhaz and Georgian rep-resentatives as well as representatives of Russia and the UNHCR, was set up to discuss repatriation of refugees.

1994 Ceasefire—Renewed Tension from 1998

On May 14, 1994, the two sides signed under Russia's auspices the "Agreement on a Ceasefire and Separation of Forces", known as the "Moscow Agreement". The agreement provides for the estab-lishment of a 12 km-wide buffer zone along the Inguri river, which separates Abkhazia from the rest of Georgia, to form a sufficiently wide security zone. The agreement also authorized the establishment of a CIS peacekeeping force (CISPKF), effectively a Russian force, of around 1,800 troops (of an authorized maxi-mum of 3,000). UNOMIG, which is currently staffed by around 100 UN military observers, is authorized to monitor the ceasefire on the ground and to observe the operations of the CISPKF, from which it operates independently. Its mandate has been renewed every six months on the basis of UN Security Council resolu-tions.

Tensions resurfaced in the spring of 1998. On March 14, 1998, Abkhazia held elections, which were declared invalid by the UN and the Russian and Georgian governments. The polling was marred by bomb explosions and violent clashes between Abkhaz and ethnic Georgians that left several people killed and wounded. In the wake of the elections, tensions on the border between Abkhazia and the rest of Georgia started to rise again. On March 20, Abkhaz guerrillas launched a cross-border artillery attack on a village in Georgia's Zugdidi region, wounding four people. On May 18, Georgian guerrillas killed some 20 Abkhaz police officers in a surprise attack. Two days later, forces of the Abkhaz Interior Ministry armed with heavy weaponry launched a counter-offensive against several Gali villages. On May 27, the Abkhaz de facto President, Vladislav Ardzinba, imposed a three-month state of emergency on Gali and parts of Ochamchira and Tkvarcheli regions, this being condemned by both Georgia and Russia as a violation of the 1994 agreement.

The growing hostilities necessitated a new ceasefire agreement, signed on May 25, 1998, in Gagra. Despite that, the situation on the ground has remained tense and unstable. The "Gali crisis" raised fears that the incidents were planned and executed by Georgian guerrilla groups, notably the White Legion and Forest Brothers, over which the Georgian central authorities are believed to have no influence or leverage. They are, rather, alleged to have links with the Abkhaz "government-in-exile" in Tbilisi, which comprises 26 ethnic Georgian deputies to the Abkhaz parliament elected in 1991. Its chairman, Tamaz Nadareishvili, has consistently espoused a tougher policy with regard to the Abkhaz conflict than is the policy of the Georgian central leadership. In December 1998, the Abkhaz "government-in-exile" created the Party for the Liberation of Abkhazia with Nadareishvili as its leader.

The chances of a political settlement diminished again in April 2001, when a sequence of arrests and retaliatory hostage-takings and detentions fuelled tensions in the border region between Abkhazia and the rest of Georgia. The incident that spurred hostilities was the arrest of three Georgian guerrillas by Abkhaz security forces in Gali on April 8. In retaliation, Georgian guerrillas abducted five Abkhaz army conscripts on April 12. Two days later, the Abkhaz authorities intercepted a Georgian fishing vessel which they said was illegally in Abkhaz territorial waters and took five crew members into custody. On April 16, the UN special envoy for Abkhazia, Dieter Boden, chaired a meeting with senior Abkhaz and Georgian government officials and UNOMIG and CISPKF representatives. A protocol was signed whereby all 13 detainees were to be handed over to law enforcement officials.

On July 9, 2001, the so-called Kodori crisis started, lasting until the end of August. The Kodori valley is the only region in Abkhazia that has remained under the control of the central Georgian government. Hostilities there flared up again in October 2002. The village of Giorgievskoe in the Kodori valley was attacked on Oct. 4 by a group of several hundred fighters, claiming the lives of up to 40 people, including five UN observers. Different hypotheses were advanced, some of them pointing to the role of Chechen detachments, though the events remained far from clear.

Efforts for Political Settlement—De Facto Independence

The unremitting tensions have had an adverse effect on the search for a political settlement of the conflict. However, since 1997, talks referred to as the Geneva peace process have been underway, chaired by the UN and in which the Russian Federation acts as a "facilitator" and the OSCE participates as an observer. Support comes from the "Group of the Friends of the Secretary-General" (France, Germany, Russia, the United Kingdom, and the United States) set up in 1994. In November 1997, the parties agreed to set up a Coordinating Council to discuss ceasefire maintenance, refugee repatriation, and economic and humanitarian issues. In parallel, a new forum on confidence-building measures was set up to develop and enhance bilateral contacts within a less official environment. In 2003, the "Group of Friends" sought to set out a three-track approach to promote progress: (1) economic projects to rehabilitate Abkhazia; (2) return of the refugees in safety, security and dignity with economic and financial support; and (3) political progress.

The discussions on the political settlement of the conflict revolve around two intertwined issues—(1) the political status of Abkhazia and forms of relations between Tbilisi and Sukhumi, and (2) the safe and secure return of internally displaced persons (IDPs) and refugees driven out of their homes during the violence of 1992-93. Dieter Boden, former Special Representative of the UN Secretary-General for Georgia, elaborated a draft proposal on "Basic Principles on Distribution of Competencies between Tbilisi and Sukhumi" known as the "Boden Paper" (Boden's successor is Ambassador Heidi Tagliavini). This document, unanimously adopted by the UN Security Council, states that the "borders of the State of Georgia…may not be altered except in accordance with the Constitution of Georgia" and that Abkhazia is a "sovereign entity…within the State of Georgia" and "enjoys a special status, within the State of Georgia, which is established by a Federal Agreement, providing for broad powers and defining the spheres of common competencies and delegated powers". The "Boden Paper" has the support of the Georgian government, the OSCE, the Council of Europe and other international organizations. On Jan. 30, 2003, the UN Security Council adopted a new resolution on Abkhazia reiterating its support for this position. The Abkhaz side has refused to accept the "Boden Paper" as it would tie them to Georgia, albeit with considerable autonomy.

At present, Abkhazia is entirely beyond Georgia's jurisdiction. Since 1994 when the Abkhaz regional government declared Abkhazia independent, Abkhazia has maintained de facto independence without formal recognition by Russia or any other state. In a referendum in 1999, 90 per cent of the population in Abkhazia at that time voted for independence. The vote, however, was not recognized by the international community, as the over 200,000 refugees outside

Abkhazia were unable to vote.

Abkhazia has become increasingly associated with Russia economically and politically, enjoying a degree of Russian support. Under the banner of the CISPKF, Russia has effectively retained its own force in the region (contrary to suggestions by the Georgian authorities that this would be withdrawn in view of its failure to guarantee the return of ethnic Georgian IDPs to Abkhazia). The currency in Abkhazia is the Russian rouble and the population is in the course of acquiring Russian citizenship and passports (estimates are at 70 per cent). The Abkhazia-Russian frontier is open for road transport, and railway communication between the Russian city of Sochi and the Abkhazian capital of Sukhumi was re-established on Dec. 25, 2002, in violation of a decision taken by the heads of the states of the CIS on Jan. 19, 1996, to restrict trade and communications with Abkhazia.

The most recent round of talks between Putin, Shevardnadze and the head of the Abkhaz government, Gennady Gagulia, took place in Sochi on March 6-7, 2003. The three sides agreed to set up working groups to facilitate repatriating Georgian IDPs to the Gali district in Abkhazia and the opening of a railway through Abkhazia, thus removing the blockade on the Georgian side. The parties proposed the rehabilitation of the Gali district and of the Ingruri hydroelectric complex. Georgia agreed to the extension of the mandate of Russian peacekeepers and to participate in a proposed economic zone led by Russia. Georgia wanted to secure an agreement on federal principles for the final status of Abkhazia within Georgia but could not get Russia's support for substantive negotiations on this point. At a press conference after the meeting, Presidents Putin and Shevardnadze sounded optimistic about the concrete economic projects and the problem of Georgian IDPs and refugees. Neither of them, however, broached on Abkhazia's status.

The peace process was frozen for much of 2003 and was effectively suspended during the Georgian political crisis in the wake of the legislative elections held in October. The resignation of Shevarnadze and consequent political changes were widely expected to give momentum to the conflict resolution efforts. The Georgian and Abkhaz sides met for security talks in January 2004.

SOUTH OSSETIA

South Ossetia is located in the southern foothills of the Caucasus mountains along Georgia's northern border with North Ossetia within the Russian Federation. The South Ossetians belong to the same ethnic group as the neighbouring North Ossetians and are descendants of tribes that migrated to the Caucasus in the early Middle Ages from Persia. Those in Georgia are primarily Orthodox Christians who speak a Persian-derived language with many Georgian borrowings but use the Cyrillic alphabet with some modifications. By 1991, when Georgia gained its independence, the ethnic composition of South Ossetia was made up of 66.2%

Ossetians, followed by 28.9% Georgians, 2.2% Russians, and 1% Armenians and others.

On April 20, 1922, after the sovietization of Georgia in 1921, the South Ossetian Autonomous Oblast (province) was formed. Georgian-Ossetian strife dates back to 1918-21, when the Menshevik government of Georgia suppressed a Bolshevik-supported South Ossetian insurgency. The division of the Soviet republics into territorial-administrative units with varying degrees of autonomy, and the segmentation of society into titular and non-titular ethnic groups with different rights and privileges, further alienated the Ossetian population in the autonomous oblast and reinforced their feeling of being politically and economically disadvantaged.

Unrest developed in the South Ossetian autonomous region in October 1989 over plans to elevate Georgian and Russian to equal status with Ossetian. On Sept. 20, 1990, the region's parliament proclaimed a "South Ossetian Soviet Democratic Republic" independent of Georgia, but on Dec. 11, 1990, this initiative was declared illegal by the Georgian parliament. The latter, by now containing a nationalist majority, also stripped South Ossetia of its autonomy (and considered doing the same to the autonomous republic of Ajara in the south-west). These moves signalled the onset of fighting between Georgian and Ossetian activists, causing the newly elected President Gamsakhurdia to declare a state of emergency in the main South Ossetian towns on Dec. 13, 1990. Around 3,000-4,000 Georgian militias were sent to the Tskhinvali and Djava regions to enforce the decision. The South Ossetians responded by demanding to be transferred from Georgia to the Russian Federation.

This turn of events alarmed the authorities in Moscow, where President Gorbachev on Jan. 7, 1991, annulled both the original South Ossetian secession declaration and the Georgian decree abolishing South Ossetian autonomy. Predictably, the Georgian parliament on Jan. 7 unanimously rejected Gorbachev's action as "gross interference" in Georgia's internal affairs. Gamsakhurdia himself accused the Soviet government of fomenting revolt in South Ossetia so that it would have an excuse to impose presidential rule throughout Georgia. Fighting then escalated between South Ossetian activists and irregular Georgian forces of the *Mkhedrioni* nationalist paramilitary movement, which itself came into conflict with the Gamsakhurdia government. Like the Abkhazians but unlike the Georgians, the South Ossetians participated in Gorbachev's referendum on decentralization of the Soviet Union on March 17, 1991, voting overwhelmingly in favour. Georgia's own declaration of independence on April 9, 1991, provoked more fighting on the ground, in which the South Ossetians were often backed by Soviet Interior Ministry forces.

In August 1991 the South Ossetian leadership, unwisely as it turned out, declared initial support for the hardliners who tried to seize power in Moscow. When the coup collapsed the South Ossetians were even more exposed to the Georgian nationalist para-militaries and to the radicalized opponents of Gamsakhurdia who also set their sights on overthrowing his government. By October 1991 the official death toll in South Ossetia since December 1990 was put at over 250 and the South Ossetian capital, Tskhinvali, was under siege by Georgian forces. In the wake of the abortive coup South Ossetian leaders repeatedly appealed to the now-ascendant Boris Yeltsin for South Ossetia to be transferred from Georgia to the Russian Federation, within which it could be unified with North Ossetia. They attracted support within Russian nationalist circles, but the Yeltsin government took a more cautious line.

On the final demise of the Soviet Union, the South Ossetian parliament on Dec. 21, 1991, voted in favour of full independence from Georgia and confirmed its desire for unification with the Russian Federation. On Dec. 23 a state of emergency and general mobilization were declared in South Ossetia in response to the massing of Georgian troops near Tskhinvali. After the overthrow of Gamsakhurdia in early January 1992, the South Ossetians held a referendum on Jan. 19, boy-cotted by local Georgians, in which 90 per cent of those taking part voted to join Russia. The vote was condemned by the new regime in Tbilisi as "a blatant attempt to violate the territorial integrity of a sovereign state". South Ossetia refused to enter into negotiations with the new regime until it pulled Georgian troops out of the region and lifted the blockade. In late April 1992 the South Ossetian leader, Torez Kolumbegov, again urged the Russian Federation to establish its sover-eignty over South Ossetia, on the grounds that most South Ossetians had declared themselves in favour of this change in the January 1992 referendum. For its part, the Georgian government remained committed to preserving Georgia's established borders and concen-trated its diplomatic efforts on securing the withdraw-al of ex-Soviet Russian troops from South Ossetia.

There was a certain lessening of combat activities in the first months of 1992 but these resumed in mid-April. A first ceasefire was agreed in Tskhinvali on May 13, only to break down a few days later. On May 20, unidentified gunmen massacred a group of Ossetian refugees near the village of Kekhvi. While the ceasefire was made more permanent on May 27, the shelling of Tskhinvali escalated through June. At the same time, hardline Russian parliamentarians issued a series of statements advocating the admission of South Ossetia into Russia. The situation had in any case been complicated by the arrival of Russian Cossack "volunteers" in the North Ossetian capital of Vladikavkaz (formerly Ordzhonikidze) with the declared intention of "protecting Russia's southern borders". That this line included South Ossetia was indicated by the penetration of a detachment of such "volunteers" to Tskhinvali in late February 1992. The ex-Soviet (now effectively Russian) military com-mander in the South Ossetian capital asserted that his forces were there "to prevent the Georgians and Ossetians...from drawing one another into war".

Towards the middle of June, Russia almost came to the brink of war with Georgia over South Ossetia when some leaders, including the Russian Supreme Soviet Chairman, Ruslan Khasbulatov, made strong state-ments and called for re-consideration of the request of South Ossetia to join Russia.

Deployment of Peacekeepers—Ceasefire Agreement

On June 22, 1992, Russian President Boris Yeltsin and Georgian President Shevardnadze met in Dagomys and, with South and North Ossetian representatives, agreed to the deployment of joint Russian, Georgian and Ossetian peacekeeping forces (JPKF). On July 14 in Sochi, an effective ceasefire agreement was con-cluded whereby the four parties agreed to provide a battalion each "to monitor the ceasefire, supervise the withdrawal of armed units, dissolve self-defence forces, and ensure security in the region".

The peacekeeping mission in South Ossetia was instituted at a time when Russia's efforts were directed towards consolidating the CIS as a platform for the implementation of its peacekeeping concept on a regional level. There was, however, no CIS authoriza-tion for he deployment of the mission but instead a bilateral agreement. At the time when peacekeeping forces were introduced in South Ossetia, Georgia was neither a CIS member state nor had it signed the Kiev Protocol on Groups of Military Observers and Collective Peacekeeping Forces. The JPKF has a spe-cific structural arrangement since it includes the direct protagonist in the warfare. Nevertheless, after the introduction of the JPKF overall security conditions in the region improved and the Russian presence was reduced to one battalion. Currently, there are thirteen peacekeeping posts under the control of the JPKF Russian commander-in-chief.

Efforts towards a Political Settlement

Conflict settlement efforts take place within the Joint Control Commission established by Yeltsin and Shevardnadze on June 23, 1992. Discussions focus mainly on economic, military and social problems within the framework of three ad hoc working groups complemented by an ad hoc committee on refugees and IDPs. Political issues, namely the status of South Ossetia and the region's relations with the central authorities, are discussed at the level of plenipoten-tiary delegations with the participation of North Ossetia as well as Russia and the OSCE as facilitators, a mechanism instituted in March 1997. In July 1996 in Moscow, the sides signed a framework agreement offi-cially entitled the "Memorandum on Measures to Provide Security and Strengthen Mutual Trust Between the Sides in the Georgian-South Ossetian Conflict". The Memorandum provides for return of refugees, negotiations on political arrangements and round-table meetings of mass media, civic organiza-tions, and intellectuals from both sides.

Despite efforts to achieve a political settlement, no progress has been made so far on the status of South Ossetia. The Georgian authorities are more preoccupied with the conflict in Abkhazia, while the South Ossetian side seems to be waiting for the outcome in Abkhazia to define the widest limit of any possible autonomy they may subsequently negotiate. In 1995, the Georgian parliament adopted a new constitution that left open the question of Georgia's territorial and administrative structure in relation to South Ossetia (as well as Abkhazia). In reality, South Ossetia is beyond Georgia's jurisdiction. Since 1992, the central Georgian government has had only minimal contacts with the secessionist leadership of South Ossetia. The unrecognized republic has survived thanks to financing from the Russian federal budget. The central Georgian authorities have made economic aid contingent on the consent of the South Ossetian leadership that the region should be an autonomous formation within a unitary Georgian state. (In 1996, Georgia changed the official name of the region from South Ossetia to Tskhinvali, which is also the name of its administrative centre.)

In September 1993, Ludvig Chbirov became chairman of the South Ossetian Supreme Soviet, later renamed State Nykhas (Council of Elders). In May 1999, South Ossetia held parliamentary elections. Four out of 33 parliamentary seats were reserved for ethnic Georgian deputies. They remained vacant, however, as the local Georgian population boycotted the poll. In a referendum held on April 8, 2001, voters in South Ossetia approved a new constitution that narrows eligibility for the post of the republic's President, designates Russian a state language together with Ossetian, and provides for the official use of Georgian in districts where Georgians form the majority of the population (South Ossetian officials claim that 60 per cent of the population of South Ossetia are citizens of Russia). The Georgian community boycotted the referendum, in which 23,540 of an estimated 45,000 voters participated. The Georgian parliament issued a statement condemning the referendum as an attempt to sabotage the ongoing search for a peaceful settlement between South Ossetia and the central Georgian authorities. On Nov. 18, 2001, South Ossetia held presidential elections, which Georgia and the international community declared illegal. Eduard Kokoyev (or Kokoita, as he is called in Ossetian), a businessman and a Russian citizen, was elected as President. He has taken a much harder line on relations with Tbilisi than his predecessor Chibirov.

The region is often referred as "no man's land", squeezed as it is between Russia and Georgia and located only 100 km west of the Pankisi gorge, which allegedly became a hideout for *Al-Qaeda* and Afghan fighters after the fall of the Taleban in Afghanistan. Upon the arrival of the first US military advisers in Tbilisi in March 2002 as part of a mission to train and equip Georgian special forces to deal with suspected *Al-Qaeda* militants hiding in the Pankisi gorge, Kokoyev called on Moscow to send more peacekeepers to South Ossetia. On March 1, 2002, the South Ossetian parliament voted to send a message to the Russian assembly, the State Duma, to demand the recognition of the independence of South Ossetia "in connection with the real threat of new armed aggression by Georgia against South Ossetia". In its turn, the State Duma passed a resolution on March 6, condemning the US military deployment in Georgia. However, the motion was milder than a previous draft, which had threatened to recognize the independence of Abkhazia and South Ossetia. The resolution adopted by the Duma warned the Tbilisi government that if it began to act more aggressively towards the two breakaway republics, the Russian parliament would respect what it called their "expressions of free choice".

JAVAKHETI

The Armenian population accounted for 8.1 percent of the total population of Georgia in 1991, dispersed across the country, including those in Abkhazia and Ajara. Armenian dissatisfaction with the existing border with Georgia centres on the southern Georgian region of Javakheti, which is mainly populated by ethnic Armenians. It is geographically as well as economically remote and isolated from Tbilisi. In 1995, the Georgian authorities merged the region with that of Meshketi (with a Georgian majority) to create the province of Samtskhe-Javakheti. This move increased the resentment and suspicion of the Armenian population but did not lead to large-scale protests.

Calls for outright autonomy for Javakheti erupted on Feb. 15, 2002, amidst allegations that the Georgian authorities intended to order out a garrison of Russian troops and replace them with units of the Turkish army. Although Tbilisi denied these allegations, the protests demonstrated the increasing fears of the ethnic Armenians in the region regarding Georgia's regional anti-terrorist policy in cooperation with Turkey and Azerbaijan and Georgia's expressed desire to join NATO.

No Georgian troops are currently in Javakheti. The last time Georgian troops tried to enter the region in 1998 to hold exercises, they were turned back by a crowd blocking the road. Georgia's Defence Minister, David Tevzadze, immediately ordered the troops to withdraw. A Russian military base is stationed in the region's capital, Akhalkalaki, which provides employment to 1,500 local residents, making it by far the largest employer in the region. There are fears that its closure would have a negative effect on the region's economy, leaving most of the population unemployed and thus more receptive to nationalistic sentiments advocated by the *Javakh* and *Virk* political movements—neither of which is registered as the Georgian Constitution bans parties based on ethnic, religious or territorial principles.

Nadia Milanova

4.17 Spain - United Kingdom (Gibraltar)

British sovereignty over Gibraltar—a strategic naval base on the tip of southern Spain ceded to Britain by Spain in 1713—has in recent decades been persistently disputed by Spain, which claims it as part of its national territory. In 1969 the land frontier between Spain and Gibraltar was closed and all other communications cut by the government of Gen. Franco. The UK government responded by upholding the self-proclaimed desire of the Gibraltarian people to retain their British status. Although the basic dispute over Gibraltar has remained unresolved, the death of Franco in 1975 and the restoration of democracy in Spain brought about an improvement in Spanish-UK relations. This in turn led to the conclusion of an agreement in Lisbon in April 1980 that the Gibraltar border would be reopened and substantive negotiations on the Gibraltar issue initiated. Although it was subsequently agreed that these provisions would be put into effect in April 1982, implementation was postponed because of the development of the Argentine-UK crisis over the Falkland Islands in that month. The border was not reopened until February 1985, after the UK government had specifically agreed the previous November to discuss the sovereignty of Gibraltar with Spain. Such discussions took place thereafter, assisted by the fact that Spain joined the United Kingdom as a member of the European Community on Jan. 1, 1986. In the early twenty-first century, however, the two sides remained fundamentally divided between the Spanish view that the Gibraltar question was one of decolonization and the British view that the right to self-determination of Gibraltar's people was paramount.

Geographical and Historical Background

Gibraltar is a narrow rocky peninsula which rises steeply from the low-lying coast of south-western Spain at the eastern end of the Strait of Gibraltar, forming one of the two Pillars of Hercules which since ancient times have been recognized as the strategically important gateway between the Mediterranean and the Atlantic Ocean. Known as the Rock, Gibraltar has a total area of 2.25 square miles (5.86 sq km), is some three miles (4.8 kilometres) long from north to south and about three-quarters of a mile wide for most of its length, although it narrows towards its southern extremity, Europa Point. The top of the Rock is a sharp ridge with a maximum height of 1,400 feet (426 metres), the northern escarpment being inaccessible, as is the whole upper length of the eastern face. The southern half slopes down to cliffs at Europa Point, while the city of Gibraltar is located on the more gen-

tly sloping western side. The Rock's porous limestone is riddled with some 35 miles of man-made tunnels and chambers, mostly dating from World War II. Gibraltar is connected to the Spanish mainland by a sandy plain about one mile long leading to the town of La Línea and the Campo de Gibraltar. The Spanish port of Algeciras lies five miles (8 kilometres) across the bay to the west, while the coast of Morocco is 13 miles (21 kilometres) distant across the Strait of Gibraltar. (Map 49, p. 517, illustrates the position of Gibraltar.)

The population in 1997 was 27,192, of whom 20,772 were Gibraltarians, 4,015 other British subjects and 2,405 non-British. Gibraltarians and British subjects in the service of the Crown (and their families) have a right of residence. All others require a residence permit. English is the official language but Spanish is also widely spoken. About four-fifths of the population is Roman Catholic and the rest largely Protestant or Jewish. There is also a Muslim community composed mainly of Moroccan workers.

It appears that there was no permanent settlement at Gibraltar before the eighth century AD, although an important Carthaginian and Roman port lay nearby. In 711 AD the Moorish leader, Tariq ibn Zeyad, built a castle on the rock, and Gibraltar's name is derived from the Arabic *Jebel Tariq* (the Mountain of Tariq). Gibraltar was held alternately by Moors and Spaniards until 1462, when the Moors were finally driven out. In 1704, during the War of the Spanish Succession, Gibraltar was captured by an Anglo-Dutch fleet under Admiral Sir George Rooke and formally ceded to Britain by the peace treaty between Spain and Britain signed at Utrecht in 1713. The terms of the Treaty of Utrecht were confirmed by the Treaty of Seville (1729), the Treaty of Vienna (1731) the Treaty of Aix-la-Chapelle (1756) and the Treaty of Paris (1763). After besieging Gibraltar unsuccessfully for more than three and a half years (1779-83), Spain agreed to withdraw its demand for Gibraltar in return for Minorca and Florida, and in the Treaty of Versailles (1783) it reaffirmed the position established by previous treaties.

Gibraltar became a Crown Colony in 1830. With the extension of the British empire in Asia and the opening of the Suez Canal, Gibraltar became increasingly important as a port of call and a strategic position controlling entry into the Mediterranean and the fast route to the East. It developed a considerable entrepôt trade and a major naval base was established there between 1895 and 1905. Gibraltar played a key role in Allied naval and military operations in the Mediterranean during the two world wars. It has remained a military base for Britain, and certain naval, air and communications facilities are made available to the North Atlantic Treaty Organization (NATO).

Gibraltar was granted a greater measure of internal self-government in 1964, and in 1967 a referendum was held in which it voted overwhelmingly to retain links with Britain. In 1969 it received a new constitution giving it a House of Assembly, executive authority being vested in a governor who represents the Queen. Gibraltar has been part of the European Community since 1973 (when the United Kingdom became a member) under Article 227(4) of the Treaty of Rome.

British and Spanish Positions on Gibraltar

The United Kingdom bases its claim to sovereignty over Gibraltar on Article X of the Treaty of Utrecht, which in the translation (from the original Latin) used by the UK government specified that "the Catholic king [of Spain] does hereby, for himself, his heirs and successors, yield to the Crown of Great Britain the full and entire propriety of the town and castle of Gibraltar, together with the port, fortifications and forts thereunto belonging…to be held and enjoyed absolutely with all manner of right for ever, without any exception or impediment whatsoever". The same article stated inter alia (i) that, so as to prevent "fraudulent importations of goods" into Spain via Gibraltar, it was understood that "the above-named propriety be yielded to Great Britain without any territorial jurisdiction [over], and without any open communication by land with, the country round about", although it would be "lawful to purchase for ready money, in the neighbouring territories of Spain, provisions and other things necessary for the use of the garrison, the inhabitants and the ships which lie in the harbour"; (ii) that at the request of the Spanish king Britain "does consent and agree that no leave shall be given under any pretence whatsoever either to Jews or Moors to reside or have their dwellings" in Gibraltar (although this seems to be contradicted by a provision allowing merchants leave to trade there); and (iii) that "in case it shall hereafter seem meet to the Crown of Great Britain to grant, sell or by any means to alienate therefrom the propriety of the said town of Gibraltar, it is hereby agreed and concluded that the preference of having the same shall always be given to the Crown of Spain before any others".

During the Second World War the base at Gibraltar was essential to Allied success in the Mediterranean, and its fervently patriotic inhabitants worked hard for the Allied cause. Spain, in contrast, where the pro-fascist Nationalists had finally been victorious in March 1939, was neutral. By the early 1950s, however, with the onset of the Cold War, the North Atlantic powers had come to tolerate the Franco dictatorship, and even to seek to make it an ally. The Franco government took advantage of the new climate of decolonization to describe the provisions of the Treaty of Utrecht as anachronistic and to accuse Britain of consistently violating them. When soon after her accession Queen Elizabeth II visited Gibraltar in May 1954, there were protests by Spanish students in Madrid, followed by the closure of the Spanish consulate in Gibraltar and the tightening of border controls by the Spanish authorities on Spanish workers crossing into Gibraltar. Since then Spain has not ceased to press for the return of Gibraltar.

After the introduction in August 1964 of a new constitution granting Gibraltar a greater measure of internal self-government, the Spanish government in October of that year began to enforce restrictions on the transit of people, traffic and goods from Spain into Gibraltar in support of its claim to Gibraltar. Meanwhile the Gibraltar issue had at the request of Spain been discussed in September 1963 for the first time within the UN Committee on Decolonization (the "Committee of 24") and again in September-October 1964. On April 5, 1965, the British government published a White Paper dealing with these and other aspects of the Gibraltar issue and reiterating Britain's full support for Gibraltar's wish to remain British. The White Paper made the following points:

Historical Background. The paper noted that "when the British captured Gibraltar in 1704 almost the entire Spanish population left the town and settled in the neighbouring countryside" and that the present population began to establish itself in Gibraltar from 1727 onwards, consisting of "time-expired British soldiers" and "Genoese and other foreign elements". By the time the Napoleonic Wars had ended, the population also comprised British, Maltese, Moroccan and Portuguese elements, and "this community has now existed in Gibraltar for over 250 years and, since 1830 when a Charter of Justice was proclaimed, has had legal recognition".

Constitutional Position. The paper said that the institutions of Gibraltar and the arrangements in force corresponded with the wishes of the Gibraltarian people and were "in accordance with modern democratic ideals and the principles of the UN Charter". The Gibraltarian people wished Gibraltar to remain in close association with Britain.

Consideration of Gibraltar at the UN. The White Paper described the proceedings in the UN Committee of 24 in September-October 1964 during which the parties concerned had put forward their positions—namely, the Spanish claim that Gibraltar formed part of Spanish territory notwithstanding the views of its inhabitants; the Gibraltarian wish to remain closely associated with Britain without becoming independent and their opposition to being handed over to Spain; and the British assertion that the grant of Gibraltar to Britain in the Treaty of Utrecht was absolute and that Spain had no right to be consulted on any change in its status or relations with Britain. The paper noted the UN Committee's conclusion of Oct. 16, 1964, that there was a dispute between Britain and Spain over the status and situation in Gibraltar, its invitation to Britain and Spain to seek a negotiated solution, and its statement that UN Declaration 1514 (XV) on the granting of independence to colonial countries and peoples was fully applicable to Gibraltar. It also noted that Britain had not accepted that there was a dispute over status, nor a conflict between the Treaty of Utrecht's provisions and the application of the principle of self-determination to the Gibraltarians.

The Situation at the Frontier. Describing the situation at the frontier since the Spanish authorities at La

Línea began enforcing procedures and regulations more strictly on Oct. 17, 1964, the White Paper said that cars and visitors had been delayed and most exports into Gibraltar stopped. Traffic, including tourist traffic, was almost at a standstill, restrictions were affecting Spanish workers commuting daily to Gibraltar, and the customs were refusing to accept as valid any British passports issued or renewed in Gibraltar, or those issued or renewed "on behalf of the government of Gibraltar".

Conclusion. The White Paper pointed out that the civilian population, who were not Spanish, had been "established there for longer than many immigrant communities in the New World" and concluded: "Great Britain has at no time renounced her title to Gibraltar or failed to defend her position there, and she will not do so now. She has no desire to quarrel with Spain but she will stand by the people of Gibraltar in their present difficulties and take whatever measures may be necessary to defend and sustain them".

In December 1965 the Spanish government in response published a Red Book on the Gibraltar issue, incorporating many maps. This said that the "sole legal basis" for the British presence in Gibraltar was Article X of the Treaty of Utrecht and that legally the cession of Gibraltar to Great Britain was therefore "subject to a series of limitations". In practice, these had been consistently ignored by Britain, it went on, notably in that since 1713 Britain had advanced its sphere of control steadily northwards "in quest of more space for the [Gibraltar] fortress over and above that stipulated at Utrecht". By the end of the 19th century Britain had advanced her frontier half a mile across the neutral zone north of Gibraltar, and as evidence of this "encroachment" the Red Book cited the construction in 1938 (i.e. during the Spanish Civil War) "of a military/civilian aerodrome, in the heart of the neutral zone, that is to say on Spanish sovereign territory". Britain had also erected a wall "which, after the Berlin manner, physically separates from Spain by walls, wire and railings a territory which is Spanish and which the British have been gradually engulfing in their advance through the so-called neutral zone".

The Red Book accused Britain of "passivity or even benevolence" towards smuggling by land and sea from the Rock in contravention of the treaty provision. It described the economic bases of the life of Gibraltar as "artificial" and added that the population of the Rock was also "artificially planned" to the prejudice of the original population, which had been driven out. After referring to the border measures taken by Spain in 1964 as normal police and customs measures, the Red Book said that in strict compliance with the Treaty of Utrecht Spain would be justified in (i) requesting the removal of the wall and fence at Gibraltar 800 metres further south "to evacuate a piece of Spanish sovereign territory which…was unjustifiably annexed by Britain on the isthmus of Gibraltar and in which the present aerodrome of Gibraltar is situated"; (ii) exercising the right to cut off land communications with Gibraltar, leaving only sea communications open; (iii) abolishing

trade with Gibraltar; and (iv) refusing to recognize the political institutions created in Gibraltar since 1950.

Commencement of UK-Spanish Talks on Gibraltar

Following the adoption by the UN General Assembly at its 20th session on Dec. 16, 1965, of a resolution (2070) inviting Spain and Britain to enter into negotiations on the Gibraltar issue without delay (both Spain and Britain voting in favour of the resolution), the two countries met for an initial round of talks in London in May 1966. In the course of the talks Spain made a formal claim to sovereignty over Gibraltar in a four-point plan. It proposed (i) that an Anglo-Spanish convention should be signed cancelling Article X of the Treaty of Utrecht and providing for "the restoration of the national unity and territorial integrity of Spain through the reversion of Gibraltar"; (ii) that Spain would accept a British military base at Gibraltar "whose structure, legal situation and co-ordination with the defence organization of Spain or the free world would be the subject of a special agreement" attached to the proposed convention; (iii) that a legal regime protecting the interests of the present citizens of Gibraltar should be the subject of an additional Anglo-Spanish agreement which would be negotiated with the UN and that it should contain, in addition to the appropriate economic and administrative formulae, a personal statute by which fundamental rights including the British nationality of the inhabitants of Gibraltar would be respected and their right of residence guaranteed, as well as the free exercise of their lawful acts and a guarantee of permanence in their place of work; and (iv) that such a convention would take effect after the additional agreements provided for under (ii) and (iii) had been regulated with the United Nations.

At the second round of talks in July 1966 Britain made counter-proposals which inter alia envisaged the exercise of internal self-government by the municipal authorities instead of by legislative and executive councils. However, no progress was made on either set of proposals at this or the next round of talks in September (which was preceded by the introduction in August 1966 of a Spanish ban on British military aircraft overflying Spanish territory).

On Oct. 5, 1966—just before a fourth round was due to commence—the Spanish government issued a decree closing the frontier with Gibraltar to all but pedestrian traffic, with the result that several thousand Spaniards who entered Gibraltar every day to work had to travel on foot. The measure took effect on Oct. 24, and in November the Spanish frontier authorities at La Línea also began to refuse to accept Gibraltarian passports issued by the governor, thus effectively placing a ban on Gibraltarians entering Spain.

The British delegation proposed at the October 1966 round of talks that the legal issues involved in the Gibraltar dispute should be referred to the International Court of Justice. However, this was rejected by Spain in a note of Dec. 14 on the grounds that it would contradict a UN Committee of 24 resolution adopted on Nov. 17 which (i) recommended that Britain should "expedite, without any hindrance and in consultation with the government of Spain, the decolonization of Gibraltar", (ii) regretted "the delay in the process of decolonization" and (iii) called on Britain and Spain to "continue their negotiations taking into account the interests of the people of the territory". A similar resolution (2231)—which did not, however, contain the latter reference to the interests of the Gibraltarian people—was adopted by the UN General Assembly on Dec. 20, 1966, with both Spain and Britain voting in favour.

The 1967 Referendum in Gibraltar

On June 14, 1967, the British government announced that a referendum would be held in Gibraltar to allow the people to decide whether to "pass under Spanish sovereignty" in accordance with the terms proposed by the Spanish government on May 18, 1966, or "voluntarily to retain their link with Britain with democratic local institutions and with Britain retaining its present responsibilities". If the majority voted in favour of the first option, Britain would, it stated, enter into further negotiations with Spain, but if the majority voted for the second option Britain would regard this choice as constituting "a free and voluntary relationship of the people of Gibraltar with Britain" and would "thereafter discuss with representatives of Gibraltar appropriate constitutional changes which may be desired".

The decision to hold a referendum was regarded by Spain as unilateral and in violation of UN resolutions and the Treaty of Utrecht, and in a note of July 3, 1967, it declined Britain's invitation to send an observer on the grounds that this would imply approval of the measure. After a Spanish complaint to the United Nations was filed on Aug. 18, 1967, the Committee of 24 on Sept. 1 adopted a resolution stating that the holding of the referendum would "contradict" previous UN resolutions. Britain denounced this resolution as "wholly partisan" and in contradiction with the spirit of the UN Charter, Chapter XI of which required the political aspirations of the people to be taken into account; the referendum, it was confirmed, would take place as planned. A similar point was made by Gibraltar's Chief Minister, Sir Joshua Hassan, who said that the resolution appeared to "disregard the interests of a colonial people and would seem to deny them the elementary human right of stating their interests through a referendum".

The referendum took place in Gibraltar on Sept. 10, 1967, and resulted in an overwhelmingly pro-British vote. Out of 12,762 registered voters (all of them normally resident in Gibraltar), 12,138 voted for continued association with Britain and 44 voted for Spanish sovereignty. A Commonwealth observer team which had been present in Gibraltar during the referendum said that it had been conducted in a fair and proper manner with adequate facilities for the free expression of views.

The UN General Assembly on Dec. 19, 1967, adopted a further resolution (2353) which had already been adopted by its Fourth Committee (on decolonization) on Dec. 16 and which (i) described the holding of the referendum as a "contravention" of Resolution 2231 and of the Committee of 24's resolution of Sept. 1, 1967; (ii) regretted the interruption of negotiations; and (iii) urged the resumption of negotiations without delay in order to put an end to the "colonial situation" in Gibraltar and to safeguard the interests of the population "upon the termination of that situation". The Spanish government meanwhile on Dec. 11, 1967, published a second Red Book reiterating its repudiation of the referendum and recapitulating the state of negotiations with Britain since May 1966.

UK-Spanish talks resumed on March 18, 1968, but broke down again on March 20. With effect from May 5 of that year Spain began what it described as a progressive implementation of the Treaty of Utrecht by closing the land frontier to all traffic including pedestrians, with the exception of those Spaniards holding work permits for Gibraltar and permanent residents of Gibraltar; the others were obliged to use the ferry from Algeciras.

1969 Constitutional Changes—Closure of the Border

In July 1968 Britain and Gibraltar held talks on proposed constitutional changes at the instigation of Gibraltar, which sought a new political status under the continued, permanent and exclusive sovereignty of Britain. It was agreed that such changes would give Gibraltarians maximum control over their domestic affairs but should not conflict with the Treaty of Utrecht or worsen UK-Spanish relations.

At the conclusion of these talks a joint communiqué was issued, which revealed that the British government believed that it could best respond to the wishes of the Gibraltarian people by inserting in the revised Gibraltar constitution a declaration to the effect that Gibraltar was "a part of Her Majesty's dominions and will remain so unless an act of parliament otherwise provides, and furthermore that HM government has made it clear that it will never hand over the people of Gibraltar to another state against their freely and democratically expressed wishes". Other constitutional changes agreed at the talks covered the replacement of the legislative and city councils of Gibraltar by a House of Assembly and the installation of an executive headed by a governor, a Gibraltar council and a council of ministers. The new constitution for Gibraltar (which was henceforth to be known as the City of Gibraltar) entered into force on May 30, 1969.

In strongly attacking the constitution, the Spanish government accused Britain of disregarding UN General Assembly Resolution 2429, adopted on Dec. 18, 1968, which declared that the "colonial situation in Gibraltar" was "incompatible with the UN Charter" and which called upon Britain to "terminate the colonial situation in Gibraltar" not later than Oct. 1, 1969. As a reprisal the Spanish government on June 8, 1969, closed the border and customs post at La Línea "to defend Spanish interests in Gibraltar", with the result that some 5,000 Spanish workers (about one-third of Gibraltar's normal labour force) were prevented from going to their jobs. On June 27 Spain suspended the ferry service from Algeciras to Gibraltar, and on July 4 it announced that Spanish nationality would be offered to all residents of Gibraltar or those born there. Finally, only hours after the expiry of the Oct. 1 deadline contained in the December 1968 UN resolution, Spain on Oct. 1 cut telephone links between the Spanish mainland and Gibraltar. Against a background of the deployment of large Spanish and British naval forces off Gibraltar, the Gibraltar government was obliged to put into effect contingency plans to deal with its new situation in the face of the Spanish restrictions.

Despite the tension which the Spanish measures caused, relations between Britain and Spain had already begun to improve by the end of 1969 and continued on a cordial basis with informal contacts taking place throughout 1970-72, although the Spanish restrictions remained in force. Eventually, formal talks resumed on May 30-31, 1974.

Later in 1974 Spanish proposals for a new regime in Gibraltar were published for the first time in Britain, although they had been handed to Sir Joshua Hassan in February 1973 (and he had described them as "utterly unacceptable" in the light of the result of the 1967 referendum). The proposals foresaw (i) that as soon as Spanish sovereignty was recognized over Gibraltar, the Gibraltar area would become a special territory with legislative, judicial, administrative and financial autonomy; (ii) that Gibraltarians would take Spanish nationality but need not renounce their British nationality; (iii) that the Spanish legal system "as developed by the special legislation of Gibraltar" would apply after the 1969 constitution had been suitably amended, and that Spanish penal and police laws would apply in all areas concerning Spain's internal and external security; (iv) that the senior authority in Gibraltar would be a civil governor appointed by the Spanish head of state; (v) that the most senior members of the executive would be Spaniards or Gibraltarians of Spanish nationality; and (vi) that Spanish would be the official language of Gibraltar, although a wide use of English would be safeguarded.

Developments following Gen. Franco's Death

Following the death of Gen. Franco on Nov. 20, 1975, King Juan Carlos stated on ascending the Spanish throne two days later that Spain's efforts to regain sovereignty over Gibraltar would continue. The following month, however, the Spanish authorities restored telephone links between Spain and Gibraltar over the Christmas-New Year period and subsequently in April 1976 for the Easter period, setting a pattern for subsequent years. In July 1977—following Spain's first general elections since 1936—the democratically-elected government headed by Adolfo Suárez González as Prime Minister stated that it would insist on resuming negotiations with Britain "with the aim of restoring Spain's territorial integrity"; and in September 1977 Dr David Owen became the first UK Foreign and Commonwealth Secretary to visit Spain since 1961. During this visit (when Dr Owen met King Juan Carlos, Suárez and the new Spanish Foreign Minister, Marcelino Oreja Aguirre) and in the course of a subsequent brief visit to London in October by Suárez in connection with Spain's recently-filed application to join the European Community, talks were held on the Gibraltar issue.

Dr Owen told a press conference on Sept. 7, 1977, after the visit that Britain had requested Spain to lift the restrictions on Gibraltar. He also said that Britain's support for Spain's application to join the European Community would not be dependent on the settlement of the Gibraltar issue and that the attitude of the Spanish government contained "a degree of sensitivity and understanding which did not exist before", and which he felt was the best ingredient for a settlement.

The Spanish Prime Minister for his part told a press conference in London on Oct. 19, 1977 (after talks with Dr Owen and James Callaghan, the Prime Minister), that he believed that Spain's political evolution and restructuring on a regional basis could permit a negotiated solution of the Gibraltar issue which would respect the "identity, culture and special characteristics of the Gibraltarian people and eventually can bring about the reintegration of Gibraltar into Spanish territory in conformity with UN resolutions". However, he ruled out the removal of restrictions, which, according to a British communiqué issued after the London talks, would have to be lifted if there was to be progress on the Gibraltar issue.

After routine talks in Madrid in November 1977 between Spanish and British representatives, later that month a meeting took place in Strasbourg between Dr Owen, his Spanish counterpart, Sir Joshua Hassan, and Maurice Xibberas (for the Gibraltar opposition). At a subsequent meeting of these four representatives in Paris in March 1978 it was agreed to set up Anglo-Spanish working groups to deal with matters including telephone communications and maritime links, and the working groups held two meetings in 1978, in July and December (a Gibraltarian delegation attending the latter).

1980 Lisbon Agreement on Reopening Border— Postponement of Implementation

After the Conservative election victory in Britain in May 1979 the new government was reported to have indicated to Spain—contrary to Dr Owen's assurance of Sept. 7, 1977—that British support for Spain's entry into the European Community would not be forthcoming as long as restrictions on Gibraltar remained in force. Publicly, it was stated that it was "inconceivable" that the frontier should remain closed when

Spain joined the Community.

With fresh moves afoot in Spain itself to reopen the frontier and negotiate over Gibraltar, Lord Carrington (the new UK Foreign and Commonwealth Secretary) and Marcelino Oreja Aguirre met in Lisbon on April 9-10, 1980, and agreed in principle that the land frontier would be reopened and that the other restrictions imposed in 1969 would be suspended. A joint communiqué issued on April 10 stated that "the British and Spanish governments, desiring to strengthen their bilateral relations and thus to contribute to European and Western solidarity, intend, in accordance with the relevant UN resolutions, to resolve, in a spirit of friendship, the Gibraltar problem" (Paragraph 1 of the Lisbon agreement), and that they had accordingly agreed to start negotiations (Paragraph 2).

The Lisbon agreement, in its subsequent paragraphs, was worded as follows: "(3) Both governments have reached agreement on the re-establishment of direct communications in the region. The Spanish government has decided to suspend the application of the measures at present in force. Both governments have agreed that future co-operation should be on the basis of reciprocity and full equality of rights. They look forward to the further steps which will be taken on both sides which they believe will open the way to closer understanding between those directly concerned in the area. (4) To this end both governments will be prepared to consider any proposals which the other may wish to make, recognizing the need to develop practical co-operation on a mutually beneficial basis. (5) The Spanish government, in reaffirming its position on the re-establishment of the territorial integrity of Spain, restated its intention that in the outcome of the negotiations the interests of the Gibraltarians should be fully safeguarded. For its part, the British government will fully maintain its commitment to honour the freely and democratically expressed wishes of the people of Gibraltar as set out in the preamble to the Gibraltar constitution. (6) Officials on both sides will meet as soon as possible to prepare the necessary practical steps which will permit the implementation of the proposals agreed to above. It is envisaged that these preparations will be completed not later than June 1".

By the end of 1980, however, the border was still closed and UK-Spanish contacts appeared deadlocked, it being reported that Spain was stipulating fresh conditions, among them that Spaniards working in Gibraltar should be granted equal status to Gibraltarians as soon as the border reopened. Gibraltar's response was that the local labour market was too complex and fragile for Spain to be given immediate access to it, and also that there were now several thousand Moroccan workers to be protected. The Gibraltar House of Assembly on Dec. 18, 1980, adopted a resolution stating that "Spanish nationals could not be granted the same rights as European Community nationals in Gibraltar, prior to Spain obtaining full membership of the Community".

In mid-1981 further difficulties in Spanish-UK relations over the Gibraltar issue arose when King Juan Carlos and Queen Sofia of Spain declined an invitation to attend the wedding of Prince Charles and Lady Diana Spencer on July 29 in view of an earlier announcement that the latter couple would embark on the royal yacht *Britannia* at Gibraltar to begin their honeymoon. Relations between the two sides subsequently improved, however, and on Jan. 8, 1982, talks in London between the UK and Spanish Prime Ministers (Margaret Thatcher and Leopoldo Calvo Sotelo) resulted in an agreement that the Gibraltar border would be reopened on April 20, 1982, and that negotiations would begin on that day to resolve the Gibraltar issue in terms of the April 1980 Lisbon agreement. However, in view of the development of a serious crisis between Argentina and Britain in early April 1982 over the Falkland Islands (for which see Section 2.3), it was agreed between the UK and Spanish governments on June 21 that implementation of the Lisbon agreement should be indefinitely postponed.

During the Falklands crisis the Spanish government consistently supported the Argentinian claim to sovereignty over the islands and abstained in UN votes calling for a cessation of hostilities and the withdrawal of Argentinian forces. In Gibraltar the Argentinian invasion of the Falklands (on April 2, 1982) gave rise to fears that similar action might be taken by Spain to recover the Rock, it being noted that extreme right-wing groups in Spain were demanding such action. However, the Spanish Council of Ministers issued a statement on April 3 giving an assurance that it regarded Gibraltar and the Falklands as separate issues.

Impasse in Negotiations—Decision to close Naval Dockyard at Gibraltar

Despite the indefinite deferment of the Lisbon agreement, the Spanish authorities in July 1982 initiated a slight relaxation of the border restrictions by allowing a small number of daily crossings into Spain for humanitarian reasons. Following the election of a Socialist government in Spain in October 1982, the border was reopened from Dec. 15 for pedestrians (restricted to one crossing a day per person) although not to vehicular and other traffic. Nevertheless, the commitment of the new Spanish government to new initiatives to achieve a settlement of the Gibraltar dispute produced no substantive movement on the diplomatic front through 1983 and most of 1984, notwithstanding the more favourable climate created by Spain's accession to NATO from May 1982 and the progress made in this period in the negotiations for full Spanish membership of the European Community.

Indeed, bilateral Spanish-UK relations deteriorated in April 1983 over a five-day visit to Gibraltar by the Royal Navy aircraft carrier HMS *Invincible* and about a dozen support vessels. The British ambassador in Madrid was twice summoned to the Spanish Foreign Ministry to receive protests against the visit (about which Spain had been notified in advance) and Spanish warships were stationed in Algeciras Bay to observe the British flotilla. While the UK government described the visit as "regular, annual and routine" since the ships were proceeding to NATO exercises in the Atlantic, Spanish spokesmen claimed that it could not be described as routine because of the number of ships involved and the fact that they had participated in the Falklands War.

The first Spanish protest note expressed "deep concern and displeasure" over the effect that the visit would have on Spanish public opinion and warned that Spain would take "appropriate diplomatic and political measures" to protect its national waters. During a subsequent visit to Gibraltar by HMS *Invincible* and six other ships in September 1983, however, the Spanish Foreign Minister made no public statements.

In an earlier significant development, the UK Defence Minister, John Nott, had announced on Nov. 22, 1981, that "changed plans for the Royal Navy no longer sustain a need for a naval dockyard in Gibraltar" and that the process of closure would commence in 1983; he had added that consultations would shortly begin with the Gibraltar government on possible economic alternatives, including the commercialization of the dockyard. In these consultations, Sir Joshua Hassan secured the postponement of the closure for one year (from the initially proposed date of Dec. 31, 1983) and the promise of a British grant of £28,000,000 to cover costs and initial losses; moreover, in the three years following the dockyard's transition to a commercial ship repair yard on Jan. 1, 1985, the UK government would pay £14,000,000 for the refitting of tankers and Royal Fleet Auxiliary landing ships and up to a further £1,000,000 for the refitting of other ships.

1984 Brussels Agreement

The impasse in Spanish-UK relations over Gibraltar was eventually unblocked by an agreement concluded in Brussels on Nov. 27, 1984, under which the 1980 Lisbon agreement was to be reactivated and applied by not later than Feb. 15, 1985, on the basis of a clarification of certain provisions which had been the subject of conflicting interpretations. The new agreement contained, for the first time, a specific British undertaking to discuss the sovereignty of Gibraltar with Spain and was seen as removing a major obstacle to Spain's entry to the European Community (the date of which was subsequently fixed for Jan. 1, 1986).

The Brussels agreement, which was the outcome of some seven months of unpublicized contacts, stated that implementation of the Lisbon agreement would involve the simultaneous application of the following measures: "(1a) The provision of equality and reciprocity of rights for Spaniards in Gibraltar and Gibraltarians in Spain. This will be implemented through the mutual concession of the rights which citizens of European Community countries enjoy, taking into account the transitional periods and derogations agreed between Spain and the Community. The necessary legislative proposals to achieve this will be intro-

duced in Spain and Gibraltar. As concerns paid employment, and recalling the general principle of Community preference, this carries the implication that during the transitional period each side will be favourably disposed to each other's citizens when granting work permits. (1b) The establishment of the free movement of persons, vehicles and goods between Gibraltar and the neighbouring territory. (1c) The establishment of a negotiating process aimed at overcoming all the differences between Spain and the United Kingdom over Gibraltar and at promoting co-operation on a mutually beneficial basis on economic, cultural, touristic, aviation, military and environmental matters. Both sides accept that the issues of sovereignty will be discussed in that process. The British government will fully maintain its commitment to honour the wishes of the people of Gibraltar as set out in the preamble of the 1969 constitution. (2) Insofar as the airspace in the region of Gibraltar is concerned, the Spanish government undertakes to take the early actions necessary to allow safe and effective air communications. (3) There will be meetings of working groups, which will be reviewed periodically in meetings for this purpose between the Spanish and British Foreign Ministers".

In a note accompanying the agreement, the Spanish government clarified the questions which, in its view, Britain had agreed to deal with regarding sovereignty. These included "both the theme of sovereignty of the territory referred to in the Treaty of Utrecht, as well as sovereignty of the isthmus, which was never ceded to Britain". The Spanish Foreign Minister, Fernando Morán, described the Brussels agreement, and particularly its reference to discussions on sovereignty, as "the biggest diplomatic success for Spain over the Rock since 1713", while stressing that Spain had "the greatest respect for the feelings of the Gibraltarians themselves".

In Gibraltar itself, Sir Joshua Hassan said that the Brussels agreement was an "honourable outcome" and a first step towards fruitful co-operation between Gibraltar and its surroundings, but added that many Gibraltarians retained deep reservations about the prospect of discussions on sovereignty. For the opposition Gibraltar Socialist Labour Party (GSLP), which had won seven of the 15 Assembly seats in the January 1984 general elections, Joe Bossano condemned the agreement and said that his party would "disown" it if it came to power. Also leader of the Transport and General Workers' Union in Gibraltar, Bossano added that he would seek to protect the jobs of some 2,000 Moroccans (representing about a third of his union membership) who had taken over from Spanish workers following the closure of the border in 1969.

Reopening of Border in 1985

After it had been announced (on Jan. 3) that the border would be reopened at midnight on Feb. 4-5, 1985, talks on border procedures, passport requirements and customs formalities opened on Jan. 10 in La Línea (the nearest Spanish town to Gibraltar) and continued the following day in Gibraltar, this being the first time since the border closure that Spanish representatives had made the crossing on official business. On Jan. 16 the Gibraltar House of Assembly adopted by eight votes to none a bill bringing forward to Feb. 5 certain of the rights which were due to accrue to Spain on its accession to the European Community, allowing Spaniards entry and residence in Gibraltar, as well as the right to purchase land, establishment of businesses, payment of family allowances and emergency medical treatment. The ruling Gibraltar Labour Party-Association for the Advancement of Civil Rights (GLA-AACR) supported the bill, on the grounds that sovereignty was "a totally unrelated question" and that Gibraltar should accept the advantages of an open border, whereas the GSLP members expressed their opposition by boycotting the vote. For its part, the Spanish Council of Ministers on Jan. 31 formally removed the 1969 border restrictions, to allow the free passage of people, vehicles and merchandise and the resumption of direct passage to Gibraltar by boat (hitherto only possible from countries other than Spain).

The frontier between Gibraltar and Spain was officially reopened as scheduled at midnight on Feb. 4-5, 1985, when the gates closed in June 1969 on the orders of Gen. Franco were ceremonially unlocked by the civil governor of Cadiz, Mariano Baquedano. Later on Feb. 5 the UK Foreign and Commonwealth Secretary, Sir Geoffrey Howe, opened talks with his Spanish counterpart in Geneva, with Sir Joshua Hassan forming part of the UK delegation. As well as signing an agreement on economic and cultural co-operation, the two sides agreed a detailed procedure for discussing issues relating to Gibraltar entailing regular annual meetings of Foreign Ministers to discuss "matters of mutual interest", including sovereignty, on which the Spanish side put forward detailed proposals. Working parties of British, Spanish and Gibraltarian officials were also to start work immediately with the aim of promoting co-operation in other spheres.

Lack of Progress in Negotiations, 1985-87

The second meeting of the Spanish and UK Foreign Ministers took place in Madrid on Dec. 5-6, 1985, with Sir Joshua Hassan in attendance for appropriate parts of the talks. A joint communiqué stated that in their exchanges on Gibraltar Sir Geoffrey Howe and Francisco Fernández Ordóñez (who had become Spanish Foreign Minister in July 1985) had had a full discussion of the issues of sovereignty, in which connection they had "reviewed the proposals put forward by the Spanish government in February 1985 and agreed that study of the issues of sovereignty should continue through diplomatic channels against the background of their shared aim of overcoming all the differences between the two governments". While not made public, the Spanish proposals were widely reported to include the possibility of a "lease-back" arrangement (under which the sovereignty of Gibraltar

would revert to Spain, which would grant Britain a lease on the Rock for an agreed period) or some form of Spanish-UK condominium over Gibraltar.

The communiqué also referred to the "common objective of developing the civilian use of Gibraltar airport on a mutually beneficial basis". Although the Spanish government had on April 1, 1985, partially lifted 18-year-old restrictions of the use of Spanish airspace over the Bay of Algeciras (in partial fulfilment of the 1984 Brussels agreement), major differences remained arising from the fact that Gibraltar's airport (used by both civil and military aircraft) had been constructed during World War II on the isthmus north of the Rock—which according to Spain was "no man's land" not covered by the Treaty of Utrecht but annexed illegally by Britain in 1908-9. Moreover, Spain was understood to be demanding that two terminals should be established at the airport, so that passengers bound for Spain would not have to pass through the UK-Gibraltar customs and immigration control.

Amid reports that the UK government was ready to make concessions on the airport issue, Sir Joshua Hassan and other Gibraltarian leaders sent an open letter to Sir Geoffrey Howe in September 1986 urging that the Spanish demands be rejected and requesting a referendum of the people of Gibraltar if any concessions were being contemplated. (Subsequently, on Dec. 17, 1986, the Gibraltar House of Assembly unanimously adopted a resolution calling for the airport to remain exclusively under the control of the British and Gibraltar authorities.) The open letter also protested against the withdrawal on July 31, 1986, of the ceremonial British military guard at the Spanish-Gibraltar border, to which Sir Geoffrey responded by stressing that he was pressing the Spanish government to reciprocate by withdrawing its own border guards.

Meanwhile, Spanish-UK relations had been subject to new tensions in March-April 1986 following an alleged incursion into Gibraltar's territorial waters by the Spanish aircraft carrier *Dédalo* during the night of March 20-21 and the launching of two helicopters into Gibraltar's airspace. In reply to a UK aide-mémoire dated April 2, the Spanish Foreign Ministry asserted that the Treaty of Utrecht recognized as Gibraltar's territorial waters only the immediate area of the port and that the surrounding waters remained Spanish.

The *Dédalo* incident preceded a state visit to Britain on April 22-25, 1986, by King Juan Carlos and Queen Sofia, the first such visit by a reigning Spanish monarch since 1905. In an address to both houses of parliament on April 23, the Spanish King said: "The recently resumed dialogue over Gibraltar is a step forward, but there remains a long way to go. I trust our respective governments may be capable of standing the test of history, and so find the formula that will transform any shadow into an element of harmony for greater co-operation between our countries and the general well-being of the international parties as well as the future of Europe".

Addressing the UN General Assembly in New York on Sept. 22, 1986, King Juan Carlos also made reference to the Gibraltar question, as follows: "Spain maintains, vigorously and with the weight of the reason inherent in its cause, the will to find a rapid solution to the problem of Gibraltar, so that the Rock can be reintegrated into the Spanish national territory. A new chapter has opened since the Brussels declaration of Nov. 27, 1984, and since the governments of the United Kingdom and Spain decided in February 1985 in Geneva to resolve the problem in all its aspects, including that of sovereignty, through negotiation. This new phase is dominated by the hope of putting an end to an unjust situation without harm for the interests of the local population".

A further meeting of the Spanish and UK Foreign Ministers took place in London on Jan. 13-14, 1987, during which Fernández Ordóñez met the UK Prime Minister, Margaret Thatcher. A communiqué issued after the session recorded that the two sides had agreed that co-operation between Gibraltar and Spain "should continue to take place on a fair and balanced basis consistent with their common Community obligations" and had noted that "contacts had developed satisfactorily in a number of fields, including tourism, the environment, culture and sport, public health and education". The statement also recorded that there had been "a full discussion of sovereignty", in which the Spanish Foreign Minister had "underlined the importance of proposals put forward by Spain in February 1985", while Sir Geoffrey Howe had "reaffirmed the British government's commitment to honour the wishes of the people of Gibraltar" and had stressed "the importance of managing any differences between Britain and Spain in a spirit consistent with their links of traditional friendship and their common membership of the European Community and NATO".

After the talks the Spanish Foreign Minister told a news conference on Jan. 14, 1987, that an "abnormal situation" existed when one NATO member country had a colony in another and when one European Community member had a colony in another. He also said that NATO military communications facilities in Gibraltar would have to be removed, on the basis that Gibraltar was part of Spain and that Spanish membership of NATO did not involve participation in its integrated military structure.

1987 Spanish-UK Agreement on Airport— Rejection by Gibraltar

In 1987 the Gibraltar airport issue represented a serious obstacle to EC moves to deregulate Community air travel. At a meeting of EC Transport Ministers on June 24-25, 1987, Spain objected to a proposed EC directive on this subject, on the grounds that Gibraltar airport was being treated as a UK regional airport under exclusive UK control. The consequence was that the directive failed to secure adoption by the specified deadline of June 30, 1987. Bilateral talks to find a solution were subsequently held within the framework of the 1984 Brussels agreement. As a result, Sir Geoffrey Howe indicated on Gibraltar television on

Nov. 16, 1987, that a compromise deal on the airport was imminent. The Gibraltar House of Assembly responded on Nov. 23 by unanimously passing a resolution calling on London not to make any concessions, while the local trade union council voted to take direct action to prevent implementation of an unacceptable agreement. In a last-minute intervention, Sir Joshua Hassan flew to London on Nov. 25 for talks with Sir Geoffrey, before further rounds of Spanish-UK negotiations took place in Madrid on Nov. 27 and in London on Dec. 2, 1987. Despite Sir Joshua's efforts, the latter session resulted in the signature of an agreement envisaging that Spain would have a separate terminal on the northern perimeter of the airport, where passengers would not be subject to Gibraltar immigration controls. As part of the agreement, both sides undertook in principle to approve the EC air transport directive, although it was accepted that, until and unless the London agreement was approved by the Gibraltar parliament, the Rock's airport was "suspended" from the scope of the directive. It was also agreed that a sea ferry service would be resumed as soon as possible between Gibraltar and Algeciras and that the flow of road traffic across the Spain-Gibraltar border would be accelerated.

A joint declaration issued by the two sides on Dec. 2, 1987, stated that (i) the aviation authorities of the two countries would hold regular discussions on the civil use of Gibraltar airport, including the establishment of new services to third countries; (ii) Spain would allow Spanish airlines to operate between Spanish airports and Gibraltar airport under EC arrangements; (iii) Spain would build a new terminal at La Línea adjacent to the northern side of the existing frontier fence, and passengers using it would have direct access to Gibraltar through a gate in the south side of the terminal; (iv) the Spanish terminal would be used by passengers going to any point north of the frontier fence and by those proceeding from this area; (v) the UK terminal would be used by all other passengers; (vi) where appropriate, passengers would be subject to customs and immigration controls in the respective terminals; (vii) a UK-Spanish committee would co-ordinate both terminals' civil air transport activities and their relations with the airport's other services; (viii) there would be close co-operation on airport security; (ix) ongoing UK-Spanish discussions would take place on further strengthening air safety and on air traffic control arrangements in the area; and (x) all arrangements would come into operation on condition that the Gibraltar House of Assembly passed the necessary legislation to give effect to the provision regarding customs and immigration controls, and not later than one year after the United Kingdom notified Spain that this had been done. On the basic issue, the declaration added that "the present arrangements and any activity or measure undertaken in applying them are understood to be without prejudice to the respective legal positions of Spain and the United Kingdom with regard to the dispute over sovereignty over the territory in which the airport is situated".

Nine days after the signature of the Spain-UK airport agreement, Sir Joshua resigned as Chief Minister of Gibraltar and leader of the GLA-AACR (on Dec. 11, 1987). His successor was the Deputy Chief Minister, Adolfo Canepa, who was regarded as more favourable to co-operation with Spain, subject to the established party line that the British link should be retained. Nevertheless, on Dec. 17, 1987, the Gibraltar House of Assembly effectively rejected the airport agreement by voting unanimously to challenge the legality of Gibraltar's exclusion from the EC directive on air traffic deregulation. The House resolution demanded that "the international use of Gibraltar's airfield should be on the basis that no special privileges are accorded to Spanish airlines, passengers with a Spanish destination or the Spanish aviation authorities". It also asserted that "Gibraltar's right to be included in the [EC] air liberalization package as a regional British airport without pre-conditions should be pursued" and added that "the concessions granted to Spain...are in conflict with the consistently-expressed views of this House and the wishes of the people of Gibraltar".

Elections to the Gibraltar House of Assembly on March 24, 1988, ended the 16-year old government of the GLP-AACR and brought to power Joe Bossano of the GSLP. In his campaign, Bossano expressed fierce opposition to both the 1984 and the 1987 UK-Spanish agreements and vowed to boycott future meetings between the Foreign Ministers of the two sides. Six weeks before the elections, in early February 1988, NATO ministers had, when approving proposals for Spanish participation in the alliance's military structure, accepted Spain's condition that it would not join in manoeuvres or operations under the command of military authorities based in Gibraltar.

Developments 1989-93—EC Dimension

During a visit to Gibraltar on Jan. 29, 1989, Sir Geoffrey Howe confirmed unofficial reports that the UK government intended to reduce its army presence on the Rock, since there was "no longer a threat from Spain". This intention was eventually clarified on Dec. 5, 1989, in a written parliamentary reply in the UK House of Commons which said that a resident infantry battalion would not be retained in Gibraltar after March 1991, when the current tour of the Third Battalion Royal Green Jackets was due to end. At the same time, the government announced plans for the permanent cadre of the Gibraltar Regiment to be more than doubled (and the Royal Navy and Air Force would maintain their presence in the colony). In 1989 Gibraltar's total revenues from the UK military presence were estimated at about £40,000,000, in addition to which the Ministry of Defence employed about 1,700 Gibraltarians, accounting for 12 per cent of the workforce. Chief Minister Bossano described the UK cutback as "not as drastic as was being postulated".

Shortly before the Howe visit, Bossano had talks with the Spanish mayor of La Línea on Jan. 10, 1989,

and discussed with him plans for joint development of the area. It was understood that such plans included Spanish use of the port of Gibraltar but not of the airport, the December 1987 agreement on which remained unimplemented because of continuing Gibraltarian opposition to it. The airport issue remained unresolved at Spanish-UK Foreign Ministers' meetings in London in February 1989 and Madrid in February 1990, which were boycotted by Bossano. In between the sessions, moreover, bilateral relations were strained by an incident on June 30, 1989, when four Spanish customs officers were arrested in Gibraltar and charged with illegal entry and possession of firearms after they had entered the colony in hot pursuit of alleged tobacco smugglers. Prior to the February 1990 talks, a UK Foreign Office minister, Francis Maude, visited the Rock in January 1990 and told Bossano that the December 1987 airport agreement in no way altered the status quo as regards sovereignty over Gibraltar. Nevertheless, the Chief Minister stood by his decision not to co-operate with the UK-Spanish negotiating process. In a subsequent interview with a Madrid newspaper, Bossano said that Britain should tell Spain that it should "abandon all hope of recovering Gibraltar through the Brussels process".

At the February 1990 talks, the Spanish Foreign Minister warned his British counterpart (by now Douglas Hurd) that, if the December 1987 agreement continued to be blocked, his government would study the feasibility of building a second airport in the area. Nevertheless, the two sides agreed to co-operate in preventing Gibraltar from becoming a base for drug trafficking and its burgeoning offshore financial sector from becoming a centre for money laundering and other crookedness. In particular, it was agreed to extend to Gibraltar the 1985 UK-Spain extradition treaty as well as a bilateral customs co-operation agreement. On the sovereignty issue, Ordóñez declared that "the colony of Gibraltar belongs to the past", while Hurd reiterated the British view that nothing could be done which went against the will of the Gibraltarians. Another UK junior Foreign Office minister, Tristan Garel-Jones, visited Gibraltar in September 1990 and found Bossano unyielding on both the Brussels process and the airport agreement as signed. Although Bossano was prepared to let Spanish aircraft use the airport, he continued to rule out any joint administration of its activities.

The Bossano government made substantial progress in its declared aim of underpinning Gibraltarians' "moral right to self-determination" with economic self-sufficiency, particularly through the development of the Rock as an offshore financial centre. By the end of 1990 there were 41,000 companies registered in Gibraltar, and a group of Danish investors was building a £100 million financial and administrative centre on reclaimed land. Against this background, many Gibraltarians envisaged the Rock's longer-term future as that of an independent city-state within the European Community, its autonomy in effect guaranteed by the process of EC economic and political integration. In this context, much publicity was given in Gibraltar in 1991 to the opinion of one British specialist in international law that the terms of the Treaty of Utrecht did not rule out independence for the colony (a view which was not shared by the Spanish government). In February 1991 Bossano again boycotted the annual session of UK and Spanish Foreign Ministers, held in London, and maintained his refusal to recommend the 1987 airport agreement to the Gibraltar House of Assembly. In May 1991 the Spanish Prime Minister, Felipe González, visited London and urged the UK government "to adopt a more imaginative approach" with a view to overcoming the deadlock over the Rock. Bossano responded by equating the attitude of González to the Gibraltarians with that once displayed by Gen. Franco. Meanwhile, the withdrawal of the last British infantry battalion from Gibraltar had commenced in March 1991, leaving the defence of the Rock to the locally-raised Gibraltar Regiment.

In a statement to the UK House of Commons on July 16, 1991, Garel-Jones said that the effort of imagination called for by the Spanish Prime Minister also had to be made by Spain and Gibraltar. He expressed the view that the future of the Rock, as of Britain and Spain, lay within the EC, adding that there was "just a chance" that the Gibraltar issue might be "resolved within the EC". The following month Spanish ministers welcomed what they described as the "imaginative" idea of "dissolving" the sovereignty dispute in a European arrangement under which Gibraltar would become in effect an EC dependency. However, Bossano and other Gibraltarian leaders quickly made it clear that, while they too attached importance to the EC dimension, they were opposed to Gibraltar becoming an "EC colony"; rather, they envisaged that Gibraltar would become fully autonomous, even independent, within an enhanced EC economic and political union. On Sept. 27, 1991, Bossano told a Commonwealth parliamentary conference in India that Britain and Spain should recognize "the right to self-determination and right to independence...of the people of Gibraltar" and explained that he was boycotting the Brussels process because he was expected to participate "as part of the UK delegation". On returning to Gibraltar he declared that, "if the people desire it", he was prepared to challenge the established UK-Spanish view that the Treaty of Utrecht ruled out the conversion of Gibraltar into an independent state.

Meanwhile, the Gibraltar issue had complicated EC efforts to formulate an agreed external frontier convention within the context of its move to greater economic and political union. In June 1991 the Spanish government warned that it would not sign the proposed convention as drafted because it would give Gibraltar (as part of the EC) the right to control entry into Spain. While Spain was prepared to cede such powers to the sovereign EC states, it demurred at Gibraltar, as a UK colony, having the same rights and demanded that there should be a separate Spanish-UK agreement on the question of the Gibraltar frontier. The UK govern-

ment responded by offering to agree to an addendum to the convention to the effect that its implementation would be without prejudice to the basic sovereignty dispute. However, the Spanish Prime Minister stated categorically that his government would not sign the convention until and unless a solution had been found to the problem of Gibraltar. In a "non-legislative" declaration adopted unanimously on Oct. 2, 1991, the foreign affairs committee of the Spanish parliament requested the Spanish government "not to make any agreement with regard to the exterior frontiers of the EC which could assume the perpetuation of [Gibraltar's] actual status nor to impair Spain's position in the negotiations for the decolonization of its national territory".

General elections in Gibraltar on Jan. 16, 1992, resulted in the return of Bossano and the GSLP with a massive 73 per cent of the popular vote (as against 58 per cent in 1988). The GSLP campaigned on a platform urging greater autonomy from the United Kingdom, especially in the economic sphere. At a victory press conference, Bossano said that the result did not mean that the Gibraltarians were hostile to Spain but was "an expression of the self-determination of the people of Gibraltar". In October 1993, addressing the UN General Assembly for the first time, he tried to persuade it to shift from the position it had adopted in the 1960s and which had been reaffirmed by Spain's Foreign Minister, Javier Solana, the previous month, that Gibraltar should be decolonized and that decolonization meant transfer to Spain.

Renewed Tightening of Border Restrictions, 1994-97

In May 1994 the Spanish government opened a new front in the dispute by lodging a formal complaint with the British embassy in Madrid accusing Britain and the Gibraltarian authorities of failing to deal adequately with an alleged increase in drug-smuggling. At the end of October, as the tenth anniversary of the Brussels declaration approached, the Spanish authorities followed this up by re-imposing elaborate checks at the border crossing at La Línea. These resulted at best in delays of up to seven hours or at worst (under orders given by the Spanish civil governor of Cadiz) in on-the-spot fines for drivers in breach of Spanish law or refusal of entry. Meanwhile the Bossano government came under criticism in London for its apparent failure to comply with EU directives on smuggling and money-laundering. This left the British Foreign Secretary, Douglas Hurd, at a disadvantage when the ninth ministerial meeting of the Brussels process took place at Chevening, Kent, on Dec. 19-20, 1994, though Solana had made it clear that the main focus of the talks would be smuggling and not the sovereignty issue. By April 27, 1995, when the cross-border group met for the second time to discuss the smuggling issue, border controls had again been tightened. Spain had taken advantage of the Schengen agreement, which had come into effect on March 28, to impose additional controls on the grounds that the Gibraltar frontier was an external entry point to the EU.

At the next meeting between the Foreign Ministers, on June 21, Javier Solana agreed to suspend a further list of sanctions Spain proposed to implement, though his government would go ahead with a formal complaint to the European Commission that smuggling based on Gibraltar was costing it some Ptas200,000m annually in lost revenue, and on June 23 the complaint was officially lodged. At this point legislation to curb money-laundering was belatedly introduced in the Gibraltar Assembly and passed on July 7, the day on which the police confiscated 50 rigid inflatable boats said to have been used for smuggling.

On April 4, 1996, general elections in Spain returned a right-wing government led by José María Aznar. He lost no time in indicating his government would continue to press its claim to the Rock. Six days later a Spanish helicopter crashed while trying to intercept a Gibraltar-based speedboat and a technician was killed. In response Spain imposed tighter controls on the border resulting in long delays, and the new Foreign Minister, Abel Matutes, promised to take a tough line on smuggling.

In Gibraltar Bossano called a general election held on May 16, but the voters rejected his policy of simultaneously confronting Spain and seeking greater independence from Britain. On a record turnout the electorate gave the Gibraltar Social Democrats an overall majority and their leader, Peter Caruana, became the new Chief Minister. He had pledged to deal with the abuses that had undermined the local economy and to seek better relations with both Britain and Spain, and his election was welcomed by the local Spanish authorities. However, the immediate response of the Aznar government was to restate that "the future of Gibraltar remains a matter to be resolved only between the governments of Spain and the United Kingdom" and to impose new checks at the frontier, resulting in delays of up to six hours.

A new British Foreign Secretary, Malcolm Rifkind, met Matutes in Madrid on June 6, and expressed the hope that cross-border talks might be resumed. Unfortunately, with Spain's declaration on Sept. 9 that it would seek integration with the NATO command structure, a new problem had been raised, as Spain had made it clear that it wished Gibraltar integrated into a new command zone covering both Spain and the Straits. (In the event the proposals were indefinitely postponed owing to a dispute between France and the USA which led to France deciding not to rejoin NATO's command structure.) Before the next meeting between the Foreign Ministers, at Madrid on Jan. 22, 1997, Spanish newspapers floated a story that Gibraltarian passports would no longer be recognized, and at the meeting itself Rifkind received assurances that the freedom of movement guaranteed by the 1960 Treaty would be maintained. A Gibraltarian delegation led by Peter Caruana visited Brussels on Jan.28 to seek voting rights for the European Parliament but proved unable to meet any of the four Commissioners involved (two of whom were Spanish) or the President of the European Parliament (who was also Spanish), despite such visits being a reg-

ular feature of EU life. Meanwhile Rifkind's assurances were somewhat tarnished by a series of border incidents in which residents of Gibraltar were delayed or denied entry to Spain.

Election of UK Labour Government—Continuing Difficulties in Relations

On May 1, 1997, a general election in the UK returned a Labour government led by Tony Blair. This was the first time Labour had held office since 1979, and Matutes immediately announced his intention to discuss his proposal for joint sovereignty over Gibraltar with the new Foreign Secretary, Robin Cook—one of whose first tasks would be to oversee the transfer of British sovereignty in Hong Kong to China on July 1.

In advance of their first meeting on July 7, Caruana announced that he would propose to Cook the same change in Gibraltar's status under British law that he had proposed to his predecessor—namely that Gibraltar be re-designated a Crown dependency like the Isle of Man, the post of Governor being abolished and the responsibility for Gibraltar being transferred from the Foreign and Commonwealth Office to the Home Office. However, despite encouraging words of support for Gibraltar from both Cook and Blair, little was changed and the annual appearances of both Spain and Gibraltar before the UN Committee on Decolonization resulted in the usual reaffirmation that the future of Gibraltar was a matter for resolution by discussion between Spain and the UK. Again the annual formal meeting between the two Foreign Ministers, which took place in London on Dec. 10, was preceded by a series of Spanish threats, coupled with a promise that under joint sovereignty Gibraltar would enjoy the same regional autonomy as Catalonia or the Basque country. For the first time in the history of negotiations, the proposal for joint sovereignty was not, however, immediately rejected, and this encouraged Spain to think that the British government's position might be changing. Robin Cook firmly rejected the preferred Gibraltarian option of integration with the UK.

Gibraltar's Chief Minister was in Brussels to lodge a complaint about Spanish intransigence on the border crossing when, on April 28, 1998, Matutes took the unprecedented step of inviting him to meet him in Madrid. On July 5 Spain made an important concession to NATO reorganization when it agreed to lift existing restrictions on the use of Gibraltar's airfield. During the whole of this time there were constant incidents involving fishing vessels in Gibraltar's coastal waters. A verbal agreement between the two Foreign Ministers proved so ambiguous as to make matters worse. Before they finally met in Luxembourg on Feb. 21, 1999, the European Court of Justice unequivocally ruled in favour of Gibraltar's right to participate in EU elections, but the meeting was still unsuccessful, with no joint communiqué being issued. On Feb. 25, at a meeting of the two Prime Ministers, José Aznar handed Tony Blair a long list of complaints alleging the Rock was a haven for drug-trafficking and money-laundering. Although the British Prime Minister backed the efforts of the Gibraltarian authorities to combat these activities, the dossier was again discussed at a meeting at Chequers on April 10, when it appeared that neither side was willing to have the Gibraltar issue become a distraction from other matters. However this did not stop Spain, as had been feared, from vetoing Britain's move to seek limited participation in the Schengen agreement. Nor did it prevent the House of Commons foreign affairs committee from criticizing the Brussels process as a whole on the grounds that it gave encouragement to the Spanish government to seek goals which could not and should not be fulfilled.

In February 2000 Gibraltarians gave Peter Caruana and the GSD a clear vote of confidence by returning them to power with 58.35 per cent of the votes cast. A month later the Aznar government was re-elected for a second term in Spain, and though Abel Matutes had retired for reasons of health, decades of policy based on trying to get Britain to cede sovereignty to Spain was not expected to change. Hence when on April 19 an agreement on Schengen between Britain and Spain was announced, Spain was satisfied because it confirmed that it was Britain and not Gibraltar that was the sovereign authority over the Rock. Spain, however, had had for the first time to agree to accept identity documents issued in Gibraltar and to recognize the Royal Gibraltar Police as the competent police authority.

The next crisis in relations came only the following month when HMS *Tireless*, a nuclear-powered "Trafalgar" class submarine, developed a fault in her reactor and put into Gibraltar for temporary repairs. A month later, however, the British Defence Ministry announced that it would be less risky to mend the reactor in Gibraltar than to try to move it. Though the Spanish government accepted this position, the new Foreign Minister, Josep Piqué, complained in advance of a meeting of the Prime Ministers at Madrid on Oct. 27 that information on the status of the repairs had been "highly inadequate". Though contradicted by Aznar himself, Piqué then used the issue to complain that the safety of Spanish citizens was at risk as long as Gibraltar remained a colony. Protests from environmental and other groups continued until the submarine's reactor was successfully restarted on May 1, 2001. It sailed for the Clyde six days later.

Failure of UK-Spanish Negotiations—Gibraltar Referendum

In April 2001 the House of Commons foreign affairs select committee criticized the UK government for failing to stand up adequately for the rights of Gibraltarians, calling on the government to threaten Spain with legal action in the European Court of Justice because of the continued border restrictions. In September 2001, however, it was reported that Tony Blair had set a deadline of 18 months to achieve a solution to the Gibraltar question, in part to cement his increasingly close relationship with Aznar on EU and

other matters. These reports produced alarm in Gibraltar, especially when Peter Hain, the Foreign Office Minister responsible for Europe, warned the Gibraltarians that "if people want to get stuck in the past, the future will leave them behind". British officials were subsequently quoted as indicating that some form of joint sovereignty was the favoured option, leading the UK Conservative Shadow Foreign Secretary, Michael Ancram, to state on Nov. 19 that the British government's conduct "has a smell of a stitch-up, has undermined confidence on the Rock and is damaging to the ties that have long existed between the UK government and Gibraltar".

Following talks held in London between the Spanish and British Foreign Ministers on Feb. 4, 2002, the Ministers stated that they aimed to conclude an agreement before the summer covering co-operation and sovereignty. British Foreign Secretary Jack Straw warned that the continuation of the present status of Gibraltar was not sustainable "in the medium term" but said that the people of Gibraltar would not lose their citizenship or way of life. The British position was that any agreement would be put to a referendum in Gibraltar. Spanish Foreign Minister Piqué said that outstanding issues could be resolved but that Spain did not accept the right of Gibraltarians to self-determination and would not renounce its claim on Gibraltar.

The talks were boycotted by Caruana, who said that the "British and the Spanish governments have already agreed between themselves an outline of principles, which include giving away half of the sovereignty of Gibraltar". Thereafter, however, the talks faltered, in particular over the British insistence that any agreement should be "durable" rather than an interim arrangement allowing Spain to continue its campaign to gain control of the territory. On July 12, 2002, Straw conceded that there was no immediate prospect of concluding an agreement with Spain, stating that while Britain favoured a settlement including co-sovereignty, this could not be used as a "stepping stone" to full Spanish sovereignty against the wishes of the people of Gibraltar. The views of the Gibraltarians themselves were left in no doubt by the result of a referendum, organized by Caruana and held on Nov. 7, 2002, in which almost 99 per cent of those who voted, on a turnout of 88 per cent, opposed any sharing of sovereignty with Spain. Although both Spain and the UK insisted that the locally organized referendum had no legal force, by this time the earlier momentum of the talks had been entirely lost.

Overall relations between Spain and the UK had meanwhile been strengthened by the strong backing they had both given to the USA in the "war against terrorism" declared after Sept. 11, 2001. By March 2003 the two governments were partially isolated from their European partners over the issue of war in Iraq. Before hostilities commenced, the two Prime Ministers met in the Azores with President George W. Bush to symbolize their common purpose. Continued frictions over Gibraltar were nonetheless demonstrated when, on Nov. 3, 2003, the Spanish government closed the border with Gibraltar for the first time since 1969, ostensibly to avoid infection from the British cruise ship *Aurora*, whose passengers had been afflicted by a virus. Straw described the measure as "unnecessary and disproportionate", and the border was reopened as soon as the ship sailed for Southampton. It was not clear whether any change in Spanish policy might be expected after Aznar's decision to stand down and the election in March 2004 of a Socialist Government.

Peter Calvert

4.18 Transcarpathia

After a thousand years of Hungarian rule, the remote region of Transcarpathia became part of the new state of Czechoslovakia at the end of World War I. Repossessed by Hungary in 1938-39, it was ceded to the Soviet Union after World War II and incorporated into the Ukrainian Soviet Socialist Republic. Like other East European boundary changes made on Stalin's direction in 1945, the transfer of Transcarpathia appeared for several decades to be immutable. However, following the restoration of democratic government in Czechoslovakia (as the Czech and Slovak Federative Republic) and the disintegration of the Soviet Union in 1990-91, the status of the region again became an issue. (Map 50, p. 517, illustrates the region.)

Geographical and Historical Background

The area in question, here called Transcarpathia for convenience, was variously known in the past as Ruthenia (although it covers only a small part of the historic province of that name), Sub-Carpathian Ruthenia, Carpatho-Ruthenia, Sub-Carpathian Russia, Carpatho-Ukraine, Transcarpathian Ukraine and Sub-Capartho Ukraine. It now forms the south-western border region of Ukraine (being known in Ukraine as Zakarpattia), bounded by Romania to the south, Hungary to the south-west, Slovakia to the west and Poland to the north-west. About 5,000 square miles (13,000 sq km) in area, it includes the south-western slopes of the northern Carpathian mountains where they descend into the Hungarian plain and a corner of the plain itself. The regional capital is Uzhgorod, the other principal towns being Mukachevo and Khust. The main population group was historically known as Ruthenes.

The Ruthenes were distinct from the other main East Slav people, namely the "Great Russians". In the interests of legitimizing their territorial expansion, the Great Russians of Muscovy, once they started to conquer surrounding areas, made a point of blurring the difference between the two main Slav branches by designating the historic Ruthenian lands as "Little

Russia" (Ukraine) and "White Russia" (Belorussia).

Transcarpathia was under continuous Hungarian rule for a thousand years until 1918. Established over the Hungarian plain in the late 9th century, Magyar dominion was extended by c.1000 to the natural frontier of the Carpathian ridges, including Transcarpathia to the north-east and Transylvania to the east. In Transcarpathia the inhabitants brought under Hungarian feudal rule were mainly Ruthenes, whose kinsmen beyond the mountains formed the south-western arm of the Kievan Rus' state. The historic forerunner of modern Ukraine, the Norse-founded Kievan Rus' reached its zenith in the 11th century under Grand Duke Yaroslav, having embraced Christianity in 988. But its disunited successor principalities were overrun by Mongol/Tatar hordes in the 13th century, after which most of Ruthenia came under Polish/Lithuanian rule in the late 14th century.

Hungary survived Mongol depradations but in 1526 succumbed to the Ottoman Turks at the Battle of Mohacs. Thereafter, unfettered Magyar rule was confined to Transylvania and Transcarpathia, with the result that these regions came to loom large in the Hungarian national consciousness. Having originally opted for the Greek Orthodox camp in the Great Schism of 1054, the Ruthenian Church switched to Roman allegiance in 1594, becoming the Uniate Catholic Church. The subject Ruthenes thereafter at least shared something of the religious faith of their Polish, Lithuanian and Hungarian masters. Those who preferred Greek Orthodoxy migrated eastwards to the empty steppes of the Dnieper and Don Basin and established semi-autonomous Cossack warrior communities, whose cultural traditions are an important component of Ukrainian national consciousness today.

Under the 1699 Treaty of Carlowitz, Hungary (with Transylvania and Transcarpathia) passed from Turkish rule to the Austrian Habsburg empire. This change of ultimate sovereignty was of only academic interest to the Ruthenes and other Slav subjects of the Hungarians, whose noblemen acquired a European reputation for feudal hauteur and reactionary tendencies. Meanwhile, the Grand Principality of Muscovy had embarked on its remarkable expansion as the self-proclaimed heir of old Kievan Rus'. By the late 17th century the Moscow-based Tsars of "all the Russias" ruled over the whole of northern and central Russia and had absorbed Kiev itself from Poland/Lithuania, together with the Cossack lands of what is now north-eastern Ukraine.

Establishing itself as a major European power under Peter the Great (r. 1689-1725), Russia made vast acquisitions in the south and west in the 18th century. Under Catherine the Great (r. 1762-96), Russian gains included the Crimea and Jedisan on the Black Sea coast as well as Lithuania, Belorussia and part of western Ukraine. Russia's main western advance came in the three partitions of the Polish kingdom between Russia, Austria and Prussia (1772-95). In that division the old Ruthenian province of Galicia, north of the Carpathians and containing many Poles, became a Habsburg province, so that Transcarpathia was no longer the political frontier region it had once been.

Russia emerged from the Napoleonic Wars in 1815 with even more of Poland. At the same time, the Congress of Vienna confirmed Habsburg dominion over a swathe of former Polish territory north and north-east of the Carpathians. This area was largely Ruthene or Polish in ethnic composition but was also contiguous with Romanian-populated Bukovina (which the Turks had ceded to the Habsburgs in 1775). The abortive Hungarian revolt against Austrian Habsburg rule of 1848-49 led to the *Ausgleich* ("compromise") of 1867, under which the ancient Hungarian kingdom was restored, although with the Habsburg emperor as king. The Hungarian part of the Austro-Hungarian dual monarchy included Transcarpathia, as well as Slovakia, Galicia, Bukovina and Transylvania, all with mixed but predominantly non-Magyar populations.

Then came World War I (1914-18). In that conflict the European continental empires were defeated—Russia by the Central powers, Germany and Austria-Hungary, in 1917, a year before in November 1918 the latter accepted defeat in the west by the Franco-British-US alliance. As the ultimate victors, the Western powers opted at the Paris peace conference for a new map of Europe governed by the principle of the national self-determination of peoples. The problem with the former Austro-Hungarian empire was to decide how this principle should determine post-war borders, given the territorial inter-mingling of former subject peoples. The solution adopted in the case of the Czech and Slovak peoples was to create a state called Czechoslovakia, as confirmed by the Treaties of St Germain (Sept. 10, 1919) and Trianon (June 4, 1920) with Austria and Hungary respectively.

Territorial Claims on Czechoslovakia—Hungarian Seizure of Transcarpathia in 1938-39

The new republic of Czechoslovakia included the Transcarparthian region of Ruthene settlement which today is part of Ukraine. Galician areas further north became part of the revived Polish state, while Bukovina was joined with Romania. Transcarpathia was not one of the regions in which a plebiscite was held to determine the wishes of the local population as to their affiliation. The priority of the Paris peacemakers was that the new Czechoslovak state should have a natural eastern frontier (the Carpathians). For a while, Transcarpathia was part of the territory claimed by the independent republic of Ukraine (set up with German backing during the war), to which Transcarpathian Ukrainians declared their allegiance in January 1919. However, complex post-1918 hostilities in the region, involving attempts by the new Polish state to recover the old borders of the Lithuanian/Polish federation, resulted in Ukraine being confirmed as a republic of the new Soviet Union (1923). Its borders left present-day western Ukraine partly within Poland and partly within Czechoslovakia.

In the 1931 Czechoslovak census, Transcarpathia was found to have a population of 750,000, of whom 65 per cent were Ruthenes/Ukrainians, 15 per cent Hungarians and 15 per cent Jews. Accounts in the inter-war period agreed that under Hungarian rule the region had been one of the most backward parts of Europe, with an illiteracy rate of 70 per cent, and that in the late 19th century conditions had been so bad that many inhabitants had emigrated to the United States and Canada. Such accounts also agreed that half of Transcarpathia was forested and that the main areas of employment were in forestry, cattle-breeding and agriculture, with the industrial workforce forming only 10 per cent of the population. As part of Czechoslovakia, Transcarpathia enjoyed local autonomy in the inter-war period but remained severely disadvantaged as compared with the Czech and Slovak areas.

International attention next focused on Transcarpathia in the late 1930s, when Czechoslovakia came under threat from Nazi Germany and its allies. In the Munich Agreement of September 1938, Britain and France concurred with Hitler's demand that the German-populated Sudetenland area of Czechoslovakia should be taken into the German Reich. This unleashed territorial claims against Czechoslovakia from Hungary (as well as from Poland). Submitted on Oct. 9, 1938, the Hungarian demand was that Czechoslovakia should cede the southern border region of Slovakia east of Bratislava (the Slovak capital) as well as the southern lowlands of Transcarpathia (including the towns of Uzhgorod and Mukachevo). The area demanded was called Felvidek by the Hungarians, who claimed that its population was 78 per cent Magyar in ethnic composition. That figure was contested by the Czechoslovaks, who pointed out that the Hungarians were using a census of 1910 to support their case (although they did not dispute that the territory demanded was predominantly Hungarian in population).

On the rejection of the Hungarian demand by the Prague government, the matter was submitted to the arbitration of the German and Italian Foreign Ministers. Their decision, known as the First Vienna Award, was announced on Nov. 2, 1938, and granted most of the Hungarian claim. The only exceptions were that Hungary's demand for territorial rights in the Danube port area of Bratislava was rejected and that Hungary did not obtain the ancient episcopal see of Nitra (north-east of Bratislava) or the area of southern Transcarpathia bordering on Romania. The award was accepted with bitterness by the Czechoslovak government and described as a "great injustice" by the Slovak leadership. The territory which Hungary received (and began occupying following the Czechoslovak withdrawal on Nov. 5-10, 1938) amounted to some 4,630 square miles (12,000 sq km), about 20 per cent of the area of Slovakia and containing the only railway line from eastern Slovakia to Prague. Its population was 1,026,000, of whom about 70 per cent were ethnic Hungarians, 10 per cent Slovaks and 10 per cent Ruthenes.

The autonomous region of Transcarpathia was particularly badly affected by the transfer, losing almost all of its fertile agricultural land, its main towns and its railway line to Bratislava and Prague. The authorities were obliged to relocate the regional capital to the town of Khust and the usage "Carpatho-Ukraine" was adopted for the region's name (although "Sub-Carpathian Russia" continued to feature in the Czechoslovak constitution). "Carpatho-Ukraine" was the preferred German appellation for the region, reflecting the Hitler regime's support for pan-Ukrainianism because it was an anti-Bolshevik movement.

During the negotiations on its claim, the Hungarian government tried to get support for an outright partition of Transcarpathia between Hungary, Romania and Poland. This plan was supported by Poland (which had in September 1938 itself succeeded in detaching the coal-rich border district of Teschen/Cieszym from Czechoslovakia) but rejected by Romania. Six months later, in March 1939, came Hungary's chance to seize the rest of Transcarpathia. On March 15, 1939, German forces occupied the Czech lands of Bohemia and Moravia (which became German-administered protectorates), as Slovakia declared itself independent under German protection. This marked the effective collapse of the Czechoslovak state, to which Hungary reacted by demanding the cession of northern Transcarpathia on the grounds that "ever-recurring frontier incidents, while endangering the security of the Hungarian population of the borderland, tend also to suggest that an attack based on that territory might be launched against the peoples of Slovakia engaged in struggling to obtain their freedom".

By now German-controlled, the Prague government accepted the Hungarian ultimatum immediately, whereupon Hungarian forces occupied the whole of Transcarpathia up to the Polish border. During the takeover, which was completed by March 18, 1939, there was heavy fighting between Hungarian troops and Ruthene/Ukrainian irregulars. An attempt by the main Ukrainian party (Christian People's Party) to declare an independent "Carpatho-Ukraine" had only a symbolic impact.

Transfer of Transcarpathia to Soviet Union after World War II

Hungary was allied with the Axis powers in World War II (1939-45) and gained further territorial benefit under the Second Vienna Award of August 1940, by which Romania was obliged to cede Northern Transylvania to Hungary (see Section 4.11). Ending up on the losing side, Hungary expected to have to revert to its pre-1938 frontiers after the war. This was duly stipulated under the Paris peace treaty between the Allies and Hungary signed on Feb. 10, 1947, except for a small adjustment in restored Czechoslovakia's favour south of Bratislava. But Hungary had perhaps not anticipated that Transcarpathia would not be returned to Czechoslovakia but instead transferred to the Soviet Union, whose forces had liberated the province in late 1944.

The change was one of many made to East European borders by Stalin, among which his annexations of Eastern Poland and of Northern Bukovina

from Romania, first instituted in November 1939 and June 1940 respectively and confirmed by the eventual victory of the Red Army, were related to the acquisition of Transcarpathia (see Sections 4.13 and 4.14). The southern part of the annexed Polish territory (East Galicia) was contiguous with Transcarpathia and with Northern Bukovina. All three areas were assigned to the Ukrainian Soviet Socialist Republic (SSR), which thus at last recovered the full territory of the historic Ruthene lands. In this, as in his other territorial dispositions, Stalin displayed a knowledge of history. The result was that the Soviet Union acquired borders with Hungary and Czechoslovakia, whereas the latter lost its pre-war border with Romania, and Hungary lost its 1939-44 border with Poland. In the case of the restored Czechoslovak-Hungarian border, the expulsion of many Hungarians from Slovakia gave it more ethnographical validity than it had possessed before the November 1938 changes.

The agreement of the Czechoslovak government to the transfer of Transcarpathia was first announced by the Prime Minister, Zdenek Fierlinger, on May 15, 1945. He said on that occasion: "The population of Sub-Carpatho Ukraine are Ukrainians speaking the language of the peasants of the Poltava and Kharkov regions [of the Ukrainian SSR]. They have now formed their own autonomous government, which expressed the desire to join the Soviet Union but in the meantime still recognizes the authority of our government. Ivan Petruscak, of the former Czechoslovak State Council in London, is now in Uzhgorod as representative of the Czechoslovak Minister of the Interior. He maintains contact with us and acts in complete harmony with both the Czechoslovak government and the Carpatho-Ukrainian National Council. President Benes and our government wish to settle the question of Sub-Carpatho Ukraine with Moscow in the most friendly atmosphere, taking into consideration the true wishes expressed by the local population".

Following the Prime Minister's statement it was confirmed on May 21, 1945, that an autonomous Transcarpathian government had been formed under the premiership of Ivan Turjanica, including Ukrainian, Russian and Jewish representatives. Fierlinger then led a Czechoslovak delegation to Moscow, where on June 29, 1945, he signed a treaty with the Soviet Foreign Minister, V. M. Molotov, specifying that "the Transcarpathian Ukraine, according to the Czechoslovak constitution called Sub-Carpathian Russia, which on the basis of the Treaty of St Germain of Sept. 10, 1919, became an autonomous unit within the Czechoslovak Republic, is reunited, in accordance with the desire of its inhabitants and on the basis of friendly agreement between the contracting parties, with the ancient mother country, the Ukraine, and incorporated in the Ukrainian SSR". The treaty also stipulated that the frontier between Czechoslovakia and the Soviet Union should be that existing between Transcarpathia and Slovakia on Sept. 29, 1938, subject to any modifications decided by a joint demarcation commission of the two countries.

The bilateral Czechoslovak-Soviet treaty on Transcarpathia was ratified in November 1945 and entered into force in January 1946. Its terms secured Western endorsement in the February 1947 peace treaty with Hungary, whose other change to Hungary's pre-1938 borders concerned the so-called "Bratislava bridgehead". This was a small area of a few square miles on the south bank of the Danube opposite the Slovak capital which Hungary was compelled to cede to Czechoslovakia for strategic reasons. In the interwar period the Danube itself had formed the border at Bratislava, so that Hungarian territory had formed a wedge between Austrian and Czechoslovak territory, enabling Hungary to exert pressure on Bratislava. The transfer of the south bank area meant that the main Budapest to Vienna highway now passed through Czechoslovak territory south of Bratislava. In accordance with the treaty provision, the three villages of Oroszvar, Horvathjarfalu and Dunaesun, with a combined population of 3,146, were formally transferred from Hungarian to Czechoslovak administration and sovereignty on Oct. 15, 1947.

Re-emergence of Transcarpathia Issue on Demise of USSR

Through more than four decades of Communist rule in Eastern Europe, territorial issues rarely surfaced in relations between the fraternal states of the Soviet bloc. In the case of Transcarpathia, its transfer to the Ukrainian SSR appeared to be immutable and was not raised even at such time of crisis in Czechoslovak-Soviet relations as the 1968 Prague Spring and its forcible suppression by Soviet-led forces (which included a Hungarian contingent). Moreover, the Communist regimes of Czechoslovakia, Hungary and the Soviet Union not only maintained a network of friendship treaties with each other but also all signed the 1975 Helsinki Final Act of the Conference on Security and Co-operation in Europe (CSCE), with its enjoinder about the inviolability of existing borders. However, the rapid post-1989 collapse of Communist rule in the Soviet satellite countries and the disintegration of the Soviet Union itself in 1991 had the effect of reviving various East European territorial issues which had been regarded as long dead. One such issue was Transcarpathia.

Before the abortive coup by Soviet hardliners in August 1991, growing strains in Czechoslovak-Ukrainian relations were mainly related to the contrast between Czechoslovakia's rapid achievement of multiparty democracy (in 1990) and the conservatism of the Communist establishment in Kiev. Although the Ukrainian Supreme Soviet declared the republic's sovereignty on July 16, 1990, Ukraine's new President, Leonid Kravchuk, took a cautious line on calls elsewhere for radical reform of Soviet structures and in consequence came under increasing pressure from the *Rukh* nationalist opposition. In Transcarpathia, popular unrest appeared to be manifested in part in a growing desire to emigrate to Czechoslovakia—a phenom-

enon which had an underlying territorial implication that was not lost on observers.

In January 1991 there were unconfirmed reports of armed clashes on the Transcarpathian border involving Ukrainians trying to cross into Czechoslovakia, to which the Czechoslovak Foreign Minister, Jiri Dienstbier, reacted by announcing a reinforcement of the border guard. Although he denied reports that Czechoslovakia was planning to build fences along the 50-mile frontier with Ukraine, he greatly upset the Ukrainian regime by claiming publicly that "120,000 people over the border in Carpatho-Ruthenia have signed a petition demanding to come to Czechoslovakia". In Kiev, such claims were dismissed as being without foundation and as indicating a desire to reopen territorial questions that had been resolved in 1945.

Following the collapse of the Moscow coup attempt, Ukraine's move to establish full independence led to further strains in relations with Czechoslovakia over Transcarpathia. In a referendum in Ukraine on Dec. 1, 1991, there was a 90 per cent vote in support of independence on a turnout officially given as 84 per cent. However, the Moscow newspaper *Pravda* published a report in early December to the effect that 60 per cent of the inhabitants of Transcarpathia supported the idea of reunion with Czechoslovakia. The same article also carried a statement by Dienstbier that "if the people of Transcarpathia show an interest in this issue and express their wish in a democratic manner, the problem can be discussed with the leaders of the Transcarpathian region and Ukraine". Predictably, these quoted remarks elicited a broadside of criticism from Ukrainian sources, which claimed that the voting in Transcarpathia had shown a clear majority in support of Ukraine's independence within its existing borders. These sources asserted that "certain forces" were trying hamper the process of Ukrainian independence and pointed out that Czechoslovakia had signed the 1975 Final Act of the CSCE which "resolutely rejects any revision of the post-war frontiers of Europe".

In a further development, a Sub-Carpathian Republican Party held its inaugural congress in Mukachevo in March 1992 and declared itself in favour of the creation of an autonomous "Transcarpathian Rus'" republic. The congress was attended by the leader of the right-wing Czechoslovak Republican Party, who said that Transcarpathia could best achieve autonomy via a restoration of the pre-1938 border. He also criticized President Vaclav Havel for not being prepared to take a firm line on the question of Transcarpathia.

Creation of the Slovak Republic and the Ruthene (Rusyn) Question

Any sentiments that the inhabitants of Transcarpathia might have had regarding the relative democracy and prosperity of pre-World War II Czechoslovakia, became irrelevant with the "velvet divorce" between Czechs and Slovaks in 1993 when independent Czech and Slovak Republics were created. The newly independent Slovak state was not in a position either to attract inhabitants of Ukrainian Transcarpathia or to challenge the territorial integrity of Ukraine, while Prague lost any interest in Transcarpathia. The main challenges for the Slovak government were an active half a million Hungarian minority and the initial difficulty of setting up a viable national economy. Indeed, the influx of illegal migrants from the East (not only Ukrainian traditional seasonal workers but immigrants from as far as South-East Asia) as well as organized crime associated with the trafficking of people and drugs, forced the Slovak and Czech authorities to strengthen their Eastern borders and introduce a visa regime with Ukraine.

The Ruthene (Rusyn) political cause was losing ground despite the fact that Bratislava recognized de facto the Rusyns as a separate people from Ukrainians. As Transcarpathia could no longer join the now defunct Czechoslovakia, the Society of Sub-Carpathian Rusyns in Ukrainian Zakarpattia (Transcarpathia) set up a "provisional government" of Ruthenia in May 1993 that appealed to the UN and foreign governments for recognition of Transcarpathia's independence. This appeal was supported by the Sub-Carpathian Republican Party with demands on the international community to recognize Rusyns as a distinct people and Transcarpathia as an independent and neutral state. Neither appeal met with an international response.

The initial years of Slovak independence were marked by self-assertion of the Slovak state, nationalism and increased hostility towards the Hungarian and Roma minorities and even the use of the Hungarian language in education and public life. The Hungarian population in Slovakia fell by 8% between 1991 and 2001, mostly due to emigration. The Ruthene (Rusyn) minority increased in the same period by 41%, from 17,000 to 24,000, while the Ukrainian minority declined 15% and was down to 11,000 in 2001.

Although the Slovak census of 2001 showed many fewer than the 120,000 Rusyns that some of the Rusyn activists claimed, such an increase suggests that this minority might have been somewhat favoured by the Slovak authorities over other groups. While ethnically the same, Ruthenes of Ukrainian nationality decreased by 15%—the increase of Ruthenes of Rusyn nationality by 41% cannot be explained by demographic factors and reflected a political struggle. Many cultural establishments belonging previously to the Ruthenes/Ukrainians united by the Union of Rusyns-Ukrainians in Slovakia (ZRUS) were handed over to the irredentist Ruthenian societies united by the Rusyn Renaissance (RO). These organizations compete with each other in efforts to persuade Rusyns/Ukrainians of their national identity and in attempts to win government support.

The Rusyn language, previously considered officially a dialect of Ukrainian, was codified as a separate literary language in 1995 and since 1997-98 some elementary schools in towns and villages teach in the Rusyn language in addition to Slovak. Rusyns also secured their own newspaper, magazine and radio pro-

grammes. Reassertion of the Rusyn heritage in place of what was regarded for decades as a Rusyn-Ukrainian one, left Ukrainian and Rusyn communities in Slovakia bitterly divided, especially when it came to the division of cultural and church property. Rusyns of non-Ukrainian orientation naturally looked for support to Bratislava and the Slovaks to Moscow, which provided a new political division between them and the Kyiv-oriented Ukrainian Rusyn minority.

The Moscow-centrism of Slovak nationalism, however, slowly decreased as Slovakia sought to join NATO and the European Union, thus undermining even further any chance of Ruthenian political mobilization in Slovakia. With Ukraine also looking westward for "Euro-Atlantic integration", relations between Kyiv and Bratislava were warming gradually. The bilateral Ukrainian-Slovak Committee for National Minorities, Education and Cultural Affairs that has met regularly since February 1995 has included since 1998 also representatives of the Union of Rusyns-Ukrainians in Slovakia and its Slovak counterpart from Ukraine (Slovak Matica), excluding from the Slovak-Ukrainian state dialogue on minorities those irredentist Ruthenian societies united by the Rusyn Renaissance (RO). Some 5,000 ethnic Slovaks living in Zakarpattia received a form of citizenship extended to them by the Slovak government in 1998.

The Ruthene (Rusyn) and Hungarian Questions in the Ukrainian Zakarpattia (Transcarpathia)

The Rusyn question in Zakarpattia (Transcarpathia) is regarded by Kyiv as a political project aimed at challenging Ukrainian territorial integrity and one supported by foreign political forces. Ever since the incorporation of Zakarpattia into the Ukrainian SSR, Kiev/Kyiv has considered Rusyns as part of the Ukrainian people, especially because the definition of who is Rusyn remains unclear and occasionally includes other ethnic groups such as Lemkos and Hutsuls that do not generally claim to be separate peoples from the Ukrainians. For centuries the name of "Ruthenes", in different variations, was used as one of the many self-given names by people living in Ukraine, who gradually shifted to the general self-designation of "Ukrainians" with the formation of the modern Ukrainian nation in the 19th and 20th centuries. In view of this, any movement to establish a Ruthenian identity as opposed to the overarching Ukrainian one is naturally perceived by Kyiv as a political project of an alternative nation-building.

Political activists of the Ruthene movement in Zakarpattia reject the classification of Rusyns as an "ethnographic" group of Ukrainians as an expression of Ukrainian cultural imperialism. They often refer to the resolution issued by the Ukrainian State Committee for Nationalities and Emigration of Oct. 7, 1996, that asked local authorities in Zakarpattia to "implement a preventive style of enlightenment work with the leadership and activists of the movement for 'political rusynism', aimed at prevention of...political structures with boldly stated separatist orientation". Ukrainian legislation does not allow political parties based on a separatist cause and hence the Society of Sub-Carpathian Ruthenes was not registered and its "provisional government" was not recognized and was later disbanded.

Although a referendum conducted in 1991 showed strong support among inhabitants of Zakarpattia for autonomy and self-government there was little political mobilization for an independent Ruthenian state. Though some Ruthenian political activists claimed there were as many as 650,000 Rusyns in Zakarpattia, most of the residents of Ruthenian origin did not insist on being Rusyn as opposed to Ukrainian. The Ukrainian census of 2001 did not list Rusyn nationality as such but counted 1,010,100 Ukrainians living in Zakarpattia, which is 80 per cent of the population. However, those respondents who insisted on being listed as Rusyns amounted only to 10,100—i.e. less than 1% of the total of 1,254,600.

With little or no Rusyn political mobilization in Transcarpathia, the main concern for the Ukrainian government was to eliminate possible political support from abroad for "Rusyn separatism". After reaching a mutual understanding with the Slovak government, Kyiv had to re-negotiate with Moscow, where some political forces in the Russian parliament openly exploited the "Rusyn card" to blackmail Ukraine. The former chairman of the Russian State Duma Committee on CIS Affairs, Konstantin Zatulin, announced in January 1995 that Russia had plans to undermine Ukrainian independence, including a plan for "an independent state on a Rusyn ethnic basis within the borders of the contemporary Transcarpathian region of Ukraine, with full support of such a state". Perhaps only the election of a more pro-Russian President, Leonid Kuchma, in 1994 prevented the Russian government from open support of Rusyn irredentism. In any case, the Rusyn card was not played openly by the Kremlin since Ukraine joined the CIS air-defence treaty and rented to Russia the vital former Soviet early warning radar station based in Mukachevo (Transcarpathia).

The Hungarian minority in the Ukrainian Zakarpattia is by far the biggest and most organized group and also lives in a fairly concentrated area. According to the last Soviet census over 150,000 Hungarians lived in Zakarpattia and the Ukrainian census of 2001 showed almost the same figure. The Hungarian cultural association has been active since February 1989 and, although not permitted to register as a political party, effectively serves this function with its members being elected as "independents" rather than on a party list. When Ukraine voted in favour of independence in December 1991, 81 per cent of Beregovo *rayon* (district), where Hungarians constitute 63 per cent of the population, voted also for Beregovo to become a "Hungarian national district" with a degree of self-government. Although this demand has not been satisfied, Ukraine has provided a broad range of opportunities for the cultural develop-ment of the Hungarian minority in Zakarpattia and self-government that was attested by the State Treaty of 1993 with Hungary.

Budapest was one of the first capitals to recognize independent Ukraine. Kyiv in return provided its Hungarian minority with the chance not only of having their education in the Hungarian language, but also to use Central European time and display Hungarian national flags and symbols in Beregovo and Chop alongside the Ukrainian. The Uzhgorod State University features a Hungarian studies department, and Hungarians may take entrance exams in their mother tongue. A Hungarian Teacher Training College in Beregovo founded as a private school in 1993 was accredited by the Ukrainian Ministry of Education in 1996. A Hungarian branch of the Nyiredyhaza Pedagogical Institute was opened later in Beregovo with the full support of the Ukrainian authorities.

Until 1999 the only divisive issue for Hungarians and the Ukrainian authorities in Zakarpattia was that of permission to erect a monument on the border of Zakarpattia and Lviv oblast to mark the millennium of Hungarian settlement in the region. This Kyiv viewed as inappropriate. More radical claims by some Hungarian activists to demand national autonomy were not supported by the representatives of the Council of Europe, who stressed in autumn 1998 during their visit to Zakarpattia that national autonomy is warrantable only if national self-preservation is not supported by regional administration, which was clearly not the case. The Hungarian consul in Uzhgorod also was careful at the time not to encourage the local Hungarian political elite to antagonise the Ukrainian establishment in the region.

In 2001 the Hungarian government extended to the Ukrainian Hungarians a form of Hungarian citizenship. It granted ethnic Hungarians the right to work for three months legally in Hungary, as well as social and health care rights, free university education, training courses and travel allowances. Although this step was criticised by Romania and Slovakia, both with sizeable Hungarian minorities, Kyiv accepted it without reservations.

Regional Co-operation and Future Prospects for Transcarpathia

One of the factors for successful interregional co-operation among countries bordering on Transcarpathia was the Carpathian Euroregion, established in February 1993. The idea, initiated by the Visegrad Triangle (Hungary, Czechoslovakia and Poland), was supported by Ukraine as a form of European integration. The Carpathian Euroregion was modelled on the Swiss-French-German Euroregion in Basel, but apart from economic co-operation was regarded from the beginning as a tool to avoid a potential "Yugoslav scenario". Although it is difficult to establish its achievement in the economic development of the region, it has certainly helped in inter-governmental coordination and solving minority issues.

Regional co-operation between Ukraine, Hungary

and Slovakia was successful in establishing a united system of water management and monitoring when the Regional Water Centre was opened in Uzhgorod in March 2000. The region has a common problem of regular flooding. Ukraine and Hungary also established a joint military battalion "Tisza" ("Tysa") that apart from peacekeeping functions could provide help in time of natural disasters. Slovakia later attached its own unit to that international military formation.

With all countries of the region aspiring to join the EU and NATO, the issue of Transcarpathia is not likely to become contentious. All parties are interested in economic, social and political integration. With the mediation and support of the Council of Europe, EU and NATO, and evidence of economic recovery, Transcarpathia may become a successful example of how EU and NATO expansion can help solve national/regional conflicts and minority issues. However, should Ukraine fail to uphold its course towards "Euro-Atlantic" integration and reorient into the Russian orbit of CIS, the Eurasian Economic Union, the Single Economic Space or similar initiatives, the historical contradictions of Transcarpathian ethnic minorities gravitating towards their kindred states may resurface.

Olexander Hryb

4.19 Yugoslavia's Successor States

Since the end of the Cold War there has been a striking change in the nature of territorial disputes in the western part of the Balkans. Earlier the parties to unresolved territorial issues were socialist Yugoslavia and its neighbouring states, in both East and West. Since the collapse of communism and the Yugoslav federation, the external borders of its former republics have been uncontested, including those borders that are not well established historically. Instead territorial disputes broke out between its successor states. At the time when other former socialist states in Eastern Europe worked hard to join the European Union, the former Yugoslav republics and emerging rebel statelets fought brutal wars over territory. Since then the conflicts have largely subsided. At present no significant political actors in the region openly support the use of force to settle potentially unresolved territorial issues and no state has a formal claim to the territory of its neighbours. Continuing political instability in the region suggests, however, that territorial disputes have not been fully resolved and that at least some of these may be revived in the future.

The common origins of all potentially unresolved disputes lay in the process of formation of Yugoslavia's successor states. The mix of the transformation of inter-republican borders into international frontiers and denial of rights and autonomy to non-dominant groups in emerging states became a hotbed for irredentist and secessionist claims in the region.

Map 51 on page 518 illustrates this section.

Uti Possidetis, National Self-Determination and Territorial
Disputes after Yugoslavia

In 1992 the former internal, administrative boundaries between Yugoslav republics were recognized as international borders on the principle of *uti possidetis*. The principle, which arose out of decolonization in former Spanish Latin America and former European Africa and South-East Asia, asserts that new states shall inherit the existing colonial administrative borders. *Uti possidetis* was resurrected at the end of the Cold War, during the disintegration of the former Soviet Union, Yugoslavia and Czechoslovakia, to reduce the likelihood of violent conflicts over territory between their successor states by providing the only clear outcome in such situations. Without the elevation in significance of existing internal boundaries into interstate frontiers, it was believed, irredentist claims by neighbours and secessionist attempts by national minorities from within emerging states would lead to armed conflicts. While the application of this principle provided for an orderly transition after the disintegration of Czechoslovakia and, to a considerable extent, the Soviet Union, it triggered large-scale violent conflicts between and within the successor states of Yugoslavia.

Yugoslavia was a multi-national state. The state's multi-national character did not find expression in its political institutions between its creation in 1918, under the name of the Kingdom of the Serbs, Croats and Slovenes, and the collapse of the interwar state in 1941. In line with attempts to create a Yugoslav nation through the integration of Serbs, Croats, Slovenes and other, smaller groups, the internal state structure largely ignored former historical and cultural boundaries. At first it consisted of 33 regions, which were later reallocated into nine provinces whose borders largely followed physical lines. The lack of collective rights and territorial autonomy for national groups remained one of the main sources of political instability throughout the interwar period and of the rapid dissolution of the state during the invasion of the Axis powers in April 1941. Likewise, the Second World War in Yugoslavia meant not only foreign military occupation, but also violent conflict between groups who identified with different nations.

The appeal of the Communist Party, which led a highly successful war of liberation, was partly based on the multi-national composition of the partisan fighting force and determination to rebuild a multi-national state by providing collective rights and territorial autonomy to various national groups. After the war the party introduced national federalism as the Soviet solution to the organization of a multi-national state and divided Yugoslavia into six republics—Bosnia-Herzegovina, Croatia, Macedonia, Montenegro, Serbia and Slovenia. In contrast to the interwar internal administrative structure, the borders corresponded more closely to pre-1918 historical boundaries. In some cases, the borders were altered to take into account the pattern of ethnic settlement.

According to the Yugoslav constitution, republics were designated as homelands of the constituent nations—Serbs, Croats, Slovenes, Macedonians, Montenegrins and, later, Muslims—and were granted the right to self-determination. Nevertheless, republics were largely multi-national in composition. The boundaries between federal units did not overlap with those of a federal society, except largely in Slovenia, and some of those who identified with one constituent nation lived outside "their" republic, such as Serbs in Croatia. Bosnia-Herzegovina was constituted as the republic of three constituent nations—Muslims, Serbs and Croats—because it lacked a majority national group. In some areas of this and other republics the population was fully intermixed. To guarantee the same level of rights to members of the constituent nations regardless of whether they resided in "their" republic or not, especially to those living in nationally highly intermixed areas, the Yugoslav constitution granted the right to self-determination not only to republics, but also to the constituent nations.

The constitution also distinguished between the constituent nations and national minorities. National minorities enjoyed extensive collective rights and, due to their numbers and territorial concentration, Albanians in Kosovo and Hungarians in Vojvodina lived in autonomous units within Serbia. National minorities were denied the right to self-determination, as they were considered to have national homelands in other states. In short, the Yugoslav Communists developed a complex web of rights and territorial autonomy to accommodate conflicting claims to self-determination of republics and constituent nations and to guarantee the protection of collective identity and interests of all national groups.

The application of the principle of *uti possidetis* in this institutional context effectively recognized the right to self-determination solely of dominant nations in the states emerging in the dissolution of Yugoslavia. The international recognition of the sovereignty and borders of the Yugoslav republics was not accompanied by their institutional restructuring to accommodate the demands of members of the constituent nations who lived outside "their" republic. As a result, they were denied the constitutional right of the same order. Their demotion to national minority status was in some of the emerging states compounded with the denial of basic rights. *Uti possidetis* also denied the right to self-determination to large national minorities that were territorially concentrated, such as Albanians. The elevation in significance of the internal borders into international frontiers left non-dominant national groups stranded in emerging national states, which

were much less likely to provide the same level of rights and autonomy than socialist Yugoslavia.

Nevertheless, *uti possidetis* did not face a serious alternative at the time because any peaceful alteration of the existing inter-republican boundaries required mutual agreement of the parties involved, which was unlikely to be reached in the context of spiralling political conflict. The international recognition of the sovereignty and borders of the former Yugoslav republics, however, could have been conditioned by their institutional restructuring to provide extensive collective rights for national groups and territorial autonomy in areas in which they constituted a majority. Since this did not happen, affected groups faced the choice between accepting the loss of rights, emigrating from emerging states or fighting them to alter the existing borders, either through non-violent resistance or by taking arms. Those who lived in territorially concentrated areas and received support from their ethnic brethren in neighbouring republics, such as Serbs in Croatia and Serbs and Croats in Bosnia-Herzegovina, chose the latter option. A relatively limited matter of the internal institutional restructuring of the former Yugoslav republics thus rapidly transformed into potentially explosive irredentist claims. Unsurprisingly, those inter-republican borders that have remained uncontested, such as the Slovenian-Croatian border and that between Serbia and Macedonia, did not feature large territorially concentrated national groups on the "wrong" side of the border.

Croatia and Serb-Croat Relations

In 1992 the European Community recognized the sovereignty and borders of newly independent Croatia. The borders of Croatia that had previously served as the international frontiers of the Yugoslav federation have since been uncontested. The greater part of the border with Hungary along the river Drava is historically well established, as it follows the northern border of the historical province of Slavonia, a part of the Habsburg polity until the creation of the Kingdom of the Serbs, Croats and Slovenes. Medjumurje and Baranja, small areas north of the Drava, were then also incorporated into the new state. Following the territorial extension of Yugoslavia after the Second World War, Croatia gained parts of the eastern Adriatic coast and most of the Dalmatian islands previously under Italian control. The former inter-republican, now international, border between Croatia and Slovenia, which largely dates from the Middle Ages, is also considered as unproblematic.

By contrast, violent conflicts involving the remaining inter-republican borders of Croatia tested the very viability of the newly independent state. The recognition of Croatia as a sovereign state in its existing administrative borders was bound to be controversial. Unlike Slovenia, Croatia was a multi-national state, both in terms of its demographic composition and constitutional provisions. According to the 1991 census, Orthodox Serbs constituted over 12 per cent of the population of this predominantly Catholic Yugoslav republic. While the majority of Serbs resided in large cities and towns across Croatia, some lived in areas in which they constituted a majority, plurality or significant minority. The roots of the territorial concentration of Serbs in Croatia were largely in the Military Frontier, a historical region closely surrounding the western and northern Bosnian border that enjoyed a special constitutional position in the Habsburg empire until its abolition in 1881. The region had long served as a defensive zone against Ottoman expansion and was largely settled by Serbs who had fled the Ottoman empire and were granted land in exchange for military service. Despite the attempts of the Ustashe regime in the Nazi-sponsored Croatian state during the Second World War to exterminate, convert or expel the Serb population, significant numbers remained in this region. The migrations during the industrialization and urbanization drive after the Second World War then triggered the move of many Serbs to cities and towns across Croatia.

Like other groups who identified with a dominant nation of another republic, Serbs in Croatia enjoyed a protected status as a part of a constituent nation under the umbrella of the Yugoslav constitution. Serbs were also explicitly designated as one of the two constituent nations in the Croatian constitution to acknowledge their suffering under the regime of the Croatian Fascists and the disproportionate role they played in the war of liberation. Following the escalation of political conflict among the Communist leaders of the Yugoslav republics in the late 1980s, the 1990 election victory of the nationalist Croatian Democratic Union (HDZ), headed by the former partisan general and nationalist historian Franjo Tudjman, brought a major change to the position of Serbs in Croatia. The new government initiated a campaign of Croatian symbolism, renaming the streets named after notable Serbs or anti-Fascists, or Serbian towns. Many Serbs lost government or public sector jobs and there were even attempts to rehabilitate the Second World War Nazi-sponsored Croatian state. The Serbs were denied the status of the constituent nation they had enjoyed under the Croatian constitution and were demoted to the status of a national minority. Simultaneously, the new government aimed to sever the links between Croatia and Yugoslavia, either through the reconstitution of Yugoslavia into a loose confederation or the creation of an independent state. For many Serbs, who saw the common Yugoslav state and the constituent nation status as the main guarantees against the replay of the Second World War, these were ominous signs.

At the time when the nationalist revival in Serbia under Slobodan Milosevic brought Serbs in Croatia and elsewhere a new sense of national identity, they looked for protection to the institutions of the Yugoslav federation and, increasingly, to Serbia. Disappointed with the vacillating leadership of the refurbished Croatian Communist Party, overwhelmingly supported by Serbs in the 1990 election, the Serb leaders set up a union of 13 municipalities with a Serbian majority or plurality, in northern Dalmatia, eastern Lika, the Kordun, Banija and western Slavonia. The Serb leaders responded to each step of the Croatian government aimed at cutting ties with Yugoslavia by severing links with Croatia, such as by creating the autonomous political unit of Krajina. Parallel with the Croatian referendum of independence, they organized a referendum to preserve the Krajina within Yugoslavia. Following increasingly frequent incidents between the Croatian police and paramilitary forces and self-organized Serbs, a full-blown war broke out in the summer of 1991. The (disproportionately Serbian) Yugoslav National Army (JNA), which initially acted as an internal peacekeeping force between the two emerging armies, gradually lost the character of a multi-national force and sided with Serbs.

Taking advantage of their powerful ally, the Serb units swiftly consolidated their grip over the Krajina and took control over eastern Slavonia, where they accounted for less then a half of the population. They exploited the fact that the area was adjacent to the border with Serbia, which provided ample assistance to the armed rebellion. This border had been established after the Second World War by the internal boundary commission mainly on the pattern of ethnic settlement. The claim of Serbs to this territory was therefore weaker than that of the Krajina Serbs. In late 1991 and early 1992 agreement was reached, with the help of UN mediators, for the arrival of a substantial peacekeeping force that would provide protection for territories under Serb control pending negotiations on their final status. The hostilities ended with the ceasefire and deployment of the UN peacekeepers, and there were few incidents in the next three years.

In May and August 1995 offensives, the Croatian army, quietly backed by the United States, broke out into the territories and regained control. Fearing reprisals, the vast majority of Serbs evacuated the area during the offensives or were expelled by the Croatian regular and paramilitary forces. Over 200,000 refugees left for Serbia or Serb-controlled areas of Bosnia-Herzegovina. Subsequently, an agreement over eastern Slavonia was reached according to which the area would gradually return to the control of the Croatian authorities. While only radical groups among Serbs in Serbia or elsewhere now put forward a claim to Krajina and eastern Slavonia, a series of obstacles to the return of Serb refugees to Croatia and the return of their property set by the Croatian government have kept the dispute alive.

In the south, following the 1992 withdrawal of the Yugoslav Army from the area surrounding Dubrovnik, a small UN mission was set up to monitor the demilitarization of the Prevlaka, a minor peninsula on the Croatian side of the border with Montenegro. In essence, the strategic position of the Prevlaka at the entrance to the Gulf of Kotor was seen as a potential threat to the common state of Serbia and Montenegro. The UN mission ended in December 2002, when the two sides reached an agreement to establish a provisional cross-border regime and keep the surrounding area demilitarized as well as to solve the outstanding issues in subsequent bilateral negotiations.

Bosnia-Herzegovina: Between Three Nations and Two Neighbours

The present borders of Bosnia-Herzegovina are based on the historical boundaries of the Ottoman empire in the region. The border with Croatia mostly dates back to the late seventeenth century and the delimitation with the Habsburg polity. In the east, along the Drina river, lies the border with Serbia, which was established in the first half of the nineteenth century, except for a small part touching Montenegro that was determined in 1913. The greater part of the border with Montenegro dates from the Congress of Berlin in 1878. These borders survived the administrative division of the Kingdom of the Serbs, Croats and Slovenes into 33 regions in 1922, although the territory of Bosnia-Herzegovina was divided into six regions. The internal structure introduced seven years later, however, did not take the historical boundaries into account; neither did its amendment in 1939, with the creation of the Croatian highly autonomous political unit. After the dismantling of the Croatian Nazi-sponsored state in 1945, which had absorbed Bosnia-Herzegovina, the Communists restored its historical borders.

The problems of Bosnia-Herzegovina since the early 1990s are not the result of border disputes with neighbouring states, but have arisen from challenges to its viability as a multi-national state in the light of the breakdown of the similarly structured, multi-national Yugoslavia. The general trend in the region has been a disintegration of multi-national polities and the formation of national states. Bosnia-Herzegovina lacked a majority national group. Unlike other Yugoslav republics, it had three constituent nations, Muslims, Serbs and Croats, comprising respectively 43.7, 31.4 and 17.3 per cent of the population in 1991. In addition to parts of the territory of this Yugoslav republic in which one nation constituted a clear majority, over a quarter of the territory had a highly inter-mixed population. Unsurprisingly, the results of the first multi-party elections in 1990, held at the time of spiralling political conflict between leaders of the Yugoslav republics, resembled the population census. Nationalist parties, namely the Party of Democratic Action (SDA), supported by Muslims, the Serbian Democratic Party (SDS) and the Croatian Democratic Union (HDZ), overwhelmed their rivals and subsequently formed a coalition government.

The impending collapse of multi-national Yugoslavia, amidst the clamour of demands for national self-determination and progressively more violent conflict in neighbouring Croatia, triggered parallel developments in Yugoslavia's most multi-national republic. Muslims ("Bosniaks"), who associated their identity and interests very closely with Bosnia-Herzegovina, aimed at the international recognition of its sovereignty and borders. Serbs and Croats, fearing Muslim domination, increasingly looked for protection to Serbia and Croatia, which they were quick to provide. International recognition of Bosnia-Herzegovina was preceded by an independence referendum, held on Feb. 29-March 1, 1992, in which over 98% of the votes on a 63% turnout—comprising overwhelmingly Muslims and Croats—supported independence. Serbs boycotted the referendum and responded by cutting ties of the areas in which they constituted a majority or plurality with the republic. The international recognition of the sovereignty and borders of Bosnia-Herzegovina in April 1992 signalled the beginning of a civil war.

Relying on the military potential of the by now exclusively Serb Yugoslav Army, the Bosnian Serb forces embarked upon the construction of their own statelet, swiftly taking over around 70 per cent of the territory of Bosnia-Herzegovina and often expelling non-Serbs. The alliance with Muslims at the referendum turned out to be little more than a tactical move of the Bosnian Croat leadership and they subsequently turned their efforts to creating their own statelet, with the thinly disguised support of Tudjman in Croatia, engaging in expulsions of non-Croats. The Bosnian Muslims found themselves squeezed mainly into territory around Sarajevo and central Bosnia. During the war, which lasted until 1995, more than half of the population was displaced, either outside or inside Bosnia-Herzegovina and the conflict led to the establishment of the International Criminal Tribunal for the former Yugoslavia by the UN under Security Council Resolution 827 of May 25, 1993.

Hostilities ended with the signing of the Dayton Peace Accords, initialled on Nov. 21, 1995, and signed the following month by Bosnian President Alija Izetbegovic, Tudjman and Milosevic (also representing the Bosnian Serbs). This agreement, achieved under US auspices, followed a shift in the military balance as a result of the August 1995 Croat offensive that won control of Krajina (with the resultant flight or expulsion of the entire Serb population) and NATO air strikes, also commenced in August, on Serb positions around Sarajevo. While confirming international recognition of the sovereignty and borders of Bosnia-Herzegovina, the Dayton agreement established a highly decentralized state. Bosnia-Herzegovina now consists of two, highly autonomous political units of roughly equal size—Republika Srpska, or the Serb Republic, and the Federation of Bosnia-Herzegovina. The boundary line between the two entities is based upon the line of military confrontation, except for some adjustments, mainly in the Sarajevo area. Effectively, however, the state is divided into three parts, each overwhelmingly dominated by one of the three major national groups, which is partly the consequence of the pre-war pattern of ethnic settlement and partly that of expulsions. In contrast to the unitary structure of Republika Srpska in the north and east, the Federation of Bosnia-Herzegovina is divided into ten highly autonomous cantons. Five cantons have mainly Bosniak populations, including those around Sarajevo,

Tuzla, Zenica, Bihac and Gorazde, while three, in western Herzegovina and a part of north-east Bosnia, are predominantly Croat. The remaining two cantons, in central Bosnia and the Neretva valley, are multi-national but are themselves divided into predominantly Bosniak and Croat areas.

After the signing of the agreement, tens of thousands of military and civilian officials from a number of international organizations descended on Bosnia-Herzegovina to engage in state- and democracy-building. This was an uphill struggle from the beginning having in mind the changes in the demographic map and the attitude of Serbs and Croats towards the new state. The vast majority of those who identify with the latter two groups, comprising around half of the state's population and controlling over two-thirds of its territory, hardly acknowledge the legitimacy of Bosnia-Herzegovina as a sovereign state, and the ethnically-based political parties have strengthened their position further in recent elections. Nonetheless, a total partition of Bosnia-Herzegovina is considered unlikely in the near future due to the opposition of the major powers and because of the new priorities of the democratic governments of Croatia and Serbia after the death of Tudjman in December 1999 and the fall of Milosevic in October 2000. Considerable powers over developments in Bosnia-Herzegovina remain in the hands of the internationally-appointed Office of the High Representative and there is a continuing international military presence.

The territorial issue left unresolved in the Dayton agreement was that of the north-east municipality of Brcko. Brcko, lying in the narrowest part of the corridor that connects western and eastern parts of Republika Srpska, has a strategic importance for Serbs; for the Bosniak-Croat federation, it is an important rail and river link with access to Croatia. The majority of the population before the war was Bosniak and Croat. By the ruling of an arbitration team, headed by an American lawyer, in March 1999, Brcko became a neutral, self-governing district.

Serbia and Montenegro

At the time when other republics declared independence and achieved international recognition, Serbia and Montenegro, the largest and smallest republics of socialist Yugoslavia, stayed together in the common state. The Federal Republic of Yugoslavia (FRY) was created in April 1992 following declarations of independence by all the other republics, i.e. Slovenia, Croatia, Bosnia-Herzegovina and Macedonia. Since the UN Security Council denied the FRY a status of the sole successor to the Socialist Federal Republic of Yugoslavia, the newly created state remained unrecognized—somewhat paradoxically, as only Serbia and Montenegro had enjoyed international recognition as sovereign states before the creation of the Kingdom of the Serbs, Croats and Slovenes. The FRY was ultimately admitted to the United Nations after the fall of Milosevic and the election of the new democratic gov-

ernment in Belgrade in 2000. Just over two years later the state was redefined and renamed Serbia and Montenegro, with the help of EU mediators.

The borders of Serbia and Montenegro that were previously the international frontiers of Yugoslavia are now regarded as unproblematic. The border with Hungary in the north, demarcated in 1919 and confirmed by the Treaty of Trianon in 1920, was initially under threat of revision due to Hungarian irredentist claims to the area lying south of the border in which Hungarians constituted a majority or plurality population. Following the Hungarian occupation of this part of Yugoslav territory during the Second World War and the restoration of the boundary in 1945, the border had been regarded as unproblematic. Further east and south lies the border with Romania, established largely on the pattern of ethnic settlement after the First World War, which has been uncontested since. The border with Bulgaria in the east mostly dates from the 19th century and the gradual extension of the territory of Serbia southwards. In the wake of the First World War Serbia gained from Bulgaria a small area with a dominant Bulgarian population. The border with Albania, in its Montenegrin section, was largely determined at the Congress of Berlin in 1878, while the part of the border touching Kosovo was for the most part established in 1913, after the Balkan Wars (1912-13) and the creation of Albania.

Serbia and Montenegro is an unusual federal polity, in which the larger republic comprises over 90 per cent of the population and resources. Nevertheless, Montenegro has enjoyed an important role in decision-making since 1992 due to constitutional arrangements that effectively secure power sharing, proportional or equal representation in government and minority veto. Regardless of the unusual composition and potentially dysfunctional constitutional arrangements, the state functioned normally so long as the ruling, refurbished Communists in the two republics shared views on the main issues of policy. After 1997 and a major row between Milosevic and Montenegrin leaders, the dominant political party in the smaller republic gradually withdrew from routine operation of the federal institutions, supported by the United States and European Union, which aimed at weakening Milosevic. While formally remaining a part of the FRY, Montenegro in reality functioned as an independent state, introducing the Deutschemark as its currency and creating paramilitary forces.

Although Montenegrin leaders justified these developments by the fear of Milosevic, the fall of Serbia's strongman from power in October 2000 only served to intensify their independence campaign. However, the European Union insisted on the preservation of the state and new Serbian leaders pointed to sharp divisions in Montenegro over the issue. As only about half of the voters seemed ready to support independence, the Montenegrin leaders scaled back their ambitious plans and reached a compromise with Serbia over the redefinition of the common state. While the new arrangement created weak central institutions and a highly decentralized polity, in some aspects resembling a confederation, the Montenegrin leadership has had to take full responsibility for the functioning of its institutions. The Constitutional Charter introduced a three-year trial period at the end of which either republic may conduct an independence referendum and, if successful, leave the union. It remains to be seen whether the freshly redefined Serbia and Montenegro can survive the trial period. If not, there is unlikely to be conflict over their common border, which has been uncontested since the demarcation of most of its course after the Balkan Wars.

The complex character of the federal state after the Second World War was to some extent replicated in the constitutional structure of Serbia by the establishment of the autonomous provinces of Vojvodina and Kosovo within its borders. The autonomous province of Vojvodina was created largely on the historical principle and consists of Serbs (now a majority of 65%), Hungarians (now a minority of 14.28%), and a number of small national groups (for details on Kosovo see the subsection below). After constitutional reforms in the late 1960s and early 1970s, Vojvodina and Kosovo, earlier little more than Serbia's administrative regions, were granted a status similar to that of republics. Following nearly a decade of political struggles over constitutional reform, the autonomy of the provinces was scaled down in 1989-90. At the time of writing a debate over the new Serbian constitution is in full swing, but Vojvodina is likely to retain its autonomy.

Kosovo: Between Serbia and Independence

The events surrounding the Kosovo problem over the past decade have confirmed the worst fears about its explosive nature and destabilizing potential. The Serb-Albanian conflict, which involved some of the most serious human rights abuses committed throughout former Yugoslavia in the 1990s, triggered NATO military intervention in March 1999 and, by way of spill over, threatened the stability of the wider region. The future status of Kosovo is the only territorial dispute in the former Yugoslavia that is still officially unresolved. While UN Security Council Resolution 1244 of June 10, 1999—adopted in the wake of the NATO intervention and Yugoslavia's agreement on June 9 to the withdrawal of its forces from the province—reaffirmed the sovereignty and territorial integrity of the FRY (now Serbia and Montenegro), Kosovo has effectively become an international protectorate after the withdrawal of the Yugoslav Army and arrival of thousands of NATO soldiers and UN civilian staff. The resolution provided a framework for both an interim administration for Kosovo and a political process leading to a final settlement, and calls for "substantial autonomy and meaningful self-administration" for the province.

The roots of the Kosovo problem lie in the mutually exclusive claims of Serbs and Albanians to this territory. The historical claim of the Serbs to Kosovo is based on the incorporation of the region into a medieval Serbian polity in the 12th century, of which it subsequently became a political and cultural centre. Kosovo has been an important marker of national identity for the Serbs. For one thing, the territory houses the most important historic and religious monuments of the Serbs; for another, the Kosovo legend, partly based on a medieval battle with the Ottomans, has long served as a source of resistance to foreign rule and as a tool for preservation of the Serb identity. The historical claim is boosted with the fact that the territory of Kosovo is a part of an internationally recognised state of Serbia and Montenegro and that Serbs, though a minority, remain in Kosovo. For Albanians, who consider themselves as having arrived in the area before the Slavs, Kosovo is the site of the creation of their national movement in the 19th century. More importantly, their claim to Kosovo is based on the contemporary predominantly Albanian population of the region.

The main sources of ethnic antagonism were the nationalist aspirations of Albanians and Serbs in the second half of the nineteenth century. The Ottoman empire was slowly losing ground in the Balkans against expanding new states, including Serbia, which strove to unite their ethnic brethren. Albanians simultaneously reacted against the irredentist plans and demanded administrative and cultural autonomy within the empire. Partly encouraged by the increasing attitude of religious intolerance of Ottoman officials and partly exploiting weak administrative controls in the region, the local Albanian warlords continually terrorized the minority Orthodox population, thus accelerating the emigration of Serbs. After the victory of the Balkan states over the Ottomans in the First Balkan War in 1912, however, Kosovo became part of a Serbian state.

Serbia, and subsequently the interwar Yugoslavia, reversed the policy of discrimination. Nationalization and land reform, designed to destroy the inherited feudal and tribal social order, were at least in part directed against Albanians, as were the attempts at discrimination in education and colonization of the sparsely populated region. During the Second World War, a large part of Kosovo was annexed by Italian-controlled Albania. Thousands of Serbs were killed and tens of thousands expelled while those aiming to challenge the occupiers, including the Communists, faced the hostility of most Kosovo Albanians. In 1944, the Communist-led partisans restored Kosovo to Yugoslav control.

Aware of the hostility of the Albanians towards the new regime, the Communist leadership sought their co-operation. The new government granted a degree of autonomy to Kosovo within Serbia, encouraged cultural emancipation of Albanians and financed development of the backward region. Some administrative restrictions on the rights of Kosovo Albanians remained for security reasons since Albania strongly supported the Soviet bloc against Yugoslavia in 1948, and Serbs remained disproportionately represented in the regional government and security apparatus. In the 1967-74 constitutional reforms Kosovo was granted a status similar to that of the federal units. The rapidly changing national composition of elites and employees in the huge public sector, largely a consequence of the strategy of positive discrimination in favour of the Albanians, coupled with decision making based on majority voting, swiftly turned the trend towards emancipation of the majority community into domination over other national groups, mainly Serbs.

Since the 1960s the national configuration of the region has changed rapidly. While the proportion of Albanians and Serbs (including Montenegrins) in the population remained relatively stable in the period between 1948 and 1961 (68.5%-67.2% and 27.5%, respectively), in the following two decades the proportion of the former increased from 67.2% to 77.4% and that of the latter decreased from 27.5% to 14.9% and fell further to a little more than 10% by the late 1980s. Critical to the changes were demographic factors, the most important of which was a much higher rate of population growth of Albanians than that of Serbs. The decreasing absolute numbers of Serbs and their shrinking territorial dispersion were caused by emigration, principally but not exclusively under pressure based on ethnicity. The popular protests of Kosovo Serbs between 1985 and 1988 triggered a shift in the policy of the Serbian government. Constitutional changes carried out by the regime of Slobodan Milosevic in 1989-90 greatly diminished the autonomy of Kosovo, and the regime responded to Albanian resistance to the implementation of these changes through a range of decrees that amounted to a gross violation of their rights.

The transformation of inter-republican borders into international frontiers left Kosovo and its Albanian community firmly within Serbia and the FRY. Initial disorientation within the Albanian population following the crackdown by the regime soon gave way to mass-based non-violent resistance, which aimed at the secession of Kosovo by way of the creation of parallel institutions. The events surrounding the end of hostilities in Croatia and Bosnia-Herzegovina and the 1995 Dayton agreement came as a surprise to many Albanians in Kosovo, who expected that a final settlement for the province would be included in the package. Since the denial of rights of this community remained largely ignored, it is hardly surprising that many Albanians started questioning the effectiveness of non-violence.

The outbreak of the Kosovo Liberation Army (KLA) insurgency in 1998 triggered a harsh response from the Serbian government, which in turn provoked NATO air strikes in March 1999. The 11-week bombing campaign ended with UN Security Council Resolution 1244 and the arrival of 40,000 NATO soldiers and UN civilian staff. Several hundred thousand Kosovo Albanians, who had been expelled during the war by Yugoslav paramilitaries and regular forces, returned to Kosovo while the majority of Serbs had to leave the province in a new wave of ethnic expulsions. Since the arrival of the international military and civilian staff violence against the remaining Serbs has produced a continuous exodus of Serbs, to Serbia proper and the remaining Serb enclaves within Kosovo, so that there are virtually no Serbs left in Albanian-dominated areas; those Serbs remaining are in isolated enclaves, except for those in and around northern Mitrovica in northern Kosovo, which is adjacent to Serbia proper.

The initial period of consolidation of the interim administration was followed by the creation of provisional self-governing institutions and sustained attempts to build an integrated multi-ethnic society. Talks on a final settlement for Kosovo are still some way off due to the UN "standards before status" policy, which states that major improvements must first be made in a number of areas, including the functioning of democratic institutions, rule of law, freedom of movement for members of non-Albanian communities, minority returns and dialogue with Belgrade. Similarly, the general lawlessness, unchecked organized crime, large-scale corruption, discrimination and violence against non-Albanian groups make the international recognition of Kosovo as a sovereign state, which is the preference of most Albanians, unlikely in the near future. Any change of international borders involving Yugoslavia's successor states is likely to be opposed by major powers for the foreseeable future for fear of again destabilizing the region.

The partition of Kosovo is another option that has its advocates. It would involve the creation of a new state through the secession of the larger part of Kosovo, in which Albanians constitute a majority, and the accession of the smaller part of the province with a Serb majority to Serbia proper. This option has been more popular among Serbs than Albanians, as most members of the latter community believe that the province must remain undivided. Radical Serb nationalists reject partition because they want to see the whole of Kosovo fully integrated into Serbia. By contrast, moderate Serb nationalists, who want to limit the damage wrought to their cause by the 1999 war and its aftermath, and some liberals, who seek a solution to the conflict that would remove obstacles to democratization and economic development, accept partition. Some Albanians propose a swap of the predominantly Serb area in northern Kosovo for "eastern Kosovo"— i.e. three municipalities in southern Serbia with an Albanian majority. Like the secession of Kosovo, however, partition remains problematic because it might endanger regional stability through a demonstration effect. Not all parts of Kosovo in which Serbs constitute a majority are adjacent to Serbia proper, which would make partition unworkable barring the exchange of populations.

Macedonia: its Albanians and Neighbouring States

On the eve of the collapse of Yugoslavia Macedonia faced serious problems because it was at least potentially involved in territorial disputes with all of its neighbours. The borders of this former Yugoslav republic were for the most part determined after the

Balkan Wars in 1912-13 during the division of an area known as Macedonia, previously under Ottoman control, among Greece, Serbia and Bulgaria. The present territory of the state of Macedonia is basically the share that Serbia received in the process. Following occupation by Bulgaria during the First World War, Macedonia was incorporated into the Kingdom of Serbs, Croats and Slovenes. In the Second World War Bulgaria reoccupied Macedonia, but the area returned to Yugoslav sovereignty in 1945, elevated by the Communist Party to the status of republic and its dominant ethnic group to that of constituent nation. The sources of potential territorial disputes between Macedonia and its neighbours include historical claims—some of which go back to centuries prior to the Ottoman conquest, when polities regarded as the precursors of modern Greece, Serbia and Bulgaria successively controlled the area—and cultural claims, rooted in linguistic and ethnic resemblances between various populations in the region.

One such potential dispute is based on the Bulgarian claim that the division of Macedonia and the Communist attempt to create a Macedonian nation have isolated the population of this area from the core of the Bulgarian linguistic and ethnic family. As a result, Bulgarian recognition of the sovereignty and borders of Macedonia in 1992 was accompanied by a refusal to acknowledge the existence of a Macedonian nation.

The sources of any potential dispute with Macedonia's northern neighbour, Serbia and Montenegro, lie in the initial control of Serbia and interwar Yugoslavia over this territory and attempts at assimilation of its population. However, after decades of sustained effort by the Communist Party at building the Macedonian nation, the vast majority of Serbs accepted both the Macedonian nation and sovereignty and the borders of the new state. The border with Serbia, established in the wake of the Second World War, has been uncontested, which is reflected in the negotiated withdrawal of Macedonia from Yugoslavia and that of the Yugoslav Army from Macedonia in 1992, at the time when other parts of Yugoslavia were engulfed in violent conflicts.

The refusal of the Greek government to recognize the name and symbols of Macedonia after the collapse of Yugoslavia proved to be the most serious obstacle to its full international recognition as a sovereign state. Considering the name Macedonia to be a geographical expression that denotes only the northern province of present-day Greece, the Greeks have seen the potential recognition of Macedonia under this name as an implicit irredentist claim to a part of their territory. Despite the legal advice of the Arbitration Commission of the EC Conference on Yugoslavia in January 1992 that Macedonia met the conditions for international recognition, the European Community, followed by the United States, withheld recognition until the resolution of the dispute between Greece and Macedonia. While the new Macedonian constitution was swiftly amended to explicitly recognize the exist-

ing borders and deny any claims to the territory of neighbouring states, the Western European states granted recognition to the newly independent state only in 1993, when it was also admitted to the United Nations under the interim name of "the Former Yugoslav Republic of Macedonia". For several years landlocked Macedonia remained under the economic blockade of Greece, which at the time of the UN economic sanctions against the FRY brought the Macedonian economy to a standstill.

The main source of potentially serious disputes over parts of the territory of Macedonia, however, is internal, rather than external. Like most former Yugoslav republics, Macedonia is a multi-national state. The censuses of 1991 and 1994 revealed that there were around 65 per cent Orthodox Macedonians, just over 20 per cent of Muslim Albanians and a few small national groups. Many Albanians live in western Macedonia, adjacent to Albania and Kosovo, where they constitute a majority population. Throughout the 1990s the relations between two major national groups were regarded as cordial and Macedonia was hailed as an "oasis of peace" in conflict-ridden former Yugoslavia. A sudden eruption of violent conflict between rebel Albanian groups and Macedonian army and paramilitary forces in 2001 therefore came as a surprise to many.

Some Albanian demands for collective rights and power sharing had been accommodated after 1992 through an informal elite agreement that provided for the representation of a dominant Albanian party in government and through recognition of a limited set of cultural rights. After the 1998 election the uneasy coalition of the hard-line nationalist parties, the Internal Macedonian Revolutionary Organization (VMRO) and Democratic Party of Albanians, survived only due to a tacit arrangement that granted the Albanian party control over trafficking routes in western Macedonia in exchange for discretionary control over the state purse by the VMRO. Simultaneously, relations between Macedonians and Albanians on the ground were hardly idyllic. Much like Albanians and Serbs in Kosovo, the two major national groups in Macedonia did not live together but mainly beside each other. The arrival of over 300,000 Albanian refugees in Macedonia as a consequence of the 1999 Kosovo War imposed a great strain on the delicate balance between Macedonians and Albanians as did the informal recruitment of Albanian youth from western Macedonia by the Kosovo Liberation Army.

In 2001 Albanian guerrilla groups launched an insurgency in Albanian majority areas. The uprising lasted less than six months and resulted in few casualties in comparison with recent conflicts throughout former Yugoslavia, but shook the very foundations of the state. The hostilities ended with the signing of a Western-brokered peace accord, the Ohrid Framework Agreement. The agreement preserves the unitary structure of Macedonia but calls for its decentralization, proportional representation in government and the civil service and proportional allocation of public funds, provisions for power sharing and minority veto and extensive language rights for the Albanian community. The insurgency to some extent exploited the fact that the uncontested border between the FRY and Macedonia had not been determined in detail and therefore had not been tightly controlled. In response, the previously established bilateral border commission swiftly completed the task allowing the Presidents of the two states to sign an agreement about the course of the border. Elections held the following year brought a new coalition into power, namely moderate Social Democrats, a Macedonian party, and the Democratic Union for Integration, the successor of the main Albanian insurgency grouping.

It remains to be seen whether the Ohrid Framework Agreement can serve as the foundation for a viable multi-national state. Despite the inclusion of the rebel leadership into the government, another insurgent group, the Albanian National Army, emerged to take responsibility for various incidents in Macedonia, southern Serbia and Kosovo, with the aim of uniting all territories populated by Albanians. Moreover, Macedonian nationalist politicians, including the former Prime Minister Ljupco Georgievski, have already sounded out the mood of their compatriots on the issue of partition of Macedonia between the two major national groups. Earlier, influential Macedonian intellectuals had proposed an arrangement according to which Albanians from western Macedonia would be free to join Albania in exchange for a small area in Albania near Lake Prespa settled by ethnic Macedonians; the territorial settlement would also include the exchange of populations that found themselves on the "wrong" side of the border. The partition of Macedonia, however, is highly unlikely in the near future, not least because it has little support among Macedonians and is strongly opposed by major powers. In the long run the stability of Macedonia, like that of Bosnia-Herzegovina, will depend much on global and regional political developments and the potential spill over effects from neighbouring states.

Nebojsa Vladisavljevic

MIDDLE EAST

5.1 The Arab-Israeli Conflict

The long-standing and still unresolved conflict between Israel and the Arab world has two main territorial dimensions. At a fundamental level, many Arabs do not accept the existence of a Jewish state within any borders and assert that the Palestinian Arabs are the rightful heirs to predominant political authority in the former British mandated territory of Palestine. On another level, the outcome of the 1967 Arab-Israeli war—which left Israel in control of large tracts of territory beyond the de facto borders resulting from the 1948-49 war—brought Israel into direct territorial dispute with Egypt, Jordan and Syria, each of which demanded the return of their Israeli-occupied territories as well as a settlement of the basic Palestinian question.

In March 1979 an historic breakthrough was achieved with the signature of an Egyptian-Israeli peace treaty, the first between Israel and an Arab state. Under this treaty the whole of Sinai (but not the formerly Egyptian-controlled Gaza Strip) was restored to Egyptian rule over the following three years and relations between the two countries were normalized (see also Section 5.4). But Israel remained in deadlock with Jordan over its continued occupation of the West Bank and with Syria over its retention (and effective annexation in December 1981) of the Golan Heights. After December 1987 Israel was also confronted by widespread unrest among the Palestinian people in the West Bank, Gaza Strip and East Jerusalem (the intifada).

Following the 1991 Gulf War, a multilateral Middle East Peace Conference was convened by the USA and USSR in Madrid in October of that year. Over successive months two distinct negotiating processes began. The first was known as the Madrid track, although most talks took place in Washington DC. These talks were bilateral in nature, essentially between Israel and its neighbouring states—Jordan, Syria and Lebanon, respectively. Most international attention, however, focused on Israel's first bilateral talks with a Palestinian delegation. All four sub-tracks dealt inter alia with matters related to borders. The second major strand originating from Madrid was launched in Moscow in January 1992. This multilateral track concerned issues of regional and cross-border concern and issues of borders and territorial disputes featured less overtly than in the bilateral Madrid track.

Initial optimism gave way to disappointment as negotiations, held in several sessions in various cities, stalled over important details. As a rule, progress in the multilateral Moscow track was impeded by lack of progress in the bilateral Madrid track. Hence the enthusiasm that greeted the surprise announcement in August 1993 that the Israeli government and the Palestine Liberation Organization (PLO) were to sign a Declaration of Principles. Initial progress on ceding limited autonomy to Palestinians would, it was hoped, culminate in a full peace between the two parties. This apparent breakthrough was the fruit of secret talks held in Oslo, outside the formal Madrid track apparatus, between delegations representing the two parties. A series of agreements resulted from the initial signing ceremony in Washington DC, in September 1993. Oslo I, as the initial agreement was termed, was signed in 1994 and mandated Palestinian rule in Jericho and Gaza. It was followed by the more ambitious Israeli-Palestinian Interim Agreement, or Oslo II, in 1995. The Oslo process also reinvigorated negotiations between Israel and Jordan, which resulted in a full peace treaty between the two nations in 1994. Significant border disputes were resolved as a result. There were occasional signs of progress in Syrian-Israeli talks, primarily concerning ownership of the Golan Heights. However, to date no agreement has been struck. Similarly there was little progress on the Lebanese-Israeli front. Ultimately Israel chose to withdraw unilaterally from its security zone in southern Lebanon in May 2000; but certain border issues remain to be formally concluded.

Meanwhile, governmental changes in Israel and rejection by certain armed Palestinian factions slowed down the Oslo process itself. The USA promoted talks in June 2000, dubbed Camp David II, to resolve outstanding issues between Israel and the Palestinians, including a final dispensation of borders. Camp David II proved a failure, and within four months a new intifada broke out in the occupied territories, which was still simmering in early 2004. Nonetheless, both Israelis and Palestinians formally adopted a new Road Map for Peace in early 2003. If successful, it should have profound implications for decisions on the ultimate borders between Israel and a now mutually accepted future State of Palestine. There also appeared a number of unofficial plans to solve the long-running dispute between Israelis and Palestinians, most notably the so-called Geneva Accords, which also addressed crucial issues of border allocations.

Historical Background

Zionism, the movement promoting Jewish settlement of Palestine, takes its name from the hill in Jerusalem on which the ancient palace of King David, and later the Temple, were built. The Zionist case for the creation of a modern Jewish state in Palestine was based pre-eminently on the postulated historical connection between the Jews and the region in question; but the extent to which Palestine can be regarded as the historic homeland of the Jewish people is a subject of considerable dispute in which both sides have their distinguished supporters. Zionist historians contend that throughout most of the last 1,200 years of the pre-Christian era Jews constituted the main settled population of what in Roman times became known as Palestine, enjoying long periods of independence in states which included coastal cities and plains (notably under the reigns of Kings David and Solomon). In contrast, Arab historians maintain that the Jews were only one of many Semitic tribes which penetrated the region in ancient times and that Jewish states were relatively short-lived and never at any time extended to the coastal plains (which were inhabited by Philistines, from whom the name "Palestine" is itself derived). What is not in dispute is that Palestine came under effective Roman control in the first century BC; that in 70 AD the (Roman puppet) Jewish state of Judaea was overthrown by the Roman Emperor Titus, who captured Jerusalem, destroyed the Jewish Temple and took many Jews as captives to Rome; and that after repeated rebellions by the Jews against their Roman overlords, Jerusalem was finally razed to the ground in 135 AD and the leaders of the surviving Jewish community in Palestine were expelled. In Zionist and mainstream Jewish historiography, this is presented as the origin of the diaspora of the Jewish people, who in the succeeding centuries became scattered throughout Europe and eventually the world in a complex sequence of large and small migrations from one country to another. Against this, some Jewish historians argue that the various Jewish communities of the world originate primarily from absorption of non-Jews through conversion, intermarriage and even conquest.

In the Arab view, the dispersion of the Jews in the second century AD marked the effective termination of the Jewish connection with Palestine; moreover, according to this viewpoint, the conquest of Jerusalem by Muslim Arabs in 636 AD and the subsequent conversion and Arabization of the Semitic inhabitants of Palestine irreversibly established the identity of the region as part of the Arab world. Against this, Zionists point out that the dispersed Jewish people never abandoned the hope—however metaphysically expressed through the centuries—of returning to the land from which their forbears had been expelled. They also cite historical evidence showing that Jews continued to live in Palestine in sizeable numbers after 135 AD—although the continuity and extent of this presence after the fifth century AD is again a matter of dispute. Certainly in the crusading era of the 11th, 12th and 13th centuries there were significant Jewish communities in several cities of the "Holy Land" and Jews are known to have fought alongside Arabs against the warriors of the cross in full awareness that, in victory, the Christian crusaders made no distinction in their treatment of Muslim and Jew.

Historians are also agreed that the Muslim reconquest of Palestine in 1291 and the relative tolerance shown thereafter to Jews stimulated a degree of Jewish migration to Palestine from European countries where anti-Jewish persecution was becoming endemic. The expulsion of the Jews from Spain in 1492 accentuated this migratory trend, which continued following the establishment of Ottoman Turkish rule over Palestine from 1517. In the early 16th century there were, for example, an estimated 10,000 Jews living in the region of Safed (north-west of the Sea of Galilee and one of the four "holy cities" of Judaism together with Jerusalem, Hebron and Tiberias) and the importance of Safed as a centre of Jewish learning is indicated by the fact that a Hebrew printing press set up there in 1563 was the first press of any language to be installed in the Asian continent. Nevertheless, as a proportion of the total population, the Jews of Palestine remained a tiny minority and formed only one non-Muslim community among the several which enjoyed a relatively tranquil existence under Turkish rule.

In 1880 there were still only 25,000 Jews in Palestine, as against an Arab population which has been variously estimated at between 150,000 and 450,000. However, over the next three decades there occurred a dramatic upsurge of Jewish immigration. Between 1880 and the outbreak of World War I in 1914 Jewish settlement of Palestine almost quadrupled to some 90,000, as over 60,000 Jews entered the country, mainly from Russia and Poland. These new arrivals were of a different type and with a different motivation than previous Jewish migrants. Inspired by the Zionist ideals of Theodor Herzl (1860-1904) and others, the new wave of Jews came as farmers and artisans, seeking to build a new Jewish society based on the land and thus to recreate a national identity for the dispersed Jewish people. As propounded by Herzl in his celebrated pamphlet *Der Judenstaat*, published in 1896, and by the first Zionist congress in 1897, Zionism called for the preservation of the Jewish people by national reunion, which was to be achieved by "establishing for the Jewish people a publicly and legally assured home in Palestine". Such ideas became particularly influential in the ghettos and Jewish villages of Eastern Europe, where millions of Jews were living in poverty and facing a mounting threat from the growth of virulent anti-semitism in the host societies.

Although efforts by Zionist leaders to secure the agreement of the Turkish Sultan to the establishment of a Jewish homeland in Palestine proved inconclusive, the piecemeal purchase of land for Jewish settlers proceeded apace, the finance being provided by wealthy Jews of Western Europe (and later the United States). Such purchases were made mainly from Arab landlords (although land owned by Europeans and Turks was also sold to Jews) and often at inflated prices, considering that the tracts acquired were usually desert wasteland or malarial marsh, which were then drained, irrigated and cultivated by Jewish settlers. In 1909 the first entirely Jewish town in modern Palestine was founded on the sandhills north of the Arab Mediterranean port of Jaffa and given the name Tel-Aviv.

Although earlier Jewish immigrants and settlers had been accepted by the Arab population, the waves of explicitly Zionist immigration starting in 1881 met with a hostile response. Major Arab opposition developed only after World War I and the establishment of the British mandate, but as early as 1882 Palestinian peasants were being evicted in order to make way for Jewish settlers, and the Turkish authorities responded to Arab disquiet at Zionist plans by seeking to prevent the entry of Jews through the Mediterranean ports. The first Arab attacks on Jewish agricultural settlements took place in the mid-1880s. In 1891 leaders of the Arab community in Jerusalem sent a petition to Constantinople demanding the prohibition of Jewish immigration and land purchase, and in the early years of the 20th century anti-Zionist newspapers and societies were founded by Arabs in several cities of Palestine and also further afield. The scene was thus set for the fundamental confrontation of national aspirations which is still with us today.

The Balfour Declaration, Arab-British Undertakings and the Sykes-Picot Agreement

Having failed to make any real progress with the Ottoman authorities, Zionist leaders concentrated their efforts on persuading European governments of the validity and desirability of establishing a Jewish homeland in Palestine. An important consideration in this respect was the realization that the days of the Ottoman empire were numbered. Ultimately, the decision of Turkey to ally itself with the central powers in World War I created a constellation of forces in which this aim became a practical proposition, given that Britain and France saw themselves as the joint post-Ottoman powers in the Middle East. In what was widely construed as a move to ensure international Jewish support for the allied war effort, the then British Foreign Secretary, Arthur Balfour, sent a letter to Lord Rothschild (a prominent British Jewish Zionist) dated Nov. 2, 1917, and worded as follows:

"I have much pleasure in conveying to you, on behalf of His Majesty's government, the following declaration of sympathy with Jewish Zionist aspirations which has been submitted to, and approved by, the Cabinet. His Majesty's government view with favour the establishment in Palestine of a national home for the Jewish people, and will use their best endeavours to facilitate the achievement of this object, it being clearly understood that nothing shall be done which may prejudice the civil and religious rights of existing non-Jewish communities in Palestine, or the rights and political status enjoyed by Jews in any other country. I should be grateful if you would bring this declaration to the knowledge of the Zionist Federation".

The Balfour Declaration, which was approved by the French government and published immediately (and subsequently reflected in the Palestine mandate given to Britain by the League of Nations—see below), is seen by Jews as a cornerstone of the legitimacy of the eventual establishment of a Jewish state in Palestine. But it was rejected then and subsequently by the Palestinian Arabs as a colonialist instrument which, by failing to take account of the wishes of the majority population, contravened the fundamental principle on which the allied powers claimed to be fighting the 1914-18 war, namely the right of self-determination of peoples. This was, indeed, recognized by Balfour himself, who wrote in a memorandum in August 1919: "in Palestine we do not propose even to go through the form of consulting the wishes of the present inhabitants of the country, though the American Commission has been going through the form of asking what they are. The four great powers are committed to Zionism and Zionism, be it right or wrong, good or bad, is rooted in age-long tradition, in present needs, in future hopes, of far profounder import than the desires and prejudices of the 700,000 Arabs who now inhabit that ancient land".

It is also claimed by the Arab side that the Balfour Declaration and other allied agreements of the time ran counter to undertakings given by Britain to its wartime Arab allies that Britain would support the independence of the Arabs once the Turks had been defeated. In the latter respect the crucial documents are the correspondence in 1915-16 between Sir Henry McMahon (the British high commissioner in Cairo) and Sharif Hussain of Mecca (head of the Hashemite dynasty of Hejaz and the father of the subsequent King of Iraq, Faisal) and also the agreement between Sir Mark Sykes of Britain and Georges Picot of France concluded in May 1916. Over both these sets of undertakings considerable controversy still flourishes.

In his first note to Sir Henry McMahon (dated July 14, 1915), Sharif Hussain requested that Britain should recognize "the independence of the Arab countries" bounded (i) in the north by a line drawn from Mersin (on the northern Mediterranean coast of Turkey) running north-east through Adana to the 37°N parallel and then eastward to the Persian frontier, (ii) on the east by the Persian frontier down to the Persian Gulf, (iii) on the south by the Indian Ocean (with the exception of Aden) and (iv) on the west "by the Red Sea and the Mediterranean Sea back to Mersin". In his reply (dated Oct. 24, 1915), Sir Henry declared on behalf of the British government that "the districts of Mersin and Alexandretta [the present Turkish port of Iskenderun], and portions of Syria lying to the west of the districts of Damascus, Homs, Hama and Aleppo, cannot be said to be purely Arab, and must on that account be excepted from the proposed delimitation". (For an account of the later dispute between Syria and Turkey over the Sanjak of Alexandretta, now the Turkish province of Hatay, see Section 5.11.) Subject to the proviso that nothing should be done to harm the interests of France, Great Britain was "prepared to recognize and uphold the independence of the Arabs in all the regions lying within the frontiers proposed by the Sharif of Mecca". Subsequent exchanges between the two correspondents achieved no clear reconciliation of these contrasting delimitations of the future independent Arab state or states, although Britain achieved its object of securing active Arab assistance in the war against Turkey.

At no point in the Hussain-McMahon correspondence was mention made of Palestine or of the Ottoman administrative unit centred on Jerusalem. Since this area was not one of potential French interest, the Arabs took the view that it had been promised as part of the territory of Arab independence, whereas the British government consistently maintained that McMahon's reservations were intended to exclude the whole of the eastern Mediterranean littoral from Turkey down to Sinai. At the centre of this particular controversy is the meaning in the correspondence of the term "district", for which both men used the Arabic word *wilaya*, and whether the term was intended to refer precisely or at all to the *vilayet*, the largest unit of Ottoman local administration. In support of the British interpretation, it is pointed out that the Ottoman *vilayet* containing the city of Damascus stretched right down to the Gulf of Aqaba in the south, on the strength of which it is argued that all the territory to the west of this *vilayet* was excluded in the undertakings given to the Arabs. On the other hand, Arab analysts have pointed out that the "districts" referred to in the correspondence did not correspond with Ottoman vilayets (either in intention or in fact) and signified only geographical areas relating to the cities mentioned. On this basis, they contend that the littoral excluded from future Arab rule was that to the north of the approximate level of the city of Damascus, and also note that even this exclusion was contested by Sharif Hussain in the course of the correspondence.

The uncertainties arising from the Hussain-McMahon correspondence will probably never be resolved to universal satisfaction. There is, however, general agreement that Britain's promises to the Arabs in 1915-16 were in conflict in certain important respects with the terms of the almost concurrent Sykes-Picot agreement under which Britain and France (with Russian concurrence) drew up a plan for the post-war dismemberment of the Ottoman empire in the Middle East. This secret agreement (which was eventually disclosed to the Arabs by the Russian Bolsheviks) divided the region into French and British spheres of influence to the north and south respectively of a line roughly corresponding with the present-day Syrian border with Jordan and Iraq (except in the east, where the Mosul region was included in the French sphere). It further specified that in these spheres the two powers would recognize and uphold "an independent Arab state or a confederation of Arab states...under the suzerainty of an Arab chief". But it also stipulated (i) that France and Britain would be allowed to establish "direct or indirect administration or control" in certain designated areas, France being allocated the eastern Mediterranean littoral north of a line just south of Safed, and Britain the Tigris-Euphrates basin (Mesopotamia); (ii) that Palestine from just south of Safed down to a line just south of Gaza (and bounded in the east by the Dead Sea and the Jordan river) would be under "an international administration, the form of which is to be decided upon after consultation with Russia, and subsequently in consultation with the other allies and the representatives of the Sharif of Mecca"; (iii) that within this international zone Britain would be "accorded" the ports of Haifa and Acre and a surrounding enclave of territory.

Establishment of British Mandate in Palestine

In the event, the post-1918 disposition of former Ottoman territories showed significant variations from both the Hussain-McMahon undertakings (such as they were) and the Sykes-Picot agreement, although it was closer to the latter than to the former. After protracted and complex negotiations accompanied by confrontations and some actual military conflict between various of the interested parties, the shape of the post-war map of the Near East was not finally determined until the signature of the Treaty of Lausanne on July 24, 1923. But already, at the San Remo conference of April 1920, Britain and France had reached agreement on the establishment of British and French mandates (as opposed to spheres of influence) over territories which extended well into the area previously designated as part of an independent Arab entity.

As eventually agreed by the new League of Nations (established in January 1920), France obtained a mandate over an area almost corresponding with the present territory of Lebanon and Syria—i.e. extending substantially to the east of the littoral designated for "direct or indirect" French rule by Sykes-Picot. Moreover, the two British mandates encompassed not only Palestine (defined as including Transjordan and the Negev desert down to the port of Eilat on the Gulf of Aqaba) but also the whole of present-day Iraq. As for the rest of the Arabian peninsula to the south, this area was recognized as independent Arab territory, but through a system of protectorates, treaties and financial subsidies it became effectively a British sphere of influence.

The mandatory instrument for Palestine differed significantly from the others in that it committed Britain to securing the establishment of a Jewish national home in the mandated territory (and also in that it contained no specific provision for the constitutional development of the inhabitants towards eventual independence). As approved by the Council of the League of Nations in 1922, the instrument said in its preamble that the principal allied powers had agreed "that the mandatory should be responsible for putting into effect the declaration originally made on Nov. 2, 1917, by the government of His Britannic Majesty, and adopted by the said powers, in favour of the establishment in Palestine of a national home for the Jewish people, it being clearly understood that nothing should be done which might prejudice the civil and religious rights of existing non-Jewish communities in Palestine, or the rights and political status enjoyed by Jews in any other country". The preamble then recorded that "recognition has thereby been given to the historical connection of the Jewish people with Palestine and to the grounds for reconstituting their national home in that country".

In its detailed provisions the instrument specified inter alia that the mandatory "shall be responsible for placing the country under such political, administrative and economic conditions as will secure the establishment of the Jewish national home…and the development of self-governing institutions, and also for safeguarding the civil and religious rights of all the inhabitants of Palestine, irrespective of race and religion" (Article 2); that "an appropriate Jewish Agency shall be recognized as a public body for the purpose of advising and co-operating with the Administration of Palestine in such economic, social and other matters as may affect the establishment of the Jewish national home and the interests of the Jewish population in Palestine, and subject always to the control of the Administration, to assist and take part in the development of the country" (Article 4); that "the Administration of Palestine, while ensuring that the rights and position of other sections of the population are not prejudiced, shall facilitate Jewish immigration under suitable conditions and shall encourage, in co-operation with the Jewish Agency referred to in Article 4, close settlement by Jews on the land, including state lands and waste lands not required for public purposes" (Article 6); and that a nationality law would be framed for Palestine "so as to facilitate the acquisition of Palestine citizenship by Jews who take up their permanent residence in Palestine" (Article 7). (The Jewish Agency referred to in the mandatory instrument was eventually set up in 1929 and recognized by Britain for the purposes of the instrument.)

The importance of the mandate's terms from a Zionist point of view was that for the first time the commitment to a Jewish national home in Palestine was enshrined within an internationally recognized instrument which superseded the ambiguous and conflicting undertakings entered into previously. For the Arabs, however, the system of British and French mandates represented a betrayal of wartime promises of independence, the Palestine mandate in particular being regarded as a device to facilitate the settlement of Arab territory by an alien people, i.e. the Jews. The regime imposed was therefore seen not only as a denial of the right of self-determination proclaimed by the allies during the war but also as a direct contravention of Article 22 of the Covenant of the League of Nations, which in its rationale of the mandatory system specifically excluded "certain communities formerly belonging to the Turkish empire" from those former colonies and territories defined as "inhabited by peoples not yet able to stand by themselves under the strenuous conditions of the modern world" and therefore as appropriate for the mandatory system.

Then and subsequently Zionists pointed out that the area allotted for the establishment of a Jewish national home amounted to only a tiny fraction of the Middle East territories taken from the Turks; mandated Palestine west of the River Jordan, it was noted, covered less than 11,000 square miles (28,500 sq km),

whereas the total area of Arab lands (including mandated territories) stretched to nearly 1,200,000 square miles (3,000,000 sq km). But this argument was not appreciated by Palestinian Arabs in the actual circumstances of the Palestine mandate, where a post-war new wave of Jewish immigration, mainly from Russia and Poland, was seen as a direct threat to their way of life and political future. In the latter context, the Arabs laid particular stress on the "European" character of the Jewish immigrants who were arriving under the impulse of Zionism. They maintained that the Ashkenazic Jews of Europe were not Semitic like the Sephardic Jews of the Arab world and had no historical connection with Palestine because they were descended from the Khazar tribes of south-east Russia who embraced Judaism in the eighth century and later spread through eastern and central Europe. (Certain more recent genetic studies suggest conversely that the Arabs and Jews, including even Ashkenazim, who currently reside west of the River Jordan share remarkably similar DNA structures, suggesting possible common racial origins in the past.)

Attacks by Arabs on Jewish settlements, previously sporadic, began in earnest in early 1920, when it became clear that British pledges on independence were to be ignored in favour of encouragement of the Zionist project. At the same time, the Jews reorganized their own previously ad hoc defence force (*Ha-Shomer*, The Guardian), establishing the *Haganah* (Defence) under the direct control of the Zionist parties. Later in the year the first Arab riots under British rule led to a decision by the British authorities in September (but later rescinded) that Jewish immigration to Palestine should not exceed 16,500 people a year; moreover, from 1921 the area east of the River Jordan was entirely closed to Jewish settlement (whereas Zionist plans of the period envisaged a Jewish national home stretching well across the Jordan, and also into southern Lebanon and south-west Syria). The latter measure was taken in the context of the separation of Transjordan from the rest of the mandate and its establishment as an autonomous state under Emir Abdullah, this process leading to semi-independence in 1928 (although Transjordan did not become fully independent until 1946). The other British mandated territory became the fully independent state of Iraq in 1932 under King Faisal, whereas Lebanon and Syria remained under French mandate until being declared independent by the Free French during World War II, at the end of which they both became founder members of the United Nations. From 1923 mandated Syria included the Golan Heights, which were ceded by Britain in that year after originally forming part of the Palestine mandate.

Development of Arab-Jewish Conflict under British Mandate

The disturbances of 1920 set the pattern of the history of the British mandate west of the Jordan, where opposing Arab and Jewish national aims not only precluded any agreement on the constitutional future of Palestine but also generated increasingly violent inter-communal conflict. As early as May 1921 the British authorities reacted to Arab rioting by placing a temporary ban on all Jewish immigration, and although this was quickly lifted, the official British position became that immigration should not exceed "the economic capacity of Palestine to absorb new immigrants". In September 1921 Britain promulgated a constitution for Palestine, but it was never implemented because the Arabs were unwilling to accept its provisions relating to the Jewish national home. Thereafter, all attempts to secure Arab-Jewish political co-operation foundered against the rocks of diametrically opposed and increasingly entrenched Jewish and Arab positions.

By 1928 the Jewish population of Palestine had reached 150,000 (and the Arab population 600,000), and increasing Arab disquiet resulted in the first large-scale Arab-Jewish clashes in 1928-29. Further serious violence occurred in 1933, when Hitler's advent to power in Germany heralded a sharp increase in Jewish immigration from Europe, taking the Jewish population of Palestine to 400,000 by 1936 and close to 30 per cent of the total. In that year the Palestinian peasantry rose in a massive revolt, initially against Zionist settlement but increasingly against British rule. Arab National Committees were set up around the country and a Higher Committee was established in Jerusalem to co-ordinate the protests; a conference on May 7 decided to call a general strike and tax boycott. The strike lasted six months; the armed revolt lasted almost three years, during much of which the National Committees were in effective control of all of the Arab parts of Palestine. The rising was eventually put down by massive British armed response—it has been estimated that, at the peak of the rising, half of the British Army was tied up in the Middle East.

In April 1936, the British government set up a royal commission under Lord Peel, charged with recommending means of implementing the Palestine mandate in such a manner as to lessen Jewish-Arab friction. In its report, published on July 7, 1937, and accepted by the British government, the Peel Commission found that "the hope of harmony between the races has proved untenable" and recommended the partition of Palestine into separate Arab and Jewish states, with Britain retaining a permanent mandate over two enclaves containing Jerusalem, Bethlehem and Nazareth. Particular features of the Peel proposals were that the Arab state would consist of Transjordan (still legally part of the mandate) united with that part of Palestine allotted to the Arabs and that there should be treaty provision for the exchange of land holdings and population between the two new states.

The Peel Commission report summarized the advantages of partition to the Arabs as follows: "(i) They obtain their national independence and can co-operate on an equal footing with the Arabs of the neighbouring countries in the cause of Arab unity and progress. (ii) They are finally delivered from the fear of being 'swamped' by the Jews and from the possibil-

ity of ultimate subjection to Jewish rule. (iii) In particular, the final limitation of the Jewish national home within a fixed frontier and the enactment of a new mandate for the protection of the Holy Places, solemnly guaranteed by the League of Nations, removes all anxiety lest the Holy Places should ever come under Jewish control. (iv) As a set-off to the loss of territory the Arabs regard as theirs, the Arab state will receive a subvention from the Jewish state [and] also, in view of the backwardness of Transjordan, obtain a grant of £2,000,000 from the British Treasury [as well as a further grant for the conversion of uncultivable land in the Arab state into productive use]".

As regards the Jews, the advantages of the Peel proposals were also summarized: "(i) Partition secures the establishment of the Jewish national home and relieves it from the possibility of its being subjected in the future to Arab rule. (ii) Partition enables the Jews in the fullest sense to call their national home their own: for it converts it into a Jewish state. Its citizens will be able to admit as many Jews into it as they themselves believe can be absorbed. They will attain the primary objective of Zionism—a Jewish nation, planted in Palestine, giving its nationals the same status in the world as other nations give theirs. They will cease at last to live a 'minority life'".

Following a debate characterized by the Chairman of the Executive, David Ben-Gurion, as being "over which of two routes would lead quicker to the shared goal", the twentieth Zionist Congress passed an ambivalent motion in August 1937, describing the partition as "unacceptable", but authorizing the Executive to negotiate with the British authorities on British proposals for the establishment of a Jewish state. In September, an Arab Conference, with the participation of delegates from nearly all Arab states, including Palestine, unanimously rejected any partition. The Palestinian rising escalated, as did Jewish armed defence and counter-attack, which developed despite reiterations by the Jewish National Council (the representative body of Jews in mandated Palestine) of the need for continued restraint in the face of Arab provocation. Various alternative partition plans were put forward over the next two years—notably those of the Woodhead Commission of 1938—but none overcame the fundamental opposition of the Arabs to any legitimation of a Zionist political entity in the territory of Palestine.

As organized guerrilla warfare by both communities developed during 1938, the British government abandoned partition as a possible solution and in May 1939 published a White Paper asserting that it was not British policy that Palestine should become either a Jewish state or an Arab state; that an independent Palestinian state should be set up within 10 years; that meanwhile Jews and Arabs should be asked to take an increasing share in the country's administration; and that Jewish immigration into Palestine should be limited to 75,000 people over the next five years (after which such entry would require Arab consent). In pursuance of this new policy, the British government on

Feb. 28, 1940, published regulations banning further land purchases by Jews in about two-thirds of the territory of Palestine, restricting such purchases in most of the remaining third and leaving only the narrow coastal plain from Haifa southward to beyond Tel Aviv as a free zone for further acquisitions.

Like earlier blueprints for the future, the 1939 White Paper failed to obtain any positive response from either community. The Arabs rejected it as failing to meet their long-standing demand for the termination of the mandate and the creation of an independent Palestinian state based on majority rule. For the Jews it represented a betrayal by Britain of its commitment under the mandate to promote the establishment of a Jewish national home in Palestine. And, throughout the late 1930s, the increasingly perilous position of Jewish communities in Europe gave particular urgency to the Zionist demand that Palestine should be open to unrestricted Jewish immigration (especially since most countries of the world were either wholly or partially closed to Jewish refugees). By 1939 the Jewish population of Palestine had risen to 445,000 (about 30 per cent of the total), but whereas over 30,000 Jews entered the country in 1939 the British authorities allowed in only 10,000 in 1940, 4,500 in 1941 and 4,200 in 1942. In this situation the Zionists sought to step up illegal immigration, but the war conditions prevailing from 1939, combined with British counter-measures, seriously hampered such activities, at the very time when millions of Jews in Europe were being liquidated by the Nazis and denied entry to other states.

Termination of the British Mandate

The constitutional position of Palestine was frozen by the British government for the duration of World War II, during which civil strife between Arab and Jew remained largely in abeyance. But the end of the war in 1945 signaled a resurgence of the political and inter-communal struggle in Palestine in ever greater intensity than before, particularly since the cause of the Palestinian Arabs now took on concrete pan-Arab dimensions. In March 1945 the independent Arab states formed the Arab League, proclaiming their intention to support Palestinian Arab aspirations. It asserted that, while the League "sympathizes as deeply as anyone with the Jews for the horrors and sufferings they have endured in Europe", it nevertheless deemed it arbitrary and unjust "to wish to resolve the question of the Jews of Europe by another injustice [against] the Arabs of Palestine". On the Jewish side, the traumatic experience of Nazi persecution massively reinforced the Zionists' determination to secure a Jewish political entity in Palestine, to which end they obtained the active support of the United States.

Despite pressure from the US government for a relaxation of immigration restrictions, the British authorities maintained the 1939 White Paper policy, at a time when settlement in Palestine was the goal of tens of thousands of survivors of the European holocaust. The Jews responded by organizing large-scale illegal immigration and also by bringing in arms supplies (notably from the Soviet bloc countries) for use in the increasingly ferocious struggle with the Arabs, whose armed groups were now often supplemented by units from the surrounding Arab countries. British soldiers and policemen attempting to control the rapidly deteriorating situation were frequently the target of extremists of both sides. Eventually, after various new partition-type proposals had again failed to move the Arabs from their demand for a unitary Palestinian state based on majority rule, the British government decided in February 1947 to refer the Palestine question to the United Nations (as the successor to the League of Nations for the purposes of the mandate).

Following the British referral, a Special Committee on Palestine (UNSCOP) was established by the UN General Assembly in May 1947 and this committee subsequently submitted a majority recommendation that Palestine should be partitioned into Arab and Jewish states (three of the 11 members favouring a federal state and one abstaining). With some frontier adjustments, the UNSCOP recommendation was eventually adopted by the UN General Assembly in an historic vote on Nov. 29, 1947, in which the required two-thirds majority was surpassed with 33 states voting in favour, 13 against, 10 abstaining and one absent. Those in favour of partition (and thus in favour of the creation of a Jewish state) included the Soviet Union and its satellites (then anxious to assist the British retreat from empire) as well as most Western and Latin American nations. Those against were Afghanistan, Cuba, Egypt, Greece, India, Iraq, Lebanon, Pakistan, Persia (Iran), Saudi Arabia, Syria, Turkey and Yemen; those abstaining were Argentina, Chile, China, Colombia, El Salvador, Ethiopia, Great Britain, Honduras, Mexico and Yugoslavia; and the absent country was Thailand.

The UN partition plan (the territorial aspects of which are shown in Map 52 (i)) provided for (i) the creation of a Jewish state in three linking segments, made up of eastern Galilee in the north, the coastal plain from Haifa south to the Rehovoth area (except Jaffa) and most of the Negev desert in the south; (ii) the creation of an Arab state in three linking areas of western Galilee, central Palestine and the southern littoral extending inland along the Egyptian border into the western Negev, with Jaffa as a coastal Arab enclave; (iii) the establishment of Jerusalem and Bethlehem as an international zone to be administered by the United Nations; and (iv) the creation of an economic union between all three parts. The Jewish state was to comprise 54 per cent of the area of Palestine, although Jews formed less than a third of the total population. Indeed, even in the Jewish state, Arabs would form 50.5 per cent of the population, while Jews would form only 1.2 per cent of the population in the Arab state. In Jerusalem, Arabs would form 51.5 per cent of the population.

The General Assembly resolution specified inter alia that the British mandate should be terminated (and the withdrawal of British forces completed) as soon as possible and not later than Aug. 1, 1948; that the independent Arab and Jewish states and the special international regime for Jerusalem should come into existence two months after the British evacuation and not later than Oct. 1, 1948; and that "the period between the adoption by the General Assembly of its recommendation on the question of Palestine and the establishment of the independence of the Arab and Jewish states shall be a transitional period". The General Assembly also appointed a five-nation UN commission (Bolivia, Czechoslovakia, Denmark, Panama and the Philippines) which was to proceed to Palestine under the aegis of the UN Security Council to take over the country's administration when the British withdrew and then to transfer power to Arab and Jewish provisional governments.

The partition resolution was immediately rejected by the Arab states and the Palestinian Arabs as a violation of the principle of self-determination expressed in the UN Charter. The six Arab states that voted against partition declared that they did not consider themselves bound by the decision, and reserved full freedom of action. The Jewish community in Palestine (the *Yishuv*) and the Zionist movement formally accepted the decision as the means of achieving internationally recognized statehood. Fighting broke out almost immediately between the two communities, with the *Haganah*, guided by its Plan 'D', seeking initially to consolidate its control over areas allocated to the Jewish state, and then to expand these areas.

On Dec. 11, 1947, the British government announced its intention to relinquish the mandate and withdraw from Palestine on May 15, 1948, and on Jan. 12, 1948, the Jewish Agency and the Jewish National Council announced that they had completed plans for a provisional government of the proposed Jewish state after the termination of the mandate. The final months of the British mandate were marked by intensifying fighting between Jewish and Arab irregular and regular forces, and by each against the British. The British government apparently hoped that, despite the UN vote, the partition decision would be rescinded and the mandate extended. Amid confusion and reported disagreements between US President Truman and the State Department, on March 19, 1948, the US requested the United Nations to establish a temporary "trusteeship" over Palestine; on March 30, this proposal was withdrawn.

Establishment of the State of Israel—1948-49 Arab-Israeli War

On May 14, 1948, a few hours before the termination at midnight of the British mandate, the Jewish National Council met in the Tel-Aviv Municipal Museum, and issued the "Declaration of the Establishment of the State of Israel", often inexactly referred to as the "Declaration of Independence". After much debate, it was decided not to include the word "independence", and the text instead declared

"the establishment of a Jewish state in the Land of Israel".

After recalling the origins and aims of Zionism in its preamble, the proclamation declared that the state of Israel "will be open to the immigration of Jews from all countries of their dispersion...will uphold the full social and political equality of all its citizens, without distinction of religion, conscience, education and culture; will safeguard the Holy Places of all religions; and will loyally uphold the principles of the United Nations Charter". It would also be "ready to co-operate with the organs and representatives of the United Nations in the implementation of the resolution of the Assembly on Nov. 29, 1947, and will take steps to bring about the economic union over the whole of Palestine". It concluded: "In the midst of wanton aggression, we yet call upon the Arab inhabitants of the state of Israel to preserve the ways of peace and play their part in the development of the state, on the basis of full and equal citizenship and due representation in all its bodies and institutions—provisional and permanent. We extend our hand in peace and neighbourliness to all the neighbouring states and their people, and invite them to co-operate with the independent Jewish nation for the common good of all. The state of Israel is prepared to make its contribution to the progress of the Middle East as a whole. Our call goes out to the Jewish people all over the world to rally to our side in the task of immigration and development and to stand by us in the great struggle for the fulfilment of the dream of generations for the redemption of Israel".

By this time, the *Haganah* had already seized large parts of the proposed Arab state, and over 300,000 Palestinian Arabs had become refugees. In the course of the fighting, there had been a number of massacres, most notoriously on April 9, 1948, at Deir Yassin on the outskirts of Jerusalem, when, according to the Red Cross, 254 Palestinian villagers were killed.

According to the terms of UN Resolution 181, Palestinians were entitled, or indeed obliged, to declare an Arab state in eastern Palestine, simultaneously with the declaration of a Jewish state in western Palestine. The near-simultaneous declaration of the twin states of India and Pakistan out of a partitioned India a year earlier served broadly as a model of what was envisaged. However, having rejected UN 181 and the partitioning of what they felt should be one Palestine, Palestinians (as the Arabs of historic Palestine came to be known) chose not to prepare for separate statehood in the area now called the West Bank.

With British withdrawal and the establishment of the state of Israel at midnight on May 14-15, 1948, the armies of Egypt, Syria, Transjordan, Lebanon and Iraq (backed by Saudi Arabian units) entered Palestine. They were supported by so-called "irregular forces" drawn from the Palestinian Arab community. The aims of these Arab armies, as proclaimed in a statement issued by the Arab League countries on May 15, was to establish the independence of Palestine for its lawful inhabitants on the basis of majority rule, which clearly implied the destruction of the new Jewish state. The Arab invasion was immediately condemned as an act of aggression by the UN Security Council, forceful statements being made to this effect by both the US and the Soviet representatives, respectively Warren Austin and Andrei Gromyko.

The Arab League statement, after a forceful reca-pitulation of the alleged infringement of Arab rights and interests during the mandate and a reiteration of the Arabs' rejection of the UN partition plan, conclud-ed as follows: "The governments of the Arab states recognize that the independence of Palestine, which has so far been suppressed by the British mandate, has become an accomplished fact for the lawful inhabi-tants of Palestine. They alone, by virtue of their absolute sovereignty, have the right to provide their country with laws and governmental institutions. They alone should exercise the attributes of their independ-ence, through their own means and without any kind of foreign interference, immediately after peace, security and the rule of law have been restored to the country. At that time the intervention of the Arab states will cease, and the independent state of Palestine will co-operate with the states of the Arab League in order to bring peace, security and prosperity to this part of the world. The governments of the Arab states empha-size...that the only just solution of the Palestine prob-lem is the establishment of a unitary Palestine state, in accordance with democratic principles, whereby its inhabitants will enjoy complete equality before the law, [and whereby] minorities will be assured of all the guarantees recognized in democratic constitutional countries, and [whereby] the Holy Places will be pre-served and the right of access thereto guaranteed. The Arab states most emphatically declare that [their] intervention in Palestine is due only to these consider-ations and objectives and that they aim at nothing more than to put an end to the prevailing conditions in [Palestine]. For this reason they have great confidence that their action will have the support of the United Nations [and that it will be] considered as an action aiming at the realization of its aims and at promoting its principles, as provided for in its Charter".

Although, on paper, the Arab armies were powerful, they were badly led and equipped, and poorly motivat-ed. Except in the battles for control of Jerusalem and its approaches, they proved no match for the combina-tion of regular and irregular forces fighting for the new Jewish state. The first phase of the war was ended by a ceasefire on June 11, 1948, by which time Israel had conquered the Arab towns of Acre and Jaffa, and ensured its control over Haifa (from which some 40,000 Palestinians are estimated to have fled). Fighting resumed on July 9, after Israel received major new arms supplies from Czechoslovakia. On July 11-12, Israel conquered the major Arab towns of Lydda and Ramle, leading to the flight of their 70,000 popu-lation, and on July 16 Nazareth was conquered. In the last case, in contrast to the situation elsewhere, most of its inhabitants did not become refugees. A further ceasefire was imposed by the UN on July 18, which

lasted until Oct. 14. During the final phase of the war, Israel conquered Beersheba, and most of the Galilee in the north and the Negev in the south. The fighting was marked by further massacres of Palestinian civilians, as in Duwayima near Hebron on Oct. 28-29, 1948, when at least 100, and possibly as many as 600, were killed.

The UN negotiated a third ceasefire on Dec. 29, 1948. Following initial talks held on the island of Rhodes, under the auspices of the UN diplomat Ralph Bunche, armistices were signed by Israel with Egypt on Feb. 24, 1949; with Lebanon on March 23; with Transjordan on April 3 and with Syria on July 20. There was no armistice with the fifth Arab nation involved in the war, Iraq, but then Iraq was not a bor-dering country.

As a result of these agreements, Israel was left in control of 73 per cent of Palestine—by contrast with its pre-war allocation of 55 per cent of the country under UN 181.(See Map 52 (ii).) Thus it held all the areas allocated by the UN to the Jewish state, plus large parts of the area intended for the Arab state. Of the major Palestinian towns, only Nablus, Hebron, Gaza and the eastern part of Jerusalem were not con-quered, while hundreds of Arab villages were also included in the Jewish state. As a result of the Armistice signed with Transjordan, the "Green Line" separated 65 Arab villages from their land; 57 of these villages remained on the Jordanian side and only eight in Israel. Jordan controlled all of Jerusalem east of the Mandelbaum Gate (currently the Tourjeman Post Museum), with the exception of an Israeli enclave on Mount Scopus, which encompassed the Hebrew University.

An important aspect of the 1948-49 war was the massive displacement of Palestinian Arabs from their homes and land. The circumstances of this displace-ment and even the numbers involved have been mat-ters of considerable dispute. The UN Economic Survey Mission estimated that 726,000 Palestinians had become refugees, while the Refugee Office of the UN Palestine Conciliation Commission placed the number at 900,000. Arab accounts have always insist-ed that the Palestinians were driven out deliberately in order to ensure that Israel should have a maximum amount of land and a clear Jewish majority. Israeli official sources have maintained that most Palestinians fled in order to escape the fighting, and in some cases were ordered to leave by Arab leaders confident of a speedy return following the destruction of the Jewish state. This last claim has never been authenticated, and in more recent years, Arab claims have been con-firmed in a number of studies by Israeli historians. By June 1950, the total number of refugees registered with the newly established UN Relief and Works Agency for Palestine Refugees (UNRWA) was 960,021 (a figure regarded as inflated by Israeli and some independent sources).

The two biggest concentrations of refugees were located in the West Bank and the Gaza Strip. Many more were relocated to the east bank of the River

Jordan, within the Hashemite Kingdom of Transjordan. Smaller numbers fled to Lebanon, Syria, Egypt and the Gulf states; certain wealthier families relocated to Western capital cities. Only some 150,000 Arabs remained within the new borders of the Jewish state (concentrated in Galilee in the north), the Jewish population of which at the end of the war was about 660,000. Though granted Israeli citizenship, many of these "Israeli Arabs" were themselves regarded as "internally displaced" (i.e. they were forced to leave their home villages or cities, and relocate to others, albeit ones that happened to fall within the borders of the state of Israel). Subsequent massive migration of Sephardi Jews from Middle Eastern states to Israel helped bolster the Jewish majority in the country.

Unsuccessful Peace Efforts—Jerusalem Declared Israeli Capital

In the immediate aftermath of the 1948-49 Arab-Israeli war UN-sponsored attempts to bring about a peace settlement between the two sides made some initial progress, the two central issues being the refugee question and the position of the borders between Israel and the neighbouring Arab states. As early as Dec. 11, 1948, the UN General Assembly established a Palestine Conciliation Commission charged with assisting the governments and authorities concerned to achieve a final settlement of all outstanding questions. The relevant resolution, UNGA 194, asserted inter alia that "refugees wishing to return to their homes and live in peace with their neighbours should be permitted to do so at the earliest practicable moment and that compensation should be paid for the property of those choosing not to return and for loss of or damage to property". It also called for peace negotiations between Israel and the Arab states.

Under the auspices of the commission, representatives of Israel, Egypt, Transjordan, Lebanon and Syria began indirect negotiations in Lausanne in April 1949 and the following month signed a protocol under which they agreed that "a basis for discussions" on the refugee and border issues should be the November 1947 UN partition plan. It has since been claimed by the Arab side that Israel's signature of this protocol amounted to acceptance of the UN partition borders, whereas Israel has pointed out that the latter were to be "a" basis for discussions rather than "the" basis. It may also be observed that the new Arab position marked a belated acceptance of the de facto reality of partition, which they had formerly rejected. In any event, the initial progress represented by the protocol quickly encountered the fundamental difficulty that Israel insisted that the Arab refugee problem should be dealt with in the context of a general peace settlement. By contrast, Arab states demanded that the refugee problem should be dealt with prior to any general settlement.

Under pressure from the US government, the Israeli side eventually made certain proposals on the refugee question. These were discussed at talks held in the Swiss city of Lausanne. Israel initially posited the "Gaza plan" under which 500,000 Arab refugees would be resettled in the Gaza Strip, provided that Egypt transferred this area to Israel. Next, it proposed that 100,000 refugees should be repatriated to Israeli territory.

However, these plans were rejected by the Arab side, which demanded in the first instance the immediate return of all refugees originating from areas designated for the Arabs under the UN partition plan and the establishment of an Arab state. Some historians have subsequently surmised that had Israel agreed to the proposed return of 100,000 refugees, and exclusively refugees originating in areas allocated to Jews under the UN partition plan, the Arabs would have been able to accept the Israeli proposal. It has been further argued that such acceptance of the UN plan (of UN 194) might have opened the way to substantive talks on a definitive settlement. At the time, however, neither side was prepared to make the requisite concessions, and talks ended in deadlock.

Since then, Israel has aired three familiar arguments against allowing refugees a "right to return". It has claimed that (i) such a return would "swamp" Israel and turn its Jewish majority into a minority; (ii) the refugee problem arose out of a war that Israel did not start; and (iii) Arab states should first accept their responsibility for driving out equivalent numbers of Jews. (Arabs contend that the departure of Jews mainly took place after the Palestinian refugee exodus. Palestinians in particular, while accepting that a wrong may have been done to these Mizrakhi Jews, reject the idea that they should pay the price for the actions of foreign Arab governments.) Finally, Israelis like to contrast the way they "absorbed" Jewish immigrants into their society, with the way Arab states tend to block Palestinian refugees from assimilating into theirs.

Notwithstanding continuous efforts by the United Nations to salvage its partition plan, the attitudes of Israelis and Arabs on both the refugee question and the border issue quickly hardened into diametrically opposed positions after 1949. All of the Arab states which had signed armistice agreements with Israel maintained that they nevertheless remained in a state of war with the Jewish state. With the partial exception of Jordan, they refused to integrate refugees under their jurisdiction on the grounds that their rightful homes were in Palestinian territory now held by the Jews. On Jan. 1, 1950, King Abdullah of Jordan (as Transjordan had been renamed in June 1949) annexed those areas of Arab Palestine held by the Arab Legion at the armistice (i.e. the West Bank and the Old City of Jerusalem). On April 24, 1950, the Jordanian Parliament adopted a resolution formally incorporating areas mentioned above into the Hashemite Kingdom of Jordan.

However, this step was strongly opposed by other Arab League states as undermining the objective of creating an independent Palestinian state. Internationally, only the UK and Pakistan recognized Jordan's annexation of the West Bank. On Jan. 23, 1950, the Israeli Knesset (parliament) had, despite UN protests, adopted a government resolution declaring that Jerusalem had resumed the status of the capital of Israel. (Down to the present day, the USA and most other nations refuse to recognize Jerusalem as Israel's capital—few embassies are located in Jerusalem; most nations that maintain relations with Israel have consulates there, but station their embassies in Tel Aviv.) The Knesset had, however, rejected an opposition amendment designed to make the resolution applicable to the Jordanian-held sector as well as to the Jewish-held New City of Jerusalem (also called West Jerusalem). In a parliamentary debate the previous month, Israel's Prime Minister David Ben-Gurion had stated that Israel regarded the 1947 UN resolution in favour of the partition of Palestine and the internationalization of Jerusalem as no longer possessing any moral force, since the United Nations had failed to implement it.

Meanwhile, following considerable secret bilateral negotiations, Jordan and Israel initialed a draft treaty concerning mutual relations and border alterations in March 1950. However the agreement was quickly shelved, following electoral setbacks in Jordan, unrest from Palestinians, enduring feelings of "betrayal" by certain Egyptian officers, including a young Gamal Abdel Nasser, and fury from fellow Arab League members when news of the treaty emerged. A Palestinian assassin, reputedly in the pay of Egypt, shot dead King Abdullah on the steps of the Mosque of Omar in Jerusalem on July 30, 1951. (More details of this and similar Israeli-Jordanian attempts to achieve peace are dealt with below.)

For their part, the Western powers quickly sought to bring about a measure of stability in the post-armistice realities in Palestine. Under a tripartite declaration issued on May 25, 1950, Britain, France and the United States affirmed "their desire to promote the establishment and maintenance of peace and stability in the area and their unalterable opposition to the use of force or threat of force between any of the states in that area". The three nations further pledged that "should they find that any of these states was preparing to violate frontiers or armistice lines [they would] immediately take action, both within and outside the United Nations, to prevent such violation". The declaration also committed the three powers to preventing an arms race between the Arab states and Israel. It laid down procedures to restrict the supply of arms to those countries deemed to require "a certain level of armed forces for the purposes of assuring their internal security and their legitimate self-defence, and to permit them to play their part in the defence of the area as a whole". In the event, France saw no contradiction between this declaration and its arms supply agreement with Israel of 1952 (albeit secret at the time and principally a response to Egyptian support for the rebels then seeking to overthrow French rule in Algeria). British attempts to construct an alliance with Iraq and Jordan in the early 1950s, which culminated in the short-lived Baghdad Pact, also involved the sup-

ply of arms.

Israel's interest in obtaining arms reflected the fact that from the territorial point of view the 1949 armistice left the Jewish state with a serious security problem. In the north-east border area Israeli settlements were frequently bombarded from positions on the Syrian Golan Heights; in the central coastal plain Israel was only nine miles wide at its narrowest point between the Jordanian-occupied West Bank and the sea. And in the south, Palestinian *fedayeen* based in the Egyptian-administered Gaza Strip mounted increasing attacks on Israeli targets across the armistice line. In addition, Palestinian peasants frequently crossed the new borders in an attempt to return to their homes and land; Israel defined them as "infiltrators". Israel responded to raids and "infiltrations" by retaliatory actions against alleged guerrilla bases. On Oct. 14, 1953, the Israeli army destroyed the Jordanian village of Qibya, killing 66 civilians. An attack on an Egyptian army base in Gaza on Feb. 28, 1955, provoked general international condemnation, and in turn led to the first major *fedayeen* raid from Egypt into Israel, in August 1955.

Advent of Nasser—1956 Arab-Israeli War

Such raids convinced the Arabs in turn of their need for a modern weapons capability, this objective being a particular preoccupation of the new Egyptian regime of Gamal Abdel Nasser which had come to power in 1954 imbued with a novel mixture of pan-Arab nationalism and revolutionary socialism. In an historic development in September 1955, Nasser concluded a major arms deal with Czechoslovakia, which marked not only the start of increased Soviet influence in the Arab world but also the final breakdown of the Western powers' attempts to prevent an arms race in the Middle East. (Paradoxically, Czechoslovakia had been one of the main arms suppliers to Israel during the 1948 war.)

Soon after the 1949 armistice Egypt had sought to impose an economic blockade on Israel by denying it the use of the Suez Canal—an action denounced as illegal by Israel but justified by Egypt on the grounds that a state of war still existed between the two countries. From 1953 Egypt also began restricting Israeli sea-borne trade through the Straits of Tiran at the entrance to the Gulf of Aqaba. Stepped up in 1955, this Egyptian blockade of the southern Israeli port of Eilat combined with increasing Israeli disquiet over Egypt's promotion of *fedayeen* activities in the Gaza Strip. These factors contributed substantially to Israel's decision to launch an attack on Egypt in October 1956—in collusion (it later transpired) with Britain and France. For the two Western powers, the key motivation was Nasser's decision of July 1956—taken partly in retaliation for the UK-US decision to withdraw financial aid from the Aswan Dam project—to nationalize the (Anglo-French) Suez Canal Company. Nationalization contravened assurances given in the 1954 Anglo-Egyptian treaty under which British forces had been withdrawn from the Canal Zone. Britain and France therefore entered into an agreement with Israel—secret at the time—that an attack by the latter on Egyptian positions in Sinai would be followed by an Anglo-French occupation of the Canal Zone. Such Anglo-French action would be justified in terms of the need to protect the waterway from the warring parties.

The sequence of events was as follows. On Oct. 29, 1956, the Israeli Army attacked Egyptian positions in the Gaza Strip and Sinai, with the declared purpose of destroying *fedayeen* bases. On the next day the British and French governments issued 12-hour ultimatums to both Israel and Egypt, under which they demanded that the two sides should cease warlike actions and withdraw their troops from the immediate vicinity of the Suez Canal, and also requested Egypt to allow Anglo-French forces to be stationed temporarily on the canal to separate the belligerents and safeguard shipping. The rejection of the ultimatum by Egypt was followed by a British and French air offensive on Egyptian airfields and other military targets from Oct. 31 to Nov. 4 and then, on Nov. 5, by Anglo-French paratroop and commando landings in the Canal Zone. Meanwhile, Israeli forces overran the Gaza Strip and most of Sinai, including Sharm el-Sheikh and the island of Tiran at the entrance to the Gulf of Aqaba.

The combined opposition of the United States and the Soviet Union brought a quick end to the 1956 Anglo-French-Israeli enterprise, principally because of the political and economic pressure which the US government was able to exert on Britain. Sir Anthony Eden (UK Prime Minister) announced acceptance of a ceasefire on Nov. 6 and a general cessation of hostilities came into effect at midnight on Nov. 6-7, following which the Anglo-French forces were quickly withdrawn. They were replaced by a UN Emergency Force (UNEF) established by the UN General Assembly on Nov. 5, the first contingents of which arrived in Egypt on Nov. 15 and whose presence was agreed to by the Egyptian government under certain conditions. In response to UN and US pressure, Israel quickly evacuated most of its conquests in Sinai but kept its forces in the Gaza Strip and in the coastal strip from Eilat down to Sharm el-Sheikh until March 1957. Its eventual withdrawal from these areas was carried out on the assumption that the UNEF units in Gaza would prevent *fedayeen* incursions into Israeli territory and on the basis of assurances from the leading maritime powers that they would support freedom of navigation in the Gulf of Aqaba.

The main beneficiary of the eclipse of Anglo-French influence in the Middle East caused by the Suez episode was the Soviet Union, which in the succeeding years consolidated its relations with the radical Arab states such as Egypt, Syria and Iraq by means of arms supply and economic aid agreements. To counter this development, the United States became increasingly drawn into the power politics of the region, principally as a supporter of Israel but also as the dominant external power in the Gulf and the ally of the conservative Arab states such as Saudi Arabia. The basic Arab-Israel conflict thus became interwoven with great-power rivalries and ambitions that increasingly threatened to transform Middle East instabilities into a wider conflict.

Arab-Israeli Relations 1957-66—Creation of PLO

With Israel restored to the borders established under the 1949 armistices, armed clashes between Arabs and Israelis continued to occur in the decade following the 1956 Suez conflict. There were a number of incidents on the Israel-Gaza border in May-June 1957, but by December of that year the area was comparatively peaceful, mainly because of the presence of UNEF. Israeli and Jordanian troops clashed in the Mount Scopus demilitarized zone of Jerusalem in August 1957 and May 1958, each side accusing the other of violation of the armistice agreement in the Jerusalem area. The main trouble area in this period, however, was the Israeli-Syrian border in the demilitarized zone south-east of the Sea of Galilee, which the Israelis claimed to be under their jurisdiction. The most serious incidents in this region took place in March 1962 and August 1963, although clashes were of frequent occurrence from 1957. In August 1963 Syria alleged that there were Israeli troop concentrations on the Syrian border, but an investigation by the UN Truce Supervision Organization (UNTSO) revealed no evidence of a military build-up.

In 1959 Egypt began a new blockade of Israeli trade through the Suez Canal, after having refrained, between 1956 and 1959, from interfering with the passage of Israeli goods when such cargoes were carried in vessels not flying the Israeli flag. During 1959 Egypt detained a number of ships of various nationalities carrying exports from Israel and impounded their cargoes. Egyptian sources justified their action on the ground that there was still a state of war between Israel and the Arab countries, and that Israel therefore had no right to ship goods through the Suez Canal.

A further cause of Arab-Israeli friction was the long-standing dispute over the waters of the River Jordan. A number of plans for an equitable division of the waters between Palestine/Israel and the riparian Arab states (Jordan, Syria, and Lebanon) were proposed between 1944 and 1955, the last of which was agreed at technical level by Israel and the Arab states under US auspices (the Johnston Plan). But it broke down at political level, largely because of Syrian opposition. Israel and Jordan subsequently went ahead with separate schemes, Israel pumping water from the Sea of Galilee to be carried by pipeline to the Negev in the south, and Jordan tapping the waters of the two tributaries, the Yarmuk and the Zarqa. Israel's action aroused the anger of the Arabs, whose heads of state, meeting in Cairo in January 1964, decided on a plan to reduce the flow of the northern tributaries of the Jordan, thus reducing the quantity of water Israel would be able to divert. It was some time before work could begin on this scheme, however, as Lebanon and Syria required assurances of their security from Israeli attack during implementation of the diversion projects.

The January 1964 Arab summit also adopted important resolutions endorsing the creation of Palestinian Arab representative bodies, on the basis of which the inaugural meeting of the Palestine National Council (PNC)—a Palestinian parliament-in-exile—was held in the Jordanian sector of Jerusalem in May-June 1964. The first session of the PNC took the decision to establish the Palestine Liberation Organization (PLO) as the armed wing of the Palestinian struggle and also adopted (on June 2) the Palestine National Charter (or "Covenant") as the basic statement of Palestinian Arab aims, which it remains today. Regarded by the Israelis as enshrining the Arab objective of destroying the Jewish state, the 33-article charter states inter alia that "Palestine is the homeland of the Palestinian Arab people…[and] is an indivisible part of the Arab homeland" (Article 1); that "Palestine, within the boundaries it had during the British mandate, is an indivisible territorial unit" (Article 2); that "the Palestinian Arab people possess the legal right to their homeland and have the right to determine their destiny after achieving the liberation of their country in accordance with their wishes and entirely of their own accord and will" (Article 3); that "the Palestinians are those Arab nationals who, until 1947, normally resided in Palestine regardless of whether they were evicted from it or have stayed there" and also all those born after that date of a Palestinian father "whether inside Palestine or outside it" (Article 5); that "the Jews who had normally resided in Palestine until the beginning of the Zionist invasion will be considered Palestinians" (Article 6).

The charter also declares that "armed struggle is the only way to liberate Palestine" (Article 9); that "the liberation of Palestine, from a spiritual point of view, will provide the Holy Land with an atmosphere of safety and tranquillity, which in turn will safeguard the country's religious sanctuaries and guarantee freedom of worship and of visit to all, without discrimination of race, colour, language or religion" (Article 16); that "the partition of Palestine in 1947 and the establishment of the state of Israel are entirely illegal, regardless of the passage of time, because they were contrary to the will of the Palestinian people and to their natural right in their homeland, and inconsistent with the principles embodied in the Charter of the United Nations, particularly the right to self-determination" (Article 19); that "the Balfour declaration, the mandate for Palestine and everything which has been based on them are deemed null and void" on the grounds that "claims of historical or religious ties of Jews with Palestine are incompatible with the facts of history and the true conception of what constitutes statehood" (Article 20); that "the Palestinian Arab people…reject all solutions which are substitutes for the total liberation of Palestine and reject all proposals aiming at the liquidation of the Palestinian problem or its internationalization" (Article 21); that "Zionism is a political movement originally associated with international imperialism and antagonistic to all action for liberation and to progressive movements in the world [and] is racist and fanatic in its nature, aggressive, expansionist and colonial in its aims and fascist in its methods" (Article 22); and that "the Palestine Liberation Organization…is responsible for the Palestinian Arab people's movement in its struggle—to retrieve its homeland, liberate and return to it and exercise the right of self-determination in it—in all military, political and financial fields and also for whatever may be required by the Palestine case on the inter-Arab and international levels" (Article 26).

As the principal guerrilla arm of the PLO, the Al Fatah ("Conquest") group led by Yasser Arafat mounted numerous incursions into Israel, initially mainly from Jordan and increasingly during 1965 from Syrian territory. An intensification of such attacks in October and November 1966 gave rise to a serious political crisis leading directly to the third Arab-Israeli war. After a resolution calling on Syria to strengthen its measures against guerrilla activities had been vetoed in the UN Security Council by the Soviet Union on Nov. 4, Israeli forces carried out a reprisal raid on a Jordanian village on Nov. 13, which was condemned by the Security Council on Nov. 25. In late November and early December 1966 violent rioting occurred in the principal towns of the Jordanian West Bank, where the population demanded arms to defend themselves against further Israeli attacks.

The Six-Day War of 1967 and its Results

By the end of 1966 both Israel and Jordan had taken military steps suggesting an anticipation of possible war, while from January 1967 tension between Israel and Syria increased sharply amid repeated armed clashes on the ground and in the air. On April 6, the Israeli air force shot down six Syrian planes in a dogfight, and later buzzed Damascus.

The sequence of events immediately prior to the June 1967 war unfolded as follows. *May 13*: The Soviet Union warned Egypt of an imminent large-scale Israeli invasion of Syria. *May 14*: Israel's Independence Day was marked by a military display in Jerusalem; Prime Minister Levi Eshkol warned that a serious confrontation with Syria was inevitable if Syrian-backed guerrilla activities continued. President Nasser put the Egyptian Army on maximum alert. *May 15*: Egyptian forces crossed the Suez Canal into Sinai. *May 16*: Nasser demanded the withdrawal of UN peacekeeping force observers from the Egyptian side of the border with Israel; the Egyptian government declared a state of emergency throughout the country and announced that its forces were "in a complete state of preparedness for war". *May 17*: Syria and Jordan similarly announced that their forces were being mobilized. *May 18*: Egypt made an official request to the UN Secretary-General, U Thant, that UNEF forces should be withdrawn from Egyptian territory and the Gaza Strip (recalling that their presence was subject to Egyptian approval) and Iraq and Kuwait announced the mobilization of their forces. *May 19*: The UNEF was officially withdrawn, with U Thant explaining that "there seemed to me to be no alternative course of action which could be taken by the Secretary-General without putting into question the sovereign authority of the [Egyptian government] within its own territory". *May 21*: Both Egypt and Israel announced the call-up of reservists, and the PLO announced that its forces had been placed under the military commands of Egypt, Syria and Iraq. *May 22*: It was announced in Cairo that President Nasser had accepted an offer of Iraqi army and air force units to assist Egypt in the event of an outbreak of hostilities. *May 23*: Nasser announced the closing of the Straits of Tiran to ships flying the Israeli flag and to any other vessel carrying strategic goods to Israel (including oil), this action being described by Eshkol as an act of aggression against Israel and as a violation of the freedom of navigation assurances given when Israel withdrew from Sharm el-Sheikh in 1957. *May 24*: Egypt announced that the Gulf of Aqaba had been effectively sealed off, while contingents of Saudi Arabian troops were reported to have arrived in Jordan. *May 26*: Following a visit by Abba Eban (Israel's Foreign Minister) to Paris, London and Washington (May 24-25), Israel warned that it had the right to break the blockade of the Gulf of Aqaba if the United Nations or the maritime powers failed to act. *May 27*: U Thant reported to the UN Security Council that Egypt had assured him that it would "not initiate offensive action against Israel" but that Israeli shipping would not be allowed to pass through the Straits of Tiran. *May 28-29*: General mobilization was proclaimed in Sudan (May 28) and Algeria announced that military units were being sent to assist Egypt (May 29). *May 30*: King Hussein of Jordan visited Cairo and signed a defence pact with Egypt under which each country would consider an attack on either as an attack on both, while Abba Eban warned that if the Gulf blockade was not lifted soon Israel would "act alone if we must…but with others if we can". *May 31*: Iraqi troops and armoured units were reported to be moving into Jordan towards the Israeli border, while several Arab countries threatened to take action against the oil interests of Western states who aided Israel. *June 1*: A National Unity coalition government was formed in Israel. Former Chief-of-Staff General Moshe Dayan replaced Eshkol as Defence Minister. *June 2-3*: More than 20 maritime nations were presented with a UK-US draft declaration affirming the right of free and innocent passage through the Gulf of Aqaba but containing no provision for any enforcement action. *June 4*: Nasser said that any such declaration would be regarded as a transgression of Egyptian sovereignty and "a preliminary to an act of war", while Iraq joined the Egypt-Jordan defence pact and Libya pledged troops to assist Egypt in the event of war. *June 5*: Early in the morning the Israeli Air Force launched pre-emptive strikes against Egypt, Jordan, Syria and Iraq. The first target was the airfields, which were put out of action; 320 of Egypt's 340 combat aircraft were destroyed on the ground. Virtually all the air capability of these four countries was destroyed on the first day of what became known

subsequently as the Six-Day War.

With the benefit of complete air supremacy, Israeli forces achieved a rapid and complete victory in the June 1967 war. By the time hostilities ended in a cease-fire on June 10 Israel had (i) captured the Gaza Strip and overrun the entire Sinai peninsula up to the Suez Canal, including Sharm el-Sheikh; (ii) gained control of the Old City of Jerusalem and overrun all Jordanian territory west of the Jordan; and (iii) captured the Golan Heights from Syria and penetrated some 12 miles into Syrian territory (this advance being achieved in the final stages of the fighting after both Israel and Syria had signified acceptance of a cease-fire). By the end of the war the Israeli armed forces were in occupation of an area more than three times greater than the territory of Israel at the outbreak of hostilities (see Map 52 (iii)), the newly occupied territories extending to some 27,000 square miles (70,000 sq km) as compared with the 8,000 square miles (20,000 sq km) of the Jewish state within the 1949 armistice lines. Israeli soldiers killed in the fighting totaled 766 while Arab losses (never definitively announced) were thought to include about 10,000 Egyptian and 6,000 Jordanian dead.

An important result of the 1967 war was a four-fold increase in the number of Palestinian Arabs under Jewish rule, from a pre-war total of some 300,000 to about 1,200,000 (as against a mid-1967 Jewish population of some 2,500,000). Although up to 200,000 Palestinians fled from the West Bank during the war, about 600,000 remained under the new Israeli administration, as did approximately 300,000 in the Gaza Strip. Virtually the entire population of the Syrian territory captured by Israel—about 60,000—fled eastwards during the fighting, leaving the Golan Heights practically uninhabited in the immediate post-war period.

Israeli Consolidation of Occupied Territories

Whereas Israel had been forced by US pressure to withdraw from the territory it had captured in the 1956 Sinai campaign, after the June 1967 war Israeli spokesmen immediately made it clear that there could be no return to the 1949 armistice lines. A final settlement of the Arab-Israeli conflict, it was stressed by Israel, was dependent on direct peace talks with the surrounding Arab states to establish definitive boundaries which took account of Israel's legitimate security interests. An eloquent exposition of the Israeli case was put during an emergency session of the UN General Assembly held from June 19 to July 21, 1967, by Foreign Minister Abba Eban, who rejected a Soviet demand that Israel should withdraw to the 1949 lines and argued as follows:

"What the Assembly should prescribe is not a formula for renewed hostilities but a series of principles for the construction of a new future in the Middle East. With the ceasefire established, our progress must not be backward to an armistice regime which has collapsed under the weight of years and the brunt of hostility. History summons us forward to permanent peace, and the peace that we envisage can only be elaborated in frank and lucid dialogue between Israel and each of the states which have participated in the attempt to overthrow her sovereignty and undermine her existence. We dare not be satisfied with intermediate arrangements which are neither war nor peace. Such patchwork ideas carry within themselves the seeds of future tragedy. Free from external pressures and interventions, imbued with a common love for a region which they are destined to share, the Arab and Jewish nations must now transcend their conflicts in dedication to a new Mediterranean future in concert with a renaissant Europe and an Africa and Asia which have emerged at last to their independent role on the stage of history. In free negotiation with each of our neighbours we shall offer durable and just solutions redounding to our mutual advantage and honour. The Arab states can no longer be permitted to recognize Israel's existence only for the purpose of plotting its elimination. They have come face to face with us in conflict. Let them now come face to face with us in peace..."

In a speech to the Knesset on Oct. 30, 1967, Prime Minister Eshkol reiterated that Israel would not allow the situation which prevailed before June 5 to be restored and stated that in the face of the Arab position of non-recognition of Israel his government would "maintain in full the situation as it was established in the ceasefire arrangements". In a further speech on Dec. 1 Eshkol enumerated five points on which Israel's policy was based: (i) permanent peace between Israel and her Arab neighbours; (ii) the achievement of peace by direct negotiations and conclusion of peace treaties between Israel and its neighbours; (iii) free passage for Israeli ships through the Suez Canal and the Straits of Tiran; (iv) agreed and secure borders between Israel and its neighbours; and (v) a settlement of the refugee problem "within a regional and international context" following the establishment of peace in the Middle East.

The Arab states, however, immediately adopted a policy of continued non-recognition of Israel and refusal to consider any form of peace negotiations. Speaking at the UN General Assembly session on June 26, 1967, King Hussein of Jordan accused Israel of having planned aggression against the Arab countries for many years and of initiating hostilities on June 5. Calling on the United Nations to condemn Israel and to enforce the return of Israeli troops to the pre-war lines, he warned that if this did not happen the Arab nation would rise again and that "the battle which began on June 5 will...become only a battle in what will be a long war". Following a summit conference of Arab nations held in Khartoum in late August 1967, on Sept. 1 delegates passed a resolution committing Arab states to neither recognizing nor negotiating with Israel. In what became known as the "three noes", delegates further vowed to "make no peace with Israel, for the sake of the rights of the Palestinian people in their homeland".

Lengthy deliberations at the United Nations eventually resulted in the unanimous adoption by the Security Council on Nov. 22, 1967, of a resolution (242) proposed by Britain which emphasized "the inadmissibility of the acquisition of territory by war and the need to work for a just and lasting peace in which every state in the area can live in security". In its substantive passages this resolution affirmed that "the fulfilment of [UN] Charter principles requires the establishment of a just and lasting peace in the Middle East which should include the application of both the following principles: (i) withdrawal of Israeli armed forces from territories occupied in the recent conflict; (ii) termination of all claims or states of belligerency and respect for and acknowledgement of the sovereignty, territorial integrity and political independence of every state in the area and their right to live in peace within secure and recognized boundaries free from threats or acts of force". It further affirmed "the necessity (i) for guaranteeing freedom of navigation through international waterways in the area; (ii) for achieving a just settlement of the refugee problem; (iii) for guaranteeing the territorial inviolability and political independence of every state in the area through measures including the establishment of demilitarized zones".

Resolution 242 was accepted both by Israel and by the front-line Arab states except Syria, although on the basis of differing interpretations of the key phrase calling for an Israeli withdrawal "from territories occupied in the recent conflict". Israel cited the absence of the definite article before the word "territories" to mean that it was not bound to carry out a complete withdrawal, particularly since the resolution also referred to the right to "secure and recognized boundaries". The Arab states, on the other hand, claimed that the resolution called for a complete Israeli withdrawal and cited the equally authentic French text, where the key phrase is rendered *"retrait des forces armées israéliennes des territoires occupés"*. It should be noted, incidentally, that such semantic arguments were of no interest to the PLO, which has always refused to accept Resolution 242 because it made no reference to the rights of the Palestinian people.

Following the 1967 war and the adoption of Resolution 242, the nature of the Arab-Israeli conflict altered. On the one hand, in place of support for the fundamental challenge to the legitimacy of the state of Israel, the neighbouring Arab states of Egypt, Jordan and Syria focused on the quest to recover their lost territories. On the other hand, the collapse of the Arab armies, the situation of the whole of Palestine under Israeli rule, and the harsh Israeli military regime imposed in the occupied territories, contributed to the growth of the PLO as an independent body, and to the almost total Palestinian identification with the PLO.

The Israelis made no immediate move to annex their conquests, which were placed under military administration pending a negotiated peace settlement with the interested Arab governments under which definitive boundaries would be agreed. But they did very quickly merge the Israeli New City of Jerusalem with the Old City, agreeing in July 1967 that Jerusalem was henceforth "one city indivisible, the capital of the state of Israel". On June 27, 1967, the Knesset passed the Protection of Holy Places Law. The following day it empowered the government to apply the law, jurisdiction and administration of the state to any part of Eretz Yisrael ("Land of Israel", effectively signifying the whole territory of Palestine). This step was condemned not only by the Arabs but also by the UN General Assembly on July 4, by 99 votes to none with 20 abstentions. The Israelis also began a controversial programme of establishing Jewish settlements in the occupied territories, which although limited in the early years and officially related to security requirements was strongly criticized by the international community, including the United States. By late 1973 Israel began allowing private acquisition of land in the West Bank, by Israeli Jews, which appeared like a departure from the earlier caution (i.e. restricting settlements to military installations). In this situation the PLO and its various member organizations increasingly resorted to extreme methods, which included a growing number of attacks on Israeli targets outside Palestine, notably the El Al airline.

From 1968-71, Israel and Egypt waged a long-range artillery battle, the "War of Attrition", across the Suez Canal. Although this caused more Israeli casualties than the 1967 war, Egypt did not succeed in its aim of forcing Israeli withdrawal from Sinai by wearing down its defences and morale.

"Yom Kippur" War of 1973

The fifth Arab-Israeli war broke out on Oct. 6, 1973, when Egyptian and Syrian forces launched major offensives across the Suez Canal and on the Golan front respectively, choosing the Day of Atonement (Yom Kippur), the holiest day in the Jewish year, to do so and thereby apparently taking the Israeli armed forces by surprise. Although Jordan did not open a third military front against Israel, units of the Jordanian Army were sent to the Syrian front, as were strong Iraqi armoured contingents and relatively token Saudi Arabian and Kuwaiti units. On the Suez front Egypt received active military assistance from Morocco and Algeria and also from the Iraqi Air Force. The declared war aims of Egypt and Syria were to recover the Arab territories lost to Israel in 1967.

After some of the bitterest and most bloody fighting since World War II, marked by great tank battles and heavy losses of men and material on both sides, a binding ceasefire came into effect on Oct. 24 in response to two successive UN Security Council resolutions. By that time the Egyptian Army had established itself along much of the eastern bank of the Suez Canal north of Ismailia and held a narrow strip of Sinai varying from three to 10 miles in width in different sectors and amounting to some 500 square miles of territory. For their part, the Israeli forces, in addition to having contained an attempted Egyptian thrust deeper into Sinai, had consolidated a successful count-

er-offensive across the Suez Canal in the southern sector, giving them control of about 500 square miles of Egyptian territory west of the Great Bitter Lake and the town of Suez.

On the northern front the Syrians also achieved initial successes, recapturing much of the Golan Heights lost in the 1967 war and advancing almost to the edge of Galilee plain. However, they were eventually checked and driven back in a powerful Israeli counter-offensive, so that when a cease-fire came into effect on Oct. 24 the Syrians had not only surrendered all their initial gains but had also lost an additional 300 square miles of territory to the Israelis, who had advanced to within 20 miles of Damascus.

Total Israeli casualties in the 1973 Arab-Israeli war included 2,400 soldiers killed. As in previous wars, the casualties of the Arab side were never officially released.

1974 and 1975 Disengagement Agreements

The UN Security Council's first 1973 ceasefire resolution (338), which was adopted on Oct. 22 but not observed until a further resolution had been passed late the following day, was proposed jointly by the United States and the Soviet Union and received the support of 14 of the 15 Security Council member states, with China refraining from voting. In addition to calling for a ceasefire, it urged the parties concerned "to start immediately...the implementation of Resolution 242 [of November 1967] in all of its parts" and decided that immediate negotiations should be initiated "aimed at establishing a just and durable peace in the Middle East".

The co-operation of the two superpowers in securing the passage of Resolution 338 reflected their joint concern that the Middle East conflict might escalate into a broader confrontation, although the situation remained tense for several days. President Richard M. Nixon disclosed on Oct. 26, 1973, that he had ordered a precautionary alert of US military forces throughout the world early the previous day after receiving information which had "led us to believe that the Soviet Union was planning to send a very substantial force" into the Middle East. In the event, the threat of a US-Soviet confrontation had been dissipated by the adoption during the night of Oct. 25-26 of a Security Council resolution providing for the creation of a UN peace-keeping force for the Middle East, the personnel of which would not be drawn from any of the five permanent members of the Security Council (i.e. the USA, the Soviet Union, Britain, France and China). On the basis of this resolution a new UN Emergency Force (UNEF) was deployed on the Suez front by early November 1973. Negotiations began at the "Kilometre 101" checkpoint on the Cairo-Suez road at the edge of the Israeli-occupied enclave west of the Suez Canal, between Egyptian Gen. Mohammed Abdel Ghani al-Gamasy and Israel's former head of military intelligence, Aharon Yariv. On Nov. 11 Egypt and Israel formally signed a ceasefire agreement at the same spot.

This was the first major agreement between Israel and an Arab country since the signature of the 1949 armistice agreements.

A feature of the complex negotiations which led over the next two years to the conclusion of military disengagement agreements between Israel on the one hand and Egypt and Syria on the other was the key diplomatic role played by the United States and in particular by the US Secretary of State, Dr Henry Kissinger. Another important and related factor was the emergence from the 1973 war onwards of the "oil weapon" as a potent means by which the Arab states, taking advantage of the near-monopoly position which they then enjoyed as oil exporters, could exert pressure on Western states with a view to securing support for Arab conceptions of a just Middle East settlement, i.e. one which involved major concessions by Israel. At the time of the 1973 war, use of this weapon took the form of an embargo on supplies to the United States and the Netherlands (because of their open support for Israel) and restrictions on supplies to other developed countries. Subsequently it took the form of massive price increases, which not only threw the economies of the industrialized states into recession but also had serious consequences for the existing international monetary system. Against this background (and with the ever-present threat of further total embargoes on Arab oil supplies), the quest for a resolution of the Arab-Israeli conflict took on added urgency for the industrialized countries, beyond their fundamental concern that Middle East instabilities represented a threat to world peace.

In December 1973 the United States and the Soviet Union made a joint effort to bring about meaningful Arab-Israeli negotiations by inviting Egypt, Jordan, Syria and Israel to a peace conference in Geneva on the basis of the UN Security Council's call for a "just and durable peace". However, Syria refused to attend (and the PLO was not invited) and the conference was adjourned inconclusively on Jan. 9, 1974. Thereafter, the Soviet Union was able to play little direct part in the overall Middle East negotiating process, particularly since President Sadat of Egypt had already reversed Nasser's policy of close alignment with the Soviet Union—a reversal culminating in his unilateral abrogation in March 1976 of the 1971 Egyptian-Soviet Treaty of Friendship and Co-operation.

With Egypt now accepting that the road to progress ran through Washington, Dr Kissinger was able to mount a direct diplomatic effort with the Middle East parties, the first fruit of which was the signature by Egypt and Israel on Jan. 18, 1974, of an initial military disengagement agreement. Under its terms Israel withdrew its forces from the areas west of the Suez Canal held since the October 1973 ceasefire and also pulled back several miles on the Sinai front east of the canal, where three roughly parallel zones were created, each about six miles wide. The first of these, immediately to the east of the canal, became an Egyptian limited-forces zone, the second a central buffer zone in which UNEF contingents were stationed and the third an Israeli limited-force zone. For Egypt the general effect of the agreement was that it regained control of all Egyptian territory west of the canal and also the whole of the eastern bank. Israel, although withdrawing 12-13 miles east of the canal, was left in control of the rest of Sinai, including the strategically important Mitla and Giddi passes in Sinai and the Bir Gafgafa defence zone behind them, as well as Sharm el-Sheikh commanding the Straits of Tiran.

Further intense shuttle diplomacy by Dr Kissinger resulted in the signature on May 31, 1974, of a similar military disengagement agreement by Syria and Israel covering the Golan front, where the two sides had continued to engage in regular hostilities notwithstanding the official existence of a ceasefire. The general effect of the agreement was that Israel withdrew from all the territory it had captured in the October 1973 war as well as from some areas occupied since the 1967 war, including the town of Quneitra. Limited-force zones were established on either side of a central buffer zone in which contingents of a newly created UN Disengagement Observer Force (UNDOF) were stationed. The agreement also provided that Syrian civilians who had fled during the hostilities would be able to return to the areas vacated by Israel, and Syrian administration restored.

As regards the Sinai front, however, a second Egyptian-Israeli disengagement agreement was signed on Sept. 4, 1975, again after protracted diplomatic efforts by Dr Kissinger. Under this agreement Israel withdrew its forces by a further 12 to 26 miles and the vacated area became the new UN buffer zone, with the old buffer zone being added to the existing Egyptian limited-forces zone. As part of this general withdrawal Israeli forces moved back to the eastern end of the Mitla and Giddi passes and a new Israeli limited-forces zone was established adjacent to the vacated area on the eastern side. Israel also vacated the Abu Rudeis and Ras Sudar oilfields on the Gulf of Suez (by February 1976), together with a narrow coastal strip running northwards to Egyptian-controlled territory south of Suez (this strip being demilitarized and placed under joint UN-Egyptian administration).

Other features of the Egyptian-Israeli agreement were that each side undertook to refrain from the use or threat of force or military blockade, to observe the ceasefire scrupulously and to renew the UNEF mandate annually. Each side also further agreed that non-military cargoes moving to and from Israel in non-Israeli vessels would be allowed to pass through the Suez Canal and that the United States would provide up to 200 civilian technicians to man electronic early-warning stations around the Mitla and Giddi passes.

In conjunction with the second Egyptian-Israeli disengagement agreement, the United States made a number of important commitments to Israel, namely (i) to be "fully responsive" to Israel's defence, energy and economic needs; (ii) to hold consultations with Israel in the event of a "world power" (i.e. the Soviet Union) interfering militarily in the Middle East; (iii) to accept the Israeli view that a further Egyptian-Israeli agreement and any negotiations with Jordan should take place within the context of an overall Middle East peace settlement; (iv) to consult and "concert" policy with Israel on the timing and procedure of a reconvened Geneva peace conference; and (v) not to recognize or negotiate with the PLO under its present orientation.

Egypt was able to comply with the provision concerning Israel's right of passage through the Suez Canal because on June 5, 1975, President Sadat had reopened the waterway on the eighth anniversary of its forcible closure by Egypt at the start of the 1967 war. On Nov. 2, 1975, the Greek freighter *Olympus* made a north-south passage of the canal bound for the Israeli port of Eilat with a cargo of cement, which thus became the first Israeli cargo shipped through the canal with the official approval of the Egyptian government since the establishment of the state of Israel in 1948.

For Egypt the 1974 and 1975 disengagement agreements were psychologically important because they confirmed and consolidated the limited territorial gains made in the 1973 war, in which the Egyptian armed forces had for the first time performed creditably against those of Israel. The attempted invasion of the new Jewish state in 1948 had ended in a debacle; in both the 1956 and the 1967 wars Nasser's forces had been comprehensively defeated; but in 1973 President Sadat became the "hero of the crossing" of the Suez Canal. Although many military analysts of the time took the view that if the fighting had continued Egypt would have been defeated for a fourth time, the ceasefire left Egyptian forces in control of the first stretch of territory wrested from Israel by military force since the creation of Israel in 1948. With Arab military honour thus restored—at least in Egyptian eyes—it became easier for Egypt to move towards its historic rapprochement with Israel.

Growing Egyptian-Israeli Rapprochement

Completion of the implementation of the second Egyptian-Israeli disengagement agreement in February 1976 was followed by protracted international negotiations aimed at reconvening the Geneva peace conference as the appropriate forum for the negotiation of an overall Middle East settlement. However, these efforts repeatedly came up against the stumbling block of Israel's refusal to accept the PLO as a participant at a reconvened conference, whereas Egypt, Jordan and Syria insisted on some form of PLO participation in accordance with a decision taken by the October 1974 Arab League summit conference held in Rabat (Morocco) to recognize the PLO as the sole legitimate representative of the Palestinian people. Moreover, the Arab states continued to insist that a settlement must not only satisfy the legitimate rights of the Palestinians but also involve an Israeli withdrawal from all the territories conquered in 1967, including the former Jordanian sector of Jerusalem.

The prospects of further accommodation appeared to recede even further when the Israeli general election of May 1977 resulted in Menachem Begin becoming Prime Minister at the head of a government dominated by his own right-wing nationalist *Likud* front. Likud's anthem stated that "The River Jordan has two banks. One of them is ours; the other one is ours too". The party's minimum position was an assertion of inalienable Israeli sovereignty over all the land between the Mediterranean Sea and the Jordan river, in which context it opposed "any plan envisaging a renunciation of the smallest piece" of the West Bank on the grounds that any such renunciation "will lead inevitably to the creation of a Palestinian state which will be a threat to the security of the civil population, will place the existence of Israel in danger and will endanger any chance of peace". The *Likud* platform also called for unrestricted Jewish settlement throughout the historic "Land of Israel" (Eretz Yisrael), including the Arab-populated West Bank. It therefore marked a significant departure from the approach pursued by the hitherto dominant Israel Labour Party, which had been prepared in principle to make territorial concessions on the West Bank as well as in Sinai and on the Golan Heights and had insisted that Jewish settlements in the occupied territories should only be authorized where security factors rendered them desirable. Yet it was to be Begin's government, apparently much less prepared to compromise than its Labour-led predecessors (but nevertheless as ready as the latter to have direct peace talks), which took Israel into a reconciliation with Egypt involving large territorial concessions (albeit not affecting the new Israeli government's conception of Jewish rights in the "Land of Israel").

In a speech to the Egyptian People's Assembly on Nov. 9, 1977, President Sadat urged other Arab states to unite in an all-out drive to reconvene the Geneva peace conference and declared that he was "ready to go to the Knesset itself" to unblock the peace-making process. Begin responded positively two days later, with the result that on Nov. 19-20, 1977, President Sadat undertook the first official visit ever made to Israel by an Arab leader and was received with the ceremonial appropriate to a head of state despite the existence of a technical state of war between the two countries. The centrepiece of the visit was an address by the Egyptian President to the Knesset in Jerusalem on Nov. 20 in which he explicitly accepted the existence of Israel as a Middle East state but reiterated his belief that a just and lasting peace depended on an Israeli withdrawal from all occupied Arab territory and on recognition of the rights of the Palestinians. The following month Menachem Begin became the first Israeli Prime Minister to be officially received in an Arab country when he had two days of talks with President Sadat in Ismailia on Dec. 25-26, 1977.

At the Ismailia meeting Begin presented Israel's proposals for "self-rule" for the Palestinian Arab residents of Judea, Samaria and Gaza, involving the election of an Administrative Council responsible for economic and social affairs, but with security and public order remaining the responsibility of the Israeli authorities. Under the proposals, which envisaged the abolition of the Israeli military administration, residents of these areas would have the option of choosing either Israeli or Jordanian citizenship, and those who chose the former would be entitled to acquire land and to settle in Israel; at the same time, residents of Israel would be entitled to acquire land and to settle in Judea, Samaria and Gaza. A tripartite committee of Israel, Jordan and the Administrative Council would determine, by unanimous decision, "the norms whereby Arab refugees residing outside Judea, Samaria and the Gaza district will be permitted to immigrate to these areas in reasonable numbers". The proposals also included the following assertion: "Israel stands by its right and its claim of sovereignty to Judea, Samaria and the Gaza district. In the knowledge that other claims exist, it proposes, for the sake of the agreement and the peace, that the question of sovereignty in these areas be left open".

In most other Arab states the reaction to the radically new departure represented by Sadat's visit to Israel was one of hostility, which mounted as it became clear that Egypt was serious about achieving a rapprochement with Israel. Particularly vociferous in its condemnation was the PLO, which saw the new policy as a means by which Egypt would seek to recover its own lost territory in desertion not only of the agreed principles of Arab solidarity but also of the interests of the dispossessed Palestinian people.

1978 Camp David Agreements—1979 Egypt-Israel Peace Treaty

The impetus towards a peace settlement created by Sadat's initiative was checked by a serious deterioration in the general Middle East situation from March 1978, when a major Palestinian guerrilla raid on Israel was immediately followed by a large-scale Israeli invasion of southern Lebanon designed to secure Israel's northern border against Palestinian incursions. However, the deployment of a UN peace-keeping force (UNIFIL) in southern Lebanon from late March 1978 and the subsequent withdrawal of Israeli forces by mid-June facilitated efforts by the United States to bring about a resumption of direct Egyptian-Israeli negotiations, culminating in talks between Sadat and Begin at Camp David (near Washington) in September 1978, with President Carter acting as intermediary. These talks resulted in the signature in Washington on Sept. 17 of two framework agreements, one on an overall Middle East settlement and the other specifically on the conclusion of a peace treaty between Egypt and Israel within three months.

The first of the Camp David agreements dealt in particular with the granting of what was termed "full autonomy" to the Palestinian Arab inhabitants of the West Bank and Gaza Strip, the following main stages being envisaged: (i) the inhabitants of the West Bank and Gaza would elect a "self-governing authority" whose powers would be defined in negotiations

between Israel, Egypt and Jordan in which the delegations of Egypt and Jordan would be open to "Palestinians from the West Bank and Gaza and other Palestinians as mutually agreed"; (ii) the self-governing authority would replace the existing Israeli administration in these areas; (iii) a five-year transitional period would begin when the self-governing authority had been established and would be marked by the withdrawal of Israeli forces or their re-deployment into "specified security locations"; (iv) not later than the third year of the transitional period negotiations would take place between Israel, Jordan, Egypt and the elected representatives of the West Bank and Gaza inhabitants "to determine the final status of the West Bank and Gaza" by the end of the transitional period. In an undertaking separate from the actual agreement, President Sadat stated that Egypt was prepared to assume "the Arab role" in these negotiations on Palestinian autonomy "following consultations with Jordan and the representatives of the Palestinian people" (i.e. if these two parties refused to participate directly—as in fact turned out to be the case).

On the broader aspects of the Middle East conflict, the first framework agreement specified inter alia (i) that parallel negotiations would take place between Israel, Jordan and elected Palestinian representatives to conclude a peace treaty between Israel and Jordan by the end of the transitional period; (ii) that Egypt and Israel would seek to conclude within three months a full peace treaty on the basis of detailed specifications set out in the second Camp David framework agreement "while inviting the other parties to the conflict to proceed simultaneously to negotiate and conclude similar peace treaties with a view to achieving a comprehensive peace in the area" ; and (iii) that peace treaties between Israel and each of its neighbours (i.e. Egypt, Jordan, Syria and Lebanon) should be based on principles establishing "relationships normal to states at peace with one another".

Contentious issues which remained unresolved under the Camp David agreements included the future of Jewish settlements in the Israeli-occupied territories and the status of East Jerusalem. In the latter connection Begin placed on the record that in July 1967 the Israeli government had decreed "that Jerusalem is one city indivisible, the capital of the state of Israel". These and other difficulties meant that the Dec. 17, 1978, target date for an Egyptian peace treaty could not be met (even though Sadat and Begin were jointly awarded the 1978 Nobel Peace Prize for their efforts at Camp David and earlier). However, further US mediation efforts, including some personal Middle East shuttle diplomacy by President Carter on March 8-13, 1979, resulted in President Sadat and Prime Minister Begin signing the first-ever Arab-Israeli peace treaty in Washington on March 26, 1979.

The draft treaty and its associated documents had been approved by the Knesset on March 22 by 95 votes to 11 (with two abstentions, three deputies not participating in the vote and two absent) and the signed text was subsequently ratified by the Israeli cabinet on April

1 (with one minister abstaining). In Egypt the draft treaty received unanimous approval from the cabinet on March 15 and its definitive text was ratified by the People's Assembly on April 10 by 328 votes to 15 (with one abstention and 16 members absent) and also by the electorate as a whole in a national referendum on April 19 (by 99.5 per cent of the valid votes cast). Instruments of ratification were exchanged at the US surveillance post at Um-Khashiba in Sinai on April 25, 1979—at which point the 31-year-old state of war between Egypt and Israel was officially terminated.

The main provisions of the Egyptian-Israeli peace treaty and the various documents associated with it were as follows: (i) Israel would evacuate its military forces and civilians from the whole of the Sinai peninsula in a phased withdrawal over a three-year period, as part of which some two-thirds of Sinai, comprising the area west of a line from El Arish in the north to Ras Mohammed in the south, would be returned to Egypt in five sub-phases within nine months of the treaty being ratified (see Map 52 (iv)); (ii) agreed security arrangements would be instituted involving the establishment of limited-force zones and the stationing of UN forces in key border areas, while the US Air Force would continue its surveillance flights over the area to verify compliance with the treaty's terms; (iii) after the completion of the Israeli withdrawal to the El Arish-Ras Mohammed line within nine months, normal diplomatic and other relations would be established between the two countries, including an exchange of ambassadors within 10 months of ratification; (iv) Israeli ships and cargoes would be granted the same right of passage in the Suez Canal and its approaches as the vessels of other countries; (v) both countries recognized the Straits of Tiran and the Gulf of Aqaba as international waterways; (vi) Egypt undertook to end its economic boycott of Israel and to sell oil from the Sinai oilfields to Israel on a non-discriminatory basis; (vii) within a month of the exchange of ratification instruments Egypt and Israel would begin negotiations with a view to implementing the provisions of the first Camp David framework agreement concerning the granting of "full autonomy" to the Palestinian Arab inhabitants of the West Bank and the Gaza Strip and the establishment of a "self-governing authority".

In letters addressed to Egypt and Israel, the US government confirmed that in the event of actual or threatened violation of the treaty the United States would, on request of one or both of the parties, consult with them and "take such other action as it may deem appropriate and helpful to achieve compliance with the treaty". The USA also agreed that if the UN Security Council failed to establish and maintain the peace-keeping arrangements called for in the treaty, the US President would be "prepared to take those steps necessary to ensure the establishment and maintenance of an acceptable alternative multinational force".

In an Israeli-US memorandum of understanding signed on March 26, 1979, the United States undertook to give strong support to Israel in certain circumstances, stating in particular: "The United States will provide support it deems appropriate for proper actions taken by Israel in response to…demonstrated violations of the treaty of peace. In particular, if a violation of the treaty of peace is deemed to threaten the security of Israel, including inter alia a blockade of Israel's use of international waterways, a violation of the provisions of the treaty of peace concerning limitation of forces or an armed attack against Israel, the United States will be prepared to consider, on an urgent basis, such measures as the strengthening of the US presence in the area, the providing of emergency supplies to Israel, and the exercise of maritime rights in order to put an end to the violation". The Egyptian government stated subsequently, however, that it would not recognize the legality of this memorandum and considered it null and void. Among 16 reasons listed by Egypt for rejecting the memorandum were that it had never been mentioned to or negotiated with Egypt; that it could be "construed as an eventual alliance between the United States and Israel against Egypt"; and that it gave the United States "the right to impose a military presence in the region for reasons agreed between Israel and the United States".

In the Arab world the price paid by Egypt for its signature of the peace treaty with Israel was virtually total political and economic isolation. Acting on preliminary decisions taken following the signature of the Camp David agreements, the Foreign and Economy Ministers of all Arab League member states except Egypt, Oman and Sudan, meeting in Baghdad on March 27-31, 1979, imposed a wide-ranging political and economic boycott on Egypt, including an embargo on oil supplies. The measures agreed to by the conference included the withdrawal of all remaining Arab ambassadors from Cairo, the suspension of Egypt from Arab League membership as well as from a large number of joint Arab organizations and projects, and the transfer of the Arab League's headquarters from Cairo to Tunis. Other international groupings which suspended Egypt's membership over the peace treaty with Israel included the Islamic Conference Organization, the Organization of African Unity, the Non-Aligned Movement and the Organization of Arab Petroleum Exporting Countries.

Implementation of Egyptian-Israeli Peace Treaty

Notwithstanding some last-minute uncertainty engendered by the Israeli bombing of Iraq's (French-supplied) Osirak nuclear reactor near Baghdad (on June 7, 1981) and by the assassination of President Sadat (on Oct. 6, 1981), the Israeli withdrawal from Sinai was carried out in accordance with the timetable laid down in the 1979 peace treaty. Completion of the fifth sub-phase on Jan. 26, 1980, took Israeli forces back to the El Arish-Ras Mohammed line, at which point the Egyptian-Israeli border was officially declared open. A month later, on Feb. 26, Israel and Egypt exchanged ambassadors—the Egyptian envoy taking up residence in Tel Aviv to signify Egypt's non-recognition of unified Jerusalem as the capital of Israel. Finally, on the third anniversary of the ratification of the 1979 treaty, Israel completed its withdrawal from the remainder of Sinai on April 25, 1982, after a core of hard-line Jewish settlers in the Yamit area of northern Sinai had been forcibly removed by the Israeli Army.

Concurrently with the final hand-over in Sinai, troops of an international peace-keeping force were deployed along the reinstated international border between Egypt and Israel. In accordance with the 1979 treaty, this force had been assembled at the instigation of the US government outside the UN framework, it having become clear that the Soviet Union would veto any move in the Security Council to designate a UN force for the purpose. Countries which had declared their willingness to contribute troops to the Sinai force included (in addition to the United States itself) Britain, France, Italy, the Netherlands, Australia, Canada and New Zealand. As agreed by Egypt and Israel on April 26, 1982, the first duties of the new force included taking control of certain sections of the international frontier where precise demarcation remained in dispute, notably a stretch of about 750 metres at Taba, to the west of Eilat on the Gulf of Aqaba (see Section 5.4).

Against a backdrop of considerable unease within Israel over the Sinai withdrawal, ministers of the *Likud*-dominated government stressed that no further territorial concessions would be made to the Arabs. Indeed, in the period since the signature of the 1979 treaty, Israel had taken several important steps to give internal legal substance to this attitude. On July 30, 1980, the Knesset had adopted legislation strengthening the status of Jerusalem as the "indivisible" capital of Israel, while on Dec. 14, 1981, the Golan Heights were effectively annexed under a government decree which extended Israeli "law, jurisdiction and administration" to that area of former Syrian territory. Both of these moves were strongly condemned by the United Nations (which had repeatedly called upon Israel to refrain from altering the status of the occupied territories), as was the Begin government's acceleration of Jewish settlement of the West Bank.

For its part, the Israeli government of that period repeatedly asserted its historic right to sovereignty over the "Land of Israel" and declared its aim of annexing the West Bank and the Gaza Strip at the end of the five-year transitional period laid down in the first Camp David framework agreement. At the time of the final Sinai withdrawal, however, this aim remained somewhat academic because the transitional period had not yet started and Israeli military administration remained in place. Despite constant efforts by the US government to bring about progress in the Palestinian "autonomy" negotiations, Egypt and Israel remained deadlocked on the nature of the Palestinian "self-governing authority", the installation of which was to initiate the five-year transitional period. Various difficulties had prevented progress being made in these negotiations (not least the refusal to participate of two directly interested parties, namely the Palestinians themselves and Jordan), but the major underlying

obstacle was the Israeli government's insistence that "full autonomy" could imply no element of Palestinian sovereignty.

The April 1982 Sinai withdrawal therefore left Israel in control of the whole of the territory of the former British Palestine mandate west of the River Jordan (plus the Golan Heights, which as explained above formed part of the original mandate) and with an estimated Arab population of some 1,700,000 (including 500,000 in Israel proper) as against a Jewish population of about 3,400,000. While Israel continued to insist that Palestinian Arab political aspirations could be reconciled with its own territorial position, this view was clearly not shared by the Palestinians themselves, among whom increasingly violent opposition to Israeli rule was accompanied by widespread open support for the PLO. Against this background, the Arab-Israeli territorial conflict continued to have important external dimensions arising from Israel's occupation of territory captured from Syria and Jordan in 1967 and from its determination to eradicate the PLO presence in Lebanon. This latter factor became the most critical aspect of the Arab-Israeli conflict after the Sinai withdrawal.

Israeli Border with Lebanon—1982 Invasion—Creation of "Security Zone"

Although the international border between Israel and Lebanon (which follows, for the most part, the border established in 1923 between the British and French mandatory territories) had been considered, until the signing of the Camp David treaty, to be Israel's only frontier not in dispute, it had in fact never been accepted by Israeli and Zionist leaders, who thirsted for Lebanon's water resources. The Zionist submission to the 1919 Paris Peace Conference had proposed a northern border at Sidon, thus including within the Jewish state Lake Karaoun and the basins of the Litani and Awali rivers, which are all now in Lebanon, as well as all the headwaters of the Jordan. Ben-Gurion had commented in his diary in 1921: "It is necessary that the water resources, upon which the future of the land depends, should not be outside the borders of the future Jewish homeland...For this reason we have always demanded that the Land of Israel include the Southern banks of the Litani river, the headwaters of the Jordan, and the Hauran region from the El Adja spring south of Damascus...The land needs this water". Such remarks had been repeated frequently by Ben-Gurion and other leaders, both before and after the establishment of Israel.

The transplantation to Lebanon of the main bulk of Palestinian activists after their forcible expulsion from Jordan in September 1970 had led to increasing Israeli concern over the security of northern Galilee in the face of guerrilla attacks mounted from southern Lebanon. Two major terror raids occurred on the northern Israeli towns of Kiryat Shemona and Ma'alot, on April 11 and May 15, 1974, respectively. Concern over the threat from across the border increased when Palestinian movements obtained substantial scope for autonomous action amid the collapse of central government authority which accompanied the 1975-76 civil war in Lebanon. There were numerous reports of shelling by the PLO of villages and towns in northern Israel. Israel responded by making frequent direct attacks on Palestinian guerrilla bases in southern Lebanon.

The most concerted military initiative, until the 1982 invasion, began on March 14-15, 1978. It was justified as retaliation for a Fatah bus hijacking on March 11 on the coastal road, near Kibbutz Ma'agan Michael, which resulted in 35 civilians being killed. Israeli forces occupied Lebanese territory up to the Litani river, and deemed it to be a "buffer zone" against future attack. On March 19 the UN Security Council passed Resolution 425, calling on Israel to withdraw. UN 425 also mandated a United Nations Interim Force in Lebanon (UNIFIL) to restore peace and "help the Lebanese government re-establish its authority in the area". According to Israel's interpretation of UN 425, withdrawal applied equally to the Syrian-dominated "Arab deterrent force" which had been stationed in Lebanon since 1976. Israel warned that it would not tolerate any move into southern Lebanon by the Syrians. At the same time, it claimed that its "buffer zone" was a temporary expedient, and it denied that it had any long-term claim on Lebanese territory.

By June 13, 1978, Israel had handed over nominal control of most of the zone to anti-PLO Lebanese forces to the north of the border, and not to UNIFIL, as demanded by the UN. Israel's ally, or "proxy army", as enemies dubbed it, was the South Lebanon Army (SLA). Led by Maj. Sa'ad Haddad, the SLA was mainly officered by Christian Lebanese, though over time its foot-soldiers included some Shiites and a few Druze.

In July 1981, following a series of Israeli air raids on Palestinian targets in southern Lebanon and retaliatory PLO shelling of targets in northern Israel, Israel bombed residential areas of Beirut, killing over 200 people. The USA sent a special envoy, Philip Habib, who negotiated a ceasefire between Israel and the PLO, which came into effect on July 24. This ceasefire held until June 4, 1982, when the attempted assassination, by a dissident Palestinian group, of the Israeli ambassador to London, Shlomo Argov, led to a further Israeli air raid on Beirut and southern Lebanon, and retaliatory Palestinian shelling (which caused no casualties) of northern Israel. Two days later, on June 6, Israel launched a full-scale invasion of Lebanon.

Code-named "Operation Peace for Galilee" (ironically, a majority of the population of Galilee was still Palestinian), the attack was officially described as an attempt to remove PLO forces from a 40-kilometre-wide belt of southern Lebanon. However, within a week the Israeli army had reached the outskirts of Beirut, 100 kilometres from the border. The siege and bombardment of Beirut lasted two months, until an agreement was reached on Aug. 19, 1982, under which the PLO forces withdrew from Beirut, with their weapons, and were dispersed to various Arab countries. Lebanese government sources claimed that 18,000 people were killed and 30,000 seriously injured (85 per cent of them civilians) during the Israeli attack.

Israel's official aim was widely disbelieved, not least in Israel itself, and it has been suggested that Israel's real aims were threefold: (i) to destroy the PLO as a political leadership for the Palestinians under Israeli rule, who had staged an uprising during May and June 1982; (ii) to fulfil Israel's long-standing ambition of taking control of Lebanon's water resources; (iii) to re-fashion the political structure of Lebanon in order to ensure the other aims, either by dividing it into rival ethnic and religious cantons or by establishing Israel's ally, the Phalangist Party, in unchallenged control of the country.

This last aim seemed to be achieved on Aug. 23 with the election as President of Phalange leader Bashir Gemayel. However, Gemayel was assassinated on Sept. 14, before he had taken office, and on the following day, in breach of the withdrawal agreement and undertakings to the US government, Israeli troops entered West Beirut. Within hours, Israel had assisted the entry of the Phalangist militia to the Palestinian refugee camps of Sabra and Shatila in Beirut, where they massacred an estimated 2,000 civilians. It was not until Sept. 18, after the first international reports of the killings, that Israel ordered the withdrawal of the militia.

The Sabra and Shatila massacre caused international outrage, and in Israel, too, tens of thousands demonstrated against the war. Under this pressure, the Israeli government established an independent judicial inquiry. The Kahan report, published in February 1983, after finding that the killings had been carried out by the Phalangists, criticized various Israeli officials including Prime Minister Menachem Begin, Foreign Minister Yitzhak Shamir, Defence Minister Ariel Sharon, Chief of Staff Rafael Eitan and others for indirect responsibility. Sharon, in particular, was criticized for permitting the Phalangists to enter the camps; following a demonstration in Tel-Aviv of an estimated 400,000 people (10 per cent of the country's population), Begin was forced to dismiss Sharon from the Defence Ministry, although he remained a member of the cabinet.

Following the PLO evacuation of Beirut, and in the face of growing international and internal criticism of the Lebanese operation, the Begin government repeatedly stated that Israeli forces would be withdrawn from southern Lebanon only in the context of an overall peace agreement with a Lebanese government restored to proper authority. Particular Israeli objectives at this time included the withdrawal of all non-Lebanese Arab forces from Lebanon and the establishment of a "PLO-free" demilitarized zone on Israel's northern border.

Against this background, talks opened in Khalde (south of Beirut) on Dec. 28, 1982, between Israeli and Lebanese officials, with the United States also represented—these being the first direct negotiations between the two countries since the conclusion of their March 1949 armistice. The Israeli team was headed by David Kimche, director-general of the Foreign Ministry, and Lieut.-Gen. Avraham Tamir, who had been Ariel Sharon's strategic advisor. The head of the Lebanese team was Antoine Fattal, a retired career diplomat and legal expert. Fattal's assistants were Brig. Abbas Hamdan, a Shiite from the south, who had led the Lebanese-Israeli Mixed Armistice Commission for several months previously, and Ghassan Tueni, editor of the *an-Nahar* newspaper and a former ambassador. Morris Draper, deputy assistant of state, headed the US negotiating team; his chief colleague was President Reagan's special envoy, Philip Habib.

The talks eventually resulted in the signature of an agreement on May 17, 1983. It provided for (i) the withdrawal of Israeli forces from Lebanon; (ii) the ending of the state of war between Israel and Lebanon; and (iii) the establishment of a security region in southern Lebanon, to prevent the re-infiltration of Palestinian guerrillas into the area.

Internal security and political conditions continued to deteriorate in Lebanon, however, and on March 5, 1984, the Lebanese government, under pressure from Syria, unilaterally abrogated the (as yet unratified) agreement with Israel. Accordingly, the Israeli government decided in January 1985 on a unilateral three-stage withdrawal from Lebanon. The first two stages were completed by mid-April 1985. On June 10, 1985, Israel announced the withdrawal of its troops from Lebanon. However, they established, or more accurately, re-established, a self-declared 10-20 kilometre-wide "security zone" inside Lebanon. The Israeli Army patrolled this area jointly with its ally, the South Lebanon Army of Gen. Antoine Lahad, who had succeeded the late Maj. Sa'ad Haddad as leader.

Over the ensuing years, Israeli forces frequently operated in the "security zone" to assist the SLA in resisting what appeared to be attempts by Palestinian guerrilla units to resume anti-Israeli operations from southern Lebanon. Moreover, Israeli aircraft and naval vessels continued to make strikes against Palestinian bases elsewhere in Lebanon, to which many of the Palestinians dispersed in 1982 had gradually returned.

Ultimately a greater threat to Israel emerged in the shape of Lebanese Shiite groups, *Amal* and particularly *Hizbullah*. When the Israelis first entered Lebanon in 1978, and even in the early days of the 1982 campaign, many Shiites cheered the invaders, as they resented the dominance of armed PLO forces in their own region. However, the mood changed, and anti-Israeli enmity grew, especially after Oct. 16, 1983, when Israeli forces clashed with a crowd of 50,000 Shiites who were publicly celebrating Ashura Muharram, the commemoration of the martyrdom of Imam Hussein, in the town of Nabatiyeh. Sheikh Mehdi Shamseddin, head of the Higher Shiite Council in Beirut, immediately issued a *fatwa* calling for "civil resistance". A National Lebanese Resistance (NLR, or *Jamoul*) was soon established, with *Amal* as its domi-

nant partner. *Hizbullah* later established its own Islamic Resistance Organization (*al-Muqawama al-Islamiyah*), which by the 1990s effectively eclipsed *Jamoul*. The Syrian-backed Taif Accords of 1990 finally ended the Lebanese civil war and ordered the disarming of all militias in Lebanon. However, Beirut did not disarm the anti-Israeli resistance coalitions, and allowed them to continue harrying Israeli occupation forces and their proxies.

Diplomatic Efforts to Unblock Negotiating Process, 1982-87

In an attempt to unblock the peace negotiating process, President Reagan of the United States on Sept. 1, 1982, announced important new US proposals for the achievement of an overall settlement, envisaging in particular the granting of self-determination to the West Bank and Gaza Palestinians within a political entity linked to Jordan. The new US proposals received a cautiously positive response from some Arab leaders, notably King Hussein of Jordan, but were immediately rejected by the Israeli government as a deviation from the 1978 Camp David framework agreement. Also rejected by Israel was a new peace plan drawn up by a summit conference of the Arab League held in Fez (Morocco) on Sept. 6-9, 1982, which appeared to hold out the prospect of Israel securing recognition in return for a withdrawal from all territories captured in 1967 (although the categoric refusal of the Arab side to negotiate directly with Israel was maintained).

The 1982 Fez summit plan was based substantially on earlier Saudi Arabian proposals (published on Aug. 8, 1981) but with certain modifications designed to meet the demands of the hard-line Arab states. The plan had the following eight points: (i) the withdrawal of Israel from all Arab territories occupied in 1967 including "Arab Jerusalem"; (ii) the dismantling of Israeli settlements established in the occupied territories since 1967; (iii) the guarantee of freedom of worship and practice of religious rites for all religions in the Holy Places; (iv) the reaffirmation of the Palestinian people's right to self-determination and "the exercise of its imprescriptible and inalienable rights under the leadership of the PLO, its sole legitimate representative, and the indemnification of all those who do not wish to return"; (v) placing the West Bank and Gaza under UN control for a transitional period not exceeding a few months; (vi) the establishment of an independent Palestinian state with Jerusalem as its capital; (vii) UN Security Council guarantees of "peace among all states of the region, including the independent Palestinian state"; and (viii) UN Security Council guarantees for the principles of the foregoing. (The Saudi Arabian plan had made no specific mention of the PLO and had envisaged an affirmation of "the right of all countries of the region to live in peace", i.e. implicitly including Israel.)

Major diplomatic and political developments arising from the formulation of the respective Reagan and

Arab League peace plans included (i) an exploration of the federation concept at a series of meetings between King Hussein and Yasser Arafat (the PLO leader); (ii) talks between President Reagan and a League delegation in Washington on Oct. 22, 1982, to evaluate the common and disparate elements in the two plans; (iii) an official visit to Washington by King Hussein on Dec. 21-23, 1982, during which he discussed with President Reagan the obstacles to future Jordanian participation in the peace negotiation process; and (iv) growing opposition within the PLO to any settlement involving an accommodation with Israel. In this process, the role of King Hussein became pivotal, in that the only realistic way forward, given Israel's determination to adhere to the Camp David agreement and its insistence on direct peace negotiations, lay in Jordan being persuaded to come to the negotiating table to discuss the future of the West Bank and Gaza. However, at his Washington talks and subsequently, King Hussein continued to reiterate his unwillingness to join in the Palestinian "autonomy" negotiations without the full backing of the PLO and the Arab League.

During 1983-85 the prospects for the Camp David peace process appeared to be improved by (i) a visit to Cairo by Arafat on Dec. 22, 1983, for talks with President Hosni Mubarak; (ii) Jordan's decision on Sept. 25, 1984, to resume full diplomatic relations with Egypt (whose gradual rehabilitation in the Arab and Islamic worlds subsequently continued with its resumption of full participation in the Islamic Conference Organization in December 1984); and (iii) an announcement on Feb. 11, 1985, that King Hussein and Arafat had reached agreement on a joint approach to peace negotiations based on the concept of a future confederal relationship between a Palestinian entity and Jordan. As regards this last development, however, seriously conflicting interpretations quickly emerged between the two sides as to what exactly had been agreed, notably whether or not the PLO had implicitly accepted UN Resolution 242 (and thus Israel's right to exist) as a basis for negotiations.

At the same time, Arafat's position came under increasing challenge from hardline PLO elements (mostly backed by Syria), who formed a Palestinian National Salvation Front, based in Damascus, in opposition to Arafat's leadership and his alleged willingness to compromise on established PLO policy principles. These and other complications resulted in King Hussein announcing on Feb. 19, 1986, that Jordan was "unable to continue to co-ordinate politically with the PLO leadership until their words become bonds, characterized by commitment, credibility and consistency". Thereafter, Jordan consolidated a rapprochement with Syria which had been under way for some months, a realignment which indirectly assisted Arafat in reasserting his authority over Syrian-backed PLO dissidents by early 1987. Nevertheless, there seemed to be no immediate prospect of a new Jordanian-PLO joint approach to peace negotiations.

Meanwhile, the Israeli general elections of July 1984 had resulted in the Labour Alignment returning to government in a national unity coalition with the *Likud* front and with the Labour Party leader, Shimon Peres, becoming Prime Minister for the first two years of the government's four-year term. In its policy platform, the Alignment had proposed that Israel should be prepared to make territorial concessions, consistent with its security requirements, in return for a peace treaty with Jordan, and had also advocated a complete freeze on all settlement activity in occupied areas of dense Palestinian population (while promising that no existing settlements would be dismantled). In contrast, *Likud* had rejected any "territorial compromise" (thus effectively reaffirming its goal of establishing full Israeli sovereignty over all the remaining occupied territories) and had urged continuing Jewish settlement throughout the West Bank and Gaza.

Against this policy background, Peres concentrated during his premiership on establishing a framework which would enable the Jordanian government to enter into some form of direct negotiations with Israel. To this end, he advanced the idea that such direct negotiations could be initiated within the framework of a wider international conference, to which the permanent members of the UN Security Council might be invited provided they had diplomatic relations with both sides of the conflict. In a surprise development, Peres had talks in Morocco on July 22-23, 1986, with King Hassan, resulting in a joint communiqué stating that they had been "essentially" concerned with the Arab League's 1982 Fez peace plan and of "a purely exploratory nature". After the meeting, the Moroccan king claimed that he had broken off the talks once it had become clear that Israel would not recognize the PLO or agree to a complete withdrawal from the occupied territories. He nevertheless added: "Arab leaders must meet directly with the leaders of Israel to know exactly what they want".

The concept of an international conference on the Arab-Israeli dispute featured prominently in talks between Peres and President Mubarak of Egypt held in Alexandria on Sept. 10-12, 1986, when both leaders agreed to make 1987 "a year of negotiations for peace". However, after Peres had vacated the Israeli premiership the following month in favour of Yitzhak Shamir (*Likud*) and succeeded the latter as Foreign Minister, the proposal for an international conference, as currently formulated, failed to command majority support in the Israeli cabinet.

Differences within the new cabinet surfaced following the visit of Peres to Cairo in February 1987, at the conclusion of which he issued a joint statement with Egyptian Foreign Minister Ahmad Abd al-Meguid calling for the convening of an international peace conference in 1987. In May, the cabinet rejected Peres' proposal, and the Labour Party failed to defeat the *Likud* on this issue in the Knesset. Peres also negotiated a secret London agreement with King Hussein, whereby Palestinians would enjoy a large measure of sovereignty under a Jordanian "umbrella"; but the Israeli cabinet scotched his plans, and he was later accused of deception for negotiating behind Prime Minister Shamir's back. (More on this putative deal may be found in the sub-section on Israel's Peace Treaty with Jordan, below.)

The growing pressure for an international peace conference, and the isolation of Shamir, were again demonstrated during Peres' visit to Washington in May 1987, where he reached agreement with Secretary of State George Shultz on the form which such a conference should take. However, in the absence of US pressure on Shamir, no progress was made. A visit to Israel by Abd al-Meguid during the summer also failed to produce any results.

Reunification of PLO—Start of Intifada

Meanwhile, the Palestinian position had strengthened with the reunification of the PLO in March 1987. The most important of the dissident groups, the Popular Front for the Liberation of Palestine (PFLP) and the Democratic Front for the Liberation of Palestine (DFLP), attended the 18th session of the Palestine National Council (PNC) in Algiers on April 20-25. At the same time, the Palestine Communist Party joined the PLO, leaving only a rump of Syrian-sponsored groups in the Salvation Front. Arafat renounced the 1985 Amman agreement, and downgraded links with Egypt, in return for which the radicals endorsed his leadership.

Demonstrations in the occupied territories in support of reunification led to a renewed cycle of violence, with students killed, universities closed, and an increase in administrative detention, house demolitions, and deportations. There were further angry demonstrations in the occupied territories during the November 1987 Arab League summit in Amman, at which Palestine was considered, for the first time, a secondary issue. Despite all these signs, there was general surprise at the eruption of the Palestinian intifada (uprising) on Dec. 9, 1987. Starting as a spontaneous protest at the death of four Gazans in a suspicious road accident, it soon became clear that this was a mass popular uprising which rapidly developed into the most serious threat yet to Israel's control of the occupied territories, and which brought the Palestinian people under Israeli rule to the centre of the political stage. By Dec. 31, 25 Palestinians had been killed in a wave of mass demonstrations that spread through the towns, and particularly the refugee camps, of the West Bank and Gaza Strip.

January 1988 saw the first communiqués of the underground United National Leadership of the Intifada (UNLI). The UNLI stressed that it was not a rival to the PLO, which remained the "sole, legitimate representative" of the Palestinian people. This was paralleled by the development of popular committees to control health, education, agriculture, defence and other aspects of life. The Israeli government tried to defeat the intifada through massive repression, leading to an unprecedentedly negative Israeli image internationally. On Dec. 22, the UN Security Council passed

Resolution 605 condemning Israel's repression of the intifada. Although the USA abstained in that vote, on Jan. 5, 1988, it voted in favour of Security Council Resolution 607, which called on Israel to observe the Fourth Geneva Convention and condemned deportations. This was the first time the United States had criticized Israel at the UN since the 1982 invasion of Lebanon.

Secretary of State Shultz visited the Middle East in February, and issued a peace plan which called for a six-month period of negotiations between Israel and a joint Jordanian/Palestinian delegation, to begin on May 1, 1988, which would determine details of a three-year transitional autonomy for the West Bank and Gaza Strip, during which period the delegations would negotiate a permanent settlement; there would be a concurrent international peace conference with the participation of the five permanent members of UN Security Council and all interested parties (including a joint Jordanian/Palestinian delegation). Peres accepted this proposal, but Shamir rejected it. It was also rejected by the PLO and the UNLI, who saw the plan as a device to outflank the PLO and defuse the intifada.

The intifada was having an impact on Israeli society, and on the Palestinians in Israel. It seemed on a number of occasions that the rioting would spill over the Green Line and unite Palestinians on both sides; this threat was met by increased repression, in particular around Land Day (March 30), on which date Palestinians commemorate six Palestinian citizens of Israel shot dead in demonstrations in 1976. Israeli Jews, too, demonstrated against the repression. In particular, reserve soldiers in the *Yesh Gvul* ("There is A Border") group refused to serve in the occupied territories; dozens went to prison rather than take part in the repression. On Aug. 17, the popular committees were banned, and deportation orders were issued against 25 Palestinian activists.

On April 16, an Israeli assassination team murdered PLO deputy leader Khalil al-Wazir (Abu Jihad) in Tunis; 16 Palestinians were killed by Israeli troops in the subsequent protests, making this the bloodiest day yet of the intifada, in which 185 Palestinians had been killed so far. Following Abu Jihad's funeral in Damascus on April 25, Arafat, on his first visit to Syria since 1983, met President Hafez al-Assad to discuss their disagreements.

An Arab League summit in June 1988 rejected the Shultz plan, demanding PLO participation in an international peace conference leading to Palestinian self-determination and an independent state. In the course of the meeting, the PLO indirectly accepted Security Council Resolutions 242 and 338. Meanwhile, on July 31 King Hussein cut Jordan's "administrative and legal links" with the West Bank. This step, which left the West Bank with no state claiming de jure rule, was welcomed by the UNLI. It was a blow to the Shultz and Peres plans, which were both premised on Jordanian representation of the Palestinians at an international peace conference; this had the effect of strengthening *Likud* vis-à-vis Labour in internal Israeli disputes.

At a speech to the European Parliament in Strasbourg on Sept. 12, Arafat stated that the PLO would be prepared to negotiate with Israel at an international peace conference conducted on the basis of Resolutions 242 and 338; he renounced armed struggle outside the occupied territories and sought mutual recognition between Israel and the PLO.

The Israeli general election on Nov. 1 resulted in a narrow victory for *Likud*. Shamir eventually established another National Unity coalition, though this time with Shamir as Prime Minister for the full term.

Declaration of "State of Palestine"

The PNC met for its 19th session in Algiers on Nov. 12-15, 1988, and on Nov. 15 declared "the establishment of the State of Palestine on our Palestinian territory with its capital, Jerusalem". The PNC did not define the borders of the state. However, its declaration was based on UN Resolution 181 of 1947 (the Partition resolution), which had defined borders between Jewish and Arab states in Palestine. These are, in effect, the only legal borders, as the 1948-49 Armistice agreements conferred no right to territories beyond the borders set out in Resolution 181. At the same meeting, the PLO accepted Security Council Resolution 242 as the basis, together with the Palestinian right of self-determination and international legitimacy on the basis of all UN resolutions, of an international peace conference.

By December 1988, when Arafat was invited to address the UN General Assembly in New York, more than 60 states had recognized Palestine. The US government, which had attempted in September 1987 to close the office of the PLO observer mission to the UN, denied him a visa, and the General Assembly eventually met in Geneva. In his speech on Dec. 13, Arafat presented a three-point programme: (i) the UN Secretary-General should establish a preparatory committee for an international peace conference; (ii) the occupied territories should come under the temporary supervision of UN forces, who would oversee Israeli withdrawal; and (iii) there should be a comprehensive settlement reached at an international peace conference to be held on the basis of Security Council Resolutions 242 and 338. In response to US demands, he explicitly recognized Israel and condemned "terrorism". Robert Pelletreau, the US Ambassador to Tunis, thereafter met PLO representatives on Dec. 16, thus conferring official US recognition on the PLO.

During 1989, there was more pressure for an international peace conference. In a visit to the Middle East in February, the Soviet Foreign Minister, Eduard Shevardnadze, proposed that preparations be made for a conference. The USA held further meetings with the PLO in March, though no agreement was reached. On April 6 Shamir, visiting Washington, set out his own peace plan, under which, in return for an end to the intifada, there would be "free and democratic" elections to a delegation which would negotiate a permanent settlement with Israel. This proposal was welcomed by the USA and rejected by the Israeli right; the Palestinians sought clarification of the proposals before taking a decision.

On a visit to Paris in May, Arafat stated that the Palestinian National Charter had been superseded by the Algiers PNC decisions, and was now "caduque" (literally, "obsolete"). In July, Shamir attempted to write further clarifications into his plan: all violence should cease before elections could be held; residents of East Jerusalem would not be able to vote; Israeli settlement in the occupied territories would continue; there would be no negotiations with the PLO and no Palestinian state west of Jordan. The Labour Party threatened to resign from the cabinet, which eventually endorsed the original plan without the changes.

In September 1989, Egyptian President Hosni Mubarak asked Israel for clarification of 10 points in the Shamir plan. He called for a commitment to the principle of "land for peace" and the participation of East Jerusalem residents in the election. The response of the Israeli government was again divided, with Peres supporting the demands and Shamir opposing them. In order to maintain the movement towards a conference, US Secretary of State James Baker proposed his own five-point plan, under which acceptance of Mubarak's 10 points would not be a precondition for participation in the conference—at which the composition of the Palestinian delegation would be decided by Israel, the USA and Egypt.

The PLO central council, meeting in Baghdad in October 1989, responded to the Shamir plan by calling for a Palestinian delegation for a dialogue with Israel, with representatives from the occupied territories and the diaspora, to be chosen by the PLO; this dialogue would be the first stage of an international peace conference. In January 1990, Peres visited Cairo, and threatened to end the coalition if no progress was made. Shamir also faced difficulties with ministers from his own *Likud* party, and on March 13 he dismissed Peres. Shamir lost the subsequent vote of confidence in the Knesset. However, Peres failed to form a new government, and in June 1990 Shamir formed a new, narrow, coalition, giving Israel the most right-wing government in its history.

A US State Department human rights report issued in February 1990 stated that 304 Palestinians had been killed by troops and settlers during 1989 (Palestinian sources claimed the figure was 366), 20,000 had been wounded and 26 deported, 164 homes had been demolished, and 9,138 Palestinians (2 per cent of the adult male population) were under detention, more than 1,000 of them without charge.

A feature of the intifada had been the growth, particularly in Gaza, of Islamic fundamentalist groups, notably Islamic Jihad and *Hamas* (the Islamic Resistance Movement). Despite tensions between these groups and the more secular PLO, leading to occasional clashes, the UNLI generally managed to maintain unity.

During 1990, Palestinians expressed growing concern at the effect of the increase in Soviet Jewish immigration (until the USA introduced new restrictions, over 90 per cent of Soviet Jewish emigrants had sought entry to the USA). The Israeli government hoped that one million would arrive during 1990. On Jan. 14 Shamir stated: "A big immigration needs a big Israel". Although few settled in the West Bank and Gaza, their arrival increased pressure on housing inside Israel. Many settled in occupied East Jerusalem, where violence over settlements was growing.

At a meeting in Geneva of the UN Security Council, Arafat claimed that Israel was seeking genocide, while at an Arab summit in Baghdad Jordan expressed its fear that Israel was seeking war in order to expel the Palestinians from the West Bank, and Iraqi President Saddam Hussein threatened chemical attack on Israel if it again attacked Iraqi nuclear sites. On June 20 the USA suspended its dialogue with the PLO after the attempt by a dissident Palestinian group to attack the Israeli coast.

The Gulf War and the Middle East Peace Conference

The Iraqi invasion of Kuwait on Aug. 2, 1990 (see Section 5.7) had a major effect on the development of the Israeli-Palestinian conflict. Saddam Hussein's calls for linkage between the Kuwait and Palestine issues, though designed to deflect criticism of his actions, found a tremendous echo among Palestinians and other Arabs. The rapid deployment of an international force to ensure implementation of the UN resolutions against the invasion was seen as hypocritical by people who had lived for 23 years under occupation, with no comparable action being taken to enforce compliance with the many UN resolutions on this issue.

The PLO's position was equivocal. While reaffirming its opposition to the acquisition of land by force and condemning the occupation, it also condemned the military action against Iraq, and in particular the US role. Although this position was shared by most Palestinians, it cost the PLO much of its financial support from the wealthy Gulf regimes, and threatened its reconciliation with Syria. Many on the Israeli left, who had been calling for negotiations with the PLO, now shifted their position, particularly after Iraq fired missiles at Israel during the war.

The US attempt to build up a coalition against Iraq was threatened by the possibility of Israeli intervention, which would embarrass the Arab states. Israel used this threat in order to extract promises that the United States would not make deals at Israel's expense. However, the USA was also obliged to persuade the Arab states to take part in the coalition, and employed a combination of financial aid and promises of pressure on Israel. While not wishing to appear to be promoting the idea of "linkage", which would be seen as a victory for Saddam Hussein, US officials spoke vaguely of the need to address the Israeli-Palestinian conflict after the end of Iraqi occupation

of Kuwait; this position was endorsed by the EC, Britain, and France.

This delicate balancing act was threatened by the Oct. 8 massacre by Israeli police of 17 Palestinian worshippers in Jerusalem's Al Aqsa mosque—Islam's third most holy site. This was the bloodiest event so far in the intifada, and led to a wave of attacks on Israeli soldiers and civilians, with several stabbed to death in Jerusalem and Tel-Aviv. At the UN Security Council, the USA voted for Resolution 672, which condemned Israel's behaviour and agreed to send a fact-finding mission to Jerusalem. Israel refused to meet the mission. Tension was raised still further following the murder in New York on Nov. 5 of Rabbi Meir Kahane, leader of Israel's extreme-right *Kach* party.

As the deadline for Iraqi withdrawal from Kuwait neared, grave concern developed in Israel. Gas masks were distributed to Israeli civilians, though despite a High Court ruling only about 1 per cent of the Palestinians were given masks. On Jan. 6, 1991, Saddam Hussein said that the coming war would become the battle to liberate Palestine.

On Jan. 14, PLO deputy leader Salah Khalaf (Abu Iyad) was assassinated in Tunis. It was not clear whether his killer was working for Israel or for the pro-Iraqi Abu Nidal group of dissident Palestinians. (Khalaf had reportedly expressed scepticism about the PLO's perceived support for Iraq, and was held responsible by Israel for the murder of Israeli athletes in Munich in 1972.)

In the course of the war, which started on Jan. 17, 1991, Iraq fired about 40 Scud missiles into Israel. These caused some physical damage, but relatively few casualties; two people were killed and about 250 injured, mostly slightly. Although these attacks attracted aid and sympathy for Israel, they also showed, as some activists and strategists in Israel pointed out, that the country's security could not be guaranteed by "defensible borders" alone. Israel imposed a total curfew lasting 33 days in the occupied territories during the war, leaving many families without income. The Palestinian economy was estimated to have lost $150-200 million—8 per cent of its annual GDP—during the curfew.

The defeat of Iraq led to a period of intense diplomatic efforts for the convening of an international peace conference on the Middle East. US Secretary of State Baker made five tours of Middle East capitals between March and August 1991. In May, Foreign Minister Aleksandr Besmertnykh became the highest ranking Soviet official to visit Israel since 1967.

On June 1, US President George Bush sent letters to all Middle East heads of state, setting out the terms of a conference. It was to be chaired jointly by the USA and the USSR; delegations would attend from Israel, Egypt, Syria, and Lebanon, with a combined Jordanian/Palestinian delegation; the UN and the EC would attend as observers; initial multilateral talks would be followed by bilateral talks between Israel and each of its neighbours. In separate letters, Bush assured President Assad of Syria that the United States would not recognize the annexation of the Golan

Heights, and that the conference would be held on the basis of UN Security Resolutions 242 and 338, while he assured Shamir that the PLO would not attend and that the Jordanian/Palestinian delegation would not include any Palestinians from East Jerusalem. He also demanded that Israel halt settlements in the occupied territories for the period of the conference.

On June 6, Shamir rejected the invitation, insisting that there be no UN involvement in the conference and that Israel should have the right to approve the Jordanian/Palestinian delegation. On June 9, the PLO, meeting in Tunis, insisted that it would not compromise on the inclusion of residents of East Jerusalem in a delegation. Following further visits by Baker, Shamir announced conditional acceptance of the invitation on Aug. 1, and on Aug. 6, Israeli Foreign Minister David Levy outlined "understandings" which had been reached with the USA. These were that (i) the conference would not be held on the basis of "land for peace"; (ii) the conference would not be empowered to take decisions; (iii) there would be direct negotiations for a treaty between Israel and Arab states; (iv) there would be no PLO participation; (v) the UN observer would remain silent; (vi) the EC representative would attend the opening session only; (vii) there would be no conference organized by the UN Security Council; and (viii) the Soviet Union would renew diplomatic relations with Israel before the conference.

The PLO stated its conditions on Aug. 2: (i) the conference should lead to the implementation of UN Security Council Resolutions 242 and 338; (ii) there should be a recognition of the national rights of the Palestinian people; (iii) there should be direct Palestinian participation in the conference; (iv) the status of East Jerusalem should be discussed; and (v) there should be a halt to Israeli settlements in the occupied territories. The PNC, meeting in Algiers on Sept. 23-28, endorsed these conditions and welcomed the invitation.

Despite disagreements between Shamir and the less intransigent Levy, and the controversy over the US refusal to release $10,000 million in loan guarantees for Israel unless it agreed to halt settlements, the first session of the Middle East Peace Conference took place in Madrid from Oct. 30 to Nov. 3, 1991. The Palestinian members of the joint Jordanian/Palestinian delegation were all residents of the West Bank or Gaza Strip; they were to be "advised" by a team of activists, many from East Jerusalem, widely recognized as being the senior PLO leaders in the occupied territories.

Madrid and Moscow Talks—Secret Oslo Talks

In his opening speech on Oct. 31 Shamir, claiming to speak "in the name of the entire Jewish people", insisted that the conflict was not primarily over territory. Dr Haidar Abd al-Shafi, for the Palestinians, reiterated the Palestinian Declaration of Independence and stressed the unity of all Palestinians, led by the PLO. In bilateral talks on Nov. 3, it was agreed to negotiate on "twin-tracks", Israel/Jordan and Israel/Palestinians,

towards a two-phase agreement for interim Palestinian self-rule before a final settlement with Israel. Further bilateral talks were held between teams from Israel and from Lebanon and Syria. However, on Nov. 4 Israel established a new settlement in the Golan Heights, and on Nov. 12 the Knesset reaffirmed that the Golan was not negotiable.

Subsequent rounds of bilateral talks were held in Washington on Dec. 10-18, in January 1992, February 1992, and April 1992. No substantive progress was made, with each side restating its known positions. The Palestinian intifada had generally died down, but continued to simmer, with occasional terror attacks and harsh Israeli reprisals, plus internecine conflict amongst Palestinian factions. Overall, more than 1,000 Palestinians had been killed by Israeli troops or settlers; many Palestinians were killed in the internal strife mentioned above; and scores of Israelis also died in sporadic incidents.

Nor was there any advance in the second round of multilateral talks, which was held in Moscow in January 1992. Known thereafter as the Moscow track, these multilateral talks concerned issues of cross-border concern to the parties mentioned above, as well as other nations in the region. The Moscow track also included participation in and "steerage" by outside powers with strong interests in the region, such as the USA, Russia, UK, Canada and Japan as well as organizations like the United Nations.

Some had hoped that the Moscow track would deliver even more positive results than the Madrid track. The Moscow track posited a free, open and peaceful Middle East, and envisaged development of the region as one strategic whole. There were five distinct sub-tracks for each of five themes under consideration: security and arms control, water, refugees, environment and regional economic development. In time, an overall steering committee co-ordinated progress across the fronts, especially in areas of overlapping jurisdiction (e.g. refugees' access to water). Matters concerning borders and territorial disputes featured less overtly than in the bilateral Madrid track, yet became pertinent as an impediment to ambitious proposals for cross-national water and transport links. In both the Madrid and Moscow tracks, no Arab state wished to strike a separate deal with Israel before Israeli and Palestinian delegations reached some semblance of an accord.

Hopes for a peace settlement rose after the Israeli election on June 23, 1992, which resulted in a serious defeat for the *Likud* and also for the *Tehiya* (Rebirth) party associated with Israeli settlers in the occupied territories. As well as the Labour Party, major gainers were two far-right parties, and the centre-left *Meretz* (Energy) party, led by civil rights activist Shulamit Aloni. The latter joined the cabinet of a new Labour-led coalition administration. Prime Minister-designate Yitzhak Rabin, who had been Chief of Staff in 1967, Prime Minister during 1974-77, and Defence Minister at the outbreak of the intifada, stated that his government would conduct continuous peace negotiations with the intention of establishing Palestinian autonomy within nine months. Although he rejected the establishment of a Palestinian state and would not negotiate the status of East Jerusalem, his victory led many observers to voice cautious optimism about the possibility of solving this apparently intractable conflict.

The arrival of the new Rabin administration in Israel initially revived negotiations in Washington DC, though problems soon re-emerged. The official Palestinian team, now operating openly in its own right, and no longer as a semi-official adjunct to the official Jordanian delegation, demanded territorial autonomy in a body to be known as the Palestinian Interim Self-Government Authority (PISGA). Israel preferred to consider PISGA as a limited organ, more executive in nature than legislative. There was a wide chasm between Israeli and Palestinian expectations over the extent of its jurisdiction. The Israeli government's decision in December 1992 to expel some 400 suspected Islamic extremists from Gaza, and to place them in southern Lebanon, infuriated the Palestinian delegation, who suspended talks.

Meanwhile, starting in late 1992, Israel's Deputy Foreign Minister, Yossi Beilin, and a Norwegian social scientist researching living conditions in Palestinian areas, Dr Terje Roed-Larsen, instigated secret talks with representatives of the PLO, notably Abu Ala (Ahmed Qurei) at first, and later Abu Mazen (Mahmoud Abbas). Their Israeli counterparts were initially Israeli academics known to Beilin. The talks began on Jan. 20, 1993, outside Oslo in Norway, with the Norwegian Foreign Ministry acting as intercessors. (Just the day before, the Knesset had repealed a long-standing ban on its citizens making contacts with the PLO.) By mid-1993 Israeli Foreign Minister Shimon Peres was apprised of developments, as was PLO Chairman Yasser Arafat, both of whom gave this "secret track" provisional support. Initially sceptical, Rabin was ultimately persuaded in August 1993 that the initiative represented the only way to break the deadlock with the Palestinians. In time Morocco, Egypt and Tunisia became peripherally involved, and the USA was also informed. The official (nominally non-PLO) Palestinian delegation in Washington was not informed, however, which gave rise to resentment when the "Oslo breakthrough" was made public in late August 1993.

Apart from mutual recognition between Israel and the PLO, and commitment to cease violence and terror, the agreements made at Oslo had territorial implications, too. In particular, they endorsed limited Palestinian autonomy in the Gaza Strip and the Jericho district of the West Bank. Known colloquially as "Gaza and Jericho First", this was to be expanded to other areas if proven successful (see below).

Oslo I: Declaration of Principles and "Gaza-Jericho First" Plan

On Sept. 13, 1993, Israel and the PLO, with the USA as guarantor, signed the Israel-Palestinian Declaration of Principles (DOP) on the White House lawn, in Washington DC. The DOP was a direct consequence of the secret agreements made at Oslo. The DOP was signed in the names of the state of Israel and the Palestine Liberation Organization, the latter as "sole representative of the Palestinian people", a description that Israel accepted for the first time with its signature to this document. In an exchange of letters with the Israelis, Arafat pledged to bring before the PNC a motion to abolish from the Palestinian National Charter those articles that called for the destruction of the state of Israel, or which denied its right to exist.

Israel's Knesset backed the DOP by 61 votes to 50 on Sept. 23; the PLO Central Council, meeting in Tunis, approved it by 63 votes to 8, on Oct. 11; and the UN General Assembly passed Resolution 48/58 on Dec. 14, in support of the DOP. An international donors' conference in October pledged billions of dollars towards establishing a Palestinian National Authority (PNA). The great breakthrough of Oslo was mutual recognition—albeit phrased in such a way as to suggest recognition between Israel and the PLO, not a Palestinian state per se. Similarly, the concept of "land for peace"—first given practical expression in the Egypt-Israel treaty—was reinforced, as Oslo incorporated UN Resolutions 242 and 338.

The question of final borders between Israel and a Palestinian entity was to be delayed until "permanent status talks", which according to the initial mutually agreed timetable were scheduled to start on Dec. 13, 1995, and to be completed on April 13, 1996. The DOP, in Annex II, specified a Protocol on Withdrawal of Israeli Forces from the Gaza Strip and Jericho, to be initiated two months after the signing of the DOP. In the event, the Gaza-Jericho agreement—colloquially known as Oslo I or the Cairo agreement, after the place of its signature—was delayed. Talks had ceased after Feb. 25, when a Jewish settler opened fired on Muslims praying in the Ibrahim Mosque in Hebron, killing about 30 people. This atrocity sparked off others by *Hamas* and similar groups, against Israeli targets. However, negotiations eventually resumed and the Cairo agreement was cemented on May 4, 1994. A last minute dispute ensued when Yasser Arafat refused to sign the map that accompanied the agreement; crisis was averted when Arafat was assured that Palestinian control would extend beyond the city centre of Jericho, to its suburbs and environs.

The DOP document included a Preamble and Articles, plus three annexes, concerning Security Arrangements, Civil Affairs and Legal Matters. Article II-1 of the agreement stated that: "Israel shall implement an accelerated and scheduled withdrawal of Israeli military forces from the Gaza Strip and from the Jericho Area, to begin immediately with the signing of this agreement. Israel shall complete such withdrawal within three weeks from this date". Annex IV, a Protocol on Economic Relations, was signed in Paris on April 29, 1994 (hence also known as the Paris Protocol).

According to Oslo I, Israel would control security at international borders and crossing points to Jordan and Egypt; it was also responsible for the Jewish settlers (who were Israeli citizens) within the territories. However, Israel did agree to "re-deploy troops outside [Palestinian] populated areas", and allow the newly established PNA to exercise control over culture, tourism, education, health, social welfare and direct taxation in its areas. Similarly, a PNA police force was to maintain public order amongst Palestinians. Oslo I was accompanied by six maps, outlining such issues as the deployment of Palestinian police in Gaza, and Maritime Activities Zones.

Palestinian opponents of Oslo I, however, criticized the agreement on numerous grounds: it gave Palestinians little more than municipal authority; it appeared to ignore the creeping extension of West Bank settlements (despite Israel's officially proclaimed "freeze"); and it postponed discussion on political prisoners, final borders, Jerusalem, water resources and refugees. To some opponents, Oslo I also forced Palestinian armed units to act as "Israeli proxies" in a simmering battle against anti-Israeli forces (notably, *Hamas*, Islamic Jihad and radical "rejectionist" militias).

Meanwhile, the constant postponement of a Palestinian constitution and bill of rights, not to mention legislative elections, as mandated by the Cairo agreement, led increasing numbers to accuse Israel of aiding and abetting an autocratic Arafat-led fiefdom. Moreover, Israel still effectively controlled 20 per cent of Gaza, including settlements, military installations and, most importantly, border crossings. Israel justified this condition on the grounds of defending security facilities, and some 12,000 Jewish settlers, distributed amongst a dozen or so small settlements. And while Israel argued that the former civic administration was no more, to the nearly one million Palestinians living in Gaza, enduring security controls rendered true autonomy a chimerical vision.

If deemed successful, the "Gaza and Jericho First" experiment was to be succeeded by Oslo II, or an interim agreement, which would extend Palestinian autonomy over wider areas. Though Oslo I and II specified Israeli "re-deployments" from areas formerly under their control, both agreements carried a clause which said that nothing in these documents should "prejudice or pre-empt" final talks over borders.

The precise nature of the Palestinian entity was also left vague; there was no explicit Israeli commitment to Palestinian statehood, although some Palestinian negotiators felt that this was implied. The methodology adopted was one of "confidence-building measures", and security co-operation, to increase trust between both sides, and prepare them for the more difficult decisions that lay ahead.

A significant milestone was reached in May 1994, when Yasser Arafat returned to the soil of "historic Palestine" for the first time in decades. This occurred after Israeli troops, after some delay, completed their initial re-deployment from Gaza and Jericho. Specifically, Arafat left PLO headquarters in Tunis for Gaza, where he began setting up a "Palestinian

National Authority" (PNA). An Agreement on the Preparatory Transfer of Powers and Responsibilities, signed by Israel and the PLO on Aug. 29, 1994, afforded the PNA further powers over various local governmental responsibilities. These included education and culture, health, social welfare, tourism and taxation.

Oslo II—Interim Agreement

With the Preparatory Transfer of Powers achieved, talks began on drafting an Interim Agreement, or Oslo II. In early January 1995 Rabin halted construction in a West Bank settlement, and stated that "Israel's future lies in territorial compromise with the Palestinians". However, his subsequent decision to construct "bypass roads" specifically for settlers, and to build and sell 4,000 new homes for West Bank settlers, dismayed Palestinians, who felt he was pre-empting the terms of the peace process—or at least acting in poor faith. Rejectionist forces, notably the *Izz al-Din al-Qassem* military wing of *Hamas*, launched a string of terror attacks. These killed 149 Israelis in the period between Oslo I and Oslo II, which unsurprisingly led many Israelis to doubt whether the peace process was living up to its name. To stifle further violence, and punish the PNA for not restricting militant groups, Israel imposed severe "closures" on Palestinian territories. As a consequence, vital supplies and monetary donations, as promised at the international post-DOP conference, were blocked; and Palestinian breadwinners lost their jobs, resulting in mounting poverty in PNA areas.

Talks between Rabin, Arafat and Egyptian President Mubarak in early February 1995 initially stalled, though a new joint commitment was issued on Feb. 12. Despite sporadic terror incidents by Palestinians, and to the chagrin of Israeli rightwingers, Rabin ordered talks to continue in late March. Following UN approbation, the Israeli government suspended plans to confiscate a plot of land in East Jerusalem, whose ultimate status was to be discussed in final status talks. Palestinians were already wary of Israeli plans for Jerusalem, after the signing of the Israeli peace treaty with Jordan (see below), on Oct. 26, 1994, which appeared to grant the Hashemite Kingdom—and thus not the Palestinians—special rights over the holy sites on the Haram al-Sharif/Temple Mount.

Following intensive talks involving large delegations of negotiators, with direct involvement by Shimon Peres, Yasser Arafat and Yitzhak Rabin, especially at the Egyptian Sinai port of Taba, Israel and the PLO eventually reached an informal agreement on the re-deployment of Israeli Defence Force (IDF) units in the West Bank on Aug. 11, 1995. The two parties initialed the Interim Agreement at Taba on Sept. 24. Yitzhak Rabin and Yasser Arafat officially signed the agreement at the White House in Washington on Sept. 28, in the presence of King Hussein and Presidents Clinton and Mubarak.

The final document was 350 pages long and went

into great detail about security and economic issues. With respect to territory, the main feature of Oslo II was the division of the West Bank into three zones, or areas. Zone A comprised 7% of the territory, and included all the main Palestinian towns apart from Hebron and East Jerusalem. This Zone A was to fall under full Palestinian control, regarding security and civilian affairs, within 100 days of the Washington signing. (Re-deployment from, or in, Hebron was to commence in March 1996.) Zone B comprised 21% of the territory under joint Israeli-Palestinian control, and included an estimated 68% of the Palestinian population of the West Bank, who lived in 400 to 450 smaller towns and villages. PNA acquisition of Zone B was to commence over a year, starting in March or April 1996, following legislative elections (see below). The remaining Zone C included Jewish settlements, and was to stay in Israeli hands until the completion of "final status talks". Israel retained responsibility for controlling international borders with Jordan and Egypt, and the borderlands of the Jordan Valley and Dead Sea. Article XIII, dealing with security, outlined modalities for Israeli re-deployments.

It was stressed that this was an interim arrangement, and did not reflect the final shape of an autonomous Palestinian entity. Nonetheless, the measure of control that the Palestinians now supposedly enjoyed in Gaza and Jericho was extended to all but two of their urban or peri-urban conurbations. Israel was also to release Palestinian prisoners, and further hand-overs followed. Oslo II also specified formalized areas of co-operation between Israeli and Palestinian security forces, with regular planning meetings and joint patrols. There were to be 12,000 Palestinian police in the West Bank, and 18,000 in Gaza.

Preparations were further launched to facilitate Palestinian elections to a Legislative Council (PLC), which would assume power and responsibilities held by the Israeli military government and Civilian Administration. The election procedures were discussed by teams led by an Israeli, Joel Singer, and a Palestinian, Sa'eb Erekat, and co-ordinated with an EU team led by the French diplomat, Jean-Luc Sibiud. Arafat approved the setting up of a Central Elections Committee to register voters (which succeeded beyond expectations) and together with Israel, the PNA joined a Joint Civil Affairs Co-ordination and Co-operation Committee (CAC) to consider, inter alia, election-related matters. Oslo II was accompanied by numerous maps, including six already stipulated in Oslo I. There were annexes on related issues, including Annex III, which recognized Palestinian rights to water that lay under the territory of the West Bank. Israel would provide Palestinians with a further 28 million cubic metres of water annually. Norway was to oversee a "People to People" programme, intended to improve relations between the Palestinian and Israeli communities. The day after Oslo II was signed, the USA, Israel and the PNA entered a Trilateral Committee. Expected to emulate the success of the Israel-US-Jordan Trilateral Committee, this one had a special brief to consider original ways of fairly distributing water.

Yasser Arafat presented the Oslo II Accords to the PLO Executive Committee in Tunis, which passed it, with some abstentions. The Israeli Knesset approved the agreement on Oct. 5, by a margin of 61 to 59 votes. Labour owed its narrow victory to two Knesset members who constituted Yi'ud, a breakaway from the far-right Tzomet faction. However, opposition grew from the right, who claimed that the passage of the bill was unconstitutional as it did not enjoy a "Jewish majority" (in addition to Yi'ud, Rabin needed the support of all the Knesset's Arab members to see it through). Likud politicians, including its leader, Benjamin Netanyahu, took part in mass street demonstrations where incendiary banners were displayed. Some called Rabin a national traitor, and likened him to a Nazi officer.

On Nov. 4 a lone assassin, Yigal Amir, shot Prime Minister Rabin dead as he was leaving a large rally, sponsored by Peace Now, in Tel Aviv that he had just addressed. Amir claimed he had assassinated Rabin because Oslo II meant that he and his government were about to give "Jewish land" to Palestinians, and was planning to create a Palestinian state. It also appeared that Amir was obeying an edict from radical nationalist rabbis, who had proclaimed that "abandoning Eretz Yisrael" was a sin worthy of death.

Some 80 international leaders attended Rabin's funeral in Jerusalem, including high-ranking representatives from Morocco, Oman, Egypt and the UAE. President Clinton and King Hussein pledged to pursue Rabin's plans for peace. Foreign Minister Peres was sworn in as acting Prime Minister, and vowed to continue the peace process initiated by his predecessor. On Nov. 20 the IDF withdrew from six West Bank towns—Tulkarm, Qalqiliyah, Nablus, Ramallah, Jenin and Tubas. As promised, the IDF also left Bethlehem by Christmas. A decision about Hebron was delayed until the outcome of further talks. Since the Hebron massacre of early 1994, a Temporary International Presence in Hebron (TIPH) had monitored the situation in the city, and they were requested to remain.

Though Palestinians were initially jubilant about IDF re-deployments, and the PNA's acquisition of full control in cities, there was disquiet over the effects of accelerated building of "bypass roads" for the sole use of settlers and IDF personnel. In 1995 alone, this exercise cost about $300m. Some 276 km of such roads were built between the signing of Oslo II and mid-1998, according to the Applied Research Institute Jerusalem, a Palestinian think-tank, and another 452 km were planned. Such roads not only discriminated against Palestinian travellers, but also appeared to split Palestinian autonomous zones into small cantons for ultimate control by Israel.

Before Oslo II's ratification by the cabinet, and then the Knesset, Shimon Peres had argued that the agreement would allow Israel to keep "73% of the land, 97% of the security and 80% of the water". This statement, and others like it, infuriated Palestinians, who felt Oslo II intended to turn a Palestinian entity into little more than a cosseted satrapy of Israel. By the same token, Israelis were upset to hear reports that Arafat and other PLO leaders had spoken of Oslo as an interim step towards the eventual replacement of Israel with one Palestine, "between the river and the sea".

A long delayed election to a Palestinian Legislative Council (PLC), pursuant to the terms of the Oslo Accords, was held on Jan. 20, 1996. It coincided with a separate presidential poll, contested by PNA Chairman Yasser Arafat and one opponent, Umm Khalil. Arafat won the executive election by taking 89 per cent of the vote, while turnout for the assembly poll topped 70 per cent. With respect to issues of borders, the PNA gained an important concession when Israel allowed Palestinian voters from East Jerusalem to cast their ballots. However, they could only do so if they had a connection to residences in other parts of the West Bank. Nonetheless, to Israeli right-wingers, this concession signified a Palestinian claim to part of Jerusalem, to them, the "united and eternal capital" of Israel and the Jewish people. Nor were they assuaged by terms of Oslo II which forbade the PNA to run offices from Jerusalem.

For the purpose of the election, the entire occupied territories, including East Jerusalem, were nominally divided into 17 multi-seat constituencies, 11 in the West Bank and six in Gaza. In all they returned 88 seats to the PLC, of which 66 were won by *Fatah* or *Fatah*-affiliated candidates. Despite a formal boycott by such groups as *Hamas* and the PFLP, international monitors assessed the elections as broadly "free and fair". Abu Ala (Ahmed Qurei) was appointed Speaker of the PLC on March 7.

However, it took some time before Arafat chose his cabinet, and there was also disquiet over the way the results were constantly "amended" after they had been initially announced. In successive months and years, many Palestinians, including PLC members, charged Arafat with ignoring the assembly, and blocking its bid to pass crucial laws, including the Basic Law—equivalent to a constitution for the PNA area. The PLC was also formally considered to be a subsection of the grander PLO Palestine National Council (PNC); its 88 seats formed a distinct minority within the 669-strong PNC. That said, by virtue of its situation in historic Palestine, and the fact that it held continuous sessions, the PLC enjoyed an intrinsic legitimacy that the parent body arguably lacked.

Israeli Prime Minister Peres was particularly insistent on one aspect of Oslo II, itself a restatement of a condition of the DOP: the PLO's revocation of those aspects of its Charter, or Covenant, which called for or implied the elimination of Israel. Yasser Arafat agreed, and during April 22-25, 1995, he convened an extraordinary session in Gaza of the full PNC, including delegates from the Palestinian "diaspora". By a surprisingly large margin of 594 votes to 54 (with 14 abstentions) the PNC voted to accept that existing agreements with Israel rendered those controversial terms of the Charter redundant. The PNC also agreed to create a new charter within six months, and PNA Attorney

General Khaled al-Kidra began considering seven plans to this end. Nonetheless, the Israeli right was sceptical about the Palestinians' sincerity in this regard.

Meanwhile, Peres had intensified the hunt for those Palestinian militants who had planned earlier bombings. On Jan. 5, 1996, IDF forces killed the legendary *Hamas* "engineer", Yehia Ayyash. After the end of the traditional Muslim mourning period, Ayyash's colleagues renewed their bombing campaign; in four suicide blasts in February and March 1996, in Jerusalem, Ashkelon and Tel Aviv, they killed 62 Israelis. Peres seemed increasingly beleaguered as popular fury grew at his failure to quell terror.

Hoping to assist him, the USA convened a Summit of Peacemakers at Sharm el-Sheikh, the easternmost port in Egyptian Sinai. Representatives from the USA, Israel, Jordan and the PNA issued a final summit statement on March 13, 1996. Meanwhile, Peres had called for early elections on May 29, 1996, so a formal start to final status talks, initiated on May 4, was soon suspended by mutual agreement, to allow for campaigning. Likewise negotiations over the future of Hebron were also postponed until after the election. In the event, Peres and Labour narrowly yet clearly lost the poll to Netanyahu's *Likud*, whose stated antipathy towards Oslo raised fears that the peace process would soon be suspended altogether.

Israel & Jordan: Genesis of 1994 Peace Treaty

Formally in a state of war for 46 years, Israel and Jordan signed a peace treaty in 1994, thereby capping a long period of alternating warfare and covert peace between the two nations. Writing in March 1995, Robert B. Satloff, executive director of the Washington Institute for Near East Policy, praised the Jordanian treaty for its "mature, creative and principled solutions to common problems". He depicted it as an advance on its Egyptian predecessor. Whereas the latter stressed "respect" between neighbours and intricate security guarantees, the Jordan-Israel treaty emphasized "partnership", argued Satloff. Likewise "cooperation" replaced "reciprocity", which he expected would facilitate a genuinely "warm peace". Such comments notwithstanding, Jordan was painfully aware that it could not ignore Palestinian sensitivities. Significantly, Jordan began its path towards peace in earnest only when it was clear that Palestinians, via the PLO, were negotiating with Israel in their own right after August 1993.

To put the Israel-Jordan peace process in context, one needs to consider its origins, and the arguably over-optimistic expectations that close though unofficial ties had generated. Jordan (then Transjordan) received its independence on March 22, 1946. Historians like Avi Shlaim have argued that there was "collusion across the Jordan" between the Kingdom and the Palestinian Jewish "Yishuv", even before Israel declared its independence on May 14, 1948. Such views are supported by reference to the memoirs of the British commander of Jordan's Arab Legion, John Glubb; and the autobiography of Israeli Prime Minister Golda Meir (in 1947-48, chief secret negotiator with Jordan).

According to this model, in the 1948 war Jordan formally joined the coalition of Arab forces that attacked the newborn Israel, yet secretly agreed to Jewish forces assuming control over the area allocated to a Jewish state by UN 181. In return Jordanian forces would take over the West Bank (formally allocated by the UN to an independent "Arab state" in Palestine). The two parties did, however, contest Jerusalem when the anticipated international *corpus separandum* failed to materialize. In the event, the war ended with Israel controlling West Jerusalem, and Jordan controlling East Jerusalem, including the Old City, with the holy Temple Mount/Haram al-Sharif complex. (There is evidence that Jordan had hardened its stance prior to the May 15 outbreak of war; in a meeting just before then, Jordan proposed that Israel defer its independence in favour of becoming an autonomous Jewish zone within an expanded Hashemite Kingdom, an offer Israel unsurprisingly declined.)

Even during the midst of war, the Jordanians and Israelis were signing agreements—witness the agreement of July 7, 1948, to demilitarize the zone around Mount Scopus in Jerusalem. Then on Nov. 30 Moshe Dayan and Abdullah Tal, respectively the Israeli and Jordanian commanders in Jerusalem, signed a "sincere truce" whereby the two men installed the world's first telephone "hot-line" between warring forces. Jordan was the first Arab state to request an armistice agreement with Israel. This it signed on April 3, 1949, but only following the Egyptian armistice, after Israelis captured all of the Negev down to Eilat, and after Jordan gave up the Wadi Ara area (the "northern triangle") held by the Iraqi expedition force. The Israel-Jordan armistice was amended slightly, after a meeting held on May 5, 1949, in Amman, between the Israeli Foreign Minister and King Abdullah. Both sides discussed rejection of the internationalization of Jerusalem.

Jordan also sought an outlet to the sea, and Israel offered the Kingdom an outlet to the port of Haifa. Jordan, for its part, seemed to prefer passage through Beersheba, in the Israeli-controlled Negev, to the port of Gaza, in the now Egyptian-occupied Gaza Strip. On Feb. 24, 1950, Israel and Jordan initialed a document of principles, towards an eventual five-year non-aggression pact between the two states. It encapsulated, amongst other points, armistice lines and no-man's land provisions, trade co-operation, compensation for those who lost property in Jerusalem after the city's partition, and a free zone for Jordan in Haifa. However, the agreement became mired after the Arab League announced on April 3 that it would expel any state that reached a separate economic, political or military agreement with Israel.

Meanwhile, Jordan annexed the West Bank in April 1950, a move opposed by fellow members of the League. King Abdullah was assassinated on July 20,

1951. At first Abdullah was replaced as ruler by his son, Talal, but on Aug. 11, 1952, his grandson, Hussein, assumed the throne. Jordan was accepted as a full member of the United Nations in 1955.

Palestinian refugees had swollen Jordan's population, and their opinion pressurized the ruling monarchy not to sign a separate peace with Israel. Throughout the 1950s Palestinian *fedayeen* used Jordan as a base from which to launch raids on Israel. There were 2,150 complaints lodged with the Israeli-Jordanian Mixed Armistice Commission (MAC) by August 1955. Retaliatory raids from Israel increased in intensity, drawing international criticism. Certain Israeli ministers suggested exploiting clashes to "correct" the borders with Jordan, though this was never adopted as formal policy.

Jordan kept out of the 1956 Suez War, reportedly at the bidding of Egyptian President Gamal Abdel Nasser. In 1957 a wave of radical Arab nationalism threatened to topple the Hashemite monarchy of Jordan. In July 1958 Israel allowed the passage of British aircraft through its airspace, thereby assisting Western powers which intervened to save the Jordanian monarchy from being toppled. That same year the Hashemites who ruled neighbouring Iraq were overthrown and killed in a coup. The short-lived union between Iraq and Jordan thus ended abruptly, leaving the latter more dependent on covert US support via the CIA. Around this time secretive ties were forged with Israeli intelligence, which apprised the young king of threats to his regime.

Even so, the 1960s saw renewed conflict with Israel over the distribution of water from the Jordan river. In 1964 Jordan and other Arab states voted to reduce the flow of water into Israel's Lake Tiberias, after Israel announced that it would divert water for irrigation. That same year Jordan joined a United Arab Command, together with Syria and Egypt; it also agreed to the setting up of a Palestine Liberation Organization, even though such a body undermined Jordan's traditional claim to represent the Palestinian people, who already constituted a majority of the Kingdom's population. Ultimately, rising regional tensions, including a large Israeli attack on the border village of Samua, in the Jordanian-ruled West Bank, resulted in a pre-emptive strike by Israel on June 5, 1967 (see above).

In the ensuing Six-Day War Jordan lost the whole of the West Bank and East Jerusalem to Israel. King Hussein subsequently confirmed rumours that Israel had requested that he not participate in the war; however, given the popular mood at the time, and deliberate misinformation from Egypt, he had little option but to commit his forces. King Hussein was a key architect of UN Resolution 242, and held intensive clandestine talks with Israel in 1968. In 1970 the Kingdom fought a virtual civil war (which became known as Black September) against militant PLO factions, who wished to overthrow the monarchy. Israel mobilized its army and air force when Syria threatened to invade Jordan in support of the PLO. It was widely understood that

Israel's friendly action helped save King Hussein.

Jordan did not participate in the Yom Kippur War of October 1973; unlike Egypt and Syria, it did not seek to reclaim territory lost in 1967 by military means. UN Resolution 338 followed the October war and reiterated the terms of UN 242. Many felt UN 338 and a restored sense of Arab honour after their performance on the battlefield would prompt new peace initiatives. However, the only one that lasted was that between Israel and Egypt. Israel hoped that Jordan would play a large role in the talks on Palestinian autonomy, part of the Camp David deal. But King Hussein, under pressure from his citizens and from Arab League states, felt he could not participate unless there was a clear role for the PLO. Hussein also objected to Menachem Begin's vision of "personal autonomy" only for Palestinians, as opposed to territorial autonomy.

On April 11, 1987, then Israeli Foreign Minister Shimon Peres and King Hussein reached a secret agreement in London to achieve regional peace. It envisaged a confederal arrangement between the Kingdom of Jordan and an autonomous Palestinian enclave in the West Bank. However, the deal soon fell apart because of opposition in the home countries. Israeli Prime Minister, Yitzhak Shamir, moreover accused Peres of negotiating behind his back. Yasser Arafat was angry about the lack of any explicit role for his PLO in the agreement. In 2003 Peres spoke of the London agreement as one of the greatest lost opportunities in Israel's history.

Following the failure of the London agreement and the outbreak of the first Palestinian intifada in the Israeli-occupied territories eight months later, King Hussein announced the abdication of Jordanian claims to the West Bank in July 1988. This unilateral decision, effectively in favour of the principle of Palestinian self-determination, led inexorably to the Palestinian National Council's Algiers Declaration that same year. The PNC thereby declared for the first time its acceptance of Palestinian rule on the West Bank and Gaza, and in effect acknowledged the existence of Israel.

As stated above, Israel and Jordan launched their first overt bilateral talks in the context of the Madrid peace process of late 1991 and these continued for two years thereafter. Jordanian Foreign Minister Kamel Abu Jabber was designated as the overall head of the joint Jordanian-Palestinian delegation. Abd al-Salaam Majali headed the Jordanian "national" delegation. (Majali later became Jordan's Prime Minister, and was replaced as delegation chief by Fayez Tarawneh, then Jordanian ambassador to the USA, for the 10th round of talks in June 1992.) Elyakim Rubinstein headed the Israeli delegates in discussion with Jordan. The new Rabin administration in Israel agreed to the requested separation of the Palestinian and Jordanian delegations in 1992—Palestinians formally negotiated under a "Jordanian umbrella" until then—though progress was slower than hoped for. King Hussein was unwilling to reach agreement with Israel before clear progress was shown in Israeli talks with Palestinians. In this he was being consistent with his long-held view that the

Palestinian issue was the key to Arab-Israeli regional peace.

On Sept. 14, 1993, however, one day after the signing of the Israel-Palestinian Declaration of Principles, Israel and Jordan signed a Common Agenda, affirming mutual commitment to a cessation of hostilities and an eventual full peace treaty between the two nations. In the words of King Hussein: "We had refused to sign [this declaration] before we saw clear and tangible progress on the Palestinian-Israeli level". Although King Hussein was reportedly upset at not being informed about the Oslo process until its final stages, he endorsed a rapid acceleration of talks with Israel. The first significant organizational innovation resulting from the Washington Declaration was a trilateral US-Jordan-Israel Economic Committee, established in Washington on Oct. 1, 1993, by US President Bill Clinton, Jordan's Crown Prince Hassan and Israeli Foreign Minister Shimon Peres. The committee met in working session on Nov. 30, and immediately set up groups to discuss issues of trade, finance, banking, Jordan valley co-operative projects and civil aviation. The outcomes of these talks were incorporated in the eventual peace treaty.

On May 28, 1994, Prime Minister Yitzhak Rabin met privately with King Hussein in London and apparently assured him that Israel would support Jordan's "special interests" in the Muslim holy sites of Jerusalem. Their first public meeting took place in Washington, on July 25, 1994, out of which emerged the Washington Declaration, which terminated the state of belligerency between the two nations. The Declaration also reaffirmed Jordan's special role in Jerusalem, and the two nations' determination to seek a just and lasting peace, based on UN Resolutions 242 and 338. It was accompanied by a string of agreements, including the establishment of direct telephone links, joint electricity grids, new border crossings, and the opening of an international air corridor between the states. The USA also agreed to forgive a major debt incurred by Jordan. This was significant, as a sign that the USA was prepared to move on from its earlier anger against Jordan for apparently favouring Saddam Hussein in 1991; and also as a boost to the Jordanian economy, which had suffered grievously from the aftermath of the 1991 Gulf War.

The final leg in the path towards a peace treaty began on July 18-19, 1994, with the first bilateral talks held in the region. They were held at Ein Avrona, north of the bordering ports, Israeli Eilat and Jordanian Aqaba. Again, Rubinstein, Majali and Tarawneh were major figures in the talks; others present included Crown Prince Hassan of Jordan, Foreign Minister Peres of Israel, former Mossad agent Ephraim Halevy, and Israeli international lawyer, Joel Singer.

Signing and Provisions of 1994 Israel-Jordan Peace Treaty

The Israeli and Jordanian Prime Ministers, Rabin and Abdul Salam al-Majali respectively, initialed a full

Treaty of Peace on Oct. 17, 1994. The treaty was finalized and publicly signed on Oct. 26, 1994, in a ceremony held at a desert border zone, known as Arava in Hebrew and Wadi al-Araba in Arabic. Ratification was required according to Article 27 of the treaty, to be followed by the establishment of interim measures and an implementation committee. The Israeli Knesset approved the treaty on Oct. 25, by 105 votes to three. The Jordanian Lower House approved the treaty on Nov. 6, 1994, by 55 votes to 23. Seventeen of the 23 "no" votes came from the Islamic Action Front, the largest single party in Jordan and in effect the chief opposition.

In an address to the nation on Nov. 5, King Hussein thanked God for "making us the builders of a…comprehensive and total peace between God's faithful creatures, the sons of Abraham…in the land of prophets and divine messages". On Nov. 9, Israel and Jordan exchanged documents of ratification. They also established the supervision committee and the joint border committee, to meet again in three months' time.

The Israel-Jordan peace treaty was the first one signed between Israel and another Arab country since Israel's Menachem Begin and Egypt's Anwar Sadat had concluded their treaty in 1979. The 1994 peace treaty consisted of a Preamble and Articles, which covered the following: (a) full diplomatic relations, (b) the agreed international boundary with minor modifications, and (c) confirmation of the end to a state of belligerency, and co-operation in prevention of terrorism. The signatories also agreed on (d) allocations of water and the development of new water resources, (e) freedom of access to religious sites, and recognition of a special role for the Hashemite Kingdom over Muslim holy shrines in Jerusalem, and (f) freedom of passage by land, sea and air.

In addition, Israel and Jordan agreed to co-operate in such areas as the economy, transportation, telecommunications, tourism, the environment, energy, health, agriculture, and the war against crime and drugs. Israel further pledged to give Jordan an extra 50m cubic metres of water from the Jordan river's annual flow. Jordanian and Israeli negotiators subsequently signed a series of protocols establishing a mutually beneficial framework of relations to jointly develop the Jordan valley and the Aqaba-Eilat region.

It was further agreed that the problem of refugees and displaced persons (referring to the "refugees of 1967") would be resolved in agreed-upon negotiating frameworks. Jordan housed an estimated 41 per cent of the world's Palestinian refugees—most of them holding Jordanian citizenship, by contrast with the position of refugees in other Arab countries. Hence a solution to the refugee issue was deemed absolutely crucial to harmonious relations between Israel, Jordan, and an eventual expected Palestinian state on the West Bank and Gaza. The 1994 treaty also enforced a Jordanian insistence that Israel never again displace Arabs under their control, and force them to flee east across the Jordanian border. Correspondingly, Israel sought and received a commitment from Jordan, that it would

never allow its territory to be used as a staging post for any other power (in particular, Iraq or Syria) to march westwards and invade Israel.

There were also five annexes, on borders, water, crime and drugs, environment, and interim measures. Annex I, on borders, was subdivided into three sections: (a) International Boundary, (b) Naharayim/Baqura area, and (c) Zofar area. The latter two areas came under Jordanian sovereignty, though Israeli farmers who over the years had worked the land were assured of private land use rights, these rights including unimpeded freedom of entry to, exit from and movement within the area. Customs and immigration legislation would not apply in these areas. The annexes further determined that these rights would remain in force for 25 years and would be renewed automatically for the same period, unless either country wished to terminate the arrangement.

With respect to Article 3 and Annex I (a), the treaty set the agreed international boundary between Israel and Jordan, including territorial waters and airspace, with reference to the old mandate-era boundary. The border was henceforth defined as consisting of four sectors. Listed from north to south, these were (i) the Jordan and Yarmouk rivers, (ii) the Dead Sea, (iii) the Arava Valley (Emek Ha'Arava in Hebrew, Wadi al-Araba in Arabic), and (iv) the Gulf of Aqaba.

Minor border modifications were made, to enable Israeli farmers in the Arava to continue to cultivate their land. As with the special stipulations made regarding Naharayim/Baqura and Zofar, the Arava compromise represented something of a legal innovation. It took into account the reality of Israeli agricultural encroachment onto Jordanian soil, on the east bank of the River Jordan, since 1967. Some international jurists hailed the arrangement as a model of pragmatism, worthy of imitation by others seeking to resolve long-standing conflicts. However, it was bitterly criticized by Syria in particular, which interpreted the compromise as a betrayal of Arab sovereignty, and even as an act of apostasy to Islam (*kufr*).

Full diplomatic relations between Israel and Jordan were established on Nov. 27, 1994. Marwan Muasher, a senior negotiator in talks with Israel, became Jordan's first ambassador to the state of Israel in April 1995. Prof. Shimon Shamir, founder and head of Tel Aviv University's Institute for Peace Studies, and previously Israel's third ambassador to Egypt, became its first ambassador to Jordan, also in 1995.

In August 1995 the Jordanian parliament rescinded its adherence to the Arab economic boycott of Israel, and on Oct. 29-31, 1995, Jordan hosted the second Middle East and North Africa economic summit (MENA) in Amman. Many Israeli business people attended the event, which was seen as a result of both the peace treaty and a revived multilateral talks process.

The assassination of Israeli Prime Minister Rabin on Nov. 4, 1995, greatly shocked King Hussein of Jordan. His memorable speech at Rabin's graveside, not far from the site of his grandfather's own assassination in 1951, was hailed as an important plea for genuine regional peace. Hussein's visit to Tel Aviv on Jan. 10, 1996, was greeted with great public enthusiasm, and his discussions with Prime Minister Peres suggested a future blossoming partnership. However, Peres lost elections in late May to Benjamin Netanyahu, who reaffirmed Israel's commitment to the treaty with Jordan. Indeed, Prime Minister Netanyahu favoured the treaty much more than the Oslo accords with the Palestinians. On Sept. 9, 1996, Israel and Jordan agreed to open consulates in the adjoining southern cities of Eilat and Aqaba. King Hussein also played a key role in mediating the Protocol Concerning the Re-deployment in Hebron, on Jan. 17, 1997 (see below).

Further Israel-Jordan Agreements—Criticism of Peace Treaty

Since 1994 the two countries have signed and ratified 15 bilateral agreements, without which the peace treaty's requirements could never be fully enacted. One was a key water agreement, signed on May 27, 1997. Another agreement, reached on Nov. 16, 1997, set up the Hassan Industrial Zone in Irbid—the first area to be granted the status of duty-free export to the USA (qualified industrial zone or QIZ). There were plans to repeat the experiment along the border of Israel and Jordan. There was some frustration at the bureaucratic, legal and political factors that delayed so many of these "enacting agreements", particularly those concerning trade. Nonetheless, once problems and misunderstandings were resolved, the path was open to the commencement of trade between Israel and Jordan in July 1996.

With regard to border issues, the signing of an Agreement on International Co-operation and Agriculture in October 1995 was significant, as it facilitated a joint enterprise for marketing agricultural produce, including the use of Israeli technology to develop farmland east of the River Jordan. Similarly, both sides aimed at flexibility regarding usage of airspace. A four-month pilot project was launched to use (Jordanian) Aqaba airport for flights from Europe bringing tourists to adjoining (Israeli) Eilat. Ultimately it was envisaged, according to an agreement signed in August 1997, that flights currently landing at Ovda and Eilat Airports would be transferred to an Aqaba-Eilat Peace Airport.

The joint airport was first mooted in the 1994 treaty. In 1999, however, an Israeli environmentalist lobby managed to stymie the Israeli end of proposed construction, arguing that the airport would damage unique natural surroundings. There are regular flights between Amman and Israel's Ben-Gurion Airport, in Lod, and also flights between Amman and Haifa. These resulted from a Civil Aviation Agreement, signed following the peace treaty.

The treaty also allowed nationals from both countries and their vehicles the freedom to move through open roads and border crossings. Similarly, vessels were granted the right to pass through territorial waters and enjoy access to ports. The Straits of Tiran and the Gulf of Aqaba were to be considered as international waterways, open to all nations for free navigation and overflight. It should be recalled that Israel had regarded Egypt's closure of the Straits of Tiran in May 1967 as a *casus belli*, and the failure to end this closure led in large part to the outbreak of war on June 5, 1967.

King Hussein took leave of treatment in the USA for a serious cancer condition, to help Israel and the PNA agree to an important re-deployment agreement at the Wye Valley Plantation, in Maine, in 1998 (for details, see below). The King died on Feb. 7, 1999, and his elder son, Abdullah, immediately succeeded him. King Abdullah II voiced his determination to honour the peace treaty with Israel when he visited the USA for the first time as monarch, on May 17-20 that year.

Notwithstanding official Jordanian support for peace with Israel, most of Jordanian civil society was opposed to normalization with its neighbour. Businessmen and cultural figures who sought to form links or joint projects with Israeli counterparts were often ostracized by the professional bodies to which they belonged. By 1997, the trade volume between Israel and Jordan stood at a disappointing $32 million, and plans to coordinate shipping at Haifa and Aqaba had failed. Thus the treaty disappointed even those Jordanians who balked at its ideological implications, yet quietly welcomed its anticipated financial dividends.

Jordanian disenchantment intensified with the outbreak of the new Palestinian intifada in late September 2000, and the election of Ariel Sharon as Israeli Prime Minister in January 2001. Bowing to public pressure, Jordan chose not to send its new ambassador-designate, Abdul Illah Kurdi, to Tel Aviv, on Oct. 8, 2000. Kurdi had been appointed to succeed Omar Rifai in August that year. After Al-Qaeda's attacks on the USA of Sept. 11, 2001, antagonism towards the US-led "war on international terrorism", widely interpreted in certain quarters as a Western battle against Islam, merely bolstered anti-Israeli sentiment in the Kingdom.

Another particular worry arose out of the effect of the Israel-Jordan treaty on the status and interests of Palestinians of the West Bank. Israeli right-wingers feared that recognizing the Kingdom of Jordan as so constituted permanently prevented Israel from annexing the whole of the West Bank—to them, Eretz Yisrael—and reconstituting what is now Jordan as "Palestine". Palestinians who held Jordanian citizenship were confused about what the treaty would imply for their personal status. The PNA in particular vocally opposed Article 9.2 of the treaty, which stated: "Israel respects the present special role of the Hashemite Kingdom of Jordan in Muslim Holy shrines in Jerusalem. When negotiations [between Israel and the PLO/PNA] on the permanent status will take place, Israel will give high priority to the Jordanian historic role in these shrines".

The PLO had staked its own claim to the Temple Mount, as an essential component of its claim to all of pre-1967 East Jerusalem. The PLO thus felt that Article 9.2 pre-empted their own negotiations to acquire sovereignty over the sensitive site. Jordan's then Crown Prince Hassan was called upon to assuage Palestinian feelings, and to a large extent succeeded in this difficult venture. He explained that Jordanian suzerainty on the Mount did not constitute permanent territorial sovereignty, but rather temporary custodianship on behalf of all Muslims. Even so, in the following months a PNA-appointed Mufti of Jerusalem ousted the Jordanian-appointed Mufti from real power, to the chagrin of both Israel and Jordan as well as many conservative, pro-Hashemite Palestinians.

That said, the Jordan-Israel border remains generally peaceful, and both sides abide strictly by the terms of the treaty. Jordan fiercely condemned two terror incidents that occurred at or near border crossings with Israel. A renegade Jordanian soldier killed seven Israeli schoolgirls in the northern Israeli town of Beit She'an in 1997; King Hussein won much credit when he visited the victims' families in Israel. On Nov. 19, 2003, a gunman wounded five South American tourists at the Eilat-Aqaba border crossing. Both sides co-operated in tightening security at such sensitive border points.

Jordan was and remains a key regional proponent of the Road Map for Peace between Israel and Palestinians (for which, see below). On Aug. 1, 2002, US President George W. Bush met King Abdullah in Washington in what was seen as major boost for the idea of such a plan. However, the shortcomings of the Road Map have exacerbated tensions between Jordan and Israel. In particular, as of early 2004, Jordan was protesting against Israel's developing "security fence". Amman fears that it may drive Palestinians into Jordan, thus contravening Israel's pledge to prevent such an eventuality in the 1994 treaty. Similarly, a 2002 meeting of the governing *Likud* party central committee in Israel decreed that there would be no Palestinian state in the West Bank, raising again the spectre of the officially discarded "Jordan is Palestine solution". Prime Minister Sharon, however, opposed the committee's vote, and since his re-election in early 2003 has reassured Jordan that Israel's 1994 treaty respects the full sovereignty of the Kingdom.

Israel & the Palestinians: 1997 Hebron Accord

As stated above, Oslo II determined that the PNA would assume full responsibility (Area A status) in all major towns in the West Bank, with the notable exception of Hebron. Here special arrangements had to be made, because Hebron was the only town with a Jewish settler community. There are settlements near other towns (like Elon Moreh, Kedumim and Itamar near Nablus, or Zufin and Alfei Menashe, just east of Qalqilya), but only in Hebron, a city of about 150,000 mainly Muslim Palestinians, do pockets of Jews live within the municipal boundaries of an Arab town.

Some 450 settlers, considered amongst the most militant and religiously devout of those living on the West Bank, reside in areas called Beit Hadassah, Beit Romano, Beit Schneerson, Avraham Avinu and Tel Rumeida, all located near the Tomb of the Patriarchs in the town centre.

Benjamin Netanyahu was narrowly elected Israeli Prime Minister in elections held on May 29, 1996. His new *Likud*-led coalition government promised to "slow down" the Oslo peace process, though not entirely abandon it. Netanyahu was also initially unwilling to meet PNA Chairman Yasser Arafat and was loath to countenance completing long-promised concessions in Hebron (as per stipulations in Oslo II). He did make a goodwill gesture by easing the closure on the territories, on July 3, but then on Aug. 2 his cabinet agreed to end the previous government's freeze on construction (mainly of settlements) in the occupied territories. On Aug. 14 talks between Israel and the PNA resumed after an eight-month hiatus, and Netanyahu and Arafat met for the first time on Sept. 4, at the Erez checkpoint, Gaza.

Later that month, Israel approved plans for building another 3,000 settler homes. This act angered Palestinians, and when Israel opened an ancient tunnel abutting the Temple Mount/Haram al-Sharif in Jerusalem, on Sept. 23, five days of rioting ensued. For the first time since 1973, Israel called in jet fighters over the territories; 14 Israelis and 56 Palestinians were killed in the clashes. Most worrying for Oslo proponents, Israeli and Palestinian security personnel exchanged gunfire. Egyptian, Jordanian and US intercession helped defuse the crisis, and a new European interest was expressed with the appointment of Ambassador Miguel Angel Moratinos as EU special envoy to the Middle East, on Oct. 25.

Increasingly, President Mubarak of Egypt pushed for a long-delayed deal on Hebron, meeting Israeli Foreign Minister David Levy in November. On Dec. 8 the USA and Egypt produced a draft agreement on Hebron. After considerable negotiation, Netanyahu and Arafat initialed the Hebron Accord at the Erez crossing point into Gaza on Jan. 14, 1997. It was finally signed on Jan. 17. US Special Peace Envoy, Dennis Ross, and Secretary of State Warren Christopher played crucial roles as arbitrators; Ross in particular drafted a "note for the record" (see below) on Jan. 15. Netanyahu and Arafat later conferred with US President Bill Clinton, President Mubarak and King Hussein, all three of whom had been intimately involved in brokering the accord.

The Hebron Accord committed Israel to giving the Palestinians control of 80 per cent of the city "within days". Israel was to maintain security control for the remaining 20 per cent, which included all Jewish-populated areas of the city. According to a simultaneous "note for the record", Israel also agreed to roll back its presence in the West Bank in three stages of further redeployments, beginning in six weeks and ending in August 1998. King Hussein prevailed upon Arafat to push back the deadline for completing the withdrawal from September 1997 to August 1998. In March 1997 Netanyahu presented his own schedule for a three-stage re-deployment. Palestinians were angry when he proposed just 9% (7% from Areas A and B, and 2% from Area C). They envisaged a first further re-deployment of 30%.

According to the previous timetable, of Oslo II, Israel was to have withdrawn from 80 per cent of Hebron by March 1996. However, this withdrawal had been postponed by then Prime Minister Shimon Peres, following his decision to go to elections shortly after-wards. Political analysts suggested that to promote such a politically sensitive concession might damage his chances for re-election. Immediately on hearing of the signing of the Accord, seven of Netanyahu's 18 ministers threatened to vote against the deal. Even so, the Knesset passed the Accord, or Protocol, by 87 votes to 17.

The peace process generally stagnated throughout 1997 and Jerusalem increasingly loomed as a bone of contention between the two parties. On Feb. 26 Israel's Ministerial Committee on Jerusalem approved con-struction at Har Homa—a major projected Jewish township in contested East Jerusalem. However, on July 27, and possibly in response to Arab and even American anger at this perceived abrogation of the Oslo spirit, Israel's government chose to delay con-struction at a similar Jerusalem site, Ras al-Amud. In September Israeli agents tried but failed to assassinate a top *Hamas* official in Amman, Jordan. To retrieve its agents, it was forced to release from incarceration Sheikh Ahmed Yassin, founder and supreme chief of *Hamas*—a major humiliation for Netanyahu.

Also in 1997, two other unofficial plans were moot-ed to resolve the controversy over future borders. One was the Abu Mazen-Yossi Beilin Plan. It proposed that a majority of settlers would live under Israeli sover-eignty, while the remainder would enjoy special status under Palestinian rule. The Jordan valley would be a special security zone for Israel, but most of the West Bank would become a demilitarized Palestinian state. The second plan, known as Allon Plus, after the previ-ous unofficial plan of former Foreign Minister Yigal Allon, of the late 1960s and early 1970s, entailed Palestinian enclaves covering 40 per cent of the West Bank. Israel would still control greater Jerusalem, the Jordan valley, large settlement blocks, areas along the Green Line, and "essential roads and waterways". Neither plan received great backing from Palestinians.

Israel & the Palestinians: Wye River Agreements, 1998-99

In late January 1998 US Secretary of State Madeleine Albright flew to the Middle East and proposed a series of simultaneous steps by the PNA (on security) and Israel (on re-deployment) to break the negotiating log-jam. She held further repeated meetings with Arafat and Netanyahu throughout the year. After arduous negotiations starting on Oct. 15, 1998, and an intense 21-hour final bargaining session, on Oct. 23

Netanyahu and Arafat signed the Wye River Memorandum, a land-for-peace deal in the West Bank. On Nov. 11, 1998, the Israeli cabinet approved the Wye River deal, by 8 votes to 5, with 4 abstentions, but added several amendments to the implementation process. The vote bespoke serious divisions within Netanyahu's ruling coalition. Arafat responded on Nov. 14 by calling for the establishment of a Palestinian state on the West Bank, with East Jerusalem as its capital, for May 4, 1999. (In the event, he postponed this call for independence, prior to May elections in Israel, in a move interpreted as a favour to Labour candidate, Ehud Barak—who won the poll, see below.)

On Nov. 30, 1998, President Clinton hosted a Middle East donors' conference in Washington, where some 40 nations pledged more than $3 billion in eco-nomic assistance to the PNA. Over Dec. 12-15 he vis-ited the PNA and Israel, addressed the PLC, and heard it vote "fully and forever" for rejecting conflict with Israel, and for revoking articles of the Charter that called for Israel's destruction. By February 1999, a newly established US-Palestinian Bilateral Committee began holding regular meetings.

The Wye Memorandum outlined an Israeli agree-ment to give the Palestinians a further 13.1 per cent of the West Bank. It also prepared modalities for a 12-week "phased hand-over" of land in return for Palestinian implementation of previous security com-mitments, including the outlawing of terrorist organi-zations, prohibition of illegal arms, and prevention of incitement. It further determined procedures for co-operation between Israeli and Palestinian security forces; and called for the Palestinian Central Committee to reaffirm the nullification of the Palestinian Charter provisions that were deemed inconsistent with the letters exchanged between Yasser Arafat and Yitzhak Rabin in September 1993. In effect, Netanyahu successfully called into question the legitimacy of the PNC's April 1996 vote to this effect (see above). With respect to the nature of the land to be transferred, approximately 1 per cent was to be desig-nated as Area A territory, and 12 per cent as Area B territory, according to the parameters of Oslo II.

Meanwhile, in December 1998, Netanyahu told Clinton and Arafat at a meeting at Erez that he wanted extra preconditions before he would undertake further re-deployments. On March 14, 1999, Netanyahu's cab-inet unanimously rejected an EU letter to Israel's Foreign Ministry on the question of Jerusalem. Issued four days previously, the letter called for re-establish-ing the city as a "corpus separandum" as per the 1947 UN partition resolution.

In elections held on May 17, 1999, Ehud Barak led his Labour Party (temporarily renamed One Israel) to a clear victory over the *Likud*, and succeeded Netanyahu as Prime Minister. He promised to con-clude final negotiations with the Palestinians, and to this end began negotiations with Egypt as an interces-sor. Barak met PNA Chairman Arafat at the Erez crossing point between Gaza and Israel, on July 27, and a joint PNA-Israel Committee began meeting two days later. The Israeli side requested a delay in implementing the Wye further re-deployments.

On Sept. 4, 1999, Barak and Arafat signed what became known as Wye II at the Egyptian Sinai port of Sharm el-Sheikh. US President Bill Clinton, US Secretary of State Madeleine Albright, Egyptian President Mubarak and Jordanian King Abdullah II all signed as witnesses. Israel's cabinet approved the accord by 21 votes to two on Sept. 5; and the Knesset approved it by 54 votes to 23 on Sept. 8.

Soon afterwards Israel released 199 Palestinian prisoners, according to the terms of Wye II, and the PNA handed over to Israel the names of its 30,000 policemen. On Sept. 10 Israel transferred 7 per cent of West Bank land from Area C to Area B (i.e. to PNA control). Exactly a month later the cabinet approved the removal of 42 settlements built since the October 1998 Wye Accord. However, Palestinians were disappointed when on Oct. 12, 1999, Barak ordered the dismantling of only 15 of these 42 sites. On Oct. 25 Israel opened a "safe passage road" from Gaza to the West Bank, through Israeli territory; 20 days earlier Israel and the PNA had signed a protocol to cover this action—safe passage having been one of the main demands of the Palestinians in the negotiations leading to Wye II.

On Oct. 26, 1999, Oded Eran became head of Israel's negotiating team on final status talks with the PNA; one of his prime responsibilities was to consider ultimate borders between Israel and the PNA entity. Several meetings ensued after Nov. 8 between Arafat and Barak on a Framework Agreement on Permanent [or Final] Status (FAPS), but problems emerged when on Nov. 11 Arafat refused to sign the map for the next further re-deployment.

Thereafter, Barak concentrated on negotiations with Syria (see below) and although he promised that this would not be "at the expense of" the Palestinian track, this is how it was perceived in Palestinian quarters. Despite Israeli and Palestinian disappointment with the gains of Oslo, it nonetheless seemed that at last the peace process was yielding dividends. The year 1999 was the first that PNA-ruled areas registered significant economic growth; it was also the first year in Israel's 51-year history that not a single Israeli citizen had died in a terror attack. (For discussion of Israeli-Palestinian negotiations after this point, see sub-section below, "Israel & the Palestinians: Camp David II", and following.)

Israel & Syria—Golan Heights Issue

Syria has consistently argued since the June 1967 war that there should be no separate peace treaty between Israel and any Arab nation, or between Israel and the Palestinians. It believes that the only acceptable formulation is a comprehensive regional settlement. Hence its opposition to the Camp David Accords of 1978 and the Israel-Egypt peace treaty of 1979. Despite participation in bilateral talks with Israel pursuant to the October 1991 Madrid Peace Conference, Syria strongly condemned the Israel-PLO agreement of 1993 and the Israel-Jordan peace treaty of 1994, on the grounds given above.

Unlike Jordan, Egypt and Israel, Syria (and the PLO) did not initially accept UN Resolution 242 as the basis for peace talks. It did, however, support UN 338 after the Yom Kippur War, in October 1973, which it fought in an abortive attempt to win back control of the Golan Heights from Israel. As UN 338 essentially reiterated the conditions of UN 242, Syria's acceptance of UN 338 signaled its belated agreement to UN 242, and thus to the principle of "land for peace". As a result, analysts determined that Syria was now prepared to recognize Israel if the latter were to hand back the Golan Heights (or Jawlan in Arabic) an area that Israel had captured during the 1967 war, and defended in the 1973 war.

From Israel's perspective, possessing the Golan Heights meant control of high ground that in the pre-1967 period Syria had used to its military advantage. Furthermore, Israeli possession ensured control of important water resources—in particular, around the Banias Springs, and access to the northern corner of the inland Sea of Tiberias (also called Galilee or, in Hebrew, Kinneret). Israel now enjoyed land rich in vineyards, orchards and cattle grazing as well as the nation's only ski resort.

Israel also encouraged its citizens to settle in the region. The first such community, Kibbutz Merom Golan, was established within a month of the June 1967 conquest of the region. As of 2003, an estimated 17,000 Israelis lived in some 30 settlements, of which the largest was the town of Katzrin, founded in 1977. Most Golan settlers are secular in outlook—by contrast with most West Bank settlers—and anecdotally include a majority of Labour voters. Although security and not ideology is the prime motivation for retaining the Golan, some Israelis claim the Heights as part of historic "Eretz Yisrael". At one stage, according to the Bible, the tribe of Manasseh lived there; and, in addition, the Heights include Gamla, a famous site of Jewish resistance against the Romans in the 1st century. Of the indigenous Druze Arabs, some left for Syria after 1967, while many remained under Israeli rule. The latter number approximately 20,000—slightly outnumbering the population of their Israeli Jewish neighbours. The Druze live in smaller villages and the larger town of Majdal Shams; a few accepted Israeli citizenship, but most remain as Syrian citizens.

Repeated UN General Assembly resolutions have criticized Israel's occupation of the Heights. UNGA 35/122, on Dec. 11, 1980, condemned Israel for imposing legislation "implying changes of condition and nature of the occupied Syrian Golan population"; and UNGA 36/147, on Dec. 16, 1980, opposed Israeli "imposition" of Israeli nationality on Syrian citizens in the occupied Golan. Similar resolutions, UNGA 42/160 and UNGA 45/83, were passed on Dec. 8, 1987, and Dec. 13, 1990, respectively. By then, the Israeli Knesset had passed the Golan Heights Law, as a constitutionally binding "basic law", on Dec. 14, 1981. This piece of legislation applied Israeli law, jurisdiction and administration to the Golan Heights. It was widely interpreted as the illegal annexation of the area; even the USA, Israel's chief ally, temporarily halted arms deliveries to Israel in protest.

Israeli-Syrian Negotiations in the 1990s

As noted above, Syria participated in the Madrid peace conference and subsequent negotiations with Israel in Washington. From the start, Syria insisted that the idea of "land for peace", as enacted in Israel's earlier successful talks with Egypt, should apply to the Golan Heights. There were hints of concessions from Syria— as when it lifted travel restrictions on its tiny Jewish community, in April 1992. But overall, during the first five rounds of talks, discussions concerned little more than procedural matters. Israel under *Likud* wanted simply "peace for peace". Syria (and Lebanon) chose to boycott the multilateral strand of talks, in the absence of an agreement with Israel.

The advent of the Rabin administration in June 1992 improved the atmosphere, as the Labour Party had conceded that the principle of territorial compromise could apply to the Golan Heights. In power, Labour was now for the first time prepared to consider a withdrawal in, though not from, this area. It was widely thought that Rabin regarded peace with Syria as a higher priority than a deal with the Palestinians, though he switched emphasis with the Oslo breakthrough. As noted above, Syria rejected the 1993 Israeli-Palestinian Declaration of Principles and subsequent Oslo Accords, and after January 1994 it hosted an alliance of ten anti-Oslo Palestinian groups. Damascus also bitterly criticized the Jordan-Israel treaty of late 1994.

Nonetheless, in time Syria resumed talks with Israel, possibly spurred on by the fear that it might be "left out" as successive parties made peace with Israel. These nations included several from the Arab Gulf, who not only agreed to suspend the secondary economic boycott of Israel, but also began establishing low level diplomatic relations with it.

The USA played a major role in encouraging an Israeli-Syrian settlement. In December 1993 US Secretary of State Warren Christopher met Syrian President Assad for intensive talks in Damascus; and on Jan. 16, 1994, President Clinton met Assad in Geneva, after which Assad said Syria was prepared for "normal, peaceful relations with Israel". Rabin responded by saying that Israel was prepared to pay a "painful price" for peace. In March Assad met a visiting delegation of Israeli Arabs, who were paying their condolences on the death of his son, Bassel.

On April 30, 1994, US Secretary of State Christopher outlined a three-phase plan over eight years, dubbed "Majdal Shams First", whereby in phase one Syria would take control of Majdal Shams and three other Druze settlements on the Heights, in phase two Israel would close all Jewish settlements, and in phase three there would be complete Israeli withdrawal. Israel suggested mutual cutbacks in the standing armies of each country (Syria and Israel having five and two divisions posted near the Golan Heights respectively). Upset by this notion, which he took as unjustified interference in Syrian internal politics, Assad broke off negotiations. Still, in January 1995 the leading Sunni cleric in Syria issued a *fatwa* supporting peace with Israel, and talks resumed in March. Then on May 24 Israel and Syria announced an apparent breakthrough: a "framework understanding on security arrangements". In diplomatic parlance, it rested on "four legs of the table"—security, normalization, withdrawal, and a timetable for implementation.

Increasingly, Israeli Foreign Minister Shimon Peres spoke about Israeli recognition of the Heights as "part of Syrian sovereignty". Such statements inspired a grassroots pro-Golan settler movement, and seven Labour parliamentary representatives became "Golan rebels", who demanded that withdrawal could only follow a national referendum on a 65 per cent majority. Some of these rebels even formed a new party, dubbed The Third Way, to "safeguard" the Golan.

As talks continued serious differences remained. Israel wanted a staged and partial withdrawal over four years (down from eight, as earlier) while Syria wanted a full withdrawal in 18 months. Rabin amplified his plan into a two-stage Israeli withdrawal that comprised four key elements: (i) an early warning station on Mt Hermon, near the Syrian border, with a similar Syrian facility near Safad in Israel; (ii) demilitarization of the entire Heights, and a limited forces zone 40 km into Syria; (iii) an international US-led monitoring force; and (iv) confidence measures, including a hotline and joint Israeli-Syrian military patrols.

In June 1995 Syrian and Iranian officials meeting in Tehran reaffirmed their strategic alliance and vowed to deny Israel a peace deal until it fully withdrew from the Heights. However, the next month Barak's successor as negotiator, Amnon Shahak, revealed a new Syrian concession: Syria would withdraw 1,000 metres for every 400 metres withdrawn by Israel. Such "assymetrical withdrawal" met a long-standing Israeli demand, predicated upon the lack of "strategic depth" that Israel enjoyed, due to its comparatively small size. But Syria balked at the idea of early warning stations. In late July Rabin narrowly defeated a bill to delay talks until a referendum was held in Israel.

The following month, faced with growing opposition at home and angry at renewed attacks by Syria's proxy, *Hizbullah*, in southern Lebanon, Rabin agreed to temporarily freeze talks with the Syrians. He concentrated instead on finalizing Oslo II with the Palestinians, but was assassinated on Nov. 4, 1995. Evidently this tragedy shocked Assad into contacting Israel's new Prime Minister, Shimon Peres, and calling for renewed and speeded-up negotiations. Peres agreed, and assumed a different approach from Rabin. He played down the incremental and security-centred strategy of his predecessor, and stressed instead a simultaneous "total package" deal, placing greater emphasis on normalization and future economic co-operation. He incorporated these ideas in a new ten-point plan. To many Arab analysts, however, Peres' approach was more threatening than Rabin's, as it raised the spectre of Israeli economic domination. It also required a greater cultural re-orientation than a simple non-belligerency pact would have called for.

Israeli-Syrian talks recommenced in late 1995, with the Israeli team originally led by the Director-General of the Foreign Ministry, Uri Savir, and the Syrian side by their ambassador to the USA, Walid Mu'alem. The negotiations took place under US auspices, with an active role for US "co-ordinator for the peace process", Dennis Ross. The location was the Aspen International Centre at the Wye River Valley, Maryland. There was also more European involve-ment: a "troika" of EU foreign ministers, from Ireland, Spain and Italy, offered Syria financial inducements in return for progress at the negotiating table.

Syrian Foreign Minister Farouk al-Sharaa promised Israel a "deep and comprehensive peace", but warned that it would be harder gained, and thus more genuine, than the peace Jordan had signed with Israel. Tunisia, Morocco, Qatar, Oman and Yemen all promised to sign full peace treaties with Israel, but only once Syria had done so. There were three sessions of talks between late December 1995 and early March 1996. However, talks then ceased, for a number of reasons. One was the sudden escalation of *Hizbullah* attacks in southern Lebanon in February 1996, leading to the subsequent Israeli mini-invasion, called Operation Grapes of Wrath (see below). *Hizbullah* belligerence was partic-ularly galling from Israel's perspective, as Sharaa had specifically promised to rein in this group. Israel had seemed prepared for the first time to consider full withdrawal in return for "full peace", as once mooted by the late Rabin. But whereas Israel meant withdraw-al to the pre-1967 de facto border, Syria favoured the international border as agreed in the 1949 armistice agreement. The latter definition afforded Syria just a few more square kilometres, but crucially it would gain access to the water of the Sea of Galilee. This was wholly unacceptable to Ehud Barak, formerly a nego-tiator with Syria, and now Israeli Foreign Minister. Apart from such impediments, the Syrian team felt unqualified to negotiate on details of trade and diplo-matic relations; and Shimon Peres was upset that the desired meeting between him and President Assad did not materialize.

After coming to power in May 1996, Benjamin Netanyahu effectively suspended the peace process with Syria. He rejected concessions made by Peres over the Golan, and refused to accept hastily written but unratified proposals as binding. In his view, true peace ought to precede territorial changes, and he ini-tially refused to cede an inch of the Golan. He also refused to negotiate until Syria disavowed its sponsor-ship of "terrorist organizations" (meaning both radical Palestinian groups and *Hizbullah*). Overall, Netanyahu believed that democracies could not make lasting, gen-uine agreements with dictatorships. Virtually no

progress was made with Syria during his tenure.

The election of Ehud Barak as new Prime Minister of Israel on May 17, 1999, revived hopes of a peace treaty with Syria. On July 22 Barak held talks in Jerusalem with Spanish Premier José Aznar, and said that Israel was prepared to restart talks with Syria from the point they left off in March 1996. Four days later Jordanian King Abdullah II briefed Barak by tele-phone of talks he had recently held with President Assad. Addressing the Knesset on Dec. 13, 1999, Barak said Israel might have to pay a "heavy territori-al price" for peace with Syria. He won a vote of confi-dence on the issue, with 47 votes for, 31 against, 24 abstentions and 18 absent. On Dec. 15 Barak met Syrian Foreign Minister Farouk al-Sharaa in Washington, to discuss administration in the Golan Heights and troop withdrawals from the Israeli-Lebanese border. This represented the highest level of negotiations between the two nations to date.

On Jan. 3, 2000, they met again—after a goodwill gesture the previous week in which Israel released five *Hizbullah* prisoners—in Shepherdstown, West Virginia, with President Bill Clinton and Secretary of State Madeleine Albright in attendance. One plan mooted the return of the Golan Heights region to Syria in exchange for new security guarantees for Israel. Clinton presented a draft Israel-Syria peace agreement to Jerusalem and Damascus on Jan. 8, henceforth dubbed the "Clinton plan". It contained nine articles: (i) establishment of peace and security within recog-nized boundaries, (ii) international boundary, (iii) nor-mal peaceful relations, (iv) security, (v) water, (vi) rights and obligations, (vii) legislation, (viii) settle-ment of disputes, and (ix) final clauses. According to a copy of this agreement held by the Haim Hertzog Centre of Ben Gurion University, in southern Israel, Article I envisaged the location of the international boundary as accommodating Syrian views. Syria favoured the June 4, 1967, line; Israel apparently broadly agreed, though wanted the line to "take into account security and other vital interests of the par-ties". Israel would withdraw (or relocate) armed forces (and possibly also citizens) behind this line. An annex outlined a timeline and modalities for implementation of such actions. Article II envisaged an international boundary that would supersede all previous demarca-tions, and a Joint Boundary Commission to oversee it.

Failure of Israeli-Syrian Negotiations

Once again, talks foundered; they ended on Jan. 10, 2000, and on Jan. 17 the US government announced that they were frozen because of "fundamental differ-ences". A major impediment proved to be Syria's opposition to Israeli plans that the Syrian army should withdraw some 100 miles from the border. This Syria regarded as unjustified interference in its internal affairs. Israel also disputed which international border to accept: Syria preferred an older plan which extend-ed the border by about a mile, and thereby afforded it access to the waters of the Sea of Galilee. Israel rejected this plan, and also lamented the fact that Syrian President Assad was unprepared to negotiate directly with Prime Minister Barak. Israel further criticized Syria for failing to curb the anti-Israeli activities of Syrian-backed *Hizbullah* guerrillas in southern Lebanon.

Barak admitted to feeling a "burden of responsibility" to reach an agreement with Syria that year. Yet the talks suspended in 2000 have never been formally resumed. With the collapse of Syria-Israel talks, the Barak administration turned its attention instead to negotiations with the Palestinians, resulting in the ill-fated Camp David II talks, whose failure led indirectly to the outbreak of a new Palestinian Al Aqsa intifada in late September 2000.

Syrian President Hafez al-Assad died on June 10, 2000, soon to be replaced as leader by his son, Bashar al-Assad. The younger Assad swore to continue his father's policies; however, he postponed bold negotiating ventures so as to concentrate on consolidating his domestic power and addressing Syria's pressing internal economic problems. The 2000 intifada and election of Ariel Sharon to power in early 2001 both reduced the likelihood of reviving negotiations with Syria. This was especially so as Sharon refused to offer the same terms as Barak and Rabin before him. He certainly was not willing to return to Syria the entire Golan Heights, however defined.

For its part, Syria reverted to its traditional policy of seeking a comprehensive peace in concert with other Arab nations. It was pivotal in helping draft the Saudi Prince Abdullah Plan, as presented to the Arab leaders' summit in Beirut in early 2002. Sharon's government was sceptical about the proposal. Later that year Syria resolutely opposed US plans to use military action against Iraq; at the same time it assured the USA that it was committed to fighting terrorism. Towards the end of the US invasion of Iraq in March-April 2003, US government officials accused Syria of harbouring wanted allies of the deposed Saddam Hussein. US Secretary of State Colin Powell extracted from Damascus promises to seal the border with Iraq, so as to prevent former Baathists from seeking refuge in Syria.

Israel capitalized on Syria's unpopularity in Washington and pro-Israeli political action groups lobbied successfully for both houses of the US Congress to pass the Syrian Accountability Act and the Lebanese Sovereignty Restoration Act (see below). Israel also accused Syria of providing sustenance and refuge to militant Palestinian groups, notably Islamic Jihad and *Hamas*, which were responsible for numerous acts of terror against Israeli citizens. (As noted above, ten Palestinian movements that rejected Oslo I had coalesced as the Damascus Front in 1993.) Re-elected in 2003, Prime Minister Sharon did not rule out a resumption of talks with Syria, but was loath to discuss withdrawal from the Golan Heights (as had his Labour predecessors, Rabin, Peres and Barak). He also demanded more concerted action from Damascus to close down "terrorist bases" in Syria, before counte-

nancing new negotiations. On Oct. 5, 2003, Israeli air force jets launched an overnight raid on alleged Islamic Jihad bases in Syria, an act that was condemned by many states, including Jordan, as "aggression" and a "dangerous escalation". Israel justified the raid as punishment for Syria's harbouring of Islamist terrorists, some of whom had the previous day killed several Israelis. There was no Syrian military retaliation.

In late November 2003 Syrian President Bashar al-Assad announced that he was willing to resume negotiations with Israel from the point where they had been suspended in early 2000 (i.e. talks held with the Barak administration). Israel's Foreign Minister Silvan Shalom welcomed his statement, but suggested that actions were preferable to fine words: "We are ready for direct negotiations without preconditions, and the first topic from our point of view will be terrorism". Israel specifically expected Damascus to take more determined action against anti-Israeli militants on Syrian soil. In the first week of 2004, however, a scandal arose in Israel when the Agriculture Minister, Yisrael Katz, spoke of a plan to double the number of settlers in the Golan Heights. Though countermanded by Deputy Prime Minister Ehud Olmert, and chided by the US administration, Katz's statement led Syrian Vice-President Abdel-Halim Khaddam to accuse Israel of trying to "abort any inclination towards peace".

On Jan. 7, 2004, Israeli analyst Ze'ev Schiff noted in the *Ha'aretz* newspaper Shalom's guarded optimism, and the advice of most Israeli security chiefs for their government to at least "test" Syria's tactical gambit. By contrast, he wrote, there was general silence from Prime Minister Sharon and Defence Minister Shaul Mofaz. UN Middle East envoy, Roed-Larsen, lent his voice to supporting the Syrian peace initiative, and Syria's officially sanctioned *Al Thawra* newspaper announced that the Assad administration was seeking the active intervention of the USA. In addition, President Assad paid his first official visit to Turkey in early 2004, and Turkish Prime Minister Recep Erdogan offered to play the role of intercessor between Israel and Syria in future negotiations.

Israel & Lebanon: Negotiations in 1990s

Direct bilateral talks between official Israeli and Lebanese delegations commenced in Madrid on Nov. 3, 1991. They resumed at "substantive" sessions held in Washington DC from Dec. 11; a new round of talks occurred on Jan. 7-16, 1992.

However, it soon became clear that Lebanon was unwilling to advance faster than Syria in its talks with their mutual neighbour, Israel. According to the Taif Accord for "national reconciliation", Syria and Lebanon were to "coordinate" their foreign policies. On Oct. 22, 1989, the Lebanese National Assembly meeting in Taif, Saudi Arabia, endorsed the accord that bears the city's name. Implementation began in October 1990. Article IV of the Accord explicitly states: "Lebanon shall not allow itself to serve as the transit point or base for any force state or organization interested in harming its own security or the security of Syria". And while it mandated a "security plan for extending government sovereignty over all Lebanese territory", it did not order Syrian troops out of the country. Instead it planned for a "withdrawal of Syrian forces *inside* Lebanon and the establishment of a joint Syrian-Lebanese mechanism for making future decisions about the positioning and functions of the Syrian troops". The subsequent Lebanese-Syrian Brotherhood Treaty of 1991 reaffirmed the principle of coordinated decision-making— a provision that some feel implies Damascus' license to control Beirut's strategic interests.

Violence increased in southern Lebanon in mid-February 1992, prompting US Secretary of State James Baker to urge Israel, Lebanon and Syria to exercise "maximum restraint". By this stage a *Hizbullah*-led Islamic militia front (*Muqawama*) had largely taken over "resistance" duties in the south from a coalition of the less radical Shiite group, *Amal*, and sundry leftists, known collectively as *Jamoul*. It should be noted that the *Muqawama* were exempted from the stipulations of the Taif Accord, which ordered all Lebanese militias to disarm. This was justified because they were "defending the nation" against external forces (i.e. Israel). Ranged against the "resistance" were Israeli forces and their local proxy militia, the South Lebanon Army (SLA). The official national army of Lebanon was largely uninvolved in the conflict. Likewise Syrian forces in Lebanon, some 35,000 strong, kept out of direct fighting, though Damascus did provide *Hizbullah* with arms, or at least acted as a conduit for Iranian weaponry to reach them.

Initial hopes for a breakthrough in Israel-Lebanon talks, with the May 1992 election of a Labour-led government in Israel, soon gave way to disappointment. In December Prime Minister Yitzhak Rabin responded to a terror attack that killed six Israeli soldiers, by deporting more than 400 suspected Palestinian Islamist militants to Lebanese soil. Beirut regarded this action as an infringement of its territorial integrity. Relations worsened after a massive Israeli blitz on southern Lebanon in 1993 that resulted in the flight of tens of thousands of southern Lebanese to the sanctuary of Beirut and other northern cities. Erosion in Lebanese-Israeli relations had a deleterious effect on multilateral talks, where many projects (e.g. transport links, water allocation, tourism development) assumed geographical contiguity across the Israeli-Lebanese border.

Furthermore, many of the 350,000 Palestinians in Lebanon, a large percentage of whom still lived in refugee camps, voiced disquiet about the Israel-PLO Oslo Accords, signed in Washington in September 1993. They particularly criticized the agreements for not explicitly addressing the future fate of refugees, and of thereby abandoning Palestinians who dwelt outside the Israeli-occupied territories. Lebanon's Palestinians also feared that the Beirut government would exploit prevailing ambiguities to intensify existing economic and political discrimination against their disenfranchised community.

On April 11, 1996, in response to increased raids by *Hizbullah* on Israeli targets, Israeli Prime Minister Shimon Peres authorized attacks on *Hizbullah* offices in southern Beirut. Operation Grapes of Wrath, as it was called, soon grew into a full-scale conflict, and terminated on April 26 following growing international anger at actions by Israel that were perceived to be excessive. In particular, Israel was blamed for a strike on or near a UNIFIL base in Qana, where about 100 Palestinian refugees who had fled from Sidon were killed. Though Israel protested that the deaths were entirely accidental, US Secretary of State Warren Christopher intervened, and helped oversee a new "understanding" on April 26. Accordingly a monitoring group was established consisting of the USA, France, Syria, Lebanon and Israel.

The terms of the understanding included: (i) no further Israeli strikes on civilians, (ii) no *Hizbullah* rocket attacks on Israel, and (iii) no *Hizbullah* raids from civilian-populated areas. The understanding drew criticism from many sides. Some felt that it illegally legitimized Israel's presence in the "buffer zone". Others, especially from Israel's *Likud* opposition, argued that it was wrong to allow *Hizbullah* a "right to self-defence". Such military action, they contended, should properly have been the province of the national defence forces of the Republic of Lebanon, and not a militia group. Within Israel, critics of Peres blamed him for stoking up an avoidable and ultimately botched confrontation, in the hope of garnering votes in forthcoming elections. In the event Peres narrowly lost the at the polls to *Likud* leader, Benjamin Netanyahu—many Israeli Arab voters, who might otherwise have voted for Peres, boycotted the elections to protest the Qana incident.

Amidst sporadic violence, on Aug. 8, 1996, the five-nation ceasefire monitoring committee held its first meeting. In 1997 Israeli Prime Minister Netanyahu and Defence Minister Yitzhak Mordechai surprised *Likud* supporters by supporting the principle of a negotiated withdrawal of Israeli troops from all of Lebanon. Mordechai reiterated this call on Jan. 2, 1998, but insisted on iron-cast security guarantees. Lebanon rejected a similar proposal from Netanyahu on March 1. On July 22, the Knesset adopted a bill requiring an absolute majority of Knesset members and a referendum majority before any territorial concessions were made on the Golan Heights. The bill won final approval on Jan. 29, 1999.

Four Israeli women whose sons were serving or had served in Lebanon formed the Four Mothers Movement, which called for total withdrawal of the IDF. They began winning popular support, as did former minister, and Labour Knesset member, Yossi Beilin, who founded a political movement to bring about a withdrawal from Lebanon. The security argument for holding on to Lebanese territory, on the ground of defending northern Israeli towns, began to look ever more untenable.

However, Lebanon seemed wary of responding

favourably, and Israeli newspapers reported that President Assad of Syria was pressurizing Lebanon not to sign such an agreement. According to an article by Ron Ben-Ishai in *Yediot Ahranot* in March 1998, Syria feared that the Netanyahu-Mordechai proposal was a trick, and a means of isolating Syria. Negotiating and then implementing an Israeli withdrawal from Lebanon would delay progress on talks over the future of the Golan Heights, it was argued. Ben-Ishai also stated that "Assad fears an Israeli withdrawal might bring international pressure on him to guarantee Israel's security".

Dissident Lebanese analysts increasingly noted that an Israeli pullout would remove Syria's justification for lodging some 35,000 of its own troops in Lebanon. According to one interpretation of UN Resolution 425, withdrawal of foreign forces applied equally to Syria as to Israel. Certainly talks failed to progress, and in November 1998 Israeli aircraft bombed an alleged *Hizbullah* centre in Iqlim al-Toufah in southern Lebanon. Ousted as Defence Minister in January 1999, Mordechai joined the newly formed Centre Party on a pledge to renew meaningful dialogue with Lebanon. In late February 1999, Israeli Air Force jets again struck at *Hizbullah* bases in Lebanon.

Ehud Barak, leader of the Labour Party in Israel, soundly defeated Netanyahu in the May 1999 elections, and pledged to withdraw Israel from Lebanon. After increased *Hizbullah* rocket attacks on Israel, outgoing Israeli Defence Minister Moshe Arens told the IDF in late June 1999 to ignore the April 1996 "understanding" and to effectively boycott the monitoring committee. Barak countermanded Arens' order in July 1999. In late January 2000, an attack on an IDF post in Lebanon prompted large Israeli retaliations on Feb. 8-11, and Israel formally left the Israel-Lebanon Monitoring Group meeting.

Israeli Withdrawal from Lebanon in 2000

On March 5, 2000, Barak's cabinet vowed to withdraw from Lebanon entirely by July 2000. In the event, Israel completed its departure from Lebanon on May 24, 2000, ahead of schedule and over barely 24 hours. In a broadcast over Israeli Army Radio, Barak promised to "re-deploy...on the international border" and added: "This 18-year tragedy is over". Israel's withdrawal was unilateral—it did not take place as a negotiated agreement with the Lebanese government. Yet it was closely co-ordinated with the United Nations Security Council, and it scrupulously adhered to UN border demarcations. In other words, in the absence of a negotiated settlement, Israel at least wanted to abide fully by UN Security Council Resolution 425.

Despite *Hizbullah* threats to "continue the struggle", Israeli forebodings about further large-scale cross-border violence proved largely unfounded. In the immediate aftermath of the departure, *Hizbullah* cadres took over vacated areas and freed 130 inmates from the Israeli-run Khiam prison. It was some time before the Lebanese National Army nominally assumed responsibility for border control; it is an open secret that the main power in southern Lebanon is *Hizbullah*, not the army. Indeed, there were reports that even some Christian communities (hitherto friendly towards Israel) welcomed *Hizbullah* as "liberators". *Hizbullah* went on to do well at national Lebanese elections in August 2000, in large part due to their perceived success at ridding Lebanon of Israeli forces.

On May 26, 2000, the BBC's Christopher Hack reported that "the Lebanese Government is reluctant to deploy the army in the south, because Syria—which dominates Lebanese politics—does not want to see Israel's border secure until Israeli troops withdraw from the Golan Heights". Israeli withdrawal proved to be a catalyst for the total collapse of the 2,500-strong SLA, most notably in Marjayoun, where the militia based its headquarters. Many SLA fighters fled to safety in Israel, fearing that Lebanese courts would convict them of collaborating with Israel. The SLA also felt that its members would face deadly retaliation from *Hizbullah* militants out for revenge. Israel had earlier demanded that Beirut should integrate the SLA into its regular national army, as a precondition for Israeli withdrawal. Lebanon angrily rebuffed this suggestion, citing numerous reports of the SLA shelling civilian centres and even UNIFIL units.

For the most part, Israelis were relieved that their 22-year presence in Lebanon was over. However, some alleged that the withdrawal was mismanaged and too hasty; that Israel had "betrayed" its SLA allies; and that withdrawal would be interpreted as surrender, and would encourage further violence. (Many right-wingers claim that the Al Aqsa intifada by Palestinians, which broke out five months later, was indirectly triggered by the "message of weakness" that the Lebanese pullout signaled.) Even from the left there was some disquiet: by unilaterally withdrawing, it was argued, Israel had squandered an opportunity to achieve a negotiated settlement, possibly a full peace treaty, with the Republic of Lebanon.

There was also disappointment after initial euphoria in Lebanon. According to a report by Rana Abouzeid of Al Jazeera on Nov. 27, 2003, "a small contingent of Lebanese forces moved into the region to fill the security vacuum created by the [May 2000] pullout. [But] the Lebanese government has refused to deploy the army along the border because it says it does not want to serve as Israel's bodyguard in the absence of a peace treaty between the two countries". Her article also reported that while southern villagers were happy to have their honour restored, and were relieved that there were no longer any irksome Israeli security restrictions, many missed the employment opportunities and civil infrastructure that Israel brought to the region. By contrast, they criticized the Lebanese government for ignoring the region, both during the Israeli occupation and now after their departure. A Council of the South, originally established in 1970, seeks to fill the administrative vacuum. However Council President Kabalan Kabalan has complained that its room for manoeuvre is restricted, as the Council falls under direct fiscal and political control of the Lebanese cabinet. "The Ministry of Energy, for example, in the past few years did not spend 1% of its budget in the South", said Kabalan.

Shebaa Farms Issue—Retention of Syrian Troops in Lebanon

A UN report concluded that Israeli forces had redeployed behind the internationally recognized border with Lebanon. On June 16, 2000, UN Secretary-General Kofi Annan certified that Israel had completed its withdrawal; on June 18 the UN Security Council endorsed this certification. However, there remained a dispute, as yet unresolved, over a 10 square kilometre area, consisting of 14 villages on the western slopes of Mount Herman and known as Shebaa Farms. Israel retained a presence there, arguing that UN maps clearly showed that the territory belonged to Syria and not to Lebanon. Thus they were unwilling to "return" the region to Lebanon. However, Annan described the border as vaguely defined in international law, and proposed that all sides should adopt the line drawn in 1974 after the Yom Kippur war of 1973, pending a permanent delineation of the border. The line forms the limit of the area monitored by UNIFIL forces under Timur Goksel. UNIFIL completed its re-deployment along the "Blue Line" on Aug. 5.

For its part, Syria supported Lebanon's claim to the small region. Israel rejected Syria's stance as a ploy to maintain tensions, to justify continued support for *Hizbullah*, and to afford it leverage in negotiations with Israel over the adjoining Golan Heights. Israeli withdrawal from a military post at Astra, in the Shebaa zone, failed to break the deadlock. Nor did a visit to the area by UN special envoy Terje Roed-Larsen (formerly a major figure in brokering the Israel-PLO Oslo Accords). In apparent contradiction of senior UN diplomatic comments, UNIFIL's Timur Goksel suggested that Shebaa was on the Syrian side of the border. On Aug. 24, 2002, after a four-month lull in fighting, *Hizbullah* launched a large mortar attack on Shebaa Farms. Another occurred on Oct. 27, 2003.

Israel continues to blame Syria for aiding and abetting *Hizbullah*. Shebaa Farms remains a location where future violence may flare up into a regional conflict. Nonetheless, in June 2002 Israel unilaterally released a *Hizbullah* prisoner it had held for 15 years, thereby setting in motion a German-brokered negotiating process with *Hizbullah* to hand over some 400 Lebanese and Palestinian prisoners in exchange for one kidnapped Israeli and the bodies of another three. On Nov. 10, 2003, the Israeli cabinet narrowly approved the final deal; though Israeli media criticized the government for talking to a guerrilla organization, albeit indirectly, and not with the official government of Lebanon. The deal was finally enacted in late January 2004.

In August 2001 another dispute flared up, over Israeli opposition to Lebanese attempts to draw irrigation water from the Hasbani and Wazzani, tributaries of the Jordan. Israel had controlled both rivers during its 22-year-long occupation of southern Lebanon. It argued that excessive and "illegal" Lebanese usage was depriving Israel of vital water, as the tributaries drained into its Sea of Galilee. Evidently 10 per cent of Israel's drinking water derived from this source. Lebanon countered that according to international law it was within its rights to pump an additional 2 million cubic metres. In December US water experts visited the region, after which the problem and the threat of military force abated.

A final issue that bears consideration is pressure on Syria to withdraw its troops from Lebanon. Currently there are estimated to be about 35,000 such troops stationed there. In 2001, responding to growing criticism from the Lebanese media and public, as well as by Christian clergy and even some Muslim leaders, Syria ordered a "re-deployment" of troops away from Beirut itself, and towards the Bek'aa Valley. However, it refuses to withdraw completely, despite arguments over the redundancy of its mission now that several years have elapsed since the last Israeli forces left the south. On Dec. 12, 2003, US President George W. Bush signed into law the Syria Accountability and Lebanese Sovereignty Restoration Act, which mandated the administration to pass sanctions on Damascus if, amongst other things, it did not remove its troops from Lebanon. The President, however, may waive the obligation to do so, if he deems it is "not in the national security interest". Furthermore, the main purpose of the bill was assumed to be to reflect American ire at Syria for allowing renegade forces to cross their borders and engage with US troops in Iraq. Nonetheless, as the title of the bill signifies, the US administration considers that the sovereignty of Lebanese borders requires the departure of all foreign forces.

Israel & the Palestinians: Camp David II

When Israeli talks with Syria failed in early 2000, Prime Minister Barak decided on a new twofold strategy: unilateral withdrawal of the IDF from Lebanon to international borders, and a speeding up of the Oslo peace process with the Palestinians. However, it appeared Barak wished to effectively glide past the interim stages and embark on a swift conclusion of talks on final status issues.

Minor re-deployments were made on Jan. 6, 2000—Israel handed over to the PNA 3% of land from Area C to Area B, and 2% of land from Area B to Area A. Following intensive meetings with Yasser Arafat, President Mubarak, King Abdullah and French Prime Minister Lionel Jospin, on March 21, 2000, Barak agreed to transfer 6.1% of Area B to Area A. Now the PNA controlled 18.2% of the West Bank, as Area A; and partially controlled 21.8% of the same, as Area B.

It was clear that tensions were increasing. On Jan. 17, for instance, Arafat rejected a Barak appeal to extend the Feb. 15 Framework Agreement on Permanent Status (FAPS) deadline; although talks later resumed at Erez and Eilat, FAPS talks at Bolling

Air Force Base, USA, failed on March 28. The PNA rejected maps that Israel revealed on May 2, although on May 15 progress revived when Israel agreed to transfer Abu Dis, Izariyah and Sawarah al-Sharqiya, all near Jerusalem, to PNA Area A control. Meanwhile Israeli Minister Shlomo Ben-Ami, it was revealed, continued holding back-channel talks with PNA officials in Stockholm, Sweden.

After some unrest in Palestinian areas, Barak's government postponed an agreement to transfer to PNA control the three above-mentioned areas in Jerusalem, as approved by the Israeli cabinet on May 15. Following an interpretation of the stipulations of Oslo I, Arafat's PNA had set Sept. 13, 2000, as the date when it would declare a Palestinian state, with or without an agreement. Fearing such an eventuality, US President Bill Clinton and Secretary of State Albright prevailed upon both parties to negotiate outstanding issues at the presidential retreat, Camp David. The talks were thereafter known as Camp David II (the first such talks being those held, ultimately successfully, between Israel and Egypt in the late 1970s).

Many aspects of Camp David II remain controversial, including whether the initiative really was Clinton's, or rather Barak's. What is clear, in hindsight, is that conditions were not exactly propitious. In Spring 2000 a pivotal party in the Labour-led government, the Russian immigrants' *Yisrael Ba'Aliyah*, left the coalition, voicing its opposition to the Oslo process. *Shas*, the National Religious Party and even some ministers from the pro-peace *Meretz* bloc, soon thereafter all left the government. On July 10 Barak flew to the USA, via Egypt, bereft of the support of numerous ministers, who had resigned in preceding weeks. Foreign Minister David Levy boycotted the talks (or was forbidden from attending). On the Palestinian side, factions such as *Hamas*, the PFLP, Islamic Jihad and the refugee lobby group, *Badil*, put pressure on Arafat not to compromise on certain important issues. The most emotive of these were Jerusalem, and the refugees' "right to return". By contrast with the talks leading to Oslo I and II, this time there was more overt participation by Palestinians of the "diaspora", who feared being "sold out" by residents of Gaza and the West Bank.

Camp David II lasted from July 11-25, and broached subjects that had never been addressed in such detail before, like final borders, Jerusalem and settlements. But it ultimately ended in failure. Clinton and Barak blamed Arafat for its demise, though his supporters countered that Israeli proposals were not as generous as was widely suggested. These proposals— though never formally published—reportedly included talk of giving the PNA control of 95 per cent of the West Bank, and sharing Jerusalem on a municipal basis. Barak, it was said, also agreed to compensate Palestinians with "equivalent" land from within pre-1967 Israel, for areas of settlements on the West Bank to be annexed to Israel.

The opposition *Likud* accused Barak of one by one abandoning all his pre-talks "red lines"—positions that he had previously deemed to be beyond discussion. Yet the PNA countered that in effect, Barak's plan divided Palestinian territories into unmanageable cantons, and left Israel in a pre-eminent position. The PNA also alleged that Israel had disrespected Oslo by willfully ignoring the refugee issue. Israel countered that by demanding a refugee "right to return" (as per UN Resolution 194, according to one interpretation), the Palestinians gave the lie to their desire for a two-state solution, as such a return would perforce end the Jewish state of Israel.

A flurry of talks ensued between Shlomo Ben-Ami (Israel's newly appointed Foreign Minister), King Abdullah, President Mubarak, Albright, and French, British and German Foreign Ministers. On Sept. 10 the PLO Central Committee again voted to postpone plans to declare Palestinian statehood, a move interpreted as a concession to Israel and a bid to revive the peace process. On Sept. 25 Barak hosted Arafat for talks at his home, and on Sept. 26 Israeli and PNA teams started new talks in Washington. Two days later, however, opposition leader Ariel Sharon visited the Temple Mount, and clashes erupted between Palestinians and Israeli security forces. These soon spread, leading to the start of the Al Aqsa Intifada.

Outbreak of Second Intifada—Israeli Reoccupation of Territories

Israel accused the PNA of planning the uprising as a cynical negotiating ploy, and the PNA accused Barak of deliberately flouting Arab and Muslim sensitivities by allowing the Sharon visit. Amidst such recriminations, international leaders tried to restore peace, but to no avail. On Oct. 12, Israeli helicopters attacked official PNA targets in Gaza and Ramallah. Five days later Barak and Arafat verbally pledged to end the uprising; yet on Oct. 22 Barak suspended the peace process, as Gilo, a Jewish suburb of East Jerusalem, came under Palestinian fire. By November Ben-Ami was describing the intifada as a "military confrontation". On Nov. 7 the USA named members of a peace-seeking mission, led by former Senator George J. Mitchell. Israel agreed to abide by its findings, on Dec. 3, and Mitchell Committee members met Barak on Dec. 11. From mid-December, Israeli and Palestinian teams revived talks in Washington, under the aegis of Secretary Albright. This led to the Clinton plan, presented on Dec. 22, which seemingly expanded on Israeli concessions in Jerusalem, and provided more contiguous borders for an autonomous Palestinian entity. Barak accepted the plan, though Arafat felt additional clarifications were necessary.

On Jan. 1, 2001, Israel tightened the closure of Palestinian areas. Five days later, CIA Director George Tenet began talks on security issues with Israeli and PLO officials. Meanwhile, Arafat proposed intensive new talks at Taba, which were held on Jan. 21-27. Both sides claimed much progress, on future borders, the division of Jerusalem, and even concessions to refugees. However, the talks were suspended on Jan.

28, pending early Israeli prime ministerial elections, scheduled for Feb. 6. Ariel Sharon soundly defeated Barak in these polls, winning 62.4 per cent of the votes cast, and became Israel's new Prime Minister. Barak refused to join a coalition government, though Labour as a party did join. Sharon ensured that the major concessions made at Taba were not binding.

Colin Powell, appointed Secretary of State in the newly elected administration of President George W. Bush, paid his first visit to Sharon in Tel Aviv and Arafat in Ramallah, on Feb. 25, 2001. On April 30, 2001, the Sharm el-Sheikh Fact-Finding Committee, chaired by Senator Mitchell, issued its final report. It called for an immediate ceasefire, renunciation of terrorism, resumption of talks, and a freeze on the building of settlements in the West Bank and Gaza. CIA Director Tenet had both sides agree to an understanding after talks held during June 7-12, 2001.

On July 19 the Group of Eight (G-8) Foreign Ministers met in Genoa, and demanded implementation of Mitchell's recommendations. On Sept. 26 Israeli Foreign Minister Shimon Peres and PNA Chairman Arafat agreed to a ceasefire, and vowed to resume joint security initiatives, as outlined in Oslo II. On Nov. 10 President Bush addressed the UN General Assembly, and called for "two states, Israel and Palestine, [who will] live peacefully together within secure and recognized borders as called for by the Security Council resolutions".

However, when attempts at resolving the conflict made little progress, from November 2001 to January 2002, President Bush sent Middle East envoy, Gen. (res.) Anthony Zinni, on repeated visits to the region, sometimes accompanied by US Assistant Secretary of State William Burns. They tried but ultimately failed to persuade the Israelis and Palestinians to enforce the Mitchell and Tenet plans. Prime Minister Sharon demanded that there be "seven [or ten] days of quiet" before Israel would consider enforcing the Mitchell Report—although, it seemed to many, his proviso allowed terror groups to continually scuttle hopes for progress.

On Feb. 18, 2002, Bush backed a Saudi proposal, from Crown Prince Abdullah, to normalize Arab relations with Israel in return for Israel's withdrawal to its 1967 borders. The Arab League, meeting in Beirut, adopted Abdullah's two-state solution, on March 27, 2002. However, that same day 22 Jewish worshippers were killed by a suicide attack during a Passover meal at a seaside hotel. This topped a month in which some 120 had died in similar circumstances. In response, the Sharon government launched Operation Defensive Shield in April, re-occupying Palestinian cities in a bid to "root out terrorist infrastructure". This marked an effective cessation of the Oslo peace process. During this period, Zinni returned to negotiate a ceasefire and resume security co-operation. Tenet visited Arafat in Ramallah on June 4, 2002, to the same end. But by this stage, Sharon was accusing Arafat of abetting terror.

In July 2002, Secretary Powell launched a major bid to discuss humanitarian relief for Palestinians, and

major reforms in Palestinian governance, prior to the granting within three years of full Palestinian independence. Powell met representatives from the UN, EU and Russia (three of the developing "Quartet"— see below) as well as senior leaders from the Arab world. On Aug. 8 he met a high-ranking Palestinian delegation in Washington. On Sept. 12 President Bush reaffirmed his commitment to Palestinian independence. He then increased donations to the UNRWA fund for refugees, and insisted that Israelis and Palestinians negotiate the status of Jerusalem. This was interpreted as an olive branch to Arabs; however, many were offended when he praised Sharon as a "man of peace".

In the interim, the intifada dragged on; numerous suicide bombings resulted in fierce Israeli retaliations, including assassinations of alleged militant leaders. From its start until January 2004, the second, Al Aqsa, intifada cost some 800 Israeli and 2,300 Palestinian lives. There was a controversial siege in Jenin and a three-month long stand-off in Manger Square, Bethlehem, both in 2002. Israeli roadblocks (*mahsoumim*) sprang up all over the West Bank, severely restricting passage of Palestinian commuters between towns. Meanwhile, Sharon appeared to encourage renewed settlement building. Some accounts suggest that the number of settlers has risen by many thousands since the start of the 2000 intifada, after an initial period when it seemed "non-ideological" settlers were deserting their posts in the face of Palestinian violence. Fatah, formerly the mainstay behind the peace process, had spawned its own militant squad which used terror against civilians, called the Al Aqsa Martyrs Brigade—presumably as a rival to *Hamas* and Islamic Jihad. Meanwhile, Arafat was restricted by Israeli military edict to his Muqata headquarters in Ramallah, and forbidden to leave, or negotiate with foreign leaders.

The Road Map for Peace

In his 2000 election campaign Bush had criticized the Clinton administration for putting too much pressure on Israel, and for generally getting too involved in a "hands-on" way with the peace process. However, things changed after the terrorist attacks in the USA of Sept. 11, 2001. In November 2001, Bush announced explicitly before the UN his support for a two-state solution. In December 2001 Elliott Abrams, a man associated with the neo-conservative lobby in Washington, became senior director for the Near and Middle East in the National Security Council, under Condoleezza Rice.

On June 24, 2002, President Bush made a major address in which he called for Palestinian economic and political reforms, and an end to corruption. He also strongly suggested that Arafat was tainted by association with terrorism, and that he should go. Despite some disquiet from Colin Powell and the State Department, this became official US policy, and was welcomed in Israel. Soon afterwards, King Abdullah met Bush and called for a Road Map, to implement the policy, so as to bring forward a Palestinian state. Abrams became the head of a division in charge of the Map. However, notwithstanding Abrams' "neocon" reputation, there was much opposition to such proposals from pro-Israeli factions in the USA.

The Road Map was expanded into a plan that was to be endorsed by a Quartet, consisting of the USA, UN, EU and Russia. During Oct. 16-30, 2002, the Assistant US Secretary of State for Near Eastern Affairs, William Burns, traveled throughout the Middle East to garner the views of Arab leaders on hopes for restored peace in Israel and Palestine. Sharon, though, was wary, and proposed postponing the declaration of the Map until after Israeli elections, President Bush agreeing to this request. In the event, Sharon's *Likud* easily won elections on Jan. 28, 2003, but unveiling the Road Map was further delayed as the re-elected Israeli Prime Minister negotiated a new coalition government.

The plan went through numerous changes and drafts, mainly in secret, but was eventually finalized. In essence it pledged a Palestinian state by 2005, and consists of three phases, in which borders were only to be addressed in the second and third. In the first phase, Israelis would freeze existing settlements and dismantle illegal "outpost settlements", while Palestinians would begin reforming their political system, draft a constitution, hold elections, revive an official and unified security service, and most importantly, dismantle the "terrorist infrastructure". This formulation was presented as an advance on Oslo, as it was "performance-based" and assumed parallel developments and reciprocity. It was to be monitored by international peace-keepers, and possibly military guarantors.

Borders for a "provisional Palestinian state"— another innovation over Oslo—would be determined in the second phase. Some described this procedure as a "way station" towards ultimate full independence for Palestine. Statehood and regional peace would be the subjects of a major international conference. This phase was intended to last until 2005, after which the third phase would commence. In the third stage, final status issues would be resolved—lasting borders, refugees, Jerusalem, settlers and water. It was hoped that full peace treaties between Israel and all Arab nations would ensue.

Certain observers noted that postponement of such issues till the end of the negotiating process was earlier criticized as a major failing of Oslo; yet here the sequence was being repeated. Defenders of the Road Map countered that the confidence generated by successful implementation of phases one and two would overcome any obstacles. They also praised the fact that the specific goal of a Palestinian state was written into the plan, whereas Oslo had left this deliberately and dangerously vague. They defended the proposed unification of Palestinian security forces, though opponents felt the main purpose behind this reform was to empower the PNA to crush dissidents, and/or those

who were deemed "anti-Israeli". From the viewpoint of the Israeli right, the Road Map augured the dismantling of the whole Greater Land of Israel project, and imperiled Jewish settlers.

Many Palestinians felt aggrieved that the Road Map did not immediately implement UN Resolution 242, as they understood it—namely, awarding Palestinians full control over the whole of pre-1967 West Bank and Gaza. Accepting 28 per cent of "historic Palestine" was enough of a concession, they contended. Finally, critics of the Map pointed out that the drafters were not specific about how final status issues would be resolved. To some extent, such feelings explain why some felt a need for independent end-status plans, like the Geneva Accord (see below), to at least suggest the architecture of a final outcome, if not to totally replace the Road Map.

From the start of the process, it was clear that the Sharon government only really trusted one of the four Quartet partners—the USA. Palestinians grew impatient while conservative forces in the USA tried to reassure Israel that the Road Map was just window-dressing, and would not lead to the feared Palestinian state. (Uzi Arad, an associate of former Israeli Prime Minister and now Finance Minister Benjamin Netanyahu, said that Israel favoured a provisional state lasting into the far future. In other words, Israel would not allow Palestinians to get as far as phase III.)

British Prime Minister Tony Blair put pressure on Bush to release the Map before the Iraq war, as a sign of good faith to Arab nations, most of which were wary about perceived bias in US Middle East policy. On March 13, 2003, Bush announced that the Road Map would begin after Mahmoud Abbas (Abu Mazen) was confirmed as PNA Prime Minister. The idea of a new Prime Minister represented a compromise on initial US demands that Arafat stand down entirely. It was envisaged that he would exercise overriding executive power, while not formally displacing Arafat as "president".

The nomination of a Palestinian Prime Minister was not, however, the first sign of Palestinian reforms. On May 30, 2002, PNA Chairman Arafat belatedly signed the PNA Basic Law—the PLC had passed the bill several years earlier, but Arafat had refused to ratify it. Salam Fayyad became PNA Finance Minister the next month and set about reforming PNA accounts. In December 2000 Israel had frozen the passage of PNA tax receipts, two-thirds of PNA taxes having flowed through Israel. However, under US pressure, and in light of Fayyad's successes, Israel unfroze Palestinian tax revenues in December 2002. On March 10, 2003, the PLO Central Committee met in Ramallah and approved Arafat's nomination of Abu Mazen as Prime Minister. The committee also condemned violence against all citizens. These decisions led directly to Bush's announcement on the Road Map three days later (see above).

Dov Weisglass, bureau chief for Prime Minister Sharon, negotiated on his government's behalf in

Washington. On April 29 the PLC elected Arafat's nominee as PNA Prime Minister, and on April 30 the USA at last formally published a revised Road Map. The Palestinians accepted it immediately but the Israelis only did so three weeks later, after they were forced to whittle down their objections from about 100 to 14. The Sharon cabinet (including parties to the right of *Likud*) eventually accepted a commitment to implement "the steps" of the Map, though this formulation was somewhat ambiguous. That said, Sharon's verbal acceptance that Palestinians were living under "occupation" (*kibush* in Hebrew), and that this was ultimately unacceptable, marked the breaking of a major taboo in the *Likud* lexicon.

Difficulties in Implementation of the Road Map

Mahmoud Abbas (Abu Mazen) officially assumed the office of Prime Minister in June 2003, after internal disputes were resolved over who should be in his cabinet. It was said that Arafat was interfering, and in particular, refusing to give up total control over the security apparatus. On June 4, 2003, Abbas attended a summit at Aqaba, with Egyptian and Jordanian officials present, and Prime Minister Sharon. Abbas revealed a 12-week plan to start reforms, and explicitly rejected violence and terror. *Hamas* and Islamic Jihad vowed to continue the violence, however, and Fatah rebels joined cadres of these two groups four days later in killing four Israeli soldiers in Gaza. Israel responded on June 10 by attempting to kill a senior *Hamas* leader; on June 11 a *Hamas* suicide attack killed 15 in Jerusalem.

Against this unpromising background, Abbas met US official Elliott Abrams and others on June 28, to determine modalities of implementing the Road Map. During the initial weeks of implementation, Israel began demolishing some outposts and released some prisoners, and IDF troops said they were re-deploying partially from Gaza, certain West Bank towns, and most notably Bethlehem. However, Palestinians called this mainly window dressing. In July Abbas protested to Bush about the Israeli "security wall", which he said was undermining the Road Map. Palestinians and the Israeli left also blamed the Quartet for failing to enact their part of the bargain—sending monitors to the region and enforcing, by military means if necessary, the promised (but as yet unenacted) Israeli further re-deployments to pre-September 2000 lines.

Some weeks of relative quiet were followed by a *Hamas* attack on a bus in Jerusalem that killed 21 on Aug. 20. Israel retaliated by assassinating a senior *Hamas* leader, Ismail Abu Shanab, the next day; and Arafat reacted by moving to replace the Abbas appointee, Mohammed Dahlan, as security chief in Gaza. Abbas resigned on Sept. 6, citing interference by Arafat, lack of encouragement from the USA, and obstruction from Israel. On Sept. 8, Abu Ala (Ahmed Qurei) was nominated as Abbas' successor, though similar cabinet problems ensued. On Oct. 9 Abu Ala, too, submitted his resignation, though later he agreed to

remain in office, and on Nov. 12 he managed to form a government. On Nov. 19 the UN Security Council passed Resolution 1515 in support of the Road Map.

Controversy accompanied the Map from the outset, as both Israelis and Palestinians were accused of subverting the scheme with ill-considered initiatives of their own. The PNA claimed that it could not dismantle "terrorist infrastructure"—or disarm militias—as long as Israeli soldiers occupied Palestinian land. To do so would risk Palestinian civil war, it claimed. In any event, Israeli retaliations against PNA security institutions over the course of the intifada had so degraded their effectiveness, argued the PNA, that even if they wished to, they lacked the resources to crack down on militants.

Instead, through the good offices of the head of Egyptian military intelligence, Omar Suleiman, various Palestinian factions agreed to a *hudna*—a temporary truce in the "war" against Israel. While Quartet members saw this as a positive step—albeit one outside the strict remit of the Road Map—Israel pointed out that its temporary nature betrayed a lack of sincerity, and merely provided an umbrella behind which exhausted militias could regroup and rearm themselves. Israelis further stressed that as they did not sign the *hudna*, they did not feel in any way obliged to obey its strictures.

The Israeli "Security Fence"

Another Israeli policy also appeared to undermine the spirit, if not the letter, of the Road Map. This was the so-called "security fence" or "wall" in the West Bank, whose formal purpose was to prevent Palestinian terrorist incursions into pre-1967 borders Israel. The idea for a wall in fact originated in the Labour Party, with the Knesset member Haim Ramon, but was adopted and adapted by Ariel Sharon. Construction of sections of the wall began in late 2002. In some places it consisted of no more than an electronic fence; in others, it was a massive 20-metre high concrete wall, with gun portals and monitoring devices.

Generally, the idea of the wall has proven popular in Israel, although there have been a range of arguments against it. One school of thought opposes the idea of any wall at all, on the grounds that it pre-empts final borders between Israel and a future Palestine. To counter this, the Sharon government insists that the wall is only a temporary measure. Another argument favours a wall in principle, out of "military necessity", yet disputes the route. Some Labour Party supporters, for instance, insist that the wall should follow the June 1967 international boundary (the "green line"). In practice, however, the wall appears to be carving out territory to the east of the green line, and meanders in such a way as to include major and long-established settlements deeper in the West Bank. In the process, the wall has cut off Arab towns from each other, and in some cases has actually bifurcated Arab municipalities (prime examples being Abu Dis, a village bordering East Jerusalem, and the town of Barta'a, whose two halves straddle the 1967 line). Thus the Israeli left regards the wall as another attempt by *Likud* to annex Palestinian territory.

Conversely, many on the Israeli right oppose the wall because it creates the likely future border between the state of Israel and an independent Palestine. To them it denotes the end of the idea of Israeli sovereignty over all of the West Bank, which they consider to be entirely part of Biblical "Eretz Yisrael". Furthermore, the wall may protect "Israel proper", but leaves many, if not most, settlers outside an Israeli security umbrella.

Unsurprisingly, Palestinians almost uniformly oppose the wall, as it divides communities, grabs land they claim, is a unilateral move, was not created in consultation with the PNA, and prejudges final borders. In January 2004 PNA Prime Minister Abu Ala (Ahmed Qurei) warned that if Israel persisted with the wall, the PNA would not negotiate with it. Responding to such arguments, the USA through Colin Powell and Condoleezza Rice chided Israel's ongoing construction. The USA even suspended a minor loan guarantee to punish Israeli actions.

On Oct. 21, 2003, the UN General Assembly passed Resolution 58/3, which inter alia condemned Israel's construction of the wall/fence. Originally, Syria had attempted to get the UN Security Council to pass a more strongly worded resolution, but the USA threatened to veto it. As a result, 58/3 was formulated in consort with EU nations. Being a General Assembly resolution, it does not have the force of law. Nonetheless, the resolution did lead to a decision to submit the legality of the wall to the International Court of Justice (ICJ) in The Hague, as the highest judicial authority of the United Nations. After wavering as to whether or not to do so, Israel submitted evidence claiming that the wall was necessary for security reasons, though simultaneously denying the court's right to judge on the issue. The USA, Britain and several other countries opposed the holding of hearings by the ICJ—US State Department spokesman Richard Boucher said that the issue should instead be resolved through negotiations between Israelis and Palestinians. The PNA Negotiations Minister Sa'eb Erekat, however, objected to the US stance as obstructing a peaceful, diplomatic resolution of the dispute.

Meanwhile, on Nov. 24, 2003, Sharon had announced his "Disengagement Plan" for unilateral withdrawal of Israeli forces if the Road Map failed to end terrorism. He amplified his new stance in December, at a conference in Hertzlia, and again at the *Likud* Central Committee conference, in early January 2004. Sharon spoke of "unilateral moves" which would entail abandoning some settlements. While his plan upset Palestinians and the USA, who saw it as a deviation from the Road Map, as well as Israeli leftists (who regarded it as mere rhetoric), right-wingers were angry, too, at what they saw as a threat to dismantle settlements. Some 120,000 right-wing protesters gathered in Tel Aviv on Jan. 11, 2004. Others flocked to outpost settlements that were about to be demolished like Migron and Tapuah B (run by supporters of the late Rabbi Meir Kahane).

Despairing of the lack of progress on the Road Map—including a severe slippage in the timetable, reminiscent of the worst failures of Oslo—many Israeli leftists and Palestinian moderates welcomed "freelance" initiatives that promised to possibly break the deadlock. Two amongst these are worth mentioning: the Nusseibeh-Ayalon Declaration of Principles, and the Geneva Accords. The former was manufactured by Prof. Sari Nusseibeh—dean of Al Quds University in Jerusalem, and at one stage after 2001 regarded as Arafat's "point-man" on the Jerusalem issue—and Ami Ayalon, former overall head of Israeli intelligence security services. Their plea was for a two-state solution, dismantling of settlements, and, controversially for Palestinians, a shelving of the demand for a refugee "right of return". Many dozens of thousands of signatures favouring the proposal have been delivered by both Israelis and Palestinians.

The Geneva plan, by contrast, goes into more detail, yet also favours a two-state solution. However, unlike the Road Map, it explicitly identifies possible solutions to final status issues, with a detailed map of future borders (incorporating swapping of territory where feasible), economic provisions, a plan for sharing sovereignty in Jerusalem (including giving Palestinians control of the Temple Mount), and a merely nominal acceptance of refugee "return". Instead, it promotes a complicated mechanism for resettling, rehabilitating and compensating refugees in the Arab and Western worlds, following extensive discussion with those who would be affected. The prime movers behind Geneva (which was signed after several delays in December 2003) are former Israeli minister and Oslo architect, Yossi Beilin, and current PNA minister Yasser Abed-Rabbo (probably best known for his role in the 1988 Algiers Declaration). Behind them, however, are an impressive array of members of the Israeli security services and opposition, including former Labour leader Amram Mitzna, and even one *Likud* Knesset member, as well as numerous leaders from Palestinian civil society. The PNA has contended that it does not oppose Geneva, while not explicitly endorsing it. This formulation was arrived at, after much protest from Palestinians who accused the Geneva framers of "abandoning the refugees". The Sharon government was more clearly opposed to Geneva, which it depicted as a "red herring", illegitimate, and obstructive to the Road Map. To the latter charge, Geneva advocates contend that their plan merely elaborates possible scenarios regarding the final stage of the Road Map, and thus would aid, rather than harm, implementation of the same.

On Feb. 1, 2004, Prime Minister Sharon shocked many in Israel by declaring that ultimately all 17 settlements and 12,000 settlers would be removed from Gaza. (Sharon had vehemently opposed such a unilateral plan when it was put forward by Labour leader, Amram Mitzna, during his unsuccessful campaign before the Israeli elections of early 2003.) The same month saw reports of another Saudi plan, which allegedly proposed, for the first time, Arab willingness to absorb all Palestinian refugees, and thus accepting (it appeared) Israeli objections regarding a "right of return" to Israel proper.

Lawrence Joffe

5.2 Bahrain - Iran

A long-standing dispute arising from an Iranian (Persian) claim to sovereignty over Bahrain—which appeared to have been settled in December 1970 when the government of the Shah of Iran endorsed a UN Security Council resolution affirming the complete independence of the state of Bahrain—was revived by Iran in September 1979 in the wake of the Iranian revolution. The Iranian claim was strongly repudiated by Bahrain and other Arab states and has not been reasserted by Iran since 1979.

During the 1980s, Iran sponsored attempted subversion by Shi'a groups in Bahrain (which has a Shi'a majority, though the ruling family are Sunni). However, full diplomatic relations were established in 1990. Bahrain again accused Iran of attempting to undermine its government in the mid-1990s and relations deteriorated once more. Since 1997 Iran has been concerned to improve relations with its Persian Gulf neighbours and by 2003 its détente policy towards Bahrain had yielded constructive results. (Map 53, p. 520, illustrates the Gulf region.)

History of the Dispute

The island of Bahrain was part of the Islamic empire between the 7th and 11th centuries and was thereafter ruled by various Arab dynasties until it was occupied by the Portuguese in 1522. It was under Persian domination from 1602 until 1783, this domination being interrupted by short periods of rule by Arab sheikhs and ended by the island's conquest by the rulers of Zubarah (on the Qatari peninsula), whose descendants have ruled Bahrain to the present day. Between 1861 and 1971 Bahrain was under British protection, with defence and external affairs being the responsibility of the United Kingdom.

An agreement concluded on Aug. 30, 1822, by the British Political Resident in the Gulf with the Persian authorities in Shiraz—which provided that Bahrain should be regarded as "subordinate to the [Persian] province of Fars" and that the British government would supply Persia with war vessels to conquer Bahrain—was disowned as "unauthorised" by the British Governor of Bombay, who denounced the admission of the King of Persia's title to Bahrain as being without "the least proof". The agreement was also denounced by the Shah of Persia, who declared

that it had been made "without his knowledge or injunction".

In 1844, however, Haji Meerza Aghassi, the Persian Prime Minister, submitted a claim to Bahrain in a note to the British government, after the Ruler of Bahrain had been expelled by his nephew and had asked the British, the Persians and the Sultan of Muscat for help to enable him to regain Bahrain. When it became known that Persia was preparing for military action in support of the expelled Sheikh, the British government informed Persia that it would actively oppose any action against the lawful government of Bahrain.

In a statement of March 15, 1844, Aghassi listed the following arguments in favour of Persia's claim to Bahrain: (i) "The Persian Gulf from the commencement of the Shatt al-'Arab to Muscat belongs to Persia and...all islands of that sea, without exception and without participation of any other government, belong entirely to Persia" (the Persians considering that the English usage of "Persian" Gulf further supported this argument); (ii) "Bahrain has always been under the authority of the Governor of Fars from 1300 AD"; (iii) "all European and Turkish books of geography as well as the books of travellers considered Bahrain as Persian"; and (iv) the 1822 agreement (see above) recognized Persia's ownership of Bahrain.

These arguments were refuted by the British East India Company, whose Secret Committee stated on July 31, 1845, inter alia (i) that the British government had treated the Sheikhs of Bahrain as independent authorities since their occupation of the island in 1783; (ii) that Bahrain might have been a dependency of Fars while the Persians were in actual possession of the island, but that to allege that the Persians had possessed it since 1300 AD was "contrary to the best evidence" that could be produced on the subject; and (iii) that the 1822 treaty had no legal significance as it had been "expressly disavowed". The committee therefore concluded that Persia had no legitimate claim to sovereignty over Bahrain.

In subsequent years the British government ignored Persia's claim to the island, but in a note dated April 29, 1869, the British government conceded that it would inform the Persian government beforehand "of any measures of coercion against himself which the conduct of the Sheikh of Bahrain may have rendered necessary" (the Sheikh having solicited military aid from Persia and Turkey and having attacked Qatar). The Persian government considered this concession as involving British recognition of Persia's claim to Bahrain.

Persia did not raise the matter again until Nov. 22, 1927, when it protested to Britain against the conclusion of a treaty (on May 27, 1927) with Saudi Arabia, in which reference was made to the maintenance of "friendly and peaceful relations with the territories of Kuwait and Bahrain, who are in special treaty relations with [the British] government". The Persian government regarded this clause, "so far as it concerns Bahrain", as "an infringement of the territorial integrity of Persia". The British Foreign Secretary, Sir Austen

Chamberlain, replying to the protest on Jan. 18, 1928, denied categorically that there were "any valid grounds upon which the claim of the Persian government to the sovereignty over Bahrain is or can be based". This exchange was followed by further notes sent respectively on Aug. 4, 1928, and Feb. 18, 1929, when the British government stated inter alia: "It would be necessary for Persia to prove that she is, or ever has been, the lawful owner of Bahrain, and that such rights as she may have acquired in former ages by conquest and the exercise of force outweigh those not only of the Portuguese but of the Arab inhabitants themselves".

Persia also protested unsuccessfully against the granting of oil concessions by the Sheikh of Bahrain (in a note to the British government on July 23, 1930, and in another note, to the United States, on May 22, 1934).

In reply to a British statement of April 5, 1956, to the effect that Bahrain was an independent sheikhdom, the Persian Foreign Minister contended on April 8 that Bahrain was "an inseparable part of Persia"; that Persia would not recognize it as a British-protected sheikhdom; that during the 19th century, Britain had several times recognized Persian sovereignty over the island; and that its ruling dynasty had on several occasions sworn fealty and paid taxes to Persia.

Following the passing of a bill by the Persian parliament declaring Bahrain the 14th Persian province, the British position of not recognizing Persian sovereignty over Bahrain was reaffirmed on Nov. 27, 1957, by the British Foreign Secretary, W. D. Ormsby-Gore, who declared that the British government would continue to fulfil its obligation to safeguard the independence of Bahrain, and that the Ruler of Bahrain had received an assurance to this effect.

Persia's claim was also rejected by the Arab League, which reaffirmed on Nov. 15, 1957, that Bahrain was "Arab territory". This was underlined by the fact that its population was overwhelmingly Arab, it being estimated in 1965 that the naturalized Iranian population of Bahrain was less than 7 per cent of the total Arab population (by 1991, this had risen to 20 per cent; one-third of the total population was non-Bahraini). Nevertheless, the Shah of Iran restated his claim on Nov. 22, 1958, when he said at a press conference in Tehran: "We consider Bahrain an integral part of Persia". He added that he would gladly accept the allegiance of its Ruler "in the capacity of the first Iranian governor-general of Bahrain".

Developments leading to 1970 Settlement

In the late 1960s the Iranian attitude towards the Bahrain question became more conciliatory. On Jan. 5, 1969, the Shah declared that Bahrain's inhabitants (numbering some 200,000 people) were welcome to decide their own fate, although Iran would not want the island to be made over to anyone else without Iranian consent. At the request of both Iran and Britain, the United Nations Secretary-General, U

Thant, agreed on March 28, 1970, to appoint a special representative to visit Bahrain in order to ascertain the wishes of its population in regard to its future status. This UN representative, Vittorio Winspeare Guicciardi (Italy), visited the island between March 30 and April 18, 1970, and in his report, issued on May 2, he declared: "My conclusions have convinced me that the overwhelming majority of the people of Bahrain wish to gain recognition of their identity in a fully independent and sovereign state free to decide for itself its relations with other states".

In this connection the Ruler of Bahrain had on March 29, 1970, declared: "The question of Bahrain's relations with Iran is a matter which needs to be tackled at its very roots, not only because it concerns these two countries, but because it has a direct bearing upon the future stability of the whole area [after the withdrawal of Britain from the Gulf at the end of 1971]...Our belief is that Bahrain is an Arab country [and] has its own independent personality and existence. We believe these to be facts which reflect the deepest feelings of the people of Bahrain, and that they should be acknowledged by all. We believe, too, that these facts are supported both in history and in the reality of the present situation; and that they allow of no doubt or of any contrary claim, which we never recognize nor admit in any way".

Meeting on May 11, 1970, at the request of Iran and the United Kingdom, the UN Security Council unanimously endorsed the report of the Secretary-General's special representative, and this endorsement was ratified by the Iranian Majlis (Lower House of Parliament) by 186 votes to 4 on May 14, and unanimously by Iran's Senate on May 18. The delimitation of the continental shelf between the two countries was agreed in a treaty of June 1971. This apparent settlement of the dispute was followed by visits to Tehran by the Prime Minister of Bahrain on May 24, 1975, and to Bahrain by the Iranian Prime Minister, Abbas Hoveyda, on Nov. 29, 1975, when the latter stated that there were no difficulties in relations between Iran and Bahrain and that co-operation between them was being fostered by a joint ministerial commission.

Revival of Iranian Claim

The 1970 settlement of the dispute was in line with the Shah's endeavours to improve Iran's relations with Arab countries, in which connection he concluded a "treaty of reconciliation" with Iraq in 1975. With the establishment of the Islamic Republic of Iran in early 1979, however, relations with most Arab countries deteriorated, in particular with Iraq. Bahrain feared that the new Iranian regime wished to export the Islamic revolution to its neighbours and felt especially vulnerable given its majority Shi'a population. In September 1979, Ayatollah Ruhani, a leading figure in the revolution, announced that Bahrain was an integral part of Iran. The claim was strongly rejected by the Bahraini government and also denounced by other Arab states.

The Bahraini Ministry of the Interior announced on Dec. 13, 1981, that it had foiled an attempted coup by members of the Islamic Front for the Liberation of Bahrain, said to have been trained in Iran. Of 73 persons charged in this connection, inter alia with possession of arms supplied from Iran, three were on May 23, 1982, sentenced to death, 60 to fifteen years in prison each and 10 to seven years each. The Iranian government denied any implication in the alleged plot. An arms cache discovered in Bahrain in 1984 was allegedly supplied by Iran to Islamic militants and an apparent attempted coup in June 1985 in Bahrain was also reportedly sponsored by Iran. In December 1987, following an alleged Iranian plot to blow up a Bahraini refinery, the US government agreed to supply 70 Stinger missiles and 14 launchers to Bahrain.

However, relations between Iran and Bahrain improved thereafter. An Iranian chargé to Bahrain was appointed on Nov. 3, 1988, and full diplomatic relations between the states were established in December 1990.

No Iranian official has revived the claim to Bahrain since 1979, although in 1992, during heated exchanges between the Arab world and Iran over recent incidents on the disputed island of Abu Musa, hardline Iranian newspapers called for a reassertion of the claim. In the mid-1990s, Bahrain was rocked by internal political dissent and violence which the government partly blamed on Iranian agitation. Decades of tension between the Shi'a majority and the ruling Sunni elite exploded in 1994 with a spate of protests, bombings and arson attacks. Many Shi'a, especially merchants, are of Iranian origin and Bahrain suspected that Iran was keen to destabilize the island state. Relations deteriorated dramatically in 1996 when Bahrain accused Iran of involvement in an armed attempt to overthrow the government. Ambassadors were recalled by both Manama and Tehran as diplomatic relations were downgraded.

Improved Relations in the Khatami Era

The election of Mohammad Khatami as President of Iran in 1997 helped usher in an era of more positive relations. In March 1998, the Iranian Foreign Minister, Dr Kamal Kharrazi, called for better relations with Iran's Gulf neighbours, and former Iranian President, Ali Akbar Hashemi Rafsanjani, visited Bahrain. Ambassadors were once again exchanged in January 1999 and President Khatami stated that the two countries shared common security goals.

Further visits by the Foreign Ministers in 2000 led to a landmark state visit to Tehran by King Hamad bin Isa al-Khalifa in August 2002, the first Bahraini head of state to do so since 1979. Dr Kharrazi described the visit as "a turning point in the history of the two countries' relations". King Hamad and President Khatami discussed regional security and bilateral relations and both sides expressed how much ties had improved over recent years. Negotiations also commenced to improve economic relations and restore commercial sea links,

closed since 1996. King Hamad hailed Iran's "positive and constructive" role in the restoration of security and stability in the region, praising President Khatami's policies of confidence building and boosting bilateral ties. In May 2003, Khatami became the first Iranian President to visit Bahrain.

Robert Lowe

5.3 Bahrain - Qatar

The ruling of the International Court of Justice (ICJ) in March 2001 on the territorial questions between Bahrain and Qatar peacefully resolved the most serious territorial dispute between Gulf Co-operation Council (GCC) member states. The competing sovereign claims of Bahrain and Qatar to the Hawar Islands, the reefs of Fasht ad Dibal and Qit'at Jaradah and the townsite of Zubarah had been the subject of exchanges between the two countries since 1938. The parameters of the dispute were largely set by decisions made by Britain as the colonial power in 1939. Following the adhesion of both countries to the GCC, established in February 1981, efforts to resolve the disagreement were pursued within that framework. However, in 1986 the two sides came into direct military confrontation over the issue. In 1991, proceedings were instituted at the ICJ. (Map 53, p. 520, illustrates the area.)

Historical Origins of the Dispute

This complicated dispute had its origins in the historical rivalries of the ruling dynasties of Bahrain and Qatar. In the 17th and 18th centuries, the houses of Al Khalifa and Al Thani were both based on the Qatar peninsula. By 1811, the Al Khalifa had taken control of Bahrain, but retained sovereign claims over parts of the Qatari peninsula and its offshore islands. The ownership of the more than 20 Hawar Islands, situated about 1.5 miles (2.4 km) off the coast of Qatar, was the most contentious issue, especially when it later emerged that this would provide control of potential oil resources. The dispute was ignited in 1938 when the Ruler of Bahrain claimed the Hawar Islands for the purposes of oil exploration and this claim was immediately rejected by the Ruler of Qatar.

The Qatari position was that the Hawar Islands were situated within the geographical boundaries of Qatar and were an extension of Qatar's territory within its territorial waters. Qatar also pointed out that the narrow channel between the islands and the peninsula is covered by Qatar's territorial waters only during a tidal period and that at low tide it is possible to walk from the coast to the islands; that Bahrain, on the other hand, is separated from the islands by a 22.5 km wide waterway used for international navigation in its various forms; and that Qatar's claim was supported by international judgements to the effect that "islands situated in the territorial waters of any state are subject by law to the sovereignty of that state...even if that state does not actually occupy these islands". Bahrain based its claim on its strong human links with the islands, claiming it had exercised sovereignty and actual occupation "continuously and uninterruptedly" for two hundred years while Qatar had never established any competing authority.

Bahrain's 1938 claim was supported by the United Kingdom (then responsible for the foreign policy of the two countries under treaty obligations). The British Political Agent in Bahrain informed the two countries' Rulers on July 11, 1939, that "having considered the claim...the British government has decided that the Hawar Islands belong to Bahrain and not to Qatar". This decision was consistently contested by the Rulers of Qatar. In 1947 the British government also endorsed a claim by Bahrain to the reefs of Fasht ad Dibal and Qit'at Jaradah, situated north-west of Qatar and considered by Qatar, on geological and geographical grounds, to be part of the Qatari peninsula.

The issue was complicated by a claim by the Sheikh of Bahrain relating to rights in Zubarah, on the north-west coast of the Qatari peninsula, on the grounds that it was his ancestral home and was inhabited by a tribe owing him allegiance. This was not regarded as a territorial claim, but as one for jurisdiction over the subjects of a state in another territory. Britain did not support the Al-Khalifa claim to Zubarah, but in the absence of any written agreement on the frontiers between the two states, Bahrain considered the matter unsettled.

In 1965 Bahrain requested that the median line drawn by Britain as the boundary between the two countries should be changed, to which request Qatar responded by proposing that the issue should be submitted to arbitration along with the territorial dispute. The governments of both Bahrain and the United Kingdom agreed to this proposal, but by March 1966 the government of Bahrain appeared to take the view that arbitration was not the best method of settling the issue.

During a visit to Qatar by the Ruler of Bahrain in March 1967, the Ruler of Qatar raised the question of the sovereignty over the Hawar Islands. The subject was later discussed within the framework of an offshore boundary settlement between the two countries, with Qatar insisting on obtaining ownership of the islands before agreeing to a settlement satisfactory to Bahrain, but the latter did not agree to this demand.

Post-Independence Acceptance of Saudi Mediation

Following the attainment of independence by both Bahrain and Qatar in 1971, the two sides agreed to accept mediation by Saudi Arabia, and in 1978 they agreed to a set of principles proposed by Saudi Arabia to guide relations between the two countries until a final solution was found. Both sides undertook (i) to

refrain from any action which would strengthen their respective legal positions, weaken the position of the other party or change the status quo in the disputed area; and (ii) to refrain from any action which would block negotiations between them or harm the brotherly atmosphere necessary to achieve the aim of the negotiations.

On March 1, 1980, Yusuf ash-Shawari, Bahrain's Minister of Industry and Development, stated that the Hawar Islands were governed by a concession agreed between the government of Bahrain and a group of US companies which were planning to drill a new experimental well in search of oil (following the failure of two earlier drilling attempts).

Sheikh Abdel Aziz bin Khalifa, the Qatar Minister of Finance and Petroleum, thereupon replied on March 4 that "all geographical, historical, legal and logical indications" categorically proved that "these islands constitute an indivisible part of Qatar, since they are situated within its territorial waters". The minister added that Bahrain had nothing to support its claim of sovereignty over these islands except the British decision made in 1939, which Qatar considered "null and void" since it contradicted "the basic norms of international law governing such matters" and also "the established geographical, material and historical facts".

On March 7, 1980, diplomatic sources in Kuwait were quoted as saying that Saudi Arabia was again to mediate between Bahrain and Qatar in order to prevent the dispute from worsening and had asked officials in the two countries not to allow the media to exacerbate the situation.

In February 1981 both Bahrain and Qatar, together with Kuwait, Oman, Saudi Arabia and the United Arab Emirates, became members of the newly established Gulf Co-operation Council (GCC) of Arab states, one of the professed functions of which was to resolve territorial disputes between member states. After the Qatari government had protested in early March 1982 against the Bahraini government's decision to name a new warship the *Hawar*, the GCC ministerial council, meeting in Riyadh on March 7-9, 1982, requested Saudi Arabia to continue its efforts to resolve the dispute. According to a statement issued at the conclusion of the meeting, both sides had agreed "to freeze the situation and not to cause an escalation of the dispute", to halt "information campaigns exchanged between the two countries" and to continue their fraternal relations on the basis of "a return to the status quo ante". However, no progress was made in subsequent discussions.

1986 Confrontation over Fasht ad Dibal

Late in 1985 Bahrain began to construct a man-made island on the low-tide elevation of Fasht ad Dibal, while it continued to erect military and other installations on the Hawar Islands. Qatar protested, but Bahrain pursued its intention of building a coastguard station on Dibal. Qatar sent gunboats to the reef and on

April 26, 1986, a small contingent of Qatari troops landed on Dibal in order to halt Bahrain's operations and arrested 29 expatriate workers (all of whom were subsequently released). On April 30 Bahrain denounced this occupation of the shoal as "a violation of good-neighbourliness". Following efforts at mediation by the leaders of Oman, Saudi Arabia and the United Arab Emirates, agreement was reached in May 1986 on the withdrawal of Qatari forces from Dibal and the removal of dredging and construction works under the supervision of a team of military officers sent by the GCC ministerial council.

The Qatari and Bahraini Defence Ministers made mutual visits, accompanied by the Saudi Defence Minister, on Oct. 5-6, 1986. The situation remained tense during 1987, despite a further visit to Bahrain by the Qatari Defence Minister in May. However, in December 1987, Saudi Arabia proposed the creation of a joint committee to study all matters relating to the dispute. This proposal, accepted by both Bahrain and Qatar, envisaged that, if it was found impossible to reach a solution acceptable to both parties, the dispute should be referred to an international arbitration commission which should settle the dispute on the basis of the principles of international law and whose judgement would be final and binding on both parties. The accord also ruled out any unilateral changes to the status of the islands.

Despite this, the conflict threatened to flare up again, with the US supplying Stinger missiles to Bahrain in December 1987, and Iran selling similar missiles (later alleged to be defective) to Qatar in June 1988.

1991 Submission to the International Court of Justice

The mediating efforts of the Gulf Co-operation Council and in particular Saudi Arabia continually failed to settle the issue, but did prevent the outbreak of open hostilities and pushed the parties towards an acceptance that international arbitration was essential. At the GCC summit in Doha in December 1990, Bahrain and Qatar agreed to refer their dispute to the International Court of Justice (ICJ), should no bilateral agreement be forthcoming in the next six months.

On July 8, 1991, Qatar unilaterally instituted proceedings at the ICJ, claiming sovereignty over the Hawar Islands, sovereign rights over Fasht ad Dibal and Qit'at Jaradah, and requesting the delimitation of the maritime area of the two states. Bahrain immediately rejected the claim, calling for recognition of the borders existing at the time of independence. As the party with most to lose from an arbitrated settlement, Bahrain was reluctant for the dispute to be tried by the ICJ and contested the basis of the jurisdiction invoked by Qatar, complaining that Qatar had broken the 1990 agreement that the submission be made jointly. By a judgement of 1994, the ICJ found that Qatar's application was admissible on the grounds of the agreements it had reached with Bahrain in 1987 and 1990.

Bahrain remained hopeful of reaching an out-of-court settlement before formal proceedings began in The Hague and was encouraged by the Manama Directive issued by the GCC summit in 1994, which urged member states to settle territorial disputes bilaterally within twelve months. Qatar was prepared to accept Saudi Arabia's reactivated role as mediator in bilateral discussions, but no further progress was made and in February 1996, Qatar formally submitted a memorial outlining its territorial claims to the ICJ. Bahrain was obliged to respond and submitted its memorial to the ICJ in the late summer of 1996.

In the course of the ICJ's consideration of the written proceedings of the case, the relationship between the two states continued to fluctuate. Qatar accused Bahrain of involvement in a failed coup attempt early in 1996 and the Amir of Bahrain boycotted the GCC Summit in Doha in December 1996. In April 1998, Bahrain challenged the authenticity of 82 documents submitted by Qatar to the ICJ. Qatar subsequently agreed that these should be disregarded. In July 1998, Bahrain announced it would proceed with plans to build a massive causeway connecting the Hawar Islands to Bahrain island. Qatar replied that Bahrain had no legal right to construct the link and said the plan constituted a clear breach of the 1987 accord.

With the prospect of the ICJ's decision looming, Bahrain and Qatar made renewed efforts to improve relations and in February 2000, the Bahrain-Qatar High Commission met for the first time, under the chairmanship of the two Crown Princes. The Heads of State made reciprocal visits and ambassadors were exchanged, but the atmosphere remained uncertain until the ICJ finished its deliberations.

Judgement of the International Court of Justice in 2001

On May 29, 2000, the ICJ started public hearings on the Bahrain-Qatar dispute and on March 16, 2001, the Court delivered its judgement. The decisions placed great importance on the judgements made by the British in 1939 and managed to share the awards sufficiently to prevent either side expressing a sense of injustice.

Bahrain was found to have sovereignty over the Hawar Islands on the grounds that both Bahrain and Qatar consented to the UK settling this dispute in 1939. While the British decision was not found to be an arbitral award, it was considered to have sufficient legal effect as the Ruler of Qatar had consented to participate in the proceedings that were to lead to the decision to award the islands to Bahrain.

Bahrain was also found to have sovereignty over Qit'at Jaradah while Qatar was awarded sovereignty over Zubarah and Fasht ad Dibal. Qatar was also found to have sovereignty over Janan Island, a small island off the south-western tip of Hawar Island proper. Qatari vessels should also enjoy the right of innocent passage in the territorial sea of Bahrain separating the Hawar Islands from the other Bahraini islands. The single maritime boundary that divides the various maritime zones of the two countries was also settled.

The ruling was greeted with great rejoicing in Bahrain and international oil companies were immediately invited to commence drilling in the Hawar area. Plans to develop the tourism potential of the area and construct the causeway were also reactivated. In accepting the decision, the Amir of Qatar described the ruling as "painful" but expressed his satisfaction that the due legal process had been carried out. Both sides stated that the dispute had now ended and looked forward to strengthening bilateral relations. These indeed improved in the following two years and Bahrain and Qatar appear to have put the conflict behind them.

Robert Lowe

5.4 Egypt - Israel (Taba Strip)

A dispute between Egypt and Israel over the ownership of a small strip of land, of some 250 acres (600 hectares), arose during the Israeli withdrawal from Sinai, as agreed in the 1979 peace treaty, which was completed in April 1982. Following international arbitration, Israel ceded the land in March 1989. (For a full account of the Egypt-Israel peace treaty, see Section 5.1; for the location of the Taba strip, see Map 54, p. 520.)

Origins of the Dispute

The dispute had its origins in 1906, when Turkish forces occupied the coastal settlement of Taba, but were subsequently forced to withdraw under British pressure. After negotiations between Anglo-Egyptian and Turkish representatives, an agreement was reached by which the border was fixed as running through Taba itself. In 1915, however, a British military survey produced a map in which the border was shown as running along a line some three-quarters of a mile to the north-east. The head of the team which produced the survey, Col. T. E. Lawrence ("Lawrence of Arabia"), admitted later that, acting under instructions, he had "invented" certain details of the map. The discrepancy resulted in an undefined area of roughly triangular shape, its southern edge extending about three-quarters of a mile eastwards along the coast from Taba, with the remaining two sides converging at a point about a mile inland. The mouth of the Taba river now lay in Egyptian territory.

The 1915 line became the boundary with Egypt under the British Palestine Mandate (established in 1920, following Britain's conquest of Turkish-ruled Palestine in 1917, and formally approved by the League of Nations in 1922). It remained as such on the establishment of the state of Israel in May 1948. In the June 1967 Arab-Israeli war Israel's capture of the Sinai peninsula from Egypt brought the Taba strip under Israeli control.

Negotiations following Israel's Withdrawal from Sinai

The question of the ownership of the Taba strip was reopened after the signature of the Egyptian-Israeli peace treaty of March 1979, under the terms of which Israel agreed to withdraw its forces from the Sinai over a three-year period. A series of negotiations held in early 1982 to resolve outstanding border questions failed to produce an agreement on Taba before the completion of the Israeli withdrawal to the pre-1967 border. Pending a final agreement being reached through further negotiations, the two sides agreed that the area would be placed under the control of the incoming Multi-National Force and Observers (MFO). Over the ensuing years, much of the coastal strip was developed as a tourist resort by Israeli businesses.

During talks in 1982 the Israeli side insisted that the 1906 agreement had provided the only valid demarcation, while the Egyptians demanded that the 1915 map should be regarded as the definitive version. One prominent Israeli geographer, Moshe Brawer, later claimed that Israel had signed the 1979 treaty with Egypt on the basis of inaccurate maps, and chided negotiators for not uncovering the original 1906 map until after signatures were exchanged.

Relations between Israel and Egypt had cooled somewhat after the assassination of President Anwar Sadat on Oct. 6, 1981. Though formally committed to the peace treaty, Sadat's successor, Hosni Mubarak, was arguably distracted by domestic problems during his early days in office, and by the need to consolidate power at home. Relations worsened after Israel's June 1982 invasion of Lebanon. Egypt responded by recalling its ambassador to Israel, Saad Murtada, and only replaced him in September 1986.

These tensions contributed to a hardening of positions over Taba. Some Egyptian commentators saw Israel's determination to hold on to the area as proof of "Zionist expansionism" (*pace* Lebanon). Such views, much aired in the Egyptian press, continued even after Israel withdrew from most territories in Lebanon in 1985. Conversely, Israeli analysts felt that Egypt's perceived obduracy over such a small tract of land confirmed that they were not interested in normalization or a "warm peace" with Israel.

Nonetheless, tripartite talks about the disputed territory, involving negotiators from Israel, Egypt and the United States, were held in Ismailia (Egypt) in March 1983; but they failed to result in any significant progress. The matter was next raised in November 1983 during talks in Cairo between Dr Boutros Boutros-Ghali (then Egyptian Foreign Minister) and David Kimche (then director-general of the Israeli Foreign Ministry). The lack of agreement on the issue was cited by President Mubarak in September 1984 as the reason for his refusal to hold a summit meeting with Shimon Peres, the Israeli Prime Minister. A meeting the same month between Yitzhak Shamir, the Israeli Foreign Minister, and his Egyptian counterpart, Dr Ahmed Esmat Abdel Meguid, similarly failed to produce an agreement.

Matters were further exacerbated when Israel created a government of national unity following hung elections in 1984. It soon emerged that the Labour component of the government, led by Shimon Peres, favoured flexibility over the Taba dispute, so as to facilitate a "package deal" that would normalize relations between Israel and Egypt. By contrast, the *Likud* component, led by Yitzhak Shamir, preferred a tougher position regarding Taba.

Position papers on the Taba dispute and an outstanding problem concerning the divided town of Rafah, on the border of Egyptian Sinai and the Israeli-occupied Gaza Strip, were exchanged at negotiations held in January 1985 (at which US observers were also present). In further talks in Cairo in May (also in the presence of US observers), the Israeli side rejected Egypt's request that the matter be referred to arbitration. (These talks did, however, produce an agreement on the Rafah question, under which residents living in the Egyptian half of the town would be allowed to cross into the Israeli zone if they wished.)

Submission of Dispute to International Arbitration Panel

From early 1985 onwards, efforts to resolve the Taba dispute were complicated by conflicting opinions within the Israeli coalition cabinet. Members of the Labour Alignment faction, led by Peres, expressed a willingness to agree to some form of arbitration; this was, however, strongly resisted by the *Likud* front, led by Shamir. These internal divisions within the Israeli government hampered the further bilateral talks on the dispute which took place in September, October and December of 1985.

On Jan. 14, 1986, however, the Israeli cabinet decided to accept binding international arbitration on the issue, this concession being welcomed as a positive step by President Mubarak. Israel simultaneously insisted that Egypt restore its ambassador to Tel Aviv; begin implementing agreements signed with Israel on commerce, tourism, transportation, culture and political dialogue; clamp down on Palestinian militants; and suppress hostile propaganda in the Egyptian media. Israel also called on Egypt to publish its report on the 1985 murder of five Israelis in Ras Burka, near Taba.

Talks concerning the details of the arbitration took place on several occasions over the ensuing months, culminating in an arbitration agreement which was endorsed by the Israeli cabinet on Aug. 13, 1986, and by the Egyptian cabinet on Sept. 10. The agreement provided for the establishment of a five-member arbitration tribunal, of whom three members would have to be mutually acceptable to Egypt and Israel, while each country would have the exclusive right to appoint one member.

The agreement cleared the way for a summit meeting between President Mubarak and Prime Minister Peres, which was held in Alexandria (Egypt) on Sept. 11-12, 1986. The Egyptians had maintained their refusal to agree to a summit until all arrangements relating to the dispute had been approved by both sides. Richard Murphy, the US special presidential envoy to the Middle East, had travelled regularly between Cairo and Jerusalem during late August and early September, in an effort to resolve the remaining differences, which in particular concerned the questions of mapping the disputed area and the composition of the arbitration tribunal. The Israeli cabinet ratified the arbitration compromise, with one minister, Ariel Sharon, objecting.

As eventually agreed, the arbitration tribunal was composed of an Israeli, an Egyptian, an American, a Swiss and a Swede, who was appointed as its president. The first meeting of the tribunal took place in Geneva on Dec. 8, 1986. Proceedings were to continue *in camera*. On Jan. 7, 1987, a team of US soldiers from the MFO opened an observation post in Taba to ensure that neither side introduced troops into the area during the arbitration process, which was expected to last about two years.

The Israeli and Egyptian governments set out their respective arguments on May 13, 1987. On Sept. 29, 1988, the tribunal issued a ruling accepting the Egyptian position by a vote of four against one (the Israeli arbitrator dissenting), and calling for the return of 700 metres of beach to Egyptian control. In January 1989 additional disagreements arose, including Israeli demands for compensation for the victims of the Ras Burka murders, and an Egyptian presidential decree that seemed to threaten absolute control over tourism in the area. On Feb. 4, US officials helped broker an agreement in Cairo that smoothed over difficulties. Egypt dropped plans for total control and agreed to pay compensation.

Egypt and Israel eventually signed a final agreement on Feb. 26, 1989, (i) reaffirming Egyptian sovereignty over Taba; (ii) agreeing Egyptian compensation to Israel for the construction of a hotel complex; (iii) arranging for Israel to continue to supply water and electricity to the area; and (iv) permitting easy access to Israeli passport holders and establishing a border crossing. Last-minute disputes about the location of the border were solved, and Nabil el-Arabi, Egypt's chief negotiator, declared that "the Taba dispute is over; it is behind us now".

On March 19, 1989, Israel evacuated Taba. Egyptian President Hosni Mubarak used the occasion of the hand-over to call for an international conference that would provide a "psychological umbrella" to enable Arab states to negotiate directly with Israel. On May 22, 1989, Egypt was re-admitted into the Arab League, from which it had been expelled nearly ten years earlier. Arguably the successful Taba deal and subsequent recovery of all of the Sinai to Egypt contributed to convincing other Arab nations that Egypt was worthy of being readmitted to the Arab fold.

Developments since the Conclusion of the Taba Dispute

Following the successful arbitration, Israel and Egypt reached two further agreements—the first established a border on the seacoast; the second provided concessions for tourists travelling from Israel and passing through the Taba terminal.

Although the border is no longer in dispute, there have been several border incidents between the two countries. For instance, in November 1990, an Egyptian policeman crossed the border and shot dead four Israelis. Such incidents have led to popular resentment and nationalist agitation in both Israel and Egypt, but have been resolved peacefully by the two governments. In May 1995 Israel's *Jerusalem Post* reported that Israel had violated an agreement with Egypt, by failing to renew the transit fee exemption for people going to Taba. Meanwhile Taba's hotel and casino facilities, just across the border from Eilat, attract thousands of Israeli and foreign tourists annually.

The Middle East peace process that began with the Madrid Conference of 1991 also promised benefits for the development of Taba. Specifically, the area demarcated by Taba in Egypt, Eilat in Israel and Aqaba in Jordan—the three cities describing an arc of the Gulf of Aqaba—became the focus for ambitious cross-border plans. These plans were discussed in multilateral talks held between Middle Eastern nations; the multilateral negotiations "stream" was launched in Moscow, in late 1991, pursuant to Madrid.

Israel's signature of a full peace treaty with Jordan on Oct. 26, 1994, further accelerated the process. Israel and Jordan signed an Agreement on Special Arrangements for Aqaba and Eilat in 1996, which entailed ambitious plans to develop joint environmental, tourist, energy and commercial enterprises. At the same time, the European Union (EU) supported a working group to co-ordinate development of the Taba-Eilat-Aqaba Macro Area (known as TEAM). In addition to complementing national development objectives, TEAM envisaged collaborative ventures, including "strengthening infrastructure links, co-ordinating environmental protection, realizing economies of scale and promoting private sector investment". In short, TEAM aimed to build on the fact that Egypt, Israel and Jordan were now three bordering nations formally linked by peace treaties.

With respect to Taba itself, TEAM planned to develop the Ras al-Naqab area as a free trade and processing zone (the area contains Taba's airport). There were also plans for improving tourism-related facilities between the border and Ras Burka, including Moqbela, Al-Homayra and the Nuweiba seaport. In a related development around Rafah, at the western end of the Egyptian-Israeli border in northern Sinai, the EU backed a plan called SEMED (South-East Mediterranean Development Project). In theory it envisaged joint ventures along a coastal strip stretching from Egyptian Sinai, through Gaza, and as far north as Israeli Ashdod. In 1996 a technical support unit chose 10 out of 42 feasibility projects as priorities; these would involve the governments of Israel, Egypt and the Palestinian Authority in various combinations.

However, recurrent political difficulties between the Israelis and Palestinians in effect postponed the multilateral "stream" and thus stymied many grand schemes devised by TEAM and SEMED. The Al Aqsa intifada, which erupted in late September 2000, has particularly strained relations between Egypt and Israel and in November 2000 Egypt withdrew its ambassador. Egypt also responded to Israel's March 2002 reoccupation of certain Palestinian towns in "Operation Defensive Shield" by suspending intergovernmental ties with Israel, apart from diplomatic channels dealing with Palestinians. That said, Egypt's intelligence chiefs in concert with the CIA played a pivotal role in engineering a ceasefire in 2003 between the Israelis and Palestinian factions.

The Al Aqsa intifada also threw up potentially worrying questions elsewhere on the Israeli-Egyptian border. Increasingly, there were reports of Palestinians smuggling arms from Egypt to Gaza via tunnels dug underneath the divided town of Rafah (see above). Retaliatory moves by Israel in Rafah met with severe international criticism. Meanwhile, Israel accused Egypt of being derelict in apparently turning a blind eye to such arms smuggling.

Despite such difficulties, Taba has largely prospered as a tourist destination. There are even plans to run road links from Taba to Jordan, Saudi Arabia, Lebanon and Turkey, via a possible $3.6bn project to build a 15.6 km suspension bridge over the Straits of Tiran. Taba has also established a role as a location for high-level international political dialogue. In part this was due to its geographical proximity to Israel and the Palestinian Authority; in part, to its symbolism as an example of a long-running dispute that was resolved by non-violent negotiation.

Lawrence Joffe

5.5 Iran - Iraq

A major source of strain in relations between Iran and Iraq has been the long-standing dispute over the Shatt al-'Arab waterway, which runs into the Gulf in the southern border area between the two countries. Whereas Iraq has traditionally claimed to have succeeded to the Ottoman empire's jurisdiction over the whole waterway and that therefore the border between the two countries in this area runs along the eastern bank, Iran has consistently maintained that such a delimitation is not only unjust but also contrary to the thalweg line principle (whereby riverine frontiers are defined as following the median line in the deepest channel). Under early partial agreements, Iran succeeded in securing the application of the thalweg principle to the vicinity of Mohammerah (now called Khorramshahr) in 1914 and to the waters off Abadan in 1937. Moreover, in return for a cessation of Iranian support for Kurdish rebels in Iraqi Kurdistan, Iraq agreed in 1975 that the entire Shatt al-'Arab should be delimited along the median line of the deepest channel.

However, the Islamic Revolution in Iran in 1979 not only served to revive Iraq's traditional suspicion of its non-Arab neighbour but also led to a reactivation of the Iraqi claim to the Shatt al-'Arab. In September 1980 Iraq unilaterally abrogated the 1975 agreement, declared its sovereignty over the whole of the Shatt al-'Arab and moved to assert its claim by force of arms. Following a bitter eight-year war a ceasefire was agreed in July 1988.

In August 1990, following the Iraqi invasion of Kuwait, Iraq accepted the 1975 agreement on the border with Iran. Iraq's continuing international isolation and Iran's realisation that the Iraqi President, Saddam Hussein, was an accomplished survivor led to slightly improved relations in the late 1990s. However, the major differences between the sides were too great to overcome and a cold peace was maintained. Iran did not support the US-led attack on Iraq in 2003 and its future relationship with a post-occupation Iraq is uncertain. The removal of Saddam's regime means that Iraq's claim to the eastern bank of the Shatt al-'Arab is unlikely to be reasserted soon.

Location and Economic Significance of Shatt al-'Arab

The Shatt al-'Arab ("Shatt" means a water border or bank), given on some modern Iranian maps as the Arvand river, is formed by the confluence of the Euphrates and Tigris rivers and flows for some 160 miles (255 kilometres) through a swampy delta before opening out into the Gulf. (Map 55, p. 521, shows its position.) From the north the land boundary between Iran and Iraq reaches the waterway about 60 miles (100 kilometres) from the coast and about 10 miles (16 kilometres) upstream from the town of Khorramshahr.

The area where the Shatt al-'Arab flows into the sea has acquired major importance for both Iran and Iraq, in particular since the development of their respective oil industries. Iran has built its major oil refinery at Abadan (its principal oil terminal being on Kharg island in the Gulf), while Iraq's main terminal is at Fao (Faw) at the southern end of the waterway and its main port at Basra upstream from Khorramshahr. This development of the Shatt al-'Arab has served to accentuate what Iran regards as the anomaly of its ports being enclosed by territorial waters claimed by Iraq, whereas Iraq has attached increasing importance to the waterway as its main outlet to the sea and has also pointed out that Iran also possesses a substantial coastline along the eastern shore of the Gulf. Because of continuing alluvial deposits, the river has a tendency to migrate north-east, into Iran.

Early Historical Background

The border between Persia (Iran) and the Ottoman empire (Turkey) was first defined in a treaty signed at Zuhab in 1639, although the boundary line remained vague because allegiance in territory between the Zagros mountains to the east of the Shatt al-'Arab and the Tigris to the west was based largely on tribal loyalties. Following the conclusion of a Russo-Ottoman agreement providing for the partition of Iran in 1724, the Ottomans invaded Persia and under the 1727 Treaty of Hamadan, were ceded the country's western provinces. Although further hostilities in the 1740s resulted in a reaffirmation of the 1639 agreement in the Treaty of Kherden of 1746, the latter treaty was itself declared invalid under the first Treaty of Erzerum signed in 1823 after renewed warfare between the Ottomans and Iran in 1821-22.

During this period, the Arab Ka'abide principality ruled on both sides of the Shatt al-'Arab, playing off the Ottomans against the Persians. In 1757, it defeated the Persians, and in 1762, a joint force of the Ottoman empire and the British East India Company. In 1837, the Ottomans attacked and demolished Mohammerah, and asserted their sovereignty over Mohammerah and Abadan.

Following the signature of the first Treaty of Erzerum in 1823, Britain and Russia exerted pressure on Turkey and Iran to achieve a resolution of their border difficulties, to which end a boundary commission was formed in 1843 comprising representatives of the four powers. As a result of the commission's work, a second Treaty of Erzerum was signed in May 1847 which delimited a boundary in the Shatt al-'Arab for the first time. Iran received the town and port of Mohammerah, the island of Abadan and its anchorage and the eastern bank of the river, but the Ottomans retained sovereignty over the waterway. (Mohammerah had been founded in 1812 by the Muhaisin tribe and was claimed by both Persia and the Ottoman empire. The Sheikh of Mohammerah had maintained his independence, however, and controlled southern Arabistan, east of the Shatt al-'Arab, where the Ottomans had also sought to enforce their suzerainty.) Although at this time the Shatt al-'Arab was of only minor importance to Persia as a trade channel, the 1847 Treaty provided that "Persian vessels have the right to navigate freely without let or hindrance on the Shatt al-'Arab from the mouth of the same to the point of contact of the frontiers of the two parties".

Under the 1847 treaty (which also settled certain other territorial issues between Persia and the Ottomans), the quadripartite boundary commission undertook to continue its work to delimit the entire frontier. However, both Persia and the Ottomans rejected the boundary line recommended by the commission in 1850 and further efforts to draw up a satisfactory border were halted by the Crimean War of 1853-56 and the 1854-56 war between Persia and Britain. Several years after the wars had ended, Britain and Russia drafted separate maps of the Ottoman-Persian border, revealing a number of discrepancies, and in a joint map (known as the *Carte identique)* produced in 1869, stretches of the border were again left uncertain. Inhabitants of the southern border region were, however, understood to have reached an informal agreement under which the boundary was regarded as running down the centre of the Shatt al-'Arab, with both sides controlling navigation.

Twentieth Century Developments prior to the 1975 Agreement

In the early 20th century, sovereignty over the Shatt al-'Arab became an important issue for Iran with the growth of the port of Mohammerah and the discovery of oil at Masjed Sulaiman in 1908, which necessitated the construction of an oil terminal. Iran was now particularly concerned that vessels carrying oil-drilling equipment and other cargo into new berths at Mohammerah had to anchor in Ottoman waters and were obliged to pay Ottoman import duties. In this situation Britain and Russia, which in 1907 had made a de facto division of Iran into Russian and British spheres of influence, again put pressure on Persia and the Ottomans to settle their differences and renewed efforts were made to work out a detailed delimitation of their boundary. A protocol was signed by representatives of the boundary commission in Constantinople in 1913 which reaffirmed Turkish sovereignty over the Shatt al-'Arab and again called for the boundary to be demarcated. In 1914, however, the commission reached a verbal agreement which recognized the changed importance of Mohammerah by moving the boundary opposite the port to the thalweg line from about a mile below to a mile above the mouth of the Karun river, although the rest of the water remained under Ottoman control. The commission also demarcated the land boundary to the north where Persia, in return for Ottoman concessions over the river boundary, ceded larger areas of territory to the Ottoman government.

From the late 19th century, Britain had exercised effective control of the Shatt al-'Arab, and at the end of World War I and the dissolution of the Ottoman empire, British forces, now occupying Iraq, set up a Basra port authority to supervise navigation of the estuary and to maintain essential services, such work being financed largely by levies on commercial shipping. The Persians were thus unable to carry out informal policing and patrolling of the river as they had done previously, even though the growth of the oil port of Abadan was rapidly increasing its strategic importance for Persia. Accordingly, the new Persian ruler, Reza Shah, repudiated Iraq's claim to the Shatt al-'Arab as the successor to Ottoman sovereignty and

urged a complete revision of the river boundary. Iran also protested that Iraq, which had become a British mandated territory in 1920, was using the bulk of revenues collected from ships using the waterway for its own benefit rather than for maintaining services on the river, and that riverine boundaries were normally determined by the thalweg line. It has been suggested that, until the 1950s, Britain was far more concerned than either of the other two parties over this issue, and opposed the thalweg concept, fearing that it would adversely affect British shipping rights. Iraq, for its part, argued that the Shatt al-'Arab was the only exit to the sea from its major port of Basra, while Iran had the potential of developing ports on the Gulf. Meanwhile, in 1924, with the assistance of the British, Reza Shah defeated the Sheikh of Mohammerah and for the first time established direct Iranian control in the area.

Iraq was accepted as a member of the League of Nations in October 1932, upon becoming an independent sovereign state. In 1934 the League of Nations was brought into the dispute on an Iraqi initiative and urged Iran and Iraq to negotiate directly, but little progress was made. In discussions in 1935, Iran accepted the 1847 treaty, but not the 1913 protocol. However, in 1936 the attitude of Iran and Iraq to one another changed following the Italian attack on Abyssinia. In mid-1937 Iran and Iraq signed an agreement on their border problems, paving the way for the signing on July 8 of the Saadabad Pact which brought Iran, Iraq, Turkey and Afghanistan together in a treaty of friendship and non-aggression.

In the border agreement, signed in Baghdad on June 29, 1937, and in Tehran on July 5, the two countries reached a compromise on the Shatt al-'Arab, over which Iran had become more amenable in view of its development on the Gulf of the new port of Bandar Shahpur (now called Bandar Khomeini). The agreement reaffirmed the boundary established by the four-party commission in 1913-14 but also applied the "Mohammerah principle" to Abadan, the border thus following the thalweg line for some four miles in the immediate vicinity and downstream of the port. The treaty also provided for both countries to reach an agreement on matters of navigation, pilotage and collection of dues in the river, and also laid down that ships using the river should fly the Iraqi flag except in the vicinity of Mohammerah and Abadan.

In the late 1950s improved technology enabled Iran to develop oil fields in the Gulf. A large oil terminal was built at Kharg island 30 miles offshore, with the result that Iran became less dependent on Abadan, which had the disadvantage of having a shallow approach channel under Iraqi control. Nevertheless, the bulk of Iran's trade still depended on Mohammerah, and the Shatt al-'Arab thus remained vital to Iran. In the mid-1960s the Shah of Iran, Mohammed Reza, reiterated his father's earlier claims that ships using Iranian ports in the Shatt al-'Arab contributed the greater part of revenues from the waterway, but that Iraq used none of these funds to benefit the river's facilities and moreover did not give a share to Iran as had been stipulated under the 1937 agreement. On April 19, 1969, Iran declared that it no longer considered the 1937 treaty valid and that Iranian vessels would henceforth neither pay Iraqi tolls nor fly the Iraqi flag in the waterway.

Iraq responded to Iran's abrogation of the 1937 treaty by declaring that the Shatt al-'Arab was Iraqi territory and by threatening to take action against any Iranian vessels contravening the terms of the treaty. Despite these warnings, no action was taken against an Iranian flagship which in April 1969 sailed down the Shatt al-'Arab to the Gulf with Iranian pilots and an Iranian escort and refused to pay dues to the Iraqi authorities. Iranian ships taking similar action were similarly unmolested, although several thousand Iranians resident in Iraq were forcibly expelled in an apparent act of retaliation.

1975 Reconciliation and Border Agreement

Strained relations between Iran and Iraq following Iran's abrogation of the 1937 treaty were exacerbated by Iran's support for Kurdish rebels fighting against the Iraqi regime, and by Iran's occupation in 1971 of Abu Musa and the Greater and Lesser Tunbs, three islands in the Strait of Hormuz disputed by the UAE, and over which Iraq broke off diplomatic relations with Iran until 1973 (see Section 5.6 for that dispute). Moreover, in the early 1970s there was a series of border incidents between the two countries. At a meeting of the UN Security Council in February 1974 both the Iranian and Iraqi governments expressed the desire to settle their border dispute peacefully and through direct negotiations, although the main obstacle to a speedy resolution of the problem remained Iran's objections to the provisions of the 1937 agreement and Iraq's insistence that Iran fulfil its obligations.

The failure of Iran and Iraq to resolve their dispute through direct talks was of concern to other oil-exporting countries, some of which attempted to mediate. At a conference of the heads of state of members of the Organization of Petroleum Exporting Countries (OPEC), held in Algiers in March 1975, Iran and Iraq, on the initiative of the Algerian President, reached an agreement which they claimed "completely eliminated the conflict between the two brotherly countries". In a joint communiqué issued on the final day of the meeting, Iran and Iraq agreed to demarcate their land boundaries on the basis of the Protocol of Constantinople of 1913 and the detailed records of the boundary commission of 1914 and to delimit the river frontier according to the thalweg line. In return for Iraqi concessions on the Shatt al-'Arab, Iran ceased its support for Iraq's Kurdish guerrillas, whose rebellion subsequently collapsed.

During a meeting of their Foreign Ministers in Tehran in March 1975, Iran and Iraq signed a protocol providing for the establishment of committees to demarcate their land boundary, delimit the river boundary and prevent any violations of the border. Under a subsequent *procès-verbal* of May 20, the two

sides agreed to draw up a final treaty on the boundary, and on June 13 they signed a Treaty Relating to the State Boundary and Good Neighbourliness. Under three protocols to this agreement the two sides established that the border between the two countries in the Shatt al-'Arab waterway should be drawn according to the thalweg line principle (defined as "the median line of the main navigable channel at the lowest level of navigation"), delineated some 670 positions on the land border between the two countries on the basis of the Protocol of Constantinople of 1913, and provided for the establishment of border security arrangements to prevent the infiltration of undesirable elements in either direction.

With regard to the river frontier, the relevant protocol provided for the boundary line to follow the thalweg line in the event of a "shift in the bed of the Shatt al-'Arab or its mouth caused by natural phenomena" and also stipulated that a survey of the river was to be conducted jointly at least every 10 years.

Iraqi Abrogation of 1975 Agreement and Outbreak of Iran-Iraq War in 1980

The Shi'a Islamic revolution in Iran in early 1979 led to a sharp deterioration in Iranian-Iraqi relations, as reflected in a number of border incidents and exchanges of hostile statements between the two states. Iraq claimed that there had been 163 Iranian hostile acts in 1979, 397 in the first three months of 1980, and 187 from June to September 1980, and argued that war began on Sept. 4 with Iranian shelling of Iraqi border posts. On Sept. 17, 1980, Saddam Hussein, who had become Iraqi head of state in mid-1979, unilaterally abrogated the agreement with Iran of June 1975 and thereupon claimed that Iraq's sovereignty over the Shatt al-'Arab had been restored. On Sept. 22 Iraq launched a large-scale offensive against Iran and rapidly gained control of part of the province of Khuzestan on the eastern side of the Shatt al-'Arab, capturing the town of Khorramshahr (formerly Mohammerah) and encircling Abadan. Oil installations in both countries suffered serious damage and ships in the Shatt al-'Arab were blocked by the ferocity of the fighting.

Three days after the outbreak of the war Iraq set conditions for a ceasefire. Iran should recognize Iraq's sovereignty over the border area, respect and recognize Iraq's sovereignty and "legitimate rights" in the Shatt al-'Arab, and return to Arab ownership the three islands which it had occupied in the Strait of Hormuz. As the Iranian government refused to fulfil these conditions, fighting persisted and various Iraqi officials made certain other territorial demands, claiming in particular that Iraq had a "historic" and "nationalist" right to the Iranian province of Khuzestan (referred to as Arabistan by Iraq). This province, with vast oil reserves, was inhabited by some 2,000,000 Arabs who had already agitated for concessions from the new Islamic regime in Iran (and also previously from the Shah) and whom Iraq now promised to help form an independent state if they so wished. In the face of Iran's total rejection of Iraqi demands, Iraq threatened to occupy more Iranian territory and also to forge closer ties with Iran's other minority groups, largely occupying border areas of the country.

Mediation efforts were undertaken by the United Nations, the Islamic Conference Organization (OIC) and the Non-Aligned Movement, but both Iran and Iraq remained intractable, the latter insisting on Iranian territorial concessions and the former refusing to accept a settlement outside the 1975 agreement. With regard to the latter agreement, Iraq maintained that Iran had invalidated it by violating at least two of its terms by refusing to restore to Iraq the areas of Zein al-Kaous and Seif-Saad (comprising some 400 square miles), which had allegedly been "usurped" some 10 years earlier but which Iran claimed it had returned in accordance with the agreement, and by permitting a Kurdish leader to return to Iran for the presumed purpose of rekindling the Kurdish rebellion in Iraq.

Course of the War, 1981-84

The Iran-Iraq war continued sporadically throughout 1981, with the military position changing little from that reached in the early stages of the fighting. Although in September 1981 Iranian forces succeeded in lifting the siege of Abadan, a military stalemate appeared to have been reached by early 1982, with Iraq still in control of substantial stretches of the eastern bank of the Shatt al-'Arab and also pockets of Iranian territory further north. However, from mid-March 1982 the situation changed dramatically when the Iranians launched a major counter-offensive in the southern war zone, driving the Iraqi forces back to the border by mid-May and recapturing Khorramshahr on May 24. With its forces having thus achieved what appeared to be a major military victory, the Iranian government stressed that it had no territorial ambitions against Iraq but insisted that the latter should pay war reparations to Iran and that the government of Saddam Hussein be removed from power.

There was then considerable speculation, fuelled by official Iranian statements, that Iran would shortly launch a "final offensive" to end the war. No operation on such a scale materialized over the following five years, however, as Iraq continued to benefit from diplomatic and financial support from many Arab states, and from increasingly sophisticated weapons supplies from the Soviet Union, France and other countries. Although there was no active intervention by other Arab armies, both Jordanian and Sudanese "volunteers" took part in the fighting in limited numbers. For its part, Iran received some diplomatic support from Libya and several radical third-world governments, but was restricted to the international and clandestine markets for its arms supplies. A report commissioned by the US Senate foreign relations committee, which was published in August 1984, asserted that both the United States and the Soviet Union had gradually shifted from their original stance

of professed neutrality to one which overtly favoured Iraq.

Evidence of the Arab world's support for Iraq was apparent in the declaration of the September 1982 Fez summit of Arab League leaders, which praised Iraq's "withdrawal" from Iranian territory, warned that "any aggression against an Arab country" would be considered an aggression "against all Arab countries", and called on all League members to "abstain from taking any measure to encourage either directly or indirectly" the prolongation of the conflict. Despite earlier support for Iran, the Syrian President, Hafez al-Assad, supported the resolution. Earlier in the year, the war had led to the postponement of the seventh summit of Non-Aligned leaders, which had been scheduled to be held in Baghdad.

From mid-1983 onwards, Iraqi aircraft flew repeated missions against Iranian oil installations, notably the Kharg island terminal, while the loan of French Super-Etendard fighter aircraft equipped with Exocet anti-ship missiles enabled Iraq to carry out accurate attacks on oil tankers travelling to and from Iranian terminals. In response, Iran threatened to "close the Gulf" to international shipping by using its naval power to prevent safe passage of ships through the narrow Strait of Hormuz at the southern end of the Gulf. The US government responded in early 1984 by warning that there should be "absolutely no doubt" that it would take steps to ensure that the Gulf remained open, to which end a US naval task force was stationed in the vicinity of the Strait.

In May 1984 Iran began attacking Kuwaiti and Saudi tankers by way of retaliation. This "Iranian aggression" against non-belligerents was condemned by meetings of the Foreign Ministers of the Arab League (not including Syrian and Libyan representatives) and the six-member Gulf Co-operation Council (GCC). The following month, the UN Security Council passed a resolution condemning the latest attacks (although it failed to condemn Iran by name, as requested by the GCC) and demanding respect for the principle of freedom of navigation in the Gulf. Commenting on the resolution, the Iranian permanent representative at the UN said: "We strongly support freedom of navigation. The Gulf should remain a zone of peace and security for all, but we cannot permit anyone to use the Gulf against us. It will either remain free and open to all of us, or nobody will be allowed to use it".

In the land war, Iran launched a major offensive, code-named "Al-Fajr" (Dawn) in February 1983, directed at the strategic town of Al Amarah, which lay on the road from Basra, Iraq's second city, to the capital. Described by Iranian spokesmen as "the final military operation which will determine the destiny of the region", the attack was beaten back by the Iraqis, who used armour and air strikes to break the "human waves" of lightly-armed Iranian soldiers. In subsequent diplomatic developments, the UN Security Council again appealed for an "immediate ceasefire", while in June 1983 Saddam Hussein also called for an end to hostilities. Iranian leaders, however, continued to insist that peace would only come after Saddam had been overthrown.

Iran gained some ground in October 1983 in the border regions of north-eastern Iraq, when its troops seized several mountains in the Penjwin area, thereby cutting communications between Iraqi units and Iranian Kurdish fighters who had been assisting them as part of their own long-running guerrilla war against the Tehran government. At the end of 1983, Iran staged a successful operation in the Majnoon oil fields, just inside the border in southern Iraq. During late 1983, evidence began to emerge of Iraqi use of chemical weapons, mostly forms of mustard gas similar to that used in Europe in World War I. Examination of wounded Iranian soldiers by international medical experts confirmed the fact that such weapons were being employed, and Iraq's use of them was specifically condemned in a resolution of the UN Security Council in March 1986.

Air attacks on civilian targets, which had become a regular feature of the war, were suspended by both sides in June 1984 as a result of a moratorium agreement arranged by the UN Secretary-General, Javier Pérez de Cuellar. Iraq resumed bombing of Iranian cities in December of that year, however, leading to retaliatory missile strikes on Iraqi towns. Throughout the war, the superiority of the Iraqi Air Force enabled it to carry out frequent raids deep into Iran.

Continuation of Hostilities, 1985-88

In an attempt to achieve a decisive breakthrough against Iraq, the Iranians launched a major offensive in the central sector in March 1985, but their forces were repulsed with heavy casualties. This apparent failure of the "human wave" tactics reportedly fuelled increasing differences within the Iranian political and military leadership over the wisdom of attempting such costly operations and over the viability of any "final offensive". Some officials started to speak of the overriding strategy as being that of a "defensive jihad", rather than offensive.

Mediation efforts were pursued without success during 1985 by the Algerian government and the Islamic Conference Organization, and also by the Indian Prime Minister, Rajiv Gandhi, on behalf of the Non-Aligned Movement. In November the Iranian Foreign Minister, Dr Ali Akbar Vellayati, held talks on possible peaceful solutions to the conflict with King Fahd of Saudi Arabia, one of Iraq's closest allies. In what was seen as an attempt to go some way towards meeting Iran's demand that the Iraqi regime should be condemned and punished as the "aggressor", the UN Security Council passed a resolution in February 1986 which "deplored the initial acts which gave rise to the conflict". In May of that year, the Iranian permanent representative at the UN suggested that negotiations could begin if Saddam Hussein was replaced as President by Ali Saleh, a former Iraqi ambassador to the UN.

In the war at sea, both sides escalated attacks on oil tankers and merchant shipping—46 tankers were attacked in 1985, while approximately double this number were fired on the following year. In September 1985 Iran began to stop and search vessels suspected of supplying Iraq with military equipment. US and Soviet ships were among those boarded and searched in 1986. In response to the increase in attacks and interceptions, naval patrols in the southern Gulf by French, British and US ships were stepped up. Iraq's attacks on Iranian oil installations became increasingly effective during 1986 and early 1987, as their pilots adopted low-level bombing tactics which increased the chances of scoring accurate hits against the target. By the latter half of 1986, Western oil experts were estimating that Iran's refined oil exports had been cut by half as a result of Iraqi air strikes. The Kharg island terminal was seriously damaged, while Iran's coastal shuttle tanker fleet, together with its terminals at Sirri and Larak in the southern Gulf, were also attacked.

Iranian ground forces gained a significant victory early in 1986 when they overwhelmed Iraqi defences at the deserted port of Faw, on the outlet of the Shatt al-'Arab. Repeated Iraqi counter-attacks failed to recapture the town. Further Iranian gains resulted from a major offensive mounted in January and February 1987, when they seized several islands in the Shatt al-'Arab opposite Basra. For a time, it appeared possible that they might succeed in capturing the city, but the attack was halted after Iranian leaders had declared that the purpose of the "Karbala-5" offensive was to "destroy the Iraqi war machine", rather than achieve territorial gains. Much of Iraq's defensive strategy in the region relied on the flooding of marshlands to impede the progress of the Iranian infantry. Following the latest attack, it was reported that Iranian engineers were constructing a system of drainage channels in an attempt to draw off the waters which fed Iraq's own complex of artificial lakes.

An element of Iran's success in the Karbala-5 operation was attributed to the arrival of US weapons and spare parts, delivered as part of the secret "arms-for-hostages" arrangement, details of which emerged during late 1986. In particular, the availability of sophisticated anti-tank missiles was thought to have hampered counter-attacks by Iraqi armoured units. Iranian forces also scored limited successes in the central and northern sectors during the opening months of 1987. Iraq responded by increasing the frequency and severity of air attacks on Iranian cities. On Feb. 19, however, the two sides agreed to a further temporary ceasefire.

In a renewed effort to satisfy Iranian diplomatic demands, Pérez de Cuellar used an address to the Islamic Conference Organization in Kuwait in January 1987 to propose the establishment of an international panel to determine the blame for the war. Saddam Hussein issued an appeal the following month for a complete and unconditional ceasefire, to be followed by a mutual withdrawal to "the internationally-recognized borders", an exchange of prisoners and an agreement by both parties to respect the political and social system of the other. The Iranian government failed to respond to the calls, however, and in April 1987 launched new attacks on the southern front.

International concern over the continuing war intensified on May 17 when the US frigate *Stark,* on patrol in the Gulf to the north of Qatar, was hit by two Exocet missiles fired by an Iraqi Mirage warplane. One missile exploded, killing 37 US sailors. The USA subsequently accepted Iraqi assurances that the attack on the USS *Stark* had been a case of mistaken identity. At the same time, it said that the US naval presence in the Gulf would be strengthened and that plans would proceed to allow Kuwaiti tankers to fly the US flag so that they could be afforded full protection from potential Iranian attacks.

The UN Security Council unanimously adopted Resolution 598 on July 20, 1987. This in effect supported the Iraqi position, calling for an immediate ceasefire and withdrawal to internationally recognized borders, the placement of observers and an exchange of prisoners of war. The resolution was rejected by Iran, which demanded that Iraq be branded the aggressor. Without any provision for sanctions, no progress was made, and several truces proved ineffective, as did a visit to the region by Pérez de Cuellar on Sept. 11-15. On Aug. 29 Iraq resumed attacks on Iranian industry, tankers, and oil installations.

There were signs at this time of an internationalization and escalation of the conflict. In August and September, the USA, Britain, France, Belgium, the Netherlands and Italy announced that they were sending minesweepers to the Gulf, to clear mines on shipping lanes to Kuwait, believed to have been laid by Iran. From September until December, Iran fired eight missiles into Kuwait. On Sept. 21, a US helicopter attacked an Iranian boat which was allegedly laying mines in the Gulf, and on Oct. 19 US boats destroyed two Iranian oil platforms. On Dec. 14, 1987, an Iraqi Exocet missile attack killed 22 sailors on an Iranian tanker.

In January 1988, with the support of dissident Kurdish groups in Iraq, Iran launched an attack in the north and centre of the front. Iraq responded with chemical attacks against the Kurds. When Iran captured the town of Halabja on March 16, 1988, it was discovered that many had died in such attacks, which continued despite international condemnation of Iraq. Some 5,000 Kurds were killed in the Halabja area. Iran resumed the "war of the cities" on Feb. 29, 1988, with attacks on Baghdad and Basra. Iraq resumed its air raids into Iran, and also attacked shipping in the Gulf, twice narrowly missing US naval units.

End of the War

By April 1988, Iraq was recouping, while war-weariness grew in Iran. On April 14 Iran mined a US warship in the Gulf, leading to a retaliatory American attack on Iranian naval platforms on April 18. On the same day, Iraq retook Faw. Iraq continued to make gains, reoccupying Iraqi territory near Basra on May 25, and the Majnoon oilfield on June 25-28. On July 13, Iraqi troops entered Iranian territory for the first time since 1986, occupying the border town of Dehloran. Meanwhile, Iraqi air attacks on Iranian tanker terminals were causing serious economic damage.

On July 18, Iran accepted UN Security Council Resolution 598, which it had rejected a year earlier. Ayatollah Khomeini stated that relinquishing his demand for the destruction of the Iraqi regime was "worse than drinking poison". On July 20, Iraq added further demands, including clearance by the UN of the Shatt al-'Arab, recognition of Iraqi freedom of navigation and peace negotiations before the conclusion of a ceasefire. Iraq also rejected the 1975 border, and demanded a border on the east bank of the river, not the thalweg line.

Kurdish mujahideen attacks on Iran during June-July 1988, which caused heavy losses on both sides, were believed to be sponsored by Iraq, which did not want to be seen in direct breach of the ceasefire. This eventually came into force on Aug. 20 and was monitored by the specially established United Nations Iran-Iraq Military Observer Group (UNIIMOG). The Foreign Ministers of both states attended peace negotiations in Geneva on Aug. 25. However, since the delimitation of the border was in dispute, it proved impossible to implement the call in UN Resolution 598 for withdrawal to internationally recognized borders and the talks became stalemated. Iraq refused to recognize the 1975 agreement, demanding full sovereignty over the Shatt al-'Arab. Iraq also demanded full freedom of navigation in the Shatt al-'Arab, and the clearing of sunken boats from the river before discussing substantive matters. Further talks in Geneva in April 1989 were also inconclusive and Iran refused to release Iraqi prisoners of war without Iraqi withdrawal from its territory, while Iraq continued to demand further concessions before withdrawing.

The ceasefire implemented in 1988 has since been maintained, but a peace treaty has still not been agreed between the two sides. The end of the war left Iraq facing huge problems, with a massive debt and a fall in oil prices. This, and other strategic considerations, turned its interest away from Iran and towards its equally long-standing dispute with Kuwait (for which see Section 5.7). This was the background to Saddam Hussein's exchange of letters with Iran in May 1990 and to the July 3 meeting in Geneva between the two Foreign Ministers. On Aug. 14, following the Iraqi invasion of Kuwait, Saddam wrote to Iranian President Rafsanjani accepting the 1975 Algiers agreement and agreeing to a withdrawal and the exchange of prisoners of war.

1991-2003: A Cold Peace

Following the 1991 Gulf War and the survival of Saddam's regime, the two countries remained wary of each other. As no peace treaty had been signed to end the 1980-88 war, and there were serious impediments to normalizing relations, a state of cold peace existed for the next decade.

The Iraqi repression of the Kurdish uprising at the end of the Gulf War caused more than one million Kurdish refugees to flee from Iraq over the Iranian border. Both countries had large Kurdish minorities and so were unable to fully exploit their potential for undermining the other's government. Instead, Iran and Iraq sheltered and supported armed dissident groups whose opposition was based on religious and ideological differences. The *Mujahideen-e Khalq* organization (People's Combatants) (MKO), a Marxist-Islamic group dedicated to the overthrow of the Iranian government, settled in Iraq in 1986 and conducted periodic attacks across the Iranian border and in Tehran. The Supreme Council for Islamic Revolution in Iraq (SCIRI), a Shi'a movement formed in 1982 in Tehran, was estimated to have 15,000 troops in Iran in the mid-1990s, plotting the overthrow of Saddam Hussein. These organizations acted almost as proxy armies for the two governments and there were regular violent incidents attributed to both throughout the 1990s.

Another major issue which hampered the restoration of relations was the return of prisoners of war from the conflict of the 1980s. At the end of the war, 50,000 Iraqi prisoners of war were held in Iran and 20,000 Iranians were held in Iraq. Iraq also demanded the return of more than 100 military and civilian aircraft it flew to Iran for safety before the allied attack on Kuwait and Iraq in 1991. Iran claimed the number was much smaller and did not return the aircraft.

In the years immediately following the 1991 Gulf War, little progress was made in improving relations as Iraq recovered from its heavy defeat and attempted to cope with the enforcement of sanctions and military restrictions. Despite Iraq's troubles, Iran remained fearful of Saddam's regime and renewed Iraqi provocation over the Shatt al-'Arab dispute. By 1998, the two sides had begun to accept that better relations might be in their interests. Iraq was suffering extreme international isolation and the new government of Mohammad Khatami in Iran was keen to improve its relations with its Arab neighbours and resolve the disputes of the past. It was reported in April 1998 that a deal was being discussed in which Baghdad would make a commitment to honour the 1975 agreement in return for Iran ceasing to claim war reparations. As part of the slight thaw in relations, the border was opened in August 1998 for the first time since 1980 to allow Iranian pilgrims to visit the great Shi'a shrines in Iraq.

These promising moves were halted in the spring of 1999, following the assassination of Lt-General Ali Sayyad-Shirazi, Iran's Deputy Chief of Staff, by the MKO and a number of murders of Shi'a clerics in Iraq which Iraq blamed on SCIRI. These killings causing increased tension as both sides deployed regular forces along the border. In May 2000, Iran complained to the UN about what it said were repeated violations by Iraq of the 1988 ceasefire, including illegal patrols, construction activities and support for subversive groups.

A rare high level meeting took place in Venezuela in September 2000 between President Khatami of Iran and the Iraqi Vice-President, Taha Yassin Ramadan,

and in October 2000, Kamal Kharrazi, the Iranian Foreign Minister, visited Baghdad for talks, the first such visit for more than a decade. The two sides agreed to resume discussions on issues including the border and the release of prisoners of war. In November 2000, Khatamai met Ezzat Ibrahim, Vice-Chairman of Iraq's Revolutionary Command Council, in Qatar and stated that Iran was willing to open a new chapter in bilateral relations.

The cycle of fluctuating relations continued in April 2001, with a sharp escalation of MKO attacks on Iranian military posts. Iran responded with strikes on a scale unprecedented since the end of the war and fired more than fifty missiles across the border at what it said were MKO training camps. Iran also paraded nine captured MKO fighters at a news conference at which the rebels spoke of their close co-operation with the Iraqi authorities.

Further efforts to resolve some of the outstanding issues were made in January 2002 at talks in Tehran, when Iraqi Foreign Minister Naji Sabri and Kamal Kharrazi spoke of their willingness to leave behind the legacy of the conflict. Iran released almost 700 Iraqi prisoners of war as a goodwill gesture while Baghdad again reopened its borders to Iranian pilgrims.

In June 2002 Iraq protested to the UN that Iran had violated the 1988 ceasefire agreement by illegal flights, construction and attacks on Iraqi troops and civilians. The issue of the return of prisoners of war remained large and Iraq claimed that Iran still held 29,000 prisoners of war, while Iran stated that 3,000 of its servicemen were still missing. The slow process of return quickened in July 2002 when Iraq returned the bodies of 570 Iranian soldiers in exchange for 1,200 Iraqi bodies from Iran. Despite this and other exchanges, the relationship remained complicated and while practical neighbourly co-operation improved on some levels, both sides continued to accuse the other of supporting subversive dissidents.

In September 2002, in the build-up to the US assault on Iraq, Iran pledged that it would not violate the Iraqi border if the USA did invade, while calling on all countries in the region not to join the attack. Iran would otherwise have welcomed the removal of Saddam's regime, but was not prepared to support an invasion by the United States. Iran also feared that the invasion could launch a repeat of the influx of more than a million Iraqi Kurd and Shi'a refugees that occurred during the war in 1991. As the likelihood of invasion increased, Iraq made some efforts to restore friendships with its neighbours and in December 2002, Iraq and Iran agreed to open a border crossing to allow Baghdad to import humanitarian goods according to the UN "oil for food" programme.

2003 War on Iraq

The USA and UK attacked Iraq on March 20, 2003, and by April 14 the Iraqi army was effectively defeated and Saddam's government had disappeared. The USA considered the MKO to be a legitimate target because of its close relationship with Saddam, but after some attacks on MKO positions, agreed a cease-fire with the organization on April 22. This greatly alarmed Iran, which demanded the extradition of its leaders and accused the USA of interfering in its internal affairs. For its part, the USA was concerned about an Iranian-style Islamic theocracy emerging in Iraq and warned Iran not to meddle in its reconstruction of the country. Iran dismissed such suggestions and Kamal Kharrazi declared that Tehran was not seeking to increase the political influence of Iraqi Shi'as at the expense of any other community. There was great anger in Iran when, on Aug. 29, at least 94 were killed in a bombing in the holy Iraqi city of Najaf, among them Ayatollah Mohammad Baqer al-Hakim, the leader of SCIRI.

The security of the Iran-Iraq border became a major issue in the summer of 2003 as border posts abandoned by the Iraqi forces were inadequately manned by US and UK troops. Deadly attacks on targets inside Iraq by (unknown) elements hostile to the occupation seriously increased and the USA became greatly concerned that such elements were crossing into Iraq through its porous borders. The Iranian border was of particular concern to the USA, given the resurgent Shi'a political activism in Iraq and suspicion of Iran's interest in stirring up anti-American unrest. On July 9, 2003, US Defence Secretary Donald Rumsfeld said that Iran had moved some border posts several kilometres inside Iraq, commenting that this was "not acceptable". Iran was concerned that Iranian pilgrims crossing the border were being killed by the mines which still litter the border area. On Sept. 3, US marines were deployed on the border.

In March 2004, as serious attacks intensified inside Iraq, the US administrator in Iraq, Paul Bremer, announced new measures to secure the Iranian border. All but three crossing points were closed and the number of border police was doubled. There were reports of a skirmish between US forces and Iranian border guards on March 15. Iranian authorities rejected US criticism that they were not doing enough to secure the border and on April 4, the Interior Minister, Abdolvahed Mussavi-Lari, emphasized that "the return of security and stability in Iraq would be in the interest of all regional states".

Robert Lowe

5.6 Iran - United Arab Emirates

A dispute has existed since the nineteenth century between Iran and the United Arab Emirates (UAE) and its predecessors, the Qasimi sheikhdoms of Sharjah and Ras al-Khaimah, over the islands of Abu Musa, Greater Tunb and Lesser Tunb, which are strategically situated at the entrance to the Persian Gulf, opposite the Strait of Hormuz (see Map 53, p. 520). The Tunb islands are respectively known to the Arabs as Tunb as-Sughra and Tunb al-Kubra, and to the Iranians as Tunb-e Bozorg and Bani Tunb. Abu Musa's population in modern times is estimated at around 600 while the Tunbs have never been permanently settled. The dispute was inflamed in 1971 when Iran occupied the islands and again in 1992 after incidents on Abu Musa. The significance of the dispute lies in the islands' strategic location and symbolism rather than their size or wealth and for much of the 1990s, it served as the focus of Arab-Iranian rivalries across the Gulf. The dispute remains the most intractable Gulf territorial issue.

Iranian Occupation of the Islands in 1971

On Nov. 30, 1971—two days before the proclamation of the United Arab Emirates as a new state, consisting of the Emirates of Abu Dhabi, Dubai, Sharjah, Ras al-Khaimah, Fujairah, Ajman and Umm al-Quwain—Iranian troops occupied the three islands of Abu Musa, Greater Tunb and Lesser Tunb. Abu Musa was occupied by Iran under an agreement reached by the government of Iran and the Ruler of Sharjah, who had held sovereignty over the island, whereas the other two islands were occupied by force after an attempt at negotiating their peaceful transfer from the Ruler of Ras al-Khaimah, under whose jurisdiction they fell, had failed.

The Memorandum of Understanding on Abu Musa, announced on Nov. 29, 1971, contained the following provisions: (i) Iranian troops would be stationed on the northern part of Abu Musa, and in this area the Iranian flag would be flown and Iran would exercise full jurisdiction; (ii) Sharjah would retain jurisdiction over the rest of the island, including the existing Sharjah police post on it; (iii) both Iran and Sharjah recognized a 12-mile territorial waters limit around the island, and both agreed to the existing concessionaire—the (US) Buttes Gas and Oil Company—continuing oil exploration both on the island and offshore; (iv) revenues accruing from oil exploration would be shared equally between Iran and Sharjah; (v) Iran would give Sharjah £1,500,000 a year in aid until Sharjah's annual revenue from oil deposits reached £3,000,000; and (vi) Iranian and Sharjah nationals would have equal fishing rights in the island's territorial waters.

Notwithstanding this agreement, the UAE Council of Ministers stated on Dec. 2, 1971, that the UAE "repudiates the principle of the use of force, rejects Iran's recent occupation of a part of the cherished Arab homeland and advocates the need to respect legitimate rights and discuss any differences that may occur among states through internationally agreed methods".

Conflicting Arab, Iranian and British Views

Iran's action against the three islands was condemned

by all Arab states as an act of aggression against Arab territories, and at the request of Algeria, Iraq, Libya and the People's Democratic Republic of Yemen (South Yemen) the United Nations Security Council met on Dec. 9, 1971, to discuss the situation.

The representative of Iraq claimed during the debate that the islands had been "under Arab jurisdiction for centuries", and he rejected as "invalid" three reasons given by Iran for its action—alleged historical rights, filling a presumed "power vacuum" in the area, and finally the strategic value to Iran of the islands. He also criticized Britain for not honouring its obligation to defend the islands although Britain's special treaty relations with the Arab rulers who held sovereignty over the islands had "not terminated at the time of Iran's occupation of the islands". The representative of South Yemen stated that Iran had never "presented any convincing evidence of its claim to the islands" and had refused to negotiate the matter with the UAE but had chosen to use force.

On the other hand, the representative of Iran declared that the Iranian title to the islands was long-standing and substantial, and that maps, both hundreds of years old and modern, and a highly authoritative encyclopaedia, treated the territories as belonging to Iran; that in line with its policy of settling disputes by peaceful means Iran had tried to settle the problem through negotiation; but that these efforts had failed and Iran had been left with no alternative but to exercise its sovereign right.

The British representative explained that his government was satisfied with the agreement reached on Abu Musa between the Ruler of Sharjah and Iran, and that it had declared that it could not protect the Tunb islands if agreement on their future was not reached before Britain's withdrawal from them (by Dec. 1, 1971). The UN Security Council subsequently decided to defer consideration of the question "in order to allow sufficient time for third-party efforts to work".

Iran's intention to occupy the islands had been stated by the Shah of Iran, who had been reported on Feb. 16, 1971, to have stressed that he would act "by force if necessary" if no peaceful agreement for the islands' transfer was reached before Britain's withdrawal from the Gulf before the end of 1971. The intention was subsequently reaffirmed by Iranian ministers, and on Nov. 10, 1971, Abbas Khalatbari, then Iran's Foreign Minister, was quoted as saying that Iran's sovereignty over the islands was "not negotiable" and that Iran had rejected Arab suggestions that they should be leased to Iran when Britain left the area.

Arguments used by Iran were (i) that the islands had been owned by Iran before they were occupied by Britain 150 years earlier "on the assumption that they were essential to combat piracy" in the Gulf; (ii) that Britain had "in pursuit of its imperial interests" considered the islands as belonging to the Arab Sheikhs of the Trucial States and had transferred them to the de facto administration of Sharjah and Ras al-Khaimah when Iran was "politically weak"; and (iii) that the islands had been shown in Iranian colours on a map which had been issued by the British Intelligence Section of the Ministry of Defence in 1886 and a copy of which had been presented to the Shah in 1888.

In the British view, however, Iran had no title to the islands which, Britain argued, had reverted to the administration of the Trucial coast state of Qawasim by the early part of the second half of the 19th century; the Rulers of Sharjah and Ras al-Khaimah had disclosed documentary evidence based on official British records, supporting their respective "prescriptive title" to the islands since 1872. On instructions from the Ruler of Sharjah on the question of Abu Musa, a firm of British counsels completed (in July 1971) a report based on the examination of "thousands of documents and hundreds of maps and charts" and concluding that Abu Musa had "from the earliest recorded date belonged to the Rulers of Sharjah". The report rebutted in particular the British map of 1886 (see above), stating that the colouring showing Abu Musa as Iranian was "in error" and had not had the consent of the Trucial Rulers.

The Iranian landing on Abu Musa was also criticized by the Arab League, which questioned the validity of the agreement between Iran and Sharjah on the grounds that the latter's Ruler had signed it under duress—i.e. under Iranian pressure and the threat to take over the island by force if no solution satisfactory to Iran were reached. In this context it should be noted that Article 52 of the Convention on the Law of Treaties of May 23, 1969, states: "A treaty is void if its conclusion has been produced by the threat of use of force in violation of the principles of international law embodied in the Charter of the United Nations". It is, however, also important to note that the agreement had been concluded with the British Foreign Secretary acting as the channel of communication between Iran and Sharjah.

The government of Iraq broke off its diplomatic relations with Iran and with Britain on Nov. 30, 1971 (i.e. after Iran's occupation of the islands), and described Iran's action as a "flagrant aggression in collusion with Britain". Iraq also warned Britain that it had "the obligation to preserve the Arab character of the islands". The Arab League, in reports published on Dec. 2, 1971, similarly declared that Britain's failure to act was contrary to its treaty obligations towards the Trucial Rulers. The British Foreign Office, however, argued that it was impossible to stop the Iranian action just one day before the treaty relations were terminated on Dec. 1, 1971—an attitude which was criticized as "hypocrisy" in *The Times* on Dec. 2 on the grounds that a treaty was "as valid on the last day as on the first".

Reaffirmation of Arab Claim to the Islands

The question of sovereignty over the islands was again raised on Oct. 31, 1979, when the Iraqi ambassador in Beirut issued a declaration containing far-reaching political demands to be fulfilled by the government of the Islamic Republic of Iran—among them a demand for the evacuation of the three islands by Iran. All these demands were, however, rejected by Iran on Nov. 1 of that year.

On April 6, 1980, the Iraqi Foreign Minister was reported to have called, in a message to the UN Secretary-General, for the immediate withdrawal of Iranian troops from the islands and to have accused Iran of pursuing "an aggressive and expansionist policy in the Gulf region". On Sept. 24, 1980, following the outbreak of war against Iran, Iraqi President Saddam Hussein announced his intention of restoring the three islands to Arab sovereignty.

The UAE government, in a message to the United Nations reported on Dec. 11, 1980, stated that while it desired to maintain good-neighbourly relations and co-operation to maintain security and stability in the Gulf area, it insisted on the restoration of its full sovereignty over the three islands and declared that it was ready to negotiate with the Iranian government to reach a solution which would fully recognize the UAE's sovereignty over the islands in accordance with the UN Charter and principles. At the same time, the UAE's representative at the United Nations asked for the distribution of this message as an official document of the UN General Assembly.

In a statement published on March 28, 1982, Sheikh Saqr bin Muhammed Al-Qasimi, the Ruler of Ras al-Khaimah and a member of the UAE Supreme Council, said that his country would not compromise or change its position on the issue of the three islands, adding: "The three islands are an Arab right about which there can be no discussion. Iran's rulers know this better than others; however, no contact on this issue has been made between them and us". From 1983 onwards, Iran made repeated patrols into the Sharjah-administered southern part of Abu Musa in breach of the 1971 Memorandum of Understanding. A serious encroachment occurred in 1987 when Iranian forces lowered the Sharjah flag for a short period before re-hoisting it and retreating.

1992 Incidents on Abu Musa

The dispute flared up in 1992 when Iranian authorities on Abu Musa refused entry to certain non-UAE nationals to the Sharjah-administered side of the island. Reports of an Iranian occupation and the expulsion of Arab inhabitants were not subsequently borne out. Sharjah had been increasingly employing non-UAE nationals in its part of Abu Musa, principally as teachers and technicians. With a greatly increased US presence in the Gulf during and after the 1991 war against Iraq, Iran was sensitive about its strategic interests in the lower Gulf and in the summer of 1992, carried out amphibious exercises in the area and strengthened its defences on Abu Musa. Iran also suspected that the UAE was offering large salaries to encourage Arab families to settle on Abu Musa and thus alter the population balance in its favour. A counter-claim of trying to alter the population balance has also been made against Iran by the UAE.

In January 1992, Iran asked Sharjah to be permitted to issue security passes to non-UAE nationals visiting the island from the Emirates, and this was refused. In April 1992, the Iranian authorities on Abu Musa prevented a group of non-national employees of Sharjah from entering the southern side of the island and in August 1992, a ferry carrying over 100 expatriates was turned back. Bilateral negotiations were held in the autumn of 1992 at which the UAE demanded that Iran end its occupation of the Tunb islands. Iran maintained that its sovereignty over the Tunbs was so well grounded that the matter was not open to discussion, and the talks immediately collapsed.

The Arab press and governments responded passionately to the incidents in 1992, strongly criticizing Iran. The Iranian government admitted a measure of responsibility, blaming the incidents on the misjudgement of junior officials, but denied having breached the 1971 Memorandum of Understanding and stated its continued support for the agreement. The UAE argued that Iran's actions had violated the Memorandum and in December 1992 the Gulf Co-operation Council (GCC) called on Iran to "abolish measures taken on Abu Musa island and to terminate the occupation of the Greater and Lesser Tunb islands". The Iranian President, Ali Akbar Hashemi Rafsanjani, responded by stating: "Iran is surely stronger than the likes of you…to reach these islands one has to cross a sea of blood…We consider this claim as totally invalid".

Iran also tried to play down the importance of the 1992 incidents, believing that Arab interests had blown the matter out of proportion. In December 1993, Iran's Interior Minister, Ali Mohammad Besharati, said that the dispute between the two countries was "minor and solvable", while the Deputy Foreign Minister, Abbas Maleki, quipped, "the volume of press coverage on Abu Musa is bigger than the island itself".

While the verbal jousting continued, daily life calmed down on Abu Musa. The ferry to Sharjah was quickly restored, Egyptian teachers who had been refused access in 1992 were able to return in 1993, and the oil-sharing arrangements were never broken. However, Iranian bureaucratic procedures and military patrols were tougher and more active and the issue of security passes remained unresolved.

Iranian Rejection of UAE Proposal for Submission of Dispute to ICJ

The UAE saw the improbability of Iran agreeing to give up the islands through bilateral negotiations and, believing in the merits of its case, announced in November 1994 that it had decided to submit the dispute to the International Court of Justice (ICJ). The UAE Foreign Ministry described this as a "peaceful and positive" step, taken after "exhausting all ways of bilateral dialogue because of Iranian intransigence".

Iran, however, argued that the issue could be solved bilaterally and has consistently opposed the involvement of the ICJ, safe in the knowledge that both parties would have to agree to the submission for the ICJ to be able to try the case. Iran has little to gain from such a submission as it is in possession of the Tunbs and well-entrenched on Abu Musa. Furthermore, the decision of the ICJ in March 2001 to base its judgement on the Bahrain-Qatar dispute on colonial-era boundaries and decisions (see Section 5.3) further reduced Iranian interest in recourse to the ICJ, as Abu Musa and the Tunbs were undeniably Arab in the British period.

The UAE's call for the ICJ to try the case was part of its strategy of Arabizing and internationalizing the issue. The GCC and Arab League became more vociferous in their support of the Emirates, broadening the scale of the dispute from national to regional. Western nations have consistently encouraged a peaceful resolution of the dispute, but have been cautious over their involvement, although the USA has raised concerns about Iranian strategic manoeuvres in the lower Gulf.

In February 1995, Iran significantly remilitarized the northern half of Abu Musa and the lower Gulf more generally. Bilateral talks resumed in Doha at the invitation of the Qatari Foreign Ministry in November 1995, aimed at the "resolution of misunderstandings". Given the clearly stated positions on both sides beforehand it was unsurprising that these quickly broke down as an agenda could not be agreed. In 1996, attempts by Iran to further consolidate its hold on the islands alarmed the UAE. Iran opened a power station on Greater Tunb and an airport on Abu Musa and it was reported that it also planned to build a university campus and stage an international football match on Abu Musa.

Continuing Stalemate

The election of Mohammad Khatami as President of Iran in 1997 helped encourage reconciliation between Iran and the Arab states of the western Gulf. However, the intractable issue of the three islands has continued to hamper moves toward warmer relations.

In November 1997, Dr Kamal Kharrazi, the Iranian Foreign Minister, held talks in Abu Dhabi with Sheikh Zayed bin Sultan al-Nahyan, the President of the UAE, and both sides spoke of reconciliation. Only one month later, however, the UAE protested to the United Nations after Iran named three naval vessels "Tunb-e Bozorg", "Bani Tunb" and "Abu Musa". The GCC summit in December 1997 again called on Iran to "put an end to the use of force to impose de facto policies, stop the building of Iranian installations on the islands...dismantle all installations built unilaterally, and pursue a peaceful resolution of the dispute in accordance with international law by referring it to the International Court of Justice".

In March 1998, Iran expressed its readiness to talk and repeated that there was no reason to refer to third party arbitration as bilateral talks could still work. In May 1998, Kharrazi held talks with his counterpart from the UAE, Sheikh Hamdan bin Zayed al-Nahyan, at which the two ministers stressed the importance of

regional stability. The following month, the Ruler of Ras al-Khaimah described how Iran had recently been exerting pressure to have the 1971 Memorandum of Understanding confirmed by the UAE. He argued the UAE could not do so because Iran had violated the clauses and furthermore the islands were UAE sovereign territory and should be returned. The Iranian Foreign Ministry replied that the islands were "an integral part of Iran's territory". The UN Secretary-General, Kofi Annan, commented that the dispute should be settled bilaterally rather than through international arbitration. Both sides at least agreed that this was the preferable method of resolving the dispute, but continually accused the other of avoiding negotiations and failing to recognize peaceful gestures.

At a meeting of the Foreign Ministers of the Gulf Co-operation Council on March 14, 1999, the UAE Foreign Minister, Rashid bin Abdullah al-Nu'aymi, said that Iran's behaviour in the dispute was "unjustified" and "exposed the region to danger and instability". The *Tehran Times* commented that the Foreign Minister's speech was part of the UAE's "futile routine" and that it should follow a "realistic approach" to the problem. In March 1999 the UAE protested to Kofi Annan over what it described as Iran's "provocative" action in opening a new municipality building on Abu Musa.

As these exchanges continued, it became apparent that there were certain tensions between the UAE and its GCC partners, especially Saudi Arabia, which the Emirates felt were too ready to forge closer relations with Iran while the issue of the three islands remained unsettled. In May 1999, Sheikh Zayed did not attend a GCC Heads of States meeting in Jeddah and in June the UAE threatened to leave the GCC unless the other states tied in progress with Iran with a resolution of the dispute over the islands. There have also been disagreements between the Emirate of Sharjah and the UAE federal government in Abu Dhabi over the handling of the dispute.

In March 2000, *Jane's Defence Weekly* reported that satellite images of Abu Musa and the Tunbs showed no evidence that Iran had fortified the islands militarily, or turned them into "unsinkable aircraft carriers capable of closing the [Hormuz] Strait during a crisis". According to *Jane's* analysis, "the most remarkable aspect about Abu Musa is its lack of major military infrastructure and fortification, despite the fact that it has been under Iranian occupation for 29 years".

On the 29th anniversary of the founding of the UAE in December 2000, Sheikh Zayed said that Iran's continued "occupation" of the islands marred Arab-Iranian relations. Iran responded that the repetition of "baseless assertions" would only intensify misunderstanding and add to regional problems. The December 2000 GCC summit supported the UAE's request that the case should be submitted to the ICJ. Iran's Foreign Ministry spokesman, Hamid Reza Assefi, again rejected such a move, stating: "Our position is clear. The Gulf islands are an integral part of Iran's territory...It is not a court matter". He added that Iran was ready to hold unconditional talks with no international arbitration and no fixed time limits. A GCC committee comprising Qatar, Oman and Saudi Arabia that had been set up in 1999 to mediate in the dispute was dissolved in January 2001 because of Iran's refusal to co-operate. Iran had described the committee as "biased".

Throughout 2001 and 2002, the UAE continued to press for referral to the ICJ and blamed Iranian intransigence for the failure to make any progress. Despite the impasse over the islands, there was a noticeable thaw in UAE-Iranian relations and in July 2002, Sheikh Hamdan bin Zayed al-Nahyan, the UAE Minister of State for Foreign Affairs, visited Tehran. His talks with President Khatami were cordial and constructive and the Iranian President accepted an invitation to visit the UAE. A senior Iranian official described ties between the countries as "good and strong" and was optimistic that a solution to the dispute over the islands was possible. Commerce between the two has grown steadily despite the political rift and in 2002, Iran was the largest market for UAE exports.

In September 2002, the UAE Foreign Minister, Rashid Abdullah, addressing the UN General Assembly, affirmed that the UAE has complete sovereignty over the islands and again called for Iran to solve the issue peacefully either through bilateral talks or the ICJ. In May 2003, the UAE stated once again that it was ready to resolve the dispute through either of these means. For its part, Iran has always stated its readiness to discuss what it describes as the "misunderstanding" over Abu Musa, but will not consider negotiations on the status of the Tunb islands.

Robert Lowe

5.7 Iraq - Kuwait

Iraq's claim to sovereignty over the Emirate of Kuwait, asserted at various times since Kuwaiti independence in 1961, arose from its contention that Kuwait had been an "integral part" of Basra province under Ottoman rule and that Iraq had inherited territorial sovereignty over Basra with the dissolution of the Ottoman empire. Kuwait has always vigorously rejected the claim, arguing that it was never directly ruled by the Ottomans and that agreements reached with Britain and Iraq guaranteed its independence and territorial integrity. Periodic Iraqi official acceptance of Kuwait's independence has in addition not prevented Iraq from attempting to gain territory at Kuwait's expense, particularly the small islands of Warba (99 sq km) and Bubiyan (924 sq km).

Iraq has long felt geographically disadvantaged in its position as a large oil-producing state with little maritime access and blamed the British and its neighbours for allowing it only limited port facilities on the Gulf. Iraqis have comment-

ed that Kuwait is the "cork in the bottle that is Iraq", and this sense of frustration increased their determination to at least acquire sufficient Kuwaiti territory to broaden access to the Gulf, if not to annex the entire Emirate. An alternative access route from Iraq to the Gulf is the Shatt al-'Arab river, ownership of which has been periodically contested by Iran and which is currently divided by a thalweg boundary (see Section 5.5). The state of Iraq's relations with Iran has therefore affected Iraq's need for access to the Gulf and influenced its policies towards Kuwait.

Despite Iraqi recognition of Kuwait as a sovereign state in 1963 and Kuwait's support for Iraq in the Iran-Iraq war in the 1980s, Saddam Hussein revived Iraq's claim to Kuwait and in 1990 invaded and annexed the Emirate. The subsequent defeat of the Iraqi forces by a US-led international coalition forced Iraq to again accept Kuwait's independence and also a new border demarcated by a United Nations commission. Iraqi relations with Kuwait and the United States then remained hostile until a US-led force invaded the country and removed Saddam's regime in March-April 2003. The establishment of a Coalition Provisional Authority under the leadership of the United States, with the expectation that an Iraqi government favourable to the USA will in time be formed, has currently removed the Iraqi threat to Kuwait's border and to the Emirate itself. (Map 56, p. 521, illustrates the Iraq-Kuwait border area.)

Historical Background

Although nominally part of the Ottoman empire from 1546, the town of Kuwait was never under direct Turkish rule. In 1756 the local tribes appointed a sheikh from the al-Sabah family, which still rules the country. In order to defend the city against Wahhabi raiders from Arabia, the al-Sabah formed an alliance with the East India Company, thus coming under British protection, although they continued to pay tribute to the Ottoman empire. In 1871 Sheikh Abdullah was appointed *Qa'immaqam* (Commandant), subject to the Ottoman *Wali* (Governor) of Basra. Sheikh Mubarak the Great seized power in 1896 after murdering his pro-Turkish half brother, Sheikh Mohammed, and asserted Kuwait's independence from the Ottoman empire, saying that his people owed no allegiance to the Turks. To this end Sheikh Mubarak sought protection from Britain and in 1899, without the approval of the Ottoman Sultan, an agreement was signed under which Britain undertook to give Kuwait protection in return for control over its foreign affairs. Under an Anglo-Turkish convention of July 29, 1913, Britain secured Turkish recognition of Kuwait's autonomy within an area formed by a 40-mile radius around the town of Kuwait, but the outbreak of World War I in 1914 prevented ratification of this agreement. On Nov. 3, 1914, Britain promised Sheikh Mubarak that it would recognize Kuwait as an "independent government under British protection" in return for his co-operation in the capture of Basra from the Turks. Kuwait retained this status until June 19, 1961, when an exchange of notes was signed between Britain and Kuwait which terminated the 1899 agreement and by which Britain recognized Kuwait as a sovereign and independent state, although a military assistance agreement remained in force.

Iraq had formerly comprised three Mesopotamian provinces (vilayet) of Baghdad, Mosul and Basra and was administered by the Ottoman empire through appointed governors (pashas) answerable to the Sultan-Caliph in Constantinople. After the dissolution of the Ottoman empire in 1918, it was agreed that Mesopotamia should form a self-governing state and on Oct. 20, 1920, Britain accepted a League of Nations mandate for Iraq until it was ready for independence. Under the Treaty of Lausanne of July 24, 1923, Turkey renounced all the territory it had previously possessed outside the borders of present-day Turkey, including Kuwait as a part of the former Ottoman province of Basra. On Jan. 28, 1932, Britain relinquished its mandate over Iraq and on Oct. 3 of that year, Iraq became an independent sovereign state and was admitted to the League of Nations.

The border between Iraq and Kuwait had first been defined in an exchange of letters, dated April 4 and 19, 1923, between Sheikh Ahmad al-Sabah and Sir Percy Cox, the British high commissioner in Iraq. In a subsequent exchange of letters, dated July 21 and Aug. 10, 1932, Sheikh Ahmad and Nuri as Said, the Iraqi Prime Minister, reaffirmed the "existing frontier between Iraq and Kuwait" on the basis of the 1923 letters as follows: "From the intersection of the Wadi al-Audja with the Batin and thence northwards along the Batin to a point just south of the latitude of Safwan; thence eastwards passing south of Safwan Wells, Jebel Sanam and Umm Qasr leaving them to Iraq and so on to the junction of the Khawr Zobeir with the Khawr Abdulla. The islands of Warba, Bubiyan, Maskan (or Mashjan), Failakah, Auhan, Kubbar, Qaru and Umm el-Maradim appertain to Kuwait". However, this early border demarcation was later regarded as invalid by Iraq on the grounds that Iraq had not been a fully independent state on the date of Nuri as Said's letter of July 21, 1932.

The Iraqi Claim to Kuwait

On June 25, 1961, the Iraqi Prime Minister, 'Abd al-Karim Qasim, claimed that Iraq held sovereignty over Kuwait, which he described as an "integral part of Iraq". A statement issued by the Iraqi Foreign Ministry the following day said that Iraq recognized neither the "secret agreement" of 1889, as it had been concluded without the authority of the Ottoman Sultan, nor the independence agreement between Britain and Kuwait which had recently been reached, as it was intended "under the new cloak of national independence...to maintain imperialist influence and to keep Kuwait sep-

arate from Iraq". The statement added that the Ottoman Sultan had formerly appointed the Sheikh of Kuwait "by a decree conferring on him the title of Qa'immaqam and making him representative of the governor of Basra in Kuwait", and that the Sheikhs of Kuwait had thus "continued to derive their administrative powers from the Ottoman Sultan until 1914". Qasim then issued a decree appointing the al-Sabah sheikh as Qa'immaqam of Kuwait, subject to the government in Baghdad.

The Kuwaiti government immediately rejected the Iraqi arguments, asserting that it had never been subject to Turkish sovereignty and that Kuwait had been governed "without direct Turkish interference" by the same dynasty since 1756. It also claimed that the title of Qa'immaqam was never used in Kuwait and "never influenced the course of life or the independence of Kuwait from the Turkish empire".

In response to a Kuwaiti request for military assistance, prompted by rumours that Iraq was moving troops southwards in the Basra area (which Iraq denied), forces from Britain and Saudi Arabia arrived in Kuwait by early July 1961 and Kuwait's own forces were mobilized. Efforts by the UN Security Council to defuse the crisis were unsuccessful and the mediation was taken on by the Arab League (which on July 20 admitted Kuwait as a member despite Iraqi opposition). On Aug. 12 the Arab League countries, Iraq alone dissenting, signed an agreement with Kuwait by which they pledged to preserve Kuwait's integrity and independence under her existing regime and in the event of any aggression, to render Kuwait immediate assistance and, if necessary, repel it with armed force. Notwithstanding this agreement, Iraq reiterated its claim to Kuwait and withdrew its representatives from all countries which afforded Kuwait recognition.

Developments Following Iraqi Recognition of Kuwait in 1963

The overthrow of 'Abd al-Karim Qasim on Feb. 3, 1963, led to an easing of the friction between Iraq and Kuwait. On Oct. 4, 1963, the new regime, under President 'Abd al-Salam 'Arif, entered into an agreement with Kuwait under which Iraq "recognized the independence and complete sovereignty of the state of Kuwait with its boundaries" as specified in the letters exchanged by Sheikh Ahmed and Nuri as Said in 1932. In addition, the two countries agreed to work towards improving relations and establishing co-operation at all levels and decided to immediately establish diplomatic relations at ambassadorial level.

Nevertheless, it became apparent that Iraqi recognition of Kuwait did not involve acceptance of the latter's frontiers, and in succeeding years long-standing Iraqi claims to certain parts of Kuwait's territory were revived. Iraq's interest lay particularly in improving its access to the Gulf through the acquisition of the islands of Warba and Bubiyan, the importance of which had increased considerably in view of Iraq's development of the north Rumailah oilfield and the expansion of its port of Umm Qasr. In March 1973, with a view to forcing the issue, Iraqi forces occupied a border post in the disputed area but were forced to withdraw when confronted with Arab disapproval of the action. Subsequently, talks between Iraq and Kuwait on the border issue were stepped up, with other Arab countries offering their assistance in mediation, and in May 1975 Iraqi officials announced that they had made concrete proposals to settle the dispute. These involved Kuwait leasing half of Bubiyan to Iraq for 99 years and ceding sovereignty over Warba in return for Iraqi recognition of Kuwait's land borders.

Negotiations reached an impasse on July 12, 1975, when the Kuwaiti National Assembly, while expressing support for the efforts latterly made, stressed "Kuwait's sovereignty over all its territory within the borders which have been approved in accordance with international and bilateral agreements between Kuwait and its neighbours". On Dec. 13, 1976, Kuwait's Minister of Information, Sheikh Jabir al-Ali, stressed that Warba and Bubiyan belonged to Kuwait as defined in the 1932 exchange of letters and the 1963 agreement between Iraq and Kuwait. He also complained that, in addition to the "previous Iraqi military presence in Kuwait territory" south of the Umm Qasr area, there were now "regular crossings by Iraqi forces all along the border between the two countries at varying depths".

Talks on the delimitation of the Iraq-Kuwait border made little progress over the following years, despite the formation in 1978 of a joint committee headed by the Interior Ministers of the two countries to work towards resolving outstanding issues. The outbreak of war between Iraq and Iran in September 1980 led to a revival of the Iraqi claim to Warba and Bubiyan in July 1981, when President Saddam Hussein repeated the Iraqi proposals of 1975 and in particular the demand that Kuwait should grant Iraq a 99-year lease of half of Bubiyan. The Kuwaiti government continued to assert its sovereignty over both islands, and in December 1981 a Kuwaiti spokesman said that no agreed date existed for a resumption of talks between the two sides.

Having become a member of the Gulf Co-operation Council (GCC) on its formation in May 1981, Kuwait followed the GCC's policy of supporting Arab Iraq's cause against Iran, a non-Arab country which was seen as having expansionist ambitions in the Gulf area. In consequence, relations with Iraq improved in the 1980s as the Gulf war dragged on and as Kuwaiti installations and ships themselves became the targets of Iranian air attacks. Moreover, with the Iraqi port of Basra on the Shatt al-'Arab waterway closed, Iraq became increasingly dependent on Kuwaiti transit facilities for access to the sea.

On the occasion of an official visit to Baghdad by Sheikh Sa'ad al-Sabah of Kuwait in mid-November 1984, Iranian radio claimed that Kuwait had reached an agreement with Iraq under which the latter obtained use of Bubiyan and two other islands in the Gulf. The broadcast also quoted a speech by the Speaker of the Iranian Parliament, Hojatolislam Hashemi Rafsanjani, warning Kuwait "not to play with fire" and to take notice that, if Iran were to capture Bubiyan, Kuwait would have no territorial claim to the island. The Kuwaiti Defence Minister responded on Dec. 2, 1984, stating that in view of recent threats Kuwaiti troops and air defences had been deployed on Bubiyan.

Following the purchase of surface-to-air missiles from the USSR in January 1985, in 1986 Kuwait signed a $230 million arms deal with the USA, thus becoming one of the few Middle East states to be armed by both superpowers. In 1987, the USA, the USSR and the UK agreed to the re-flagging of Kuwaiti tankers as a defence against continuing Iranian attacks, while several European countries sent minesweepers to clear the approaches to Kuwait harbour. Meanwhile, Iran fired a number of missiles into Kuwait, threatening to embroil it in the Iran-Iraq war.

Aftermath of the Iran-Iraq War—Build-up to 1990 Invasion

At the end of the Iran-Iraq war in July 1988, Iraq faced immense problems. Although Saddam Hussein proclaimed himself the victor, his country was almost bankrupt. Iraq's total international debt was estimated at $80-85,000 million and debt servicing required an annual $8,000 million, while its foreign reserves were no more than $2,000 million. Further huge sums were needed for post-war reconstruction, while the fading of the Iranian threat removed the incentive for other Gulf states to support the Iraqi economy. Added to this, the fall in world oil prices, from about $28 per barrel in July 1985 to half this in 1988-89, caused further economic damage to Iraq.

About $16,000 million of this debt was owed to Kuwait, which had provided much of Iraq's finance during the war with Iran. Iraq, which claimed that it had fought the war on behalf of the whole Arab world, argued that Kuwait had recouped this money through an increase in oil production, to compensate for the fall in Iraqi production. The Iraqi government stated that this sum should therefore be considered as the Kuwaiti contribution to a common struggle, rather than as a loan.

An additional source of conflict between Kuwait and Iraq was the apparent willingness of the latter to reach an agreement with Iran for joint control of the Shatt al-'Arab, leaving Iraq without full control over access to the port of Basra. Umm Qasr would thereby replace Basra as Iraq's major port, thus reinforcing Iraq's demand for concessions over the key islands of Warba and Bubiyan. In 1989, Iraq protested at Kuwaiti plans to build a causeway linking Bubiyan island to the mainland, and to build a new city, Subiya, on Bubiyan.

The continuing over-production of oil exacerbated relations between the two countries. At a meeting of the Organization of Petroleum Exporting Countries (OPEC) in March 1990, both Kuwait and the UAE refused to reduce their production to within agreed quotas, and although they agreed on cuts at an emergency meeting in May, they did not observe them. Kuwait's OPEC quota for 1990 was 1,500,000 barrels per day (bpd), but its actual production reached 2,150,000 bpd in March, dropping to 1,750,000 bpd in July. The price of oil fell from $19.60 per barrel on Feb. 20 to $15.60 on June 5. Iraq claimed that a fall of $1 per barrel cost its economy $1,000 million per year, and an independent report in July 1990 argued that if the OPEC agreed price of $18 per barrel was reached, Iraq's deficit would be halved.

Iraq believed that Kuwait was deliberately weakening the Iraqi economy in support of its Western allies. On July 17, 1990, the Iraqi Foreign Minister, Tariq Aziz, accused unnamed Arab states of helping the USA to undermine Iraqi security and complained to the Arab League that Kuwait had encroached on Iraqi territory, stolen oil from the Iraqi Rumailah oil field to the value of $2,400 million and refused to cancel Iraqi debts. He also claimed that over-production of oil had cost the Arab world $25,000 million since 1987. These complaints were accompanied by troop movements in the south of the country and on July 18 Kuwait placed its army on a state of alert and called on the Arab League to arbitrate in the border dispute. Despite mediation attempts by Saudi Arabia and Yemen, by July 24 Iraq had massed 30,000 troops on the border with Kuwait. However, neither the other Arab states nor the USA responded strongly to this Iraqi threat. Indeed, the US ambassador to Iraq, April Glaspie, was reported to have told Saddam Hussein in a meeting in Baghdad on July 25 that "we have no opinion on the Arab-Arab conflicts, like your border disagreement with Kuwait".

At a meeting of OPEC oil ministers on July 27, Kuwait and the UAE agreed to reduce their production by twenty per cent and to observe the quota. Iraq demanded that the basic reference price be raised to $25 per barrel and it was agreed to set a new price of $21. At a meeting in Jeddah on July 31, by which date there were 100,000 Iraqi troops on the Kuwaiti border, Iraq demanded $2,400 million compensation for the allegedly stolen oil, cancellation of $20,000 million in debts, $10,000 million in development aid and the cession of Bubiyan and Warba. Despite some Kuwaiti concessions, the talks broke down after only two hours and it was agreed to hold further talks a few days later in Baghdad.

Iraqi Invasion of Kuwait—International Response

On Aug. 2, 1990, Iraq invaded Kuwait, claiming that Kuwaiti popular revolutionaries had invited its forces in. The United Nations Security Council immediately passed Resolution 660 stating that the UN: "Condemns the Iraqi invasion of Kuwait; demands that Iraq withdraw immediately and unconditionally all its forces to the positions in which they were located on 1 August 1990; calls on Iraq and Kuwait to begin immediately intensive negotiations for the resolution of their differences".

On Aug. 3, Arab League Foreign Ministers meeting in Cairo also called for an immediate and unconditional Iraqi withdrawal. Saudi Arabia, fearing that Saddam had designs on its vast oil reserves, invited "friendly forces" to strengthen its defences. On Aug. 10, an emergency Arab League summit called for the withdrawal of Iraqi troops, the restoration of Kuwaiti sovereignty and the reinstatement of the legitimate government, and agreed to send a pan-Arab force to defend Saudi Arabia.

Iraq established a Provisional Kuwaiti Free Government on Aug. 4. All of its members were Iraqi officers, and its head, Colonel Ala Hussein Ali, was Saddam Hussein's son-in-law. Iraq annexed Kuwait on Aug. 8 and on Aug. 28 declared it the 19th province of Iraq. Warba and Bubiyan, the border area around Abdali, and the southern part of the Rumailah oil field were separated from the rest of Kuwait and attached to Basra Province, as the region of Saddamiyat al-Mitla'a. Iraq also ordered the closure of all embassies in Kuwait, and started to round up and arrest all foreign nationals.

The UN Security Council passed further resolutions imposing sanctions on Iraq, condemning the annexation of Kuwait, calling on Iraq to release all foreigners and allowing the use of force against shipping in order to enforce sanctions. Iraq insisted on "linkage" between the questions of Kuwait and Palestine, and on Aug. 12 Saddam Hussein proposed that if Israel withdrew from the occupied territories and Syria from Lebanon, he would then be prepared to discuss Iraqi withdrawal, taking into account Iraq's claim to Kuwait.

In an attempt to gain support and reduce the impact of sanctions, Saddam tried to bribe some of his neighbours with promises of cheap oil and territorial gain. He proposed the partition of Saudi Arabia, with Jordan receiving the Hijaz and Yemen receiving 'Asir, and called on the Egyptian and Saudi people to overthrow their governments. Meanwhile, Kuwait was plundered, with much of its property being removed to Iraq. Kuwaiti resistance was quickly crushed, though there were occasional reports of guerrilla activity. Several more resolutions were passed by the UN Security Council, most notably Resolution 678, agreed on Nov. 29, which authorized the use of "all necessary means" against Iraq unless it fully implemented Resolution 660 and all subsequent resolutions on or before Jan. 15, 1991.

The first US troops had arrived in Saudi Arabia on Aug. 8, 1990. By the end of the year they had been joined by forces from a vast international coalition, including the Gulf Co-operation Council countries, bringing the number of troops lined up against Iraq to 580,000. The Kuwaiti government was re-established in exile in Ta'if, Saudi Arabia. Iraq crushed any internal resistance, with about 7,000 Kuwaitis killed and 20,000 missing, and 400,000 Kuwaitis fled the country. A fresh-water canal linking Kuwait to the Shatt al-'Arab and new roads and railways were built, connecting the country to Iraq. Kuwaiti oil production dropped to about 50,000-100,000 bpd, much of which was being used to flood defensive ditches. The Kuwaiti government estimated the total damage at $64,000 million.

Gulf War of 1991

By Jan. 15, 1991, despite intensive diplomatic activity, Iraq showed no sign of complying with the UN resolutions requiring its withdrawal from Kuwait. On Jan. 17 the allied forces launched an intense air and missile attack on targets in Iraq and Kuwait, at the start of the war code-named Operation "Desert Storm". Iraq responded by firing Scud missiles into Israel, in the hope that an Israeli military intervention would unite the Arab world against the allied attack on Iraq. Contrary to earlier fears, these missiles did not contain chemical warheads, and caused only minor casualties. The USA supplied Israel with Patriot anti-missile missiles and Israel was prevailed upon not to jeopardize the allied war effort.

The US Commander-in-Chief of the allied forces, General Norman Schwarzkopf, stated on Jan. 18 that 2,000 bombing sorties a day were being flown. Iraq was also subject to heavy missile attack. The main targets included military bases and airfields, command headquarters, industrial and oil installations, fixed and mobile missile launchers, transport and communications. The Iraqi airforce avoided combat and over 100 planes were flown across the border into Iran in order to avoid destruction. It was alleged that allied bombing caused thousands of civilian deaths and 314 people were killed in an attack on a Baghdad air-raid shelter on Feb. 13.

The first Kuwaiti territory to be recaptured was the island of Qaru, taken by the British Royal Navy on Jan. 24. Umm al-Maradim was recaptured five days later. Iraq then conducted a number of small raids into Saudi Arabia, but these were quickly beaten back. Continuing international diplomatic efforts, including peace proposals by the USSR, Pakistan and Iran, failed to end the war. The UN Security Council met from Feb.13-15 and for the first time Iraq indicated willingness to co-operate with Resolution 660. However, it ignored a US deadline of Feb. 23 to withdraw from Kuwait.

The aerial war continued for 39 days until Feb. 24, when a massive ground offensive was launched against Iraq. On Feb. 25 Iraq announced that it accepted the Soviet peace proposal and would withdraw from Kuwait. The allied governments refused a ceasefire, however, claiming that the Iraqi proposal amounted to a conditional withdrawal only. On Feb. 26 Iraqi forces retreated from Kuwait City, and Kuwaiti troops re-entered the city the following day. By this time, Iraq had reportedly totally withdrawn from Kuwait, and the Iraqi ambassador to the UN indicated Iraq's willingness to accept all twelve relevant Security Council resolutions. However, the war continued with allied governments convinced that Iraq was still playing for time. Large numbers of Iraqi troops were killed while retreating from Kuwait and more than 600 of Kuwait's oil wells were set on fire before the withdrawal.

On Feb. 28 the USA announced the suspension of offensive operations and on March 3 the Security Council adopted Resolution 686, reaffirming all previous resolutions and laying down conditions for a permanent ceasefire: the immediate release of all POWs and other foreign detainees; Iraqi co-operation in the clearance of mines from Kuwait; compliance with all UN resolutions and an Iraqi agreement to pay compensation. This was accepted by Iraq. A United Nations Iraq-Kuwait Observer Mission (UNIKOM) was set up to supervise the ceasefire, and a demilitarized zone 240 km long was established extending ten miles north and five miles south of the border. 1,400 troops were deployed by UNIKOM in the demilitarized zone by May 6, 1991.

The United Nations Iraq-Kuwait Boundary Commission

Under the terms of Security Council Resolution 687 of April 3, 1991, the UN set up the United Nations Iraq-Kuwait Boundary Commission (UNIKBC) to demarcate the border between Iraq and Kuwait. The demarcation would take place without negotiation, but in accordance with Resolution 687, which asked both countries to respect the security of the international borders agreed upon by the two states in 1963. Iraq complained that Resolution 687 and the establishment of UNIKBC were unfair as the Commission's remit conflicted with earlier UN assurances that border issues would be solved by negotiation and not by enforcement.

The commission was chaired by an Indonesian, two members were nominated by Kuwait and Iraq, and two were from New Zealand and Sweden. Having considered the location of features identified vaguely in earlier agreements—such as "a point just south of the latitude of Safwan" and the identity of a particular date palm—the commission proposed in April 1992 that the border be moved northwards, in effect accepting the Kuwaiti position. On April 16 Iraq rejected the proposals. Some experts believed that, by reallocating Iraqi territory to Kuwait, and in particular by further restricting Iraq's access to the sea, the ruling, which would become mandatory once ratified by the Security Council, might lead to further conflict in the future.

UNIKBC demarcated the border with permanent pillars by November 1992. In March 1993 it announced a median line delimitation for the Khawr Abdullah and the Khawr Shetana, the water channels separating Iraq's Faw Peninsula from Warba and Bubiyan, and in doing so placed the principal navigation lanes from Umm Qasr to the Gulf, which Iraq had dredged and deepened, in Kuwaiti territorial waters. UNIKBC's final report to the Security Council was presented on May 20, 1993. A list of geographic co-ordinates precisely delimiting the whole boundary was released which pushed the land boundary 600 metres north. Kuwait stated on May 23 that it felt "profound satisfaction" with the UN delineated boundary and affirmed its "complete adherence to the decisions and results of the (UN) committee". Iraq rejected the demarcation complaining that it would "keep the embers burning forever in the Gulf powder keg". The Iraqi Parliamentary Speaker, Sa'di Mahdi Salih, stated that the UN had made its "biggest mistake ever" in redrawing the boundary. The UN Security Council responded that it had not reallocated territory but technically demarcated a border agreed to by both parties in 1963. Iraq organized demonstrations and stone throwing along the border and there were incidents of shooting.

In late May 1993, Kuwait announced the construction of a trench along the new 130-mile border with Iraq in accordance with the UN demarcation line. Skirmishes followed in the autumn of 1993 as Iraqis tried to prevent the trench being built. After spending eighteen months denouncing the border demarcation, Iraq's Revolutionary Command Council issued a decree on Nov. 10, 1994, which recognized "Kuwait's sovereignty, territorial integrity and political independence" and the international borders between Iraq and Kuwait as demarcated by UNIKBC, and stated its respect for "the inviolability of the above borders". Kuwait reacted cautiously, pointing out that previous agreements had been broken by Iraq and demanding the return of Kuwaiti prisoners held in Iraq; it refused to consider normalizing relations while Saddam Hussein's regime remained in power.

Continued Poor Iraq-Kuwait Relations

Through the mid and late 1990s there were continual protests by both sides against border violations and infringements of territorial waters, with accusations of hostile fire common, mostly at sea. Kuwait continued to warn of Iraqi troop deployments near the border although in June 1998, Iraq wrote to the UN Security Council reaffirming its recognition of the country's border with Kuwait as determined by UNIKBC in 1993. Despite US and British air strikes on Iraq in December 1998, UNIKOM reported that Iraq was still fully co-operating in its operations on the border. Iraqi aircraft were unable to operate anywhere near the Kuwaiti border from 1992 because of the enforcement of a no-fly zone across the south of the country by the USA and UK. The zone was patrolled from bases in Kuwait and Saudi Arabia.

In June 1999 Iraq called on the UN to halt what it described as aggression by Kuwait along the land and sea border, and in September 1999 Kuwait said that two of its guards had been killed by shots fired from the Iraqi side. In July 2000 Iraq announced it would not accept a maritime deal agreed between Kuwait and Saudi Arabia, arguing that it took no account of Iraq's "legitimate interests" in the Gulf. Iraq also stated it would not accept any deal reached between Kuwait and Iran on their maritime boundary. Kuwait continued to rule out a resumption of ties with Iraq while the latter continued its "hostile behaviour" and detained Kuwaiti prisoners, estimated by the Kuwaiti government to number 605. Baghdad persistently denied

holding any Kuwaitis. In September 2000, Iraq repeated charges that Kuwait was stealing its oil from disputed border oilfields. An editorial in the ruling Ba'ath Party newspaper *al-Thawra* in April 2001 called for the UN to halve the demilitarized zone. In November 2001 Iraq fired a mortar into Kuwait and Iraqi Prime Minister Tariq Aziz renewed the claim that Kuwait was part of Iraq.

Qatar attempted to broker a deal between the two states at the Arab League summit in Beirut in March 2002 and secured a promise from Iraq not to invade Kuwait again. The head of the Iraqi delegation, Ezzat Ibrahim, stated that "we wish to reach a brotherly accord and re-establish relations between Iraq and Kuwait" and that Iraq "respects the security of Kuwait". In October 2002 Iraq began returning Kuwait's national archive, which had been seized during the seven-month occupation in 1990-91. The Kuwaiti Foreign Minister, Sheikh Sabah al-Ahmed al-Sabah, said: "Even though it [the return of the archives] is important, there is something more important to us, which is the issue of the POWs".

The 2003 War on Iraq

By September 2002 it was apparent that the United States was seriously considering removing Saddam's regime by force. While Iraq was making some conciliatory noises towards Kuwait, the USA and UK were gravely concerned about Iraq's possible capability to launch chemical or biological weapons in addition to its appalling human rights record and ongoing breach of UN resolutions. UN weapons inspectors returned to Iraq in November to resume operations which had been suspended in 1998 when Iraq ended co-operation. After three months, the USA and UK lost patience with Iraq's continued lack of co-operation and argued that Iraq's "material breach" of UN Resolution 1441 provided grounds for war.

Kuwait supported the subsequent invasion of Iraq and allowed US and UK forces to prepare the air and land assault from its territory. Air strikes were launched on March 20, 2003, and were followed by an attack by ground forces with UK troops concentrating on Basra and US troops moving north towards Baghdad, which fell on April 9. US-backed Kurdish forces took Kirkuk and Mosul, and Tikrit fell to US forces on April 14. Senior figures in the Iraqi regime were quickly killed or captured although Saddam Hussein himself disappeared and remained at liberty for several months. A Coalition Provisional Authority was established to govern Iraq until elections could be held for a new Iraqi government.

UN Resolution 1490 on July 3, 2003, recognized that the continued operation of UNIKOM and the demilitarized zone established under Resolution 687 were no longer necessary and noted that UNIKOM had successfully fulfilled its mandate from 1991 to 2003.

In the year following the war, relations between Kuwait and Iraq entered a new phase as the Iraqi Governing Council expressed its hope that the countries could be reconciled as friendly neighbours. Kuwaiti public opinion was highly sensitive to the development of bilateral ties with Iraq and continuing security problems and uncertainty over Iraq's political direction made the government cautious. The fate of Kuwaiti prisoners captured by Iraq in 1990 remained an important issue and the Iraqi authorities stated their willingness to investigate.

Robert Lowe

5.8 Iraq - Saudi Arabia

Following the collapse of Ottoman power in Arabia during World War I, the emergence of what were to become the independent states of Iraq and Saudi Arabia was accompanied by bitter territorial rivalry between the two centres of power, exacerbated by the general absence of defined borders in the vast desert territories of the region. Under the aegis of Britain as the dominant post-Ottoman external power, the boundary between present-day Iraq and Saudi Arabia was first defined under agreements signed in 1922, which also created a neutral zone in the contentious eastern border area between the two states.

Although the status quo established by the 1922 agreements prevailed over the next sixty years, the question of the demarcation of the border and the delimitation of the neutral zone remained a potential source of dispute between the two states, especially after the 1958 revolution in Iraq and that country's gravitation to the radical Arab camp opposed to the conservative line of the Saudi leadership. However, the new constellation of interests created by the 1979 revolution in Iran and the outbreak of the Iran-Iraq war the following year, led Iraq and Saudi Arabia to sign an agreement in December 1981 defining their common border and also providing for the division of the neutral zone between the two countries. Despite subsequent hostile relations between the states, especially during the wars of 1990-91 and 2003, the line of the border was not contested. Iraq did, however, threaten to invade Saudi Arabia in 1990 and this belligerent but impractical threat was only removed with the defeat of Saddam Hussein's regime by a US-led force in April 2003. (Map 55, p. 521, shows the Iraq-Saudi neutral zone.)

Historical Background

By the early 19th century much of Arabia was under the control of the powerful Wahhabi army associated with the al-Saud family, which had risen to power in the sultanate of Najd, centred on Riyadh in central Arabia. In the latter part of the 19th century the al-Rashid family from Hail in the northern Najd defeated the al-Saud, but by the outbreak of World War I Abd al-Aziz (Ibn Saud) had recaptured Riyadh and consolidated his authority in Najd and Hasa further south. Under the 1915 Treaty of Qatif, Britain recognized the independence and territorial integrity of Najd and acknowledged Ibn Saud as ruler of both Najd and Hasa.

After World War I territorial problems and tribal rivalries re-emerged and Ibn Saud sought to take control of Hail. In 1921-22 Ibn Saud, his tribesmen now organized in Ikhwan brotherhoods, defeated the al-Rashids in Hail and spread his sphere of control up to the borders of Transjordan and Iraq, surrounding the kingdom of Hijaz, where the al-Hashimi tribe had latterly become serious rivals to the al-Sauds. Ibn Saud now posed a threat not only to Hijaz but also to Iraq, the new country for which Britain had accepted a League of Nations mandate in 1920—Iraq having previously been administered by the Ottoman empire as the three Mesopotamian provinces of Baghdad, Mosul and Basra. In 1921, Faisal, the son of Sharif Hussein al-Hashimi, the ruler of Hijaz, was crowned King of Iraq with the support of the British.

British interest in eliminating the potential for conflict in Arabia gave rise to the signing of the Treaty of Mohammerah (Khorramshahr) on May 5, 1922, between Ibn Saud and the British high commissioner for Iraq, Sir Percy Cox. This treaty did not define a boundary between Iraq and Najd (Ibn Saud having objected to the "attempt to curb, by an imaginary line in the open desert, the movement of tribes who are accustomed to roam widely in search of pasturage and water"), but agreement was reached on the assignment of the Muntafiq, Dhafir and Amarat tribes to Iraq and the Shammar Najd tribe to Najd. Both sides undertook to prevent mutual aggression by the tribes, whose traditional wells and lands were allocated relative to the respective host government. It was further agreed to "determine the location of these lands and wells and to fix a boundary line in accordance with this principle".

Under two protocols to the Uqair Convention of Dec. 2, 1922, the British defined the Iraq-Najd boundary and also established a neutral zone on the eastern side of the border. The boundary was based on the vague affiliations of nomadic tribes and was essentially a series of straight lines linking identifiable natural features such as palm trees, outcrops or wadis. The protocols stated that the neutral zone "will remain neutral and common to the two governments of Iraq and Najd who will enjoy equal rights to it for all purposes", that border wells would be accessible for tribes from either side and would not be used for military purposes, and that the tribes could choose whether to give allegiance to Iraq or Najd. This rhomboid-shaped zone began at the extremity of Kuwait's western frontier at the junction of the Wadi al-Audja and the Wadi al-Batin, its northern border with Iraq running for some 119 miles and its southern border with Saudi Arabia some 125 miles. At its widest north-south point, the zone measured about 40 miles and had a total area of some 2,500 square miles.

Further Agreements between Ibn Saud and King Faisal

The conclusion of the agreements of 1922 did not put an end to the deep-seated rivalry between Ibn Saud and King Faisal or to tribal conflicts. In 1924-25 Ibn Saud succeeded in annexing Hijaz, while Najd's expansionist policies also threatened Transjordan, which was ruled by Faisal's brother, Abdullah. On Jan. 8, 1926, Ibn Saud was proclaimed King of Hijaz and was recognized as such by Britain in the Treaty of Jeddah signed on May 20, 1927.

Following their conquest of Hijaz, the Ikhwan forces made a series of raids on tribes inside Iraqi territory and Iraq used aircraft to ward of such attacks. In 1929 Ibn Saud was threatened by rebellious Najdi tribes, with the result that he took steps to reach an understanding with King Faisal. In February 1930 the two leaders met on board a ship at the mouth of the Shatt al-'Arab river and as a result of their discussions a Treaty of Friendship and Good Neighbourliness was signed the following year. Under this treaty both parties undertook to take steps to prevent tribal raiding and agreed at the same time that tribes of either country were to be permitted free movement within the territory of the other for pasturage or for purchasing provisions. A permanent frontier committee was established to oversee these matters.

There were no further serious incidents of raiding after the 1930 treaty and generally friendly relations prevailed between the two powers, assisted by the growth of the oil industry in both countries and consequent economic advances and by the gradual extension of administrative control throughout their respective territories. In 1932 the dual kingdom of Hijaz and Najd became the Kingdom of Saudi Arabia and in the same year Iraq was admitted to the League of Nations as an independent state. Four years later the two countries concluded a Treaty of Arab Brotherhood and Alliance.

The 1981 Border Agreement

An agreement concerning the administration of the neutral zone was signed between Iraq and Saudi Arabia in May 1938 but there were no further important developments relating to the zone for many years. In July 1975 the two countries agreed to divide the zone equally by a line drawn as straight as possible, but the agreement remained unratified. However, the potential threat to the stability of the Gulf area posed by the Islamic Revolution in Iran in 1979 and the outbreak of war between Iran and Iraq in September 1980, impelled Saudi Arabia and Iraq to seek closer relations and in particular to achieve a settlement of their common border and the question of the neutral zone.

Talks on these matters reached a positive outcome on Dec. 26, 1981, when the Saudi Interior Minister,

Prince Nayef ibn Abdul Aziz, signed a boundary treaty in Baghdad with his Iraqi counterpart, Sa'adoun Shaker. The treaty equally divided the neutral zone and straightened out the whole boundary to the west of the zone, removing some rather jagged edges which had been drawn under the Uquair protocols. Both sides expressed satisfaction that the frontier had been stabilized. The ratifications of the treaty were exchanged in February 1982, but it was not until 1992 that the text, containing the border co-ordinates, was registered with the United Nations.

Uncertain Relations through Three Wars

During the 1980s, Saudi Arabia strongly supported Iraq in its war with Iran. It did not become militarily involved in the conflict, but provided financial and diplomatic assistance. Following the Iraqi invasion of Kuwait in August 1990, however, fears were expressed that Iraq now threatened Saudi Arabia. On Aug. 6, President Saddam Hussein of Iraq promised to honour the 1981 agreement, but he subsequently made a number of threats of military action against Saudi Arabia and proposed the division of the Kingdom, with Jordan gaining Hijaz, Yemen gaining 'Asir and Iraq controlling the rest of the country. Saudi Arabia allowed US and other forces to use its territory and contributed troops of its own to the multinational force which expelled the Iraqis from Kuwait in January-February 1991. In January 1991 the Iraqi Revolutionary Command Council cancelled all charters and agreements signed with Saudi Arabia since 1968, including the 1981 border treaty. This probably contributed to Saudi Arabia's decision to register the text of the 1981 treaty with the United Nations in the summer of 1991.

Following the war, relations between Iraq and Saudi Arabia failed to improve and the border remained closed other than for the annual passage of pilgrims performing the Haj. Iraq was furious that US and UK aircraft were allowed to use bases in Saudi Arabia to patrol the southern no-fly zone in Iraq, and about 5,000 US troops were stationed in Saudi Arabia from the end of the 1991 war. In January 1999, Saddam stated that the "Saudi rulers have caused great catastrophes for the Arab nation and violated its rights ever since they became a bridge to the foreigner". He also complained that the price of oil had been driven down by Kuwait and Saudi Arabia to deliberately harm Iraq. In August 2000, Saddam denounced the Saudis as "traitors" for helping the US and UK launch attacks on Iraq.

In November 2000, Saudi Arabia announced plans to open its land border with Iraq for the first time in nine years in order to export Saudi goods which were being transported through other countries, mainly Jordan. The UN Security Council's Sanctions Committee on Iraq agreed to open the Ar'ar crossing on the border on Jan. 20, 2001 for the passage of Saudi goods under the "oil-for-food" programme. The border reopened in October 2002, but diplomatic relations between the states remained suspended. On June 10,

2001, Saudi Arabia seized control of an Iraqi crude oil pipeline that crosses its territory to the Red Sea and alleged that Iraq had recently staged a series of raids on Saudi border outposts and killed Saudi border guards. Iraq made similar accusations in return.

In March 2003, during the build-up to war with Iraq, US troops were deployed in Saudi Arabia near the Iraqi border, but the Saudi government stated that the troops were there to receive refugees and it did not allow any attacks from its territory in the subsequent invasion. The USA and its coalition partners launched a military attack on Iraq from Kuwait on March 20 and Baghdad was captured on April 9 (for a fuller account of the conflict, see Section 5.7). The USA then announced it was pulling almost all its forces out of Saudi Arabia as Iraq was no longer considered a threat. In the months following the war, the policing of the Iraq-Saudi Arabia border became a serious issue as the USA claimed that citizens of Saudi Arabia and other countries were crossing it to fight against American forces in Iraq. The Saudis blamed the USA for not effectively occupying abandoned Iraqi border posts.

Robert Lowe

5.9 Kuwait - Saudi Arabia

The Uqair Protocol of 1922 between Kuwait, then a British protectorate, and the Sultanate of Najd, subsequently part of Saudi Arabia, provided for the establishment of a neutral zone immediately to the south of Kuwait over which both sides would have joint sovereignty pending a final settlement. In the 1960s Kuwait and Saudi Arabia reached agreement on the partitioning of the zone and a new international land boundary came into effect. The maritime border between the states and the sovereignty of the Gulf islands of Qaru and Umm al-Maradim were not settled until 2000. (Map 55, p. 521, shows the territorial relationship between Kuwait and Saudi Arabia.)

Historical Background

During the centuries of Ottoman rule over Arabia, the current border region of Kuwait and Saudi Arabia was virtually uninhabited desert, although as a historic route for tribes moving northwards to the more fertile areas of the Tigris and Euphrates rivers, it was the scene of frequent tribal rivalry. In the early 1900s, the territory was disputed by Abd al-Aziz (Ibn Saud), the Sultan of Najd, and Sheikh Salim of Kuwait. Under an Anglo-Turkish convention of July 1913, Kuwaiti autonomy was agreed up to a 40-mile (64-kilometre) radius from the port of Kuwait, but this agreement was never ratified and Ibn Saud did not recognise Kuwaiti sovereignty as extending anywhere beyond the walls of Kuwait town.

The final eclipse of Ottoman authority during World War I gave rise to a fluid situation in which Ibn Saud's forces engaged in armed hostilities with Sheikh Salim. Following a particularly serious raid by Ibn Saud on the Kuwaiti oasis area of Jahra in October 1920, Sir Percy Cox, the British high commissioner in Iraq, decided that a permanent and peaceful boundary should be established. Reports that oil had been found around Khawr Maqtah in the disputed area increased the urgency for an arrangement to be reached.

Upon the death of Sheikh Salim in 1921 and the accession of his nephew, Sheikh Ahmad, Ibn Saud declared that he had no further dispute with Kuwait and that there was thus no need to determine a boundary. The British nonetheless proceeded with their efforts to define lasting borders in the area and at a conference at Al Uqair in December 1922 decided to establish neutral zones between Kuwait and Najd and between Iraq and Najd (for the Iraq-Najd agreement, see Section 5.8). This was the first time the device of a neutral zone had been used in Arabia. The neutral zone between Kuwait and Najd consisted of some 2,500 square miles (6,500 sq km) of desert with a coastline about 40 miles (64 kilometres) long on the Gulf. The Uqair Protocol gave Kuwait and Najd equal rights in the zone "until through the good offices of the government of Great Britain a further agreement is made between Najd and Kuwait".

Najd subsequently became part of the larger Kingdom of Saudi Arabia established by Ibn Saud in 1932, while Kuwait continued as a British protectorate until achieving full independence in 1961.

Partition of the Neutral Zone

The granting of joint sovereignty to both parties in the neutral zone meant that they were obliged to exploit any natural resources there on an equal basis. After the discovery of oil in Kuwait's southern fields in 1938, attention was given to exploration in the neutral zone itself and towards the end of the following decade Kuwait and Saudi Arabia granted exploration rights in the territory to two private companies which later exploited the oil under a joint agreement. In 1948 Kuwait signed a contract with the American Oil Company (Aminoil) and the following year Saudi Arabia reached a similar agreement with the Pacific Western Oil Company (later renamed Getty Oil Company). Both these agreements applied to the area of the neutral zone. In 1957-58 Kuwait and Saudi Arabia granted the Japanese Oil Company separate concessions for offshore fields.

In view of the administrative problems caused by the construction of oil installations and the increased number of workers in the zone, Saudi Arabia and Kuwait began discussions in the late 1950s on the legal status of the zone and its offshore area. By the end of 1960 the parties had agreed that the land area of the neutral territory should be divided into two parts, one to be annexed by Kuwait and the other by Saudi Arabia, and that each country should form a committee of experts to draft boundary lines for the partitioned zone. Although progress was slowed by Kuwaiti protests that Saudi Arabia was exerting excessive control over the zone, further deliberations finally led to an exchange of notes on Aug. 5, 1963. Saudi Arabia and Kuwait reaffirmed their agreement in principle to divide the zone and, on the basis of a Kuwaiti proposal, decided that one government would administer each separate part. Kuwait had rejected an earlier suggestion by Saudi Arabia that a system of joint administration be introduced.

Kuwait and Saudi Arabia signed a Partition Agreement at Jeddah on July 7, 1965, by which the neutral zone was divided into equal shares with the proviso that the "equal rights of the two parties shall be preserved in full in the whole partitioned zone as this had originally been decided by the convention made at Al Uqair". Kuwait and Saudi Arabia would "exercise the rights of administration, legislation and defence" over their own part of the zone, while undertaking to respect the rights of the other to the "shared natural resources" which exist, or might exist, in its own annexed part. Citizens of each country were also guaranteed the freedom to work in the other's part of the zone.

Each country was given the same rights to the territorial waters adjoining both parts of the zone as it had over the land areas of the zone annexed to them. It was agreed that "for the purpose of exploiting natural resources" in the partitioned zone, "not more than six marine miles of the seabed and subsoil adjoining the partitioned zone shall be annexed to the principal land of that partitioned zone". With a view to safeguarding the continued efforts of both parties in exploiting natural resources in the zone, it was agreed that a joint permanent committee would be established, composed of an equal number of representatives from both sides. A demarcation agreement on the dividing line through the zone was formally concluded on Dec. 18, 1968, and became effective almost immediately.

The Maritime Boundary

Talks between Kuwait and Saudi Arabia in the 1960s on the boundaries of the neutral zone had also covered the islands of Qaru and Umm al-Maradim, situated respectively some 23 miles (37 kilometres) and 16 miles (26 kilometres) off the coast of the northern part of the zone. On the basis of an exchange of letters between Iraq and Kuwait in 1923 and 1932 both these islands belonged to Kuwait, but Saudi Arabia contested their sovereignty. In 1961 Kuwait's offer of a share in any oil proceeds from the islands in return for acknowledgement of sovereignty was declined by Saudi Arabia.

Upon its invasion of Kuwait in August 1990, Iraq occupied Qaru and Umm al-Maradim. The allies recaptured the islands in January 1991 and they were returned to Kuwaiti control, although Saudi Arabia had not formally abandoned its claim to sovereignty.

Overlapping Iranian claims in the maritime area contested by Kuwait and Saudi Arabia complicated the

issue of the border. Kuwait and Iran agreed that talks should not begin until an agreement had been reached between the former and Saudi Arabia. In January 2000, Iran began drilling in the offshore Al-Dorra gas field, an area claimed by all three countries. Work was stopped three months later after protests from Kuwait and Saudi Arabia, but Iran maintained it was drilling in its own territorial waters and expressed its readiness to discuss the division of the tripartite zone.

On July 2, 2000, an agreement was reached between Kuwait and Saudi Arabia on their maritime borders, giving Kuwait sovereignty over Qaru and Umm al-Maradim with a one-mile radius around each. It was agreed that the submarine gas reserves, estimated at 370 billion cubic metres, would continue to be shared between the two states. Iraq protested and announced it would not recognize any deal that did not consider its territorial rights. Kuwait and Saudi Arabia signed maps demarcating the maritime border on Jan. 30, 2001, after their completion by a Swedish surveying company. Discussions between Kuwait and Iran on the demarcation of their maritime border were ongoing in 2003.

Robert Lowe

5.10 Other Arabian Peninsula Border Relationships

The international borders of the south and east of the Arabian peninsula remained largely undemarcated until the 1990s, when great progress was made in settling vague or disputed boundaries. Saudi Arabia's borders with Qatar, Oman and the United Arab Emirates and Oman's borders with Yemen and the United Arab Emirates have now been definitively agreed. (Map 57, p. 522, shows location of borders in the peninsula; for Saudi Arabia's border with Yemen, see Section 5.13.)

Saudi Arabia and Qatar

The border between Saudi Arabia and Qatar unexpectedly became a live issue in 1992 after a fatal incident at a border post. In 1965 this land boundary was demarcated across the base of the Qatari peninsula from Duhat as-Salwa in the west to Khawr al-Udaid in the east. Although the text of the 1965 agreement was not made public until 1992, the matter appeared settled between Doha and Riyadh and maps produced in the two countries showed the same boundary.

On Sept. 30, 1992, a serious clash occurred at Khafus on the eastern stretch of the border which left two Qataris and one Saudi dead. Qatar accused Saudi Arabia of attacking the border post, while the Saudi version stated that the clash took place inside Saudi territory between Bedouins from the two countries.

Diplomatic relations between the countries were briefly suspended and the unity of the Gulf Co-operation Council (GCC) was threatened. Mediation by President Hosni Mubarak of Egypt encouraged both sides to agree at the end of 1992 to establish a joint committee to demarcate the boundary in accordance with the 1965 agreement.

The cause of the incident appears to have been political rather than territorial. Neither side contested the alignment of the boundary, but existing political tensions were channelled into an increased sensitivity on the mutual border. Improvements in Saudi-Qatari relations were slow, but in April 1996 the two governments finally announced they had reached agreement on a procedure to demarcate the boundary. On March 22, 2001, the process was completed when the two Foreign Ministers signed the final border demarcation agreement.

Saudi Arabia, United Arab Emirates and Oman

In 1952 a long-standing dispute between Saudi Arabia and Abu Dhabi (subsequently part of the UAE) and Muscat (subsequently part of Oman) over the oil-rich Al Buraimi/Al Ain oasis led to the occupation by Saudi Arabia of the oasis. In 1955 a British-led force comprising troops from Abu Dhabi and Muscat evicted the Saudi force. In 1971 Saudi Arabia ceded three of the villages to Oman, and in 1974, ceded the remaining six to the UAE. The details of the Saudi-UAE border delimitation agreement of 1974 were only made public in 1995. In return for relinquishing its claim to Buraimi, Saudi Arabia secured from the UAE a long-desired land corridor to the Gulf coast southeast of Qatar.

The north-western boundary of Abu Dhabi had long been contested by Saudi Arabia. In 1971 Britain supported the UAE's claim to territory as far as the inlet at Khawr Udaid at the base of the Qatari peninsula. Saudi Arabia also claimed the territory around Khawr Udaid and argued that the newly formed UAE should not stretch as far as the Qatari border. The 1974 agreement gave Saudi Arabia a 15-mile coastline east from Khawr Udaid and removed the land boundary between the UAE and Qatar. The agreement also gave Saudi Arabia sole rights over the 14 billion barrel Shaibah oil field (referred to as Zarara by the UAE), even though 20 per cent of the field lies beneath Abu Dhabi.

This exclusion from the oil field left Abu Dhabi with a sense of injustice and in 1993 Saudi Arabia allowed the UAE to extend its territorial limits slightly to the west at the expense of the Kingdom's territory. In 1995 Saudi Arabia registered the 1974 border agreement with Abu Dhabi at the United Nations. The UAE boycotted a Saudi-hosted GCC oil ministers' meeting held in March 1999, at the same time as the inauguration of the Shaibah field, requesting that the output of the field be shared. Relations were already strained at this time because of the UAE's disapproval of Saudi Arabian moves to improve relations with Iran while the dispute over Abu Musa and the Tunbs remained unresolved (see Section 5.6).

An agreement ratifying the border between Saudi Arabia and Oman was signed on March 21, 1990. This had apparently been agreed some years earlier as a Saudi Military Survey map of 1986 showed the same line for the Omani boundary as Omani maps. In 1995 a ceremony was held in Riyadh to celebrate the joint signature of a series of detailed official maps of the Saudi-Omani border.

Oman and the United Arab Emirates

The territorial limits of the Sultanate of Muscat and the Qasimi sheikhdoms of the Trucial Coast were ill-defined until the mid-1960s when, with British encouragement and technical support, most disagreements were resolved. Disputes later resurfaced in the 1970s between the successor states of Oman and the UAE. Oman claimed Umm al-Zamul in Abu Dhabi and a northern portion of Ras al-Khaimah, the most northerly of the seven emirates, where offshore oil deposits had been found. However, it was announced in Abu Dhabi on Sept. 18, 1979, that full agreement had been reached on the border dispute between the two countries and that in the Omani view, "all principles and bases pertaining to the ending of all border problems had been adopted within a framework of full understanding".

The UAE government announced on April 7, 1981, that the two sides had "agreed on specific bases for the re-demarcation of the border" between Oman and Ras al-Khaimah. This agreement would "finally resolve the issues which have recently been raised" and would preserve "the historic ties between the two fraternal countries". In April 1993, the Omani Foreign Minister, Yusuf bin Alawi bin Abdullah, announced that "the frontier dispute is completely settled", following the signing of a "lasting agreement" between the two states. An accord signed by Oman's Sultan Qaboos and UAE President Sheikh Zayed bin Sultan al-Nahyan in May 1999 formally demarcated the border. In October 2003, the two governments exchanged authenticated documents on the agreement, finally bringing to an end the process of border demarcation.

Oman and Yemen

At independence in 1967, South Yemen (the People's Democratic Republic of Yemen, PDRY) inherited from the British Aden Protectorate an undemarcated border with Oman. Relations between Oman and South Yemen were seriously strained by the support given by the latter to the military activities of the Popular Front for the Liberation of Oman (PFLO) in the Dhofar region of Oman, to which South Yemen had itself laid claim from time to time. Efforts by Kuwait to mediate in the Oman-South Yemen dispute collapsed in 1980 after the Omani government had agreed to make military facilities available to the United States.

Oman reported a number of border incidents in 1981, leading to renewed mediation efforts by Kuwait. In December of that year, South Yemen claimed that

Oman had conducted a helicopter raid on a border village, involving the "abduction" of some South Yemeni citizens.

In 1981 the Foreign Ministers of Kuwait and the United Arab Emirates were entrusted by the Supreme Council of the Gulf Co-operation Council with the task of "exerting efforts to ease tension" between the two states. The Ministers arranged a series of meetings with Omani and South Yemeni officials, culminating in direct talks between the two sides in July 1982. A four-point agreement on normalizing relations, concluded in November 1982, included the decision to form a "technical committee", including Kuwaiti and UAE representatives, to discuss outstanding border problems.

The border committee held two meetings during 1983, in the UAE and Kuwait respectively, and in a joint statement issued in late October of that year the Omani and South Yemeni governments declared that they had agreed to establish diplomatic relations and would shortly exchange ambassadors. Members of the South Yemeni delegation who travelled to Muscat for the third meeting of the border committee in January 1985, were the first official South Yemeni visitors to Oman since relations between the two countries began to deteriorate in the late 1960s.

The fourth meeting of the border committee took place in Aden on Feb. 28-March 2, 1987, at the end of which a press statement recorded that "discussions on the question of the borders between the two countries continued in a cordial and fraternal atmosphere". Further border clashes were reported in October 1987, but these were apparently quickly resolved. President al-Attas became the first head of the PDRY to visit Oman in October 1988, and returned in November 1989, following which Sultan Qaboos of Oman was invited to visit Aden. The two sides signed a co-operation agreement, and agreed all but minor elements of the border dispute.

Following the unification of North and South Yemen in March 1990, the new government of the Republic of Yemen stated that resolution of the border dispute would be a priority. In October 1992, the land boundary delimitation between Oman and Yemen was finalized and a procedure agreed for its demarcation and the manner by which the territorial limit would be extended offshore into the Arabian Sea. In 1995 the demarcation of the boundary delimitation was completed and the official documentation was registered with the Arab League Secretariat.

Former North and South Yemen

The border between the former Yemen Arab Republic (North Yemen) and the People's Democratic Republic of Yemen (South Yemen)—which were unified as the Republic of Yemen in 1990—was never fully demarcated, and the two states had a long-standing border dispute, particularly over the Shabura oil field straddling the border. Brief border wars in 1972 and 1979 had led to failed unification agreements on Oct. 28, 1972, and March 30, 1979.

From March 1979, the two states initiated serious negotiations with a view to eventual unification. Despite Saudi opposition, agreement was reached in late 1981 on the creation of a "Yemen Council" and other joint bodies which were to prepare for the establishment of a unified state.

Following a failed coup and civil war in the PDRY in January 1986, President Ali Nasser Mohammed and several thousand supporters fled to the YAR. The subsequent treason trials provoked tension between the two states. In July 1986, Presidents Ali Abdullah Saleh of the YAR and Haidar Abu-Bakr al-Attas of the PDRY met in Libya to discuss unification.

Both states denied reports of border clashes in December 1987, though in April 1988 both were reported to be reinforcing their border troops. However, during a visit to Sana'a (the capital of North Yemen) in May 1988 by Ali Salim al-Beid, the secretary-general of the ruling Yemen Socialist Party in South Yemen, a declaration was signed. The main terms were: (i) the refusal to recognize any colonial borders, or those drawn up by the former Imam; (ii) an agreement to replace the existing border posts, and start joint running of the new posts; (iii) unrestricted cross-border movement between the states; (iv) the joint withdrawal of troops; and (v) joint exploitation of the cross-border Marib/Shabura oil fields, which would be demilitarized. It was also agreed to reconstitute the Higher Yemeni Council, the Joint Ministerial Committee, and other joint bodies. Former South Yemen President Mohammed, in exile in the North, welcomed the agreements, and pledged not to disrupt the moves; at the end of 1989, he announced his withdrawal from politics.

In November 1989, against the background of growing financial problems in both states, President Saleh met secretary-general al-Beid in South Yemen. They declared a union of their countries within 12 months. A 136-article draft constitution (based on the 1979 agreement) was drawn up and agreed, and a multi-party government established in Sana'a. The two agreed on immediate mergers of their Interior Ministries and the state airlines, a joint currency, a new press law, joint cabinet meetings, and the release of political prisoners (there were also many refugees from the PDRY in the YAR).

The moves to unity were opposed by some communists in the PDRY and Islamic fundamentalists in the YAR. Further, although Saudi Arabia formally accepted unification, in private it was concerned at the prospect of a large and populous multiparty democracy on its borders. Following several clashes during March-April 1990, and in order to forestall internal or external opposition to the merger, the date was brought forward. On May 21, 1990, the PDRY parliament in Aden voted unanimously for immediate unification. In the YAR parliament in Sana'a on the same day, three Islamic fundamentalists walked out of the vote and a further five abstained.

On May 22, 1990, the two parliaments met together to establish the Republic of Yemen, and elected a

Joint Presidential Council with Saleh as President and al-Beid as Vice-President. The two parliaments were merged, with elections were to be held during 1992. A referendum on unity, held on May 15, 1991, was boycotted by the fundamentalist Yemen Reform Group. Less than 50 per cent of the population voted, of whom 98.3 per cent voted for unification.

In August 1993, Vice-President al-Beid withdrew to Aden, claiming that the south was being marginalized in the new united state. The armies of either side had failed to fully integrate and began mobilizing as relations between their leaders continued to deteriorate. In May 1994, al-Beid announced the secession of the Democratic Republic of Yemen. President Saleh declared the illegality of the move and announced a state of emergency. After a brief civil war, northern forces took control of Aden in July 1994 and the secessionist leaders fled abroad and were sentenced to death in absentia.

Qatar and Iran

Although the two states had signed an agreement in 1969 on their maritime boundary, in 1989 Iran claimed that 30 per cent of Qatar's North Field lay under Iranian territorial waters, and announced plans to extract it. The gasfield, known in Iran as the South Pars Field, is the largest natural gas field in the world. The amicable relations that currently exist between the countries have helped ease potential tensions over these resources and have allowed for technical co-operation rather than confrontation.

Robert Lowe

5.11 Syria - Turkey (Hatay)

The separation of the Sanjak of Alexandretta from the French mandated territory of Syria and its incorporation into Turkey in 1939 has never been formally accepted by Syria and has caused periodic tensions between the two countries. The Sanjak became the Turkish province of Hatay, its principal towns being the Mediterranean port of Iskenderun (formerly Alexandretta) and Antakya (formerly Antioch). (Map 58, p. 522, illustrates the position of Hatay.)

Historical Background—Establishment of Autonomous State of Hatay

The Sanjak of Alexandretta (including Antioch) was a province of the Ottoman empire from 1516 until the empire's demise at the end of World War I. Occupied by French forces in 1918, the Sanjak was subsequently, under the 1921 Franklin-Bouillon agreement, incorporated into the territory of greater Syria which had been mandated to France by the newly established

League of Nations in 1920. It thereafter formed one of the five "natural anthropo-geographical regions" into which the French divided the mandated territory, the others being (i) Arab Syria, (ii) the coastal territory of Latakia (present-day Al Ladhiqiyah), (iii) Christian Lebanon and (iv) the region further south inhabited by the semi-nomadic Jebel Druse. Of these components, areas (i) and (ii) subsequently became the independent state of Syria and areas (iii) and (iv) the independent state of Lebanon. The Sanjak of Alexandretta, however, was regarded by the French as a special case because of its substantial Turkish population.

Although Turkey formally renounced its former possessions under the 1923 Treaty of Lausanne, the conclusion in September 1936 of a treaty between France and Syrian representatives, providing for Syria to become independent after a transitional period, led the Turkish government of Kemal Ataturk to raise the question of the Sanjak of Alexandretta at the League of Nations. Whereas France envisaged at that stage that the Sanjak would be under the sovereignty of an independent Syria, the Turkish government claimed that a majority of its population were Turks and that it should therefore be administered completely separately from Syria. At a meeting of the League's Council in December 1936, the French representative stated that when Syria achieved independence (the date of which had not yet been determined) the existing special administration of the Sanjak would be observed, with the rights of Turks in the region being guaranteed; he also rejected Turkish demands for the Sanjak to be granted separate independence, maintaining that such a course would be contrary to the terms of the French mandate. The meeting concluded with Turkey and France reaching a provisional agreement that ratification of the Franco-Syrian independence treaty would be postponed to allow time for a League committee to investigate and report on the situation in the Sanjak— until such ratification, Hatay's future remaining technically within France's jurisdiction.

The report of the League's investigating committee (which included French and Turkish members) was presented on May 24, 1937, and contained a draft statute for an autonomous Sanjak of Alexandretta which was endorsed in all essentials by France and Turkey on May 28. Under the statute (i) the Sanjak would have full control over its internal affairs; (ii) Syria would have responsibility for foreign, diplomatic and consular affairs; (iii) the Sanjak and Syria would have the same customs and monetary administrations; (iv) the Sanjak and Syria would each accredit a commissioner to the other in order to maintain liaison; (v) the Sanjak would be completely demilitarized and compulsory military conscription prohibited, with public order being maintained by a gendarmerie of 1,500 men; (vi) the rights of minorities would be guaranteed without distinction as to birth, nationality, language, race or religion; (vii) Turkey would be guaranteed full use of the port of Alexandretta and leased an area for its customs administration; (viii) a unicameral Assembly of 40 members would be elected in the

Sanjak, which would have an Executive consisting of a President and a four-member executive council; (ix) Turkish and Arabic would have equal status as the Sanjak's official languages; and (x) elementary education would be compulsory and freedom of the press would be guaranteed.

The adoption of the statute provoked serious inter-communal violence in the Sanjak, where martial law was declared on June 6, 1937, in response to a general strike by Arabs (both Muslim and Christian) and Armenians in protest in particular against the acceptance of Turkish as an official language. Disturbances continued over the following year and intensified in the early months of 1938 as the authorities attempted to accomplish the registration of voters for elections to the new Assembly. During this period there were several reports of Turkish troop concentrations on the northern border and the Turkish government repeatedly protested against the alleged mistreatment of Turks in the Sanjak. On Dec. 7, 1937, Turkey unilaterally abrogated its treaty of friendship and non-aggression with Syria (originally concluded on May 30, 1926, for five years and subsequently renewed annually).

A central issue at this time was whether, as claimed by the Turkish government, Turks constituted a majority of the Sanjak's population, or whether, as claimed by Syrian nationalists, there were over 100,000 Muslim Arabs, about 25,000 Christian Arabs and Armenians and only 85,000 Turks. A census conducted by the French authorities early in 1938 (on a system advocated by the Turkish government) found that Turks constituted 46 per cent of the population, a finding subsequently disputed both by Turkey and by the Syrians (the latter because it gave the Turks as being the largest single population group in the Sanjak). Syrian and internal Arab protests mounted when it became known in June 1938 that France and Turkey had agreed, on the basis of the "preponderance" of the Turkish population, that Turks would have 22 of the 40 Assembly seats and also that Turkish army officers had arrived in the Sanjak to co-operate with French forces in the maintenance of order. Actions taken by deputies in the Syrian parliament in Damascus included the sending of telegrams to independent Arab rulers urging them to intervene to preserve the Sanjak as part of the Arab world.

Notwithstanding Syrian Arab opposition, France proceeded to sign a series of four agreements with Turkey on July 3-4, 1938, effectively recognizing Turkish predominance in the Sanjak as well as Turkey's special interest in the province. The first of these agreements was a military convention (signed in Antioch on July 3) providing that, pending the normal functioning of the Sanjak's new statute, the province would be garrisoned by 2,500 French troops, 2,500 Turkish troops and 1,000 men raised locally; it was specified that the Turkish forces (which entered the Sanjak on July 5) would be stationed in the predominantly Turkish parts of the province. The other three agreements (all signed in Ankara on July 4) were (i) a declaration that France and Turkey would apply the

new statute on the basis of the preponderance of the Turkish element of the Sanjak, but on the understanding that Turkey had no territorial claim; (ii) a protocol concerning the rights and interests of persons of Turkish, Syrian or Lebanese origin residing in the territory of the other party and wishing to adopt the nationality of their country of residence; and (iii) a treaty of friendship affirming the desire of both parties to maintain peace in the eastern Mediterranean.

Prior to the signature of these agreements, it had been announced from the League of Nations headquarters in Geneva on June 24, 1938, that the Assembly elections had been postponed and that a League commission sent to supervise them had been withdrawn principally because the Turkish government opposed its presence in the Sanjak and no longer recognized its status. On June 13, 1938, the British member of the League commission had resigned, reportedly because he disapproved of actions being taken by the French authorities against the non-Turkish sections of the Sanjak's population.

The Assembly elections were eventually held at the end of August 1938 and Turkish representatives duly obtained 22 of the 40 seats. At the Assembly's inaugural session on Sept. 5 a former deputy in the Turkish National Assembly, Tayfour Seukmen, was elected President and the Sanjak was officially renamed Hatay. The same session declared (i) that Hatay was "a republican state upheld by a Turkish majority and enjoying absolute independence in its internal affairs"; (ii) that the capital and seat of government would be at Antakya (Antioch); (iii) that all citizens would have equal rights before the law, irrespective of race or religion; (iv) that public order would be maintained by a gendarmerie of not more than 1,500 men; and (v) that the flag of Hatay would be a white crescent and star on a red background, modelled closely on Turkey's own flag. In a message to the Turkish National Assembly, President Seukmen stated that the political principles of the new state would be those of "Kemalism" as practised in Turkey itself.

Incorporation of Hatay into Turkey

In terms of sovereignty, the autonomous state of Hatay remained part of French mandated Syria, the proposed independence of which under the 1936 Franco-Syrian treaty was repeatedly postponed by France in view of the worsening international situation. On the basis of the July 1938 agreements, France subsequently developed its relations with Turkey, principally with the aim of ensuring that in the event of another European war Turkey would not follow the example of the Ottoman empire (in World War I) by taking the side of Germany. This process culminated in the signature in Paris on June 23, 1939, of a Franco-Turkish declaration of mutual assistance "in the event of an act of aggression leading to war in the Mediterranean" (a similar UK-Turkish agreement having been signed on May 12). On the same day, a separate Franko-Turkish agreement was concluded in Ankara providing for the cession of Hatay to Turkey.

Ratified by the Turkish National Assembly on June 30, 1939, and backed by a local plebiscite, the Hatay agreement contained the following main provisions: (i) Turkish sovereignty over Hatay would be unconditional; (ii) Turkey recognized the inviolable character of the newly drawn Syrian frontiers and undertook to refrain from any form of activity likely to compromise either the territorial integrity of Syria or peace within its borders; (iii) non-Turkish elements who did not wish to become naturalized Turkish citizens would have the right to opt for Syrian or Lebanese nationality within the space of six months, those so opting being obliged to leave Hatay within 18 months (and being entitled to take their moveable property with them); and (iv) the strategically important heights of Jebel Akra to the south of Antakya would remain within the Syrian borders.

In accordance with the agreement, the evacuation of the French administration from Hatay was completed on July 23, 1939, and a new Turkish governor formally assumed control the same day. Celebrations were held throughout Turkey to mark the completion of the transfer. Among Syrian Arab nationalists, however, the cession was vigorously condemned as an illegal act, protest demonstrations being held in Damascus and other Syrian cities. When Syria finally achieved independence during World War II, the cession continued to be regarded as illegal by the Syrian government, although it received no support in this position from governments outside the Arab world. In the event, the frontier established between Syria and Turkey in the west followed the old boundary of the Sanjak of Alexandretta, so that the Jebel Akra heights formed part of Turkish territory.

Continued Maintenance of Syrian Claim to Hatay

The Turkish government announced its recognition of the independence of Syria (and of Lebanon) on March 6, 1946, but in subsequent years Syrian-Turkish relations underwent periods of severe strain, particularly after Turkey became a member of the North Atlantic Treaty Organization (NATO) in 1952. While Syria did not actively prosecute its claim to Hatay, it did not renounce its view that the 1939 cession by France was illegal, and the issue remained a source of friction.

From time to time Syria published official maps showing the province as part of its territory. After one such map had been published by Syria in a brochure for the 1987 Mediterranean Games, Hasan Celal Guzel (Turkish Minister of State) said in answer to a parliamentary question on March 19, 1987, that Syria's claim on Hatay constituted "one of the negative factors in Turkish-Syrian relations". He continued: "We, on every occasion, remind Syria that Hatay is an inseparable part of Turkey and that claims on this province damage Turkish-Syrian relations, which both countries wish to develop". He added that in response to Turkey's protest, the offending brochure had been withdrawn and a new version issued with a map showing Hatay as part of Turkey.

A *Daily Telegraph* report of mid-1998 stated that barbed wire fencing and "millions of land mines" still separated Turkish Hatay from Syria. During a cross-border crisis in 1998 resulting from Turkish allegations of Syrian support for Kurdish Workers' Party (PKK) guerrillas, Turkish President Suleyman Demirel explicitly warned Damascus not to raise the Hatay issue; and at the same time, Turkish Prime Minister Mesut Yilmaz pointedly used a visit to Hatay to denounce Syrian claims on the province.

The province of Hatay contains a large minority of Alawite Arabs, whose treatment particularly concerned Syrian Presidents Hafez al-Assad and, after his death, his son and successor, Bashar al-Assad. The Assads are members of the Alawite religio-ethnic community, a considerable minority in Syria. Alawites follow a syncretist faith that split from Shiite Islam. Most live in or originate from Syria's Latakia province, bordering Hatay. Since 1970 they have enjoyed disproportionate power in Damascus' Baath regime. Many Syrian Alawites claim that their brethren in Hatay suffer officially sanctioned discrimination from the province's majority Sunnis, both Turkish and Arab in ethnicity.

Access to water has been a source of continuing strain in relations between Turkey and Syria. The Euphrates originates in Turkey and wends through Syria before entering Iraq, and Turkish damming and irrigation schemes have threatened the flow in Syria. The Syrian government has called for a permanent accord, whereas Turkey has resisted such an arrangement until the Hatay dispute is resolved. There is also a more direct connection between water politics and Hatay, in that Turkey opposes dams that Syria has built on the smaller al-'Asi River. Better known by its ancient name, Orontes, this waterway rises in Lebanon, passes through Syria, and curves back into Turkish territory before emptying into the sea through the province of Hatay. In this instance, the roles are reversed, with Turkey fearing that Syria has the power to deprive Hatay of its right to river water.

Lawrence Joffe

5.12 Turkey - Iraq

Although the border between Iraq and Turkey was agreed by a treaty in 1926, following arbitration by the International Court of Justice, Turkish nationalists did not accept the incorporation of the Mosul area into Iraq. The issue was raised during the 1990-91 Gulf War (for an account of which see Section 5.7) although Turkey has not officially sought to reopen the border issue. Relations have also been complicated by the existence of a large Kurdish population on both sides of the border. Turkey made regular incursions into Kurdish areas in northern Iraq throughout the

1990s and early 2000s and was closely watching developments in northern Iraq in the aftermath of the 2003 Iraq war.

Historical Background—Incorporation of Mosul into Iraq

Mosul was conquered by the Mongols in the 13th century and later incorporated into the Ottoman empire, subordinate to Baghdad. In 1879, it became an independent province (*vilayet*), equal in status to Baghdad. It was populated mainly by Kurds and Arabs and also by small Turkish and Assyrian communities.

In the course of World War I, Britain occupied the provinces of Baghdad and Basra and the Kirkuk area, but before Mosul could be occupied, an armistice was signed with the Ottoman empire. Under the Treaty of Sèvres, signed on Aug. 10, 1920, but never ratified, an independent Kurdish state was to be established in the region. Following the abolition of the Caliphate in 1923, the new Turkish Republic relinquished its Arab provinces but laid claim to the Kurdish areas, insisting that the Kurds were not a separate nation, but merely "mountain Turks". Under pressure from Persian and Turkish nationalists, Britain reneged on the commitment to form an independent Kurdistan and the discovery of oil in the Mosul region led Britain to support the incorporation of the area into Iraq, for which it had been granted a mandate by the League of Nations in 1920.

The Treaty of Lausanne of July 24, 1923, called for a friendly agreement to be reached on the border between Turkey and Iraq, failing which the matter would be referred to the League of Nations. On Oct. 29, 1924, the Council of the League of Nations issued a ruling establishing a provisional border on the "Brussels line", equivalent to the northern border of the Mosul *vilayet*. From November 1924 to March 1925, a commission of the League of Nations studied the border, and in June 1925 it recommended that a permanent border be established on the Brussels line. The matter was then referred to the International Court of Justice (ICJ), which in June 1925 recommended the award of Mosul to Iraq. Iraq, Turkey and the UK signed the Treaty of Ankara on June 5, 1926, establishing the border between Iraq and Turkey along the Brussels line, with some slight modifications.

The Kurds

The Kurdish issue has greatly complicated Turkish-Iraqi relations and their dealings over the border area. The vast majority of inhabitants on both sides of the border are Kurds and their relations with Ankara and Baghdad have been troubled and often very violent. After 1984, Kurdish groups in Turkey, particularly the Kurdish Workers' Party (PKK), fought a long and bloody struggle with the Turkish state for an ethnic homeland in south-eastern Turkey. This has made Turkey highly sensitive to developments in the Kurdish areas in Iraq, Iran and Syria.

At the close of the Gulf War in 1991, the Iraqi government brutally suppressed a Kurdish uprising, leading to the flight of hundreds of thousands of refugees into the border regions and across the border into Turkey. Following the establishment of a "safe haven" for Kurds in northern Iraq, the border areas of the region were frequently attacked by Turkey, which alleged that PKK guerrillas had established bases there. These assaults regularly caused high casualties and were loudly denounced by both Kurdish leaders and the Iraqi government. The official Turkish position was that there was no intention of gaining territory through these operations and in July 1992, the government stated that Iraq's problems could only be solved if the country's territorial integrity was maintained.

In March 1995 Turkey carried out a major operation in northern Iraq in which 30,000 troops pushed deep into Iraqi territory across a 150-mile front. The stated aim was to "clean out the area used by the PKK" in retaliation for a Kurdish ambush of Turkish troops the previous week. Iraq denounced the operation as a violation of its sovereignty. Most Turkish units withdrew by early May, claiming to have killed 568 PKK guerrillas and destroyed much of the organization's infrastructure. Turkey maintained its right to carry out such activities, President Demirel stating: "If the region is occupied by terrorists, Turkey will go into northern Iraq again. There is no other solution". There were reports that Demirel was planning to redefine the border with Iraq in an attempt to prevent further infiltration by the PKK. This brought strong protests from Iraq, Iraqi Kurdish autonomous leaders and the Arab League. The Turkish position was clarified by the Turkish chargé d'affaires to Iraq on May 4, 1995, when he stated that "the Iraqi-Turkish borders are not correct but settling this issue is not subject to discussion at the present moment". He described any suggestions that Turkey was seeking to alter the border as being "completely out of context".

In September 1996 Turkey and Iraq held talks on establishing a Turkish security zone in northern Iraq to prevent Kurdish guerrillas crossing the border. The PKK agreed to a ceasefire in 1998 and its leader, Abdullah Ocalan, was captured and imprisoned in 1999. More than 30,000 have died in the conflict.

Recent Developments in Turkish-Iraqi Relations

During the Gulf crisis of 1990-91, Turkey closed the oil pipeline from Kirkuk to Ceyhan in Turkey, and ended all commerce with Iraq. The Turkish parliament voted to authorize the use of force if Turkey were to be attacked and agreed to allow foreign troops into the country. Although the Turkish government officially denied having any territorial ambitions in Iraq, President Turgut Ozal spoke of the need to "redraw the map" of the Middle East, mentioning the Turkish claims to Mosul and to Kirkuk.

Through the late 1990s and early 2000s, Ankara and Baghdad improved commercial and diplomatic ties. This happened despite continuing disagreements over water resources and Iraqi anger that US and UK patrols of the northern no-fly zone in Iraq were carried out from Turkish bases. In December 1996 the Iraq-Turkey oil pipeline was reopened.

Although Turkey had no desire to see Saddam Hussein's regime survive, it did not support the US-led invasion of Iraq in 2003, as public opinion was overwhelmingly against the action and Ankara was also concerned about the possibility of Iraq becoming partitioned. Turkey maintained the right to protect its interests in Iraqi Kurdistan during and after the war in March-April 2003. Thousands of troops were deployed on the border and there were reports of some military movement into Iraqi territory. On March 25, Turkey announced that it was planning to deploy troops in a 12-mile buffer zone inside northern Iraq should a "crisis situation" develop as refugees fled the fighting.

The border area remained tense in the aftermath of the war as the parties jostled to protect their interests in the new Iraq. Turkey's offer in October 2003 to send troops to help keep the peace in Iraq was strongly rejected by Iraqi leaders, who argued that that the presence of a neighbouring country's forces would create further instability. The opposition, particularly from Iraqi Kurds, was so intense that the USA was forced to turn down the offer.

The political stability of Iraq was of great importance to Turkey, which was concerned that the Iraqi Kurds might be able to turn their enclave into an independent Kurdish state and thus unsettle its own large Kurdish population. Turkey's Deputy Chief of Staff, General Ilker Basburg, warned in January 2004 that, "Iraq's future might be very bloody if there was a federal structure, especially based on ethnicity". Turkey also demanded that the USA take action against Turkish Kurdish rebels who remained in hiding in northern Iraq.

The leader of the Kurdistan Democratic Party, Massoud Barzani, stated on March 16, 2004: "As a nation, the Kurds not only deserve federalism, they have all the rights for independence. But we do realise the circumstances and realities of the day". The other main Iraqi Kurdish party, the Patriotic Union of Kurdistan, held a similar position. Its leader, Jalal Talabani, said on Feb. 2, 2004, that it would work with the KDP and others, "seriously towards uniting our government ...in order to live in a democratic, federal Iraq".

Robert Lowe

5.13 Saudi Arabia - Yemen

The last disputed land border in the Arabian peninsula appears to have been settled by an agreement signed in June 2000. The Jeddah Treaty provides for the demarcation of the 1,500-km frontier between Saudi Arabia and Yemen,

one of the longest undemarcated borders in the world, and was intended to mark the end of Arabia's most heated and intractable territorial dispute.

The modern states of Saudi Arabia, North Yemen and South Yemen (merged in 1990 to form the Republic of Yemen) inherited complex territorial claims and a legacy of often hostile mutual relations from their predecessors. The countries held vastly different opinions on the course of their borders, leading to substantially overlapping territorial claims. The unification of Yemen in 1990 increased the possibility of a settlement, but because the border dispute was as much a symptom as a cause of Saudi-Yemeni ill-feeling, it took ten difficult years before sufficient will enabled a resolution to be found. (For resolution of other Arabian peninsula disputes, see Section 5.10; see also Map 57, p. 522.)

The Ta'if Treaty

By 1930 the expanding Saudi state had effectively annexed the 'Asir region to the north of Yemen and the provinces of Jizan and Najran which Yemen had disputed with 'Asir. A short war between Saudi Arabia and the Imamate of Yemen in the spring of 1934 ended with the first attempt to settle the border between the two modern states. Under the Treaty of Islamic Friendship and Brotherhood signed on May 20, 1934, in the Yemeni village of Ta'if, the border was defined from the Red Sea coast to a point in the high mountains of 'Asir, but the eastern section was left undetermined. The location of Jabal al-Thar, the mountain at which the line stopped, was also disputed. Demarcation of the Ta'if line was carried out in 1935-36. Yemen was the less happy of the two states with the boundary, but as the defeated party in the 1934 war, had to be content that it did not run even further south. The Ta'if treaty contained the unusual requirement that it be renewed every twenty lunar years and both sides consented to this in 1953.

North and South Yemen

The border between the British Aden Protectorate and Saudi Arabia had not been agreed by 1967, when South Yemen gained independence. A series of lines had been drawn by the British across the southern rim of the Rub' al Khali desert in agreements made with the Ottomans and later offers made to the Saudis. The Saudis themselves presented the "Hamza" line in 1935, marking the minimum extent of their claims in south and south-east Arabia and significantly overlapping territory claimed by the Aden Protectorate.

After Yemen's long civil war in the 1960s, the People's Democratic Republic of Yemen (South Yemen) was governed by a Marxist regime while the Yemen Arab Republic (North Yemen) was heavily influenced by Saudi Arabia, which became a major aid provider and offered crucial employment opportunities. In 1974 Saudi Arabia and North Yemen agreed to extend the Ta'if treaty for another twenty years, but this was never ratified by North Yemen.

In armed confrontations in early 1980, five North Yemeni soldiers were said to have been killed by the Saudis. Western press reports suggested that the clashes were related to the Saudis' construction of a new road in the Boa district and may also have reflected their desire to exert pressure against North Yemen's proposed merger with South Yemen and gravitation towards closer relations with the Soviet Union. A Saudi airliner was hijacked to Tehran in November 1984 by North Yemeni nationals protesting at what they alleged was Saudi "interference" in the internal affairs of North Yemen.

Saudi Arabia was hostile to South Yemen following its creation in 1967 and made frequent attempts to disrupt it either by encouraging northern tribes to make raids or by giving refuge and support to South Yemeni exiles opposed to the Marxist regime in Aden. The Saudi-South Yemen border was also undemarcated and the two sides held overlapping territorial claims. There were unconfirmed reports during December 1983 and January 1984 of border clashes between Saudi and South Yemeni troops. After the South Yemeni civil war of January 1986, there were further reports that Saudi Arabia was supplying arms and equipment to rebel forces loyal to ex-President Mohammed based in North Yemen.

1990s Negotiations and Border Incidents

Following the unification of North and South Yemen in March 1990, the new government of the Republic of Yemen stated that resolution of the border dispute would be a priority. However, Saudi Arabia responded to Yemen's perceived support of Iraq during the 1990-91 Gulf crisis by expelling around one million Yemeni migrant workers and suspending aid. In March 1992, the government in Riyadh sent stern letters to four oil companies which had been granted concessions by Yemen, advising them to cease operations in areas where the border had not been agreed. Saudi Arabia also backed the failed attempt by South Yemenis to secede from the union in 1994. The accompanying deterioration in relations between Sana'a and Riyadh was further exacerbated when Yemeni and Saudi forces clashed around the border town of al-Buqa', near the eastern end of the Ta'if line.

The increased tension forced the two sides to negotiate and in February 1995 a Memorandum of Understanding was signed in Mecca, reaffirming the Ta'if line and establishing a procedural framework for negotiating the indeterminate border in the desert wastes further east. In June 1995 the Ta'if treaty was renewed for another twenty lunar years. In the summer of 1996 Yemen formally submitted a territorial claim on the disputed border, the first time this had been precisely articulated. The claim was for a boundary running along the 20th parallel, considerably further north

of the territorial claims Britain had made for the Aden Protectorate.

In the two years following the signing of the Memorandum of Understanding, the two sides met regularly and by the summer of 1997, it appeared that the line of the border had been essentially agreed. A map published in the *Yemen Times* in August 1997 showed a boundary very similar to that finally agreed in 2000. A meeting between President Ali Abdullah Saleh of Yemen and Crown Prince Abdullah of Saudi Arabia, at Como in Italy in September 1997, indicated that a settlement was near. However, negotiations failed to reach a conclusion in 1997 and this was probably not due to disagreements over the coordinates of the border, but rather because of a disagreement on the inclusion of an economic component in the final agreement. Yemen was keen to gain an agreement on Saudi economic aid and access to the Saudi employment market for its large workforce, but the Saudis were determined to avoid any such provisions.

As negotiations stalled, the fractious relationship became further troubled as a result of a number of incidents along the border. Saudi and Yemeni forces had clashed in 1997, and tensions increased in the summer of 1998 after the Saudis lodged objections at the UN over a border agreement between Yemen and Oman (see Section 5.10). Yemen accused Saudi Arabia of violating its border 73 times in the four weeks from June 15 to July 15. The Interior Minister, Hussein Arab, said that these included military deployments, the shelling of soldiers and civilians and violations of Yemeni air space and territorial waters, commenting: "Our Saudi brothers are eating up the land in a big way".

The most serious incident occurred on the disputed island of Al-Duwaima in the Red Sea. On July 20, Yemeni President Ali Abdullah Saleh accused Saudi Arabian forces of attacking and occupying the island, killing three Yemeni coastguards and wounding nine others. He said nine Saudi naval vessels using long range artillery had bombarded the island, and that Saudi Arabia was "pouring oil on the fire". The Saudi Interior Minister, Prince Nayef bin Abdul Aziz, described the incident on Al-Duwaima as a border skirmish in which Saudi forces had acted in self-defence and dismissed the accusation that Saudi Arabia had occupied the island. Talks between the respective Foreign Ministers were immediately held in Jeddah to defuse the situation, and it was agreed that any solution to the border problem must prevent both countries from endangering each other's interests and that recent incidents must not be repeated. A joint military committee met in Riyadh on Aug. 5 and both sides expressed goodwill in resolving the border issue.

In April 1999, the Joint Border Demarcation Committee met in Sana'a to examine the results of fieldwork carried out by survey teams on the land and sea borders. In November 1999, there were further armed clashes on the border in Hadramout province. According to the Yemeni press, two Yemeni soldiers were killed by Saudi forces as revenge for the killing of two Saudi soldiers the previous week. Despite this, the Saudi attitude towards Yemen appeared to be warming, most noticeably in May 2000, when Crown Prince Abdullah attended the celebrations of the 10-year anniversary of the unification of Yemen.

The Jeddah Treaty, 2000

The breakthrough was finally made on June 12, 2000, when an International Border Treaty on the "final and permanent demarcation line" of the border was signed in Jeddah. President Saleh met Crown Prince Abdullah and said they had "reached a peaceful, cordial, brotherly and satisfactory solution". The definition of the border further north of that long claimed by Saudi Arabia gave Yemen territory in the eastern sector of the disputed region as well as four disputed islands in the Red Sea. Most of the known oilfields in the border area lie in territory agreed to be Yemeni. For its part, Saudi Arabia received reaffirmation of the Ta'if treaty and so Yemen's claims to its former northern provinces were finally dropped. The Saudis also managed to avoid the insertion of any economic provisions although Prince Nayef encouraged Saudi employers to hire Yemenis. The Jeddah Treaty also stipulated that the forces of the two countries should withdraw 20 km on both sides of the line and bound the parties to prevent their territories from being used for aggression against the other. A German firm, Hansa Luftbild, was commissioned to carry out the demarcation of the 1,318 km of border in question by surveying the lines and erecting marker columns, with the expectation that this will be completed in 2005.

It should be noted that while the Jeddah Treaty confirms the Ta'if line and fixes the coordinates of Jabal al-Thar, the remaining eastern line of the border towards Oman "has not yet been defined, but the two contracting parties have agreed to define this part amicably". It would appear that while a number of fixed points have been marked, the demarcation of the line between them remains to be formally agreed. There were also reports in 2000 that tribes inhabiting the border area did not accept the agreement. Daham tribe officials in north Yemen said they would not allow the surveyors to enter their territory, fearing that the demarcation would lead to part of their traditional land being awarded to Saudi Arabia. The Wa'ila tribe in north Yemen also opposed the demarcation because they feared it would interfere with an agreement marking tribal boundaries which they reached with the Yam tribe on the Saudi side in 1759.

Saudi Arabia suffered a series of terrorist attacks in 2003, including suicide bombings in Riyadh on May 12 which killed 34 people and on Nov. 8 which killed 17. Saudi officials believed that many of the weapons used in the attacks were smuggled into the Kingdom from Yemen and also expressed concern that militants were crossing from Yemen with the intention of carrying out further attacks. Steps were taken to tighten border security including commenc-

ing the construction of a fence in January 2004. A project to establish an electronic surveillance system around all the Kingdom's frontiers had been planned for some years. Talal Anqawi, head of Saudi Arabia's border guard, said the intention was not to construct a barrier, but a "security screen" on the Saudi side of the border which would stem the flow of arms and militants into the country.

The Yemeni government protested that the fence violated the treaty of 2000 as construction was taking place inside the 20 km neutral zone. Tribes on the Yemeni side of the border, including the Wa'ila, claimed that parts of the fence were actually within Yemeni territory and warned that they were ready to fight Saudi forces unless the structure was dismantled. In February 2004, following talks between President Saleh and Crown Prince Abdullah, Saudi Arabia agreed to cease construction. Yemeni Foreign Minister Abubakr al-Qirbi said the two countries had agreed to strengthen co-ordinated efforts to control the border and that both had agreed to abide by the treaty signed in 2000.

Robert Lowe

5.14 Yemen - Eritrea

The Hanish islands are located approximately 65 miles north of the strategically critical Bab al-Mandab strait which joins the Red Sea to the Indian Ocean.(See Map 57, p 522.) The archipelago consists of around 40 hot, dry, mostly uninhabited islands, islets, rocks and low-tide elevations. Despite their location in one of the world's major shipping lanes, the ownership of the Hanish islands and other small islands and rocks was not established by international convention until 1998.

The legal status of these islands was of little concern until the 1990s when newly independent Eritrea pressed its claim of sovereignty. Yemen, which maintained a light presence on the islands, contested the claim. Competition over oil and fishing rights and developing tourist projects helped trigger a brief conflict in 1995, which resulted in Eritrea gaining control of the largest island and subsequent intervention by the international community. Negotiations sponsored by France led to the submission of the dispute to an independent arbitral tribunal which delivered its ruling in 1998. The Hanish islands were awarded to Yemen while Eritrea was given other small islands and security in its fishing rights. The decision by both countries to accept the ruling without complaint won praise from the international community, which held it up as a model for the resolution of other territorial disputes.

Historical Background

The Ottoman empire was the unchallenged ruler of the Red Sea until the Italian colony of Eritrea was established in 1890. The Italians maintained an active presence in the Red Sea, but did not consider occupying the Hanish islands until the 1910s when the weakness of the Ottoman empire became apparent. Britain briefly occupied the islands in 1915 during the First World War and the Italians again considered annexing the islands after the war, but failed to do so. Turkey renounced its title to Ottoman Red Sea possessions in the 1923 Treaty of Lausanne. Britain then intended to prevent other European countries from acquiring the islands by ceding them to local Arab rulers, but the plan was not realized. In 1936, Britain and Italy agreed a treaty which gave the British responsibility for protecting fishing vessels and maintaining the lighthouses on the islands and gave Italy the right to an official presence on Hanish al-Kabir (Greater Hanish), Hanish al-Saghir (Lesser Hanish) and Jabal Zuqar. The agreement also prohibited either side from establishing sovereignty or erecting any defences on the islands.

British forces occupied Eritrea in 1941 and subsequently administered the country as a United Nations trust territory. In 1952, the UN resolved to establish Eritrea as an autonomous entity federated with Ethiopia as a compromise between Ethiopian claims of sovereignty and Eritrean demands for independence. However, Ethiopia annexed Eritrea as its northernmost province in 1962, instantly triggering a war of independence. At the time, Yemen was divided into two parts, South Yemen (which gained independence from the British in 1967) and North Yemen, which had not been colonized. North Yemen's coastline faced the Hanish islands.

An international agreement which renewed Britain's responsibility for the upkeep of the lighthouses was signed by the UK, USA, USSR and France in 1962. North Yemen and Ethiopia did not sign this treaty. Britain retained responsibility for the Hanish lighthouses until 1989, when the role was handed over to North Yemen.

In 1982, following the signing of the UN Law of the Sea treaty, North Yemen and Ethiopia began to assert claims to the various islands between them in the Red Sea. The treaty created a 12-mile territorial sea drawn from a state's coastal baseline, meaning that control of the Hanish islands in the narrow southern reaches of the Red Sea became even more significant. North Yemen claimed sovereignty over all the islands in the Red Sea that had been under Ottoman rule while Ethiopia protested and made a "non-specific" claim of sovereignty over the Red Sea islands.

Competing Claims

In 1991, the Eritrean People's Liberation Front captured the Eritrean capital, Asmara, and formed a pro-visional government. Two years later, after a referendum which provided overwhelming backing for secession from Ethiopia, Eritrea became independent and joined the United Nations. North and South Yemen united to form the Republic of Yemen in 1990.

The young Eritrean state was infused with nationalism and pursued a more vigorous territorial policy in the Red Sea than had the Ethiopian government. Eritrea asserted that it had inherited the title to the Hanish islands that Ethiopia had inherited from Italy—arguing that Italy had acquired sovereignty over the islands through "effective occupation" by the end of the 1920s. Eritrea believed that the 11 years of British control of the country from 1941 did not break the chain of title as this had been a belligerent occupation. The 31-year period between Eritrea's incorporation into the Ethiopian empire and independence in 1993 was characterized as one of extensive exercise of Ethiopian sovereignty over the islands. Eritrea also argued that there was no Yemeni presence on or around the islands during the Italian period and that the Yemenis had shown no interest in the islands until the 1970s, when false reports claimed that Ethiopia had leased the islands to Israel.

Yemen based its claim to the Hanish islands on the "original, historic, or traditional Yemeni title", which could be traced back to the Bilad el-Yemen (Realm of Yemen) in the 6th Century AD. Yemen contended that its incorporation into the Ottoman empire did not remove its historic title to the territory, which was in any case considered part of the Ottoman *vilayet* of Yemen. It also emphasized that Italy and Britain had never claimed sovereignty over the islands, and maintained that the 1923 Treaty of Lausanne had no effect on the Yemeni title because Yemen was not party to the treaty and because Turkey's renunciation of rights could not prejudice the interests of third parties. Furthermore, Yemen claimed to find acknowledgment of its right to the islands in British and French "practice and internal thinking". Yemen also emphasized that its armed forces had been active on the islands since the early 1970s, that Yemeni fishermen had enjoyed virtually exclusive use of the islands, and that the islands were home to a number of Yemeni holy sites and shrines.

The 1995 Clash on Hanish al-Kabir

Eritrea made it clear that it would not accept any moves by Yemen to increase its control over the islands. The growing tension was heightened by competition over fishing and oil rights in the vicinity of the islands, rights which were both relatively little exploited and possibly of great potential to these two poor countries. The development of a Yemeni hotel and diving complex on Hanish al-Kabir in 1995 prompted Petros Solomon, Eritrea's Foreign Minister, to issue an ultimatum on Nov. 11 giving Yemen one month to withdraw military forces and civilians from the island. The Eritrean navy then attempted to land on Hanish al-Kabir but was repelled and Yemen responded by increasing its military presence throughout the islands. The two sides attempted to resolve the crisis diplomatically and Petros Solomon visited Sana'a on Nov. 22. The Yemeni Foreign Minister, Abdul al-Karim al-Iryani, made a return visit to Asmara on Dec. 7 when it was agreed that negotiations would begin in February 1996. Should the negotiations fail, the two sides agreed that the case would be referred to the International Court of Justice (ICJ).

It was therefore a considerable surprise that just eight days later, on Dec. 15, 1995, Eritrean forces attacked the garrison of some 200 Yemeni troops on Hanish al-Kabir. Yemen immediately accused Eritrea of a "treacherous act of aggression". The Eritreans captured the island after three days of fighting in which six Yemeni and twelve Eritrean soldiers were killed and 213 Yemenis were taken prisoner. A ceasefire was agreed on Dec. 17 after a conversation between President Ali Abdullah Saleh of Yemen and President Isaya Afewerki of Eritrea. However, only the next day, Yemen claimed that Eritrea had completed the occupation of the island after the agreement of the truce while Eritrea contended that the island had been captured before the ceasefire came into force. On Dec. 29, the UN Secretary-General, Boutros Boutros-Ghali, arrived in Yemen to mediate the dispute. Two days later, he was able to announce that Yemen had agreed to withdraw its forces and accept international arbitration. Eritrea immediately released its Yemeni prisoners of war and the two sides maintained diplomatic relations.

With a large military presence in neighbouring Djibouti, France agreed to take on the role of mediator and Yemen and Eritrea signed an agreement in Paris in May 1996 to accept the verdict of a special arbitration tribunal. The French effort appeared in vain when Eritrean forces occupied Hanish al-Saghir on Aug. 10, 1996. Yemen threatened to respond militarily and the UN Security Council ordered Asmara to remove its troops from the island. The Eritrean force withdrew on Aug. 27, leaving Hanish al-Saghir unoccupied, Hanish al-Kabir still under Eritrean control and Jabal Zuqar in Yemeni hands. A second agreement was signed in Paris on Oct. 3, 1996, committing Eritrea and Yemen to submit the dispute to an international tribunal that would sit in London.

The Eritrea-Yemen Arbitral Tribunal, 1998

By January 1997, the panel of judges had been chosen for the tribunal to be held under the auspices of the Permanent Court of Arbitration. Eritrea appointed an American and a British judge, Yemen selected an Egyptian and an American judge and both agreed to the appointment of a British judge, Sir Robert Jennings, to chair the panel. While the tribunal hearings were being prepared, the two states worked to improve their bilateral relations and avoided statements or actions which might compromise the legal process.

On Oct. 9, 1998, the Eritrea-Yemen Arbitral Tribunal announced its decision. The Mohabbakah islands, the Haycock islands and the South West Rocks (all closer to the Eritrean coast and historically administered from Africa) were found to be subject to the territorial sovereignty of Eritrea. The larger Hanish islands and the Zuqar group of islands were awarded to Yemen, as the tribunal found that the weight of evidence supported Yemen's assertions of the exercise of state authority on these islands. The traditional fishing rights of both sides in the areas covered by the tribunal were also preserved. Phase II of the arbitration was completed on Dec. 17, 1999, and delimited the international maritime boundary, taking into account the territorial settlement achieved in the first stage of arbitration.

Eritrea welcomed the ruling and reaffirmed its commitment to comply with and implement the tribunal's decisions. The Eritrean Foreign Minister, Haile Weldensae, hoped that the ruling would "make the Red Sea a sea of peace and a sea of co-operation". Yemen was also content with the decision and the Foreign Minister, Abdel Kader Bajammal, stated: "The Hanish islands will not be used under Yemeni sovereignty for military purposes. They will be a bridge of friendship between all the countries which border the Red Sea". With the dispute resolved, the two sides expressed their eagerness to improve relations and on Nov. 1, 1998, Eritrea formally returned Hanish al-Kabir to Yemen. Eritrea also expressed its hope that the settlement of the dispute would help lead to a similar arbitral resolution of its bloody border conflict with Ethiopia—for which see Section 1.6.

Robert Lowe

MAPS

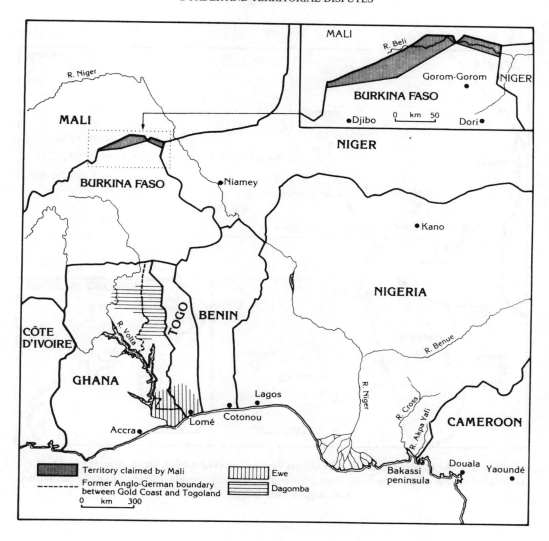

Territory claimed by Mali

Former Anglo-German boundary
between Gold Coast and Togoland

Ewe

Dagomba

0   km   300

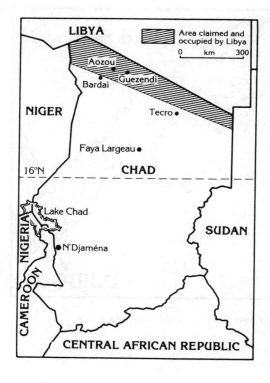

Area claimed and
occupied by Libya

0   km   300

Map 1 (above) illustrates the disputes between Burkina Faso and Mali, Cameroon and Nigeria, and Ghana and Togo.

Map 2 (opposite) illustrates the Chad-Libya dispute.

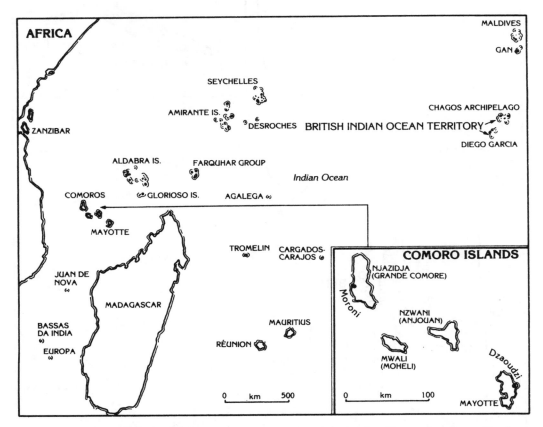

Map 3   The Indian Ocean islands off the eastern coast of Africa, illustrating the residual territorial claims of the Comoros, Madagascar and Mauritius against France and the Mauritius-UK dispute over Diego Garcia.

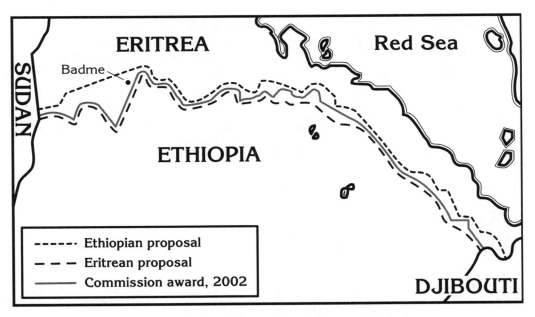

Map 4   Ethiopian and Eritrean claims and 2002 Border Commission line.

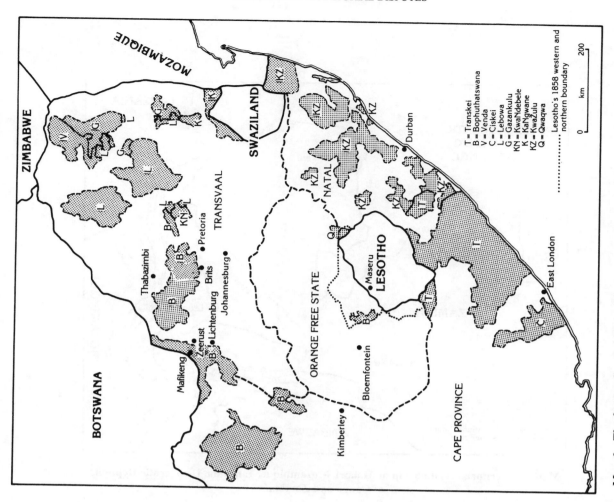

Map 6   The former South African Black homelands, also showing the disputed Lesotho-South Africa border and Swaziland.

T = Transkei
B = Bophuthatswana
V = Venda
C = Ciskei
L = Lebowa
G = Gazankulu
KN = KwaNdebele
K = KaNgwane
KZ = KwaZulu
Q = Qwaqwa

.... Lesotho's 1858 western and northern boundary

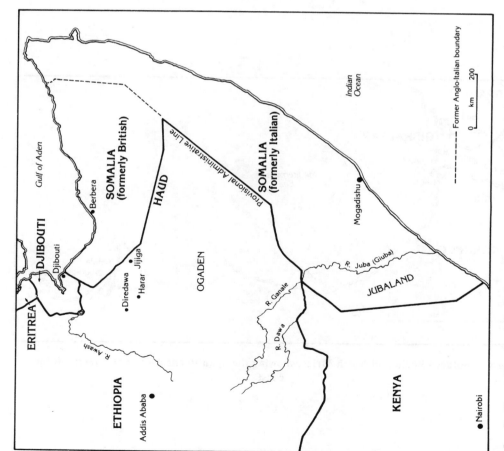

Map 5   Present territorial relationship of Somalia with Djibouti, Ethiopia and Kenya.

---- Former Anglo-Italian boundary

495

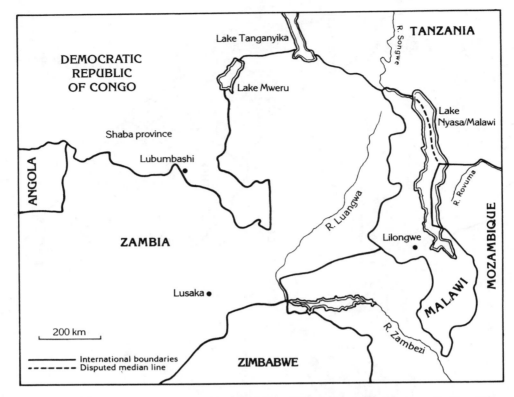

Map 7   Territorial relationship of Malawi, Mozambique, Tanzania, Democratic Republic of Congo and Zambia.

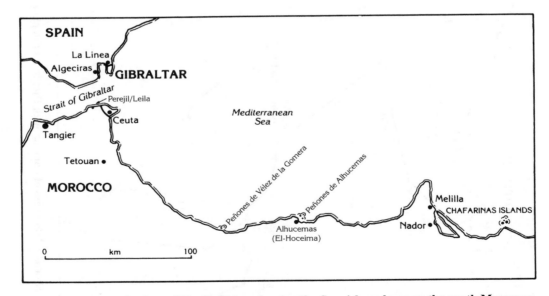

Map 8   Southern Spain and North Africa, showing the Spanish enclaves on the north Moroccan coast.

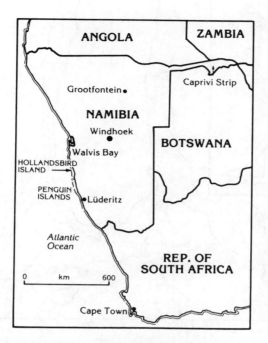

Map 9   Nambia-South Africa and Caprivi Strip.

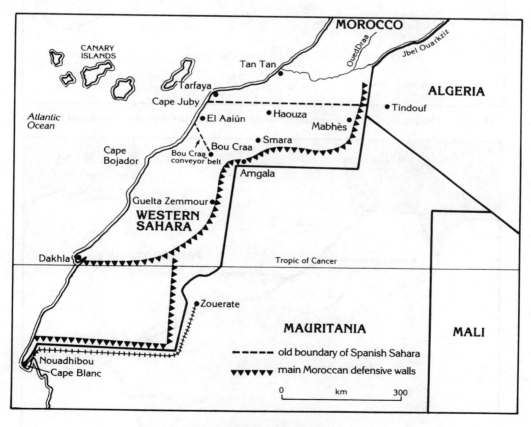

Map 10   Western Sahara.

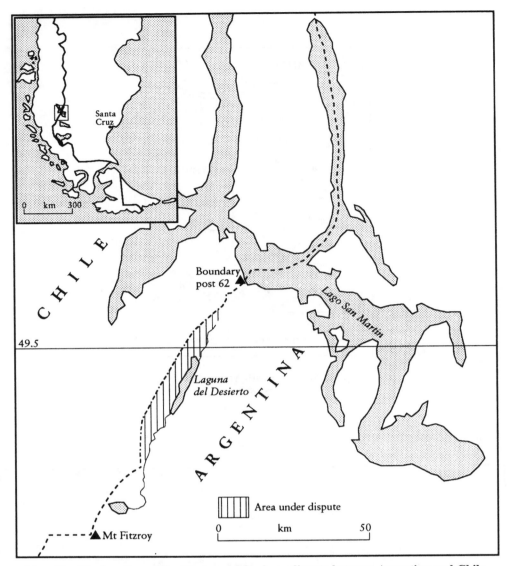

Map 11   The location of the Laguna del Desierto dispute between Argentina and Chile.

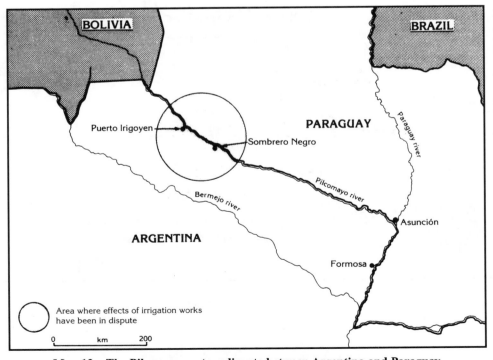

Map 12   The Pilcomayo waters dispute between Argentina and Paraguay.

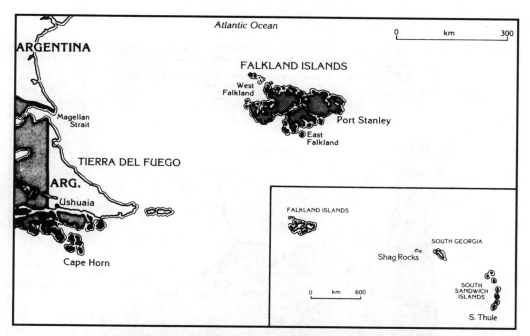

Map 13   The disputed Falkland Islands, South Georgia and the South Sandwich Islands.

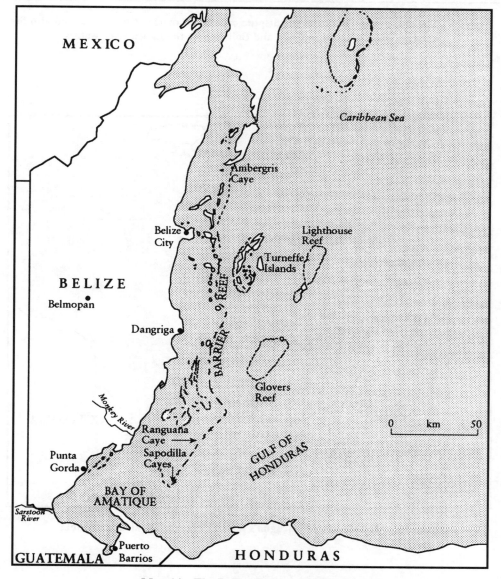

Map 14   The Belize-Guatemala dispute.

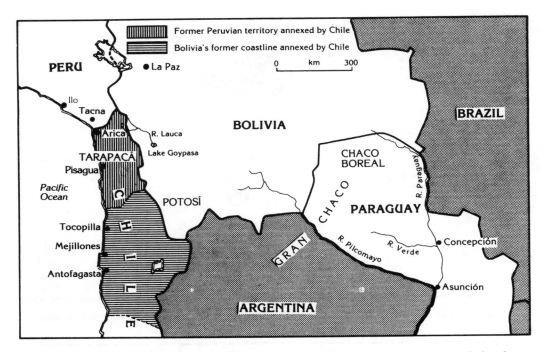

Map 15   The above map illustrates the dispute over Bolivian access to the sea, and also the separate dispute between Chile and Bolivia over the Lauca river waters.

Map 16   Map showing Nicaragua's territorial claims against Columbia.

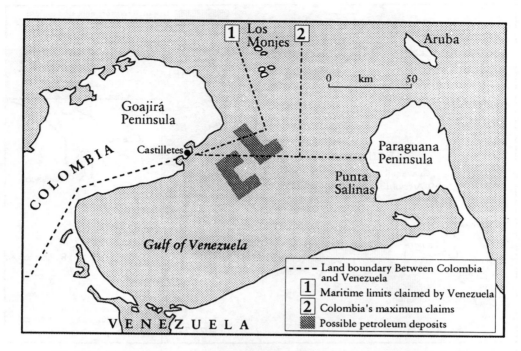

Map 17   The Los Monjes islands and Colombian and Venezuelan claims in the Gulf of Venezuela.

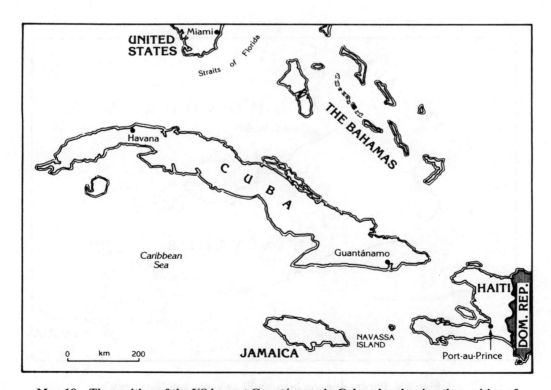

Map 18   The position of the US base at Guantánamo in Cuba, also showing the position of Navassa Island (US), which is claimed by Haiti.

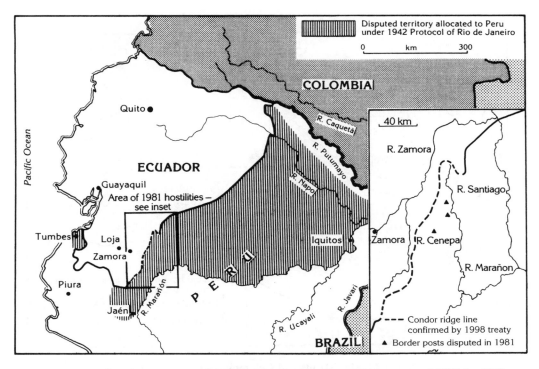

Map 19   Ecuador's territorial claim against Peru, with inset showing area of 1981 hostilities.

Map 20   Border disputes between El Salvador and Honduras.

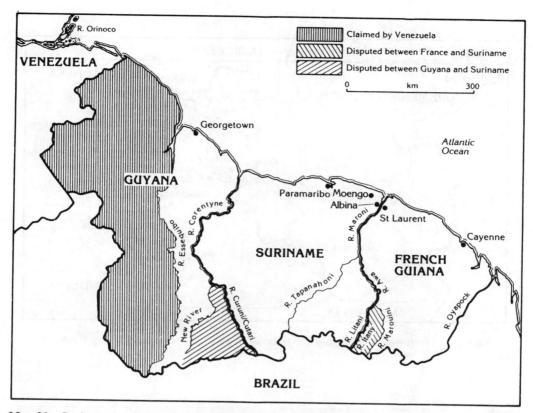

Map 21 Suriname's territorial disputes with France (French Guiana) and Guyana, also showing Venezuela's claim to the Essequibo region of Guyana.

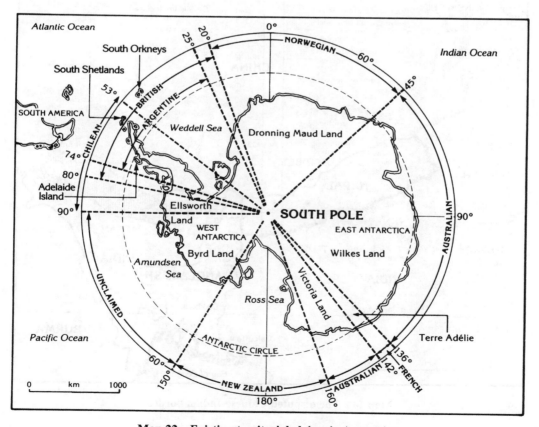

Map 22 Existing territorial claims in Antarctica.

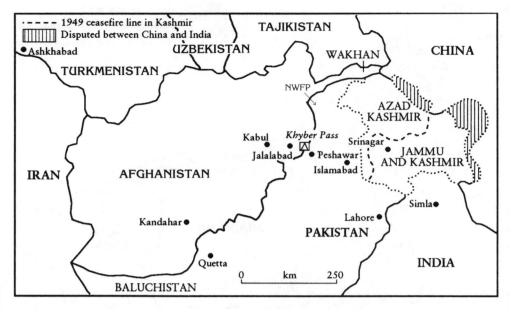

Map 23   Territorial relationship of Afghanistan and Pakistan, also showing Kashmir.

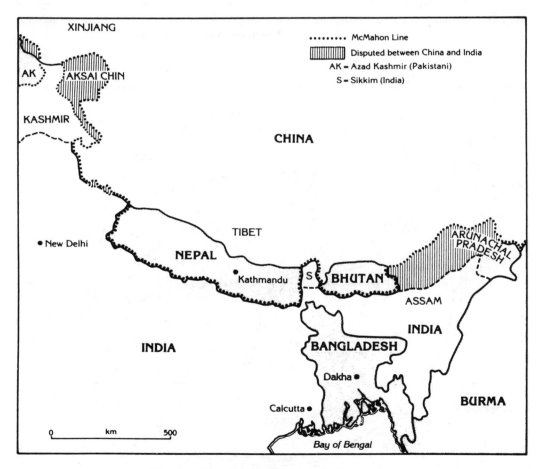

Map 24   The disputed Chinese-Indian border.

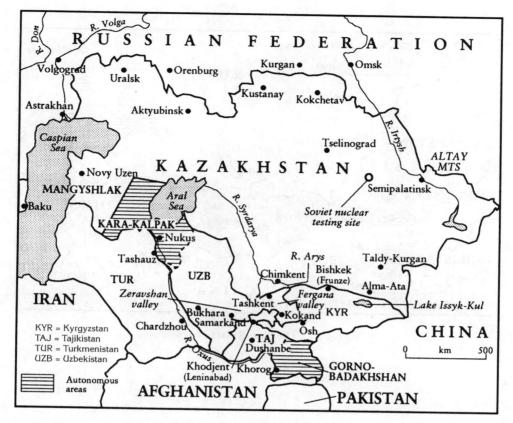

Map 25   Ex-Soviet Central Asia.

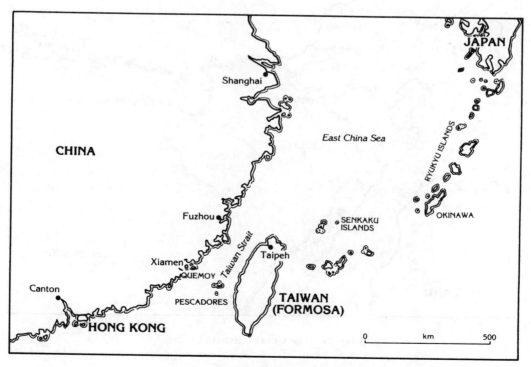

Map 26   The location of the Senkaku Islands.

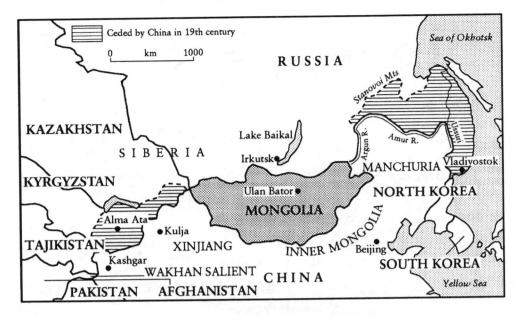

Map 27   The Sino-Russian border.

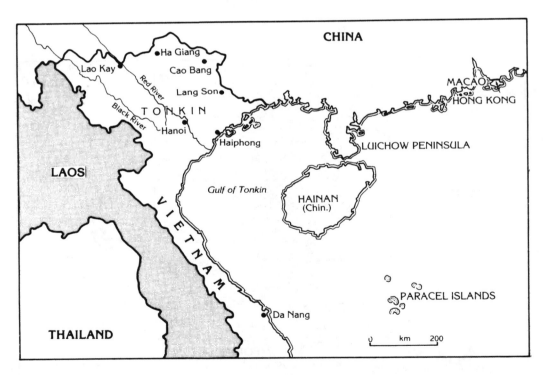

Map 28   The China-Vietnam border.

Map 29   The division of Korea.

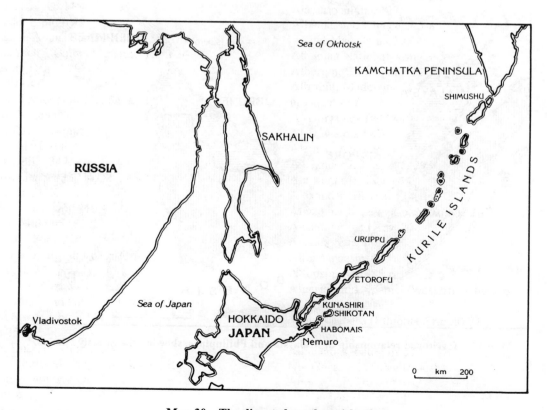

Map 30   The disputed northern islands.

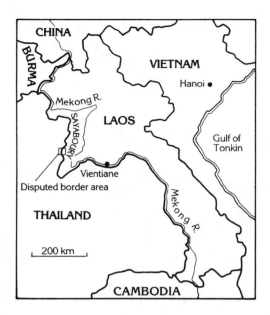

Map 31   The Laos-Thailand border.

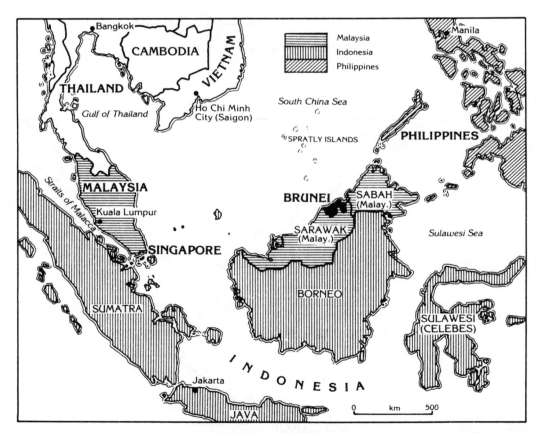

Map 32   Territorial relationship of Malaysia and Philippines, showing the Spratly Islands.

Map 33   Albania, Greece and Macedonia.

Map 34   Armenia, Azerbaijan and Nagorno-Karabakh.

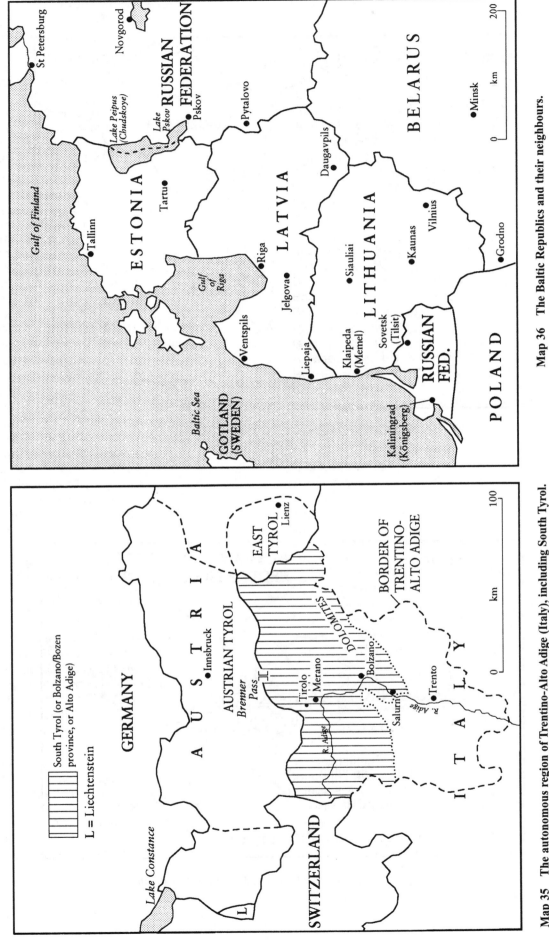

Map 36   The Baltic Republics and their neighbours.

Map 35   The autonomous region of Trentino–Alto Adige (Italy), including South Tyrol.

Map 37   Historic province of Bessarabia and Republic of Moldova.

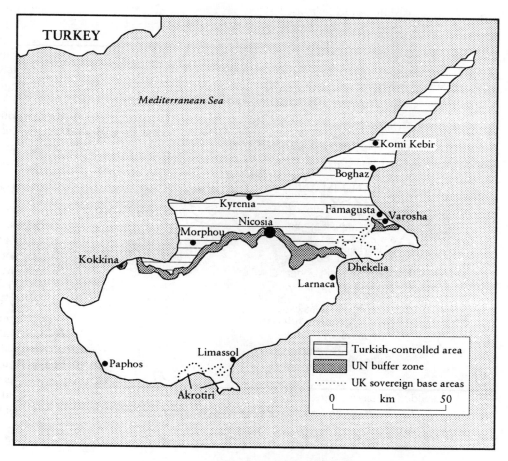

Map 38   The de facto partition of Cyprus.

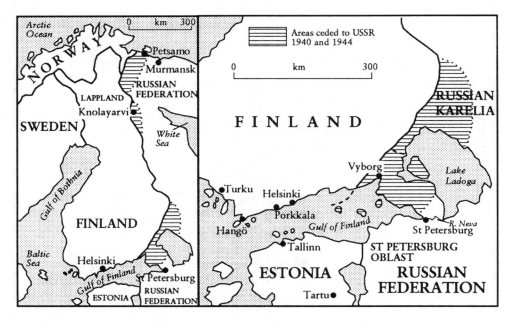

Map 39   Finnish cessions to USSR in 1940 and 1944.

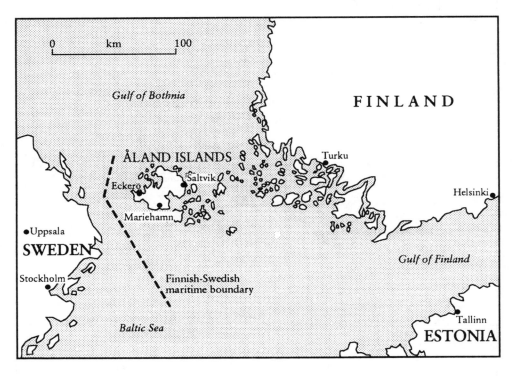

Map 40   The Åland (Ahvenanmaa) Islands.

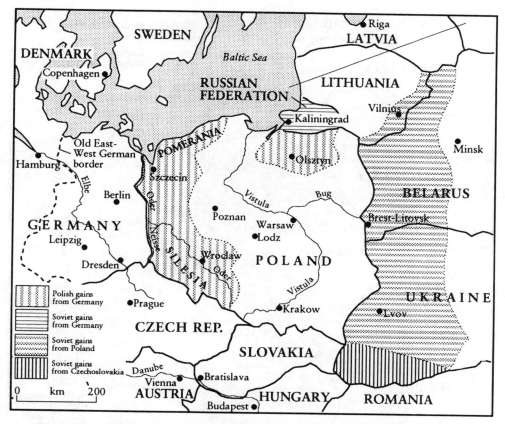

Map 41   Polish-German and related territorial changes following World War II.

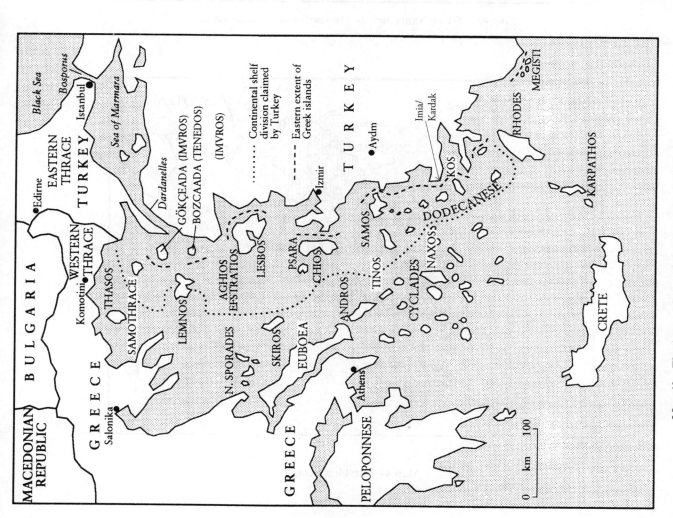

Map 42   The Aegean Sea and the Greek-Turkish border.

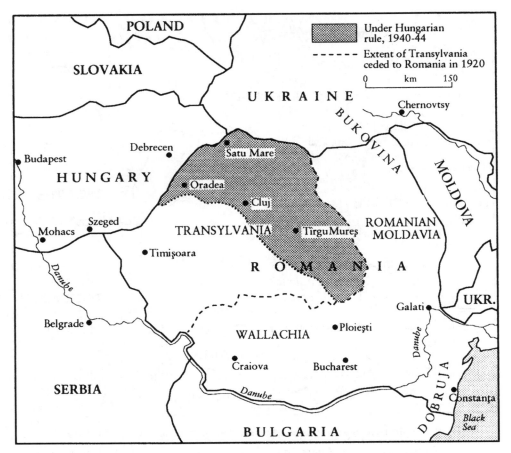

Map 43   Transylvania and the Hungarian-Romanian border.

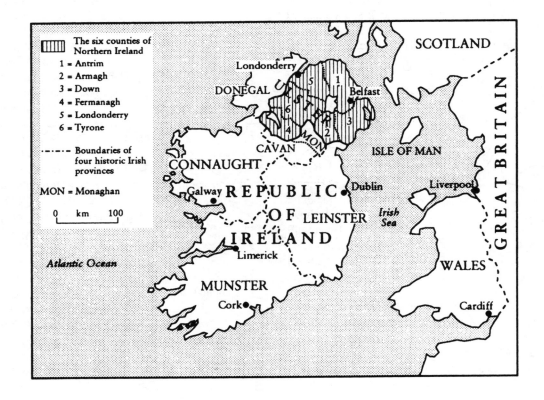

Map 44   Divided Ireland.

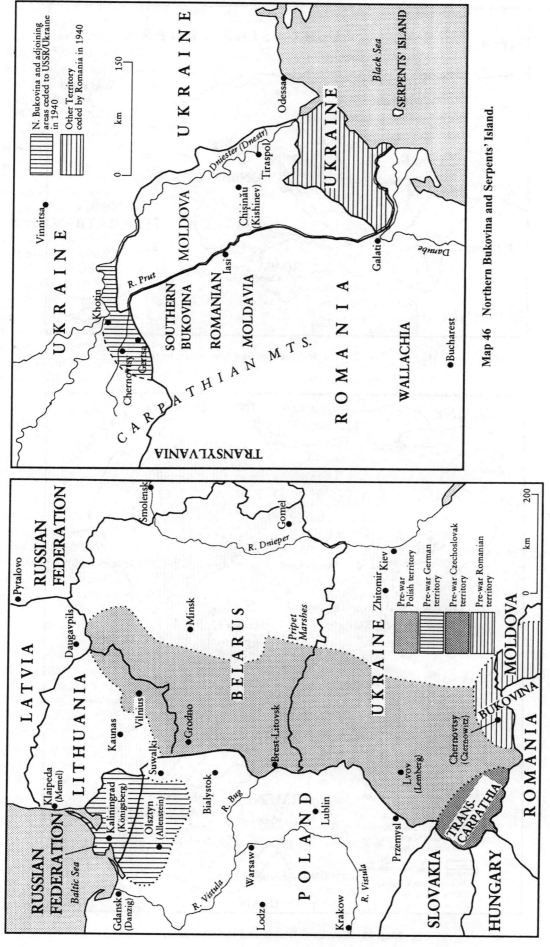

Map 46   Northern Bukovina and Serpents' Island.

Map 45   World War II changes in Poland's eastern borders.

Map 47   The Crimea and the Russian-Ukrainian border.

Map 48   Southern Russia and the Caucasus.

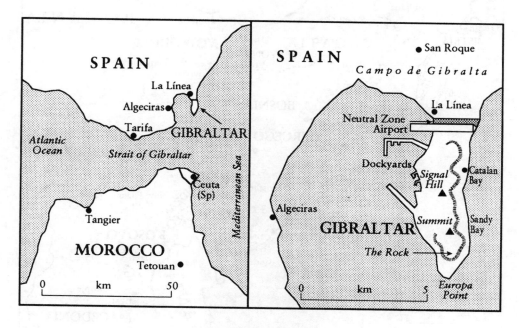

Map 49   Gibraltar.

Map 50   Transcarpathia.

Map 51(i)   Former Yugoslavia: external and internal borders.

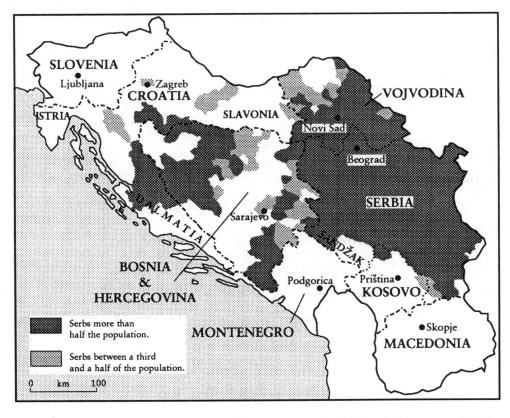

Map 51(ii)   Distribution of Serbs by local government units in Yugoslavia: census of 1981.

Map 52(i)   The UN partition plan, 1947.

Map 52(ii)   Armistice boundaries, 1949.

Map 52(iii)   1967 Arab-Israeli War.

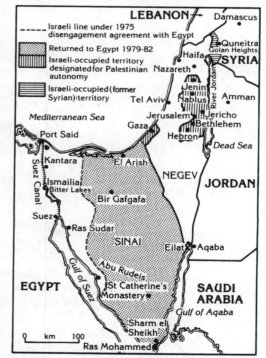

Map 52(iv)   Boundary changes since 1973 war.

Maps 52(i–iv)   The Arab-Israeli conflict.

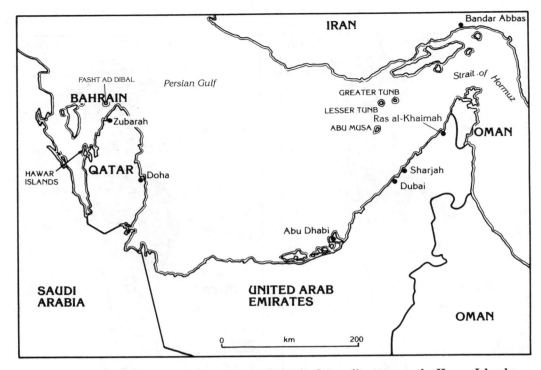

Map 53   The Persian Gulf, illustrating the Bahrain-Qatar dispute over the Hawar Islands and also showing Abu Musa and the Tunbs, which are disputed by Iran and the United Arab Emirates.

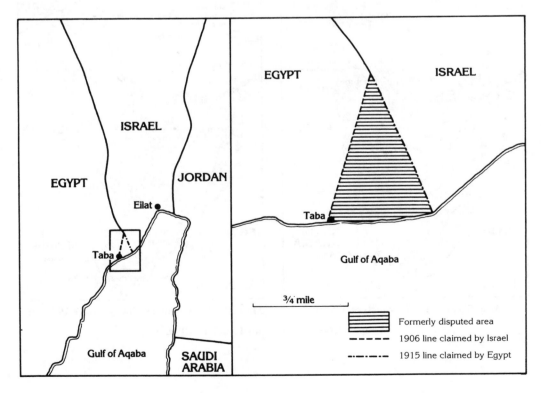

Map 54   The Taba strip dispute between Egypt and Israel.

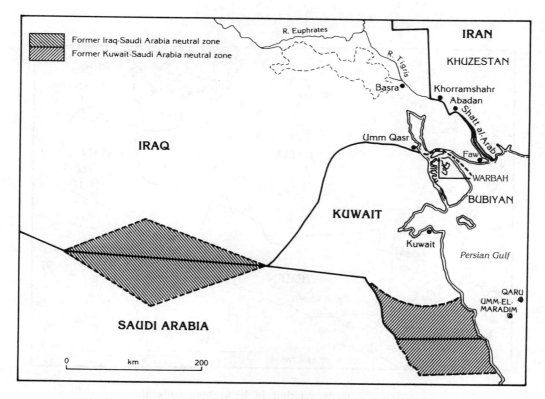

Map 55   Territorial relationships of Iran, Iraq, Kuwait and Saudi Arabia.

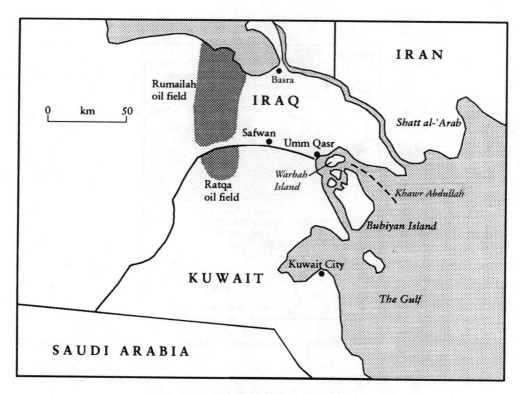

Map 56   The Iraq-Kuwait border area.

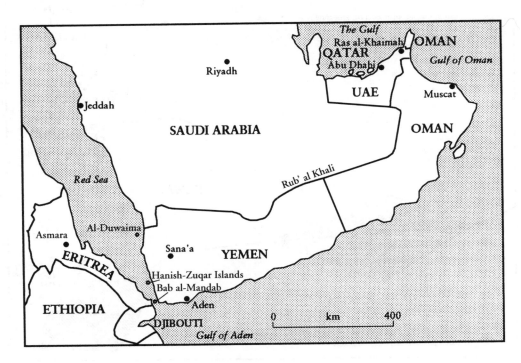

Map 57   Border relations in the Arabian peninsula.

Map 58   The province of Hatay.

INDEX

INDEX